DICTIONARY OF
LAW

English–German

DICTIONARY OF

LAW

English–German

P. H. Collin
Sigrid Janssen
Anke Kornmüller
Rupert Livesey

PETER COLLIN PUBLISHING

First published in Great Britain 1990
by Peter Collin Publishing Ltd
8 The Causeway, Teddington, Middlesex, TW11 0HE

© English text P.H. Collin 1986, 1990
© German translation copyright Ernst Klett Verlag für Wissen und
Bildung GmbH & Co. KG, Stuttgart 1990

British Library Cataloguing in Publication Data

Collin, P.H. (Peter Hodgson), *1935*–
English – German dictionary of law.
  1. Law
  I. Title
  340

  ISBN 0-948549-18-1

Computer processing by Compulexis, Charlton-on-Otmoor, Oxford
Text computer typeset by Systemset, Stotfold, Hertfordshire

Printed in West Germany

Preface

The ENGLISH-GERMAN LAW DICTIONARY contains some 6000 English words and phrases with their German equivalents. The subject matter covers criminal, civil, commercial and international law, dealing with situations as varied as the solicitor's office, the courtroom, and the prison. The level of languages ranges from the very formal (including many Latin terms) to prison slang.

The words and phrases are clearly defined in simple English and only 500 words are used in the definitions which do not appear in the dictionary as main words. Because of the differences between the English or American and German legal systems, in cases where terms or institutions do not correspond, an explanation or approximate equivalent in German is given.

Many examples are given to show how the words are used in normal contexts and some entries have simple grammar notes to remind the user of irregular verbs or plural forms, constructions used with particular words, differences between British and American usage and other useful points. In addition, many entries are followed by comments relating to the judicial system or to particular points of law.

In the second part of the dictionary a Glossary lists the translated German terms in alphabetical order, together with their English equivalents, thus enabling the user to refer to words both in English and in German.

The Supplement gives information in tabular form about legal systems, writs, judgements, conveyances, wills and other legal documents. We are particularly grateful to the Office for Official Publications, acting on behalf of the institutions of the European Communities, to Her Majesty's Stationery Office, and to the Solicitors' Law Stationery Society Plc for giving permission to reproduce copyright documents in the Supplement. We would also like to acknowledge the specialist assistance rendered by Ulrich Sabiel in the translating of the dictionary.

Preface

Englisch-Deutsches
Wörterbuch

Aa

A *first letter of the alphabet* **category "A" prisoners** = prisoners who are dangerous, and would be a danger to the public if they escaped from prison **Häftlinge der höchsten Gefährlichkeitsstufe; Schedule A** = schedule to the Finance Acts under which tax is charged on income from land *or* buildings **Einkommenssteuergruppe A; Table A** = model articles of association of a limited company set out in the Companies Act, 1985 **Mustersatzung einer AG; "A" shares** = ordinary shares with limited voting rights **dividendenberechtigte Aktien mit beschränktem Stimmrecht**

◊ **A1** *adjective*
(a) best **1A, erstklassig;** *we sell only goods in A1 condition*
(b) ship which is A1 at Lloyd's = ship which is in best condition according to Lloyd's Register **Schiff, das von Lloyd's als in erstklassigem Zustand befindlich beschrieben wird**

A.B.A. = AMERICAN BAR ASSOCIATION

abandon *verb*
(a) to give up *or* not to continue **aufgeben; to abandon an action** = to give up a court case **eine Klage zurückziehen**
(b) to leave (something *or* a person) **verlassen, aufgeben;** *he abandoned his family and went abroad; the crew abandoned the sinking ship*

◊ **abandonment** *noun* act of giving something up voluntarily (such as the right to a property) **Aufgabe; Verlassen; abandonment of a claim** = giving up a claim in a civil action **Aufgabe eines Rechtsanspruchs**

> COMMENT: abandoning a child under two years old is a notifiable offence

abate *verb*
(a) to remove *or* stop a nuisance **beseitigen, abstellen**
(b) (i) to reduce (a legacy); (ii); *(of a legacy)* to be reduced (because there is not enough money in the estate to pay in full) **(i) kürzen; (ii) gekürzt sein**

◊ **abatement** *noun*
(a) removal *or* stopping of a nuisance **Beseitigung; noise abatement** = stopping someone who is making an unpleasant loud noise **Lärmbekämpfung;** *a noise abatement notice was served on the club*
(b) reducing a legacy *or* legacies, where the deceased person has not left enough money to pay them all in full **Kürzung**

◊ **abator** *noun* person who abates a nuisance **jd, der einen Mißstand abstellt**

abduct *verb* to take (someone, especially a woman *or* child) away by force **entführen;** *the bank manager was abducted at gunpoint; the robbers abducted the heiress and held her to ransom*

◊ **abduction** *noun* notifiable offence of taking someone (especially a woman *or* child) away by force **Entführung**

◊ **abductor** *noun* person who takes someone away by force **Entführer/-in**

abet *verb* to encourage someone to commit a crime **anstiften, begünstigen; aiding and abetting** = offence of helping and encouraging someone to commit a crime **Beihilfe (bei einer Straftat)**
NOTE: abetting - abetted

abeyance *noun*
(a) this law is in abeyance = this law in not being enforced at the present time **dies Gesetz ist zeitweilig außer Kraft gesetzt**
(b) situation where there is no owner of a piece of land **besitzloser Zustand**
NOTE: no plural

ABH = ACTUAL BODILY HARM

abide by *verb* to obey (an order *or* a rule) **sich halten an;** *he promised to abide by the decision of the court; she did not abide by the terms of the agreement*

ab initio *Latin phrase meaning* "from the beginning" **von Anfang an**

abjure *verb*
(a) to renounce under oath **unter Eid schwören, zu verzichten;** *US* to swear not to bear allegiance to another country **auf die Treue gegenüber einem anderen Land verzichten**

◊ **abjuration** *noun* act of abjuring **Verzichtleistung unter Eid**

abnormal *adjective* not normal *or* not usual **anormal**

abode *noun* residence *or* place where someone lives **Wohnsitz; right of abode** = right to live in a country **Aufenthaltsrecht**

abolish *verb* to cancel *or* to remove (a law *or* a rule) **abschaffen, aufheben;** *the Chancellor of the Exchequer refused to ask Parliament to abolish the tax on alcohol; the Senate voted to abolish the death penalty*
◊ **abolition** *noun* act of abolishing **Abschaffung, Aufhebung;** *to campaign for the abolition of the death penalty*

abortion *noun* ending of a pregnancy before the natural term **Schwangerschaftsabbruch, Abtreibung**

> COMMENT: illegal abortion is a notifiable offence

abrogate *verb* to end (a law *or* a treaty) **außer Kraft setzen**
◊ **abrogation** *noun* ending (of a law *or* a treaty) **Außerkraftsetzung**

abscond *verb* to go away without permission *or* not to return to the court after being released on bail *or* to escape from prison **sich (durch Flucht) entziehen;** *he was charged with absconding from lawful custody*

absence *noun* not being at a meeting *or* hearing **Abwesenheit; in the absence of** = when someone is not there **in Abwesenheit von;** *in the absence of the chairman, his deputy took the chair; the trial took place in the absence of the defendant; she was sentenced to death in her absence;* **leave of absence** = being allowed to be absent from work **Beurlaubung;** *see also* IN ABSENTIA
◊ **absent** *adjective* not at a meeting *or* hearing **abwesend**
◊ **absentee** *noun* person who is not able to attend a meeting *or* hearing **Abwesender**

absolute *adjective* complete *or* total **absolut; absolute discharge** = letting a convicted person go free without any punishment **unbeschränkte Entlassung (nach Verurteilung); absolute monopoly** = situation where only one producer or supplier produces or supplies something **unumschränktes Monopol; absolute privilege** = privilege which protects a person from being sued for defamation (such as an MP speaking in the House of Commons, a judge making a statement in judicial proceedings) **absoluter Rechtfertigungsgrund; absolute Immunität;** *see also* DECREE, FORECLOSURE

abstain *verb* to refrain from doing something (especially voting) **sich enthalten;** *sixty MPs abstained in the vote on capital punishment*
◊ **abstention** *noun*
(a) refraining from doing something (especially voting) **Enthaltung;** *the motion was carried by 200 votes to 150, with 60 abstentions*
(b) *US* situation where a federal court refuses to hear a case and passes it to a state court **Verweigerung**

abstract
1 *noun* short form of a report *or* document **Auszug, Abriß;** *to make an abstract of the deeds of a property;* **abstract of title** = summary of the details of the ownership of a property which has not been registered **Eigentumsnachweis**
2 *verb* to make a summary **einen Auszug machen**

abuse
1 *noun*
(a) using something wrongly **Mißbrauch; abuse of power** = using legal powers in an illegal *or* harmful way **Machtmißbrauch; abuse of process** = suing someone in bad faith *or* without proper justification *or* for malicious reasons **Verfahrensmißbrauch; drug abuse** = being mentally and physically dependent on taking a drug regularly **Drogenmißbrauch**
(b) rude *or* insulting words **Beschimpfung;** *the prisoner shouted abuse at the judge*
(c) bad treatment (usually sexual) of a person **Mißbrauch; Mißhandlung;** *child abuse or sexual abuse of children* (NOTE: no plural for (b) or (c))
2 *verb*
(a) to use something wrongly **mißbrauchen; to abuse one's authority** = to use authority in an illegal *or* harmful way **sein Amt mißbrauchen**
(b) to say rude words to (someone) **beschimpfen;** *he abused the police before being taken to the cells*
(c) to treat someone badly (usually in a sexual way) **mißbrauchen; mißhandeln;** *he had abused small children*

abut (on) *verb (of a piece of land)* to touch another property **grenzen an**
NOTE: **abutting - abutted**

ACAS = ADVISORY CONCILIATION AND ARBITRATION SERVICE

ACC = ASSISTANT CHIEF CONSTABLE

accept *verb*
(a) to take something which is being offered **akzeptieren, annehmen**
(b) to say "yes" *or* to agree to something **akzeptieren;** *she accepted the offer of a job in Australia; he accepted £200 for the car;* **to accept an offer conditionally** = to accept provided that certain conditions apply **ein Angebot unter Vorbehalt annehmen**

◊ **acceptable** *adjective* which can be accepted **akzeptabel, annehmbar;** *the offer is not acceptable to both parties*

◊ **acceptance** *noun* one of the main conditions of a contract, where one party agrees to what is proposed by the other party **Annahme, Zustimmung; acceptance of an offer** = agreeing to an offer (and therefore entering into a contract) **Annahme eines Angebotes; we have his letter of acceptance** = we have received a letter from him accepting the offer **wir haben seine Annahmeerklärung erhalten;** *see note at* CONTRACT

◊ **accepting house** *noun* firm which accepts bills of exchange (i.e. promises to pay them) and is paid a commission for this **Akzepthaus**

◊ **acceptor** *noun* person who accepts an offer **Annehmer/-in; Akzeptant**

access
1 *noun*
(a) right of the owner of a piece of land to use a public road which is next to the land **Zugang, Zutritt;** *he complained that he was being denied access to the main road*
(b) **to have access to something** = to be able to obtain *or* reach something **zu etwas Zugang haben; to gain access to something** = to reach *or* to get hold of something **sich zu etwas Zugang verschaffen;** *access to the courts should be open to all citizens; the burglar gained access through the window*
(c) right of a child to see a parent regularly *or* of a parent or grandparent to see a child regularly, where the child is in the care of someone else **Besuchsrecht;** (NOTE: no plural)
2 *verb* to call up (data) which is stored in a computer **aufrufen, zugreifen auf**

◊ **accession** *noun* joining something *or* taking up a position **Beitritt; Antritt, Übernahme; accession to the throne** = becoming King *or* Queen **Thronbesteigung; Treaty of Accession** = treaty whereby the UK joined the EC **EG-Beitrittsvertrag**

◊ **accessory** *noun* person who helps *or* advises someone who is committing a crime **Mittäter/-in, Komplize/Komplizin; to be an accessory after the fact** = person who helps a criminal after the crime has been committed **nach der Tat Beteiligter (z.B. Begünstiger, Hehler); to be an accessory before the fact** = person who helps a criminal before the crime is committed **sich der Beihilfe schuldig machen**

accident *noun* something unpleasant which happens by chance (such as the crash of a plane) **Unfall, Unglück; industrial accident** = accident which takes place at work **Betriebs-, Arbeitsunfall; accident insurance** = insurance which will pay when an accident takes place **Unfallversicherung**

◊ **accidental** *adjective* which happens by accident **durch Unfall, Unfall-;** *a case of accidental death*

accommodation *noun*
(a) money lent for a short time **kurzfristiges (ungesichertes) Darlehen, Dispo-Kredit**
(b) something done to help someone **Gefälligkeit; to reach an accommodation with creditors** = to agree terms for settlement **mit Gläubigern zu einer Übereinkunft kommen; accommodation address** = address used for receiving messages but which is not the real address of the company **Briefkastenadresse; accommodation bill** = bill of exchange where the person signing is helping someone to raise a loan **Gefälligkeitswechsel; accommodation maker** = person who signs a promissory note for no fee, but who expects to lend the creditor money **Aussteller eines Gefälligkeitswechsels**

accompany *verb* to go with **begleiten;** *they sent a formal letter of complaint, accompanied by an invoice*
NOTE: accompanied **by** something

accomplice *noun* person who helps another to commit a crime **Komplize/Komplizin, Mittäter/-in**

accord and satisfaction *noun* payment by a debtor of (part of) a debt *or* the performing by a debtor of some act or service which is accepted by the creditor in full settlement, so that the debtor can no longer be sued **vergleichsweise Erfüllung (einer Verbindlichkeit)**

accordance *noun* **in accordance with** = in agreement with *or* according to **in Übereinstimmung mit;** *in accordance with your instructions we have deposited the money in your current account; I am submitting the claim for damages in* *accordance with the advice of our legal advisers*

◊ **according to** *preposition* as someone says *or* writes **gemäß, nach, laut;** *according to the witness, the accused carried the body on the back seat of his car; the payments were made according to the maintenance order*

◊ **accordingly** *adverb* in agreement with what has been decided **(dem)entsprechend;** *we have received your letter and have altered the contract accordingly*

account

1 *noun*

(a) invoice *or* record of money paid *or* owed **Abrechnung; Konto;** *please send me your account or a detailed or an itemized account;* **accounts payable =** money owed to creditors **Verbindlichkeiten; accounts receivable =** money owed by debtors **Außenstände; action for an account =** court action to establish how much money is owed by one party to another **Rechnungslegungsklage**

(b) *(in a shop)* arrangement which a customer has with the shop to buy goods and pay for them at a later date (usually the end of the month) **Kundenkreditkonto**

(c) customer who does a large amount of business with a firm and has a credit account with that firm **Kreditkunde**

(d) the accounts of a business *or* **a company's accounts =** detailed record of a company's financial affairs **Geschäftsbücher, Bücher**

(e) bank account *or* **US banking account =** arrangement to keep money in a bank **Bankkonto**

(f) *(Stock Exchange)* period of credit (usually fourteen days) at the end of which all people who have traded must pay for shares bought **(14-tägige) Abrechnung**

(g) notice *or* attention; **to take account of the age of the accused** *or* **to take the accused's age into account when passing sentence =** to pass a certain sentence because the accused is very old *or* very young **das Alter des Angeklagten (bei der Urteilsfällung) berücksichtigen**

2 *verb* **to account for =** to explain and record a money deal **Rechenschaft ablegen;** *to account for a loss or a discrepancy*

◊ **accountable** *adjective* (person) who has to explain what has taken place *or* who is responsible for something **verantwortlich;** *if money is lost, the person at the cash desk is held accountable; the group leader will be held accountable for the actions of the group*

◊ **accountability** *noun* being accountable *or* responsible **Verantwortlichkeit**

◊ **accountant** *noun* person trained in keeping *or* drawing up accounts *or* arranging systems of accounts **Buchhalter/-in;** **Chartered Accountant =** accountant who

has passed the professional examinations and is a member of the Institute of Chartered Accountants; *entspricht* **beeidigter Wirtschaftsprüfer**

◊ **accounting** *noun* preparing the accounts of a business **Buchführung, Buchhaltung, Rechnungswesen; false accounting =** notifiable offence of changing *or* destroying *or* hiding financial records for money **vorsätzlich inkorrekte Buchführung**

accredited *adjective* (agent) who is appointed by a company to act on its behalf **akkreditiert, autorisiert, bevollmächtigt**

accrual *noun* slow increase by addition **Auflaufen, Zuwachs; accrual of interest =** automatic addition of interest to capital **Auflaufen von Zinsen, Zinsthesaurierung**

◊ **accrue** *verb (of interest or dividends)* to increase and be due for payment at a later date **auflaufen, anwachsen**

accumulate *verb* to grow larger by adding **akkumulieren, anhäufen**

accuse *verb* to say that someone has committed a crime *or* to charge someone with a crime **beschuldigen, anklagen;** *she was accused of stealing £25 from her boss; he was accused of murder; of what has she been accused? or what has she been accused of?* NOTE: you accuse someone **of** a crime

◊ **accusation** *noun* act of saying that someone has committed a crime **Beschuldigung, Anklage**

◊ **accused** *noun* **the accused =** person *or* persons charged with a crime **der/die Beschuldigte; der /die Angeklagte;** *all the accused pleaded not guilty; the police brought the accused into the court* NOTE: can be singular or plural: **the six accused all pleaded guilty**

acknowledge *verb*

(a) to accept that something is true **anerkennen, eingestehen; acknowledged and agreed =** words written on an agreement to show that it has been read and approved **geprüft und genehmigt**

(b) to confirm that (a letter) has been received **bestätigen; to acknowledge service =** to confirm that a legal document (such as a writ) has been received **die Zustellung bestätigen**

◊ **acknowledgement** *noun* act of acknowledging **Bestätigung; acknowledgement of service =** document whereby a defendant confirms that a writ *or* a legal document has been received and that he intends to defend the case **Zustellungsbestätigung**

acquire *verb* to buy *or* to obtain **erwerben**

◇ **acquisition** *noun* (i) thing bought; (ii) act of obtaining *or* buying something (i) **Anschaffung**; (ii) **Erwerb; the acquisition of Smith & Sons by Jones Ltd** = the takeover of Smith & Sons **Acquisition/Übernahme von Smith & Sons durch Jones Ltd**

acquit *verb* to set a person free because he has been found not guilty **freisprechen;** *he was acquitted of the crime; the court acquitted two of the accused*
NOTE: **acquitting - acquitted** Note also that you acquit someone **of** a crime

◇ **acquittal** *noun* act of acquitting someone of a crime **Freispruch;** *after his acquittal he left the court smiling*

act
1 *noun*
(a) statute which has been approved by a law-making body (in Great Britain, by Parliament) **Gesetz; Erlaß; Act of Parliament** = decision which has been approved by Parliament and so becomes law **Parlamentsgesetz;** *(GB)* **Companies Act** = British Act which rules how companies should do their business *entspricht* **Unternehmensrecht; Finance Act** = annual Act of the British Parliament which gives the government power to raise taxes as proposed in the budget *(GB)* **Finanzgesetz;** (NOTE: use **under** when referring to an Act of Parliament: **a creditor seeking a receiving order under the Bankruptcy Act; she does not qualify under section 2 of the 1979 Act)**

> COMMENT: before an Act becomes law, it is presented to Parliament in the form of a Bill. See notes at BILL

(b) act of God = natural disaster which you do not expect to happen, and which cannot be avoided (such as a storm *or* a flood) **höhere Gewalt**

> COMMENT: acts of God are usually not covered by an insurance policy

2 *verb*
(a) to work **fungieren, agieren;** *to act as an agent for an American company; to act for someone or to act on someone's behalf*
(b) to do something **handeln;** *the lawyers are acting on our instructions;* **to act on a letter** = to do what a letter asks to be done **etwas auf einen Brief hin unternehmen**

action *noun*
(a) thing which has been done **Handlung, Vorgehen; to take action** = to do something **etwas/Schritte unternehmen**
(b) court action = civil case in a law court where a person sues another person **Prozeß; letter before action** = letter written by a lawyer to give a party the chance to pay his client before he sues **anwaltliches Anspruchs-, Anforderungsschreiben; action in personam** = court case in which one party claims that the other should do some act *or* should pay damages **obligatorische Klage; action in rem** = court case in which one party claims property *or* goods in the possession of the other **dingliche Klage; action in tort** = case brought by a plaintiff who alleges he has suffered damage *or* harm caused by the defendant **Schadensersatzklage; to take legal action** = to begin a legal case (such as to instruct a solicitor *or* to sue someone) **gerichtlich vorgehen, Klage erheben;** *action for damages; action for libel or libel action; to bring an action for damages against someone;* **chose in action** = personal right which can be enforced or claimed as if it were a property (such as a patent *or* copyright) **obligatorischer Anspruch; civil action** = case brought by a person *or* company (the plaintiff) against someone who is alleged to have harmed them (the defendant) **Zivilprozeß, zivilrechtliche Klage;** *(US)* **class action** = legal action brought on behalf of a group of people **Gruppenklage; criminal action** = case brought usually by the state against someone who is charged with a crime **Strafverfahren, strafrechtliche Verfolgung; personal action** = (i) legal action brought by a person himself; (ii) common law term for an action against a person arising out of a contract *or* tort **(i) persönlich erhobene Klage; (ii) Leistungsklage**

◇ **actionable** *adjective* (writing *or* speech *or* act) which could provide the grounds for bringing an action against someone **belangbar, (ein)klagbar; torts which are actionable per se** = torts which are in themselves sufficient grounds for bringing an action without the need to prove that damage has been suffered **Delikte, die selbstständig einen Klagegrund bilden (ohne Schadensnachweis)**

◇ **active** *adjective* working *or* busy **aktiv; active partner** = partner who works in the firm **geschäftsführender Teilhaber**

◇ **actively** *adverb* in a busy way **aktiv**

◇ **activity** *noun* being active **Aktivität**

actual *adjective* real **tatsächlich, effektiv; actual bodily harm (ABH)** = assault which causes injury to the victim **Körperverletzung; actual loss** *or* **damage** = real loss *or* damage which can be shown to have been suffered **tatsächlich entstandener Verlust od Schaden; actual notice** = real knowledge which someone has of something **tatsächliche Kenntnis; actual value** = real value of something if sold on the open market **Realwert**

actuary *noun* person employed by an insurance company to calculate premiums **Versicherungsmathematiker**

◊ **actuarial** *adjective* calculated by an actuary **versicherungsmathematisch;** *the premiums are worked out according to actuarial calculations;* **actuarial tables** = lists showing how long people of certain ages are likely to live, used to calculate life assurance premiums **Sterbetabellen**

actus reus *Latin phrase meaning* "guilty act": act which is forbidden by the criminal law, one of the two elements of a crime **Tatbestand;** *compare* MENS REA. *See note at* CRIME

addict *noun* **drug addict** = person who is physically and mentally dependent on taking drugs regularly **Drogenabhängiger, Drogensüchtiger**

◊ **addicted** *adjective* **to be addicted to alcohol** *or* **drugs** = being unable to live without taking alcohol *or* drugs regularly **Alkoholiker od Drogenabhängiger sein**

◊ **addiction** *noun* **drug addiction** = being mentally and physically dependent on taking a drug regularly **Drogenabhängigkeit, Drogensucht**

address
1 *noun* details of number, street and town where an office is or where a person lives **Adresse, Anschrift; address for service** = address where court documents (such as pleadings) can be sent to a party in a case **Zustellungsadresse**
2 *verb*
(a) to write the details of an address on an envelope, etc. **adressieren;** *an incorrectly addressed package*
(b) to speak to **anreden, sprechen zu;** *the defendant asked permission to address the court*

adduce *verb* to bring before the court **vorlegen, erbringen; to adduce evidence** = to bring evidence before a court **Beweismaterial vorlegen**

adeem *verb* to remove a legacy from a will because it no longer exists **(ein Vermächtnis) wegfallen lassen/entziehen**

◊ **ademption** *noun* removing a legacy from a will, because the item concerned no longer exists **Wegfall/Entziehung eines Vermächtnisses**

adequate *adjective* large enough **adäquat; ausreichend; to operate without adequate cover** = to act without being protected by insurance **ohne hinreichenden Versicherungsschutz handeln; he made adequate provision for his wife** = in his will he left his wife enough money to live on **er traf für seine Frau ausreichend Vorsorge**

ad hoc *Latin phrase meaning* "for this particular purpose" **zu diesem Zweck, ad hoc; an ad hoc committee** = a committee set up to study a particular problem **ein ad hoc-Ausschuß;** *see also* STANDING

ad idem *Latin phrase meaning* "in agreement" **in Übereinstimmung mit**

adjoin *verb (of a property)* to touch another property **angrenzen;** *the developers acquired the old post office and two adjoining properties; the fire spread to the adjoining property*

adjourn *verb* to stop a meeting for a period *or* to put off a legal hearing to a later date **vertagen;** *to adjourn a meeting; the chairman adjourned the tribunal until three o'clock; the meeting adjourned at midday; the appeal was adjourned for affidavits to be obtained;* **the hearing was adjourned sine die** = the hearing was adjourned without saying when it would meet again **die Verhandlung wurde auf unbestimmte Zeit vertagt**

◊ **adjournment** *noun* act of adjourning; *the adjournment lasted two hours; the defendant has applied for an adjournment* **Vertagung; adjournment debate** = debate in the House of Commons on a motion to adjourn the sitting **formlose Debatte über die Vertagung der Parlamentssitzung**

adjudicate *verb* to give a judgment between two parties in law; to decide a legal problem **entscheiden; ein Urteil fällen;** *to adjudicate a claim; to adjudicate in a dispute; magistrates may be paid expenses when adjudicating;* **he was adjudicated bankrupt** = he was declared legally bankrupt **über ihn wurde der Konkurs verhängt**

◊ **adjudication** *noun* act of giving a judgment *or* of deciding a legal problem **Entscheidung; Gerichtsentscheidung; adjudication order** *or* **adjudication of bankruptcy** = order by a court making someone bankrupt **Konkurseröffnungsbeschluß; adjudication tribunal** = group which adjudicates in industrial disputes **Schlichtungskommission**

◊ **adjudicator** *noun* person who gives a decision on a problem **Schlichter;** *an adjudicator in an industrial dispute*

adjust *verb* to change something to fit new conditions, especially to calculate and settle an insurance claim **anpassen, angleichen**

◊ **adjuster** *noun* person who calculates losses for an insurance company **Schadenssachverständiger; average adjuster** *or* **loss adjuster** = person who calculates how much is due to the insured when he makes a claim under his policy **Schadenregulierer**

◊ **adjustment** *noun* act of adjusting; slight change **Anpassung, Angleichung; average adjustment** = calculation of the share of cost of damage or loss of a ship **Dispache**

◊ **adjustor** *noun* = ADJUSTER

ad litem *Latin phrase meaning* "referring to the case at law" **für den Rechtsstreit; guardian ad litem** = person who acts on behalf of a minor who is a defendant in a court case **Prozeßpfleger**

administer *verb*
(a) **to administer justice** = to provide justice **Recht sprechen; to administer an oath** = to make someone swear an oath **(jdn) vereidigen**
(b) to organize *or* to manage **verwalten;** *he administers a large pension fund*
(c) to give someone a medicine *or* a drug **verabreichen;** *she was accused of administering a poison to the old lady*

◊ **administration** *noun*
(a) organization *or* control *or* management, especially the management of the affairs of someone who has died **Verwaltung; letters of administration** = document given by a court to allow someone to deal with the estate of a person who has died without leaving a will *or* where the executor appointed under the will cannot act **Bestallungsurkunde zum Nachlaßverwalter;** (NOTE: not used in the singular) **administration bond** = oath sworn by an administrator that he will pay the state twice the value of the estate being administered, if it is not administered in accordance with the law **Sicherheitsleistung des Nachlaßverwalters; administration order** = order by a court, appointing someone to administer the estate of someone who is not able to meet the obligations of a court order **Verteilungsanordnung der Nachlaßverwalter**
(b) government **Regierung;** *the Act became law under the previous administration; she was Minister of Education in the last administration*

◊ **administrative** *adjective* referring to administration **administrativ, verwaltungstechnisch; administrative law** = laws which regulate how government organizations affect the lives and property of individuals **Verwaltungsrecht; administrative tribunal** = tribunal which decides in cases where government regulations affect and harm the lives and property of individuals **Verwaltungsgericht**

◊ **administrator** *noun*
(a) person who arranges the work of other employees in a business so that the business functions well **Verwalter; Bürovorsteher**
(b) person appointed by a court to represent a person who has died without making a will or without naming executors, and who is recognized in law as able to manage the estate **Nachlaßverwalter**

◊ **administratrix** *noun* woman appointed by a court to administer the estate of a person who has died **Erbschaftsverwalterin**

Admiralty *noun* British government office which is in charge of the Navy **britisches Marineministerium;** Admiralty **Court** = court which decides in disputes involving ships; *GB* **Seegericht;** Admiralty **law** = law relating to ships and sailors, and actions at sea **Seerecht**

admit *verb*
(a) to allow someone to go in **Zutritt gewähren;** *children are not admitted to the bank; old age pensioners are admitted at half price*
(b) to allow someone to practise as a solicitor **zulassen;** *he was admitted in 1978*
(c) to allow evidence to be used in court **zulassen;** *the court agreed to admit the photographs as evidence*
(d) to agree that an allegation is correct *or* to say that something really happened **zugeben;** *he admitted his mistake or his liability; she admitted having stolen the car; he admitted to being in the house when the murder took place*
NOTE: **admitted - admitting.** Note also that you admit **to** something, or admit **having done** something

◊ **admissibility** *noun* being admissible **Zulässigkeit;** *the court will decide on the admissibility of the evidence*

◊ **admissible** *adjective* (evidence) which a court will admit *or* will allow to be used **zulässig;** *the documents were not considered relevant to the case and were therefore not admissible*

◊ **admission** *noun*
(a) allowing someone to go in **Eintritt, Zutritt;** *there is a £1 admission charge; admission is free on presentation of this card; free admission on Sundays*
(b) making a statement that you agree that certain facts are correct *or* saying that

something really happened **Eingeständnis, Geständnis**

adopt *verb*
(a) to become the legal parent of a child who was born to other parents **adoptieren**
(b) to agree to (something) *or* to accept (something) so that it becomes law **annehmen**; *to adopt a resolution; the proposals were adopted unanimously*

◊ **adoption** *noun*
(a) act of becoming the legal parent of a child which is not your own **Adoption; adoption order** = order by a court which legally transfers the rights of the natural parents to the adoptive parents **Adoptionsbeschluß; adoption proceedings** = court action to adopt someone **Adoptionsverfahren**
(b) act of agreeing to something so that it becomes legal **Annahme, Billigung**; *he moved the adoption of the resolution*

◊ **adoptive** *adjective* **adoptive child** = child who has been adopted **Adoptivkind; adoptive parents** = people who have adopted a child **Adoptiveltern**

> COMMENT: if a child's parents divorce, or if one parent dies, the child may be adopted by a step-father or step-mother

adult *noun* person who is eighteen years old *or* who has reached majority **Erwachsener**

adultery *noun* sexual intercourse by consent between a married person and someone of the opposite sex who is not that person's spouse **Ehebruch**; *his wife accused him of committing adultery with Miss X*
NOTE: no plural

◊ **adulterous** *adjective* referring to adultery **ehebrecherisch**; *he had an adulterous relationship with Miss X*

ad valorem *Latin phrase meaning* "according to value" **dem Wert nach; ad valorem duty** *or* **ad valorem tax** = tax calculated according to the value of the goods taxed **Wertsteuer**

advance
1 *noun*
(a) money paid as a loan *or* as a part of a payment which is to be completed later **Vorschuß; Anzahlung**; *a cash advance; to receive an advance from the bank; an advance on account; to make an advance of £100 to someone*
(b) **in advance** = early *or* before something happens **im voraus, vorab**; *to pay in advance; freight payable in advance*

(c) early **im voraus, vorab**; *advance booking; advance payment; you must give seven days' advance notice of withdrawals from the account*
2 *verb*
(a) to lend (money) **vorschießen**; *the bank advanced him £10,000 against the security of his house*
(b) to increase **steigen, anziehen**; *prices generally advanced on the stock market*
(c) to make something happen earlier **vorverlegen**; *the date of the hearing has been advanced to May 10th*

advantage *noun* something useful which may help you to be successful **Vorteil; to learn something to your advantage** = to hear news which is helpful to you, especially to hear that you have been left a legacy **etwas für sich Vorteilhaftes erfahren; obtaining a pecuniary advantage by deception** = offence of deceiving someone so as to derive a financial benefit **einen Vermögensvorteil durch Betrug erlangen**

adversary *noun* opponent *or* the other side (in a court case) **Gegner, Prozeßgegner**

adverse *adjective* contrary *or* which goes against one party **gegnerisch; nachteilig; adverse possession** = occupation of property (such as by squatters) contrary to the rights of the real owner **rechtswidrige Besetzung; adverse witness** = hostile witness *or* witness called by a party, whose evidence goes unexpectedly against that party and who can then be cross-examined by his own side as if he were giving evidence for the other side **Gegenzeuge**

advert *verb* to refer to **hin-, verweisen**; *this case was not adverted to in Smith v. Jones Machines Ltd*

advice *noun*
(a) **advice note** = written notice to a customer giving details of goods ordered and shipped but not yet delivered **Versandanzeige, Avis; as per advice** = according to what is written on the advice note **laut Mitteilung/Avis**
(b) opinion as to what action should be taken **Rat, Empfehlung; to take legal advice** = to ask a lawyer to advise about a problem in law **sich juristisch beraten lassen; counsel's advice** = opinion of a barrister about a case; *(GB)* **Rechtsgutachten (eines Barristers)**; *we sent the documents to the police on the advice of the solicitor or we took the solicitor's advice and sent the documents to the police*

advise *verb*
(a) to tell someone what has happened in **Kenntnis setzen, informieren, unterrichten;** *we are advised that the shipment will arrive next week*
(b) to suggest to someone what should be done **raten, empfehlen;** *we are advised to take the shipping company to court; the solicitor advised us to send the documents to the police*

◊ **advise against** *verb* to suggest that something should not be done **abraten;** *the bank manager advised against closing the account; our lawyers have advised against suing the landlord*

◊ **adviser** *or* **advisor** *noun* person who suggests what should be done **Berater/-in, Ratgeber/-in;** *he is consulting the company's legal adviser;* **financial adviser** = person *or* company which gives advice on financial problems for a fee **Finanzberater**

◊ **advisory** *adjective* as an adviser **beratend;** *he is acting in an advisory capacity;* **an advisory board** = a group of advisers **Beratungsgremium, Beirat;** *(GB)* the **Advisory Conciliation and Arbitration Service (ACAS)** = government body which assists in settling industrial and employment disputes **Beratungs-, Schlichtungs- und Schiedsgerichtsdienst (bei Streit zwischen Sozialpartnern)**

advocacy *noun* (i) skill of pleading a case orally before a court; (ii) support for a cause **(i) juristische Wortgewandtheit; (ii) Eintreten, Befürwortung;** *his advocacy of the right of illegal immigrants to remain in the country*

advocate
1 *noun (in Scotland)* barrister **Rechtsanwalt;** *(US)* lawyer **Rechtsbeistand;** **Faculty of Advocates** = legal body to which Scottish barristers belong **Anwaltskammer;** **Judge Advocate-General** = lawyer appointed by the state to advise on all legal matters concerning the army **Oberster Militärstaatsanwalt**

◊ **Advocate General** *noun*
(a) one of the two Law Officers for Scotland **Rechtsberater der Krone**
(b) *(in the European Court of Justice)* officer of the court who summarizes and presents a case to the judges to assist them in coming to a decision **juristischer Berater eines Richters am Europäischen Gerichtshof**

advowson *noun* right to nominate a person to be a parish priest **Recht zur Besetzung einer Pfründe**

affair *noun*

(a) business *or* dealings **Geschäft, Handel, Sache, Angelegenheit;** *are you involved in the copyright affair? his affairs were so difficult to understand that the lawyers had to ask accountants for advice*
(b) adulterous relationship *or* sexual relationship where one party (or both parties) is married to someone else **Verhältnis, Affäre; to have an affair with someone** = to commit adultery **mit jdm ein Verhältnis/eine Affäre haben**

affect *verb* to change *or* to have a bad effect on (something) **betreffen, sich auswirken auf, angehen;** *the new government regulations do not affect us; the company's sales in the Far East were seriously affected by the embargo*

◊ **affection** *noun* love (for another person) **Zuneigung;** *see also* ALIENATION

affidavit *noun* written statement which is signed and sworn before a solicitor and which can then be used as evidence in court hearings **Affidavit, schriftliche unter Eid abgegebene Erklärung**

affiliation *noun* **affiliation order** = court order which makes the father of an illegitimate child pay for the child's maintenance **Unterhaltsverfügung; affiliation proceedings** = court case to order the father of an illegitimate child to provide for the child's maintenance **Vaterschaftsprozeß (mit Feststellung der Unterhaltspflicht)**

affirm *verb*
(a) to state that you will tell the truth, but without swearing an oath **an Eides Statt versichern**
(b) to confirm that something is correct **bestätigen**

◊ **affirmation** *noun* statement in court that you will say the truth, though this is not sworn on oath **eidesstattliche Erklärung**

◊ **affirmative** *adjective* meaning "yes" **affirmativ, bejahend, zustimmend; the answer was in the affirmative** = the answer was "yes" **die Antwort war positiv**

affray *noun* public fight which frightens other people **Schlägerei**

COMMENT: a person is guilty of affray if he uses or threatens to use unlawful violence towards another, and his conduct is such that a reasonable person who happened to be present might fear for his safety

aforementioned *adjective* which has been mentioned earlier **vorher erwähnt;** *the aforementioned company*

aforesaid *adjective* said earlier **vorher erwähnt; as aforesaid** = as was stated earlier **wie schon erwähnt**

aforethought *adjective* **with malice aforethought** = with the intention of committing a crime (especially murder) **mit Vorsatz; böswillig**

a fortiori *Latin phrase meaning* "for a stronger reason" **offensichtlich;** *if the witness was present at the scene of the crime, then a fortiori he must have heard the shot*

against *preposition*
(a) against the law = which breaks the law **gegen das Gesetz, gesetzwidrig;** *lighting fires in the street is against the law; the company went against the law by sending dangerous goods through the post*
(b) relating to *or* part of **gegen;** *to pay an advance against next month's salary; the bank advanced him £10,000 against the security of his house*

agency *noun*
(a) (i) arrangement where one person *or* company acts on behalf of another person in contractual matters; (ii) office *or* job of representing another company in an area **(i) Stellvertretung; Bevollmächtigung; (ii) Agentur, Geschäftsstelle;** *they signed an agency agreement or an agency contract*
(b) branch of government **Behörde, Amt;** *the Atomic Energy Agency; a counter-intelligence agency*

agenda *noun* list of things to be discussed at a meeting **Tagesordnung;** *the committee meeting agenda or the agenda of the committee meeting; after two hours we were still discussing the first item on the agenda; the Secretary put finance at the top of the agenda*

agent *noun*
(a) person who represents a company *or* another person in matters relating to contracts **Stellvertreter; Bevollmächtigter; land agent** = person who manages a farm *or* large area of land for someone; *GB* **Gutsverwalter**
(b) person in charge of an agency **Makler/-in, Agent/-in;** *advertising agent; estate agent; travel agent;* **commission agent** = agent who is paid by commission, not by fee **Provisionsagent**

(c) person who works for a government agency, especially in secret **Agent; secret agent** = person who tries to find out information in secret about other countries *or* other governments *or* other armed forces **Geheimagent**

◊ **agent provocateur** *French words meaning* "agent who provokes": person who provokes others to commit a crime (often by taking part in it himself) in order to find out who is not reliable *or* in order to have his victim arrested **Lockspitzel, Agent provocateur**

aggravation *noun* something (usually the carrying of a weapon) which makes a crime more serious **Erschwerung, Verschärfung**

◊ **aggravated** *adjective* made worse **erschwert, verschärft; aggravated assault** = assault causing serious injury *or* carried out in connection with another serious crime **schwere Körperverletzung; aggravated burglary** = burglary where guns or other weapons are used **erschwerter Diebstahl; aggravated damages** = damages awarded by a court against a defendant who has behaved maliciously *or* wilfully **erhöhter Schadensersatz**

aggrieved *adjective* (party) who has been damaged *or* harmed by a defendant's actions **beschwert**

AGM = ANNUAL GENERAL MEETING

agree *verb*
(a) to approve **genehmigen;** *the figures were agreed between the two parties; terms of the contract are still to be agreed*
(b) to say "yes" *or* to accept **zustimmen, vereinbaren;** *it has been agreed that the lease will run for twenty-five years; after some discussion he agreed to our plan; the bank will never agree to lend the company £250,000*
(c) to agree to do something = to say that you will do something **sich einverstanden/bereit erklären, etwas zu tun**
NOTE: you agree **to** or **on** a plan or agree **to do** something

◊ **agree with** *verb*
(a) to say that your opinions are the same as someone else's **übereinstimmen mit**
(b) to be the same as **übereinstimmen mit;** *the witness' statement does not agree with that of the accused*

◊ **agreed** *adjective* which has been accepted by everyone **vereinbart, abgemacht;** *an agreed amount; on agreed terms or on terms which have been agreed upon*

◊ **agreement** *noun* document setting out the contractual terms agreed between two parties *or* contract between two parties where one party makes an offer, and the other party accepts it **Vereinbarung, Abkommen, Abmachung;** *written agreement; unwritten or verbal agreement; to draw up or to draft an agreement; to break an agreement; to sign an agreement; to witness an agreement; an agreement has been reached or concluded or come to; to reach an agreement or to come to an agreement on prices or salaries; an international agreement on trade; collective wage agreement; an agency agreement; a marketing agreement;* **blanket agreement =** agreement which covers many different items **Gesamtvereinbarung; exclusive agreement =** agreement where a company is appointed sole agent for a product in a market **Alleinvertretungsvereinbarung; shareholders' agreement =** agreement showing the rights of shareholders in a company **(verbriefte) Aktionärsrechte; agreement in principle =** agreement with the basic conditions of a proposal **Grundsatzvereinbarung; gentleman's agreement =** verbal agreement between two parties who trust each other **Gentleman's Agreement, Vereinbarung auf Treu und Glauben**

COMMENT: a gentleman's agreement is not usually enforceable by law

aid
1 *noun* help; **Legal Aid =** British government scheme whereby a person with very little money can have legal representation and advice paid for by the state **Beratungs- und Prozeßkostenhilfe; to pray in aid =** to rely on something when pleading a case **sich berufen auf;** *I pray in aid the Statute of Frauds in support of the defendant's case*
2 *verb* to help; **to aid and abet =** to help and encourage someone to commit a crime **Beihilfe leisten**

◊ **aiding and abetting** *noun* offence of helping and encouraging someone to commit a crime **Beihilfe (bei einer Straftat)**

a. k. a. = ALSO KNOWN AS

al. *see* ET AL.

alarm *noun* device which gives a warning, usually by ringing a bell **Alarm;** *as he put his hand through the window he set off an alarm bell;* **burglar alarm =** bell which is set to ring when someone tries to break into a house *or* shop **Alarmanlage; fire alarm =** bell which is set to sound if it detects fire **Feuermelder, Feueralarm**

aleatory *adjective* not certain *or* which carries a risk **aleatorisch, zufallsbedingt; aleatory contract =** bargain (such as a wager) where what is done by one party depends on something happening which is not certain to happen **aleatorischer Vertrag**

alia *see* ET ALIA, INTER ALIA

alias
1 *noun* name which you take to hide your real name **Deckname;** *the confidence trickster used several aliases*
2 *adverb* otherwise known as *or* using the name of **alias;** *John Smith, alias Reginald Jones*

alibi *noun* plea that a person charged with a crime was somewhere else when the crime was committed **Alibi**

alien *noun* person who is not a citizen of a country **Ausländer/-in;** *(in the UK)* person who is not a UK citizen, not a citizen of a Commonwealth country and not a citizen of the Republic of Ireland **Ausländer/-in**

alienation *noun* the transfer of property (usually land) to someone else **Übertragung, Umschreibung; alienation of affection =** making one of the partners in a marriage stop loving the other **Entfremdung**

alimony *noun* money which a court orders a husband to pay regularly to his separated *or* divorced wife **Unterhaltszahlung; alimony pending suit *or* pendente lite =** money paid by a husband to his wife while their divorce case is being prepared **vorläufige Unterhaltszahlung;** *see also* PALIMONY (NOTE: no plural; in GB English is usually referred to as **maintenance**)

COMMENT: can occasionally be applied to a wife who is ordered to support her divorced husband

all *adjective & pronoun* everything *or* everyone **alle; alles, alle;** *all the witnesses say they saw the accused with the can of petrol; all the evidence suggests that it was a gang of three people who held up the bank;* **on all fours with =** exactly similar to **identisch sein (mit einem früheren Rechtsstreit);** *this case is on all fours with Donoghue v. Stevenson*

◊ **All England Law Reports (All E.R.)** *plural noun* reports of cases in the higher courts **Rechtsprechungsübersicht der höheren Gerichte**

◊ **all-in** *adjective* including everything **Inklusiv-**

allege *verb* to state (usually in evidence) that something has happened *or* is true **(bei Gericht) vorbringen; behaupten;** *the prosecution alleged that the accused was in the house when the crime was committed*

◊ **allegation** *noun* statement (usually in evidence) that something has happened *or* is true **Vorbringen; Behauptung**

allegiance *noun* obedience to the State *or* the Crown **Treuepflicht; oath of allegiance =** oath which is sworn to put the person under the orders *or* rules of a country *or* an army, etc. **Treueeid;** *he swore an oath of allegiance to the new president*

All E. R. = ALL ENGLAND LAW REPORTS

allocate *verb* to divide (something) in various ways and share it out **zuteilen, zuweisen**

◊ **allocation** *noun*
(a) dividing a sum of money in various ways **Zuteilung, Zuweisung;** *allocation of funds to research into crime*
(b) share allocation *or* **allocation of shares =** spreading a small number of shares among a large number of people who have applied for them **Aktienzuteilung**

◊ **allocatur** *Latin word meaning* "it is allowed": court document confirming the amount of costs to be paid by one party to another after a court action **Kostenverteilung**

allot *verb* to share out **zuteilen, zuweisen; to allot shares =** to give a certain number of shares to people who have applied for them **Aktien zuteilen**
NOTE: allotting - allotted

◊ **allotment** *noun*
(a) sharing out funds by giving money to various departments **Zuteilung**
(b) giving some shares in a new company to people who have applied to buy them **Zuteilung (von Aktien)**

allow *verb*
(a) to say that someone can do something **gestatten, erlauben;** *the law does not allow you to drive on the wrong side of the road; begging is not allowed in the station; visitors are not allowed into the prisoners' cells*
(b) to give (someone) time *or* a privilege **gewähren, geben;** *the court adjourned to allow the prosecution time to find the missing witness; you are allowed thirty days to pay the fine*
(c) to agree *or* to accept legally **anerkennen, zugestehen;** *to allow a claim or an appeal*

◊ **allow for** *verb* to give a discount for *or* to add an extra sum to cover something **einrechnen; delivery is not allowed for =** delivery charges are not included **Liefergebühren sind nicht inklusive; allow twenty-eight days for delivery =** calculate that delivery will take at least 28 days **Lieferzeit bis zu 28 Tagen**

◊ **allowable** *adjective* legally accepted **zulässig, erlaubt; allowable expenses =** expenses which can be claimed against tax **abzugsfähige Unkosten**

◊ **allowance** *noun*
(a) money which is given for a special reason **Zuschuß;** *travel allowance or travelling allowance; foreign currency allowance;* **cost-of-living allowance =** addition to normal salary to cover increases in the cost of living **Lebenshaltungskostenzuschuß**
(b) personal allowances = part of a person's income which is not taxed **Steuerfreibetrag;** *allowances against tax or tax allowances;* **wife's earned income allowance =** tax allowance to be set against money earned by the wife of the main taxpayer **zusätzlicher Steuerfreibetrag für Erwerbseinkünfte der Ehefrau**
(c) proportion of money removed **Ausgleich; Nachlaß; Toleranz;** *to make an allowance for legal expenses or an allowance for exchange loss*

alphabet *noun* the 26 letters used to make words **Alphabet**

◊ **alphabetical order** *noun* arrangement of records (such as files, index cards) in the order of the letters of the alphabet (A,B,C,D, etc.) **alphabetische Reihenfolge;** *the names of the accused were read out in alphabetical order*

alter *verb* to change **ab-, verändern;** *to alter the terms of a contract; he has altered his will six times in the last ten years*

◊ **alteram** *see* AUDI

◊ **alteration** *noun* change which has been made **Änderung, Abänderung;** *we made some alterations to the terms of a contract*

alternative
1 *noun* thing which can be done instead of another **Alternative**
2 *adjective* other *or* which can take the place of something **Alternativ-; to find someone alternative employment =** to find someone another job **für jdn eine andere Arbeitsstelle finden**

a.m. *or* **ante meridiem** *Latin phrase meaning* "in the morning" *or* "before 12 midday" **vormittags;** *the flight leaves at 9.20* *a.m.; telephone calls before 6 a.m. are charged at the cheap rate*

ambiguous *adjective* (words) which can mean two or more things *or* which can be misleading **zwei-, mehrdeutig;** *the wording of the clause is ambiguous and needs clarification*

◊ **ambiguity** *noun*
(a) being ambiguous **Zwei-, Mehrdeutigkeit**
(b) words which are ambiguous **Zwei-, Mehrdeutigkeit; latent ambiguity** = words in a contract which can mean two or more things, but which do not appear to be misleading at first sight **versteckte Mehrdeutigkeit**

amend *verb* to change *or* correct **(ab)ändern, berichtigen;** *please amend your copy of the contract accordingly*

◊ **amendment** *noun*
(a) change made in a document **Änderung, Abänderung;** *to propose an amendment to the draft agreement; to make amendments to a contract*
(b) change proposed to a Bill which is being discussed in Parliament **Novellierung**

◊ **amends** *plural noun* **to make amends** = to do something to compensate for damage *or* harm done **etwas wiedergutmachen, Schadensersatz leisten; offer of amends** = offer (by a libeller) to write an apology **schriftliches Wiedergutmachungs-, Entschädigungsangebot**

American Bar Association *noun* association of lawyers practising in the USA **US-Bundesanwaltskammer**

amicus curiae *Latin phrase meaning* "friend of the court": lawyer who does not represent a party in a case but who is called upon to address the court to help clear up a difficult legal point *or* to explain something which is in the public interest; *(GB)* **juristischer Berater des Gerichts**

amnesty
1 *noun* pardon, often for political crimes, given to several people at the same time **Amnestie; general amnesty** = pardon granted to all prisoners **Generalamnestie**
2 *verb* to grant convicted persons a pardon **amnestieren; begnadigen;** *they were amnestied by the President*

anarchy *noun* lack of law and order, because the government has lost control **Anarchie;** *when the President was assassinated, the country fell into anarchy*
NOTE: no plural

◊ **anarchical** *adjective* with no law or order **anarchisch;** *the anarchical state of the country districts*

ancestor *noun* person living many years ago from whom someone is descended **Vorfahr, Ahne; common ancestor** = person from whom two or more people are descended **gemeinsamer Vorfahr;** *Mr Smith and the Queen have a common ancestor in King Henry VIII*

ancient lights *plural noun* claim by the owner of a property that he has the right to enjoy light in his windows, which light must not be blocked by a neighbour's buildings; *(GB)* **Lichtrecht**

ancillary *adjective* which gives help *or* support **Hilfs-; ancillary relief** = financial provision *or* adjustment of property rights ordered by a court for a spouse or child in divorce proceedings **Unterhaltsregelung; Wohnungs- und Haushaltsregelung**

animus *noun* intention **Vorsatz, Absicht; animus cancellandi** = the intention to cancel **Kündigungs-, Stornierungsabsicht; animus furandi** = the intention to steal **Diebstahlsvorsatz; animus revocandi** = the intention to revoke (a will) **Widerrufsabsicht**
NOTE: when used to mean "with the intention of", use **animo: animo revocandi** = with the intention of revoking a will

annexe *or US* **annex**
1 *noun* document added *or* attached to a contract **Anhang; Anlage**
2 *verb* to attach (a document) **anhängen**

announce *verb* to tell something to the public **ankündigen, bekanntgeben;** *the foreman of the jury announced their verdict*

◊ **announcement** *noun* telling something in public **Ankündigung, Bekanntmachung;** *the chairman made an announcement about the takeover bid*

annual *adjective* for one year **jährlich; Annual General Meeting** = meeting of the shareholders of a company which takes place once a year to approve the accounts **ordentliche Jahreshauptversammlung; annual return** = form to be completed by each company once a year, giving details of the directors and the financial state of the company **jährlicher Geschäftsbericht; on an annual basis** = each year **auf jährlicher Basis**

◊ **annually** *adverb* each year **jährlich;** *the figures are revised annually*

annuity *noun* money paid each year to a person, usually as the result of an investment **Jahresrente;** *he has a government annuity or an annuity from the government; to buy or to take out an annuity*

◊ **annuitant** *noun* person who receives an annuity **Empfänger einer Jahresrente**

annul *verb* (i) to cancel *or* to stop something having any legal effect; (ii) to declare that something never existed *or* that something never had legal effect **(i) annullieren, für nichtig erklären; rückgängig machen; (ii) annullieren;** *the contract was annulled by the court; their marriage has been annulled*

NOTE: **annulling - annulled**

◊ **annullable** *adjective* which can be cancelled **annullier-, aufhebbar**

◊ **annulling**
1 *adjective* which cancels **Annullierungs-, Aufhebungs-;** *annulling clause*
2 *noun* act of cancelling **Annullieren, Aufheben;** *the annulling of a contract*

◊ **annulment** *noun* act of cancelling **Annullierung, Aufhebung; annulment of adjudication** = cancelling of an order making someone bankrupt **Konkursaufhebungsbeschluß; annulment of marriage** = ending of a marriage, by saying that it never existed; *entspricht* **Eheaufhebung**

annum *see* PER ANNUM

answer
1 *noun*
(a) reply *or* letter or conversation coming after someone else has written or spoken **Antwort;** *I am writing in answer to your letter of October 6th; my letter got no answer or there was no answer to my letter; I tried to phone his office but there was no answer*
(b) formal reply to an allegation made in court, especially defence made by a respondent to a divorce petition **Klageerwiderung, Replik**
2 *verb*
(a) to speak *or* write after someone has spoken or written to you **antworten; to answer a letter** = to write a letter in reply to a letter which you have received **einen Brief beantworten; to answer the telephone** = to lift the telephone when it rings and listen to what the caller is saying **das Telefon abnehmen**
(b) to reply formally to an allegation made in court **auf eine Klage Stellung nehmen; to answer charges** = to plead guilty *or* not guilty to a charge **sich wegen einer Klage od Beschuldigung verantworten;** *the judge ruled*

there was no case to answer = the judge ruled that the prosecution *or* the plaintiff had not shown that the accused *or* the defendant had done anything wrong **der Richter wies die Anklage zurück (ohne Eröffnung des Hauptverfahrens)**

◊ **answerable** *adjective* having to explain why actions have been taken *or* being responsible for one's actions **verantwortlich;** *he is answerable to the Police Commissioner for the conduct of the officers in his force; she refused to be held answerable for the consequences of the police committee's decision*
NOTE: you are answerable **to** someone **for** an action

ante *Latin adverb meaning* "which has taken place earlier" *or* "before" **vor; status quo ante** = the situation as it was before **vorheriger Zustand**

antecedents *plural noun* details of the background of a convicted person given to a court before sentence is passed **Vorleben**

antedate *verb* to put an earlier date on a document **zurückdatieren;** *the invoice was antedated to January 1st*

anti- *prefix* against **Anti-, anti-;** *an anti-drug campaign; the anti-terrorist squad*

◊ **anti-trust** *adjective* which attacks monopolies and encourages competition **Antitrust-;** *anti-trust laws or legislation*

anticipation *noun* doing something before it is due to be done **Vorwegnahme**

◊ **anticipatory** *adjective* done before it is due **vorwegnehmend, vorweggenommen; anticipatory breach** = refusal by a party to a contract to perform his obligations under the contract at a time before they were due to be performed **vorweggenommene Vertragsverletzung**

Anton Piller order *noun* order by a court in a civil case allowing a party to inspect and remove a defendant's documents, especially where the defendant might destroy evidence **spezielle Entscheidung, die Akten und Unterlagen des Beklagten unter gewissen Voraussetzungen einzusehen**

COMMENT: called after the case of *Anton Piller K.G. v. Manufacturing Processes Ltd*

AOB = ANY OTHER BUSINESS

apologize *verb* to say you are sorry **sich entschuldigen;** *to apologize for the delay in answering; she apologized for being late; he apologized to the court for the absence of the chief witness*

◊ **apology** *noun* saying you are sorry **Entschuldigung;** *to write a letter of apology; I enclose a cheque for £10 with apologies for the delay in answering your letter; the writer of the libel was ordered to print a full apology*

a posteriori *Latin phrase meaning* "from what has been concluded afterwards" **a posteriori; a posteriori argument** = argument based on observation **a posteriori-Argument**

apparent *adjective* which can be seen **sichtbar, offensichtlich; apparent defect** = defect which can be easily seen **sichtbarer Fehler/Schaden; heir apparent** = heir who will certainly inherit if a person dies before him **gesetzlicher/rechtmäßiger Erbe**

appeal
1 *noun* asking a higher court to change a decision of a lower court *or* asking a government department to change a decision **Berufung, Revision;** *the appeal from the court order or the appeal against the planning decision will be heard next month; he lost his appeal for damages against the company;* **she won her case on appeal** = her case was lost in the first court, but the appeal court said that she was right **sie gewann den Prozeß in der Berufung/Rechtsmittelinstanz; appeal against conviction** = asking a higher court to change the decision of a lower court that a person is guilty **Berufung/Revision gegen den Schuldspruch allgemein einlegen; appeal against sentence** = asking a higher court to reduce a sentence imposed by a lower court **Berufung unter Beschränkung auf das Strafmaß; Appeal Court** *or* **Court of Appeal** = civil or criminal court to which a person may go to ask for a sentence to be changed and of which the decisions are binding on the High Court and lower courts **Berufungs-, Revisionsgericht; Lord of Appeal in Ordinary** = one of the eleven lords who sits as a member of the House of Lords when it acts as a Court of Appeal **Mitglied des höchsten britischen Rechtsmittelgerichts**
2 *verb* to ask a government department to change its decision *or* a high law court to change a sentence **Berufung einlegen;** *the company appealed against the decision of the planning officers; he has appealed to the Supreme Court* (NOTE: you appeal **to** a court or **against** a decision; an appeal is **heard** and **allowed** or **dismissed**)

COMMENT: in English law, in the majority of cases decisions of lower courts and of the High Court can be appealed to the Court of Appeal. The Court of Appeal is divided into the Civil Division and the Criminal Division. The Civil Division hears appeals from the County Court and the High Court; the Criminal Division hears appeals from the Crown Court. From the Court of Appeal, appeal lies to the House of Lords. When the remedies available under English law are exhausted, it is in certain cases possible to appeal to the European Court of Justice. For many countries (especially Commonwealth countries) appeals may be heard from the highest court of these countries by the Privy Council

appear *verb*
(a) to seem **scheinen;** *the witness appeared to have difficulty in remembering what had happened*
(b) to come to court to stand trial **erscheinen**
(c) to come to court to represent a client **auftreten;** *Mr A. Clark QC is appearing on behalf of the defendant*

◊ **appearance** *noun* act of coming to court to defend *or* prosecute a case **Auftreten; to enter an appearance** = to register with a court that a defendant intends to defend an action **die Verteidigungsbereitschaft (des Beklagten) dem Gericht gegenüber schriftlich anzeigen; entry of appearance** = lodging by the defendant of a document in court to confirm his intention to defend an action **schriftliche Anzeige der Verteidigungsbereitschaft (des Beklagten) gegenüber dem Gericht**

appellant *noun* person who appeals *or* who goes to a higher court to ask it to change a decision *or* a sentence imposed by a lower court **Berufungs-, Revisionskläger**

appellate *adjective* referring to appeal **Berufungs-, Revisions-; appellate jurisdiction** = jurisdiction of the House of Lords to hear appeals **Berufungsgerichtsbarkeit**

appendix *noun* additional text at the end of a document **Appendix, Anhang;** *the markets covered by the agency agreement are listed in the Appendix; see Appendix B for the clear-up rates of notifiable offences* NOTE: plural is **appendices**

apply *verb*
(a) to ask for something, usually in writing **beantragen;** *(Aktien)* **zeichnen;** *to apply for a job; to apply for shares; to apply in writing; to apply in person; my client wishes to apply*

for Legal Aid; he applied for judicial review or for compensation or for an adjournment; **to apply to the Court** = to ask the court to make an order **das Gericht bitten;** *he applied to the Court for an injunction*
(b) to affect *or* to touch **gelten;** *this clause applies only to deals outside the EC; the legal precedent applies to cases where the parents of the child are divorced*

◊ **applicant** *noun* person who applies for something **Antragsteller/-in; Bewerber/-in;** *(für Aktien)* **Zeichner;** *applicant for a job or job applicant; there were thousands of applicants for shares in the new company*

◊ **application** *noun*
(a) asking for something, usually in writing **Antrag, Gesuch; Bewerbung;** *(für Aktien)* **Zeichnung;** *application for shares; shares payable on application; application for a job or job application;* **application form** = form to be filled in when applying **Antragsformular; Bewerbungsformular;** *to fill in an application (form) for a job or a job application (form);* **letter of application** = letter in which someone applies for a job *or* applies for shares in a new company **Bewerbungsschreiben; Antrag auf Aktienzuteilung**
(b) act of asking the Court to make an order **Gesuch, Antrag;** *his application for an injunction was refused; solicitors acting for the wife made an application for a maintenance order*

appoint *verb* to choose someone for a job **ernennen; einsetzen; berufen;** *to appoint James Smith to the post of manager; the government has appointed a QC to head the inquiry; the court appointed a receiver*
NOTE: you appoint a person **to** a job or **to do** a job

◊ **appointee** *noun* person who is appointed to a job **Ernannter, Kandidat/-in**

◊ **appointment** *noun*
(a) arrangement to meet **Termin;** *to make or to fix an appointment for two o'clock; to make an appointment with someone for two o'clock; he was late for his appointment; she had to cancel her appointment;* **appointments book** = desk diary in which appointments are noted **Terminkalender**
(b) being appointed to a job **Ernennung; Einsetzung; Berufung; on his appointment as magistrate** = when he was made a magistrate **bei seiner Ernennung zum Richter; letter of appointment** = letter in which someone is appointed to a job **Ernennungsurkunde; Einstellungsschreiben**
(c) job; **legal appointments vacant** = list in a newspaper of legal jobs which are vacant **juristische Stellenausschreibung**

apportion *verb* to share out (property *or* rights *or* liabilities) in proportion **zuteilen,**

zumessen; *costs are apportioned according to planned revenue*

◊ **apportionment** *noun* sharing out of (property *or* rights *or* liabilities) **Zuteilung, Zumessung**

appraise *verb* to make an estimate of the value of something **ab-, einschätzen, bewerten**

◊ **appraiser** *noun* person who appraises something **Schätzer/-in**

appreciate *verb*
(a) to notice how good something is **zu schätzen wissen, schätzen;** *a judge always appreciates a well-documented case*
(b) to increase in value **steigen;** *property values have appreciated by 20% over the last two years*

◊ **appreciation** *noun*
(a) increase in value **Wertsteigerung, Wertzuwachs**
(b) act of valuing something highly **Anerkennung, Würdigung, Wertschätzung; in appreciation of** = to show how much something is valued **in Anerkennung**

apprehend *verb (formal)*
(a) to understand **verstehen;** *I apprehend that you say your client has a reference*
(b) to arrest **festnehmen;** *the suspect was apprehended at the scene of the crime*

◊ **apprehension** *noun (formal)* arrest (of a person) **Festnahme**

approach
1 *noun*
(a) getting in touch with someone with a proposal **Herantreten;** *the company has had an approach from an Australian consortium*
(b) method of dealing with something **Herangehensweise;** *he has a professional approach to his work*
2 *verb*
(a) to get in touch with someone with a proposal **herantreten an;** *he approached the bank with a request for a loan; the company was approached by an American publisher with the suggestion of a merger*
(b) to come closer *or* to bring closer **sich nähern;** *the offer does not approach the figure my client seeks*

appropriate
1 *adjective* suitable *or* which fits **angemessen, passend;** *is a fine an appropriate punishment for sex offences?*
2 *verb* to take control of (something) for one's own use **sich aneignen, beschlagnahmen;** *the town council appropriated the land to build the new municipal offices*

◊ **appropriation** *noun* allocating of money for a particular purpose **Zuweisung; Bewilligung; appropriations committee =** committee which examines government expenditure **Bewilligungsausschuß**

approve *verb*
(a) to approve of = to think something is good **billigen, gutheißen**
(b) to agree to something officially **genehmigen; ratifizieren;** *to approve the terms of a contract; the proposal was approved by the board; the motion was approved by the committee*

◊ **approval** *noun*
(a) agreement **Genehmigung;** *to submit a budget for approval;* **certificate of approval =** document showing that an item has been approved officially **Genehmigungszertifikat**
(b) on approval = sale where the buyer pays for goods only if they are satisfactory **zur Probe, versuchsweise**

◊ **approved school** *noun* old name for a school for young delinquents **Besserungsanstalt**

appurtenant *adjective* connected to *or* belonging to **zugehörig**
◊ **appurtenances** *plural noun* land *or* buildings attached to *or* belonging to a property **Grundstücksbestandteile**

a priori *Latin phrase meaning* "from the first" **a priori; a priori argument =** reasoning based on ideas *or* assumptions, not on real examples **a priori-Argument**

arbitrate *verb* to settle a dispute between parties by referring it to an arbitrator instead of going to court (usually used in building *or* shipping *or* employment disputes) **schlichten;** *to arbitrate in a dispute*
◊ **arbitration** *noun* settling of a dispute by an outside person *or* persons, chosen by both sides **Schlichtung;** *to submit a dispute to arbitration; to refer a question to arbitration; to take a dispute to arbitration; to go to arbitration;* **arbitration agreement =** agreement by two parties to submit a dispute to arbitration **Schiedsvertrag; arbitration award =** ruling given by an arbitrator **Schiedsspruch; arbitration board** *or* **arbitration tribunal =** group which arbitrates **Schlichtungsausschuß; industrial arbitration tribunal =** court which decides in industrial disputes **Schiedsgericht für arbeitsrechtliche Streitigkeiten (im industriellen Bereich);** *to accept the ruling of the arbitration board*
NOTE: no plural
◊ **arbitrator** *noun* person not concerned with a dispute who is chosen by both sides

to try to settle it **Schlichter/-in;** *industrial arbitrator; to accept* or *to reject the arbitrator's ruling*

argue *verb*
(a) to discuss something about which there is disagreement **(sich) streiten, (lebhaft) diskutieren;** *they argued over* or *about the price; counsel spent hours arguing about the precise meaning of the clause; the union officials argued among themselves over the best way to deal with the ultimatum from the management*
(b) to give reasons for something **argumentieren;** *prosecuting counsel argued that the accused should be given exemplary sentences; the police solicitor argued against granting bail*
NOTE: you argue **with** someone **about** *or* **over** something

◊ **argument** *noun*
(a) discussing something without agreeing **Streit, Auseindandersetzung;** *they got into an argument with the judge over the relevance of the documents to the case; he sacked his solicitor after an argument over costs*
(b) (speech giving) reasons for something **Argumentation, Beweisführung;** *the judge found the defence arguments difficult to follow; counsel presented the argument for the prosecution; the Court of Appeal was concerned that the judge at first instance had delivered judgment without proper argument*
NOTE: can be used without **the**

arise *verb* to happen *or* to come as a result **sich ergeben, entstehen;** *the situation has arisen because neither party is capable of paying the costs of the case; the problem arises from the difficulty in understanding the VAT regulations;* **matters arising =** section in an agenda, where problems *or* questions which refer to items in the minutes of the previous meeting can be discussed **Tagesordnungspunkt (Genehmigung und Diskussion des Protokolls der letzten Sitzung)**
NOTE: **arising - arose - arisen**

arm's length *noun* **at arm's length =** not closely connected *or* dealt with in an official and not a personal way **auf rein geschäftlicher Basis; auf Distanz;** *the directors were required to deal with the receiver at arm's length*

armourer *noun (slang)* criminal who supplies guns to other criminals **illegaler Waffenhändler/Beschaffer von Waffen**

arraign *verb* to make the accused person appear in the court and to read the indictment to him **jdn vor Gericht stellen, Anklage erheben**

◊ **arraignment** *noun* reading of the indictment to the accused and hearing his plea **Anklageerhebung**

arrange *verb*
(a) to put in order **(an)ordnen;** *the office is arranged as an open-plan area with small separate rooms for meetings; the files are arranged in alphabetical order; arrange the documents in order of their dates*
(b) to organize **arrangieren, einrichten;** *the hearing was arranged for April; we arranged to have the meeting in their offices; she arranged for a car to meet him at the airport*
NOTE: you arrange **for** someone to do something or you arrange **for** something to be done

◊ **arrangement** *noun*
(a) way in which something is organized **Arrangement, Plan;** *the company secretary is making all the arrangements for the AGM*
(b) settling of a financial dispute, especially by proposing a plan for repaying creditors **Vergleich;** *to come to an arrangement with the creditors;* **deed of arrangement** = agreement made between a debtor and his creditors whereby the creditors accept an agreed sum in settlement of their claim rather than make the debtor bankrupt **Vergleichsvertrag; Vereinbarung; scheme of arrangement** = agreement between a company and its creditors whereby the creditors accept an agreed sum in settlement of their claim rather than force the company into insolvency **Vergleichsregelung (zur Abwendung des Konkurses)**

arrears *plural noun* money which is owed, but which has not been paid at the right time **Rückstände;** *to allow the payments to fall into arrears;* **in arrears** = owing money which should have been paid earlier **im Rückstand;** *the payments are six months in arrears; he is six weeks in arrears with his rent*

arrest
1 *noun*
(a) act of taking and keeping someone legally, so that he can be kept in custody and charged with a crime **verhaften, festnehmen; a warrant is out for his arrest** = a magistrate has signed a warrant, giving the police the power to arrest someone for a crime **gegen ihn wurde Haftbefehl erlassen; under arrest** = kept and held by the police in **Haft;** *six of the gang are in the police station under arrest;* **citizen's arrest** = right of a private person to arrest without a warrant

someone who he suspects has committed a crime **(jedermann zustehendes) vorläufiges Festnahmerecht; house arrest** = being ordered by a court to stay in your own house and not to leave it **Hausarrest;** *the opposition leader has been under house arrest for six months;* **summary arrest** = arrest without a warrant **vorläufige Festnahme**
(b) **arrest of judgment** = situation where a judgment is held back because there appears to be an error in the documentation **Verfahrensaufschub**
2 *verb*
(a) to hold someone legally so as to keep him in custody and charge him with a crime **verhaften;** *two of the strikers were arrested; the constable stopped the car and arrested the driver*
(b) to seize a ship *or* its cargo **mit Beschlag belegen**

◊ **arrestable offence** *noun* crime for which someone can be arrested without a warrant (usually an offence which carries a penalty of at least five years' imprisonment) **schweres Verbrechen (,das für Verhaftung ohne Haftbefehl hinreichend ist)**

◊ **arrest warrant** *noun* warrant signed by a magistrate which gives the police the power to arrest someone for a crime **Haftbefehl**

COMMENT: any citizen may arrest a person who is committing a serious offence, though members of the police force have wider powers, in particular the power to arrest persons on suspicion of a serious crime or in cases where an arrest warrant has been granted. Generally a policeman is not entitled to arrest someone without a warrant if the person does not know or is not told the reason for his arrest

arson *noun* notifiable offence of setting fire to property **Brandstiftung;** *he was charged with arson; during the riot there were ten cases of looting and two of arson; the police who are investigating the fire suspect arson;* **an arson attack on a house** = setting fire to a house **ein Brandanschlag auf ein Haus**
NOTE: no plural

◊ **arsonist** *noun* person who commits arson **Brandstifter/-in**

article *noun*
(a) product *or* thing for sale **Artikel, Ware;** *a black market in imported articles of clothing*
(b) section of a legal agreement **Artikel, Paragraph, Absatz;** *see article 8 of the contract*
(c) **articles of association** *or (US)* **articles of incorporation** = document which regulates

the way in which a company's affairs are managed **Gesellschaftsvertrag, Satzung; articles of partnership** = document which sets up the legal conditions of a partnership **Gesellschaftsvertrag (einer Personengesellschaft);** *he is a director appointed under the articles of the company; this procedure is not allowed under the articles of association of the company* **(d) articles** = time when a clerk is working in a solicitor's office learning the law **Anwaltsreferendarzeit; articles of indenture** = contract by which a trainee craftsman works for a master for some years to learn a trade **Ausbildungsvertrag; to serve articles** = to work in a solicitor's office to learn the law **seine Rechtsreferendarzeit ableisten**

◊ **articled** *adjective* **articled clerk** = clerk who is bound by contract to work in a solicitor's office for some years to learn the law; *(GB)* **Anwaltsreferendar**

artificial person *noun* body (such as a company) which is a person in the eyes of the law **juristische Person**

aside *adverb* to one side *or* out of the way **zur Seite, beiseite; to put aside** *or* **to set aside** = to say that something no longer applies **aufheben;** *the appeal court set aside the earlier judgment*

ask *verb*
(a) to put a question to someone **fragen;** *prosecuting counsel asked the accused to explain why the can of petrol was in his car* **(b)** to tell someone to do something **auffordern; bitten;** *the police officers asked the marchers to go home; she asked her secretary to fetch a file from the managing director's office; the customs officials asked him to open his case; the judge asked the witness to write the name on a piece of paper*

◊ **ask for** *verb*
(a) to say that you want *or* need something **verlangen;** *he asked for the file on 1984 debtors; counsel asked for more time to consult with his colleagues; there is a man on the phone asking for Mr Smith;* **to ask for bail to be granted** = to ask a court to allow a prisoner to be remanded on bail **einen Kautionsantrag stellen**
(b) to put a price on something for sale **verlangen, fordern;** *they are asking £24,000 for the car*

assassin *noun* murderer of a public figure **Mörder/-in, Attentäter/-in**

◊ **assassinate** *verb* to murder (a public figure) **einen Mordanschlag/ein Attentat verüben**

◊ **assassination** *noun* murder of a public figure **(geglücktes) Attentat, Mord**

assault
1 *noun* crime *or* tort of acting in such a way that someone is afraid he will be attacked and hurt **gewaltsame Drohung; (tätlicher) Angriff;** *he was sent to prison for assault; the number of cases of assault is increasing; see also* BATTERY (NOTE: as a crime *or* tort, assault has no plural; when it has a plural this means "cases of assault")
2 *verb* to attack someone **(tätlich) angreifen;** *she was assaulted by two muggers*

COMMENT: assault should be distinguished from battery, in that assault is the threat of violence, whereas battery is actual violence. However, because the two are so closely connected, the term "assault" is frequently used as a general term for violence to a person. "Aggravated assault" is assault causing serious injury or carried out in connection with another serious crime. The term "common assault" is frequently used for any assault which is not an aggravated assault

assay *noun* test (especially of gold *or* silver) to see if a metal is of the right quality **Feststellung des Feingehalts; assay mark** = hallmark *or* mark put on gold or silver items to show that the metal is of correct quality **Feingehaltsstempel**

assemble *verb*
(a) to put something together from various parts **zusammentragen;** *the police are still assembling all the evidence*
(b) to come together *or* to gather **sich versammeln;** *the crowd assembled in front of the police station*

◊ **assembly** *noun* coming together in a group **Versammlung; the Assembly of the EC** = the European Parliament **das Europa-Parlament; freedom of assembly** = being able to meet as a group without being afraid of prosecution **Versammlungsfreiheit; unlawful assembly** = notifiable offence when a number of people come together to commit a breach of the peace or any other crime **unerlaubte Versammlung**

assent *noun* agreement to something **Zustimmung; Royal Assent** = formal passing of a Bill into law to become an Act of Parliament **königliche Genehmigung**

assert *verb* to state in a strong way *or* to insist **behaupten; beteuern;** *he asserted that the damage suffered was extremely serious*

◊ **assertion** *noun* strong statement **Behauptung; Beteuerung;** *counsel made a series of assertions which were disputed by the witness*

assess *verb* to calculate the value of something, especially for tax *or* insurance purposes **schätzen; veranlagen;** *to assess damages at £1,000; to assess a property for the purposes of insurance*

◊ **assessment** *noun* calculation of value **Schätzung;** *assessment of damages; assessment of property; tax assessment*

◊ **assessor** *noun* expert who can help a judge in a particularly difficult case **sachverständiger Beisitzer**

asset *noun* thing which belongs to company or person, and which has a value **Aktiva, Vermögenswert;** *he has an excess of assets over liabilities; her assets are only £640 as against liabilities of £24,000;* **concealment of assets** = hiding assets so that creditors do not know that they exist **Vermögensverschleierung; capital assets** *or* **fixed assets** = property *or* machinery which a company owns and uses **Anlagevermögen; current assets** = assets used by a company in its ordinary work (such as materials, finished goods, cash) **Umlaufvermögen; fictitious assets** = assets which do not really exist, but are entered as assets to balance the accounts **Scheinaktiva; frozen assets** = assets of a company which cannot be sold because someone has a claim against them **eingefrorene/blockierte Vermögenswerte; intangible assets** = assets which have a value, but which cannot be seen (such as goodwill *or* a patent *or* a trademark) **immaterielle Vermögenswerte; liquid assets** = cash, or bills which can be quickly converted into cash **flüssige Mittel; personal assets** = moveable assets which belong to a person **bewegliches Privatvermögen; tangible assets** = assets which are solid (such as furniture *or* jewels *or* cash) **materielle Vermögenswerte, bilanzierbare Sachwerte; asset value** = value of a company calculated by adding together all its assets **Vermögenswert**

assign *verb*
(a) to give *or* transfer **übertragen, übereignen, abtreten;** *to assign a right to someone; to assign shares to someone; to assign a debt to someone*
(b) to give someone a piece of work to do **beauftragen, betrauen;** *he was assigned the job of checking the numbers of stolen cars; three detectives have been assigned to the case*

◊ **assignee** *noun* person who receives something which has been assigned **Abtretungsempfänger**

◊ **assignment** *noun*
(a) legal transfer of a property *or* of a right **Übereignung, Übertragung;** *assignment of a patent or of a copyright; assignment of a lease;* **deed of assignment** = agreement which legally transfers a property from a debtor to a creditor **Abtretungs-, Übereignungsurkunde**
(b) document whereby something is assigned **Abtretungs-, Übertragungsurkunde**
(c) particular job of work **Aufgabe;** *we have put six constables on that particular assignment*

◊ **assignor** *noun* person who assigns something to someone **Abtretender**

◊ **assigns** *plural noun* people to whom property has been assigned **Rechtsnachfolger; his heirs and assigns** = people who have inherited his property and had it transferred to them **seine Erben und Rechtsnachfolger**

assist *verb* to help **unterstützen, helfen;** *the accused had to be assisted into the dock;* **assisted person** = person who is receiving Legal Aid **Empfänger von Beratungs- und Prozeßkostenhilfe**

◊ **assistance** *noun* help **Unterstützung, Hilfe;** *litigants who receive assistance under the Legal Aid scheme;* **financial assistance** = help in the form of money **finanzielle Unterstützung, Finanzhilfe**

Assizes *or* **Assize Courts** *plural noun* old name for what is now the Crown Court; *(GB)* **Assisen(gericht)**

associate
1 *adjective* joined together with something **assoziiert; associate company** = company which is partly owned or controlled by another **Beteiligungsgesellschaft; associate director** = director who attends board meetings, but does not enjoy the full powers of a director; *entspricht* **außerordentliches Verwaltungsratsmitglied**
2 *noun* person who works in the same business as someone **Teilhaber; Mitarbeiter;** *in his testimony he named six associates;* **associate of the Crown Office** = official who is responsible for the clerical and administrative work of a court **(oberster) Geschäftsstellenbeamter eines Gerichts**
3 *verb* to mix with *or* to meet (people) **verkehren; she associated with criminals** = she was frequently in the company of criminals **sie verkehrte mit Kriminellen**

◊ **associated** *adjective* joined to *or* controlled by **assoziiert, Beteiligungs-;** *Smith*

Ltd and its associated company, Jones Brothers

◊ **association** *noun*
(a) group of people *or* of companies with the same interest **Gesellschaft; Verband; Bund;** *trade association; employers' association;* **freedom of association** = being able to join together in a group with other people without being afraid of prosecution **Vereinsfreiheit; Koalitionsfreiheit; guilt by association** = presumption that a person is guilty because of his connection with a guilty person **Strafbarkeit durch Verbindung zu einer schuldigen Person**
(b) **articles of association** = document which regulates the way in which a company's affairs are managed (such as the appointment of directors and rights of shareholders) **Gesellschaftsvertrag, Satzung; memorandum of association** = document setting up a limited company, giving details of its aims, the way it is financed and its registered office **Gründungsurkunde einer AG**
(c) *(in prison)* time when prisoners can move about and meet other prisoners **Freigang**

assume *verb*
(a) to believe something without any proof **annehmen;** *everyone assumed he was guilty*
(b) to take **übernehmen;** *to assume all risks; he has assumed responsibility for marketing*

◊ **assumption** *noun* taking **Übernahme; assumption of risks** = situation where someone sees that risks exist but still takes the risks **Risikoübernahme**

assure *verb* to insure *or* to have a contract with a company where if regular payments are made, the company will pay compensation if you die *or* suffer harm or damage **versichern; the assured** = person whose interests are assured *or* who is entitled to the benefit in an insurance policy **der/die Versicherte/Versicherungsnehmer/-in**

◊ **assurance** *noun* insurance *or* agreement that in return for regular payments, one party will pay another party compensation for loss of life **Versicherung**

◊ **assurer** *or* **assuror** *noun* insurer *or* company which insures **Versicherungsträger**

COMMENT: assure and assurance are used in Britain for insurance policies relating to something which will certainly happen (such as death or the end of a given period of time); for other types of policy use insure and insurance

asylum *noun*

(a) hospital for people who are mentally ill **Nervenheilanstalt**
(b) safe place **Asyl; to ask for political asylum** = to ask to be allowed to remain in a foreign country because it would be dangerous to return to the home country for political reasons **um politisches Asyl bitten**

at issue *see* ISSUE

attach *verb*
(a) to fasten *or* to join **anhängen, beiheften;** *I am attaching a copy of my previous letter; attached is a copy of my letter of June 24th*
(b) to arrest (a person *or* a property) **festnehmen, verhaften; pfänden, beschlagnahmen**

◊ **attachment** *noun*
(a) holding a debtor's property to prevent it from being sold until debts are paid **dinglicher Arrest, Beschlagnahme; Pfändung; attachment of earnings** = legal power to take money from a person's salary to pay money, which is owed, to the courts **Lohn- und Gehaltspfändung; attachment of earnings order** = court order to make an employer pay part of an employee's salary to the court to pay off debts **Lohn- und Gehaltspfändungsbeschluß**
(b) **warrant of attachment** = warrant which authorizes the bailiff to arrest a person in contempt of court **Festnahmeanordnung**

attack
1 *verb*
(a) to try to hurt *or* harm someone **angreifen, überfallen;** *the security guard was attacked by three men carrying guns*
(b) to criticize **angreifen;** *MPs attacked the government for not spending enough money on the police*
2 *noun*
(a) act of trying to hurt *or* harm someone **Angriff, Überfall;** *there has been an increase in attacks on police or in terrorist attacks on planes*
(b) criticism **Angriff;** *the newspaper published an attack on the government*
NOTE: you attack someone, but make an attack **on** someone

◊ **attacker** *noun* person who attacks **Angreifer/-in;** *she recognized her attacker and gave his description to the police*

attainder *noun* **bill of attainder** = obsolete way of punishing a person legally without holding a trial, by passing a law to convict and sentence him; *(GB)* **Bestreitung durch Dekret ohne Gerichtsverhandlung (durch das Ehrverlust, Vermögenseinziehung und Todesurteil ausgesprochen werden)**

attempt

1 *noun*
(a) trying to do something **Versuch;** *the company made an attempt to break into the American market; the takeover attempt was turned down by the board; all his attempts to get a job have failed*
(b) trying to do something illegal *or* to commit an offence **Versuch; Anschlag**

> COMMENT: attempt is a crime even if the attempted offence has not been committed

2 *verb* to try **versuchen;** *the solicitor attempted to have the charge dropped; he was accused of attempting to contact a member of the jury;* **attempted murder =** notifiable offence of trying to murder someone **Mordversuch**

◊ **attend** *verb* to be present at **beiwohnen, anwesend sein;** *the witnesses were subpoenaed to attend the trial*

◊ **attend to** *verb* to give careful thought to (something) and deal with it **sich kümmern um;** *the managing director will attend to your complaint personally*

◊ **attendance** *noun* being present **Anwesenheit; attendance centre =** place where a young person may be sent by a court to take part in various types of sport or do hard work as a punishment; *(GB)* **Jugendarrestanstalt**

◊ **attention** *noun* careful thought **Beachtung, Kenntnisnahme;** *for the attention of the Managing Director; your orders will have our best attention*

attest *verb* to sign (a document such as a will) in the presence of a witness who also signs as evidence that the signature is real **bescheinigen, bestätigen, beglaubigen**

◊ **attestation** *noun* signing a document (such as a will) in the presence of a witness to show that the signature is genuine **Bescheinigung, Bestätigung, Beglaubigung; attestation clause =** clause showing that the signature of the person signing a legal document has been witnessed **Beglaubigungsvermerk**

> COMMENT: the attestation clause is usually written: "signed sealed and delivered by ... in the presence of ..."

attorn *verb* to transfer **übertragen**

◊ **attorney** *noun*
(a) person who is legally allowed to act on behalf of someone else **Bevollmächtigter, gesetzlicher Vertreter; letter of attorney =** document showing that someone has power of attorney **Vollmacht(sbescheinigung); power of attorney**

= official power giving someone the right to act on someone else's behalf in legal matters **Handlungsvollmacht;** *his solicitor was granted power of attorney*
(b) *US* lawyer **Rechtsanwalt**

◊ **Attorney-General** *noun GB* one of the Law Officers, a Member of Parliament, who prosecutes for the Crown in certain cases, advises government departments on legal problems and decides if major criminal offences should be tried; **Kronanwalt;** *entspricht* **Generalstaatsanwalt;** *US* minister of legal affairs in a (i) state or (ii) federal government **(i) (ii) Justizminister**

> COMMENT: in the US Federal Government, the Attorney-General is in charge of the Department of Justice

attribute *verb* to suggest that something came from a source **zuschreiben;** *remarks attributed to the Chief Constable*

◊ **attributable** *adjective* **to be attributable to somebody =** originating from somebody **jdm zuzuschreiben sein**

auction

1 *noun* selling of goods where people offer bids, and the item is sold to the person who makes the highest offer **Auktion, Versteigerung; to put something up for auction =** to offer an item for sale at an auction **etwas zur Versteigerung anbieten**
2 *verb* to sell to the person who makes the highest offer **versteigern;** *the factory was closed and the machinery was auctioned off*

◊ **auctioneer** *noun* person who conducts an auction **Auktionator/-in**

audi alteram partem *Latin phrase*

meaning "hear the other side": a rule in natural justice that everyone has the right to speak in his own defence and to have the case against him explained to him **Grundsatz des rechtlichen Gehörs**

audience *noun* right to speak to a court,

which can be used by the parties in the case or their legal representatives **Rederecht (vor Gericht); Auftrittsrecht (für Rechtsanwälte);** *a barrister has right of audience in any court in England and Wales*

audit

1 *noun* examination of the books and accounts of a company **Buch-, Rechnungsprüfung, Revision;** *to carry out an annual audit;* **external audit** *or* **independent audit =** audit carried out by an independent auditor **unabhängige Rechnungsprüfung/Revision; general audit =** examining of all the books and accounts of

a company **ordentliche Buchprüfung; internal audit** = audit carried out by a department inside the company **betriebsinterne Rechnungsprüfung/Revision**
2 *verb* to examine the books and accounts of a company **Rechnungsprüfungen vornehmen;** *to audit the accounts; the books have not yet been audited*
◊ **auditor** *noun* person who audits **Rechnungsprüfer, Revisor;** *the AGM appoints the company's auditors;* **Comptroller and Auditor General** = official whose duty is to examine the accounts of ministries and government departments **Rechnungsprüfer des Rechnungshofes; external auditor** = independent person who audits the company's accounts **unabhängiger Rechnungsprüfer/Revisor; internal auditor** = member of staff who audits a company's accounts **betriebsinterner Rechnungsprüfer/Revisor**

authenticate *verb* to show that something is true **bestätigen, beglaubigen, für echt erklären**

authority *noun*
(a) official power given to someone to do something **Befugnis, Vollmacht;** *he has no authority to act on our behalf; she was acting on the authority of the court; on whose authority was the charge brought?*
(b) local authority = section of elected government which runs a small area of a country **örtliche Behörde;** *a court can give directions to a local authority; a decision of the local authority pursuant to the powers and duties imposed upon it by the statutory code; the Bill aims at giving protection to children in the care of a local authority*
(c) the authorities = the government *or* those who are in control **die Behörden**

authorize *verb*
(a) to give official permission for something to be done **bewilligen, genehmigen, ermächtigen;** *to authorize payment of £10,000*
(b) to give someone the authority to do something **autorisieren, ermächtigen, bevollmächtigen;** *to authorize someone to act on your behalf*
◊ **authorization** *noun*
(a) official permission *or* power to do something **Bewilligung, Genehmigung, Ermächtigung;** *do you have authorization for this expenditure? he has no authorization to act on our behalf*
(b) document showing that someone has official permission to do something **Genehmigung;** *he showed the bank his authorization to inspect the contents of the safe*

◊ **authorized** *adjective* permitted **autorisiert, befugt, bevollmächtigt; authorized capital** = amount of capital which a company is allowed to have, according to its memorandum of association **genehmigtes Grundkapital; authorized dealer** = person *or* company (such as a bank) which is allowed to buy and sell foreign currency **Geldhändler**

automatic *adjective* which works *or* takes place without any special action *or* instruction **(voll)automatisch;** *there is an automatic increase in salaries on January 1st*
◊ **automatically** *adverb* working without a person giving instructions **automatisch;** *unpaid fines are automatically increased by 15%*
◊ **automatism** *noun* defence to a criminal charge whereby the accused states he acted involuntarily; *(im Strafverfahren)* **Schuldunfähigkeit**

autopsy *noun* examination of a dead person to see what was the cause of death **Autopsie**

autrefois acquit *French phrase* meaning "previously acquitted": plea that an accused person has already been acquitted of the crime with which he is charged **Einspruch des Freispruchs in gleicher Sache**
◊ **autrefois convict** *French phrase* meaning "previously convicted": plea that an accused person has already been convicted of the crime with which he is charged **Einwand der Verurteilung in gleicher Sache**

available *adjective* which can be used *or* which is ready to be used **erhältlich, verfügbar;** *the right of self-defence is only available against unlawful attack*

aver *verb* to make a statement *or* an allegation in pleadings **beteuern, versichern; behaupten**
NOTE: averring - averred
◊ **averment** *noun* statement *or* allegation made in pleadings **Beteuerung, Versicherung; Behauptung**

average
1 *noun*
(a) number calculated by adding together several figures and dividing by the number of figures added **Durchschnitt, Mittelwert;** *the average for the last three months or the last three months' average; sales average or average of sales;* **on an average** = in general

im Durchschnitt, durchschnittlich; *on an average, £15 worth of goods are stolen every day*
(b) sharing of the cost of damage or loss of a ship between the insurers and the owners **Havarie, Havarei; average adjuster** = person who calculates how much is due to the insured when he makes a claim under his policy **Schadenregulierer; general average** = sharing of the cost of the lost goods by all parties to an insurance **große Havarie; particular average** = situation where part of a shipment is lost or damaged and the insurance costs are borne by the owner of the lost goods and not shared among all the owners of the shipment **besondere Havarie**
2 *adjective*
(a) middle (figure) **durchschnittlich;** *average cost of expenses per employee; the average figures for the last three months; the average increase in prices*
(b) not very good **durchschnittlich, Durchschnitts-;** *the company's performance has been only average; he is an average worker*
3 *verb* to produce as an average figure **sich durchschnittlich belaufen auf, durchschnittlich betragen;** *price increases have averaged 10% per annum; days lost through sickness have averaged twenty-two over the last four years*

◊ **averager** *noun* person who buys the same share at various times and at various prices to give an average price **Person, die zu verschiedenen Kursen und Zeitpunkten Aktien kauft, um so einen besseren Durchschnittskurs zu erzielen**

avoid *verb* to try not to do something **vermeiden, umgehen;** *the company is trying to avoid bankruptcy; my aim is to avoid paying too much tax; we want to avoid direct competition with Smith Ltd;* **to avoid creditors** = to make sure that creditors cannot find you so as not to pay them **Gläubigern aus dem Weg gehen**
NOTE: you avoid something or someone or avoid **doing** something

◊ **avoidance** *noun*
(a) trying not to do something **Vermeidung, Umgehung;** *avoidance of an agreement or of a contract;* **tax avoidance** = trying (legally) to pay as little tax as possible **legale Steuerumgehung/Steuerverkürzung;** *see also* EVASION
(b) confession to a charge, but suggesting it should be cancelled **Widerruf**

await *verb* to wait for **warten auf, erwarten;** *we are awaiting the decision of the planning department; they are awaiting a decision of the court; the solicitor is awaiting our instructions*

award
1 *noun* decision which settles a dispute **Schiedsspruch; außergerichtliche Entscheidung;** *an award by an industrial tribunal; the arbitrator's award was set aside on appeal;* **arbitration award** = ruling given by an arbitrator **Schiedsspruch**
2 *verb* to decide the amount of money to be given to someone **zusprechen, gewähren;** *to award someone a salary increase; to award damages; the judge awarded costs to the defendant;* **to award a contract to a company** = to decide that a company will have the contract to do work for you **einen Auftrag/Vertrag an ein Unternehmen vergeben**

Bb

B *second letter of the alphabet* **category "B" prisoners** = less dangerous prisoners, who still have to be guarded carefully to prevent them from escaping **Häftlinge der zweithöchsten Gefährlichkeitsstufe; Schedule B** = schedule to the Finance Acts under which tax is charged on income from woodlands **Einkommenssteuergruppe B; Table B** = model memorandum of association of a limited company set out in the Companies Act, 1985 **Mustersatzung einer AG; "B" shares** = ordinary shares with special voting rights **Aktien mit besonderem Stimmrecht**

back
1 *noun* opposite side to the front **Rückseite;** *the conditions of sale are printed on the back of the invoice; please endorse the cheque on the back*
2 *adjective* referring to the past **zurück, Rück-; back interest** = interest not yet paid **Zinsrückstand; back rent** = rent owed **Mietrückstand; back taxes** = taxes which have not been paid **Steuerrückstand; back wages** *or* **back pay** = wages which are owed to a worker **Lohnrückstand**
3 *adverb* as things were before **zurück;** *he will pay back the money in monthly instalments; the store sent back the cheque because the date was wrong; he went back on his promise not to see the girl*
4 *verb*
(a) to back someone = to help someone financially **jdn (finanziell) unterstützen**
(b) to back a bill = (i) to sign a bill promising to pay it if the person it is addressed to is not able to do so; (ii) to support a Bill in Parliament **(i) (als Dritter)**

einen Wechsel unterzeichnen; (ii) einen Gesetzesentwurf unterstützen

◊ **backdate** *verb* to put an earlier date on a cheque *or* an invoice **zurückdatieren;** *backdate your invoice to April 1st; the pay increase is backdated to January 1st*

◊ **backer** *noun* backer of a bill = person who backs a bill **Wechselgarant**

◊ **background** *noun*
(a) past work *or* experience *or* family connections **Werdegang; Herkunft; Verhältnisse;** *the accused is from a good background; can you tell us something of the girl's family background?*
(b) past details **Hintergründe, Hintergrund, Zusammenhänge;** *he explained the background to the claim; the court asked for details of the background to the case; I know the contractual situation as it stands now, but can you fill in the background details?*

◊ **backsheet** *noun* last sheet of paper in a legal document which, when folded, becomes the outside sheet and carries the endorsement

bad *adjective* not good **schlecht; bad debt** = debt which will never be paid **uneinbringliche Forderung, nicht einziehbare Außenstände; in bad faith** = dishonestly; *(Zivilrecht)* **bösgläubig**

bail
1 *noun* releasing an arrested person from custody after payment has been made to a court as guarantee that the person will return to face trial **Kaution; Bürgschaft;** *to stand bail of £3,000 for someone; he was granted bail on his own recognizance of £1,000; the police opposed bail on the grounds that the accused might try to leave the country;* **police bail** = bail granted by the police **gegen Sicherheitsleistung von der Polizei gewährte Haftverschonung; he was remanded on bail of £3,000** = he was released on payment of £3,000 as a guarantee that he would return to the court to face trial **er wurde gegen £3.000 Kaution freigelassen; to jump bail** = not to appear in court after having been released on bail **die Kaution (durch Nichterscheinen) verfallen lassen; bail bond** = signed document which is given to the court as security for payment of a judgment; *(GB)* **Kautionsurkunde;** (NOTE: no plural)
2 *verb* to bail someone out = to pay a debt on behalf of someone **jdm aus (finanziellen) Schwierigkeiten helfen;** *she paid £3,000 to bail him out*

◊ **bailee** *noun* person who receives property by way of bailment **Verwahrer; Treuhänder**

◊ **bailment** *noun* transfer of goods by someone (the bailor) to someone (the bailee) who then holds them until they have to be returned to the bailor (as when leaving a coat in a cloakroom *or* at the cleaner's) **Hinterlegung; Besitzübertragung**

◊ **bailor** *noun* person who transfers property by way of bailment **Hinterleger; Übergeber**

Bailey *see* OLD BAILEY

bailiff *noun*
(a) *GB* person employed by the court, whose responsibility is to see that documents (such as summonses) are served, and that court orders are obeyed **Gerichtsdiener; Gerichtsvollzieher;** *the court ordered the bailiffs to seize his property because he had not paid his fine*
(b) *US* deputy to a sheriff **Stellvertreter des Sheriffs**

balance
1 *noun*
(a) amount in an account which makes the total debits and credits equal **Saldo; credit balance** = balance in an account showing that more money has been received than is owed **Kredit-, Aktivsaldo; debit balance** = balance in an account showing that more money is owed than has been received **Sollsaldo**
(b) rest of an amount owed **Restbetrag, Differenz;** *you can pay £100 deposit and the balance within sixty days*
(c) bank balance = state of an account at a bank at a particular time **Kontostand**
(d) balance of mind = good mental state **psychisches Gleichgewicht; disturbed balance of mind** = state of mind when someone is temporarily incapable of rational action (as because of illness *or* depression) **gestörtes psychisches Gleichgewicht;** *the verdict of the coroner's court was suicide while the balance of mind was disturbed*
2 *verb*
(a) to calculate the amount needed to make the two sides of an account equal **saldieren;** *I have finished balancing the accounts for March*
(b) to plan a budget so that expenditure and income are equal **ausgleichen**

◊ **balance sheet** *noun* statement of the financial position of a company at a particular time, such as the end of the financial year or the end of a quarter **Bilanz;** *the company balance sheet for 1984 shows a substantial loss; the accountant has prepared the balance sheet for the first half-year*

ballot
1 *noun*
(a) election where people vote for someone

by marking a cross on a paper with a list of names **(geheime) Wahl; ballot paper** = paper on which the voter marks a cross to show for whom he wants to vote **Wahl-, Stimmzettel; ballot box** = sealed box into which ballot papers are put **Wahlurne; postal ballot** = election where the voters send their ballot papers by post **Briefwahl; secret ballot** = election where the voters vote in secret **geheime Wahl**
(b) selecting by taking papers out of a box **Losverfahren;** *the share issue was oversubscribed, so there was a ballot for the shares*
2 *verb* to take a vote by ballot **abstimmen, eine (geheime) Wahl abhalten;** *the union is balloting for the post of president*

◊ **ballot-rigging** *noun* illegal arranging of the votes in a ballot, so that a particular candidate *or* party wins **Manipulation der Wahlresultate**

ban

1 *noun* order which forbids someone from doing something *or* which makes an act against the law **Verbot;** *a government ban on the sale of weapons; a ban on the copying of computer software;* **to impose a ban on smoking** = to make an order which forbids smoking **Rauchverbot erlassen; to lift the ban on smoking** = to allow people to smoke **das Rauchverbot aufheben**
2 *verb* to forbid something *or* to make something illegal **verbieten, mit einem Verbot belegen;** *the government has banned the sale of alcohol; the sale of pirated records has been banned*
NOTE: **banning - banned**

bandit *noun* person who robs people in lonely country areas **Bandit, Räuber;** *after the coup groups of bandits came down from the mountains to attack police stations*

◊ **banditry** *noun* act of robbing people **Banditentum**
NOTE: no plural

banish *verb* to send (someone) to live a long distance away (usually out of the country, or to a distant part of the country) as a punishment **verbannen;** *he was banished for ten years*

◊ **banishment** *noun* being banished **Verbannung**
NOTE: no plural

bank

1 *noun* business which holds money for its clients, which lends money at interest, and trades generally in money **Bank; central bank** = main government-controlled bank

in a country, which controls the financial affairs of the country by fixing main interest rates, issuing currency and controlling the foreign exchange rate **Zentral-, Notenbank; clearing bank** = bank which clears cheques by transferring money from the payer's account to another account; *GB* **Clearing-Bank**
2 *verb* to deposit money into a bank or to have an account with a bank **bei einer Bank einzahlen; ein Konto bei einer Bank haben**

◊ **bankable** *adjective* (paper) which a bank will accept as security for a loan **bankfähig**

◊ **bank account** *noun* account which a customer has with a bank, where the customer can deposit and withdraw money **Bankkonto**

◊ **bank draft** *noun* cheque payable by a bank **Bankwechsel; Banktratte**

◊ **banker** *noun* person who carries on the business of a bank **Bankier, Banker; banker's draft** = cheque payable by a bank **Bankwechsel; Banktratte**

◊ **bank holiday** *noun* a weekday which is a public holiday when the banks are closed **Feiertag;** *Easter Monday is a bank holiday*

◊ **bank note** *or* **banknote** *noun* piece of printed paper money **Banknote, Schein**
NOTE: US English is **bill**

◊ **bank statement** *noun* document showing payments into and out of a bank account **Kontoauszug**

bankrupt

1 *noun* (person) who has been declared by a court not to be capable of paying his debts and whose affairs are put into the hands of a trustee **Konkursschuldner;** *he was adjudicated or declared bankrupt; a bankrupt property developer; he went bankrupt after two years in business*
2 *adjective* not capable of paying debts **bankrott, insolvent; certificated bankrupt** = bankrupt who has been discharged from bankruptcy with a certificate to show he was not at fault **rehabilitierter Konkursschuldner; discharged bankrupt** = person who has been released from being bankrupt **entlasteter Konkursschuldner; undischarged bankrupt** = person who has been declared bankrupt and has not been released from that state **nicht entlasteter Konkursschuldner**
2 *verb* to make someone become bankrupt **ruinieren, in den Konkurs treiben;** *the recession bankrupted my father*

COMMENT: a bankrupt cannot serve as a Member of Parliament, a Justice of the Peace, a director of a limited company, and cannot sign a contract or borrow money

◊ **bankruptcy** *noun* state of being bankrupt **Bankrott, Konkurs;** *the recession has caused thousands of bankruptcies;* **bankruptcy notice** = notice warning someone that he faces bankruptcy if he fails to pay money which he owes **Konkursanzeige; bankruptcy petition** = petition to the Court asking for an order making someone bankrupt **Konkursantrag; bankruptcy proceedings** = court case to make someone bankrupt **Konkursverfahren; adjudication of bankruptcy** *or* **declaration of bankruptcy** = legal order making someone bankrupt **Konkurseröffnungsbeschluß; criminal bankruptcy** = bankruptcy of a criminal in the Crown Court as a result of crimes of which he has been convicted **betrügerischer Bankrott/Konkurs; discharge in bankruptcy** = being released from bankruptcy **Entlastung des Konkursschuldners; to file a petition in bankruptcy** = to apply to the Court to be made bankrupt *or* to ask for someone else to be made bankrupt **den Konkurs anmelden, Antrag auf Konkurseröffnung stellen**

◊ **Bankruptcy Court** *noun* court which deals with bankruptcies **Konkursgericht**

banns *plural noun* declaration in church that a couple intend to get married **Aufgebot;** *to publish the banns of marriage between Anne Smith and John Jones*

bar
1 *noun*
(a) place where you can buy and drink alcohol **Lokal, Bar;** *the solicitors for the plaintiffs met in the bar of the hotel*
(b) snack bar = small restaurant where you can get simple meals **Imbiß-Stube**
(c) thing which stops you doing something **Hindernis, Hemmnis;** *government legislation is a bar to foreign trade*
(d) the Bar = (i) the profession of barrister; (ii) all barristers *or* lawyers **(i) Anwaltsberuf (vor Gericht); (ii) Anwaltschaft; to be called to the bar** = to pass examinations and fulfil certain requirements to become a barrister **als Anwalt (vor Gericht) zugelassen werden; the Bar Council** = the ruling body of English and Welsh barristers **Anwaltskammer; the American Bar Association** = the ruling body of American lawyers **US-Bundesanwaltskammer**
(e) rails in a court, behind which the lawyers and public have to stand or sit **Gerichtsschranke; prisoner at the bar** = prisoner being tried in court *or* the accused **Angeklagter**
2 *verb* to forbid something *or* to make something illegal **ausschließen; verbieten, untersagen;** *he was barred from attending the meeting; the police commissioner barred the use of firearms*

barely *adverb* almost not **kaum;** *there is barely enough money left to pay the staff; she barely had time to call her lawyer*

bargain
1 *noun*
(a) agreement between two parties (such as when one sells and the other buys something) **Handel, Geschäft**
(b) thing which is cheaper than usual **Gelegenheitskauf, Schnäppchen; bargain hunter** = person who looks for cheap deals **jd, der auf Sonderangebote aus ist**
(c) sale of one lot of shares on the Stock Exchange **Börsengeschäft, Abschluß; bargains done** = number of deals made on the Stock Exchange during a day **Anzahl der Abschlüsse/Börsengeschäfte**
2 *verb* to discuss a price for something **(aus)handeln;** *you will have to bargain with the dealer if you want a discount; they spent two hours bargaining about or over the discount*

◊ **bargaining** *noun* act of discussing a price, usually wage increases for workers **Handeln, Aushandeln; (free) collective bargaining** = negotiations between employers and workers' representatives over wages and conditions **(autonome) Tarifverhandlungen; bargaining power** = strength of one person or group when discussing prices *or* wage settlements **Verhandlungsstärke; bargaining position** = statement of position by one group during negotiations **Verhandlungsposition; plea bargaining** = arrangement where the accused pleads guilty to some charges and the prosecution drop other charges *or* ask for a lighter sentence **Absprache zwischen Anklage und Verteidigung (hinsichtlich der Beschränkung der Anklage auf einzelne Punkte oder des Strafmaßes)**

baron *noun (slang)* prisoner who has power over other prisoners because he sells tobacco and runs other rackets in a prison **Pate**

barrier *noun* thing which stops someone from doing something, especially sending goods from one place to another **Barriere, Sperre, Schranke; customs barriers** *or* **tariff barriers** = customs duty intended to make trade more difficult **Zollschranken; to impose trade barriers on certain goods** = to restrict the import of certain goods by charging high duty **bestimmte Güter mit Handelsschranken belegen; to lift trade barriers from imports** = to remove restrictions on imports **Handelsschranken für Importe aufheben**

barrister *noun* lawyer (especially in England) who can plead *or* argue a case in one of the higher courts **Rechtsanwalt, Barrister**

COMMENT: in England and Wales, a barrister is a member of one of the Inns of Court; he has passed examinations and spent one year in pupillage before being called to the bar. Barristers have right of audience in all courts in England and Wales. Note also that barristers are instructed only by solicitors and never by members of the public. A barrister or a group of barristers is referred to as "counsel"

base
1 *noun*
(a) lowest *or* first position **Basis, Ausgangspunkt, Grundlage; base year =** first year of an index, against which later years' changes are measured **Basisjahr**
(b) place where a company has its main office or factory *or* place where a businessman has his office **Sitz, Standort;** *the company has its base in London and branches in all European countries; he has an office in Madrid which he uses as a base while he is travelling in Southern Europe*
2 *verb*
(a) to start to calculate *or* to negotiate from a position **basieren, gründen;** *we based our calculations on last year's turnover;* **based on** = calculating from **basieren auf, auf der Grundlage von**
(b) to set up a company *or* a person in a place **stationieren; a London-based salesman ein Vertreter mit Sitz in London;** *the European manager is based in our London office; our foreign branch is based in the Bahamas*

basic
1 *adjective*
(a) normal **Grund-, Basis-; eigentlich; basic pay** *or* **basic salary** *or* **basic wage** = normal salary without extra payments **Ecklohn; Grundgehalt; Grundlohn; basic rate tax =** lowest rate of income tax **niedrigster Einkommensteuersatz**
(b) most important **wesentlich, hauptsächlich, Haupt-; basic commodities =** ordinary farm produce, produced in large quantities (such as corn, rice, sugar) **Grundstoffe**
(c) simple *or* from which everything starts **Grund-, elementar;** *he has a basic knowledge of the market; to work at the cash desk, you need a basic qualification in maths*
◊ **basics** *plural noun* simple and important facts **Grundlagen,**

Grundsachverhalt; to get back to basics = to start discussing the basic facts again **zum Kern der Sache/zu den Grundlagen zurückkommen**
◊ **basically** *adverb* seen from the point from which everything starts **im Grunde**
◊ **BASIC** *noun* = BEGINNER'S ALL-PURPOSE SYMBOLIC INSTRUCTION CODE simple language for writing computer programs **BASIC**

basis *noun*
(a) point *or* number from which calculations are made **Grundlage, Basis;** *we have calculated the turnover on the basis of a 6% price increase*
(b) general terms of agreement *or* general principles on which something is decided **Basis, Grundlage; on a short-term** *or* **long-term basis =** for a short *or* long period **kurzfristig; langfristig;** *he has been appointed on a short-term basis; we have three people working on a freelance basis*

bastard *noun* illegitimate child *or* child born to an unmarried mother **uneheliches Kind**

batter *verb* to hit someone *or* something hard **schlagen, prügeln;** *the dead man had been battered to death with a hammer; police were battering on the door of the flat;* **battered child** *or* **battered wife =** child who is frequently beaten by one of its parents *or* wife who is frequently beaten by her husband **mißhandeltes Kind; mißhandelte Ehefrau**
◊ **battery** *noun* crime *or* tort of using force against another person **Körperverletzung; Mißhandlung; tätlicher Angriff**
NOTE: no plural *compare* ASSAULT

battle *noun* fight **Kampf; courtroom battles =** arguments between lawyers in court **Auseinandersetzungen zwischen Anwälten im Gerichtssaal**

beak *noun (slang)* magistrate **Kadi**

bear *verb*
(a) to pay (costs) **tragen;** *the company bore the legal costs of both parties*
(b) **to bear on** *or* **to have a bearing on =** to refer to *or* to have an effect on **betreffen, sich auswirken aus;** *the decision of the court bears on or has a bearing on future cases where immigration procedures are disputed*
NOTE: **bearing - bore - borne**
◊ **bearer** *noun* person who holds a cheque *or* certificate **Inhaber/-in, Überbringer/-in; the cheque is payable to bearer =** is paid to the person who holds it, not to any particular

name written on it **der Scheck ist zahlbar an den Überbringer/Inhaber**
◊ **bearer bond** *noun* bond which is payable to the bearer and does not have a name written on it **Inhaberschuldverschreibung**
◊ **bearer cheque** *noun* cheque which entitles the person who has it to be paid **Überbringer-, Inhaberscheck**

beat
1 *noun* area which a policeman patrols regularly **Revier; the constable on the beat** = the ordinary policeman on foot patrol **der Streifenpolizist**
2 *verb*
(a) to hit **schlagen;** *the prisoners were beaten with sticks; the warders beat the prisoner to make him confess*
(b) to win in a fight against someone **schlagen;** *they have beaten their competitors into second place in the computer market*
(c) to beat a ban = to do something which is going to be forbidden by doing it rapidly before the ban is enforced **ein Verbot umgehen**
NOTE: **beating - beat - has beaten**

beforehand *adverb* in advance **im voraus;** *the terms of the payment will be agreed beforehand*

begin *verb* to start **beginnen, anfangen;** *the case began with the reading of the indictment; the auditors' report began with a description of the general principles adopted*
NOTE: **beginning - began - begun**

behalf *noun* **on behalf of** = acting for (someone *or* a company) **für; in Namen von; im Auftrag von;** *I am writing on behalf of the minority shareholders; she is acting on my behalf; solicitors acting on behalf of the American company*

behead *verb* to cut off someone's head **enthaupten, köpfen;** *the accused was found guilty of treason and beheaded*

believe *verb* to think that something is true **glauben;** *we believe he has offered to buy 25% of the shares; the chairman is believed to be in South America on business*

belli *see* CASUS BELLI

bellman *noun (slang)* criminal who specializes in stopping alarm signals **Alarmanlagenspezialist**

belong *verb*

(a) to belong to = to be the property of **gehören zu;** *the company belongs to an old American banking family; the patent belongs to the inventor's son*
(b) to belong with = to be part of (a group) **gehören zu;** *those documents belong with the sales reports*

bench *noun* place where judges *or* magistrates sit in court **Richterstuhl, Richterbank; bench of magistrates** = group of magistrates in an area **Richterschaft; he is on the bench** = he is a magistrate **er ist Richter; bench warrant** = warrant issued by a court for the arrest of an accused person who has not appeared to answer charges **(richterlicher) Haftbefehl; Queen's Bench Division** = one of the main divisions of the High Court **Abteilung des High Court; Masters of the Bench** = senior members of an Inn of Court **Ältere Mitglieder der Rechtsanwaltskammer (in London)**
◊ **Bencher** *noun* one of the senior members of an Inn of Court **Vorsitzender Richter**

benefactor *noun* person who gives property or money to others, especially in a will **Wohltäter, Gönner**
◊ **benefactress** *noun* woman who leaves property or money to others, especially in her will **Wohltäterin, Gönnerin**

Nutzungsrechte

beneficial *adjective* **beneficial interest** = interest of the beneficiary of a property *or* shares *or* trust, which allows someone to occupy or receive rent from a property, while the property is owned by a trustee **Nießbrauch; beneficial occupier** = person who occupies a property but does not own it **Nießbrauchberechtigter; beneficial owner** = true *or* ultimate owner (whose interest may be concealed by a nominee) **wirtschaftlicher Eigentümer; beneficial use** = right to use *or* occupy *or* receive rent from a property which is owned by a trustee **unbeschränktes Nutzungsrecht**
◊ **beneficiary** *noun*
(a) person who is left property in a will **Begünstigter, Erbe/Erbin;** *the main beneficiaries of the will are the deceased's family*
(b) person whose property is administered by a trustee **Nutznießer/-in; Berechtigter**

COMMENT: in a trust, the trustee is the legal owner of the property, while the beneficiary is the equitable owner who receives the real benefit of the trust

benefit
1 *noun*
(a) money *or* advantage gained from

something **Nutzen; Vorteil;** *the estate was left to the benefit of the owner's grandsons*
(b) payments which are made to someone under a national or private insurance scheme **Leistung; Beihilfe;** *she receives £20 a week as unemployment benefit; the sickness benefit is paid monthly; the insurance office sends out benefit cheques each week;* **death benefit** = money paid to the family of someone who dies in an accident at work **Sterbegeld**
2 *verb* **to benefit from** *or* **by something** = to be improved by something *or* to gain more money because of something **profitieren von, den Nutzen ziehen aus**

bent *adjective slang* corrupt *or* stolen *or* illegal **korrupt; krumm; bent copper** = corrupt policeman **korrupter Polizist; bent job** = illegal deal **krummes Ding**

bequeath *verb* to leave (property, but not freehold land) to someone in a will **vermachen, vererben;** *he bequeathed his shares to his daughter*

◊ **bequest** *noun* giving of property, money, etc. (but not freehold land) to someone in a will **Vermächtnis, testamentarische Zuwendung;** *he made several bequests to his staff*

> COMMENT: freehold land given in a will is a **devise**

BES = BUSINESS EXPANSION SCHEME

best
1 *adjective* very good **bester; best evidence** = original document used as evidence (as opposed to a copy) **primäres Beweismaterial**
2 *noun* very good effort **der/die/das beste;** *the lawyers did their best, but the jury was not convinced by the evidence*

bet
1 *noun* amount deposited when you risk money on the result of a race *or* of a game **Wetteinsatz, Wette**
2 *verb* to risk money on the result of something **wetten;** *he bet £100 on the result of the election; I bet you £25 the accused will get off with a fine;* **betting duty** *or* **tax** = tax levied on betting on horses, dogs, etc. **Wettsteuer**

betray *verb* to give away a secret **verraten; preisgeben;** *he betrayed the secret to the enemy;* **to betray one's country** *or* **a friend** = to give away one's country's *or* friend's secrets to an enemy **sein Vaterland od einen Freund verraten**

◊ **betrayal** *noun* **betrayal of trust** = acting against something with which you have been entrusted **Vertrauensbruch**

beware *verb* to be careful **sich vorsehen; beware of imitations** = be careful not to buy cheap low-quality items which are made to look like more expensive items **vor Imitationen wird gewarnt**

beyond *preposition* further than **über... hinaus; außer(halb); it is beyond question that** = it is certain that **es steht außer Frage, daß; beyond reasonable doubt** = almost certain proof needed to convict a person in a criminal case **unzweifelhaft**

bi- *prefix* twice **Bi-, bi-; bi-monthly** = (i) twice a month; (ii) every two months *or* six times a year **(i) zweimal monatlich; (ii) jeden zweiten Monat, sechsmal jährlich; bi-annually** = twice a year **zweimal jährlich, halbjährlich**

◊ **bicameralism** *noun* system of government where there are two houses of parliament, one senior to the other **Zweikammersystem**

bias *noun* leaning towards *or* favouring one party in a case **Parteilichkeit, Befangenheit; likelihood of bias** = possibility that bias will occur because of a connection between a member of the court and a party in the case **Besorgnis der Befangenheit**

◊ **biased** *adjective* (judge *or* juror) who favours one of the parties in a case **parteiisch, befangen**

bid
1 *noun*
(a) offer to buy something at a certain price (especially at an auction) **Gebot, Angebot; to make a bid for something** = to offer to buy something **ein Angebot/Gebot für etwas machen; to put in a bid for something** *or* **to enter a bid for something** = to offer to buy something **ein Angebot abgeben/machen**
(b) offer to do some work at a certain price **Angebot;** *he made the lowest bid for the job; US* offer to sell something at a certain price **Angebot;** *they asked for bids for the supply of spare parts*
(c) takeover bid = offer to buy all or a majority of shares in a company so as to control it **Übernahmeangebot; to make a takeover bid for a company** = to offer to buy a majority of the shares in a company **ein Übernahmeangebot für ein Unternehmen machen; to withdraw a takeover bid** = to say that you no longer offer to buy the majority of the shares in a company **ein Übernahmeangebot zurückziehen**

2 *verb (at an auction)* **to bid for something =** to offer to buy something **für/auf etwas bieten; he bid £1,000 for the jewels =** he offered to pay £1,000 for the jewels **er bot £1000 für den Schmuck**
NOTE: **bidding - bid**

◊ **bidder** *noun* person who makes a bid **Bieter, Bietender; the lot was sold to the highest bidder =** to the person who has offered the most money **das Los ging an den Meistbietenden**

bigamy *noun* notifiable offence of going through a ceremony of marriage to someone when you are still married to someone else **Bigamie;** *see also* MONOGAMY, POLYGAMY
NOTE: no plural

◊ **bigamist** *noun* person who is married to two people at the same time **Bigamist**

◊ **bigamous** *adjective* referring to bigamy **bigamistisch;** *they went through a bigamous marriage ceremony*

bilateral *adjective* (agreement) between two parties *or* countries **bilateral, zweiseitig;** *the minister signed a bilateral trade agreement*

bilking *noun* offence of removing goods without paying for them *or* of refusing to pay a bill **Prellerei**

bill
1 *noun*
(a) written list of charges to be paid **Rechnung;** *the salesman wrote out the bill; does the bill include VAT? the bill is made out to Smith Ltd; the builder sent in his bill; he left the country without paying his bills;* **to foot the bill =** to pay the costs **die Rechnung begleichen/bezahlen**
(b) list of charges in a restaurant **Rechnung;** *can I have the bill please? the bill comes to £20 including service; does the bill include service? the waiter has added 10% to the bill for service*
(c) written paper promising to pay money **Wechsel; Tratte; bill of exchange =** document which orders one person to pay another person a sum of money **Wechsel; Tratte**
(d) bill of health = document given to the master of a ship showing that the ship is free of disease **Quarantäneattest; bill of indictment =** (i) draft of an indictment which is examined by the court, and when signed becomes an indictment; (ii); *US* list of charges given to a grand jury, asking them to indict the accused **(i) (dem Gericht vorgelegte) Anklageschrift; (ii) (der Grand Jury vorgelegte) Anklageschrift; bill of lading =** list

of goods being shipped, which the shipper gives to the person sending the goods to show that the goods have been loaded **Konnossement**
(e) *US* piece of paper money **Banknote, Schein**
(f) bill of sale = (i) document which the seller gives to the buyer to show that the sale has taken place; (ii) document given to a lender by a borrower to show that the lender owns the property as security for the loan **Kaufvertrag; (ii) Pfandverschreibung**
(g) draft of a new law which will be discussed in Parliament **Gesetzesvorlage, Gesetzesentwurf;** *the house is discussing the Noise Prevention Bill; the Finance Bill had its second reading yesterday;* **Private Member's Bill =** Bill which is drafted and proposed by an ordinary Member of Parliament, not by a government minister **Gesetzesvorlage eines Abgeordneten; Private Bill =** Bill relating to a particular person *or* corporation *or* institution **Gesetzesvorlage für ein Einzelfallgesetz; Public Bill =** ordinary Bill relating to a matter applying to the public in general, introduced by a government minister **Gesetzesvorlage für ein allgemeines Gesetz**
(h) *US* **Bill of Rights =** those sections (the first ten amendments) of the constitution of the United States which refer to the rights and privileges of the individual **Zusatzklauseln 1-10 zu den Grundrechten**
2 *verb* to present a bill to someone so that it can be paid **in Rechnung stellen;** *the builders billed him for the repairs to his neighbour's house*

COMMENT: a Bill passes through the following stages in Parliament: First Reading, Second Reading, Committee Stage, Report Stage and Third Reading. The Bill goes through these stages first in the House of Commons and then in the House of Lords. When all the stages have been passed the Bill is given the Royal Assent and becomes law as an Act of Parliament. In the USA, a Bill is introduced either in the House or in the Senate, passes through **Committee Stage** with public hearings, then to general debate in the full House. The Bill is debated section by section in **Second Reading** and after being passed by both House and Senate is engrossed and sent to the President as a joint resolution for signature (or veto)

bind *verb* to tie *or* to attach (someone) so that he has to do something **binden, verpflichten;** *the company is bound by its articles of association; he does not consider himself bound by the agreement which was signed by his predecessor; High Court judges are bound by the decisions of the House of Lords*

◊ **binder** *noun*
(a) stiff cardboard cover for papers **Hefter, Mappe; ring binder** = cover with rings in it which fit into special holes made in sheets of paper **Ringbuch**
(b) *US* temporary agreement for insurance sent before the insurance policy is issued **vorläufige Deckungszusage**
NOTE: the British English for this is **cover note**

◊ **binding** *adjective* which legally forces someone to do something **bindend, verbindlich;** *this document is legally binding or it is a legally binding document;* **the agreement is binding on all parties** = all parties signing it must do what is agreed **die Vereinbarung ist für alle Parteien verbindlich/bindend; binding precedent** = decision of a higher court which has to be followed by a judge in a lower court **bindender Präzedenzfall**

◊ **bind over** *verb*
(a) *GB* to make someone promise to behave well and not commit another offence *or* to return to court at a later date to face charges **Verwarnen mit Strafvorbehalt;** *he was bound over (to keep the peace or to be of good behaviour) for six months*
(b) *US* to order a defendant to be kept in custody while a criminal case is being prepared **Untersuchungshaft anordnen**

◊ **bind-over order** *noun* court order which binds someone over **gerichtliche Verwarnung mit Strafvorbehalt;** *the applicant sought judicial review to quash the bind-over order*

birth *noun* being born **Geburt; he is British by birth** = he has British nationality because his parents are British **er ist Brite von Geburt, er ist gebürtiger Brite; date and place of birth** = day of the year when someone was born and the town where he was born **Geburtstag und Geburtsort; birth certificate** = document giving details of a person's date and place of birth **Geburtsurkunde; concealment of birth** = offence of hiding the fact that a child has been born **Personenstandsunterdrückung, Verletzung der Anzeigepflicht (der Geburt eines Kindes)**

black
1 *adjective*
(a) **black market** = buying and selling goods in a way which is not allowed by law **Schwarzmarkt;** *there is a lucrative black market in spare parts for cars; you can buy gold coins on the black market; they lived well on black-market goods;* **to pay black market prices** = to pay high prices to get items which are not easily available **Schwarzmarktpreise bezahlen; black marketeer** = person who sells goods on the black market **Schwarzmarkthändler**

(b) **black economy** = work which is paid for in cash *or* goods, and therefore not declared to the tax authorities **Schattenwirtschaft**
2 *verb* to forbid trading in certain goods or with certain suppliers **boykottieren;** *three firms were blacked by the government; the union has blacked a shipping firm*

◊ **blackleg** *noun* worker who goes on working when there is a strike **Streikbrecher**

◊ **black list** *noun* list of goods *or* people *or* companies which have been blacked **schwarze Liste**

◊ **blacklist** *verb* to put goods *or* people *or* a company on a black list **auf die schwarze Liste setzen;** *his firm was blacklisted by the government*

◊ **Black Maria** *noun* (*informal*) van used by the police to take prisoners from one place to another **grüne Minna**

blackmail
1 *noun* notifiable offence of getting money from someone, by threatening to make public facts about him which he does not want revealed *or* by threatening violence **Erpressung;** *he was charged with blackmail; they got £25,000 from the managing director by blackmail; she was sent to prison for blackmail*
NOTE: no plural
2 *verb* to threaten someone that you will make public facts about him *or* to do violence to him unless he pays you money **erpressen;** *he was blackmailed by his former secretary*

◊ **blackmailer** *noun* person who blackmails someone **Erpresser/-in**

blag *noun* (*slang*) robbery by an armed gang **bewaffneter Raubüberfall**

blame
1 *noun* saying that someone has done something wrong *or* that someone is responsible **Schuld;** *the sales staff got the blame for the poor sales figures*
2 *verb* to say that someone has done something wrong *or* is responsible for a mistake **beschuldigen, verantwortlich machen;** *the magistrate blamed the social services for not reporting the case quickly; the lack of fire equipment was blamed by the coroner for the deaths*

◊ **blameworthy** *adjective* which is likely to attract blame *or* to be blamed **schuldig; verantwortlich**

blanche *see* CARTE

blank
1 *adjective* with nothing written **leer,**

unausgefüllt; **a blank cheque** = a cheque with the amount of money and the payee left blank, but signed by the drawer **ein Blankoscheck**
2 *noun* space on a form which has to be completed **Lücke**

blanket *noun* thick woollen cover for a bed **Decke; blanket agreement** = agreement which covers many items **Gesamtvereinbarung; blanket insurance policy** = policy covering several items **Kombination mehrerer Versicherungsarten; blanket refusal** = refusal to accept many different items **allgemeine Ablehnung**

blasphemy *noun* formerly the crime of ridiculing *or* denying God *or* the Christian religion in a scandalous way **Blasphemie, Gotteslästerung**
◊ **blaspheme** *verb* to ridicule *or* deny God *or* the Christian religion **lästern; Gott lästern**

block
1 *noun*
(a) series of items grouped together **Paket;** *he bought a block of 6,000 shares;* **block booking** = booking of several seats *or* rooms at the same time **Gruppenbuchung;** *the company has a block booking for twenty seats on the plane or for ten rooms at the hotel;* **block vote** = casting of a large number of votes at the same time (such as of trade union members) by a person who has been delegated by the holders of the votes to vote for them in this way **einheitliches Votum; Sammelstimme**
(b) series of buildings forming a square with streets on all sides **Häuserblock; a block of offices** *or* **an office block** = a large building which contains only offices **Bürohauskomplex**
(c) building in a prison **Block; H-block** = building in a prison built with a central section and two end wings, forming the shape of the letter H **H-Block, H-Trakt; hospital block** = section of a prison which contains the hospital **Krankenhaustrakt**
(d) block capitals *or* **block letters** = capital letters (as A,B,C) **Druck-, Blockschrift, Versalien;** *write your name and address in block letters*
2 *verb* to stop something taking place **blockieren, vereiteln;** *he used his casting vote to block the motion; the planning committee blocked the plan to build a motorway through the middle of the town;* **blocked currency** = currency which cannot be taken out of a country because of exchange controls **nicht frei konvertierbare und transferierbare Währung**

blockade

1 *noun* act of preventing goods *or* people going into or out of a place **Blockade;** *the government brought in goods by air to beat the blockade; the enemy lifted the blockade of the port for two months to let emergency supplies in*
2 *verb* to prevent goods *or* food *or* people going into or coming out of a place **eine Blockade verhängen; belagern;** *the town was blockaded by the enemy navy*

blood *noun* red liquid in the body **Blut; blood relationship** = relationship between people who have a common ancestor **Blutsverwandtschaft; blood sample** = small amount of blood taken from someone for a blood test (such as to establish the alcohol level in the blood) **Blutprobe; blood test** *or* **blood grouping test** = test to establish the paternity of a child **Blut(gruppen)untersuchung, Vaterschaftstest**

blotter *noun (US)* book in which arrests are recorded at a police station **Tagebuch**

blue bag *noun* blue bag in which a junior barrister carries his gown **Tasche des Barristers für seinen Talar;** *(GB) see also* RED BAG
◊ **Blue Book** *noun* official report of a Royal Commission
◊ **blue laws** *plural noun (US)* laws relating to what can *or* cannot be done on a Sunday **(puritanische) Sonntagsgesetze**

board
1 *noun* **board of directors** = group of directors elected by the shareholders to run a company **Board of Directors;** *entspricht* **Firmenvorstand, Aufsichtsrat (nach britischem Recht);** *the bank has two representatives on the board; he sits on the board as a representative of the bank; two directors were removed from the board at the AGM;* **board meeting** = meeting of the directors of a company; *entspricht* **Vorstands-, Aufsichtsratssitzung**
(b) group of people who run a trust *or* a society **Ausschuß; advisory board** = group of advisors **Beratungsgremium, Beirat; editorial board** = group of editors **Redaktion, Redaktionskomitee; parole board** = group of people who advise the Home Secretary if a prisoner should be released on parole before the end of his sentence **Ausschuß zur Gewährung der bedingten Haftentlassung; board of visitors** = group of people appointed by the Home Secretary to visit and inspect the conditions in prisons **Inspektionskomitee**

2 *verb* to go on to a ship *or* plane **an Bord gehen;** *(Zug)* **einsteigen;** *customs officials boarded the ship in the harbour*

◊ **boarding card** *or* **boarding pass** *noun* card given to passengers who have checked in for a flight *or* voyage to allow them to board the plane *or* ship **Bordkarte**

bobby *noun (informal) GB* policeman **Bobby**

bodily *adverb* to the body **körperlich; actual bodily harm (ABH)** = really hitting and hurting someone **Körperverletzung; grievous bodily harm (GBH)** = crime of causing serious injury to someone **schwere Körperverletzung**

bodyguard *noun* person who protects someone **Leibwächter;** *the minister was followed by his three bodyguards*

bona fides *or* **bona fide** *Latin phrase meaning* "good faith" *or* "in good faith" **in gutem Glauben;** *he acted bona fide; the respondent was not acting bona fides;* **a bona fide offer** = an offer which is made honestly *or* which can be trusted **ein Bona-fide Angebot**

bona vacantia *noun* property with no owner *or* which does not have an obvious owner and which usually passes to the Crown **"herrenlose" Sachen**

bond *noun*
(a) contract document promising to repay money borrowed by a company *or* by the government **Schuldverschreibung; Obligation;** *government bonds or treasury bonds*
(b) contract document promising to repay money borrowed by a person **Schuldschein; bearer bond** = bond which is payable to the bearer and does not have a name written on it **Inhaberschuldverschreibung; debenture bond** = certificate showing that a debenture has been issued **Schuldverschreibung, Obligation; mortgage bond** = certificate showing that a mortgage exists and that the property is security for it **Pfandbrief**
(c) signed legal document which binds one or more parties to do *or* not to do something **Ab-, Übereinkommen; bail bond** = signed document which is given to the court as security for payment of a judgment; *GB* **Kautionsurkunde; goods (held) in bond** = goods held by the customs until duty has been paid **Waren unter Zollverschluß; entry of goods under bond** = bringing goods into a country in bond **Einfuhr von Waren unter Zollverschluß; to take goods out of bond** = to pay duty on goods so that they can be

released by the customs **Waren aus dem Zollverschluß nehmen/verzollen**

◊ **bonded** *adjective* held in bond **unter Zollverschluß; bonded goods** = goods which are held by the customs under a bond until duty has been paid **Waren unter Zollverschluß; bonded warehouse** = warehouse where goods are stored in bond until duty is paid **Zollager**

◊ **bondholder** *noun* person who holds government bonds **Obligations-, Pfandbriefinhaber**

◊ **bondsman** *noun* person who has stood surety for another person **Bürge**

book
1 *noun*
(a) set of sheets of paper attached together **Buch; a company's books** = the financial records of a company **die Geschäftsbücher (einer Firma); book value** = value of a company's assets as shown in the company accounts **Buch-, Bilanzwert**
(b) phone book *or* **telephone book** = book which lists names of people or companies with their addresses and telephone numbers **Telefonbuch**
(c) to bring someone to book = to find a suspect and charge him with a crime **jdn zur Rechenschaft ziehen; jdn aufschreiben**
2 *verb*
(a) to order *or* to reserve something **bestellen; buchen; reservieren;** *to book a room in a hotel or a table at a restaurant or a ticket on a plane; I booked a table for 7.45; he booked a ticket through to Cairo;* **to book someone into a hotel** *or* **onto a flight** = to order a room *or* a plane ticket for someone **für jdn ein Zimmer od ein Flugticket buchen**
(b) *informal* to charge someone with a crime **aufschreiben; einen Strafzettel verpassen;** *he was booked for driving on the wrong side of the road*

◊ **booking** *noun* act of ordering a room *or* a seat **Bestellung; Buchung; Reservierung**

bootleg *adjective* illicit (alcohol, record or tape) **schwarz gebrannt; illegal**

◊ **bootlegger** *noun* person who makes *or* supplies illicit alcohol **Schwarzbrenner/-in; Schwarzhändler (mit Alkohol); Alkoholschmuggler**

◊ **bootlegging** *noun*
(a) making illicit alcohol **Schwarzbrennerei, Schwarzbrennen**
(b) making illegal records *or* tapes from live concerts **Aufnehmen von Raubdrucken**

borough *noun* town which has been incorporated **Stadtgemeinde; borough council** = representatives elected to run a borough **Stadtrat**

borrow *verb*
(a) to take money from someone for a time, possibly paying interest for it, and repaying it at the end of the period **leihen, borgen;** *he borrowed £1,000 from the bank; the company had to borrow heavily to repay its debts; they borrowed £25,000 against the security of the factory*
(b) *slang* to steal **ausborgen**
◊ **borrower** *noun* person who borrows **Entleiher/-in ; Kreditnehmer/-in;** *borrowers from the bank pay 12% interest*
◊ **borrowing** *noun*
(a) action of borrowing money **Leihen; Kreditaufnahme;** *the new factory was financed by bank borrowing;* **borrowing power** = amount of money which a company can borrow **Kreditfähigkeit**
(b) borrowings = money borrowed **aufgenommene Schulden; Fremdkapital;** *the company's borrowings have doubled;* **bank borrowings** = loans made by banks **Kreditvergaben**

borstal *noun* formerly a centre where a young offender was sent for training if he had committed a crime which would normally be punishable by a prison sentence **Jugendstraf-, Erziehungsanstalt**

boss *noun* head of a Mafia family *or* criminal gang **Boss**

bottleneck *noun* position when activity is slowed down because one section of the operation cannot cope with the amount of work **Engpaß;** *there are serious bottlenecks in the divorce courts*

bottomry *noun* mortgage of a ship *or* cargo **Schiffshypothek, Bodmerei; bottomry bond** = bond which secures a ship *or* cargo against a loan **Bodmereibrief**
NOTE: no plural

bounce *verb slang (of a cheque)* to be returned to the person who has tried to cash it, because there is not enough money in the payer's account to pay it **platzen;** *he paid for the car with a cheque that bounced*

bound *see* BIND, DUTY

boundary (line) *noun* line marking the edge of a piece of land owned by someone **Grenze;** *the boundary dispute dragged through the courts for years*
◊ **Boundary Commission** *noun* committee which examines the area and population of constituencies for the House of Commons and recommends changes to make each

Member of Parliament represent similar numbers of people **Grenzkommission**

bounty *noun* (i) government subsidy made to help an industry; (ii) payment made by government to someone who has saved lives *or* found treasure **(i) Subvention; (ii) Belohnung**

box *noun*
(a) container **Schachtel, Kasten;** *the goods were sent in thin cardboard boxes; the drugs were hidden in boxes of office stationery;* **envelopes come in boxes of two hundred** = packed two hundred to a box **Briefumschläge sind in Schachteln zu zweihundert erhältlich; box file** = file (for papers) made like a box **kastenförmiger Aktenordner**
(b) witness box = place in a courtroom where the witnesses give evidence **Zeugenstand;** (NOTE: American English is **witness stand**)
(c) box number = reference number used in a post office or an advertisement to avoid giving an address **Chiffre;** *(beim Postamt)* **Postfach;** *please reply to Box No. 209; our address is: P.O. Box 74209, Edinburgh*

boycott
1 *noun* refusal to buy *or* to deal in goods from a certain country *or* company, used as a punishment **Boykott;** *the union organized a boycott against or of imported cars*
2 *verb* to refuse to buy *or* to deal in goods from a certain country *or* company, as a punishment **boykottieren;** *the company's products have been boycotted by the main department stores; we are boycotting all imports from that country;* **the management has boycotted the meeting** = has refused to attend the meeting **das Management hat die Sitzung boykottiert**

bracelets *plural noun (slang)* handcuffs **Handschellen**

bracket
1 *noun* group of items *or* people of a certain type taken together **Gruppe, Klasse, Stufe; income bracket** *or* **tax bracket** = level of income where a certain percentage tax applies **Einkommensstufe; Steuerklasse**
2 *verb* **to bracket together** = to treat several items together in the same way **zusammenfassen**

branch
1 *noun*
(a) local office of a bank or large business; local shop of a large chain of shops **Filiale, Geschäfts-, Zweigstelle, Niederlassung;** *the*

bank or the store has branches in most towns in the south of the country; the insurance company has closed its branches in South America; he is the manager of our local branch of Lloyds bank; we have decided to open a branch office in Chicago; the manager of our branch in Lagos or of our Lagos branch;* **branch manager** = manager of a branch **Filial-, Geschäftsstellenleiter**
(b) part *or* separate section (of the law) **Rechtsgebiet;** *the Law of Contract and the Law of Tort are branches of civil law*
2 *verb* **to branch out** = to start a new (but usually related) type of business **in fremde/andere Branchen einsteigen;** *from dealing in stolen bicycles, the gang branched out into car theft*

brand

1 *noun* make of product, which can be recognized by a name *or* by a design **Marke**
2 *verb* to mark with a special mark **markieren; brandmarken**
◊ **branded** *adjective* **branded goods** = goods sold under brand names **Markenartikel**

breach *noun*

(a) failure to carry out the terms of an agreement **Verletzung, Verstoß; breach of duty** = failing to do something which was agreed **Pflichtverletzung; breach of contract** = failing to do something which is in a contract **Vertragsbruch; the company is in breach of contract** = the company has failed to carry out what was agreed in the contract **das Unternehmen ist vertragsbrüchig geworden; breach of promise** = formerly, complaint in court that someone had promised to marry the plaintiff and then had not done so **Bruch des Eheversprechens; breach of trust** = failure to act properly on the part of a trustee in regard to a trust **Verletzung von Treuhänderpflichten; breach of warranty** = supplying goods which do not meet the standards of the warranty applied to them **Garantieverletzung; Verletzung der Gewährleistungspflicht**
(b) failure to obey the law **Vergehen; Übertretung;** *the soldier was charged with a serious breach of discipline;* **breach of the peace** = creating a disturbance which is likely to annoy *or* frighten people **Störung der öffentlichen Sicherheit und Ordnung**

break

1 *noun* short space of time, when you can rest **Pause;** *the court adjourned for a ten-minute break*
2 *verb*
(a) to do something which is against the law **verletzen, brechen, übertreten;** *if you hit a policeman you will be breaking the law; he*

is breaking the law by selling goods on Sunday; the company broke section 26 of the Companies Act
(b) to fail to carry out the duties of a contract **nicht einhalten, brechen, verletzen;** *the company has broken the contract or the agreement;* **to break an engagement to do something** = not to do what has been agreed **eine Verpflichtung nicht einhalten**
(c) to cancel (a contract) **brechen; (auf)lösen;** *the company is hoping to be able to break the contract*
NOTE: **breaking - broke - broken**

◊ **breakages** *plural noun* breaking of items **Bruchschaden; Bruch;** *customers are expected to pay for breakages*

◊ **break down** *verb*
(a) to stop working because of mechanical failure **ausfallen;** *(Auto)* **stehenbleiben;** *the two-way radio has broken down; what do you do when your squad car breaks down?*
(b) to stop **scheitern;** *negotiations broke down after six hours; their marriage broke down and they separated*
(c) to show all the items in a total list **auschlüsseln, spezifizieren;** *we broke the crime figures down into crimes against the person and crimes against property; can you break down this invoice into spare parts and labour?*

◊ **breakdown** *noun*
(a) stopping work because of mechanical failure **Betriebsstörung, Ausfall;** *we cannot communicate with our squad car because of the breakdown of the radio link*
(b) stopping work *or* discussion **Scheitern;** *a breakdown in wage negotiations; she petitioned for divorce on account of the breakdown of their marriage;* **irretrievable breakdown of a marriage** = situation where the two spouses can no longer live together, where the marriage cannot be saved and therefore divorce proceedings can be started **endgültige Zerrüttung einer Ehe**
(c) showing details item by item **Aufschlüsselung;** *give me a breakdown of the latest clear-up figures*

◊ **break in** *verb* to go into a building by force in order to steal **einbrechen;** *burglars broke in through a window at the back of the house*

◊ **break-in** *noun (informal)* crime of breaking into a house **Einbruch;** *there have been three break-ins in our street in one week*

◊ **breaking and entering** *noun* crime of going into a building by force and stealing things **Einbruch;** *he was charged with breaking and entering; see also* HOUSEBREAKING

◊ **break into** *verb* to go into (a building) by force to steal things **einbrechen in;** *their* *house was broken into while they were on holiday; looters broke into the supermarket*

◇ **break off** *verb* to stop **abbrechen;** *we broke off the discussion at midnight; management broke off negotiations with the union*

◇ **break up** *verb*
(a) to split something large into small sections **aufteilen;** *the company was broken up and separate divisions sold off*
(b) to come to an end *or* to make something come to an end **sich auflösen;** *the meeting broke up at 12.30; the police broke up the protest meeting*

breath *noun* air which a person takes into his body to live **Atem; breath test** = test where a person's breath is sampled to establish the amount of alcohol he has drunk **(Atem-)Alkoholtest**

◇ **breathalyse** *verb* to test someone's breath using a breathalyser **einen Alkoholtest machen**

◇ **breathalyser** *noun* device for testing the amount of alcohol a person has drunk by testing his breath **Alcotest (zur Atemalkoholbestimmung)**

bribe
1 *noun* money offered corruptly to someone to get him to do something to help you **Bestechungsgeld;** *the police sergeant was dismissed for taking bribes*
2 *verb* to give someone money corruptly to get him to help you **bestechen;** *he bribed the police sergeant to get the charges dropped*

◇ **bribery** *noun* crime of paying someone money corruptly to get him to do something to help you **Bestechung;** *bribery in the security warehouse is impossible to stamp out*
NOTE: no plural

bridewell *noun (slang)* cells in a police station; house of correction for minor offenders **Zellen; Strafanstalt; Zuchthaus**

bridging loan *noun* short term loan to help someone buy a new house when he has not yet sold his old one **Überbrückungskredit**

bridleway *noun* path used by people on horseback **Reitweg**

brief
1 *noun*
(a) details of a client's case, prepared by his solicitor and given to the barrister who is going to argue the case in court **Informationen für den Prozeßanwalt**
(b) *slang* lawyer *or* barrister **Rechtsverdreher, Winkeladvokat, (abschätzig)**

2 *verb* to explain something to someone in detail **unterrichten, informieren;** *the superintendent briefed the press on the progress of the investigation;* **to brief a barrister** = to give a barrister all the details of the case which he will argue in court **einem Anwalt eine Darstellung des Sachverhalts geben**

◇ **briefcase** *noun* case with a handle for carrying papers and documents **Aktenkoffer;** *he put all the files into his briefcase*

◇ **briefing** *noun* telling someone details **Besprechung;** *all the detectives on the case attended a briefing given by the commander*

bring *verb* to come to a place with someone *or* something **bringen;** *he brought his documents with him; the solicitor brought his secretary to take notes of the meeting;* **to bring a lawsuit** *or* **proceedings against someone** = to sue someone **jdn verklagen, gegen jdn ein gerichtliches Verfahren einleiten**
NOTE: **bringing - brought**

◇ **bring forward** *verb* to make earlier **vorverlegen;** *to bring forward the date of repayment; the date of the hearing has been brought forward to March*

◇ **bring in** *verb* **to bring in a verdict of guilty** *or* **not guilty** = **jdn für schuldig od nicht schuldig erklären**

◇ **bring up** *verb* to refer to something for the first time **aufbringen, zur Sprache bringen;** *the chairman brought up the question of corruption in the police force*

broker *noun* person who buys *or* sells on behalf of others **Makler, Händler; insurance broker** = person who sells insurance to clients **Versicherungsvertreter**

brothel *noun* house where sexual intercourse is offered for money **Bordell**

budget *noun*
(a) plan of expected spending and income (usually for one year) **Budget, Etat; Haushaltsplan;** *to draw up a budget; we have agreed the budgets for next year*
(b) the Budget = the annual plan of taxes and government spending proposed by a finance minister **der Staatshaushalt;** *the minister put forward a budget aimed at slowing down the economy;* **to balance the budget** = to plan income and expenditure so that they balance **den Etat ausgleichen;** *the President is planning for a balanced budget*

◇ **budgetary** *adjective* referring to a budget **Finanz-, Budget-, Etat-, Haushalts-; budgetary policy** = policy of planning income and expenditure **Budgetpolitik; budgetary control** = keeping check on spending **Budgetkontrolle; budgetary requirements** = spending or income required to meet the expected budget **Budgetbedarf**

◊ **budgeting** *noun* preparing of budgets to help plan expenditure and income **Budgetierung, Finanzplanung; Kalkulation**

bug

1 *noun* small device which can record conversations secretly and send them to a secret radio receiver **Wanze;** *the cleaners planted a bug under the lawyer's desk* **2** *verb* to place a secret device in a place so that conversations can be heard and recorded secretly **verwanzen;** *the agents bugged the President's office;* **bugging device** = bug **Abhörgerät;** *police found a bugging device under the lawyer's desk*

buggery *noun* notifiable offence of sexual intercourse with animals *or* rectal intercourse with man or woman **Sodomie; Analverkehr**

building society *noun (GB)* financial institution which accepts and pays interest on deposits and lends money to people who are buying property **Bausparkasse**

bumping *noun (US)* situation were a senior employee takes the place of a junior (in a restaurant *or* in a job) **Verdrängung eines untergeordneten Angestellten vom Tisch im (Betriebs-)Restaurant; Personalpolitik nach dem LIFO-Prinzip**

bunco *noun (slang)* swindle *or* cheating someone out of money (usually at cards) **Trickbetrügerei, Betrug, Schwindel**

burden of proof *noun* duty to prove that something which has been alleged in court is right **Beweislast; to discharge a burden of proof** = to prove something which has been alleged in court **den Beweis antreten; the burden of proof is on the prosecution** = the prosecution must prove that what it alleges is true **die Anklage trägt die Beweisführungspflicht**

bureau *noun* office which specializes **Büro; computer bureau** = office which offers to do work on its computers for companies which do not own their own computers **Rechenzentrum; EDV-Servicebüro; employment bureau** = office which finds jobs for people **Stellenvermittlung; information bureau** = office which gives information **Information, Auskunft;** *US* **Federal Bureau of Investigation (FBI)** = American government office, a section of the Department of Justice, which investigates crimes against federal law and subversive acts in the USA **Bundeskriminalamt, FBI**

NOTE: the plural is **bureaux**

burglar *noun* person who steals (or tries to steal) goods from property *or* who enters property intending to commit a crime **Einbrecher/-in; burglar alarm** = bell which is set to ring when someone tries to break into a house *or* shop **Alarmanlage;** *as he put his hand through the window he set off the burglar alarm*

◊ **burglarize** *verb US informal* to steal things from (a building *or* a household) **einbrechen in; Einbruchsdiebstahl begehen**

◊ **burglary** *noun* crime of going into a building (usually by force) and stealing things **Einbruch; Einbruchsdiebstahl;** *he was charged with burglary; there has been a series of burglaries in our street;* **aggravated burglary** = burglary where guns or other offensive weapons are carried or used **erschwerter Diebstahl**

◊ **burgle** *verb* to steal things from (a building *or* a household) **einbrechen in; Einbruchsdiebstahl begehen;** *the school was burgled when the caretaker was on holiday*

burn *verb* to destroy by fire **verbrennen;** *the chief accountant burned the documents before the police arrived*

NOTE: **burning - burned** *or* **burnt**

◊ **burn down** *verb* to destroy completely in a fire **abbrennen**

business *noun*
(a) work in buying or selling **Geschäft, Gewerbe; on business** = on commercial work **geschäftlich**
(b) commercial company **Unternehmen, Geschäft, Betrieb;** *he owns a small car repair business; she runs a business from her home; he set up in business as an insurance broker;* **Business Expansion Scheme (BES)** = government scheme to encourage investment by making money invested for some years in a new company to be free of tax **Steuerbefreiung bei Investitionen in Betriebsneugründung; business hours** = time (usually 9 a.m. to 5 p.m.) when a business is open **Geschäftszeit; Schalterstunden; business name** = name under which a firm *or* company trades **Firmenname**
(c) affairs discussed **Angelegenheit, Sache;** *the main business of the meeting was finished by 3 p.m.;* **any other business (AOB)** = item at the end of an agenda, where any matter can be raised **Verschiedenes**

NOTE: no plural for meanings (a) and (c); (b) has the plural **businesses**

busy *adjective* occupied in doing something *or* in working **beschäftigt;** *the police were kept busy dealing with the crowds; the court has a busy schedule;* **the line is busy** = the telephone line is being used **die Leitung ist besetzt**

buy
1 *verb* to get something by paying money **kaufen;** *he bought 10,000 shares; the company has been bought by its leading supplier; to buy wholesale and sell retail;* **to buy forward** = to buy foreign currency before you need it, in order to be sure of the exchange rate **auf Termin kaufen/am Terminmarkt kaufen;**
2 *noun* **good buy** *or* **bad buy** = thing bought which is *or* is not worth the money paid for it **guter Kauf; schlechter Kauf;** *that watch was a good buy; this car was a bad buy*

◊ **buy back** *verb* to buy something which you have sold **zurückkaufen;** *he sold the shop last year and is now trying to buy it back*

◊ **buyer** *noun*
(a) person who buys **Käufer/-in**
(b) person who buys a certain type of goods wholesale, which are then stocked by a large store **Einkäufer/-in; head buyer** = most important buyer in a store **Einkaufsleiter/-in**

by-election *noun* election for Parliament *or* for a council during a term of office (because of the death *or* retirement of the person first elected) **Nachwahl**

bylaw *or* **byelaw** *or* **by-law** *or* **bye-law** *noun* rule *or* law made by a local authority *or* public body and not by central government **städtische/örtliche Verordnung;** *the bylaws forbid playing ball in the public gardens; according to the local bylaws, noise must be limited in the town centre*

COMMENT: bylaws must be made by bodies which have been authorized by Parliament, before they can become legally effective

Cc

C *third letter of the alphabet* **category "C" prisoners** = prisoners who are not likely to try to escape, but who cannot be kept in open prisons **relativ ungefährliche Häftlinge, die trotzdem nicht als Freigänger beschrieben werden können; Schedule C** = schedule to the Finance Acts under which tax is charged on profits from government stock **Einkommenssteuergruppe C; Table C** = model memorandum and articles of association set out in the Companies Act 1985 for a company limited by guarantee having no share capital **Mustersatzung einer AG**

cabinet *noun*
(a) piece of furniture for storing records or for display **Schrank, Vitrine;** *last year's correspondence is in the bottom drawer of the filing cabinet*
(b) committee formed of the most important members of the government, chosen by the Prime Minister or President to be in charge of the main government departments **Kabinett; Cabinet Office** = section of the British Civil Service which works for the Prime Minister and the Cabinet **Kanzleramt**

cadaver *noun (US)* dead body **Leiche**
NOTE: GB English is **corpse**

cadet *noun* trainee police officer **Kadett;** *he has entered the police cadet college; she joined the police force as a cadet*

calculate *verb*
(a) to find the answer to a problem using numbers **(be)rechnen, ermitteln;** *the bank clerk calculated the rate of exchange for the dollar*
(b) to estimate **kalkulieren, schätzen;** *he calculated that they had six minutes left to escape before the police patrol would arrive*

◊ **calculating** *adjective* (person) who plans clever schemes in a careful way **berechnend;** *the judge called the prisoner a cool calculating villain*

◊ **calculation** *noun* answer to a problem in mathematics **Berechnung, Kalkulation;** *I made some rough calculations on the back of an envelope; according to my calculations, the detection rate has increased by 20% over the last six months*

◊ **calculator** *noun* electronic machine which works out the answers to problems in mathematics **Rechenmaschine; Taschenrechner**

calendar *noun*
(a) book *or* set of sheets of paper showing the days and months in a year, often attached to pictures **Kalender; calendar month** = a whole month as on a calendar, from the 1st to the 30th or 31st **Kalendermonat; calendar year** = year from the 1st January to 31st December **Kalenderjahr**

(b) *US* list of Bills for consideration by the House of Representatives *or* the Senate **Sitzungskalender**

call

1 *noun*
(a) conversation on the telephone **Anruf; Gespräch; local call** = call to a number on the same exchange **Ortsgespräch; trunk call** *or* **long-distance call** = call to a number in a different zone *or* area **Ferngespräch; overseas call** *or* **international call** = call to another country **Auslandsgespräch; person-to-person call** = call where you ask the operator to connect you with a named person **Gespräch mit namentlicher Voranmeldung**
(b) (i) demand for repayment of a loan by a lender; (ii) demand by a company to pay for shares **(i) Zahlungsaufforderung; (ii) Einzahlungsaufforderung; money at call** *or* **money on call** *or* **call money** = money loaned for which repayment can be demanded without notice **Tagesgeld; call option** = option to buy shares at a certain price **Kaufoption**
(c) (i) admission of a barrister to the bar; (ii) number of years a barrister has practised at the bar **(i) Zulassung, Bestallung; (ii) Dienstzeit; he is ten years' call** = he has been practising for ten years **er ist seit zehn Jahren (als Anwalt) zugelassen**
(d) visit **Besuch;** *the salesmen make six calls a day;* **business call** = visit to talk to someone on business **Geschäftsbesuch**
2 *verb*
(a) to telephone to someone **anrufen;** *I shall call you at your office tomorrow*
(b) to admit someone to the bar to practise as a barrister **zulassen;** *he was called (to the bar) in 1980*

◊ **call box** *noun* outdoor telephone kiosk **Telefonzelle**

◊ **called** *adjective* named *or* with a certain name **mit Namen, genannt;** *a property called "High Trees"*

◊ **caller** *noun*
(a) person who telephones **Anrufer/-in**
(b) person who visits **Besucher/-in**

◊ **call in** *verb*
(a) to visit **vorbeigehen, vorbeikommen;** *the sales representative called in twice last week*
(b) to ask someone to come to help **hinzuziehen;** *the local police decided to call in the CID to help in the murder hunt*
(c) to ask for plans to be sent to the ministry for examination **anfordern;** *the minister has called in the plans for the new supermarket*
(d) to ask for a debt to be paid **einfordern**

◊ **call off** *verb* to ask for something not to take place **abbrechen; absagen;** *the search for the missing children has been called off*

◊ **call on** *verb*
(a) to visit someone **besuchen;** *the probation officers call on their clients twice a month*
(b) to ask someone to do something **bitten; appellieren; auffordern;** *the minister called on community leaders to help prevent street crime*

camera *see* BICAMERALISM, IN CAMERA

campaign

1 *noun* planned method of working **Kampagne, Aktion;** *the police have launched a campaign against drunken drivers*
2 *verb* to try to change something by writing about it *or* by organizing protest meetings *or* by lobbying Members of Parliament **sich einsetzen, sich stark machen;** *they are campaigning for the abolition of the death penalty or they are campaigning against the death penalty; he is campaigning for a revision of the Official Secrets Act*

cancel *verb*

(a) to stop something which has been agreed *or* planned **absagen; annullieren; aufheben;** *to cancel an appointment or a meeting; to cancel a contract*
(b) to cancel a cheque = to stop payment of a cheque which you have signed **einen Scheck stornieren**
NOTE: GB English is **cancelling - cancelled** but US English **canceling - canceled**

◊ **cancellandi** *see* ANIMUS

◊ **cancellation** *noun* stopping something which has been agreed *or* planned **Absage; Annullierung; Aufhebung;** *cancellation of an appointment; cancellation of an agreement;* **cancellation clause** = clause in a contract which states the terms on which the contract may be cancelled **Rücktrittsklausel**

candidate *noun* person who applies for a job *or* person who puts himself forward for election **Kandidat/-in; Bewerber/-in;** *there are six candidates for the post of security guard; we interviewed ten candidates for the post; all the candidates in the election appeared on television; which candidate are you voting for?*

canon law *noun* law applied by the church to priests; also formerly to other members of the church in cases of marriage, legitimacy and personal property **kanonisches Recht**

canvass *verb* to visit people to ask them to buy goods *or* to vote *or* to say what they think **werben; Wahlwerbung betreiben; befragen**

◊ **canvasser** *noun* person who canvasses **Vertreter/-in; Wahlhelfer; Meinungsforscher**

◊ **canvassing** *noun* action of asking people to buy goods *or* to vote *or* to say what they think **Vertreterbesuche; Wahlwerbung; Meinungsforschung**

capable *adjective* efficient *or* (person) who works well **fähig; leistungsfähig;** *she is a very capable divorce barrister;* **capable of** = able *or* clever enough to do something **können, fähig sein zu;** *she is capable of very fast typing speeds; he is capable of very complicated frauds*

capacity *noun*
(a) amount which can be produced *or* amount of work which can be done **Kapazität**
(b) amount of space **Inhalt, Fassungsvermögen; storage capacity** = space available for storing goods *or* information **Lagerkapazität**
(c) ability **Befähigung, Eignung;** *he has a particular capacity for business*
(d) ability to enter into a legal contract, one of the essential elements of a contract **Rechtsfähigkeit; Geschäftsfähigkeit; person of full age and capacity** = person who is over eighteen years of age and of sound mind, and therefore able to enter into a contract **volljährige und geschäftsfähige Person**
(e) in his capacity as chairman = acting as chairman **in seiner Eigenschaft als Vorsitzender; the manager, speaking in his official capacity, said** = speaking officially **er sagte in seiner Eigenschaft als Manager**

capax *see* DOLI

capita *see* PER CAPITA

capital
1 *noun*
(a) money, property and assets used in a business **Kapital; capital gains** = money made by selling a fixed asset *or* by selling shares at a profit **Veräußerungsgewinne; (realisierte) Kursgewinne; capital gains tax** = tax paid on capital gains **Veräußerungsgewinnsteuer; capital transfer tax** = tax paid on the transfer of capital *or* assets from one person to another **Kapitaltransfersteuer**
(b) capital letters *or* **block capitals** = letters written as A, B, C, D, etc., and not a, b, c, d **Druck-, Blockschrift, Versalien;** *write your name in block capitals at the top of the form* (NOTE: no plural for (a))
2 *adjective* **capital crime** *or* **offence** = crime for which the punishment is death **Kapitalverbrechen; capital punishment** =

punishment of a criminal by execution **Todesstrafe**

COMMENT: in the UK the only capital crime is now treason

◊ **capitalization** *noun* **market capitalization** = value of a company calculated by multiplying the price of its shares on the Stock Exchange by the number of shares issued **Börsenkapitalisierung**

caption *noun* formal heading of an indictment *or* affidavit or other court document **Rubrum; Einleitungsformel**

captive *noun* prisoner, especially a soldier captured in war **(Kriegs-)Gefangener**

◊ **captivity** *noun* being held captive **Gefangenschaft;** *the guerillas were held in captivity for three months* NOTE: no plural

capture *verb* to take *or* to get control of something **erobern;** *the castle was captured by the enemy; the opposition captured six seats in the general election*

care *noun*
(a) act of looking after someone **Obhut, Fürsorge;** *the children were put in the care of the social services department;* **care and control** = responsibility for day-to-day decisions relating to the welfare of a child **(elterliche) Sorgepflicht;** *compare* CUSTODY; **child in care** = child who has been put into the care of the local social services department **Fürsorgekind; care order** = order from a juvenile court, putting a child into the care of a local authority **Anordnung öffentlicher Fürsorge; care proceedings** = action in court to put a child into the care of someone **Fürsorgeverfahren**
(b) making sure that someone is not harmed **Aufsicht; Betreuung; duty of care** = duty which everyone has not to act negligently **Sorgfaltspflicht; driving without due care and attention** = driving a car in a careless way, so that other people are in danger **fahrlässiges Verhalten im Straßenverkehr**

◊ **careless** *adjective* without paying attention to other people **gleichgültig; achtlos; careless driving** = driving without due care and attention **fahrlässiges Fahren**

◊ **carelessly** *adverb* in a careless way **gleichgültig; achtlos; fahrlässig**

◊ **care of** *phrase (in an address)* words to show that the person lives at the address, but only as a visitor **bei;** *Herr Schmidt, care of Mr W Brown*

caretaker *noun* person whose job is to look after property **Hausmeister/-in; caretaker Prime Minister** *or* **caretaker chairman** = Prime Minister *or* chairman who occupies the office temporarily until a newly elected *or* appointed official arrives **Übergangs-, Interimsministerpräsident; geschäftsführender Vorsitzender**

carry *verb*
(a) to take from one place to another **befördern;** *to carry goods; the train was carrying a consignment of cars;* **carrying offensive weapons** = offence of holding a weapon or something (such as a bottle) which could be used as a weapon **unerlaubtes Führen von Angriffswaffen**
(b) to vote to approve **annehmen; the motion was carried** = the motion was accepted after a vote **der Antrag wurde angenommen**
(c) the offence carries a maximum sentence of two years' imprisonment **auf dieses Vergehen steht maximal zwei Jahre Gefängnis**
◊ **carriage** *noun* act of carrying goods from one place to another **Transport;** *carriage charges; carriage by air* NOTE: no plural
◊ **carriageway** *noun* way where the public have a right to go in vehicles **Fahrbahn**
◊ **carrier** *noun* company which takes goods from one place to another **Spedition, Transport-, Fuhrunternehmen; common carrier** = firm which carries goods *or* passengers, which cannot normally refuse to do so, and which can be used by anyone **öffentliches Transportunternehmen; öffentliches Verkehrsunternehmen; private carrier** = firm which carries goods *or* passengers, but which is not contractually bound to offer the service to anyone **privates Transportunternehmen; carrier's lien** = right of a carrier to hold goods until he has been paid for carrying them **Spediteurpfandrecht**
◊ **carry off** *verb* to steal *or* to kidnap **wegtragen;** *the looters carried off all the stock of television sets*
◊ **carry out** *verb* to do a job which has been assigned **durchführen; ausführen, erfüllen;** *the police carried out the raid with great speed; the bailiffs had to carry out the order of the court and seize the woman's property*

carte blanche *French phrase meaning* "white card": permission given by someone to another person, allowing him to do anything *or* to act in any way **Blankovollmacht;** *he has carte blanche to act on behalf of the company or the company has given him carte blanche to act on its behalf*

case
1 *noun*
(a) suitcase *or* box with a handle for carrying clothes and personal belongings when travelling **Koffer;** *the customs made him open his case; she had a small case which she carried onto the plane*
(b) (i) cardboard *or* wooden box for packing and carrying goods; (ii) box containing twelve bottles of alcohol **(i)(ii) Kiste; a packing case** = large wooden box for carrying items which can be easily broken **Kiste**
(c) possible crime and its investigation by the police **Fall;** *we have three detectives working on the case; the police are treating the case as murder or are treating it as a murder case; we had six cases of looting during the night*
(d) **court case** = legal action *or* trial **Prozeß; Gerichtsverfahren; the case is being heard next week** = the case is coming to court **der Fall wird nächste Woche verhandelt; case law** = law as established by precedents, that is by the decisions of courts in earlier cases **Präzedenz-, Einzelfallrecht**
(e) arguments *or* facts put forward by one side in legal proceedings **Klage: Sache;** *defence counsel put his case; there is a strong case against the accused;* **case stated** = statement of the facts of a case which has been heard in a lower court, drawn up so that a higher court can decide on an appeal **Revisionsvorlage;** *he appealed by way of case stated; the Appeal Court dismissed the appeal by way of case stated;* **the case rests** = all the arguments for one side have been put forward **die Beweisführung ist abgeschlossen; no case to answer** = submission by the defence (after the prosecution has put its case) that the case should be dismissed **Antrag auf Verfahrenseinstellung**
2 *verb (slang)* **to case the joint** = to look at a building carefully before deciding how to break into it **sich den Laden ansehen**

COMMENT: a case is referred to by the names of the parties, the date and the reference source where details of it can be found: *Smith v. Jones [1985] 2 W.L.R. 250* This shows that the case involved Smith as plaintiff and Jones as defendant, it was heard in 1985, and is reported in the second volume of the Weekly Law Reports for that year on page 250

cast *verb* **to cast a vote** = to vote **eine Stimme abgeben;** *the number of votes cast in the election was 125,458; under proportional representation, the number of seats occupied by each party is related to the number of votes cast for that party;* **casting vote** = vote used by the chairman in a case where the votes for and against a proposal

are equal **entscheidende Stimme;** *the chairman has a casting vote; he used his casting vote to block the motion*
NOTE: **casting - cast - has cast**

casual *adjective*
(a) not permanent *or* not regular **Aushilfs-, flüchtig; casual labour** = workers who are hired for a short period **Aushilfsarbeiter; casual work** = work where the workers are hired for a short period **Aushilfsarbeit; casual labourer** *or* **casual worker** = worker who can be hired for a short period **Aushilfsarbeiter**
(b) not formal **lässig, leger;** *he appeared in court wearing casual clothes*

casus belli *Latin phrase meaning* "case for war": reason which is used to justify a declaration of war **Casus belli, kriegsauslösendes Ereignis**

category *noun* type *or* sort of item **Kategorie, Klasse;** *the theft comes into the category of petty crime;* **category "A" prisoners** = prisoners who are dangerous, and would be a danger to the public if they escaped from prison **Häftlinge der höchsten Gefährlichkeitsstufe; category "B" prisoners** = less dangerous prisoners, who still have to be guarded carefully to prevent them from escaping **Häftlinge der zweithöchsten Gefährlichkeitsstufe; category "C" prisoners** = prisoners who are not likely to try to escape, but who cannot be kept in open prisons **relativ ungefährliche Häftlinge, die trotzdem nicht als Freigänger beschrieben werden können; category "D" prisoners** = reliable prisoners who can be kept in open prisons **Freigänger**

cater for *verb* to deal with *or* to provide for **sich befassen mit; ausgerichtet sein auf;** *the police station has to cater for every type of crime*

causa *see* DONATIO

cause
1 *noun*
(a) thing which makes something happen **Ursache, Grund; cause of action** = reason why a case is brought to court **Klagegrund; challenge for cause** *or* **without cause** = objection to a proposed juror, stating *or* not stating the reasons for the objection **Ablehnung unter Angabe von Gründen; Ablehnung ohne Angabe von Gründen; contributory causes** = causes which help something to take place **mitverursachende Umstände;** *the report listed bad community relations as one of the contributory causes to*

the riot; **to show cause** = to give a reason for something **Gründe vorlegen;** *the judgment debtor was given fourteen days in which to show cause why the charging order should not be made absolute*
(b) legal proceedings **Prozeß, Sache, Rechtsfall, Rechtsstreit; cause list** = list of cases which are to be heard by a court **Verhandlungsliste,   Terminkalender; matrimonial causes** = cases referring to the rights of partners in a marriage **Ehesachen**
2 *verb* to make something happen **verursachen;** *the recession caused hundreds of bankruptcies*

caution
1 *noun*
(a) warning from a policeman, telling someone not to repeat a minor crime **Verwarnung, Verweis;** *the boys were let off with a caution*
(b) warning by a police officer, that someone will be charged with a crime, and that what he says will be used in evidence **Rechtsmittelbelehrung;** *he typed his confession under caution*
(c) document lodged at the Land Registry to prevent land *or* property being sold without notice to the cautioner **Vormerkung;** (NOTE: in meaning (b) and (c) can be used without **the** or **a: to lodge caution)**
2 *verb*
(a) to warn (someone) that what he has done is wrong and should not be repeated **verwarnen;** *the policeman cautioned the boys after the he caught them stealing fruit*
(b) to warn (someone) that he will be charged with a crime, and that what he says will be used as evidence at his trial **auf (jds) Rechte hinweisen;** *the accused was arrested by the detectives and cautioned*

> COMMENT: the person who is cautioned has the right not to answer any question put to him

◊ **cautioner** *noun* person who lodges caution at the Land Registry **Vormerkungsbegünstigter**

caveat *noun* warning **Warnung; to enter a caveat** = to warn legally that you have an interest in a case, and that no steps can be taken without notice to you (especially warning to a probate court not to grant probate) **Einspruch einlegen**

◊ **caveat emptor** *Latin phrase meaning* "let the buyer beware": phrase meaning that the buyer is himself responsible for checking that what he buys is in good order **Ausschluß der Gewährleistung**

◊ **caveator** *noun* person who warns the court not to give probate without asking his consent **Einspruch Erhebender**

CB *(in the armed forces)* = CONFINED TO BARRACKS

CC = CHIEF CONSTABLE

cell *noun* small room in a prison *or* police station where a criminal can be kept locked up **Zelle**; *she was put in a small cell for the night; he shares a cell with two other prisoners;* **condemned cell** = cell where a prisoner is kept who has been condemned to death **Todeszelle**
NOTE: often used in the plural, meaning the cells in a police station: **he spent the night in the cells**

◊ **cellmate** *noun* person who shares a prison cell with someone else **Zellengenosse**

censor
1 *noun* official whose job is to say whether books *or* films *or* TV programmes, etc., are acceptable and can be published or shown to the public **Zensor**; *the film was cut or was banned or was passed by the censor*
2 *verb* to say that a book *or* film *or* TV programme, etc. cannot be shown *or* published because it is not considered right to do so **zensieren**; *all press reports are censored by the government; the news of the riots was censored; the TV report has been censored and only parts of it can be shown*

◊ **censorship** *noun* act of censoring **Zensur**; *TV reporters complained of government censorship; the government has imposed strict press censorship or censorship of the press*
NOTE: no plural

censure
1 *noun* **vote of censure** *or* **censure vote** = vote which criticizes someone, especially a vote in parliament which criticizes the government **Mißbilligungsvotum**; *the meeting passed a vote of censure on the minister*
2 *verb* to criticize **tadeln, rügen**; *the opposition put forward a motion to censure the government*

central *adjective* organized at one main point **zentral, Zentral-**; **central office** = main office which controls all smaller offices **Hauptbüro, Zentrale**; **Central Criminal Court** = the Crown Court sitting in London **Zentralstrafgericht** (= THE OLD BAILEY)

◊ **centralization** *noun* organization of everything from a central point **Zentralisierung**

◊ **centralize** *verb* to organize from a central point **zentralisieren**; *the gathering of all criminal records has been centralized in the police headquarters*

◊ **centre** *noun*

(a) business centre = part of a town where the main banks, shops and offices are **Geschäftsviertel**
(b) important town **Zentrum**; *an industrial centre; the centre for the shoe industry*
(c) office **Zentrum**; **Job Centre** = government office which lists jobs which are vacant; *entspricht* **Arbeitsamt; Stellenvermittlung; Law Centre** = local office (mainly in London) with full-time staff who advise and represent clients free of charge; *entspricht* **Rechtsbeistandberatung; Legal Aid Centre** = local office giving advice to clients with legal problems, giving advice on obtaining Legal Aid and recommending clients to solicitors; *entspricht* **Rechtsberatungsstelle**

certain *adjective*
(a) sure **sicher, gewiß**; *the superintendent is certain that the head of the gang is still at large*
(b) a certain = one particular **ein bestimmter; a certain number** *or* **a certain quantity** = some **eine bestimmte Anzahl**

◊ **certainty** *noun* thing which is certain **Gewißheit**

certificate *noun* official document which shows that something is true **Zertifikat, Urkunde, Bescheinigung; clearance certificate** = document showing that goods have been passed by customs **Zollabfertigungs-, Ausklarierungsschein; fire certificate** = document from the municipal fire department to say that a building is properly protected against fire **Brandschutzbescheinigung; land certificate** = document which shows who owns a piece of land, and whether there are any charges on it **(beglaubigter) Grundbuchauszug; practising certificate** = certificate from the Law Society allowing someone to work as a solicitor **Bestallungsurkunde, Anwaltszulassung; share certificate** = document proving that you own shares **Aktienzertifikat, Anteilschein; certificate of approval** = document showing that an item has been officially approved **Genehmigungszertifikat; certificate of deposit** = document from a bank showing that money has been deposited **Depositenquittung; Depotschein; certificate of incorporation** = document showing that a company has been officially registered **Gründungsurkunde; certificate of judgment** = official document showing a decision of a court **Urteilsschrift; certificate of origin** = document showing where goods were made *or* produced **Herkunftsbescheinigung; certificate of registration** = document showing that an item has been registered **Eintragungsbescheinigung; Meldeschein;**

certificate of registry = document showing that a ship has been officially registered **Schiffsbrief**

◊ **certificated** *adjective* **certificated bankrupt** = bankrupt who has been discharged from bankruptcy with a certificate to show that he was not at fault **rehabilitierter Konkursschuldner**

certify *verb* to make an official declaration in writing **bescheinigen, bestätigen, beglaubigen;** *I certify that this is a true copy; the document is certified as a true copy;* **certified accountant** = accountant who has passed the professional examinations and is a member of the Association of Certified Accountants; *entspricht* **amtlich zugelassener Wirtschaftsprüfer; certified cheque** *or (US)* **certified check** = cheque which a bank says is good and will be paid out of money put aside from the bank account **bestätigter Scheck; certified copy** = copy which is certified as being the same as the original **beglaubigte Kopie**

certiorari *Latin word meaning* "to be informed" **Vorlage der Akten an ein höheres Gericht; order of certiorari** = order which transfers a case from a lower court to the High Court for investigation into its legality **Aktenanforderung (durch ein höheres Gericht);** *he applied for judicial review by way of certiorari; the court ordered certiorari following judicial review, quashing the order made by the juvenile court*

cessate grant *noun* special grant of probate made because of the incapacity of an executor *or* grant made to renew a grant which has expired **erneute gerichtliche Bestätigung (z.B. eines Testaments)**

cession *noun* giving up property to someone (especially a creditor) **Abtretung, Zession**

CGT = CAPITAL GAINS TAX

chair
1 *noun*
(a) piece of furniture for sitting on **Stuhl; electric chair** *or* **the chair** = chair attached to a powerful electric current, used in the USA for executing criminals **elektrischer Stuhl**
(b) position of the chairman, presiding over a meeting **Vorsitz;** *to be in the chair; she was voted into the chair;* **Mr Jones took the chair** = Mr Jones presided over the meeting **Herr Jones übernahm den Vorsitz; to address the chair** = in a meeting, to speak to the

chairman and not to the rest of the people at the meeting **sich an den Vorsitzenden wenden**
2 *verb* to preside over a meeting **den Vorsitz führen bei;** *the meeting was chaired by Mrs Smith*

◊ **chairman** *noun*
(a) person who is in charge of a meeting **Vorsitzender;** *chairman of the magistrates or of the bench; Mr Howard was chairman or acted as chairman;* **Mr Chairman** *or* **Madam Chairman** = way of speaking to the chairman **Herr Vorsitzender; Frau Vorsitzende**
(b) person who presides over the board meetings of a company **Vorstandsvorsitzender; Vorsitzender des Aufsichtsrates;** *the chairman of the board or the company chairman*

◊ **chairmanship** *noun* being a chairman **Vorsitz, Leitung; the committee met under the chairmanship of Mr Jones** = Mr Jones chaired the meeting of the committee **das Komitee trat unter dem Vorsitz von Herrn Jones zusammen**

◊ **chairperson** *noun* person who is in charge of a meeting **Vorsitzender**

◊ **chairwoman** *noun* woman who is in charge of a meeting **Vorsitzende**

challenge
1 *noun* act of objecting to a decision, and asking it to be set aside **Anfechtung; Ablehnung; challenge for cause** *or* **challenge without cause** = objecting to a juror, stating *or* not stating the reason for the objection **Ablehnung unter Angabe von Gründen; Ablehnung ohne Angabe von Gründen; peremptory challenge** = challenge without cause **unbegründete Ablehnung**
2 *verb* to object to *or* to refuse to accept (a juror *or* evidence) **ablehnen; anfechten; in Frage stellen;** *to challenge a sentence passed by magistrates by appeal to the Crown Court*

Chamber of Commerce *noun* group of local businessmen who meet to discuss problems which they have in common, and to promote business in the town **Handelskammer**

◊ **chambers** *plural noun*
(a) offices of barristers **Anwaltsbüros**
(b) office of a judge **Richterzimmer; the judge heard the case in chambers** = in his private rooms, without the public being present and not in open court **der Richter verhandelte den Fall im Richterzimmer (unter Ausschluß der Öffentlichkeit)**

champerty *noun* financial help given to a person starting proceedings against a party, where the person giving help has a

share in the damages to be recovered **Beteiligung an einem Prozeß gegen Beteiligung am Prozeßerlös**
NOTE: no plural

chance

(a) being possible **Möglichkeit, Chance;** *is there any chance of the hearing taking place before the summer?*
(b) opportunity to do something **Gelegenheit, Chance;** *the prosecuting counsel seized his chance and asked the witness to repeat the conversation which he had had with the accused*

Chancellor *noun*

(a) *(in the United Kingdom)* **Chancellor of the Exchequer** = chief finance minister in the government **Finanzminister, Schatzkanzler; the Lord Chancellor** = chief minister of justice **Lordkanzler**

> COMMENT: the Lord Chancellor is a member of the Cabinet; he presides over debates in the House of Lords; he is the head of the judicial system and advises on the appointment of judges

(b) *(in the US)* judge who presides over a court of equity **vorsitzender Richter an einem Billigkeitsgericht**

Chancery *noun* the **Chancery Bar** = barristers who specialize in the Chancery Division **Anwaltschaft der Chancery Division; Chancery Court** = formerly the court presided over by the Lord Chancellor, which established case law *or* equity **Gericht des Lordkanzlers; Chancery Division** = one of the three divisions of the High Court, dealing with wills, partnerships and companies, taxation, bankruptcies, etc. **Chancery-Abteilung des High Court**

channel *noun* way in which information or goods are passed from one place to another **Kanal, Weg; to go through the official channels** = to deal with government officials (especially when making a request) **den Amtsweg/Dienstweg gehen; to open up new channels of communication** = new ways of communicating with someone **neue Kommunikationswege erschließen**

chaos *noun* disorder *or* disorderly state **Chaos;** *after the coup the country was in chaos; chaos reigned in the centre of the town until the police and fire engines arrived*

◊ **chaotic** *adjective* in a disorderly state **chaotisch;** *the situation was chaotic until the police arrived to control the traffic*

chapter *noun* official term for an Act of Parliament **Artikel; Abschnitt**

character *noun* general qualities of a person which make him different from others **Charakter, Wesen; he is a man of good character** = he is an honest *or* hard-working *or* decent man **er hat einen guten Charakter; to give someone a character reference** = to say that someone has good qualities **jdm Referenzen geben; to introduce character evidence** = to produce witnesses to say that a person is of good *or* bad character **Leumundsbeweise aufbieten**

charge

1 *noun*
(a) money which must be paid *or* price of a service **Gebühr, Kosten;** *to make no charge for delivery; to make a small charge for rental; there is no charge for service or no charge is made for service;* **admission charge** *or* **entry charge** = price to be paid before going into an exhibition, etc. **Eintritt(sgebühr); scale of charges** = list showing various prices **Gebührenordnung; free of charge** = free *or* with no payment to be made **gebührenfrei, kostenlos; solicitors' charges** = payments to be made to solicitors for work done on behalf of clients **Anwaltsgebühren, Anwaltskosten**
(b) charge on land *or* **charge over property** = mortgage *or* liability on a property which has been used as security for a loan **Grundschuld; fixed charge** = charge over a particular asset *or* property **Fixbelastung; floating charge** = charge over changing assets of a business **variable Belastung; charge by way of legal mortgage** = way of borrowing money on the security of a property, where the mortgagor signs a deed which gives the mortgagee an interest in the property **formelle Hypothekenbestellung**
(c) official statement in a court accusing someone of having committed a crime **Anklage;** *he appeared in court on a charge of embezzling or on an embezzlement charge; the clerk of the court read out the charges;* **charge sheet** = document listing the charges which a magistrate will hear *or* listing the charges against the accused together with details of the crime committed **polizeiliches Anklageblatt; to answer charges** = to appear in court to plead guilty *or* not guilty to a charge **sich wegen einer Klage/Beschuldigung verantworten; the charges were withdrawn** *or* **dropped** = the prosecution decided not to continue with the trial **die Anklage wurde zurückgezogen/fallengelassen; to press charges against someone** = to say formally that someone has committed a crime **jdn anzeigen;** *he was very angry when his neighbour's son set fire to his car, but*

decided not to press charges; **holding charge** = minor charge brought against someone so that he can be held in custody while more serious charges are being prepared **Nebenbeschuldigung, die dazu dient, jdn während der Hauptermittlungen in Haft zu halten**
(d) instructions given by the judge to the jury, summing up the evidence and giving advice on the points of law which have to be considered **Rechtsbelehrung**
2 *verb*
(a) to ask someone to pay for services; to ask for money to be paid **berechnen; verlangen;** *to charge £5 for delivery; how much does he charge?;* **he charges £6 an hour** = he asks to be paid £6 for an hour's work **er nimmt £6 pro Stunde**
(b) *(in a court)* to accuse someone formally of having committed a crime **anklagen;** *he was charged with embezzling his clients' money; they were charged with murder*
NOTE: you charge someone **with** a crime

◇ **chargeable** *adjective* which can be charged **gebührenpflichtig; anrechenbar**

◇ **chargee** *noun* person who holds a charge over a property **Hypothekengläubiger**

◇ **charging order** *noun* court order made in favour of a judgment creditor granting him a charge over a debtor's property **Beschlagnahmeverfügung**

charity *noun* body which aims not to make money, but to benefit the general public by helping the poor *or* by promoting education or religion *or* by doing other useful work **karitative Organisation; the Charity Commissioners** = body which governs charities and sees that they follow the law and use their funds for the purposes intended **Stiftungsaufsichtsamt**

◇ **charitable trust** *or (US)* **charitable corporation** *noun* trust which benefits the public as a whole, which promotes education or religion *or* which helps the poor *or* or which does other useful work **gemeinnützige Stiftung**

chart *noun* diagram showing information as a series of lines *or* blocks, etc. **Diagramm; flow chart** = diagram showing the arrangement of various work processes in a series **Fluß-, Arbeitsablaufdiagramm; organization chart** = diagram showing how a company *or* an office is organized **Organisationsplan**

charter
1 *noun*
(a) document from the Crown establishing a town *or* a corporation *or* a university *or* a company **Charter; Urkunde; bank charter** =

official government document allowing the establishment of a bank **Bankenkonzession**
(b) hiring transport for a special purpose **Chartern; Charterung; charter flight** = flight in an aircraft which has been hired for that purpose **Charterflug; charter plane** = plane which has been chartered **Charterflugzeug; boat on charter to Mr Smith** = boat which Mr Smith has hired for a voyage **Boot, das von Herrn Smith gechartert wurde**
2 *verb* to hire for a special purpose **chartern; mieten;** *to charter a plane or a boat or a bus*

◇ **chartered** *adjective*
(a) **chartered accountant** = accountant who has passed the professional examinations and is a member of the Institute of Chartered Accountants; *entspricht* **beeidigter Wirtschaftsprüfer**
(b) (company) which has been set up by royal charter, and not registered as a company; *(GB)* **durch königlichen Hoheitsakt geschaffen**
(c) **chartered ship** *or* **plane** *or* **bus** = ship *or* bus *or* plane which has been hired for a special purpose **gechartertes Schiff od Flugzeug; gemieteter Bus**

◇ **charterer** *noun* person who hires a ship, etc., for a special purpose **Charterer; Mieter/-in**

◇ **chartering** *noun* act of hiring for a special purpose **Chartern; Mieten**

◇ **charterparty** *noun* contract where the owner of a ship charters his ship to someone for carrying goods **Befrachtungsvertrag**

chattel mortgage *noun (US)* mortgage using personal property as security **Mobiliarhypothek**

◇ **chattels** *plural noun* **goods and chattels** = moveable property (but not freehold real estate) **bewegliches Eigentum, Mobiliar; chattels real** = leaseholds **Grundstücksrechte; chattels personal** = any property that is not real property **persönliche Habe; incorporeal chattels** = intangible properties (such as patents *or* copyrights) **immaterielle Vermögenswerte**

cheat
1 *noun* person who tricks someone so that he loses money *or* property **Betrüger/-in**
2 *verb* to trick someone so that he loses money *or* property **betrügen;** *he cheated the Income Tax out of thousands of pounds; she was accused of cheating clients who came to ask her for advice*
NOTE: you cheat someone **out of** money

check
1 *noun*
(a) sudden stop **Einhalt; Hemmnis, Hindernis;**

to put a check on the sale of firearms = to stop some firearms being sold **den Verkauf von Schußwaffen kontrollieren**
(b) **check sample** = sample to be used to see if a consignment is acceptable **Stichprobe**
(c) investigation *or* examination **Überprüfung, Kontrolle;** *the auditors carried out checks on the petty cash book; a routine check of the fire equipment;* **baggage check** = examination of passengers' baggage to see if it contains bombs **Gepäckkontrolle**
(d) *US* = CHEQUE
2 *verb*
(a) to stop *or* to delay **lahmlegen; hemmen, bremsen;** *to check the entry of contraband into the country*
(b) to examine *or* to investigate **überprüfen, kontrollieren;** *to check that an invoice is correct; to check and sign for goods;* **he checked the computer printout against the invoices** = he examined the printout and the invoices to see if the figures were the same **er verglich den Computerausdruck mit den Rechnungen**
(c) *US* to mark with a sign to show that something is correct **abhaken**

◊ **checking** *noun* examination *or* investigation **Überprüfung;** *the inspectors found some defects during their checking of the building*

cheque *noun* order to a bank to pay money from your account to the person whose name is written on it **Scheck; cheque account** = bank account which allows the customer to write cheques **laufendes Konto, Girokonto; crossed cheque** = cheque with two lines across it showing that it can only be deposited at a bank and not exchanged for cash **Verrechnungsscheck; open** *or* **uncrossed cheque** = cheque which can be exchanged for cash anywhere **Barscheck; blank cheque** = cheque written with the amount of money and the payee left blank, but signed by the drawer **Blankoscheck; traveller's cheques** = cheques used by a traveller which can be exchanged for cash in a foreign country **Reiseschecks**
(b) **to endorse a cheque** = to sign a cheque on the back to make it payable to someone else **einen Scheck girieren/indossieren; to make out a cheque to someone** = to write out a cheque to someone **jdm einen Scheck ausstellen; to pay by cheque** = to pay by writing a cheque, and not by using cash or a credit card **mit (einem) Scheck bezahlen; to pay a cheque into your account** = to deposit a cheque **einen Scheck auf das Konto einzahlen; to dishonour a cheque** *or informal* **to bounce a cheque** = to refuse to pay a cheque because there is not enough money in the account to pay it **einen Scheck platzen lassen; the bank referred the cheque to**

drawer = returned the cheque to the person who wrote it because there was not enough money in the account to pay it **die Bank gab den Scheck zurück an den Aussteller; to sign a cheque** = to sign on the front of a cheque to show that you authorize the bank to pay the money from your account **einen Scheck unterschreiben; to stop a cheque** = to ask a bank not to pay a cheque which you have written **einen Scheck sperren lassen**

chief *adjective*
(a) most important **erster, Haupt-;** *he is the chief accountant of an industrial group; (GB)* **Lord Chief Justice** = chief judge of the Queen's Bench Division of the High Court who is also a member of the Court of Appeal **Lordoberrichter;** *(US)* **Chief Justice** = main judge in a court **Oberrichter; Chief Constable** = person in charge of a police force **Kommandeur der Polizei; Assistant Chief Constable** *or* **Deputy Chief Constable** = ranks in the police force below Chief Constable **stellvertretender Polizeipräsident; Chief Inspector** *or* **Chief Superintendent** = ranks in the police force above Inspector *or* Superintendent **Hauptkommissar**
(b) **in chief** = in person **persönlich; examination in chief** = examining of a witness by counsel for his side **Befragung von eigenen Zeugen durch den Anwalt**

child *noun* person under the age of majority **Kind; child destruction** = notifiable offence of a killing an unborn child capable of being born alive **Kindestötung (durch Abtreibung); child stealing** = notifiable offence of taking away a child from its parents *or* guardian **Kindesraub**

COMMENT: In Great Britain a child does not have full legal status until the age of eighteen. A contract is not binding on a child, and a child cannot own land, cannot make a will, cannot vote, cannot drive a car (under the age of seventeen). A child cannot marry before the age of sixteen. A child who is less than ten years old is not considered capable of committing a crime; a child between ten and fourteen years of age may be considered capable to committing a crime if there is evidence of malice or knowledge.

chose *French word meaning* "item" *or* "thing" **Objekt, Gegenstand; chose in action** = personal right which can be enforced or claimed as if it were property (such as a patent *or* copyright *or* debt *or* cheque) **obligatorischer Anspruch; chose in possession** = physical thing which can be owned (such as a piece of furniture) **bewegliche Sache**

Christmas Day *noun* 25th December, one of the four quarter days when rent is payable on land **1. Weihnachtstag**

chronic *adjective* permanently bad **chronisch**

chronological order *noun* arrangement of records (files, invoices, etc.) in order of their dates **chronologische Reihenfolge**

c.i.f. = COST, INSURANCE, FREIGHT contract for the sale of goods where the seller arranges the export licence, loading, carriage, and insurance and provides a bill of lading, and the purchaser pays on delivery of documents and pays duties and the unloading **cif, Kosten, Versicherung und Fracht**

circuit *noun* one of six divisions of England and Wales for legal purposes **Kreis; Bezirk; Gerichtsbezirk;** *he is a judge on the Welsh Circuit;* **circuit judge** = judge in the Crown Court or a County Court; *(Strafrecht)* **Richter an einem Crown Court;** *(Zivilrecht)* **Richter an einem County Court**

COMMENT: the six circuits are: Northern, North-Eastern, Midland and Oxford, Wales and Chester, South-Eastern, and Western

circular
1 *adjective* (letter) sent to many people **Rund-; circular letter of credit** = letter of credit sent to all branches of the bank which issues it **Akkreditiv**
2 *noun* leaflet *or* letter sent to many people **Rundschreiben;** *they sent out a circular offering a 10% discount*
◇ **circularize** *verb* to send a circular to **Rundschreiben verschicken;** *the committee has agreed to circularize the members; they circularized all their customers with a new list of prices*
◇ **circulate** *verb* to send information to **zirkulieren lassen, in Umlauf bringen;** *they circulated a new list of prices to all their customers*
◇ **circulating** *adjective* which is moving about freely **zirkulierend**
◇ **circulation** *noun*
(a) movement **Verbreitung; Umlauf;** *the company is trying to improve the circulation of information between departments;* **circulation of capital** = movement of capital from one investment to another **Kapitalverkehr; free circulation of goods** = movement of goods from one country to another without import quotas or other restrictions **freier Güterumlauf**

(b) to put money into circulation = to issue new notes to business and the public **Geld in Umlauf bringen;** *the amount of money in circulation increased more than had been expected*
(c) *(von Zeitungen)* number of copies sold **Auflage, Auflagenhöhe; a circulation battle** = competition between two newspapers to try to sell more copies in the same market **Kampf um die Auflagenhöhe verschiedener Zeitungen**

circumstances *plural noun* situation as it is when something happens **Umstände;** *the police inspector described the circumstances leading to the riot; see also* EXTENUATING
◇ **circumstantial** *adjective* which allows someone to infer facts **indirekt; circumstantial evidence** = evidence which suggests that something happened, but does not give firm proof of it **Indizienbeweis**

cite *verb*
(a) to summon someone to appear in court **vorladen**
(b) to quote *or* to refer to something **anführen, zitieren;** *the judge cited several previous cases in his summing up*
◇ **citation** *noun*
(a) official request asking someone to appear in court **Vorladung;** (NOTE: used mainly in the Scottish and US courts)
(b) quotation of a legal case *or* authority *or* precedent **Anführung, Zitat**

citizen *noun*
(a) person who lives in a city **Bürger/-in**
(b) person who has the nationality of a certain country **Staatsbürger;** *he is a French citizen by birth;* **Citizens' Advice Bureau** = office where people can go to get free advice on legal and administrative problems **öffentliche Beratungsstelle (für Verwaltungs- und Rechtsfragen); citizen's arrest** = arrest of a suspected criminal by an ordinary citizen without a warrant **Festnahme durch eine Zivilperson**
◇ **citizenship** *noun* state of being a citizen of a country **Staatsbürgerschaft**

city *noun*
(a) large town **Stadt;** *the largest cities in Europe are linked by hourly flights;* **capital city** = main town in a country, where the government and parliament are situated **Hauptstadt**
(b) the City = old centre of London, where banks and large companies have their main offices; *the London financial centre* **die City**

civil *adjective* referring to the rights and duties of private persons *or* corporate bodies (as opposed to criminal, military or ecclesiastical) **Zivil-, bürgerlich; civil action** = court case brought by a person *or* a company (the plaintiff) against someone who is alleged to have done them wrong (the defendant) **Zivilprozeß, zivilrechtliche Klage; civil disorder** = riots *or* fighting in public places **(innere) Unruhen, Aufruhr; civil law** = laws relating to people's rights and agreements between individuals (as opposed to criminal law) **Zivilrecht, bürgerliches Recht; civil liberties** = freedom to act within the law (liberty of the press, liberty of the individual, etc.) **Grund-, Bürgerrechte, staatsbürgerliche Freiheiten; civil rights** = rights and privileges of each individual person according to the law **Grundrechte, staatsbürgerliche Rechte; civil strife** = trouble where gangs of people fight each other, usually over matters of principle **(innere) Unruhen; civil war** = situation in a country where the nation is divided into two or more sections which fight each other **Bürgerkrieg**

◊ **civil service** *noun* organization which administers a country **öffentlicher Dienst, Staatsdienst;** *he has a job in the civil service; you have to pass an examination to get a job in the civil service or to get a civil service job*

◊ **civil servant** *noun* person who works in the civil service **Beamter im öffentlichen Dienst, Staatsbeamter**

CJ = CHIEF JUSTICE

claim
1 *noun*
(a) (i) assertion of a legal right; (ii) document used in the County Court to start a legal action **(i) Klagebegehren; (ii) Klageschrift; particulars of claim** = County Court pleading setting out the plaintiff's claim **Klagebegründung**
(b) statement that someone has a right to property held by another person **Rechtsanspruch, Forderung; legal claim to something** = statement that you think you own something legally **einen Rechtsanspruch auf etwas haben;** *he has no legal claim to the property or to the car*
(c) asking for money **Forderung; wage claim** = asking for an increase in wages **Lohnforderung; the union put in a 6% wage claim** = the union asked for a 6% increase in wages for its members **die Gewerkschaft forderte 6% mehr Lohn;** *she put in a claim for £250,000 damages against the driver of the other car*
(d) insurance claim = asking an insurance company to pay for damages *or* for loss **Versicherungsanspruch; no claims bonus** = reduction of premiums to be paid because no claims have been made against the

insurance policy **Schadenfreiheitsrabatt; to put in a claim** = to ask the insurance company officially to pay for damage *or* loss **einen Anspruch geltend machen, Schadensansprüche stellen; claim form** = form which has to be completed when making an insurance claim **Schadensformular;** *she put in a claim for repairs to the car; he filled in the claim form and sent it to the insurance company;* **to settle a claim** = to agree to pay what is asked for **eine Forderung regulieren**
(e) small claim = claim for less than £500 in the County Court **Bagatellsache; small claims court** = court which deals with disputes over small amounts of money **Gericht, das für Geldansprüche bis zu einer bestimmten Höhe zuständig ist;** *entspricht* **Amtsgericht**
2 *verb*
(a) to state a grievance in court **eine Forderung geltend machen**
(b) to ask for money **fordern, einfordern;** *he claimed £100,000 damages against the cleaning firm; she claimed for repairs to the car against her insurance*
(c) to say that you have a right to property held by someone else **beanspruchen; fordern;** *he is claiming possession of the house; no one claimed the umbrella found in my office*
(d) to state that something is a fact **behaupten;** *he claims he never received the goods; she claims that the shares are her property*
(e) *slang* (i) to attack someone in prison; (ii) to arrest someone **(i) angreifen; (ii) verhaften**

◊ **claimant** *noun* person who claims **Antrags-, Anspruchsteller/-in; Kläger/-in; rightful claimant** = person who has a legal claim to something **Anspruchsberechtigter**

◊ **claim back** *verb* to ask for money to be paid back **zurückfordern**

clandestine
adjective secret *or* hidden **geheim, heimlich**

clarify
verb to make something clear *or* easy to understand **klarstellen;** *the opposition asked the minister to clarify his statement*

◊ **clarification** *noun* making something clear *or* easy to understand **Klarstellung;** *the wording of the clause is ambiguous and needs clarification*

class
1 *noun* category *or* group into which things are classified **Klasse, Kategorie; first-class** = top quality *or* most expensive **erstklassig; Class F charge** = charge on a property registered by a spouse who is not an owner, claiming the right to live in the property; *entspricht* **Belastung in Abteilung 6; class gift**

= gift to a defined group of people **Schenkung an eine bestimmte Personengruppe;** *US* **class action** *or* **class suit** = legal action brought on behalf of a group of people **Gruppenklage**

2 *verb* to put into a category *or* to classify **einordnen, klassifizieren;** *the magazine was classed as an obscene publication*

classify *verb* to put into classes *or* categories **klassifizieren, einstufen; classified directory** = book which lists businesses grouped under various headings (such as computer shops, newsagents, hairdressers) **Branchenverzeichnis; classified information** = information which is secret and can be told only to certain people **Verschlußsache, Geheimsache**

◊ **classification** *noun* way of putting into classes **Klassifizierung, Einstufung**

clause *noun* section of a contract *or* of a constitution **Klausel, Paragraph, Absatz;** *there are ten clauses in the contract; according to clause six, payment will not be due until next year;* **exclusion clause** = clause in an insurance policy *or* contract which says which items are not covered by the policy *or* gives details of circumstances where the insurance company will refuse to pay **Ausschluß-, Freizeichnungsklausel; forfeit clause** = clause in a contract which says that goods *or* a deposit will be forfeited if the contract is not obeyed **Verfalls-, Verwirkungsklausel; liability clause** = clause in the articles of association of a company which states that the liability of its members is limited **Haftungsklausel; penalty clause** = clause which lists the penalties which will be imposed if the terms of the contract are not fulfilled **Strafklausel; termination clause** = clause which explains how and when a contract can be terminated **Kündigungsklausel**

claw back *verb* (i) to take back money which has been allocated **(i) sich zurückholen** (ii); *(of the Inland Revenue)* to take back tax relief which was previously granted **zurückfordern; sich zurückholen;** *income tax claws back 25% of pensions paid out by the government; of the £1m allocated to the development of the system, the government clawed back £100,000 in taxes*

◊ **clawback** *noun* (i) money taken back; (ii) loss of tax relief previously granted **(i) (ii) Rückforderung**

clean hands *plural noun* **the plaintiff must have clean hands** = the plaintiff cannot claim successfully if his motives or actions are dishonest *or* if he has not

discharged his own obligations to the defendant **Motive und Handlungen des Klägers müssen aufrichtig sein**

> COMMENT: from the maxim: "he who comes to equity must come with clean hands"

clear

1 *adjective*

(a) easily understood **klar, deutlich;** *he made it clear that he wanted the manager to resign; there was no clear evidence or clear proof that he was in the house at the time of the murder*

(b) clear profit = profit after all expenses have been paid **Reingewinn;** *we made $6,000 clear profit on the sale;* **to have a clear title to something** = to have a right to something with no limitations *or* charges **ein unbestrittenes Recht auf etwas haben**

(c) free *or* total period of time **frei; ganz; three clear days** = three whole working days **drei ganze/volle Tage;** *allow three clear days for the cheque to be paid into your account*

2 *verb*

(a) to sell cheaply in order to get rid of stock **räumen, ausverkaufen**

(b) to clear goods through the customs = to have all documentation passed by the customs so that goods can leave the country **Güter zollamtlich abfertigen lassen**

(c) to clear 10% *or* **$5,000 on the deal** = to make 10% *or* $5,000 clear profit **bei einem Geschäft 10% od $5000 Gewinn machen; we cleared only our expenses** = the sales revenue paid only for the costs and expenses without making any profit **wir konnten nur unsere Unkosten decken**

(d) to clear a cheque = to pass a cheque through the banking system, so that the money is transferred from the payer's account to another account **einen Scheck einlösen;** *the cheque took ten days to clear or the bank took ten days to clear the cheque*

(e) to clear someone of charges = to find that someone is not guilty of the charges against him **jdn freisprechen;** *he was cleared of all charges or he was cleared on all counts*

◊ **clearance** *noun* **customs clearance** = act of clearing goods through the customs **Zollabfertigung; clearance certificate** = document which shows that goods have been passed by customs **Zollabfertigungsschein**

◊ **clearing** *noun*

(a) clearing of goods through the customs = passing of goods through the customs **Verzollung von Waren**

(b) clearing of a debt = paying all of a debt **Schuldenbegleichung**

(c) clearing bank = bank which clears cheques, one of the major British High

Street banks **Clearingbank; clearing house =** central office where clearing banks exchange cheques **Clearing House, Abrechnungsstelle**

◊ **clear up** *verb* to solve a crime *or* to discover who has committed a crime and arrest him **aufklären;** *half the crimes committed are never cleared up;* **clear-up rate =** number of crimes solved, as a percentage of all crimes committed **Aufklärungsrate**

> COMMENT: clear up can be divided into two categories: primary clear up, when a crime is solved by arresting the suspect, and secondary clear up, where a person charged with one crime then confesses to another which had not previously been solved

clemency *noun* pardon *or* mercy **Gnade; Begnadigung; Milde;** *as an act of clemency, the president granted an amnesty to all political prisoners*
NOTE: no plural

clerical *adjective*
(a) (work) done in an office *or* done by a clerk **Büro-, Schreib-; clerical error =** mistake made in an office **Schreibfehler; clerical staff =** staff of an office **Büropersonal, Schreibkräfte; clerical work =** paperwork done in an office **Schreib-, Büroarbeit; clerical worker =** person who works in an office **Büroangestellter**
(b) referring to the church **geistlich, klerikal**

clerk *noun*
(a) person who works in an office **Büroangestellter; Sachbearbeiter;** *accounts clerk; sales clerk; wages clerk;* **articled clerk =** trainee who is bound by a contract to work in a solicitor's office for some years to learn the law; *(GB)* **Anwaltsreferendar; chief clerk** *or* **head clerk =** most important clerk **Bürochef, Bürovorsteher; Clerk of the House (of Commons** *or* **of Lords) =** head of the administrative staff which runs the House of Commons *or* House of Lords **Verwaltungschef des Unter- od Oberhauses; clerk to the justices =** official of a magistrates' court (a qualified lawyer) who advises the magistrates on legal questions **juristischer Berater des Amtsrichters;** *the functions of a justices' clerk include giving advice about law, practice and procedure; the clerk advised the magistrates that the case had to be passed to the Crown Court for trial*

◊ **clerkess** *noun (in Scotland)* woman clerk **Büroangestellte; Sachbearbeiterin**

◊ **clerkship** *noun (in the US)* time when a student lawyer is working in the office of a lawyer before being admitted to the bar **Vorbereitungszeit bei einem Anwalt**

clever *adjective* intelligent *or* able to learn quickly **klug, schlau;** *he is very clever at spotting a bargain; clever shareholders have made a lot of money on the deal*

client *noun*
(a) person who pays for a service carried out by a professional person (such as an accountant *or* a solicitor) **Klient/-in, Mandant/-in; Kunde/Kundin**
(b) person who is represented by a lawyer **Klient/-in, Mandant/-in;** *the solicitor paid the fine on behalf of his client*

◊ **clientele** *noun* all the clients of a business; all the customers of a shop **Klientel; Kundschaft**
NOTE: no plural

clinch *verb* to settle (a business deal) *or* to come to an agreement **abschließen, besiegeln;** *he offered an extra 5% to clinch the deal; they need approval from the board before they can clinch the deal*

close
1 *noun* end **Schluß;** *at the close of the day's trading the shares had fallen 20%*
2 *adjective* **close to =** very near *or* almost **nahe daran, fast;** *the company was close to bankruptcy; we are close to solving the crime*
3 *verb*
(a) to stop doing business for the day **schließen;** *the office closes at 5.30; we close early on Saturdays*
(b) **to close the accounts =** to come to the end of an accounting period and make up the profit and loss account **die Bücher abschließen**
(c) **to close an account =** (i) to stop supplying a customer on credit; (ii) to take all the money out of a bank account and stop the account **(i) ein Kundenkonto sperren; (ii) ein Konto auflösen**
(d) **the shares closed at $15 =** at the end of the day's trading the price of the shares was $15 **die Aktien erreichten eine Schlußnotierung von $15**

◊ **close company** *or (US)* **close(d) corporation** *noun* privately owned company where the public may own a small number of shares; *entspricht* **Personengesellschaft**

◊ **closed** *adjective*
(a) shut *or* not open *or* not doing business **geschlossen;** *the office is closed on Mondays; all the banks are closed on the National Day*

(b) restricted to a few people **nichtöffentlich; closed shop** = system where a company agrees to employ only union members in certain jobs **gewerkschaftspflichtiger Betrieb;** *a closed shop agreement; the union is asking the management to agree to a closed shop;* **closed market** = market where a supplier deals only with one agent and does not supply any others direct **geschlossener Markt;** *they signed a closed market agreement with an American company;* **closed session** = meeting which is not open to the public or to journalists **geschlossene/nichtöffentliche Sitzung;** *the town council met in closed session to discuss staff problems in the Education Department; the public gallery was cleared when the meeting went into closed session*

◊ **close down** *verb* to shut a shop *or* factory for a long period or for ever **schließen; stillegen;** *the company is closing down its London office; the strike closed down the railway system*

◊ **closing**
1 *adjective*
(a) final *or* coming at the end **Abschluß-, Schluß-, abschließend; closing speech** = final speech for prosecution and defence at the end of a trial **Schlußplädoyer**
(b) at the end of an accounting period **Abschluß-**
2 *noun*
(a) shutting of a shop *or* being shut **Schließung; Sunday closing** = not opening a shop on Sundays **geschäftsfreier Sonntag; closing time** = time when a shop or office stops work **Geschäftsschluß; Ladenschluß; early closing day** = weekday (usually Wednesday or Thursday) when many shops close in the afternoon **Tag mit frühem Ladenschluß**
(b) closing of an account = act of stopping supply to a customer on credit **Sperrung eines Kunden(kredit)kontos**

◊ **closure** *noun*
(a) act of closing **Schließung**
(b) *(in the House of Commons)* **closure motion** = proposal to end a debate **Antrag auf Schluß der Debatte**

clue *noun* thing which helps someone solve a crime **Spur; Anhaltspunkt; Hinweis;** *the police have searched the room for clues; the police have several clues to the identity of the murdered*

Cmnd = COMMAND PAPERS

c/o = CARE OF

Co = COMPANY *J. Smith & Co Ltd*

co- *prefix* working *or* acting together **Mit-, mit; co-creditor** = person who is a creditor of the same company as you are **Solidargläubiger; co-defendant** = person who appears in a case with another defendant **Mitbeklagter; co-director** = person who is a director of the same company as you **Mitdirektor; co-insurance** = insurance policy where the risk is shared among several insurers **Mitversicherung**

c.o.d. = CASH ON DELIVERY, *(US)* COLLECT ON DELIVERY

code
1 *noun*
(a) official set of laws *or* regulations **Kodex; Vorschriften; the Highway Code** = rules which govern the behaviour of people and vehicles using roads **Straßenverkehrsordnung; the penal code** = set of laws governing crime and its punishment **Strafgesetzbuch;** *failure to observe the code does not render anyone liable to proceedings*
(b) set of laws of a country **Gesetzbuch;** *(US)* **the Louisiana Code** = laws of the state of Louisiana **Gesetze des Staates Louisiana; Code Napoleon** = civil laws of France (introduced by Napoleon) **Code Napoléon**
(c) set of semi-official rules **Regeln, Kodex; code of conduct** = informal (sometimes written) rules by which a group of people work **Verhaltenskodex; code of practice** = (i) rules to be followed when applying a law; (ii) rules drawn up by an association which the members must follow when doing business **(i) Verfahrensrecht; (ii) Richtlinien;** *the Code of Practice on Picketing has been issued by the Secretary of State*
(d) system of signs *or* numbers *or* letters which mean something **Code, Chiffre;** *the spy sent his message in code;* **area code** = numbers which indicate an area for telephoning **Vorwahl, Ortsnetzkennzahl; machine-readable codes** = sets of signs or letters (such as bar codes *or* post codes) which can be read by computers **maschinenlesbare Codes; post code** *or* *(US)* **zip code** = letters and numbers used to indicate a town *or* street in an address on an envelope **Postleitzahl**
2 *verb* to write (a message) using secret signs **verschlüsseln, chiffrieren;** *we received coded instructions from our agent in New York*

◊ **coding** *noun* act of putting a code on something **Verschlüsselung, Chiffrierung;** *the coding of invoices*

codicil *noun* document executed in the same way as a will, making additions *or* changes to an existing will **Kodizill, Testamentsnachtrag**

codify *verb* to put (laws) together to form a code **kodifizieren**

◊ **codification** *noun*
(a) putting all laws together into a formal legal code **Kodifizierung von Gesetzen**
(b) bringing together all statutes and case law relating to a certain issue, to make a single Act of Parliament **Vereinigung von Gesetzen;** *see also* CONSOLIDATION

coercion *noun* forcing someone by pressure to commit a crime *or* do some act **Nötigung, Zwang**
NOTE: no plural

cohabit *verb (of a man and a woman)* to live together as man and wife **in eheähnlicher Gemeinschaft leben**

◊ **cohabitation** *noun* living together as man and wife (whether married or not) **eheähnliche Gemeinschaft**

◊ **cohabiter** *or* **cohabitee** *noun* person who lives with another person of the opposite sex without being married **in eheähnlicher Gemeinschaft Lebender**

coin *noun* piece of metal money **Münze, Geldstück;** *he gave me two 10-cent coins in my change; I need some 10p coins for the telephone*

◊ **coinage** *noun* system of metal money used in a country **Hartgeldwährung**
NOTE: no plural

collaborate *verb* to work together **zusammenarbeiten;** *to collaborate with a French firm on building a bridge; they collaborated on the new aircraft*

◊ **collaboration** *noun* working together **Zusammenarbeit;** *their collaboration on the development of the computer system was very profitable*

collateral
1 *noun* (security) used to provide a guarantee for a loan **zusätzliche Sicherheit/Deckung**
2 *adjective*
(a) in addition **zusätzlich, zusatz-, Neben-; collateral contract** contract which induces a person to enter into a more important contract **Nebenvertrag**
(b) **collateral issue** = issue which arises from a plea in a criminal court **Nebenfrage**

collation *noun* comparing a copy with the original to see if it is perfect **Kollation, Vergleich**

colleague *noun* person who works with someone else **Kollege/Kollegin;** *counsel asked for more time to consult his colleagues*

collect
1 *verb*
(a) to make someone pay money which is owed **einziehen, eintreiben; to collect a debt** = to go and make someone pay a debt **Schulden einziehen/eintreiben**
(b) to take goods away from a place **abholen;** *we have to collect the stock from the warehouse; can you collect my letters from the typing pool?;* **letters are collected twice a day** = the post office workers take them from the letter box to the post office so that they can be sent off **die Briefkästen werden zweimal täglich geleert**
2 *noun US* phone call where the person receiving the call agrees to pay for it **R-Gespräch;** *to make a collect call; he called his office collect*

◊ **collecting** *noun* **collecting agency** = agency which collects money owed to other companies for a commission **Inkassobüro**

◊ **collection** *noun*
(a) getting money together *or* making someone pay money which is owed **Einziehung, Eintreibung; debt collection** = collecting money which is owed **Schuldeneinziehung; debt collection agency** = company which collects debts for other companies for a commission **Inkassobüro; bills for collection** = bills where payment is due **fällige Rechnungen; Inkassowechsel**
(b) fetching of goods **Abholung;** *the stock is in the warehouse awaiting collection;* **collection charges** *or* **collection rates** = charge for collecting something **Abholgebüren; to hand something in for collection** = to leave something for someone to come and collect **etwas für jdn hinterlegen**
(c) **collections** = money which has been collected **Sammlung; Kollekte**
(d) taking of letters from a letter box or mail room to the post office to be sent off **Leerung;** *there are six collections a day from the letter box*

◊ **collective** *adjective* working together **gemeinsam, kollektiv, Gemeinschafts-, Kollektiv-; (free) collective bargaining** = negotiations about wages and working conditions between management and workers' representatives **(autonome) Tarifverhandlungen; collective ownership** = ownership of a business by the workers who work in it **Kollektivinhaberschaft; collective responsibility** = doctrine that all members of a group (such as the British cabinet) are responsible together for the actions of the group **Kollektivverantwortung;** *they signed a collective wage agreement* =

an agreement was signed between management and the trade union about wages **sie haben einen Lohntarifvertrag unterzeichnet**

◊ **collector** *noun* person who makes people pay money which is owed **Einnehmer/-in; Inkassobeauftragter;** *collector of taxes or tax collector; debt collector*

college *noun*
(a) place where people can study after they have left school **College, Institut; Hochschule; business college** *or* **commercial college** = college which teaches general business methods **Wirtschafts-, Handelsinstitut; correspondence college** = college where the teaching is done by mail (sending work to the students who then return it to be marked) **Fernhochschule; secretarial college** = college which teaches shorthand, typing and word-processing **Sekretärinnenschule**
(b) electoral college = group of people elected by larger groups to vote on their behalf in an election **Wahlausschuß, Wahlmännergremium**

collision *noun* crash *or* accident between vehicles **Kollision, Zusammenstoß;** *six people were injured in the collision*

collusion *noun* illicit co-operation between people *or* agreement between parties in order to cheat another party *or in* order to defraud another party of a right **Kollusion, (unerlaubte) geheime Absprache;** *he was suspected of (acting in) collusion with the owner of the property*
NOTE: no plural

◊ **collusive action** *noun* action which is taken in collusion with another party **in (unerlaubter) geheimer Absprache erfolgte Handlung**

column *noun* list of figures one written underneath the other **Spalte, Kolonne; debit column** *or* **credit column** = lists of figures in accounts, showing money paid to others *or* owed by others **Debetspalte; Kreditspalte**

comfort *noun* **letter of comfort** *or* **comfort letter** = letter supporting someone who is trying to get a loan *or* letter which reassures someone on a particular point **Bonitätsbestätigung**

comity (of nations) *noun* custom whereby the courts of one country acknowledge and apply the laws of another country in certain cases **Anerkennung ausländischer Gesetze und Gerichtsentscheidungen**

command
1 *noun* order **Befehl; by Royal Command** = by order of the Queen *or* King **durch königliche Order; Command papers** = papers (such as White papers *or* Green Papers *or* reports of Royal Commissions) which are presented to Parliament by the government **Regierungsvorlagen**
2 *verb* to order someone to do something **befehlen;** *the judge commanded that the public gallery should be cleared; the President commanded the Chief of Police to arrest the Members of Parliament*

commander *noun* high rank in the Metropolitan Police force (equivalent to Assistant Chief Constable) **Kommandeur der Londoner Polizei**

commence *verb* to begin **beginnen;** *the proceedings commenced with the swearing-in of witnesses; the police inspector commenced the questioning of the suspect*

◊ **commencement** *noun* beginning **Beginn; date of commencement** = date when an Act of Parliament takes effect **Datum des Inkrafttretens (eines Gesetzes)**

comment
1 *noun* remark *or* spoken *or* written opinion **Be-, Anmerkung; Kommentar;** *the judge made a comment on the evidence presented by the defence; the newspaper has some short comments about the trial;* **fair comment** = remark which is honestly made on a matter of public interest and so is not defamatory **sachliche Kritik**
2 *verb* to remark *or* to express an opinion **sich äußern;** *the judge commented on the lack of evidence; the newspapers commented on the result of the trial*

◊ **commentary** *noun* (i) textbook which comments on the law; (ii) brief notes which comment on the main points of a judgment **(i) Erläuterungswerk; (ii) Kommentar**

commerce *noun* business *or* buying and selling of goods and services **Handel; Handelsverkehr; Chamber of Commerce** = group of local businessmen who meet to discuss problems which they have in common and to promote business in their town **Handelskammer**

◊ **commercial**
1 *adjective*
(a) referring to business **Handels-, Geschäfts-, geschäftlich, kommerziell; commercial college** = college which teaches business studies **Wirtschafts-, Handelsinstitut; commercial course** = course where business skills are studied **kaufmännischer Lehrgang; Commercial Court** = court in the Queen's

Bench Division which hears cases relating to business disputes; *(GB)* **Handelsgericht; entspricht Kammer für Handelssachen; commercial directory** = book which lists all the businesses and business people in a town **Branchenadreßbuch; commercial law** = laws regarding business **Handelsrecht (Teil des Wirtschaftsrechts)**
(b) profitable **wirtschaftlich; kommerziell; not a commercial proposition** = not likely to make a profit **kein gewinnbringendes Geschäft**

◊ **commercialization** *noun* making something into a business enterprise **Kommerzialisierung**

◊ **commercialize** *verb* to make something into a business **kommerzialisieren**

◊ **commercially** *adverb* in a business way **geschäftlich, kommerziell; not commercially viable** = not likely to make a profit **unrentabel**

commission *noun*
(a) official order to someone, giving him authority and explaining what his duties are **Auftrag; Amt; he has a commission in the armed forces** = he is an officer in the armed forces **er ist Offizier der Streitkräfte**
(b) payment (usually a percentage of turnover) made to an agent **Provision, Maklergebühr;** *he has an agent's commission of 15% of sales*
(c) group of people officially appointed to examine some problem **Kommission, Ausschuß;** *the government has appointed a commission of inquiry to look into the problems of prison overcrowding; he is the chairman of the government commission on football violence;* **Commission of the European Community** = main executive body of the EC, made up of members of each state **Europäische Kommission; Law Commission** = permanent committee which reviews English law and recommends changes to it **ständiger Rechtsausschuß; Royal Commission** = group of people specially appointed by a minister to examine and report on a major problem **königlicher Untersuchungsausschuß**

◊ **commissioner** *noun* member of an official commission; person who has an official commission; member of the Commission of the European Community **Ausschußmitglied; Kommissar; EG Kommissar; the Commissioners of the Inland Revenue** = the Board of the Inland Revenue **Aufsichtsbehörde des Finanzamts; commissioner for oaths** = solicitor appointed by the Lord Chancellor to administer affidavits which may be used in court **Anwalt, der befugt ist, Eide abzunehmen;** *entspricht* **Notar; commissioner of police** *or* **police commissioner** = highest rank in a

police force **Polizeikommandeur; Metropolitan Police Commissioner** = head of the Metropolitan Police in London **Chef der Londoner Polizei**

commit *verb*
(a) to send (someone) to prison *or* to a court **einweisen; einliefern; überstellen;** *he was committed for trial in the Central Criminal Court; the magistrates committed her for trial at the Crown Court*
(b) to carry out (a crime) **begehen;** *the gang committed six robberies before they were caught*
NOTE: **committing - committed**

◊ **commitment** *noun*
(a) order for sending someone to prison **Überstellung; Einweisung; Einlieferung**
(b) commitments = obligations *or* things which have to be done **Verpflichtungen; to honour one's commitments** = to do what one is obliged to do **zu seinen Verpflichtungen stehen; financial commitments** = money which is owed *or* debts which have to be paid **finanzielle Verpflichtungen**

◊ **committal** *noun* sending someone to a court *or* to prison **Überstellung; Inhaftierung; committal order** = order sending someone to prison for contempt of court **Haftanordnung; committal proceedings** = preliminary hearing of a case before the magistrates' court, to decide if it is serious enough to be tried before a jury in a higher court **gerichtliche Voruntersuchung; committal for trial** = sending someone to be tried in a higher court following committal proceedings in a magistrates' court **Übergabe der Sache an eine höhere Instanz; committal for sentence** = sending someone who has been convicted in a magistrates court to be sentenced in a higher court **Überweisung an eine höhere Instanz zur Aburteilung; committal warrant** = order sending someone to serve a prison sentence **Nachricht zum Strafantritt, Einlieferungsbefehl**

committee *noun*
(a) official group of people who organize or plan for a larger group **Komitee, Ausschuß, Gremium;** *to be a member of a committee or to sit on a committee; he was elected to the committee of the staff club; the new plans have to be approved by the committee members;* **to chair a committee** = to be the chairman of a committee **einem Ausschuß vorsitzen, bei einem Ausschuß den Vorsitz führen;** *he is the chairman of the planning committee; she is the secretary of the finance committee*
(b) *(in the House of Commons)* **Committee Stage** = one of the stages in the discussion of a Bill, where each clause is examined in

detail **Prüfung eines Gesetzentwurfes im dafür zuständigen Ausschuß; select committee =** special committee of the House of Commons (with members representing various political parties) which examines the work of a ministry **Sonderausschuß; standing committee =** permanent committee which examines Bills not sent to other committees **ständiger Ausschuß; Committee of the Whole House =** the House of Commons acting as a committee to examine the clauses of a Bill **Unterhausausschuß zur Prüfung von Gesetzentwürfen; Plenarausschuß; Committee of Privileges** special committee of the House of Commons which examines cases of breach of privilege **Ausschuß zur Untersuchung von Privilegien; Public Accounts Committee =** committee of the House of Commons which examines the spending of each ministry and department **Rechnungsprüfungsausschuß; Committee of Ways and Means =** committee of the whole House of Commons which considers a Supply Bill (i.e. a Bill relating to public finance) **Finanzausschuß**

commodity *noun* thing sold in very large quantities, especially raw materials and food such as metals or corn **Ware; primary** *or* **basic commodities =** farm produce grown in large quantities, such as corn, rice, cotton **Grundstoffe; commodity market =** place where people buy and sell commodities **Warenbörse; commodity futures =** trading in commodities for delivery at a later date **Warentermingeschäft;** *silver rose 5% on the commodity futures market yesterday;* **commodity trader =** person whose business is buying and selling commodities **Warenterminhändler**

common
1 *noun* land on which anyone can walk, and may have the right to keep animals, pick wood, etc. **Gemeindeland;** (NOTE: now usually used in place names such as **Clapham Common**)
2 *adjective*
(a) which happens very often **häufig, weitverbreitet, allgemein;** *putting the carbon paper in the wrong way round is a common mistake; being caught by the customs is very common these days*
(b) referring to *or* belonging to several different people or to everyone **gemeinsam, Gemeinschafts-, Gemein-; common assault =** crime *or* tort of acting in such a way that another person is afraid he will be attacked and hurt **Bedrohung, unqualifizierte Gewaltandrohung; common carrier =** firm which carries goods or passengers, which

cannot normally refuse to do so and which can be used by anyone **öffentliches Transportunternehmen; öffentliches Verkehrsunternehmen; common land =** land on which anyone can walk and may have the right to keep animals, pick wood, etc. **Gemeindeland; common nuisance =** criminal act which causes harm *or* danger to members of the public in general *or* to their rights **grober Unfug; öffentliches Ärgernis; common ownership =** ownership of a company *or* a property by a group of people who each own a part **Miteigentum; common pricing** illegal fixing of prices by several businesses so that they all charge the same price **Preisabsprache; common seal** seal which a corporation must possess, and which is used to seal official papers; *(GB)* **Gesellschaftssiegel**
(c) in common = together **gemeinsam; gemeinschaftlich; ownership in common =** COMMON OWNERSHIP; **tenancy in common** = situation where two or more persons jointly lease a property and each can leave his interest to his heirs when he dies **Bruchteilsgemeinschaft;** *compare* JOINT TENANCY

◊ **common law** *noun*
(a) law as laid down in decisions of courts, rather than by statute **nicht-kodifiziertes Recht**
(b) general system of laws which formerly were the only laws existing in England, and which in some cases have been superseded by statute; *(GB)* **früheres englisches Gesetzessystem**
NOTE: you say **at common law** when referring to something happening according to the principles of common law

◊ **common-law** *adjective* according to the old unwritten system of law **nach gemeinem Recht; common-law marriage =** situation where two people live together as husband and wife without being married **eheähnliche Gemeinschaft; she is his common-law wife =** woman who is living with a man as his wife, although they have not been legally married **sie lebt mit ihm in eheähnlicher Gemeinschaft**

◊ **Common Market** *noun* **the Common Market =** the European Community *or* organization which joins several European countries for the purposes of trade **der Gemeinsame Markt; the Common Market finance ministers =** the finance ministers of all the Common Market countries meeting as a group **die Finanzminister der Europäischen Gemeinschaft**

◊ **Commons** *plural noun* = HOUSE OF COMMONS *the Commons voted against the Bill; the majority of the Commons are in favour of law reform*

◊ **Common Serjeant** *noun* senior barrister who sits as a judge in the City of London and acts as adviser to the City of London Corporation; *(in London)* **ranghöherer Barrister**

◊ **Commonwealth** *noun* the **Commonwealth** = association of independent countries which were once ruled by the UK **das Commonwealth**

commorientes *plural noun* people who die at the same time (as a husband and wife who die in an accident) **Kommorienten, gleichzeitig Versterbende**

> COMMENT: the law assumes that the younger person has died after the older one

communicate *verb* to pass information to someone **sich besprechen, sich verständigen;** *the members of the jury must not communicate with the witnesses*

◊ **communication** *noun*
(a) passing of information **Besprechung, Verständigung; to enter into communication with someone** = to start discussing something with someone, usually in writing **mit jdm in Verbindung treten;** *we have entered into communication with the relevant government department*
(b) official message **Mitteilung; Nachricht;** *we have had a communication from the local tax inspector;* **privileged communication** = letter which could be libellous, but which is protected by privilege (such as a letter from a client to his lawyer) **der Rechtsverfolgung entzogene Mitteilungen**
(c) **communications** = being able to contact people *or* to pass messages **Kommunikationsverbindungen;** *after the flood all communications with the outside world were broken*

community *noun*
(a) group of people living or working in the same place **Gemeinde; Gemeinschaft; the local business community** = the business people living and working in the area **die örtliche Geschäftswelt; community home** = house which belongs to a local authority, where children in care can be kept **kommunales Kinderheim; community policing** = way of policing a section of a town, whereby the people in the area and the local police force act together to prevent crime and disorder **Zusammenarbeit zwischen Bürgern und Kontakt(bereichs)beamten; community service** = working on behalf of the local community **gemeinnützige Arbeit; community service order** = punishment where a criminal is sentenced to do unpaid work in the local community **Verurteilung zu gemeinnütziger Arbeit**
(b) **the European Community** = the Common Market **die Europäische Gemeinschaft; Community legislation** = regulations *or* directives issued by the EC Council of Ministers *or* the EC Commission **Bestimmungen der Europäischen Gemeinschaft; the Community ministers** = the ministers of member states of the Common Market **die Minister der Europäischen Gemeinschaft**
(c) *(in the USA, Canada, France and many other countries)* **Öffentlichkeit; Volk; Bevölkerung; community property** = situation where the husband and wife jointly own any property which they acquire during the course of their marriage **Gütergemeinschaft**

commute *verb*
(a) to travel to work from home each day **pendeln;** *he commutes from the country to his office in the centre of town*
(b) to change a right into cash **umwandeln**
(c) to reduce a harsh sentence to a lesser one **umwandeln; mildern, herabsetzen;** *the death sentence was commuted to life imprisonment*
◊ **commutation** *noun* reducing a harsh sentence to a lesser one **Umwandlung; Milderung, Herabsetzung**
◊ **commuter** *noun* person who commutes to work **Pendler/-in; he lives in the commuter belt** = area of country where the commuters live round a town **er lebt im städtischen Einzugsbereich; commuter train** = train which commuters take in the morning and evening **Pendler-, Nahverkehrszug**

compact *noun* agreement **Vertrag; Abkommen**

company *noun*
(a) business *or* group of people organized to buy, sell or provide a service **Firma, Unternehmen**
(b) group of people organized to buy or sell or provide a service which has been legally incorporated, and so is a legal entity separate from its individual members **Gesellschaft; to put a company into liquidation** = to close a company by selling its assets to pay its creditors **ein Unternehmen liquidieren; to set up a company** = to start a company legally **eine Firma gründen; associate company** = company which is partly owned by another company **Beteiligungsgesellschaft; close company** = privately owned company where the public may own a small number of shares **Personengesellschaft;** *entspricht* **GmbH; family company** = company where most of

the shares are owned by members of the same family **Familiengesellschaft; holding company** = company which exists only to own shares in subsidiary companies **Dach-, Holdinggesellschaft; joint-stock company** = company whose shares are held by many people; *entspricht* **(nicht an der Börse notierte) Aktiengesellschaft; limited (liability) company** = company where a shareholder is responsible for repaying the company's debts only to the face value of the shares he owns **Gesellschaft mit beschränkter Haftung; listed company** = company whose shares can be bought or sold on the Stock Exchange **börsenfähiges Unternehmen, an der Börse notierte Gesellschaft; parent company** = company which owns more than half of another company's shares **Muttergesellschaft; private (limited) company** = company with a small number of shareholders, whose shares are not traded on the Stock Exchange **Personengesellschaft (mit beschränkter Haftung);** *entspricht* **GmbH; public limited company (plc)** = company whose shares can be bought on the Stock Exchange; *entspricht* **Aktiengesellschaft; subsidiary company** = company which is owned by a parent company **Tochtergesellschaft**

(c) finance company = company which provides money for hire-purchase **Finanzierungsgesellschaft; insurance company** = company whose business is insurance **Versicherungsgesellschaft; shipping company** = company whose business is in carrying goods by sea **Reederei; a tractor** *or* **chocolate company** = company which makes tractors *or* chocolate **Traktorenhersteller; Schokoladenhersteller**

(d) company director = person appointed by the shareholders to run a company; *entspricht* **geschäftsführender Direktor/Manager;** *(bei AG)* **Vorstandsvorsitzender; company law** = laws which refer to the way companies may work **Unternehmensrecht; company member** = shareholder in a company **Gesellschafter; company secretary** = person responsible for the company's legal and financial affairs; *(GB)* **Manager mit Aufgabenbereich Finanzen und Verwaltung;** *(GB)* **the Companies Act** = Act of the British parliament which states the legal limits within which a company may do business **Gesellschaftsrecht; Registrar of Companies** = official who keeps a record of all incorporated companies, the details of their directors and financial state; *entspricht* **Registerbevollmächtigter; register of companies** *or* **companies' register** = list of companies showing details of their directors and registered addresses **Firmenregister; Companies House** = office

which keeps details of incorporated companies; *entspricht* **Registerbüro**

(e) organization in the City of London which does mainly charitable work, and is derived from one of the former trade associations **Gesellschaft, Wohltätigkeitsorganisation;** *the Drapers' Company; the Grocers' Company*

compare *verb* to look at several things to see how they differ **vergleichen;** *the finance director compared the figures for the first and second quarters; the detective compared the fingerprints on the bottle and those on the knife*

◊ **compare with** *verb* to put two things together to see how they differ **vergleichen mit;** *compared with that of some major cities, our crime rate is quite low*

◊ **comparable** *adjective* which can be compared **vergleichbar;** *the two crimes are not comparable;* **which is the nearest company comparable to this one in size?** = which company is of a roughly similar size and can be compared with this one? **welches Unternehmen ist von der Größe her, am nähesten vergleichbar?**

◊ **comparison** *noun* way of comparing **Vergleich;** *sales are down in comparison with those of last year;* **there is no comparison between export and home sales** = export and home sales are so different they cannot be compared **die Verkaufszahlen des Inlandes lassen sich nicht mit den Exportziffern vergleichen**

◊ **comparative** *adjective* which compares one thing with another **vergleichend; comparative law** = study which compares the legal systems of different countries **vergleichende Rechtswissenschaft**

compel *verb* to force (someone) to do something **zwingen;** *the Act compels all drivers to have adequate insurance*
NOTE: **compelling - compelled**

◊ **compellable** *adjective* **a compellable witness** (person) who can be forced to do something **aussagepflichtiger Zeuge**

◊ **compellability** *noun* being compellable **Zwang**

compensate *verb* to pay for damage done **entschädigen;** *to compensate a manager for loss of commission*

◊ **compensation** *noun*
(a) payment made by someone to cover the cost of damage *or* hardship which he has caused **Entschädigung;** *unlimited compensation may be awarded in the Crown Court;* **compensation for damage** = payment for damage done **Schadensersatz; compensation for loss of office** = payment to

a director who is asked to leave a company before his contract ends **Entlassungsabfindung; compensation for loss of earnings** = payment to someone who has stopped earning money *or* who is not able to earn money **Verdienstausfallentschädigung; compensation fund** = special fund set up by the Law Society to compensate clients for loss suffered because of the actions of solicitors **Ausgleichsfonds; compensation order** = order made by a criminal court to compel a criminal to pay money to his victim **Urteil auf Schadensersatz**
(b) *US* salary *or* payment made to someone for work which he has done **Lohn, Gehalt; Vergütung; compensation package** = salary, pension and other benefits offered with a job **Lohn und weitere Sozialleistungen**

◊ **compensatory** *adjective* **compensatory damages** = damages which compensate for loss *or* harm suffered **ausgleichender Schadensersatz**

compete *verb* **to compete with someone** *or* **with a company** = to try to do better than another person *or* another company **mit jdm od einem Unternehmen konkurrieren;** *the gangs were competing for control of the drugs market*

◊ **competition** *noun* competing with another company *or* trying to do better than another company **Wettbewerb, Konkurrenz; free competition** = being free to compete without government interference **freier Wettbewerb; unfair competition** = trying to do better than another company by bringing cheap foreign products into the country *or* by making incorrect criticisms of the other company's products **unlauterer Wettbewerb**

◊ **competitor** *noun* person *or* company which competes **Konkurrent/-in;** *two German firms are our main competitors; the contract of employment forbids members of staff from leaving to go to work for competitors*

competence *or* **competency** *noun*
(a) state of a witness who is permitted to give evidence **Wertigkeit der Zeugenaussage**
(b) the case falls within the competence of the court = the court is legally able to deal with the case **der Rechtsfall fällt in die Zuständigkeit des Gerichts**

◊ **competent** *adjective*
(a) able to do something; efficient **kompetent, fähig;** *she is a competent secretary or a competent manager*
(b) legally able to do something **befugt, zuständig; the court is not competent to deal with this case** = the court is not legally able to deal with the case **das Gericht ist nicht zuständig für diesen Rechtsfall**

complain *verb* to say that something is no good *or* does not work properly **sich beschweren;** *the office is so cold the staff have started complaining; she complained about the service; they are complaining that our prices are too high; if you want to complain, write to the manager*

◊ **complainant** *noun* person who makes a complaint *or* who starts proceedings against someone **Beschwerdeführer; Kläger/-in**

◊ **complaint** *noun*
(a) statement that you feel something is wrong **Beschwerde;** *when making a complaint, always quote the reference number; she sent her letter of complaint to the managing director;* **to make** *or* **lodge a complaint against someone** = to write and send an official complaint to someone's superior **gegen jdn Beschwerde einlegen; complaints procedure** = agreed way for workers to make complaints to the management about working conditions **Beschwerdeverfahren; Police Complaints Committee** = group of people who investigate complaints made by members of the public against the police **Ausschuß zur Untersuchung polizeilicher Vergehen**
(b) document signed to start proceedings in a Magistrates' Court **Klageschrift**
(c) statement of the case made by the plaintiff at the beginning of a civil action **Strafanzeige**

complete
1 *adjective* whole *or* with nothing missing **komplett, vollständig;** *the order is complete and ready for sending; the order should be delivered only if it is complete*
2 *verb*
(a) to finish **beenden, fertigstellen;** *the factory completed the order in two weeks; how long will it take you to complete the job?*
(b) to complete a conveyance = to convey a property to a purchaser, when the purchaser pays the purchase price and the vendor hands over the signed conveyance and the deeds of the property **eine Eigentumsübertragung abschließen**

◊ **completely** *adverb* all *or* totally **völlig, vollkommen;** *the cargo was completely ruined by water; the warehouse was completely destroyed by fire*

◊ **completion** *noun* act of finishing something **Abschluß, Beendigung; Fertigstellung; completion date** = date when something will be finished **Fertigstellungstermin; Abschlußtermin; completion of a conveyance** = last stage in the sale of a property when the solicitors for the two parties meet, when the purchaser pays and the vendor passes the conveyance and the deeds to the purchaser

Vertragsabschluß (bei Eigentumsübertragung); **completion statement** = statement of account from a solicitor to a client showing all the costs of the sale *or* purchase of a property **Abschlußrechnung nach Vertragsabschluß**

complex
1 *noun* series of large buildings **Komplex;** *a large industrial complex*
2 *adjective* with many different parts **komplex, kompliziert;** *a complex system of import controls; the regulations governing immigration are very complex*

compliance *noun* agreement to do what is ordered **Einhaltung; Befolgung; Erfüllung;** *the documents have been drawn up in compliance with the provisions of the Act;* **declaration of compliance** = declaration made by a person forming a limited company, that the requirements of the Companies' Act have been met **Erklärung der Richtigkeit von Angaben im Sinne des Companies Act zur Gesellschaftsgründung**
◊ **compliant** *adjective* which agrees with something **übereinstimmend; not compliant with** = not in agreement with **nicht übereinstimmend mit;** *the settlement is not compliant with the earlier order of the court*

complicated *adjective* with many different parts *or* sections which make things difficult to understand **kompliziert;** *the VAT rules are very complicated; the judge warned the jury that the case was a complicated one and might last several weeks*

comply *verb* **to comply with something** = to obey **etwas einhalten; etwas befolgen;** *the company has complied with the court order; she refused to comply with the injunction*

composition *noun* agreement between a debtor and creditors to settle a debt immediately by repaying only part of it **Vergleich**

compos mentis *Latin phrase meaning* "of sound mind" *or* "sane" **bei gesundem Verstand**

compound
1 *adjective* **compound interest** = interest which is added to the capital and then itself earns interest **Zinseszins(en)**
2 *verb*
(a) to agree with creditors to settle a debt by paying part of what is owed **einen Vergleich schließen**

(b) to compound an offence = to agree (in return for payment) not to prosecute someone who has committed an offence **Einstellung des Verfahrens gegen Geldauflage**

comprehensive *adjective* which includes everything **umfassend;** *(GB)* **comprehensive insurance** = insurance policy which covers you against a large number of possible risks **kombinierte Haftpflicht- und Vollkaskoversicherung**

compromise
1 *noun* agreement between two sides, where each side gives way a little in order to reach a settlement **Kompromiß;** *management offered £5 an hour, the union asked for £9, and a compromise of £7.50 was reached; after some discussion a compromise solution was reached*
2 *verb*
(a) to reach an agreement by giving way a little **einen Kompromiß schließen;** *he asked £15 for it, I offered £7 and we compromised on £10*
(b) to involve someone in something which makes his reputation less good **kompromittieren;** *the minister was compromised in the bribery case*

comptroller *noun* person in charge, especially referring to accounts **Rechnungsprüfer;** *(GB)* **Comptroller and Auditor General** = official whose duty is to examine the accounts of ministries and government departments **Rechnungsprüfer des Rechnungshofes**

compulsory *adjective* which is forced *or* ordered **obligatorisch, verbindlich; compulsory liquidation** *or* **compulsory winding up** = liquidation which is ordered by a court **Zwangsliquidation; compulsory purchase** = buying of a property by the local council *or* the government even if the owner does not want to sell **Enteignung; compulsory purchase order** = official order from the local council *or* from the government ordering an owner to sell his property **Enteignungsbeschluß; compulsory winding up order** = order from a court saying that a company must be wound up **Zwangsliquidationsbeschluß**

computer *noun* electronic machine which calculates *or* stores information and processes it automatically **Computer, Rechner; computer bureau** = office which offers to do work on its computers for companies which do not have their own computers **Rechenzentrum; EDV-Service; computer error** = mistake made by a

computer **Computerfehler; computer file =** section of information on a computer (such as a list of addresses *or* customer accounts) **Computerdatei; computer fraud =** fraud committed by using computer files (such as in a bank) **Computerbetrug; computer language =** system of signs, letters and words used to instruct a computer **Computersprache; computer program =** instructions to a computer, telling it to do a particular piece of work **Computerprogramm**
◊ **computerize** *verb* to change from a manual system to one using computers **computerisieren, auf Computer/Datenverarbeitung/EDV umstellen;** *the police criminal records have been completely computerized*

con
1 *noun*
(a) *informal* trick done to try to get money from someone **Schwindel, Trick;** *trying to get us to pay him for ten hours' overtime was just a con*
(b) *slang* (i) convict *or* prisoner; (ii) conviction **(i) Knastbruder, Knacki; (ii) Verurteilung**
2 *verb (informal)* to trick someone to try to get money **jdn durch einen Trick dazu bringen, etwas zu tun; hereinlegen;** *they conned the bank into lending them £25,000 with no security; he conned the finance company out of £100,000*
NOTE: **con - conning - conned** Note also you con someone **into** doing something

conceal *verb* to hide **verbergen; verschweigen; unterdrücken;** *he was accused of concealing information; the accused had a gun concealed under his coat*
◊ **concealment** *noun* hiding for criminal purposes **Veschweigung; Unterdrückung; concealment of assets =** hiding assets so that creditors do not know they exist **Vermögensverschleierung; concealment of birth =** notifiable offence of hiding the fact that a child has been born **Personenstandsunterdrückung, Verletzung der Anzeigepflicht (der Geburt eines Kindes)**

concede *verb* to admit (that the opposing party is right) **zugeben, zugestehen;** *counsel conceded that his client owed the money; the witness conceded under questioning that he had never been near the house;* **to concede defeat =** to admit that you have lost **sich geschlagen geben**

concern
1 *noun*
(a) business *or* company **Konzern; his business is a going concern =** the company is working (and making a profit) **er hat ein**

dynamisches Unternehmen; **sold as a going concern =** sold as an actively trading company **als rentables Unternehmen verkauft**
(b) state of being worried about a problem **Besorgnis, Sorge; Anteil, Interesse;** *the management showed no concern at all for the workers' safety*
2 *verb* to deal with *or* to be connected with **betreffen, angehen, sich befassen mit;** *the court is not concerned with the value of the items stolen; the report does not concern itself with the impartiality of the judge; he has been asked to give evidence to the commission of inquiry concerning the breakdown of law and order; the contract was drawn up with the agreement of all parties concerned*

concert party *noun* two or more people who act together in secret to take over a company **Konsortium, das die verdeckte Übernahme eines Unternehmens plant**

concession *noun*
(a) right to use someone else's property for business purposes **Konzession; mining concession =** right to dig a mine on a piece of land **Abbaurechte, Bergbaukonzession**
(b) right to be the only seller of a product in a place **Alleinvertrieb, Konzession;** *she runs a jewellery concession in a department store*
(c) allowance **Vergünstigung; tax concession =** allowing less tax to be paid **Steuervergünstigung**
(d) admission **Zugeständnis, Einräumung**
◊ **concessionaire** *noun* person who has the right to be the only seller of a product in a place **Konzessionär/-in**
◊ **concessionary** *adjective* **concessionary fare =** reduced fare for certain types of passenger (such as employees of the transport company) **Vorzugsfahrpreis**

conciliation *noun* bringing together the parties in a dispute so that the dispute can be settled **Schlichtung; the Conciliation Service =** ADVISORY, CONCILIATION AND ARBITRATION SERVICE

conclude *verb*
(a) to complete successfully **abschließen;** *to conclude an agreement with someone*
(b) to believe from evidence **schließen, schlußfolgern;** *the police concluded that the thief had got into the building through the main entrance*
◊ **conclusion** *noun*
(a) deciding from evidence **Schluß, Schlußfolgerung;** *the police have come to the conclusion or have reached the conclusion that the bomb was set off by radio control*

conclusion 63 conduct

(b) final completion **Abschluß;** *the conclusion of the defence counsel's address;* **in conclusion** = finally *or* at the end **abschließend, zum Schluß/Abschluß;** *in conclusion, the judge thanked the jury for their long and patient service*

◊ **conclusive** *adjective* which proves something **schlüssig; zwingend;** *the fingerprints on the gun were conclusive evidence that the accused was guilty*

◊ **conclusively** *adverb* in a way which proves a fact **schlüssig; zwingend;** *the evidence of the eye witness proved conclusively that the accused was in the town at the time the robbery was committed*

concur *verb* to agree **zustimmen; übereinstimmen;** *Smith LJ dismissed the appeal, Jones and White LJJ concurring*

◊ **concurrence** *noun* agreement **Zustimmung; Übereinstimmung;** *in concurrence with the other judges, Smith LJ dismissed the appeal*

concurrent *adjective* taking place at the same time **gleichzeitig; concurrent sentence** = sentence which takes place at the same time as another **gleichzeitig zu verbüßende Freiheitsstrafe;** *he was given two concurrent jail sentences of six months*

◊ **concurrently** *adverb* taking place at the same time **gleichzeitig;** *he was sentenced to two periods of two years in prison, the sentences to run concurrently; see also* CONSECUTIVE, CONSECUTIVELY

condemn *verb*
(a) to sentence someone to suffer punishment **verurteilen; schuldig sprechen;** *the prisoners were condemned to death;* **condemned cell** = cell where a prisoner is kept who has been sentenced to death **Todeszelle**
(b) to say that a house is not fit for people to live in **für unbewohnbar erklären**

◊ **condemnation** *noun*
(a) sentencing of someone to a certain punishment **Verurteilung**
(b) forfeiting a piece of property when it has been legally seized **Beschlagnahme; Enteignung**

condition *noun*
(a) term of a contract *or* duty which has to be carried out as part of a contract *or* something which has to be agreed before a contract becomes valid **Kondition, Bedingung, Auflage; conditions of service** = terms of a contract of employment **Arbeitsvertrags-, Anstellungsbedingungen; conditions of sale** = agreed ways in which a

sale takes place (such as discounts *or* credit terms) **Verkaufsbedingungen; on condition that** = provided that **unter der Bedingung, daß;** *they were granted the lease on condition that they paid the legal costs;* **condition precedent** = condition which says that a right will not be granted until something is done **aufschiebende Bedingung; Vorbedingung; condition subsequent** = condition which says that a contract will be modified *or* annulled if something is not done **auflösende Bedingung**
(b) general state **Zustand;** *item sold in good condition; what was the condition of the car when it was sold?*

◊ **conditional** *adjective* provided that certain things take place *or* (agreement) which is dependent on something **mit Auflagen, unter Vorbehalt, bedingt; to give a conditional acceptance** = to accept, provided that certain things happen *or* certain terms apply **unter Vorbehalt annehmen; the offer is conditional on the board's acceptance** = provided the board accepts **das Angebot hängt von der Annahme des Vorstands ab; he made a conditional offer** = he offered to buy, provided that certain terms applied **er machte ein bedingtes Angebot; conditional discharge** = allowing a prisoner to be set free, with no punishment, provided that he does not commit a crime for a period of time **bedingte Strafaussetzung**

◊ **conditionally** *adverb* provided certain things take place **unter Vorbehalt; to accept an offer conditionally** = to accept provided certain conditions are fulfilled **ein Angebot unter Vorbehalt annehmen**

condominium *noun (US)* system of ownership, where a person owns an apartment in a building, together with a share of the land and common parts (stairs, roof, etc.); *entspricht* **Eigentumswohnung**

condone *verb* to forgive (criminal behaviour) **entschuldigen; dulden;** *the court cannot condone your treatment of your children*

◊ **condonation** *noun* the forgiving by one spouse of the acts of the other (especially forgiving adultery) **Verzeihung**

conducive *adjective* which is likely to produce **förderlich, dienlich;** *the threat of strike action is not conducive to an easy solution to the dispute*

conduct
1 *noun*
(a) way of behaving **Verhalten;** *he was arrested for disorderly conduct in the street;*

code of conduct = informal (sometimes written) rules by which a group of people work **Vehaltenskodex**
(b) bad way of behaving **Verhalten; Benehmen;** *she divorced her husband because of his conduct;* **conduct conducive to a breach of the peace** = way of behaving (using rude or threatening language in speech or writing) which seems likely to cause a breach of the peace **Verhalten, das zu Erregung öffentlichen Ärgernisses führen kann**
2 *verb* to carry on **leiten, führen;** *to conduct discussions or negotiations; the chairman conducted the proceedings very efficiently*

confer *verb*
(a) to give power *or* responsibility to someone **übertragen; verleihen;** *the discretionary powers conferred on the tribunal by statute*
(b) to discuss **konferieren, sich besprechen;** *the Chief Constable conferred with the Superintendent in charge of the case*

conference *noun* meeting of a group of people to discuss something **Konferenz;** *the Police Federation is holding its annual conference this week;* **conference proceedings** = written report of what has been discussed at a conference **Konferenzbericht; press conference** = meeting where reporters from newspaper and TV are invited to hear news of a police investigation *or* the result of a court case, etc. **Pressekonferenz**

confess *verb* to admit that you have committed a crime **geständig sein;** *after six hours' questioning by the police the accused man confessed*
◊ **confession** *noun* (i) admitting that you have committed a crime; (ii) document in which you admit that you have committed a crime **(i) Geständnis; (ii) Geständnis;** *the police sergeant asked him to sign his confession; the accused typed his own confession statement; the confession was not admitted in court, because the accused claimed it had been extorted*

confidence *noun*
(a) feeling sure *or* being certain *or* having trust in (someone) **Vertrauen;** *the sales teams do not have much confidence in their manager; the board has total confidence in the managing director;* **confidence vote** *or* **vote of no confidence** = vote to show that a person *or* group is *or* is not trusted **Vertrauensvotum; Mißtrauensvotum;** *he proposed a vote of confidence in the government; the chairman resigned after the motion of no confidence was passed at the AGM*

(b) trusting someone with a secret **Vertrauen; breach of confidence** = betraying a secret which someone has told you **Vertrauensbruch; in confidence** = in secret **vertraulich;** *I will show you the report in confidence*

◊ **confidence trick** *or* *(US)* **confidence game** *noun* business deal where someone gains another person's confidence and then tricks him **Schwindel, Betrug, Bauernfängerei**
◊ **confidence trickster** *or (US)* **confidence man** *noun* person who carries out confidence tricks on people **Schwindler, Betrüger, Bauernfänger**

◊ **confident** *adjective* certain *or* sure **zuversichtlich;** *I am confident the turnover will increase rapidly; are you confident the sales team is capable of handling this product?*

◊ **confidential** *adjective* secret *or* not to be told or shown to other people **vertraulich;** *he sent a confidential report to the chairman; please mark the letter "Private and Confidential"*
◊ **confidentiality** *noun* being secret **Vertraulichkeit; he broke the confidentiality of the discussions** = he told someone about the secret discussions **er brach die Vertraulichkeit der Unterredungen**
NOTE: no plural

confine *verb* to keep (a criminal) in a room or area **einsperren, gefangen halten; confined to barracks** = (soldier) who is sentenced to stay in the barracks for a set period of time and not to go outside **Kasernenarrest haben**
◊ **confinement** *noun* being kept in a place as a punishment **Haft; Arrest; solitary confinement** = being kept alone in a cell, without being able to speak to other prisoners **Einzelhaft;** *he was kept in solitary confinement for a week*
NOTE: no plural

confirm *verb* to say that something is certain *or* is correct **bestätigen; bekräftigen;** *the Court of Appeal has confirmed the judge's decision; his secretary phoned to confirm the hotel room or the ticket or the agreement or the booking;* **to confirm someone in a job** = to say that someone is now permanently in the job **jdn nach einer Probezeit fest anstellen**
◊ **confirmation** *noun*
(a) being certain **Bestätigung; Bekräftigung; confirmation of a booking** = checking that a booking is certain **eine Buchung bestätigen**
(b) document which confirms something **Bestätigung;** *he received confirmation from the bank that the deeds had been deposited*

confiscate *verb* to take away private property into the possession of the state **konfiszieren, beschlagnahmen;** *the court ordered the drugs to be confiscated*

◊ **confiscation** *noun* act of confiscating **Konfiszierung, Beschlagnahme**

conflict
1 *noun* **conflict of interest** = situation where a person may profit personally from decisions which he takes in his official capacity *or* may not be able to act properly because of some other person or matter with which he is connected **Interessenkonflikt; Conflict of Laws** = section in a country's legal statutes which deals with disputes between that country's laws and those of another country **Kollisionsrecht; Gesetzeskonflikt**
2 *verb* not to agree **widersprechen; im Widerspruch stehen;** *the evidence of the wife conflicts with that of her husband; the UK legislation conflicts with the directives of the EC;* **conflicting evidence** = evidence from different witnesses which does not agree **widersprüchliche Zeugenaussagen;** *the jury has to decide who to believe among a mass of conflicting evidence*

conform *verb* to act in accordance with something **entsprechen;** *the proposed Bill conforms to the recommendations of the Royal Commission*

◊ **conformance** *noun* acting in accordance with a rule **Übereinstimmung;** *in conformance with the directives of the Commission; he was criticized for non-conformance with the regulations*

◊ **conformity** *noun* **in conformity with** = agreeing with **in Übereinstimmung mit;** *he has acted in conformity with the regulations*

Congress *noun* elected federal legislative body of the USA (formed of the House of Representatives and the Senate) **Kongreß**

◊ **Congressional** *adjective* referring to Congress **Kongreß-;** *a Congressional subcommittee*

◊ **Congressman** *noun* member of the House of Representatives **Kongreßabgeordneter**

conjugal *adjective* referring to marriage **ehelich, Ehe-;** **conjugal rights** = rights of a husband and wife in relation to each other **eheliche Rechte**

conman *noun (informal)* = CONFIDENCE TRICKSTER

connect *verb*
(a) to link *or* to join **verbinden;** *the company is connected to the government because the chairman's father is a minister;* **connected persons** = people who are closely related to *or* have a close business association with a certain company director **Vertrauensperson**

◊ **connection** *noun* link *or* something which joins **Verbindung;** *is there a connection between the loss of the documents and the death of the lawyer?;* **in connection with** = referring to **im Zusammenhang mit;** *the police want to interview the man in connection with burglaries committed last November*

connive *verb* **to connive at something** = to shut one's eyes to wrongdoing *or* to know that a crime is being committed, but not to report it **mit Absicht übersehen**

◊ **connivance** *noun* shutting one's eyes to wrongdoing *or* knowing that a crime is being committed, but not reporting it **stillschweigende Duldung, Nachsicht;** *with the connivance of the customs officers, he managed to bring the goods into the country*

consecutive *adjective* which follows **aufeinanderfolgend; fortlaufend; consecutive sentences** = two or more sentences which follow one after the other **mehrere nacheinander zu verbüßende Freiheitsstrafen**

◊ **consecutively** *adverb* which follows **aufeinanderfolgend; fortlaufend;** *he was sentence to two periods of two years in jail, the sentences to run consecutively; see also* CONCURRENT, CONCURRENTLY

consensus *noun* general agreement **Konsens, Übereinstimmung;** *there was a consensus between all parties as to the next steps to be taken; in the absence of a consensus, no decisions could be reached;* **consensus politics** = way of ruling a country, where the main political parties agree in general on policy **Politik des Miteinander**

◊ **consensus ad idem** *Latin phrase* meaning "agreement to this same thing": real agreement to a contract by both parties **Einmütigkeit**

◊ **consensual** *adjective* which happens by agreement **durch Konsens; consensual acts** = sexual acts which both parties agree should take place **einverständlicher Verkehr**

consent
1 *noun* agreeing that something should happen **Einwilligung;** *he borrowed the car without the owner's consent;* **the age of consent** = sixteen years old (when a girl can agree to have sexual intercourse)

Einwilligungsalter (zur Ehe od zum Sexualverkehr); **consent order** = court order that someone must not do something without the agreement of another party **Beschluß aufgrund der Zustimmung der beschwerten Partei**
2 *verb* to agree that something should be done **einwilligen;** *the judge consented to the request of the prosecution counsel*

consider *verb*

(a) to think seriously about something **bedenken, überlegen; to consider the terms of a contract** = to examine and discuss if the terms are acceptable **die Vertragsbedingungen prüfen; the judge asked the jury to consider their verdict** = he asked the jury to discuss the evidence they had heard and decide if the accused was guilty or not **der Richter forderte die Geschworenen auf, über das Urteil zu beraten**
(b) to believe **halten für; betrachten als;** *he is considered to be one of the leading divorce lawyers; the law on libel is considered too lenient*

◊ **consideration** *noun*
(a) serious thought **Überlegung, Erwägung;** *we are giving consideration to moving the head office to Scotland;* **to take something into consideration** = to think about something when deciding what to do **etwas berücksichtigen; to ask for other offences to be taken into consideration** = to confess to other offences after being accused *or* convicted of one offence, so that the sentence can cover all of them **bitten um Gesamtstrafenbildung;** *the accused admitted six other offences, and asked for them to be taken into consideration; having taken the age of the accused into consideration, the court has decided to give him a suspended sentence*
(b) the price (but not necessarily money) paid by one person in exchange for the other person promising to do something, an essential element in the formation of a contract **Gegenleistung; for a small consideration** = for a small fee *or* payment **für geringes Entgelt; executed consideration** = consideration where one party has made a promise in exchange for which the other party has done something for him **erbrachte Gegenleistung; executory consideration** = consideration where one party makes a promise in exchange for a counter-promise from the other party **wechselseitiges Leistungsversprechen**

considerable *adjective* quite large **beträchtlich, erheblich;** *we sell considerable quantities of our products to Africa; they lost a considerable amount of money on the commodity market*

◊ **considerably** *adverb* quite a lot **beträchtlich, erheblich;** *crime figures are considerably higher than they were last year*

consign *verb* to consign goods to someone
= to send goods to someone for him to use or to sell for you **Waren in Kommission geben**
◊ **consignation** *noun* act of consigning **Versand, Versenden;** *(Überseehandel)* **Konsignation**
◊ **consignee** *noun* person who receives goods from someone for his own use or to sell for the person who sends them **Empfänger;** *(Überseehandel)* **Konsignatar**
◊ **consignment** *noun*
(a) sending of goods to someone who will hold them for you and sell them on your behalf **Versand, Versenden;** *(Überseehandel)* **Konsignation; consignment note** = note saying that goods have been sent **Versandanzeige; goods on consignment** = goods kept for another company to be sold on their behalf for a commission **Kommissionsware**
(b) certain quantity of goods sent for sale **Warensendung, Lieferung;** *a consignment of goods has arrived; we are expecting a consignment of cars from Japan*
◊ **consignor** *noun* person who consigns goods to someone **Ab-, Versender;** *(Überseehandel)* **Konsignatant**

COMMENT: the goods remain the property of the consignor until the consignee sells them

consist of *verb* to be formed of **bestehen aus, sich zusammensetzen aus;** *the Magistrates' Court consists normally of three justices; a delegation consisting of all the heads of department concerned*

consistent *adjective* which does not contradict *or* which agrees with **entsprechend;** *the sentence is consistent with government policy on the treatment of young offenders*

consolidate *verb* to bring several Acts of Parliament together into one act; to hear several sets of proceedings together **vereinfachen, verbinden (von schon bestehenden Gesetzen);** *the judge ordered the actions to be consolidated*
◊ **Consolidating Act** *noun* Act of Parliament which brings together several previous Acts which relate to the same subject **Kodifizierungsgesetz;** *see also* CODIFICATION
◊ **consolidation** *noun* (i) bringing together various Acts of Parliament which deal with one subject into one single Act; (ii)

procedure whereby several sets of proceedings are heard together by the court **(i) Kodifikation; (ii) Verbindung; Zusammenfassung**

consortium *noun*
(a) group of different companies which work together on one project **Konsortium**
(b) right of a husband and wife to the love and support of the other **Recht der ehelichen Gemeinschaft**

conspire *verb* to agree with another person *or* other people to commit a crime *or* tort **konspirieren, sich verschwören**

◊ **conspiracy** *noun* agreeing with another person *or* other people to commit a crime *or* tort **Konspiration, Verschwörung**

COMMENT: conspiracy to commit a crime is itself a crime

constable *noun* **police constable** *or* **woman police constable** = lowest rank of police officer **Polizist/-in;** *the sergeant and six constables searched the premises*
NOTE: constable can be used to address a policeman; also used with a name: **Constable Smith;** it is usually abbreviated to PC or WPC

constituency *noun* area of a country which is represented by a Member of Parliament **Wahlkreis;** *he represents one of the northern constituencies*

constitute *verb* to make *or* to form **darstellen;** *the documents constitute primary evidence; this Act constitutes a major change in government policy; conduct tending to interfere with the course of justice constitutes contempt of court*

constitution *noun*
(a) (usually written) laws under which a country is ruled **Verfassung; Grundgesetz;** *the freedom of the individual is guaranteed by the country's constitution; the new president asked the assembly to draft a new constitution*
(b) written rules *or* regulations of a society *or* association *or* club **Satzung; Statut;** *under the society's constitution, the chairman is elected for a two-year period; payments to officers of the association are not allowed by the constitution*

◊ **constitutional** *adjective*
(a) referring to a country's constitution **Verfassungs-; verfassungsmäßig;** *censorship of the press is not constitutional;* **constitutional law** = laws under which a country is ruled *or* laws relating to government and its function

Verfassungsrecht; constitutional lawyer = lawyer who specializes in constitutional law *or* in drafting or interpreting constitutions **ein auf Verfassungsrecht spezialisierter Jurist; constitutional right** = right which is guaranteed by a constitution **Grundrecht**
(b) according to a constitution **verfassungsgemäß; satzungsgemäß;** *the re-election of the chairman for a second term is not constitutional*

construct *verb* to build **bauen; konstruieren;** *the company has tendered for the contract to construct the new airport*

◊ **construction** *noun*
(a) building **Bau; Konstruktion; construction company** = company which specializes in building **Bauunternehmen; construction** = being built **in/im Bau befindlich;** *the airport is under construction*
(b) interpreting the meaning of words **Deutung; to put a construction on words** = to suggest a meaning for words which is not immediately obvious **einen Wortlaut auslegen**

◊ **constructive** *adjective* which helps in the making of something **konstruktiv;** *she made some constructive suggestions for improving management-worker relations; we had a constructive proposal from a shipping company in Italy;* **constructive dismissal** = situation when a worker leaves his job voluntarily but because of pressure from the management **erzwungene Kündigung; constructive knowledge** = knowledge of a fact *or* matter which the law says a person has, whether or not that person actually has it **gesetzlich unterstellte Kenntnis; constructive notice** = knowledge which the law says a person has of something (whether or not the person actually has it) because certain information is available to him if he makes reasonable inquiry **zumutbare Kenntnis; constructive trust** = trust arising by reason of a person's behaviour **fingiertes Treuhandverhältnis**

construe *verb* to interpret the meaning of words *or* of a document **auslegen;** *the court construed the words to mean that there was a contract between the parties; written opinion is not admissible as evidence for the purposes of construing a deed of settlement*

consult *verb* to ask an expert for advice **konsultieren, zu Rate ziehen;** *he consulted his solicitor about the letter*

◊ **consultancy** *noun* act of giving specialist advice **Beratung; Konsultation;** *a consultancy firm; he offers a consultancy service*

◊ **consultant** *noun* specialist who gives advice **Berater/-in; Gutachter/-in;** *engineering consultant; management consultant; tax consultant*

◊ **consultation** *noun* meeting between a client and his professional adviser, such as between a QC (and often a junior barrister) and a solicitor and clients **Beratung; Treffen**

◊ **consulting** *adjective* person who gives specialist advice **beratend;** *consulting engineer*

consumer *noun* person *or* company which buys and uses goods and services **Verbraucher/-in, Konsument/-in;** *gas consumers are protesting at the increase in prices; the factory is a heavy consumer of water;* **consumer council** = group representing the interests of consumers **Verbraucherberatung; consumer credit** = provision of loans by finance companies to help people buy goods **Kundenkredit; Abzahlungskredit; consumer goods** = goods bought by the general public and not by businesses **Verbrauchs-, Konsumgüter; consumer legislation** = laws which give rights to people who buy goods *or* who pay for services **Verbraucherschutzgesetze; consumer protection** = protecting consumers from unfair *or* illegal business practices **Verbraucherschutz**

consummation *noun* having sexual intercourse for the first time after the marriage ceremony **Vollzug**

consumption *noun* buying or using goods or services **Verbrauch; Konsum;** *a car with low petrol consumption; the factory has a heavy consumption of coal*

contact
1 *noun*
(a) person you know *or* person you can ask for help or advice **Kontakt(person), Verbindung;** *he has many contacts in the city; who is your contact in the Ministry?*
(b) act of getting in touch with someone **Kontakt, Verbindung; I have lost contact with them** = I do not communicate with them any longer **ich habe den Kontakt zu ihnen verloren; he put me in contact with a good lawyer** = he told me how to get in touch with a good lawyer **er hat mir einen guten Anwalt vermittelt**
2 *verb* to get in touch with someone *or* to communicate with someone **Kontakt/Verbindung aufnehmen;** *he tried to contact his office by phone; can you contact the solicitors representing the vendors?*

contain *verb* to hold something inside **enthalten;** *the contract contains some clauses which are open to misinterpretation; some of the instructions contained in the will are quite impossible to carry out*

contemnor *noun* person who commits a contempt of court **Störer (der Ordnung) im Gerichtssaal**

contempt *noun* being rude *or* showing lack of respect to a court *or* Parliament **Verachtung, Geringschätzung; to be in contempt** = to have shown disrespect to a court, especially by disobeying a court order **das Gericht/die Würde des Gerichts mißachten; contempt of court** = being rude to a court, as by bad behaviour in court, or by refusing to carry out a court order **Mißachtung des Gerichts;** *at common law, conduct tending to interfere with the course of justice in particular legal proceedings constitutes criminal contempt;* **contempt of Parliament** *or* **contempt of the House** = conduct which may bring the authority of Parliament into disrepute **Mißachtung der Parlamentshoheit; to purge one's contempt** = to apologize *or* to do something to show that you are sorry for the lack of respect shown **sich für ein ungebührliches Verhalten entschuldigen**

content *noun* the ideas inside a letter, etc. **Gehalt; the content of the letter** = the real meaning of the letter **der Gehalt des Briefes**

◊ **contents** *plural noun* things contained *or* what is inside something **Inhalt;** *the contents of the bottle poured out onto the floor; the customs officials inspected the contents of the box;* **the contents of the letter** = the words written in the letter **der Inhalt des Briefes** Hausrat (a. Möbel)

contentious *adjective* disputable **streitig, strittig; contentious business** *noun* legal business where there is a dispute **streitige Zivilsache**

contest
1 *noun* competition, especially in an election **Kampf; Wettbewerb**
2 *verb*
(a) to argue that a decision *or* a ruling is wrong **anfechten; bestreiten;** *I wish to contest the statement made by the witness*
(b) to fight (an election) **kämpfen um;** *the seat is being contested by five candidates;* **contested takeover** = takeover where the directors of the company being bought do not recommend the bid and try to fight it **angefochtene Übernahme**

context *noun* other words which surround a word or phrase; general situation in which something happens **Kontext, Zusammenhang;** *the words can only be understood in the context of the phrase in which they occur; the action of the police has to be seen in the context of the riots against the government*

contingency *noun* possible state of emergency when decisions will have to be taken quickly **unvorhergesehenes Ereignis, Eventualität; contingency fund** *or* **contingency reserve** = money set aside in case it is needed urgently **Not-, Sonderfonds; contingency plan** = plan which will be put into action if something happens which is expected to happen **Krisenplan**

◊ **contingent** *adjective* **contingent expenses** = expenses which will be incurred only if something happens **unvorhergesehene Sonderausgaben;** *(US)* **contingent fee** = fee paid to a lawyer which is a proportion of the damages recovered in the case **Erfolgshonorar; contingent policy** = policy which pays out only if something happens (as if the person named in the policy dies before the person due to benefit) **Risikoversicherung; Eventualversicherung**

continue *verb* to go on doing something *or* to do something which you were doing earlier **andauern; fortsetzen, fortfahren mit**

◊ **continual** *adjective* which happens again and again **ständig, ununterbrochen**

◊ **continually** *adverb* again and again **ständig, ununterbrochen**

◊ **continuation** *noun* act of continuing **Fortsetzung, Fortführung**

◊ **continuous** *adjective* with no end *or* with no breaks **kontinuierlich; gleichmäßig; fortlaufend; to be in continuous employment** = to work for a period of time (possibly for several different employers) with no time when you are not employed in **ständiger Beschäftigung sein; continuous feed** = device which feeds continuous stationery into a printer **Endlospapiereinzug; continuous stationery** = paper made as one long sheet, used in computer printers **Endlospapier**

◊ **continuously** *adverb* without stopping **kontinuierlich, ununterbrochen;** *the meeting discussed the problem of budgets continuously for five hours*

contra
1 *preposition* against *or* differing **Kontra-, Gegen-**
2 *noun* **contra account** = account which offsets another account **Gegenkonto; contra entry** = entry made in the opposite side of

an account to make an earlier entry worthless (i.e. a debit against a credit) **Gegenbuchung; per contra** *or* **as per contra** = words showing that a contra entry has been made **als Gegenbuchung**
3 *verb* **to contra an entry** = to enter a similar amount in the opposite side of an account **einen Eintrag zurückbuchen**

◊ **contra proferentem** *Latin phrase meaning* "against the one making the point": rule that an ambiguity in a document is construed against the party who drafted it **Unklarheiten in Geschäftsbedingungen gehen zu Lasten des Verfassers**

contraband *noun* **contraband (goods)** = goods brought into or taken out of a country illegally, without paying customs duty **Schmuggelware**

contract
1 *noun*
(a) legal agreement between two or more parties **Vertrag;** *to draw up a contract; to draft a contract; to sign a contract;* **the contract is binding on both parties** = both parties signing the contract must do what is agreed **der Vertrag ist für beide unterzeichnende Parteien bindend; under contract** = bound by the terms of a contract **unter Vertrag stehen; vertraglich gebunden sein;** *the firm is under contract to deliver the goods by November;* **to void a contract** = to make a contract invalid **einen Vertrag aufheben/für nichtig erklären; contract of service** *or* **of employment** = contract between management and employee showing all conditions of work **Arbeitsvertrag; service contract** = contract between a company and a director *or* employee showing all conditions of work **Dienstvertrag; exchange of contracts** = point in the conveyance of a property when the solicitors for the buyer and seller hand over the contract of sale which then becomes binding **Unterzeichnung des Kaufvertrages (bei Grundbesitz)**
(b) **contract law** *or* **law of contract** = laws relating to agreements **Vertragsrecht; Schuldrecht; by private contract** = by private legal agreement **durch Privatvertrag; contract note** = note showing that shares have been bought or sold but not yet paid for **Ausführungsanzeige**
(c) **contract for services** = agreement for supply of a service or goods **Dienstleistungsvertrag;** *contract for the supply of spare parts; to enter into a contract to supply spare parts; to sign a contract for £10,000 worth of spare parts;* **to put work out to contract** = to decide that work should be done by another company on a contract,

rather than employing members of staff to do it **Auftragsarbeit vergeben; to award a contract to a company** *or* **to place a contract with a company** = to decide that a company shall have the contract to do work for you **einen Auftrag an eine Firma vergeben; to tender for a contract** = to put forward an estimate of cost for work to be carried out under contract **ein Angebot/eine Offerte unterbreiten;** *conditions of contract or contract conditions;* **breach of contract** = breaking the terms of a contract **Vertragsbruch; the company is in breach of contract** = the company has failed to do what was agreed in the contract **die Firma ist vertragsbrüchig geworden; contract work** = work done according to a written agreement **Auftragsarbeit**
(d) *slang* agreement to kill someone for a payment **Auftrag; there is a contract out for him** = someone has offered money for him to be killed **auf seinen Kopf ist Geld aufgesetzt**

COMMENT: a contract is an agreement between two or more parties to create legal obligations between them. Some contracts are made "under seal", i.e. they are signed and sealed by the parties; most contracts are made orally or in writing. The essential elements of a contract are: (a) that an offer made by one party should be accepted by the other; (b) consideration; (c) the intention to create legal relations. The terms of a contract may be express or implied. A breach of contract by one party entitles the other party to sue for damages or in some cases to seek specific performance

2 *verb* to agree to do some work by contract **sich vertraglich verpflichten; einen Vertrag abschließen;** *to contract to supply spare parts or to contract for the supply of spare parts;* **the supply of spare parts was contracted out to Smith Ltd** = Smith Ltd was given the contract for supplying spare parts **der Vertrag für den Ersatzteilvertrieb wurde an Smith Ltd vergeben; to contract out of an agreement** = to withdraw from an agreement with written permission of the other party **sich von einer vertraglichen Verpflichtung befreien**

◊ **contracting** *adjective* **contracting party** = person or company which signs a contract **Vertragspartner**

◊ **contractor** *noun* person who enters into a contract, especially a person *or* company which does work according to a written agreement **Auftragnehmer; Unternehmer**

◊ **contractual** *adjective* according to a contract **vertraglich, vertragsmäßig; contractual liability** = legal responsibility for something as stated in a contract **Vertragshaftung; to fulfil your contractual obligations** = to do what you have agreed to

do in a contract **seine vertraglichen Verpflichtungen erfüllen; he is under no contractual obligation to buy** = he has signed no agreement to buy **er ist vertraglich nicht verpflichtet zu kaufen**
◊ **contractually** *adverb* according to a contract **vertraglich, durch Vertrag;** *the company is contractually bound to pay his expenses*

contradict *verb* not to agree with *or* to say exactly the opposite **widersprechen;** *the statement contradicts the report in the newspapers; the witness contradicted himself several times*
◊ **contradiction** *noun* statement which contradicts **Widerspruch;** *the witness' evidence was a mass of contradictions; there is a contradiction between the Minister's statement in the House of Commons and the reports published in the newspapers*
◊ **contradictory** *adjective* which does not agree **widersprüchlich;** *a mass of contradictory evidence*

contrary *noun* opposite instructions **Gegenteil; failing instructions to the contrary** = unless different instructions are given **sofern Sie nichts Gegenteiliges hören; on the contrary** = quite the opposite **im Gegenteil;** *counsel was not annoyed with the witness - on the contrary, he praised her*

contravene *verb* to break *or* to go against (rules, regulations) **verstoßen gegen; übertreten;** *the workshop has contravened the employment regulations; the fire department can close a restaurant if it contravenes the safety regulations*
◊ **contravention** *noun* act of breaking a regulation **Verstoß; Übertretung; to be in contravention of** = which contravenes **verstoßen gegen;** *the restaurant is in contravention of the safety regulations; the management of the cinema locked the fire exits in contravention of the fire regulations*

contribute *verb*
(a) to give money *or* to add to money **beisteuern, einen Beitrag leisten;** *to contribute 10% of the profits; he contributed to the pension fund for ten years*
(b) to contribute to = to help something **beitragen zu;** *the public response to the request for information contributed to the capture of the gang*
◊ **contribution** *noun* money paid to add to a sum **Beitrag; employer's contribution** = money paid by an employer towards a worker's pension **Arbeitgeberanteil; National Insurance contributions** = money paid each month by a worker and the company to the

National Insurance **Sozialversicherungsbeiträge; pension contributions** = money paid by a company or worker into a pension fund **Rentenbeiträge**

◊ **contributor** *noun* **contributor of capital** = person who contributes capital **Investor**

◊ **contributory**
1 *adjective* **contributory pension plan** *or* **scheme** = pension plan where the employee has to contribute a percentage of salary **beitragspflichtige Rentenversicherung; contributory causes** = causes which help something to take place **mitverursachende Umstände; contributory factor** = something which contributes to a result **beitragender Faktor; contributory negligence** = negligence partly caused by the plaintiff and partly by the defendant, which results in harm done to the plaintiff **Mitverschulden**
2 *noun* shareholder who is liable in respect of partly paid shares to a company being wound up **nachschußpflichtiger Aktionär**

con trick *noun* *(informal)* = CONFIDENCE TRICK

control
1 *noun*
(a) power *or* being able to direct something **Leitung, Kontrolle; Aufsicht;** *the company is under the control of three shareholders; the family lost control of its business;* **to gain control of a business** = to buy more than 50% of the shares so that you can direct the business **die Aktienmehrheit an einem Unternehmen erwerben; to lose control of a business** = to find that you have less than 50% of the shares in a company, and so are not longer able to direct it **die Aktienmehrheit an einem Unternehmen verlieren; control test** = test to decide if someone is an employee or is selfemployed (used for purposes of tax assessment) **Überprüfung**
(b) restricting *or* checking something *or* making sure that something is kept in check **Kontrolle, Überwachung; under control** = kept in check **unter Kontrolle; out of control** = not kept in check **außer Kontrolle**
(c) exchange **controls** = government restrictions on changing the local currency into foreign currency **Devisenkontrollen;** *the government imposed exchange controls to stop the rush to buy dollars;* **price controls** = legal measures to prevent prices rising too fast **Preisbindung; Preisüberwachung; rent controls** = government regulation of rents charged by landlords **Mietpreisbindung**
(d) control systems = systems used to check that a computer system is working correctly **Steuerungssysteme**

2 *verb*
(a) to control a business = to direct a business **die Mehrheit an einem Unternehmen haben;** *the business is controlled by a company based in Luxembourg; the company is controlled by the majority shareholder*
(b) to make sure that something is kept in check *or* is not allowed to develop **unter Kontrolle halten, steuern;** *the government is fighting to control inflation or to control the rise in the cost of living*

◊ **controlled** *adjective* ruled *or* kept in check **unter Kontrolle gehalten, gesteuert; government-controlled** = ruled by a government **staatlich gelenkt; unter staatlicher Aufsicht; controlled economy** = economy where most business activity is directed by orders from the government **staatlich gelenkte Wirtschaft**

◊ **controller** *noun*
(a) person who controls (especially the finances of a company) **Controller**
(b) *US* chief accountant in a company **Leiter der Buchhaltung**

◊ **controlling** *adjective* **to have a controlling interest in a company** = to own more than 50% of the shares so that you can direct how the company is run **die Mehrheitsbeteiligung an einem Unternehmen haben**

convene *verb* to ask people to come together **zusammenrufen; einberufen;** *to convene a meeting of shareholders*

convenience *noun* **at your earliest convenience** = as soon as you find it possible **baldmöglichst; ship sailing under a flag of convenience** = ship flying the flag of a country which may have no ships of its own but allows ships of other countries to be registered in its ports **Schiff, das unter Billigflagge fährt**

◊ **convenient** *adjective* suitable *or* handy **genehm, passend; praktisch;** *a bank draft is a convenient way of sending money abroad; is 9.30 a.m. a convenient time for the meeting?*

convenor *noun* person who convenes a meeting, especially a trade unionist who organizes union meetings **Gewerkschaft(l)er**

convention *noun*
(a) general way in which something is usually done, though not enforced by law **Konvention, Brauch, Sitte;** *it is the convention for American lawyers to designate themselves "Esquire"*
(b) international treaty **Abkommen; Konvention;** *the Geneva Convention on Human Rights*

conversion *noun* tort of dealing with a person's property in a way which is not consistent with that person's rights over it **widerrechtliche Aneignung; conversion of funds** = using money which does not belong to you for a purpose for which it is not supposed to be used **Veruntreuung von Geldern**

◊ **convert** *verb*
(a) to change property into another form (as into cash) **umwandeln; realisieren, flüssig machen**
(b) to change money of one country for money of another **(um)tauschen;** *we converted our pounds into Swiss francs;* **to convert funds to one's own use** = to use someone else's money for yourself **Geldmittel für eigene Zwecke umleiten, Geldmittel veruntreuen**

◊ **convertible** *adjective* which can be changed into something else (such as cash) **umwandelbar; realisierbar; convertible loan stock** = money which can be exchanged for shares at a later date **Wandelanleihe**

convey *verb* to carry goods from one place to another **befördern; to convey a property to a purchaser** = to pass the ownership of the property to the purchaser **einem Käufer Eigentum übertragen**

◊ **conveyance** *noun* legal document which transfers the ownership of land from the seller to the buyer **Übertragungsurkunde; fraudulent conveyance** = putting a property into someone else's possession to avoid it being seized to pay creditors **Vollstreckungsvereitelung durch Eigentumsübertragung**

◊ **conveyancer** *noun* person who draws up a conveyance **Notar**

◊ **conveyancing** *noun* (i) drawing up the document which legally transfers a property from a seller to a buyer; (ii) law and procedure relating to the purchase and sale of property **(i) Aufsetzen eines Eigentumsübertragungsdokuments; (ii) Eigentumsübertragungsverfahren; do-it-yourself conveyancing** = drawing up a legal conveyance without the help of a lawyer **Aufsetzen einer Übertragungsurkunde ohne notarielle Hilfe**

convict
1 *noun* person who is kept in prison as a punishment for a crime **Strafgefangener; convict settlement** = prison camp where convicts are sent **Strafkolonie**
2 *verb* **to convict someone of a crime** = to find that someone is guilty of a crime **jd eines Verbrechens überführen; jdn verurteilen;** *he was convicted of manslaughter and sent to prison;* **convicted criminal** = criminal who

has been found guilty and sentenced **verurteilter Straftäter**

◊ **conviction** *noun*
(a) being sure that something is true **Überzeugung;** *it is his conviction that the plaintiff has brought the case maliciously*
(b) finding that a person accused of a crime is guilty **Überführung; Verurteilung;** *he has had ten convictions for burglary;* compare SENTENCE

convince *verb* to make someone believe something is true **überzeugen;** *counsel tried to convince the jury that the accused was not guilty; he convinced the owner of the shop that the building needed painting; the two conmen convinced the woman that they were plainclothes policemen*

cooling off period *or US* **cooling time** *noun* (i) during an industrial dispute, a period when negotiations have to be carried on and no action can be taken by either side; (ii) period when a person is allowed to think about something which he has agreed to buy on hire-purchase and possibly change his mind **(i) Friedenspflicht (bei Arbeitskämpfen); (ii) Rücktrittsfrist**

co-operate *verb* to work together **kooperieren, zusammenarbeiten;** *the governments are co-operating in the fight against piracy; the two firms have co-operated on planning the computer system*

◊ **co-operation** *noun* working together **Kooperation, Zusammenarbeit;** *the work was completed ahead of schedule with the co-operation of the whole staff*

◊ **co-operative**
1 *adjective* willing to work together **kooperativ;** *the staff have not been co-operative over the management's reorganization plan ;* **co-operative society** = society where the customers and workers are partners and share the profits **Genossenschaft**
2 *noun* business run by a group of workers who are the owners and who share the profits **Kooperative;** *industrial co-operative; to set up a workers' cooperative*

co-opt *verb* **to co-opt someone onto a committee** = to ask someone to join a committee without being elected **kooptieren, hinzuwählen**

co-owner *noun* person who owns something jointly with another person or persons **Miteigentümer; Mitinhaber;** *the two sisters are co-owners of the property*

◊ **co-ownership** *noun*
(a) arrangement where two or more

persons own a property **Mitinhaberschaft; Miteigentum**
(b) arrangement where partners *or* workers have shares in a company **Bruchteilseigentum**

cop
1 *noun (informal)*
(a) policeman; *(umg)* **Bulle**
(b) it's a fair cop = you have caught me **jetzt hat's mich erwischt**
2 *verb (slang)* to get *or* to receive **erwischen, schnappen; to cop a plea** = to plead guilty to a lesser charge and so hope the court will give a shorter sentence to save the time of a full trial **auf Strafmaß plädieren**

co-partner *noun* person who is a partner in a business with another person **Teilhaber/-in, Partner/-in**
◊ **co-partnership** *noun* arrangement where partners *or* workers have shares in the company **Teilhaber-, Partnerschaft**

cope *verb* to deal with **zurechtkommen, fertigwerden;** *the judges have difficulty in coping with all the divorce cases; how can the police cope with inner city violence when they do not have enough staff?*

copper *noun GB (informal)* policeman **Bulle**
◊ **copper-bottomed** *adjective* (guarantee) which cannot possibly be broken **handfest, solide**

co-property *noun* ownership of property by two or more people together **Miteigentum**
◊ **co-proprietor** *noun* person who owns a property with another person or several other people **Miteigentümer**

copy
1 *noun*
(a) document which looks the same as another **Kopie; carbon copy** = copy made with carbon paper **Durchschlag; certified copy** = document which is certified as being exactly the same in content as the original **beglaubigte Kopie; file copy** = copy of a document which is filed in an office for reference **Aktenkopie**
(b) document **(Abschrift einer) Urkunde; fair copy** *or* **final copy** = document which is written or typed with no changes or mistakes **Reinschrift; hard copy** = printout of a text which is on a computer *or* printed copy of something which is on microfilm **Ausdruck, Abzug; rough copy** = draft of a document which, it is expected, will have changes made to it before it is complete

Entwurf, Konzept; top copy = first or top sheet of a document which is typed with carbon copies **Original**
(c) a book *or* a newspaper **Ausgabe;** *have you kept yesterday's copy of "The Times"? I read it in the office copy of "Fortune"; where is my copy of the telephone directory?*
2 *verb* to make a second document which is like the first **kopieren; einen Durchschlag/eine Abschrift machen;** *he copied the company report at night and took it home*
◊ **copier** *or* **copying machine** *noun* machine which makes copies of documents **Kopierer**

copyright
1 *noun* legal right (lasting for fifty years after the death of an artist whose work has been published) which a writer *or* film maker *or* musician has in his own work allowing him not to have it copied without the payment of royalties **Copyright, Urheberrecht; Copyright Act** = Act of Parliament making copyright legal, and controlling the copying of copyright material **Urheberrechtsgesetz; copyright law** = laws concerning the protection of copyright **Urheberrecht; work which is out of copyright** = work by a writer, etc., who has been dead for fifty years, and which anyone can publish **Werk, das nicht mehr urheberrechtlich geschützt ist; work still in copyright** = work by a living writer, or by a writer who has not been dead for fifty years **urheberrechtlich geschütztes Werk; infringement of copyright** *or* **copyright infringement** = act of illegally copying a work which is in copyright **Verletzung des Urheberrechts; copyright notice** = note in a book showing who owns the copyright and the date of ownership **Urheberrechtsvermerk; copyright owner** = person who owns the copyright in a work **Urheberrechtsinhaber**
2 *verb* to confirm the copyright of a written work by printing a copyright notice and publishing the work **urheberrechtlich schützen**
3 *adjective* covered by the laws of copyright **urheberrechtlich geschützt;** *it is illegal to take copies of a copyright work*
◊ **copyrighted** *adjective* in copyright **urheberrechtlich/verlagsrechtlich geschützt**

cordon
1 *noun* **a police cordon** = barriers and policemen put round an area to prevent anyone getting near it **eine Polizeikette**
2 *verb* **to cordon off** = to put barriers and policemen round (an area) so that no one can get near it **absperren, abriegeln;** *the street was cordoned off after the bomb was discovered*

co-respondent *noun* party to divorce proceedings who has committed adultery with another person **Mitbeklagter;** *see also* CORRESPONDENT

coroner *noun* public official (either a doctor or a lawyer) who investigates sudden violent deaths and also treasure trove **richterlicher Beamter (zur Klärung von gewaltsamen Todesursachen und Schatzfunden); coroner's court** = court presided over by a coroner **Untersuchungsgericht (zur Klärung von gewaltsamen Todesursachen und Schatzfunde); coroner's inquest** = inquest carried out by a coroner into a death *or* case of treasure trove **gerichtliche Untersuchung (zur Klärung von gewaltsamen Todesursachen und Schatzfunden)**

COMMENT: coroners investigate deaths which are violent or unexpected, deaths which may be murder *or* manslaughter, deaths of prisoners and deaths involving the police

corporal punishment *noun* punishing a criminal by whipping him **Prügelstrafe**

corporate *adjective* referring to a company **Firmen-, Unternehmens-; corporate personality** = legal status of a company, so that it can be treated as a person **juristische Körperschaft; corporate planning** = planning the future work of a whole company **Unternehmensplanung; corporate profits** = profits of a corporation **Unternehmensgewinne**

◊ **corporation** *noun*
(a) legal body (such as a limited company *or* town council) which has been incorporated **Kapitalgesellschaft;** *(GB)* **Körperschaft;** *(US)* company which is incorporated in the United States **Kapital-, Aktiengesellschaft**
(b) generally, any large company **Unternehmen; finance corporation** = company which provides money for hire purchase **Finanzierungsgesellschaft**

corporeal hereditaments *plural noun* rights of property which physically exist, such as houses and furniture **vererbbare materielle Gegenstände**

corpse *noun (GB)* body of a dead person **Leiche**
NOTE: US English is **cadaver**

corpus *noun* body (of laws) **Gesetzessammlung, Korpus;** *see also* HABEAS CORPUS
NOTE: plural is **corpora**

◊ **corpus delicti** *Latin phrase meaning* "the body of the crime": the real proof that a crime has been committed **Corpus delicti, Beweisstück**

◊ **corpus legis** *Latin phrase meaning* "body of laws": books containing Roman civil law **Corpus legis, Gesetzessammlung Römischen Rechts**

correct
1 *adjective* accurate *or* right **korrekt, richtig;** *the published accounts do not give a correct picture of the company's financial position*
2 *verb* to remove mistakes from something **korrigieren, verbessern;** *the secretary will have to correct all these typing errors before you send the contract*
◊ **correction** *noun* act of making something correct; change which makes something correct **Korrektur, Verbesserung;** *he made some corrections to the draft contract*
◊ **corrective** *adjective* which punishes (a criminal) in such a way that he becomes a better person **Besserungs-;** *he was sent to the detention centre for corrective training*

correspond *verb*
(a) to correspond with someone = to write letters to someone **mit jdm korrespondieren/in Briefwechsel stehen**
(b) to correspond with something = to fit *or* to match something **(sich) entsprechen, übereinstimmen**
◊ **correspondence** *noun* letters which are exchanged **Korrespondenz, Briefwechsel; business correspondence** = letters concerned with a business **Geschäftskorrespondenz, Schriftwechsel; to be in correspondence with someone** = to write letters to someone and receive letters back **mit jdm korrespondieren/in Briefwechsel stehen**
NOTE: no plural
◊ **correspondent** *noun*
(a) person who writes letters **Korrespondent/-in, Briefeschreiber/-in**
(b) journalist who writes articles for a newspaper on specialist subjects **Korrespondent/-in;** *a financial correspondent; "The Times" legal correspondent; he is the Paris correspondent of the "Telegraph";* *see also* CO-RESPONDENT

corrigendum *noun* correction *or* word which has been corrected **Berichtigung**
NOTE: plural is **corrigenda**

corroborate *verb* to prove evidence which has already been given **bestätigen; erhärten;** *the witness corroborated the* *accused's alibi, saying that at the time of the murder he had seen him in Brighton*

◊ **corroboration** *noun* evidence which confirms and supports other evidence **Bestätigung; Erhärtung;** *the witness was unable to provide corroboration of what he had told the police*

◊ **corroborative** *adjective* which corroborates **bestätigend; erhärtend;** *the letter provides corroborative evidence, showing that the accused did know that the victim lived alone*

corrupt

1 *adjective* (person, especially an official) who takes bribes **korrupt, bestechlich**
2 *verb* **to corrupt someone's morals** = to make someone willing to commit a crime *or* to act against normal standards of behaviour **jds Moral korrumpieren/verderben**

◊ **corruption** *noun* paying money *or* giving a favour to someone (usually an official) so that he does what you want **Korruption, Bestechung;** *the government is keen to stamp out corruption in the police force; bribery and corruption are difficult to control*
NOTE: no plural

◊ **corruptly** *adverb* in a corrupt way **durch Bestechung;** *he corruptly offered the officer money to get the charges dropped*

Cosa Nostra = MAFIA

cosh

1 *noun* heavy stick for hitting people **Totschläger, Knüppel**
2 *verb* to hit someone with a stick **mit einem Knüppel schlagen;** *the burglars coshed the shopkeeper and stole money from the till*

cost

1 *noun*
(a) amount of money which has to be paid for something **Preis; Kosten;** *computer costs are falling each year; we cannot afford the cost of two telephones;* **to cover costs** = to produce enough money in sales to pay for the costs of production **die Kosten decken**
(b) costs = expenses involved in a court case, which can be awarded by the judge to the party which wins (so that the losing side pays the expenses of both sides) **Prozeß-, Gerichtskosten;** *the judge awarded costs to the defendant; costs of the case will be borne by the prosecution; the court awarded the plaintiff £2,000 in damages, with costs;* **to pay costs** = to pay the expenses of a court case **die Kosten (des Rechtsstreits) tragen; costs order** = court order requiring someone to pay costs **Kostenentscheidung (durch das Gericht); fixed costs** = set amount

of money to which a plaintiff is entitled in legal proceedings **feststehende Kosten; taxed costs** = varying amount of costs which can be awarded in legal proceedings **festgesetzte Kosten (aus einem Gebührenrahmen)**
2 *verb*
(a) to have a price **kosten;** *how much does the machine cost? rent of the room will cost £50 a day*
(b) to cost a product = to calculate how much money will be needed to make a product, and so work out its selling price **den Preis eines Produktes kalkulieren**

◊ **cost of living** *noun* money which has to be paid for food, heating, rent etc. **Lebenshaltungskosten;** *to allow for the cost of living in salaries;* **cost-of-living allowance** = addition to normal salary to cover increases in the cost of living **Lebenshaltungskostenzuschuß; cost-of-living increase** = increase in salary to allow it to keep up with the increased cost of living **Teuerungszulage; cost-of-living index** = way of measuring the cost of living which is shown as a percentage increase on the figure for the previous year **Lebenshaltungskostenindex**

coterminous

adjective (two things) which terminate at the same time **gleichzeitig auslaufend;** *the leases are coterminous*

council *noun*

(a) official group chosen to run something *or* to advise on a problem **Rat; Behörde; consumer council** = group representing the interests of consumers **Verbraucherberatung; borough council** *or* **town council** = representatives elected to run a town **Gemeinderat; Stadtrat; Council of Ministers** = body made up of the foreign ministers of the member states of the EC **Ministerrat; Security Council** = permanent ruling body of the United Nations **Sicherheitsrat**
(b) = PRIVY COUNCIL; **Order in Council** = legislation made by the Queen in Council, which is allowed by an Act of Parliament and does not have to be ratified by Parliament **königlicher Erlaß**

◊ **councillor** *noun* member of a council, especially member of a town council **Ratsmitglied; Stadtrat;** *see also* PRIVY COUNCILLOR

counsel *noun* barrister (or barristers) acting for one of the parties in a legal action **Anwalt/Anwältin;** *defence counsel; prosecution counsel; the plaintiff appeared in court with his solicitor and two counsel;* **counsel's advice** *or* **opinion** = written opinion of a barrister about a case

Rechtsgutachten (eines Barristers); **leading counsel** = main barrister (usually a QC) in a team appearing for one side in a case **führender Anwalt (unter mehreren Vertretern der jeweiligen Partei); Queen's Counsel** = senior British lawyer appointed to the rank of Queen's Counsel by the Lord Chancellor **Kronanwalt**

NOTE: **Queen's Counsel** is usually abbreviated to **QC**. Note that there is no plural for counsel which is always used in the singular whether it refers to one barrister or several, and it is never used with the article **the** or **a**. On the other hand the abbreviation QC can have a plural: **two QCs represented the defendant**

◊ **counsellor** *noun (US)* lawyer *or* person who gives legal advice **Rechtsanwalt; Rechtsberater**

count

1 *noun* separate charge against an accused person read out in court in the indictment **Anklagepunkt;** *he was found guilty on all four counts*
2 *verb*
(a) to add figures together to make a total **(zusammen)zählen;** *he counted up the sales for the six months to December*
(b) to include **(mit)rechnen, (mit)zählen;** *did the defence count the accused's theft of money from the till as part of the total theft?*

◊ **count on** *verb*
(a) to expect something to happen **rechnen mit;** *the defence seems to be counting on winning the sympathy of the jury*
(b) to rely on someone *or* something **sich verlassen auf;** *you can count on Mr Jones, he is an excellent solicitor*

counter

1 *noun* long flat surface in a shop for displaying and selling goods **Tresen, Ladentisch;** over the counter = legally **legal (verkaufen), über den Ladentisch; goods sold over the counter** = retail sales of goods in shops **im Einzelhandel gegen bar verkaufte Ware; over-the-counter market (OTC)** = legal selling of shares which are not listed in the official Stock Exchange list **Freiverkehr(smarkt) (für nicht im offiziellen Börsenhandel zugelassene Aktien); under the counter** = illegally **unter dem Ladentisch; illegal; under-the-counter sales** = black market sales **ungesetzliche Verkäufe**
2 *adverb* **counter to** = against *or* opposite **gegen;** *the decision of the court runs counter to the advice of the clerk to the justices*

counter- *prefix* against **Gegen-**

◊ **counterclaim**
1 *noun*
(a) claim in a court by a defendant against the plaintiff who has already brought in a claim against him **Widerklage**
(b) claim for damages made in reply to a previous claim **Gegenanspruch, Gegenforderung;** *Jones claimed £25,000 in damages against Smith, and Smith entered a counterclaim of £50,000 for loss of office*
2 *verb* to put in a counterclaim **eine Gegenforderung erheben;** *Jones claimed £25,000 in damages and Smith counterclaimed £50,000 for loss of office*

◊ **counterfeit**
1 *adjective* false *or* imitation (money) **gefälscht, Falsch-;** *he was charged with passing counterfeit notes in shops*
2 *verb* to make imitation money **fälschen**

◊ **counterfeiting** *noun* crime of making imitation money **Fälschung**

◊ **counter-intelligence** *noun* organization of secret agents whose job is to work against the secret agents of another country **Spionageabwehr;** *the offices were bugged by counter-intelligence agents*

◊ **countermand** *verb* **to countermand an order** = to say that an order must not be carried out **eine Anordnung aufheben**

◊ **counteroffer** *noun* offer made in reply to another offer **Gegenangebot**

◊ **counterpart** *noun*
(a) copy of a lease **Kopie/Duplikat (einer Originalurkunde)**
(b) person who has a similar job in another company **Kollege; Pendant, Gegenstück; John is my counterpart in Smith's** = he has a similar post at Smith's as I have here **John ist mein Pendant bei Smith's**

◊ **counter-promise** *noun* promise made in reply to a promise **Gegenversprechen**

◊ **countersign** *verb* to sign a document which has already been signed by someone else **gegenzeichnen;** *the payment has to be countersigned by the mortgagor*

country *noun* land which is an entity and governs itself **Land, Staat;** *the contract covers sales in the countries of the Common Market; some African countries export oil;* **country of origin** = country where the goods have been produced or made **Herkunftsland**

county *noun* one of the administrative divisions of a country **Kreis; Bezirk;** *(GB)* **Grafschaft; county council** = group of people elected to run a county **Kreistag; Bezirksrat;** *(GB)* **Grafschaftsrat; County Court** = one of the types of court set up in England and Wales which hears local civil cases **Amtsgericht;** *(GB)* **Grafschaftsgericht; County Court Rules** = book of procedural rules for County Courts; *(GB)* **Richtlinien eines Grafschaftsgerichts;** *see also* GREEN BOOK

COMMENT: the County Court hears most civil cases up to a value of £5,000

coup (d'état) *noun* rapid revolution which removes one government and replaces it by another **Coup d'état, Staatsstreich;** *after the coup, groups of students attacked the police stations*

course *noun*
(a) in the course of = during *or* while something is happening **während, im Verlauf/Lauf;** *in the course of the hearing, several new allegations were made by the defendant*
(b) series of lessons **Kurs(us), Lehrgang;** *he is taking a management course; she has finished her secretarial course; the company has paid for her to attend a course for trainee sales managers*
(c) course of action = action which has been taken *or* which can be taken **Vorgehen;** *what is the best course of action the defendant should take?;* **in the course of employment** = done as part of the work of the person concerned **während der Arbeit; als Teil der Arbeit**
(d) of course = naturally **natürlich, selbstverständlich;** *of course the company is interested in profits; are you willing to go on a sales trip to Australia? - of course!*

court *noun*
(a) court of law *or* **law court** = place where a trial is held **Gericht; Gerichtshof;** *the law courts are in the centre of the town; she works in the law courts as an usher;* **court action** *or* **court case** = legal action or trial **gerichtliches Vorgehen; Gerichtsverfahren; Prozeß; to take someone to court** = to start legal proceedings against someone **gegen jdn gerichtlich vorgehen; in court** = present during a trial **vor Gericht;** *the defendant was in court for three hours;* **in open court** = in a courtroom with members of the public present **in öffentlicher Verhandlung;** *a settlement was reached out of court or* **the two parties reached an out-of-court settlement** = the dispute was settled between the two parties privately without continuing the court case **es kam zu einem außergerichtlichen Vergleich; contempt of court** = being rude to a court, or by bad behaviour in the courtroom or by refusing to carry out a court order **Mißachtung des**

Gerichts; court order = legal order made by a court, telling someone to do *or* not to do something **Gerichtsbeschluß, gerichtliche Verfügung;** *the court made an order for maintenance or made a maintenance order; he refused to obey the court order and was sent to prison for contempt*
(b) Criminal Court *or* **Civil Court** = court where criminal *or* civil cases are heard **Strafgericht; Zivilgericht; Court of Appeal** *or* **Appeal Court** = civil *or* criminal court to which a person may go to ask for an award *or* a sentence to be changed **Berufungs-, Revisionsgericht; court of first instance** = court where a case is heard first **Gericht erster Instanz; Court of Protection** = court which administers the property of people suffering from a disability **Gericht, das das Vermögen von Entmündigten verwaltet; High Court (of Justice)** = main civil court in England and Wales **Oberstes Zivilgericht; International Court of Justice** = the court of the United Nations, which sits in the Hague, Netherlands **Internationaler Gerichtshof; magistrates' court** = court presided over by magistrates **Amtsgericht;** *(GB)* **Gericht erster Instanz; Supreme Court (of Judicature)** = (i) highest court in England and Wales (except for the House of Lords), formed of the High Court and the Court of Appeal; (ii) highest federal court in the USA **(i) Oberster Gerichtshof; (ii) oberstes US Bundesgericht;** *(in Scotland)* **Court of Session** = highest civil court in Scotland **Oberstes Gericht in Zivilsachen**
(c) the judges *or* magistrates in a court **Gericht;** *the court will retire for thirty minutes*

◊ **court-martial**
1 *noun*
(a) court which tries someone serving in the armed forces for offences against military discipline **Disziplinargericht für Bundeswehrangehörige;** *(GB)* **Militärgericht**
(b) trial of someone serving in the armed forces by the armed forces authorities **Militärgerichtsprozeß;** *the court-martial was held in the army headquarters; he was found guilty by the court-martial and sentenced to imprisonment* (NOTE: plural is **courts-martial**)
2 *verb* to try someone who is serving in the armed forces; *(GB)* **vor das Militärgericht stellen**
NOTE: **court-martialled**

◊ **courtroom** *noun* room where a judge listens to a trial **Gerichtssaal**

COMMENT: in England and Wales the main courts are: **the Magistrates' Court:** petty crime; adoption; affiliation; maintenance and domestic violence; licensing; **the County Court:** most civil actions up to a value of £5,000; **the High Court:** most civil claims where the value exceeds £5,000; **the Crown Court:** major crime; **the Court of Appeal:** appeals from lower courts; **the House of Lords:** the highest court of appeal in the country; **the Privy Council:** appeals on certain matters from England and Wales, and appeals from certain Commonwealth countries; **the European Court of Justice:** appeals where EEC legislation is involved. Other courts include **Industrial tribunals:** employment disputes; **courts-martial:** military matters

covenant

1 *noun* agreement *or* undertaking to do something or not to do something, contained in a deed *or* contract **Vertrag, Abkommen;** *he signed a covenant against underletting the premises;* **deed of covenant** = official signed agreement to do something (such as to pay someone a sum of money each year) **Vertrags-, Versprechensurkunde (über die Zahlung einer festen jährlichen Summe); covenant to repair** = agreement by a landlord *or* tenant to keep a rented property in good repair **Instandsetzungsvertrag; restrictive covenant** = clause in a contract which prevents someone from doing something **einschränkende Vereinbarung (über Unterlassungspflichten in Verträgen)**

COMMENT: examples of restrictive covenants could be a clause in a contract of employment which prevents the employee from going to work for a competitor, or a clause in a contract for the sale of a property which prevents the purchaser from altering the building

2 *verb* to agree to pay a sum of money each year by contract **vertraglich vereinbaren (jährlich eine bestimmte Summe zu zahlen);** *to covenant to pay £10 per annum to a charity*

COMMENT: there is a tax advantage to the recipient of covenanted money; a charity pays no tax, so it can reclaim tax at the standard rate on the money covenanted

cover

1 *noun*

(a) insurance cover = protection guaranteed by an insurance policy **Versicherungsschutz;** *do you have cover against theft?;* **to operate without adequate cover** = without being protected by insurance **ohne ausreichenden Versicherungsschutz handeln; to ask for additional cover** = to ask the insurance company to increase the amount for which you are insured **Erhöhung der Versicherungssumme beantragen; full cover** = insurance against all types of risk **voller Versicherungsschutz; cover note** = letter from an insurance company giving basic details of an insurance policy and confirming that the policy exists **vorläufige Deckungszusage**

(b) security to guarantee a loan **Sicherheit;** *do you have sufficient cover for this loan?*

(c) to send something under separate cover = in a separate envelope **etwas mit getrennter Post schicken; to send a document under plain cover** = in an ordinary envelope with no company name printed on it **ein Dokument in neutralem Umschlag verschicken**

2 *verb*

(a) to deal with *or* to refer to something completely **(ab)decken;** *the agreement covers all agencies; the newspapers have covered the murder trial; the fraud case has been covered by the consumer protection legislation*

(b) to cover a risk = to be protected by insurance against a risk **ein Risiko decken; to be fully covered** = to have insurance against all risks **vollen Versicherungsschutz haben;** *the insurance covers fire, theft and loss of work*

(c) to have enough money to pay; to ask for security against a loan which you are making **decken, abdecken;** *the damage was* **covered by the insurance** = the insurance company paid for the damage **der Schaden wurde von der Versicherung bezahlt; to cover a position** = to have enough money to be able to pay for a forward purchase **eine Position abdecken**

(d) to earn enough money to pay for costs, expenses, etc. **(ab)decken; sichern;** *we do not make enough sales to cover the expense of running the shop; we hope to reach the point soon when sales will cover all costs;* **the dividend is covered four times** = profits are four times the dividend paid out **das Verhältnis Gewinn-Dividende ist 4:1**

◇ **coverage** *noun*
(a) press coverage *or* **media coverage** = reports about something in the newspapers *or* on TV, etc. **Berichterstattung durch die Presse od die Medien;** *the company had good media coverage for the launch of its new model*
(b) *US* protection guaranteed by insurance **Versicherungsschutz;** *do you have coverage against fire damage?*

◇ **covering** *adjective* **covering letter** *or* **covering note** = letter or note sent with documents to say why you are sending them **Begleitschreiben**

covert *adjective* hidden *or* secret **versteckt; geheim; covert action** = action which is secret (such as spying) **geheime Aktion;** *see also* FEME COVERT

◇ **coverture** *noun* state of being married (of a woman) **Ehestand (einer Frau)**

cracksman *noun (slang)* criminal who specializes in breaking safes **Safeknacker**

create *verb* to make something new **schaffen;** *by acquiring small unprofitable companies he soon created a large trading group; the government scheme aims at creating new jobs for young people*

◇ **creation** *noun* making **Schaffung; job creation scheme** = government-backed scheme to make work for the unemployed **Arbeitsbeschaffungs-, Beschäftigungsprogramm**

credere *see* DEL CREDERE

credit
1 *noun*
(a) time given to a debtor before he has to pay **Kredit, Darlehen;** *to give someone six months' credit; to sell on good credit terms;* **credit account** = account which a customer has with a shop which allows him to buy goods and pay for them later **Kundenkreditkonto; credit agency** *or (US)* **credit bureau** = company which reports on the ability of customers to pay their debts and shows whether they should be allowed credit **Kreditauskunftei; credit bank** = bank which lends money **Kreditbank; credit card** = plastic card which allows the owner to borrow money, and to buy goods without paying for them immediately **Kreditkarte;**

credit facilities = arrangement with a bank or supplier to have credit so as to buy goods **Kreditmodalitäten; letter of credit** = letter from a bank, allowing someone credit and promising to repay at a later date **Akkreditiv; irrevocable letter of credit** = letter of credit which cannot be cancelled **unwiderrufliches Akkreditiv; credit limit** = fixed amount which is the most a customer can owe **Kreditlinie; credit rating** = amount which a credit agency feels a customer should be allowed to borrow **Bonitätsbeurteilung; to buy on credit** = without paying immediately **auf Kredit kaufen**
(b) money received by a person *or* company and recorded in the accounts **Kredit, Haben;** *to enter £100 to someone's credit; to pay in £100 to the credit of Mr Smith;* **debit and credit** = money which a company owes and which it is entitled to receive **Soll und Haben, Debet und Kredit; credit side** = right side of accounts which records money received **Habenseite**
2 *verb* to put money into someone's account; to note money received in an account **gutschreiben;** *to credit an account with £100 or to credit £100 to an account*

◇ **creditor** *noun* person who is owed money **Gläubiger; creditors' meeting** = meeting of all persons to whom a company in receivership owes money **Gläubigerversammlung; judgment creditor** = person who has been given a court order making a debtor pay a debt **Vollstreckungsgläubiger; preferential creditor** = creditor who must be paid first if a company is in liquidation **bevorrechtigter Gläubiger; secured** *or* **unsecured creditor** = creditor who holds *or* does not hold a mortgage *or* charge against the debtor's property as security for the loan **gesicherter Gläubiger; ungesicherter Gläubiger**

crime *noun*
(a) act which is against the law and which is punishable by law **Straftat, Verbrechen;** *there has been a 50% increase in crimes of violence*
(b) illegal acts in general **Kriminalität;** *crime is on the increase; there has been an increase in violent crime;* **crime rate** = number of crimes committed, shown as a percentage of the total population **Kriminalität; crime wave** = sudden increase in crime **Verbrechenswelle;** NOTE: no plural for (b)

COMMENT: a crime is an illegal act which may result in prosecution and punishment by the state if the accused is convicted. Generally, in order to be convicted of a crime, the accused must be shown to have committed an unlawful act (**actus reus**) with a criminal state of mind (**mens rea**). The main types of crime are: 1. **crimes against the person**: murder; manslaughter; assault, battery, wounding; grievous bodily harm; abduction; 2. **crimes against property**: theft; robbery; burglary; obtaining property *or* services *or* pecuniary advantage by deception; blackmail; handling stolen goods; going equipped to steal; criminal damage; possessing something with intent to damage *or* destroy property; forgery; 3. **sexual offences**: rape; buggery; bigamy; indecency; 4. **political offences**: treason; terrorism; sedition; breach of the Official Secrets Act; 5. **offences against justice**: assisting an offender; conspiracy; perjury; contempt of court; perverting the course of justice; 6. **public order offences**: obstruction of the police; unlawful assembly; obscenity; possessing weapons; misuse of drugs; breach of the peace; 7. **road traffic offences**: careless *or* reckless driving; drunken driving; driving without a licence *or* insurance. Most minor crime is tried before the Magistrates' Courts; more serious crime is tried at the Crown Court which has greater powers to sentence offenders. Most crimes are prosecuted by the police or the Crown Prosecutors, though private prosecutions brought by individuals are possible

criminal

1 *adjective*

(a) illegal **strafbar; kriminell;** *misappropriation of funds is a criminal act;* **criminal offence** = action which is against the law **strafbare Handlung**

(b) referring to crime **Straf-; criminal action** = court case brought by the state against someone who is charged with a crime **Strafverfahren, strafrechtliche Verfolgung; criminal bankruptcy** = bankruptcy of a criminal in the Crown Court as a result of crimes of which he has been convicted **betrügerischer Konkurs/Bankrott; criminal court** = court (such as a Crown Court) which hears criminal cases **Strafgericht; criminal damage** = notifiable offence of causing serious damage **strafbare Sachbeschädigung; criminal law** = laws relating to acts committed against the laws of the land, and which are punished by the state **Strafrecht; criminal libel** = serious libel which might cause a breach of the peace **strafbare Verleumdung; criminal negligence** = acting recklessly with the result that harm is done to other people **strafbare/grobe**

Fahrlässigkeit; the criminal population = all people who have committed crimes **die Kriminellen; to have a criminal record** = to be in police files for having previously committed a crime **vorbestraft sein;** *the accused had no criminal record; he has a criminal record going back to the time when he was still at school;* **age of criminal responsibility** = age at which a person is considered to be capable of committing a crime **Strafmündigkeit**

COMMENT: the age of criminal responsibility is ten years. Children under ten years old cannot be charged with a crime

2 *noun* person who has committed a crime *or* person who often commits crimes **Krimineller;** *the police have contacted known criminals to get leads on the gangland murder;* **a hardened criminal** = a person who has committed many crimes **Gewohnheitsverbrecher**

◊ **Criminal Injuries Compensation Board** *noun* committee which administers the awarding of compensation to victims of crime **Entscheidungsbehörde für Verbrechensopfer**

criminology *noun* academic study of crime **Kriminologie**
NOTE: no plural

criterion *noun* standard by which something can be judged **Kriterium;** *using the criterion of the ratio of cases solved to cases reported, the police force is becoming more efficient*
NOTE: plural is **criteria**

criticize *verb* to say that something *or* someone is wrong *or* is working badly, etc. **kritisieren;** *the judge criticized the police for their handling of the rape case*

◊ **criticism** *noun* words showing that you consider that someone *or* something is wrong **Kritik;** *the judge made some criticisms of the way in which the police handled the case*

crook *noun (slang)* criminal *or* person who has committed a crime, especially involving deceit **Gauner**

cross *verb*

(a) to go across **überqueren;** *Concorde takes only three hours to cross the Atlantic; to get to the bank, you turn left and cross the street at the post office*

(b) to cross a cheque = to write two lines across a cheque to show that it has to be paid into a bank **einen Scheck zur**

Verrechnung ausstellen; **crossed cheque** = cheque with two lines across it to show that it can only be deposited at a bank and not exchanged for cash **Verrechnungsscheck**

◊ **cross off** *verb* to remove something from a list **streichen;** *he crossed my name off his list; you can cross him off our mailing list*

◊ **cross out** *verb* to put a line through something which has been written **durchstreichen;** *she crossed out £250 and put in £500*

cross-examine *verb* to question witnesses called by the other side in a case, in the hope that you can destroy their evidence **ins Kreuzverhör nehmen**

◊ **cross-examination** *noun* questioning witnesses called by the other side in a case **Kreuzverhör**

Crown *noun GB*
(a) the Crown = the King *or* Queen as representing the State **die Krone;** *Mr Smith is appearing for the Crown; the Crown submitted that the maximum sentence should be applied in this case; the Crown case or the case for the Crown was that the defendants were guilty of espionage*
NOTE: in legal reports, the Crown is referred to as **Rex** *or* **Regina** (abbreviated to **R.**) depending on whether there is a King or Queen reigning at the time: **the case of** *R. v. Smith Limited*
(b) associate of the **Crown Office** = official who is responsible for the clerical and administrative work of a court **Geschäftsstellenbeamter; Crown Lands** *or* **Crown property** = land *or* property belonging to the King *or* Queen **Ländereien od Eigentum der Krone; Crown copyright** = copyright in government publications **Urheberrecht der Krone**

◊ **Crown Court** *noun* court, above the level of the magistrates' courts, which has centres all over England and Wales and which hears criminal cases; *(GB)* **Höheres Gericht für Strafsachen**

COMMENT: a Crown Court is formed of a circuit judge and jury, and hears major criminal cases

◊ **Crown privilege** *noun* right of the Crown *or* the government not to have to produce documents to a court by reason of the interest of the state **Vorrecht der Krone od Regierung (, die Vorlage von Urkunden vor Gericht abzulehnen)**

◊ **Crown prosecutor** *noun* official of the Director of Public Prosecution's department who is responsible for prosecuting criminals in a local area **Staatsanwalt;** *(GB)* **Kronanwalt**

cruelty *noun*
(a) hurting a person *or* animal **Mißhandlung; Grausamkeit**
(b) acting harshly to a spouse **Grausamkeit**
NOTE: no plural

CTT = CAPITAL TRANSFER TAX

culpable *adjective* which is likely to attract blame **schuldhaft; culpable homicide** = murder *or* manslaughter **Totschlag; Mord; culpable negligence** = negligence which is so bad that it amounts to an offence **schuldhafte/grobe Fahrlässigkeit**

◊ **culpability** *noun* being culpable **Strafbarkeit**
NOTE: no plural

culprit *noun* person who is responsible for a crime *or* for something which has gone wrong **Täter/-in; Schuldiger**

curiam *see* PER CURIAM

currency *noun* money in coins and notes which is used in a particular country **Währung; blocked currency** = money which cannot be taken out of a country because of exchange controls **nicht frei konvertier- und transferierbare Währung; foreign currency** = currency of another country **Fremdwährung; free currency** = currency which a government allows to be bought or sold without restriction **frei konvertierbare Währung; hard currency** = currency of a country which has a strong economy and which can be changed into other currencies easily **harte Währung; legal currency** = money which is legally used in a country **gesetzliche Währung; soft currency** = currency of a country with a weak economy, which is cheap to buy and difficult to exchange for other currencies **weiche Währung**

current *adjective* referring to the present time **derzeitig, gegenwärtig; current account** = ordinary account in a bank into which money can be deposited and on which cheques can be drawn **laufendes Konto, Girokonto; current liabilities** = debts which a company has to pay within the next accounting period **kurzfristige Verbindlichkeiten**

◊ **currently** *adverb* at the present time **gegenwärtig, zur Zeit;** *six murders which are currently being investigated*

curriculum vitae *noun* summary of a person's life story showing details of education and work experience **Lebenslauf;**

candidates should send a letter of application with a curriculum vitae to the administrative office
NOTE: the US English is **résumé**

curtilage *noun* land round a house **eingezäuntes Land eines Anwesens**

custody *noun*
(a) being kept in prison *or* in a cell **Gewahrsam; Untersuchungshaft;** *the young men were kept in police custody overnight;* **remand in custody** = kept in prison until the trial starts **Untersuchungshaft**
(b) right and duty of a parent to keep and bring up a child after a divorce **Sorgerecht;** *custody of the children was awarded to the mother; the court granted the mother custody of both children*
NOTE: no plural

◊ **custodial** *adjective* **custodial establishment** *or* **institution** = prison *or* other institution where criminals are kept **Strafanstalt; custodial sentence** = sentence which involves sending someone to prison **Freiheitsstrafe**

◊ **custodian** *noun* person who guards a museum or public building **Aufseher/-in, Wächter/-in**

custom *noun*
(a) unwritten law which lays down how things are usually done and have been done since time immemorial **Brauch, Sitte;** *it is the custom that everyone stands up when the magistrates enter the courtroom;* **local custom** = way in which things are usually done in a particular place **örtliche Gepflogenheit; the customs of the trade** = general way of working in a trade **Handelsbrauch, Usance**
(b) use of a shop by regular shoppers **Kundschaft; to lose someone's custom** = to do something which makes a regular customer go to another shop **jdn als Kunden verlieren**

◊ **customs** *or* **Customs and Excise** *plural noun* the government department which organizes the collection of taxes on imports; office of this department at a port *or* airport **Zoll(behörde); Behörde für Zölle und Verbrauchssteuern; to go through the customs** = to pass through the area of a port or airport where customs officials examine goods **den Zoll passieren;** *he was stopped by the customs; her car was searched by the customs;* **customs barrier** = customs duty intended to prevent imports **Zollschranke; customs clearance** = act of clearing goods through the customs **Zollabfertigung; customs declaration** = statement showing goods being imported on which duty will have to be paid **Zollerklärung; customs union**

= agreement between several countries that goods can travel between them without paying duty, while goods from other countries have to pay special duties **Zollunion**

cut
1 *noun*
(a) sudden lowering of a price *or* salary *or* numbers of jobs **Senkung; Kürzung;** *price cuts or cuts in prices; salary cuts or cuts in salaries*
(b) share in a payment **Anteil, Teil;** *he introduces new customers and gets a cut of the salesman's commission*
2 *verb*
(a) to lower suddenly **senken; kürzen;** *we are cutting prices on all our models;* **to cut (back) production** = to reduce the quantity of products made **die Produktion zurückschrauben**
(b) to stop *or* to reduce the number of something **streichen; abbauen; reduzieren; to cut jobs** = to reduce the number of jobs by making people redundant **Arbeitsplätze abbauen**

◊ **cut in on** *verb* **to cut someone in on a deal** = to offer someone part of the profits of a deal **jdn an einem Geschäft beteiligen**

CV *noun* = CURRICULUM VITAE *please apply in writing, enclosing a current CV*

cycle *noun* period of time when something leaves its original position and then returns to it **Zyklus, Kreislauf**

◊ **cyclical** *adjective* which happens in cycles **zyklisch; cyclical factors** = way in which a trade cycle affects businesses **zyklische Faktoren** *adjective & adverb* as near as possible **so nahe wie möglich;** rule that if a charity cannot apply its funds to the purposes for which they were intended, a court can apply the funds to a purpose which is as close as possible to the original intention **Änderung im anzunehmenden Sinn (eines Stiftungsgebers)**

Dd

D *fourth letter of the alphabet* **category "D" prisoners** = reliable prisoners who can be kept in open prisons **Freigänger/-in; Schedule D** = schedule to the Finance Acts under which tax is charged on income from trades, professions, interest and other earnings which do not come from employment **Einkommenssteuergruppe D;**

Table D = model memorandum and articles of association of a public company with share capital limited by guarantee, set out in the Companies Act, 1985 **Mustersatzung einer AG**

DA *US* = DISTRICT ATTORNEY

dabs *plural noun slang* fingerprints **Fingerabdrücke**

damage

1 *noun*
(a) harm done to things **Schaden, Beschädigung; fire damage** = damage caused by a fire **Brandschaden; malicious damage** = deliberate and intentional harming of property **böswillige Sachbeschädigung; storm damage** = damage caused by a storm **Sturmschaden; to suffer damage** = to be harmed **Schaden erleiden/nehmen; to cause damage** = to harm something **beschädigen, Schaden verursachen/anrichten; causing criminal damage** = notifiable offence where serious damage is caused **Verursachung strafbarer Sachbeschädigung; damage feasant** = situation where the animals of one person damage the property of another person **Schadenstiftung durch fremde Tiere;** (NOTE: no plural)
(b) **damages** = money claimed by a plaintiff from a defendant as compensation for harm done **Schadensersatz, Entschädigung;** *to claim £1,000 in damages; to be liable for or in damages; to pay £25,000 in damages;* **to bring an action for damages against someone** = to take someone to court and claim damages **jdn auf Schadensersatz verklagen; aggravated damages** = damages awarded by court against a defendant who has behaved maliciously *or* wilfully **erhöhter Schadensersatz; compensatory damages** = damages which compensate for the loss *or* harm suffered **ausgleichender Schadensersatz; exemplary damages** = damages which punish the defendant for the loss *or* harm caused to the plaintiff *or* heavy damages awarded to show that the court feels the defendant has behaved badly towards the plaintiff **verschärfter Schadensersatz; general damages** = damages awarded by court to compensate for a loss which cannot be calculated (such as an injury) **genereller Schadensersatz; measure of damages** = calculation of how much money a court should order one party to pay another to compensate for a tort *or* breach **Schadensbemessung; mitigation of damages** = reduction in the extent of damages awarded **Herabsetzung des Schadensersatzes; nominal damages** = very small amount of damages, awarded to show that the loss *or* harm suffered was

technical rather than actual **nomineller Schadensersatz; special damages** = damages awarded by court to compensate for a loss which can be calculated (such as the expense of repairing something) **Schadensersatz für konkreten Schaden;** NOTE: damages are noted at the end of a report on a case as: *Special damages: £100; General damages: £2,500*
2 *verb* to harm **beschädigen;** *the storm damaged the cargo; stock which has been damaged by water; he alleged that the newspaper article was damaging to the company's reputation*

◊ **damaged** *adjective* which has suffered damage *or* which has been harmed **beschädigt, schadhaft; fire-damaged goods** = goods harmed in a fire **brandgeschädigte Waren**

danger *noun*
(a) possibility of being harmed *or* killed **Gefahr, Risiko;** *there is danger to the workers in using old machinery*
(b) likelihood *or* possibility **Wahrscheinlichkeit; there is no danger of the case being heard early** = it is not likely that the case will be heard early **es ist unwahrscheinlich, daß der Fall schon bald verhandelt wird; to be in danger of** = which may easily happen **Gefahr laufen;** *he is in danger to being in contempt of court*

◊ **danger money** *noun* extra money paid to workers in dangerous jobs **Gefahrenzulage;** *the workers have stopped work and asked for danger money*

◊ **dangerous** *adjective* which can be harmful **gefährlich, riskant; dangerous drugs** = drugs which may be harmful to people who take them, and so can be prohibited from import and general sales **gesundheitsgefährdende Drogen, Rauschgifte; dangerous job** = job where the workers may be killed *or* hurt **gefährlicher Beruf; dangerous weapon** = weapon which can hurt someone **gefährliche Waffe**

data *noun* information (letters *or* figures) which is available on computer **Daten; data bank** *or* **bank of data** = store of information in a computer **Datenbank; data processing** = selecting and examining data in a computer to produce special information **Datenverarbeitung; data protection** = protecting information (such as records about private people) in a computer from being copied or used wrongly **Datenschutz** NOTE: **data** is usually singular: **the data is easily available**

◊ **database** *noun* store of information in a large computer **Datenbank;** *the police maintain a database of fingerprints*

date

1 *noun*

(a) number of day, month and year **Datum; date of commencement** = date when an Act of Parliament takes effect **Tag des Inkrafttretens; date stamp** = rubber stamp for marking the date on letters received **Datumsstempel; date of receipt** = date when something is received **Eingangs-, Empfangsdatum**

(b) at an early date = very soon **früh, frühzeitig; up to date** = current *or* recent *or* modern **aktuell, auf dem neuesten Stand; to bring something up to date** = to add the latest information to something **etwas auf den neuesten Stand bringen; to keep something up to date** = to keep adding information to something so that it is always up to date **etwas auf dem laufenden halten/aktualisieren**

(c) to date = up to now **bis jetzt/heute; interest to date** = interest up to the present time **Zinsen bis auf den heutigen Tag**

2 *verb* to put a date on a document **datieren;** *the cheque was dated March 24th; he forgot to date the cheque*

◊ **dated** *adjective* with a date written on it **datiert;** *the murderer's letter was dated June 15th*

day *noun*

(a) period of 24 hours **Tag;** *there are thirty days in June; the first day of the month is a public holiday;* **three clear days** = three whole working days **drei (volle) Werk-/Arbeitstage;** *to give ten clear days' notice; allow four clear days for the cheque to be paid into the account;* **early day motion** = motion proposed in the House of Commons for discussion at an early date (usually used to introduce the particular point of view of the MP proposing the motion, without necessarily going to a full debate) **frühzeitig gestellter Antrag (im Unterhaus)**

(b) period of work during a 24 hour day **Tag;** *the trial lasted ten days*

◊ **day-to-day** *adjective* ordinary *or* which goes on all the time **täglich, Tages-;** *the clerk organizes the day-to-day running of the courts*

◊ **day training centre** *noun* centre where young offenders attend courses as a condition of being on probation **Tagesausbildungsstätte**

DC = DETECTIVE CONSTABLE

DCC = DEPUTY CHIEF CONSTABLE

dead *adjective*

(a) not alive **tot, verstorben;** *six people were dead as a result of the accident; we inherited the house from my dead grandfather*

(b) not working **unproduktiv, ertraglos; dead account** = account which is no longer used **umsatzloses Konto; dead letter** = regulation which is no longer valid **außer Kraft getretene Verordnung;** *this law has become a dead letter;* **dead loss** = total loss **Totalverlust;** *the car was written off as a dead loss*

◊ **deadline** *noun* date by which something has to be done **(letzter) Termin, Stichtag; to meet a deadline** = to finish something in time **eine Frist einhalten; to miss a deadline** = not to finish something in time **eine Frist nicht einhalten**

◊ **deadlock**

1 *noun* point where two sides in a dispute cannot agree **Stillstand; to break a deadlock** = to find a way to start discussions again **aus einer Sackgasse herausfinden**

2 *verb* to be unable to agree to continue discussing **zum Stillstand kommen; talks have been deadlocked for ten days** = after ten days the talks have not produced any agreement **nach zehn Tagen sind die Gespräche an einem toten Punkt angekommen**

deal

1 *noun*

(a) business agreement *or* affair *or* contract **Abkommen, Abschluß, Geschäft, Handel;** *to arrange a deal or to set up a deal or to do a deal; to sign a deal;* **to call off a deal** = to stop an agreement **ein Abkommen rückgängig machen; package deal** = agreement where several different items are agreed at the same time **Pauschalarrangement, Verhandlungspaket**

(b) a great deal *or* **a good deal of something** = a large quantity of something **viel, eine Menge;** *he has made a good deal of money on the stock market; counsel wasted a great deal of time cross-examining the dead man's father*

2 *verb* **to deal with** = to be busy with *or* to have to do with **sich befassen mit, etwas bearbeiten;** *Crown Courts do not deal with civil cases*

◊ **dealer** *noun* person who buys and sells **Händler/-in, Kaufmann/Kauffrau;** *a wine dealer or a foreign exchange dealer*

◊ **dealing** *noun*

(a) buying and selling on the Stock Exchange **Effektenhandel; fair dealing** = (i) legal trade *or* legal buying and selling of shares; (ii) legal quoting of small sections of a copyright work **(i) legaler Handel; geordneter Effektenhandel; (ii) legales Zitat (eines kleinen Auszuges) aus einem urheberrechtlich geschützten Werk; foreign exchange dealing** = buying and selling

foreign currencies **Devisenhandel; forward dealings** = buying or selling commodities forward **Termingeschäfte; insider dealing** = illegal buying or selling of shares, such as by staff of a company who have secret information about the company's plans **Insiderhandel**
(b) buying and selling goods **Handel; to have dealings with someone** = to do business with someone **mit jdm Geschäfte machen, mit jdm in Geschäftsbeziehungen stehen**

dear *adjective*
(a) expensive *or* costing a lot of money **teuer, kostspielig;** *property is very dear in this area;* **dear money** = money which has to be borrowed at a high rate of interest **teures Geld**
(b) way of starting a letter **Liebe(r); Sehr geehrte(r); Dear Sir** *or* **Dear Madam** = addressing a man or woman whom you do not know, or addressing a company **Sehr geehrte Damen und Herren; Dear Sirs** = addressing a firm **Sehr geehrte Damen und Herren; Dear Mr Smith** *or* **Dear Mrs Smith** *or* **Dear Miss Smith** = addressing a man or woman whom you know **Lieber/Sehr geehrter Herr Smith; Liebe/Sehr geehrte Frau Smith; Liebes/Sehr geehrtes Fräulein Smith; Dear James** *or* **Dear Julia** = addressing a friend *or* a person you do business with **Lieber James; Liebe Julia**

death *noun* act of dying **Tod, Sterben; death benefit** = insurance benefit paid to the family of someone who dies in an accident at work **Sterbegeld; death certificate** = official certificate signed by a doctor, stating that a person has died and giving details of the person **Sterbeurkunde, Totenschein; death grant** = state grant to the family of a person who has died, which is supposed to contribute to the funeral expenses **Sterbegeld; death in service** = insurance benefit *or* pension paid when someone dies while employed by a company **Versicherungszahlung im Todesfall eines Betriebsangehörigen; death penalty** = sentence of a criminal to be executed **Todesstrafe;** *US* **death duty** *or* **death tax** = tax paid on the property left by a dead person **Erbschaftssteuer; presumption of death** = situation where a person has not been seen for seven years and is presumed to be legally dead **Todesvermutung**

debate
1 *noun* discussion leading to a vote, especially the discussion of a motion in Parliament **Debatte;** *several MPs criticized the government in* *or* *during the debate on the Finance Bill; the Bill passed its Second Reading after a short debate; the debate continued until 3 a.m.*
2 *verb* to discuss a proposal, especially in Parliament **debattieren, erörtern;** *the MPs are still debating the Data Protection Bill*

debenture *noun* document whereby a company acknowledges it owes a debt, and gives the company's assets as security **Schuldverschreibung; Schuldschein; mortgage debenture** = debenture where the lender can be repaid by selling the company's property **Hypothekenpfandbrief; debenture issue** *or* **issue of debentures** = borrowing money against the security of the company's assets **Ausgabe/Emission von Schuldverschreibungen; debenture bond** = certificate showing that a debenture has been issued **Schuldverschreibung, Obligation; debenture capital** *or* **debenture stock** = capital borrowed by a company, using its fixed assets as security **Anleihekapital; debenture holder** = person who holds a debenture for money lent **Obligationär; Pfandbriefinhaber; debenture register** *or* **register of debentures** = list of debenture holders of a company **Verzeichnis der Obligationäre**

debit
1 *noun* money which a company owes **Schuldposten, Soll, Debet; debit and credit** = money which a company owes and money it is entitled to receive **Soll und Haben; debit column** = left-hand column in accounts showing the money paid or owed to others **Debetspalte; debit entry** = entry on the debit side of an account **Sollbuchung, Lastschrift; debit side** = left-hand side of an account showing the money paid or owed to others **Debetseite; debit note** = note showing that a customer owes money **Lastschriftanzeige; direct debit** = system where a customer allows a company to charge costs to his bank account automatically and where the amount charged can be increased or decreased automatically, the customer being informed of the change by letter **Direktabbuchung;** *compare* STANDING ORDER
2 *verb* **to debit an account** = to charge an account with a cost **ein Konto belasten;** *his account was debited with the sum of £25*
◊ **debitable** *adjective* which can be debited **belastbar**

debt *noun*
(a) money owed for goods or services **Schulden;** *the company stopped trading with debts of over £1 million;* **to be in debt** = to owe money **Schulden haben; to get into debt** = to start to borrow more money than you can pay back **sich verschulden, Schulden**

machen; **to be out of debt** = not to owe money any more **schuldenfrei sein, aus den Schulden heraus sein; to pay back a debt** = to pay all the money owed **eine Schuld zurückzahlen; to pay off a debt** = to finish paying money owed **Schulden begleichen/tilgen; to service a debt** = to pay interest on a debt **für Schulden Zinsen bezahlen; bad debt** = money owed which will never be paid back **uneinbringliche Forderung, nicht einziehbare Außenstände; debt collection** or **collecting** = collecting money which is owed **Forderungseinziehung, Schuldeneintreibung; debt collection agency** or **collecting agency** = company which collects debts for other companies for a commission **Inkassofirma; debt collector** = person who collects debts **Inkassobeauftragter; debt factor** = person who buys debts at a discount and enforces them for himself or person who enforces debts for a commission **Factor**

◊ **debtor** noun person who owes money **Schuldner/-in, Kreditnehmer; debtor side** = debit side of an account **Soll-, Debetspalte; debtor nation** = country whose foreign debts are larger than money owed to it by other countries **Schuldnerland; judgment debtor** = person who has been ordered by a court to pay a debt **Vollstreckungsschuldner**

decapitate verb to cut off someone's head **enthaupten**

◊ **decapitation** noun act of cutting off someone's head **Enthauptung;** he was sentenced to death by decapitation
NOTE: no plural

decease noun (formal) death **Ableben, Tod;** on his decease all his property will go to his widow

◊ **deceased** adjective & noun (person) who has died **verstorben; Verstorbener;** the deceased left all his property to his widow; she inherited the estate of a deceased aunt

deceive verb to trick (someone) or to make someone think something is true when it is not **betrügen, hintergehen, täuschen**

◊ **deceit** or **deception** noun making a wrong statement to someone in order to trick him into paying money or in order to make him do something which will harm him **Betrug, Betrügerei, Täuschung;** she obtained £10,000 by deception; **obtaining a pecuniary advantage by deception** = crime of tricking someone into handing over money **durch Täuschung einen Vermögensvorteil erlangen; obtaining property by deception** = tricking someone into handing over possession of property **Besitz betrügerisch erwerben**

◊ **deceiver** noun person who deceives **Betrüger/-in**

◊ **deceptive** adjective which deceives **betrügerisch, täuschend, irreführend**

decent adjective which does not shock other people or which is accepted by society in general **anständig;** this book should be banned - it will shock any decent citizen

◊ **decency** noun being decent **Anstand, Anständigkeit, Sittlichkeit;** the film shocked public decency

decide verb
(a) to give a judgment in a civil case **entscheiden;** the judge decided in favour of the plaintiff
(b) to make up your mind to do something **sich entschließen/entscheiden, beschließen;** we have decided to take our neighbours to court; the tribunal decided against awarding any damages

◊ **decided case** noun case where a court has decided, and where that decision then becomes a precedent **entschiedener Fall**

◊ **decidendi** see RATIO

◊ **deciding** adjective **deciding factor** = most important factor which influences a decision **entscheidender Faktor**

◊ **decision** noun
(a) judgment in a civil court **Urteil;** the decision of the House of Lords is final = there is no appeal against a decision of the House of Lords **das Urteil des Oberhauses ist rechtskräftig/endgültig**
(b) making up one's mind to do something **Entschluß, Entscheidung, Beschluß;** to come to a decision or to reach a decision; **decision making** = act of coming to a decision **Entscheidungsfindung, Beschlußfassung; the decision-making processes** = ways in which decisions are reached **Entscheidungsprozeß; decision maker** = person who has to decide **Person, die Entscheidungen trifft; Entscheidungsträger**

◊ **decisis** see STARE DECISIS

declare verb to make an official statement or to announce to the public **Erklärung abgeben, erklären, bekanntgeben;** to declare someone bankrupt; to declare a dividend of 10%; **to declare goods to the customs** = to state that you are importing goods which are liable to duty **Waren deklarieren, Waren verzollen; to declare an interest** = to state in public that you own shares in a company being investigated **seine Beteiligungen offenlegen**

◊ **declared** adjective which has been made public or officially stated **erklärt; declared**

value = value of goods entered on a customs declaration **angemeldeter/angegebener Wert**

◇ **declaration** *noun* official statement **Erklärung, Deklaration; declaration of association** = statement in the articles of association of a company, saying that the members have agreed to form the company and buy shares in it **Gründungserklärung einer Kapitalgesellschaft; declaration of bankruptcy** = official statement that someone is bankrupt **Konkurseröffnungsbeschluß; declaration of income** = statement declaring income to the tax office **Einkommenssteuererklärung; customs declaration** = statement declaring goods brought into a country on which customs duty may be paid **Zolldeklaration; statutory declaration** = (i) statement made to the Registrar of Companies that a company has complied with certain legal conditions; (ii) statement made, signed and witnessed for official purposes **(i) Anmeldung zum Handelsregister über bestimmte, die Firma betreffende Änderungen; (ii) eidesstattliche Erklärung/Versicherung; VAT declaration** = statement declaring VAT income to the VAT office **Mehrwertsteuererklärung**

◇ **declaratory judgment** *noun* judgment where a court states what the legal position of the various parties is **Feststellungsurteil**

decline
1 *noun* slow fall **Rückgang, Abnahme, Abschwächung, Sinken;** *the decline in the value of the franc; a decline in buying power; the last year has seen a decline in real wages*
2 *verb* to refuse to do something **ablehnen;** *the witness declined to take the oath*

decontrol *verb* to stop *or* remove controls from something **freigeben; to decontrol the price of petrol** = to stop controlling the price of petrol so that a free market price can be reached **den Benzinpreis freigeben**
NOTE: **decontrolled - decontrolling**

decrease *verb* to make smaller *or* to become smaller **vermindern, reduzieren, herabsetzen; zurückgehen, abnehmen;** *the government proposes to decrease the rate of VAT*

decree
1 *noun*
(a) order made by a head of state, but which is not passed by a parliament **Verordnung, Erlaß; to govern by decree** = to rule a country by issuing orders without having them debated and voted in a parliament **auf dem Verordnungswege regieren**

(b) decree nisi = order from a court which ends a marriage for the time being, and becomes final when decree absolute is pronounced **vorläufiges Scheidungsurteil; decree absolute** = order from a court which ends a marriage finally **(rechtskräftiges) Scheidungsurteil**
2 *verb* to make an order **verordnen, verfügen, gerichtlich anordnen;** *the President decreed that June 1st should be a National Holiday*

deduce *verb* to conclude *or* to come to a decision based on observing something **schließen, folgern;** *from his clothes, we can deduce that the victim was a rich man*

◇ **deducing title** *noun* proving (by the vendor) of his title to the property being sold **Nachweis des Eigentumtitels**

deduct *verb* to remove money from a total **abziehen;** *to deduct £3 from the price; to deduct a sum for expenses; to deduct 5% from salaries;* **tax deducted at source** = tax which is removed from a salary, interest payment or dividend payment on shares before the money is paid **Quellensteuer**

◇ **deductible** *adjective* which can be deducted **abziehbar; tax-deductible** = which can be deducted from an income before tax is paid **steuerlich absetzbar/abzugsfähig; these expenses are not tax-deductible** = tax has to be paid on these expenses **diese Ausgaben sind nicht (von der Steuer) absetzbar**

◇ **deduction** *noun*
(a) conclusion which is reached by observing something **Schluß, Folgerung, Deduktion;** *by deduction, the detective came to the conclusion that the dead person has not been murdered*
(b) removing of money from a total *or* money removed from a total **Abziehen, Abzug;** *net salary is salary after deduction of tax and social security contributions;* **deductions from salary** *or* **salary deductions** *or* **deductions at source** = money which a company removes from salaries to give to the government as tax, national insurance contributions, etc. **Lohnabzüge; tax deductions** = (i) money removed from a salary to pay tax; (ii); *US* business expenses which can be claimed against tax **(i) Steuerabzüge; (ii) (von der Steuer) absetzbare Ausgaben**

deed *noun* legal document which has been signed, sealed and delivered by the person making it **gesiegelte Urkunde; deed of arrangement** = agreement made between a debtor and his creditors whereby the creditors accept an agreed sum in settlement of their claim rather than make the debtor bankrupt **Vergleichsvereinbarung (zwischen Schuldner und Gläubiger); deed of**

assignment = agreement which legally transfers a property from a debtor to a creditor **Übereignungs-, Abtretungsurkunde; deed of covenant** = signed legal agreement to do something (such as to pay someone a sum of money every year) **Vertragsurkunde, Versprechensurkunde; deed of partnership** = agreement which sets up a partnership **Gesellschaftsvertrag; deed of transfer** = agreement which transfers the ownership of shares **(Aktien)übertragungsurkunde; title deeds** = document showing who owns a property **Grundeigentumsurkunde;** *entspricht* **Grundbucheintrag;** *we have deposited the deeds of the house in the bank*

◊ **deed poll** *noun* document made under seal, to which there is only one party **einseitige (gesiegelte) Urkunde; to change one's name by deed poll** = to sign a legal document by which you change your name **seinen Namen durch eine einseitige Rechtserklärung ändern**

deem *verb* to believe *or* to consider **glauben, halten (für), betrachten (als);** *the judge deemed it necessary to order the court to be cleared; if no payment is made, the party shall be deemed to have defaulted*

de facto *Latin phrase meaning* "in fact": as a matter of fact, even though the legal title may not be certain **faktisch, de facto;** *he is the de facto owner of the property; see also* DE JURE

defalcation *noun* illegal use of money by someone who is not the owner but who has been trusted to look after it **Veruntreuung, Unterschlagung**

defame *verb* to say *or* write things about the character of someone so as to damage his reputation **verleumden, diffamieren**

◊ **defamation** *noun* **defamation of character** = act of ruining someone's reputation by maliciously saying *or* writing things about him **Ehrabschneidung, Ehrverletzung**

COMMENT: defamation is a tort and may be libel (if it is in a permanent form, such as printed matter) or slander (if it is spoken)

◊ **defamatory** *adjective* **defamatory statement** = statement which is made to defame someone's character **beleidigende Äußerung, üble Nachrede**

default
1 *noun* failure to carry out the terms of a contract, especially failure to pay back a debt **Nichterfüllung, Versäumnis,** Unterlassung, Vertragsverletzung, Nichtzahlung; **in default of payment** = if no payment is made **bei Zahlungsverzug; the company is in default** = the company has failed to carry out the terms of the contract **die Firma befindet sich in Verzug; by default** = because no one else will act **im Unterlassungsfall; he was elected by default** = he was elected because all the other candidates withdrew *or* because there were no other candidates **er wurde in Ermangelung anderer Kandidaten gewählt; judgment by default** *or* **default judgment** = judgment against a defendant who fails to defend his case **Versäumnisurteil; default action** = County Court action to get back money owed **Klage auf geschuldeten Geldbetrag, Mahnverfahren; default summons** = County Court summons to someone to pay what is owed **Mahnbescheid**
2 *verb* to fail to carry out the terms of a contract, especially to fail to pay back a debt **nicht erfüllen, nicht einhalten, in (Zahlungs)verzug geraten; to default on payments** = not to make payments which are due under the terms of a contract **mit Zahlungen in Verzug geraten**

◊ **defaulter** *noun* person who defaults **jd, der seinen Verpflichtungen nicht nachkommt; säumiger Schuldner**

defeasance *noun* clause (in a collateral deed) which says that a contract *or* bond *or* recognizance will be revoked if something happens *or* if some act is performed **Aufhebung(sklausel), Verwirkung(sklausel), Annullierung**

defeat
1 *noun* failure to get a majority in a vote **Niederlage;** *the minister offered to resign after the defeat of the motion in the House of Commons*
2 *verb*
(a) to beat someone *or* something in a vote **schlagen, besiegen; zu Fall bringen;** *the bill was defeated in the Lords by 52 to 64; the government was defeated in a vote on law and order*
(b) to revoke *or* to render invalid (an agreement *or* a contract *or* a bond) **aufheben, annullieren, rückgängig machen**

defect
1 *noun* something which is wrong *or* which stops a machine from working properly **Defekt, Fehler, Mangel**
2 *verb (of a spy or agent or government employee)* to leave your country and go to work for an enemy country **zum Feind überlaufen, sich absetzen**

◊ **defective** *adjective*

(a) faulty *or* not working properly **defekt, fehlerhaft, schadhaft;** *the machine broke down because of a defective cooling system* **(b)** not legally valid **unzulänglich, ungültig;** *his title to the property is defective*

defence *or US* **defense** *noun*
(a) protecting someone *or* something against attack **Verteidigung, Abwehr;** *the merchant bank is organizing the company's defence against the takeover bid*
(b) (i) party in a legal case which is sued by the plaintiff; (ii) party in a criminal case which is being prosecuted; (iii) lawyers representing a party being sued *or* prosecuted **(i) Beklagter; (ii) Angeklagter; (iii) Verteidigung, Verteidiger; defence counsel =** lawyer who represents the defendant *or* the accused **Verteidiger**
(c) arguments used when fighting a case **Klageerwiderung, Einspruch;** *his defence was that he did not know the property was stolen;* **to file a defence =** to state that you wish to defend a case, and outline the reasons for doing so **eine Klage beantworten**
(d) document *or* a pleading setting out the defendant's case; *compare* PROSECUTION **Verteidigungsvorbringen; Klageerwiderung**

◊ **defend** *verb*
(a) to fight to protect someone *or* something which is being attacked **verteidigen, sich wehren;** *the company is defending itself against the takeover bid*
(b) to speak on behalf of someone who has been charged with a crime **verteidigen;** *he hired the best lawyers to defend him against the tax authorities;* **to defend an action =** to appear in court to state your case when accused of something **sich auf eine Klage einlassen, einen Prozeß in der Verteidigungsposition führen**

◊ **defendant** *noun* (i) person who is sued in a civil case; (ii) person who is accused of a crime in a criminal case **(i) Beklagter; (ii) Angeklagter;** *compare* PLAINTIFF

defer *verb* to put back to a later date *or* to postpone **ver-, aufschieben, zurückstellen, vertagen;** *to defer judgment; the decision has been deferred until the next meeting*
NOTE: **deferring - deferred**

◊ **deferment** *noun* postponement *or* putting back to a later date **Aufschub, Zurückstellung, Vertagung;** *deferment of payment; deferment of a decision;* **deferment of sentence =** putting back the sentencing of a convicted criminal until a later date to see how he behaves **Aufschub der Urteilsverkündung**

◊ **deferred** *adjective* put back to a later date **aufgeschoben, vertagt; deferred creditor =** person who is owed money by a bankrupt but who is paid only after all other creditors **nachrangiger (Konkurs)gläubiger; deferred payment =** payment for goods by instalments over a long period **Ratenzahlung; deferred stock** *or* **shares =** shares which receive a dividend after all other dividends have been paid **Nachzugsaktien**

define *verb* to say clearly what a word *or* phrase means **definieren;** *immigrant persons as defined in Appendix 3; the judge asked counsel to define what he meant by "incapable"*

deforce *verb* to take wrongfully and hold land which belongs to someone else **widerrechtlich Grundbesitz entziehen**

◊ **deforcement** *noun* wrongful taking and holding of another person's land **widerrechtliche Entziehung von Grundbesitz, verbotene Eigenmacht**

defraud *verb* to trick someone so as to obtain money illegally **betrügen, unterschlagen;** *he defrauded the Inland Revenue of thousands of pounds*
NOTE: you defraud someone **of** something

defray *verb* to provide money to pay (costs) **aufkommen für, tragen, übernehmen;** *the company agreed to defray the costs of the prosecution*

degree *noun*
(a) level *or* measure of a relationship **Verwandtschaftsgrad; prohibited degrees =** relationships which make it illegal for a man and woman to marry (such as father and daughter) **verbotene Verwandtschaftsgrade**
(b) *US* system for classifying murders **Grad; first degree murder =** premeditated and deliberate murder **vorsätzlicher Mord; second degree murder =** murder without premeditation **Totschlag**

COMMENT: in the US, the penalty for first degree murder can be death

de jure *Latin phrase meaning* "by law": as a matter of law, where the legal title is clear **rechtlich, de jure, von Rechts wegen;** *he is the de jure owner of the property; see also* DE FACTO

delay
1 *noun* time when someone *or* something is later than planned **Verspätung, Verzögerung, Verzug;** *there was a delay of thirty minutes before the hearing started or the hearing started after a thirty minute delay*

2 *verb* to be late; to make someone late **sich verspäten/verzögern; jdn aufhalten;** *judgment was delayed while the magistrates asked for advice*

del credere agent *noun* agent who receives a high commission because he guarantees payment by customers to his principal **Delkredereagent**

delegate
1 *noun* person who is elected by others to put their case at a meeting **Delegierter, Bevollmächtigter;** *the management refused to meet the trade union delegates*
2 *verb* to pass authority or responsibility to someone else **delegieren, bevollmächtigen, Vollmacht erteilen; delegated legislation =** orders, which have the power of Acts of Parliament, but which are passed by a minister to whom Parliament has delegated its authority **durch delegierte Gesetzgebung entstandene Normen**

◊ **delegation** *noun*
(a) group of delegates **Delegation, Abordnung;** *a Chinese trade delegation; the management met a union delegation*
(b) act of passing authority or responsibility to someone else **Bevollmächtigung, Übertragung, Delegierung**
NOTE: no plural for (b)

◊ **delegatus non potest delegare** *Latin phrase meaning* "the delegate cannot delegate to someone else"

delete *verb* to remove words in a document **streichen;** *the court ordered the newspaper to delete all references to the divorce case; the lawyers have deleted clause two from the contract*

deliberate
1 *adjective* done on purpose **absichtlich, vorsätzlich, bewußt;** *the police suggest that the letter was a deliberate attempt to encourage disorder*
2 *verb* to consider *or* to discuss a problem **bedenken, beraten, überlegen;** *the committee deliberated for several hours before reaching a decision*

◊ **deliberately** *adverb* on purpose *or* done intentionally **absichtlich, vorsätzlich, bewußt;** *he was accused of deliberately setting fire to the shop*

◊ **deliberations** *plural noun* discussions **Beratungen;** *the result of the committee's deliberations was passed to the newspapers*

delicti *see* CORPUS

delicto *see* IN FLAGRANTE DELICTO

delinquency *noun* the act of committing crime, usually minor crime **Vergehen, Kriminalität**

◊ **delinquent** *noun* **Delinquent/-in, Täter/-in;** *a juvenile delinquent or US a delinquent =* young criminal who commits minor crimes, especially crimes against property **jugendlicher Täter**

deliver *verb* to transport goods to a customer **liefern, zustellen; goods delivered free** *or* **free delivered goods =** goods carried to the customer's address at a price which includes transport costs **frei Haus gelieferte Waren; goods delivered on board =** goods carried free to the ship or plane but not to the customer's warehouse **frei Bord gelieferte Waren**

◊ **delivery** *noun*
(a) delivery of goods = transport of goods to a customer's address **Warenlieferung, Warenzustellung; delivery note =** list of goods being delivered, given to the customer with the goods **Lieferschein; delivery order =** instructions given by the customer to the person holding his goods, to tell him to deliver them **Lieferauftrag; recorded delivery =** mail service where the letters are signed for by the person receiving them **Einschreiben; cash on delivery =** payment in cash when the goods are delivered **gegen Nachnahme; to take delivery of goods =** to accept goods when they are delivered **eine Lieferung abnehmen/übernehmen**
(b) goods being delivered **Lieferung;** *we take in three deliveries a day; there were four items missing in the last delivery*
(c) transfer of a bill of exchange **Übertragung**
(d) formal act whereby a deed becomes effective **Aushändigung, Übergabe;** *deeds take effect only from the time of delivery*

demand
1 *noun*
(a) asking for payment **Forderung, Aufforderung; payable on demand =** which must be paid when payment is asked for **zahlbar auf Verlangen/bei Vorlage; demand bill =** bill of exchange which must be paid when payment is asked for **Sichtwechsel; final demand =** last reminder from a supplier, after which he will sue for payment **letzte Mahnung; letter of demand =** letter issued by a party *or* lawyer demanding payment before taking legal action **Mahnschreiben, Mahnbrief**
(b) need for goods at a certain price **Nachfrage, Bedarf; supply and demand =** amount of a product which is available at a certain price and the amount which is wanted by customers at that price **Angebot und Nachfrage; law of supply and demand =** general rule that the amount of a product

which is available is related to the needs of possible customers **Gesetz von Angebot und Nachfrage**
2 *verb* to ask for something and expect to get it **fordern, verlangen;** *they were accused of demanding payment with threats*
◊ **demanding with menaces** *noun* crime of demanding money by threatening someone **(räuberische) Erpressung**

de minimis non curat lex *Latin phrase meaning* "the law does not deal with trivial things" **das Gericht befaßt sich nicht mit Geringfügigem**

demise *noun*
(a) death **Tod, Ableben;** *on his demise the estate passed to his daughter* (NOTE: no plural)
(b) granting of property on a lease **Verpachtung; demise charter** = charter of a ship without the crew **Miete/Chartern eines Schiffes ohne Besatzung**

demonstrate *verb*
(a) to show **vorführen, demonstrieren;** *the police demonstrated how the bomb was planted; counsel was able to demonstrate how it was impossible for the accused to climb through the window*
(b) to make a public protest about something **demonstrieren;** *crowds of students were demonstrating against the government*
◊ **demonstration** *noun* act of demonstrating **Demonstration;** *police broke up the student demonstration*
◊ **demonstrative legacy** *noun* gift in a will which is ordered to be paid out of a special account **beschränktes Gattungsvermächtnis**
◊ **demonstrator** *noun* person who demonstrates **Demonstrant/-in**

demur
1 *noun* objection **Einwand, Einwendungen;** *counsel made no demur to the proposal*
2 *verb*
(a) not to agree **Einwand erheben, Einwendungen machen, beanstanden;** *counsel stated that there was no case to answer, but the judge demurred*
(b) to make a formal objection that the facts as alleged are not sufficient to warrant the civil action **auf mangelnde Schlüssigkeit hinweisen**
NOTE: **demurring - demurred**
◊ **demurrage** *noun* money paid to the owner of a cargo when a ship is delayed in a port **Liegegeld**
NOTE: no plural
◊ **demurrer** *noun* plea that although the facts of the case are correct, they are not sufficient to warrant the action **Abweisungsbegehren**

denomination *noun* unit of money (on a coin *or* stamp *or* banknote) **Nennwert, Stückelung;** *small denomination banknotes; coins of all denominations*

de novo *Latin phrase meaning* "starting again"

deny *verb*
(a) not to allow something **verweigern, abschlagen;** *he was denied the right to see his lawyer*
(b) to say that you have not done something **bestreiten, abstreiten, leugnen;** *he denied being in the house at the time of the murder*
NOTE: you deny someone something or deny doing or having done something
◊ **denial** *noun*
(a) act of not allowing something **Verweigerung, Ablehnung; denial of human rights** = refusing someone a right which is generally accepted as fair **Nichtanerkennung der Menschenrechte; denial of justice** = situation where justice appears not to have been done **Rechtsverweigerung**
(b) act of stating that you have not done something **Leugnen, Dementi;** *in spite of his denials he was found guilty*

depart *verb*
(a) to leave **abreisen, abfahren; abfliegen;** *the plane departs at 11.15*
(b) to depart from normal practice = to act in a different way from the normal practice **von der üblichen Verfahrensweise abweichen**
◊ **department** *noun*
(a) specialized section of a large company **Abteilung;** *complaints department; legal department;* **accounts department** = section which deals with money paid or received **Buchhaltung; head of department** *or* **department head** *or* **department manager** = person in charge of a department **Abteilungsleiter**
(b) section of a large store selling one type of product **Abteilung; furniture department** = department in a large store which sells furniture **Möbelabteilung**
(c) Department of State = major section of the British government headed by a Secretary of State **Ministerium;** *the Department of Trade and Industry; the Department of Education and Science*

departure *noun*
(a) going away **Abreise, Abfahrt; Abflug;** *the plane's departure was delayed by two hours*
(b) new type of business **Neubeginn, Start;** *selling records will be a departure for the local bookshop*
(c) departure from = thing which is different from what happened before

Abweichen von; this forms a departure from established practice; any departure from the terms and conditions of the contract must be advised in writing

depend *verb*
(a) **to depend on** = to need someone *or* something to exist **angewiesen sein auf;** *the company depends on efficient service from its suppliers; we depend on government grants to pay the salary bill*
(b) to happen because of something **abhängig sein von;** *the success of the anti-drug campaign will depend on the attitude of the public;* **depending on** = happening as a result of something **je nach, abhängig von;** *depending on the circumstances, the accused may receive a fine or be sent to prison*
◊ **dependant** *noun* person who is supported financially by someone else **finanziell abhängiger Angehöriger, Unterhaltsberechtigter;** *he has to provide for his family and dependants out of a very small salary*
◊ **dependent** *adjective* (person) who is supported financially by someone else **finanziell abhängig;** *tax relief is allowed for dependent relatives*

deponent *noun* person who makes a statement under oath *or* by affidavit **vereidigter Zeuge**

deport *verb* to send (someone) away from a country **ausweisen, abschieben, deportieren;** *the illegal immigrants were deported*
◊ **deportation** *noun* sending of someone away from a country **Ausweisung, Abschiebung, Deportation;** *the convicts were sentenced to deportation;* **deportation order** = official order to send someone away from a country **Ausweisungsbeschluß;** *the minister signed the deportation order*
NOTE: no plural

depose *verb*
(a) to state under oath **unter Eid aussagen/zu Protokoll geben**
(b) to remove (a king) from the throne **absetzen, entthronen**
◊ **deposition** *noun* written statement of evidence of a witness **(beeidigte) schriftliche Zeugenaussage**

deposit
1 *noun*
(a) money placed in a bank for safe keeping or to earn interest **Einzahlung, Einlage, eingezahltes Geld; certificate of deposit** = certificate from a bank to show that money

has been deposited **Depositenquittung; Depotschein; deposit account** = bank account which pays interest but on which notice has to be given to withdraw money **Sparkonto; licensed deposit-taker** = business (such as a bank) which takes deposits from individuals and lends the money to others **Einlagenbank, amtlich zugelassener Hinterleger**
(b) **safe deposit** = bank safe where you can leave jewellery or documents **Tresor; safe deposit box** = small box which you can rent, in which you can keep jewellery or documents in a bank's safe **Bankschließfach**
(c) money given in advance so that the thing which you want to buy will not be sold to someone else **Anzahlung;** *to leave £10 as deposit;* **to forfeit a deposit** = to lose a deposit because you have decided not to buy the item **eine Anzahlung einbüßen/verwirken**
(d) money paid by a candidate when nominated for an election, which is forfeited if the candidate does not win enough votes **Hinterlegung;** *he polled only 25 votes and lost his deposit*
2 *verb*
(a) to put documents somewhere for safe keeping **in Verwahrung geben, deponieren;** *we have deposited the deeds of the house with the bank; he deposited his will with his solicitor*
(b) to put money into a bank account **einzahlen;** *to deposit £100 in a current account*
◊ **depositary** *noun* *(US)* person *or* company with whom money or documents can be deposited **Verwahrer; Depot, Hinterlegungsstelle**
◊ **depositor** *noun* person who deposits money in a bank **Einzahler, Einleger**
◊ **depository** *noun*
(a) **furniture depository** = warehouse where you can store household furniture **Möbellager**
(b) person or company with whom money or documents can be deposited **Verwahrer; Hinterlegungsstelle**

deprave *verb* to make someone's character bad **verderben;** *TV programmes which may deprave the minds of children who watch them*

deprive *verb* **to deprive someone of something** = to remove something from someone *or* not to allow someone to have something **jdm etwas entziehen; jdm etwas vorenthalten;** *the prisoners were deprived of contact with their families; the new Bill deprives aliens of the right to appeal*

dept = DEPARTMENT

deputy *noun*
(a) person who takes the place of a higher official *or* who assists a higher official **(Stell)vertreter;** *to act as deputy for someone or to act as someone's deputy*
(b) *US* person who acts for *or* assists a sheriff **Stellvertreter des Sheriffs**

◊ **deputize** *verb* to deputize for someone = to take the place of someone who is absent **jdn vertreten, als Stellvertreter für jdn fungieren**

deregulation *noun* reducing government control over an industry **Deregulation, Abbau von Kontrollen, Freigabe;** *the deregulation of the airlines*

derelict *noun* abandoned floating boat **(treibendes) Wrack**
◊ **dereliction of duty** *noun* failure to do what you ought to do **Pflichtverletzung;** *he was found guilty of gross dereliction of duty*

derive *verb*
(a) to come from **(sich) herleiten, (sich) ableiten;** *this law derives from or is derived from the former Roman law of property*
(b) to obtain **erlangen, erzielen;** *he derived financial benefit from the transaction*

derogate *verb* **to derogate from something which has been agreed** = to act to prevent something which has been agreed from being fully implemented **eine Vereinbarung beeinträchtigen, einer Sache Abbruch tun**
◊ **derogation** *noun* act of avoiding *or* destroying something **Abbruch; derogation of responsibility** = avoiding doing a duty **Ablehnung der Verantwortung**

descended from *adjective* having a person as an ancestor **abstammend von;** *he is descended from William I*
◊ **descendant** *noun* person who is descended from an ancestor **Nachkomme;** *his wife is a descendant of King Charles I*
◊ **descent** *noun* family ties of inheritance between parents and children **Abstammung; (gesetzliche) Erbfolge; he is British by descent** *or* **he is of British descent** = one (or both) of his parents is British **er ist britischer Abstammung/Herkunft; lineal descent** = direct descent from parent to child **Abstammung in gerader Linie, direkte Abstammung**

describe *verb* to say what someone *or* something is like **beschreiben, ausführen, schildern;** *she described her attacker to the police; he described the judge as a silly old man*

◊ **description** *noun* words which show what something is like **Beschreibung, Schilderung;** *the police circulated a description of the missing boy or of the wanted man;* **false description of contents** = wrongly stating the contents of a packet to trick customers into buying it **unkorrekte Inhaltsbeschreibung; trade description** = description of a product to attract customers **Warenkennzeichnung;** *GB* **Trade Descriptions Act** = Act of Parliament which limits the way in which products can be described so as to protect consumers from wrong descriptions made by the makers **Warenkennzeichnungsgesetz**

desert *verb*
(a) to leave the armed forces without permission **desertieren, fahnenflüchtig werden;** *he deserted and went to live in South America*
(b) to leave a family *or* spouse **verlassen;** *the two children have been deserted by their father*
◊ **deserter** *noun* person who has left the armed forces without permission **Deserteur/-in, Fahnenflüchtiger**
◊ **desertion** *noun*
(a) leaving the armed forces without permission **Desertion, Fahnenflucht**
(b) leaving one's spouse **(böswilliges) Verlassen;** *he divorced his wife because of her desertion*

designate
1 *adjective* person who has been appointed to a job but who has not yet started work **designiert;** *the chairman designate* (NOTE: always follows a noun)
2 *verb* to name *or* to appoint officially **ernennen, bestimmen;** *the area was designated a National Park*

destruction *noun* action of killing someone *or* ending something completely **Tötung; Vernichtung, Zerstörung, Ausrottung;** *the destruction of the evidence in the fire at the police station made it difficult to prosecute;* **child destruction** = notifiable offence of killing an unborn child capable of being born alive **Kindestötung durch Abtreibung**

detail
1 *noun* small part of a description **Detail, Einzelheit; in detail** = giving many particulars **detailliert;** *the contract lists all the markets in detail*
2 *verb*
(a) to list in detail **detailliert beschreiben, einzeln aufführen;** *the document details the arrangements for maintenance payments;*

the terms of the licence are detailed in the contract
(b) to tell someone to do something **abkommandieren, abstellen;** *six officers were detailed to search the premises*

◊ **detailed** *adjective* in detail **detailliert, ausführlich; detailed account** = account which lists every item **spezifizierte/detaillierte Rechnung**

detain *verb* to hold a person so that he cannot leave **festnehmen, in Haft nehmen; in Haft halten;** *the suspects were detained by the police for questioning*

◊ **detainee** *noun* person who has been detained **Häftling, Festgenommener, Inhaftierter**

◊ **detainer** *noun* act of holding a person **Inhaftierung**

detect *verb* to notice *or* to discover (something which is hidden or difficult to see) **aufspüren, ausfindig machen, entdecken;** *the machine can detect explosives*

◊ **detection** *noun* discovering something, especially discovering who has committed a crime *or* how a crime has been committed **Entlarvung; Entdeckung, Aufdeckung; detection rate** = number of crimes which are solved, as a percentage of all crimes **Aufklärungsquote**

◊ **detective** *noun* person, usually a policeman, who tries to solve a crime **Ermittler; Detektiv; Polizeibeamter; private detective** = person who for a fee will try to solve mysteries *or* to find missing people *or* will keep watch on someone **Privatdetektiv; detective agency** = office which hires out the services of private detectives **Detektivbüro, Detektei**

COMMENT: the ranks of detectives in the British Police Force are Detective Constable, Detective Sergeant, Detective Inspector, Detective Chief Inspector, Detective Superintendent, and Detective Chief Superintendent

---

detention *noun*
(a) keeping someone so that he cannot escape **Haft, Inhaftierung, Gewahrsam;** *the suspects were placed in detention;* **detention centre** = place where young offenders (aged between 14 and 21) can be kept for corrective training, instead of being sent to prison, if they are convicted of crimes which would normally carry a sentence of three months' imprisonment or more **Jugendstrafanstalt; detention order** = court order asking for someone to be kept in detention **Haftbefehl**

(b) wrongfully holding goods which belong to someone else **(widerrechtliche) Vorenthaltung, Einbehaltung**

deter *verb* to make someone not eager to do something **abhalten, abschrecken;** *it is hoped that long jail sentences will deter others from smuggling drugs*
NOTE: **deterring - deterred.** Note also that you deter someone **from** doing something

◊ **deterrence** *noun* idea that the harsh punishment of one criminal will deter other people from committing crimes **Abschreckung**

◊ **deterrent**
1 *noun* punishment which will deter people from committing crimes **Abschreckungsmittel;** *a long prison sentence will act as a deterrent to other possible criminals*
2 *adjective* **deterrent sentence** = harsh sentence which the judge hopes will deter other people from committing crimes **abschreckende Strafe**

determine *verb*
(a) to fix *or* to arrange *or* to decide **bestimmen, festlegen, festsetzen;** *to determine prices or quantities; the conditions of the contract are still to be determined*
(b) to bring to an end **beendigen;** *the tenancy was determined by a notice to quit*

detinue *noun* tort of wrongfully holding goods which belong to someone else **(widerrechtliche) Vorenthaltung (von Besitz); action in detinue** = action formerly brought to regain possession of goods which were wrongfully held by someone **Herausgabeklage**

detriment *noun* damage *or* harm **Schaden, Beeinträchtigung; without detriment to his claim** = without harming his claim **ohne Beeinträchtigung seines Anspruches; his action was to the detriment of the plaintiff** = his action harmed the plaintiff **sein Vorgehen gereichte dem Kläger zum Nachteil**

◊ **detrimental** *adjective* which may harm **schädlich, nachteilig;** *action detrimental to the maintenance of public order*

develop *verb*
(a) to plan and produce **entwickeln;** *to develop a new product*
(b) to plan and build an area **erschließen;** *to develop an industrial estate*

◊ **developer** *noun* **a property developer** = person who plans and builds a group of new houses *or* new factories **Bauunternehmer**

◊ **development** *noun*

(a) planning the production of a new product *or* new town **Entwicklung; Erschließung; industrial development** = planning and building of new industries in special areas **industrielle Erschließung; development area** *or* **development zone** = area which has been given special help from a government to encourage businesses and factories to be set up there **Förderungsgebiet**
(b) change which has taken place **Entwicklung;** *the case represents a new development in the law of libel*

deviate *verb* **to deviate from a course of action** = to do something different *or* to act in a different way **vom Kurs abweichen**

device *noun* small useful machine; way of doing something **Gerät; Trick;** *a device to avoid paying tax or a tax-saving device*

devil
1 *noun* barrister to whom another barrister passes work because he is too busy **Anwaltsvertreter**
2 *verb* to pass instruction to another barrister because you are too busy to deal with the case yourself **einen Fall an einen Anwaltsvertreter weitergeben; to devil for someone** = to do unpleasant *or* boring work for someone **für jdn Handlangerdienste tun/untergeordnete Arbeiten verrichten**

devise
1 *noun* giving freehold land to someone in a will **letztwillige Verfügung von Grundbesitz**
2 *verb* to give freehold property to someone in a will **Grundbesitz vermachen**

> COMMENT: giving of other types of property is a bequest

◊ **devisee** *noun* person who receives freehold property in a will **testamentarischer Erbe von Grundbesitz**

diary *noun* book in which you can write notes or appointments for each day of the week and record events which have taken place **Terminkalender, Tagebuch**

dictate *verb* to say something to someone who then writes down your words **diktieren; dictating machine** = machine which records what someone dictates, which a secretary can play back and then type out the text **Diktiergerät**

◊ **dictation** *noun* act of dictating **Diktat; to take dictation** = to write down what someone is saying **ein Diktat aufnehmen; dictation speed** = number of words per

minute which a secretary can write down in shorthand **Silbenzahl pro Minute**

dictum *noun* saying *or* statement made by a judge **richterlicher Ausspruch; obiter dicta** = part of a judgment which does not form an essential part of it **beiläufige Bemerkung, nicht tragende Entscheidungsgründe;** *see also* RATIO DECIDENDI
NOTE: plural is **dicta**

differ *verb* not to agree with **nicht übereinstimmen, anderer Meinung sein;** *one of the appeal judges differed from the others;* **I beg to differ** = I want to say that I do not agree **ich bin anderer Ansicht**
◊ **difference** *noun* way in which two things are not the same **Unterschied**
◊ **different** *adjective* not the same **unterschiedlich, verschieden**

digest *noun* book which collects summaries of court decisions together, used for reference purposes by lawyers **Fallsammlung (in Auszügen)**

dilatory *adjective* too slow **hinhaltend, verzögernd, dilatorisch; dilatory motion** = motion in the House of Commons to delay the debate on a proposal **Verzögerungsantrag**

diminish *verb* to get *or* to make smaller **abnehmen, sich verringern/vermindern; verringern, vermindern; diminished responsibility** *or* *US* **diminished capacity** = mental state of a criminal (inherited *or* caused by illness or injury) which means that he cannot be held responsible for a crime which he has committed **verminderte Zurechnungsfähigkeit**

DInsp = DETECTIVE INSPECTOR

dip *noun (slang)* pickpocket **Langfinger, Taschendieb**

diplomat *or* **diplomatist** *noun* person (such as an ambassador) who is the official representative of his country in another country **Diplomat/-in**
◊ **diplomatic** *adjective* referring to diplomats **diplomatisch; diplomatic immunity** = not being subject to the laws of the country in which you are living, because you are a diplomat **diplomatische Immunität;** *he claimed diplomatic immunity to avoid being arrested;* **to grant someone diplomatic status** = to give someone the rights of a diplomat **jdn in den Diplomatenstand erheben**

direct

1 *verb* to order *or* to give an order to (someone) **anweisen, anordnen; Rechtsbelehrung erteilen;** *the judge directed the jury to acquit all the defendants; the Crown Court directed the justices to rehear the case*
2 *adjective* straight *or* with no interference **direkt, unmittelbar; direct debit** = system where a customer allows a company to charge costs to his bank account automatically and where the amount charged can be increased or decreased automatically, the customer being informed of the change by letter **(Direkt)abbuchung; direct evidence** = first hand evidence, such as the testimony of an eye witness or the production of original documents **unmittelbarer Beweis; direct examination** = asking a witness questions (by lawyers for his side) so that he gives oral evidence in court **Befragung eines Zeugen durch die benennende Partei; direct mail** = selling a product by sending advertising material by post to possible buyers **Direktversand; Direktwerbung; direct selling** = selling a product direct to the customer without going through a shop **Direktverkauf; direct taxation** = tax, such as income tax, which is paid direct to the government **direkte Besteuerung**
3 *adverb* straight *or* with no third party involved **direkt, unmittelbar;** *we pay income tax direct to the government; the fine is paid direct to the court*

◊ **direction** *noun*
(a) way in which something is going **Verlauf, Richtung;** *the new evidence changed the direction of the hearing*
(b) organizing *or* managing **Leitung, Führung;** *he took over the direction of a large bank*
(c) directions = (i) order which explains how something should be done; (ii) instructions from a judge to a jury; (iii) orders given by a judge concerning the general way of proceeding with a case **(i) Anweisung; (ii) Rechtsbelehrung (der Geschworenen); (iii) prozeßleitende Verfügungen;** *the court is not able to give directions to the local authority*

◊ **directive** *noun* order *or* command to someone to do something (especially order from the Council *or* Commission of the European Community) **Richtlinie, Direktive;** *the Commission issued a directive on food prices*

◊ **directly** *adverb*
(a) immediately **sofort, gleich;** *the summons was served directly after the magistrate had signed the warrant*
(b) in a straight way **direkt, unmittelbar;** *the Metropolitan Police Commissioner is directly responsible to the Home Secretary*

◊ **director** *noun*
(a) person appointed by the shareholders to manage a company **Direktor/-in, Aufsichtsratsmitglied; managing director** = the most senior executive director in a company **Generaldirektor, geschäftsführender Direktor; chairman and managing director** = managing director who is also chairman of the board of directors **Vorsitzender und geschäftsführender Direktor; board of directors** = all the directors of a company **Board of Directors;** *entspricht* **Aufsichtsrat (nach britischem Recht), (Firmen)vorstand; directors' report** = annual report from the board of directors to the shareholders **Jahresbericht des Verwaltungsrates; executive director** = director who actually works full-time in the company **geschäftsführender Direktor; non-executive director** = director who attends board meetings and gives advice, but does not work full-time for the company; *entspricht* **Aufsichtsratsmitglied; outside director** = director who is not employed by the company **unternehmensfremder Direktor, Unternehmensorgan ohne Anstellung beim Unternehmen**
(b) person who is in charge of a programme of work, an official institute, etc. **Leiter/-in, Direktor/-in;** *he is the director of a government institute; she was appointed director of the charity;* **Director-General of Fair Trading** = official in charge of the Office of Fair Trading, dealing with consumers and the law **Leiter des Amtes für Verbraucherschutz**

◊ **directorate** *noun* group of directors **Direktion, Direktorium, Geschäftsleitung; Verwaltungsrat**

◊ **Director of Public Prosecutions (DPP)** *noun* government official in charge of a group of lawyers (working under the Attorney-General), who prosecutes in important cases and advises other government departments if prosecutions should be started **Leiter der Anklagebehörde, (General)staatsanwalt;** *the papers in the fraud case have been sent to the Director of Public Prosecutions*

◊ **directorship** *noun* post of director **Direktorenstelle;** *he was offered a directorship with Smith Ltd*

directory *noun* list of people *or* businesses with information about their addresses and telephone numbers **Adreßbuch; Telefonbuch; classified directory** = list of businesses grouped under various headings, such as computer shops or newsagents **Branchenverzeichnis; commercial directory** *or* **trade directory** = book which lists all the businesses and business people in a town

Branchenadreßbuch; street directory = (i) list of people living in a street; (ii) map of a town which lists all the streets in alphabetical order in an index **(i) Adreßbuch; (ii) Stadtplan (mit Index); telephone directory** = book which lists all people and businesses who have telephones, in alphabetical order with their phone numbers **Telefonbuch**

disability *noun*
(a) being unable to use one's body properly (as because you are blind *or* cannot walk, etc.) **Behinderung**
(b) lack of legal capacity to act in one's own right (such as because of one's age *or* mental state) **Geschäftsunfähigkeit; person under a disability** = person who is not capable to taking legal action for himself **Prozeßunfähiger**

◊ **disabled person** *noun* person who is physically handicapped in some way (such as being blind or not capable of walking) **Behinderter**

disadvantage *noun* something which makes you less successful **Nachteil;** *it is a disadvantage for a tax lawyer not to have studied to be an accountant;* **to be at a disadvantage** = to be in a more awkward position (than another person) **benachteiligt/im Nachteil sein;** *not having studied law puts him at a disadvantage*

disagree *verb* not to agree **nicht übereinstimmen;** *the jury disagreed and were* **not able to return a verdict** = there were not enough jurors who were in agreement to be able to form even a majority verdict **die Geschworenen waren sich nicht einig und konnten kein Urteil aussprechen**

◊ **disagreement** *noun* not agreeing **Uneinigkeit, Differenz;** *there was disagreement among the MPs about how the police should deal with terrorist attacks*

disallow *verb* to reject *or* not to accept **zurückweisen, nicht anerkennen;** *the judge disallowed the defence evidence; he claimed £2000 for fire damage, but the claim was disallowed*

disapprove *verb* to show doubt about (a decision made by a lower court), but not to reverse *or* overrule it **mißbilligen;** *the Appeal Court disapproved the County Court decision;* **to disapprove of something** = to show that you do not approve of something *or* that you do not think something is good **etwas mißbilligen;** *the judge openly disapproves of juries*

◊ **disapproval** *noun* act of disapproving a decision made by a lower court **Mißbilligung; Ablehnung**

disbar *verb* to stop a barrister from practising **von der Anwaltsliste streichen** NOTE: **disbarring - disbarred**

disburse *verb* to pay money **aus(be)zahlen, ausgeben**

◊ **disbursement** *noun* payment of money **Auszahlung, Ausgabe, Auslage**

discharge
1 *noun*
(a) ending of a contract by performing all the conditions of the contract *or* by releasing a party from the terms of the contract *or* by being in breach of contract **Erlöschen (durch Erfüllung, Befreiung, Vertragsverletzung); discharge by agreement** = situation where both parties agree to end a contract **einverständliche Vertragsbeendigung; discharge by performance** = situation where the terms of a contract have been fulfilled **Leistungserfüllung; discharge in** *or* **of bankruptcy** = order of a court to release someone from bankruptcy **Konkursaufhebung, Entlastung eines Konkursschuldners**
(b) payment of debt **Tilgung, Begleichung, Bezahlung; in full discharge of a debt** = paying a debt completely *or* paying less than the total amount owed, by agreement **Schuldentilgung in voller Höhe; Schuldentilgung durch Zahlung eines Teilbetrages; final discharge** = final payment of what is left of a debt **letzte Tilgungsrate**
(c) release from prison *or* from military service **Entlassung, Abschied; absolute discharge** = letting an offender go free without any punishment **unbeschränkte Entlassung; conditional discharge** = allowing an offender to be set free without any immediate punishment on condition that he does not commit an offence during the following period **Strafaussetzung zur Bewährung**
(d) in discharge of his duties as director = carrying out his duties as director **bei der Wahrnehmung seiner Pflichten als Direktor**
2 *verb*
(a) to let (someone) go free **entlassen, freilassen;** *the prisoners were discharged by the judge;* **the judge discharged the jury** = the judge told the jury that they were no longer needed **der Richter entließ die Geschworenen**
(b) **to discharge a bankrupt** = to release someone from bankruptcy (as when a

person has paid his debts) **einen Konkursschuldner entlasten**
(c) to discharge a debt or **to discharge one's liabilities** = to pay a debt or one's liabilities in full **eine Schuld begleichen, eine Verbindlichkeit erfüllen**
(d) to dismiss or to sack **entlassen**; to discharge an employee

discipline verb to punish (an official) **disziplinarisch bestrafen**; the clerk was disciplined for leaking the report to the newspapers
◊ **disciplinary** adjective **disciplinary procedure** = way of warning a worker officially that he is breaking rules or that he is working badly **Disziplinarverfahren; to take disciplinary action against someone** = to punish someone **ein Disziplinarverfahren gegen jdn anstrengen**

disclaim verb to refuse to admit **abstreiten, bestreiten, ablehnen**; he disclaimed all knowledge of the bomb; the management disclaims all responsibility for customers' property
◊ **disclaimer** noun
(a) legal refusal to accept responsibility or to accept a right **Haftungsablehnungserklärung; Aufgabe eines Anspruches**
(b) clause in a contract where a party disclaims responsibility for something **Haftungsausschlußklausel**

disclose verb to tell details **preisgeben, aufdecken, enthüllen**; the bank has no right to disclose details of my account to the tax office
◊ **disclosure** noun act of telling details or of publishing a secret **Preisgabe, Aufdeckung, Enthüllung**; the disclosure of the takeover bid raised the price of the shares; the defendant's case was made stronger by the disclosure that the plaintiff was an undischarged bankrupt

discount noun percentage by which a full price is reduced by the seller to a buyer **Rabatt, Preisnachlaß**; we give a 30% discount for large orders; he buys stock at a discount and sells at full price to the public

discover verb to find something new **entdecken, ausfindig machen, herausfinden**; the auditors discovered some errors in the accounts
◊ **discovery** noun disclosure of each party's documents to the other before a hearing starts in the civil courts (usually done by preparing a list of documents) **Offenlegung/Bekanntgabe von Urkunden**

discredit verb to show that a person is not reliable **diskreditieren**; the prosecution counsel tried to discredit the defence witnesses

discrepancy noun difference between two sets of figures **Diskrepanz**; there is a discrepancy between the crime figures released by the Home Office and those of the Metropolitan Police Force

discretion noun being able to decide correctly what should be done **Ermessen, Entscheidungsgewalt**; magistrates have a discretion to allow an accused person to change his election from a summary trial to a jury trial; the judge refused the application, on the ground that he had a judicial discretion to examine inadmissible evidence; **to exercise one's discretion** = to decide which of several possible ways to act **nach eigenem Ermessen handeln; the court exercised its discretion** = the court decided what should be done **das Gericht handelte nach eigenem Ermessen; I leave it to your discretion** = I leave it for you to decide what to do **ich stelle es in Ihr Ermessen, ich lasse Ihnen freie Hand; at the discretion of someone** = if someone decides **nach jds Ermessen**; membership is at the discretion of the committee; sentencing is at the discretion of the judge; the granting of an injunction is at the discretion of the court
◊ **discretionary** adjective which can be done if someone wants **beliebig; the minister's discretionary powers** = powers which the minister could use if he thought he should do so **die Ermessensbefugnis/Ermessensfreiheit des Ministers; the tribunal has wide discretionary power** = the tribunal can decide on many different courses of action **das Gericht hat unbeschränkte Vollmacht; discretionary trust** = trust where the trustees decide how to invest the income and when and how much income should be paid to the beneficiaries **uneingeschränktes Treuhandverhältnis**

discrimination noun treating people in different ways because of class, religion, race, language, colour or sex **Diskriminierung; sexual discrimination** or **sex discrimination** or **discrimination on grounds of sex** = treating men and women in different ways **Diskriminierung aufgrund des Geschlechts**

discuss verb to talk about a problem **diskutieren, erörtern, besprechen**; they spent two hours discussing the details of the *contract; the lawyers discussed the possibility of an acquittal*

◊ **discussion** *noun* talking about a problem **Diskussion, Besprechung, Erörterung, Debatte;** *after some discussion the magistrates agreed to an adjournment*

disenfranchise *or* disfranchise *verb*
to take away someone's right to vote **das Wahlrecht entziehen;** *the company has tried to disenfranchise the ordinary shareholders*

disguise
1 *noun* change of clothes *or* hair style, etc., which makes someone difficult to recognize **Verkleidung;** *the spy crossed the border in disguise*
2 *verb* **to disguise yourself as someone** = to change your clothes and appearance so as to look like someone else **sich als jd verkleiden;** *he entered the country disguised as a policeman*

dishonest *adjective* not honest *or* trying
to deceive **unehrlich, unredlich;** *the public has been warned to look out for dishonest shopkeepers; he assisted the trustees to commit a dishonest breach of trust*

◊ **dishonestly** *adverb* in a deceiving way **unehrlich, unredlich;** *he was accused of dishonestly acquiring the jewels*

dishonour
1 *verb* to refuse to pay a cheque *or* bill of exchange because there is not enough money in the account to pay it **nicht einlösen/honorieren;** *the bank dishonoured his cheque*
2 *noun* act of dishonouring a cheque **Nichthonorierung;** *the dishonour of the cheque brought her business to a stop;* **notice of dishonour** = letter *or* document warning a person to pay a cheque or risk being sued **Mitteilung der Nichthonorierung/Nichtzahlung**

disinherit *verb* to make a will which
prevents someone from inheriting **enterben;** *he was disinherited by his father*

disk *noun* round flat object, used to store
information in computers **Diskette; floppy disk** = small disk for storing information for a computer **Floppy Disk; hard disk** = solid disk which will store a large amount of computer information in a sealed case **Festplatte; disk drive** = part of a computer which makes a disk turn round in order to read it or store information on it **Diskettenlaufwerk**

◊ **diskette** *noun* very small floppy disk **Diskette**

dismiss *verb*
(a) to dismiss an employee = to remove an employee from a job **einen Angestellten entlassen;** *he was dismissed for being late*
(b) to refuse to accept **abweisen;** *the court dismissed the appeal or the application or the action; the justices dismissed the witness' evidence out of hand*

◊ **dismissal** *noun* removal of an employee from a job **Entlassung; dismissal procedure** = correct way of dismissing an employee, following the rules in the contract of employment **Entlassungsverfahren; constructive dismissal** = situation where an employee leaves his job voluntarily but because of pressure from the management **erzwungene Kündigung; unfair dismissal** = removing someone from a job for reasons which are not fair **ungerechtfertigte Entlassung; wrongful dismissal** = removing someone from a job for a reason which does not justify dismissal and which is in breach of the contract of employment **unrechtmäßige/widerrechtliche Entlassung**

COMMENT: an employee can complain of unfair dismissal to an industrial tribunal, or of wrongful dismissal to the County Court

disobey *verb* not to obey **nicht befolgen,
verstoßen;** *the husband disobeyed the court order to pay maintenance to his children*

◊ **disobedience** *noun* not obeying **Ungehorsam;** *the prisoners were put in solitary confinement as punishment for their disobedience of the governor's orders;* **civil disobedience** = disobeying orders by civil authorities (such as the police) as an act of protest **passiver Widerstand, ziviler/bürgerlicher Ungehorsam;** *the group planned a campaign of civil disobedience as a protest against restrictions on immigrants*
NOTE: no plural

disorder *noun* lack of order *or* of control
Unordnung, Durcheinander; civil disorder *or* **public disorder** *or* **public disorders** = riots *or* disturbances *or* fighting in the streets **(öffentliche) Unruhen, Aufruhr; mental disorder** = sickness of the mind **Geistesgestörtheit**

◊ **disorderly** *adjective* badly behaved *or* wild **öffentliches Ärgernis erregend, ordnungswidrig;** *he was charged with disorderly conduct or with being drunk and disorderly;* **to keep a disorderly house** = to be the proprietor *or* manager of a brothel **ein Bordell betreiben**

dispense *verb*
(a) to dispense justice to give out justice **Recht sprechen**

(b) to dispense with something = not to use *or* to do without something **auf etwas verzichten;** *the chairman of the tribunal dispensed with the formality of taking minutes; the accused decided to dispense with the services of a lawyer*
◊ **dispensation** *noun*
(a) act of giving out justice **Rechtsprechung**
(b) special permission to do something which is normally not allowed or is against the law **Befreiung, Ausnahmebewilligung**

display *verb* to show **zeigen, ausstellen; aushängen;** *all cars must display a valid parking permit*

dispose *verb* **to dispose of** = to get rid of *or* to sell cheaply **veräußern, losschlagen;** *to dispose of excess stock; to dispose of one's business*
◊ **disposable** *adjective*
(a) which can be used and then thrown away **Wegwerf-, Einweg-**
(b) disposable income = income left after tax and national insurance have been deducted **verfügbares Einkommen (nach Steuerabzug)**
◊ **disposal** *noun* sale **Verkauf, Veräußerung, Absatz;** *disposal of securities or of property;* **lease** *or* **business for disposal** = lease *or* business for sale **langfristiger Pachtvertrag zu verkaufen; Unternehmen zu verkaufen**
◊ **disposition** *noun* act of passing property (land *or* goods) to another person, especially in a will **Verfügung;** *to make testamentary dispositions*

dispossess *verb* to deprive someone wrongfully of his possession of land **(rechtswidrig) den Grundbesitz entziehen**
◊ **dispossession** *noun* act of wrongfully depriving someone of possession of land **(widerrechtliche) Entziehung des Grundbesitzes**

dispute
1 *noun* disagreement *or* argument **Kontroverse, Disput, Streit;** **industrial dispute** *or* **labour dispute** = argument between management and workers **Arbeitskampf; to adjudicate** *or* **to mediate in a dispute** = to try to settle a dispute between other parties **einen Disput schlichten**
2 *verb* to argue against something **bestreiten, anfechten; the defendant disputed the claim** = the defendant argued that the claim was not correct **der Beklagte bestritt die Forderung; she disputed the policeman's version of events** = she said that the policeman's story of what had happened was wrong **sie bestritt die von dem Polizisten gegebene Schilderung der Ereignisse**

disqualify *verb* to make (someone) not able to do something **disqualifizieren, ausschließen;** *being a judge disqualifies you from being a Member of Parliament; after the accident he was fined £1000 and disqualified from driving for two years; he was convicted for driving a motor vehicle while disqualified*
◊ **disqualification** *noun*
(a) being disqualified from driving a car **Entzug der Fahrerlaubnis**
(b) disqualification from office = rule which forces a director to be removed from a directorship if he does not fulfil certain conditions **Unfähigkeit zur Bekleidung eines Amtes**

disrepute *noun* bad reputation **schlechter Ruf; to bring something into disrepute** = to give something a bad reputation **etwas in Verruf bringen;** *he was accused of bringing the club into disrepute by his bad behaviour*

disrespect *noun* lack of respect **Respektlosigkeit;** *he was accused of showing disrespect to the judge*

disseisin *noun* dispossession *or* wrongfully depriving someone of possession of land **widerrechtlicher Entzug des Grundbesitzes**

dissemination *noun* act of passing information *or* slanderous or libellous statements to other members of the public **Weitergabe, Verbreitung**

dissent
1 *noun* not agreeing **Dissens, Meinungsverschiedenheit;** *the opposition showed its dissent by voting against the Bill*
2 *verb* not to agree with someone **nicht übereinstimmen, differieren, anderer Ansicht/Meinung sein;** *one of the appeal judges dissented;* **dissenting judgment** = judgment of a judge, showing that he disagrees with other judges in a case which has been heard by several judges **abweichendes Urteil**

dissolve *verb* to bring to an end **auflösen, aufheben;** *to dissolve a marriage or a partnership or a company;* **to dissolve Parliament** = to end a session of Parliament, and so force a general election **das Parlament auflösen**
◊ **dissolution** *noun* ending (of a partnership *or* a marriage) **Auflösung, Aufhebung; dissolution of Parliament** = ending of a Parliament, so forcing a general election **Auflösung des Parlaments**

distinction *noun* difference between two things **Unterschied, Unterscheidung;** *the judge made no distinction between the parties; I see no distinction between the two claims*

◊ **distinguish** *verb* to state the difference between two things **unterscheiden; to distinguish a case** = to point to differences between a case and a previously decided case so as not to be bound by the precedent **den Unterschied zu einem Präzedenzfall herausstellen**

NOTE: you distinguish one thing **from** another, or you distinguish **between** two things

distrain *verb* to seize (goods) to pay for debts **beschlagnahmen, in Besitz nehmen**

◊ **distress** *noun* taking someone's goods to pay for debts **Beschlagnahme, Inbesitznahme; distress sale** = selling of someone's goods to pay his debts **Pfandverkauf, Verkauf der beschlagnahmten Gegenstände**

distribute *verb* to share out *or* to give out (to various people) **verteilen;** *the money in the estate is to be distributed among the members of the deceased's family*

◊ **distribution** *noun* sharing out property in an estate **Verteilung/Aufteilung des Nachlasses; distribution of assets** = sharing the assets of a company among the shareholders **Verteilung des Vermögens**

district *noun* section of a town *or* of a country **Stadtteil; Gebiet**

◊ **district attorney** *noun US* (i) prosecuting attorney in a federal district; (ii) state prosecuting attorney **(i) Staatsanwalt; (ii) Staatsanwalt eines Einzelstaates, Bezirksstaatsanwalt**

◊ **district court** *noun US* court in a federal district **Bezirksgericht, Bundesgericht**

disturb *verb* **to disturb the peace** = to make a noise which annoys people in the area **die Ruhe stören**

◊ **disturbance** *noun* noise *or* movement of people which annoys other people **Ruhestörung; Störung der öffentlichen Ordnung; Unruhen;** *street disturbances forced the government to resign; he was accused of making a disturbance in the public library*

divide *verb*
(a) to cut into separate sections **aufteilen,**

teilen; *England and Wales are divided into six court circuits; the two companies agreed to divide the market between them*
(b) *(in the House of Commons)* to vote **abstimmen/abstimmen lassen (durch Hammelsprung);** *the House divided at 10.30*

dividend *noun* payment to shareholders of a proportion of a company's profits **Dividende; final dividend** = dividend paid at the end of a year **Schlußdividende; interim dividend** = dividend paid at the end of a half-year **Abschlags-, Zwischendividende**

division *noun*
(a) main section of something large, especially the separate sections of the High Court (the Queen's Bench Division, the Family Division and the Chancery Division) or the separate sections of the Appeal Court (Civil Division and Criminal Division) **(Gerichts)abteilung, Kammer, Senat**
(b) company which is part of a large group **Tochtergesellschaft;** *Smith's is now a division of the Brown group of companies*
(c) to have a division of opinion = to disagree **anderer Meinung sein, eine Meinungsverschiedenheit haben**
(d) vote in the House of Commons **Abstimmung (durch Hammelsprung);** *in the division on the Law and Order Bill, the government had a comfortable majority*

◊ **divisional** *adjective* referring to a division **Abteilungs-; divisional court** = one of courts of the High Court **Abteilungsgericht, Rechtsmittelkammer; divisional judge** = judge in a division of the High Court **Richter in einer Gerichtsabteilung**

divorce
1 *noun* legal ending of a marriage **Scheidung; divorce petition** = official request to a court to end a marriage **Scheidungsantrag;** *she was granted a divorce on the grounds of unreasonable behaviour by her husband*
2 *verb* to stop being married (to someone) **sich scheiden lassen;** *he divorced his wife and married his secretary*

◊ **Divorce Registry** *noun* court which deals with divorce cases in London **für Scheidungen zuständiges Gericht in London**

COMMENT: under English law, the only basis of divorce is the irretrievable breakdown of marriage. This is proved by one of five grounds: (a) adultery; (b) unreasonable behaviour; (c) one of the parties has deserted the other for a period of two years; (d) the parties have lived apart for two years and agree to a divorce; (e) the parties have lived apart for five years. In the context of divorce proceedings the court has wide powers to make orders regarding custody and care and control of children, and ancillary relief. Divorce proceedings are normally dealt with by the County Court, or in London at the Divorce Registry. Where divorce proceedings are defended, they are transferred to the High Court, but this is rare and most divorce cases are now conducted by what is called the "special procedure"

divulge *verb* to tell a secret **preisgeben, enthüllen;** *he refused to divulge any information about his bank account; she divulged that she had been with the accused on the evening of the murder*

dock

1 *noun*
(a) part of a court where an accused prisoner stands **Anklagebank; the prisoner in the dock** = the prisoner who is being tried for a crime **der Häftling auf der Anklagebank; dock brief** = former system where an accused person could choose a barrister from those present in court to represent him for a small fee **Beauftragung eines (im Gericht anwesenden) Anwaltes mit der Verteidigung**
(b) harbour *or* place where ships can load or unload **Hafen, Anlegestelle, Kai; the docks** = part of a town where the harbour is **Hafen(anlagen); dock dues** = money paid by a ship going into or out of a dock, used to keep the dock in good repair **Dockgebühren**
2 *verb*
(a) to go into dock **ins Dock gehen; am Kai festmachen;** *the ship docked at 17.00*
(b) to remove money from someone's wages **einbehalten, kürzen;** *we will have to dock his pay if he is late for work again; he had £20 docked from his pay for being late*

docket *noun*
(a) list of contents of a package which is being sent **Warenbegleitschein, Verzeichnis**
(b) *US* list of cases for trial **Prozeßliste**

doctrine *noun* general principle of law **Doktrin, Prinzip;** *(US)* **the Monroe Doctrine** = the principle that the USA has an interest in preventing outside interference in the internal affairs of other American states **die Monroe-Doktrin**

document *noun* paper with writing on it **Dokument, Urkunde, Akte;** *deeds, contracts and wills are all legal documents;* **list of documents** = list prepared by parties in a civil action giving discovery of documents relevant to the action **Verzeichnis des schriftlichen Beweismaterials**
◊ **documentary** *adjective* in the form of documents **dokumentarisch, urkundlich;** *documentary evidence; documentary proof*
◊ **documentation** *noun* all documents referring to something **Dokumentation;** *please send me the complete documentation concerning the sale*
NOTE: no plural

doli capax *or* **doli incapax** *Latin phrases meaning* "capable of crime" *or* "incapable of crime" **strafmündig; strafunmündig**

COMMENT: children under ten years of age are doli incapax and cannot be prosecuted for criminal offences; children aged between 10 and 14 are presumed to be doli incapax but the presumption can be reversed if there is evidence of malice or knowledge

domain *noun* area of responsibility **Bereich; public domain** = land *or* property *or* information which belongs to and is available to the public **öffentliches Eigentum, Gemeingut; work which is in the public domain** = work which is no longer in copyright **Werke, die der Allgemeinheit zugänglich sind/die nicht mehr geschützt sind**

Domesday Book *noun* record made for King William I in 1086, which recorded lands in England and their owners and inhabitants for tax purposes **Domesday Book**

domestic *adjective*
(a) referring to a family **häuslich, Familien-; domestic premises** = house *or* flat, etc., used for private accommodation **Privathaus, Privatwohnung, Privathaushalt; domestic proceedings** = court case which involves a man and his wife, or parents and children **familienrechtliches Verfahren**
(b) referring to the market of the country where a business is situated **Innen-, Binnen-, einheimisch, inländisch; domestic consumption** = consumption on the home market **Inlandsverbrauch; domestic market** = market in the country where a company is based **Binnen-, Inlandsmarkt; domestic**

production = production of goods in the home country **Inlandsproduktion**

domicile
1 *noun* country where someone is deemed to live permanently *or* where a company's office is registered (especially for tax purposes) **Wohnsitz; Sitz, Niederlassung; domicile of origin** = domicile which a person has from birth (usually the domicile of the father) **Ursprungswohnsitz; domicile of choice** = country where someone has chosen to live, which is not the domicile of origin **gewählter Wohnsitz**
2 *verb* **he is domiciled in Denmark** = he lives in Denmark officially **er ist in Dänemark ansässig/wohnhaft; bills domiciled in France** = bills of exchange which have to be paid in France **in Frankreich zahlbare Wechsel**

dominant tenement *noun* land which has been granted an easement over another property **herrschendes Grundstück**

COMMENT: the grantor of the easement is the servient tenement

donatio mortis causa *Latin phrase meaning "gift because of death":* transfer of property made when death is imminent **Schenkung wegen bevorstehenden Todes**
◊ **donation** *noun* gift (especially to a charity) **Spende, Schenkung, Stiftung**
◊ **donee** *noun* person who receives a gift from a donor **Spendenempfänger, Schenkungsempfänger, Beschenkter**
◊ **donor** *noun* person who gives property to another **Spender, Schenkungsgeber, Stifter**

dormant *adjective* not active **ruhend, still, untätig; dormant account** = bank account which is not used **umsatzloses Konto; dormant partner** = SLEEPING PARTNER

double
1 *adjective*
(a) twice as large *or* two times the size **doppelt; double taxation** = taxing the same income twice **Doppelbesteuerung; double taxation agreement** *or* **treaty** = agreement between two countries that a person living in one country shall not be taxed in both countries on the income earned in the other country **Doppelbesteuerungsabkommen**
(b) which happens twice **zweifach; in double figures** = with two figures *or* 10 to 99 **zweistellig;** *inflation is in double figures; we have had double-figure inflation for some years;* **double jeopardy** = right of a citizen not to be tried twice for the same crime **Verbot der zweimaligen Strafverfolgung (wegen des gleichen Vergehens)**

2 *verb* to become twice as big; to make something twice as big **sich verdoppeln; verdoppeln**

doubt *noun* not being sure that something is correct **Zweifel; beyond reasonable doubt** *or US* **beyond a reasonable doubt** = proof needed to convict a person in a criminal case **jeden Zweifel ausschließend**

down *adverb & preposition* in a lower position *or* to a lower position **unten, herunter, hinunter, niedrig, gefallen;** *the crime rate is gradually coming down; the price of petrol has gone down;* **to pay money down** = to make a deposit **Geld anzahlen**
◊ **downgrade** *verb* to reduce the importance of someone *or* of a job **herunterstufen, niedriger einstufen;** *his job was downgraded in the company reorganization*

dowry *noun* money *or* property brought by a wife to her husband when she marries him **Aussteuer, Mitgift**

DPP = DIRECTOR OF PUBLIC PROSECUTIONS

draft
1 *noun*
(a) order for money to be paid by a bank **Tratte, (gezogener) Wechsel; to make a draft on a bank** = to ask a bank to pay money for you **einen Wechsel auf eine Bank ziehen; bank draft** *or* **banker's draft** = cheque payable by a bank **Bankwechsel, Banktratte; sight draft** = bill of exchange which is payable when it is presented **Sichtwechsel, Sichttratte**
(b) first rough plan *or* document which has not been finished **Entwurf, Fassung, Konzept;** *draft of a contract or draft contract; he drew up the draft agreement on the back of an envelope; the first draft of the contract was corrected by the managing director; the draft Bill is with the House of Commons lawyers;* **rough draft** = plan of a document which may have changes made to it before it is complete **Rohentwurf, Konzept**
2 *verb* to make a first rough plan of a document **entwerfen, konzipieren;** *to draft a contract or a document or a bill; the contract is still being drafted or is still in the drafting stage*
◊ **drafter** *noun* person who makes a draft **Verfasser/-in**
◊ **drafting** *noun* act of preparing the draft of a document **Verfassen, Formulieren;** *the drafting of the contract took six weeks; the drafting stage of a parliamentary Bill*
◊ **draftsman** *noun* person who drafts documents **Entwerfer, Urkundenverfasser;**

costs draftsman = person who draws up a bill of costs for taxation **Kostensachbearbeiter; parliamentary draftsman** = lawyer who drafts Bills going before Parliament **Jurist, der Gesetzesentwürfe formuliert**

draw verb
(a) to take money away **abheben;** to draw money out of an account; **to draw a salary** = to have a salary paid by a company **ein Gehalt beziehen**
(b) to write a cheque **ausstellen;** to draw a cheque on a bank; he paid the invoice with a cheque drawn on an Egyptian bank

◊ **drawee** noun person or bank asked to make a payment by a drawer **Bezogener, Trassat**

◊ **drawer** noun person who writes a cheque or a bill asking a drawee to pay money to a payee **Aussteller, Trassant; the bank returned the cheque to drawer** = the bank could not pay the cheque because the person who wrote his did not have enough money in his account to pay it **die Bank schickte den Scheck an den Aussteller zurück;** see also RD

◊ **drawings** plural noun money taken out of a partnership by a partner as his salary **(Privat)entnahmen**

◊ **draw up** verb to write a legal document **aufsetzen, abfassen, konzipieren;** to draw up a contract or an agreement; to draw up a company's articles of association

drive
1 noun
(a) energetic way of working **Elan, Schwung; economy drive** = vigorous effort to save money or materials **Sparkampagne;** the government has launched a drive against tax evaders
(b) part of a machine which makes other parts work **Antrieb; disk drive** = part of a computer which makes the disk turn round in order to store information on it **Diskettenlaufwerk**
2 verb
(a) to make a car or lorry, etc. go in a certain direction **fahren;** he was driving to work when he heard the news on the car radio; she drives a company car; **careless driving** or **driving without due care and attention** = offence of driving in such a way that other people and property may be harmed **fahrlässiges Fahren; drunken driving** = offence of driving a car when under the influence of alcohol **Trunkenheit am Steuer; reckless driving** = offence of driving a car in a wild way where the driver does not think that he is causing a risk to other people **rücksichtsloses/verkehrsgefährdendes Fahren**

(b) **he drives a hard bargain** = he is a difficult negotiator **er schließt bei Verhandlungen keine Kompromisse**
NOTE: **driving - drove - driven**

drop
1 noun
(a) fall **Rückgang, Sturz;** drop in sales; sales show a drop of 10%; a drop in prices
(b) **drop shipment** = delivery of a large order from the factory direct to a customer's shop or warehouse without going through an agent or wholesaler **Direktlieferung, Streckengeschäft**
2 verb
(a) to fall **zurückgehen, stürzen, fallen;** sales have dropped by 10% or have dropped 10%; the pound dropped three points against the dollar
(b) to stop a case **einstellen, fallen lassen;** the prosecution dropped all charges against the accused; the plaintiff decided to drop the case against his neighbour
NOTE: **dropping - dropped**

◊ **drop ship** verb to deliver a large order direct to a customer **direkt an den Kunden liefern**

drug noun medicine, especially substances which can be harmful if taken regularly **Arzneimittel, Medikament; dangerous drugs** = drugs which may be harmful to people who take them, and so can be prohibited from import and general sale **gesundheitsgefährdende Drogen, Rauschgifte; drug addiction** = being mentally and physically dependent on taking a drug regularly **Drogenabhängigkeit; the Drug Squad** = section of the police force which investigates crime related to drugs **Rauschgiftdezernat; drug trafficking** = buying and selling drugs illegally **Rauschgifthandel**

drunk adjective incapable because of having drunk too much alcohol **betrunken; drunk and disorderly** = incapable and behaving in a wild way because of having drunk too much alcohol **betrunken und öffentliches Ärgernis erregend**

◊ **drunkard** noun person who is frequently drunk **Trinker;** see also HABITUAL

DSgt = DETECTIVE SERGEANT

dual adjective referring to two things **doppelt; person of dual nationality** or **person who has dual nationality** = person who is a citizen of two countries **jd mit doppelter Staatsangehörigkeit**

dud
1 noun (informal) false coin or banknote **Blüte;** the £50 note was a dud

2 *adjective* false *or* not good **falsch, gefälscht, wertlos; dud cheque** = cheque which the bank refuses to pay because the person writing it has not enough money in his account to pay it **ungedeckter Scheck**

due *adjective*
(a) owed **fällig; to fall due** *or* **to become due** = to be ready for payment **fällig sein/werden; bill due on May 1st** = bill which has to be paid on May 1st **eine am 1. Mai fällige Rechnung; balance due to us** = amount owed to us which should be paid **fälliger Rechnungsbetrag**
(b) the plane is due to arrive at 10.30 *or* **is due at 10.30** it is expected to arrive at 10.30 **das Flugzeug soll um 10.30 Uhr ankommen**
(c) proper *or* as is right **ordnungsgemäß; in due form** = written in the correct legal form **vorschriftsmäßig, rechtsgültig;** *receipt in due form; contract drawn up in due form; driving without due care and attention* = offence of driving in such a way that other people and property may be harmed **Fahren ohne gehörige Sorgfalt; after due consideration** = after thinking seriously **nach reiflicher Überlegung; the due process of the law** = the formal work of a fair legal action **ordnungsgemäßes/ordentliches Verfahren**
(d) due to = caused by **aufgrund, wegen;** *supplies have been delayed due to a strike at the warehouse; the company continues to pay the wages of staff who are absent due to illness*
◊ **dues** *plural noun*
(a) dock dues *or* **port dues** *or* **harbour dues** = payment which a ship makes to the harbour authorities for the right to use the harbour **Dockgebühren; Hafengebühren**
(b) orders taken but not supplied until new stock arrives **Vorbestellungen**

duly *adverb*
(a) properly **vorschriftsmäßig, ordnungsgemäß;** *duly authorized representative*
(b) as was expected **erwartungsgemäß;** *we duly received his letter of 21st October*

dungeon *noun* underground prison (often in a castle) **Verlies, Kerker**

duplicate
1 *noun* copy **Duplikat, Zweitschrift, Kopie;** *he sent me the duplicate of the contract;* **duplicate receipt** *or* **duplicate of a receipt** = copy of a receipt **Quittungsduplikat; in duplicate** = with a copy **in doppelter/zweifacher Ausfertigung; receipt in duplicate** = two copies of a receipt **Quittung in doppelter Ausfertigung;** *to print an invoice in duplicate*

2 *verb*
(a) *(of entry in accounts)* **to duplicate with another entry** = to repeat another entry *or* to be the same as another entry **mit einem anderen Eintrag übereinstimmen**
(b) to duplicate a letter = to make a copy of a letter **einen Brief kopieren, von einem Brief ein Duplikat anfertigen**

◊ **duplicating** *noun* copying **Kopieren; duplicating machine** = machine which makes copies of documents **Vervielfältigungsgerät, Kopiergerät; duplicating paper** = special paper to be used in a duplicating machine **Saugpostpapier, Matrizenpapier**

◊ **duplication** *noun* copying of documents **Vervielfältigung; duplication of work** = work which is done twice without being necessary **doppelte Arbeit**

◊ **duplicator** *noun* machine which makes copies of documents **Vervielfältigungsapparat, Kopiergerät**

duress *noun* force *or* illegal threat to use force on someone to make him do something **Nötigung, Zwang;** *duress provides no defence to a charge of murder;* **under duress** = being forced to do something **durch Nötigung, genötigt, unter Zwang;** *they alleged they had committed the crime under duress from another defendant;* **he signed the confession under duress** = he signed the confession because he was threatened **er unterschrieb das Geständnis unter Zwang**
NOTE: no plural

duty *noun*
(a) work which a person has to do **Pflicht, Aufgabe;** *it is the duty of every citizen to serve on a jury if called; the government has a duty to protect the citizens from criminals;* **duty of care** = duty which every citizen has not to act negligently **Sorgfaltspflicht**
(b) official work which you have to do in a job **Dienst; to be on duty** = to be doing official work at a special time **Dienst haben; night duty** = work done at night **Nachtdienst;** *PC Smith is on night duty this week;* **point duty** = work of a policeman *or* traffic warden to direct the traffic at crossroads **Verkehrsdienst; duty sergeant** = police sergeant who is on duty at a particular time **Polizeibeamter vom Dienst; duty solicitor** = solicitor who is on duty at a magistrates' court and can be contacted at any time by a party who is appearing in that court *or* by a party who has been taken to a police station under arrest *or* for questioning **abrufbereiter Pflichtverteidiger im Magistrates' Court**
(c) tax which has to be paid **Steuer;** *to take the duty off alcohol; to put a duty on*

cigarettes; **ad valorem duty** = duty calculated on the sales value of the goods **Wertsteuer; customs duty** *or* **import duty** = tax on goods imported into a country **Zoll, Einfuhrzoll; excise duty** = tax on the sale of goods (such as alcohol and petrol) which are produced in the country *or* on imports where the duty was not paid on entry into the country **Verbrauchssteuer; goods which are liable to duty** = goods on which customs or excise tax has to be paid **zu verzollende Güter; duty-paid goods** = goods where the duty has been paid **verzollte Waren; stamp duty** = tax on legal documents (such as the conveyance of a property to a new owner) **Stempelgebühr; estate duty** *or* (*US*) **death duty** = tax paid on the property left by a dead person **Erbschaftssteuer**

◊ **duty bound** *adjective* bound to do something because it is your duty **gesetzlich verpflichtet;** *witnesses under oath are duty bound to tell the truth*

◊ **duty-free** *adjective & adverb* sold with no duty to be paid **zollfrei;** *he bought a duty-free watch at the airport* or *he bought the watch duty-free;* **duty-free shop** = shop at an airport *or* on a ship where goods can be bought without paying duty **Duty-free-Shop**

◊ **dutiable** *adjective* **dutiable goods** *or* **dutiable items** = goods on which a customs or excise duty has to be paid **zollpflichtige Waren**

dwelling *noun* place where someone lives (such as a house *or* flat) **Wohnung, Wohnhaus;** *the tax on dwellings has been raised*

Ee

E *fifth letter of the alphabet* **Schedule E** = schedule to the Finance Acts under which tax is charged on wages, salaries and pensions **Einkommenssteuergruppe E; E list** = list of the names of prisoners who frequently try to escape from prison **Liste der Häftlinge, bei denen Ausbruchsgefahr besteht; Table E** = model memorandum and articles of association of an unlimited company with share capital set out in the Companies Act **Muster der Gründungsurkunde und Satzung einer AG mit unbeschränkter Haftung**

e. & o.e. = ERRORS AND OMISSIONS EXCEPTED

early *adjective & adverb*

(a) before the usual time **frühzeitig, früher, vorzeitig; early closing day** = weekday, usually Wednesday or Thursday, when most shops in a town close in the afternoon **Tag, an dem die Geschäfte nachmittags geschlossen sind; at your earliest convenience** = as soon as you find it possible **so bald wie möglich; at an early date** = very soon **bald; early day motion** = motion proposed in the House of Commons for discussion at an early date (usually used to introduce a particular point of view without necessarily going to a full debate) **frühzeitiger Antrag (im Unterhaus)**

(b) at the beginning of a period of time **früh;** *he took an early flight to Paris;* **we hope for an early resumption of negotiations** = we hope negotiations will start again soon **wir hoffen, daß die Verhandlungen schon bald wieder aufgenommen werden werden**

earmark *verb* to reserve for a special purpose **vorsehen, bereitstellen;** *to earmark funds for a project; the grant is earmarked for computer systems development*

earn *verb*

(a) to be paid money for working **verdienen;** *to earn £150 a week; our agent in Paris certainly does not earn his commission;* **wife's earned income allowance** = tax allowance to be set against money earned by the wife of the main taxpayer **Freibetrag für Erwerbseinkommen der Ehefrau**

(b) to produce interest *or* dividends **(ein)bringen;** *what level of dividend do these shares earn? account which earns interest at 10%*

◊ **earnings** *plural noun* money which someone receives for work done **Einkommen, Einkünfte; attachment of earnings** = legal power to take money from a person's salary to pay money which is owed to the courts *or* to a judgment creditor **Lohn-, Gehaltspfändung;** *see also* GARNISHEE ORDER

earnest *noun* money paid as a down payment to show one's serious intention to proceed with a contract **Hand-, Draufgeld;** *he deposited £1,000 with the solicitor as earnest of his intention to purchase*

easement *noun* right which someone has to use land belonging to someone else (such as for a path) **Grunddienstbarkeit**

Easter *noun* one of the four sittings of the Law Courts; one of the four law terms **Gerichtstermine vom 15. April bis 8. bzw. 13. Mai; Vorlesungszeit vom 15. April bis 8. bzw. 13. Mai**

easy *adjective* not difficult **einfach, leicht; easy terms** = credit terms which are not difficult to accept *or* instalments which are easy to pay **günstige Bedingungen, Zahlungserleichterungen; the loan is repayable in easy payments** = with very small sums paid back regularly **das Darlehen ist unter erleichterten Bedingungen zurückzuzahlen**

◊ **easily** *adverb*
(a) without any difficulty **einfach, leicht;** *the motion was passed by the Commons easily*
(b) much *or* a lot **bei weitem;** *he is easily the most important international criminal to have been arrested this year; the firm is easily the biggest in the market; this is easily the largest consignment of drugs we have seized*

EC = EUROPEAN COMMUNITY

ecclesiastical *adjective* referring to the church **kirchlich, geistlich; ecclesiastical court** = court which hears matters referring to the church **Kirchengericht**

economy *noun*
(a) being careful not to waste money *or* materials **Sparsamkeit, Wirtschaftlichkeit; an economy measure** = action to try to save money *or* materials **Sparmaßnahme; economies of scale** = making a product more cheaply by producing it *or* buying it in large quantities **Kosten-, Größendegression**
(b) financial state of a country *or* the way in which a country makes and uses its money **Wirtschaft; black economy** = work which is paid for in cash *or* goods but not declared to the tax authorities **Schattenwirtschaft; free market economy** = system where the government does not interfere in business activity in any way **freie Marktwirtschaft**

◊ **economic** *adjective* referring to economy **Wirtschafts-; economic sanctions** = restrictions on trade with a country in order to influence its political situation *or* in order to make its government change its policy **Wirtschaftssanktionen**

edict *noun* public announcement of a law **Erlaß, Edikt**

editor *noun* (i) person in charge of a newspaper or a section of a newspaper; (ii) person who is responsible for a reference book; (iii) person who checks the work of a writer **(i) Redakteur/-in; (ii) Herausgeber/-in; (iii) Lektor/in; the city editor** = business *or* finance editor of a British newspaper **Wirtschaftsredakteur**

◊ **editorial**
1 *adjective* referring to an editor **redaktionell, Redaktions-; editorial board** = group of editors (on a newspaper, etc.) **Redaktion**
2 *noun* main article in a newspaper, written by the editor **Leitartikel**

EC = EUROPEAN COMMUNITY *EC ministers met today in Brussels; the USA is increasing its trade with the EC*

effect
1 *noun*
(a) result **Auswirkung, Effekt; terms of a contract which take effect** *or* **come into effect from January 1st** = terms which start to operate on January 1st **Vertragsbedingungen, die am 1. Januar in Kraft treten; prices are increased 10% with effect from January 1st** = new prices will apply from January 1st **mit Wirkung vom 1. Januar werden die Preise um 10% erhöht; to remain in effect** = to continue to be applied **wirksam/gültig bleiben**
(b) meaning **Sinn; clause to the effect that** = clause which means that **Klausel, die ... beinhaltet; we have made provision to this effect** = we have put into the contract terms which will make this work **wir haben dementsprechende Vorkehrungen getroffen**
(c) **personal effects** = personal belongings **Gegenstände des persönlichen Gebrauchs**
2 *verb* to carry out **aus-, durchführen; to effect a payment** = to make a payment **eine Zahlung leisten; to effect customs clearance** = to clear something through customs **zollamtlich abfertigen lassen; to effect a settlement between two parties** = to bring two parties together and make them agree to a settlement **einen Vergleich zustande bringen**

◊ **effective** *adjective* which works well *or* which gives the correct result **effektiv, wirksam;** *the police are trying to find an effective means of dealing with young offenders;* **effective date** = date on which a rule *or* a contract starts to be applied **Tag des Inkrafttretens; clause effective as from January 1st** = clause which starts to be applied on January 1st **Klausel mit Wirkung vom 1. Januar**

efficient *adjective* working well **tüchtig, leistungsfähig, wirksam, effizient;** *an efficient secretary; the efficient policing of city centres*

◊ **efficiently** *adverb* which works well **gut, effizient;** *the police coped efficiently with the crowds of protesters*

e.g. = for example *or* such as **z.B.** *the contract is valid in some countries (e.g. France and Belgium) but not in others*

EGM = EXTRAORDINARY GENERAL MEETING

eject *verb* to make (someone) leave a property which he is occupying illegally **zwangsräumen, Zwangsräumung durchführen, zur Räumung zwingen**

◊ **ejection** *noun* action of making someone leave a property which he is occupying illegally **(Zwangs)räumung**

◊ **ejectment** *noun* **action of ejectment** = court action to force someone to leave a property which he is occupying illegally **Räumungsklage**

> COMMENT: ejection of someone who is legally occupying a property is an ouster

ejusdem generis *or* **eiusdem generis** *Latin phrase meaning* "of the same kind": a rule of legal interpretation, that when a word or phrase follows two or more other words or phrases, it is construed to be of the same type as the words or phrases which precede it **derselben Art**

> COMMENT: in the phrase houses, flats and other buildings other buildings can mean only other dwellings, and would not include, for example, a church

elapse *verb (of time)* to pass **vergehen, verstreichen;** *six weeks elapsed before the court order was put into effect; we must allow sufficient time to elapse before making a complaint*

elect *verb*
(a) to choose someone by a vote **wählen;** *to elect the officers of an association; she was elected president*
(b) to choose to do something **sich entscheiden für, (er)wählen;** *he elected to stand trial by jury*

◊ **-elect** *suffix* person who has been elected but has not yet started the term of office **designiert;** *she is the president-elect*
NOTE: the plural is **presidents-elect**

◊ **election** *noun*
(a) act of electing **Wahl; general election** = choosing of a Parliament by all the voters in a country **Parlamentswahl**
(b) act of choosing **Wahl;** *his election as president of the society; the accused made his election for jury trial; see also* BY-ELECTION

elector *noun* person who votes *or* is eligible to vote in an election **Wähler/-in; register of electors** = official list of names and addresses of people living in a certain area who are eligible to vote in local or national elections **Wählerliste**

◊ **electoral** *adjective* referring to an election **Wahl-; electoral roll** = REGISTER OF ELECTORS; **electoral college** = group of people elected by a larger group to vote on their behalf in an election **Wahlausschuß**

> COMMENT: the President of the USA is elected by an electoral college made up of people elected by the states of the USA

◊ **electorate** *noun* all electors taken as a group **Wählerschaft**

electric chair *noun* chair attached to a powerful electric current, used in some states of the USA for executing criminals **elektrischer Stuhl**

eleemosynary *adjective* referring to charity **wohltätig, karitativ**

element *noun* basic part **Grundlage, Grundbestandteil;** *the elements of a settlement*

eligible *adjective* person who can be chosen **wählbar;** *she is eligible for re-election*
◊ **eligibility** *noun* being eligible **Wählbarkeit, Qualifikation;** *the chairman questioned her eligibility to stand for re-election*

embargo
1 *noun* government order which stops a type of trade **Embargo, Handelsverbot; to lay** *or* **put an embargo on trade with a country** = to say that trade with a country must not take place **ein Handelsembargo über ein Land verhängen; to lift an embargo** = to allow trade to start again **ein Embargo aufheben; to be under an embargo** = to be forbidden **einem Embargo unterliegen;** (NOTE: plural is **embargoes**)
2 *verb* to stop trade *or* not to allow trade **ein Embargo verhängen;** *the government has embargoed trade with the Eastern countries*

embark *verb*
(a) to go on a ship **einschiffen;** *the passengers embarked at Southampton*
(b) **to embark on** = to start **(mit) etwas beginnen;** *the company has embarked on a development programme*

◊ **embarkation** *noun* going on to a ship **Einschiffung; port of embarkation** = port at which you get on to a ship **Einschiffungshafen; embarkation card** = card given to passengers getting on to a ship (or plane) **Bordkarte**

embezzle *verb* to use illegally *or* steal money which is not yours, or which you are looking after for someone **unterschlagen, veruntreuen;** *he was sent to prison for six months for embezzling his clients' money*
◊ **embezzlement** *noun* act of embezzling **Unterschlagung, Veruntreuung;** *he was sent to prison for six months for embezzlement* NOTE: no plural
◊ **embezzler** *noun* person who embezzles **jd, der Geld unterschlagen hat; Veruntreuer**

emblements *plural noun* vegetable products which come from farming **Feldfrüchte, Ernteertrag, Ernte auf dem Halm**

embracery *noun* offence of corruptly seeking to influence jurors **Bestechung von Geschworenen**

emergency *noun* dangerous situation where decisions have to be taken quickly **Notlage, Notfall, Notstand; the government declared a state of emergency** = the government decided that the situation was so dangerous that the police *or* army had to run the country **die Regierung hat den Notstand ausgerufen; to take emergency measures** = to take action rapidly to stop a serious state of affairs developing **Krisenmaßnahmen ergreifen; emergency powers** = special powers granted by law to a minister to deal with an emergency **Notstandsermächtigung, Ermächtigung zur Anwendung außerordentlicher Maßnahmen; emergency reserves** = ready cash held in case it is needed suddenly **Notfonds**

emigrate *verb* to go to another country to live permanently **auswandern, emigrieren**
◊ **emigration** *noun* leaving a country to go to live permanently in another country **Auswanderung, Emigration**
◊ **emigrant** *noun* person who emigrates **Auswanderer/-in, Emigrant/-in**

empanel *verb* **to empanel a jury** = to choose and swear in jurors **die Geschworenenliste aufstellen** NOTE: empanelling - empanelled

employ *verb* to give someone regular paid work **beschäftigen, an-, einstellen; to employ twenty staff** = to have twenty people working for you **zwanzig Angestellte haben; to employ twenty new staff** = to give work to twenty people who did not work for you before **zwanzig neue Mitarbeiter einstellen**

◊ **employed**
1 *adjective*
(a) in regular paid work **beschäftigt, angestellt; he is not gainfully employed** = he has no regular paid work **er ist nicht erwerbstätig; self-employed** = working for yourself **selbständig;** *he worked in a bank for ten years but now is selfemployed*
(b) (money) used profitably **arbeitend, gewinnbringend angelegt;** *return against capital employed*
2 *plural noun* people who are working **Arbeitnehmer/-in;** *the employers and the employed;* **the self-employed** = people who work for themselves **die Selbständigen**
◊ **employee** *noun* worker *or* person employed by someone **Arbeitnehmer/-in, Angestellter;** *employees of the firm are eligible to join a profitsharing scheme; relations between management and employees have improved; the company has decided to take on new employees*
◊ **employer** *noun* person *or* company which has employees and pays them **Arbeitgeber; employers' organization** *or* **association** = group of employers with similar interests **Arbeitgeberverband; employer's contribution** = money paid by an employer towards an employee's pension **Arbeitgeberanteil**
◊ **employment** *noun* contractual relationship between an employer and his employees **Arbeits-, Angestellten-, Dienstverhältnis, Beschäftigung; conditions of employment** = terms of a contract whereby someone is employed **Arbeitsvertrags-, Anstellungsbedingungen; contract of employment** *or* **employment contract** = contract between an employer and an employee showing all the conditions of work **Arbeits-, Dienstvertrag; security of employment** = feeling by a worker that he has the right to keep his job until he retires **Arbeitsplatzsicherheit; employment office** *or* **bureau** *or* **agency** = office which finds jobs for people **Stellenvermittlung, Arbeitsvermittlungsstelle; Employment Appeal Tribunal** = court which hears appeals from industrial tribunals **(Landes)arbeitsgericht, Appellationstribunal**

empower *verb* to give someone the power to do something **ermächtigen, Vollmacht erteilen;** *the agent is empowered to sell the property; she was empowered by the company to sign the contract; a constable is empowered to arrest a person whom he suspects of having committed an offence*

emptor *see* CAVEAT

enable *verb* to make it possible for something to happen **ermöglichen,**

befähigen; enabling legislation *or* **statute** = Act of Parliament which gives a minister the power to put other legislation into effect **Ermächtigungsgesetz**

enact *verb* to make (a law) **erlassen, zum Gesetz erklären, gesetzlich verfügen**

◊ **enactment** *noun* (i) making a law; (ii) an Act of Parliament **(i) Erlaß eines Gesetzes; (ii) Gesetz, gesetzliche Bestimmung, Rechtsverordnung**

enclose *verb* to put something inside an envelope with a letter **beilegen, beifügen;** *to enclose an invoice with a letter; I am enclosing a copy of the contract; a letter enclosing two cheques; please find the cheque enclosed herewith*

◊ **enclosure** *noun* document enclosed with a letter **An-, Beilage**

encourage *verb* to help someone to do something *or* to help something to happen **ermutigen, anregen, unterstützen, anstiften, fördern;** *the probation service encourages ex-offenders to settle in new jobs; leaving windows open only encourages burglars; some people believe that lenient sentences encourage crime*

encroachment *noun* illegally taking over someone's property little by little **Übergriff, Eingriff**

encumbrance *noun* liability (such as a mortgage *or* charge) which is attached usually to a property *or* land **Grundstücksbelastung, Hypothekenschulden**

endanger *verb* to put someone in danger of being killed *or* hurt **gefährden; endangering railway passengers** *or* **endangering life at sea** *or* **criminal damage endangering life** = notifiable offences where human life is put at risk **Bahnreisende in Gefahr bringen; Leben auf hoher See in Gefahr bringen; Gefährdung durch strafbare Sachbeschädigung**

endorse *verb*
(a) to agree with **billigen, zustimmen;** *the court endorsed counsel's view*
(b) to endorse a bill *or* **a cheque** = to sign a bill *or* a cheque on the back to make it payable to someone else **einen Wechsel indossieren, einen Scheck girieren**
(c) to make a note on a driving licence that the holder has been convicted of a traffic offence **(eine Strafe auf dem Führerschein) vermerken**
(d) to write a summary of the contents of a legal document on the outside of the folded

document **den Inhalt einer Urkunde auf der Vorderseite vermerken**

◊ **endorsee** *noun* person in whose favour a bill *or* a cheque is endorsed **Indossat**

◊ **endorsement** *noun*
(a) act of endorsing; signature on a document which endorses it; summary of a legal document noted on the outside of the folded document **Indossament; Inhaltsvermerk**
(b) note on an insurance policy which adds conditions to the policy **Zusatzklausel, Versicherungsnachtrag**
(c) note on a driving licence to show that the holder has been convicted of a traffic offence **Strafvermerk auf dem Führerschein**

◊ **endorser** *noun* person who endorses a bill *or* cheque **Indossant**

endowment *noun* giving money to provide a regular income **Stiftung, Dotation; endowment assurance** *or* **endowment policy** = assurance policy where a sum of money is paid to the insured person on a certain date, *or* to his heirs if he dies **Versicherung auf den Erlebens- und Todesfall, gemischte Lebensversicherung; endowment mortgage** = mortgage backed by an endowment policy **durch eine gemischte Lebensversicherung gesicherte Hypothek**

enforce *verb* to make sure something is done *or* is obeyed **erzwingen, Geltung verschaffen, durchsetzen, vollstrecken;** *to enforce the terms of a contract;* **to enforce a debt** = to make sure a debt is paid **eine Schuld beitreiben**

◊ **enforceable** *adjective* which can be enforced **erzwingbar, durchsetzbar, vollstreckbar, einklagbar**

◊ **enforcement** *noun* making sure that something is obeyed **Erzwingung, Durchsetzung, Vollstreckung;** *enforcement of the terms of a contract;* **law enforcement** = making sure that a law is obeyed **Gesetzesvollzug; law enforcement officers** = members of the police force, the Drug Squad, etc. **Vollstreckungsbeamten**
NOTE: no plural

enfranchise *verb* to give (someone) the right to vote **das Wahlrecht verleihen**

◊ **enfranchisement** *noun* action of giving someone a vote **Verleihung des Wahlrechts; leasehold enfranchisement** = right of a leaseholder to buy the freehold of the property which he is leasing **Erwerbsrecht des Eigentums an einem Grundstück durch den Pächter**

engage *verb*

(a) **to engage someone to do something** = to bind someone contractually to do something **jdn zu etwas verpflichten;** *the contract engages the company to purchase minimum annual quantities of goods*
(b) to employ **jdn an-, einstellen, engagieren;** *we have engaged the best commercial lawyer to represent us*
(c) **to be engaged in** = to be busy with **sich befassen mit, tätig sein;** *he is engaged in work on computers; the company is engaged in trade with Africa*

◊ **engaged** *adjective* busy (telephone) **besetzt;** *you cannot speak to the manager - his line is engaged*

◊ **engagement** *noun*
(a) agreement to do something **Verpflichtung, Vereinbarung; to break an engagement to do something** = not to do what you have legally agreed to do **eine Verbindlichkeit nicht erfüllen, eine Abmachung nicht einhalten**
(b) **engagements** = arrangements to meet people **Termine;** *I have no engagements for the rest of the day; she noted the appointment in her engagements diary*

engross *verb* to draw up a legal document in its final form ready for signature **ausfertigen;** *(US)* **engrossed Bill** = Bill which has been passed by both House and Senate, and is written out in its final form with all amendments for the President's signature **gedruckte Gesetzesvorlage**

◊ **engrossment** *noun* (i) drawing up of a legal document in its final form; (ii) legal document in its final form **(i) Ausfertigung (von Urkunden); (ii) Urkunde; engrossment paper** = thick heavy paper on which court documents are engrossed **Urkundenpapier**

enjoyment *noun* **quiet enjoyment of land** = right of an occupier to occupy a property under a tenancy without anyone interfering with that right **ungestörter Grundbesitz**

enquire = INQUIRE
◊ **enquiry** = INQUIRY

ensuing *adjective* which follows **(nach)folgend;** *in the ensuing argument, the defendant hit the plaintiff with a bottle*

entail
1 *noun* interest in land where the land is given to another person and the heirs of his body, but reverts to the donor when the donee and his heirs have all died **festgelegte Erbfolge für Grundbesitz, Fideikommiß**

2 *verb* to involve **erforderlich machen, zur Folge haben;** *itemizing the sales figures will entail about ten days' work*

enter *verb*
(a) to go in **hereinkommen, hineingehen, einsteigen;** *they all stood up when the judges entered the courtroom; the company has spent millions trying to enter the do-it-yourself market*
(b) to write **eintragen;** *to enter a name on a list; the clerk entered the objection in the records; the defendant entered defence of justification;* **to enter appearance** = to register with a court that a defendant intends to defend an action **die Verteidigungsbereitschaft dem Gericht schriftlich anzeigen; to enter a bid for something** = to offer (usually in writing) to buy something **für etwas ein Angebot machen; to enter a caveat** = to warn legally that you have an interest in a case or a grant of probate, and that no steps can be taken without notice to you **Einspruch einlegen; to enter judgment for someone** = to make a legal judgment on someone's behalf **in jds Namen ein Urteil erlassen/eintragen;** *judgment was entered for the plaintiff;* **the plaintiff entered judgment** = the plaintiff took judgment (usually because the defendant failed to defend an action) **für den Kläger erging ein Versäumnisurteil**
(c) **to enter into** = (i) to begin to do something; (ii) to agree to do something **(i) aufnehmen; (ii) (Verpflichtungen) eingehen, abschließen;** *to enter into relations with someone; to enter into negotiations with a foreign government; to enter into a partnership with a friend; to enter into an agreement or a contract*

◊ **entering** *noun* act of writing items in a record **Eintragung**

enterprise *noun*
(a) system of carrying on a business **Unternehmertum; free enterprise** = system of business free from government interference **freies Unternehmertum; enterprise zone** = area of a country, where the government offers special subsidies to firms to encourage them to set up businesses **Förderungsgebiet**
(b) business which is carried on **Unternehmen;** *she runs a mail order enterprise*

entertain *verb*
(a) to offer meals *or* hotel accommodation *or* theatre tickets, etc. to business visitors **unterhalten, bewirten**
(b) to be ready to consider a proposal **in Erwägung/Betracht ziehen, erwägen;** *the judge*

will not entertain any proposal from the prosecution to delay the start of the hearing

entice *verb* to try to persuade someone to do something (by offering money) **verleiten;** *they tried to entice the managers to join the new company*

◊ **enticement** *noun* trying to persuade someone to do something (especially trying to persuade a worker to leave his job *or* a wife to leave her husband) **Verlockung; Abwerbung**

entitle *verb* to give (someone) the right to something **berechtigen; he is entitled to four weeks' holiday** = he has the right to take four weeks' holiday **ihm stehen vier Wochen Urlaub zu**

◊ **entitlement** *noun* right *or* thing to which you are entitled **Anspruch, Berechtigung, Anrecht; holiday entitlement** = number of days' paid holiday which a worker has the right to take **Urlaubsanspruch; pension entitlement** = amount of pension which someone has the right to receive when he retires **Rentenanspruch**

entity *noun* thing which exists in law **Rechtsträger, Rechtssubjekt;** *his private company is a separate entity*

entrust *verb* **to entrust someone with something** *or* **to entrust something to someone** = to give someone the responsibility for looking after something **jdm etwas anvertrauen**

entry *noun*
(a) act of going into a building *or* onto land **Eintritt, Betreten;** *there is no right of entry through this door*
(b) written information entered in a record **Eintrag;** *the sergeant copied the entries into the report*
(b) **entry of appearance** = lodging by the defendant of a document in court to confirm his intention to defend an action **schriftliche Anzeige der Verteidigungsbereitschaft; entry of judgment** = recording the judgment of a court in the official records **Eintragung des Urteils**

equal
1 *adjective* exactly the same **gleich;** *male and female workers have equal pay;* **Equal Opportunities Commission** = official committee set up to make sure that men and women have equal chances of employment and to remove discrimination between the sexes **Kommission für die Gleichberechtigung am Arbeitsplatz; equal opportunities programme** = programme to avoid discrimination in employment **Chancengleichheitsplan;** (NOTE: in US English this is **affirmative action program**)
2 *verb* to be the same as **gleichkommen;** *production this month has equalled our best month ever*
NOTE: **equalling - equalled** but US English is **equaling - equaled**

◊ **equalize** *verb* to make equal **aus-, angleichen;** *to equalize dividends*

◊ **equalization** *noun* *(GB)* **Exchange Equalization Account** = account with the Bank of England used by the government when buying or selling foreign currency to influence the exchange rate for the pound **Währungsausgleichsfonds**

◊ **equally** *adverb* in the same way **gleichmäßig, gleichermaßen;** *costs will be shared equally between the two parties*

equitable *adjective* fair and just *or* referring to equity **gerecht, billig, fair; nach dem Equity-Recht; equitable jurisdiction** = power of a court to enforce a person's rights **Billigkeitsgerichtsbarkeit; equitable lien** = right of someone to hold property (which legally he does not own) until the owner pays money due **Sicherungspfandrecht; equitable mortgage** = mortgage which does not give the mortgagee a legal estate in the land mortgaged **auf Equity-Recht beruhende Hypothek, formlose Hypothek**

equity *noun*
(a) fair system of laws *or* system of British law which developed in parallel with the common law to make the common law fairer, summarized in the maxim "equity does not suffer a wrong to be without a remedy" **Billigkeitsrecht, Equity-Recht; equity of redemption** = right of a mortgagor to redeem the estate by paying off the principal and interest **Tilgungs-, Auslösungsrecht des Hypothekenschuldners**
(b) right to receive dividends as part of the profit of a company in which you own shares **Dividendenanspruch**
(c) **shareholders' equity** *or* **equity capital** = amount of a company's capital which is owned by shareholders **Eigenkapital**
NOTE: no plural

◊ **equities** *plural noun* ordinary shares **Stammaktien**

equivalence *noun* being equivalent **Gleichwertigkeit, Äquivalenz**

◊ **equivalent** *adjective* **to be equivalent to** = to have the same value as *or* to be the same as **gleichkommen, gleich/gleichwertig sein;** *the total dividend paid is equivalent to one quarter of the total profits*

equivocal *adjective* not certain *or* ambiguous **unklar, zweideutig, doppeldeutig;** *the court took the view that the defendant's plea was equivocal*

error *noun* mistake **Fehler;** *he made an error in calculating the total; the secretary must have made a typing error;* **clerical error** = mistake made in an office **Schreibfehler; computer error** = mistake made by a computer **Computerfehler; errors and omissions excepted (e. & o.e.)** = words written on an invoice to show that the company has no responsibility for mistakes in the invoice **Irrtümer und Auslassungen vorbehalten**

escalate *verb* to increase at a constant rate **eskalieren, ansteigen**
◊ **escalation** *noun* **escalation of prices** = constant increase in prices **Preiseskalation, Preisanstieg; escalation clause** = ESCALATOR CLAUSE
◊ **escalator clause** *noun* clause in a contract allowing for regular price increases because of increased costs **Preisgleitklausel**

escape
1 *noun* getting away from a difficult situation **Ausbruch, Entkommen; escape clause** = clause in a contract which allows one of the parties to avoid carrying out the terms of the contract under certain conditions **Befreiungs-, Rücktrittsklausel**
2 *verb* to get away from (a prison) **ausbrechen, entweichen, flüchten;** *three prisoners escaped by climbing over the wall*

escrow *noun* deed which the parties to it deliver to an independent person who hands it over only when certain conditions have been fulfilled **treuhänderisch hinterlegte Vertragsurkunde; in escrow** = held in safe keeping by a third party **treuhänderisch hinterlegt; document held in escrow** = document given to a third party to keep and to pass on to someone when, for example, money has been paid **bei einem Treuhänder hinterlegtes Dokument;** *(US)* **escrow account** = account where money is held in escrow until a contract is signed *or* until goods are delivered, etc. **Treuhandkonto**
NOTE: no plural

espionage *noun* spying **Spionage; industrial espionage** = trying to find out the secrets of a competitor's work or products, usually by illegal means **Werks-, Wirtschaftsspionage**
NOTE: no plural

esquire *noun*
(a) *GB* **J. Smith, Esq.** title written after the name of a man, in an address; *entspricht* **Herrn J. Smith;** NOTE: you can use **Mr** before a name, or **Esq.** after it; both are titles, but **Esq.** is more formal and suggests that the man is more important. **Esq.** is used by lawyers, bank managers, etc., when writing to clients
(b) *US* title given to an American lawyer **Titel für Anwälte**

essential *adjective* very important **wesentlich, unerläßlich, unbedingt notwendig;** *it is essential that all the facts of the case should be presented as clearly as possible; mens rea is one of the essential elements of a crime*

establish *verb*
(a) to set up *or* to make *or* to open **gründen, schaffen, bilden, einrichten;** *the company has established a branch in Australia; the business was established in Scotland in 1823;* **established post** = permanent post in the civil service or similar organization **feste Beamtenstelle, Planstelle; to establish oneself in business** = to become successful in a new business **sich geschäftlich durchsetzen/etablieren**
(b) to decide what is correct *or* what is fact **ermitteln, feststellen, nachweisen;** *the police are trying to establish his movements on the night of the murder; it is an established fact that the car could not have been used because it was out of petrol*
◊ **establishment** *noun*
(a) commercial business **Firma, Geschäft, Betrieb, Unternehmen;** *he runs an important printing establishment*
(b) *(in the EC)* **right of establishment** = right of an EC citizen to live and work in any EC country **Niederlassungsrecht**
(c) number of people working in a company **Personalbestand; establishment charges** = cost of people and property, in a company's accounts **Unternehmens-Fixkosten; to be on the establishment** = to be a full-time employee **zum Personal gehören, fest angestellt sein; office with an establishment of fifteen** = office with a permanent staff of fifteen **Büro mit fünfzehn Mitarbeitern**

estate *noun*
(a) interest in *or* right to hold and occupy land **Besitzrecht**
(b) **real estate** = property (land *or* buildings) **Grundbesitz, Immobilien; estate agency** = office which arranges for the sale of property **Grundstücks- und Immobilienfirma; estate agent** = person in charge of an estate agency **Grundstücks- und Immobilienmakler**

(c) **industrial estate** or **trading estate** = area of land near a town specially for factories and warehouses **Gewerbe-, Industriegebiet**
(d) property left by a dead person **Nachlaß;** *his estate was valued at £100,000 or he left estate valued at £100,000;* **estate duty** or US **estate tax** = tax on property left by a person now dead **Erbschaftssteuer**

estimate

1 *noun*
(a) calculation of probable cost or size or time of something **Schätzung; rough estimate** = very approximate calculation **grobe Schätzung/Berechnung; at a conservative estimate** = calculation which probably underestimates the final figure **bei vorsichtiger Schätzung;** *the crime rate has risen by at least 20% in the last year, and that is a conservative estimate;* **these figures are only an estimate** = these are not the final accurate figures **diese Beträge sind nur Schätzwerte; estimate of expenditure** = calculation of future expenditure prepared for each government department by the minister **Voranschlag der Ausgaben**
(b) calculation of how much something is likely to cost in the future, given to a client so as to get him to make an order **Kostenvoranschlag;** *before we can give the grant we must have an estimate of the total costs involved; to ask a builder for an estimate for building the warehouse;* **to put in an estimate** = to give someone a written calculation of the probable costs of carrying out a job **einen Kostenvoranschlag machen**
2 *verb*
(a) to calculate the probable cost or size or time of something **schätzen;** *to estimate that it will cost £1m or to estimate costs at £1m*
(b) **to estimate for a job** = to state in writing the future costs of carrying out a piece of work so that a client can make an order **einen Kostenvoranschlag für einen Auftrag einreichen**

◊ **estimation** *noun* judgment **Einschätzung;** *in my estimation, he is the best commercial lawyer in town*

◊ **estimator** *noun* person whose job is to calculate estimates for the carrying out of work **Schätzer/-in**

estoppel *noun* rule of evidence whereby someone is prevented from denying or asserting a fact in legal proceedings **(Rechts)verwirkung, Hinderung, rechtshemmender Einwand; estoppel of** or **by record** = rule that a person cannot reopen a matter which has already been decided by a court **Unzulässigkeit einer Einrede aufgrund eines bereits existierenden Urteils; estoppel by deed** = rule that a person cannot deny having done something which is recorded in a deed **Unzulässigkeit einer Einrede gegen Tatsachen, die urkundlich belegt sind; estoppel by conduct** or **in pais** = rule that no one can deny things which he has done or failed to do which have had an effect on other persons' actions if that person has acted in a way which relied on the others' behaviour **Unzulässigkeit der Rechtsausübung aufgrund eines Widerspruches gegenüber eigenem Verhalten;** *see also* PROMISSORY

estovers *plural noun* wood and timber taken from land **Holzentnahme**

estreat *verb* to get a copy of a record of bail or a fine awarded by a court **eine Abschrift aus einem Gerichtsprotokoll anfordern; estreated recognizance** = recognizance which is forfeited because the person making it has not come to court **verwirkte Kaution wegen Nichterscheinens vor Gericht**

et al. or **et alia** *Latin phrase meaning* "and others" or "and other things" **und andere**

etc. or **etcetera** and so on **usw., etc.** *the import duty is to be paid on expensive items including cars, watches, etc.*

etiquette *noun* rules governing the way people should behave, such as the way in which a solicitor or barrister behaves towards clients in court **Etikette**

et seq. or **et sequenter** *Latin phrase meaning* "and the following" **und folgende**

Euro- *prefix* referring to Europe or the European Community **Euro-**
◊ **European** *adjective* referring to Europe **europäisch; the European Community** = the Common Market **die Europäische Gemeinschaft; European Community Law** = law created by the European Community and enforceable in EC states **EG-Recht; European Court of Justice** = court responsible for settling disputes relating to European Community Law **Europäischer Gerichtshof; European Court of Human Rights** = court considering the rights of citizens of states which are parties to the European Convention for the Protection of Human Rights **Europäischer Gerichtshof für Menschenrechte; the European Monetary System** = system of controlled exchange rates between some member countries of the Common Market **das Europäische Währungssystem; the European Parliament** = parliament of delegates elected in each

member country of the EC **das Europäische Parlament**

euthanasia *noun* mercy killing *or* killing of a sick person to put an end to his suffering **Euthanasie**
NOTE: no plural

evade *verb* to try to avoid something **ausweichen, entgehen, sich entziehen; to evade tax** = to try illegally to avoid paying tax **Steuer hinterziehen**

evaluate *verb* to calculate a value **ab-, einschätzen, festsetzen, berechnen;** *to evaluate costs*
◊ **evaluation** *noun* calculation of value **Ein-, Abschätzung, Festsetzung; job evaluation** = examining different jobs within a company to see what skills and qualifications are needed to carry them out with a view to establishing appropriate salaries **Arbeitsplatzbewertung**

evasion *noun* avoiding **Umgehung, Ausweichen; tax evasion** = illegally trying not to pay tax **Steuerhinterziehung;** *see also* AVOIDANCE
◊ **evasive** *adjective* which tries to avoid **ausweichend; to give evasive answers** = to avoid answering questions directly **ausweichende Antworten geben**

event *noun* thing which has happened **Ereignis, Vorfall;** *the police are trying to piece together the events of the previous evening; the newspaper reports covered the events following the football match;* **in the event of** *or* **in the event that** = if something should happen **im Falle;** *in the event of a disagreement or in the event that the parties fail to agree, the case will be submitted to arbitration*

evict *verb* to force (someone) to leave a property **zwangsräumen, zur Räumung zwingen;** *all the tenants were evicted by the new landlords*
◊ **eviction** *noun* forcing someone to leave a property **Zwangsräumung**

evidence
1 *noun* written or spoken statement of facts which helps to prove something at a trial **Aussage; Beweis;** *all the evidence points to arson;* **circumstantial evidence** = evidence which suggests that something must have happened, but does not give firm proof of it **Indizienbeweis; direct evidence** = first-hand evidence, such as the testimony of an eye witness *or* the production of original documents **unmittelbarer Beweis;**

documentary evidence = evidence in the form of documents **Urkundenbeweis; the secretary gave evidence against her former employer** = the secretary was a witness, and her statement suggested that her former employer was guilty **die Sekretärin sagte gegen ihren ehemaligen Vorgesetzten aus; to plant evidence** = to put items at the scene of a crime after the crime has taken place, so that a person is incriminated and can be arrested **Beweismaterial unterschieben; rule of evidence** = rule established by law which determines the type of evidence which a court will consider and how such evidence must be given **Beweisregeln; to turn Queen's evidence** *or* *(US)* **to turn state's evidence** = to confess to a crime and then act as witness against the other criminals involved, in the hope of getting a lighter sentence **als Kronzeuge/Belastungszeuge aussagen;** (NOTE: no plural; to refer to a single item say **a piece of evidence**)
2 *verb* to show **nachweisen, bestätigen;** *the lack of good will, as evidenced by the defendant's behaviour in the witness stand*

ex *preposition & prefix*
(a) out of *or* from **ab; price ex warehouse** = price for a product which is to be collected from the factory or from an agent's warehouse and so does not include delivery **Preis ab Lager; price ex works** *or* **ex factory** = price not including transport from the maker's factory **Preis ab Werk**
(b) **share quoted ex dividend** = share price not including the right to receive the next dividend **ex Dividende notierte Aktie**
(c) former *or* formerly **ehemalig, Ex-;** *Mr Smith, the ex-chairman of the company; she claimed maintenance from her ex-husband*
(d) **ex-directory number** = telephone number which is not printed in the list of people having telephone numbers **eine nicht im Telefonbuch verzeichnete Nummer**

examine *verb* to look at someone *or* something very carefully to see if it can be accepted **untersuchen, (über)prüfen;** *the customs officials asked to examine the inside of the car; the police are examining the papers from the managing director's safe;* **examining justice** *or* **magistrate** = magistrate who hears a case when it is presented for the first time, and decides if there should be a prosecution **Untersuchungsrichter**
◊ **examination** *noun*
(a) asking someone questions to find out facts, such as the questioning of a prisoner by a magistrate **Vernehmung, Verhör**
(b) **examination in chief** *or* *US* **direct examination** = asking a witness questions (by counsel for his side) to give oral

evidence in court **Befragung eines Zeugen durch die benennende Partei**
(c) looking at something very carefully to see if it is acceptable **Untersuchung, Prüfung; customs examination** = looking at goods *or* baggage by customs officials **Zollkontrolle**
(d) test to see if someone has passed a course **Prüfung, Examen;** *he passed his law examinations; she came first in the final examination for the course; he failed his examination and so had to leave his job; see also* CROSS-EXAMINE, CROSS-EXAMINATION

◊ **examiner** *noun* person who conducts a test **Prüfer/-in**

example *noun*
(a) thing chosen to show something **Beispiel;** *these sentences are a good example of the harshness of the military tribunals; new laws on computer copying provide an example of how the law changes to keep in step with new inventions;* **for example (e.g.)** = to show one thing out of many **zum Beispiel (z.B.);** *the government took steps to control drugs, and, for example, increased the numbers of policemen in the Drug Squad*
(b) thing which shows how something ought to be **Beispiel, Muster, Modell; to set a good example to someone** = to show someone how to behave **jdm mit gutem Beispiel vorangehen;** *the police ought to set an example to the community; the rioters were sentenced to periods of imprisonment as an example to others;* **to make an example of someone** = to punish someone harshly so that others will be warned not to do the same **jdn exemplarisch bestrafen**

exceed *verb* to be more than **übersteigen, überschreiten, hinausgehen über; to exceed one's powers** = to act in a way which one is not legally entitled to do **seine Befugnisse überschreiten;** *the judge exceeded his powers in criticizing the court of appeal;* **he was arrested for exceeding the speed limit** = he was arrested for driving faster than was permitted **er wurde wegen Überschreitens der Geschwindigkeitsbegrenzung verhaftet; he has exceeded his credit limit** = he has borrowed more money than he is allowed to do **er hat seinen Kredit überzogen**

excellent *adjective* very good **ausgezeichnet, hervorragend, vorzüglich;** *the accused is a person of excellent character*

except *preposition & conjunction* not including **außer;** *VAT is levied on all goods and services except books, newspapers and children's clothes; sales are rising in all markets except the Far East; the rule applies in all cases, except where otherwise stated*

◊ **excepted** *adverb* not including **ausgenommen; errors and omissions excepted** = note on an invoice to show that the company has no responsibility for mistakes in the invoice **Irrtümer und Auslassungen vorbehalten; excepted persons** = types of workers listed in an insurance policy as not being covered by the insurance **ausgenommene Personen**

◊ **exception** *noun*
(a) thing which is not included with others **Ausnahme;** *all the accused were acquitted with the exception of Jones who was sent to prison for three months*
(b) objection raised to the ruling of a judge **Einrede, Einwendung; to take exception to something** = to object to something *or* to protest against something **an etwas Anstoß nehmen; gegen etwas Einwand erheben;** *counsel for the defence took exception to the witness' remarks; he has taken exception to the reports of the trial in the newspapers*

◊ **exceptional** *adjective* not usual *or* different **außergewöhnlich; exceptional items** = items in a balance sheet which do not appear there each year **Sonderposten; exceptional needs payment** = payment made by the social services to a claimant who has a particular urgent need (such as for clothes) **außergewöhnliche Sozialleistungen**

excess *noun*
(a) amount which is more than what is allowed **Überschuß; excess alcohol in the blood** = more alcohol in the blood than a driver is permitted to have **zu hoher Blutalkoholgehalt; excess fare** = extra fare to be paid (such as for travelling first class with a second class ticket) **Nachlösegebühr; excess of jurisdiction** = case where a judge or magistrate has exceeded his powers **Kompetenzüberschreitung, Unzuständigkeit; excess profits** = profits which are more than is considered to be normal **Mehrgewinn; in excess** = above *or* more than **über, mehr als;** *quantities in excess of twenty-five kilos*
(b) amount to be paid by the insured as part of any claim made under the terms of an insurance policy **Selbstbehalt;** *he has to pay a £50 excess, and the damage amounted to over £1,000*

◊ **excessive** *adjective* too large **übermäßig;** *we found the bill for costs excessive and applied to have it reduced; the driver had an excessive amount of alcohol in his blood*

exchange
1 *noun*
(a) giving of one thing for another **Tausch,**

Austausch; to offer *or* take something in part exchange = giving *or* taking an old product as part of the payment for a new one **etwas in Zahlung geben od nehmen; exchange of contracts** = point in the conveyance of a property when the solicitors for the buyer and the seller hand over the contract which then becomes binding **Unterzeichnung des Kaufvertrages (bei Grundbesitz)**
(b) foreign exchange = (i) exchanging the money of one country for that of another; (ii) money of another country **(i) Geldwechsel; (ii) Devisen; foreign exchange broker** = person who buys and sells foreign currency on behalf of other people **Devisenhändler, Devisenmakler; foreign exchange market** = dealings in foreign currencies **Devisenmarkt, Devisenbörse; rate of exchange** *or* **exchange rate** = price at which one currency is exchanged for another **Wechselkurs; exchange controls** = government instructions on changing the local currency for foreign currency **Devisenkontrolle;** *the government had to impose exchange controls to stop the rush to buy dollars; (GB)* **Exchange Equalization Account** = account with the Bank of England used by the government when buying or selling foreign currency to influence the exchange rate for the pound **Währungsausgleichsfonds**
(c) bill of exchange = document ordering the person to whom it is directed to pay a person money on demand *or* at a certain date **Wechsel, Tratte**
(d) Stock Exchange = place where stocks and shares are bought and sold **Börse; commodity exchange** = place where commodities are bought and sold **Warenbörse**
2 *verb*
(a) to exchange an article for another = to give one thing in place of something else **einen Artikel gegen einen anderen umtauschen**
(b) to exchange contracts = to hand over a contract when buying or selling a property (done by both buyer and seller at the same time) **beim Kauf von Grundbesitz den Kaufvertrag unterschreiben**
(c) to change money of one country for money of another **wechseln, tauschen**

◊ **exchangeable** *adjective* which can be exchanged **austauschbar, umtauschbar**

◊ **exchanger** *noun* person who buys and sells foreign currency **Devisenhändler**

Exchequer *see* CHANCELLOR

excise
1 *noun*
(a) excise duty *or* **tax** = tax on certain goods produced in a country (such as alcohol) **Verbrauchssteuer**

(b) Customs and Excise *or* **Excise Department** = government department which deals with VAT and with taxes on imports and on products, such as alcohol, produced in the country **Behörde für Zölle und Verbrauchsteuern**
2 *verb* to cut out **herausschneiden;** *the chairman ordered the remarks to be excised from the official record*

◊ **exciseman** *noun* person who works in the Excise Department **Steuereinnehmer**

exclude *verb* to keep out *or* not to include **ausschließen**

◊ **excluding** *preposition* not including **außer, ausgenommen, ausschließlich, unter Ausschluß von;** *the regulations apply to members of the public, excluding those serving in the emergency services;* **not excluding** = including **einschließlich;** *government servants, not excluding judges, are covered by the Bill*

◊ **exclusion** *noun* not including **Ausschluß; exclusion clause** = clause in a contract which limits the liability of a party, for example a clause in an insurance policy which says which items are not covered **Ausschlußklausel, Freizeichnungsklausel; to the exclusion of** = not including *or* without including **unter Ausschluß von; exclusion order** = court order in matrimonial proceedings which stops a wife *or* husband from going into the matrimonial home **Ausschließung aus dem Familienheim; exclusion zone** = area (usually an area of sea) near a country, which is forbidden to military forces of other countries **Sperrgebiet**

◊ **exclusive** *adjective*
(a) exclusive agreement = agreement where a person *or* firm is made sole agent for a product in a market **Alleinvertretungsvereinbarung; exclusive licence** = licence where the licensee is the only person to be able to enjoy the licence **Alleinlizenz; exclusive right to market a product** = right to be the only person to market the product **Recht zum Alleinvertrieb eines Produktes**
(b) exclusive of = not including **exklusive, ausschließlich**

◊ **exclusivity** *noun* exclusive right to market a product **Alleinvertrieb**

excuse
1 *noun* reason for doing something wrong *or* for omitting to do something **Entschuldigung;** *what was his excuse for arriving late in court? the judge refused to*

accept the defendant's excuse; see also IGNORANCE
2 *verb*
(a) to forgive a small mistake **entschuldigen**
(b) to allow someone not to do something **befreien;** *he was excused jury service because he was deaf*

execute *verb*
(a) to carry out (an order); to carry out (the terms of a contract) **ausführen; erfüllen; executed consideration** = consideration where one party has made a promise in exchange for which the other party has done something for him **erbrachte Gegenleistung**
(b) to kill someone who has been sentenced to death by a court **hinrichten;** *he was executed by firing squad*

◊ **execution** *noun*
(a) carrying out of a court order *or* of the terms of a contract **Ausführung; Erfüllung; stay of execution** = temporary stopping of a legal order **Vollstreckungsaufschub, vorläufge Einstellung der Zwangsvollstreckung;** *the court granted the company a two-week stay of execution;* **warrant of execution** = warrant issued by a court which gives the bailiffs *or* sheriffs the power to seize goods from a debtor in order to pay his debts **Vollstreckungsbefehl; Pfändungsauftrag**
(b) killing of someone who has been sentenced to death by a court **Hinrichtung**

◊ **executioner** *noun* person who executes people who have been sentenced to death **Henker, Scharfrichter**

◊ **executive**
1 *adjective*
(a) which puts decisions into action **exekutiv, Exekutiv-, vollziehend; executive committee** = committee which runs a society *or* a club **Vorstand; executive director** = director who works full-time in the company **geschäftsführender Direktor; executive powers** = right to put decisions into actions **ausübende Gewalt, Exekutivgewalt, Exekutive**
(b) *US* **executive order** = order by the president of the USA *or* of a state governor **Exekutivorder, Vollzugsanordnung**
2 *noun*
(a) person in a business who takes decisions *or* manager *or* director **Führungskraft, leitender Angestellter; chief executive** = executive director in charge of a company; *entspricht* **geschäftsführender Direktor; legal executive** = clerk in a solicitor's office who is not a solicitor and is not articled to become one, but has passed the examinations of the Institute of Legal Executives **(qualifizierter) Mitarbeiter in einem Anwaltsbüro**

(b) the Executive = (i) section of a government which puts into effect the laws passed by Parliament; (ii); *US* the President **(i) die Exekutive, die vollziehende Gewalt; (ii) der Präsident**

executor *noun* someone who is appointed by a person making his will who will see that the terms of the will are carried out **Testamentsvollstrecker;** *he was named executor of his brother's will*

◊ **executory** *adjective* which is still being carried out **noch zu erfüllen/vollziehen; executory consideration** = consideration where one party makes a promise in exchange for a counter-promise from the other party **wechselseitiges Leistungsversprechen**

◊ **executrix** *noun* female executor **Testamentsvollstreckerin**

exemplary *adjective* which is so good that it serves as an example to others **vorbildlich;** *her conduct in the case was exemplary;* **exemplary damages** = damages which punish the defendant for loss or harm caused to the plaintiff *or* heavy damages which show that a court feels that the defendant has behaved badly towards the plaintiff **verschärfter Schadensersatz; exemplary sentence** = particularly harsh sentence which aims at deterring others from committing the same type of crime **abschreckende/exemplarische Strafe**

exempt
1 *adjective* not covered by a law; not forced to obey a law **ausgenommen, befreit; exempt from tax** *or* **tax-exempt** = not required to pay tax **steuerfrei; exempt supplies** = sales of goods or services which are exempt from VAT **nicht mehrwertsteuerpflichtige Waren oder Dienstleistungen**
2 *verb* to free something from having tax paid on it or from having to pay tax **befreien;** *non profit-making organizations are exempt(ed) from tax; food is exempt(ed) from sales tax; the government exempted trusts from tax*

◊ **exemption** *noun* act of exempting something from a contract *or* from a tax **Befreiung; exemption clause** = clause in a contract exempting a party from certain liabilities **Freizeichnungsklausel; exemption from tax** *or* **tax exemption** = being free from having to pay tax **Steuerbefreiung;** *as a non profit-making organization you can claim tax exemption*

exercise
1 *noun* use (of a power) **Ausübung, Anwendung;** *a court can give directions to a*

local authority as to the exercise of its powers in relation to children in care; **exercise of an option** = using an option *or* putting an option into action **Ausübung einer Option**
2 *verb* to use *or* to put into practice **anwenden, ausüben, gebrauchen; to exercise one's discretion** = to decide which of several courses to take **nach eigenem Ermessen handeln;** *the magistrates exercised their discretion and let the accused off with a suspended sentence;* **to exercise an option** = to put an option into action **eine Option ausüben;** *he exercised his option to acquire sole marketing rights for the product; not many shareholders exercised their option to buy the new issue of shares*

ex gratia *Latin phrase meaning* "as a favour" **freiwillig; an ex gratia payment** = payment made as a gift, with no obligations **Kulanzzahlung, Zahlung ohne Anerkennung einer Rechtspflicht**

exhaust *verb* to wear out *or* to use up **erschöpfen, aufbrauchen;** *the appellant has exhausted all channels of appeal; the company has exhausted all its development budget*

exhibit *noun* object (such as a gun *or* coat *or* document) which is shown as evidence to a court **Beweisstück**

exile
1 *noun*
(a) being sent to live in another country as a punishment **Exil, Verbannung;** *the ten members of the opposition party were sent into exile* (NOTE: no plural)
(b) person who has been sent to live in another country as a punishment **Verbannter**
2 *verb* to send someone to live in another country as a punishment **verbannen;** *he was exiled for life; she was exiled to an island in the North Sea*

exist *verb* to be **existieren;** *the right of way has existed since the early nineteenth century*

◊ **existence** *noun* being **Existenz; to come into existence** = to start to be **entstehen;** *the custom came into existence during the eighteenth century;* **immemorial existence** = before 1189, the date from which events are supposed to be remembered **vorhanden seit undenklichen Zeiten**

ex officio *Latin phrase meaning* "because of an office held" **von Amts wegen;** *the treasurer is ex officio a member or an ex officio member of the finance committee*

exonerate *verb* to say that someone who has been blamed, should not be blamed **entlasten;** *the judge exonerated the driver from all responsibility for the accident*

◊ **exoneration** *noun* act of exonerating **Entlastung**

ex parte *Latin phrase meaning* "on behalf of" **einseitig, auf Antrag, seitens einer Partei; an ex parte application** = application made to a court where only one side is represented and no notice is given to the other side (often where the application is for an injunction) **Antrag (nur) einer Partei;** *the wife applied ex parte for an ouster order against her husband; see also* INTER PARTES
NOTE: in legal reports, abbreviated to **ex p** as in: *Williams v. Smith, ex p White* showing that White was the party which applied for the hearing to take place

expatriate
1 *noun* person who lives abroad **im Ausland Lebender;** *there is a large expatriate community or a large community of expatriates in Geneva*
2 *verb* to force someone to leave the country where he is living **ausbürgern**

◊ **expatriation** *noun* forcing someone to leave the country where he is living **Ausbürgerung**

expect *verb* to hope that something is going to happen **erwarten;** *we are expecting him to arrive at 10.45; they are expecting a cheque from their agent next week; the house was sold for more than the expected price*

◊ **expectancy** *or* **expectation** *noun* hope that you will succeed to a property **Anwartschaft,, Erbaussicht; expectation of life** *or* **life expectancy** = number of years a person is likely to live **Lebenserwartung**

expenditure *noun* amounts of money spent **Ausgaben, Aufwendungen; capital expenditure** = money spent on assets (such as property or machinery) **Investitionen**
NOTE: no plural

◊ **expense** *noun*
(a) money spent **Ausgabe, Kosten; at great expense** = having spent a lot of money **mit hohen Kosten, kostenintensiv**
(b) expense account = money which a businessman is allowed by his company to spend on travelling and entertaining clients in connection with his business **Spesenkonto**

◇ **expenses** *plural noun* money paid for doing something **Unkosten, Spesen; all expenses paid** = with all costs paid by the company **mit Vergütung aller Unkosten; allowable expenses** = business expenses which are allowed against tax **abzugsfähige Ausgaben; business expenses** = money spent on running a business, not on stock or assets **Betriebskosten; entertainment expenses** = money spent on giving meals to business visitors **Bewirtungsspesen; fixed expenses** = money which is spent regularly (such as rent, electricity, telephone) **Fixkosten; incidental expenses** = small amounts of money spent at various times, in addition to larger amounts **Nebenausgaben; legal expenses** = money spent on fees to lawyers **Anwaltskosten; overhead expenses** *or* **general expenses** *or* **running expenses** = money spent on the day-to-day costs of a business **Betriebskosten, allgemeine Unkosten, Festkosten; travelling expenses** = money spent on travelling and hotels for business purposes **Reisespesen**

experience

1 *noun*
(a) having lived through various situations and therefore knowing how to make decisions **Erfahrung;** *he is a lawyer of considerable experience; she has a lot of experience of dealing with divorce cases; he gained most of his legal experience in the Far East*
(b) something one has lived through **Erfahrung;** *the accident was a terrible experience for her* NOTE: no plural for (a)
2 *verb* to live through a situation **durchmachen, erleben, erfahren**

◇ **experienced** *adjective* person who has lived through many situations and has learnt from them **erfahren, sachkundig;** *he is the most experienced negotiator I know; we have appointed a very experienced woman as sales director*

expert *noun* person who knows a lot about something **Experte/Expertin, Fachmann, Sachverständiger;** *an expert in the field of fingerprints or a fingerprints expert; the company asked a financial expert for advice or asked for expert financial advice;* **expert's report** = report written by an expert (usually for a court case) **Sachverständigengutachten, Expertise; expert witness** = witness who is a specialist in a subject and is asked to give his opinion on technical matters **sachverständiger Zeuge**

◇ **expertise** *noun* specialist knowledge **Fachwissen, Sachkenntnis;** *we hired Mr Smith because of his financial expertise or*

because of his expertise in the African market
NOTE: no plural

expiration *noun* coming to an end **Ablauf, Fälligwerden, Erlöschen;** *expiration of an insurance policy; to repay before the expiration of the stated period;* **on expiration of the lease** = when the lease comes to an end **nach Ablauf des Mietvertrages**
NOTE: no plural

◇ **expire** *verb* to come to an end **ablaufen, fällig werden, erlöschen;** *the lease expires in 1987;* **his passport has expired** = his passport is no longer valid **sein Paß ist abgelaufen**

◇ **expiry** *noun* coming to an end **Ablauf, Verfall, Erlöschen;** *expiry of an insurance policy;* **expiry date** = date when something will end **Ablauf-, Verfallsdatum, Fälligkeitstag**

explain *verb* to give reasons for something **erklären;** *he explained to the customs officials that the two computers were presents from friends; can you explain to the jury how you came to be in the house on Thursday 13th July?*

◇ **explanation** *noun* reason for something **Erklärung;** *the VAT inspector asked for an explanation of the invoices; he could give no explanation of how the drugs came to be in his suitcase*

◇ **explanatory** *adjective* which explains **erklärend, erläuternd;** *read the explanatory notes before filling in the form*

explicit *adjective* which is clearly stated **deutlich, klar, ausdrücklich;** *his explicit intention was to leave his house to his wife*

◇ **explicitly** *adverb* in a clear way **deutlich, klar, ausdrücklich;** *the contract explicitly prohibits sale of the goods in Europe*

explore *verb* to examine carefully **untersuchen, sondieren;** *we are exploring the possibility of opening an office in London*

explosive

1 *noun* substance which can blow up and damage property **Sprengstoff;** *the car was full of explosives*
2 *adjective* which can blow up and damage property **explosiv, Explosiv-; an explosive device** = a bomb **ein Sprengkörper**

export

1 *noun* sending of goods to a foreign country to be sold **Export, Ausfuhr; export licence** = permit which allows a company to send a certain type of product abroad to be sold **Exportlizenz**

2 *verb* to send goods abroad to be sold **exportieren, ausführen;** *most of the company's products are exported to the USA*

expose *verb* to show something which had previously been hidden **aufdecken, enthüllen;** *the police investigation exposed corruption in the government; he was exposed as the boss of the gang of forgers*
◊ **exposure** *noun* act of showing something which was hidden **Aufdeckung, Enthüllung;** *the report's exposure of corruption in the police force;* **indecent exposure** = offence where a male person shows his sexual organs to a woman **unsittliche Entblößung**

ex post facto *Latin phrase meaning* "after the event" **rückwirkend, retrospektiv**

express
1 *adjective*
(a) rapid *or* very fast **Express-, Eil-, per Express;** *express letter; express delivery*
(b) clearly shown in words **ausdrücklich;** *the contract has an express condition forbidding sale in Africa;* **express term** = term in a contract which is clearly stated (as opposed to an implied term) **ausdrückliche Vertragsvereinbarung**
2 *verb*
(a) to put into words *or* diagrams **ausdrücken;** *this chart shows crime in London expressed as a percentage of total crime in the UK*
(b) to send very fast; *we expressed the order to the customer's warehouse* **per Express/als Eilsendung schicken**
◊ **expressly** *adverb* clearly in words **ausdrücklich;** *the contract expressly forbids sales to the United States; the franchisee is expressly forbidden to sell goods other than those supplied by the franchisor*

expressio unius est exclusio alterius *Latin phrase meaning* "the mention that one thing is included implies that another thing is expressly excluded"

expunge *verb* to remove (from a record) **löschen, (aus)streichen;** *inadmissible hearsay evidence was expunged from the report*

extend *verb*
(a) to make available *or* to give **gewähren;** *to extend credit to a customer*
(b) to make longer **verlängern, prolongieren;** *to extend a contract for two years; the court extended the defendant's time for serving his defence by fourteen days; he was sentenced to five years imprisonment, extended;* **extended credit** = credit allowing

the borrower a longer time to pay **verlängerter Kredit; extended family** = group of related people, including distant relatives and close friends **Großfamilie; extended sentence** = sentence which is made longer than usual because the criminal is likely to repeat the offence **verlängerte Strafe**
◊ **extension** *noun*
(a) allowing longer time **Verlängerung, Prolongation; to get an extension of credit** = to get more time to pay back **eine Kreditverlängerung gewährt bekommen; extension of a contract** = continuing the contract for a further period **Vertragsverlängerung; extension of time** = allowance by court to a party of more time in which to do something **Fristverlängerung, Nachfrist;** *the defendant applied for an extension of time in which to serve her defence*
(b) *(in an office)* individual telephone linked to the main switchboard **(Neben)anschluß, Apparat;** *can you get me extension 21? extension 21 is engaged; the legal department is on extension 53*
◊ **extensive** *adjective* very large *or* covering a wide area **umfangreich, ausgedehnt, weit, breit, umfassend;** *he has an extensive knowledge of drugs; she has extensive contacts in the underworld*
◊ **extent** *noun* amount *or* area covered by something **Umfang, Ausmaß;** *they are assessing the extent of the damage after the fire;* **to a certain extent** = partly *or* not completely **in gewissem Maße, teilweise;** *he was correct to a certain extent; the recommendations of the report were carried out to a certain extent*

extenuating circumstances *plural noun* factors which excuse a crime in some way **mildernde Umstände**
◊ **extenuation** *noun* **in extenuation of something** = in order to excuse something **zur Milderung von;** *counsel pleaded the accused's age in extenuation of his actions*

extinction *noun* coming to an end **Erlöschen;** *the extinction of a legal right*

extinguishment *noun* act of cancelling a right *or* a power (especially the right to sue for non-payment once payment has been made) **Löschung, Aufhebung**

extort *verb* to get money *or* promises *or* a confession from someone, by using threats **erpressen, erzwingen;** *he extorted £20,000 from local shopkeepers*
◊ **extortion** *noun* getting money by threats **Erpressung, Erzwingung; extortion racket** =

racket to make money by threatening people **(Schutzgeld)erpressung, verbrecherische Erpressung**

NOTE: no plural

◊ **extortionate** *adjective* at very high cost *or* too much **Wucher-; extortionate credit bargain** = transaction whereby money is lent at a very high rate of interest, thereby rendering the transaction illegal **Wucherkreditgeschäft**

◊ **extortionist** *noun* person who extorts money from people **Erpresser/-in**

extra- *prefix* outside **außer-, extra-**

◊ **extra-territoriality** *noun* being outside the territory of the country where you are living, and so not subject to its laws (used of diplomats) **Exterritorialität**

extract
1 *noun* printed document which is part of a larger document **Auszug**; *the solicitor sent an extract of the deeds*
2 *verb* to force someone to say something which he does not want to say **herausholen, herauspressen, entlocken**; *the confession was extracted under torture; the magistrate extracted an admission from the witness that he had not seen the accident*

extradite *verb* to bring an arrested person from another country to your country because he is wanted for trial for a crime which he committed in your country **ausliefern**; *he was arrested in France and extradited to stand trial in Germany*

◊ **extradition** *noun* bringing an arrested person from another country to be tried for a crime he committed in your country **Auslieferung**; *the USA requested the extradition of the leader of the drug gang;* **extradition treaty** = agreement between two countries that a person arrested in one country can be sent to the other to stand trial for a crime committed there **Auslieferungsvertrag**

extraordinary *adjective* different from normal **außerordentlich, außergewöhnlich; Extraordinary General Meeting (EGM)** = special meeting of shareholders *or* members of a club, etc., to discuss an important matter which cannot wait until the next Annual General Meeting **außerordentliche Hauptversammlung; extraordinary items** = items in accounts which do not appear each year **Sonderposten**; *the auditors noted several extraordinary items in the accounts*

extrinsic evidence *noun* evidence used in the interpretation of a document which is not found in the document itself **Beweis,** der nicht aus einer Urkunde ableitbar ist; *compare* INTRINSIC

eye witness *noun* person who saw something happen (such as an accident *or* a crime) **Augenzeuge**; *he gave an eye witness account of the bank hold-up*

Ff

F *sixth letter of the alphabet* **Class F charge** = charge on a property registered by a spouse who is not the owner, claiming a right to live in the property **Steuergruppe F; Schedule F** = schedule to the Finance Acts under which tax is charged on income from dividends **Einkommenssteuergruppe F**

face
1 *noun* front part of something **Gesicht; face value** = value written on a coin *or* share certificate *or* banknote **Nominal-, Nennwert**
2 *verb* **to face a charge** = to appear in court and be charged with a crime **angeklagt sein, sich vor Gericht zu verantworten haben**; *he faces three charges relating to firearms*

facie *see* PRIMA FACIE

facsimile (copy) *noun* exact copy of a document **Faksimile**

Sachverhalt

fact *noun* something which is true and real, especially something which has been proved by evidence in court **Tatsache, Faktum**; *the chairman of the tribunal asked to see all the facts on the income tax claim;* **in fact** *or* **in point of fact** = really **eigentlich; tatsächlich; matters of fact** = facts relevant to a case which is being tried at court **Tatsachen**; *see also* ACCESSORY

◊ **fact-finding** *noun & adjective* looking for information **Tatsachenermittlung; Ermittlungs-; a fact-finding delegation** = group of people who visit to search for information about a problem **Ermittlungskommission; Untersuchungsausschuß**

facto *see* DE FACTO, IPSO FACTO

factor *noun*
(a) thing which is important *or* which influences things **Faktor**; *the rise in unemployment is an important factor in the increased crime rate;* **cyclical factors** = way in which a trade cycle affects businesses **zyklische**

Faktoren; **contributory factor** = something which contributes to a result **fördernder Umstand; deciding factor** = most important factor which influences a decision **entscheidender Faktor; factors of production** = things needed to produce a product (land, labour and capital) **Produktionsfaktoren**
(b) agent *or* person who buys or sells as an agent for another in exchange for a commission **Factor, Kommissionär; debt factor** = person who buys debts at a discount, and enforces them for himself *or* enforces them for a commission **Factor**

◊ **factoring** *noun* selling debts to a debt factor **Factoring**

faculty *noun* special permission to do something, granted by a church (such as permission to get married without publishing banns) **Dispens; Vollmacht**

◊ **Faculty of Advocates** *noun* legal body to which Scottish barristers belong **Anwaltskammer**

fail *verb*
(a) not to do something which you were trying to do **keinen Erfolg haben; unterlassen; scheitern;** *he failed to appear at the probation office; counsel failed to persuade the jury that his client was innocent*
(b) to be unsuccessful commercially **keinen Erfolg haben; the company failed** = the company became insolvent **das Unternehmen ging bankrott**

◊ **failing**
1 *noun* being weak *or* weakness **Schwäche, Fehler;** *the chairman has one failing - he goes to sleep at board meetings*
2 *preposition* if something does not happen **mangels; ansonsten, widrigenfalls; failing instructions to the contrary** = unless different instructions are given **falls keine gegenteiligen Instruktionen erfolgen; failing prompt payment** = if the payment is not made on time **bei nicht termingerechter Zahlung; failing that** = if that does not work **sonst, widrigenfalls;** *try the company secretary, and failing that the chairman*

◊ **failure** *noun*
(a) breaking down *or* stopping **Scheitern; Versagen;** *the failure of the negotiations*
(b) not doing something which should be done **Unterlassung; Nichteinhaltung;** *his failure to comply with the court order; their failure to meet the deadline; her failure to pay a bill*
(c) commercial failure = bankruptcy of a person *or* insolvency of a company **kommerzieller Mißerfolg/Zusammenbruch;** *he lost all his money in the bank failure*

fair
1 *noun* **trade fair** = large exhibition and meeting for advertising and selling a certain type of product **Handels-, Fachmesse**
2 *adjective*
(a) honest *or* correct **fair, gerecht; fair comment** = remark which is honestly made on a matter of public interest and so is not defamatory **sachliche Kritik; fair dealing** = legal buying and selling of shares **geordneter Effektenhandel; fair price** = good price for both buyer and seller **angemessener Preis; fair trade** = international business system where countries agree not to charge import duties on certain items imported from their trading partners **Nichtdiskriminierung im Außenhandel; fair trading** *or* **fair dealing** = way of doing business which is reasonable and does not harm the consumer **lauterer Wettbewerb; Office of Fair Trading** = British government department which protects consumers against unfair *or* illegal business **Amt für Verbraucherschutz; fair wear and tear** = acceptable damage caused by normal use **Abnutzungs- und Verschleißerscheinungen;** *the insurance policy covers most damage, but not fair wear and tear to the machine*
(b) fair copy = document which is written *or* typed with no corrections or mistakes **Reinschrift**

faith *noun* **to have faith in something** *or* **someone** = to believe that something *or* a person is good or will work well **in etwas/jdn Vertrauen setzen; in good faith** = in an honest way **in gutem Glauben; he acted in good faith** *or* **in bad faith** = he acted honestly *or* dishonestly **er handelte in gutem Glauben od böswillig; to buy something in good faith** = to buy something honestly *or* in the course of an honest transaction **etwas in gutem Glauben kaufen;** *he bought the car in good faith, not knowing it had been stolen*

◊ **faithfully** *adverb* **yours faithfully** = used as an ending to a formal business letter not addressed to a named person **Mit freundlichen Grüßen, Hochachtungsvoll** ·

fake
1 *noun* forgery *or* copy made for criminal purposes **Fälschung, Imitation;** *the shipment came with fake documentation*
2 *verb* to make an imitation for criminal purposes **fälschen; fingieren; vortäuschen;** *they faked a break-in to make the police believe the documents had been stolen*

fall *verb* to happen *or* to take place **fallen;** *the national holiday falls on a Monday;* **the bill fell due** = the bill was due to be paid **die Rechnung wurde fällig; to fall outside** = not to be part of a list *or* not to be covered by a rule **nicht gehören zu; fallen aus;** *the case falls* *outside the jurisdiction of the court;* **to fall within** = to become part of a list *or* to be covered by a rule **gehören zu; fallen unter;** *the newspaper report falls within the category of defamation; the case falls within the competence of the court*

false *adjective* not true *or* not correct **falsch;** *to make a false entry in the record;* **false accounting** = notifiable offence of changing *or* destroying *or* hiding records for money **vorsätzlich inkorrekte Buchführung; false imprisonment** = (i) tort of keeping someone imprisoned wrongfully; (ii) sending someone to prison for a wrong reason **(i) Freiheitsberaubung; (ii) ungesetzliche Festnahme; false pretences** = doing *or* saying something to cheat someone **Vorspiegelung falscher Tatsachen;** *he was sent to prison for obtaining money by false pretences;* **false representation** = offence of making a wrong statement **falsche Angabe; false weight** = weight on shop scales which is wrong and so cheats customers **falsches Gewicht**

◊ **falsehood** *noun* lie *or* incorrect statement **Unwahrheit; injurious falsehood** *or* **malicious falsehood** = tort of making a wrong statement about someone so as to harm his reputation (usually in relation to his business *or* property) **Rufschädigung**

◊ **falsify** *verb* to change something to make it wrong **fälschen; to falsify accounts** = to change *or* destroy a record **die Bücher od Unterlagen fälschen**

◊ **falsification** *noun* **falsification of accounts** = action of making false entries in a record *or* of destroying a record **Fälschung von Konten od Unterlagen**

family *noun*
(a) group of people who are related (including husband, wife, mother, father, children) **Familie; extended family** = group of related people including distant relatives and close friends **Großfamilie; family company** = company where most of the shares are owned by members of the same family **Familienunternehmen; Family Division** = one of the three divisions of the High Court which deals with divorce cases and cases involving parents and children **Abteilung für Familiengerichtssachen (des High Court); family law** = laws relating to families *or* to the rights and duties of the members of a family **Familienrecht**
(b) *slang* group of organized Mafia gangsters, ruled by a boss or godfather **Clan**

fatal *adjective* which causes a death **tödlich;** *he took a fatal dose of drugs; there were six fatal accidents in the first week of the year*

fault *noun*
(a) being to blame for something which is wrong **Verschulden; Schuld;** *the witness said the accident was the fault of defective machinery; was it the fault of the police if the protest march developed into a riot?*
(b) wrong working **Fehler, Defekt;** *the technical staff are trying to correct a fault in the computer; we think there is a basic fault in the construction of the product*

◊ **faulty** *adjective* which does not work properly *or* which has not been done in the correct way **fehlerhaft, defekt;** *the accident was caused by faulty brakes or by faulty repairs to the brakes*

favour *or US* **favor**
1 *noun*
(a) **as a favour** = to help *or* to be kind to someone **aus Gefälligkeit;** *he asked the secretary for a loan as a favour*
(b) **in favour of** = in agreement with *or* feeling that something is right **für;** *most of the workers are in favour of shorter working hours; six members of the cabinet are in favour of the proposal, and three are against it*
2 *verb* to agree that something is right *or* to vote for something **bevorzugen; begünstigen;** *judges favour deterrent sentences for hooligans*

◊ **favourable** *adjective* which helps someone *or* which approves of something **günstig, vorteilhaft; to buy on favourable terms** = to buy on terms which make it easier to pay **zu günstigen Bedingungen kaufen**

FBI = FEDERAL BUREAU OF INVESTIGATION

feasant *see* DAMAGE FEASANT

federal *adjective* referring to a system of government where a group of states are linked together in a federation **Bundes-; federal court** *or* **federal laws** = court *or* laws of the USA *or* FRG, as opposed to state courts *or* state laws **Bundesgericht; Bundesrecht**

◊ **Federal Bureau of Investigation (FBI)** *noun* section of the US Department of Justice, which investigates crimes against federal law and subversive acts in the USA **FBI;** *entspricht* **Bundeskriminalamt**

◊ **federation** *noun* group of societies *or* companies *or* organizations which have a central organization which represents them and looks after their common interests **Verband; Syndikat**

fee *noun*
(a) money paid for work carried out by a professional person (such as an accountant *or* a doctor *or* a lawyer) **Honorar;** *we charge a small fee for our services; a barrister's fees;* *(US)* **contingent fee** = fee paid to a lawyer which is a proportion of the damages recovered in a case **Erfolgshonorar**
(b) money paid for something **Gebühr;** *entrance fee or admission fee; registration fee*
(c) fee simple = freehold ownership of land with no restrictions to it **freier Eigenbesitz;** *to hold an estate in fee simple;* **fee tail** = interest in land which is passed on to the owner's direct descendants, and which cannot be passed to anyone else **Grundbesitz mit Erbbeschränkungen**

feed
1 *noun* device which puts paper into a printer *or* into a copying machine **Einzug, Vorschub; continuous feed** = device which feeds in continuous computer stationery into a printer **Endlospapiereinzug; sheet feed** = device which puts in one sheet at a time into a printer **Einzelblatteinzug**
2 *verb* to put information into a computer **speisen, eingeben**
NOTE: **feeding - fed - has fed**

felony *noun* old term for a serious crime **Kapitalverbrechen;** *to commit a felony*
NOTE: still used in **treason felony**
◊ **felonious** *adjective* criminal **verbrecherisch; strafbar;** *he carried out a felonious act*

feme covert *French phrase meaning* "married woman" **verheiratete Frau**
◊ **feme sole** *French phrase meaning* "unmarried woman" **unverheiratete Frau**

fence
1 *noun (informal)* person who receives and sells stolen goods **Hehler**
2 *verb* to receive stolen goods to sell **hehlen**

fiat *noun*
(a) agreement (as of the Attorney-General) to bring a prosecution **Dekret, Anordnung**
(b) fiat money = coins or notes which are not worth much as paper or metal, but are said by the government to have a value **ungedecktes Geld**
◊ **fiat justicia** *Latin phrase meaning* "let justice be done" **fiat justicia; das Recht muß seinen Gang gehen**

fiction *noun* **fiction of law** *or* **legal fiction** = assuming something to be true, even if it is not proved to be so (a procedural device by

courts to get round problems caused by statute) **Gesetzesfiktion; Rechtsfiktion**
◊ **fictitious** *adjective* false *or* which does not exist **falsch; fiktiv; Schein-; fictitious assets** = assets which do not really exist, but are entered as assets to balance the accounts **Scheinaktiva**

fiddle
1 *noun (informal)* cheating **Schiebung, Trickserei;** *it's all a fiddle;* **he's on the fiddle** = he is trying to cheat **er macht faule Geschäfte/dreht ein krummes Ding**
2 *verb (informal)* to cheat **frisieren, manipulieren;** *he tried to fiddle his tax returns; the salesman was caught fiddling his expense account*

fide *see* BONA FIDE

fieri facias *Latin phrase meaning* "make it happen" **Vollstreckung; writ of fieri facias** = court order to a sheriff telling him to seize the goods of a debtor against whom judgment has been made **Vollstreckungsbefehl**
NOTE: often abbreviated to **fi. fa.**

fiduciary *noun* (person) acting as trustee for someone else *or* being in a position of trust **Treuhänder; Vertrauensmann** *adjective* relating to a trust *or* a trustee **treuhänderisch; he was acting in a fiduciary capacity** = he was acting as a trustee **er handelte in seiner Eigenschaft als Treuhänder;** *a company director owes a fiduciary duty to the company*

fi. fa. *see* FIERI FACIAS

figure *noun*
(a) number *or* cost written in numbers **Zahl, Ziffer; Summe; he put a very low figure on the value of the lease** = he calculated the value of the lease as very low **er setzte im Pachtvertrag eine sehr niedrige Summe an**
(b) figures = written numbers **Zahlen, Ziffern; sales figures** = total sales **Verkaufs-, Absatzzahlen; to work out the figures** = to calculate **Berechnungen vornehmen; his income runs into five figures** *or* **he has a fivefigure income** = his income is more than £10,000 **er hat ein fünfstelliges Einkommen; in round figures** = not totally accurate, but correct to the nearest 10 or 100 **rund; ab- od aufgerundet;** *the number of prisoners in jail is 45,000 in round figures*
(c) figures = results for a company **Zahlen(werk);** *the figures for last year or last year's figures*

file

1 *noun*
(a) cardboard holder for documents, which can fit in the drawer of a filing cabinet **Aktenordner;** *put these letters in the unsolved cases file; look in the file marked "Scottish police forces";* **box file** = cardboard box for holding documents **kastenförmige Mappe**
(b) documents kept for reference **Akte;** *the police keep a file of missing vehicles; look up her description in the missing persons' file;* **to place something on file** = to keep a record of something **etwas zu den Akten nehmen, ablegen; to keep someone's name on file** = to keep someone's name on a list for reference **jdn in den Akten führen; file copy** = copy of a document which is kept for reference in an office **Aktenkopie; card file** = information kept on filing cards **Karteikarte; computer file** = section of information on a computer (such as a list of addresses *or* of customer accounts) **Computerregister**
(c) section of data on a computer (such as staff salaries, address list, customer accounts) **Computerdatei;** *how can we protect our computer files?*
2 *verb*
(a) to file documents = to put documents in order so that they can be found easily **Unterlagen abheften;** *the correspondence is filed under "complaints"*
(b) to make an official request **einreichen, vorlegen; anmelden; erheben; to file a petition in bankruptcy** = to ask officially to be made bankrupt *or* to ask officially for someone else to be made bankrupt **Antrag auf Konkurseröffnung stellen**
(c) to send a document to court **etwas (bei Gericht) einreichen/registrieren; the defence must be filed and served in seven days** = the defence must be sent to court and to the other party within seven days **die Klagebeantwortung muß binnen sieben Tagen zugestellt werden**
(d) to register something officially **(offiziell) einreichen;** *to file an application for a patent; to file a return to the tax office*

◊ **filing** *noun*
(a) delivering a legal document to court **Vorlage, Einreichung; Erhebung**
(b) documents which have to be put in order **Ablage;** *there is a lot of filing to do at the end of the week; the manager looked through the week's filing to see what letters had been sent;* **filing basket** *or* **filing tray** = container kept on a desk for documents which have to be filed **Ablage; filing cabinet** = metal box with several drawers for keeping files **Aktenschrank; filing card** = card with information written on it, used to classify information into the correct order **Karteikarte; filing system** = way of putting documents in order for reference **Ablagesystem**

final *adjective* last *or* coming at the end of a period **letzter, Schluß-, End-, Abschluß-;** *to pay the final instalment; to make the final payment; to put the final details on a document;* **final date for payment** = last date by which payment should be made **letzter Zahlungstermin; final demand** = last reminder from a supplier, after which he will sue for payment **letzte Mahnung; final discharge** = last payment of what is left of a debt **letzte Tilgungsrate; final dividend** = dividend paid at the end of the year **Schlußdividende; final judgment** = judgment which is awarded at the end of an action after trial, as opposed to an interlocutory judgment **rechtskräftiges Urteil**

◊ **finally** *adverb* in the end **schließlich, endlich;** *the contract was finally signed yesterday; after ten hours of discussions, the House of Commons finally rose at two o'clock in the morning*

finance
1 *noun* money used by a company, club, etc. **Finanzen, Geldmittel;** *where will the authority find the finance to pay the higher salaries? he is the secretary of the local authority finance committee;* **Finance Act** = annual Act of Parliament which gives the government the power to raise taxes to spend as proposed in the Budget; *(GB)* **Finanzgesetz**
2 *verb* to pay for something **finanzieren;** *the new building must be financed by the local authority;* a *government-financed programme of prison construction*

◊ **financial** *adjective* referring to money *or* finance **finanziell;** *he has a financial interest in the company;* **financial assistance** = help in the form of money **finanzielle Unterstützung, Finanzhilfe;** *she receives financial assistance from the local authority;* **financial institution** = bank *or* other company which provides finance **Geld-, Finanzinstitut; to make financial provision for someone** = to give someone money to live on **für jdn finanzielle Vorsorge treffen**

◊ **financially** *adverb* in the form of money **finanziell;** *he is financially involved in the property company; the company is financially very strong*

find *verb*
(a) to get something which was not there before **finden;** *to find backing for a project*
(b) to make a legal decision in court **befinden für, erklären (für);** *the tribunal found that both parties were at fault; the court found the accused guilty on all charges;* **the judge found for the defendant** = the judge decided that the defendant was right **der**

Richter entschied zugunsten des Angeklagten/Beklagten
NOTE: **finding - found**

◇ **findings** *noun* decision reached by a court **Urteil(sspruch); the findings of a commission of enquiry** = the conclusions of the commission **die Ergebnisse einer Untersuchungskommission**

fine

1 *noun* money paid as a punishment because something wrong has been done **Geldstrafe;** *the court sentenced him to pay a £25,000 fine; we had to pay a £10 parking fine; the sentence for dangerous driving is a £1,000 fine or two months in prison*
2 *verb* to punish someone by making him pay money **zu einer Geldstrafe verurteilen;** *to fine someone £2,500 for obtaining money by false pretences*

fingerprint

1 *noun* mark left on a surface by fingers, from which a person may be identified **Fingerabdruck;** *they found his fingerprints on the murder weapon; the court heard evidence from a fingerprint expert;* **to take someone's fingerprints** = to take a copy of a person's fingerprints (by printing them with ink on a filing card) so that he can be identified in future **jds Fingerabdrücke nehmen**
2 *verb* to take someone's fingerprints **Fingerabdrücke nehmen;** *the police fingerprinted the suspect after charging him*

fire

1 *noun*
(a) thing which burns **Feuer;** *the shipment was damaged in the fire on board the cargo boat; half the stock was destroyed in the warehouse fire;* **to catch fire** = to start to burn **Feuer fangen;** *the papers in the waste paper basket caught fire;* **fire certificate** = certificate from the municipal fire department to say that a building is properly protected against fire **Brandschutzbescheinigung; fire damage** = damage caused by fire **Brandschaden;** *he claimed £250 for fire damage;* **fire-damaged goods** = goods which have been damaged in a fire **brandgeschädigte Waren; fire door** = special door to prevent fire going from one part of a building to another **Feuertür; fire escape** = door *or* stairs which allow staff to get out of a building which is on fire **Feuertreppe, Feuerleiter; fire hazard** *or* **fire risk** = situation *or* goods which could start a fire **Feuergefahr;** *that warehouse full of paper is a fire hazard;* **fire insurance** = insurance against damage by fire **Feuer-, Brandversicherung; fire regulations** = local or national regulations which owners of

buildings used by the public have to obey in order to be granted a fire certificate **Feuerschutzbestimmungen**
(b) act of shooting **Feuer; the police opened fire on the crowd** = the police started to shoot at the crowd **die Polizei eröffnete das Feuer auf die Menge**
2 *verb*
(a) to shoot (with a gun) **abschießen, schießen, feuern;** *he fired two shots at the crowd*
(b) to fire someone = to dismiss someone from a job **jdn entlassen;** *the new managing director fired half the sales force*

◇ **firearm** *noun* gun *or* other weapon used to shoot **Schußwaffe; firearms certificate** = official document saying that someone has permission to own a gun **Waffenschein**

◇ **fireproof** *adjective* which cannot be damaged by fire **feuerfest, feuersicher;** *we packed the papers in a fireproof safe; it is impossible to make the office completely fireproof*

◇ **fire-raiser** *noun* person who sets fire to property **Brandstifter/-in**

◇ **fire-raising** *noun* setting fire to property on purpose **Brandstiftung;** *see also* ARSON, ARSONIST

◇ **firing squad** *noun* group of soldiers who execute someone by shooting **Exekutionskommando**

firm

1 *noun* partnership *or* any other business which is not a company **Firma; Unternehmen;** *he is a partner in a law firm; a firm of accountants; an important publishing firm* (NOTE: **firm** is often used when referring to incorporated companies, but this is not correct)
2 *adjective*
(a) which cannot be changed **fest; sicher; endgültig;** *to make a firm offer for something; to place a firm offer for two aircraft; they are quoting a firm price of £1.22 per case*
(b) not dropping in price, and possibly going to rise **stabil;** *the pound was firmer on the foreign exchange markets; shares remained firm*
3 *verb* to remain at a price and seem likely to go up **sich festigen;** *the shares firmed at £1.50*

◇ **firmness** *noun* remaining at a price *or* being likely to rise **Stabilität;** *the firmness of the pound*

first *noun* person *or* thing which is there at the beginning *or* earlier than others **der/die/das erste;** *our company was one of the first to sell into the European market;* **first quarter** = three months' period from January to the end of March **erstes Quartal; first half** *or* **first half-year** = six months' period from January to the end of June **erste Hälfte; erstes Halbjahr; first in first out =** (i) redundancy policy, where the people who have been working longest are the first to be made redundant; (ii) accounting policy where stock is valued at the price of the oldest purchases **(i) Personalpolitik nach der FIFO-Methode; (ii) FIFOAbschreibungsmethode; case of first impression =** case which raises points of law for which there are no precedents **Präzedenzfall; first offence =** committing an offence for the first time **Straftat eines Ersttäters/nicht vorbestraften Täters; first offender =** person who has committed an offence for the first time **noch nicht vorbestrafter Täter, Ersttäter; First Reading =** formal introduction of a Bill into the House of Commons, after which it is printed **erste Lesung**

◊ **first-class** adjective
(a) top quality or most expensive **erstklassig, Spitzen-;** he is a first-class accountant
(b) most expensive and comfortable type of travel or type of hotel **Erster Klasse; erstklassig;** to travel first-class; first-class travel provides the best service; a first-class ticket; to stay in first-class hotels; **first-class mail =** (i) (in Britain) most expensive mail service, planned to be faster; (ii) (in the USA) mail service for letters and postcards **(i) (ii) Briefpost erster Klasse;** a first-class letter should get to Scotland in a day

◊ **first degree murder** noun (US) premeditated and deliberate murder **vorsätzlicher Mord**

◊ **first instance** noun **court of first instance =** court in which a case is tried first **Gericht erster Instanz**

fiscal adjective referring to tax or to government revenue **Finanz-, Steuer-, steuerlich;** the government's fiscal policies; **fiscal measures =** tax changes made by a government to improve the working of the economy **steuerpolitische Maßnahmen; fiscal year =** twelve-month period on which taxes are calculated (in the UK, April 6th to April 5th) **Steuerjahr; Procurator Fiscal =** Scottish law officer who decides whether an alleged criminal should be prosecuted; (bei geringeren Straftaten) **Amtsanwalt;** (bei Strafandrohung von mehr als einem Jahr) **Staatsanwalt**

fit adjective physically or mentally able to do something **fit, gesund; tauglich;** the solicitor stated that his client was not fit to plead

◊ **fitness** noun state of being of the necessary standard **Tauglichkeit; fitness for purpose =** implied contractual term that goods sold will be of the necessary standard to be used for the purpose for which they were bought **Zweckdienlichkeit, Eignung**

◊ **fittings** see FIXTURE

fix verb
(a) to arrange or to agree **beschließen; festlegen, festsetzen;** to fix a budget; to fix a meeting for 3 p.m.; the date of the hearing has still to be fixed; the price of gold was fixed at $300; the punishment for drug offences has been fixed by Parliament
(b) to mend **reparieren;** the maintenance staff are coming to fix the telephone; can you fix the copying machine?

◊ **fixed** adjective permanent or which cannot be removed **fest, Fest-, gebunden; fixed assets =** property or machinery which a company owns and uses **Anlagevermögen; fixed capital =** capital in the form of buildings and machinery **Anlagekapital; fixed charge =** charge over a particular asset or property **Fixbelastung;** (see also FLOATING CHARGE); **fixed costs =** (i) set amount of money to which a plaintiff is entitled in legal proceedings (as opposed to taxed costs); (ii) cost of producing a product, which does not increase with the amount of product made (such as rent) **(i) feststehende Kosten; (ii) Fix-, Gemeinkosten; fixed deposit =** deposit which pays a stated interest over a set period **Festgeld; fixed expenses =** money which is spent regularly (such as rent, electricity, telephone) **Fixkosten; fixed income =** income which does not change (such as from an annuity) **festes Einkommen; fixed-interest investments =** investments producing an interest which does not change **festverzinsliche Kapitalanlagen; fixed-price agreement =** agreement where a company provides a service or a product at a price which stays the same for the whole period of the agreement **Festpreisvereinbarung; fixed scale of charges =** rate of charging which cannot be altered **verbindliche Gebührenordnung; fixed term =** period which is fixed when a contract is signed and which cannot be changed afterwards **festgesetzte Dauer (eines Vertrages)**

◊ **fixing** noun
(a) arranging **Festsetzung, Festlegung;** fixing of charges; fixing of a mortgage rate
(b) price fixing = illegal agreement between companies to charge the same price for competing products **Preisabsprache**
(c) the London gold fixing = system where the world price for gold is set each day in London **London Gold Fixing**

◊ **fixture** noun item in a property which is permanently attached to it (such as a sink or lavatory) and which passes to a new owner with the property itself **Einbauten;**

fixtures and fittings = objects in a property which are sold with the property (both those which cannot be removed and those which can) **Installationen und Einbauten**

flag *noun* piece of coloured cloth which is used to represent a country **Flagge, Fahne; flag of convenience** = flag of a country which may have no ships of its own but allows ships of other countries to be registered in its ports **Billigflagge; to fly a flag** = to attach the flag in an obvious position to show that you belong to a certain country **eine Flagge führen;** *ship flying the British flag; ship flying a flag of convenience*

flagrant *adjective* clear and obvious **offenkundig, flagrant;** *a flagrant case of contempt of court; a flagrant violation of human rights*

◊ **flagrante** *see* IN FLAGRANTE DELICTO

flat
1 *adjective*
(a) falling because of low demand **lustlos;** *the market was flat today*
(b) fixed *or* not changing **Pauschal-; flat rate** = charge which always stays the same **Pauschal-, Einheitssatz;** *we pay a flat rate for electricity each quarter; he is paid a flat rate of £2 per thousand*
2 *noun* set of rooms for one family in a building with other sets of similar rooms **Wohnung;** *he has a flat in the centre of town; she is buying a flat close to her office;* **company flat** = flat owned by a company and used by members of staff from time to time **Dienstwohnung**
NOTE: US English is **apartment**

floating charge *noun* a charge over the changing assets (such as debts or stock) of a business, as opposed to a fixed charge **variable Belastung**

flotsam *noun* rubbish floating in the water after a ship has been wrecked **Treib-, Strandgut**

flout *verb* to break *or* to go against (a rule *or* the law) **mißachten;** *by selling alcohol to minors, the shop is deliberately flouting the law*

f.o.b. = FREE ON BOARD

follow *verb* to act in accordance with (a rule) **folgen;** *the court has followed the precedent set in the 1972 case*

◊ **follow up** *verb* to examine something further **nachgehen; nachfassen;** *the police are following up several leads;* **to follow up an initiative** = to take action once someone else has decided to do something **eine Initiative aufgreifen**

foolscap *noun* large size of writing paper 13 1/4 x 16 1/2 inches; *the letter was on six sheets of foolscap;* **a foolscap envelope** = large envelope which takes foolscap paper

forbear *verb* **to forbear from doing something** = not to do something which you intended to do **unterlassen; Abstand nehmen von;** *he forbore from taking any further action*
NOTE: **forbearing - forbore - has forborne**

◊ **forbearance** *noun* not doing something which was intended **Unterlassung; Abstandnahme**
NOTE: no plural

forbid *verb* to tell someone not to do something *or* to say that something must not be done **verbieten;** *the contract forbids sale of the goods to the USA; the staff are forbidden to use the front entrance; the judge forbade any reference to the defendant in the media*
NOTE: **forbidding - forbade - has forbidden**

force
1 *noun*
(a) strength **Kraft; to be in force** = to be operating *or* working **in Kraft sein;** *the rules have been in force since 1946;* **to come into force** = to start to operate *or* work **in Kraft treten;** *the new regulations will come into force on January 1st;* **the new regulations have the force of law** = they are the same as if they had been voted into law by parliament **die neuen Bestimmungen sind rechtsverbindlich**
(b) labour force = all the workers in a company *or* in an area **Arbeitskräfte; Belegschaft;** *the management has made an increased offer to the labour force; we are opening a new factory in the Far East because of the cheap local labour force;* **police force** = group of policemen organized in an area **Polizei(einheit);** *members of several local police forces have collaborated in searching for the murderer*
(c) force majeure = something which happens which is out of the control of the parties who have signed a contract (such as strike, war, storm) and which prevents the contract being fulfilled **höhere Gewalt**
2 *verb* to make someone do something **zwingen;** *competition has forced the company to lower its prices*

◊ **forced** *adjective* **forced sale** = sale which takes place because a court orders it *or* because it is the only way to avoid insolvency **Zwangsverkauf**

◊ **forcible** *adjective* by force *or* using force **gewaltsam; forcible entry** = formerly, the criminal offence of entering a building *or* land and taking possession of it by force **gewaltsames Eindringen; forcible feeding** = giving food by force to a prisoner on hunger strike **Zwangsernährung**

foreclose *verb* to take possession of a property because the owner cannot repay money which he has borrowed (using the property as security) **(aus einer Hypothek) zwangsvollstrecken lassen;** *to foreclose on a mortgaged property*

◊ **foreclosure** *noun* act of foreclosing **Zwangsvollstreckung (aus einer Hypothek); foreclosure order nisi** = court order which makes a mortgagor pay outstanding debts to a mortgagee within a certain period of time **vorläufige Verfallserklärung; foreclosure order absolute** = court order giving the mortgagee full rights to the property **endgültige Verfallserklärung**

foreign *adjective* not belonging to one's own country **ausländisch, Auslands-;** *foreign cars have flooded our market; we are increasing our trade with foreign countries;* **foreign currency** = money of another country **Fremdwährung; Devisen; foreign goods** = goods produced in other countries **Auslandsprodukte; foreign investments** = money invested in other countries **Auslandsinvestitionen; foreign trade** = trade with other countries **Außenhandel**

◊ **foreign exchange** *noun* exchanging the money of one country for that of another **Geldwechsel; foreign exchange broker** *or* **dealer** = person who deals on the foreign exchange market **Devisenhändler, Devisenmakler; foreign exchange dealing** = buying and selling foreign currencies **Devisenhandel; the foreign exchange markets** = market where people buy and sell foreign currencies **die Devisenmärkte; foreign exchange reserves** = foreign money held by a government to support its own currency and pay its debts **Devisenreserven; foreign exchange transfer** = sending of money from one country to another **Devisentransfer**

◊ **foreigner** *noun* person from another country **Ausländer/-in**

◊ **Foreign (and Commonwealth) Office** *noun* British government department dealing with relations with other countries **Außenministerium**

◊ **Foreign Secretary** *noun* British government minister in charge of relations with other countries **Außenminister**

COMMENT: in most countries, the government department dealing with other countries is called the Foreign Ministry, with the Foreign Minister in charge. In the UK, these are the Foreign Office and Foreign Secretary; in the USA, they are the State Department and the Secretary of State

foreman of the jury *noun* person elected by the other jurors, who chairs the meetings of a jury, and pronounces the verdict in court afterwards **Obmann, Sprecher**

forensic *adjective* referring to courts *or* the law *or* pleading a case *or* punishing crime **forensisch; forensic medicine** = medical science concerned with solving crimes against people (such as autopsies of murdered people, taking blood samples from clothes) **Gerichtsmedizin; forensic science** = science used in solving legal problems and criminal cases **Kriminalistik**

foresee *verb* to imagine (correctly) what is going to happen in the future **voraussehen, vorhersehen;** *he did not foresee that his letter could be taken as a threat; the closure of the company was not foreseen by the staff*
NOTE: **foreseeing - foresaw - has foreseen**

◊ **foreseeability** *noun* ability of something to be foreseen **Voraussehbarkeit; foreseeability test** = test for calculating liability on the part of a person who should have foreseen the consequences of his action, especially in cases of negligence **Prüfung, ob Fahrlässigkeit vorliegt**

◊ **foresight** *noun* seeing what effects an action will have in the future **Weitblick**

forfeit
1 *noun* taking something away as a punishment **Verfall, Verwirkung; forfeit clause** = clause in a contract which says that goods *or* a deposit will be taken away if the contract is not obeyed **Verfalls-, Verwirkungsklausel; the goods were declared forfeit** = the court said that the goods had to be taken away from their owner **die Waren wurden für verlustig erklärt**
2 *verb* to have something taken away as a punishment **konfiszieren; verwirken; to forfeit a deposit** = to lose a deposit which was left for an item because you have decided not to buy that item **eine Anzahlung verwirken/einbüßen**

◊ **forfeiture** *noun* act of forfeiting a property *or* a right **Konfiskation; Verwirkung; forfeiture of shares** = losing the right to shares which a shareholder has not claimed **Forfaitierung von Aktien**

forge *verb* to copy money *or* a signature illegally *or* to make a document which looks like a real one **fälschen;** *he tried to enter the country with forged documents; she wanted to pay the bill with a forged £10 note*

◊ **forgery** *noun*
(a) crime of making an illegal copy of a document *or* recording *or* banknote to use as if it were a real one **Fälschen; Fälschung;** *he was sent to prison for forgery*
(b) illegal copy **Fälschung;** *the signature was proved to be a forgery*
NOTE: no plural for (a)

forget *verb* not to remember **vergessen;** *she forgot to put a stamp on the envelope; don't forget we're having lunch together tomorrow; he forgot to come to the hearing*
NOTE: **forgetting - forgot - forgotten**

fori *see* LEX FORI

form
1 *noun*
(a) form of words = words correctly laid out for a legal document **Form; Formulierung; receipt in due form** = correctly written receipt **ordnungsgemäße Quittung/Rechnung**
(b) official printed paper with blank spaces which have to be filled in with information **Formular, Formblatt, Vordruck;** *you have to fill in form A20; customs declaration form; a pad of order forms;* **application form** = form which has to be filled in to apply for something **Bewerbungsformular; Antragsformular; claim form** = form which has to be filled in when making an insurance claim **Schadensformular**
2 *verb* to start *or* to organize **gründen;** *the brothers have formed a new company*
◊ **formation** *or* **forming** *noun* act of organizing **Gründung;** *the formation of a new company*

forma *see* PRO FORMA

formal *adjective* clearly and legally written **formell; förmlich; offiziell;** *to make a formal application; to send a formal order*
◊ **formality** *noun* procedure *or* thing which has to be done to obey the law or because it is the custom **Formalität;** *the chairman dispensed with the formality of reading the minutes;* **customs formalities** = declaration of goods by the shipper and examination of them by the customs **Zollformalitäten**

◊ **formally** *adverb* in a formal way **förmlich, formell;** *we have formally applied for planning permission for the new shopping precinct*

formulate *verb* to put down *or* state clearly **formulieren**

forthwith *adverb* immediately **umgehend**

fortiori *see* A FORTIORI

forum *noun* court *or* place where matters are discussed **Gerichtsstand; Forum;** *the magistrates' court is not the appropriate forum for this application*

forward
1 *adjective* in advance *or* to be paid at a later date **im voraus, Voraus-; forward buying** *or* **buying forward** = buying shares *or* currency *or* commodities at today's price for delivery at a later date **Terminkauf; forward contract** = agreement to buy foreign currency *or* shares *or* commodities at a later date at a certain price **Abschluß auf Termin; forward market** = market for purchasing foreign currency *or* oil *or* commodities for delivery at a later date **Terminmarkt; forward (exchange) rate** = rate for purchase of foreign currency at a fixed price for delivery at a later date **Devisenterminkurs; forward sales** = sales for delivery at a later date **Terminverkäufe**
2 *adverb*
(a) to date an invoice forward = to put a later date than the present one on an invoice **eine Rechnung vordatieren; carriage forward** *or* **freight forward** = deal where the customer pays for shipping the goods **Frachtnachnahme; charges forward** = charges which will be paid by the customer **Gebühr bezahlt Empfänger**
(b) to buy forward = to buy foreign currency *or* gold *or* commodities before you need them, in order to be certain of the exchange rate **auf Termin kaufen/am Terminmarkt kaufen; to sell forward** = to sell foreign currency *or* gold *or* commodities for delivery at a later date **auf Termin verkaufen**
(c) balance brought forward *or* **carried forward** = balance which is entered in an account at the end of a period *or* page and is then taken to be the starting point of the next period *or* page **Saldovortrag**
3 *verb* **to forward something to someone** = to send something to someone **jdm etwas nachschicken; please forward** *or* **to be forwarded** = words written on an envelope, asking the person receiving it to send it on to the person whose name is written on it **bitte nachsenden**

foster *verb* to look after and bring up (a child who is not your own) **in Pflege nehmen; foster child** = child brought up by people who are not its own parents **Pflegekind; foster home** = home where a foster child is brought up **Pflegeheim; foster mother** *or* **foster father** *or* **fosterparents** = woman *or* man who looks after a child and brings it up **Pflegemutter; Pflegevater; Pflegeeltern**

foul *adjective* **foul bill of lading** = bill of lading which says that the goods were in bad condition when received by the shipper **unreines Konnossement**

founder *noun* person who starts a company **Gründer/-in; founder's shares** = shares issued to the founder of a company, which carry special rights **Gründeraktien**

fours *see* ALL

frais *see* SANS FRAIS

frame *verb* (*informal*) to arrange for someone to appear to be guilty **in eine Falle locken, eine Falle stellen; he has been framed** = he is innocent, but the situation has been arranged in such a way that he appears guilty **er wurde reingelegt**

franchise
1 *noun*
(a) right granted to someone to do something, especially the right to vote in local *or* general elections **Vorrecht; Wahlrecht; universal franchise** = right to vote which is given to all adult members of the population **allgemeines Wahlrecht**
(b) licence to trade using a brand name and paying a royalty for it **Franchise; he has bought a printing franchise** *or* **a hot dog franchise** NOTE: no plural for (a)
2 *verb* to sell licences for people to trade using a brand name and paying a royalty **auf Franchise-Basis vergeben;** *his sandwich bar was so successful that he decided to franchise it*

◊ **franchisee** *noun* person who runs a franchise **Franchisenehmer**

◊ **franchiser** *noun* person who licenses a franchise **Franchisegeber**

◊ **franchising** *noun* act of selling a licence to trade as a franchise **Franchising;** *he runs his sandwich chain as a franchising operation*
NOTE: no plural

◊ **franchisor** *noun* = FRANCHISER

franco *adverb* free **franko; portofrei**

frank *verb* to stamp the date and postage on a letter **frankieren; franking machine** = machine which marks the date and postage on letters so that the person sending them does not need to use stamps **Frankiermaschine**

fraud *noun*
(a) harming someone (by obtaining property *or* money from him) after making him believe something which is not true **Betrug;** *he got possession of the property by fraud; he was accused of frauds relating to foreign currency;* **to obtain money by fraud** = to obtain money by saying or doing something to cheat someone **auf betrügerische Weise Geld erlangen; Fraud Squad** = special police department which investigates frauds **Betrugsdezernat**
(b) act of deceiving someone in order to make money **Betrügereien;** *he was convicted of a series of frauds against insurance companies;* **computer fraud** = fraud committed by using computer files (as in a bank) **Computerbetrug**

COMMENT: frauds are divided into fraud by a director and other fraud

◊ **fraudulent** *adjective* not honest *or* aiming to cheat people **betrügerisch; fraudulent conveyance** = putting a property into someone else's possession to avoid it being seized to pay creditors **Vermögensveräußerung (zur Vollstreckungsvereitelung); fraudulent misrepresentation** = false statement made to trick someone *or* to persuade someone to enter into a contract **arglistige Täuschung; fraudulent preference** = payment made by an insolvent company to a particular creditor in preference to other creditors **Gläubigerbegünstigung; fraudulent trading** = carrying on the business of a company, knowing that the company is insolvent **betrügerisches Geschäftsgebaren**

◊ **fraudulently** *adverb* not honestly **auf betrügerische Weise;** *goods imported fraudulently*

free
1 *adjective & adverb*
(a) not costing any money **kostenlos, gratis; Frei-;** *he was given a free ticket to the exhibition; the price includes free delivery; goods are delivered free; price list sent free on request;* **free gift** = present given by a shop to a customer who buys a certain amount of goods **Werbegeschenk; free sample** = sample given free to advertise a product **Gratisprobe; free trial** = testing of a machine with no payment involved **kostenlos zur Probe;** *to send a piece of equipment for two weeks' free trial;* **free of**

charge = with no payment to be made **kostenlos; free on board (f.o.b.)** = (i) international contract whereby the seller promises to deliver goods on board ship and notify the buyer of delivery, and the buyer arranges freight, pays the shipping cost and takes the risk once the goods have passed onto the ship; (ii); *US* contract for sale whereby the price includes all the seller's costs until the goods are delivered to a certain place **(i) Frei an Bord, f.o.b. (ii) f.o.b. inkl. Fracht**

(b) not in prison **frei, auf freiem Fuß; to set someone free** = to let someone leave prison **jdn befreien; jdn freilassen;** *the crowd attacked the police station and set the three prisoners free*

(c) with no restrictions **frei; free circulation of goods** = movement of goods from one country to another without import quotas or other restrictions **freier Warenverkehr; free collective bargaining** = negotiations over wages and working conditions between the management and the workers' representatives without government interference **autonome Tarifverhandlungen; free competition** = being free to compete without government interference **freier Wettbewerb; free currency** = currency which is allowed by the government to be bought and sold without restriction **frei konvertierbare Währung; free enterprise** = system of business with no interference from the government **freies Unternehmertum; free market economy** = system where the government does not interfere in business activity in any way **freie Marktwirtschaft; free movement of capital** = ability to transfer capital from one EC country to another **freier Kapitalverkehr; free port** *or* **free trade zone** = port *or* area where there are no customs duties **Freihafen; Freihandelszone; free of tax** *or* **tax-free** = with no tax having to be paid **steuerfrei; interest-free credit** *or* **loan** = credit *or* loan where no interest is paid by the borrower **zinsloses Darlehen; free of duty** *or* **duty-free** = with no duty to be paid **zollfrei; free trade** = system where goods can go from one country to another without any restrictions **Freihandel; free trade area** = group of countries practising free trade **Freihandelszone**

(d) not busy *or* not occupied **frei; unbesetzt;** *are there any tables free in the restaurant? the solicitor will be free in a few minutes; the hearing was delayed because there was no courtroom free*

2 *verb* to release someone from prison **freilassen;** *the new president freed all political prisoners*

◊ **freelance** *adjective & adverb, noun, verb* independent worker who works for several different companies without being employed by any of them **freiberuflich; freier Mitarbeiter; freiberuflich tätig sein;** *she is a freelance reporter for the local newspaper; he works freelance as an advertising agent*

◊ **freely** *adverb* with no restrictions **frei;** *money should circulate freely within the Common Market*

◊ **free pardon** *noun* pardon given to a convicted person where both the sentence and conviction are recorded as void **unbeschränkte Begnadigung**

freedom *noun*
(a) being free *or* not being held in custody **Freiheit;** *the president gave the accused man his freedom*
(b) being free to do something without restriction **Freiheit; freedom of association** = being able to join together in a group with other people without being afraid of prosecution, provided that you do not break the law **Vereinsfreiheit; Koalitionsfreiheit; freedom of assembly** *or* **of meeting** = being able to meet as a group without being afraid of prosecution, provided that you do not break the law **Versammlungsfreiheit; freedom of the press** = being able to write and publish in a newspaper what you wish without being afraid of prosecution, provided that you do not break the law **Pressefreiheit; freedom of speech** = being able to say what you want without being afraid of prosecution, provided that you do not break the law **Redefreiheit**

freehold *noun* absolute right to hold land *or* property for an unlimited time without paying rent **unbeschränkter/uneingeschränkter Besitz; freehold property** = property which the owner holds in freehold **unbeschränkter Grundbesitz**

◊ **freeholder** *noun* person who holds a freehold property **Grundeigentümer/-in**

freeze *verb* to order a person not to move money *or* not to sell assets **einfrieren, sperren, blockieren;** *the court ordered the company's bank account to be frozen;* **frozen assets** = assets of a company which cannot be sold because a person has a claim against them **eingefrorene Vermögenswerte**

freight *noun* cargo *or* goods which are carried by land *or* sea *or* air **Fracht; freight charges** *or* **freight rates** = money charged for carrying goods **Frachtkosten**

French *noun* language spoken in France **französisch**

COMMENT: French was used in England together with Latin as the language of the law courts for some centuries after the conquest by King William I. It still survives in some legal words and phrases, such as chose, tort, oyez, puisne, autrefois convict, feme covert

fresh pursuit *noun* chasing a thief, etc., to get back what he has stolen **sofortige Verfolgung**

friendly society *noun* group of people who pay regular contributions which are used to help members of the group when they retire, are ill or in financial difficulty **Versicherungsverein auf Gegenseitigkeit**

frisk *verb* to search someone by passing your hands over his clothes to see if he is carrying a weapon *or* a package **durchsuchen**

frivolous *adjective* **frivolous complaint** *or* **frivolous action** = complaint *or* action which is not brought for a serious reason **leichtfertig erhobene Beschwerde; leichtfertige erhobene Klage**

frolic *noun* **frolic of his own** = situation where an employee does damage outside the normal course of his employment, and for which his employer cannot be held responsible **zum eigenen Vergnügen**

frozen *see* FREEZE

frustrate *verb* to prevent something (especially the terms of a contract) being fulfilled **vereiteln**
◊ **frustration** *noun* situation where the terms of a contract cannot possibly be fulfilled (as where the contract requires the use of something which then is destroyed) **Vereitelung**

fugitive *noun* (person) who is running away from justice **Flüchtiger** *adjective* running away from justice **flüchtig; fugitive offender** = person running away from the police who, if he is caught, is sent back to the place where the offence was committed **flüchtiger Straftäter**

fulfil *verb* to do everything which is promised in a contract **erfüllen;** *the company has fulfilled all the terms of the agreement*

full *adjective*
(a) with as much inside it as possible **voll;** *prisoners have to share cells because the*

prisons are too full; the court has to deal with a full list of cases
(b) complete *or* including everything **voll; we are working at full capacity** = we are doing as much work as possible **wir arbeiten unter voller Kapazitätsausnutzung; full costs** = all the costs of manufacturing a product, including both fixed and variable costs **Vollkosten; full cover** = insurance cover against all types of risk **voller Versicherungsschutz; in full discharge of a debt** = paying a debt completely *or* paying less than the total amount owed by agreement **völlige Schuldentilgung;** *the plaintiff accepted £500 in full and final settlement of his claim for £600, to avoid going to court;* **full title** = complete title of an Act of Parliament **Haupttitel; full trial** = properly organized trial according to the correct procedure **Hauptverfahren**
(c) **in full** = completely **voll, ganz, vollständig;** *give your full name and address or your name and address in full; he accepted all our conditions in full; full refund or refund paid in full; he got a full refund when he complained about the service; the clerk read out the charges in full;* **full payment** *or* **payment in full** = paying all money owed **Zahlung in voller Höhe**
◊ **fully** *adverb* completely **voll, ganz, vollständig; fully paid-up shares** = shares where the full face value has been paid **voll bezahlte Aktien; fully paid-up capital** = all money paid for the issued capital shares **voll einbezahltes Kapital**

function
1 *noun* duty *or* job **Funktion, Aufgabe; a management function** = one part of the duties of management, such as sales *or* financial planning **eine der Aufgaben der Betriebsleitung; the function of management** = the duties of being a manager **die Aufgaben der Manager**
2 *verb* to work **funktionieren;** *the advertising campaign is functioning smoothly; the new management does not seem to be functioning very well*

functus officio *Latin phrase meaning* "no longer having power *or* jurisdiction" (because the power has been exercised) **seines Amtes entbunden;** *the justices' clerk asserted that the justices were functi officio*
NOTE: plural is **functi officio**

fundamental *adjective* basic *or* essential **fundamental, grundlegend; wesentlich; fundamental breach** = breach of an essential *or* basic term of a contract by one party, entitling the other party to treat the contract as terminated **(zum Vertragsrücktritt berechtigender) schwerer Vertragsbruch**

fund *noun*
(a) amount of money collected for a special purpose **Fonds, zweckgebundene Mittel; pension fund** = money which provides pensions for retired members of staff **Rentenfonds**
(b) funds = money available for a purpose **Mittel, Gelder; conversion of funds** = using money which does not belong to you for a purpose for which it is not supposed to be used **Veruntreuung von Geldern; to convert funds to one's own use** = to use someone else's money for yourself **Gelder veruntreuen**

fungible goods *or* **fungibles** *plural noun* goods (such as seeds *or* coins) which are measured by weight *or* counted **vertretbare Sachen**

furandi *see* ANIMUS

furnish *verb*
(a) to supply *or* to provide **beliefern, versorgen;** *he was asked to furnish the court with proof of his identity*
(b) to put furniture into an office *or* room **möblieren;** *he furnished his office with secondhand chairs and desks; the company spent £10,000 on furnishing the chairman's office;* **furnished accommodation** = flat, house, etc., which is let with furniture in it **möblierte Unterkunft**

future
1 *adjective* referring to time to come *or* to something which has not yet happened **zukünftig; future delivery** = delivery at a later date **Terminlieferung; future estate** = old term for the possession and enjoyment of an estate at some time in the future **zukünftiges Vermögen**
2 *noun* time which has not yet happened **Zukunft;** *try to be more careful in future; in future all reports must be sent to Australia by air*

◊ **futures** *plural noun* trading in shares *or* currencies *or* commodities for delivery at a later date **Termingeschäfte**

the fuzz *noun (slang)* the police **die Bullen**

Gg

gain
1 *noun*
(a) increase *or* becoming larger **Zuwachs,** Zunahme; **gain in experience** = act of getting more experience **Gewinn an Erfahrung**
(b) increase in profit *or* price *or* value **Gewinn, Profit; Anstieg; to deal in stolen goods for gain** = to buy and sell stolen goods to make a profit **des Profits wegen hehlen; capital gains** = money made by selling a fixed asset *or* by selling shares at a profit **Veräußerungsgewinne; capital gains tax** = tax paid on capital gains **Veräußerungsgewinnsteuer**
2 *verb* to get *or* to obtain **erwerben, erlangen;** *he gained some useful experience working in a bank;* **to gain control of a business** = to buy more than 50% of the shares so that you can direct the business **die Aktienmehrheit an einem Unternehmen erlangen**

◊ **gainful** *adjective* **gainful employment** = employment which pays money **Erwerbstätigkeit**

◊ **gainfully** *adverb* **he is not gainfully employed** = he has no regular paid work **er ist nicht erwerbstätig**

gallows *plural noun* wooden support from which criminals are executed by hanging **Galgen**

game *noun*
(a) birds and animals which are hunted, especially for food **Wild; game licence** = official permit which allows someone to shoot game **Jagdschein**
(b) game of chance = game (such as roulette) where the result depends on luck **Glücksspiel**
NOTE: no plural for (a)

◊ **gaming** *noun* playing games of chance for money **Spielen (um Geld); gaming licence** = official permit which allows someone *or* a club to organize games of chance **Erlaubnis zum Betrieb von Glücksspielen**

gang *noun* group of criminals working together **Bande;** *a drugs gang; a gang of jewel thieves*

◊ **gangland** *noun* all gangs considered as a group **die Unterwelt; a gangland murder** = murder of a gangster by another gangster **Mord in der Unterwelt**

◊ **gangster** *noun* person who is a member of a gang of criminals **Gangster, Verbrecher;** *the police shot six gangsters in the bank raid*

gaol
1 *noun (GB)* prison **Gefängnis**
2 *verb (GB)* to put someone in prison **jdn inhaftieren**

◊ **gaoler** *noun (GB)* person who works in a prison *or* who is in charge of a prison

Gefängniswärter; **Leiter der Haftanstalt;** *for examples see* JAIL, JAILER

garnish *verb* to warn (a debtor) to pay his debts, not to the creditor, but to a creditor of the creditor who has a judgment **einem Drittschuldner einen Pfändungsbeschluß zukommen lassen**

◊ **garnishee** *noun* person who owes money to a creditor and is ordered by a court to pay that money to a creditor of the creditor, and not to the creditor himself **Drittschuldner; garnishee order** = court order, making a garnishee pay money to a judgment creditor **Pfändungs- (und Überweisungs)beschluß**

gas chamber *noun* room in which a convicted prisoner is executed by poisonous gas **Gaskammer**

COMMENT: used in some states in the USA

gather *verb*
(a) to collect together *or* to put together **zusammenpacken, (zusammmen)sammeln;** *he gathered his papers together before the meeting started; she has been gathering information on import controls from various sources*
(b) to understand *or* to find out **schließen, folgern; entnehmen;** *I gather he has left the office; did you gather who will be at the meeting?*

GATT = GENERAL AGREEMENT ON TARIFFS AND TRADE

gazump *verb* he was gazumped = his agreement to buy the house was cancelled because someone offered more money before exchange of contracts **entgegen mündlicher Zusage, wurde das Haus, das er kaufen wollte, an einen Höherbietenden verkauft**

◊ **gazumping** *noun (of a buyer)* offering more money for a house than another buyer has done, so as to be sure of buying it **das akzeptierte Angebot eines Käufers für ein Haus überbieten;** *(of a seller)* removing the house from a sale which has been agreed, so as to accept a higher offer **vom Verkauf eines Hauses zugunsten eines höheren Angebotes zurücktreten**

GBH = GRIEVOUS BODILY HARM

general *adjective*
(a) ordinary *or* not special **allgemein, generell; general expenses** = all kinds of minor expenses *or* money spent on the day-to-day costs of running a business

allgemeine Unkosten; **general manager** = manager in charge of the administration of a company **geschäftsführender Direktor;** *(US)* **Generaldirektor; general office** = main administrative office of a company **Zentrale**
(b) dealing with everything *or* with everybody **allgemein; general audit** = examining all the books and accounts of a company **ordentliche Buchprüfung; general average** = sharing of the cost of lost goods between all parties to an insurance **große Havarie; general damages** = damages awarded by a court to compensate for an unquantifiable loss (such as an injury) **allgemeiner Schadensersatz; general election** = election of a parliament by all the voters in a country **Bundestagswahlen;** *(GB)* **Parlamentswahlen; general lien** = holding goods or property until a debt has been paid **allgemeines Zurückbehaltungsrecht, Pfandrecht;** *compare also* PARTICULAR AVERAGE, PARTICULAR LIEN; **general meeting** = meeting of all the shareholders of a company **ordentliche Hauptversammlung; general strike** = strike of all the workers in a country **Generalstreik; Annual General Meeting (AGM)** = meeting of all the shareholders *or* all the members of a club, which takes place once a year to approve the accounts **ordentliche Jahreshauptversammlung; Extraordinary General Meeting (EGM)** = special meeting of shareholders *or* members of a club to discuss an important matter which cannot wait until the next Annual General Meeting **außerordentliche Hauptversammlung**
(c) the **General Agreement on Tariffs and Trade (GATT)** = international treaty which aims to try to reduce restrictions in trade between countries **Allgemeines Zoll- und Handelsabkommen**

◊ **generally** *adverb* normally *or* usually **im allgemeinen;** *the office is generally closed between Christmas and the New Year; political crimes are generally dealt with more harshly in the military courts*

generation *noun* all people born at about the same time; members of the same family born at about the same time **Generation; the jewels have been in our family for several generations** = the family has owned the jewels for many years **der Schmuck ist seit mehreren Generationen im Besitz unserer Familie; generation gap** = age difference between one generation and another, usually making it difficult for them to understand each other **Generationskonflikt**

generous *adjective* (person) who is glad to give money **großzügig;** *the staff contributed a generous sum for the retirement present for the manager*

Geneva Convention(s) *noun* international treaties governing behaviour of countries at war **Genfer Konventionen**; *the attacking army was accused of violating the Geneva Convention*

genocide *noun* killing of a whole race *or* religious group **Völkermord, Genozid**
NOTE: no plural

gentleman *noun*
(a) "gentlemen" = (i) way of starting to talk to a group of men **"Meine Herren"** (ii); *US* way of starting a letter to a firm **"Sehr geehrte Herren"**; "ladies and gentlemen" = way of starting to talk to a group of women and men **"Meine (sehr geehrten) Damen und Herren"**
(b) man **Gentleman; gentleman's agreement** *or US* **gentlemen's agreement** = verbal agreement between two parties who trust each other (not usually enforceable by law) **Gentleman's Agreement, Vereinbarung auf Treu und Glauben**

genuine *adjective* true *or* real **echt**; *this old table is genuine; a genuine leather purse;* **the genuine article** = real article, not an imitation **Markenartikel; genuine purchaser** = someone who is really interested in buying **ernsthafter Käufer**

◊ **genuineness** *noun* being real *or* not being an imitation **Echtheit**

get *verb*
(a) to receive **bekommen, erhalten**; *we got a letter from the solicitor this morning; he got a £25 fine or a parking ticket*
(b) to arrive at a place **ankommen**; *the shipment got to Canada six weeks late; she finally got to the courtroom at 10.30*
NOTE: **getting - got - has got** *or US*

◊ **get back** *verb* to receive something which you had had before **zurückbekommen**; *I got my money back after I had complained to the manager; he got his initial investment back in two months*

◊ **get off** *verb* not to be punished **davonkommen**; *the boys got off with a reprimand from the magistrate*

◊ **get on** *verb*
(a) to work *or* to manage **zurechtkommen**; *how is the new secretary getting on?*
(b) to succeed **Fortschritte machen, sich machen**; *my son is getting on well - he has just been promoted*

◊ **get on with** *verb*
(a) to be friendly *or* to work well with someone **auskommen mit, sich verstehen mit**; *she does not get on with her new boss*

(b) to go on doing work **vorankommen mit; weitermachen mit**; *the staff got on with the work and finished the order on time*

◊ **get out** *verb*
(a) to produce something (on time) **herausbringen; vorlegen**; *the Royal Commission got out the report in time for the meeting*
(b) to sell an investment **aussteigen**; *he didn't like the annual report, so he got out before the company became insolvent*

◊ **get round** *verb* to avoid **umgehen**; *we tried to get round the embargo by shipping from Canada; can you advise me how we can get round the quota system?*

get *or* **gett** *noun* divorce according to Jewish religious custom **Get; Scheidung (nach jüdischem Ritus)**

gift
1 *noun* thing given to someone **Geschenk; gift inter vivos** = present given by a living person to another living person **Schenkung zu Lebzeiten; free gift** = present given by a shop to a customer who buys a certain amount of goods **Werbegeschenk**

| COMMENT: a gift is irrevocable |

2 *verb* to give **schenken**

gilt-edged securities *or* **gilts** *plural noun* British government securities (assumed to be a safe investment) **mündelsichere Staatspapiere**

give *verb*
(a) to pass something to someone as a gift **schenken; überreichen**; *the office gave him a clock when he retired*
(b) to pass something to someone **geben**; *she gave the documents to the accountant; can you give me some information about the new computer system? do not give any details to the police*
(c) to organize **geben; veranstalten**; *the company gave a party after they won their appeal*
NOTE: **giving - gave - given**

◊ **give away** *verb* to give something as a free present **vergeben, verschenken**; *we are giving away a pocket calculator with each £10 of purchases*

◊ **giveaway**
1 *adjective* **to sell at giveaway prices** = to sell at very cheap prices **zu Schleuderpreisen verkaufen**
2 *noun* thing which is given as a free gift when another item is bought **Werbegeschenk**

◊ **give rise to** *verb* to be the cause of something **hervorrufen; Anlaß geben zu;** *the* *decision has given rise to complaints from the family of the defendant*

gloss *noun* interpretation *or* meaning given to a word or phrase **Erläuterung**

go *verb*
(a) to move from one place to another **gehen;** *the cheque went to your bank yesterday; the plane goes to Frankfurt, then to Rome; he is going to our Lagos office*
(b) to be placed **hingehören;** *the date goes at the top of the letter*
NOTE: going - went - has gone

◊ **go back on** *verb* not to do what has been promised **zurücknehmen; rückgängig machen;** *two months later they went back on the agreement*

◊ **going concern** *noun* business which is actively trading **dynamisches, rentables Unternehmen**

◊ **going equipped for stealing** *noun* notifiable offence of carrying tools which could be used for burglary **für einen Diebstahl ausgerüstet sein;** *(kein Straftatbestand in der BRD)*

◊ **go into** *verb*
(a) to go into business = to start in business **ins Geschäftsleben eintreten;** *he went into business selling cars; she went into business in partnership with her son*
(b) to examine carefully **überprüfen, untersuchen;** *the bank wants to go into the details of the intercompany loans; the fraud squad is going into the facts behind the property deals*

◊ **go on** *verb*
(a) to continue **weitermachen, weiter-;** *the staff went on working in spite of the fire; the chairman went on speaking for two hours*
(b) to work with **sich stützen auf;** *two fingerprints are all the police have to go on*

◊ **go to law** *verb* to start legal proceedings about something **vor Gericht gehen, klagen;** *we went to law to try to regain our property*

godfather *noun (slang)* Mafia boss **Pate**

good *adjective*
(a) not bad **gut; a good buy** = excellent item which has been bought cheaply **ein guter Kauf**
(b) a good deal of = a large quantity of **viel, eine Menge;** *we wasted a good deal of time discussing the arrangements for the AGM; the company had to pay a good deal of money for the building;* **a good many** = very many **ziemlich viele;** *a good many staff members have joined the union*

◊ **good behaviour** *noun* behaving well *or* acting in a peaceful and lawful way **gute Führung;** *the magistrates bound him over to be of good behaviour; she was sentenced to four years in prison, but was released early for good behaviour*
NOTE: no plural

◊ **good cause** *noun* reason which is accepted in law **hinreichender Grund;** *the court asked the accused to show good cause why he should not be sent to prison*
NOTE: not used with **the**

◊ **good consideration** *noun* proper consideration **reifliche Überlegung**

◊ **good faith** *noun* general honesty **Redlichkeit; in good faith** = in an honest way **in gutem Glauben; redlich, ehrlich; he acted in good faith** = he did it honestly **in guter Absicht handeln; to buy something in good faith** = to buy something honestly *or* in the course of an honest transaction **etwas in gutem Glauben kaufen;** *he bought the car in good faith, not knowing that it had been stolen*

◊ **goods** *plural noun*
(a) goods and chattels = moveable personal possessions **bewegliches Eigentum, Mobiliar; household goods** = items which are used in the home **Haushaltsartikel**
(b) items which can be moved and are for sale **Waren, Güter; goods (held) in bond** = imported goods held by the customs until duty is paid **Waren unter Zollverschluß; capital goods** = machinery, buildings and raw materials which are used to make other goods **Anlagegüter; consumer goods** = goods bought by the general public and not by businesses **Konsum-, Verbrauchsgüter; goods train** = train for carrying freight **Güterzug**

◊ **good title** *noun* title to a property which gives the owner full rights of ownership **einwandfreier Rechtstitel; unbestrittenes Eigentum**

◊ **goodwill** *noun* good reputation of a business and its contacts with its customers (such as the name of the product which it sells *or* its popular appeal to customers) **Firmenansehen; Goodwill;** *he paid £10,000 for the goodwill of the shop and £4,000 for the stock*

govern *verb*
(a) to rule a country **regieren;** *the country is governed by a group of military leaders*
(b) to rule *or* to be in authority **bestimmen, beeinflussen;** *the amount of damages is governed by the seriousness of the injuries suffered*

◊ **government** *noun*
(a) organization which administers a country **Regierung; central government** = main organization dealing with the affairs of the whole country **Zentralregierung; local government** = organizations dealing with the affairs of a small area of the country **örtliche Verwaltung**

(b) coming from the government *or* referring to the government **staatlich; Staats-, Regierungs-;** *government intervention or intervention by the government; a government ban on the import of arms; a government investigation into organized crime; government officials prevented him leaving the country; government policy is outlined in the book; government regulations state that import duty has to be paid on expensive items;* **government contractor** = company which supplies goods or services to the government on contract **Betrieb mit Staatsaufträgen**

◇ **governmental** *adjective* referring to a government **staatlich, Staats-, Regierungs-**

◇ **governor** *noun* (i) person in charge of a prison; (ii) person representing the government as the official in charge of a colony **(i) Direktor; (ii) Gouverneur;** *a prison governor; the prisoners applied to the governor for parole*

gown *noun* long black item of clothing worn by a lawyer *or* judge, etc., over normal clothes when appearing in court **Robe; Talar** *see also* SILK

grace *noun* favour shown by granting a delay **Aufschub, Nachfrist; to give a creditor a period of grace** *or* **two weeks' grace** = to allow a creditor two weeks to pay **einem Gläubiger zwei Wochen Zahlungsfrist gewähren**

graft *noun (informal)* corruption of officials **Bestechung**
NOTE: no plural

grand
1 *adjective* important **großartig, bedeutend; grand plan** = major plan **großer/wichtiger Plan; grand total** = final total made by adding several smaller totals **Gesamtsumme, Endbetrag**
2 *noun (informal)* one thousand pounds *or* dollars **tausend Pfund; tausend Dollar;** *they offered him fifty grand for the information*
NOTE: no plural

◇ **grand jury** *noun (US)* group of jurors (between twelve and twenty-four) who assemble as a preliminary to a trial to decide if an indictment should be issued to start criminal proceedings **Anklagejury (, die sich aus der Zeit ernannten Bürgern zusammensetzt und die die öffentliche Anklage ablehnt oder für recht befindet)**

◇ **grand larceny** *noun (US)* theft of goods valued at more than a certain price **schwerer Diebstahl**

grant
1 *noun*
(a) act of giving something to someone (permanently *or* temporarily) by a written document, where the object itself cannot be transferred **urkundliche Übertragung;** *he made a grant of land to his son;* **grant of letters of administration** = giving of documents to administrators to enable them to administer the estate of a dead person who has not made a will **Anordnung der Nachlaßverwaltung; grant of probate** = official document proving that a will is genuine, given to the executors so that they can act on the terms of the will **Erbschein;** *(GB)* **gerichtliche Testamentsbestätigung**
(b) money given by the government to help pay for something **Zuschuß; Beihilfe; Subvention;** *the institute has a government grant to cover the cost of the development programme; the local authority has allocated grants towards the costs of the scheme;* **grant-aided scheme** = scheme which is backed by funds from the government **bezuschußtes/subventioniertes Programm; death grant** = state grant to the family of a person who has died, which is supposed to contribute to the funeral expenses **Sterbegeld**
2 *verb* to agree to give someone something *or* to agree to allow someone to do something **gewähren, bewilligen;** *to grant someone permission to build a house or to leave the country; the local authority granted the company an interest-free loan to start up the new factory; he was granted parole; the government granted an amnesty to all political prisoners*

◇ **grantee** *noun* person who is assigned an interest in a property *or* who receives a grant **Begünstigter; Empfänger**

◇ **grantor** *noun* person who assigns an interest in a property (especially to a lender) *or* who makes a grant **Bewilligender; urkundlich Übertragender**

grass *(slang)*
1 *noun* criminal who gives information to the police about other criminals **Spitzel, Informant/-in;** *see also* SUPERGRASS
2 *verb* **to grass on someone** = to give information to the police about someone **jdn verpfeifen**

grata *see* PERSONA

gratia *see* EX GRATIA

gratis *adverb* free *or* not costing anything *or* without paying anything **gratis, umsonst;** *we got into the exhibition gratis*

gratuitous *adjective* free *or* with no money being offered **gratis, unentgeltlich; gratuitous promise** = promise which cannot be enforced because no money has been involved **(unentgeltliches) Versprechen ohne Verpflichtung**

gratuity *noun* tip *or* money given to someone who has helped you **Geldgeschenk;** *the staff are instructed not to accept gratuities*

Gray's Inn *noun* one of the four Inns of Court in London **einer der Inns of Court (Barristerinnung in London)**

great *adjective* large **groß; a great deal of** = very much **sehr viel;** *he made a great deal of money on the Stock Exchange; there is a great deal of work to be done before the company can be made really profitable*

◊ **Great Seal** *noun* seal, kept by the Lord Chancellor, used for sealing important public documents on behalf of the Queen **Staatssiegel**

Green Book *noun* the County Court Rules (book of procedural rules of county courts) **Prozeßordnung der County Courts**

green card *noun*
(a) special British insurance certificate to prove that a car is insured for travel abroad **grüne Versicherungskarte**
(b) work permit for a person going to live in the USA **Arbeitserlaubnis**

green form *noun* form for giving free or subsidized legal advice to clients who are eligible for Legal Aid **Beratungshilfeformular; Prozeßkostenhilfeformular; the green form scheme** = scheme where a solicitor will give advice to someone free of charge or at a subsidized rate, if the client has filled in the green form **Beratungshilfe; Prozeßkostenhilfe**

Green Paper *noun* report from the British government on proposals for a new law to be discussed in Parliament; *entspricht* **Enquetekommissionsbericht**

grievance *noun* complaint made by a trade union *or* an employee to the management **Beschwerde; Klage; grievance procedure** = agreed way of presenting complaints from a trade union *or* an employee to the management of a company **Beschwerdeverfahren (bei Arbeitsstreitigkeiten)**

grievous bodily harm (GBH) *noun* crime of causing serious injury to someone **schwere Körperverletzung**

gross *adjective*
(a) total *or* with no deductions **brutto, Brutto-; gross domestic product** = annual value of goods sold and services paid for inside a country **Bruttoinlandsprodukt; gross earnings** *or* **gross income** *or* **gross salary** = total earnings before tax and other deductions **Bruttoverdienst, Bruttoeinnahmen; gross margin** = percentage difference between sales income and the cost of sales **Bruttomarge; gross national product** = annual value of goods and services in a country including income from other countries **Bruttosozialprodukt; gross profit** = profit calculated as sales income less the cost of the goods sold **Brutto-, Rohgewinn; gross receipts** = total amount of money received before expenses are deducted **Brutto-, Roheinnahmen; gross weight** = weight of both the container and its contents **Brutto-, Rohgewicht**
(b) serious **schwer, grob; gross indecency** = crime entailing unlawful sexual contact between men or with a child **schwere Unzucht; gross negligence** = act showing very serious neglect of duty towards other people **grobe Fahrlässigkeit**

ground *noun*
(a) soil *or* earth **Boden; ground landlord** = person *or* company which owns the freehold of a property which is then leased and subleased **Grundeigentümer; ground lease** = first lease on a freehold building **Grundstückspacht; ground rent** = rent paid by a lessee to the ground landlord; *entspricht* **Erbpachtzins; Nutzungsentgelt**
(b) grounds = basic reasons **Grund;** *does he have good grounds for complaint? there are no grounds on which we can be sued; what are the grounds for the claim for damages?*
NOTE: (b) can be used in the singular if only one reason exists: **the judge refused the application on the ground that he had discretion to remove the hearsay evidence from the report**

group
1 *noun*
(a) several things *or* people together **Gruppe;** *a group of staff members has sent a memorandum to the chairman complaining about noise in the office*
(b) group several companies linked together in the same organization **Gruppe, Konzern;** *the group chairman or the chairman of the group; group turnover or turnover for the group;* **group results** = results of a group of companies taken together **Konzernergebnisse**

2 *verb* **to group together** = to put several items together **zusammenfassen;** *civil wrongs against persons and their property are grouped together under the heading "torts"*

guarantee
1 *noun*
(a) document handed to a buyer of goods which promises that a machine will work properly *or* that an item is of good quality **Garantie(schein);** *certificate of guarantee or guarantee certificate; the guarantee lasts for two years; the typewriter is sold with a two-year guarantee;* **the car is still under guarantee** = the car is still covered by the maker's certificate of guarantee **das Auto hat noch Garantie**

COMMENT: in English law, a guarantee must usually be in writing

(b) promise made by a person that he will do what someone else is obliged to do if that other person fails to do it **Garantie; Bürgschaft**
(c) thing given as a security **Sicherheit;** *to leave share certificates as a guarantee*

COMMENT: the person making a guarantee is secondarily liable if the person who is primarily liable defaults. Compare INDEMNITY

2 *verb* to give a promise that something will happen **garantieren; sich verbürgen; to guarantee a debt** = to promise that you will pay a debt incurred by someone else if that person fails to pay it **sich für eine Schuld verbürgen; to guarantee an associated company** = to promise that an associate company will pay its debts **sich für ein Partnerunternehmen verbürgen; to guarantee a bill of exchange** = to promise to pay a bill **eine Wechselbürgschaft leisten; the product is guaranteed for twelve months** = the maker states that the product will work well for twelve months, and promises to mend it free of charge if it breaks down within that period **die Ware hat zwölf Monate Garantie**

◇ **guarantor** *noun* person who gives a guarantee **Garant; Bürge/Bürgin; to stand guarantor for someone** = to promise to pay someone's debts **eine Bürgschaft für jdn leisten**

guard
1 *noun*
(a) person whose job is to protect people *or* property **Wachmann, Wächter;** *there were three guards on duty at the door of the bank or three bank guards were on duty; the prisoner was shot by the guards as he tried to escape;* **security guard** = person whose job is to protect money *or* valuables *or* buildings against theft **Wachmann, Wächter**
(b) state of being protected by a guard **Bewachung;** *the prisoners were brought into the courtroom under armed guard*
2 *verb* to protect someone *or* to prevent someone being harmed *or* to prevent someone escaping **schützen; beschützen; bewachen;** *the building is guarded by a fence and ten guard dogs; the prisoners are guarded night and day*

◇ **guardian** *noun* person appointed by law to act on behalf of someone (such as a child) who cannot act on his own behalf **Vormund; guardian ad litem** = person who acts on behalf of a minor who is a defendant in a court case **Prozeßpfleger;** *see also* NEXT FRIEND

◇ **guardianship** *noun* state of being a guardian **Vormundschaft; guardianship order** = court order appointing a local authority to be the guardian of a child **Vormundschaftsbeschluß**

guerilla *noun* armed person (not a regular soldier) who engages in unofficial war **Guerilla;** *the train was attacked by guerillas; the appeal was made by a guerilla radio station*

guidelines *plural noun* unofficial suggestions from the government or some other body as to how something should be done **Richtlinien;** *the government has issued guidelines on increases in wages and prices; the Law Society has issued guidelines to its members on dealing with rape cases; the Secretary of State can issue guidelines for expenditure; the Lord Justice said he was not laying down guidelines for sentencing*

guillotine
1 *noun*
(a) machine used in France for executing criminals by cutting off their heads **Guillotine, Fallbeil**
(b) motion in the House of Commons to end a debate at a certain time **Antrag auf Schluß der Debatte**
2 *verb* to execute someone by cutting his head off with a guillotine **mit der Guillotine/dem Fallbeil hinrichten**

guilt *noun* being guilty *or* state of having committed a crime or done some other legal wrong **Schuld; Strafbarkeit; guilt by association** = presumption that a person is guilty because of his connection with another guilty person **Strafbarkeit durch Verbindung zu einer schuldigen Person; he admitted his guilt** = he admitted that he had committed the crime **er war geständig**

NOTE: no plural

◊ **guilty** *adjective* (person) who has done something which is against the law **schuldig; strafbar;** *he was found guilty of libel; the company was guilty of evading the VAT regulations;* **guilty knowledge** = MENS REA *(of a judge or jury)* **to find someone guilty** *or* **to return a verdict of guilty** *or* **to return a guilty verdict** = to say at the end of the trial that the accused is guilty **jdn schuldig sprechen; einen Schuldspruch verkünden;** *(of an accused person)* **to plead guilty** *or* **not guilty** = to say at the beginning of a trial that you did *or* did not commit the crime of which you are accused **sich schuldig bekennen; sich nicht schuldig bekennen;** *the accused pleaded not guilty to the charge of murder, but pleaded guilty to the lesser charge of manslaughter*

gun *noun* weapon used for shooting **Schußwaffe;** *the police are not allowed to carry guns; they shouted to the robbers to drop their guns*

◊ **gun down** *verb* to kill someone with a gun **erschießen;** *he was gunned down in the street outside his office*
NOTE: gunned - gunning

◊ **gunman** *noun* man who carries and uses a gun **Bewaffneter;** *the security van was held up by three gunmen*

◊ **gunpoint** *noun* **at gunpoint** = with a gun pointing at you **mit vorgehaltener Schußwaffe;** *he was forced at gunpoint to open the safe*

◊ **gunshot** *noun* result of shooting with a gun **Schuß;** *he died of gunshot wounds*

Hh

habeas corpus *Latin phrase meaning* "may you have the body": legal remedy against being wrongly imprisoned **Habeaskorpusakte; writ of habeas corpus** = writ to obtain the release of someone who has been unlawfully held in prison or in police custody, or to make the person holding him bring him to court to explain why he is being held **Anordnung eines Haftprüfungstermins**

habendum *noun* section of a conveyance which gives details of how the property is to be assigned to the purchaser; *entspricht* **Auflassungsklausel; die das Eigentumsrecht des Käufers erläuternde Klausel einer Übertragungsurkunde**

habitual *adjective* (person) who does something frequently **gewohnheitsmäßig, Gewohnheits-; habitual criminal** *or* **habitual offender** = person who has been convicted of a similar crime at least twice before **Gewohnheitsverbrecher; habitual drunkard** = person who drinks alcohol so frequently that he is almost always dangerous or incapable **Gewohnheitstrinker; habitual residence** = (i) fact of living normally in a place; (ii) the place where someone normally lives **(i) gewöhnlicher Aufenthalt; (ii) gewöhnlicher Aufenthaltsort**

hallmark
1 *noun* mark put on gold *or* silver items to show that the metal is of the correct quality **Feingehaltsstempel**
2 *verb* to put a hallmark on a piece of gold *or* silver **mit einem Feingehaltsstempel versehen;** *a hallmarked spoon*

hand *noun*
(a) to shake hands = to hold someone's hand when meeting to show you are pleased to meet him *or* to show that an agreement has been reached **sich die Hand geben; to shake hands on a deal** = to shake hands to show that a deal has been agreed **einen Abschluß mit Handschlag besiegeln**
(b) by hand = using the hands, not a machine **von Hand, hand-; to send a letter by hand** = to ask someone to carry and deliver a letter personally, not sending it through the post **einen Brief durch Boten überbringen lassen**
(c) in hand = kept in reserve **vorrätig, zur Verfügung; balance in hand** *or* **cash in hand** = cash held to pay small debts and running costs **Kassen-, Barbestand; Bargeld; work in hand** = work which is in progress but not finished **noch nicht fertiggestellte Arbeit**
(d) goods left on hand = goods which have not been sold and are left with the retailer or producer **unverkaufte Ware**
(e) out of hand = immediately *or* without taking time to think **unverzüglich, umgehend;** *the justices dismissed his evidence out of hand*
(f) to hand = here *or* present **zur Hand; I have the invoice to hand** = I have the invoice in front of me **ich habe die Rechnung zur Hand**
(g) show of hands = way of casting votes where people show how they vote by raising their hands **Abstimmung durch Handheben;** *the motion was carried on a show of hands*
(h) to change hands = to be sold to a new owner **in andere Hände übergehen, den Besitzer wechseln;** *the shop changed hands for £100,000*
(i) note of hand = document where someone promises to pay money at a stated time

without conditions **Schuldschein; in witness whereof, I set my hand** = I sign as a witness **ich bestätige die Richtigkeit durch meine Unterschrift**

◊ **handcuffs** *plural noun* two metal rings chained together which are locked round the wrists of someone who is being arrested **Handschellen**

◊ **handcuffed** *adjective* wearing handcuffs *or* attached with handcuffs **mit Handschellen (versehen)/gefesselt;** *the accused appeared in court handcuffed to two policemen*

◊ **hand down** *verb*
(a) to pass (property) from one generation to another **vererben;** *the house has been handed down from father to son since the nineteenth century*
(b) to hand down a verdict = to announce a verdict **ein Urteil verkünden**

◊ **handgun** *noun* small gun which is carried in the hand **Handfeuerwaffe;** *the police found six handguns when they searched the car*

◊ **hand over** *verb* to pass something to someone **übergeben, überreichen;** *she handed over the documents to the lawyer;* **he handed over to his deputy** = he passed his responsibilities to his deputy **er übergab (die Verantwortung) an seinen Stellvertreter**

◊ **hand up** *verb* to pass to someone who is in a higher place **hinaufreichen;** *the exhibit was handed up to the judge*

◊ **handwriting** *noun*
(a) writing done by hand **Handschrift; to send a letter of application in your own handwriting** = written by you with a pen, and not typed **einen handgeschriebenen Bewerbungsbrief schicken; handwriting expert** = person who is able to identify a person by examining his handwriting **Schriftsachverständiger**
(b) *slang* particular way of committing a crime which identifies a criminal **Handschrift, Markenzeichen**

◊ **handwritten** *adjective* written by hand, not typed **von Hand geschrieben, handgeschrieben;** *it is more professional to send in a typed rather than a handwritten letter of application*

handle *verb*
(a) to deal with something *or* to organize something **bearbeiten, sich befassen mit, erledigen;** *the courts had difficulty in handling all the cases; the fraud squad handles cases of business malpractice*
(b) to sell *or* to trade in (a sort of product) **führen, handeln mit;** *we do not handle foreign cars; they will not handle goods produced by other firms*

◊ **handling** *noun* moving something *or* dealing with something **Beförderung,**

Umschlag; Bearbeitung, Erledigung, Handhabung; **handling charges** = money to be paid for packing and making invoices *or* for dealing with something in general *or* for moving goods from one place to another **Bearbeitungsgebühr; Umschlagspesen; handling stolen goods** = notifiable offence of dealing with goods (receiving them or selling them) which you know to have been stolen **Hehlerei**

| COMMENT: handling stolen goods is a more serious crime than theft, and the penalty can be higher |

hang *verb*
(a) to attach something to a hook, nail, etc. **(auf)hängen;** *hang your coat on the hook behind the door; he hung his umbrella over the back of his chair*
(b) to execute someone by hanging him by a rope round his neck **hängen;** *see also* HUNG
NOTE: **hanging - hung** for meaning (a) and **hanging - hanged** for meaning (b)

◊ **hanging** *noun* act of executing someone by hanging **Erhängen, Hinrichtung durch den Strang;** *the hangings took place in front of the prison*

◊ **hangman** *noun* man who executes criminals by hanging them **Henker**

Hansard *noun* official report of what is said and done in the House of Commons and the House of Lords **offizielles Parlamentsprotokoll**

harass *verb* to worry *or* to bother someone, especially by continually checking on him *or* taking him into custody **belästigen, schikanieren**

◊ **harassment** *noun* action of harassing someone **Belästigung, Schikane;** *he complained of police harassment or of harassment by the police*
NOTE: no plural

harbour *verb* to give shelter and protection to (a criminal) **Unterschlupf gewähren**

hard *adjective*
(a) strong *or* not weak **hart; to take a hard line in trade union negotiations** = to refuse to accept any proposal from the other side **in Verhandlungen mit der Gewerkschaft hart sein/eine harte Linie verfolgen**
(b) difficult **schwierig, schwer; a hard case** = a criminal *or* an addict who cannot be reformed **ein unverbesserlicher/aussichtsloser Fall**
(c) solid *or* real **hart, fest; hard cash** = money in notes and coins which is ready at hand

Bargeld; *he paid out £100 in hard cash for the chair;* **hard copy** = printout of a text which is on computer *or* printed copy of a document which is on microfilm **Ausdruck; Kopie; Abzug; hard disk** = computer disk which has a sealed case and can store large quantities of information **Festplatte**
(d) hard bargain = bargain with difficult terms **ein Abkommen mit harten Bedingungen; to drive a hard bargain** = to be a difficult negotiator **hart verhandeln, harte Bedingungen stellen; to strike a hard bargain** = to agree a deal where the terms are favourable to you **ein gutes Geschäft machen**
(e) hard currency = currency of a country which has a strong economy and which can be changed into other currencies easily **harte Währung**

◊ **hardened criminal** *noun* criminal who has committed many crimes and who will never go straight **Gewohnheitsverbrecher**

◊ **hard labour** *noun* punishment of sending someone to prison to do hard manual labour there **Zwangsarbeit**

◊ **hardship** *noun* difficulty in living (because of lack of money *or* house, etc.) **Not(lage), Härte, Elend;** *the court order may cause hardship to the family of the defendant; in hardship cases or in cases of hardship, the local authority may offer temporary accommodation*
NOTE: no plural

harm
1 *noun* damage done to (someone) **Schaden;** *the newspaper report has done a lot of harm to the firm's reputation* (NOTE: no plural)
2 *verb* to damage **schaden;** *the news that the chairman has been arrested for fraud has harmed the company's reputation*

harsh *adjective* severe *or* which does not treat someone in a kind way **streng, hart;** *the magistrate gave harsh sentences to the rioters; they complained of harsh treatment on the part of the warders*

◊ **harshly** *adverb* in a harsh way *or* not in a kind way **streng, hart;** *the prisoners have complained that they are harshly treated in the military prisons*

◊ **harshness** *noun* being harsh **Strenge, Härte;** *the newspapers commented on the harshness of the sentence*

hatred *noun* violent dislike of someone *or* something **Haß;** *his hatred of injustice or of inequality;* **racial hatred** = violent dislike of someone because of his race **Rassenhaß**
NOTE: no plural

hazard *noun* danger **Gefahr, Risiko; fire hazard** = situation *or* goods which could start a fire **Feuergefahr**

head
1 *noun*
(a) most important person **Leiter/-in, Chef/-in, Vorstand; head of department** *or* **department head** = person in charge of a department **Abteilungsleiter**
(b) top part *or* first part **Spitze, oberes Ende;** *write the name of the company at the head of the list*
(c) person **Kopf;** *allow £10 per head for expenses; representatives cost on average £25,000 per head per annum*
(d) heads of agreement = draft agreement containing the most important points but not all the details **Hauptaspekte eines Abkommens; head of damage** = item of damage in a pleading *or* claim **beschädigter Gegenstand**
2 *adjective* most important *or* main **Haupt-, Ober-;** *head clerk; head porter; head salesman; head waiter;* **head office** main office, where the board of directors works and meets **Hauptgeschäftsstelle, Zentrale, Direktion**
3 *verb*
(a) to be the manager *or* to be the most important person **leiten, vorstehen;** *to head a department; he is heading a government delegation to China*
(b) to be first **anführen, an der Spitze stehen;** *the list of cases to be heard is headed by two murder cases; the two largest oil companies head the list of stock market results*

◊ **headed** *adjective* **headed paper** = notepaper with the name of the company and its address printed on it **Papier mit Briefkopf**

◊ **headhunt** *verb* to look for managers and offer them jobs in other companies **nach Führungskräften suchen; he was headhunted** = he was approached by a headhunter and offered a new job **er wurde abgeworben**

◊ **headhunter** *noun* person *or* company which looks for top managers and offers them jobs in other companies **Headhunter; jd, der für Firmen nach Führungskräften sucht**

◊ **heading** *noun*
(a) words at the top of a piece of text, especially words at the beginning of a section of a statute **Überschrift;** *items are listed under several headings; look at the figure under the heading "Costs 85-86"*
(b) letter heading *or* **heading on notepaper** = name and address of a business, firm or company printed at the top of its notepaper **Briefkopf**

◊ **head lease** *noun* first lease given by a freeholder to a tenant **Hauptmietvertrag;**

Hauptpachtvertrag; Hauptvermietung; Hauptverpachtung

◊ **head licence** *noun* first licence given by the owner of a patent *or* copyright to someone who will use it **Hauptlizenz**

◊ **headnote** *noun* note at the beginning of a law report, giving a summary of the case **zusammenfassende Sachverhaltsdarstellung; Leitsatz**

◊ **headquarters** *plural noun* main office **Hauptsitz, Hauptgeschäftsstelle, Zentrale; police headquarters** = central office of a police force **Polizeipräsidium**

hear *verb*
(a) to sense a sound with the ears **hören;** *you can hear the printer in the next office; the traffic makes so much noise that I cannot hear my phone ringing*
(b) to have a letter *or* a phone call from someone **hören;** *we have not heard from them for some time; we hope to hear from the lawyers within a few days*
(c) to listen to the arguments in a court case **verhandeln;** *the judge heard the case in chambers; the case will be heard next month; the court has heard the evidence for the defence*
NOTE: **hearing - heard**

◊ **hearing** *noun* case which is being heard in court **(Gerichts)verhandlung, (Gerichts)sitzung;** *the hearing lasted ten days;* **hearing in camera** = court case which is heard in private with no member of the public present **Verhandlung unter Ausschluß der Öffentlichkeit; preliminary hearing** = court proceedings where the witnesses and the defendant are examined to see if there are sufficient grounds for the case to proceed *or* to try a specific issue rather than the whole case **Voruntersuchung**

◊ **hearsay evidence** *noun* evidence by a witness who has heard it from another source, but did not witness the acts himself **Beweis vom Hörensagen**

heavy
1 *adjective* harsh *or* not treating someone in a kind way **hart, schwer, hoch;** *the looters were given heavy jail sentences; he was sentenced to pay a heavy fine*
2 *noun (slang)* strong man employed to frighten people **Schläger**

◊ **heavily** *adverb* **he had to borrow heavily to pay the fine** = he had to borrow a lot of money **er hat viel Geld aufnehmen müssen, um die Strafe zu bezahlen**

heir *noun* person who receives *or* will receive property when someone dies **Erbe;** *his heirs split the estate between them;* **heirs and assigns** = people who have inherited

property and had it transferred to them **Erben und Rechtsnachfolger; heir apparent** = heir who will certainly inherit if a person dies before him **gesetzlicher/rechtmäßiger Erbe; heir presumptive** = heir who will inherit if a person dies at this moment, but whose inheritance may be altered in the future **mutmaßlicher Erbe**

◊ **heiress** *noun* female heir **Erbin**

◊ **heirloom** *noun* piece of family property (such as silver *or* a painting *or* a jewel) which has been handed down for several generations **Erbstück;** *the burglars stole some family heirlooms*

heist *noun (slang)* holdup **Raubüberfall**

help
1 *noun* thing which makes it easy to do something **Hilfe, Unterstützung;** *she finds the computer a great help in writing letters; the company was set up with help from the government; counsel did not get much help from the witness*
2 *verb* to make it easy for something to be done **helfen, unterstützen, zuträglich sein;** *his evidence did not help the case for the defendant; his case was not helped by the evidence of the expert witness;* **to help police with their inquiries** = to be taken to the police station for questioning **von der Polizei vernommen werden**

henceforth *adverb* from this time on **künftig, fortan;** *henceforth it will be more difficult to avoid customs examinations*

here- *prefix* this point **hier-**

◊ **hereafter** *adverb* from this time *or* point on **künftig, in Zukunft, im folgenden, nachstehend**

◊ **hereby** *adverb* in this way *or* by this letter **hiermit;** *we hereby revoke the agreement of January 1st 1982*

hereditament *noun* property, including land and buildings, which can be inherited **vererbbare Vermögensgegenstände, vererbbarer Grundbesitz; corporeal hereditaments** = rights of property which physically exist, such as houses, furniture **materielle vererbbare Vermögensgegenstände; incorporeal hereditaments** = rights (such as patents *or* copyrights) which can form part of an estate and be inherited **immaterielle vererbbare Vermögenswerte**

hereditary *adjective* which is inherited *or* which is passed from one member of a family to another **ererbt; erblich, vererbbar, Erb-; hereditary office** = official position which is inherited **ererbtes Amt; hereditary**

peer = member of the House of Lords who has inherited his title **Peer mit ererbtem Adelstitel**

herein *adverb* in this document **hierin;** *the conditions stated herein; see the reference herein above*

◊ **hereinafter** *adverb* stated later in this document **nachstehend, im folgenden;** *the conditions hereinafter listed*

◊ **hereof** *adverb* of this **hiervon; in confirmation hereof we attach a bank statement** = to confirm this we attach a bank statement **zur Bestätigung (hiervon) fügen wir einen Kontoauszug bei**

◊ **hereto** *adverb* **according to the invoice attached hereto** = according to the invoice attached to this **entsprechend der beigefügten Rechnung; as witness hereto** = as a witness of this fact **als Zeuge hiervon; the parties hereto** = the parties to this agreement **die beteiligten Parteien**

◊ **heretofore** *adverb* previously *or* earlier **bisher, vorher;** *the parties heretofore acting as trustees*

◊ **hereunder** *adverb* under this heading *or* below this phrase **untenstehend;** *see the documents listed hereunder*

◊ **herewith** *adverb* together with this letter **anbei;** *please find the cheque enclosed herewith*

Her Majesty's pleasure *noun* **detention at** *or* **during Her Majesty's pleasure** = detention for an indefinite period, until the Home Secretary decides that a prisoner can be released **Haft auf unbestimmte Zeit**

COMMENT: used as a punishment for people under a disability and children who commit murder

hesitate *verb* not to be sure what to do next **zögern, unschlüssig sein;** *the jury is hesitating about its verdict; she hesitated for some time before answering the question*

hidden *adjective* which cannot be seen **versteckt, verdeckt, verborgen; hidden assets** = assets which are valued in the company's accounts at much less than its true market value **stille Reserven; hidden reserves** = illegal reserves which are not declared in the company's balance sheet **stille Reserven; hidden defect in the program** = defect which was not noticed when a computer program was tested **versteckter/verdeckter Mangel im Programm**

high
1 *adjective*
(a) tall **hoch, höher;** *the shelves are 30 cm*

high; the top of the table is 20 inches high; the door is not high enough to let us get the machines into the building; they are planning a 30-storey high office block
(b) large *or* not low **höher; highest bidder** = person who offers the most money at an auction **Meistbietender; high flier** = (i) person who is very successful *or* who is likely to get a very important job; (ii) share whose market price is rising rapidly **(i) Senkrechtstarter; (ii) schnell steigende Aktie; high sales** = large amount of revenue produced by sales **hoher Absatz; high taxation** = taxation which imposes large taxes on wages *or* profits **hohe Besteuerung; high volume (of sales)** = large number of items sold **hoher Absatz**
2 *adverb* **prices are running high** = prices are above their usual level **die Preise sind gestiegen**
3 *noun* point where prices *or* sales are very large **Höchststand; sales volume has reached an all-time high** = has reached the highest point at which it has ever been **das Umsatzvolumen hat einen absoluten Höchststand erreicht**

◊ **High Court (of Justice)** *noun* main civil court in England and Wales **Oberstes Zivilgericht (in England und Wales)**

COMMENT: in England and Wales, the High Court is divided into three divisions: the Queen's Bench, the Chancery and the Family Divisions; the Court hears most civil claims where the value exceeds £5,000

◊ **High Court of Justiciary** *noun* the supreme criminal court of Scotland **Oberstes Strafgericht (in Schottland)**

◊ **high seas** *plural noun* part of the sea which is further than three miles *or* five kilometres from a coast, and so is under international jurisdiction **hohe See**
NOTE: usually used with "the": **an accident on the high seas**

◊ **High Sheriff** *noun* senior representative appointed by the government in a county **höchster Verwaltungsbeamter einer Grafschaft**

◊ **highway** *noun* road *or* path with a right of way which anyone may use **(öffentliche) Straße; the Highway Code** = rules which govern the behaviour of people and vehicles using roads **Straßenverkehrsordnung**

COMMENT: the Highway Code is not itself part of English law

hijack
1 *noun* act of taking control of a plane *or* ship *or* train *or* lorry which is moving **Entführung;** *the hijack was organized by a group of opponents to the government*
2 *verb* to take control of a moving plane *or*

ship *or* train *or* lorry, with passengers on board, by threatening the crew **entführen, überfallen;** *the plane was hijacked by six armed terrorists; the bandits hijacked the lorry and killed the driver*

◊ **hijacker** *noun* person who hijacks a vehicle **Entführer/-in**

◊ **hijacking** *noun* act of taking control of a moving plane *or* ship *or* train *or* lorry by force **Entführung;** *the hijacking took place just after the plane took off; there have been six hijackings so far this year*

Hilary *noun* one of the four sittings of the law courts; one of the four law terms **Gerichtstermine vom 11. Januar bis Mittwoch vor Ostern; Vorlesungszeit vom 11. Januar bis Mittwoch vor Ostern**

hire
1 *noun*
(a) paying money to rent a car *or* boat *or* piece of equipment for a time **Mieten, Leihen; car hire firm** *or* **equipment hire firm** = company which owns cars *or* equipment and lends them to customers for a payment **Autoverleih(firma); Geräteverleih; hire car** = car which has been rented **Leih-, Mietwagen**
(b) **"for hire"** = sign on a taxi showing it is empty **"frei"**
2 *verb*
(a) **to hire staff** = to engage new staff to work for you **Personal einstellen;** *we have hired the best lawyers to represent us; they hired a small company to paint the offices*
(b) **to hire a car** *or* **a crane** = to pay money to use a car *or* a crane for a time **einen Wagen/einen Kran mieten**
(c) **to hire out cars** *or* **equipment** = to lend cars *or* equipment to customers who pay for their use **Wagen/Geräte vermieten**

◊ **hired** *adjective* **a hired car** = car which has been rented **ein Mietwagen; hired killer** = person who will kill someone for a fee **gedungener Mörder**

◊ **hire purchase** *noun* system of buying something by paying a sum regularly each month until you own it completely **Raten-, Teilzahlungskauf;** *to buy a refrigerator on hire purchase;* **to sign a hire-purchase agreement** = to sign a contract to pay for something by instalments **einen Teilzahlungskaufvertrag unterschreiben; hire-purchase company** = company which provides money for hire purchase **Teilzahlungsfinanzierungsgesellschaft**
NOTE: the US English is **installment plan**

◊ **hirer** *noun* person who hires something **Mieter/-in**

hit *verb (slang)* to kill **umlegen, killen**

◊ **hit man** *noun (slang)* hired killer *or* person who will kill for a fee **Killer, gedungener Mörder**

hoard *verb* to buy and store food in case of need *or* to keep cash instead of investing it **horten, ansammeln;** *umg* **hamstern**

◊ **hoarder** *noun* person who buys and stores food in case of need **Hamsterer**

◊ **hoarding** *noun*
(a) **hoarding of supplies** = buying large quantities of food to keep in case of need **Horten von Vorräten**
(b) **advertisement hoarding** = large board for sticking advertisements **Reklametafel, Plakatwand**

hoc *see* AD HOC

hold *verb*
(a) to own *or* to keep *or* to possess **(be)halten, besitzen;** *he holds 10% of the company's shares; she holds the land under a lease from the property company*
(b) to contain **enthalten, fassen;** *the tin holds twenty packets; each box holds 250 sheets of paper; a bag can hold twenty kilos of sugar*
(c) to occupy land **besitzen;** *he holds fifty acres in South Scotland*
(d) to make something happen **(ab)halten, stattfinden;** *to hold a meeting or a discussion; the hearings were held in camera; the receiver will hold an auction of the company's assets; the inquiry will be held in London in June*
(e) to keep (someone) in custody **gefangenhalten, festhalten;** *the prisoners are being held in the police station; twenty people were held in the police raid; she was held for six days without being able to see her lawyer*
(f) to decide *or* to make a judgment **beschließen, entscheiden;** *the court held that there was no case to answer; the appeal judge held that the defendant was not in breach of his statutory duty*
NOTE: **holding - held**

◊ **hold back** *verb* to wait *or* not to go forward **(sich) zurückhalten, zögern;** *he held back from signing the lease until he had checked the details* = he delayed signing the lease until he had checked the details **er wartete mit der Unterzeichnung des Pachtvertrages, bis er einzelne Punkte überprüft hatte; payment will be held back until the contract has been signed** = payment will not be made until the contract has been signed **die Zahlungen werden zurückgehalten, bis der Vertrag unterschrieben ist**

◊ **holder** *noun*
(a) person who owns *or* keeps something

Besitzer/-in, Inhaber/-in; *holders of government bonds or bondholders; holder of stock or of shares in a company; holder of an insurance policy or policy holder; she is a British passport holder or she is the holder of a British passport;* **credit card holder** = person who has a credit card **Kreditkarteninhaber; debenture holder** = person who holds a debenture for money lent **Obligationär**
(b) person to whom a cheque is made payable and who has possession of it **Scheckinhaber**
(c) person who is holding a bill of exchange *or* promissory note **Wechselinhaber, Schuldscheininhaber; holder in due course** = person who takes a bill *or* promissory note *or* cheque before it becomes overdue *or* is dishonoured **(gutgläubiger) rechtmäßiger/legitimierter Inhaber**
(d) thing which keeps something *or* which protects something **Halter, Hülle; card holder** = frame which protects a card **Kartenhülle; credit card holder** = plastic wallet for keeping credit cards **Kreditkartenhülle**

◊ **holding** *noun* group of shares owned **Anteil, Beteiligung, Aktienbesitz;** *he has sold all his holdings in the Far East; the company has holdings in German manufacturing companies;* **cross holdings** = situation where two companies own shares in each other in order to stop each from being taken over **wechselseitiger Aktienbesitz, gegenseitige Beteiligung;** *the two companies have protected themselves from takeover by a system of cross holdings*

◊ **holding charge** *noun* minor charge brought against someone so that he can be held in custody while more serious charges are being prepared **Nebenbeschuldigung, die dazu dient, jdn während der Hauptermittlungen in Haft zu halten**

◊ **holding company** *noun* company which exists only to own shares in subsidiary companies **Holding-, Dachgesellschaft**

◊ **holding over** *noun* situation where a person who had a lease for a certain period continues to occupy the property after the end of the lease **Inbesitzhalten (einer Pacht-/Mietsache nach Vertragsablauf)**

◊ **hold out** *verb*
(a) to behave in a way which misleads others **sich ausgeben;** *he held himself out as a director of the company* = he behaved like a director **er gab sich als ein Direktor des Unternehmens aus**
(b) **to hold out for** = to ask for something and refuse to act until you get what you asked for **bestehen auf;** *he held out for a 50% discount; the union is holding out for a 10% wage increase*

◊ **hold over** *verb*
(a) to postpone *or* to put back to a later date **vertagen, verschieben;** *discussion of item 4 was held over until the next meeting*
(b) to allow someone who has had a lease to continue to occupy the property after the lease has ended **die Pacht-/Mietsache nicht zurückverlangen**

◊ **hold to** *verb* not to allow something to change **festhalten an, einhalten; we will try to hold him to the contract** = we will try to stop him going against the contract **wir werden versuchen, ihn zur Einhaltung des Vertrages zu zwingen; the government hopes to hold wage increases to 5%** = the government hopes that wage increases will not be more than 5% **die Regierung hofft, an Lohnerhöhungen unter 5% festhalten zu können**

◊ **hold up** *verb*
(a) to go into a bank *or* to stop a lorry, in order to steal money **überfallen (und berauben);** *six gunmen held up the bank or the security van*
(b) to stay at a high level **hochbleiben;** *share prices have held up well; sales held up during the tourist season*
(c) to delay **verzögern, aufhalten;** *the shipment has been held up at the customs; payment will be held up until the contract has been signed; the strike will hold up delivery for some weeks*

◊ **holdup** *noun* act of holding up a bank, etc. **Raubüberfall;** *the gang committed three armed holdups on the same day*

◊ **hold-up** *noun* delay **Verzögerung;** *the strike caused hold-ups in the shipment of goods*

holiday *noun*

(a) **bank holiday** = weekday which is a public holiday when the banks are closed **Feiertag;** *Easter Monday is a bank holiday;* **public holiday** = day when all workers rest and enjoy themselves instead of working **Feiertag; statutory holiday** = holiday which is fixed by law **gesetzlicher Feiertag**
(b) period when a worker does not work, but rests, goes away and enjoys himself **Urlaub;** *to take a holiday or to go on holiday; when is the manager taking his holidays? my secretary is off on holiday tomorrow; he is away on holiday for two weeks;* **the job carries five weeks' holiday** = one of the conditions of the job is that you have five weeks' holiday **in dieser Stellung bekommt man fünf Wochen Urlaub; the summer holidays** = holidays taken by the workers in the summer when the weather is good and children are not at school **Sommerferien, Sommerurlaub; holiday entitlement** = number of days' paid holiday which a worker has the right to take **Urlaubsanspruch; holiday pay** = salary which is still paid during the holiday **Urlaubsgeld**

(c) tax holiday = period when a new business is exempted from paying tax **steuerfreie Jahre; Steuerbefreiung**

holograph *noun* document written by hand **eigenhändig geschriebene Urkunde;** *he left a holograph will*

home *noun* place where a person lives *or* country where a company is based **Wohnung, Zuhause; Heimatland; home-produced products** = products which are not imported **einheimische Erzeugnisse**

◊ **Home Office** *noun* British government ministry dealing with internal affairs, including the police and prisons **Innenministerium**

◊ **Home Secretary** *noun* member of the British government, the minister in charge of the Home Office, dealing with law and order, the police and prisons **Innenminister**

COMMENT: in most countries the government department dealing with the internal order of the country is called the Ministry of the Interior, with a Minister of the Interior in charge

◊ **homestead** *noun US* house and land where a family lives **Familienheim**

COMMENT: a homestead cannot be the subject of a sale by court order

homicide *noun*
(a) killing of a person (either accidental or illegal) **Tötung;** *he was found guilty of homicide; the homicide rate has doubled in the last ten years;* **culpable homicide** = murder *or* manslaughter **Mord; Totschlag; justifiable homicide** = killing of a person for an acceptable reason (such as in self-defence) **Tötung bei Vorliegen von Rechtfertigungsgründen**
(b) murder **Mord; the Homicide Squad** = special section of the police force which investigates murders **Mordkommission**

COMMENT: homicide covers the crimes of murder, manslaughter and infanticide

◊ **homicidal** *adjective* (person) who is likely to commit murder **mörderisch veranlagt**

honest *adjective* truthful *or* saying what is right **ehrlich, redlich; to play the honest broker** = to act for the parties in a negotiation to try to help them agree to a solution **die Rolle des Vermittlers spielen**

◊ **honestly** *adverb* saying what is right *or* not cheating **ehrlich**

◊ **honesty** *noun* being honest *or* telling the truth **Ehrlichkeit;** *the court praised the witness for her honesty in informing the police of the crime*

honorarium *noun* money paid to a professional person, such as an accountant *or* a lawyer, which is less than a full fee **freiwillig gezahltes Honorar**

◊ **honorary** *adjective* person who is not paid a salary **ehrenamtlich, Ehren-;** *honorary secretary; honorary president;* **honorary member** = member of a club *or* group who does not have to pay a subscription **Ehrenmitglied**

honour *verb* to accept and pay a cheque *or* bill of exchange **anerkennen und bezahlen; to honour a debt** = to pay a debt because it is owed and is correct **eine Schuld begleichen; to honour a signature** = to pay something because the signature is correct **seine Unterschrift einlösen**

hoodlum *noun US* gangster **Ganove**

hooligan *noun* person who behaves violently in public **Rowdy;** *the police put up barriers to prevent the football hooligans from damaging property*

hospital *noun* place where sick people can be kept and treated **Krankenhaus; hospital order** = court order putting an insane offender in hospital instead of in prison **gerichtliche Verfügung der Unterbringung eines Straftäters in einer psychiatrischen Klinik**

hostage *noun* person captured by an enemy *or* by criminals and kept until a ransom is paid **Geisel;** *he was taken hostage by the guerillas; the bandits took away the bank manager and kept him hostage; the terrorists released three hostages*

hostile *adjective* not friendly **feindselig, feindlich; hostile witness** = witness called by a party, whose evidence goes unexpectedly against that party, and who can then be cross-examined by his own side as if he were giving evidence for the other side **Zeuge, der unerwartet gegen die eigene Partei aussagt;** *she was ruled a hostile witness by the judge*

hot *adjective*
(a) very warm **heiß;** *the staff complain that the office is too hot in the summer and too cold in the winter; the drinks machines sells coffee, tea and hot soup; switch off the machine if it gets too hot*
(b) not safe *or* very bad **unsicher; schwierig; to make things hot for someone** = to make it

difficult for someone to work *or* to trade **jdm einheizen;** *customs officials are making things hot for the drug smugglers;* **hot money** = money which is moved from country to country to get the best interest rates **heißes Geld; he is in the hot seat** = his job involves making many difficult decisions **er sitzt auf dem Schleudersitz**
(c) *informal* stolen *or* illegal **heiß;** *hot jewels; a hot car*

◊ **hot pursuit** *noun* right in international law to chase a ship into international waters *or* to chase suspected criminals across an international border into another country **Nacheile, Verfolgungsrecht**

hotchpot *noun* bringing together into one fund money to be distributed under a will **Gütervereinigung zum Zweck gleicher Vererbung**

house *noun*
(a) building in which someone lives **Haus; house property** = private houses, not shops, offices or factories **Hausbesitz; house agent** = estate agent who deals in buying or selling houses **Häuser-, Immobilienmakler**
(b) one of the two parts of the British Parliament **Unterhaus; Oberhaus; the Houses of Parliament** (i) the building where the British Parliament meets; (ii) the British Parliament **(i) die Parlamentsgebäude; (ii) das Parlament**
(c) *US* **the House** = the House of Representatives **das Repräsentantenhaus**

◊ **house arrest** *noun* being ordered by a court to stay in your house and not to leave it **Hausarrest;** *the opposition leader has been under house arrest for six years*

◊ **housebreaker** *noun* burglar *or* person who breaks into houses and steals things **Einbrecher/-in**

◊ **housebreaking** *noun* burglary *or* entering a house and stealing things **Einbruch**

◊ **household** *noun* people living in a house **Haushalt; household effects** = furniture and other items used in a house, and moved with the owner when he moves house **Hausrat**

◊ **householder** *noun* person who occupies a private house **Hausbesitzer**

◊ **House of Commons** *noun* lower house of the British Parliament, made up of about 650 elected members **Unterhaus**

◊ **House of Lords** *noun* upper house of the British Parliament made up of hereditary lords, life peers, leading judges and bishops **Oberhaus; Judicial Committee of the House of Lords** = highest court of appeal in both civil and criminal cases in England and Wales **Rechtsausschuß des Oberhauses**

COMMENT: as a court, the decisions of the House of Lords are binding on all other courts, and the only appeal from the House of Lords is to the European Court of Justice

◊ **House of Representatives** *noun* lower house of the Congress of the United States **Repräsentantenhaus**

◊ **house-to-house** *adjective* **house-to-house selling** going from one house to the next asking people to buy something **Direktverkauf, Verkauf an der Haustür; house-to-house search** searching all the houses in an area **Durchsuchung von Häusern;** *the police carried out a house-to-house search for the escaped prisoners*

human *adjective* referring to men and women **menschlich; human error** = mistake made by a person, not by a machine **Fehler aufgrund menschlichen Versagens; human rights** = rights of individual men and women to basic freedoms, such as freedom of association, freedom of speech **Menschenrechte**

hung *adjective* with no majority **ohne Mehrheit; hung jury** = jury which cannot arrive at a unanimous *or* majority verdict **nicht entscheidungsfähige Jury; hung parliament** = parliament where no single party has enough votes to form a government **Parlament ohne Mehrheit;** *see also* HANG

hunger strike *noun* protest (often by a prisoner), where the person refuses to eat until his demands have been met **Hungerstreik;** *he went on hunger strike until the prison authorities allowed him to receive mail*

hunt
1 *noun* looking for something *or* someone **Suche;** *the police have organized a hunt for the stolen gold or for the escaped prisoners or for the murder weapon;* **murder hunt** = search for a suspected murderer **Suche/Jagd nach dem Mörder**
2 *verb* to look for **suchen;** *the police are hunting for clues to the murder*

hurdle *noun* thing which prevents something happening **Hürde;** *the defendant will have to overcome two hurdles if his appeal is to be successful*

hurry
1 *noun* doing things fast **Eile;** *there is no hurry for the figures, we do not need them until next week;* **in a hurry** = very fast **schnell**

2 *verb* to do something *or* to make something *or* to go very fast **sich beeilen; eilen; antreiben;** *the government whips are trying to hurry the bill through the committee stages; the chairman does not want to be hurried into making a decision; the directors hurried into the meeting*

hurt *verb* to harm *or* to damage **schaden, Schaden zufügen;** *the criticism in the newspapers did not hurt our sales; sales of summer clothes were hurt by the bad weather; the company has not been hurt by the recession*

husband *noun* male spouse **Ehemann**

hush money *noun (informal)* money paid to someone to stop him talking **Schweigegeld**

hybrid offence *noun* offence which can be tried either by magistrates or by a judge and jury **Delikt, das in einem summarischen Verfahren oder durch förmliche Anklage abgeurteilt werden kann**

Ii

ibid *or* **ibidem** *adverb* just the same *or* in the same place in a book **ib., ibd., am selben Ort**

ID = IDENTITY; **ID card** = IDENTITY CARD

idem *pronoun* the same thing *or* the same person **dasselbe; derselbe, dieselbe; ad idem** = in agreement **übereinstimmend**

identify *verb* to say who someone is *or* what something is **identifizieren;** *she was able to identify her attacker; passengers were asked to identify their suitcases; the dead man was identified by his fingerprints*
◊ **identification** *noun* act of identifying someone *or* something **Identifizierung; proof of identification** = (i) proving that something is what the evidence says it is; (ii) proving that someone is who he says he is **(i) Nachweis der Identifizierung; (ii) Identitätsnachweis;** *the policeman asked him for proof of identification;* **identification parade** = arranging for a group of people (including a suspect) to stand in line at a police station so that a witness can point out the criminal **Gegenüberstellung zur Identifikation des Täters**

◊ **identikit picture** *noun* method of making a picture of a criminal from descriptions given by witnesses, using pieces of photographs and drawings of different types of faces **Phantombild;** *the police issued an identikit picture of the mugger*
◊ **identity** *noun*
(a) who someone is **Identität; he changed his identity** = he assumed a different name, changed his appearance, etc., (usually done to avoid being recognized) **er änderte seine Identität; he was asked for proof of identity** = he was asked to prove he really was the person he said he was **er wurde aufgefordert, sich auszuweisen; identity card** *or* **ID card** *or* **identity disk** = card *or* disk carried to show who the holder is **Personalausweis; Erkennungsmarke; identity parade** = IDENTIFICATION PARADE; **case of mistaken identity** = situation where a person is wrongly thought to be someone else **ein Fall von Personenverwechslung**
(b) being the same **Gleichheit, Identität; identity of parties** = situation where the parties in different actions are the same **Parteiengleichheit**

i.e. that is **i.e., d.h.** *the largest companies, i.e. Smith's and Brown's, show very good profits; the import restrictions apply to expensive items, i.e. items costing more than $2,500*

ignorance *noun* not knowing **Unwissenheit, Unkenntnis; ignorance of the law is no excuse** = the fact that someone does not know that he has committed an offence does not make the offence any the less **Unkenntnis des Gesetzes schützt nicht vor Strafe**

ignorantia legis non *or* **neminem** *or* **haud excusat** *Latin phrase meaning* "ignorance of the law is not an excuse for anyone" **Unkenntnis des Gesetzes schützt nicht vor Strafe**

illegal *adjective* not legal *or* against criminal law **illegal, ungesetzlich, rechtswidrig, unrechtmäßig;** *the illegal carrying of arms; illegal immigrants are deported;* **illegal contract** = contract which cannot be enforced in law (such as a contract to commit a crime) **sittenwidriger/rechtswidriger Vertrag**
◊ **illegality** *noun* being illegal **Illegalität, Gesetzwidrigkeit, Rechtswidrigkeit, Ungesetzlichkeit**
◊ **illegally** *adverb* against the law **illegal;** *he was accused of illegally bringing firearms into the country*

illegitimate *adjective*
(a) against the law **unzulässig, unrechtmäßig, gesetzwidrig**
(b) (person) born to parents who are not married to each other **un-, nichtehelich**
◊ **illegitimacy** *noun* being illegitimate **Unrechtmäßigkeit, Gesetzwidrigkeit; Un-, Nichtehelichkeit**
NOTE: no plural

illicit *adjective* not legal *or* not permitted **verboten, unerlaubt;** *illicit sale of alcohol; trade in illicit alcohol*

imitate *verb* to do what someone else does **nachmachen, kopieren, imitieren;** *this new gang is imitating all the tricks of the famous Chinese gang of the 1930s*
◊ **imitation** *noun* thing which copies another **Nachahmung, Kopie, Imitation; beware of imitations** = be careful not to buy low quality goods which are made to look like other more expensive items **vor Imitationen wird gewarnt**

immediate *adjective* happening at once **umgehend, prompt, sofort;** *he wrote an immediate letter of complaint; the magistrate ordered her immediate release*
◊ **immediately** *adverb* at once **umgehend, gleich, sofort;** *as soon as she arrived in the country, she was immediately arrested by the airport police; as soon as he heard the news he immediately phoned his office; can you phone immediately you get the information?*

immemorial *adjective* so old it cannot be remembered **unvordenklich; immemorial existence** *or* **time immemorial** = before 1189, the date from which events are supposed to be remembered **unvordenkliche Zeit; from time immemorial** = for so long that no one can remember when it started **seit Urzeiten/Menschengedenken**

immigrate *verb* to move to this country to live permanently **einwandern**
◊ **immigration** *noun* moving to this country to live permanently **Einwanderung; Immigration Laws** = legislation regarding immigration into a country **Einwanderungsgesetze**
◊ **immigrant** *noun* person who moves to this country to live permanently **Einwanderer/-in, Immigrant/-in; illegal immigrant** = person who enters a country to live permanently without having the permission of the government to do so **illegaler Immigrant;** *see also* EMIGRATE, EMIGRANT

immoral earnings *plural noun* money earned from prostitution **Einkünfte aus gewerbsmäßiger Unzucht; living off immoral earnings** = offence of making a living from money obtained from prostitutes **von Zuhälterei leben**

immovable *adjective* which cannot be moved **unbeweglich; immovable property** *or* **immovables** = land, and houses and other buildings on land **unbewegliches Vermögen, Immobilien**

immunity *noun* protection against arrest *or* prosecution **Immunität; diplomatic immunity** = not being subject to the laws of the country in which you are living because of being a diplomat **diplomatische Immunität; when he offered to give information to the police, he was granted immunity from prosecution** = he was told he would not be prosecuted **als er anbot, der Polizei Informationen zukommen zu lassen, wurde ihm Freiheit von Strafverfolgung gewährt; judicial immunity** = safety from prosecution granted to judges when acting in a judicial capacity **Immunität des Richters**

COMMENT: immunity from prosecution is also granted to magistrates, counsel and witnesses as regards their statements in judicial proceedings. Families and servants of diplomats may be covered by diplomatic immunity

impanel = EMPANEL

impartial *adjective* not partial *or* not biased *or* not prejudiced **unvoreingenommen, unparteiisch, vorurteilslos;** *a judgment must be impartial; to give someone a fair and impartial hearing*
◊ **impartiality** *noun* state of being impartial **Unvoreingenommenheit, Unparteilichkeit, Objektivität;** *the newspapers doubted the impartiality of the judge*
◊ **impartially** *adverb* not showing any bias *or* favour towards someone **unvoreingenommen, unparteiisch, vorurteilslos;** *the adjudicator has to decide impartially between the two parties*

impeach *verb*
(a) formerly to charge a person with treason before Parliament **wegen Verrats anklagen**
(b) to charge a head of state with treason **ein Staatsoberhaupt unter Amtsanklage stellen**
(c) *US* to discredit (a witness) **die Glaubwürdigkeit eines Zeugen anzweifeln**
◊ **impeachment** *noun* charge of treason brought against a head of state **Anklage**

gegen ein Staatsoberhaupt wegen eines Amtsvergehens, Impeachment

impending *adjective* which will happen soon **bevorstehend;** *the newspapers carried stories about the impending divorce case*

imperfect *adjective* not perfect **fehlerhaft;** *sale of imperfect items; to check a shipment for imperfect products*
◊ **imperfection** *noun* part of an item which is not perfect **Mangel, Fehler;** *to check a shipment for imperfections*

impersonal *adjective* without any personal touch *or* as if done by machines **unpersönlich;** *an impersonal style of management*

impersonate *verb* to pretend to be someone else **sich ausgeben für;** *he gained entrance to the house by impersonating a local authority inspector*
◊ **impersonation** *noun* pretending to be someone else; *he was charged with impersonation of a police officer* **Vortäuschung einer falschen Identität**

implement
1 *noun* tool *or* instrument used to do some work **Gerät, Arbeitsgerät, Werkzeug;** *he was hit on the head with a heavy implement*
2 *verb* to put into action **aus-, durchführen, vollziehen;** *to implement an agreement or a decision*
◊ **implementation** *noun* putting into action **Aus-, Durchführung, Vollzug;** *the implementation of new rules*

implicit *adjective* implied *or* not clearly stated **impliziert, (stillschweigend) mit inbegriffen**

imply *verb* to suggest (that something may be true) **implizieren, andeuten, zu verstehen geben;** *counsel implied that the witness had not in fact seen the accident take place; do you wish to imply that the police acted improperly?*
◊ **implied** *adjective* which is presumed to exist *or* which can be established by circumstantial evidence **mit inbegriffen, stillschweigend angenommen, impliziert; gefolgert, konkludent; implied contract =** agreement which is considered to be a contract, because the parties intended it to be a contract *or* because the law considers it to be a contract **(durch konkludentes Handeln) als abgeschlossen geltender Vertrag; implied malice =** intention to commit grievous bodily harm on someone **vermutete böse**

Absicht; **implied terms and conditions =** terms and conditions which are not written in a contract, but which are legally taken to be present in the contract **stillschweigend mit eingeschlossene Bedingungen; implied trust =** trust which is implied by the intentions and actions of the parties **stillschweigend als bestehend angenommenes Treuhandverhältnis**

import
1 *noun* bringing foreign goods into a country to be sold **Einfuhr, Import;** *the import of firearms is forbidden;* **import levy =** tax on imports, especially in the EC a tax on imports of farm produce from outside the EC **Einfuhrzoll,** *EG* **Abschöpfung; import licence =** permit which allows a company to bring a certain type of product into a country **Importlizenz, Importgenehmigung**
2 *verb* to bring foreign goods into a country **einführen, importieren**
◊ **imports** *plural noun* goods brought into a country **Einfuhren, Importe;** *all imports must be declared to the customs*

importance *noun* having a value *or* mattering a lot **Bedeutung, Wichtigkeit;** *the bank attaches great importance to the deal*
◊ **important** *adjective* which matters a lot **bedeutend, wichtig;** *he left a pile of important papers in the taxi; she has an important meeting at 10.30; he was promoted to a more important position*

importuning *noun* crime of asking someone to have sexual relations with you (for money) **sexuelle Belästigung**

impose *verb* to ask someone to pay a fine; to put a tax *or* a duty on goods **verhängen, auferlegen; erheben, belegen mit;** *the court imposed a fine of £100; to impose a tax on bicycles; they tried to impose a ban on smoking; the government imposed a special duty on oil; the customs have imposed a 10% tax increase on electrical items; the unions have asked the government to impose trade barriers on foreign cars*
◊ **imposition** *noun* putting a tax on goods or services **Verhängung**

impossible *adjective* which cannot be done **unmöglich;** *it is impossible for the police force to work harder than they are working already; getting skilled staff is becoming impossible; government regulations make it impossible for us to sell our computer parts*
◊ **impossibility of performance** *noun* situation where a party to a contract is unable to perform his part of the contract **Unmöglichkeit der Leistung/Erfüllung**

impound *verb* to take something away and keep it until a tax is paid *or* until documents are checked to see if they are correct **beschlagnahmen, in gerichtliche Verwahrung nehmen;** *the customs impounded the whole cargo*

◊ **impounding** *noun* act of taking something and keeping it **gerichtliche Verwahrung**

impression *noun* effect which something *or* someone makes on a person **Eindruck;** *counsel's speech made a strong impression on the jury; the judge got the impression that the witness worked in a bank ;* **case of first impression** = case which raises points of law for which there are no precedents **erstmaliger Rechtsfall**

imprison *verb* to put (someone) in prison **inhaftieren, einsperren, gefangenhalten;** *he was imprisoned by the secret police for six months*

◊ **imprisonment** *noun* being put in prison **Inhaftierung; Haft, Freiheitsstrafe, Gefängnis;** *the penalty for the first offence is a fine of £200 or six weeks' imprisonment;* **a term of imprisonment** = time which a prisoner has to spend in prison **Gefängnis-, Freiheitsstrafe, Strafzeit;** *he was sentenced to the maximum term of imprisonment;* **false imprisonment** = (i) tort of keeping someone wrongly imprisoned; (ii) sending someone to prison for a wrong reason **(i) Freiheitsberaubung; (ii) ungesetzliche Festnahme;** **life imprisonment** = being put in prison for a long time (the penalty for murder) **lebenslängliche Freiheitsstrafe**

COMMENT: life imprisonment is a term of many years, but not necessarily for the rest of the prisoner's life

improper *adjective* not correct *or* not as it should be **unrichtig, unzutreffend, nicht vorschriftsmäßig; unpassend**

◊ **improperly** *adverb* not correctly **unrichtig, unzutreffend, nicht vorschriftsmäßig;** *the police constable's report was improperly made out; he was accused of acting improperly in going to see the prisoner's father*

impulse *noun* strong wish to do something **Impuls; irresistible impulse** = strong wish to do something which you cannot resist because of insanity **unwiderstehlicher Drang**

impunity *noun* **with impunity** = without punishment **ungestraft;** *no one can flout the law with impunity*

impute *verb* to suggest **bezichtigen, unterstellen, zuschreiben; to impute a motive to someone** = to suggest that someone had a certain motive in acting as he did **jdm ein Motiv zuschreiben**

◊ **imputation** *noun* suggestion (that someone has done something wrong) **Bezichtigung, Beschuldigung, Unterstellung; imputation of malice** = suggestion that someone acted out of malice **Unterstellung des Vorsatzes/der bösen Absicht**

in absentia *adverb* in someone's absence **in Abwesenheit;** *she was tried and sentenced to death in absentia*

inadmissible *adjective* (evidence) which a court cannot admit **unzulässig, nicht zugelassen**

inalienable *adjective* (right) which cannot be taken away *or* transferred **unveräußerlich, nicht übertragbar**

Inc = INCORPORATED

in camera *adverb* in private *or* with no members of the public permitted to be present **unter Ausschluß der Öffentlichkeit;** *the case was heard in camera*

incapable *adjective* not able **unfähig, nicht in der Lage;** *he was incapable of fulfilling the terms of the contract; a child is considered legally incapable of committing a crime;* **drunk and incapable** = offence of having drunk so much alcohol that you are not able to act normally **betrunken und unzurechnungsfähig**

◊ **incapacity** *noun* not being legally able to do something **(Geschäfts)unfähigkeit;** *the court had to act because of the incapacity of the trustees*

incapax *see* DOLI INCAPAX

incarcerate *verb* to put in prison **einsperren;** *he was incarcerated in a stone tower*

◊ **incarceration** *noun* imprisonment *or* act of putting a criminal in prison **Freiheitsentzug, Inhaftierung**

incest *noun* notifiable offence of having sexual intercourse with a close relative (daughter, son, mother, father) **Inzest, Blutschande**

in chambers *adverb* in the office of a judge, and not in court **im Amtszimmer des**

Richters; *the judge heard the application in chambers*

inchoate *adjective* started, but not complete **unfertig, unvollständig, im Entstehen begriffen; inchoate instrument** = document which is not complete **unvollständige Urkunde; inchoate offences** = offences (such as incitement *or* attempt *or* conspiracy to commit a crime) which are offences even though the substantive offence may not have been committed **einleitende/unvollendete Straftaten**

incidence *noun* how often something happens **Häufigkeit;** *the incidence of cases of rape has increased over the last years; a high incidence of accidents relating to drunken drivers*

incident *noun*
1 thing which has happened (especially a crime *or* accident) **Vorfall, Zwischenfall;** *three incidents were reported when police vehicles were attacked by a crowd;* **incident room** = special room in a police station to deal with a particular crime *or* accident **Einsatzzentrale**
2 *adjective* **incident to something** = which depends on something else **mit etwas verbunden**

◊ **incidental** *adjective* not important *or* depending on someone else **nebensächlich, Neben-; verbunden, abhängig; incidental expenses** = small amounts of money spent at various times, in addition to larger amounts **Nebenausgaben**

incite *verb* to encourage *or* persuade *or* advise (someone) to commit a crime **verleiten, anstiften**

◊ **incitement** *noun* crime of encouraging *or* persuading *or* advising someone to commit a crime **Verleitung, Anstiftung; incitement to racial hatred** = offence of encouraging (by words *or* actions *or* writing) people to attack others because of their race **Aufhetzung zum Rassenhaß**

◊ **inciter** *noun* person who incites someone to commit a crime **Anstifter/-in**

> COMMENT: it is not necessary for a crime to have been committed for incitement to be proved

include *verb* to count something along with other things **einschließen, einbeziehen, enthalten;** *the charge includes VAT; the total comes to £1,000 including freight; the total is £140 not including insurance and freight; the account covers services up to and including the month of June;* **including, but**

not limited to = counting this item, but not excluding other items **einschließlich, aber nicht darauf beschränkt**

◊ **inclusive** *adjective* which counts something in with other things **inklusive, einschließlich;** *inclusive of tax or not inclusive of VAT;* **inclusive sum** *or* **inclusive charge** = charge which includes all costs **Pauschale, Gesamtgebühr; the meeting runs from the 12th to the 16th inclusive** = it starts on the morning of the 12th and ends on the evening of the 16th **die Sitzung geht vom 12. bis einschließlich 16.**

income *noun* money which a person receives as salary *or* dividend *or* interest **Einkommen, Einkünfte; income tax** = tax on a person's income **Einkommenssteuer**

incompetent *adjective*
(a) who cannot work well *or* who is not able to do something **inkompetent, unfähig, unzulänglich;** *the sales manager is quite incompetent; the company has an incompetent sales director*
(b) not legally able to do something **nicht befugt; geschäftsunfähig;** *he is incompetent to sign the contract*

◊ **incompetency** *noun* state of not being legally competent to do something **Geschäftsunfähigkeit**

inconvenience
1 *noun* situation which someone finds awkward *or* difficult **Unannehmlichkeit, Ungelegenheit;** *the protest march caused some inconvenience to the local shopkeepers*
2 *verb* to make things difficult *or* awkward for someone **Umstände/Unannehmlichkeiten bereiten**

incorporate *verb*
(a) to bring something in to form part of a main group *or* to make a document part of another document **integrieren, einbeziehen, aufnehmen;** *income from the 1984 acquisition is incorporated into the accounts; the list of markets is incorporated into the main contract*
(b) to form a registered company **eine Kapitalgesellschaft gründen, amtlich eintragen;** *a company incorporated in the USA; an incorporated company; J. Doe Incorporated*

◊ **incorporation** *noun* act of incorporating a company **Gesellschaftsgründung, amtliche Eintragung; articles of incorporation** = document which regulates the way in which a company's affairs are managed **Satzung; certificate of incorporation** = certificate issued by the Registrar of Companies showing that a company has been officially incorporated and the date at

which it came into existence
Gründungsurkunde

incorporeal *adjective* which is not physical *or* which cannot be touched **immateriell, nicht körperlich; incorporeal chattels** = properties like patents *or* copyrights **immaterielle Vermögenswerte; incorporeal hereditaments** = rights (such as patents *or* copyrights) which can form part of an estate and be inherited **immaterielle vererbbare Vermögenswerte**

incorrect *adjective* wrong *or* not correct **ungenau, fehlerhaft;** *the minutes of the meeting were incorrect and had to be changed*

◊ **incorrectly** *adverb* wrongly *or* not correctly **falsch, ungenau;** *the indictment was incorrectly worded*

increase
1 *noun*
(a) growth *or* becoming larger **Erhöhung, Steigerung, Zunahme, Zuwachs;** *increase in tax or tax increase; increase in price or price increase; profits showed a 10% increase or an increase of 10% on last year ;* **increase in the cost of living** = rise in the annual cost of living **Steigerung der Lebenshaltungskosten**
(b) higher salary **Lohnzulage, Gehaltserhöhung, Gehaltsaufbesserung;** *increase in pay or pay increase; increase in salary or salary increase; the government hopes to hold salary increases to 3%;* **cost-of-living increase** = increase in salary to allow it keep up with the increased cost of living **Teuerungszulage; merit increase** = increase in pay given to a worker whose work is good **Leistungszulage**
(c) on the increase = growing larger *or* becoming more frequent **(ständig) zunehmen, im Wachsen begriffen sein;** *stealing from shops is on the increase*
2 *verb*
(a) to grow bigger *or* higher **(sich)erhöhen/steigern, zunehmen, wachsen, (an)steigen; to increase in price** = to cost more **teurer werden; to increase in size** *or* **in value** = to become larger *or* more valuable **größer werden; im Wert steigen**
(b) *his salary was increased to £20,000* = he had a rise in salary to £20,000 **sein Gehalt wurde auf £20.000 erhöht**

◊ **increasing** *adjective* which is growing bigger **wachsend, steigend, zunehmend;** *increasing profits; the company has an increasing share of the market*

◊ **increasingly** *adverb* more and more **immer mehr, zunehmend;** *the company has to depend increasingly on the home consumer market*

incriminate *verb* to show that a person has committed a criminal act **beschuldigen, belasten;** *he was incriminated by the recorded message he sent to the victim*

◊ **incriminating** *adjective* which shows that someone has committed a crime **belastend;** *incriminating evidence was found in his car*

incumbent *adjective* **it is incumbent upon him** = he has to do this, because it is his duty **es ist seine Pflicht, es obliegt ihm;** *it is incumbent upon justices to give some warning of their doubts about a case*

incumbrance = ENCUMBRANCE

incur *verb* to make yourself liable to **übernehmen, auf sich nehmen, eingehen; to incur the risk of a penalty** = to make it possible that you risk paying a penalty **das Risiko einer Geldstrafe eingehen; to incur debts** *or* **costs** = to do something which means that you owe money *or* that you will have to pay costs **Schulden machen; sich Unkosten aufladen;** *the company has incurred heavy costs to implement the development programme* = the company has had to pay large sums of money to put the development programme into effect **das Unternehmen hat zur Durchführung des Expansionsprogrammes hohe Aufwendungen gemacht**
NOTE: **incurring - incurred**

incuriam *see* PER INCURIAM

indebted *adjective* owing money to someone **verschuldet;** *to be indebted to a property company*

◊ **indebtedness** *noun* amount of money owed by someone **Schulden; state of indebtedness** = being in debt *or* owing money **Verschuldung**

indecent *adjective* rude *or* not decent *or* which an ordinary person would find shocking **unanständig, anstößig, unzüchtig; indecent assault** = crime of assaulting a person together with an indecent act *or* proposal **Nötigung zur Unzucht, unzüchtige Handlung unter Gewaltandrohung; indecent exposure** = offence where a male person shows his sexual organs to a woman **unsittliche Entblößung**

◊ **indecency** *noun* being indecent **Unanständigkeit, Anstößigkeit, Unzucht;** *(of a man)* **to commit an act of gross indecency** = to have unlawful sexual contact with another man *or* with a child **schwere Unzucht begehen**
NOTE: no plural

indefeasible right *noun* right which cannot be made void **unangreifbares/unverletzliches Recht**

indefinite *adjective* not defined, especially with no stated end **unbestimmt, unbegrenzt; for an indefinite period of time =** for a period with no stated termination **für unbegrenzte Zeit, mit unbestimmter Dauer**

indemnification *noun* payment for damage **Entschädigung, Schadensersatz**

◊ **indemnify** *verb* to pay for damage suffered **entschädigen, Schadensersatz leisten;** *to indemnify someone for a loss*

◊ **indemnity** *noun* (i) statement of liability to pay compensation for a loss *or* for a wrong in a transaction to which you are a party; (ii); *(in general)* compensation for a loss *or* a wrong **(i) Versprechen der Schadloshaltung; (ii) Entschädigung;** *he had to pay an indemnity of £100;;* **letter of indemnity =** letter promising payment of compensation for a loss **(schriftliche) Schadloshaltungserklärung; Ausfallbürgschaftserklärung**

COMMENT: the person making an indemnity is primarily liable and can be sued by the person with whom he makes the transaction. Compare GUARANTEE

indent
1 *noun*
(a) order placed for goods at a certain price (especially by a company which imports goods from overseas) **Warenbestellung (aus dem Ausland), Indentgeschäft;** *he put in an indent for a new stock of spare parts*
(b) line of typing which starts several spaces from the left-hand margin **Einrückung, Einzug**
2 *verb*
(a) **to indent for something =** to put in an order for something **einen Auslandsauftrag erteilen, etwas aus dem Ausland bestellen;** *the department has indented for a new computer*
(b) to start a line of typing several spaces from the lefthand margin **einrücken, einziehen;** *indent the first line three spaces*

indenture
1 *noun* deed made between two or more parties **(von mindestens zwei Parteien ausgefertigte) Vertragsurkunde; indentures** *or* **articles of indenture =** contract by which a trainee craftsman works for a master for some years to learn a trade **Ausbildungsvertrag, Lehrvertrag**
2 *verb* to contract with a trainee who will work for some years to learn a trade **in die Lehre nehmen;** *he was indentured to a builder*

independent *adjective* free *or* not controlled by anyone **unabhängig, ungebunden; independent company =** company which is not controlled by another company **unabhängiges Unternehmen; independent contractor =** person *or* company working independently, which is told what to do by a person *or* company giving a contract, but not how to do the work **selbständiger Unternehmer; independent trader** *or* **independent shop =** shop which is owned by an individual proprietor, not by a chain **selbständiger Händler; unabhängiges Geschäft**

◊ **independently** *adverb* alone *or* without the help of anyone else **unabhängig;** *the two detectives reached the same conclusion independently of each other*

index *noun*
(a) list of items classified into groups or put into order **Index, Register, Verzeichnis;** *we keep a card index of clients*
(b) regular report which shows rises and falls in prices, etc. **Index; cost-of-living index =** way of measuring the cost of living shown as a percentage increase on the figure for the preceding period **Lebenshaltungskostenindex**

indicate *verb* to show **(an)zeigen, hinweisen auf;** *the latest figures indicate a fall in the crime rate*

◊ **indication** *noun* act of indicating **(An)zeichen, Hinweis;** *he gave no indication that he was lying =* he did not show that he was lying **nichts wies darauf hin, daß er log**

◊ **indicator** *noun* thing which indicates **Indikator; government economic indicators =** figures which show how the country's economy is going to perform in the short or long term **staatliche Konjunkturindikatoren**

indict *verb* to charge (someone) with a crime **anklagen, Anklage erheben;** *he was indicted for murder*

◊ **indictable offence** *noun* formerly, a serious offence which could be tried in the Crown Court **schweres Vergehen** NOTE: now called **notifiable offence**

◊ **indictment** *noun* written statement of the details of the crime with which someone is charged in the Crown Court **(formelle) Anklageschrift;** *the clerk to the justices read out the indictment;* **bill of indictment =** (i) draft of an indictment which is examined by the court and, when signed, becomes an indictment; (ii); *US* list of charges given to a grand jury, asking them to indict the accused **(i) (dem Gericht vorgelegte) Anklageschrift; (ii)** *USA* **(der Grand Jury vorgelegte) Anklageschrift**

individual
1 *noun* single person **Einzelperson, Individuum;** *he was approached by two individuals in white coats*
2 *adjective* referring to a single person **Einzel-, individuell;** *the prisoners are kept in individual cells*

indorse *verb* to write something on the back of a document, especially to note details of a plaintiff's claim on a writ **mit Rückseitenvermerken versehen, auf der Rückseite vermerken;** *the writ was indorsed with details of the plaintiff's claim;* **he indorsed the cheque over to his solicitor** = he signed the cheque on the back so as to make it payable to his solicitor **er übertrug den Scheck durch Indossament auf seinen Anwalt**

◊ **indorsement** *noun* writing notes on a document, especially writing the details of a plaintiff's claim on a writ **(Rückseiten)vermerk; special indorsement** = full details of a claim involving money *or* land *or* goods which a plaintiff is trying to recover **Vollindossament;** *see also* ENDORSE, ENDORSEMENT

induce *verb* to help persuade someone to do something **veranlassen, anstiften;** *he was induced to steal the plans by an offer of a large amount of money*

◊ **inducement** *noun* thing which helps to persuade someone to do something **Anreiz, Ansporn;** *they offered him a company car as an inducement to stay;* **inducement to break contract** = tort of persuading someone to break a contract he has entered into **Überredung zum Vertragsbruch**

industrial *adjective* relating to work **Industrie-, industriell; industrial dispute** = argument between management and workers **Arbeitskampf; industrial property** = property owned by a company such as patents, trademarks, copyrights, etc. **gewerbliches Eigentum; industrial tribunal** = court which decides in disputes between employers and employees or trade unions **Arbeitsgericht**

in esse *Latin phrase meaning* "in being" **tatsächlich vorhanden**

inevitable *adjective* (accident) which cannot be avoided even if you try to avoid it **unvermeidlich, unvermeidbar**

infant *noun* person aged less than eighteen years **Minderjähriger**
NOTE: this is an old term, now replaced by **minor**

◊ **infanticide** *noun* notifiable offence of killing a child, especially the killing of a child by its mother before it is twelve months old **Kindestötung**

infer *verb* to reach an opinion about something **folgern, schließen;** *he inferred from the letter that the accused knew the murder victim; counsel inferred that the witness had not been present at the time of the accident*

inferior *adjective* not as good as others **minderwertig, zweitklassig;** *inferior products or products of inferior quality;* **inferior court** = lower court (such as a magistrates' court or County Court) **unteres Gericht**

in flagrante delicto *Latin phrase meaning* "(caught) in the act of committing a crime" **auf frischer Tat, in flagranti**

inflation *noun* situation where prices rise to keep up with production costs **Inflation; rate of inflation** *or* **inflation rate** = percentage increase in prices over the period of one year **Inflationsrate**

influence
1 *noun* effect which is had on someone *or* something **Einfluß, Einwirkung, Auswirkung;** *he was charged with driving under the influence of alcohol; we are suffering from the influence of a high exchange rate;* **undue influence** = pressure put on someone which prevents that person from acting independently **unzulässige Beeinflussung, Einschüchterung**
2 *verb* to have an effect on someone *or* something **beeinflussen;** *the court was influenced in its decision by the youth of the accused; the price of oil has influenced the price of industrial goods; he was accused of trying to influence the magistrates*

inform *verb* to tell someone officially **informieren, mitteilen, benachrichtigen, unterrichten, in Kenntnis setzen;** *I regret to inform you that your tender was not acceptable; we are pleased to inform you that your offer has been accepted; we have been informed by the Department of Trade that new tariffs are coming into force;* **to inform on someone** = to tell the police that someone has committed a crime **jdn denunzieren/anzeigen**

◊ **informant** *noun* person who informs *or* who gives information to someone

Informant/-in, **Gewährsmann;** *is your informant reliable?*

◊ **information** *noun*
(a) details which explain something **Information, Informationsmaterial, Unterlagen;** *have you any information on or about deposit accounts? I enclose this leaflet for your information; to disclose a piece of information; to answer a request for information; for further information, please write to Department 27;* **disclosure of confidential information** = telling someone information which should be secret **Enthüllung/Weitergabe vertraulicher Informationen**
(b) details of a crime given to a magistrate **Strafanzeige, Anklage; laying (an) information** = starting criminal proceedings in a magistrates' court by informing the magistrate of the offence **Erstattung der Anzeige;** *the justices were ordered to rehear the information*
(c) information technology = working with computer data **Informationstechnologie; information retrieval** = storing and then finding data in a computer **Datenabruf, Wiederauffinden von Information**
(c) information bureau or **information office** = office which gives information to tourists or visitors **Fremdenverkehrsamt; Auskunft, Information; information officer** = person whose job is to give information about a company or an organization or a government department to the public **Pressereferent**
NOTE: no plural: to indicate one item use **a piece of information**

◊ **informer** *noun* person who gives information to the police about a crime or about criminals **Denunziant/-in, Spitzel**

informal *adjective* not formal or not strictly official **informell, inoffiziell;** *the head of the CID had an informal meeting with officers from Interpol*

in forma pauperis *Latin phrase* meaning "as a poor person" **im Armenrecht**

COMMENT: a term formerly used to allow a person who could prove that he had little money to bring an action even if he could not pay the costs of the case; now replaced by Legal Aid

infringe *verb* to break a law or a right **verletzen, übertreten; to infringe a copyright** = to copy a copyright text illegally **ein Urheberrecht verletzen; to infringe a patent** = to make a product which works in the same way as a patented product and not pay a royalty to the patent holder **ein Patentrecht verletzen**

◊ **infringement** *noun* breaking a law or a right **Verletzung, Übertretung; infringement of copyright** or **copyright infringement** = act of illegally copying a work which is in copyright **Verletzung des Urheberrechts; infringement of patent** or **patent infringement** = act of illegally using or making or selling an invention which is patented without the permission of the patent holder **Patentverletzung**

inherit *verb* to succeed to an estate in realty; to acquire something from a person who has died **erben;** *when her father died she inherited the shop; he inherited £10,000 from his grandfather*

◊ **inheritance** *noun* property which is received from a dead person **Erbe, Erbschaft** NOTE: no plural

◊ **inheritor** *noun* person who receives something from a person who has died **Erbe/Erbin**

initial
1 *adjective* first or starting **anfänglich, Anfangs-; initial capital** = capital which is used to start a business **Start-, Gründungskapital;** *he started the business with an initial expenditure or initial investment of £500*
2 *noun* **initials** = first letters of the words in a name **Initialen, Anfangsbuchstaben;** *what do the initials QC stand for? the chairman wrote his initials by each alteration in the contract he was signing*
3 *verb* to write your initials on a document to show you have read it and approved **abzeichnen, paraphieren;** *to initial an amendment to a contract; please initial the agreement at the place marked with an X*

initio *see* AB INITIO

injunction *noun* court order compelling someone to stop doing something or not to do something **einstweilige Verfügung;** *he got an injunction preventing the company from selling his car; the company applied for an injunction to stop their competitor from marketing a similar product;* **interim injunction** = injunction which prevents someone from doing something until a certain date **einstweilige Verfügung; interlocutory** or **temporary injunction** = injunction which is granted until a case comes to court **einstweilige Verfügung; prohibitory injunction** = injunction which prevents someone from doing an illegal act **einstweilige Verfügung auf Unterlassung;** *see also* MAREVA INJUNCTION

injure *verb* to hurt (someone) **verletzen;** *two workers were injured in the fire*

◊ **injured party** *noun* party in a court case which has been harmed by another party **der/die Geschädigte, geschädigte Partei**

◊ **injurious** *adjective* which can cause an injury **verletzend, schädlich; injurious falsehood** = tort of making a wrong statement about someone so as to affect his reputation **Rufschädigung**

◊ **injury** *noun* hurt caused to a person **Verletzung; injury benefit** = money paid to a worker who has been hurt at work **Unfallgeld, Versehrtenrente; industrial injuries** = injuries caused to workers at work **Berufsschäden, Betriebsunfälle; personal injury** = injury to the body suffered by the victim of an accident **Körperverletzung, Personenschaden**

injustice *noun* lack of justice **Ungerechtigkeit, Unrecht**
NOTE: no plural

inland *adjective*
(a) inside a country **Binnen-, Inlands-; inland postage** = postage for a letter to another part of the country **Inlandsporto; inland freight charges** = charges for carrying goods from one part of the country to another **Inlandsfrachtkosten**
(b) **the Inland Revenue** = British government department dealing with income tax **Finanzamt, Finanzverwaltung**

in loco parentis *Latin phrase meaning* "in the place of a parent" **an Stelle eines Elternteils;** *the court is acting in loco parentis*

Inn *noun* **the Inns of Court** = four societies in London, of which the members are lawyers and who are called to the bar as barristers; *entspricht* **Berufsorganisation der Barrister**

COMMENT: the four societies are Gray's Inn, Lincoln's Inn, Inner Temple and Middle Temple

innocent *adjective* not guilty of a crime **unschuldig, nicht schuldig;** *the accused was found to be innocent; in English law, the accused is presumed to be innocent until he is proved to be guilty*

◊ **innocence** *noun* being innocent *or* not being guilty **Unschuld;** *he tried to establish his innocence*
NOTE: no plural

innuendo *noun* spoken words which are defamatory because they have a double meaning **versteckte Andeutung;** *an apparently innocent statement may be defamatory if it contains an innuendo*

in personam *Latin phrase meaning* "against a person" **gegen eine Person; action in personam** = action against an individual person **obligatorische Klage;** *see* IN REM

input
1 *noun* material *or* information put into something **Einsatz; (Daten)eingabe; input tax** = VAT paid on goods or services bought **Vorsteuer**
2 *verb* to put information into a computer **Daten eingeben**
NOTE: **inputting - inputted**

inquest *noun* inquiry (by a coroner) into a death *or* into treasure trove **(amtliche) Leichenschau, gerichtliche Untersuchung der Todesursache; gerichtliche Untersuchung**

COMMENT: an inquest has to take place where death is violent or unexpected, where death could be murder *or* manslaughter, where a prisoner dies and when police are involved

inquire *verb* to ask questions about something **sich erkundigen, Erkundigungen einziehen;** *he inquired if anything was wrong; she inquired about the rate of crimes solved; the commission is inquiring into corruption in the police force*

◊ **inquiry** *noun* official investigation **Untersuchung, Ermittlung;** *there has been a government inquiry into the loss of the secret documents*

inquorate *adjective* without a quorum **nicht beschlußfähig, beschlußunfähig;** *the meeting was declared inquorate and had to be abandoned*

in re *Latin phrase meaning* "concerning" *or* "in the case of" **in Sachen**

in rem *Latin phrase meaning* "against a thing" **dinglich; action in rem** = action against a property, not a person **dingliche Klage;** *see* IN PERSONAM

insane *adjective* mad *or* suffering from a state of mind which makes it impossible for you to know that you are doing wrong, and so you cannot be held responsible for your actions **geisteskrank, geistesgestört**

◊ **insanity** *noun* being mad *or* not being sane **Geisteskrankheit, Geistesgestörtheit**
NOTE: no plural

COMMENT: where an accused is found to be insane, a verdict of "not guilty by reason of insanity" is returned and the accused is ordered to be detained at Her Majesty's pleasure

inside

1 *adjective & adverb*
(a) in, especially in a company's office or building **Innen-, betriebsintern; innen; inside job** = crime which has been committed on a company's property by one of the employees of the company **von einem Betriebsangehörigen (in der Firma) begangene Straftat; inside worker** = worker who works in the office or factory (not in the open air, not a salesman) **Angestellter/Arbeiter im Innendienst**
(b) *slang* in prison **im Gefängnis/Knast**
2 *preposition* in **in, innerhalb;** *there was nothing inside the container; we have a contact inside our main competitor's production department who gives us very useful information*
◊ **insider** *noun* person who works in an organization and therefore knows its secrets **Insider; insider dealing** *or* **insider trading** = illegal buying or selling of shares by staff of a company who have secret information about the company's plans **Insiderhandel**

insist *verb* to state firmly *or* to demand **bestehen;** *he insisted on something being done or he insisted that something should be done to help the family of the plaintiff*

insolvent *adjective* not able to pay debts **zahlungsunfähig, insolvent;** *the company was declared insolvent*
◊ **insolvency** *noun* not being able to pay debts **Zahlungsunfähigkeit, Insolvenz; the company was in a state of insolvency** = it could not pay its debts **das Unternehmen war zahlungsunfähig**
NOTE: no plural. **Insolvent** and **insolvency** are general terms, but are usually applied to companies; individuals are usually described as **bankrupt** once they have been declared so by a court

inspect *verb* to examine in detail **prüfen, kontrollieren, untersuchen; besichtigen; Einsicht nehmen;** *to inspect a machine or a prison; to inspect the accounts of a company;* **to inspect products for defects** = to look at products in detail to see if they have any defects **Produkte auf Mängel prüfen**
◊ **inspection** *noun*
(a) close examination of something, especially the examination of the site of a crime by the judge and jury **Prüfung,**

Kontrolle, Untersuchung; Besichtigung; *to make an inspection or to carry out an inspection of a machine or a new prison; inspection of a product for defects;* **to carry out a tour of inspection** = to visit various places *or* offices *or* factories to inspect them **eine Inspektionstour/Besichtigungsreise machen; to issue an inspection order** = to order a defendant to allow a plaintiff to inspect documents, which the plaintiff thinks the defendant might want to destroy **einen Beschluß auf Urkundeneinsicht erlassen; inspection stamp** = stamp placed on something to show it has been inspected **Kontrollsiegel**
(b) the examination of documents after discovery **Urkundeneinsicht;** *inspection was ordered to take place seven days after discovery*
◊ **inspector** *noun*
(a) official who inspects **Kontrolleur/-in, Prüfer/-in, Aufsichtsbeamter; inspector of factories** *or* **factory inspector** = government official who inspects factories to see if they are safely run **Gewerbeaufsichtsbeamter; inspector of taxes** *or* **tax inspector** = official of the Inland Revenue who examines tax returns and decides how much tax people should pay **Leiter des Finanzamtes; Steuerprüfer; inspector of weights and measures** = government official who inspects weighing machines and goods sold in shops to see if the quantities and weights are correct **Eichmeister**
(b) (police) **inspector** = rank in the police force above a sergeant and below chief inspector **Polizeikommissar**
◊ **inspectorate** *noun* all inspectors **Aufsichtsbehörde; the factory inspectorate** = all inspectors of factories **Gewerbeaufsichtsamt**

inst = INSTANT; **your letter of the 6th inst** = your letter of the 6th of this month **Ihr Brief vom 6.d.M.**

instalment *noun* payment of part of the total purchase price *or* of part of the sum due **Rate;** *he paid off his creditors in twelve instalments; you pay £25 down and twelve monthly instalments of £20*
◊ **installment plan** *noun US* system of buying something by paying a sum regularly each month until the purchase is completed **Ratenzahlung, Teilzahlungssystem**
NOTE: GB English is **hire purchase**

instance *noun* particular example *or* case **Fall;** *in this instance we will overlook the delay;* **court of the first instance** = court where a case is heard first **Gericht erster Instanz**

instant *adjective*
(a) at this point **gegenwärtig, laufend; our letter of the 6th instant** = our letter of the 6th of this current month **unser Brief vom 6. dieses Monats; the instant case** = the case now being considered by the court **der vorliegende Fall**
(b) immediately available **sofortig;** *instant credit*

institute
1 *noun* official organization **Institut; research institute** = organization set up to do research **Forschungsinstitut**
2 *verb* to start **einleiten, einrichten, gründen, einsetzen;** *to institute proceedings against someone*
◊ **institution** *noun*
(a) organization *or* society set up for a particular purpose **Institut, Gesellschaft; financial institution** = bank *or* investment trust *or* insurance company whose work involves lending or investing large sums of money **Finanz-, Kreditinstitut**
(b) building for a special purpose **Anstalt; mental institution** = special hospital for patients suffering from mental disorders **psychiatrische Klinik; penal institution** = place (such as a prison) where convicted criminals are kept **Strafanstalt**
◊ **institutional** *adjective* referring to a financial institution **institutionell; institutional buying** *or* **selling** = buying or selling shares by financial institutions **Effektenkauf od Effektenverkauf von Finanzinstituten; institutional investors** = financial institutions who invest money in securities **Kapitalsammelstellen**

instruct *verb*
(a) to give an order to someone **anweisen, beauftragen; to instruct someone to do something** = to tell someone officially to do something **jdm Anweisung geben, etwas zu tun;** *he instructed the credit controller to take action*
(b) **to instruct a solicitor** = to give information to a solicitor and to ask him to start legal proceedings on your behalf **einen Anwalt beauftragen;** *(of a solicitor)* **to instruct a barrister** = to give a barrister all the details of a case which he will plead in court **einen Barrister mit Informationen versehen; einen Barrister hinzuziehen**
◊ **instructions** *plural noun* order which tells what should be done *or* how something is to be used, especially details of a case given by a client to a solicitor, or by a solicitor to a barrister **Instruktionen, Anweisungen, Verhaltensmaßregeln; Weisungen an einen Anwalt;** *he gave instructions to his stockbroker to sell the shares immediately;* **to await instructions** =

to wait for someone to tell you what to do **auf Anweisungen warten; to issue instructions** = to tell everyone what to do **Anweisungen geben; in accordance with** *or* **according to instructions** = as the instructions show **vorschriftsmäßig, laut Vorschrift; failing instructions to the contrary** = unless someone tells you to do the opposite **falls nichts Gegenteiliges angewiesen; forwarding instructions** *or* **shipping instructions** = details of how goods are to be shipped and delivered **Versandvorschriften, Versandanweisungen;** *US* **instructions to the jury** = speech by a judge at the end of a trial where he reviews all the evidence and arguments and notes important points of law for the benefit of the jury **Zusammenfassung der Verhandlung und der Beweisergebnisse (durch den Vorsitzenden) für die Geschworenen**
NOTE: GB English is **summing up**
◊ **instructor** *noun* person who shows how something is to be done **Ausbilder/-in, Lehrer/-in**

instrument *noun*
(a) tool *or* piece of equipment **Gerät, Apparat, Instrument;** *the technical staff have instruments to measure the output of electricity*
(b) legal document **Urkunde (von rechtlicher Bedeutung); inchoate instrument** = document which is not complete **unvollständige Urkunde; negotiable instrument** = document (such as a bill of exchange *or* a cheque) which can be exchanged for cash **übertragbares/begebbares Wertpapier; statutory instrument** = order (which has the force of law) made under authority granted by an Act of Parliament **Rechts-, Ausführungsverordnung**

insult *verb* to say rude things about someone **beleidigen; insulting behaviour** = offence of acting (shouting *or* making rude signs) in a way which shows that you are insulting someone **beleidigendes Verhalten**

insure *verb* to have a contract with a company where, if regular small payments are made, the company will pay compensation for loss, damage, injury *or* death **versichern, Versicherung abschließen;** *to insure a house against fire; to insure someone's life; he was insured for £100,000; to insure baggage against loss; to insure against bad weather; to insure against loss of earnings;* **the life insured** = the person whose life is covered by a life assurance **der/die Versicherte (in einer Lebensversicherung); the sum insured** = the largest amount of money that an insurer will pay under an insurance **die Versicherungssumme**

◇ **insurable** *adjective* which can be insured **versicherungsfähig, versicherbar; insurable interest** = interest which a person taking out an insurance policy must have in what is being insured **versicherbares Interesse**

◇ **insurance** *noun*
(a) agreement that in return for regular small payments, a company will pay compensation for loss *or* damage *or* injury *or* death **Versicherung; to take out an insurance against fire** = to pay a premium, so that if a fire happens, compensation will be paid **eine Feuerversicherung abschließen**
(b) **accident insurance** = insurance which will pay if an accident takes place **Unfallversicherung; car insurance** *or* **motor insurance** = insuring a car, the driver and passengers in case of accident **Kraftfahrzeugversicherung; legal expenses insurance** = insurance which will pay the costs of a court case **Rechtsschutzversicherung; life insurance** = situation which pays a sum of money when someone dies **Lebensversicherung; medical insurance** = insurance which pays the cost of medical treatment, especially when travelling abroad **Krankenversicherung; National Insurance** = state insurance which pays for medical care, hospitals, unemployment benefits, etc. **Sozialversicherung; term insurance** = life assurance which covers a person's life for a fixed period of time **zeitlich begrenzte Lebensversicherung; third-party insurance** = insurance which pays compensation if someone who is not the insured person incurs loss or injury **Haftpflichtversicherung; whole-life insurance** = insurance where the insured person pays premiums for all his life and the insurance company pays a sum when he dies **Lebensversicherung auf den Todesfall**

◇ **insurer** *noun* company which insures **Versicherer, Versicherungsträger**
NOTE: for life insurance, GB English prefers to use **assurance, assure, assurer**

intangible *adjective* which cannot be touched **immateriell, nicht greifbar; intangible assets** = assets which have a value, but which cannot be seen (such as goodwill *or* a patent *or* a trademark) **immaterielle Vermögenswerte**

intellectual *adjective* belonging to the mind **geistig, intellektuell; intellectual property** = ownership of something (a copyright *or* patent *or* design) which is intangible **geistiges Eigentum**

intend *verb* to plan *or* to want to do something **beabsichtigen, vorhaben;** *the company intends to sue for damages; we intend to offer jobs to 250 unemployed young people;* **intended murder** = murder which was planned in advance **vorsätzlicher Mord**

◇ **intent** *noun* what is planned **Absicht, Vorsatz; letter of intent** = letter which states what someone intends to do if a certain thing takes place **Absichtserklärung;** *see also* LOITERING

◇ **intention** *noun*
(a) wanting *or* planning to do something **Absicht, Zweck;** *he was accused of perjury with the intention of incriminating his employer*
(b) knowing that something will happen as the result of an action **Vorsatz**
(c) meaning of the words in a document such as a will (which may not be the same as what the maker of the document had actually written) **tatsächliche Absicht; Bedeutung, Sinn**

COMMENT: intention to create a legal relationship is one of the essential elements of a contract

◇ **intentional** *adjective* which is intended **absichtlich; vorsätzlich;** *an act of intentional cruelty*

◇ **intentionally** *adverb* on purpose *or* as intended **absichtlich; vorsätzlich;** *he intentionally altered the date on the contract*

inter- *prefix* between **Zwischen-, zwischen-; inter-bank loan** = loan from one bank to another **Bank-an-Bank-Kredit; the inter-city rail services are good** = train services between cities are good **die Intercity-Verbindungen sind gut; inter-company dealings** = dealings between two companies in the same group **konzerninterne/zwischenbetriebliche Abmachungen; inter-company comparisons** = comparing the results of one company with those of another in the same product area **Vergleiche zwischen Unternehmen aus dem gleichen Bereich**

inter alia *Latin phrase meaning* "among other things" **unter anderem**

intercourse *noun* **sexual intercourse** = sexual act between man and woman **Geschlechtsverkehr;** *sexual intercourse with a girl under sixteen is an offence*

interdict *noun (in Scotland)* ban *or* written court order, telling someone not to do something **(gerichtliches)** **Verbot, einstweilige Verfügung**

interest

1 *noun*
(a) special attention **Interesse;** *the managing director takes no interest in the staff club; the police showed a lot of interest in the abandoned car*
(b) payment made by a borrower for the use of money, calculated as a percentage of the capital borrowed **Zinsen; simple interest** = interest calculated on the capital only, and not added to it **einfache Zinsen; compound interest** = interest which is added to the capital and then itself earns interest **Zinseszins; accrual of interest** = automatic addition of interest to capital **Auflaufen von Zinsen; accrued interest** = interest which is accumulating and is due for payment at a later date **aufgelaufene Zinsen; back interest** = interest which has not yet been paid **Zinsrückstand; fixed interest** = interest which is paid at a set rate **feste Zinsen; high** *or* **low interest** = interest at a high or low percentage rate **hohe Zinsen; niedrige Zinsen**
(c) money paid as income on investments or loans **Zinsen, Kapitalertrag;** *the bank pays 10% interest on deposits; to receive interest at 5%; the loan pays 5% interest; deposit which yields or gives or produces or bears 5% interest; account which earns interest at 10% or which earns 10% interest;* **interest-bearing deposits** = deposits which produce interest **zinstragende Spareinlagen**
(d) percentage to be paid for borrowing **Zinsfuß; interest charges** = cost of paying interest **Zinsbelastung; interest rate** *or* **rate of interest** = percentage charge for borrowing money **Zinssatz, Zinsfuß; interest-free credit** *or* **loan** = credit or loan where no interest is paid by the borrower **zinsfreies Darlehen;** *the company gives its staff interest-free loans*
(e) right *or* title to a property *or* money invested in a company *or* financial share in, and part control over, a company **(An)recht; Beteiligung, Anteil; beneficial interest** = (i) interest of the beneficiary of a property *or* trust, which allows someone to occupy or receive rent from a property, while the property is owned by a trustee; (ii) situation where someone has an interest in shares even though the shares may be held in the name of another person **(i) Nutzungsrecht, Nießbrauch; (ii) Nutzungsrecht; conflict of interest** = situation where a person may profit personally from decisions which he takes in his official capacity *or* may not be able to act properly because of some other person or matter with which he is connected **Interessenkonflikt; he has a controlling interest in the company** = he owns more than 50% of the shares and so can direct

how the company is run **er hat eine Mehrheitsbeteiligung an dem Unternehmen; life interest** = situation where someone benefits from a property as long as he is alive **Nutzungsrecht auf Lebensdauer; majority interest** *or* **minority interest** = situation where someone owns a majority *or* a minority of shares in a company **Mehrheitsbeteiligung; Minderheitsbeteiligung;** *he has a majority interest in a supermarket chain;* **to acquire a substantial interest in the company** = to buy a large number of shares in a company **einen beträchtlichen Anteil an einem Unternehmen erwerben; to declare** *or* **disclose an interest** = to state in public that you own shares in a company which is being investigated *or* that you are connected with someone who may benefit from your contacts **seine Beteiligungen offenlegen**
2 *verb* to attract someone's attention **interessieren, Interesse hervorrufen X/ he tried to interest several companies in his new invention; interested in** = paying attention to **sich interessieren für, Interesse haben an;** *the managing director is interested only in increasing profitability;* **interested party** = person *or* company with a financial interest in a company **Beteiligter**

◊ **interesting** *adjective* which attracts attention **interessant;** *they made us a very interesting offer for the factory*

interfere *verb* to get involved *or* to try to change something which is not your concern **sich einmischen, eingreifen, intervenieren; to interfere with witnesses** = to try to get in touch with witnesses to influence their evidence **Zeugen beeinflussen**

◊ **interference** *noun* the act of interfering **Einmischung, Eingriff, Beeinträchtigung, Intervention;** *the local authority complained of continual interference from the central government*

interim *adjective* temporary *or* not final **Übergangs-, Interims-, Zwischen-, vorläufig; interim dividend** = dividend paid at the end of a half-year **Abschlags-, Zwischendividende; interim injunction** = injunction which prevents someone from doing something until a certain date **einstweilige Verfügung; interim order** = order given which has effect while a case is still being heard **einstweilige Anordnung; interim payment** = part payment of a dividend *or* of money owed **Abschlags-, Interimszahlung; interim report** = report (from a commission) which is not final *or* financial report given at the end of a half-year **Zwischenbericht; in the interim** = meanwhile *or* for the time being **einstweilig, in der Zwischenzeit**

interior *noun* what is inside **Inneres; Ministry of the Interior** *or* **Interior Ministry** = government department dealing with law and order, usually including the police **Innenministerium**

> COMMENT: in the UK, this ministry is called the Home Office

interlocutory *adjective* temporary *or* provisional *or* happening at a court hearing which takes place before full trial **Zwischen- , vorläufig, einstweilig; interlocutory injunction** = injunction which is granted for the period until a case comes to court **einstweilige Verfügung; interlocutory judgment** = judgment given during the course of an action before full trial (as opposed to a final judgment) **vorläufiges Urteil; interlocutory matter** = subsidiary dispute which is dealt with before full trial **Vorverfahren; Erörterung; interlocutory proceedings** = hearings that take place before the court before full trial **Vorverfahren, Zwischenverfahren**

intermediary *noun* person who is the link between parties who do not agree or who are negotiating **Vermittler/-in;** *he refused to act as an intermediary between the two directors*

intern *verb* to put (someone) in prison *or* in a camp without trial (usually for political reasons) **internieren**

◊ **internee** *noun* person who is interned **Internierter**

◊ **internment** *noun* being put in prison *or* in a camp without trial **Internierung**
NOTE: no plural

international *adjective* working between countries **international; International Bar Association** = international lawyers' organization formed to promote international law **Internationale Anwaltsvereinigung; international call** = telephone call to another country **Auslandsgespräch; International Court of Justice** = the court of the United Nations, which sits in the Hague, Netherlands **Internationaler Gerichtshof; International Labour Organization** = section of the United Nations, an organization which tries to improve working conditions and workers' pay in member countries **Internationale Arbeitsorganisation; international law** = laws governing relations between countries **internationales Recht, Völkerrecht**

inter partes *Latin phrase meaning* "between the parties": case heard where both parties are represented **im Innenverhältnis der Parteien;** *the court's opinion was that the case should be heard inter partes as soon as possible; see also* EX PARTE

interpleader *noun* court action started by a person who has property which is not his, but which is claimed by two or more people *or* by a person who may be sued by two different parties **Drittwiderspruchsklage, Verfahren zur Herbeiführung eines Beansprucherstreits**

Interpol *noun* international police organization whereby the member countries co-operate in solving crimes **Interpol;** *they warned Interpol that the criminals might be disguised as women*
NOTE: used without **the**

interpret *verb*
(a) to say what you think a law *or* precedent means **interpretieren, auslegen**
(b) to translate what someone has said into another language **dolmetschen;** *my assistant knows Greek, so he will interpret for us*

◊ **interpretation** *noun* what someone thinks is the meaning of a law *or* precedent **Interpretation, Auslegung; to put an interpretation on something** = to make something have a different meaning **etwas anders auslegen;** *his ruling puts quite a different interpretation on the responsibility of trustees;* **Interpretation Act** = Act of Parliament which rules how words used in other Acts of Parliament are to be understood **Gesetz über die Auslegung von gesetzlichen Bestimmungen; interpretation clause** = clause in a contract stating the meaning to be given to terms in the contract **Auslegungsklausel**

◊ **interpreter** *noun* person who translates what someone has said into another language **Dolmetscher/-in;** *my secretary will act as interpreter; the witness could not speak English and the court had to appoint an interpreter*

interrogate *verb* to ask questions in a severe manner **verhören, vernehmen;** *the prisoners were interrogated for three hours*

◊ **interrogation** *noun* severe questioning **Verhör, Vernehmung;** *he confessed to the crime during his interrogation; under interrogation, she gave the names of her accomplices*

◊ **interrogator** *noun* person who interrogates **Vernehmungsbeamter**

◊ **interrogatories** *plural noun* questions put in writing during a civil action by one side to the other, and which have to be answered on oath **schriftliche Beweisfragen (die unter Eid zu beantworten sind)**

intervene *verb*
(a) to come between people *or* things so as to make a change **intervenieren, eingreifen, dazwischentreten, sich einmischen; to intervene in a dispute** = to try to settle a dispute **bei einem Streit vermitteln**
(b) to become a party to an action **einem Prozeß beitreten**

◊ **intervener** *noun* person who intervenes in an action to which he was not originally a party **Nebenkläger, Nebenintervenient**

◊ **intervention** *noun* acting to make a change **Intervention, Eingriff, Einschreiten, Einmischung;** *the government's intervention in the foreign exchange markets; the central bank's intervention in the banking crisis; the association's intervention in the labour dispute;* **intervention price** = price at which the EC will buy farm produce which farmers cannot sell, in order to store it **Interventionspreis, garantierter Mindestpreis**

interview *verb* to talk to a person who is applying for a job *or* who is able to give information **ein Vorstellungsgespräch führen; befragen; interviewen;** *we interviewed ten candidates for the post of Chief Constable; the police want to interview a man in connection with the burglary;* **interview room** = room where a person is asked questions *or* is interviewed **Besprechungszimmer**

inter vivos *Latin phrase meaning* "among living people" **unter Lebenden; gift inter vivos** = gift given by a living person to another living person **Schenkung zu Lebzeiten**

intestate *adjective* **to die intestate** = to die without having made a will **ohne Hinterlassung eines Testamentes sterben; intestate succession** = rules which apply when someone dies without having made a will **gesetzliche Erbfolge**

COMMENT: when someone dies intestate, the property automatically goes to the surviving partner, unless there are children

◊ **intestacy** *noun* dying without having made a will **Sterben ohne Hinterlassung eines Testamentes**
NOTE: no plural

intimidate *verb* to frighten someone to make him do something *or* to prevent him from doing something **einschüchtern;** *the accused was said to have intimidated the witnesses*

◊ **intimidation** *noun* act of frightening someone to make him do something *or* to prevent him from doing something **Einschüchterung**

intoxicated *adjective* drunk *or* under the effects of alcohol **betrunken**

◊ **intoxication** *noun* state of being drunk **(Be)trunkenheit**

in transit *adverb* **goods in transit** = goods being carried from one place to another **Transitgüter**

intra vires *Latin phrase meaning* "within the permitted powers" **innerhalb der rechtlichen Befugnisse;** *the minister's action was ruled to be intra vires; see* ULTRA VIRES

intrinsic evidence *noun* evidence used to interpret a document which can be found in the document itself **aus einer Urkunde abgeleiteter Beweis;** *see also* EXTRINSIC

introduce *verb* to present *or* to put forward **einführen, vorstellen; einbringen;** *he is introducing a Bill in Parliament to prevent the sale of drugs; the prosecution has introduced some new evidence*

◊ **introduction** *noun* presenting *or* putting forward **Einführung, Vorstellung; Einbringung;** *the introduction of new evidence into the case;* **introduction of a Bill** = putting forward a Bill for discussion in Parliament **Einbringung eines Gesetzentwurfes**

invalid *adjective* not valid *or* not legal **ungültig, nichtig, rechtsunwirksam;** *permit that is invalid; claim which has been declared invalid*

◊ **invalidate** *verb* to make something invalid **für ungültig erklären;** *because the company has been taken over, the contract has been invalidated*

◊ **invalidation** *noun* making invalid **Ungültigkeitserklärung, Kraftloserklärung, Annullierung**

◊ **invalidity** *noun* being invalid **(Rechts)ungültigkeit, Nichtigkeit;** *the invalidity of the contract*
NOTE: no plural

invasion of privacy *noun* action (such as being followed by newspaper reporters) which does not allow someone to live a

normal private life **Verletzung der Privatsphäre**
NOTE: no plural

invent *verb* to make something which has never been made before **erfinden;** *she invented a new type of computer keyboard; who invented shorthand? the chief accountant has invented a new system of customer filing*
◊ **invention** *noun* thing which has been invented **Erfindung;** *she filed a patent application for her invention; he tried to sell his latest invention to a US car company*
◊ **inventor** *noun* person who invents something **Erfinder/-in;** *he is the inventor of the all-plastic car*

invest *verb* to put money somewhere (in a bank *or* by buying shares) where it should increase in value **investieren, (Geld) anlegen;** *he invested all his money in a shop; she was advised to invest in real estate*
◊ **investment** *noun* money which has been invested **Investition, Kapital-, Vermögensanlage;** *he lost all his money in risky investments on the Stock Exchange*
◊ **investor** *noun* person *or* company which invests money **Investor, Kapitalanleger**

investigate *verb* to examine something which may be wrong **untersuchen, überprüfen, ermitteln**
◊ **investigation** *noun* examination to find out what is wrong **Untersuchung, Überprüfung, Ermittlung;** *to conduct an investigation into irregularities in share dealings;* **preliminary investigation** = examining of the details of a case by a magistrate who then has to decide if the case should be committed to a higher court for trial **Voruntersuchung**
◊ **investigator** *noun* person who investigates **Untersuchungs-, Ermittlungsbeamter;** *a government investigator*

invite *verb* to ask someone to do something **einladen, auffordern;** *to invite someone to a meeting; to invite someone to join the board; to invite shareholders to subscribe to a new issue; to invite tenders for a contract*
◊ **invitation** *noun* asking someone to do something **Einladung, Aufforderung;** *to issue an invitation to someone to join the board or an invitation to tender for a contract or an invitation to subscribe to a new issue;* **invitation to treat** = asking someone to make an offer to buy (as by putting items for sale in a shop window) **Aufforderung zur Abgabe eines Angebotes**

◊ **invitee** *noun* person who has accepted an invitation to go into a property **jd, der mit Genehmigung des Besitzers ein Gebäude betritt**

invoice *noun* note asking for payment of goods *or* services supplied **Rechnung**

involuntary *adjective* not done willingly **unfreiwillig, nicht vorsätzlich; involuntary conduct** = conduct beyond a person's control (a defence to a criminal charge) **Verhalten, das nicht willensmäßig beherrscht werden kann; involuntary manslaughter** = killing someone without having intended to do so **fahrlässige Tötung**
◊ **involuntarily** *adverb* not willingly **unfreiwillig, nicht vorsätzlich;** *the accused's defence was that he acted involuntarily*

involve *verb* to be concerned with **beteiligen, verwickeln, betreffen, mit etwas verbunden sein;** *there is an increase of crimes involving young girls; his claim involves money spent on trips abroad; deaths involving policemen or deaths where policemen are involved are always the subject of an inquest*

IOU *noun* = I OWE YOU signed document promising that you will pay back money borrowed **Schuldschein;** *to pay a pile of IOUs*

ipso facto *Latin phrase meaning* "by this very fact" *or* "the fact itself shows" **automatisch;** *the writing of the letter was ipso facto an admission of guilt; he was found in the vehicle at the time of the accident and ipso facto was deemed to be in charge of it*

irreconcilable *adjective* (differences between husband and wife) which cannot be reconciled, usually leading to a divorce **unversöhnlich, unüberbrückbar, unheilbar**

irrecoverable *adjective* which cannot be recovered **nicht einziehbar/beitreibbar; irrecoverable debt** = debt which will never be paid **uneinbringliche Forderung**

irredeemable *adjective* which cannot be redeemed **nicht einlösbar, nicht rückzahlbar, untilgbar; irredeemable bond** = bond which has no date of maturity and which therefore provides interest but can never be redeemed at full value **untilgbare Anleihe**

irregular *adjective* not correct *or* not done in the correct way **vorschriftswidrig, nicht ordnungsgemäß, unstatthaft;** *irregular*

documentation; this procedure is highly irregular
◊ **irregularity** *noun*
(a) not being regular *or* not being on time **Unregelmäßigkeit, Vorschriftswidrigkeit;** *the irregularity of the postal deliveries*
(b) irregularities = things which are not done in the correct way and which are possibly illegal **Unregelmäßigkeiten, Verstöße;** *to investigate irregularities in the share dealings*

irresistible *adjective* which cannot be resisted **unwiderstehlich; irresistible impulse** = impulse to do something which you cannot resist due to insanity **unwiderstehlicher Trieb;** *his irresistible impulse to set fire to shoe shops*

irresponsible *adjective* not responsible *or* wild (behaviour) **unverantwortlich, verantwortungslos**
◊ **irresponsibility** *noun* lack of responsibility *or* not acting in a responsible way **Unverantwortlichkeit, Verantwortungslosigkeit**

irretrievable *adjective* which cannot be brought back to its former state **nicht wiedergutzumachen, unwiderbringlich; irretrievable breakdown of a marriage** = situation where a marriage cannot be saved, and therefore divorce proceedings can be started **(unheilbare) Zerrüttung der Ehe**
◊ **irretrievably** *adverb* in an irretrievable way **unwiderbringlich, unheilbar;** *it was agreed that the marriage had broken down irretrievably*

irrevocable *adjective* which cannot be changed **unwiderruflich; irrevocable acceptance** = acceptance which cannot be withdrawn **unwiderrufliche Annahme; irrevocable letter of credit** = letter of credit which cannot be cancelled or changed **unwiderrufliches Akkreditiv**

Islam *noun* the religion of the Muslims, based on the teachings of the prophet Mohammed **Islam**
◊ **Islamic** *adjective* referring to Islam **islamisch; Islamic Law** = law of Muslim countries set out in the Koran and the teachings of the prophet Mohammed; the law itself cannot be changed, but it can be interpreted in different ways **islamisches Recht**

issue
1 *noun*
(a) child *or* children of a parent **Kind, Kinder, Nachkommen;** *he had issue two sons and one*

daughter; she died without issue; they have no issue (NOTE: in this meaning issue is either singular or plural and is not used with **the**)
(b) subject of a dispute **Streitpunkt, Streitfrage; collateral issue** = issue which arises from a plea in a criminal court **Nebenfrage; point at issue** = the point which is being disputed **strittiger Punkt, zu entscheidende Frage;** *the point at issue is the ownership of the property*
(c) giving out new shares **Emission, Ausgabe; bonus issue** *or* **scrip issue** = new shares given free to shareholders **Ausgabe von Gratisaktien; issue of debentures** *or* **debenture issue** = borrowing money against the security of the company's assets **Ausgabe von Schuldverschreibungen; issue of new shares** *or* **share issue** = selling new shares in a company to the public **Aktienausgabe, Emission neuer Aktien; rights issue** = giving shareholders the right to buy more shares **Bezugsrechtsemission**
2 *verb* to put out *or* to give out **ausstellen, herausgeben, erlassen , ausgeben, emittieren;** *to issue a letter of credit; to issue shares in a new company; to issue a writ against someone; the government issued a report on London's traffic; the Secretary of State issued guidelines for expenditure; he issued writs for libel in connection with allegations made in a Sunday newspaper*
◊ **issuance** *noun* act of issuing **Erlaß; Ausgabe, Emission;** *upon issuance of the order, the bailiffs seized the property*
◊ **issued** *adjective* **issued capital** = amount of capital which is given out as shares to shareholders **ausgegebenes Kapital; issued price** = price of shares in a new company when they are offered for sale for the first time **Emissions-, Ausgabekurs**
◊ **issuing** *adjective* organizing an issue of shares **Emissions-, Ausgabe-; issuing bank** *or* **issuing house** = bank which organizes the selling of shares in a new company **Emissionsbank**

item *noun*
(a) thing for sale **Artikel, Gegenstand; cash items** = goods sold for cash **Barposten**
(b) piece of information **Posten, Artikel; extraordinary items** = items in accounts which do not appear each year and need to be noted **Sonderposten; item of expenditure** = goods or services which have been paid for and appear in the accounts **Ausgabeposten**
(c) point on a list **Punkt; we will now take item four on the agenda** = we will now discuss the fourth point on the agenda **wir gehen jetzt zu Punkt vier der Tagesordnung über**
◊ **itemize** *verb* to make a detailed list of things **einzeln aufführen, spezifizieren;**

itemizing the sales figures will take about two days; **itemized account** = detailed record of money paid or owed **spezifizierte Abrechnung**

Jj

J *abbreviation* Justice: often put after the name of a High Court judge **Richter;** *Smith J said he was not laying down guidelines for sentencing*
NOTE: **Smith J** is spoken as "Mr Justice Smith"

jactitation *noun* boasting *or* saying proudly that something is true when it is not **Berühmung; jactitation of marriage** = boasting that you are married to someone when you are not; *(GB)* **Vortäuschung der Ehe, Ehebetrug**

jail *or* gaol
1 *noun* prison *or* place where criminals are kept **Gefängnis;** *he spent ten years in jail*
2 *verb* to put someone in prison **inhaftieren;** *she was jailed for three years; he was jailed for manslaughter*

◊ **jailbird** *noun* person who is in prison *or* who has often been sent to prison **Knastbruder, Knacki**

◊ **jailbreak** *noun* escape from prison **Ausbruch (aus dem Gefängnis); mass jailbreak** = escape from prison of several prisoners at the same time **Massenausbruch**

◊ **jailer** *noun* person who works in a jail *or* who is in charge of a jail **Gefängniswärter; Leiter der Haftanstalt**

jaywalker *noun* person who walks across a street at a place which is not a proper crossing place **Verkehrssünder (Fußgänger)**

◊ **jaywalking** *noun* offence of walking across a street at a place which is not a proper crossing point for pedestrians **verkehrswidriges Verhalten (eines Fußgängers)**

jeopardy *noun* **to be in jeopardy** = to be in danger of punishment *or* of harm **gefährdet sein, Gefahr laufen;** *his driving licence is in jeopardy* = he may lose his driving licence **er läuft Gefahr, seinen Führerschein zu verlieren;** *see also* DOUBLE JEOPARDY

◊ **jeopardize** *verb* to be likely to harm **gefährden;** *her arrest for drunken driving may jeopardize her work as a doctor specializing in child care*

jetsam *noun* cargo which is thrown off a sinking ship **über Bord geworfene Ladung; flotsam and jetsam** = rubbish floating in the water after a ship has been wrecked and rubbish washed on to the land **Treib-, Strandgut**

jettison *verb* to throw cargo from a ship into the sea to make the ship lighter **(Ladung) über Bord werfen**

jobber *noun* **(stock) jobber** = person who buys and sells shares from other traders on the Stock Exchange **Jobber, Börsenhändler**

join *verb*
(a) to put things together **verbinden, anfügen;** *the offices were joined together by making a door in the wall; the appendix is joined to the contract;* **to join someone to an action** = to attach someone's name as one of the parties to an action **jdn veranlassen, einem Rechtsstreit beizutreten**
(b) to join a firm of solicitors = to start work with a firm **eine Stelle in einer Anwaltskanzlei antreten; he joined on January 1st** = he started work on January 1st **er trat seine Stelle am 1. Januar an; to join an association** *or* **a group** = to become a member of an association *or* a group **einem Verband/einer Gruppe beitreten;** *all the staff have joined the company pension plan; he was asked to join the board; Smith Ltd has applied to join the trade association*

◊ **joinder** *noun* bringing together several actions *or* several parties in one action **Klageverbindung, Klagehäufung;** *see also* MISJOINDER, NONJOINDER

joint
1 *adjective*
(a) with two or more organizations or people linked together **Gemeinschafts-, Mit-, Joint-, gemeinschaftlich; joint account** = bank account for two people **gemeinsames Konto; joint commission of inquiry** *or* **joint committee** = commission *or* committee with representatives of various organizations on it **gemischter Untersuchungsausschuß; gemischter Ausschuß; joint discussions** = discussions between management and workers before something is done; *entspricht* **Betriebsratsgespräch; joint management** = management done by two or more people **gemeinsame Geschäftsführung; joint ownership** = situation where two or more persons own the same property **Miteigentum;** *(US)* **joint resolution** = Bill which has been passed by both House and Senate, and is sent to the President for signature **gemeinsame Entschließung/Resolution; joint-stock bank** =

bank which is a public company quoted on the Stock Exchange **Aktienbank; joint-stock company** = public company whose shares are owned by many people; *(GB)* **Aktiengesellschaft; joint venture** *or (US)* **joint adventure** = very large business partnership where two or more companies join together as partners for a limited period **Joint-venture, Gemeinschaftsunternehmen**
(b) one of two or more people who work together *or* who are linked **Mit-, Partner-, Gemeinschafts-;** *joint beneficiary; joint managing director; joint owner; joint signatory;* **joint heir** = person who is an heir with someone else **Miterbe; joint tortfeasors** = two or more people who are responsible and liable for a tort **Mittäter**
2 *noun (slang)* place *or* building **Laden; to case a joint** = to investigate a building carefully before breaking into it **sich den Laden genauer ansehen**

◊ **joint and several** *adjective* as a group together and also separately **gesamtschuldnerisch; joint and several liability** = situation where someone who has a claim against a group of people can sue them separately or together as a group **gesamtschuldnerische Haftung**

◊ **jointly** *adverb* together with one or more other people **gemeinsam; zusammen;** *to own a property jointly; to manage a company jointly; they are jointly liable for damages;* **jointly and severally liable** = liable both as a group and as individuals **gesamtschuldnerisch haftbar**

◊ **joint tenancy** *noun* situation where two or more persons acquire an interest in a property together, where if one of the joint tenants dies, his share goes to the others who survive him **gemeinschaftlich ausgeübtes Miet- od Pachtrecht; Gesamthandeigentum;** *see also* TENANCY IN COMMON

joy riding *noun* offence of taking a car without the permission of the owner and using it to drive about **unbefugtes Benutzen eines Fahrzeugs**

JP *noun* = JUSTICE OF THE PEACE
NOTE: the plural is **JPs**

judge
1 *noun* official who presides over a court and in civil cases decides which party is in the right **Richter/-in;** *a County Court judge; a judge in the Divorce Court; the judge sent him to prison for embezzlement;* **judge in chambers** = judge who hears a case in his private room without the public being present and not in open court **Einzelrichter ohne Öffentlichkeit; Judges' Rules** = informal

set of rules governing how the police may question a suspect **Vernehmungsrichtlinien**
2 *verb* to decide **entscheiden;** *he judged it was time to call an end to the discussions*

◊ **Judge Advocate-General** *noun* lawyer appointed by the state to advise on all legal matters concerning the Army **Oberster Militärstaatsanwalt**

◊ **Judge Advocate of the Fleet** *noun* lawyer appointed by the state to advise on all legal matters concerning the Royal Navy; *(GB)* **Oberster Marinestaatsanwalt**

COMMENT: In England, judges are appointed by the Lord Chancellor. The minimum requirement is that one should be a barrister or solicitor of ten years' standing. The majority of judges are barristers but they cannot practise as barristers. Recorders are practising barristers who act as judges on a part-time basis The appointment of judges is not a political appointment, and judges remain in office unless they are found guilty of gross misconduct In the USA, state judges can be appointed by the state governor or can be elected; in the federal courts and the Supreme Court, judges are appointed by the President, but the appointment has to be approved by Congress

judgment *or* **judgement** *noun* legal decision *or* official decision of a court **Gerichtsurteil; certificate of judgment** = official document showing the decision of a court **Urteilsschrift; judgment by default** *or* **default judgment** = judgment against a defendant who fails to defend his case **Versäumnisurteil; final judgment** = judgment which is given at the end of an action after trial **rechtskräftiges Urteil; interlocutory judgment** = judgment given during the course of an action before full trial **vorläufiges Urteil; to pronounce judgment** *or* **to give one's judgment on something** = to give an official *or* legal decision about something **ein Urteil verkünden; to enter judgement** *or* **to take judgment** = to record an official judgment on a case **ein Urteil eintragen; to enter judgment for** *or* **against the plaintiff** = to make a legal judgment that the plaintiff's claim is accepted *or* not accepted **einer Klage stattgeben; eine Klage abweisen; the plaintiff entered judgment in default** = the plaintiff took judgment (because the defendant failed to defend the case) **für den Kläger erging ein Versäumnisurteil; entry of judgment** = recording the judgment of the court in the official records **Eintragung/Erlaß des Urteils; judgment creditor** = person who has been given a court order making a debtor pay him a debt **Vollstreckungsgläubiger; judgment debtor** = debtor who has been ordered by a court to pay a debt **Vollstreckungsschuldner; judgment summons** = summons by a court to enforce a court order, such as ordering a judgment debtor to pay or to go to prison **gerichtliche Vorladung (z.B. des Vollstreckungsschuldners)** NOTE: the spelling **judgment** is used by lawyers

judicata *see* RES

judicature *noun* administration of justice **Gerichtswesen; Justiz; Rechtspflege; judicature paper** = thick heavy paper on which court documents are engrossed **Urkundenpapier;** *see also* SUPREME COURT

judice *see* SUB JUDICE

judicial *adjective* referring to a judge *or* the law; done in a court *or* by a judge **richterlich; Justiz-, rechts-; Gerichts-, gerichtlich; the Judicial Committee of the House of Lords** = the highest appeal court in England and Wales **Rechtsausschuß des Oberhauses; the Judicial Committee of the Privy Council** = the appeal court for appeals from some Commonwealth countries and colonies **Rechtsausschuß des Kronrates; judicial immunity** = safety from prosecution granted to a judge when acting in a judicial capacity **Immunität des Richters; judicial notice** = facts and matters which a judge is presumed to know, so that evidence does not have to be produced to prove them (such as that New Year's Day is January 1st, that a small baby is not capable of walking) **Kenntnis des Gerichts; judicial precedent** = precedent set by a court decision, which can be reversed only by a higher court **Präzedenzfall; judicial process** = the way in which the law works **Verfahrensformeln; Rechtsweg; judicial review** = (i) examination of a case a second time by a higher court because a lower court has acted wrongly; (ii) examination of administrative decisions by a court **(i) Revision; (ii) richterliche Überprüfung von Verwaltungsakten und Verwaltungsentscheidungen; Normenkontrolle; judicial separation** = legal separation of man and wife, ordered by the court, where each becomes separated, but neither is allowed to marry again **gerichtlich angeordnetes Getrenntleben, Aufhebung der ehelichen Gemeinschaft**

judiciary *noun* **the judiciary** = all judges **die Richterschaft** NOTE: no plural

junior
1 *adjective* younger *or* lower in rank **junior;**

junior clerk = clerk, usually young, who has lower status than a senior clerk **Bürogehilfe, untere Angestellter; junior executive** *or* **junior manager** = less important manager in a company **Nachwuchsmanager; junior partner** = person who has a small part of the shares in a partnership **Juniorpartner; John Smith, Junior** = the younger John Smith (i.e. the son of John Smith, Senior) **John Smith, junior**
2 *noun*
(a) (i) barrister who is not a Queen's Counsel; (ii) barrister appearing with a leader **(i) Juniorgerichtsanwalt; (ii) Nebenanwalt**
(b) office junior = young man or woman who does all types of work in an office **Bürohilfe**

jurat *noun* words at the end of an affidavit, showing the details of when and by whom it was sworn **Eidesformel in einem Affadavit**

juridical *adjective* referring to the law *or* to judges **Rechts-, juristisch, rechtlich; richterlich**

jurisdiction *noun* legal power over someone *or* something **Jurisdiktion; Zuständigkeit; within the jurisdiction of the court** = in the legal power of a court **zur Zuständigkeit des Gerichts gehören; outside the jurisdiction of the court** = not covered by the legal power of the court **außerhalb der Zuständigkeit des Gerichts; the prisoner refused to recognize the jurisdiction of the court** = the prisoner said that he did not believe that the court had the legal right to try him **der Häftling weigerte sich, die Zuständigkeit des Gerichtes anzuerkennen; equitable jurisdiction** = power of a court to enforce a person's rights **Billigkeitsgerichtsbarkeit**

jurisprudence *noun* study of the law and the legal system **Jura, Rechtswissenschaft** NOTE: no plural

jurist *noun* person who has specialized in the study and practice of law **Rechtswissenschaftler, Jurist/-in**

◊ **juristic** *adjective* according to the practice of law **juristisch, rechtswissenschaftlich; juristic person** = ARTIFICIAL PERSON

juror *noun* member of a jury **Schöffe/Schöffin**

COMMENT: jurors can be selected from registered electors who are between eighteen and sixty-five years old and who have been resident in the UK for five years. Barristers, solicitors, judges, priests, doctors, Members of Parliament, people who are insane are among the categories of people disqualified from being jurors

jury *noun* group of twelve citizens who are sworn to decide whether someone is guilty or not guilty on the basis of the evidence they hear in court **Schöffen;** *(GB)* **Geschworene; trial by jury** *or* **jury trial** = proceedings where an accused is tried by a jury and judge **Schöffengerichtsverhandlung; he has been called for jury service** *or (US)* **called for jury duty** = he has been asked to do his duty as a citizen and serve on a jury **er wurde als Schöffe einberufen; "Members of the jury"** = way of speaking to a jury in court **Schöffen; the foreman of the jury** = the chief juror, elected by the other jurors, who chairs the discussions of the jury and pronounces the verdict in court afterwards; *(GB)* **Obmann, Sprecher; jury vetting** = examination of each of the proposed members of a jury to see if he is qualified to be a juror; *(GB)* **Schöffenüberprüfung;** *(US)* **grand jury** = group of between twelve and twenty-four jurors who meet as a preliminary to a trial to decide if an indictment should be issued to start criminal proceedings **Anklagejury (, die sich aus auf Zeit ernannten Bürgern zusammensetzt und die die öffentliche Anklage ablehnt oder für recht befindet)**
NOTE: the word jury can take a plural verb

◊ **jury box** *noun* place where the jury sit in the courtroom **Schöffenbank; Geschworenenbank**

◊ **juryman** *noun* member of a jury **Schöffe/Schöffin; Geschworener**
NOTE: plural is **jurymen**

◊ **jury room** *noun* room where a jury meet to discuss the trial and reach a verdict **Beratungszimmer**

jus *Latin word meaning* "law" *or* "right" **Recht**

just *adjective* fair *or* right **fair, gerecht; to show just cause** = to show a reason which is fair and acceptable in law **eine rechtlich einwandfreie Begründung haben**

justice *noun*
(a) fair treatment (in law) **Gerechtigkeit; to administer justice** = to make sure that the laws are correctly and fairly applied **Recht sprechen; to bring a criminal to justice** = to find a criminal and charge him with an offence **einen Straftäter der Gerichtsbarkeit überantworten; natural justice** = the general principles of justice **Naturrecht;** *(US)* **Department of Justice** *or* **Justice Department** = department of the US government responsible for federal legal cases, headed by the Attorney-General **Justizministerium;** *see also note at* MINISTRY
(b) magistrate; *entspricht* **Amtsrichter; chairman of the justices** = chief magistrate in a magistrates' court; *entspricht* **Vorsitzender Amtsrichter; justices' clerk** *or* **clerk to the justices** = official of a Magistrates' Court who gives advice to the justices on law *or* practice *or* procedure; *(GB)* **juristischer Berater des Amtsrichters; Lord Chief Justice** = chief judge of the Queen's Bench Division of the High Court, and second most senior judge after the Lord Chancellor; *(GB)* **Lordoberrichter;** *(US)* **Chief Justice** = senior judge in a court **Oberrichter**
(c) title given to a High Court judge **Richter;** *Mr Justice Adams;* **Lord Justice** = title given to a judge who is a member of the House of Lords **Lordrichter**
NOTE: usually written as **J** or **LJ** after the name: **Adams J; Smith LJ**

◊ **justice of the peace** *noun* magistrate *or* local judge **entspricht Amtsrichter**

justicia *see* FIAT

justiciary *noun* all judges **die Richterschaft; High Court of Justiciary** = supreme criminal court in Scotland **Oberstes Strafgericht**

justify *verb* to give an excuse for **rechtfertigen; the end justifies the means** = if the result is right, the means used to reach it are acceptable **der Zweck heiligt die Mittel**

◊ **justifiable** *adjective* which can be excused **gerechtfertigt; vertretbar; justifiable homicide** = killing of a person for an acceptable reason (such as in self-defence) **Tötung bei Vorliegen von Rechtfertigungsgründen**

◊ **justification** *noun* showing an acceptable reason for an act **Rechtfertigung; Verteidigung; in justification** = as an acceptable excuse **zur Rechtfertigung;** *in justification, the accused claimed that the burglar had attacked him with an axe; the defendant entered defence of justification*

juvenile *noun & adjective* young person under seventeen years of age **Jugendlicher; jugendlich, Jugend-; juvenile court** = court which tries young offenders **Jugendgericht;** *the appeal court quashed the care order made by the juvenile court;* **juvenile**

delinquent = young criminal who commits minor crimes, especially against property **jugendlicher Straftäter; juvenile offender** = person under the age of sixteen, tried in a juvenile court **jugendlicher Straftäter**

Kk

kangaroo court *noun* unofficial and illegal court set up by a group of people **Scheingericht, illegales Gericht**
KC = KING'S COUNSEL

keep *verb*
(a) to go on doing something **etwas weiter tun;** *they kept working, even when the boss told them to stop; the other secretaries complain that she keeps singing when she is typing*
(b) to do what is necessary **(ein)halten, befolgen; to keep an appointment** = to be there when you said you would be **eine Verabredung einhalten; to keep the books of a company** *or* **to keep a company's books** = to note the accounts of a company **die Bücher einer Firma führen; to keep the law** = to make sure the law is obeyed **das Gesetz einhalten; to keep the peace** = to obey the law, to behave well and not to create a disturbance **die öffentliche Sicherheit und Ordnung bewahren;** *he was bound over to keep the peace*
(c) to hold items for sale *or* for information **auf Lager halten, führen; we always keep this item in stock** = we always have this item in our warehouse *or* shop **wir haben diesen Artikel immer auf Lager; to keep someone's name on file** = to have someone's name on a list for reference **jds Namen in den Akten führen**
(d) to hold things at a certain level **halten;** *we must keep our mailing list up to date; to keep spending to a minimum; the price of oil has kept the pound at a high level; the government is encouraging firms to keep prices low; lack of demand for typewriters has kept prices down*
NOTE: **keeping - kept**

◊ **keeper** *noun* person who keeps something **Inhaber/-in; Verwahrer; Wärter/-in, Aufseher/-in; Keeper of the Great Seal** = the Lord Chancellor **Staatssiegelbewahrer = Lordkanzler**

◊ **keeping** *noun* **safe keeping** = being looked after carefully **Verwahrung, sichere Aufbewahrung;** *we put the documents into the bank for safe keeping;* **keeping a disorderly house** = offence of being the proprietor *or* manager of a brothel **ein Bordell betreiben**

key *noun*
(a) piece of metal used to open a lock **Schlüssel;** *he has taken the office keys home with him, so no one can get in; we have lost the keys to the computer room;* **key money** = premium paid when taking over the keys of a flat or office which you are renting **Abstand, Mietvorauszahlung**
(b) part of a computer *or* typewriter which you press with your fingers **Drucktaste;** *there are sixty-four keys on the keyboard;* **control key** = key on a computer which works part of a program **Kontrolltaste; shift key** = key which makes a typewriter *or* computer move to capital letters **Umschalt-, Shifttaste**
(c) important **Haupt-, Schlüssel-;** *a key witness has disappeared*

◊ **keyboard** *noun* part of a computer *or* typewriter with a series of keys which are pressed to make letters or figures **Tastatur**

kickback *noun* illegal commission paid to someone (especially a government official) who helps in a business deal **Schmiergeld, geheime Provision**

kidnap *verb* to take away (a child *or* a person) and keep him alone by force (usually asking for money to be paid before he is released) **entführen, kidnappen**
◊ **kidnapper** *noun* person who kidnaps someone **Entführer/-in, Kidnapper/-in**
◊ **kidnapping** *noun* notifiable offence of taking away a person by force **Entführung, Menschenraub, Kidnapping**

kill *verb* to make someone die **töten;** *he was accused of killing his girl friend with a knife*
◊ **killer** *noun* person who kills **Mörder/-in;** *the police are searching for the girl's killer*

kin *plural noun* relatives *or* close members of the family **Verwandtschaft, Verwandten, Angehörigen;** *see also* NEXT OF KIN

kind *noun* sort *or* type **Art, Gattung, Sorte;** *the printer produces two kinds of printout; the law distinguishes several kinds of crime against the person;* **payment in kind** = payment made by giving goods but not money **Sachleistung, Bezahlung in Naturalien**

kite mark *noun* mark put on British goods to show that they meet official standards **Gütezeichen**

kleptomania *noun* mental illness which makes someone steal things **Kleptomanie**
NOTE: no plural

◊ **kleptomaniac** *noun* person who steals things because he suffers from kleptomania **Kleptomane/Kleptomanin**

knock *verb*
(a) to hit something **stoßen, anschlagen;** *she knocked her head on the filing cabinet*
(b) **to knock the competition** = to hit competing firms hard by vigorous selling **die Konkurrenz schlagen; knocking copy** = advertising material which criticizes competing products **herabsetzender Werbetext**

◊ **knock down** *verb* **to knock something down to a bidder** = to sell something at an auction **jdm etwas zuschlagen, jdm für etwas den Zuschlag erteilen;** *the stock was knocked down to him for £10,000*

◊ **knockdown** *noun* **knockdown prices** = very low prices **Spottpreise, Werbepreise;** *he sold me the car at a knockdown price*

◊ **knock-for-knock agreement** *noun* agreement between two insurance companies that they will not take legal action against each other, and that each will pay the claims of their own clients **gegenseitige Regreßverzichtsvereinbarung, Schadensteilungsvereinbarung**

◊ **knock off** *verb*
(a) to stop work **Feierabend machen**
(b) to reduce a price by an amount **nachlassen;** *he knocked £10 off the price for cash*
(c) *slang* to steal **klauen**

◊ **knock-on effect** *noun* effect which an action will have on other situations **Schneeballeffekt, Anstoßwirkung;** *the strike by customs officers has had a knock-on effect on car production by slowing down exports of cars*

know *verb*
(a) to learn *or* to have information about something **wissen;** *I do not know how a computer works; does he know how long it takes to get to the airport? the senior partner's secretary does not know where he is*
(b) to have met someone **kennen;** *do you know Mr Jones, our new sales director?*
NOTE: **knowing - known**

◊ **know-how** *noun* knowledge about how something works *or* how something is made **Know-how, Fachkenntnisse;** *you need some legal know-how to do this job; he needs to acquire computer know-how*
NOTE: no plural

◊ **knowingly** *adverb* deliberately *or* on purpose **wissentlich, absichtlich;** *it was charged that he knowingly broke the Official Secrets Act by publishing the document in his newspaper*

◊ **knowledge** *noun* what is known to be true **Kenntnis, Wissen; he had no knowledge of the contract** = he did not know that the contract existed **er wußte nichts von dem Vertrag; to the best of my knowledge** = I am reasonable certain of the fact **meines Wissens, nach bestem Wissen;** *the witness said that to the best of his knowledge the accused had never left the room;* **constructive knowledge** = knowledge of a fact *or* matter which the law says a person has whether or not that person actually has such knowledge **gesetzlich unterstelltes/präsumptives Wissen, zumutbare Kenntnis**
NOTE: no plural

Ll

labour *or US* **labor** *noun*
(a) heavy work **(schwere) Arbeit; manual labour** = work done by hand **körperliche Arbeit; to charge for materials and labour** = to charge for both the materials used in a job and also the hours of work involved **Material und Arbeitslohn in Rechnung stellen; hard labour** = punishment of sending someone to prison to do hard manual work **schwere körperliche Arbeit, Zwangsarbeit**
(b) workers in general **Arbeiter, Arbeitskräfte; casual labour** = workers who are hired for a short period **Aushilfsarbeiter; cheap labour** = workers who do not earn much money **billige Arbeitskräfte; local labour** = workers recruited near a factory, not brought in from somewhere else **ortsansässige Arbeitskräfte; organized labour** = workers who are members of trade unions **gewerkschaftlich organisierte Arbeiter; skilled labour** = workers who have special knowledge or qualifications **Facharbeiter; labour-intensive industry** = industry which needs large numbers of workers *or* where labour costs are high in relation to turnover **arbeitsintensive Industrie**
(c) **labour disputes** = arguments between management and workers **Arbeitskämpfe; labour law** *or* **labour laws** *or* **labour legislation** = laws relating to the employment of workers **Arbeitsgesetz(e); Arbeitsrecht; Arbeitsgesetzgebung; labour relations** = relations between management and workers **Arbeitgeber-Arbeitnehmer-Beziehungen;** *(US)* **labor union** = organization which represents workers who are its members in discussions about

wages and conditions of work with management **Arbeitergewerkschaft**
(d) International Labour Organization = section of the United Nations which tries to improve working conditions and workers' pay in member countries **Internationale Arbeitsorganisation**

◊ **labourer** *noun* person who does unskilled work **Arbeiter, Lohnarbeiter; casual labourer** = worker who can be hired for a short period **Aushilfsarbeiter; manual labourer** = person who does work with his hands **ungelernte Arbeitskraft**

laches *noun* long delay *or* neglect in asserting a legal right **zum Rechtsverlust führendes Versäumnis gesetzlicher Ausschluß- und Versäumnisfristen;** *see also* STATUTE OF LIMITATIONS

lack

1 *noun* not having enough **Mangel;** *the investigation has been held up by lack of information; charges cannot be brought for lack of evidence;* **lack of data** *or* **lack of information** = not having enough information **fehlende Daten; fehlende Information;** *the decision has been put back for lack of up-to-date information;* **lack of funds** = not enough money **fehlende Geldmittel;** *the project was cancelled because of lack of funds*
2 *verb* not to have enough of something **mangeln an, fehlen an;** *the police lack any clues to the murder; the fraud squad lacks the necessary staff to undertake the investigation*

lading *see* BILL

Lady Day *noun* 25th March, one of the quarter days when rent is paid for land **Mariä Verkündigung**

lag *noun* old **lag** = criminal who has served many (short) prison sentences *or* who will never go straight **alter Knacki**

land

1 *noun*
(a) area of earth **Land; land agent** = person who manages a farm *or* a large area of land for someone; *(GB)* **Gutsverwalter; land certificate** = document which shows who owns a piece of land, and whether there are any charges on it **(beglaubigter) Grundbuchauszug; land charges** = covenants, mortgages, etc. which are attached to a piece of land **Grundschuld; land register** = register of land, showing who owns it and what buildings are on it **Grundbuch; land registration** = system of registering land and its owners **Grundbucheintragung; Land Registry** = British government office where land is registered **Kataster-, Grundbuchamt; land taxes** = taxes on the amount of land owned by someone **Grundsteuern**
(b) lands = estate *or* large area of land owned by one owner **Land, Ländereien; Crown Lands** = estates belonging to the King or Queen **Ländereien der Krone**
2 *verb*
(a) to put goods *or* passengers on to land after a voyage by sea *or* by air **löschen, ausladen; von Bord gehen lassen; landed costs** = costs of goods which have been delivered to a port *or* airport, unloaded and passed through customs **Fracht- und Löschungskosten**
(b) to come down to earth after a flight **landen;** *the plane landed ten minutes late*

COMMENT: under English law, the ownership of all land is vested in the Crown; individuals or other legal persons may however hold estates in land, the most important of which are freehold estates (which amount to absolute ownership) and leasehold estates (which last for a fixed period of time). Ownership of land usually confers ownership of everything above and below the land. The process of buying and selling land is "conveyancing". Any contract transferring land or any interest in land must be in writing. Interests in land can be disposed of by a will

---

◊ **landing** *noun* **landing card** = card given to passengers who have passed customs and can land from a ship *or* an aircraft **Einreisekarte; landing charges** = payment for putting goods on land and for customs duties **Löschgebühren und Löschungszölle;** *(Flugzeug)* **Landegebühren; landing order** = permit which allows goods to be unloaded into a bonded warehouse without paying customs duty **Zollpassierschein**

◊ **landlady** *noun* woman who owns a property which she lets **Vermieterin**

◊ **landlord** *noun* person *or* company which owns a property which is let **Vermieter; ground landlord** = person *or* company which owns the freehold of a property which is then let and sublet **Grundeigentümer;** *our ground landlord is an insurance company;* **the Landlord and Tenant Act** = Act of Parliament which regulates the letting of property **Mieterschutzgesetz**

◊ **landmark decision** *noun* legal *or* legislative decision which creates an important legal precedent **eine einen Wendepunkt markierende Entscheidung**

◊ **landowner** *noun* person who owns large areas of land **Grundbesitzer**

◊ **Lands Tribunal** *noun* court which deals with compensation claims relating to land;

(GB) **Schiedsstelle für Entschädigungsentscheidungen bei Enteignungen**

language *noun* words spoken or written by people in a certain country **Sprache; he was accused of using offensive language to a policeman** = he was accused of saying rude words **er wurde beschuldigt, einen Polizisten beleidigt zu haben; computer language** *or* **programming language** = system of signs, letters and words used to instruct a computer **Computersprache; Programmiersprache**

lapse

1 *noun*
(a) a lapse of time = a period of time which has passed **Zeitspanne**
(b) ending of a right *or* a privilege *or* an offer (such as the termination of an insurance policy because the premiums have not been paid) **Erlöschen; Verfall; Ablaufen (c)** failure of a legacy because the beneficiary has died before the testator **Hinfälligkeit**
2 *verb* to stop being valid *or* to stop being active **verfallen; ablaufen; to let an offer lapse** = to allow time to pass so that an offer is no longer valid **ein Angebot verstreichen lassen; lapsed legacy** = legacy which cannot be put into effect because the person who should have received it died before the person who made the will **hinfällig gewordenes Vermächtnis; lapsed passport** = passport which is out of date **abgelaufener Paß; lapsed (insurance) policy** = insurance which is no longer valid because the premiums have not been paid **verfallene Versicherungspolice**

larceny *noun* crime of stealing goods which belong to another person **Diebstahl;** *he was convicted of larceny;* **petty larceny** *or* **grand larceny** = minor thefts *or* very large thefts **einfacher Diebstahl; schwerer Diebstahl;** (NOTE: no plural)

COMMENT: larceny no longer exists in English law, having been replaced by the crime of theft

large *adjective*
(a) very big *or* important **groß;** *our company is one of the largest suppliers of computers to the government; he is our largest customer; why has she got an office which is larger than mine?*
(b) at large = not in prison **auf freiem Fuß;** *three prisoners escaped - two were recaptured, but one is still at large*
◊ **largely** *adverb* mainly *or* mostly **zum größten Teil;** *our sales are largely in the home market; they have largely pulled out of the American market*

last

1 *adjective & adverb*
(a) coming at the end of a series **letzter; zuletzt;** *out of a queue of twenty people, I was served last; this is our last board meeting before we move to our new offices; this is the last case which the magistrates will hear before lunch;* **last quarter** = period of three months to the end of the financial year **letztes Quartal; court of last resort** = highest court from which no appeals are allowed **Gericht letzter Instanz; lender of the last resort** = central bank which lends money to commercial banks **Kreditgeber letzter Instanz**
(b) most recent *or* most recently **letzter;** *the last case was one of attempted murder, this one is for theft;* **last week** *or* **last month** *or* **last year** = the week *or* month *or* year before this one **letzte Woche; letzten Monat; letztes Jahr;** *last year's accounts have to be ready by the AGM;* **last will and testament** = statement written by a person of what he wants to be done with his property after he dies **letzter Wille; Testament**
(c) the week *or* month *or* year before last = the week *or* month *or* year before the one before this **vorletzte Woche; vorletzten Monat; vorletztes Jahr**
2 *verb* to go on *or* to continue **dauern, andauern; halten;** *the hearing started in December and lasted until the second week of January*
◊ **last in first out** *phrase*
(a) redundancy policy, where the people who have been most recently appointed are the first to be made redundant **Personalpolitik nach der LIFO-Methode**
(b) accounting method where stock is valued at the price of the latest purchases **LIFO-Abschreibungsmethode der Vorratsbewertung**

late

1 *adjective*
(a) after the time stated or agreed **spät; verspätet;** *we apologize for the late arrival of the plane from Amsterdam;* **there is a penalty for late delivery** = if delivery is later than the agreed date, the supplier has to pay a fine **verspätete Lieferungen werden mit einer Strafe belegt**
(b) at the end of a period of time **letzter; latest date for signature of the contract** = the last acceptable date for signing the contract **der letzte Termin für die Vertragsunterzeichnung**
(c) latest = most recent **letzter, jüngster;** *he always drives the latest model of car; here are the latest accident figures*
2 *adverb* after the time stated or agreed **spät; verspätet;** *the hearing started late; the shipment was landed late; the plane was two hours late*

◊ **late-night** *adjective* happening late at night **Nacht-, spät am Abend;** *they had a late-night meeting at the airport; their late-night negotiations ended in an agreement which was signed at 3 a.m.*

latent *adjective* hidden *or* which cannot immediately be seen **latent, verborgen; latent ambiguity** = words in a contract which can mean two or more things, but which do not at first sight seem to be misleading **versteckte Mehrdeutigkeit**

Latin *noun* language used by the Romans **Latein(isch)**

> COMMENT: Latin was used as the language of the law courts for centuries, and its use still exists in many common legal phrases, such as habeas corpus, in flagrante delicto, de jure and de facto

launch *verb* to begin *or* to start **beginnen, starten;** *the police have launched a campaign against drunken drivers*

launder *verb (slang)* to transfer illegal *or* stolen money into an ordinary bank account, usually by a complex process to avoid detection **waschen;** *the proceeds of the robbery were laundered through a bank in the Caribbean*

law *noun*
(a) rule (which may be written or unwritten) by which a country is governed and the activities of people and organizations controlled **Gesetz, Gesetze;** *a law has to be passed by Parliament; the government has proposed a new law to regulate the sale of goods on Sundays;* **Conflict of Laws** = section in a country's statutes which deals with disputes between that country's laws and those of another country **Gesetzeskonflikt; Kollisionsrecht; labour laws** = laws concerning the employment of workers **Arbeitsgesetze; Arbeitsrecht**
(b) law = all the statutes of a country taken together **Recht; case law** = law as established by precedents, that is by decisions of courts in earlier cases **Präzedenz-, Einzelfallrecht; civil law** = laws relating to people's rights, and agreements between individuals **bürgerliches Recht, Zivilrecht; commercial law** = laws regarding business **Handelsrecht (Teil des Wirtschaftsrechts); company law** = laws which refer to the way companies work **Unternehmensrecht; constitutional law** = laws under which a country is ruled *or* laws relating to government and its function **Verfassungsrecht; contract law** *or* **the law of contract** = laws relating to agreements

Vertragsrecht; Schuldrecht; copyright law = laws concerning the protection of copyright **Urheberrecht; criminal law** = laws relating to acts committed against the laws of the land and which are punishable by the state **Strafrecht; international law** = laws referring to the way countries deal with each other **Völkerrecht, internationales Recht; maritime law** *or* **the law of the sea** = laws referring to ships, ports, etc. **Seerecht; mercantile law** *or* **law merchant** = law relating to commerce **Handelsrecht; Handelsgesetz (Teil des Wirtschaftsrechts); private law** = law relating to relations between individual persons (such as the law of contract) **Privat-, Zivilrecht; public law** = law which refers to people in general (such as administrative and constitutional law) **öffentliches Recht; law and order** = situation where the laws of a country are being obeyed by most people **Ruhe und Ordnung, Law and Order;** *there was a breakdown of law and order following the assassination of the president;* **law reform** = continuing process of revising laws to make them better suited to the needs of society **Rechtsreform; to take someone to law** = to sue someone **jdn vor Gericht bringen, jdn verklagen; inside the law** *or* **within the law** = obeying the laws of a country **im Rahmen des Gesetzes; against the law** *or* **outside the law** = not according to the laws of a country **gegen das Gesetz od außerhalb des Gesetzes;** *dismissing a worker without reason is against the law; the company is operating outside the law;* **in law** = according to the law **gesetzlich, gesetzmäßig;** *what are the duties in law of a guardian?;* **to break the law** = to do something which is not allowed by law **gegen das Gesetz verstoßen;** *he is breaking the law by selling goods on Sunday; you will be breaking the law if you try to take that computer out of the country without an export licence*
(c) general rule **Gesetz(mäßigkeit); law of supply and demand** = general rule that the amount of a product which is available is related to the needs of the possible customers **Gesetzmäßigkeit von Angebot und Nachfrage**
(d) *informal* **the law** = the police and the courts **die Polente, das Gesetz;** *the law will catch up with him in the end; if you don't stop making that noise I'll have the law on you;* **the strong** *or* **long arm of the law** = ability of the police to catch criminals and deal with crime **der starke od lange Arm des Gesetzes**

◊ **lawbreaker** *noun* person who breaks the law **Gesetzesbrecher/-in**

◊ **law-breaking** *noun* act of doing something which is against the law **Gesetzesübertretung**

◊ **Law Centre** *noun* local office (mainly in London) with full-time staff who advise and represent clients free of charge; *(GB)* **Rechtsberatungsstelle**

◊ **Law Commission** *noun* permanent committee which reviews English law and recommends changes to it; *(GB)* **ständiger Rechtsausschuß**

◊ **law court** *noun* place where a trial is held *or* place where a judge listens to cases **Gericht(shof)**

> COMMENT: in civil cases he decides which party is right legally; in criminal cases the decision is made by a jury

◊ **lawful** *adjective* acting within the law **rechtmäßig; lawful practice** = action which is permitted by the law **rechtmäßiges Handeln; lawful trade** = trade which is allowed by law **erlaubter Handel**

◊ **lawfully** *adverb* acting within the law **rechtmäßig**

◊ **lawless** *adjective* not controlled by the law *or* by the police **gesetzwidrig; gesetzlos;** *the magistrates criticized the lawless behaviour of the football crowd*

◊ **lawlessness** *noun* being lawless **Gesetzwidrigkeit; Gesetzlosigkeit;** *the government is trying to fight lawlessness in large cities*
NOTE: no plural

◊ **Law List** *noun* annual published list of barristers and solicitors **Anwaltsverzeichnis**

◊ **Law Lords** *plural noun* members of the House of Lords who are or were judges **derzeitige und ehemalige Revisionsrichter des Oberhauses**

◊ **law-making** *noun* making of laws **Gesetzgebung;** *Parliament is the law-making body in Great Britain*

◊ **lawman** *noun (US)* policeman **Polizist**
NOTE: plural is **lawmen**

◊ **Law Officers** *plural noun* British government posts: the Attorney-General and Solicitor-General in England and Wales, and the Lord Advocate and Solicitor-General in Scotland **(höchste) Rechtsberater des Staates**

◊ **Law Reports** *plural noun* regular reports of new cases and legislation; *(GB)* **Urteils-und Entscheidungssammlung**

◊ **law school** *noun* school where lawyers are trained; *entspricht* **juristische Fakultät**

◊ **Law Society** *noun* organization of solicitors in England and Wales, which represents and regulates the profession **Anwaltskammer**

◊ **Laws of Oleron** *plural noun* the first maritime laws, drawn up in 1216 and used as a base for subsequent international laws **Gesetze von Oleron**

◊ **lawsuit** *noun* case brought to a court by a private person **Klage; Zivilprozeß; to bring a lawsuit against someone** = to tell someone to appear in court to settle an argument **jdn verklagen; to defend a lawsuit** = to appear in court to state your case **einen Prozeß in der Verteidigungsposition führen**

◊ **lawyer** *noun* person who has studied law and can act for people on legal business **Rechtsanwalt; commercial lawyer** *or* **company lawyer** = person who specializes in company law *or* who advises companies on legal problems **ein auf Handelsrecht od Unternehmensrecht spezialisierter Jurist; constitutional lawyer** = lawyer who specializes in constitutional law *or* in interpreting constitutions **ein auf Verfassungsrecht spezialisierter Jurist; international lawyer** = person who specializes in international law **ein auf internationales Recht spezialisierter Jurist; maritime lawyer** = person who specializes in laws concerning ships **ein auf Seerecht spezialisierter Jurist**

lay
1 *verb*
(a) to put *or* to place **legen; to lay an embargo on trade with a country** = to forbid trade with a country **ein Handelsembargo über ein Land verhängen; to lay (an) information** = to start criminal proceedings in a magistrates' court by informing the magistrate of the offence **Anzeige erstatten; to lay a proposal before the House** = to introduce a new Bill before Parliament for discussion **einen Gesetzesvorschlag ins Parlament einbringen**
(b) to lay down = to state clearly **festlegen, festsetzen;** *the conditions are laid down in the document; the guidelines lay down rules for dealing with traffic offences* (NOTE: **laying - laid - has laid**)
2 *adjective* not belonging to a certain profession **Laien-; lay assessor** = person (not a lawyer) with technical knowledge who advises a court on specialized matters **Laienbeisitzer; lay magistrate** = magistrate who is not usually a qualified lawyer (as opposed to a stipendiary magistrate) **Laienrichter (am Magistrates' Court)**

◊ **layman** *noun* person who does not belong to the legal profession **Laie**
NOTE: plural is **laymen**

LC = LORD CHANCELLOR

LCJ = LORD CHIEF JUSTICE

lead
1 *noun* clue *or* piece of information which may help solve a crime **Hinweis, Anhaltspunkt; Spur;** *the police are following up several leads in the murder investigation*

2 *verb*

(a) to be the first *or* to be in front **führen; anführen;** *the company leads the market in cheap computers*

(b) to be the main person in a group (especially in a team of barristers appearing for one side in a case) **(die Prozeßvertretung als erster Anwalt) führen;** *the prosecution is led by J.M. Jones, QC; Mr Smith is leading for the Crown*

(c) to start to do something (especially to start to present a case in court) **eröffnen;** *Mr Jones led for the prosecution; the Home Secretary will lead for the Government in the emergency debate*

(d) to bring evidence before a court **Beweis antreten/erbringen**

(e) to try to make a witness answer a question in court in a certain way **Suggestivfragen stellen;** *counsel must not lead the witness*

NOTE: **leading - led - has led**

◊ **leader** *noun*

(a) person who manages *or* directs others **Leiter/-in; Führer/-in;** *the leader of the construction workers' union or the construction workers' leader; an employers' leader; she is the leader of the trade delegation to Nigeria; the minister was the leader of the party of lawyers on a tour of American courts*

(b) main barrister (usually a QC) in a team appearing for one side in a case **führender Anwalt**

(c) product which sells best **Spitzenreiter, führender Artikel; a market leader** = product which sells most in a market *or* company which has the largest share of a market **ein Marktführer; loss-leader** = article which is sold very cheaply to attract customers **Lockartikel**

(d) important share *or* share which is often bought or sold on the Stock Exchange **Blue Chip, Spitzenwert**

◊ **Leader of the House** *noun* main government minister and member of the cabinet, who is responsible for the administration of legislation in the House of Commons **Führer des Unterhauses**

◊ **Leader of the Opposition** *noun* head of the largest party opposing the government **Oppositionsführer**

◊ **leading** *adjective*

(a) most important **maßgebend, entscheidend; führend;** *leading businessmen feel the end of the recession is near; leading shares rose on the Stock Exchange; leading shareholders in the company forced a change in management policy; they are the leading company in the field;* **leading cases** = important cases which have set precedents **Präzedenzfälle; leading counsel** = main barrister (usually a QC) in a team

appearing for one side in a case **führender Anwalt (unter mehreren Vertretern der jeweiligen Partei)**

(b) leading question = question put by a barrister to a witness which suggests to the witness what his answer ought to be *or* which can only be answered "Yes" or "No" **Suggestivfrage**

COMMENT: leading questions may be asked during cross-examination or during examination in chief

◊ **lead time** *noun* time between placing an order and receiving the goods **Lieferzeit;** *the lead time on this item is more than six weeks*

◊ **lead (up) to** *verb* to be the cause of **führen zu;** *the discussions led to a big argument between the management and the union; we received a series of approaches leading up to the takeover bid*

leak

1 *noun* passing secret information (to the newspapers *or* TV stations, etc.) **Indiskretion; undichte Stelle;** *the government is investigating the latest leak of documents relating to the spy trial*

2 *verb* to pass secret information (to the newspapers *or* TV stations, etc.) **zuspielen;** *information about the government plans has been leaked to the Sunday papers*

lease

1 *noun*

(a) written contract for letting or renting of a building *or* a piece of land *or* a piece of equipment for a period of time, against payment of a fee **Mietvertrag; Pachtvertrag; long lease** *or* **short lease** = lease which runs for fifty years or more *or* for up to two or three years **Mietvertrag od Pachtvertrag mit langer od kurzer Laufzeit;** *to take an office building on a long lease; we have a short lease on our current premises; to rent office space on a twenty-year lease;* **full repairing lease** = lease where the tenant has to pay for all repairs to the property **Miet- od Pachtvertrag mit Reparaturklausel; head lease** = lease from the freeholder to a tenant **Hauptmietvertrag; Hauptpachtvertrag; Hauptvermietung; Hauptverpachtung; sublease** *or* **underlease** = lease from a tenant to another tenant **Untermietvertrag; Unterpachtvertrag; Untervermietung; Unterverpachtung; the lease expires** *or* **runs out in 1995** = the lease comes to an end in 1995 **der Mietvertrag od die Pacht läuft 1995 aus; on expiration of the lease** = when the lease comes to an end **bei Ablauf des Mietvertrages od der Pacht;** *see also* DEMISE

(b) to hold a lease in the North Sea = to have a lease on a section of the North Sea to explore for oil **eine (Öl)konzession in der Nordsee haben**

2 *verb*

(a) to let or rent offices *or* land *or* machinery for a period **vermieten; verpachten;** *to lease offices to small firms; to lease equipment*

(b) to use an office *or* land *or* machinery for a time and pay a fee to the landlord *or* lessee **mieten; pachten;** *to lease an office from an insurance company; all our company cars are leased*

◊ **lease back** *verb* to sell a property *or* machinery to a company and then take it back on a lease **verkaufen und wieder anmieten;** *they sold the office building to raise cash, and then leased it back for twenty-five years*

◊ **lease-back** *noun* arrangement where property is sold and then taken back on a lease **Eigentumsübertragung mit anschließender Rückvermietung an den Verkäufer;** *they sold the office building and then took it back under a lease-back arrangement*

◊ **leasehold** *noun* possessing property on a lease, for a fixed time **Miete; Pacht;** *leasehold property; the company has some valuable leaseholds; to purchase a property leasehold;* **leasehold enfranchisement** = right of a leaseholder to buy the freehold of the property he is leasing **Vorkaufsrecht des Mieters od Pächters**

◊ **leaseholder** *noun* person who holds a property on a lease **Mieter/-in; Pächter/-in**

◊ **leasing** *noun* which leases *or* working under a lease **Leasing;** *the company has branched out into car leasing; a computer-leasing company; to run a copier under a leasing arrangement*

leave

1 *noun*

(a) permission to do something **Erlaubnis;** *counsel asked leave of the court to show a film taken of the accident;* **"by your leave"** = with your permission **"mit Ihrer Erlaubnis"**

(b) to be away from work **Urlaub; leave of absence** = being allowed to be away from work **Beurlaubung; maternity leave** = period when a woman is away from work to have a baby **Mutterschaftsurlaub; sick leave** = period when a worker is away from work because of illness **Krankenurlaub; to go on leave** *or* **to be on leave** = to be away from work **sich beurlauben lassen ; beurlaubt sein;** *she is away on sick leave or on maternity leave*

2 *verb*

(a) to go away from **verlassen; gehen;** *he left his office early to go to the meeting; the next plane leaves at 10.20*

(b) to give property to someone when you die **hinterlassen;** *he left his house to his wife;*

I was left £5,000 by my grandmother in her will

(c) to resign **aufgeben; kündigen;** *he left his job and bought a farm*

NOTE: **leaving - left - has left**

◊ **leave out** *verb* not to include **aus-, weglassen;** *she left out the date on the letter; the contract leaves out all details of marketing arrangements*

legacy *noun* money or personal property (but not land) given by someone to someone else in his will **Vermächtnis;** *she received a small legacy in her uncle's will*

> COMMENT: freehold land left to someone in a will is a **devise**

legal *adjective*

(a) according to the law *or* allowed by the law **legal, rechtmäßig;** *the company's action was completely legal*

(b) referring to the law **juristisch, rechtlich, Rechts-; to take legal action** *or* **to start legal proceedings** = to sue someone *or* to take someone to court **gerichtlich vorgehen; Klage erheben; to take legal advice** = to ask a lawyer to advise about a problem in law **sich juristisch beraten lassen; legal adviser** = person who advises clients about problems in law **Rechtsberater;** *(US)* **legal age** = age at which a person can sue *or* can be sued *or* can undertake business **Volljährigkeit, Eintritt der Geschäfts- und Prozeßfähigkeit; Legal Aid scheme** = British government scheme where a person with very little money can have legal representation and advice paid for by the state **Beratungs- und Prozeßkostenhilfe; Legal Aid Centre** = local office giving advice to clients about applications for Legal Aid and recommending clients to solicitors **Rechtsberatungsstelle; legal charge** = charge created over property by a legal mortgage (as opposed to an equitable charge) **Grundschuld; legal claim** = statement that someone owns something legally **Rechtsanspruch;** *he has no legal claim to the property;* **legal costs** *or* **legal charges** *or* **legal expenses** = money spent on fees to lawyers **Anwaltskosten; legal currency** = money which is legally used in a country **gesetzliche Währung; legal department** *or* **legal section** = section of a company dealing with legal matters **Rechtsabteilung; legal executive** = clerk in a solicitor's office who is not a solicitor and is not articled to become one but has passed the examinations of the Institute of Legal Executives **(qualifizierter) Anwalts- und Notarmitarbeiter; legal expert** = person who has a wide knowledge of the law **juristischer Sachverständiger; legal fiction** = assuming

legal interest = dingliches Recht

something to be true, even if it is not proved to be so (a procedural device used by courts to get round problems caused by statute) **Rechtsfiktion; legal holiday** = day when banks and other businesses are closed **gesetzlicher Feiertag; legal personality** = existence as a body and so ability to be affected by the law **Rechtspersönlichkeit; legal separation** = legal separation of man and wife, ordered by the court, where each becomes separated, but neither is allowed to marry **gerichtlich angeordnetes Getrenntleben; legal tender** = coins or notes which can be legally used to pay a debt (small denominations cannot be used to pay large debts) **gesetzliches Zahlungsmittel; legal writer** = person who writes and publishes commentaries on legal problems **juristischer Kommentator**

◊ **legality** *noun* being allowed by law **Legalität, Gesetzmäßigkeit;** *there is doubt about the legality of the company's action in dismissing him*
NOTE: no plural

◊ **legalize** *verb* to make something legal **legalisieren**

◊ **legalization** *noun* making something legal **Legalisierung;** *the campaign for the legalization of abortion*

◊ **legally** *adverb* according to the law **gesetzlich; rechtlich; the contract is legally binding** = according to the law, the contract has to be obeyed **der Vertrag ist rechtsverbindlich; the directors are legally responsible** = the law says that the directors are responsible **die Direktoren sind gesetzlich verantwortlich**

◊ **legal memory** *noun* time when things are supposed to be remembered in law, taken to be 1189 **rechtlich erfaßte Vergangenheit;** *this practice has existed from before the time of legal memory; see also* IMMEMORIAL

legatee *noun* person who receives a legacy from someone who has died **Vermächtnisnehmer**

legis *see* CORPUS

legislate *verb* to make a law **Gesetze erlassen;** *Parliament has legislated against the sale of drugs*

◊ **legislation** *noun* laws *or* written rules which are passed by Parliament and implemented by the courts **Gesetzgebung; labour legislation** = laws concerning the employment of workers **Arbeitsgesetzgebung**
NOTE: no plural

◊ **legislative** *adjective* used to make laws **legislativ, gesetzgebend;** *the legislative*

processes; Parliament has a legislative function

◊ **legislature** *noun* group of people (such as a Parliament) which makes laws **Legislative**

legitimate
1 *adjective*
(a) allowed by law **legitim; gesetzmäßig;** *he has a legitimate claim to the property*
(b) born to parents who are married to each other **ehelich;** *he left his property to his legitimate offspring; see also* ILLEGITIMATE
2 *verb* to make (a child) legitimate **für ehelich erklären; für rechtmäßig erklären**

◊ **legitimacy** *noun*
(a) state of being legitimate **Prozeß zur Entscheidung über jds Ehelichkeit;** *the court doubted the legitimacy of his claim*
(b) court case to make someone legitimate **Recht-, Gesetzmäßigkeit**

◊ **legitimation** *or* **legitimization** *noun* making a person legitimate (as by the marriage of the parents) **Legitimierung; Legalisierung**

lend *verb* to allow someone to use something for a period **ver-, ausleihen;** *to lend something to someone or to lend someone something; he lent the company money or he lent money to the company; she lent the company car to her daughter; to lend money against security; the bank lent him £50,000 to start his business*

◊ **lender** *noun* person who lends money **Gläubiger; lender of the last resort** = central bank which lends money to commercial banks **Kreditgeber letzter Hand**

◊ **lending** *noun* act of letting someone use money for a time **Ver-, Ausleihung; lending limit** = limit on the amount of money a bank can lend **Kreditlimit**

lenient *adjective* not severe *or* kind (sentence) **mild; nachsichtig;** *the judge took a lenient view of the offence; because of the accused's age, the court passed a lenient sentence*

◊ **leniently** *adverb* in a kind way **mild; nachsichtig;** *the accused were treated leniently by the military tribunal*

lessee *noun* person who has a lease *or* who pays money for a property he leases **Mieter/-in; Pächter/-in**

lessen *verb* to make less *or* to make smaller **vermindern; senken; verkleinern;** *the government is taking steps to lessen the overcrowding in prisons*

lesser *adjective* smaller *or* less important (of two things) **vermindert; gesenkt; verkleinert;** *he pleaded guilty to the lesser charge of manslaughter*

lessor *noun* person who grants a lease on a property **Vermieter/-in; Verpächter/-in**

let
1 *verb*
(a) to allow someone to do something **lassen;** *the magistrate let the prisoner speak to his wife*
(b) to lend a house *or* an office *or* a farm to someone for a payment **vermieten; to let an office** = to allow someone to use an office for a time in return for payment of rent **ein Büro vermieten; offices to let** = offices which are available to be leased by companies **Büroräume zu vermieten;** (NOTE: **letting - let - has let**)
2 *noun*
(a) they took the office on a short let they rented the office for a short time **sie mieteten das Büro für kurze Zeit**
(b) without let or hindrance = without any obstruction **ungehindert**

◊ **let off** *verb* not to punish someone **davonkommenlassen; erlassen;** *the magistrate let the boys off with a warning*

◊ **let-out clause** *noun* clause which allows someone to avoid doing something in a contract **Rücktrittsklausel; Umwandlungsklausel;** *he added a let-out clause to the effect that the payments would be revised if the exchange rate fell by more than 5%*

letter *noun*
(a) piece of writing sent from one person *or* company to another to give information **Brief; business letter** = letter which deals with business matters **Geschäftsbrief; circular letter** = letter sent to many people **Rundschreiben; Umlauf; covering letter** = letter sent with documents to say why they are being sent **Begleitschreiben; follow-up letter** = letter sent to someone after a previous letter *or* after a visit **Nachfaß-, Folgeschreiben; private letter** = letter which deals with personal matters **persönlicher Brief; standard (form) letter** = letter which is sent without change to various correspondents **Standard-, Formbrief**
(b) letter before action = letter written by a lawyer to give a party the chance to pay his client before he sues **anwaltliches Anspruchs-, Aufforderungsschreiben; letter of acknowledgement** = letter which says that something has been received **Bestätigungsschreiben; letters of administration** = document given by a

court to allow someone to deal with the estate of someone who has died without leaving a will *or* where the executor appointed under the will cannot act **Bestallungsurkunde zum Nachlaßverwalter; letter of allotment** *or* **allotment letter** = letter which tells someone how many shares in a new company he has been allotted **Zuteilungsanzeige; letter of application** = letter in which someone applies for a job *or* applies for shares in a new company **Bewerbungsschreiben; Antrag (auf Aktienzuteilung); letter of appointment** = letter in which someone is appointed to a job **Einstellungsschreiben; Ernennungsschreiben; Bestallungsurkunde; letter of attorney** = document showing that someone has power of attorney **Vollmacht; letter of comfort** *or* **comfort letter** = letter supporting someone who is trying to get a loan *or* letter which reassures someone on a certain point **Bonitätsbestätigung; letter of complaint** = letter in which someone complains **Beschwerdebrief; letter of credit** = letter from a bank allowing someone credit and promising to repay at a later date **Akkreditiv; letter of demand** = letter issued by a party *or* by a lawyer demanding payment before taking legal action **Zahlungsaufforderung, Mahnschreiben; letter of indemnity** = letter promising payment of compensation for a loss **Ausfallbürgschaftserklärung; letter of intent** = letter which states what someone intends to do if something happens **Absichtserklärung; letters patent** = official document from the Crown, which gives someone the exclusive right to do something (such as becoming a lord *or* making and selling an invention) **Urkunde, durch die ein Recht od Amt verliehen wird; Patenturkunde; letter of reference** = letter in which an employer or former employer recommends someone for a new job **Zeugnis, Referenz**
(c) air letter = special thin blue paper which when folded can be sent by air without an envelope **Luftpostbrief(papier); airmail letter** = letter sent by air **Luftpostbrief; registered letter** = letter which is noted by the Post Office before it is sent, so that compensation can be claimed if it is lost **Einschreiben**
(d) to acknowledge receipt by letter = to write a letter to say that something has been received **den Empfang schriftlich bestätigen**
(e) written or printed sign (such as A, B, C) **Buchstabe;** *write your name and address in block letters or in capital letters*

◊ **letterhead** *noun* name and address of a company printed at the top of a piece of notepaper **Briefkopf**

letting *noun* letting agency = agency which deals in property to let **Wohnungs-, Immobilienmakler; furnished lettings** = furnished property to let **möblierte Unterkunft zu vermieten;** *see also* LET

levy
1 *noun* money which is demanded and collected by the government *or* by an agency *or* by an official body **Steuer; Abgabe; capital levy** = tax on the value of a person's property and possessions **Vermögenssteuer; import levy** = tax on imports, especially in the EC a tax on imports of farm produce from outside the EC **Einfuhrzoll; training levy** = tax to be paid by companies to fund the government's training schemes **Ausbildungsabgabe**
2 *verb* to demand payment of a tax *or* an extra payment and to collect it **erheben; einziehen;** *the government has decided to levy a tax on imported cars; to levy a duty on the import of computer parts*

lex *Latin word meaning* "law" **Gesetz; lex fori** = law of the place where the case is being heard **Recht des Gerichtsortes/Gerichtsstandes; lex loci actus** = law of the place where the act took place **Recht des Handlungsortes; lex loci contractus** = law of the place where the contract was made **Recht des Vertragsortes; lex loci delicti** = law of the place where the crime was committed **Recht des Tatortes**

liability *noun*
(a) being legally responsible for paying for damage *or* loss, etc. **Haftung;** *his insurers have admitted liability but the amount of damages has not yet been agreed;* **to accept** *or* **to admit liability for something** = to agree that you are responsible for something **für etwas Haftung übernehmen; to refuse liability for something** = to refuse to agree that you are responsible for something **sich weigern, für etwas zu haften; contractual liability** = legal responsibility for something as stated in a contract **Vertragshaftung; limited liability** = principle that by forming a limited liability company, individual members are liable for that company's debts only to the value of their shares **beschränkte Haftung; limited liability company** = company where a member is responsible for repaying the company's debts only up to the face value of the shares he owns; *entspricht* **Gesellschaft mit beschränkter Haftung; liability clause** = clause in the articles of association of a company which states that the liability of its members is limited **Haftungsklausel; vicarious liability** = liability of one person for torts committed by another, especially the liability of an employer for acts committed by an employee in the course of his work **stellvertretende Haftung**
(b) liabilities = debts of a business **Verbindlichkeiten; Schulden;** *the balance sheet shows the company's assets and liabilities;* **current liabilities** = debts which a company should pay within the next accounting period **kurzfristige Verbindlichkeiten; long-term liabilities** = debts which are not due to be repaid for some years **langfristige Verbindlichkeiten; he was not able to meet his liabilities** = he could not pay his debts **er konnte seinen Zahlungsverpflichtungen nicht nachkommen; to discharge one's liabilities in full** = to repay all debts **seinen Verbindlichkeiten nachkommen**
◊ **liable** *adjective*
(a) liable (for) = legally responsible (for) **haften (für), haftbar (für);** *the customer is liable for breakages; the chairman was personally liable for the company's debts; he was found by the judge to be liable for the accident; he will be found liable if he assists a trustee to commit a dishonest breach of trust*
(b) liable to = which is officially due to be paid **unterliegen, unterworfen;** *sales which are liable to stamp duty; such an act renders him liable to a fine*

libel
1 *noun*
(a) untrue written and published or broadcast statement which damages someone's character **(schriftliche/öffentliche) Verleumdung, Beleidigung;** *he claimed that the newspaper report was a libel;* **criminal libel** = serious libel which might cause a breach of the peace **strafbare Verleumdung;** *see also* DEFAMATION, SLANDER
(b) libel act of making a libel **Verleumdung, Beleidigung; action for libel** *or* **libel action** = case in a law court where someone says that another person has written a libel about him **Verleumdungs-, Beleidigungsklage;** (NOTE: no plural for (b))
2 *verb* to damage someone's character in writing or in a broadcast **(schriftlich/öffentlich) verleumden**
NOTE: **libelling - libelled** but US **libeling - libeled**
◊ **libeller** *noun* person who has libelled someone **Verleumder/-in**
◊ **libellous** *adjective* which libels someone's character **verleumderisch;** *he said that the report was libellous*

liberate *verb* to set free **befreien; aus der Haft entlassen;** *three prisoners were liberated*

liberty *noun* being free **Freiheit; at liberty =** free *or* not in prison **frei, in Freiheit;** *they are* *still at liberty while waiting for charges to be brought;* **civil liberties** = freedom for people to work *or* write *or* speak as they want, providing they keep within the law **Grundrechte; Bürgerrechte; liberty of the individual** = freedom for each person to act within the law **persönliche/individuelle Freiheit; liberty of the press** = freedom of newspapers to publish what they want within the law without censorship **Pressefreiheit; liberty of the subject** = right of a citizen to be free unless convicted of a crime which is punishable by imprisonment **Bürgerfreiheit**

licence *or US* **license** *noun*
(a) official document which allows someone to do something *or* to use something; permission given by someone to another person to do something which would otherwise be illegal **Genehmigung; Erlaubnis; Konzession; Lizenz;** *he granted his neighbour a licence to use his field;* **driving licence** = document which shows that you have passed a driving test and can legally drive a car *or* truck, etc. **Führerschein;** *applicants for the police force should hold a valid driving licence;* **gaming licence** = document which allows someone *or* a club to organize games of chance, such as roulette **Erlaubnis zum Betrieb von Glücksspielen; import licence** *or* **export licence** = document which allows goods to be imported *or* exported **Einfuhrlizenz; Ausfuhrlizenz; licence to sell liquor** *or* **liquor licence** = document given by the Magistrates' Court allowing someone to sell alcohol **Schankkonzession;** *(GB)* **off licence** = (i) licence to sell alcohol to be drunk away from the place where it is bought; (ii) shop which sells alcohol to be taken away for drinking elsewhere **(i) Konzession zum Alkoholverkauf; (ii) Wein- und Spirituosenhandlung; on licence** = licence to sell alcohol for drinking on the premises (as in a bar *or* restaurant) **Schankkonzession im Hause; occasional licence** = licence to sell alcohol at a certain place and time only **Sonderkonzession**
(b) permission for someone to leave prison before the end of his sentence **(bedingter) Straferlaß; release on licence** = being allowed to leave prison on parole **bedingter Haftentlassung;** *the appellant will be released on licence after eight months*
(c) goods manufactured under licence = goods made with the permission of the owner of the copyright *or* patent **Lizenzwaren**

◊ **license**
1 *noun (US)* = LICENCE
2 *verb* to give someone official permission to do something **amtlich genehmigen: eine**

Konzession od Lizenz erteilen; *licensed to sell beers, wines and spirits; to license a company to produce spare parts; he is licensed to drive a lorry; she is licensed to run an employment agency;* **licensed premises** = inn *or* restaurant *or* bar *or* shop which has a licence to sell alcohol **konzessionierter Betrieb**

◊ **licensee** *noun* person who has a licence, especially a licence to sell alcohol *or* to manufacture something **Lizenzinhaber; Konzessionsinhaber**

◊ **licensing** *noun* which refers to licences **Schank-; Lizenz-; Konzessions-; licensing agreement** = agreement where a person is granted a licence to manufacture something *or* to use something, but not an outright sale **Lizenzabkommen;** *(GB)* **licensing hours** = hours of the day where alcohol can be bought to be drunk on the premises **Ausschankzeiten; licensing magistrate** = magistrate who grants licences to persons *or* premises for the sale of alcohol **zuständiger Beamter für Schankkonzessionserteilungen**

licit *adjective* legal **zulässig, gesetzlich erlaubt**

lien *noun* legal right to hold someone's goods and keep them until a debt has been paid **Pfandrecht; Zurückbehaltungsrecht;** *the garage had a lien on her car until she paid the repair bill;* **lien on shares** = right of a company to sell shares which have not been fully paid up, and where the shareholder refuses to pay for them fully **Zurückbehaltungsrecht von Aktien; carrier's lien** = right of a carrier to hold goods until he has been paid for carrying them **Spediteurpfandrecht; equitable lien** = right of someone to hold property (which legally he does not own) until the owner pays money due **Sicherungspfandrecht; general lien** = holding goods *or* property until a debt has been paid **allgemeines Pfandrecht; maritime lien** = right to seize a ship against an unpaid debt **Schiffspfandrecht; particular lien** = right of a person to keep possession of another person's property until debts relating to that property have been paid **Pfandrecht an einer bestimmten Sache; repairer's lien** = right of someone who has been carrying out repairs to keep the goods until the repair bill has been paid **Zurückbehaltungsrecht von Reparaturwerkstätten**
NOTE: you have a lien **on** an item

lieu *noun* **in lieu of** = instead of **anstelle von; to give someone two months' salary in lieu of notice** = to give an employee money equivalent to the salary for two months' work and ask him to leave immediately **jdm zwei Monatsgehälter anstelle einer Kündigungsfrist geben**

life *noun*
(a) time when a person is alive **Leben, Lebensdauer; for life** = for as long as someone is alive **lebenslang, auf Lebenszeit;** *his pension gives him a comfortable income for life;* **life annuity** *or* **annuity for life** = annual payments made to someone as long as he is alive **Leibrente; life assurance** *or* **life insurance** = insurance which pays a sum of money when someone dies, or at a certain date if he is still alive then **Lebensversicherung; the life assured** *or* **the life insured** = the person whose life has been covered by the life assurance **der Versicherte (in einer Lebensversicherung); life expectancy** = number of years a person is likely to live **Lebenserwartung; life imprisonment** *or* **life sentence** = being sent to prison as a punishment for a serious crime, but not necessarily for the whole of your life (the penalty for murder) **lebenslängliche Freiheitsstrafe**

COMMENT: life imprisonment lasts on average ten years

life interest = interest in a property which comes to an end when a person dies **lebenslanges Nutzungsrecht; life peer** = member of the House of Lords who is appointed for life **Peer auf Lebenszeit;** *(slang)* **life preserver** = heavy club *or* cosh **Totschläger**
(b) period of time when something is in existence **Laufzeit, Dauer;** *the life of a loan; during the life of the agreement;* **shelf life of a product** = length of time when a product can stay in the shop and still be good to use **Haltbarkeit od Lagerfähigkeit eines Produktes**
◊ **lifer** *noun (slang)* person serving a life sentence **Lebenslänglicher**

lift *verb*
(a) to take away *or* to remove **aufheben;** *the government has lifted the ban on imports of technical equipment; the minister has lifted the embargo on the export of firearms*
(b) *informal* to steal **klauen**

light *noun* **ancient lights** = claim by the owner of a property that he has the right to enjoy light in his windows, which must not be blocked by a neighbour's buildings; *(GB)* **Lichtrecht**

likelihood *noun* being probable *or* being likely **Wahrscheinlichkeit; Plausibilität; likelihood of bias** = being probable that bias will occur **Besorgnis der Befangenheit**

likewise *adverb* in a similar way **gleichermaßen, ebenso;** *the principal agrees to reimburse the agent, and likewise the agent agrees to reimburse his principal*

limit
1 *noun* point at which something ends *or* point where you can go no further **Grenze, Limit; to set limits to imports** *or* **to impose limits on imports** = to allow only a certain amount of goods to be imported **Importbeschränkungen einführen; age limit** = top age at which you are permitted to do something **Altersgrenze; credit limit** = fixed amount of money which is the most a client can owe **Kreditlinie; he has exceeded his credit limit** = he has borrowed more money than is allowed **er hat seine Kreditlinie überzogen; lending limit** = restriction on the amount of money a bank can lend **Kreditlimit; time limit** = maximum time which can be taken to do something **Frist; weight limit** = maximum permitted weight **Höchstgewicht**
2 *verb* to stop something from going beyond a certain point **begrenzen; be-, einschränken;** *the court limited damages to £100;* **the banks have limited their credit** = the banks have allowed their customers only a certain amount of credit **die Banken haben ihre Kreditrahmen begrenzt**
◊ **limitation** *noun*
(a) act of allowing only a certain amount of something **Begrenzung; Be-, Einschränkung;** *the contract imposes limitations on the number of cars which can be imported;* **limitation of liability** = (i) making someone liable for only a part of the damage *or* loss; (ii) making shareholders in a limited company liable for the debts of the company only in proportion to their shareholding **(i) Haftungsbeschränkung; (ii) Haftungsbeschränkung; time limitation** = amount of time which is available **zeitliche Begrenzung; Verjährung; Klagefrist**
(b) **limitation of actions** *or* **statute of limitations** = law which allows only a certain amount of time (usually six years) for someone to start legal proceedings to claim property *or* compensation for damage, etc. **prozessuales Verjährungs-, Ausschlußgesetz**
◊ **limited** *adjective* restricted *or* not open **begrenzt; beschränkt; limited liability** = principle that by forming a limited liability company, individual members are liable for that company's debts only to the value of their shares **beschränkte Haftung; limited market** = market which can take only a certain quantity of goods **begrenzter Absatzmarkt; limited partnership** = partnership where the liability of some of the partners is limited to the amount of

capital they have each provided to the business, and where these partners may not take part in the running of the business, while other working partners are fully liable for all the obligations of the partnership; *entspricht* **Kommanditgesellschaft; limited liability company** = company where a shareholder is responsible for repaying the company's debts only to the face value of the shares he owns; *entspricht* **Gesellschaft mit beschränkter Haftung; private limited company** = company with a small number of shareholders, whose shares are not traded on the Stock Exchange; *entspricht* **Gesellschaft mit beschränkter Haftung; Public Limited Company** = company whose shares can be bought on the Stock Exchange **Aktiengesellschaft**

NOTE: a private limited company is called **Ltd** or **Limited**; a Public Limited Company is called **Plc** or **PLC** or **plc**

◊ **limiting** *adjective* which limits **be-, einschränkend;** *a limiting clause in a contract; the short holiday season is a limiting factor on the hotel trade*

Lincoln's Inn *noun* one of the four Inns of Court in London **einer der Inns of Court (Barristerinnung in London)**

lineal descent *noun* direct descent from parent to child **direkte Abstammung, Abstammung in gerader Linie**

liquid assets *noun* cash, or bills which can be quickly converted into cash **flüssige Mittel**

◊ **liquidate** *verb* **to liquidate a company** = to wind up a company *or* to close down a company and sell its assets **ein Unternehmen liquidieren/auflösen; to liquidate a debt** = to pay a debt in full **eine Schuld begleichen; to liquidate assets** *or* **stock** = to sell assets *or* stock to raise cash **Vermögenswerte und Lagerbestände flüssigmachen; liquidated damages** = specific amount which has been calculated as the loss suffered **bezifferter Schaden**

◊ **liquidation** *noun*
(a) liquidation of a debt = payment of a debt in full **Begleichung einer Schuld**
(b) winding up *or* closing of a company and selling of its assets **Liquidation, Auflösung; the company went into liquidation** = the company was closed and its assets sold **das Unternehmen ging in Liquidation; compulsory liquidation** = liquidation which is ordered by a court **Zwangsliquidation; voluntary liquidation** = situation where a company itself decides to close down **freiwillige Liquidation/Auflösung**

◊ **liquidator** *noun* person who administers the assets and supervises the winding up of a company **Liquidator; Konkursverwalter**

◊ **liquidity** *noun* having cash *or* assets which can easily be sold to raise cash **Liquidität**

lis *Latin word meaning* "lawsuit" **Rechtsstreit; lis alibi pendens** = legal action has been started in another place **Einrede der Rechtshängigkeit; lis pendens** = pending suit **anhängiger Rechtsstreit;** *see also* AD LITEM

list
1 *noun*
(a) several items written one after the other **Liste;** *list of debtors; list of products or product list; to add an item to a list; to cross someone's name off a list; list of cases to be heard;* **list of members** = annual return made by a company listing its shareholders **Aktionärsverzeichnis; address list** *or* **mailing list** = list of names and addresses of people and companies **Adressenliste; black list** = list of goods *or* companies *or* countries which are banned for trade **schwarze Liste; Law List** = annual published list of barristers and solicitors **Anwaltsverzeichnis**
(b) catalogue **Liste, Verzeichnis; list price** = price as shown in a catalogue **Listenpreis**
2 *verb*
(a) to write a series of items one after the other **auflisten;** *the catalogue lists products by category; the case is listed to be heard next week*
(b) listed building = building of special interest (usually because it is old), which the owners cannot alter or demolish **unter Denkmalschutz stehendes Gebäude; listed company** = company whose shares can be bought *or* sold on the Stock Exchange **an der Börse notiertes Unternehmen; listed securities** = shares which can be bought on the Stock Exchange *or* shares which appear on the official Stock Exchange list **an der Börse notierte Wertpapiere**

litem *see* AD LITEM

litigate *verb* to go to law *or* to bring a lawsuit against someone to have a dispute settled **prozessieren**

◊ **litigant** *noun* person who brings a lawsuit against someone **Prozeßführender, Prozeßpartei; litigant in person** = person bringing a lawsuit who also speaks on his own behalf in court without the help of a lawyer **Naturalpartei**

◊ **litigation** *noun* going to law *or* bringing of a lawsuit against someone to have a dispute settled **Prozeß, Rechtsstreit;** *he has got into litigation with the county council*

◊ **litigious** *adjective* (person) who likes to bring lawsuits against people **prozeßsüchtig**

LJ = LORD JUSTICE
NOTE: written after the surname of the judge in legal reports: **Smith LJ said he was not laying down any guidelines for sentencing** but **Smith LJ** is spoken as "Lord Justice Smith"

◊ **LJJ** = LORD JUSTICES

LL.B. *or* **LL.M.** *or* **LL.D.** letters written after someone's name, showing that he has the degree of Bachelor of Laws *or* Master of Laws *or* Doctor of Laws

Lloyd's *noun* central London market for underwriting insurances **Lloyd's; Lloyd's Register** = classified list showing details of all the ships in the world **Lloyd's Register; ship which is A1 at Lloyd's** = ship in very good condition **Schiff, das von Lloyd's als in erstklassigem Zustand befindlich beschrieben wird**

loan
1 *noun* money which has been lent **Kredit, Darlehen; loan capital** = part of a company's capital which is a loan to be repaid at a later date, and is not equity or preference shares **Fremd-, Anleihekapital; loan stock** = money lent to a company at a fixed rate of interest **festverzinsliche Anleihe; convertible loan stock** = money which can be exchanged for shares at a later date **Wandelanleihe; bank loan** = money lent by a bank **Bankkredit, Bankdarlehen; bridging loan** = short-term loan to help someone buy a new house when he has not yet sold his old one **Überbrückungskredit; short-term loan** *or* **long-term loan** = loans which have to be repaid within a few weeks or some years **kurzfristiges od langfristiges Darlehen; soft loan** = loan (from a company to an employee *or* from one government to another) with no interest payable **zinsloses Darlehen; unsecured loan** = loan made with no security **ungesichertes Darlehen**
2 *verb* to lend **(aus)leihen, verleihen**

lobby
1 *noun* part of the House of Commons, where MPs go to vote **Lobby**
2 *verb* to ask someone (such as an MP, local official) to do something on your behalf **beeinflussen (durch Lobbies), als Lobbyist tätig sein;** *a group of local businessmen has gone to London to lobby their MPs on the problems of unemployment in the area*

local *adjective* relating to a certain area *or* place **Orts-, örtlich, lokal; local authority** = section of elected government which runs a certain area (such as a district council) **örtliche Behörde; local court** = court (such as a magistrates' court) which hears cases coming from a certain area; *entspricht* **Amtsgericht;** *a court can give instructions to a local authority as to the exercise of its powers in relation to children in care; a decision of the local authority pursuant to the powers and duties imposed on it by the Act*

loc. cit. *Latin phrase meaning* "in the place which has been mentioned" **am angegebenen Ort, a.a.O.**
NOTE: used when referring to a point in a legal text: **"see also Smith J in** *Jones v. Associated Steel Ltd*

lock
1 *noun* device for closing a door *or* box so that it can be opened only with a key **Schloß;** *the lock is broken on the petty cash box; I have forgotten the combination of the lock of the safe;* **time lock** = lock which will open only at a certain time of day (such as in a bank vault) **Zeitschloß**
2 *verb* to close a door with a key, so that it cannot be opened **ver-, abschließen;** *the manager forgot to lock the door of the computer room; the petty cash box was not locked*

◊ **lock out** *verb* to lock out workers = to shut the factory door so that workers cannot get in and so make them unable to work until the conditions imposed by the management are met **Arbeiter aussperren**

◊ **lockout** *noun* industrial dispute where the management will not let the workers into the factory until they have agreed to the management's conditions **Aussperrung**

◊ **lock up** *verb*
(a) to put (someone) in prison *or* in a psychiatric hospital **einsperren**
(b) to lock up a shop *or* an office = to close and lock the door at the end of the day's work **ein Geschäft od ein Büro abschließen; to lock up capital** = to have capital invested in such a way that it cannot be used for other investments **Kapital fest anlegen**

◊ **locking up** *noun* the locking up of money in stock = investing money in stock so that it cannot be used for other, possibly more profitable, investments **die Festlegung von Geldern in Wertpapieren**

◊ **lock-up**
1 *adjective* **lock-up shop** = shop which has no living accommodation which the proprietor locks at night when it is closed **Geschäft ohne Wohnräume**

2 *noun (informal)* prison **Haftanstalt;** *(umg)* **Knast**

loco *see* IN LOCO PARENTIS

locum (tenens) *noun* person who takes the place of another person for a time **Stellvertreter;** *locums wanted in South London*

locus *Latin word meaning* "place" **Ort**

◊ **locus standi** *Latin phrase meaning* "place to stand": right to be heard in a court **Recht, bei Gericht gehört zu werden;** *the taxpayer does not have locus standi in this court*

lodge *verb* to put *or* to deposit (officially) **hinterlegen, deponieren; to lodge caution** = to deposit a document with the Land Registry which prevents land *or* property being sold without notice **eine Vormerkung eintragen; to lodge a complaint against someone** = to make an official complaint about someone **gegen jdn Beschwerde einlegen; to lodge money with someone** = to deposit money with someone **Geld bei jdm hinterlegen/deponieren; to lodge securities as collateral** = to put securities into a bank to be used as collateral for a loan **Wertpapiere als Sicherheit hinterlegen**

loiter *verb* **loitering (with intent)** = offence of walking slowly, stopping frequently, especially to solicit sexual relations **sich mit Belästigungsabsicht (auffällig lange) aufhalten**

long

1 *adjective* for a large period of time **lang; long credit** = credit terms which allow the borrower a long time to pay **Kredit mit langer Laufzeit; in the long term** = over a long period of time **langfristig, auf lange Sicht; to take the long view** = to plan for a long period before current investment becomes profitable **etwas langfristig betrachten**

2 *noun* **longs** = government stocks which mature in over fifteen years' time **Langläufer, Longs**

◊ **long-dated** *adjective* **long-dated bills** *or* **paper** = bills of exchange which are payable in more than three months' time **langfristige Wechsel od Wertpapiere**

◊ **longhand** *noun* handwriting where the words are written out in full and not typed or in shorthand **Langschrift, normale Schreibschrift;** *applications should be written in longhand and sent to the recruitment officer*

◊ **long-standing** *adjective* (agreement) which has been arranged for a long time **schon lange bestehend, alt**

◊ **long-term** *adjective* **on a long-term basis** = for a long period of time **langfristig; long-term debts** = debts which will be repaid many years later **langfristige Verbindlichkeiten; long-term forecast** = forecast for a period of over three years **langfristige Prognose; long-term loan** = loan to be repaid many years later **langfristiges Darlehen; long-term objectives** = aims which will take years to fulfil **langfristige Ziele**

◊ **Long Vacation** *noun* summer holiday of the law courts and universities **Sommersemesterferien; Gerichtsferien**

loophole *noun* **to find a loophole in the law** = to find a means of doing what you want to do, by finding a way of getting round a law which otherwise would prevent you from acting **eine Gesetzeslücke finden; to find a tax loophole** = to find a means of legally not paying tax **eine Lücke in der Steuergesetzgebung finden**

loot

1 *noun* valuables which have been stolen (by gangs of rioters *or* soldiers, etc.) **Beute;** (NOTE: no plural)

2 *verb* to steal valuable goods from shops *or* warehouse *or* homes (especially during a riot) **plündern;** *the stores were looted by a mob of hooligans*

◊ **looter** *noun* person who steals valuables from shops *or* warehouses *or* homes during a riot **Plünderer**

◊ **looting** *noun* act of stealing valuable goods **Plünderung;** *the police cordoned off the area to prevent looting*
NOTE: no plural

lord *noun* member of the House of Lords **Lord; Lord of Appeal in Ordinary** = one of eleven lords who are paid to sit as members of the House of Lords when it acts as a court of appeal **Mitglied des höchsten britischen Rechtsmittelgerichts; Lord Chancellor** = member of the government and cabinet who presides over the debates in the House of Lords and is responsible for the administration of justice and the appointment of judges **Lordkanzler; Lord Chief Justice** = chief judge of the Queen's Bench Division of the High Court who is also a member of the Court of Appeal **Lordoberrichter; Lord Justice** = title given to a judge who is a member of the Court of Appeal **Lordrichter**
NOTE: written **LJ** after the name: **Smith LJ** = Lord Justice Smith

◊ **Lords** *plural noun*
(a) the House of Lords **Oberhaus;** *the Lords voted to amend the Bill*
(b) members of the House of Lords **Lords; Mitglieder des Oberhauses; Lords Spiritual** =

archbishops and bishops who are members of the House of Lords **geistliche Oberhausmitglieder; Lords Temporal =** members of the House of Lords who are not bishops **weltliche Oberhausmitglieder; the Law Lords =** members of the House of Lords who are or were judges, and are entitled to sit on the Court of Appeal **derzeitige und ehemalige Revisionsrichter des Oberhauses**

◊ **Lord Advocate** *noun* member of the government who is one of the two Law Officers in Scotland **Generalstaatsanwalt**

◊ **Lord Ordinary** *noun* judge of first instance in the outer house of the Scottish Court of Session **erstinstanzlicher Richter**

◊ **Lord President** *noun* judge of the Scottish Court of Session **Präsident des Court of Session**

lose *verb*
(a) not to win (in legal proceedings) **verlieren;** *he lost his appeal to the House of Lords; she lost her case for compensation*
(b) not to have something any more **verlieren; to lose an order =** not to get an order which you were hoping to get **einen Auftrag verlieren;** *during the strike, the company lost six orders to American competitors;* **to lose control of a company =** to find out that you have less than 50% of the shares and so are no longer able to direct the company **die Aktienmehrheit an einem Unternehmen verlieren; she lost her job when the factory closed =** she was made redundant **sie verlor ihre Arbeitsstelle, als die Fabrik geschlossen wurde; lost profits =** profits which would have been made from a transaction which is the subject of an action for breach of contract **Gewinnverlust, Gewinnausfall**
(c) to have less money **verlieren;** *he lost £25,000 in his father's computer company;* **the pound has lost value =** the pound is worth less **das Pfund hat an Wert verloren**
(d) to drop to a lower price **verlieren, einbüßen;** *the dollar lost two cents against the pound; gold shares lost 5% on the market yesterday*
NOTE: **losing - lost - has lost**

◊ **lose out** *verb* to suffer as a result of something **Verluste hinnehmen müssen; den kürzeren ziehen;** *the company has lost out in the rush to make cheap computers*

loss *noun*
(a) not having something which was had before **Verlust; compensation for loss of earnings =** payment to someone who has stopped earning money *or* who is not able to earn money **Verdienstausfallentschädigung;**

compensation for loss of office = payment to a director who is asked to leave a company before his contract ends **Entlassungsabfindung**
(b) having less money than before *or* not making a profit **Verlust, Einbuße; the company suffered a loss =** the company did not make a profit **das Unternehmen mußte (finanzielle) Verluste hinnehmen; to report a loss =** not to show a profit in the accounts at the end of the year **Verluste ausweisen; capital loss =** loss made by selling assets **Kapitalverlust; the car was written off as a dead loss** *or* **a total loss =** the car was so badly damaged that the insurers said it had no value **der Wagen wurde als Totalschaden abgeschrieben; trading loss =** situation where the company's receipts are less than its expenditure **Verlust; at a loss =** making a loss *or* not making any profit **mit Verlust;** *the company is trading at a loss; he sold the shop at a loss;* **to cut one's losses =** to stop doing something which was losing money **seine Verluste verringern**
(c) loss in weight = goods which weigh less than when they were packed **Gewichtsverlust, Gewichtsschwund; loss in transport =** amount of weight which is lost while goods are being shipped **Transportverlust; Transportschaden**

◊ **loss-leader** *noun* article which is sold at a loss to attract customers **Lockartikel**

lot *noun*
(a) large quantity **Menge;** *a lot of people or lots of people are out of work*
(b) group of items sold together at an auction **Los;** *he put in a bid for lot 23; at the end of the auction half the lots had not been sold*
(c) group of shares which are sold **Aktienpaket;** *to sell shares in small lots*
(d) *US* piece of land, especially one to be used for development **Bauplatz**

lottery *noun* game of chance, where numbered tickets are sold and prizes given for certain numbers **Lotterie**

lucrative *adjective* which makes a lot of money **lukrativ, einträglich;** *there is a lucrative black market in car spare parts; he signed a lucrative contract with a TV company*

lump sum *noun* money paid in one single payment, not in several small amounts **Pauschalbetrag;** *he received a lump sum payment of £500; the company offer a lump sum of £1,000 as an out-of-court settlement*

lynch *verb* to catch an accused person and kill him (usually by hanging) without a trial **lynchen**

◊ **lynch law** *noun* killing of accused persons by a mob without a trial **Lynchjustiz**

Mm

machine *noun*
(a) device which works with power from a motor **Maschine; copying machine** *or* **duplicating machine** = machine which makes copies of documents **Kopiergerät; Vervielfältigungsgerät; dictating machine** = machine which records what someone dictates, which a typist can then play back and type out **Diktiergerät**
(b) **machine code** *or* **machine language** = instructions and information shown as a series of figures (0 and 1) which can be read by a computer **Maschinencode; Maschinensprache; machine-readable codes** = sets of signs or letters (such as bar codes *or* post codes) which a computer can read **maschinenlesbare Codes**

◊ **machinery** *noun*
(a) machines **Maschinen;** *the inspector found that the machinery in the factory was dangerous*
(b) organization *or* system *or* method of organizing **Apparat, Maschinerie;** *the local government machinery or the machinery of local government; administrative machinery; the machinery for awarding government contracts*

Madam *noun* formal way of addressing a woman, especially one whom you do not know **gnädige Frau; Dear Madam** = beginning of a letter to a woman whom you do not know **Sehr geehrte gnädige Frau; Madam Chairman** = way of addressing a woman who is in the chair at the meeting **Frau Vorsitzende**

Mafia *noun* the Mafia = Italian secret society, working on criminal activities in Italy and the USA **die Mafia**

magistrate *noun* usually unpaid official who tries cases in a police court **richterlicher Beamter, Polizeirichter; magistrates' clerk** = official of a magistrates' court who gives advice to the magistrates on law *or* practice *or* procedure **Magistratsbeamter; magistrates' court** = (i) building where magistrates try cases; (ii) court presided over by magistrates **(i) (ii) Amtsgericht;** *GB* **erstinstanzliches Gericht; lay magistrate** = unpaid magistrate who is usually not a qualified lawyer **Laienrichter (am Magistrates' Court); stipendiary magistrate** = magistrate who is a qualified lawyer and receives a salary **Berufsrichter (am Magistrates' Court);** (NOTE: unpaid magistrates are also called **Justices of the Peace** or **JPs**)

COMMENT: the Magistrates' Court hears cases of petty crime, adoption, affiliation, maintenance and violence in the home; it can commit someone for trial or for sentence in the Crown Court. A stipendiary magistrate is a qualified lawyer who usually sits alone; lay magistrates usually sit as a bench of three

Magna Carta *noun* the Great Charter, granted by King John in 1215, which gave his subjects certain political and personal freedoms **Magna Charta**

magnetic tape *or (informal)* **mag tape** *noun* plastic tape for recording information on a large computer **Magnetband**

mail
1 *noun*
(a) system of sending letters and parcels from one place to another **Post; by mail** = using the postal services, not sending something by hand or by messenger **per Post; by surface mail** = by land or sea, not by air **auf dem Land- od Seeweg, mit gewöhnlicher Post; by sea mail** = sent by post abroad, using a ship **auf dem Seeweg; by air mail** = by post using a plane **per Luftpost; electronic mail** = system of sending messages from one computer to another, using the telephone lines **elektronische Post, E-Mail**
(b) letters sent or received **Post;** *your cheque arrived in yesterday's mail; my secretary opens my mail as soon as it arrives; the receipt was in this morning's mail*
(c) **direct mail** = selling a product by sending advertising material to possible buyers through the post **Direktversand; Direktwerbung; mail shot** = advertising material sent by mail to possible customers **Rundschreiben; Briefwerbeaktion**
2 *verb* to send something by post **(per Post) (ver)schicken**

◊ **mailing** *noun* sending something in the post **Verschicken, Versenden; direct mailing** = sending of advertising material by post to possible buyers **Direktversand; Direktwerbung; mailing list** = list of names and addresses of people who might be interested in a product *or* list of names and addresses of members of a society **Adressenliste, Versandliste; to buy a mailing list** = to pay a society, etc. money to buy the list of members so that you can use it to mail advertising material **eine Adressenliste kaufen; mailing piece** = leaflet suitable for sending by direct mail **Postwurfsendung; mailing shot** = advertising material sent by mail to possible customers **Rundschreiben; Briefwerbeaktion**

◊ **mail-order** *noun* system of buying and selling from a catalogue, placing orders and sending goods by mail **Postversand; mail-order business** *or* **mail-order firm** *or* **mail-order house** = company which sells a product by mail **Versandhaus; mail-order catalogue** = catalogue from which a customer can order items to be sent by mail **Versandhauskatalog**

maintain *verb*
(a) to keep something going *or* working **aufrechterhalten, unter-, erhalten;** *to maintain good relations with one's customers; to maintain contact with an overseas market; mounted police were brought in to maintain law and order*
(b) to keep something working at the same level **(aufrechter)halten;** *the company has maintained the same volume of business in spite of the recession; to maintain an interest rate at 5%;* **to maintain a dividend** = to pay the same dividend as in the previous year **eine Dividende in gleicher Höhe ausschütten**
(c) to pay for the food and clothing, etc., for a child *or* a person **unterhalten;** *the ex-husband was ordered to maintain his wife and three children*

◊ **maintenance** *noun*
(a) keeping things going *or* working **Aufrechterhaltung, Erhaltung;** *the maintenance of law and order is in the hands of the local police force*
(b) keeping a machine in good working order **Wartung; Instandhaltung; maintenance contract** = contract by which a company keeps a piece of equipment in good working order **Wartungsvertrag**
(c) payment made by a divorced or separated husband *or* wife to the former spouse, to help pay for living expenses and the cost of bringing up the children **Unterhalt; maintenance order** = court order which orders a divorced or separated husband *or* wife to pay maintenance to the former spouse **Unterhaltsurteil; maintenance pending suit** = maintenance obtained by a spouse in matrimonial proceedings until there is a full hearing to deal with the couple's financial affairs **vorläufige Unterhaltszahlung;** (NOTE: US English is **alimony)**

(d) formerly, the crime *or* tort of unlawfully providing someone with money to help that person to pay the costs of suing a third party **widerrechtliche Unterstützung einer prozeßführenden Partei**

Majesty *see* HER MAJESTY'S PLEASURE

majeure *see* FORCE MAJEURE

major *adjective* important **bedeutender, Haupt-; major shareholder** = shareholder with a large number of shares **Hauptaktionär**
◊ **majority** *noun*
(a) larger group than any other **Mehrheit, Majorität; majority of the shareholders** = more than 50% of the shareholders **die Mehrheit der Aktionäre; the board accepted the proposal by a majority of three to two** = three members of the board voted to accept and two voted against **der Vorschlag nahm den Vorschlag mit einer Mehrheit von drei zu zwei Stimmen an; majority vote** *or* **majority decision** = decision made after a vote according to the wishes of the larger group **Mehrheitsbeschluß; majority shareholding** *or* **majority interest** = group of shares which is more than 50% of the total **Mehrheitsbeteiligung; a majority shareholder** = person who owns more than half the shares in a company **ein Mehrheitsaktionär; majority verdict** = verdict reached by a jury where at least ten jurors vote for the verdict **Mehrheitsvotum der Geschworenen**
(b) age at which someone becomes responsible for his actions *or* can sue *or* can be sued *or* can undertake business transactions **Volljährigkeit**

COMMENT: the age of majority in the UK and US is eighteen

maladministration *noun* incompetent *or* illegal administration **schlechte Verwaltung; Mißwirtschaft**

mala in se *Latin phrase meaning* "wrongs in themselves": acts (such as murder) which are in themselves crimes **Unrecht od Verbrechen per se**
◊ **mala prohibita** *Latin phrase meaning* "forbidden wrongs": acts (such as walking on the grass in a park) which are not crimes in themselves, but which are forbidden **Verbote**

malfeasance *noun* unlawful act **rechtswidrige Handlung**

malice *noun* intentionally committing an act from wrong motives *or* intention to commit a crime **Vorsatz; with malice**

aforethought = with the intention of committing a crime (especially murder or grievous bodily harm) **mit Vorsatz, böswillig; express malice** = intention to kill someone **ausdrückliche böse Absicht (bei Tötungen); implied malice** = intention to cause grievous bodily harm to someone **vermutete böse Absicht**

◊ **malicious** *adjective* without a lawful reason *or* with an improper motive **böswillig; vorsätzlich; malicious damage** = deliberate and intentional damage to property **böswillige Sachbeschädigung; malicious falsehood** = lie which is said with the intention of harming someone's business interests **Rufschädigung; Wirtschaftsschädigung; malicious prosecution** = tort of charging someone with a crime out of malice and without proper reason **böswillige Rechtsverfolgung**

◊ **maliciously** *adverb* in a malicious way *or* with the intention of causing harm **böswillig; vorsätzlich;** *he claimed that he had been prosecuted maliciously*

malpractice *noun* acting in an unprofessional *or* illegal way (by a doctor *or* lawyer *or* accountant, etc.) **Sorgfaltspflichtverletzung; ärztlicher Kunstfehler**

manage *verb*
(a) to direct *or* to be in charge of **leiten, führen;** *to manage a department; to manage a branch office*
(b) **to manage property** = to look after rented property for the owner **Immobilienbesitz verwalten**
(c) **to manage to** = to succeed (with some difficulty) in doing something **es schaffen, es fertigbringen;** *did you manage to see the solicitor? counsel managed to have the hearing adjourned; she managed to write six orders and take three phone calls all in two minutes*

◊ **manageable** *adjective* which can be dealt with easily **zu bewältigen, zu handhaben**

◊ **management** *noun*
(a) directing *or* running a business **Management, Unternehmensführung;** *to study management; good management or efficient management;* **line management** = organization of a business where each manager is directly responsible for a stage in the operation of the business **Linienmanagement; management accountant** = accountant who prepares specialized information (especially budgets) for managers so that they can make decisions **Finanzbuchhalter (für besondere Zwecke der Unternehmensleitung); management accounts** = financial information (on sales, costs, credit, profitability) prepared for a

manager *or* director of a company **Rechnungswesen für besondere Zwecke der Unternehmensleitung; management consultant** = person who gives advice on how to manage a business **Unternehmensberater; management course** = training course for managers **Managementkurs; management by objectives** = way of managing a business by planning work for the managers and testing to see if it is completed correctly and on time **zielorientiertes Management; management team** = a group of managers working together **Management-Team; management training** = training managers by making them study problems and work out ways of solving them **Management-Ausbildung; management trainee** = young person being trained to be a manager **Führungsnachwuchs**
(b) group of managers or directors **Management, Unternehmensleitung; top management** = the main directors of a company **Top-Management, Unternehmensspitze; middle management** = the department managers of a company who carry out the policy set by the directors and organize the work of a group of workers **mittleres Management; junior management** = managers of small departments *or* deputies to departmental managers **unteres Management**

◊ **manager** *noun*
(a) head of a department in a company **Abteilungsleiter; accounts manager** = head of the accounts department **Leiter/-in der Buchhaltung; area manager** = manager who is responsible for the company's work (usually sales) in an area **Bezirks-, Gebietsleiter; general manager** = manager in charge of the administration in a large company **geschäftsführender Direktor;** *(US)* **Generaldirektor**
(b) person in charge of a branch or shop **Geschäftsleiter; bank manager** = person in charge of a branch of a bank **Bankdirektor; branch manager** = person in charge of a branch of a company **Geschäftsstellen-, Filialleiter**

◊ **manageress** *noun* woman who runs a shop, or a department **Managerin; Abteilungsleiterin**

◊ **managerial** *adjective* referring to managers *or* to management **Management-, Führungs-; to be appointed to a managerial position** = to be appointed a manager **auf eine Managerposition berufen werden; decisions taken at managerial level** = decisions taken by managers **auf der oberen Geschäftsebene getroffene Entscheidungen**

◊ **managing** *adjective* **managing clerk** = former term for a legal executive **Bevollmächtigter; Vollzugsbeamter; managing director** = director who is in charge of a whole company **geschäftsführender Direktor; chairman and managing director =** managing director who is also chairman of the board of directors **Vorsitzender und geschäftsführender Direktor**

mandamus *Latin word meaning* "we command": court order from the Divisional Court of the Queen's Bench Division, ordering a body (such as a lower court *or* tribunal) to do a certain legal duty **(schriftliche) gerichtliche Verfügung an ein untergeordnetes Gericht;** *the Chief Constable applied for an order of mandamus directing the justices to rehear the case*

mandate *noun* written authority given to a person authorizing and requiring him to act on behalf of the writer **Vollmacht; bank mandate =** written order allowing someone to sign cheques on behalf of a company **Bankvollmacht**

mandatory *adjective* which has to be done *or* to take place **obligatorisch; mandatory injunction =** order from a court which compels someone to do something **einstweilige Verfügung (zur Regelung eines einstweiligen Zustandes); mandatory meeting =** meeting which must be held *or* which all members have to attend **verbindliche/obligatorische Versammlung**

manendi *see* ANIMUS

manifest
1 *adjective* obvious **offenkundig;** *a manifest injustice*
2 *noun* list of goods in a shipment **Ladeliste; passenger manifest =** list of passengers on a ship or plane **Passagierliste**

manipulate *verb* **to manipulate the accounts =** to make false accounts so that the company seems profitable **die Bücher schönen; to manipulate the market =** to work to influence share prices in your favour **Börsenkurse beeinflussen/manipulieren**
◊ **manipulation** *noun* **stock market manipulation =** trying to influence the price of shares **Kursmanipulation**
◊ **manipulator** *noun* **stock market manipulator =** person who tries to influence the price of shares in his own favour **Kursmanipulant**

manslaughter *noun* notifiable offence of killing someone without having intended to do so *or* of killing someone intentionally but with mitigating circumstances **Totschlag;** *he was accused of manslaughter; she was convicted of the manslaughter of her husband;* **involuntary manslaughter =** killing someone without having intended to do so **fahrlässige Tötung; voluntary manslaughter =** killing someone intentionally, but under mitigating circumstances (such as provocation *or* diminished responsibility) **vorsätzliche Tötung**
NOTE: no plural

Maria *see* BLACK

Mareva injunction *noun* court order to freeze the assets of a person who has gone overseas *or* of a company based overseas to prevent them being taken out of the country **dinglicher Arrest**

COMMENT: called after the case of *Mareva Compania Naviera SA v. International BulkCarriers SA*

margin *noun* difference between the money received from selling a product and the money paid for it **Marge; Gewinnspanne; gross margin =** percentage difference between sales income and cost of sales **Bruttomarge**

marine
1 *adjective* referring to the sea *or* ships **See-; Meer(es)-; Schiffs-; marine insurance =** insurance of ships and their cargoes **See(transport)versicherung; marine underwriter =** person who insures ships and their cargoes **See(transport)versicherer**
2 *noun* **the merchant marine =** all the commercial ships of a country **die Handelsmarine**
◊ **maritime** *adjective* referring to the sea *or* ships **See-; Schiffahrts-; maritime law =** laws referring to ships, ports, etc. **Seerecht; maritime lawyer =** lawyer who specializes in legal matters concerning ships and cargoes **ein auf Seerecht spezialisierter Jurist; maritime lien =** right to seize a ship against an unpaid debt **Schiffspfandrecht; maritime perils =** PERILS OF THE SEA; **maritime trade =** carrying commercial goods by sea **Seehandel**

marital *adjective* referring to a marriage **Ehe-, ehelich; marital privileges =** privilege of a spouse not to give evidence against the other spouse in certain criminal proceedings **Aussageverweigerungsrecht eines Ehegatten**

mark
1 *noun*
(a) sign put on an item to show something

Markierung, Zeichen; **assay mark** = hallmark *or* mark put on gold or silver items to show that the metal is of the correct quality **Feingehaltsstempel; kite mark** = mark on British goods to show that they meet official standards **(dreieckiges) Gütezeichen (b)** cross ("X") put on a document in place of a signature by someone who cannot write **Kreuz**

2 *verb* to put a sign on something **markieren;** *to mark a product "for export only"; article marked at £1.50; to mark the price on something; because he could not write he marked an "X" in place of his signature*

◊ **marksman** *noun* (i) person who can shoot a gun very accurately; (ii) person who cannot write, and who has to put an "X" in place of a signature **(i) Scharfschütze; (ii) mit Kreuz Unterzeichnender**

market

1 *noun*
(a) place (often in the open air) where farm produce is sold **Markt; market day** = day when a market is regularly held **Markttag; market dues** = rent for a place in a market **Standmiete**
(b) the **Common Market** = the European Economic Community **der Gemeinsame Markt; the Single Market** = european market within the Common Market where no restrictions exist **der Binnenmarkt;** *the Common Market policy on trade restrictions; the Common Market ministers*
(c) place where a product might be sold *or* group of people who might buy a product **Markt, Absatzgebiet; home** *or* **domestic market** = market in the country where the selling company is based **Binnen-, Inlandsmarkt**
(d) possible sales of a certain type of product *or* demand for a certain type of product **Markt, Absatzmarkt; a growth market** = market where sales are likely to rise rapidly **ein Wachstumsmarkt**
(e) black market = buying and selling goods in a way which is not allowed by law **Schwarzmarkt; to pay black market prices** = to pay high prices to obtain items which are not easily available **Schwarzmarktpreise bezahlen;** *there is a lucrative black market in spare parts for cars; he bought gold coins on the black market*
(f) a buyer's market = market where goods are sold cheaply because there is little demand **Käufermarkt; a seller's market** = market where the seller can ask high prices because there is a large demand for the product **Verkäufermarkt**
(g) closed market = market where a supplier deals with only one agent and does not supply any others direct **geschlossener Markt; free market economy** = system where

the government does not interfere in business activity in any way **freie Marktwirtschaft; open market** = market where anyone can buy and sell **offener Markt; market overt** = market which is open to all, in which a sale gives good title to a buyer, even though the seller's title may be defective **offener Markt**
(h) capital market = place where companies can look for investment capital **Kapitalmarkt; the foreign exchange market** = place where currencies are bought or sold **der Devisenmarkt; forward market** = place where foreign currency or commodities can be bought or sold for delivery at a later date **Terminmarkt**
(i) stock market = place where shares are bought and sold **Börse; to buy shares in the open market** = to buy shares on the Stock Exchange, not privately **Aktien im Freiverkehr kaufen; over-the-counter market** = secondary market in shares which are not listed on the main Stock Exchange **Freiverkehr(smarkt) (für nicht im offiziellen Börsenhandel zugelassene Aktien); market capitalization** = value of a company calculated by multiplying the price of its shares on the Stock Exchange by the number of shares issued **Börsenkapitalisierung; market maker** = person who trades in stocks and shares on the Stock Exchange **Market-maker; market price** = price at which a product can be sold **Marktpreis**
2 *verb* to sell (products) **verkaufen, absetzen;** *this product is being marketed in all European countries*

marriage *noun* act *or* state of being joined together as husband and wife **Heirat; Ehe; by marriage** = because of being married **durch (die) Eheschließung;** *she became a British citizen by marriage;* **marriage settlement** = agreement which is made before marriage where money *or* property is given on trust for the benefit of the future spouse **Güterrechtsvertrag über treuhänderische Zuwendungen anläßlich der Eheschließung; sham marriage** *or* **marriage of convenience** = form of marriage arranged for the purpose of acquiring the nationality of a spouse *or* for some other financial reason **Scheinehe, (nicht vollzogene) Zweckheirat**

marshal *noun*
(a) Marshal of the Admiralty Court = official in charge of the Admiralty Court; *GB* **Amtmann beim Admiralitätsgericht**
(b) *US* official who carries out the orders of a court **Vollstreckungsbeamter**

martial *adjective* relating to the armed services **Militär-, militärisch; martial law** =

rule of a country *or* part of a country by the army on the orders of the main government, the ordinary civil law having been suspended **Kriegsrecht;** *the president imposed or declared martial law in two provinces; the government lifted martial law; see also* COURT-MARTIAL

master *noun*
(a) official in the Queen's Bench Division or Chancery Division of the High Court whose work is to examine and decide on preliminary matters before trial **Rechtspfleger; Practice Master =** master on duty in the High Court, who will hear solicitors without appointment and give directions in relation to the general conduct of proceedings **Rechtspfleger (im High Court); Taxing Master =** official of the Supreme Court who assesses the costs of a court action **Kostenfestsetzungsbeamter**
(b) **Masters of the Bench =** senior members of one of the Inns of Court **ältere Mitglieder der Rechtsanwaltskammer (in London)**
(c) **master and servant =** employer and employee **Arbeitgeber und Arbeitnehmer, Dienstherr und Angestellter; the law of master and servant =** employment law **das Arbeitsrecht**
(d) main *or* original **Original; master copy of a file =** main copy of a computer file, kept for security purposes **Stamm-, Bestandsdatei**
◊ **Master of the Rolls** *noun* judge who presides over the Court of Appeal and is responsible for admitting solicitors to the Roll of Solicitors **Vorsitzender des Court of Appeal**

material
1 *noun*
(a) **materials =** substances which can be used to make a finished product **Material; building materials =** bricks, cement, etc., used in building **Baustoffe, Baumaterial(ien); raw materials =** substances which have not been made in a factory (such as wool, wood, sand) **Rohstoffe**
(b) **display material =** advertisements, photographs, etc., which can be used to attract attention to goods which are for sale **Dekorationsmaterial;** (NOTE: no plural for (b))
2 *adjective* important *or* relevant **wesentlich; material alteration =** change made to a legal document which alters the rights *or* duties in it **rechtserhebliche Änderung; material evidence =** evidence which has important relevance to a case **stichhaltige Zeugenaussage od Beweise; material witness =** witness whose evidence is important to the case **Hauptzeuge**

matricide *noun* murder of one's mother **Muttermord**

matrimony *noun* marriage *or* state of being joined together as husband and wife **Heirat; Ehe**
◊ **matrimonial** *adjective* referring to marriage **Heirats-; Ehe-, ehelich; matrimonial cause =** proceeding concerned with rights of partners in a marriage (such as divorce *or* separation proceedings) **Ehesache; matrimonial home =** place where a husband and wife live together **eheliche Wohnung**

matter
1 *noun*
(a) problem **Problem; Sache, Angelegenheit; it is a matter of concern to the members of the committee =** the members of the committee are worried about it **die Mitglieder des Komitees nehmen die Angelegenheit sehr ernst**
(b) **printed matter =** printed books, newspapers, advertising material, etc. **Drucksache;** (NOTE: no plural)
(c) question *or* problem to be discussed **Frage; Sache, Dinge;** *the most important matter on the agenda; we shall consider first the matter of last month's fall in prices ;* **interlocutory matter =** subsidiary dispute which is dealt with before a full trial **Vorverfahren; matter of fact =** question of fact which has to be decided **Tatfrage; matters of fact =** facts relevant to a case which is tried at court **Tatbestände; matters of law =** law relevant to a case which is tried at court **Rechtsfrage;** *it is a matter of fact whether the parties entered into the contract, but it is a matter of law whether or not the contract is legal*
2 *verb* to be important **von Bedeutung/wichtig sein;** *does it matter if one month's sales are down?*

mature *verb* to be due for payment **fällig sein;** *bill which will mature in three months*
◊ **maturity** *noun* time when a bill *or* government stock *or* insurance is due for payment **Fälligkeitstermin**

maxim *noun* short phrase which formulates a principle, such as "let the buyer beware" **Maxime, Grundsatz**

maximum
1 *noun* largest possible number *or* price *or* quantity **Maximum; up to a maximum of £10 =** no more than £10 **bis zu maximal £10;** (NOTE: plural is **maxima**)
2 *adjective* largest possible **maximal-, Höchst-;** *maximum income tax rate or maximum rate of tax; he was sentenced to the maximum sentence of imprisonment;* **to increase production to the maximum level =**

as much as possible **die Produktion auf das Maximum erhöhen**

mayhem *noun* (i) general riot *or* disturbance; (ii) violent removal of a person's arm or leg **(i) Chaos; (ii) Verstümmelung**

McNaghten *see* M'NAGHTEN

means *plural noun* money which is available **Mittel, Gelder; statement of means** = statement attached to an application for Legal Aid which shows the financial position of the claimant **Armenrechtserklärung; Bedürftigkeitsnachweis**

measure
1 *noun*
(a) way of calculating size *or* quantity **Maß; cubic measure** = volume in cubic feet or metres, calculated by multiplying height, width and length **Hohlmaß; dry measure** = way of calculating the quantity of loose dry goods (such as corn) **Trockenmaß; square measure** = area in square feet or metres, calculated by multiplying width and length **Flächenmaß; inspector of weights and measures** = government inspector who inspects weighing machines and goods sold in shops to see if the quantities and weights are correct **Eichmeister; measure of damages** = calculation of how much money a court should order one party to pay another to compensate for a tort or breach **Schadensbemessung**
(b) type of action, especially a law passed by Parliament or statutory instrument **(gesetzliche) Maßnahme; Gesetz;** *a government measure to reduce crime in the inner cities;* **to take measures to prevent something happening** = to act to stop something happening **Maßnahmen ergreifen, um etwas zu verhindern; to take emergency measures** = to act rapidly to stop a dangerous situation developing **Krisenmaßnahmen ergreifen; an economy measure** = an action to save money **eine Sparmaßnahme; fiscal measures** = tax changes made by the government to improve the working of the economy **steuerpolitische Maßnahmen; as a precautionary measure** = to prevent something taking place **als Vorsichtsmaßnahme; safety measures** = actions to make sure that something is *or* will be safe **Sicherheitsvorkehrungen**
2 *verb*
(a) to find out the size *or* quantity of something; to be of a certain size *or* quantity **(ab)messen; aus-, vermessen;** *to measure the size of a package; a package*

which measures 10cm by 25cm or a package measuring 10cm by 25cm
(b) to measure the government's performance = to judge how well the government is doing **die Leistung der Regierung beurteilen**

◊ **measurement** *noun*
(a) measurements = size (in inches, centimetres, etc.) **Maße;** *to write down the measurements of a package*
(b) way of judging something **Beurteilung, Einschätzung;** *performance measurement or measurement of performance;* **measurement of profitability** = way of calculating how profitable something is **Rentabilitätsberechnung**

mechanical reproduction rights *plural noun* right to make a recording of a piece of music *or* to make a copy of something by photographing it, etc. (usually against payment of a fee) **(mechanische) Reproduktionsrechte**

mediate *verb* to try to make the two sides in an argument come to an agreement **vermitteln;** *to mediate between the manager and his staff; the government offered to mediate in the dispute*

◊ **mediation** *noun* attempt by a third party to make the two sides in an argument agree **Vermittlung;** *the employers refused an offer of government mediation; the dispute was ended through the mediation of union officials*

◊ **mediator** *noun* **official mediator** = government official who tries to make the two sides in an industrial dispute agree **Unterhändler; Schlichter**

medical *noun* referring to the study or treatment of illness **medizinisch; ärztlich; medical certificate** = certificate from a doctor to show that a worker has been ill **ärztliches Attest; medical inspection** = examining a place of work to see if the conditions are safe **Gesundheits- und Sicherheitsüberprüfung; medical insurance** = insurance which pays the cost of medical treatment especially when travelling abroad **Krankenversicherung; medical officer of health (MOH)** = person responsible for the health services in a town **Amtsarzt; he resigned for medical reasons** = he resigned because he was too ill to work **er trat aus gesundheitlichen Gründen zurück**

◊ **medicine** *noun* scientific study of diseases and health **Medizin; forensic medicine** = medical science concerned with solving crimes against people (such as autopsies of murdered persons, taking

autopsies of murdered persons, taking blood samples from clothes) **Gerichtsmedizin**

meet *verb*

(a) to come together with someone **(sich) treffen;** *to meet a negotiating committee; to meet an agent at his hotel; the two sides met in the lawyer's office*

(b) to be satisfactory for **erfüllen, entsprechen;** *to meet a customer's requirements; he failed to meet the conditions of the court order;* **to meet the demand for a new product =** to fill the demand for a product **die Nachfrage nach einem neuen Produkt befriedigen; we will try to meet your price =** we will try to offer a price which is acceptable to you **wir werden uns bemühen, Ihnen preislich entgegenzukommen; they failed to meet the deadline =** they were not able to complete in time **sie haben die Frist nicht einhalten können**

(c) to pay for **bezahlen, begleichen; decken;** *to meet someone's expenses; the company will meet your expenses; he was unable to meet his mortgage repayments;* **to meet your obligations =** to pay your debts **seinen Verpflichtungen nachkommen**

NOTE: **meeting - met - has met**

◊ **meeting** *noun*

(a) coming together of a group of people **Versammlung, Sitzung, Besprechung;** *management meeting; staff meeting;* **board meeting =** meeting of the directors of a company; *entspricht* **Vorstands-, Aufsichtsratssitzung; general meeting** *or* **meeting of shareholders** *or* **shareholders' meeting =** meeting of all the shareholders of a company *or* meeting of all the members of a society **ordentliche Hauptversammlung; Annual General Meeting =** meeting of all the shareholders of a company which takes place once a year to agree the accounts **ordentliche Jahreshauptversammlung; Extraordinary General Meeting =** special meeting of shareholders to discuss an important matter which cannot wait until the next Annual General Meeting **außerordentliche Hauptversammlung**

(b) freedom of meeting **=** being able to meet as a group without being afraid of prosecution **Versammlungsfreiheit; to hold a meeting =** to organize a meeting of a group of people **eine Versammlung abhalten;** *the meeting will be held in the committee room;* **to open a meeting =** to start a meeting **eine Sitzung eröffnen; to conduct a meeting =** to be in the chair for a meeting **eine Sitzung leiten; to close a meeting =** to end a meeting **eine Sitzung schließen; to put a resolution to a meeting =** to ask a meeting to vote on a

proposal **einer Versammlung einen Resolutionsentwurf vorlegen**

member *noun*

(a) person who belongs to a group *or* a society **Mitglied; ordinary member =** person who pays a subscription to belong to a club *or* group **ordentliches Mitglied; honorary member =** special person who does not have to pay a subscription **Ehrenmitglied**

(b) shareholder *or* person who owns shares in a company **Gesellschafter**

(c) organization which belongs to a society **Mitglied;** *the member countries or the member states of the EEC; the members of the United Nations; the member companies of a trade association*

◊ **Member of Parliament** *noun* person elected to represent a constituency in Parliament **Abgeordnete(r);** *(GB)* **Mitglied des Unterhauses**

NOTE: often abbreviated to **MP**. The plural is **MPs**

◊ **membership** *noun*

(a) belonging to a group **Mitgliedschaft;** *membership qualifications; conditions of membership; to pay your membership or your membership fees; is Austria going to apply for membership of the Common Market?*

(b) all the members of a group **Mitglieder;** *the membership was asked to vote for the new president;* **the club's membership secretary =** committee member who deals with the ordinary members of a society **der Vereinsschriftführer/Clubsekretär; the club has a membership of five hundred =** the club has five hundred members **der Verein hat 500 Mitglieder**

memorandum *noun* short note **Mitteilung; memorandum of association =** legal document setting up a limited company and giving details of its aims, capital structure, and registered office **Gründungsurkunde (einer AG); memorandum of satisfaction =** document showing that a company has repaid a mortgage *or* charge **Löschungsbewilligung**

NOTE: plural is **memoranda**

menace *noun* threat *or* action which frightens someone **Drohung; Bedrohung; demanding money with menaces =** crime of getting money by threatening another person **Geld erpressen**

mens rea *Latin phrase meaning* "guilty mind": mental state required to be guilty of committing a crime (intention *or* recklessness *or* guilty knowledge) **Zurechnungsfähigkeit;** *see note at* CRIME *and compare* ACTUS REUS

mental *adjective* referring to the mind **geistig; mental disorder** = sickness of the mind **Geistesgestörtheit**

◊ **mentally** *adverb* in the mind **geistig;** *mentally ill criminals are committed to special establishments*

mention
1 *noun* short hearing at court **kurze Erörterung (der Rechtslage)**
2 *verb* to talk about something for a short time **erwähnen;** *the judge mentioned the need for the jury to examine all the documents; can you mention to the secretary that the date of the next meeting has been changed?*

mentis *see* COMPOS MENTIS

mercantile law *or* **law merchant** *noun* law relating to commerce **Handelsrecht, Handelsgesetz (Teil des Wirtschaftsrechts)**

mercy *noun* showing that you forgive **Gnade; prerogative of mercy** = power (used by the Home Secretary) to commute or remit a sentence **Begnadigungsrecht**

◊ **mercy killing** *noun* euthanasia *or* killing of someone who is ill to put an end to his suffering **Gnadentod; Euthanasie**

merge *verb* to join together **fusionieren, zusammenschließen;** *the two companies have merged; the firm merged with its main competitor*

◊ **merger** *noun* (i) joining of a small estate to a large one; (ii) joining together of two or more companies **(i) (ii) Fusion, Zusammenschluß;** *as a result of the merger, the company is the largest in the field*

meridiem *see* A.M., P.M.

merit *noun* being good or efficient **Leistung, Verdienst; merit award** *or* **merit bonus** = extra money given to a worker because he has worked well **Leistungsprämie; merit increase** = increase in pay given to someone because his work is good **Leistungszulage; merit rating** = judging how well a worker does his work, so that he can be paid according to merit **Leistungsbeurteilung**

◊ **merits of the case** *plural noun* main question which is at issue in an action **Klagegrund**

mesne *adjective* in the middle **Mittel-; Zwischen-; mesne process** = process in a legal action, which comes after the first writ but before the outcome of the action has been decided **Zwischenverfahren; action for mesne profits** = action to recover money that should be paid to a landowner in place of rent by a person who is in wrongful possession **Klage auf Entgeld für unrechtmäßige Nutzung**

messenger *noun* person who brings a message **Bote;** *he sent the package by special messenger or by motorcycle messenger;* **office messenger** = person who carries messages from one person to another in a large office **Bürobote; messenger boy** = young man who carries messages **Laufbursche, Botenjunge**

Messrs *noun* plural form of Mr, used in names of firms **Firma, Herren;** *Messrs White, White & Smith*

messuage *noun* house where people live, and the land and buildings attached to it **Anwesen**

Met *noun (informal)* **the Met** = the Metropolitan Police **Abkürzung für die Londoner Polizei**

metropolitan *adjective* referring to a large city **weltstädtisch; der Hauptstadt; the Metropolitan Police** = the police force of Greater London, which is directly responsible to the Home Secretary **die Londoner Polizei; the Metropolitan Police Commissioner** = the head of the Metropolitan Police, appointed directly by the Home Secretary **Chef der Londoner Polizei; solicitor for the Metropolitan Police** = solicitor responsible for prosecutions brought by the Metropolitan Police **Anwalt für Fälle der Londoner Polizei**

COMMENT: the higher ranks in the Metropolitan Police are Deputy Assistant Commissioner, Assistant Commissioner, and Commissioner. See also DETECTIVE, POLICE

Michaelmas *noun*
(a) 29th September: one of the quarter days when rent is payable on land **Michaelis(tag), Quartalszahltag**
(b) one of the four sittings of the law courts; one of the four law terms **Michaelis(tag); Herbstsitzungsperiode**

microfiche *noun* index sheet, made of several microfilm photographs **Mikrofiche;** *we hold our records on microfiche*

◊ **microfilm**

1 *noun* roll of film on which a document is photographed in very small scale **Mikrofilm;** *we hold our records on microfilm*
2 *verb* to make a very small scale photograph **auf Mikrofilm aufnehmen;** *send the 1980 correspondence to be microfilmed or for microfilming*

middle *adjective* in the centre *or* between two points **mittlerer, Mittel-;** **middle management** = department managers in a company, who carry out the policy set by the directors and organize the work of a group of workers **mittleres Management**
◊ **Middle Temple** *noun* one of the four Inns of Court in London **einer der Inns of Court (Barristerinnung in London)**

Midland and Oxford Circuit *noun* one of the six circuits of the Crown Court, to which barristers belong, with its centre in Birmingham **Gerichtsbezirk Midland und Oxford**

Midsummer day *noun* 24th June: one of the four quarter days when rent is payable on land **Sommersonnenwende; Johanni(stag)**

minder *noun (slang)* bodyguard *or* person employed to protect someone **Leibwächter**

minimal *adjective* the smallest possible **minimal;** *there was a minimal quantity of imperfections in the new stock; the head office exercises minimal control over the branch offices*
◊ **minimis** *see* DE MINIMIS
◊ **minimize** *verb* to make something seem to be very small and not very important **bagatellisieren; herabsetzen;** *do not minimize the risks involved; he always minimizes the difficulty of the project*
◊ **minimum**
1 *noun* smallest possible quantity *or* price *or* number **Minimum;** *to keep expenses to a minimum; to reduce the risk of a loss to a minimum*
2 *adjective* smallest possible **Mindest-;** **minimum dividend** = smallest dividend which is legal and accepted by the shareholders **Mindestdividende; minimum payment** = smallest payment necessary **Mindestbetrag; minimum sentence** = shortest possible sentence allowed in law for a certain offence **Mindeststrafe; minimum wage** = lowest hourly wage which a company can legally pay its workers **Mindestlohn**

minister *noun* member of a government who is in charge of a ministry **Minister/-in;** *a*

government minister; the Minister of Information or the Information Minister; the Minister of Foreign Affairs or the Foreign Minister; the Minister of Justice or the Justice Minister; **Minister of State** = person who is in charge of a section of a government department **Staatsminister; Staatssekretär**

COMMENT: in the USA, heads of government departments are called secretary: the Secretary for Commerce; in the UK, heads of government departments (see below) are called Secretary of State: the Secretary of State for Defence

◊ **ministerial** *adjective* referring to a minister **ministeriell, Ministerial-, Minister-; ministerial tribunal** = tribunal set up by a government minister to hear appeals from local tribunals **parlamentarischer Anhörungsausschuß**
◊ **ministry** *noun*
(a) department in the government **Ministerium;** *he works in the Ministry of Finance or the Finance Ministry; he is in charge of the Ministry of Information or of the Information Ministry; a ministry official or an official from the ministry*
(b) government **Regierung; during the Wilson ministry** = when the government headed by Prime Minister Wilson was in office **während der Amtszeit der Regierung Wilson**

COMMENT: in Britain and the USA, important ministries are called departments: the Department of Trade and Industry; the Commerce Department. Note also that the UK does not have a government department called the "Ministry of Justice", and the duties of supervising the administration of justice fall to the Lord Chancellor's office and the Home Office

minor
1 *adjective* less important **unbedeutend, unwichtig;** *minor expenditure; minor shareholders;* **a loss of minor importance** = not a very serious loss **ein Verlust von geringer Bedeutung**
2 *noun* person less than eighteen years old **Minderjähriger**
◊ **minority** *noun*
(a) being less than eighteen years old *or* time when someone is less than eighteen years old **Minderjährigkeit;** *a person is not liable for debts contracted during his minority*
(b) number *or* quantity which is less than half of the total **Minorität, Minderheit;** *a minority of board members opposed the chairman;* **minority shareholding** *or*

minority interest = group of shares which are less than one half of the shares in a company **Minderheitsbeteiligung; minority shareholder** = person who owns a group of shares but less than half of the shares in a company **Minderheitsaktionär; in the minority** = being fewer than half **in der Minderheit;** *the small parties are in the minority on the local council*

minute
1 *noun*
(a) one sixtieth part of an hour **Minute;** *counsel cross-examined the witness for fifty minutes*
(b) minutes = the record of what happened at a meeting, especially the record of a general meeting of a company **Protokoll; to take the minutes** = to write notes of what happened at a meeting **Protokoll führen; the chairman signed the minutes of the last meeting** = he signed them to show that they were a correct record of what was said and what decisions were taken **der Vorsitzende zeichnete das Protokoll der letzten Sitzung ab; this will not appear in the minutes of the meeting** = this is unofficial and will not be noted as having been said **dies wird nicht in das Protokoll aufgenommen**
(c) minutes of order = a draft order submitted to a court when a party wishes the court to make an order **Verfügungsentwurf**
2 *verb* to put something into the minutes of a meeting **zu Protokoll nehmen, protokollieren;** *the chairman's remarks about the auditors were minuted;* **I do not want that to be minuted** *or* **I want that not to be minuted** = do not put that remark into the minutes of the meeting **ich möchte nicht, daß das in das Protokoll aufgenommen wird**

◊ **minutebook** *noun* book in which the minutes of a meeting are kept **Protokollbuch**

misadventure *noun* accident **Unglück; death by misadventure** = accidental death **Unfalltod;** *the coroner's verdict was death by misadventure*

misappropriate *verb* to steal *or* to use illegally money which is not yours, but with which you have been trusted **unterschlagen; veruntreuen**

◊ **misappropriation** *noun* illegal use of money by someone who is not the owner but who has been trusted to look after it **Unterschlagung; Veruntreuung**

misbehaviour *noun* bad behaviour, especially a criminal offence committed by a public official **ungebührliches Betragen**

miscalculate *verb* to calculate wrongly **falsch berechnen;** *the salesman miscalculated the discount, so we hardly broke even on the deal*

◊ **miscalculation** *noun* mistake in calculating **Fehlberechnung**

miscarriage of justice *noun* decision wrongly *or* unjustly reached by a court *or* decision which goes against the rights of a party in a case, in such a way that the decision may be reversed on appeal **Justizirrtum; Rechtsbeugung**

miscellaneous *adjective* various *or* mixed *or* not all of the same sort **verschieden;** *miscellaneous items; a box of miscellaneous pieces of equipment; miscellaneous expenditure*

misconduct *noun* illegal action *or* action which can harm someone **Verfehlung; Amtspflichtverletzung; professional misconduct** = behaviour by a member of a profession (such as a lawyer *or* accountant *or* doctor) which the body which regulates that profession considers to be wrong **Berufsvergehen (z.B. standeswidriges Verhalten); wilful misconduct** = doing something which harms someone while knowing it is wrong **vorsätzliches Fehlverhalten**
NOTE: no plural

miscount
1 *noun* mistake in counting **Rechenfehler**
2 *verb* to count wrongly **falsch (aus)zählen; sich verzählen;** *the votes were miscounted, so the ballot had to be taken again*

misdeed *noun* crime **Untat; Verbrechen**

misdemeanour *noun* minor crime **Vergehen, Übertretung;** *he was charged with several misdemeanours, including driving without a valid licence and creating a disturbance*

misdirect *verb* to give wrong directions to a jury on a point of law **irreführen; irreleiten**

◊ **misdirection** *noun* giving wrong directions to a jury on a point of law **Irrreführung; Irreleitung**

misfeasance *noun* doing something improperly **Vergehen, Delikt**
NOTE: no plural

misinterpret *verb* to understand something wrongly **mißverstehen,**

mißinterpretieren; *the rioters misinterpreted the instructions of the police*

◇ **misinterpretation** *noun* wrong interpretation *or* understanding of something **falsche Auslegung/Interpretation; clause which is open to misinterpretation** = clause which can be wrongly interpreted **Klausel, die falsch ausgelegt werden kann**

misjoinder *noun* wrongly joining someone as a party to an action **unzulässige Einbeziehung eines Streitgenossen**

mislead *verb* to make someone understand something wrongly **irreführen;** *the instructions in the document are quite misleading; the wording of the will is misleading and needs to be clarified; the judge misled the jury in his summing up* NOTE: *misleading - misled*

mismanage *verb* to manage badly **schlecht verwalten**

◇ **mismanagement** *noun* bad management **Mißwirtschaft;** *the company failed because of the chairman's mismanagement*

misprision *noun* generally, a mistake in doing something **Vergehen; Versäumnis; misprision of treason** = crime of knowing that treason has been committed **strafbares Unterlassen der Anzeige von Hochverrat**

misrepresent *verb* to report facts wrongly **falsch darstellen**

◇ **misrepresentation** *noun* making a wrong statement with the intention of persuading someone to enter into a contract **falsche Darstellung; fraudulent misrepresentation** = false statement made wilfully to trick someone *or* to persuade someone to enter into a contract **arglistige Täuschung**

mistake *noun* wrong action *or* wrong decision **Fehler; to make a mistake** = to do something wrong **einen Fehler machen;** *the shop made a mistake and sent the wrong items; there was a mistake in the address; she made a mistake in addressing the letter;* **by mistake** = in error *or* wrongly **irrtümlich, versehentlich, aus Versehen;** *they sent the wrong items by mistake; she put my letter into an envelope for the chairman by mistake;* **mistake in venue** = starting legal proceedings in the wrong court **örtliche Unzuständigkeit (eines Gerichts)**

◇ **mistaken identity** *noun* situation where someone is wrongly thought to be another person **Personenverwechslung;** *he was arrested for burglary, but released after it*

had been established that it was a case of mistaken identity

mistrial *noun* trial which is not valid **Prozeß mit Verfahrensmängeln**

misunderstanding *noun* lack of agreement *or* mistake **Meinungsverschiedenheit; Mißverständnis;** *there was a misunderstanding over my tickets*

misuse *noun* wrong use **Mißbrauch; falsche Anwendung; Zweckentfremdung;** *misuse of funds or of assets*

mitigate *verb* to make (a crime) less serious **mildern; mitigating circumstances** *or* **factors** = things which make a crime less serious *or* which can excuse a crime **mildernde Umstände**

◇ **mitigation** *noun* reduction of a sentence *or* of the seriousness of a crime **Milderung;** *in mitigation, counsel submitted evidence of his client's work for charity; defence counsel made a speech in mitigation;* **plead in mitigation** = things said in court on behalf of a guilty party to persuade the court to impose a lenient sentence **auf Strafmilderung plädieren; mitigation of damages** = reduction in the extent of damages awarded **Herabsetzen des Schadensersatzes** NOTE: used in the construction **in mitigation of**

M'Naghten Rules *noun* rules which a judge applies in deciding if a person charged with a crime is insane **Regeln zur Überprüfung der Schuldfähigkeit**

COMMENT: to prove insanity, it has to be shown that because of a diseased mind, the accused did not know what he was doing *or* did not know that his action was wrong. Based on the case of *R v. M'Naghten* (1843) in which the House of Lords considered and ruled on the defence of insanity

mob *noun (US)* the Mafia **die Mafia**

◇ **mobster** *noun (US)* member of the mob **Gangster**

modify *verb* to change *or* to make something fit a different use **modifizieren, ändern;** *the chairman modified the reporting system; this is the new modified agreement; the car will have to be modified to pass the government tests*

◇ **modification** *noun* change **Modifizierung, Änderung;** *to make or to carry out modifications to the plan; we asked for modifications to the contract*

modus operandi *Latin phrase meaning* "way of working": especially a particular way of committing crimes which can identify a criminal **Modus operandi**

MOH = MEDICAL OFFICER OF HEALTH

moiety *noun* half **Hälfte**

molest *verb* to threaten violent behaviour against (a child *or* a woman, especially a spouse) in a sexual way **belästigen; nötigen;** *he was accused of molesting children in the park*
◊ **molestation** *noun* act of threatening violent behaviour towards a child *or* a woman, especially a spouse **Belästigung; Nötigung; non-molestation order** = order made by a court in matrimonial proceedings to prevent one spouse from molesting the other **gerichtliche Verfügung, jdn nicht mehr zu belästigen**
◊ **molester** *noun* person who molests **Belästiger; Nötiger;** *a convicted child molester*

money *noun*
(a) coins and notes used for buying and selling **Geld; cheap money** = money which can be borrowed at a low rate of interest **billiges Geld; danger money** = extra salary paid to workers in dangerous jobs **Gefahrenzulage; dear money** = money which has to be borrowed at a high rate of interest **teures Geld; hot money** = (i) money which is moved from country to country to get the best returns; (ii) illegal money **(i) (ii) heißes Geld; paper money** = money in notes, not coins **Papiergeld; ready money** = cash *or* money which is immediately available **Bargeld, flüssige Mittel; money had and received** = cause of action where one party has had money which really belongs to someone else **Klage auf Herausgabe ungerechtfertigter Bereicherung**
(b) money supply = amount of money which exists in a country **Geldreserve, Geldvolumen; money markets** = markets for buying and selling short-term loans **Geldmärkte; money rates** = rates of interest for borrowers or lenders **Geldmarktsätze**
(c) money order = document which can be bought for sending money through the post **Postanweisung; foreign money order** *or* **international money order** *or* **overseas money order** = money order in a foreign currency which is payable to someone living in a foreign country **Auslandszahlungsanweisung**
(d) monies = sums of money **Gelder;** *monies owing to the company; to collect monies due*
◊ **moneylender** *noun* person who lends money at interest **Geldverleiher**

monitor
1 *noun* screen (like a TV screen) on a computer **Monitor, Bildschirm**
2 *verb* to check *or* to examine how something is working **überwachen;** *they are monitoring the new system of dealing with young offenders*

monogamy *noun* system of society where a man is married to one woman at a time **Monogamie**

monopoly *noun* situation where one person *or* company controls all the market in the supply of a product *or* right given to one person *or* company to control all the market in the supply of a product **Monopol;** *to have the monopoly of alcohol sales or to have the alcohol monopoly; the company has the absolute monopoly of imports of French wine;* **public monopoly** *or* **state monopoly** = situation where the state is the only suppliers of a product or service (such as the Post Office, the Coal Board) **staatliches Monopol; the Monopolies (and Mergers) Commission** = British body which examines takeovers and mergers to make sure that a monopoly is not being created; *entspricht* **das Bundeskartellamt**
NOTE: American English uses **trust** more often
◊ **monopolize** *verb* to create a monopoly *or* to get control of all the supply of a product **monopolisieren; den Markt beherrschen**
◊ **monopolization** *noun* making a monopoly **Monopolisierung**

monopsony *noun* situation where one person *or* company controls all the purchasing in a certain market **Nachfragemonopol**

Monroe doctrine *noun (US)* principle that the USA has an interest in preventing outside interference in the internal affairs of other American states **Monroe Doktrin**

COMMENT: so called because it was first proposed by President Monroe in 1823

monthly *adjective* happening every month **monatlich;** *she paid off the debt in monthly instalments; he was ordered to pay a sum of money to his wife monthly*

moonlight *verb (informal)* to do a second job for cash (often in the evening) as well as a regular job, and usually not declaring the money earned to the income tax authorities **schwarzarbeiten**
◊ **moonlighter** *noun* person who moonlights **Schwarzarbeiter**

◊ **moonlighting** *noun* doing a second job **Schwarzarbeit;** *he makes thousands a year from moonlighting*

mooring *noun* place where boats can be tied up in a harbour **Liegeplatz**

moral *adjective* referring to the difference between what is right and what is wrong **moralisch, Moral-;** *the high moral standard which should be set by judges*

◊ **morals** *plural noun* standards of behaviour **Moral; to corrupt someone's morals** = to make someone behave in a way which goes against the normal standard of behaviour **jdn korrumpieren**

moratorium *noun* temporary stop to repayments of money owed **Moratorium, Zahlungsaufschub;** *the banks called for a moratorium on payments*
NOTE: plural is **moratoria**

mortality *noun* **mortality tables** = chart, used by insurers, which shows how long a person of a certain age can be expected to live, on average **Sterbetabellen**

mortgage
1 *noun* (i) agreement where someone lends money to another person so that he can buy a property, the property being used as the security; (ii) money lent in this way **(i) (ii) Hypothek;** *to take out a mortgage on a house; to buy a house with a £20,000 mortgage;* **mortgage (re)payments** = money paid each month as interest on a mortgage, together with repayment of a small part of the capital borrowed **Hypothekentilgungen; endowment mortgage** = mortgage backed by an endowment policy **durch eine Lebensversicherung abgesicherte Hypothek; equitable mortgage** = mortgage which does not give the mortgagee a legal estate in the land mortgaged **formlose Hypothek, auf Equity-Recht beruhende Hypothek; first mortgage** = main mortgage on a property **Ersthypothek; puisne mortgage** = mortgage where the deeds of the property have not been deposited with the lender **nachstehende Hypothek; second mortgage** = further mortgage on a property which is already mortgaged, the first mortgage always having a prior claim **Zweithypothek; to foreclose on a mortgaged property** = to take possession of a property because the owner cannot repay money which he has borrowed, using the property as security **aus einer Hypothek zwangsvollstrecken; to pay off a mortgage** = to pay back the principal and all the interest on a loan to buy a property **eine Hypothek abzahlen; mortgage**

bond = certificate showing that a mortgage exists and that property is security for it **Pfandbrief; mortgage debenture** = debenture where the lender can be repaid by selling the company's property **Hypothekenpfandbrief**
2 *verb* to accept a loan with a property as security **hypothekarisch belasten;** *the house is mortgaged to the bank; he mortgaged his house to set up in business*

◊ **mortgagee** *noun* person or company which lends money for someone to buy a property and takes a mortgage of the property as security **Hypothekengläubiger**

◊ **mortgagor** *noun* person who borrows money, giving a property as security **Hypothekenschuldner**

mortem *see* POST MORTEM

mortis *see* DONATIO, RIGOR

most favoured nation *noun* country which has the best trade terms **meistbegünstigtes Land; most-favoured-nation clause** = agreement between two countries that each will offer the best possible terms in commercial contracts **Meistbegünstigungsklausel**

motion *noun*
(a) moving about **Bewegung; time and motion study** = study in an office *or* factory of the time taken to do certain jobs and the movements workers have to make to do them **Zeit- und Bewegungsstudie;** *entspricht* **REFA-Studie**
(b) proposal which will be put to a meeting for that meeting to vote on **Antrag;** *to propose or to move a motion; the meeting voted on the motion; to speak against or for a motion;* **the motion was carried** *or* **was defeated by 220 votes to 196** = the motion was approved *or* not approved **der Antrag wurde mit 220 zu 196 Stimmen angenommen od abgelehnt; to table a motion** = to put forward a proposal for discussion by putting details of it on the table at a meeting **einen Antrag einbringen**
(c) application to a judge in court, asking for an order in favour of the person making the application **Antrag; notice of motion** = document telling the other party to a case that an application will be made to the court **Antragsschrift, Antragsschriftsatz (an den Prozeßgegner in einem schwebenden Verfahren)**

motive *noun* reason for doing something **Motiv, Beweggrund**

mounted *adjective* **mounted police berittene Polizei;** *mounted police were brought in to control the crowd*

◊ **mounting** *adjective* which is going up *or* rising **steigend, zunehmend;** *there is mounting pressure on the police to solve the murder or to combat inner city crime*

move *verb*
(a) to go from one place to another **umziehen; verlegen;** *the company is moving from London Road to the centre of town; we have decided to move our factory to a site near the airport*
(b) to propose formally that a motion be accepted by a meeting **beantragen;** *he moved that the accounts be agreed; I move that the meeting should adjourn for ten minutes*
(c) to make an application to the court **einen Antrag stellen**

◊ **movable** *or* **moveable**
1 *adjective* which can be moved **beweglich; movable property** = chattels and other objects which can be moved (as opposed to land) **Mobilien, bewegliches Vermögen**
2 *plural noun* **movables** = movable property **Mobilien**

◊ **movement** *noun*
(a) changing position *or* going up or down **Bewegung;** *movements in the money markets; cyclical movements of trade;* **movements of capital** = changes of investments from one country to another **Kapitalverkehr; free movement of capital** = ability to transfer capital from one EC country to another without any restrictions **freier Kapitalverkehr; stock movements** = passing of stock into or out of the warehouse **Warenbewegung**
(b) group of people working towards the same aim **Bewegung**

◊ **mover** *noun* person who proposes a motion **Antragsteller/-in**

MP = MEMBER OF PARLIAMENT, MILITARY POLICE

MR = MASTER OF THE ROLLS
NOTE: usually written after the surname: **Lord Smith, MR** but spoken as "the Master of the Rolls, Lord Smith"

Mr Big *noun (informal)* important criminal whose name is not known, but who is supposed to be in control of a large criminal operation **Mr. X**

mug
1 *noun (informal)*
(a) person who is easily cheated **Trottel**

(b) face **Visage; mug shot** = photograph of a criminal taken, after he has been detained, for the police records **Verbrecherfoto**
2 *verb* to attack and rob someone **berauben;** *the tourists were mugged in the station; he was accused of mugging an old lady in the street*
NOTE: **mugging - mugged**

◊ **mugger** *noun* person who attacks and robs someone **Räuber**

◊ **mugging** *noun* attacking and robbing someone **Straßenraub;** *the number of muggings has increased sharply over the last few years*

multiple *adjective* many **mehr-, vielfach; multiple entry visa** = visa which allows a visitor to enter a country many times **Visum zur mehrmaligen Einreise; multiple ownership** = situation where something is owned by several parties **Gemeinschaftseigentum**

municipal *adjective*
(a) referring to a town **städtisch, Stadt-, kommunal, Kommunal-;** *municipal taxes; municipal offices*
(b) **municipal law** = law which is in operation within a state, as opposed to international law **Landesgesetz**

◊ **municipality** *noun* corporation of a town **Stadtverwaltung**

murder
1 *noun*
(a) notifiable offence of killing someone illegally and intentionally **Mord;** *he was charged with murder or he was found guilty of murder; the murder rate has fallen over the last year* (NOTE: no plural)
(b) an act of killing someone illegally and intentionally **Mord;** *three murders have been committed during the last week*
2 *verb* to kill someone illegally and intentionally **morden**

◊ **murderer** *noun* person who commits a murder **Mörder**

◊ **murderess** *noun* woman who commits a murder **Mörderin**

Muslim *adjective* relating to religion and law following the commands of the prophet Mohammed **mohammedanisch, moslemisch**

mutiny
1 *noun* agreement between two or more members of the armed forces to disobey commands of superior officers and to try to take command themselves **Meuterei, Rebellion**
2 *verb* to carry out a mutiny **meutern, rebellieren**

◊ **mutineer** *noun* person who takes part in a mutiny **Meuterer, Rebell**

mutual *adjective* belonging to two or more people **gemeinsam; mutual (insurance) company** = company which belongs to insurance policy holders **Versicherungsverein auf Gegenseitigkeit;** *(US)* **mutual funds** = organizations which take money from small investors and invest it in stocks and shares for them, the investment being in the form of shares in the fund **Investmentfondsgesellschaft; mutual wills** = wills made by two people, where each leaves his property to the other **gegenseitige Testamente**

◊ **mutuality** *noun* state where two parties are bound contractually to each other **Reziprozität**

Nn

name
1 *noun* word used to call a thing *or* a person **Name; brand name** = name of a particular make of product **Markenname; corporate name** = name of a large corporation **Firmenname; under the name of** = using a particular name **unter dem Namen; trading under the name of "Best Foods"** = using the name "Best Foods" as a commercial name for selling a product, but not as the name of the company **unter der Bezeichnung "Best Foods" verkaufen**
2 *verb* to give someone a name *or* to mention someone's name **nennen; erwähnen;** *the Chief Constable was named in the divorce case; (of the speaker)* **to name a Member of Parliament** = to say that an MP has been guilty of misconduct **ein Mitglied des Parlamentes namentlich zur Ordnung rufen**

◊ **named** *adjective* **person named in the policy** = person whose name is given on an insurance policy as the person insured **der Versicherte**

nark *noun (slang)* informer *or* person who gives information to the police **Spitzel**

nation *noun* country and the people living in it **Nation; Volk**

◊ **national**
1 *adjective* referring to a particular country **national, National-; National Insurance** = state insurance which pays for medical care, hospitals, unemployment benefits, etc. **Sozialversicherung; National Insurance contributions** = money paid into the National Insurance scheme by the employer and the worker **Sozialversicherungsbeiträge; gross national product** = annual value of goods and services in a country including income from other countries **Bruttosozialprodukt; National Savings** = savings scheme for small investors run by the Post Office (including a savings bank, savings certificates and premium bonds) **britisches Sparsystem**
2 *noun* person who is a citizen of a state **Staatsbürger;** *the government ordered the deportation of all foreign nationals*

◊ **nationality** *noun* being the citizen of a state **Nationalität; he is of United Kingdom nationality** = he is a citizen of the United Kingdom **er hat britische Staatsangehörigkeit; dual nationality** = to be a citizen of two countries at the same time **doppelte Staatsangehörigkeit**

◊ **nationalize** *verb* to put a privately-owned industry under state ownership and control **verstaatlichen; nationalized industry** = industry which was once privately owned, but now belongs to the state **verstaatlichter Wirtschaftszweig**

◊ **nationalization** *noun* taking over of a private industry by the state **Verstaatlichung;** *compare* NATURALIZATION

nature *noun* kind *or* type **Beschaffenheit, Natur;** *what is the nature of the contents of the parcel? the nature of his business is not known*

◊ **natural** *adjective*
(a) found in the earth **natürlich, Natur-; natural resources** = raw materials (such as coal, gas, iron) which are found in the earth **Bodenschätze**
(b) not made by people **Natur-; natural fibre** = fibre made from animal hair *or* plants, etc. **Naturfasern**
(c) normal **natürlich, Natur-; natural child** = child (especially an illegitimate child) of a particular parent **leibliches Kind; natural justice** = the general principles of justice **Naturrecht; natural parents** = actual mother and father of a child (as opposed to step-parents, adoptive parents, foster parents, etc.) **leibliche Eltern; natural person** = human being (as opposed to an artificial person such as a company) **natürliche Person; natural right** = general right which people have to live freely, usually stated in a written constitution **Natur-, Grundrecht; natural wastage** = losing workers because they resign or retire, not through redundancy or dismissals **natürliche Fluktuation**

◊ **natural-born subject** *noun* term formerly applied to a person born in the

UK or a Commonwealth country who was a British citizen by birth **britischer Staatsbürger kraft Geburt**

◇ **naturalization** *noun* granting of citizenship of a state to a foreigner **Einbürgerung;** *she has applied for naturalization; you must fill in the naturalization papers;* compare NATIONALIZATION

◇ **naturalized** *adjective* (person) who has become a citizen of another country **eingebürgert;** *he is a naturalized American citizen*

necessary *adjective* which has to be done *or* which is needed **nötig, notwendig;** *it is necessary to fill in the form correctly; you must have all the necessary documentation before you apply for a subsidy*

◇ **necessaries** *plural noun* things which are needed by a child *or* mentally ill person to live on **Notwendiges**

◇ **necessarily** *adverb* in an unavoidable way **notwendigerweise; unbedingt;** *the imposition of a fine is not necessarily the only course open to the court*

◇ **necessity** *noun*
(a) thing which is absolutely important, without which nothing can be done **Notwendigkeit; das Notwendigste; the necessities of life** = things which every person needs to live **das Notwendigste zum Leben**
(b) situation which makes it impossible not to do something **Notwendigkeit; of necessity** = unavoidably **notwendigerweise;** *a judge must of necessity be impartial*

negative *adjective* meaning "no" **negativ, verneinend; the answer was in the negative** = the answer was "no" **der Bescheid war negativ; the breathalyser test was negative** = the test showed that there was not an excessive amount of alcohol in the blood **der Alkoholtest war negativ**

neglect
1 *noun* (i) not doing a duty; (ii) lack of care towards someone *or* something **(i) Versäumnis; Unterlassung; (ii) Vernachlässigung; Verwahrlosung;** *the children had suffered from neglect;* **wilful neglect** = intentionally not doing something which it is your duty to do **vorsätzliche Unterlassung;** (NOTE: no plural)
2 *verb*
(a) to fail to take care of someone **vernachlässigen; verwahrlosen lassen;** *he neglected his three children*
(b) to neglect to do something = to forget *or* omit to do something which has to be done

versäumen, etwas zu tun; *he neglected to return his income tax form*

◇ **neglected** *adjective* not well looked after **vernachlässigt; verwahrlost;** *the local authority applied for a care order for the family of neglected children*

negligence *noun* lack of proper care *or* not doing a duty (with the result that a person *or* property is harmed) *or* tort of acting carelessly towards others so as to cause harm entitling the injured party to claim damages **Nachlässigkeit; Fahrlässigkeit; contributory negligence** = negligence partly caused by the plaintiff and partly by the defendant, resulting in harm done to the plaintiff **Mitverschulden; criminal negligence** = acting recklessly with the result that harm is done to other people **strafbare/grobe Fahrlässigkeit; culpable negligence** = negligence which is so bad that it amounts to an offence **schuldhafte/grobe Fahrlässigkeit; gross negligence** = act showing very serious neglect of duty towards other people **grobe Fahrlässigkeit**
NOTE: no plural

◇ **negligent** *adjective* showing negligence *or* not taking proper care **nachlässig; fahrlässig;** *the defendant was negligent in carrying out his duties as a trustee*

◇ **negligently** *adverb* in a way which shows negligence **nachlässig; fahrlässig;** *the guardian acted negligently towards his ward*

◇ **negligible** *adjective* very small *or* not worth bothering about **unwesentlich; unerheblich; not negligible** = quite large **nicht unbedeutend**

negotiable *adjective* **not negotiable** = which cannot be exchanged for cash **unverkäuflich; "not negotiable"** = words written on a cheque to show that it can be paid only to a certain person **nicht übertragbar; negotiable cheque** = cheque made payable to bearer (i.e. to anyone who holds it) **Inhaberscheck; negotiable instrument** = document (such as a bill of exchange *or* cheque) which can be legally transferred to another owner simply by passing it to him or by endorsing it *or* which can be exchanged for cash **übertragbares/begebbares Wertpapier**

◇ **negotiability** *noun* ability of a document to be legally transferred to a person simply by passing it to him **Übertragbarkeit**

◇ **negotiate** *verb* **to negotiate with someone** = to discuss a problem formally with someone, so as to reach an agreement **mit jdm verhandeln;** *the management refused to negotiate with the union;* **to negotiate terms and conditions** *or* **to negotiate a contract** = to discuss and agree the terms of a contract **Bedingungen aushandeln; einen Vertrag aushandeln; negotiating committee** = group of representatives of management or unions who negotiate a wage settlement **Verhandlungsausschuß**

◊ **negotiation** *noun* discussion of terms and conditions to reach an agreement **Verhandlung; contract under negotiation** = contract which is being discussed **Vertrag wird verhandelt; a matter for negotiation** = something which must be discussed before a decision is reached **Verhandlungssache; to enter into negotiations** *or* **to start negotiations** = to start discussing a problem **in die Verhandlungen eintreten; Verhandlungen aufnehmen; to resume negotiations** = to start discussing a problem again, after talks have stopped for a time **die Verhandlungen wiederaufnehmen; to break off negotiations** = to refuse to go on discussing a problem **die Verhandlungen abbrechen; to conduct negotiations** = to negotiate **Verhandlungen führen**

◊ **negotiator** *noun* person who discusses with the aim of reaching an agreement **Verhandelnder; Unterhändler; Verhandlungsführer**

neighbour *noun* person who lives near to someone **Nachbar/-in;** *he was accused of setting fire to his neighbour's car; she sued her next door neighbour for damages*

◊ **neighbourhood** *noun* district and the people living in it **Nachbarschaft;** *we live in a very quiet neighbourhood;* **in the neighbourhood of** = near to **in der Nähe von;** *the factory is in the neighbourhood of the prison;* **neighbourhood watch** = system where the people living in an area are encouraged to look out for criminals *or* to report any breakdown of law and order **Nachbarschaftsinitiative zur Kriminalitätsbekämpfung**

◊ **neighbouring** *adjective* placed next to something **benachbart; angrenzend;** *he lives in the neighbouring street; the factory is in the neighbouring town*

nemine contradicente *or* **nem con** *Latin phrase meaning* "with no one contradicting": phrase used to show that no one voted against the proposal **ohne Gegenstimme, ohne Widerspruch;** *the motion was adopted nem con*

nemo dat quod non habet *Latin phrase meaning* "no one can give what he does not have": rule that no one can pass *or* sell to another person something to which he has no title (such as stolen goods) **niemand kann übertragen, was er nicht besitzt;** Verbot, unrechtmäßig erworbenes Gut zu veräußern

new *adjective* recent *or* not old **neu; under new management** = with a new owner **unter neuer Leitung; new for old policy** = insurance policy which covers the cost of buying a new item to replace an old one which has been stolen *or* damaged **Wiederbeschaffungspreis zum Neuwert-Police; new issue** = issues of new shares **Neuemission; new trial** = trial which can be ordered to take place in civil cases, when the first trial was improper in some way **Wiederaufnahmeverfahren**

◊ **news** *noun* information about things which have happened **Nachrichten; news agency** = office which distributes news to newspapers and television companies **Nachrichtenagentur; news release** = sheet giving information about a new event which is sent to newspapers and TV and radio stations so that they can use it **Pressenotiz**

next *adjective & adverb*
(a) coming afterwards in time **nächster;** *on Wednesday he arrived in London and the next day tried to assassinate the Prime Minister; the first case this morning was one of murder, the next of attempted murder; the court's next decision was judged to be unconstitutional*
(b) nearest (in place) **am nächsten; neben; nächster;** *the trial was adjourned to the next courtroom; the plaintiff sat next to his solicitor*

◊ **next friend** *noun* person who brings an action on behalf of a minor **Prozeßpfleger**

◊ **next of kin** *noun* person *or* persons who are most closely related to someone **nächster Angehöriger;** *his only next of kin is an aunt living in Scotland; the police have informed the next of kin of the people killed in the accident*
NOTE: can be singular or plural

nick *(slang)*
1 *noun* police station **Wache**
2 *verb*
(a) to steal **klauen**
(b) to arrest **einlochen**

nil *noun* zero *or* nothing **Null, Nichts; to make a nil return** = to report the figure zero on a form **keinerlei Erträge angeben, Nullsatz eintragen**

nisi *see* DECREE, FORECLOSURE

nobble *verb (slang)* to interfere with *or* to bribe *or* to influence (a jury) **(sich) kaufen,**

bestechen; **mit unlauteren Mitteln für sich gewinnen;** *he tried to nobble one of the jurors*

no-claims bonus *noun* reduction of premiums paid because no claims have been made against an insurance policy **Schadenfreiheitsrabatt**

nolle prosequi *Latin phrase meaning* "do not pursue": power used by the Attorney-General to stop a criminal trial **Einstellungsverfügung**

nominal *adjective*
(a) very small (payment) **unbedeutend; nominell;** *we make a nominal charge for our services; they are paying a nominal rent;* **nominal damages** = very small damages, awarded to show that the loss *or* harm suffered was technical rather than actual **geringer/nomineller Schadensersatz**
(b) nominal capital = the total of the face value of all the shares which a company is allowed to issue according to its memorandum and articles of association **Nominalkapital; nominal value** = face value *or* value written on a share *or* a coin *or* a banknote **Nenn-, Nominalwert**

nominate *verb* to suggest someone *or* to name someone for a job **nominieren, aufstellen; to nominate someone to a post** = to appoint someone to a post without an election **jdn auf eine Stelle berufen; to nominate someone as proxy** = to name someone as your proxy **jdn als Stellvertreter nominieren**

◊ **nomination** *noun* act of nominating **Nominierung, Aufstellung**

◊ **nominee** *noun* person who is nominated, especially someone who is appointed to deal with financial matters on behalf of a person **Nominierte(r), Kandidat/-in; nominee account** = account held on behalf of someone **Anderkonto, Mündelkonto; nominee shareholder** = person named as the owner of shares, when the shares are in fact owned by another person **als Strohmann auftretender Aktionär**

non- *prefix* not **nicht-, Nicht-**

◊ **non-acceptance** *noun* situation where the person who should pay a bill of exchange does not accept it **Akzeptverweigerung**

◊ **non-arrestable offence** *noun* crime for which a person cannot be arrested without a warrant **Bagatelldelikt**

COMMENT: non-arrestable offences are usually crimes which carry a sentence of less than five years imprisonment

◊ **non-capital crime** *or* **offence** *noun* crime *or* offence for which the punishment is not death **Verbrechen unterhalb der Todesstrafe**

◊ **non compos mentis** *Latin phrase meaning* "mad" *or* "not fully sane" **unzurechnungsfähig**

◊ **non-conformance** *noun* act of not conforming **Nichteinhaltung;** *he was criticized for non-conformance with the regulations*

◊ **non-consummation** *noun* **non-consummation of marriage** = not having sexual intercourse (between husband and wife) **Nichtvollzug der Ehe**

◊ **non-contributory** *adjective* **non-contributory pension scheme** = pension scheme where the employee does not make any contributions and the company pays everything **beitragsfreie Rentenversicherung**

◊ **non-direction** *noun (of a judge)* not giving direction to a jury **ohne Rechtsbelehrung an die Geschworenen**

◊ **non-executive director** *noun* director who attends board meetings and gives advice, but does not work full time for the company; *entspricht* **nichtgeschäftsführender Direktor**

◊ **nonfeasance** *noun* not doing something which should be done by law **pflichtwidrige Unterlassung**

◊ **nonjoinder** *noun* plea that a plaintiff has not joined all the necessary parties to his action **unterlassene Einführung eines wichtigen Streitgenossen in einen Prozeß**

◊ **non-molestation order** *noun* order made by a court in matrimonial proceedings to prevent one spouse from molesting the other **gerichtliche Verfügung, jdn nicht mehr zu belästigen**

◊ **non-negotiable instrument** *noun* document (such as a crossed cheque) which is not payable to bearer and so cannot be exchanged for cash **nicht begebbares/übertragbares Wertpapier, Rektapapier**

◊ **non-payment** *noun* **non-payment of a debt** = not paying a debt due **Nichtbezahlung einer Verpflichtung**

◊ **non profit-making organization** *or (US)* **non-profit corporation** *noun* organization (such as a club) which is not allowed by law to make a profit **gemeinnütziges Unternehmen**

◊ **non-recurring items** *noun* special items in a set of accounts which appear only once **einmalige Posten**

◊ **non-refundable** *adjective* which will not be refunded **nicht erstattungsfähig**

◊ **non-resident** *noun* person who is not considered a resident of a country for tax purposes **Nichtansässiger; Ausländer/-in**

◊ **non-returnable** *adjective* which cannot be returned **Einweg-; non-returnable packing** = packing which is to be thrown away when it has been used and not returned to the person who sent it **Einweg(ver)packung**

◊ **nonsuit** *or* **nonsuited** *adjective* **to be nonsuit** *or* **nonsuited** = (i) situation in civil proceedings where a plaintiff fails to establish a cause of action and is forced to abandon his proceedings; (ii) situation in criminal proceedings where a judge directs a jury to find the defendant not guilty **(i) Klagerücknahme; (ii) Klageabweisung**

◊ **non-taxable** *adjective* which is not subject to tax **steuerfrei**

◊ **non-voting shares** *plural noun* shares which do not allow the shareholder to vote at meetings **stimmrechtslose Aktien**

normal *adjective* usual *or* which happens regularly **normal, üblich;** *normal deliveries are made on Tuesdays and Fridays; now that the strike is over we hope to resume normal service as soon as possible;* **under normal conditions** = if things work in the usual way **unter normalen Bedingungen**

North-Eastern Circuit, Northern Circuit *noun* two of the six circuits of the Crown Court to which barristers belong, with centres in Leeds and Manchester **Gerichtsbezirk Nord-Ost; Gerichtsbezirk Nord**

noscitur a sociis *Latin phrase meaning* "the meaning of the words can be understood from the words around them": ambiguous words *or* phrases can be clarified by referring to the context in which they are used **Auslegung nach dem Zusammenhang**

notary public *noun* lawyer (usually but not necessarily a solicitor) who has the authority to witness and draw up certain documents, and so make them official **Notar**
NOTE: plural is **notaries public**

◊ **notarial** *adjective* referring to notaries **notariell, Notariats-; notarial act** = act which can be carried out only by a notary public **notarielle Handlung**

note
1 *noun*
(a) short document *or* short piece of information **Bescheid; Mitteilung; advice note** = written notice to a customer giving details of goods ordered and shipped but not yet delivered **Versandanzeige, Avis; contract note** = note showing that shares have been bought *or* sold but not yet paid

for **Ausführungsanzeige; cover note** = letter from an insurance company giving details of an insurance policy and confirming that the policy exists **vorläufige Deckungszusage; covering note** = letter sent with documents to explain why you are sending them **Begleitschreiben; credit note** = note showing that money is owed to a customer **Gutschriftsanzeige, Kreditnote; debit note** = note showing that a customer owes money **Lastschriftanzeige, Debetnote; note of costs** = bill *or* invoice **Rechnung; note of hand** *or* **promissory note** = document stating that someone promises to pay an amount of money on a certain date **Schuldschein**
(b) short letter *or* short piece of information **Notiz;** *the foreman of the jury passed a note to the judge;* **to make a note of something** = to write something down in a few words **(sich) etwas notieren; to take notes of a meeting** = to write down details of a meeting in a few words, so that the details can be remembered later **sich Notizen/Anmerkungen zur Sitzung machen**
(c) to take note of something = to pay attention to something *or* to take something into account **etwas berücksichtigen; etwas zur Kenntnis nehmen;** *the jury was asked to take note of the evidence given by the pathologist*
(d) bank note *or* **currency note** = piece of printed paper money **Banknote**
2 *verb*
(a) to pay attention to something **zur Kenntnis nehmen; berücksichtigen;** *members of the jury will note that the defendant does not say he was at home on the night of the crime*
(b) to write down details of something and remember them **notieren, vermerken;** *the policeman noted the number of the car in his notebook; your complaint has been noted*
(c) to note a bill = to attach a note to a dishonoured bill of exchange, explaining why it has not been honoured **einen Wechsel protestieren**

◊ **notebook** *noun* book for writing notes **Notizbuch**

◊ **notepad** *noun* pad of paper for writing short notes **Notizblock**

notice *noun*
(a) piece of written information **Mitteilung; Anschlag;** *the company secretary pinned up a notice about the pension scheme;* **copyright notice** = note in a book showing who owns the copyright and the date of ownership **Urheberrechtsvermerk**
(b) official passing of information to someone (such as a warning that a contract is going to end *or* that terms are going to be changed *or* that an employee will leave his

job at a certain date *or* that a tenant must leave the property he is occupying) **Benachrichtigung; Bescheid; Kündigung; to give someone notice** *or* **to serve notice on someone** = to give someone a legal notice **jdm ein (rechtlich relevantes) Dokument zustellen; to give a tenant notice to quit** *or* **to serve a tenant with notice to quit** = to inform a tenant officially that he has to leave the premises by a certain date **einem Mieter kündigen; einem Mieter die Kündigung zustellen; she has handed in** *or* **given her notice** = she has said she will quit her job at a certain date **sie hat gekündigt; period of notice** = time stated in the contract of employment which the worker or company has to allow between resigning or being fired and the worker actually leaving his job **Kündigungsfrist; until further notice** = until different instructions are given **bis auf weiteres; at short notice** = with very little warning **kurzfristig; you must give seven days' notice of withdrawal** = you must ask to take money out of the account seven days before you want it **Sie haben sieben Tage Kündigungsfrist; notice of motion** = document telling the other party to a case that an application will be made to the court **Antragsschrift, Antragsschriftsatz (an den Prozeßgegner in einem schwebenden Rechtsstreit); to give notice of appeal** = to start official proceedings for an appeal to be heard **Revision einlegen; notice of opposition** = document opposing a patent application **Einspruchseinlegung**
(c) knowledge of a fact **Kenntnis; actual notice** = real knowledge which a person has of something **tatsächliche Kenntnis; constructive notice** = knowledge which the law says a person has of something (whether or not the person actually has it) because the information is available to him if he asks for it **gesetzlich unterstellte Kenntnis; judicial notice** = facts and matters which a judge is presumed to know, so that evidence does not have to be provided for them **Kenntnis des Gerichts**

◊ **noticeboard** *noun* board fixed to a wall where notices can be put up **Schwarzes Brett, Anschlagbrett;** *the list of electors is put up on the noticeboard in the local offices*

notify *verb* **to notify someone of something** = to tell someone something formally **jdn von etwas in Kenntnis setzen/unterrichten;** *they were notified of the impending court action*

◊ **notifiable** *adjective* which must be notified **(an)melde-, anzeigepflichtig; notifiable offence** = serious offence which can be tried in the Crown Court **anzeigepflichtiges Vergehen**

◊ **notification** *noun* informing someone **Benachrichtigung; Anzeige**

not proven *adjective (in Scotland)* (verdict) that the prosecution has not produced sufficient evidence to prove the accused to be guilty **(Freispruch) mangels Beweisen**

notwithstanding *adverb* in spite of **trotzdem, dennoch** *preposition* in spite of **trotz, ungeachtet;** *the case proceeded notwithstanding the objections of the defendant* or *the defendant's objections notwithstanding*
NOTE: can be used before or after the phrase

novation *noun* transaction in which a new contract is agreed by all parties to replace an existing contract (as where one of the parties to the old contract is released from his liability under the old contract, and this liability is assumed by a third party) **Erneuerung**

noxious *adjective* unpleasant *or* which offends **übel; schädlich; giftig;** *noxious substance; noxious smell*

nuisance *noun* something which causes harm *or* inconvenience to someone *or* to property **Ärgernis; public nuisance** *or* **common nuisance** = criminal act which causes harm *or* damage to members of the public in general *or* their rights **öffentliches Ärgernis; grober Unfug; private nuisance** = nuisance which causes harm *or* damage to a particular person *or* his rights **(Besitz)störung od Beeinträchtigung (einer Einzelperson)**

null *adjective* with no meaning *or* which cannot legally be enforced **nichtig, ungültig; the contract was declared null and void** = the contract was said to be no longer valid **der Vertrag wurde für (null und) nichtig/ungültig erklärt; to render a decision null** = to make a decision useless *or* to cancel a decision **eine Entscheidung für nichtig erklären/aufheben**
◊ **nullification** *noun* act of making something invalid **Annullierung; Aufhebung**
◊ **nullify** *verb* to make something invalid *or* to cancel something **für nichtig erklären; annullieren**
◊ **nullity** *noun* situation where a marriage is ruled never to have been in effective existence **Nichtigkeit, Ungültigkeit**

numerical order *noun* arrangement (of records) in order of their numbers **Zahlenfolge;** *the documents are filed in numerical order*

nuncupative will *noun* will made orally in the presence of a witness (as by a soldier in time of war) **mündliches Zeugentestament**

Oo

oath *noun* solemn legal promise that someone will say *or* write only what is true **Eid; he was on oath** *or* **under oath** = he had promised in court to say what was true **er stand unter Eid; to administer an oath to someone** = to make someone swear an oath **jdn vereidigen, jdm den Eid abnehmen; commissioner for oaths** = solicitor appointed by the Lord Chancellor to administer affidavits which will be used in court **Anwalt, der befugt ist, Eide abzunehmen**

obey *verb* to do what someone asks you to do **gehorchen, befolgen, Folge leisten, nachkommen;** *the crowd refused to obey the police instructions; he was asked to give an undertaking that he would obey the court order*

◊ **obedience** *noun* doing what someone asks you to do **Gehorsam;** *the army swore obedience to the president; every citizen should show obedience to the laws of the state*

obiter dicta *Latin phrase meaning* "things which are said in passing": part of a judgment which is not essential to the decision of the judge and does not create a precedent **beiläufige Bemerkungen, nicht tragende Entscheidungsgründe;** *see also* RATIO DECIDENDI
NOTE: the singular is **obiter dictum**

object
1 *noun* purpose **Ziel, Zweck; objects clause** = section in a company's memorandum of association which says what work the company will do **Gesellschaftszweckbestimmung (der Satzung)**
2 *verb* to refuse to do something *or* to say that you do not accept something **ablehnen, protestieren, Einwand/Einspruch erheben;** *to object to a clause in a contract;* **to object to a juror** = to ask for a juror not to be appointed because he or she may be biased **einen Geschworenen ablehnen**
NOTE: you object **to** something or someone

◊ **objection** *noun* **to raise an objection to something** = to object to something **gegen etwas Einspruch/einen Einwand erheben;** *the union delegates raised an objection to the wording of the agreement*

objective
1 *noun* something which you try to do **Ziel; long-term objective** *or* **short-term objective** = aim which you hope to achieve within a few years or a few months **langfristige Zielsetzung; kurzfristige Zielsetzung; management by objectives** = way of managing a business by planning work for the managers to do and testing if it is completed correctly and on time **Unternehmensführung mit Zielvorgabe**
2 *adjective* considered from a general point of view and not from that of the person involved **objektiv, sachlich;** *the judge asked the jury to be objective in considering the evidence put before them; you must be objective in assessing the performance of the staff; to carry out an objective review of current legislation*

obligate *verb especially US* **to be obligated to do something** = to have a legal duty to do something **verpflichtet sein, etwas zu tun**

◊ **obligation** *noun*
(a) duty to do something **Verpflichtung; to be under an obligation to do something** = to feel it is your duty to do something **sich verpflichtet fühlen, etwas zu tun; he is under no contractual obligation to buy** = he has signed no contract to buy **er ist vertraglich nicht zum Kauf verpflichtet; to fulfil one's contractual obligations** = to do what is stated in a contract **seine Vertragspflicht/vertraglichen Verpflichtungen erfüllen; two weeks' free trial without obligation** = situation where the customer can try the item at home for two weeks without having to buy it at the end of the test **zwei Wochen Probezeit ohne Kaufzwang**
(b) debt **Verbindlichkeit, Schuld; to meet one's obligations** = to pay one's debts **seinen Verbindlichkeiten nachkommen**

◊ **obligatory** *adjective* necessary according to the law or rules **obligatorisch, bindend, verpflichtend;** *each person has to pass an obligatory medical examination*

◊ **oblige** *verb* **to oblige someone to do something** = to make someone feel he must do something **jdn zu etwas verpflichten;** *he felt obliged to cancel the contract*

◊ **obligee** *noun* person who is owed a duty **Forderungsberechtigter**

◊ **obligor** *noun* person who owes a duty to someone **Verpflichteter**

obscene *adjective* (play, book, etc.) which is likely to deprave *or* corrupt someone who sees or reads it *or* offend public morals and decency **obszön, unzüchtig;** *the magazine was classed as an* *obscene publication; the police seized a number of obscene films*

◊ **obscenity** *noun* being obscene **Obszönität;** *the magistrate commented on the obscenity of some parts of the film;* **obscenity laws** = law relating to obscene publications *or* films **Gesetze gegen Veröffentlichungen pornographischen Inhalts**

observe *verb*
(a) to obey (a rule *or* a law) **einhalten, befolgen;** *failure to observe the correct procedure; all members of the association should observe the code of practice*
(b) to watch *or* to notice what is happening **beobachten;** *officials have been instructed to observe the conduct of the election*

◊ **observance** *noun* doing what is required by a law **Einhaltung, Befolgung;** *the government's observance of international agreements*

◊ **observation** *noun*
(a) noticing what is happening **Beobachten, Beobachtung**
(b) remark **Bemerkung, Äußerung;** *the judge made some observations about the conduct of the accused during the trial*

◊ **observer** *noun* person who observes **Beobachter/-in;** *two official observers attended the meeting*

obsolete *adjective* no longer used *or* no longer in force **überholt, veraltet; nicht mehr angewandt/gültig;** *the law has been made obsolete by new developments in forensic science*

obstruct *verb* to get in the way *or* to stop something progressing **versperren, blockieren;** *the parked cars are obstructing the traffic;* **obstructing the police** = offence of doing something which prevents a policeman carrying out his duty **die Polizei an der Ausübung ihrer Pflichten hindern, Widerstand gegen die Staatsgewalt**

◊ **obstruction**
(a) thing which gets in the way **Hindernis;** *the car caused an obstruction to the traffic*
(b) act of obstructing someone **(vorsätzliche) Behinderung;** *obstruction of the police is an offence*

obtain *verb*
(a) to get **erhalten, beziehen, bekommen; erwirken;** *to obtain supplies from abroad; we find these items very difficult to obtain; to obtain an injunction against a company; he obtained control by buying the family shareholding;* **obtaining by deception** = acquiring money *or* property by tricking someone into handing it over **durch Betrug erlangen, betrügerisch erwerben; obtaining**

credit = offence whereby an undischarged bankrupt obtains credit above a limit of £50 **Kreditbetrug; to obtain a property by fraud** *or* **by deception** = to trick someone into handing over possession of property **ein Vermögen durch Betrug/Täuschung erlangen; obtaining a pecuniary advantage by deception** = crime of tricking someone into handing over money **einen Vermögensvorteil durch Täuschung erlangen**
(b) to be a rule *or* to have a legal status **gelten;** *this right does not obtain in judicial proceedings; a rule obtaining in international law*

◊ **obtainable** *adjective* which can be got **erhältlich, zu bekommen;** *prices fall when raw materials are easily obtainable; our products are obtainable in all computer shops*

occasion
1 *noun* time when something takes place **Anlaß, Gelegenheit;** *the opening of the trial was the occasion of protests by the family of the accused*
2 *verb* to make something happen **verursachen, veranlassen;** *he pleaded guilty to assault occasioning actual bodily harm*

◊ **occasional** *adjective* which happens from time to time **gelegentlich; occasional licence** = licence to sell alcohol at a certain place and time **Sonderkonzession**

◊ **occasionally** *adverb* from time to time **gelegentlich;** *he admitted that he occasionally visited the house*

occupancy *noun*
(a) act of occupying a property (such as a house, an office, a room in a hotel) **Besitz, Belegung, Bewohnen; with immediate occupancy** = empty and available to be occupied immediately **sofort beziehbar**
(b) occupying a property which has no owner, and so acquiring title to the property **Aneignung, Besitzergreifung**
NOTE: no plural

◊ **occupant** *noun* person *or* company which occupies a property **Bewohner/-in; Besitzer/-in**

◊ **occupation** *noun*
(a) **occupation of a building** = act of occupying a building **Bewohnen eines Gebäudes; Besitz eines Gebäudes**
(b) job *or* work **Beruf, Tätigkeit;** *what is her occupation? his main occupation is house building;* **occupations** = types of work **Tätigkeiten;** *people in professional occupations*

◊ **occupational** *adjective* referring to a job **Berufs-, beruflich; occupational accident** = accident which takes place at work **Arbeitsunfall; occupational disease** = disease which affects people in certain jobs **Berufskrankheit; occupational hazards =** dangers which apply to certain jobs **Berufsrisiko; occupational pension scheme =** pension scheme where the worker gets a pension from the company he has worked for **Betriebsaltersversorgung**

◊ **occupier** *noun* person who lives in a property **Bewohner/-in; beneficial occupier =** person who occupies a property but does not own it **Nießbrauchberechtigter; occupier's liability =** duty of an occupier to make sure that visitors to a property are not harmed **Haftung des Besitzers (gegenüber Personen, die sein Grundstück betreten); owner-occupier =** person who owns the property which he occupies **Bewohner des eigenen Grundbesitzes**

> COMMENT: the occupier has the right to stay in or on a property, but is not necessarily an owner

◊ **occupy** *verb*
(a) to live *or* work in a property (such as a house *or* office *or* hotel room) **bewohnen, belegen;** *all the rooms in the hotel are occupied; the company occupies three floors of an office block*
(b) to enter and stay in a property illegally **besetzen;** *the rebels occupied the Post Office; squatters are occupying the building*
(c) to occupy a post = to be employed in a job **eine Stelle innehaben**

occur *verb* to happen *or* to take place **geschehen, sich ereignen, vorkommen;** *the witness described how the argument occurred; no infringements have occurred since the court order was made*

off
1 *adverb*
(a) not working *or* not in operation **abgesagt, ausgefallen, nicht mehr geltend;** *the agreement is off; they called the strike off*
(b) taken away from a price **ermäßigt, mit Ermäßigung;** *these carpets are sold at £25 off the marked price; we give 5% off for quick settlement*
2 *preposition*
(a) to take £25 off the price= to take it away from the price **etwas 25£ billiger verkaufen, den Preis um 25£ herabsetzen;** *we give 10% off our normal prices*
(b) away from work **frei;** *to take time off work; to take three days off; we give the staff four days off at Christmas; it is the secretary's day off tomorrow*

offence *or US* **offense** *noun* crime *or* act which is against the law **Straftat, strafbare Handlung, Delikt, Vergehen;** *he was charged with three serious offences; the minister was*

arrested and charged with offences against the Official Secrets Act; **offence against the person =** criminal act which harms a person physically (such as murder *or* manslaughter) **Straftat gegen die Person; offence against property =** criminal act which damages *or* destroys property (such as theft *or* forgery *or* criminal damage) **Straftat gegen das Eigentum, Vermögensdelikt; offence against public order =** criminal act which disturbs the general calm of society (such as riot *or* affray) **Straftat gegen die öffentliche Ordnung, Störung der öffentlichen Ordnung; offence against the state =** act of attacking the lawful government of a country (such as sedition *or* treason) **Staatsschutzdelikt; first offence =** committing an illegal act for the first time **Straftat eines Ersttäters/nicht vorbestraften Täters;** *as it was a first offence, he was fined and not sent to prison;* **inchoate offences =** offences (such as incitement *or* attempt *or* conspiracy to commit a crime) which are offences even though the substantive offence may not have been committed **einleitende/unvollendete Straftaten; notifiable offence =** serious offence which can be tried in the Crown Court **anzeigepflichtiges Vergehen; offence triable either way =** offence which can be tried before the Magistrates' Court *or* before the Crown Court **Vergehen, über das im Magistrates' Court oder im Crown Court gleichermaßen verhandelt werden kann**

◊ **offend** *verb* to commit a crime **eine Straftat begehen**

◊ **offender** *noun* person who commits a crime **Täter/-in; first offender =** person who has been charged with an offence for the first time **Ersttäter, nicht vorbestrafter Täter; fugitive offender =** criminal running away from the police who, if he is caught, is sent back to the place where the offence was committed **flüchtiger Täter; persistent offender =** person who has been convicted of a crime several times before **Gewohnheitsverbrecher; young offenders =** young persons who commit crimes **jugendliche Täter**

◊ **offensive weapon** *noun* object which can be used to harm a person *or* property **Angriffs-/Offensivwaffe; carrying offensive weapons =** offence of holding a weapon or something (such as a bottle) which could be used as a weapon **Besitz von Angriffswaffen**

> COMMENT: many things can be considered as offensive weapons if they are used as such: a brick *or* a bottle *or* a piece of wire

offer
1 *noun*
(a) statement by one party to a contract

that he proposes to do something **Vertragsangebot**

> COMMENT: the offer (and acceptance by the other party) is one of the essential elements of a contract

(b) offer to buy = statement that you are willing to pay a certain amount of money to buy something **Kaufangebot**; *to make an offer for a company; he made an offer of £10 a share; we made a written offer for the house; £1,000 is the best offer I can make; to accept an offer of £1,000 for the car;* **the house is under offer = für das Haus liegt ein Kaufangebot vor** someone has made an offer to buy the house and the offer has been accepted provisionally; **we are open to offers** = we are ready to discuss the price which we are asking **Angebote werden entgegengenommen; cash offer** = being ready to pay in cash **Barangebot; or near offer (o.n.o.)** = or an offer of a price which is slightly less than the price asked **oder gegen Höchstgebot; VB**; *asking price: £200 o.n.o.*

(c) offer to sell = statement that you are willing to sell something **Verkaufsangebot; offer for sale** = situation where a company advertises new shares for sale **Zeichnungsangebot; offer price** = price at which new shares are put on sale **Emissionskurs; bargain offer** = sale of a particular type of goods at a cheap price **Sonderangebot; special offer** = goods put on sale at a specially low price **Sonderangebot**

(d) he received six offers of jobs *or* **six job offers** = six companies told him he could have a job with them **ihm wurden sechs Stellen angeboten**

2 *verb*

(a) to propose something to someone *or* to propose to do something **anbieten, ein Angebot machen;** *he offered to buy the house; to offer someone £100,000 for his house; he offered £10 a share;* **to offer someone a job** = to tell someone that he can have a job in your company **jdm eine Stelle anbieten**

(b) to say that you are willing to sell something **anbieten;** *we offered the house for sale*

◊ **offeree** *noun* person who receives an offer **Angebotsempfänger, Antragsempfänger**

◊ **offeror** *noun* person who makes an offer **Anbietender, Offerent**

office *noun*

(a) set of rooms where a company works *or* where business is done **Büro, Geschäftsstelle; Kanzlei; branch office** = less important office, usually in a different town or country from the main office **Filiale, Geschäftsstelle, Niederlassung; head office** *or* **main office** = office building where the board of directors works and meets

Hauptgeschäftsstelle, Zentrale, Direktion; registered office = in Britain, the office address of a company which is officially registered with the Companies' Registrar and to which certain legal documents must normally be sent **eingetragener Sitz**

(b) office block *or* **a block of offices** = building which contains only offices **Bürohaus; office hours** = time when an office is open **Dienstzeit, Bürostunden; office junior** = young man or woman who does all types of work in an office **Bürohilfe; office space** *or* **office accommodation** = space available for offices or occupied by offices **Büroräume; office staff** = people who work in offices **Büropersonal**

(c) room where someone works and does business **Büro;** *come into my office; she has a pleasant office which looks out over the park; the senior partner's office is on the third floor*

(d) booking office = office where you can book seats at a theatre *or* tickets for the railway **Vorverkaufsstelle; Fahrkartenschalter; box office** = office at a theatre where tickets can be bought **(Theater)kasse; general office** = main administrative office in a company **Zentrale; information office** *or* **inquiry office** = office where someone can answer questions from members of the public **Auskunft, Information; ticket office** = office where tickets can be bought **Kasse; Fahrkartenschalter**

(e) British government department **Ministerium; the Foreign Office** = ministry dealing with foreign affairs **Außenministerium, Auswärtiges Amt; the Home Office** = ministry dealing with the internal affairs of the country, including the police and the prisons **Innenministerium; Office of Fair Trading** = government body which protects consumers against unfair *or* illegal business **Amt für Verbraucherschutz**

(f) post *or* position **Amt, Posten;** *he holds or performs the office of treasurer;* **high office** = important position or job **hohe amtliche Stellung; office of profit (under the Crown)** = government post which disqualifies someone from being a Member of Parliament **Amtstätigkeit gegen Bezahlung; compensation for loss of office** = payment to a director who is asked to leave a company before his contract ends **Entlassungsentschädigung**

officer *noun*

(a) police officer = policeman *or* member of a police force **Polizist/-in;** (NOTE: used in US English with a name: **Officers Smith and Jones went to the scene of the accident**; GB English is constable)

(b) person who has an official position **Beamter/Beamtin; Angestellte(r) im**

öffentlichen Dienst; **customs officer** = person working for the customs **Zollbeamter; fire safety officer** = person responsible for fire safety in a building **Betriebsfeuerwehrmann; information officer** = person who gives information about a company *or* about a government department to the public **Pressereferent; personnel officer** = person who deals with the staff and their conditions of employment, especially interviewing new workers **Personalchef, Personalreferent; training officer** = person who deals with the training of staff **Ausbildungsleiter; the company officers** *or* **the officers of a company** = the main executives or directors of a company **die Führungskräfte eines Unternehmens**
(c) official (usually unpaid) of a club *or* society, etc. **Vorstandsmitglied;** *the election of officers of an association*

◊ **Law Officers** *plural noun* the posts of Attorney-General and Solicitor-General (in England and Wales) and Lord Advocate and Solicitor-General (in Scotland) **(höchste) Rechtsberater des Staates**

official

1 *adjective*
(a) done because it has been authorized by a government department *or* organization **amtlich, Amts-; dienstlich, Dienst-;** *on official business; he left official documents in his car; she received an official letter of explanation;* **official secret** = piece of information which is classified as important to the state and which it is a crime to reveal **Staatsgeheimnis; Official Secrets Act** = Act of Parliament which governs the publication of secret information relating to the state **Gesetz über die Wahrung von Staatsgeheimnissen; speaking in an official capacity** = speaking officially **in Ausübung seines Amtes sprechen; to go through official channels** = to deal with officials, especially when making a request **den Amtsweg/Dienstweg beschreiten**
(b) done or approved by a director *or* by a person in authority **offiziell, genehmigt;** *this must be an official order - it is written on the company's notepaper;* **the strike was made official** = the local strike was approved by the main trade union office **der Streik wurde genehmigt**
(c) **Official Journal** = publication which lists the regulations, statutory instruments and directives of the EC **Amtsblatt der Europäischen Gemeinschaft; the Official Receiver** = government official who is appointed to close down a company which is in liquidation *or* to deal with affairs of bankrupts **Konkursverwalter; official referee** = expert judge appointed by the High Court to try complicated. usually technical,

cases where specialist knowledge is required **(als Sachverständiger) beauftragter Richter; Official Solicitor** = solicitor who acts in the High Court for parties who have no one to act for them, usually because they are under a legal disability **Anwalt, der im High Court für Parteien tätig wird, die von niemand anders vertreten werden**
2 *noun* person working in a government department **Beamter/Beamtin; Angestellte(r);** *airport officials inspected the shipment; government officials stopped the import licence;* **customs official** = person working for the customs **Zollbeamter; high official** = important person in a government department **höherer Beamter; minor official** = person in a low position in a government department **unterer Beamter**

◊ **officialese** *noun* language used in government documents and which can be difficult to understand **Beamtendeutsch, Amtsjargon**

◊ **officially** *adverb* in an official way **offiziell;** *officially he knows nothing about the problem, but unofficially he has given us a lot of advice about it*

officio *see* EX OFFICIO, FUNCTUS OFFICIO

off-licence *noun*

(a) licence to sell alcohol for drinking away from the place where you buy it **Konzession zum Alkoholverkauf**
(b) shop which sells alcohol for drinking at home **Wein- und Spirituosenhandlung**

offspring *noun* child *or* children of a parent **Kind, Kinder, Nachkommen;** *his offspring inherited the estate; they had two offspring*
NOTE: offspring is both singular and plural

old *adjective* having existed for a long time **alt;** *the company is 125 years old next year; we have decided to get rid of our old computer system and put in a new one*

◊ **old age** *noun* period when a person is old **Alter; old age pension** = state pension given to a man who is 65 or a woman who is 60 **Altersversorgung, Altersrente; old age pensioner** = person who receives the old age pension **Rentner/-in**

◊ **Old Bailey** *noun* Central Criminal Court in London **Gericht für Strafsachen von Bedeutung in London**

Oleron *noun* **Laws of Oleron** = first international maritime laws, drawn up in 1216 **die Gesetze von Oleron**

ombudsman *noun* official who investigates complaints by the public against government departments *or* other large organizations **Ombudsmann**

> COMMENT: although the ombudsman may make his recommendations public, he has no power to enforce them

omit *verb*
(a) to leave something out *or* not to put something in **aus-, weglassen;** *the secretary omitted the date when typing the contract*
(b) not to do something **unterlassen, versäumen;** *he omitted to tell the managing director that he had lost the documents*
NOTE: **omitting - omitted**

◊ **omission** *noun* thing which has been omitted **Aus-, Unterlassung, Versäumnis; errors and omissions excepted** = words written on an invoice to show that the company has no responsibility for mistakes in the invoice **Irrtümer und Auslassungen vorbehalten**

onerous *adjective* heavy *or* needing a lot of effort or money **beschwerlich, lästig; the repayment terms are particularly onerous** = the loan is particularly difficult to pay back **die Rückzahlungsbedingungen sind extrem schwer**

o.n.o. = OR NEAR OFFER

onus *noun* responsibility for doing something difficult **Last, Bürde; onus of proof** *or* **onus probandi** = duty to prove that what has been alleged in court is correct **Beweislast;** *the onus of proof is on the plaintiff; if there is a prosecution the onus will normally be on the prosecutor to prove the case; see also* BURDEN

op. cit. *Latin phrase meaning* "in the work mentioned" **a.a.O., am angegebenen Ort**
NOTE: used when referring to a legal text: **"see Smith LJ in** *Jones v. Amalgamated Steel Ltd* **op. cit. p. 260"**

open
1 *adjective*
(a) at work *or* not closed **geöffnet;** *the store is open on Sunday mornings; our offices are open from 9 to 6; they are open for business every day of the week*
(b) ready to accept something **offen, offenstehend; the job is open to all applicants** = anyone can apply for the job **die Stelle steht allen Bewerbern offen; open to offers** = ready to accept a reasonable offer **Angebote werden entgegengenommen; the company is open to offers for the empty factory** = the company is ready to discuss an offer which is lower than the suggested price **die Firma zieht Angebote für die leerstehende Fabrik in Betracht**
(c) **open account** = unsecured credit *or* amount owed with no security **Kontokorrentkonto; open cheque** = cheque which is not crossed and can be exchanged for cash anywhere **Barscheck; open court** = court where the hearings are open to the public **öffentliche Verhandlung; in open court** = in a courtroom with members of the public present **in öffentlicher Verhandlung; open credit** = bank credit given to good customers without security up to a certain maximum sum **Blanko-, Kontokorrentkredit; open market** = market where anyone can buy or sell **freier/offener Markt; open policy** = marine insurance policy, where the value of what is insured is not stated **Police ohne Wertangabe, untaxierte Police; open prison** = prison with minimum security where category "D" prisoners can be kept **offene Strafvollzugsanstalt; open ticket** = ticket which can be used on any date **offenes Ticket; open verdict** = verdict in a coroner's court which does not decide how the dead person died **richterliche Feststellung auf unbekannte Todesursache;** *the court recorded an open verdict on the two policemen*
2 *verb*
(a) to start a new business working **eröffnen, aufmachen;** *she has opened a shop in the High Street; we have opened an office in London*
(b) to start work *or* to be at work **aufmachen, öffnen, geöffnet sein;** *the office opens at 9 a.m.; we open for business on Sundays*
(c) to begin speaking **öffnen, beginnen;** *counsel for the prosecution opened with a description of the accused's family background;* **to open negotiations** = to begin negotiating **Verhandlungen aufnehmen;** *he opened the discussions with a description of the product; the chairman opened the meeting at 10.30*
(d) to start *or* to allow something to start **eröffnen, einrichten;** *to open a bank account; to open a line of credit; to open a loan*

◊ **open-ended** *or US* **open-end** *adjective* with no fixed limit *or* with some items not specified **offen, unbeschränkt, unbefristet, Blanko-;** *an open-ended agreement*

◊ **opening**
1 *noun*
(a) act of starting a new business **Eröffnung;** *the opening of a new branch or of a new market or of a new office*
(b) **opening hours** = hours when a shop *or* business is open **Öffnungs-, Geschäftszeit**
(c) **job openings** = jobs which are empty and need filling **freie Stellen; a market**

opening = possibility of starting to do business in a new market **Markterschließung**
2 *adjective* at the beginning *or* first **Eröffnungs-, einleitend;** *the judge's opening remarks; the opening speech from the defence counsel or from the Home Secretary;* **opening balance** = balance at the beginning of an accounting period **Eröffnungsbetrag; opening bid** = first bid at an auction **Eröffnungsgebot; opening entry** = first entry in an account **Eröffnungsbuchung**

◊ **openly** *adverb* in an open way **offen;** *he openly admitted that he had sold drugs*

operandi *see* MODUS

operate *verb*
(a) to work **gelten, wirksam werden;** *the new terms of service will operate from January 1st; the rules operate on inland postal services*
(b) to operate a machine = to make a machine work **eine Maschine bedienen**

◊ **operating** *noun* general running of a business *or* of a machine **Betrieb; operating budget** = income and expenditure which is expected to be incurred over a period of time **Betriebswirtschaftsplan; operating costs** *or* **operating expenses** = costs of the day-to-day organization of a company **Betriebskosten, betriebliche Aufwendungen; operating profit** *or* **operating loss** = profit *or* loss made by a company in its usual business **Betriebsgewinn; Betriebsverlust; operating system** = the main program which operates a computer **Betriebssystem**

◊ **operation** *noun*
(a) business organization and work **Geschäft, Tätigkeit, Geschäftstätigkeit;** *the company's operations in West Africa; he heads up the operations in Northern Europe;* **operations review** = examining the way in which a company or department works to see how it can be made more efficient and profitable **Betriebsanalyse; a franchising operation** = selling licences to trade as a franchise **Franchisevergabe**
(b) Stock Exchange operation = buying *or* selling of shares on the Stock Exchange **Börsengeschäft, Effektenhandel**
(c) in operation = working *or* being used **in Betrieb, in Kraft;** *the system will be in operation by June; the new system came into operation on June 1st*

◊ **operational** *adjective*
(a) referring to how something works **betrieblich, Betriebs-, Funktions-; operational budget** = expenditure which is expected to be made in running a business *or* an office *or* a police force **Betriebsbudget; operational costs** = costs of running a business *or* a police force **Betriebskosten; operational planning** = planning how something is to be

run **Betriebsplanung; operational research** = study of a method of working to see if it can be made more efficient and cost-effective **Unternehmensforschung, Operational-Research**
(b) the system became operational on June 1st = the system began working on June 1st **das System war ab 1. Juni einsatzbereit**

◊ **operative**
1 *adjective* referring to the working of a system **wirksam; to become operative** = to start working **wirksam/gültig werden, in Kraft treten; operative words** = words in a conveyancing document which transfer the land *or* create an interest in the land **rechtsgestaltende Worte**
2 *noun* person who operates a machine which makes a product **Fabrikarbeiter, Maschinist/-in**

opinion *noun*
(a) public opinion = what people think about something **öffentliche Meinung; opinion poll** *or* **opinion research** = asking a sample group of people what their opinion is, so as to guess the opinion of the whole population **Meinungsumfrage; to be of the opinion** = to believe *or* to think **der Meinung sein;** *the judge was of the opinion that if the evidence was doubtful the claim should be dismissed*
(b) piece of expert advice **Ansicht, Stellungnahme; Gutachten;** *the lawyers gave their opinion; to ask an adviser for his opinion on a case; counsel prepared a written opinion;* **counsel's opinion** = a barrister's written advice about a case **Anwaltsgutachten**

opponent *noun* person who is against you *or* who votes against what you propose **Gegner/-in, Gegenseite;** *the prosecution tried to discredit their opponents in the case*

oppose *verb* to try to stop something happening; to vote against something **ablehnen, Einspruch erheben, sich widersetzen, bekämpfen;** *a minority of board members opposed the motion; we are all opposed to the takeover; counsel for the plaintiff opposed the defendant's application for an adjournment;* **the police opposed bail** *or* **opposed the granting of bail** = the police said that bail should not be granted to the accused **die Polizei lehnte eine Kaution/Sicherheitsleistung ab**

◊ **opposition** *noun*
(a) action of trying to stop something *or* of not agreeing to something **Opposition, Widerstand;** *there was considerable opposition to the plan for reorganizing the divorce courts; the voters showed their opposition to the government by voting*

against the proposal in the referendum;
notice of opposition = document opposing a
patent application **Einspruchseinlegung**
(b) (i) the largest political party which
opposes the government; (ii) group of
parties which oppose the government **(i)
Oppositionspartei; (ii) Opposition;** *the
opposition tried to propose a vote of censure
on the Prime Minister;* **Leader of the
Opposition** = head of the largest political
party opposing the government
Oppositionsführer

optimal *adjective* best **optimal**

◊ **optimum** *adjective* best **optimal;** *the
market offers optimum conditions for sales*

option *noun*
(a) offer to someone of the right to enter
into a contract at a later date **Option; option
to purchase** *or* **to sell** = giving someone the
possibility to buy or sell something within a
period of time *or* when a certain event
happens **Optionsrecht auf Kauf, Kaufoption;
Optionsrecht auf Verkauf, Verkaufsoption; first
option** = allowing someone to be the first to
have the possibility of deciding something
**Vorhand; to grant someone a six-month
option on a product** = to allow someone six
months to decide if he wants to be the agent
or if he wants to make the product **jdm für ein
Produkt ein sechsmonatiges Optionsrecht
einräumen; to take up an option** *or* **to exercise
an option** = to accept the option which has
been offered and to put it into action **sein
Optionsrecht ausüben;** *he exercised his
option or he took up his option to acquire
sole marketing rights to the product;* **I want
to leave my options open** = I want to be able
to decide what to do when the time is right
**ich will mir alle Möglichkeiten offenhalten; to
take the soft option** = to decide to do
something which involves the least risk,
effort or problems **den Weg des geringsten
Widerstandes wählen**
(b) *(Stock Exchange)* **call option** = option to
buy shares at a certain price **Kaufoption; put
option** = option to sell shares at a certain
price **Verkaufsoption; share option** = right to
buy or sell shares at a certain price at a time
in the future **Aktienoption; stock option** =
right to buy shares at a cheap price given by
a company to its employees **Anrecht auf
Belegschaftsaktien; option contract** = right to
buy or sell shares at a fixed price
Optionsvertrag; option dealing *or* **option
trading** = buying and selling share options
Optionsgeschäfte, Optionshandel

◊ **optional** *adjective* which can be added if
the customer wants **wahlweise, fakultativ, auf
Wunsch erhältlich;** *the insurance cover is
optional*

oral *adjective* spoken **mündlich; oral
evidence** = spoken evidence (as opposed to
written) **mündliche Zeugenaussage**

◊ **orally** *adverb* in speaking, not writing
mündlich

order
1 *noun*
(a) general state of calm, where everything
is working as planned and ruled **Ordnung;**
*there was a serious breakdown of law and
order;* **public order** = situation were the
general public is calm *or* where there are no
riots **öffentliche (Sicherheit und) Ordnung;
offence against public order** *or* **public order
offence** = riot *or* street fight, etc. **Verstoß
gegen die öffentliche Ordnung, Störung der
öffentlichen Ordnung**
(b) court order = command (which has no
bearing on the final decision in a case)
made by a court for someone to do
something **gerichtliche Verfügung,
Gerichtsbeschluß;** *the prisoner was removed
by order of the court; the factory was sold by
order of the receiver ;* **committal order** =
order sending someone to prison for
contempt of court **Haftanordnung;
compensation order** = order made by a
criminal court which forces a criminal to
pay compensation to his victim **Urteil auf
Schadensersatz; delivery order** =
instructions given by the customer to the
person holding his goods, telling him to
deliver them **Lieferauftrag; order of
discharge** = court order releasing a person
from bankruptcy **Aufhebung des
Konkursverfahrens; interim order** = order of
a court which has effect while a case is still
being heard **einstweilige Anordnung;
preservation order** = court order which
prevents a building from being knocked
down *or* a tree from being cut down
**Verfügung, die etwas unter Denkmalschutz
oder unter Naturschutz stellt**
(c) orders = legislation made by ministers,
under powers delegated to them by Act of
Parliament, but which still have to be
ratified by Parliament before coming into
force **Rechtsverordnungen; Order in Council**
= legislation made by the Queen in
Council, which is allowed by an Act of
Parliament and which does not have to be
ratified by Parliament **königlicher Erlaß**
(d) arrangement of records (filing cards,
invoices, etc.) **Anordnung, Reihenfolge;
alphabetical order** = arrangement by the
letters of the alphabet (A, B, C, etc.)
**alphabetische Reihenfolge; chronological
order** = arrangement by the order of the
dates **zeitliche/chronologische Reihenfolge;
numerical order** = arrangement by numbers
zahlenmäßige Reihenfolge

(e) arrangement of business in the House of Commons **Geschäftsordnung; order book =** list showing the House of Commons business for the term of Parliament **Liste der Anträge und Fragen; order paper =** agenda of business to be discussed each day in the House of Commons **schriftliche Tagesordnung, Sitzungsprogramm**
(f) standing orders = rules *or* regulations governing the way in which a meeting *or* a debate in Parliament is conducted **Geschäftsordnung; to call a meeting to order** = to start proceedings officially **eine Sitzung eröffnen; to bring a meeting to order =** to get a meeting back to discussing the agenda again (after an interruption) **eine Sitzung zur Rückkehr zur Tagesordnung aufrufen; order !** **order! =** call by the Speaker of the House of Commons to bring the meeting to order **Ruhe! Ruhe!; zur Tagesordnung!; point of order** = question relating to the way in which a meeting is being conducted **Anfrage zur Geschäftsordnung;** *he raised a point of order; on a point of order, Mr Chairman, can this committee approve its own accounts? the meeting was adjourned on a point of order*
(g) working arrangement **Zustand; machine in full working order =** machine which is ready and able to work properly **Maschine, die voll betriebsfähig ist; the telephone is out of order =** the telephone is not working **das Telefon funktioniert nicht; is all the documentation in order? =** are all the documents valid and correct? **sind alle Dokumente in Ordnung?**
(h) pay to Mr Smith or order = pay money to Mr Smith or as he orders **zahlbar an Herrn Smith oder dessen Order; pay to the order of Mr Smith =** pay money directly into Mr Smith's account **zahlbar an Herrn Smith, auf Order Smith lautend**
(i) official request for goods to be supplied **Bestellung, Auftrag;** *to give someone an order or to place an order with someone for twenty filing cabinets;* **to fill** *or* **to fulfil an order =** to supply items which have been ordered **eine Bestellung ausführen; purchase order =** official paper which places an order for something **Auftrag, Bestellung; items available to order only =** items which will be made only if someone orders them **nur auf Bestellung erhältliche Ware; on order =** ordered but not delivered **bestellt; back orders** *or* **outstanding orders =** orders received in the past and not yet supplied **noch ausstehende Lieferungen, unerledigte Aufträge; order book =** record of orders **Bestellbuch, Auftragsbuch; telephone orders** = orders received over the telephone **telefonische Bestellungen**
(j) document which allows money to be paid to someone **Zahlungsanweisung, Order;** *he sent us an order on the Chartered Bank;* **banker's order** *or* **standing order =** order

written by a customer asking a bank to make a regular payment **Dauerauftrag; money order =** document which can be bought for sending money through the post **Postanweisung**
2 *verb*
(a) to tell someone to do something **anordnen, befehlen;** *he ordered the police to search the premises; the government ordered the army to occupy the radio station*
(b) to ask for goods to be supplied **bestellen;** *to order twenty filing cabinets to be delivered to the warehouse; they ordered a new Rolls Royce for the managing director*
(c) to put in a certain way **anordnen, ordnen;** *the address list is ordered by country; that filing cabinet contains invoices ordered by date*

ordinance *noun*
(a) special decree of a government **Verordnung**
(b) *US* rule made by a municipal authority, and effective only within the jurisdiction of that authority **Gemeindesatzung, städtische Verordnung**

ordinary *adjective* normal *or* not special **normal, gewöhnlich; ordinary member =** person who pays a subscription to belong to a club *or* group **ordentliches Mitglied; ordinary resolution =** resolution which can be passed by a simple majority of shareholders **Beschluß mit einfacher Mehrheit; ordinary shares =** normal shares in a company, which have no special benefits or restrictions **Stammaktien; ordinary shareholder =** person who owns ordinary shares in a company **Stammaktionär**
◊ **ordinarily** *adverb* normally *or* usually **normalerweise, gewöhnlich; ordinarily resident =** usually resident in a certain country **normalerweise wohnhaft**

organize *verb* to arrange (a meeting *or* a business *or* a demonstration) so that it is run properly and efficiently **organisieren, planen; organized crime =** crime which is run as a business, with groups of specialist criminals, assistants, security staff, etc., all run by a group of directors or by a boss **organisiertes Verbrechen; organized labour =** workers who are members of trade unions **gewerkschaftlich organisierte Arbeitnehmer**
◊ **organization** *noun*
(a) way in which something is arranged **Organisation, Planung;** *the organization of a protest meeting; the organization of an appeal to the House of Lords*
(b) group which is organized for a purpose **Organisation;** *he runs an organization for the rehabilitation of criminals*

origin *noun* where something comes from **Herkunft, Provenienz;** *spare parts of European origin;* **certificate of origin** = document showing where goods were made *or* produced **Herkunftsbescheinigung, Herkunftszertifikat; country of origin** = country where certain goods are produced **Herkunftsland**
◊ **original**
1 *adjective* which was used *or* made first **original, Original-;** *they sent a copy of the original invoice;* **original evidence** = evidence given by a witness, based on facts which he knows to be true (as opposed to hearsay) **unmittelbarer Beweis, originäres Beweismittel**
2 *noun* first copy made **Original;** *send the original and file two copies*
◊ **originally** *adverb* first *or* at the beginning **ursprünglich**
◊ **originate** *verb* to start *or* to begin **entstehen; originating application** = way of beginning certain types of case in the County Court **verfahrenseinleitender Antrag; originating summons** = official document which begins certain types of case in the High Court **Klage mit Ladung, Form der Klageerhebung**

orphan *noun* child whose parents have died **Waise, Waisenkind**

ostensible *adjective* appearing to be something, but not really so **angeblich, scheinbar; ostensible partner** = person who appears to be a partner (by allowing his name to be used as such) but really has no interest in the partnership **Scheingesellschafter**

OTC = OVER-THE-COUNTER

otherwise *adverb* in another way **sonst, ansonsten;** *John Smith, otherwise known as "the Butcher";* **except as otherwise stated** = except where it is stated in a different way **sofern nicht anders angegeben; otherwise agreed** = unless different terms are agreed **falls nichts anderes vereinbart ist**

ouster *noun* removal of an occupier from a property so that he has to sue to regain possession (especially used against a violent spouse in matrimonial proceedings) **Zwangsräumung, zwangsweise Entfernung eines Bewohners (aus einer Wohnung);** *he had to apply for an ouster order; the judge made an ouster order; compare* EJECT

outcome *noun* result **Ergebnis, Resultat;** *we are waiting for the outcome of the enquiry; the outcome of the trial was in doubt*

outlaw
1 *noun* old term for a person who was thrown out of society as a punishment **Geächteter**
2 *verb* to say that something is unlawful **für ungesetzlich erklären, verbieten;** *the government has proposed a bill to outlaw drinking in public*

outline
1 *noun* general description, without giving many details **Überblick, Abriß, Entwurf;** *they drew up the outline of a plan or an outline plan;* **outline planning permission** = general permission to build a property on a piece of land, but not final because there are no details **vorläufige Baugenehmigung**
2 *verb* to make a general description **skizzieren, entwerfen, einen Überblick geben;** *the chairman outlined the company's plans for the coming year*

out of court *adverb & adjective* **a settlement was reached out of court** = a dispute was settled between two parties privately without continuing a court case **es kam zu einem außergerichtlichen Vergleich;** *they are hoping to reach an out-of-court settlement*

out of pocket *adjective & adverb* having paid out money personally **aus eigener Tasche; out-of-pocket expenses** = amount of money to pay a worker back for his own money which he has spent on company business **Spesen, Auslagen**

output
1 *noun*
(a) amount which a company *or* a person *or* a machine produces **Produktion, Ausstoß, Output;** *output has increased by 10%; 25% of our output is exported;* **output tax** = VAT charged by a company on goods *or* services sold **(Brutto)mehrwertsteuer**
(b) information which is produced by a computer **Ausgabe, Ausgang, Output**
2 *verb* to produce (by a computer) **ausgeben;** *the printer will output colour charts; that is the information outputted from the computer*
NOTE: **outputting - outputted**

outright *adverb & adjective* completely **total, ganz, vollständig; to purchase something outright** *or* **to make an outright purchase** = to buy something completely, including all rights in it **etwas komplett kaufen**

outside *adjective & adverb* not in a company's office or building **außer Haus, extern; to send work to be done outside** = to send work to be done in other offices **Arbeit außer Haus geben; outside office hours** = when the office is not open **außerhalb der Bürozeit; outside dealer** = person who is not a member of the Stock Exchange but is allowed to trade **nicht zur Börse zugelassener Wertpapierhändler; outside director** = director who is not employed by the company **unternehmensfremder Direktor; Unternehmensorgan ohne Anstellung beim Unternehmen; outside line** = line from an internal office telephone system to the main telephone exchange **Verbindung außer Haus/nach außen; outside worker** = worker who does not work in a company's offices **Angestellter außer Haus; Angestellter im Außendienst**

outstanding *adjective* not yet paid or completed **ausstehend, unbezahlt; outstanding debts** = debts which are waiting to be paid **Außenstände; outstanding offences** = offences for which a person has not yet been convicted, which can be considered at the same time as a similar offence for which he faces sentence **Straftatsbestände, die im laufenden Verfahren zu einer Gesamtstrafe zusammengefaßt werden können; outstanding orders** = orders received but not yet supplied **ausstehende Lieferungen, unerledigte Aufträge; matters outstanding from the previous meeting** = questions which were not settled at the previous meeting **von der vorhergehenden Besprechung noch offenstehende Punkte**

outvote *verb* to defeat in a vote **überstimmen; the chairman was outvoted** = the majority voted against the chairman **der Vorsitzende wurde überstimmt**

overcharge
1 *noun* charge which is higher than it should be **zuviel berechneter Betrag; *to pay back an overcharge***
2 *verb* to ask too much money **zuviel berechnen;** *the hotel overcharged us for meals; we asked for a refund because we had been overcharged*

overcome *verb* to defeat *or* to win against **überwinden, meistern, bezwingen;** *the defendant will have to overcome two hurdles if his appeal is to succeed*
NOTE: **overcame - has overcome**

overdue *adjective* which has not been paid on time **überfällig; interest payments are three weeks overdue** = interest

payments which should have been made three weeks ago **die Zinszahlungen sind seit drei Wochen fällig**

overestimate *verb* to think something is larger *or* worse than it really is **überschätzen, zu hoch ansetzen;** *he overestimated the amount of time needed to prepare his case*

overlook *verb*
(a) to look out over **überblicken;** *his chambers overlook the garden of the Middle Temple*
(b) not to pay attention to **übersehen;** *in this instance we will overlook the delay; the court overlooked the fact that the defendant's car was not insured*

overreaching *noun* legal principle where an interest in land is replaced by a direct right to money **lastenfreie Auflassung, lastenfreie Übertragung von Grundbesitz unter pfandmäßiger Belastung des Kaufpreises**

override *verb* to pay no attention to *or* to be more important than **nicht berücksichtigen; vorgehen, sich hinwegsetzen über;** *the appeal court overrode the decision of the lower court;* **overriding interest** = interest which comes before that of another party **vorrangige Rechte;** *his wife established an overriding interest in the property against the bank's charge on it*
NOTE: **overriding - overrode - has overridden**
◊ **overrider** *or* **overriding commission** *noun* special extra commission which is above all other commissions **außerordentliche Provision**

overrule *verb (of a higher court)* to set a new precedent by deciding a case on a different principle from one laid down by a lower court **außer Kraft setzen, aufheben**

overrun *noun* to go beyond a limit **überschreiten, überziehen;** *the construction company overran the time limit set to complete the factory*
NOTE: **overrunning - overran - has overrun**

overt *adjective* open *or* obvious (as opposed to covert) **offen, offenkundig; overt act** = act which is obviously aimed at committing a criminal offence **offenkundige Handlung;** *see also* MARKET OVERT

over-the-counter *adjective* **over-the-counter market** = secondary stock market dealing in shares which are not listed on the Stock Exchange **Freiverkehr(smarkt) (für nicht im offiziellen Börsenhandel zugelassene Aktien); over-the-counter sales** = legal selling of shares which are not listed in the official Stock Exchange list **Verkauf im Freiverkehr**

overtime
1 *noun* hours worked more than the normal working time **Überstunden;** *to work six hours' overtime; the overtime rate is one and a half times normal pay;* **overtime ban** = order by a trade union which forbids overtime work by its members **Überstundenverbot; overtime pay** = pay for extra time worked **Überstundenlohn**
2 *adverb* **to work overtime** = to work longer hours than in the contract of employment **Überstunden machen**

owe *verb* to have to pay money **schulden; he owes the company for the stock he purchased** = he has not paid for the stock **er schuldet der Firma für die gekauften Waren**
◇ **owing** *adjective*
(a) which is owed **offenstehend;** *money owing to the directors; how much is still owing to the company?*
(b) owing to = because of **wegen;** *the plane was late owing to fog; I am sorry that owing to pressure of work, we cannot supply your order on time*

own *verb* to have *or* to possess **besitzen; a wholly-owned subsidiary** = a subsidiary which belongs completely to the parent company **eine hundertprozentige Tochtergesellschaft; a state-owned industry** = industry which is nationalized **ein staatseigener/verstaatlichter Industriebetrieb**
◇ **owner** *noun* person who owns something **Eigentümer/-in; beneficial owner** = true *or* ultimate owner (whose interest may be concealed by a nominee) **wirtschaftlicher Eigentümer; sole owner** = person who owns something alone **Alleineigentümer; owner-occupier** = person who owns and lives in a house **Bewohner des eigenen Grundbesitzes; goods sent at owner's risk** = situation where it is the owner of the goods who has to insure them while they are being shipped **Warensendung mit Gefahr beim Absender**
◇ **ownership** *noun* act of owning something **Eigentum; collective ownership** = situation where a business is owned by the workers who work in it **Kollektiveigentum; common ownership** *or* **ownership in common** = ownership of a company *or* of a property by a group of people who each own a part **Miteigentum; joint ownership** = situation where two or more persons own the same property **gemeinschaftliches Eigentum, Eigentum zur gesamten Hand; public ownership** *or* **state ownership** = situation where an industry is nationalized **Staatseigentum;** *the company has been put*

into state ownership; **private ownership** = situation where a company is owned by private shareholders **Privateigentum; the ownership of the company has passed to the banks** = the banks have become owners of the company **das Eigentumsrecht an dem Unternehmen ist auf die Banken übergegangen** NOTE: no plural

oyez *French word meaning* "hear!": used at the beginning of some types of official proceedings **Achtung**

Pp

pais *see* ESTOPPEL

palimony *noun* money which a court orders a man to pay regularly to a woman with whom he has been living and from whom he has separated **Unterhalt**

panel *noun*
(a) flat surface standing upright **Tafel, Brett; display panel** = flat area for displaying goods in a shop window **Auslage-, Anschlagfläche; advertisement panel** = special large advertising space in a newspaper **Kasten**
(b) panel of experts = group of people who give advice on a problem **Sachverständigenausschuß, Expertengruppe;** *see also* EMPANEL

paper *noun*
(a) thin material for writing on or for wrapping **Papier; carbon paper** = sheet of paper with a black coating on one side used in a typewriter to make a copy **Kohlepapier; duplicating paper** = special paper to be used in a duplicating machine **Saugpost-, Matrizenpapier; headed paper** = notepaper with the name and address of the company printed on it **Papier mit Briefkopf; engrossment paper** *or* **judicature paper** = thick heavy paper on which court documents are engrossed **Urkundenpapier; lined paper** = paper with thin lines printed on it **liniertes Papier; typing paper** = thin paper for use in a typewriter **Schreibmaschinenpapier; paper feed** = device which puts paper into a printer *or* copying machine **Papiervorschub, Papiereinzug;** (NOTE: no plural)
(b) papers = documents **Papiere, Unterlagen;** *the solicitor sent me the relevant papers on the case; the police have sent the papers on the fraud to the Director of Public*

Prosecutions; he has lost the customs papers; the office is asking for the VAT papers
(c) on paper = as explained in writing, but not tested in practice **auf dem Papier, theoretisch;** *on paper the system is ideal, but we have to see it working before we will sign the contract;* **paper loss** = loss made when an asset has fallen in value but has not been sold **nicht realisierter Verlust; paper profit** = profit made when an asset has increased in value but has not been sold **nicht realisierter Gewinn, Buchgewinn**
(d) documents which can represent money (bills of exchange, promissory notes, etc.) **Geldmarktpapiere; bankable paper** = document which a bank will accept as security for a loan **bankfähiges Papier; negotiable paper** = document which can be transferred from one owner to another for money **begebbares Wertpapier**
(e) paper money *or* **paper currency** = banknotes **Papiergeld**
(f) newspaper **Zeitung; trade paper** = newspaper aimed at people working in a certain industry **Fachzeitschrift; free paper** *or* **giveaway paper** = newspaper which is given away free, and which relies for its income on its advertising **Werbe-, Anzeigenblatt**

◇ **paperwork** *noun* office work, especially writing memoranda and filling in forms **Schreibarbeiten**
NOTE: no plural

parade *noun* **identification** *or* **identity parade** = arrangement where a group of people (including a suspect) stand in line at a police station so that a witness can point out a person whom he recognizes **Gegenüberstellung zur Identifikation des Täters**

paragraph *noun* group of several lines of writing which makes a separate section **Abschnitt, Absatz;** *the first paragraph of your letter or paragraph one of your letter; please refer to the paragraph in the contract on "shipping instructions"*

paralegal
1 *adjective* connected with, but not part of, the law **paralegal**
2 *noun* person with no legal qualifications who works in a lawyer's office **Anwaltsassistent**

parcel *noun* area of land **Grundstück, Stück Land;** *for sale: a parcel of land in the Borough of Richmond*

pardon
1 *noun* official ending of a prison sentence

which a criminal is serving for a crime **Begnadigung, Straferlaß; free pardon** = pardon given to a convicted person where both the sentence and the conviction are recorded as void **unbeschränkte Begnadigung**
2 *verb* to end the prison sentence which a criminal is serving **begnadigen;** *the political prisoners were pardoned by the president*

parent *noun* **parents** = father and mother **Eltern; parent company** = company which owns more than 50% of the shares of another company **Muttergesellschaft, Dachgesellschaft**

parentis *see* IN LOCO PARENTIS

pari passu *Latin phrase meaning* "equally" *or* "with no distinction between them" **gleichrangig, gleichwertig;** *the new shares will rank pari passu with the existing ones*

parish *noun* area which surrounds a church and which is served by that church **Gemeinde**

parity *noun* being equal **Gleichheit; Parität; the female staff want parity with the men** = they want to have the same rates of pay and conditions as the men **die weibliche Belegschaft will mit der männlichen gleichgestellt werden; the pound fell to parity with the dollar** = the pound fell to a point where one pound equalled one dollar **das Pfund fiel, bis es den Kurs von 1:1 zum Dollar erreichte**
NOTE: no plural

parliament *noun* elected group of representatives who form the legislative body which votes the laws of a country (in the UK formed of the House of Commons and House of Lords) **Parlament; Act of Parliament** = decision which has been approved by Parliament and so becomes law **Gesetz; contempt of Parliament** = conduct which may bring the authority of Parliament into disrepute **Mißachtung der Parlamentshoheit; Member of Parliament** = person elected to represent a constituency in Parliament **Abgeordnete(r);** *GB* **Mitglied des Unterhauses; the European Parliament** = parliament made up of delegates elected by each member state of the EC **das Europäische Parlament**
NOTE: often used without **"the": Parliament voted to abolish the death penalty; this is one of the Bills which will shortly be coming before Parliament**

◊ **parliamentary** *adjective* referring to parliament **parlamentarisch; parliamentary agents** = persons (usually solicitors) who advise private individuals who wish to promote a Bill in Parliament **Anwälte, die Rat zu Privatvorlagen geben; Parliamentary Commissioner** = the Ombudsman *or* official who investigates complaints by the public against government departments; **Ombudsmann; jd, der für Beschwerden über Behörden zuständig ist; parliamentary draftsman** = lawyer who is responsible for drafting Bills going before Parliament **Jurist, der Gesetzesentwürfe formuliert; Parliamentary privilege** = right of a Member of Parliament to speak freely to the House of Commons without possibility of being sued for defamation **Abgeordnetenimmunität**

parol *adjective* done by speaking **mündlich; parol agreement** *or* **contract** = simple contract *or* informal or oral contract **formloser Vertrag; parol evidence** = evidence given orally **mündlicher Beweis**

parole
1 *noun* (i) allowing a prisoner to leave prison for a short time, on condition that he behaves well; (ii) allowing a prisoner who has behaved well to be released from prison early on condition that he continues to behave well **(i) Straf-, Hafturlaub; (ii) bedingte Entlassung;** *he was given a week's parole to visit his mother in hospital; after six month's good conduct in prison she is eligible for parole; he was let out on parole and immediately burgled a house;* **parole board** = group of people who advise the Home Secretary if a prisoner should be released on parole before the end of his sentence **Ausschuß zur Gewährung der bedingten Entlassung**
2 *verb* to let a prisoner out of prison on condition that he behaves well **bedingt entlassen;** *if you're lucky you will be paroled before Christmas*

part
1 *noun*
(a) piece *or* section **Teil;** *part of the shipment was damaged; part of the staff is on overtime; part of the expenses will be refunded*
(b) in part = not completely **teilweise, zum Teil;** *to contribute in part to the costs; to pay the costs in part*
(c) spare part = small piece of machinery used to take the place of a piece which is broken **Ersatzteil**
(d) part-owner = person who owns something jointly with one or more other persons **Miteigentümer; part-ownership** =

situation where two or more persons own the same property **Miteigentum**
(e) to offer something in part exchange = giving an old product as part of the payment for a new one **etwas in Zahlung geben; part payment** = paying of part of a whole payment **Teilzahlung; part performance** = situation where a party has carried out part of a contract, but not complied with all the terms of it **Teilleistung, Teilerfüllung**
2 *verb* to part with something = to give something which you possess to someone else **sich trennen von, etwas aufgeben;** *he was tricked into parting with the keys to the safe*

parte *see* EX PARTE, INTER PARTES, AUDI ALTERNAM PARTEM

partial *adjective*
(a) not complete **Teil-, teilweise, partiell; partial loss** = situation where only part of the insured property has been damaged or lost **Teilverlust, Teilschaden;** *he was awarded partial compensation for the damage to his house* = he was compensated for part of the damage **der Schaden an seinem Haus wurde zum Teil ersetzt**
(b) biased *or* showing favour towards one party **parteiisch, voreingenommen;** *the defendant complained that the judge was partial*

particular
1 *adjective* special *or* different from others **besonderer, speziell; particular average** = situation where part of a shipment is lost or damaged and the insurance costs are borne by the owner of the lost goods and not shared among all the owners of the shipment **besondere Havarie; particular lien** = right of a person to keep possession of another person's property until debts relating to that property have been paid **Pfandrecht an einer bestimmten Sache;** *compare* GENERAL AVERAGE, GENERAL LIEN
2 *noun*
(a) particulars = details, especially a statement of the facts of a case made by a party in civil proceedings *or* a County Court pleading setting out the plaintiff's claim **nähere Angaben, Einzelheiten; Spezifizierungen im Schriftsatz;** *sheet which gives particulars of the items for sale; the inspector asked for particulars of the missing car;* **to give full particulars of something** = to list all the known details about something **genaue/detaillierte Angaben zu etwas machen; request for further and better particulars** = pleading served by one party on another in civil proceedings, asking for information about the other

party's claim *or* defence **Antrag einer Partei (an die andere Partei) auf Erteilung ausführlicherer Angaben über den Inhalt der gegnerischen Klagebegründung od Klagebeantwortung; particulars of claim** = County Court pleading setting out the plaintiff's claim **Klagebegründung (b) in particular** = specially *or* as a special point **besonders, insbesondere, vor allem;** *goods which are easily damaged, in particular glasses, need special packing*

partition *noun* dividing up of land which is held by joint tenants *or* tenants in common **Grundstücksteilung**

partly *adverb* not completely **teilweise, zum Teil; partly-paid capital** = capital which represents partly-paid shares **teilweise eingezahltes Aktienkapital; partly-paid up shares** = shares where the shareholders have not paid the full face value **teilweise eingezahlte Aktien; partly-secured creditors** = creditors whose debts are not fully covered by the value of the security **nur zum Teil gesicherte Gläubige**

partner *noun* person who works in a firm and has a share in it with other partners **Partner/-in, Gesellschafter/-in, Teilhaber/-in;** *he became a partner in a firm of solicitors;* **active partner** *or* **working partner** = partner who works in a partnership **geschäftsführender Teilhaber; junior partner** *or* **senior partner** = person who has a small *or* large part of the shares in a partnership **Juniorpartner, Seniorpartner, Hauptteilhaber; limited partner** = partner who has only limited liability for the partnership debts **beschränkt haftender Gesellschafter; sleeping partner** *or* **dormant partner** = partner who has a share in a business but does not work in it; *entspricht* **stiller Teilhaber**

◇ **partnership** *noun*
(a) unregistered business where two or more people share the risks and profits equally **Partnerschaft, Teilhaberschaft, Personengesellschaft, offene Handelsgesellschaft, Sozietät;** *to go into partnership with someone; to join with someone to form a partnership;* **articles of partnership** = document which sets up the legal conditions of a partnership **Gesellschaftsvertrag; to offer someone a partnership** *or* **to take someone into partnership with you** = to have a working business and bring someone in to share it with you **jdn zum Teilhaber machen; to dissolve a partnership** = to bring a partnership to an end **eine Gesellschaft/Partnerschaft auflösen; partnership at will** = partnership with no

fixed time limit stated **jederzeit kündbare Partnerschaft**
(b) **limited partnership** = registered business where the liability of some of the partners is limited to the amount of capital they have each provided to the business and where these partners may not take part in the running of the business, while other, working partners, are fully liable for all the obligations of the partnership **Kommanditgesellschaft**

party *noun*
(a) company *or* person involved in a legal dispute *or* legal agreement *or* crime **Partei;** *one of the parties to the suit has died; the company is not a party to the agreement;* **identity of parties** = situation where the parties in different actions are the same **Parteiengleichheit; party and party costs** = normal basis for taxation of costs which includes all costs incurred in the party's case **erstattungsfähige Kosten, Prozeßkosten**
(b) **third party** = any third person, in addition to the two main parties involved in a contract **Dritter, dritte Person; third party insurance** *or* **third party policy** = insurance which pays compensation if someone who is not the insured person incurs loss or injury **Haftpflichtversicherung**
(c) **working party** = group of experts who study a problem **Arbeitsausschuß;** *the government has set up a working party to study the problems of industrial waste; Professor Smith is the chairman of the working party on drug abuse*
(d) **political party** = organized group of people who believe a country should be run in a certain way **politische Partei**

◇ **party wall** *noun* wall which separates two adjoining properties (houses *or* land) and belongs to both owners equally **(gemeinsame) Grenzmauer, Brandmauer**

pass
1 *noun* permit to allow someone to go into a building **Ausweis, Passierschein;** *you need a pass to enter the ministry offices; all members of staff must show a pass*
2 *verb*
(a) to vote to approve *or* to vote to make a law **annehmen, verabschieden;** *Parliament passed the Bill which has now become law; the finance director has to pass an invoice before it is paid; the loan has been passed by the board;* **to pass a resolution** = to vote to agree to a resolution **eine Resolution annehmen;** *the meeting passed a proposal that salaries should be frozen*
(b) **to pass sentence on someone** = to give a convicted person the official legal punishment **über jdn ein Urteil fällen;** *the jury*

returned a verdict of guilty, and the judge will pass sentence next week
(c) to pass a dividend = to pay no dividend in a certain year **keine Dividende ausschütten, eine Dividende ausfallen lassen**
(d) to be successful **bestehen;** *he passed his typing test; she has passed all her exams and now is a qualified solicitor*

◊ **pass off** *verb* **to pass something off as something else** = to pretend that it is another thing in order to cheat a customer **etwas für/als etwas anderes ausgeben**

◊ **passing off** *noun* tort of pretending that goods are someone else's, using that other person's reputation to make a sale **Ausgeben eigener Ware als die eines anderen, Warenzeichenmißbrauch**

passport *noun* official document proving that you are a citizen of a country, which you have to show when you travel from one country to another **Paß;** *we had to show our passports at the customs post; his passport is out of date; the passport officer stamped my passport;* **passport holder** = person who holds a passport **Paßinhaber;** *she is a British passport holder*

patent
1 *noun*
(a) official document showing that a person has the exclusive right to make and sell an invention **Patent;** *to take out a patent for a new type of light bulb; to apply for a patent for a new invention; he has received a grant of patent for his invention;* **patent applied for** *or* **patent pending** = words on a product showing that the inventor has applied for a patent for it **Patent angemeldet; to forfeit a patent** = to lose a patent because payments have not been made **ein Patent verfallen lassen/verwirken; to infringe a patent** = to make and sell a product which works in the same way as a patented product and not pay a royalty for it **ein Patent verletzen; patent agent** = person who advises on patents and applies for patents on behalf of clients **Patentanwalt; to file a patent application** = to apply for a patent **ein Patent anmelden; patent examiner** = official who checks patent applications to see if the inventions are really new **Patentprüfer; patent holder** = person who has been granted a patent **Patentinhaber; infringement of patent** *or* **patent infringement** = act of illegally using *or* making *or* selling an invention which is patented without the permission of the patentee **Patentverletzung; patent number** = reference number given to a patented invention **Patentnummer; patent office** = government office which grants patents and supervises them **Patentamt; patent rights** = rights which an inventor

holds under a patent **Patentrecht; patent specification** = full details of an invention which is the subject of a patent application **Patentbeschreibung**
(b) letters patent = official document from the Crown, which gives someone the exclusive right to do something (such as becoming a lord *or* granting a patent to make and sell an invention) **Urkunde, durch die ein Recht verliehen wird; Berufungsurkunde; Patenturkunde**
2 *verb* **to patent an invention** = to register an invention with the patent office to prevent other people from copying it **eine Erfindung patentieren lassen**
3 *adjective* obvious *or* clear to see **offensichtlich;** *the prisoner's statement is a patent lie*

◊ **patented** *adjective* which is protected by a patent **patentiert, patentrechtlich geschützt**
◊ **patentee** *noun* person who has been granted a patent **Patentinhaber**
◊ **patently** *adverb* clearly *or* obviously **offensichtlich;** *he made a patently false statement to the court*

paternity *noun* **paternity leave** = permission for a man to be away from work when his wife is having a baby **Arbeitsfreistellung zur Geburt**
◊ **paternity action** *or* **suit** *noun* lawsuit brought by the mother of an illegitimate child to force the putative father to maintain the child **Vaterschaftsprozeß**

pathology *noun* study of disease **Pathologie**
◊ **pathologist** *noun* doctor who specializes in pathology, especially a doctor who examines corpses to find out the cause of death **Pathologe/Pathologin; Home Office pathologist** = official government pathologist employed by the Home Office to examine corpses **vom Innenministerium angestellter Pathologe**

patrial *noun* person who has the right to live in the UK because he has close family ties with the country (for example, if his grandfather was British) **jd mit Wohnsitzrecht in GB, der keinen Ein- und Ausreisebeschränkungen unterworfen ist**

patricide *noun* murder of one's father **Vatermord**

patrol
1 *noun* group of people who walk through an area to see what is happening **Streife; Patrouille; a police patrol** = group of policemen who are patrolling an area **Polizeistreife; on patrol** = walking through

an area to see what is happening **auf Streife;** *we have six squad cars on patrol in the centre of the town;* **on foot patrol** = patrolling an area on foot, not in a car **auf Streifengang**
2 *verb* to walk regularly through an area to see what is happening **Streife gehen; patrouillieren;** *groups of riot police were patrolling the centre of the town*

◊ **patrol car** *noun* car used by police on patrol **Streifenwagen**

◊ **patrolman** *noun* US lowest rank of policeman **Polizist im Streifendienst;** *Patrolman Jones was at the scene of the accident*

pattern *noun*
(a) pattern book = book showing examples of design **Musterbuch**
(b) general way in which something usually happens **Struktur,(übliches) Schema;** *the pattern of crime in the inner cities is different from the pattern in the country*

pauperis *see* IN FORMA PAUPERIS

pawn
1 *noun* transfer of a piece of property to someone as security for a loan **Verpfändung; to put something in pawn** = to leave a valuable object with someone in exchange for a loan which has to be repaid if you want to take back the object **etwas verpfänden; to take something out of pawn** = to repay the loan and so get back the object **ein Pfand auslösen; pawn ticket** = receipt given by the pawnbroker for the object left in pawn **Pfandschein;** (NOTE: no plural)
2 *verb* **to pawn a watch** = to leave a watch with a pawnbroker who gives a loan against it **eine Uhr verpfänden/in Pfand geben**

◊ **pawnbroker** *noun* person who lends money against the security of valuable objects **Pfandleiher/-in**

◊ **pawnshop** *noun* pawnbroker's shop **Leihhaus, Pfandleihanstalt**

pay
1 *noun*
(a) salary *or* wage *or* money given to someone for regular work **Gehalt, Lohn; back pay** = salary which has not been paid **Lohnrückstand; basic pay** = normal salary without extra payments **Grundgehalt, Ecklohn; take-home pay** = pay left after tax and insurance have been deducted **Nettoverdienst; unemployment pay** = money given by the government to someone who is unemployed **Arbeitslosengeld; Arbeitslosenhilfe**
(b) pay cheque = monthly cheque which pays a salary to a worker **Gehalts-,**

Lohnscheck; pay day = day on which wages are paid to workers (usually Friday for workers paid once a week, and during the last week of the month for workers who are paid once a month) **Zahltag; pay negotiations** *or* **pay talks** = discussions between management and workers about pay increases **Lohnverhandlungen**
2 *verb*
(a) to give money to buy an item or a service **(be)zahlen; to pay in advance** = to give money before you receive the item bought or before the service has been completed **im voraus bezahlen; to pay in instalments** = to give money for an item by giving small amounts regularly **in Raten zahlen; to pay cash** = to pay the complete sum in cash **bar zahlen; "pay cash"** = words written on a crossed cheque to show that it can be paid in cash if necessary; *GB* **Barauszahlung; to pay on demand** = to pay money when it is asked for, not after a period of credit **auf Anforderung bezahlen; to pay a dividend** = to give shareholders a part of the profits of a company **eine Dividende ausschütten; to pay interest** = to give money as interest on money borrowed or invested **Zinsen zahlen;** *building societies pay interest of 10%;* **pay as you earn** *or* US **pay-as-you-go** = tax system, where income tax is deducted from the salary before it is paid to the worker **Lohnsteuerabzug vor Auszahlung des Lohns, Quellenabzugssystem**
(b) to give a worker money for work done **(be)zahlen;** *the workers have not been paid for three weeks; we pay good wages for skilled workers; how much do they pay you per hour?;* **to be paid by the hour** = to get money for each hour worked **einen Stundenlohn erhalten, stundenweise bezahlt werden; to be paid at piece-work rates** = to get money calculated on the number of pieces of work finished **einen Akkordlohn erhalten, im Akkord bezahlt werden**
NOTE: **paying - paid - has paid**

◊ **payable** *adjective* which is due to be paid **zahlbar, fällig; payable in advance** = which has to be paid before the goods are delivered **im voraus zahlbar; payable on delivery** = which has to be paid when the goods are delivered **zahlbar bei Lieferung; payable on demand** = which must be paid when payment is asked for **zahlbar bei Sicht/auf Verlangen; payable at sixty days** = which has to be paid by sixty days after the date of invoice **zahlbar innerhalb von sechzig Tagen; cheque made payable to bearer** = cheque which will be paid to the person who has it, not to any particular name written on it **an den Überbringer zahlbarer Scheck; shares payable on application** = shares which must be paid for when you apply to buy them **bei Antragstellung zahlbare Wertpapiere; accounts payable** =

money owed to creditors **Verbindlichkeiten; bills payable** = bills which a debtor will have to pay **Wechselverbindlichkeiten, zu zahlende Wechsel; electricity charges are payable by the tenant** = the tenant (and not the landlord) must pay for the electricity **Elektrizitätskosten sind vom Mieter zu tragen**

◊ **pay back** verb to give money back to someone **zurückzahlen;** to pay back a loan; I lent him £50 and he promised to pay me back in a month; he has never paid me back the money he borrowed

◊ **payback** noun paying back money which has been borrowed **Rückzahlung; payback clause** = clause in a contract which states the terms for repaying a loan **Rückzahlungsklausel; payback period** = period of time over which a loan is to be repaid or an investment is to pay for itself **Tilgungszeitraum; Amortisationszeit**

◊ **pay cheque** or **paycheck** noun salary cheque given to an employee **Lohn-, Gehaltsscheck**

◊ **pay down** verb to pay money down = to make a deposit **Geld anzahlen;** he paid £50 down and the rest in monthly instalments

◊ **PAYE** = PAY AS YOU EARN

◊ **payee** noun person who receives money from someone or person whose name is on a cheque or bill of exchange **Zahlungsempfänger**

◊ **payer** noun person who gives money to someone **Zahler; slow payer** = person or company which does not pay debts on time **säumiger Schuldner**

◊ **pay in** or **into** verb (of a defendant) to pay in or to pay money into court = to deposit money with the court at the beginning of a case, so that if the case is lost you cannot be charged with the plaintiff's costs **Geld bei Gericht hinterlegen**

COMMENT: if at trial the plaintiff fails to recover more than the amount the defendant has paid in, he will have to pay the defendant's costs from the date of the payment in

◊ **payment** noun
(a) transfer of money from one person to another to satisfy a debt or obligation **(Be)zahlung, Begleichung;** payment in cash or cash payment; payment by cheque; payment of interest or interest payment; **payment on account** = paying part of the money owed before a bill is delivered **Anzahlung;** the solicitor asked for a payment of £100 on account; **full payment** or **payment in full** = paying all money owed **Zahlung in voller Höhe; payment on invoice** = paying money as soon as an invoice is received **Zahlung bei Erhalt der Rechnung; payment in** or **payment into court** = depositing money into the court before the case starts, so that if the

case is lost, the defendant will not have to pay the plaintiff's costs **Hinterlegung (einer Geldsumme) bei Gericht**
(b) money paid **Zahlung; back payment** = paying money which is owed **Nach-, Rückzahlung; deferred payments** = money paid later than the agreed date **aufgeschobene Zahlung; down payment** = part of a total payment made in advance **Anzahlung; interim payment** = payment of part of a sum owed **Abschlagszahlung; part payment** = paying part of a whole payment **Teilzahlung**

◊ **pay off** verb
(a) to finish paying money which is owed **vollständig abbezahlen, tilgen;** to pay off a mortgage; to pay off a loan
(b) to pay all the money owed to someone and terminate his employment **auszahlen;** when the company was taken over the factory was closed and all the workers were paid off

◊ **payoff** noun money paid to finish paying something which is owed **Tilgungssumme**

◊ **pay up** verb to give money which is owed **voll/ganz bezahlen;** the company paid up only when we sent them a letter from our solicitor; he finally paid up six months late

PC = PERSONAL COMPUTER, POLICE CONSTABLE, PRIVY COUNCIL, PRIVY COUNCILLOR
NOTE: the plural is **PCs**

peace noun
(a) being quiet or calm; calm existence **Ruhe; öffentliche Sicherheit und Ordnung; breach of the peace** = creating a disturbance which is likely to annoy people **Störung der öffentlichen Sicherheit und Ordnung**
(b) state of not being at war **Frieden;** after six years of civil war, the country is now at peace; the peace treaty was signed yesterday; both sides claimed the other side broke the peace agreement

pecuniary adjective referring to money **finanziell, pekuniär; obtaining a pecuniary advantage by deception** = crime of deceiving someone so as to derive a financial benefit from the deception **durch Täuschung einen Vermögensvorteil erlangen;** he gained no pecuniary advantage = he made no profit **er erlangte keinen Vermögensvorteil/finanziellen Vorteil**

peer noun
(a) member of the House of Lords **Mitglied des Oberhauses; hereditary peer** = member of the House of Lords who has inherited his title **Peer mit ererbtem Adelstitel; life peer** =

member of the House of Lords who is appointed for life **Peer auf Lebenszeit** (b) person who is in the same group or rank as another **Gleichrangiger, Gleichgestellter; peer group** = group of persons of the same level or rank **Gleichrangigengruppe**

◊ **peeress** noun female peer **Peeress**

penal adjective referring to punishment **Straf-, strafrechtlich; penal code** = set of laws governing crime and its punishment **Strafgesetzbuch; penal colony** = prison camp in a distant place, where prisoners are sent for long periods **Strafkolonie; penal institution** = place (such as a prison) where convicted criminals are kept **Strafvollzugsanstalt; penal laws** or **the penal system** = system of punishments relating to different crimes **Strafgesetz, Strafrecht; Strafrechtssystem; penal servitude** = former punishment by imprisonment with hard labour **Zwangsarbeit; Zuchthaus**

◊ **penalize** verb to punish or to fine **bestrafen; mit einer Strafe belegen;** to penalize a supplier for late deliveries; they were penalized for bad service

penalty noun punishment (such as a fine) which is imposed if something is not done or if a law is not obeyed **Geldstrafe; Strafe;** the penalty for carrying an offensive weapon is a fine of £2,000 and three months in prison; **death penalty** = sentence of a criminal to be executed **Todesstrafe;** the president has introduced the death penalty for certain crimes against the state; **penalty clause** = clause which lists the penalties which will be imposed if the terms of the contract are not fulfilled **Strafklausel, Bestimmung einer Vertragsstrafe;** the contract contains a penalty clause which fines the company 1% for every week the completion date is late

COMMENT: penalty clauses in a contract are sometimes unenforceable

pendens see LIS

◊ **pendente lite** Latin phrase meaning "during the lawsuit" **in einem schwebenden Verfahren, während der Anhängigkeit des Rechtsstreits;** see also ALIMONY

pending
1 adjective waiting **schwebend, anstehend; pending action** = action concerned with land which has not been heard **anhängiger Rechtsstreit; pending suit** = while a lawsuit is being heard **für die Dauer des Prozesses; maintenance pending suit** = maintenance obtained by a spouse in matrimonial proceedings until there is a full hearing to deal with the couple's financial affairs **vorläufige Unterhaltszahlung; patent pending** = words printed on a product to show that its inventor has applied for a grant of patent **Patent angemeldet**
2 adverb **pending advice from our lawyers** = while waiting for advice from our lawyers **bis zur Benachrichtigung durch unsere Anwälte**

penitentiary noun US large prison **Strafanstalt, Gefängnis;** the Pennsylvania State Penitentiary

penology noun study of sentences in relation to crimes **Strafvollzugswissenschaft** NOTE: no plural

pension
1 noun
(a) money paid regularly to someone who no longer works **Rente, Pension, Ruhegehalt; retirement pension** or **old age pension** = state pension given to a man who is over 65 or and woman who is over 60 **Altersrente, Altersversorgung; occupational pension** = pension which is paid by the company by which a worker has been employed **betriebliche Altersversorgung, Betriebsrente**
(b) **pension contributions** = money paid by a company or worker into a pension fund **Rentenversicherungsbeiträge; pension entitlement** = amount of pension which someone has the right to receive when he retires **Rentenanspruch; pension fund** = money which provides pensions for retired members of staff **Rentenfonds; pension plan** or **pension scheme** = plan worked out by an insurance company which arranges for a worker to pay part of his salary over many years and receive a regular payment when he retires **Altersversorgungssystem, Rentenversicherungssystem; contributory pension scheme** = scheme where the worker has to pay a proportion of his salary **beitragspflichtige Rentenversicherung; graduated pension scheme** = pension scheme where the benefit is calculated as a percentage of the salary of each person in the scheme **gestaffeltes Rentensystem; noncontributory pension scheme** = scheme where the employer pays in all the money on behalf of the worker **beitragsfreie Rentenversicherung; personal pension plan** = pension plan which applies to one worker only, usually a self-employed person, not to a group **private Rentenversicherung**
2 verb **to pension someone off** = to ask someone to retire and take a pension **jdn vorzeitig pensionieren, jdn in den Ruhestand versetzen**

◊ **pensionable** adjective able to receive a pension **pensionsberechtigt; rentenberechtigt;**

pensionable age = age after which someone can take a pension **Pensionsalter; Rentenalter**

◊ **pensioner** *noun* person who receives a pension **Rentner/-in; old age pensioner** = person who receives the retirement pension **Rentner/-in, Rentenempfänger**

peppercorn rent *noun* very small *or* nominal rent **nominelle Miete; nominelle Pacht;** *to pay a peppercorn rent; to lease a property for or at a peppercorn rent*

per *preposition*
(a) as per = according to **gemäß, laut; as per invoice** = as stated in the invoice **laut Rechnung; as per sample** = as shown in the sample **gemäß dem Muster; as per previous order** = according to the details given in our previous order **gemäß der vorausgegangenen Bestellung**
(b) at a rate of **pro; per hour** *or* **per day** *or* **per week** *or* **per year** = for each hour *or* day *or* week *or* year **pro Stunde; pro Tag; pro Woche; pro Jahr;** *the rate is £5 per hour; he makes about £2,500 per month;* **we pay £10 per hour** = we pay £10 for each hour worked **wir bezahlen £10 pro Stunde; the earnings per share** = dividend received by each share **der Gewinn pro Aktie; per head** = for each person **pro Kopf/Person;** *allow £15 per head for expenses; reliable staff cost on average £15,000 per head per annum*
(c) out of **pro;** *the rate of imperfect items is about twenty-five per thousand; the birth rate has fallen to twelve per hundred*

◊ **per annum** *adverb* in a year *or* annually **im/pro Jahr;** *the rent is £2,500 per annum; what is their turnover per annum?*

◊ **per autre vie** *French phrase meaning* "for the lifetime of another person" **auf die Lebenszeit eines Dritten**

◊ **per capita** *adjective & adverb*
(a) divided among beneficiaries individually **nach Köpfen**
(b) per head *or* for each person **pro Person/Kopf; average income per capita** *or* **per capita income** = average income of one person **Pro-Kopf-Einkommen; per capita expenditure** = total money spent divided by the number of people involved **Pro-Kopf-Ausgaben**

◊ **per curiam** *Latin phrase meaning* "by a court": decision correctly made by a court, which can be used as a precedent **durch das Gericht**

◊ **per diem** *Latin phrase meaning* "for each day" **pro Tag**

◊ **per incuriam** *Latin phrase meaning* "because of lack of care": decision wrongly made by a court (which does not therefore set a precedent) **wegen mangelnder Sorgfalt**

◊ **per my et per tout** *French phrase meaning* "by half and by all": used to indicate the relationship between joint tenants **gesamthänderisch**

◊ **per procurationem** *Latin phrase meaning* "with the authority of" **in Vollmacht, in Vertretung**

◊ **per quod** *Latin phrase meaning* "by which" *or* "whereby" **wodurch**

◊ **per se** *Latin phrase meaning* "on its own" *or* "alone" **für sich (allein), von selbst, schlechthin; actionable per se** = which is in itself sufficient grounds for bringing an action **für sich genommen ein Klagegrund sein**

◊ **per stirpes** *Latin phrase meaning* "by branches": phrase used in wills where the entitlement is divided among branches of a family rather than among individuals **nach Stämmen**

per cent *noun* out of each hundred *or* for each hundred **Prozent;** *eighty per cent (80%) of crimes are solved*
NOTE: usually written % after figures

◊ **percentage** *noun* amount shown as a proportion of one hundred **Prozentsatz, Prozent; percentage increase** = increase calculated on the basis of a rate per hundred **prozentualer Anstieg; a percentage point** = one per cent **ein Prozentpunkt;** *what is the percentage of crimes committed at night? the number of crimes of violence has fallen by two percentage points over the last three years*

peremptory challenge *noun* objecting to a juror without stating any reason **Ablehnung (eines Geschworenen) ohne Angabe von Gründen**

perfect
1 *adjective* completely correct *or* with no mistakes **perfekt, fehlerlos, vollkommen;** *we check each shipment to make sure it is perfect; she did a perfect typing test;* **perfect right** = correct and legally acceptable right **vollkommenes Recht**
2 *verb* to make something which is completely correct **vervollkommnen, perfektionieren;** *he perfected the process for making high quality steel*

◊ **perfectly** *adverb* with no mistakes *or* correctly **perfekt, fehlerlos;** *she typed the letter perfectly*

perform *verb*
(a) to do well *or* badly **abschneiden; the company** *or* **the shares performed badly** = the company's share price fell **das Unternehmen hat/die Aktien haben schlecht abgeschnitten**

(b) to do (a duty) *or* to do what one is obliged to do by a contract **erfüllen, leisten**

◊ **performance** *noun*
(a) way in which someone *or* something acts **Leistung; the poor performance of the shares on the stock market** = the fall in the share price on the stock market **das schlechte Abschneiden der Aktien an der Börse; as a measure of the company's performance** = as a way of judging if the company's results are good or bad **als Maßstab für die Leistung/den Erfolg des Unternehmens; performance of personnel against objectives** = how personnel have worked, measured against the objectives set **Leistung des Personals gemessen an den Zielen; performance review** = yearly interview between a manager and each worker to discuss how the worker has worked during the year **Leistungsbeurteilung**
(b) carrying out of something, such as a duty *or* the terms of a contract **Ausführung, Erfüllung, Leistung; they were asked to put up a £1m performance bond** = they were asked to deposit £1m as a guarantee that they would carry out the terms of the contract **von ihnen wurde £1 Million Erfüllungsgarantie verlangt; discharge by performance** = situation where the terms of a contract have been fulfilled **Erfüllung; impossibility of performance** = situation where a party to a contract is unable to perform his part of the contract **Unmöglichkeit der Erfüllung; part performance** = situation where a party has carried out part of a contract, but not complied with all the terms of it **Teilleistung, Teilerfüllung; specific performance** = court order to a party to carry out his obligations in a contract **Leistung der Vertragsschuld**

◊ **performing right** *noun* right to allow the playing of a copyright piece of music **Aufführungsrecht**

peril *noun* danger (especially possible accident covered by an insurance policy) **Gefahr, Risiko; perils of the sea** *or* **maritime perils** = accidents which can happen at sea **Seerisiken**

period *noun*
(a) length of time **Zeit, Zeitspanne, Zeitraum, Periode;** *for a period of time or for a period of months or for a six-year period; to deposit money for a fixed period*
(b) accounting period = period of time at the end of which the firm's accounts are made up **Abrechnungszeitraum**

◊ **periodic** *or* **periodical**
1 *adjective* happening regularly from time to time **periodisch, periodisch erscheinend; periodical payments** = regular payments (such as maintenance paid to a divorced spouse) **regelmäßig wiederkehrende Zahlungen; periodic tenancy** = tenancy where the tenant rents for several short periods but not for a fixed length of time **sich automatisch verlängerndes Mietverhältnis od Pachtverhältnis**
2 *noun* **periodical** = magazine which comes out regularly **Zeitschrift, Magazin**

perjure *verb* **to perjure yourself** = to tell lies when you have made an oath to say what is true **meineidig werden, einen Meineid leisten**

◊ **perjury** *noun* notifiable offence of telling lies when you have made an oath to say what is true in court **Meineid;** *he was sent to prison for perjury; she appeared in court on a charge of perjury or on a perjury charge*
NOTE: no plural

permanent *adjective* which will last for a very long time *or* for ever **dauerhaft, fest, unbefristet, ständig;** *he has found a permanent job; she is in permanent employment; the permanent staff work a thirty-five hour week*

◊ **permanency** *noun* being permanent **Dauerhaftigkeit, Beständigkeit**
NOTE: no plural

◊ **permanently** *adverb* for ever **fest, ständig;** *he was permanently disabled by the accident*

permission *noun* being allowed to do something **Erlaubnis, Genehmigung, Bewilligung; written permission** = document which allows someone to do something **schriftliche Genehmigung; verbal permission** = telling someone that he is allowed to do something **mündliche Genehmigung; to give someone permission to do something** = to allow someone to do something **jdm gestatten, etwas zu tun; jdm die Erlaubnis erteilen**

permit
1 *noun* official document which allows someone to do something **Genehmigung, Erlaubnis(schein); building permit** = official document which allows someone to build on a piece of land **Baugenehmigung; entry permit** = document allowing someone to enter a country **Einreiseerlaubnis; export permit** *or* **import permit** = official document which allows goods to be exported or imported **Exportgenehmigung; Importgenehmigung; work permit** = official document which allows someone who is not a citizen to work in a country **Arbeitserlaubnis**
2 *verb* to allow someone to do something **genehmigen, erlauben, gestatten;** *this*

document permits the export of twenty-five computer systems; the ticket permits three people to go into the exhibition

perpetrate *verb* to commit (a crime) **begehen, verüben**

◊ **perpetrator** *noun* person who does something (especially person who commits a crime) **Täter/-in**

per pro = PER PROCURATIONEM with the authority of **in Vollmacht, in Vertretung; the secretary signed per pro the manager** = the secretary signed on behalf of, and with the authority of, the manager **der Sekretär unterzeichnete per Vollmacht**

persistent offender *noun* person who has been convicted of a crime at least three times before, and is likely to commit the crime again **Gewohnheitsverbrecher**

person *noun*
(a) someone *or* man or woman **Person;** *insurance policy which covers a named person;* **the persons named in the contract** = people whose names are given in the contract **die im Vertrag genannten Personen; the document should be witnessed by a third person** = someone who is not named in the document **das Dokument sollte von einem Dritten/einer dritten Person als Zeuge unterschrieben werden; in person** = someone himself *or* herself **persönlich; this important package is to be delivered to the chairman in person** = the package has to be given to the chairman himself (and not to his secretary, assistant, etc.) **dieses wichtige Paket muß dem Vorsitzenden persönlich übergeben werden; he came to see me in person** = he himself came to see me **er kam persönlich zu mir; litigant in person** = person bringing a lawsuit who also speaks on his own behalf in court without the help of a lawyer **Naturalpartei**
(b) legal person *or* **artificial person** = company *or* corporation considered as a legal body **juristische Person**

◊ **persona** *noun*
(a) thing (such as a company) which has personality **Einrichtung mit Rechtsfähigkeit**
(b) persona non grata = foreign person who is not acceptable to a government (used especially of diplomats) **Persona non grata, unerwünschte Person**

◊ **personal** *adjective*
(a) referring to one person **persönlich; personal action** = (i) legal action brought by a person himself; (ii) common law term for an action against a person arising out of a contract *or* tort; (iii) = ACTION IN PERSONAM **(i) vom Geschädigten erhobene Klage; (ii) Leistungsklage; (iii)** = ACTION IN PERSONAM; **personal allowances** = part of a person's income which is not taxed **persönlicher Steuerfreibetrag; personal assets** = moveable assets which belong to a person **bewegliches Privatvermögen; personal chattels** *or* **chattels personal** = things (furniture, clothes, cars) which belong to a person and which are not land **persönliche Habe, bewegliches Privatvermögen; personal computer** = small computer which can be used at home **Personal-Computer, PC; personal estate** *or* **personal property** = things which belong to someone (excluding land) which can be inherited by his heirs **beweglicher Nachlaß; personal income** = income received by an individual person before tax is paid **Privateinkommen; personal injury** = injury to the body suffered by the victim of an accident **Personenschaden; Körperverletzung; personal representative** = person who is the executor of a will *or* the administrator of the estate of a deceased person **Testamentsvollstrecker, Nachlaßverwalter; personal service** = act of giving legal documents to someone as part of a legal action (such as serving someone with a writ) **persönliche Zustellung**
(b) private **privat, Privat-;** *I want to see the director on a personal matter;* **personal assistant** = secretary who can take on responsibility in various ways when the boss is not there **Privatsekretär, persönlicher Assistent**

◊ **personally** *adverb* in person **persönlich, eigenhändig;** *he personally opened the envelope; she wrote to me personally*

◊ **personality** *noun* **legal personality** = legal existence *or* status of a person **Rechtspersönlichkeit; corporate personality** = legal existence of an incorporated company which can be treated as a person **juristische Körperschaft**

◊ **personalty** *noun* personal property *or* chattels (as opposed to land) **bewegliches Privatvermögen**

◊ **personam** *see* ACTION

◊ **personation** *noun* crime of fraudulently pretending to be someone else **Identitätstäuschung**

personnel *noun* staff *or* people who work in an office *or* company *or* department **Personal, Belegschaft;** *all the personnel have to sign the Official Secrets Act;* **personnel officer** = manager who deals with the staff and their conditions of employment **Personalchef**
NOTE: no plural; personnel usually takes a plural verb

persuade *verb* to talk to someone and get him to do what you want **überreden,**

dazubringen; *after ten hours of discussion, they persuaded the plaintiff to accept an out-of-court settlement; we could not persuade the French company to sign the contract*

◊ **persuasive precedent** *or* **authority** *noun* precedent which a judge is not obliged to follow but is of importance in reaching a judgment, as opposed to a binding precedent **nicht bindender Präzedenzfall**

pertain *verb* **to pertain to** = to refer to *or* to relate to **etwas betreffen, zu etwas gehören, sich beziehen auf;** *the law pertaining to public order*

perverse *adjective* strange *or* odd **pervers, widernatürlich; perverse verdict** = verdict by a jury which goes against what anyone would normally feel to be the right decision *or* which goes against the direction of the judge **auf ungewöhnlichem Rechtsverständnis basierendes Geschworenenurteil; gegen die Rechtsbelehrung des Richters verstoßendes Geschworenenurteil**

pervert *verb* to change *or* to interfere **verzerren, verdrehen; to attempt to pervert the course of justice** = to try to influence the outcome of a trial by tampering with the evidence *or* bribing the jurors, etc. **versuchen, das Recht zu beugen/Rechtsbeugung zu begehen**

COMMENT: perverting the course of justice is a notifiable offence

petition
1 *noun*
(a) written application to a court **Antrag, Klage; bankruptcy petition** = application to a court asking for an order making someone bankrupt **Konkurseröffnungsantrag; to file a petition in bankruptcy** = to apply to the court to be made bankrupt *or* to ask for someone else to be made bankrupt **einen Konkursantrag stellen, die Konkurseröffnung beantragen; divorce petition** = application to a court to end a marriage **Scheidungsklage; winding up petition** = application to a court for an order that a company be put into liquidation **Konkurseröffnungsantrag**
(b) written request accompanied by a list of signatures of people supporting it **Petition;** *they presented a petition with a million signatures to Parliament, asking for the law to be repealed*
2 *verb* to make an official request **ein Gesuch/eine Petition einreichen, beantragen;** *he petitioned the government for a special pension; the marriage had broken down and the wife petitioned for divorce*

◊ **petitioner** *noun* person who puts forward a petition **Antrag-, Gesuchsteller; Kläger/-in (in Scheidungsprozessen)**

petty *adjective* small *or* not important **unwichtig, belanglos, unbedeutend; petty cash** = small amount of money kept in an office to make small purchases **Portokasse, Kasse für kleinere Auslagen; petty crime** = small crimes which are not very serious **Vergehen; petty sessions** = magistrates' court summarisches Gericht mit zwei oder mehreren Friedensrichtern; Amtsgericht; petty theft = stealing small items *or* small amounts of money **Bagatelldiebstahl**

◊ **petty-sessional division** *noun* area of the country covered by a magistrates' court **Amtsgerichtsbezirk**

physical *adjective* referring to objects *or* to the body, as opposed to ideas **physisch, körperlich;** *the court was told of acts of physical violence committed against the police*

◊ **physically** *adverb* referring to the body *or* to the laws of nature **körperlich, physisch; physikalisch;** *the testator was physically fit, but mentally incapable of understanding the terms of the will*

pick
1 *noun* thing which is chosen **Wahl; take your pick** = choose what you want **suchen Sie sich etwas aus; the pick of the group** = the best item *or* person in the group **das/der/die Allerbeste**
2 *verb*
(a) to choose **auswählen, aussuchen;** *the government has picked a leading QC to be the new chairman of the tribunal; the board picked the finance director to succeed the retiring managing director; the Association has picked Paris for its next meeting*
(b) **to pick someone's pocket** = to steal something from someone's pocket **bei jdm Taschendiebstahl begehen; to pick a lock** = to open a lock using a piece of wire, etc. **ein Schloß mit einem Draht/Dietrich öffnen**

◊ **pickpocket** *noun* person who steals things from people's pockets **Taschendieb**

◊ **picker** *noun (slang)* one of a group of pickpockets, who actually picks the victim's pocket **(in einer Bande arbeitender) Taschendieb;** *compare* RUNNER

◊ **pick up** *verb*
(a) to get better *or* to improve **sich erholen;** *business or trade is picking up*
(b) *informal* to arrest **festnehmen, hopsnehmen;** *he was picked up by the police at the airport*

picket
1 *noun* striking worker who stands at the

gate of a factory to try to persuade other workers not to go to work **Streikposten; picket line** = line of pickets at the gate of a factory **Streikpostenkette**
2 *verb* **to picket a factory** = to put pickets at the gate of a factory to try to prevent other workers from going to work **vor einer Fabrik Streikposten aufstellen**

◊ **picketing** *noun* action of standing at the gates of a factory to prevent workers going to work **Streikpostenstehen; lawful** *or* **peaceful picketing** = picketing which is allowed by law **rechtmäßiges Aufstellen von Streikposten; mass picketing** = picketing by large numbers of pickets who try to frighten workers who want to work **massives Aufgebot an Streikposten; secondary picketing** = picketing of another factory *or* place of work, not directly connected with the strike, to prevent it supplying the striking factory *or* receiving supplies from it **Bestreikung eines nur indirekt beteiligten Betriebes**
NOTE: no plural

pilfer *verb* to steal small objects *or* small amounts of money **stehlen, klauen**

◊ **pilferage** *or* **pilfering** *noun* stealing small amounts of money *or* small items **geringfügiger Diebstahl**
NOTE: no plural

◊ **pilferer** *noun* person who steals small objects *or* small amounts of money **kleiner Dieb**

pimp *noun* man who organizes prostitutes and lives off their earnings **Zuhälter**

pinch *verb informal*
(a) to steal **klauen**
(b) to arrest **verhaften, einsperren**

pirate
1 *noun*
(a) person who attacks a ship at sea to steal cargo **Seeräuber, Pirat**
(b) person who copies a patented invention *or* a copyright work and sells it **Markenpirat, Plagiator; Hersteller von Raubdrucken;** *a pirate copy of a book;* **pirate radio station** = radio station which broadcasts without a licence from outside a country's territorial waters **Piratensender**
2 *verb* to copy a copyright work **plagiieren, Markenpiraterie betreiben; unerlaubt nachdrucken;** *a pirated book or a pirated design; the drawings for the new dress collection were pirated in the Far East*

◊ **piracy** *noun*
(a) robbery at sea, by attacking ships **Seeräuberei, Piraterie**

(b) copying of patented inventions *or* copyright works **Markenpiraterie, Plagiat; Raubdruck, unerlaubter Nachdruck;** *laws to ban book piracy*
NOTE: no plural

place
1 *noun*
(a) where something is *or* where something happens **Platz, Ort, Stelle; to take place** = to happen **stattfinden;** *the meeting will take place in our offices;* **meeting place** = room *or* area where people can meet **Treffpunkt; place of performance** = place where a contract is to be performed **Erfüllungsort, Leistungsort; place of work** = office *or* factory, etc., where people work **Arbeitsplatz; public place** = place (such as a road *or* park) where the public in general have a right to be **öffentlicher Ort**
(b) job; *he was offered a place with an insurance company; she turned down three places before accepting the one we offered* **Stelle, Stellung**
(c) position (in a text) **Stelle;** *she marked her place in the text with a red pen; I have lost my place and cannot remember where I have reached in my filing*
2 *verb* to put **legen, setzen, stellen; to place money in an account** = to deposit money **Geld auf ein Konto einzahlen; to place a block of shares** = to find a buyer for a block of shares **ein Aktienpaket plazieren; to place a contract with a company** = to decide that a certain company shall have the contract to do work **einen Auftrag an eine Firma vergeben; to place an order** = to order something **eine Bestellung aufgeben; to place something on file** = to file something **etwas abheften**
(b) **to place staff** = to find jobs for staff **Personal unterbringen/vermitteln**

◊ **placement** *noun* finding work for someone **Unterbringung**

◊ **placing** *noun* **the placing of a line of shares** = finding a buyer for a large number of shares in a new company *or* a company which is going public **die Plazierung eines Aktienpaketes**

plagiarism *noun* copying the text of a work created by someone else and passing it off as your own **Plagiat, Diebstahl geistigen Eigentums**
NOTE: no plural

◊ **plagiarize** *verb* to copy the text of a work created by someone else and pass it off as your own **plagiieren**

plainclothes *adjective* (person) who is working in ordinary clothes, not in uniform **Zivil-, in Zivil;** *a group of plainclothes police went into the house; a plainclothes detective travelled on the train*

plain cover *noun* **to send something under plain cover** = to send something in an ordinary envelope with no company name printed on it **etwas in einem neutralen Umschlag schicken**

plaint *noun* claim brought by one party (the plaintiff) against another party (the defendant) **Klage; plaint note** = note issued by a County Court at the beginning of a County Court action **Klageschrift**

◊ **plaintiff** *noun* person who starts an action against someone in the civil courts **Kläger/-in;** *compare* DEFENDANT

plan

1 *noun*
(a) organized way of doing something **Plan; contingency plan** = plan which will be put into action if something happens which is expected to happen **Krisenplan; the government's economic plans** = the government's proposals for running the country's economy **das Wirtschaftsprogramm der Regierung; a Five-Year Plan** = proposals for running a country's economy over a fiveyear period **ein Fünfjahresplan**
(b) drawing which shows how something is arranged *or* how something will be built **Plan, Entwurf; floor plan** = drawing of a floor in a building, showing where different departments are **Raumverteilungsplan; street plan** *or* **town plan** = map of a town showing streets and buildings **Stadtplan**

2 *verb* to organize carefully how something should be done **planen;** *the bank robbery was carefully planned in advance; he plans to disguise himself as a policeman ;* **to plan for an increase in bank interest charges** = to change a way of doing things because you think there will be an increase in bank interest charges **sich einstellen auf eine Erhöhung der Bankzinsen; to plan investments** = to propose how investments should be made **Investitionen planen**

◊ **planned** *adjective* **planned economy** = system where the government plans all business activity **Planwirtschaft**

◊ **planner** *noun*
(a) person who plans **Planer/-in; the government's economic planners** = people who plan the future economy of the country for the government **die Wirtschaftsplaner der Regierung; town planner** = person who supervises the design of a new town *or* the way the streets and buildings are laid out **Stadtplaner**
(b) desk planner *or* **wall planner** = book or chart which shows days *or* weeks *or* months so that the work of an office can be shown by coloured lines **Tischkalender od Wandkalender zur Arbeitsplanung**

◊ **planning** *noun*
(a) organizing how something should be done, especially how a company should be run to make increased profits **Planung; economic planning** = planning the future financial state of the country for the government **Wirtschaftsplanung**
(b) organizing how land and buildings are to be used **Erschließung; Planung; planning authority** = local body which gives permission for changes to be made to existing buildings or for new use of land **Planungsbehörde; planning department** = section of a local government office which deals with requests for planning permission **Bauordnungsamt; planning inquiry** = hearing before a government inspector relating to the decision of a local authority in planning matters **Planungsanhörung; planning permission** = official document allowing a person or company to plan new buildings on empty land *or* to alter existing buildings **Baugenehmigung; outline planning permission** = general permission to build a property on a piece of land, but not the final approval because there are no details given **vorläufige Baugenehmigung;** *to be refused planning permission; we are waiting for planning permission before we can start building; the land is to be sold with outline planning permission for four houses*

plant

1 *noun* machinery *or* goods and chattels needed for a business **Maschinenanlage, Anlage**

2 *verb* **to plant evidence** = to put items at the scene of a crime after the crime has been discovered, so that a person can be incriminated and arrested **jdm Beweismaterial unterschieben**

plc *or* **PLC** *or* **Plc** = PUBLIC LIMITED COMPANY

plea *noun* (i) in civil law, answer made by a defendant to the case presented by the plaintiff; (ii) in criminal law, statement made by a person accused in court in answer to the charge **(i) Klageerwiderung; (ii) Verteidigung; to enter a plea of not guilty** = to answer the charge by stating that you are not guilty **sich nicht schuldig bekennen; plea in mitigation** = things said in court on behalf of a guilty party to persuade the court to impose a lenient sentence **Bitte um Strafmilderung/milde Beurteilung**

◊ **plea bargaining** *noun* arrangement where the accused pleads guilty to some charges and the prosecution drop other charges *or* ask for a lighter sentence **Absprache (zwischen Anklage und**

Verteidigung) hinsichtlich der Beschränkung der Anklage auf einzelne Punkte oder hinsichtlich des Strafmaßes

plead *verb*
(a) (i) to make *or* answer an allegation in legal proceedings; (ii) to answer a charge in a criminal court **(i) vorbringen; (ii) sich verteidigen, sich zur Anklage äußern; fit** *or* **unfit to plead** = mentally capable *or* not capable of being tried **prozeßfähig; prozeßunfähig; to plead guilty** *or* **not guilty** = to say at the beginning of a trial that you did *or* did not commit the crime of which you are accused **sich schuldig bekennen; sich nicht schuldig bekennen**
(b) to speak on behalf of a client in court **plädieren**

◊ **pleading** *noun*
(a) pleadings = documents setting out the claim of the plaintiff or the defence of the defendant *or* giving the arguments which the two sides will use in proceedings **(vorbereitende) Schriftsätze, Parteiausführungen;** *the damage is itemized in the pleading; the judge found that the plaintiff's pleadings disclosed no cause of action; pleadings must be submitted to the court when the action is set down for trial*
(b) action of speaking in court on someone's behalf **Plädieren, Plädoyer**
NOTE: no plural for (b)

pleasure *see* HER MAJESTY'S PLEASURE

pledge
1 *noun*
(a) transfer of objects *or* documents to someone as security for a loan **Verpfändung**
(b) object given by someone (especially to a pawnbroker) as security for a loan **Pfand(sache); to redeem a pledge** = to pay back a loan and interest and so get back the security **ein Pfand einlösen; unredeemed pledge** = pledge which the borrower has not claimed back by paying back his loan **nicht eingelöstes Pfand**
2 *verb* **to pledge share certificates** = to deposit share certificates with the lender as security for money borrowed **Aktienzertifikate verpfänden**

◊ **pledgee** *noun* person who receives objects or documents as security for money lent **Pfandnehmer**

◊ **pledger** *noun* person who gives objects or documents as security for money borrowed **Pfandgeber, Verpfänder**

plenipotentiary *noun* official person acting on behalf of a government in international affairs **Bevollmächtigte(r), bevollmächtigter Gesandter**

plunder
1 *noun* valuable things taken when a place is attacked **Beute;** (NOTE: no plural)
2 *verb* to attack and rob (a place), taking valuable things away **rauben, plündern**

p.m. *or* **post meridiem** *Latin phrase meaning* "after 12 o'clock midday" **nachmittags;** *the train leaves at 6.50 p.m.; if you phone New York after 6 p.m. the calls are at a cheaper rate*

PM = POST MORTEM, PRIME MINISTER

PO = POST OFFICE

poaching *noun* (i) crime of killing game which belongs to another person *or* trespassing on someone's land to kill game; (ii) enticing workers to work for another company *or* enticing workers to leave one trade union and join another **(i) Wilderei, Wildern; (ii) Abwerben von Arbeitskräften; Abwerben von Gewerkschaftsmitgliedern**

point *noun* question relating to a matter **Punkt; point of fact** = question which has to be decided regarding the facts of a case **Tatfrage; in point of fact** = really *or* actually **tatsächlich; point of law** = question relating to the law as applied to a case **Rechtsfrage;** *counsel raised a point of law; the case illustrates an interesting point of legal principle;* **point of order** = question regarding the way in which a meeting is conducted **Anfrage zur Geschäftsordnung;** *he raised an interesting point of order; on a point of order, Mr Smith asked the chairman to give a ruling on whether the committee could approve its own accounts*

poison
1 *noun* substance which can kill if eaten or drunk **Gift;** *she killed the old lady by putting poison in her tea*
2 *verb* to kill someone using poison **vergiften;** *he was not shot, he was poisoned*

police
1 *noun* group of people who keep law and order in a country *or* town **Polizei;** *the police have cordoned off the town centre; the government is relying on the police to keep law and order during the elections; the bank robbers were picked up by the police at the railway station;* **military police** = soldiers who act as policemen to keep order among other soldiers **Militärpolizei; secret police** = policemen who work in secret, especially dealing with people working against the state **Geheimpolizei; police cordon** = barriers and policemen put round an area to

prevent anyone moving in or out of the area **Polizeikordon; police court =** magistrates' court; *entspricht* **Amtsgericht;** (NOTE: no plural. **Police** is usually followed by a plural verb)

2 *verb*

(a) to keep law and order in a place **polizeilich überwachen;** *the meeting was policed by plainclothes men; the council is debating the Chief Constable's policing policy*

(b) to make sure that regulations *or* guidelines are carried out **kontrollieren**

COMMENT: under English law, a policeman is primarily an ordinary citizen who has certain powers at common law and by statute The police are organized by area, each area functioning independently with its own police force. London, and the area round London, is policed by the Metropolitan Police Force under the direct supervision of the Home Secretary Outside London, each police force is answerable to a local police authority, although day-to-day control of operations is vested entirely in the Chief Constable

◊ **police authority** *noun* local committee which supervises a local police force **Polizei(behörde)**

◊ **Police Commissioner** *noun* highest rank in certain police forces **Polizeikommandeur; Metropolitan Police Commissioner =** person in charge of the Metropolitan Police in London **Chef der Londoner Polizei**

◊ **Police Complaints Board** *noun* group which investigates complaints made by members of the public against the police **Ausschuß zur Untersuchung polizeilicher Vergehen**

◊ **police constable** *noun* ordinary member of the police **Polizist/-in;** *Police Constables Smith and Jones are on patrol; Woman Police Constable MacIntosh was at the scene of the accident* NOTE: usually abbreviated to **PC** and **WPC**

◊ **police force** *noun* group of policemen organized in a certain area **Polizei(einheit);** *the members of several local police forces have collaborated in the murder hunt; the London police force is looking for more recruits; see also* DETECTIVE, METROPOLITAN

COMMENT: the ranks in a British police force are: Police Constable, Police Sergeant, Inspector, Chief Inspector, Superintendent, Chief Superintendent, Assistant Chief Constable, Deputy Chief Constable and Chief Constable

◊ **police headquarters** *noun* main offices of a police force **Polizeipräsidium**

◊ **police inspector** *noun* rank in the police force above a sergeant **Polizeikommissar**

◊ **policeman** *noun* man who is a member of the police **Polizist** NOTE: the plural is **policemen**

◊ **police officer** *noun* member of the police **Polizeibeamter, Polizist/-in**

◊ **police precinct** *noun* US section of a town with its own police station **Polizeibezirk, Polizeirevier**

◊ **police sergeant** *noun* rank in the police force above constable and below inspector **Polizeibeamter (einem Kommissar untergeordnet)**

◊ **police station** *noun* local office of a police force **Polizeirevier, Polizeiwache**

◊ **policewoman** *noun* woman member of a police force **Polizistin** NOTE: the plural is **policewomen**

◊ **policing** *noun* keeping law and order in a place, using the police force **polizeiliche Überwachung, Aufrechterhaltung von Ruhe und Ordnung; community policing =** way of policing a section of a town, where the members of the local community and the local police force act together to prevent crime and disorder, with policemen on foot patrol, rather than in patrol cars **Zusammenarbeit zwischen Bürgern und Kontaktbereichsbeamten** NOTE: no plural

policy *noun*

(a) decisions on the general way of doing something **Kurs, Politik, Linie, Taktik;** *government policy on wages or government wages policy; the government's prices policy; the country's economic policy; our policy is to submit all contracts to the legal department;* **the government made a policy statement** *or* **made a statement of policy =** the government declared in public what its plans were **die Regierung gab eine Grundsatzerklärung ab; budgetary policy =** policy of expected income and expenditure **Budgetpolitik;** *see also* PUBLIC POLICY

(b) insurance policy = document which shows the conditions of an insurance contract **Versicherungspolice; accident policy =** insurance against accidents **Unfallversicherung(spolice); comprehensive** *or* **all-risks policy =** insurance policy which covers risks of any kind, with no exclusions **Universalversicherung(spolice), Allgefahrendeckung; contingent policy =** policy which pays out only if something happens (as if the person named in the policy dies before the person due to benefit) **Eventualversicherung; Risikoversicherung; endowment policy =** policy where a sum of money is paid to the insured person on a certain date, or to his estate if he dies earlier **gemischte Lebensversicherung, Versicherung auf den Erlebens- und Todesfall; open policy =**

marine insurance policy where the value of what is insured is not stated **Police ohne Wertangabe; policy holder** = person who is insured by an insurance company **Versicherungsnehmer**

political *adjective* referring to a certain idea of how a country should be run **politisch; political crime** = crime (such as assassination) committed for a political reason **politisches Verbrechen; political fund** = part of the funds of a trade union which is allocated to subsidize a political party **Sonderfonds (einer Gewerkschaft) zur Unterstützung einer Partei; political levy** = part of the subscription of a member of a trade union which the union then pays to support a political party; *GB* **Abgaben für politische Zwecke; political party** = group of people who believe a country should be run in a certain way **politische Partei; political prisoner** = person kept in prison because he is an opponent of the political party in power **politischer Häftling**

poll
1 *noun*
(a) voting to choose something **Wahl, Abstimmung; to go to the polls** = to vote to choose a Member of Parliament *or* a local councillor **zur Wahl gehen**
(b) **opinion poll** = asking a sample group of people what they feel about something, so as to guess the opinion of the whole population **Meinungsumfrage**
(c) **deed poll** = legal agreement which refers only to one party **einseitige Erklärung; she changed her name by deed poll** = she executed a legal document to change her name **sie hat ihren Namen durch eine einseitige Rechtserklärung geändert**
2 *verb*
(a) to receive a certain number of votes in an election **(Stimmen) erhalten;** *he polled only 123 votes in the general election*
(b) **to poll a sample of the population** = to ask a sample group of people what they feel about something **eine repräsentative Bevölkerungsgruppe fragen; to poll the members of the club on an issue** = to ask the members for their opinion on an issue **die Klubmitglieder zu einem Punkt befragen**
◊ **pollster** *noun* expert in understanding what polls mean **Meinungsforscher**
◊ **poll tax** *noun* tax levied equally on each member of the population **Kopf-, Bürgersteuer**

polygamy *noun* state of having more than one wife **Polygamie**
NOTE: no plural
◊ **polygamous** *adjective* referring to polygamy **polygam; a polygamous society** = a

society where men are allowed to be married to more than one wife at the same time **eine polygame Gesellschaft**

popular *adjective* liked by many people **beliebt, populär;** *this is our most popular model; the South Coast is the most popular area for holidays;* **popular prices** = prices which are low and therefore liked **erschwingliche Preise; popular vote** = vote of the people **national abgegebene Stimmen; the president is elected by popular vote** = the president is elected by a majority of all the voters in the country (as opposed to being elected by parliament) **der Präsident wird von der Wählerschaft gewählt**

pornography *noun* obscene publications *or* films **Pornographie**
NOTE: no plural

porridge *noun (slang)* imprisonment **Knast; to do porridge** = to serve a term of imprisonment **Strafzeit verbüßen**

portfolio *noun*
(a) all the shares owned by someone **Aktienportefeuille;** *his portfolio contains shares in the major oil companies*
(b) office of a minister in the government **Ressort, Geschäftsbereich; Minister without Portfolio** = minister who does not have responsibility for any particular department **Minister ohne Geschäftsbereich**

portion *noun* money *or* property given to a young person to provide money for him *or* her as income **Ausstattung eines Kindes mit Vermögen**

position *noun*
(a) situation *or* state of affairs **Lage, Situation; bargaining position** = statement of position by one group during negotiations **Verhandlungsposition; to cover a position** = to have enough money to pay for a forward purchase **eine Position abdecken**
(b) job *or* paid work in a company **Stellung, Stelle, Position;** *to apply for a position as manager; we have several positions vacant; all the vacant positions have been filled; she retired from her position in the accounts department;* **position of trust** = job where the employee is trusted with money *or* confidential documents, etc. **Vertrauensstellung**

positive *adjective* meaning "yes" **bejahend, positiv, zustimmend;** *the board gave a positive reply;* **the breath test was positive** = the breath test showed that he had too much alcohol in his blood **der Alkoholtest fiel**

positiv aus; positive vetting = discovery after examination that a person working with classified information may not be reliable **Feststellung, daß jd, der mit Geheiminformationen zu tun hat, trotz vorheriger Überprüfung möglicherweise nicht vertrauenswürdig ist**

possess verb to own or to be in occupation of or to be in control of **besitzen;** the company possesses property in the centre of the town; he lost all he possessed when his company was put into liquidation

◊ **possession** noun
(a) control over property **Eigentum, Besitz, Sachherrschaft;** actual possession = occupying and controlling land and buildings **unmittelbarer Besitz; chose in possession** = physical thing which can be owned **bewegliche Sache; possession in law** = ownership of land or buildings without actually occupying them **rechtlicher/mittelbarer Besitz; adverse possession** = occupation of property (such as by a squatter) contrary to the rights of the real owner **Besetzung; vacant possession** = being able to occupy a property immediately after buying it because it is empty **sofort beziehbar;** the property is to be sold with vacant possession
(b) physically holding something (which does not necessarily belong to you) **Innehabung, Besitz; the documents are in his possession** = he is holding the documents **die Unterlagen befinden sich in seinem Besitz; how did it come into his possession or how did he get possession of it?** = how did he acquire it? **wie ist es in seinen Besitz gelangt?; possession of drugs** = offence of having drugs **Besitz von Rauschgift**
(c) possessions = property or things owned **Besitz(tümer), Habe;** they lost all their possessions in the fire
NOTE: no plural for (a) and (b)

◊ **possessive action** noun action to regain possession of land or buildings **Besitzklage**

◊ **possessory** adjective referring to possession of property **Besitz-, besitzrechtlich, possessorisch; possessory title** = title to land acquired by occupying it continuously, usually for twelve years **Besitztitel**

post
1 noun
(a) system of sending letters and parcels from one place to another **Post;** to send an invoice by post; he put the letter in the post; the cheque was lost in the post; **to send a reply by return of post** = to reply to a letter immediately **postwendend antworten; letter post** or **parcel post** = service for sending letters or parcels **Briefpost; Paketpost; post room** = room in an office where the post is sorted and sent to each department or collected from each department for sending **Poststelle**
(b) letters sent or received **Post;** has the post arrived yet? my secretary opens the post as soon as it arrives; the receipt was in this morning's post; the letter did not arrive by first post this morning
(c) job or paid work in a firm or company **Stelle, Stellung, Posten;** to apply for a post as legal executive; we have three posts vacant; all our posts have been filled; we advertised three posts in "The Times"
2 verb
(a) to send something by post **(ab)schicken, mit der Post schicken;** to post a letter or to post a parcel
(b) to post an entry = to transfer an entry to an account **einen Posten buchen**
(c) to post up a notice = to put a notice on a wall or on a noticeboard **einen Anschlag machen; to post an increase** = to let people know that an increase has taken place **eine Erhöhung bekanntgeben**

post- prefix later **nach-, Nach-, post-, Post-**

postage noun payment for sending a letter or parcel by post **Porto, Postgebühren**

postal adjective referring to the post **Post-; postal packet** = small parcel sent by post **Postpaket; postal service** = (i) sending letters by post; (ii) service of legal documents by post **(i) Postdienst, Postverkehr; (ii) Postzustellung**

post code noun letters and numbers used to indicate a town or street in an address on an envelope **Postleitzahl**
NOTE: US English is **zip code**

postdate verb to put a later date on a document **vordatieren;** he sent us a postdated cheque; his cheque was postdated to June

poste restante noun counter where letters addressed to someone at a post office can be collected **Schalter für postlagernde Sendungen;** send any messages to "Poste Restante, Athens"

posteriori see A POSTERIORI

post free adverb without having to pay any postage **portofrei;** the leaflet is obtainable post free from the Law Society

posthumous adjective (child) born after the death of its father **nachgeboren, postum**

post mortem *noun* examination of the body of a dead person to see how he died **Obduktion;** *the post mortem was carried out or was conducted by the police pathologist*

post obit bond *noun* agreement where a borrower will repay a loan when he receives money as a legacy from someone **nach Erhalt einer Erbschaft fälliger Schuldschein**

post office *noun*
(a) (i) building where the postal services are based; (ii) shop where you can buy stamps, send parcels, etc. **(i) Post(amt); (ii);** *GB* **Zweigstelle der Post; sub-post office** = small post office, usually part of a general store **Zweigstelle der Post**
(b) the Post Office = national organization which deals with sending letters and parcels; *entspricht* **Deutsche Bundespost;** *Post Office officials or officials of the Post Office;* **Post Office box number** = reference number given for delivering mail to a post office, so as not to give the actual address of the person who will receive it **Postfach**

postpone *verb* to arrange for something to take place later than planned **auf-, verschieben, vertagen;** *he postponed the meeting until tomorrow; they asked if they could postpone payment until the cash situation was better*

◊ **postponement** *noun* arranging for something to take place later than planned **Aufschub, Vertagung;** *I had to change my appointments because of the postponement of the board meeting*

post scriptum *see* P.S.

power *noun*
(a) strength *or* ability *or* capacity **Macht, Stärke, Kraft, Vermögen, Fähigkeit; bargaining power** = strength of one person or group when discussing prices *or* wages *or* contracts **Verhandlungsstärke; borrowing power** = amount of money which a company can borrow **Kreditfähigkeit; earning power** = amount of money someone should be able to earn **Verdienstmöglichkeit**
(b) authority *or* legal right **Vollmacht, Ermächtigung, Befugnis;** *the powers of a local authority in relation to children in care; the powers and duties conferred on the tribunal by the statutory code; the president was granted wide powers under the constitution;* **executive power** = right to act as director *or* to put decisions into action **Entscheidungsgewalt, Exekutive, ausübende Gewalt; power of attorney** = official power which gives someone the right to act on someone's behalf in legal matters

Handlungsvollmacht; the full power of the law = the full force of the law when applied **die volle Gesetzeskraft;** *we will apply the full power of the law to regain possession of our property*

p.p. *verb* **to p.p. a receipt** *or* **a letter** = to sign a receipt *or* a letter on behalf of someone **eine Quittung od einen Brief i.V. von jemandem unterschreiben;** *the secretary p.p.'d the letter while the manager was at lunch; see also* PER PROCURATIONEM

PR = PROPORTIONAL REPRESENTATION, PUBLIC RELATIONS

practice *noun*
(a) way of doing things **Gewohnheit, Gepflogenheit, Verfahrensweise;** *his practice was to arrive at work at 7.30 and start counting the cash;* **business practices** *or* **industrial practices** *or* **trade practices** = ways of managing or working in business, industry or trade **Geschäftspraktiken, Geschäftsgepflogenheiten; Industriepraktiken; Handelspraktiken; restrictive practices** = ways of working which exclude free competition in relation to the supply of goods or labour in order to maintain prices or wages **wettbewerbsbeschränkende Geschäftspraktiken; sharp practice** = way of doing business which is not honest, but is not illegal **unsauberes/unlauteres Geschäftsgebaren; code of practice** = rules drawn up by an association which the members must follow when doing business **Richtlinien; practice direction** = notes made by judges as to how certain procedures *or* formalities should be carried out **(allgemeine) Verfahrensanweisungen**
(b) in practice = when actually done **in der Praxis;** *the scheme for dealing with young offenders seems very interesting, but what will it cost in practice?*
(c) office and clients (of a professional person) **Praxis;** *he has set up in practice as a solicitor or a patent agent; he is a partner in a country solicitor's practice*
(d) carrying on of a profession **Berufsausübung, Berufspraxis;** *he has been in practice for twenty years*

◊ **Practice Master** *noun* Master on duty in the High Court, who will hear solicitors without appointment and give directions in relation to the general conduct of proceedings **Rechtspfleger im High Court**

practise *verb* to work (in a profession) **praktizieren, ausüben;** *he is a practising solicitor;* **practising certificate** = certificate from the Law Society allowing someone to work as a solicitor **Bestallungsurkunde**

praecipe *noun* written request addressed to a court, asking that court to prepare and issue a document (such as a writ of execution *or* a subpoena) **schriftlicher Antrag an das Gericht, eine Urkunde auszustellen**

pray *verb* to ask **ersuchen, bitten; to pray in aid** = to rely on something in pleading a case **sich berufen auf;** *I pray in aid the Statute of Frauds*

◊ **prayer** *noun* words at the end of a petition *or* pleading, which summarize what the litigant is asking the court to do **Klageantrag**

pre- *prefix* before **Vor-, vor-, Prä-, prä-;** *pre-contract discussion; a pre-stocktaking sale; there will be a pre-AGM board meeting*

preamble *noun* first words in an official document (such as a Bill before Parliament *or* contract) introducing the document and setting out the main points in it **Präambel, Einleitung**

precatory *adjective* which requests **bittend, ersuchend; precatory words** = words (such as in a will) which ask for something to be done **einen Wunsch ausdrückende Worte**

precautionary *adjective* **as a precautionary measure** = in case something takes place **als Vorsichtsmaßnahme**

◊ **precautions** *plural noun* care taken to avoid something unpleasant **Vorkehrungen, Vorsichtsmaßnahmen;** *to take precautions to prevent thefts in the office; the company did not take proper fire precautions;* **safety precautions** = actions to try to make sure that something is safe **Sicherheitsvorkehrungen**

precede *verb* to go before *or* to come earlier **vorangehen;** *see the preceding paragraph of my letter; the preceding clause gives details of the agency arrangements*

precedent
1 *noun* something (such as a judgment) which has happened earlier than the present, and which can be a guide as to what should be done in the present case **Präzedenzfall; to set a precedent** = to make a decision in court which will show other courts how to act in future **einen Präzedenzfall schaffen; to follow a precedent** = to decide in the same way as an earlier decision in the same type of case **einem Präzedenzfall folgen;** *the judge's decision sets a precedent for future cases of contempt of court; the tribunal's ruling has established a*

precedent; *the court followed the precedent set in 1926;* **binding precedent** = decision of a higher court which has to be followed by a judge in a lower court **bindender Präzedenzfall; judicial precedent** = precedent set by a court decision which can be reversed only by a higher court **Präzedenzfall; persuasive precedent** = precedent which a judge does not have to follow but which is of importance in reaching a decision **nicht bindender Präzedenzfall**
2 *adjective* **condition precedent** = condition which says that a right will not be granted until something is done **aufschiebende Bedingung; Vorbedingung**

COMMENT: although English law is increasingly governed by statute, the doctrine of precedent still plays a major role. The decisions of higher courts bind lower courts, except in the case of the Court of Appeal, where the court has power to change a previous decision reached per incuriam. Cases can be distinguished by the courts where the facts seem to be sufficiently different

precept *noun* order asking for rates to be paid **Zahlungsbefehl für Kommunalsteuern**

precinct *noun*
(a) pedestrian precinct *or* shopping precinct = part of a town which is closed to traffic so that people can walk about and shop **Fußgängerzone**
(b) *US* administrative district in a town **(Verwaltungs)bezirk;** *police precinct*

precise *adjective* clear and with correct details **genau, präzis;** *the will gives precise instructions about the settlement of the estate; the pathologist was unable to give a precise time for the murder*

preclude *verb* to forbid *or* to prevent **ausschließen;** *the High Court is precluded by statute from reviewing such a decision; this agreement does not preclude a further agreement between the parties in the future*

predecease *verb* to die before someone **sterben vor, früher sterben als;** *he predeceased his father; his estate is left to his daughter, but should she predecease him, it will be held in trust for her children*

◊ **predecessor** *noun* person who had a job *or* position before someone else **Vorgänger/-in;** *he took over from his predecessor last May; she acquired her predecessor's list of clients*

pre-empt *verb* to act before someone else can act **zuvorkommen**

◊ **pre-emption** *noun* right of first refusal to purchase something before it is sold to someone else **Vorkaufsrecht; pre-emption clause** = clause in a private company's articles of association which requires any shares offered for sale to be offered first to existing shareholders **Bezugsrechtsklausel**

prefer *verb*
(a) to like something better than another thing **vorziehen, bevorzugen**; *he prefers to deal directly with his clients himself; most people prefer to avoid taking their neighbours to court*
(b) to pay one creditor before any others **bevorzugt befriedigen**
(c) to bring something before a court **einreichen, erheben, vorbringen; to prefer charges** = to charge someone with an offence **anklagen, Anklage erheben**
NOTE: **preferring - preferred**

◊ **preference** *noun* (i) thing which is preferred; (ii) the payment of one creditor before other creditors **(i) Wahl, Vorzug; (ii) Gläubigerbegünstigung; fraudulent preference** = payment made by an insolvent company to a particular creditor before other creditors **Gläubigerbegünstigung; preference shares** = shares (often with no voting rights) which receive their dividend before all other shares and which are repaid first (at face value) if the company is liquidated **Vorzugsaktien; preference shareholders** = owners of preference shares **Vorzugsaktienbesitzer; cumulative preference shares** = preference shares where the dividend will be paid at a later date even if the company cannot pay a dividend in the current year **nachzugsberechtigte/kumulative Vorzugsaktien**

◊ **preferential** *adjective* showing that something is preferred more than another **bevorzugt, Vorzugs-; preferential creditor** = creditor who must be paid first if a company is in liquidation **bevorrechtigter Gläubiger; preferential debt** = debt which is paid before all others **bevorrechtigte Forderung; preferential duty** *or* **preferential tariff** = special low rate of tax **Vorzugszoll, Vorzugstarif; preferential payment** = payment made to one creditor before others **bevorrechtigte Zahlung, bevorzugte Befriedigung; preferential terms** *or* **preferential treatment** = terms or way of dealing which is better than usual **Vorzugskonditionen; bevorzugte Behandlung**

◊ **preferment** *noun* **preferment of charges** = act of charging someone with a criminal offence **Anklageerhebung**

◊ **preferred** *adjective* **preferred creditor** = creditor who must be paid first if a company is in liquidation **bevorrechtigter Gläubiger; preferred shares** *or* *US* **preferred stock** = shares which receive their dividend before all other shares, and which are repaid first (at face value) if the company is in liquidation **Vorzugsaktien;** *US* **cumulative preferred stock** = preference shares where the dividend will be paid at a later date even if the company cannot pay a dividend in the current year **kumulative Vorzugsaktie**

pregnancy *noun* period when a woman is expecting a baby **Schwangerschaft; to terminate a pregnancy** = to give a woman an abortion **eine Schwangerschaft abbrechen**

◊ **pregnant** *adjective* (woman) with an unborn child in her body **schwanger**

prejudge *verb* to judge an issue before having heard the evidence **im voraus/vorschnell urteilen**; *do not prejudge the issue - hear what defence counsel has to say*

prejudice
1 *noun*
(a) bias *or* unjust feelings against someone **Vorurteil; racial prejudice** = feelings against someone because of his race **Rassenvorurteil**
(b) harm done to someone **Schaden;** *forgery is the copying of a real document, so that it is accepted as genuine to someone's prejudice;* **without prejudice** = phrase spoken *or* written in letters when attempting to negotiate a settlement, meaning that the negotiations cannot be referred to in court *or* relied upon by the other party if the discussions fail **ohne Verbindlichkeit/Anerkennung einer Rechtspflicht; to act to the prejudice of a claim** = to do something which may harm a claim **zum Nachteil/Schaden einer Forderung handeln**
2 *verb* to harm **beeinträchtigen, schädigen;** *to prejudice someone's claim*

◊ **prejudiced** *adjective* biased *or* with unjust feelings against someone **voreingenommen, befangen;** *the judge seemed to be prejudiced against foreigners*

preliminary *adjective* early *or* happening before anything else **vorbereitend, vorausgehend, Vor-; preliminary discussion** *or* **a preliminary meeting** = discussion or meeting which takes place before the main discussion or meeting starts **Vorbesprechung; preliminary hearing** = court proceedings where the witnesses and the defendant are examined to see if there are sufficient grounds for the case to proceed *or* court proceedings to try a specific issue rather than the whole case

Voruntersuchung; **preliminary inquiries** = investigation by the solicitor for the purchaser addressed to the vendor's solicitor concerning the vendor's title to the property for which the purchaser has made an offer **Voranfragen; preliminary investigation** = first examination of the details of a case by a magistrate who then has to decide if the case should be committed to a higher court for trial **Voruntersuchung; preliminary ruling** = provisional decision of the European Court **Vorabentscheidung**

premeditated *adjective* which has been thought about carefully *or* which has been planned **mit Vorbedacht, vorsätzlich;** *the crime was premeditated; a premeditated murder*

◊ **premeditation** *noun* thinking about and planning a crime (such as murder) **Vorbedacht, Überlegung**
NOTE: no plural

premises *plural noun*
(a) building and the land it stands on **bebautes Gelände, Besitz, Haus mit Grund; business premises** *or* **commercial premises** = building used for commercial use **Geschäftsräume; office premises** *or* **shop premises** = building which houses an office or shop **Bürogebäude; Ladenräume; lock-up premises** = shop which is locked up at night when the owner goes home **Laden mit offener Front, der durch Rolläden verschlossen wird; Geschäft/Laden** (*ohne Nebenräume*); **licensed premises** = shop *or* restaurant *or* public house which is licensed to sell alcohol **Laden od Gaststätte mit Schankkonzession; on the premises** = in the building **im Gebäude, an Ort und Stelle;** *there is a doctor on the premises at all times*
(b) things that have been referred to previously **Vorstehendes, Vorangehendes, Obenerwähntes**
NOTE: used at the end of a pleading: **in the premises the defendant denies that he is indebted to the plaintiff as alleged or at all**

premium *noun*
(a) sum of money paid by one person to another, especially one paid regularly **Beitrag, Prämie; insurance premium** = annual payment made by the insured person or a company to an insurance company **Versicherungsprämie; additional premium** = extra payment made to cover extra items in an existing insurance **Prämienzuschlag;** *the annual premium is £150; you pay either an annual premium of £360 or twelve monthly premiums of £32*
(b) amount to be paid to a landlord or a tenant for the right to take over a lease

Abstandssumme; *flat to let with a premium of £10,000; annual rent: £8,500 - premium: £25,000*
(c) extra charge **Zuschlag, Aufgeld; exchange premium** = extra cost above the normal rate for buying foreign currency **Agio, Aufgeld;** *the dollar is at a premium;* **shares sold at a premium** = shares whose price is higher than their face value; new shares whose market price is higher than their issue price **mit Aufgeld verkaufte Aktien**
(d) premium bonds = government bonds, part of the national savings scheme, which pay no interest, but give the owner the chance to win a weekly or monthly prize and which can be redeemed at face value **Sparprämienanleihe**

prerogative *noun* special right which someone has **Vorrecht, Vorrang, Prärogative; royal prerogative** = right of the king *or* queen to do something **Königliches Hoheitsrecht; prerogative order** *or* **writ** = writ which requests a body to do its duty *or* not to do some act *or* to conduct an inquiry into its own actions **außerordentliches Rechtsmittel**

prescribe *verb* to claim rights which have been enjoyed for a long time **Gewohnheitsrechte geltend machen; Rechte auf Grund von Ersitzung geltend machen**
◊ **prescription** *noun* acquiring a right *or* exercising a right over a period of time **Erwerb durch ständigen Genuß; Ersitzung**

presence *noun* being present *or* being at a place when something happens **Anwesenheit, Gegenwart, Präsenz;** *the will was signed in the presence of two witnesses*

present
1 *noun*
(a) thing which is given **Geschenk;** *these calculators make good presents; the office gave her a present when she got married*
(b) these presents = this document itself **vorliegende Urkunde; know all men by these presents** = be informed by this document **hiermit wird kundgetan**
2 *adjective*
(a) happening now **gegenwärtig, augenblicklich, derzeitig, jetzig;** *the shares are too expensive at their present price; what is the present address of the company?*
(b) being there when something happens **anwesend;** *two police officers were present when the bailiffs seized the property; only six directors were present at the board meeting*
3 *verb*
(a) to give someone something **überreichen, übergeben; schenken;** *he was presented with*

*a watch on completing twenty-five years'
service with the company*
(b) to bring *or* send and show a document
vorlegen; to present a bill for acceptance = to
send a bill for payment by the person who
has accepted it **einen Wechsel zur Annahme
vorlegen; to present a bill for payment** =
send a bill to be paid **eine Rechnung zur
Zahlung vorlegen**

◊ **presentation** *noun*
(a) showing a document **Vorlage;**
presentation of a bill of exchange; **cheque
payable on presentation** = cheque which
will be paid when it is presented **Scheck bei
Vorlage zahlbar; free admission on
presentation of this card** = you do not pay to
go in if you show this card **Eintritt kostenlos
bei Vorlage dieser Karte**
(b) demonstration *or* exhibition of a
proposed plan **Präsentation, Vorführung;** *the
marketing company made a presentation of
the services they could offer; we have asked
two PR firms to make presentations of
proposed advertising campaigns*

◊ **presentment** *noun* showing a document
Vorlage, Vorlegung, Präsentation;
presentment of a bill of exchange

◊ **present value** *noun* the value something
has now **gegenwärtiger Wert;** *in 1974 the
pound was worth five times its present value*

preservation order *noun* court order
which prevents a building from being
knocked down *or* a tree from being cut
down **Verfügung, die etwas unter
Denkmalschutz oder unter Naturschutz stellt**

preside *verb* to be chairman **den Vorsitz
führen/haben;** *to preside over a meeting; the
meeting was held in the committee room,
Mr Smith presiding*

◊ **president** *noun*
(a) head of a company *or* a club *or* a court
Generaldirektor, Vorsitzender, Präsident/-in; *he
was elected president of the sports club;
A.B.Smith has been appointed president of
the company;* **President of the Family
Division** = judge who is responsible for the
work of the Family Division of the High
Court **Präsident der Familiengerichtsabteilung**

COMMENT: in Britain "president" is a title
sometimes given to a non-executive former
chairman of a company; in the USA, the
president is the main executive director of
a company

(b) head of a republic **Präsident/-in;** *the
President of the United States*
NOTE: as a title of a head of state, President can be
used with a surname: **President Ford, President
Wilson**

COMMENT: the President of the United
States is both head of state and head of
government. He is elected by an electoral
college, and holds the executive power
under the United States constitution. The
legislative power lies with Congress, and
the President cannot force Congress to
enact legislation, although he can veto
legislation which has been passed by
Congress

press
1 *noun* newspapers and magazines **Presse;
the local press** = newspapers which are sold
in a small area of the country **Lokalblätter;
the national press** = newspapers which sell
in all parts of the country **die überregionale
Presse; press conference** = meeting where
reporters from newspapers are invited to
hear news of a new product *or* of a court
case *or* of a takeover bid, etc.
Pressekonferenz; Press Council = body
concerned with regulation of the press
Presserat; press coverage = reports about
something in the press **Berichterstattung
durch die Presse; press release** = sheet giving
news about something which is sent to
newspapers and TV and radio stations so
that they can use the information
Pressemitteilung; freedom of the press =
being able to write and publish in a
newspaper what you wish without being
afraid of prosecution, provided that you do
not break the law **Pressefreiheit**
2 *verb* **to press charges against someone** = to
say formally that someone has committed a
crime **Beschuldigungen gegen jdn erheben;** *he
was very angry when his neighbour's son set
fire to his car, but decided not to press
charges*

◊ **pressing** *adjective* urgent **dringend;
pressing engagements** = meetings which
have to be attended **dringende Termine;
pressing bills** = bills which have to be paid
dringende Rechnungen

presume *verb* to suppose something is
correct **annehmen, vermuten;** *the court
presumes the maintenance payments are
being paid on time; the company is
presumed to be still solvent; we presume the
shipment has been stolen; two sailors are
missing, presumed drowned*

COMMENT: in English law, the accused is
presumed to be innocent until he is proved
to be guilty, and presumed to be sane until
he is proved to be insane

◊ **presumption** *noun* thing which is
assumed to be correct, because it is
assumed from other facts **Annahme,
Vermutung; presumption of death** = situation
where a person has not been seen for seven

years, and is legally presumed to be dead **Todesvermutung; presumption of innocence** = assuming that someone is innocent, until he has been proved guilty **Nichtschuld-/Unschuldvermutung**

◊ **presumptive** *adjective* **presumptive evidence** = circumstantial evidence **Indizienbeweis; heir presumptive** = heir who will inherit if someone dies at this moment, but whose inheritance may be altered in the future **mutmaßlicher Erbe**

pretence *noun* **false pretences** = doing *or* saying something to cheat someone **Vorspiegelung falscher Tatsachen;** *he was sent to prison for obtaining money by false pretences*

pretend *verb* to act like someone else in order to trick *or* to act as if something is true when it really is not **vorgeben, vortäuschen;** *he got in by pretending to be a telephone engineer; she pretended she had 'flu and asked to have the day off*

pretrial review *noun* meeting of the parties before a civil action, to examine what is likely to arise during the action, so that ways can be found of making it shorter and so reduce costs **Vorverfahren**

prevail *verb* **to prevail upon someone to do something** = to persuade someone to do something **jdn veranlassen/bewegen, etwas zu tun;** *counsel prevailed upon the judge to grant an adjournment*

prevaricate *verb* to be evasive *or* not to give a straight answer to a question **Ausflüchte machen**

prevent *verb* to stop something happening **verhindern, verhüten, hindern;** *we must try to prevent the takeover bid; the police prevented anyone from leaving the building; we have changed the locks on the doors to prevent the former managing director from getting into the building*

◊ **prevention** *noun* stopping something taking place **Verhinderung, Verhütung; prevention of corruption** = stopping corruption taking place **Verhütung von Bestechung; the prevention of terrorism** = stopping terrorist acts taking place **Bekämpfung des Terrorismus**

◊ **preventive** *adjective* which tries to stop something happening **vorbeugend, verhütend, präventiv; to take preventive measures against theft** = to try to stop things from being stolen **vorbeugende Maßnahmen gegen Diebstahl ergreifen; preventive detention** = formerly,

imprisonment of someone who frequently committed a certain type of crime, so as to prevent him from doing it again **Sicherheitsverwahrung, Präventivhaft**

COMMENT: now replaced by extended sentence

previous *adjective* which has happened earlier **vorig, vorhergehend, Vor-; he could not accept the invitation because he had a previous engagement** = because he had earlier accepted another invitation to go somewhere **er konnte die Einladung nicht annehmen, weil er anderweitig verabredet war; to ask for six previous convictions to be taken into consideration** = to ask the court to note that the accused has been convicted earlier of similar crimes **die Beachtung von sechs Vorstrafen beantragen; a person of previous good character** = person with no criminal record **eine Person mit gutem Leumund/ohne Vorstrafe**

◊ **previously** *adverb* happening earlier **vorher**

price
1 *noun*
(a) money which has to be paid to buy something **Preis; agreed price** = price which has been accepted by both the buyer and seller **vereinbarter Preis; all-in price** = price which covers all items in a purchase (goods, insurance, delivery, etc.) **Pauschalpreis, Gesamtpreis; asking price** = price which the seller is hoping to be paid for the item when it is sold **geforderter Preis; Verhandlungsbasis; fair price** = good price for both buyer and seller **fairer/angemessener Preis; firm price** = price which will not change **Festpreis; net price** = price which cannot be reduced by a discount **Nettopreis; retail price** = price at which the retailer sells to the final customer **Einzelhandelspreis; spot price** = price for immediate delivery of a commodity **Lokopreis; price controls** = legal measures to stop prices rising too fast **Preiskontrollen; price fixing** = illegal agreement between companies to charge the same price for competing products **Preisabsprache**
(b) *(on the Stock Exchange)* **asking price** = price which sellers are asking for shares **Briefkurs; closing price** = price at the end of a day's trading **Schlußkurs; opening price** = price at the start of a day's trading **Eröffnungskurs; price/earnings ratio** = ratio between the market price of a share and the current earnings it produces **Kurs-Gewinn-Verhältnis**
2 *verb* to give a price to a product **einen Preis festsetzen;** *car priced at £5,000*

◊ **pricing** *noun* giving a price to a product **Preisfestsetzung, Preiskalkulation; pricing policy** = a company's policy in setting prices for its products **Preispolitik; common pricing** = illegal fixing of prices by several businesses so that they all charge the same price **Preisabsprache**

prima facie *Latin phrase meaning* "on the face of it *or* as things seem at first" **beim ersten Anschein; there is a prima facie case to answer** = one side in a case has shown that there is a case to answer, and so the action should be proceeded with **ein Fall mit glaubhaft gemachtem Sachverhalt ist zu entscheiden**

primary *adjective* in the first place **primär, Primär-, hauptsächlich, Haupt-; primary evidence** = best evidence (such as original documents, evidence from eye witnesses) **Beweismittel erster Ordnung**

◊ **primarily** *adverb* in the first place **in erster Linie, hauptsächlich;** *he is primarily liable for his debts; see also* SECONDARY, SECONDARILY

prime *adjective*
(a) most important **Haupt-, wesentlich; prime time** = most expensive advertising time for TV advertisements **Hauptsendezeit**
(b) basic **ursprünglich; prime bills** = bills of exchange which do not involve any risk **erstklassige Wechsel; prime cost** = cost involved in producing a product, excluding overheads **Gestehungs-, Herstellungskosten; prime rate** = best rate of interest at which a bank lends to its customers **Prime Rate, Leitzins (für erste Adressen)**

◊ **Prime Minister** *noun* head of a government **Premierminister, Ministerpräsident;** *the Australian Prime Minister or the Prime Minister of Australia*

> COMMENT: the British Prime Minister is not the head of state, but the head of government. The Prime Minister is usually the leader of the party which has the majority of the seats in the House of Commons, and forms a cabinet of executive ministers who are either MPs or members of the House of Lords

primogeniture *noun* former rule that the oldest son inherits all his father's estate **Primogenitur, Erstgeburt(srecht)**
NOTE: no plural

principal
1 *noun*
(a) person who is responsible for something (especially person who is in charge of a

company *or* person who commits a crime) **Leiter, Chef, Vorgesetzter; Anführer, Haupttäter**
(b) person *or* company which is represented by an agent **Auftraggeber/-in;** *the agent has come to London to see his principals*
(c) money invested *or* borrowed on which interest is paid **Kapital(summe), Hauptsumme; Darlehensbetrag;** *to repay principal and interest*
2 *adjective* most important **Haupt-, wichtigster;** *the principal shareholders asked for a meeting; the country's principal products are paper and wood; compare* PRINCIPLE

principle *noun* basic point *or* general rule **Prinzip; in principle** = in agreement with a general rule **prinzipiell, im Prinzip; agreement in principle** = agreement with the basic conditions of a proposal **grundsätzliche Übereinstimmung; it is against his principles** = it goes against what he believes to be the correct way to act **das ist gegen seine Prinzipien;** *compare* PRINCIPAL

printout *noun* printed copy of information produced by a computer **Ausdruck**

prior *adjective* earlier **früher, vorausgehend; prior agreement** = agreement which was reached earlier **frühere Vereinbarung; prior charge** = charge which ranks before others **vorrangige Belastung; without prior knowledge** = without knowing before **ohne es zuvor zu wissen**

◊ **priori** *see* A PRIORI

◊ **priority** *noun* right to be first (such as the right to be paid first before other creditors) **Vorrang, Priorität; to have priority** = to have the right to be first **Vorrang haben; to have priority over** *or* **to take priority over something** = to be more important than something **vor etwas Vorrang haben, vorgehen;** *debenture holders have priority over ordinary shareholders;* **to give something top priority** = to make something the most important item **etwas vorrangig behandeln;** *the government has given the maintenance of law and order top priority*

prison *noun*
(a) safe building where criminals can be kept locked up after they have been convicted *or* while they await trial **Gefängnis;** *the government has ordered the construction of six new prisons; the prison was built 150 years ago;* **prison officer** *or* **prison governor** = member of staff *or* person in charge of a prison **Gefängnisaufseher, Strafvollzugsbeamter; Gefängnisdirektor; open prison** = prison with minimum security

where category "D" prisoners can be kept **offene Strafvollzugsanstalt; top security prison** = prison with very strict security where category "A" prisoners are kept **mit besonderen Sicherungsvorkehrungen versehenes Gefängnis**
(b) place where prisoners are kept as a punishment **Strafvollzugsanstalt, Gefängnis;** *he was sent to prison for six years; they have spent the last six months in prison; he escaped from prison by climbing over the wall*
NOTE: no plural for (b), which is also usually written without the article: **in prison; out of prison; sent to prison**

◊ **prisoner** *noun* person who is in prison **Häftling, Gefangener; prisoner of war** = member of the armed forces captured and put in prison by the enemy **Kriegsgefangener; prisoner at the bar** = the accused person in the dock *or* being tried in court **Häftling auf der Anklagebank**

◊ **prison visitor** *see* VISITOR

privacy *noun* private life **Privatleben, Privat-, Intimsphäre; invasion of privacy** = action (such as being followed by newspaper reporters) which prevents someone from living a normal private life **Einbruch in die Privatsphäre**
NOTE: no plural

private *adjective*
(a) belonging to a single person, not a company or the state **privat, Privat-; letter marked "private and confidential"** = letter which must not be opened by anyone other than the person to whom it is addressed **ein Brief mit der Aufschrift "streng vertraulich"; Private Bill** = Bill relating to a particular person *or* corporation *or* institution **Gesetzesvorlage für ein Einzelfallgesetz;** *see below* PRIVATE MEMBER'S BILL; **private business** = business dealing with the members of a group *or* matters which cannot be discussed in public **Privatbetrieb, Privatangelegenheit;** *the committee held a special meeting to discuss some private business;* **private client** *or* **private customer** = client dealt with by a professional man *or* by a salesman as a person, not as a company **Privatkunde; private effects** = goods which belong to someone and are used by him **persönliche Habe/Gebrauchsgegenstände;** **private detective** *or* *(informal)* **private eye** = person who for a fee will try to solve mysteries *or* to find missing persons *or* to keep watch on someone **Privatdetektiv; private law** = law as it refers to individuals **Zivil-, Privatrecht; Private Member's Bill** = Bill which is drafted and proposed in the House of Commons by an ordinary Member of

Parliament, not by a government minister on behalf of the government **Gesetzesvorlage eines Abgeordneten; private nuisance** = act which can harm a particular person or his rights **(Besitz)störung einer Einzelperson; private property** = property which belongs to a private person, not to the public **Privatbesitz; Privatgrundstück; private prosecution** = prosecution for a criminal act, brought by an ordinary member of the public and not by the police **Privatklage**
(b) in private = away from other people **unter vier Augen;** *he asked to see the managing director in private*
(c) private limited company = company with a small number of shareholders whose shares are not traded on the Stock Exchange; *entspricht* **Gesellschaft mit beschränkter Haftung; private enterprise** = economic system where businesses are owned by private shareholders, not by the state **freie Marktwirtschaft; private sector** = all companies which are owned by private shareholders, not by the state **Privatsektor, Privatwirtschaft**

◊ **privately** *adverb* away from other people **unter vier Augen;** *the deal was negotiated privately*

privilege *noun* protection from the law given in certain circumstances **Sonderrecht, Privileg; absolute privilege** = privilege which protects a person from being sued for defamation (such as an MP speaking in the House of Commons, a judge *or* a lawyer making a statement during judicial proceedings) **absolute Immunität; absoluter Rechtfertigungsgrund; breach of parliamentary privilege** = speaking in a defamatory way about Parliament *or* about a Member of Parliament **Verletzung des Parlamentsfriedens; Committee of Privileges** = special committee of the House of Commons which examines cases of breach of privilege **Ausschuß zur Untersuchung von Privilegienbrüchen; Crown privilege** = right of the Crown *or* of the government not to have to produce documents in court **Vorrecht der Krone od der Regierung, die Vorlage von Urkunden vor Gericht abzulehnen; qualified privilege** = protection from being sued for defamation which is given to someone only if it can be proved that the statements were made without malice **eingeschränkte Indemnität**

◊ **privileged** *adjective* protected by privilege **privilegiert, bevorrechtigt; immun; privileged communication** = letter which could be libellous but which is protected by privilege (such as a letter from a client to his lawyer) **der Rechtsverfolgung entzogene Mitteilung; privileged meeting** = meeting where what is said will not be repeated outside **geheime Sitzung**

privity of contract *noun* relationship between the parties to a contract, which makes the contract enforceable as between them **Vertragsbeziehung, unmittelbares Vertragsverhältnis**

Privy Council *noun* body of senior advisers who advise the Queen on certain matters **Geheimer Staatsrat, Kronrat; Judicial Committee of the Privy Council** = appeal court for appeals from some Commonwealth countries and the colonies **Rechtsausschuß des Kronrates**
◊ **Privy Councillor** *noun* member of the Privy Council **Mitglied des Kronrates**

prize *noun* enemy ship *or* cargo captured in war **Prise**

pro for *or* on behalf of **für, namens, an Stelle von; per pro** = with the authority of **per Prokura, in Vertretung**

probable *adjective* likely to happen *or* to be true **wahrscheinlich, zu erwarten;** *he is trying to prevent the probable takeover of the company; a heart attack was the probable cause of death*
◊ **probably** *adverb* likely **wahrscheinlich, vermutlich;** *the judge is probably going to retire next year; his death was probably caused by a heart attack*

probate *noun* legal acceptance that a document, especially a will, is valid **gerichtliche (Testaments)bestätigung; grant of probate** = official document proving that a will is genuine, given to the executors so that they can act on the terms of the will **Erbschein;** *GB* **gerichtliche Testamentsbestätigung; the executor was granted probate** *or* **obtained a grant of probate** = the executor was told officially that the will was valid **der Testamentsvollstrecker erwirkte eine gerichtliche Testamentsbestätigung; Probate Registry** = court office which deals with the granting of probate **Geschäftsstelle des Nachlaßgerichts N/ NOTE: no plural**

probation *noun*
(a) legal system for dealing with criminals (often young offenders) where they are not sent to prison provided that they continue to behave well under the supervision of a probation officer **Strafaussetzung zur Bewährung, Bewährung;** *she was sentenced to probation for one year;* **probation officer** = official of the social services who supervises young people on probation **Bewährungshelfer; probation order** = court order putting someone on probation **Strafaussetzung zur Bewährung**
(b) period when a new worker is being tested before being confirmed as having a permanent job **Probezeit**
(c) on probation = (i) being tested; (ii) being under a probation order from a court **(i) auf Probe; (ii) auf Bewährung;** *he is on three months' probation; to take someone on probation* NOTE: no plural
◊ **probationary** *adjective* while someone is being tested **Probe-, auf Probe;** *a probationary period of three months; after the probationary period the company decided to offer him a full-time contract*
◊ **probationer** *noun* person who has been put on probation **auf Probe Angestellter; Strafentlassener auf Bewährung**

problem *noun* thing to which it is difficult to find an answer **Problem;** *the company suffers from cash flow problems or staff problems;* **to solve a problem** = to find an answer to a problem **ein Problem lösen; problem area** = area of work which is difficult to manage **Problembereich;** *drug-related crime is a problem area in large cities*

procedure *noun* way in which something is done, especially steps taken to bring an action to the court **Verfahren, Vorgehen;** *to follow the proper procedure;* **this procedure is very irregular** = this is not the set way to do something **diese Vorgehensweise ist unvorschriftsmäßig; disciplinary procedure** = way of warning a worker that he is breaking the rules of a company *or* working badly **Disziplinarverfahren; complaints procedure** *or* **grievance procedure** = agreed way of presenting complaints formally from a trade union *or* from an employee to the management of a company **Beschwerdeverfahren; dismissal procedures** = correct way of dismissing someone, following the rules in the contract of employment **Entlassungsverfahren**
◊ **procedural** *adjective* referring to legal procedure **prozessual, verfahrensrechtlich; procedural law** = rules governing how the civil *or* criminal law is administered by the courts **Verfahrensrecht; procedural problem** *or* **question** = question concerning procedure **Verfahrensfrage;** *the hearing was held up while counsel argued over procedural problems*

proceed *verb* to go on *or* to continue **fortfahren, fortsetzen;** *the negotiations are proceeding slowly;* **to proceed against**

someone = to start a legal action against someone **jdn verklagen, gegen jdn gerichtlich vorgehen; to proceed with something** = to go on doing something **mit etwas weitermachen/fortfahren;** *the hearing proceeded after the protesters were removed from the courtroom*

◇ **proceedings** *plural noun*
(a) conference proceedings = written report of what has taken place at a conference **Konferenzprotokoll**
(b) legal proceedings = legal action *or* lawsuit **Gerichtsverfahren, Prozeß;** *to take proceedings against someone; the court proceedings were adjourned;* **to institute** *or* **to start proceedings against someone** = to start a legal action against someone **gegen jdn gerichtlich vorgehen; committal proceedings** = preliminary hearing of a case before the magistrates' court, to decide if it is serious enough to be tried before a jury in a higher court **gerichtliche Voruntersuchung; interlocutory proceedings** = hearing that takes place before a court before full trial **Vorverfahren, Zwischenverfahren**

◇ **proceeds** *plural noun* **the proceeds of a sale** = money received from a sale after deducting expenses **der Verkaufserlös**

process
1 *noun*
(a) industrial processes = processes involved in manufacturing products in factories **Herstellungsprozeß; decision-making processes** = ways in which decisions are reached **Entscheidungsprozeß**
(b) (i) way in which a court acts to assert its jurisdiction; (ii) writs issued by a court to summon the defendant to appear in court; (iii) legal procedure **(i) Verfahren, Prozeß; (ii) Vorladung, Ladung des Beklagten; (iii) Verfahrensweise; the due process of the law** = the formal work of a fair legal action **ordentliches Gerichtsverfahren, ordnungsgemäßes Verfahren; abuse of process** = suing someone in bad faith *or* without proper justification *or* for malicious reasons **Verfahrensmißbrauch**
2 *verb*
(a) to process figures = to sort out information to make it easily understood **Zahlen aufbereiten;** *the sales figures are being processed by our accounts department; data is being processed in our computer*
(b) to deal with something in the usual routine way **bearbeiten;** *to process an insurance claim; the incident room is processing information received from the public*

◇ **processing** *noun*
(a) sorting of information **Aufarbeitung, Verarbeitung;** *processing of information or of figures;* **data processing** *or* **information**

processing = selecting and examining data in a computer to produce information in a special form **Datenverarbeitung; word processing** *or* **text processing** = working with words, using a computer to produce, check and amend texts, contracts, reports, letters, etc. **Textverarbeitung**
(b) the processing of a claim for insurance = putting a claim for compensation through the usual office routine in the insurance company **Schadensbearbeitung der Versicherung**

◇ **process-server** *noun* person who delivers legal documents (such as a writ *or* summons) to people in person **Zusteller (einer gerichtlichen Verfügung)**

proctor *noun (in a university)* official who is responsible for keeping law and order **Aufsichtsbeamter in einer Universität; Queen's Proctor** = solicitor acting for the Crown in matrimonial and probate cases **in Scheidungsprozessen und Nachlaßdisputen tätig werdender Kronanwalt**

procurantionem *see* PER PROCURANTIONEM

Procurator Fiscal *noun (in Scotland)* law officer who decides whether an alleged criminal should be prosecuted; *(bei Strafandrohung von mehr als einem Jahr)* **Staatsanwalt;** *(bei geringen Straftaten)* **Amtsanwalt**

procure *verb* to get someone to do something, especially to arrange for a woman to provide sexual intercourse for money **veranlassen, anstiften; Kuppelei betreiben, verkuppeln**

◇ **procuring** *or* **procurement** *noun* notifiable offence of getting a woman to provide sexual intercourse for money **Kuppelei; Zuhälterei**

◇ **procurer** *noun* person who procures women **Kuppler/-in; Zuhälter**

produce *verb* to show *or* to bring out **vorzeigen, vorlegen;** *the police produced a number of weapons seized during the riot; the summons required him to produce a certain document before the court*

product *noun*
(a) thing which is made **Produkt, Erzeugnis; basic product** = main product made from a raw material **Grundprodukt; end product** *or* **final product** *or* **finished product** = product made at the end of a production process **Endprodukt; product liability** = liability of the maker of a product for negligence in the

design or production of the product **Produkthaftung, Produzentenhaftung** (b) **gross domestic product** = annual value of goods sold and services paid for inside a country **Bruttoinlandsprodukt; gross national product** = annual value of goods and services in a country, including income from other countries **Bruttosozialprodukt**

production *noun*

(a) showing something **Vorlage, Vorzeigen; on production of** = when something is shown **bei Vorlage von;** *the case will be released by the customs on production of the relevant documents; goods can be exchanged only on production of the sales slip*

(b) making *or* manufacturing of goods for sale **Herstellung, Produktion, Erzeugung, Fertigung;** *production will probably be held up by industrial action; we are hoping to speed up production by putting in new machinery;* **domestic production =** production of goods in the home market **Inlandsproduktion; mass production =** manufacturing of large quantities of goods **Massenproduktion, serienmäßige Herstellung, Serienfertigung; rate of production** *or* **production rate** = speed at which items are made **Produktionsleistung**

◊ **productive** *adjective* which produces **produktiv; productive capital** = capital which is invested to give interest **arbeitendes/gewinnbringendes Kapital; productive discussions** = useful discussions which lead to an agreement or decision **produktive Gespräche**

◊ **productively** *adverb* in a productive way **produktiv**

proferentem *see* CONTRA

profession *noun*

(a) work which needs special learning over a period of time **Beruf; the managing director is a lawyer by profession** = he trained as a lawyer **der geschäftsführende Direktor ist von Beruf Anwalt**

(b) group of specialized workers **Berufsstand; the legal profession** = all lawyers **der Anwaltsstand, die Anwälte; the medical profession** = all doctors **die Ärzteschaft**

◊ **professional**

1 *adjective*

(a) referring to one of the professions **beruflich, Berufs-; fachlich;** *the accountant sent in his bill for professional services; we had to ask our lawyer for professional advice on the contract;* **a professional man** = man who works in one of the professions (such as a lawyer, doctor, accountant) **Angehöriger der**

gehobenen/freien/akademischen Berufe; professional misconduct = action which is considered wrong by the body which regulates a profession (as an action by a solicitor which is considered wrong by the Law Society) **Berufsvergehen (z.B. standeswidriges Verhalten); professional qualifications** = documents showing that someone has successfully finished a course of study which allows him to work in one of the professions **fachliche Qualifikationen**

(b) expert **professionell, fachmännisch; professional witness** = witness who is a specialist in a subject and is asked to give evidence to a court on technical matters **Sachverständiger, sachverständiger Zeuge**

2 *noun* skilled person *or* person who does skilled work for money **Fachmann**

profit *noun* money gained from a sale which is more than the money spent on making the item sold **Gewinn, Profit, Erlös; clear profit** = profit after all expenses have been paid **Rein-, Nettogewinn; gross profit** = profit calculated as sales income less the cost of the goods sold **Bruttogewinn; net profit** = result where income from sales is larger than all expenditure **Nettogewinn; operating profit** = result where sales from normal business activities are higher than the costs **Betriebsgewinn; trading profit** = result where the company' receipts are higher than its expenditure **Geschäftsgewinn; profit and loss account** = accounts for a company which show expenditure and income balanced to show a final profit or loss **Gewinn- und Verlustrechnung; profit before tax** *or* **pretax profit** = profit before any tax has been paid **Gewinn vor (Abzug der) Steuern; profit after tax** = profit after tax has been paid **Gewinn nach Steuern**

◊ **profitability** *noun*

(a) ability to make a profit **Rentabilität**

(b) amount of profit made as a percentage of costs **Profitabilität; measurement of profitability** = way of calculating how profitable something is **Rentabilitätsberechnung**

◊ **profitable** *adjective* which makes a profit **rentabel, gewinnbringend, ertragreich, einträglich**

◊ **profitably** *adverb* making a profit **rentabel, gewinnbringend, ertragreich** *noun* right to take something from land (such as game, or fish from a river passing through the land) **Nutzungs- und Entnahmerecht an einem fremden Grundstück**

◊ **profiteer** *noun* person who makes too much profit, especially when goods are rationed or in short supply **Geschäftemacher**

◇ **profiteering** noun making too much profit **Geschäftemacherei, Preistreiberei**

pro forma Latin phrase meaning "for the sake of form" **pro forma; pro forma (invoice)** = invoice sent to a buyer before the goods are sent, so that payment can be made or that business documents can be produced **Proforma-Rechnung; pro forma letter** = formal letter which informs a court of a decision of another court **Gerichtsrundschreiben**

program
1 noun **computer program** = instructions to a computer telling it to do a particular piece of work **Computer-, Rechnerprogramm**
2 verb to write a program for a computer **programmieren;** the computer is programmed to search the police records for a certain type of fingerprint; **programming language** = system of signs, letters and words used to instruct a computer **Programmiersprache**

progress
1 noun movement of work forward **Fortschreiten, Verlauf, Fortschritt;** the superintendent briefed the press on the progress of the investigation; the fraud squad is making progress in the false insurance case
2 verb to move forward **Fortschritte machen;** the investigation progressed rapidly once the details were put onto the police computer

prohibit verb to forbid or to say that something must not happen **verbieten, untersagen;** parking is prohibited in front of the garage; the law prohibits the sale of alcohol to minors; **prohibited degrees** = relationships which make it illegal for a man and woman to marry (such as father and daughter) **verbotene Verwandtschaftsgrade; prohibited goods** = goods which are not allowed to be imported **Schmuggelware**
◇ **prohibition** noun
(a) act of forbidding something **Verbot, Untersagung**
(b) High Court order forbidding a lower court from doing something which exceeds its jurisdiction **Zuständigkeitsentziehung durch ein höheres Gericht**
◇ **prohibitive** adjective with a price so high that you cannot afford to pay it **unerschwinglich, untragbar**
◇ **prohibitory injunction** noun order from a court preventing someone from doing an illegal act **einstweilige Verfügung auf Unterlassung**

promise
1 noun statement that you will do something or not do something **Versprechen, Zusage; to keep a promise** = to do what you said you would do **ein Versprechen halten; to go back on a promise** = not to do what you said you would do **ein Versprechen brechen; a promise to pay** = a promissory note **ein Zahlungsversprechen; breach of promise** = formerly, a complaint in court that someone had promised to marry the plaintiff and then had not done so **Bruch des Eheversprechens; gratuitous promise** = promise that cannot be enforced because no money has been involved **unentgeltliches Versprechen**
2 verb to say that you will do something **versprechen, zusagen;** they promised to pay the last instalment next week; the personnel manager promised to look into the grievances of the office staff
◇ **promisee** noun person to whom a promise is made **Versprechensempfänger**
◇ **promisor** noun person who makes a promise **Versprechensgeber**
◇ **promissory** adjective which promises **versprechend, ein Versprechen enthaltend; promissory estoppel** = promise made by one person to another, so that the second person relies on the promise and acts to his detriment, and the first person is stopped from denying the validity of the promise **Rechtscheinbindung aufgrund eines Versprechens; promissory note** = document stating that someone promises to pay an amount of money on a certain date **Schuldschein**

promote verb
(a) to introduce a new Bill into Parliament **(eine Gesetzesvorlage) einbringen**
(b) to give someone a more important job **befördern;** he was promoted from salesman to sales manager
(c) to advertise **werben, Reklame machen; to promote a new product** = to increase the sales of a new product by a sales campaign or TV advertising or free gifts **durch Werbung den Verkauf eines neuen Produktes fördern**
(d) to encourage something to grow **fördern; to promote a new company** = to organize the setting up of a new company **eine neue Firma gründen**
◇ **promoter** noun person who introduces a new Bill into Parliament **jd, der eine Gesetzesvorlage einbringt; company promoter** = person who organizes the setting up of a new company **Firmengründer**
◇ **promotion** noun
(a) moving up to a more important job **Beförderung; to earn promotion** = to work hard and efficiently and so be promoted **sich seine Beförderung verdienen**

(b) promotion of a company = setting up a new company **Firmengründung**
(c) promotion of a product = selling a new product by advertising *or* sales campaigns *or* free gifts **Werbekampagne für ein Produkt**

◊ **promotional** *adjective* used in an advertising campaign **Werbe-; promotional budget** = expected cost of promoting a new product **Werbeetat**

prompt
1 *adjective* rapid *or* done immediately **prompt, sofortig;** *the minister issued a prompt denial of the allegations against him;* **failing prompt payment** = if the payment is not made on time **bei nicht pünktlicher/unpünktlicher Zahlung**
2 *verb* to tell someone what to say **vorsagen;** *the judge warned counsel not to prompt the witness*

◊ **promptly** *adverb* rapidly **prompt, pünktlich;** *the defendant promptly counterclaimed against the plaintiff*

proof *noun*
(a) thing *or* evidence which shows that something is true **Beweismittel; Beweis; documentary proof** = proof in the form of a document **Urkundenbeweis; burden of proof** *or* **onus of proof** = duty to prove that what has been alleged in court is correct **Beweislast;** *the onus of proof is on the plaintiff*
(b) statement *or* evidence of a creditor to show that he is owed money by a bankrupt *or* by a company in liquidation **Anmeldung/Nachweis einer Konkursforderung; proof of debt** = proceedings for a creditor to claim payment from a bankrupt's assets **Anmeldung einer Konkursforderung; proof of evidence** = written statement of what a witness intends to say in court **schriftliche Zeugenaussage; proof of service** = showing that legal documents have been delivered to someone **Zustellungsnachweis**

◊ **-proof** *suffix* which prevents something getting in or out *or* harming **-dicht, -sicher;** *burglarproof door; inflation-proof pension; escapeproof prison*

proper *adjective* correct *or* appropriate **richtig, ordnungsgemäß, rechtmäßig; angebracht, passend, angemessen; proper law of the contract** = law which the parties signing a contract agree should govern that contract *or* its formation **das auf den Vertrag anzuwendende Recht**

property *noun*
(a) ownership *or* right to own something **Eigentum, Eigentumsrecht; law of property** = branch of the law dealing with the rights of ownership **Sachenrecht, Liegenschaftsrecht**
(b) anything which can be owned **Vermögensgegenstand, Vermögenswert; industrial property** = intangible property owned by a company (such as copyrights *or* patents *or* trademarks) **gewerbliches Eigentum; intellectual property** = ownership of something (such as a copyright *or* patent *or* trademark) which is intangible **geistiges Eigentum; personal property** = things (but not land) which belong to a person and can be inherited by his heirs **bewegliche Sachen, bewegliches Vermögen; beweglicher Nachlaß;** *the storm caused considerable damage to personal property; the management is not responsible for property left in the hotel rooms*
(c) (real) property = land and buildings **Grundbesitz, Grundstücke, Immobilien, Liegenschaften;** *property tax or tax on property; damage to property or property damage; the commercial property market is declining;* **property company** = company which buys *or* constructs buildings to lease them **Immobiliengesellschaft; property developer** = person who buys old buildings *or* empty land and builds new buildings for sale *or* rent **Bauunternehmer, der zum Wiederverkauf baut od renoviert; private property** = land *or* buildings which belong to a private person and not to the public **Privatgrundstück, Privatbesitz**
(d) a building **Gebäude;** *we have several properties for sale in the centre of the town*
NOTE: no plural for (a), (b) or (c)

proportion *noun* part (of a total) **Teil, Anteil;** *a proportion of the pretax profit is set aside for contingencies; only a small proportion of our sales comes from retail shops;* **in proportion to** = showing how something is related to something else **im Verhältnis zu**

◊ **proportional** *adjective* directly related **proportional; proportional representation** = system of electing representatives where each political party is allocated a number of places which is directly related to the number of votes cast for the party **Verhältniswahl**

◊ **proportionately** *adverb* in proportion **verhältnismäßig**

proposal *noun*
(a) suggestion *or* thing suggested **Vorschlag, Antrag;** *to make a proposal or to put forward a proposal;* **to lay a proposal before the House** = to introduce a new Bill before Parliament **eine Gesetzesvorlage im Parlament einbringen; the committee turned down the proposal** = the committee refused

to accept what had been suggested **der Ausschuß hat den Antrag abgewiesen**
(b) proposal form = official document with details of a property *or* person to be insured which is sent to the insurance company when asking for an insurance **Versicherungsantrag**

◊ **propose** *verb*
(a) to suggest that something should be done **vorschlagen;** *the Bill proposes that any party to the proceedings may appeal;* **to propose a motion** = to ask a meeting to vote for a motion and explain the reasons for this **einen Antrag stellen; to propose someone as president** = to ask a group to vote for someone to become president **jdn als Vorsitzenden vorschlagen**
(b) to propose to = to say that you intend to do something **vorhaben;** *I propose to repay the loan at £20 a month*

proprietary *adjective*
(a) product (such as a medicine) which is made and owned by a company **gesetzlich geschützt, Marken-; proprietary drug** = drug which is made by a particular company and marketed under a brand name **patentrechtlich geschütztes Arzneimittel; proprietary right** = right of someone who owns a property **Eigentumsrecht**
(b) *(in South Africa and Australia)* **proprietary company (Pty)** = private limited company **Gesellschaft mit beschränkter Haftung**

◊ **proprietor** *noun* owner of a property **Eigentümer, Inhaber;** *the proprietor of a hotel or a hotel proprietor*

◊ **proprietorship** *noun* act of being the proprietor of land **Eigentumsrecht an Grundbesitz; proprietorship register** = land register which shows the details of owners of land **Verzeichnis der Grundstückseigentümer, Grundbuch**

◊ **proprietress** *noun* woman owner **Eigentümerin, Besitzerin;** *the proprietress of an advertising consultancy*

pro rata *adjective & adverb* at a rate which changes according to the importance of something **anteilmäßig, anteilig;** *a pro rata payment; to pay someone pro rata*

prorogation *noun* end of a session of Parliament **Ende einer Sitzungsperiode**

◊ **prorogue** *verb* to end a session of Parliament **eine Sitzungsperiode beenden;** *Parliament was prorogued for the summer recess*

proscribe *verb* to ban **verbieten;** *a* **proscribed political party** = political party

which has been banned **eine verbotene politische Partei**

prosecute *verb*
(a) to bring (someone) to court to answer a criminal charge **anklagen, strafrechtlich verfolgen;** *he was prosecuted for embezzlement*
(b) to speak against the accused person on behalf of the party bringing the charge **die Anklage vertreten, als Kläger auftreten;** *Mr Smith is prosecuting, and Mr Jones is appearing for the defence*

◊ **prosecution** *noun*
(a) act of bringing someone to court to answer a charge **Anklage, Strafverfolgung;** *his prosecution for embezzlement;* **Director of Public Prosecutions** = government official in charge of a group of lawyers (working under the Attorney-General), who prosecutes in important cases and advises other government departments if prosecutions should be started **Leiter der Anklagebehörde, Generalstaatsanwalt**
(b) (i) party who brings a criminal charge against someone; (ii) lawyers representing the party who brings a criminal charge against someone **(i) Anklagebehörde, Staatsanwaltschaft, Ankläger; (ii) Anklagevertretung;** *the costs of the case will be borne by the prosecution;* **prosecution counsel** *or* **counsel for the prosecution** = lawyer acting for the prosecution **Anklagevertreter;** *see also* DEFENCE

◊ **prosecutor** *noun* person who brings criminal charges against someone **Staatsanwalt, Vertreter der Anklage; Crown prosecutor** = official of the Director of Public Prosecutions' department who is responsible for prosecuting criminals in a local area **Staatsanwalt;** *(GB)* **Kronanwalt; public prosecutor** = government official who brings charges against alleged criminals (in the UK, the Director of Public Prosecutions) **Staatsanwalt, öffentlicher Ankläger; Generalstaatsanwalt**

prosequi *see* NOLLE

prospectus *noun*
(a) document which gives information to attract buyers *or* customers **Prospekt;** *the restaurant has girls handing out prospectuses in the street*
(b) document which gives information about a company whose shares are being sold to the public for the first time **Emissions-, Subskriptionsprospekt**
NOTE: plural is **prospectuses**

prostitution *noun* providing sexual intercourse in return for payment **Prostitution, gewerbsmäßige Unzucht**

◊ **prostitute** *noun* person who provides sexual intercourse in return for payment **Prostituierte**

protect *verb* to defend something against harm **schützen, absichern**; *the workers are protected from unfair dismissal by government legislation; the computer is protected by a plastic cover; the cover protects the machine from dust;* **to protect an industry by imposing tariff barriers** = to stop a local industry from being hit by foreign competition by stopping foreign products from being imported **eine Industrie durch die Einführung von Zollschranken schützen; protected tenancy** = tenancy where the tenant is protected from eviction **Mietverhältnis mit Mieterschutz; Pachtverhältnis mit Pächterschutz**

NOTE: you protect someone **from** something or **from having** something done to him

◊ **protection** *noun* thing which protects **Schutz; consumer protection** = protecting consumers against unfair *or* illegal traders **Verbraucherschutz; Court of Protection** = court which administers the property of people suffering from a disability **Gericht, das das Vermögen von Entmündigten verwaltet; data protection** = protecting information (such as records about private people) in a computer from being copied or used wrongly **Datenschutz; police protection** = services of the police to protect someone who might be harmed **Polizeischutz;** *the minister was given police protection;* **protection racket** = illegal organization where people demand money from someone (such as a small businessman) to pay for "protection" against criminal attacks **Erpressung von Schutzgeld**

NOTE: no plural

◊ **protective** *adjective* which protects **Schutz-; protective tariff** = tariff which tries to ban imports to stop them competing with local products **Schutzzoll**

pro tem *or* **pro tempore** *adverb* temporarily *or* for a time **zur Zeit, gegenwärtig, vorübergehend**

protest
1 *noun*
(a) statement *or* action to show that you do not approve of something **Protest;** *to make a protest against high prices;* **sit-down protest** = action by members of the staff who occupy their place of work and refuse to leave **Sit-in, Sitzstreik; protest march** = demonstration where protesters march through the streets **Protestmarsch; in protest**

at = showing that you do not approve of something **aus Protest gegen;** *the staff occupied the offices in protest at the low pay offer;* **to do something under protest** = to do something, but say that you do not approve of it **etwas unter Protest tun**
(b) official document from a notary public which notes that a bill of exchange has not been paid **Wechselprotest**
2 *verb*
(a) **to protest against something** = to say that you do not approve of something **gegen etwas protestieren/Einspruch erheben;** *the retailers are protesting against the ban on imported goods* (NOTE: in this meaning GB English is **protest against something**, but US English is **to protest something**)
(b) **to protest a bill** = to draw up a document to prove that a bill of exchange has not been paid **Wechselprotest einlegen, einen Wechsel zu Protest gehen lassen**

◊ **protester** *noun* person who protests **Protestierender; Demonstrant/-in**

protocol *noun*
(a) (i) draft memorandum; (ii) list of things which have been agreed **(i) Protokoll; (ii) Verhandlungsniederschrift**
(b) correct diplomatic behaviour **Protokoll**

prove *verb* to show that something is true **beweisen, nachweisen;** *the tickets proved that he was lying; dispatch of the packet was proved by the Post Office receipt; the claim was proved to be false;* **to prove a debt** = to show that a bankrupt owes you money **eine (Konkurs)forderung anmelden; to prove a will** = to show that a will is valid and obtain a grant of probate **ein Testament bestätigen lassen**

◊ **provable** *adjective* which can be proved **beweisbar, nachweisbar; provable debts** = debts which a creditor can prove against a bankrupt estate **anmeldbare Forderungen**

◊ **proven** *adjective (in Scotland)* **not proven** = verdict that the prosecution has not produced sufficient evidence to prove the accused to be guilty **Freispruch mangels Beweisen**

provide *verb*
(a) **to provide for something** = to allow for something which may happen in the future **für etwas Vorsorge treffen;** *the contract provides for an annual increase in charges; £10,000 has been provided for in the budget; these expenses have not been provided for; payments as provided in schedule 6 attached;* **to provide for someone** = to put aside money to give someone enough to live on **für jdn sorgen;** *he provided for his daughter in his will*

(b) to put money aside in accounts to cover expenditure or loss in the future **bereitstellen;** £25,000 is provided against bad debts
(c) to provide someone with something = to supply something to someone **jdm etwas liefern/zur Verfügung stellen, jdn mit etwas versorgen;** the defendant provided the court with a detailed account of his movements; duress provides no defence to a charge of murder

◊ **provided that** or **providing** conjunction on condition that **vorausgesetzt, daß;** the judge will sentence the convicted man next week provided (that) or providing the psychiatrist's report is received in time
NOTE: in deeds, the form **provided always that** is often used

provision noun
(a) to make provision for = to see that something is allowed for in the future **Vorsorge/Vorkehrungen treffen für; to make financial provision for someone** = to give someone enough money to live on **für jds Unterhalt sorgen; there is no provision for** or **no provision has been made for car parking in the plans for the office block** = the plans do not include space for cars to park **in den Plänen für das Bürogebäude sind keine Parkplätze vorgesehen**
(b) money put aside in accounts in case it is needed in the future **Rücklage, Rückstellung;** the company has made a £2m provision for bad debts
(c) legal condition **Klausel, Bestimmung; the provisions of a Bill** = conditions listed in a Bill before Parliament **Gesetzesbestimmungen; we have made provision to this effect** = we have put into the contract terms which will make this work **wir haben für diesen Fall Klauseln eingebaut**

◊ **provisional** adjective temporary or not final or permanent **vorläufig, provisorisch, Interims-;** provisional budget; they wrote to give their provisional acceptance of the contract; **provisional liquidator** = official appointed by a court to protect the assets of a company which is the subject of a winding up order **vorläufiger Konkursverwalter; provisional injunction** = temporary injunction granted until a full court hearing can take place **einstweilige Verfügung**

◊ **provisionally** adverb not finally **vorläufig, provisorisch;** the contract has been accepted provisionally; he was provisionally appointed director

proviso noun condition in a contract or deed **Vorbehalt, Vorbehaltsklausel;** we are signing the contract with the proviso that the terms can be discussed again in six months' time
NOTE: the proviso usually begins with the phrase **"provided always that"**

provocation noun being provoked to commit a crime or to carry out an action which you had not intended **Provokation, Herausforderung;** he acted under provocation
NOTE: no plural

◊ **provoke** verb to make someone do something or to make something happen **provozieren, herausfordern;** the strikers provoked the police to retaliate; the murders provoked a campaign to increase police protection for politicians
NOTE: you provoke someone **to do** something

◊ **provocateur** see AGENT PROVOCATEUR

proxy noun
(a) document which gives someone the power to act on behalf of someone else **Vollmachtsurkunde;** to sign by proxy; **proxy vote** = votes made by proxy **durch Stellvertreter abgegebene Stimmen**
(b) person who acts on behalf of someone else, especially a person appointed by a shareholder to vote on his behalf at a company meeting **Bevollmächtigter, Stimmrechtsvertreter;** to act as proxy for someone

P.S. = POST SCRIPTUM additional note at the end of a letter **PS;** did you read the P.S. at the end of the letter?

psychiatry noun study of diseases of the mind **Psychiatrie**

◊ **psychiatric** adjective referring to psychiatry **psychiatrisch; psychiatric hospital** = hospital where mentally ill people are treated **psychiatrische Klinik;** he was sent to hospital for psychiatric treatment; the court was shown a psychiatric report

◊ **psychiatrist** noun doctor specializing in diseases of the mind **Psychiater/-in**

Pty = PROPRIETARY COMPANY

public
1 adjective
(a) referring to all the people in general **öffentlich; Public Bill** = Bill referring to a matter applying to the public in general which is introduced in Parliament by a government minister **Gesetzesvorlage für ein allgemeines Gesetz; public domain** = land or property or information which belongs to and is available to the public **Gemeingut; work in the public domain** = written work

which is no longer in copyright **nicht länger (durch das Urheberrecht) geschützte Werke; public holiday** = day when all workers rest and enjoy themselves instead of working **gesetzlicher Feiertag; public house** = building which has been licensed for the sale of alcohol to be drunk on the premises **Gaststätte; public image** = idea which the people have of a company *or* a person **Image;** *the police are trying to improve their public image;* **public law** = law which affects the people *or* the public as a whole (such as administrative and constitutional law) **öffentliches Recht; public nuisance** = criminal act which can harm members of the public *or* their rights **öffentliches Ärgernis; public order** = situation where the general public is calm *or* where there are no riots **öffentliche (Sicherheit und) Ordnung; offence against the public order** *or* **public order offence** = riot *or* street fight *or* looting, etc. **Verstoß gegen die öffentliche Ordnung, Störung der öffentlichen Ordnung; public place** = place (such as a road *or* park *or* pavement) where the public in general have a right to be **öffentlicher Ort; public policy** = general good of all the people **Gemeinwohl, öffentliches Interesse; public transport** = transport (such as buses, trains) which is used by any member of the public **öffentliche Verkehrsmittel; Public Trustee** = official who is appointed as a trustee of an individual's property **öffentlich bestellter Treuhänder**

(b) referring to the government *or* the state **staatlich; Public Accounts Committee** = committee of the House of Commons which examines the spending of each department and ministry **Rechnungsprüfungsausschuß; public administration** = (i) means whereby government policy is carried out; (ii) people responsible for carrying out government policy **(i) öffentliche Verwaltung; (ii) Beamte; public expenditure** = spending of money by the local or central government **öffentliche Ausgaben, Staatsausgaben; public finance** = the raising of money by governments (by taxes or borrowing) and the spending of it **Staatsfinanzen; public funds** = government money available for expenditure **öffentliche Mittel/Gelder; public ownership** = situation where an industry is nationalized **Staatsbesitz, Eigentum der öffentlichen Hand**

(c) public limited company (plc) = company whose shares can be bought on the Stock Exchange **Aktiengesellschaft; the company is going public** = the company is going to place some of its shares for sale on the Stock Exchange so that anyone can buy them **das Unternehmen wird in eine Aktiengesellschaft umgewandelt**

2 *noun* **the public** *or* **the general public** = the people in general **die Öffentlichkeit; in public** = in front of everyone **öffentlich, in der Öffentlichkeit**

◊ **publication** *noun*
(a) (i) making something public (either in speech or writing); (ii) making a libel known to people other than the person libelled **(i) Veröffentlichung, Bekanntgabe, Bekanntmachung; (ii) Verbreitung (von Verleumdungen), Zurkenntnisbringung;** *publication of Cabinet papers takes place after thirty years*
(b) printed work shown to the public **Publikation, Veröffentlichung, (Druck)schrift; obscene publication** = book *or* magazine which is liable to deprave or corrupt someone who sees or reads it **pornographische Veröffentlichung;** *the magazine was classed as an obscene publication and seized by the customs*

◊ **public relations (PR)** *noun* keeping good links between an organization *or* a company *or* a group and the public so that people know what the organization is doing and approve of it **PR-Arbeit, Public Relations, Öffentlichkeitsarbeit; public relations department** = section of an organization which deals with relations with the public **Public Relations-Abteilung; public relations officer** = official who deals with relations with the public **Public Relations-Fachmann**

◊ **public sector** *noun* nationalized industries and services **öffentlicher Bereich, staatlicher Sektor;** *a report on wage rises in the public sector or on public sector wage settlements;* **public sector borrowing requirement** = amount of money which a government has to borrow to pay for its own spending **Kreditbedarf der öffentlichen Hand**

publish *verb* to have a document (such as a catalogue *or* book *or* magazine *or* newspaper *or* piece of music) written and printed and then sell or give it to the public **veröffentlichen, herausgeben, verlegen;** *the society publishes its list of members annually; the government has not published the figures on which its proposals are based; the company publishes six magazines for the business market*

◊ **publisher** *noun* person or company which publishes **Verleger, Verlag**

puisne *adjective* lesser *or* less important **nachstehend, untergeordnet, Unter-; puisne judge** = High Court judge **(beisitzender) Richter; puisne mortgage** = mortgage where the deeds of the property have not been deposited with the lender **nachstehende Hypothek**

punish *verb* to make (someone) suffer for a crime which he has committed **(be)strafen;** *you will be punished for hitting the policeman*

◊ **punishable** *adjective* (crime) which can be punished **strafbar;** *crimes punishable by imprisonment*

◊ **punishment** *noun*
(a) act of punishing someone **Bestrafung; corporal punishment** = punishing someone by hitting him **körperliche Züchtigung; capital punishment** = punishing someone by execution **Todesstrafe**
(b) treatment of someone as a way of making him suffer for a crime **Strafe;** *the punishment for treason is death*

pupillage *noun* training period of one year after completing studies at university and passing all examinations which a person has to serve before he can practise independently as a barrister; *entspricht* **Referendarzeit**
NOTE: no plural

purchase
1 *noun* (i) action of buying something; (ii) thing which has been bought **(i) Kauf, Erwerb; (ii) gekaufter Gegenstand; purchase order** = official order made out by a purchasing department for goods which a company wants to buy **Auftrag, Bestellung; purchase price** = price paid for something **Kaufpreis, Anschaffungspreis; purchase tax** = tax paid on things which are bought **Kaufsteuer; compulsory purchase** = buying of a property by a local authority *or* by the government, even if the owner does not wish to sell **Enteignung; compulsory purchase order** = official order from a local authority *or* from the government ordering an owner to sell his property **Enteignungsverfügung; hire purchase** = system of buying something by paying a sum regularly each month **Raten-, Teilzahlungskauf; hire purchase agreement** = contract to pay for something by instalments **Teilzahlungskaufvertrag**
2 *verb* to buy **kaufen, erwerben, erstehen, einkaufen, käuflich erwerben; to purchase something for cash** = to pay cash for something **etwas bar/gegen Barzahlung kaufen**

◊ **purchaser** *noun* person *or* company which purchases something **Käufer/-in, Erwerber/-in**

purge *verb* **to purge one's contempt** *or* **to purge a contempt of court** = to do something (such as make an apology) to show that you are sorry for the lack of respect you have shown **sich für Mißachtung des Gerichts entschuldigen**

purpose *noun* aim *or* plan *or* intention **Ziel, Zweck, Absicht; on purpose** = intentionally **absichtlich;** *she hid the knife on purpose;* **we need the invoice for tax purposes** *or* **for the purpose of declaration to the tax authorities** = in order for it to be declared to the tax authorities **wir benötigen die Rechnung zu Steuerzwecken; fitness for purpose** = implied contractual term that goods sold will be of the necessary standard to be used for the purpose for which they were bought **Eignung für einen besonderen Zweck**

pursue *verb* to continue with (proceedings in court *or* debate in Parliament, etc.) **fortsetzen, fortfahren, weiterführen**

◊ **pursuant to** *adverb* relating to *or* concerning **gemäß, laut, entsprechend;** *matters pursuant to Article 124 of the EC treaty; pursuant to the powers conferred on the local authority*

pursuit *noun* **in pursuit** = following *or* chasing **hinterher(jagend);** *the bank robbers escaped in a car with the police in pursuit; see also* FRESH, HOT

purview *noun* general scope of an Act of Parliament **Geltungsbereich**

put
1 *noun* **put option** = right to sell shares at a certain price at a certain date **Verkaufsoption**
2 *verb* to place *or* to fix **festsetzen, festlegen, setzen; to put a proposal to the vote** = to ask a meeting to vote for or against the proposal **über einen Antrag abstimmen lassen; to put a proposal to the board** = to ask the board to consider a suggestion **dem Vorstand einen Antrag unterbreiten**
NOTE: **putting - put - has put**

◊ **put away** *verb* to send to prison **einsperren;** *he was put away for ten years*

◊ **put down** *verb*
(a) to make a deposit **anzahlen;** *to put down money on a house*
(b) to write an item in an account book **eintragen, aufschreiben;** *to put down a figure for expenses*

◊ **put in** *verb* **to put an ad in a paper** = to have an ad printed in a newspaper **ein Inserat aufgeben; to put in a bid for something** = to offer (usually in writing) to buy something **für etwas ein Angebot machen; to put in an estimate for something** = to give someone a written calculation of the probable costs of carrying out a job **für etwas einen Kostenvoranschlag machen; to put in a claim for damage** *or* **loss** = to ask an insurance company to pay for damage *or* loss **einen Schadensersatzanspruch stellen**

◊ **put into** *verb* **to put money into a business** = to invest money in a business **Geld in ein Geschäft stecken**

◊ **put off** *verb* to arrange for something to take place later than planned **ver-, aufschieben;** *the hearing was put off for two weeks; he asked if we could put the visit off until tomorrow*

◊ **put on** *verb* **to put an item on the agenda** = to list an item for discussion at a meeting **einen Punkt auf die Tagesordnung setzen; to put an embargo on trade** = to forbid trade **ein Handelsembargo verhängen**

◊ **put out** *verb* to send out **vergeben, außer Haus geben;** *to put work out to freelance workers; we put all our typing out to a bureau;* **to put work out to contract** = to decide that work should be done by a company on a contract, rather than employ members of staff to do it **Unteraufträge vergeben**

putative *adjective* **putative father** = man who is supposed to be *or* who a court decides must be the father of an illegitimate child **mutmaßlicher Vater**

Qq

QB *or* **QBD** = QUEEN'S BENCH DIVISION

QC = QUEEN'S COUNSEL
NOTE: written after the surname of the lawyer: **W. Smith QC.** Note also that the plural is written **QCs**

qua *conjunction* as *or* acting in the capacity of **als;** *a decision of the Lord Chancellor qua head of the judiciary*

quadruplicate *noun* **in quadruplicate** = with the original and three copies **in vierfacher Ausfertigung;** *the invoices are printed in quadruplicate*
NOTE: no plural

qualification *noun*
(a) proof that you have completed a specialized course of study **Qualifikation;** *to have the right qualifications for the job;* **professional qualifications** = documents which show that someone has successfully finished a course of study which allows him to work in one of the professions **fachliche Qualifikationen**

(b) period of qualification = time which has to pass before something qualifies for something **Zulassungsfrist; qualification shares** = number of shares which a person has to hold to be a director of a company **Pflichtaktien**

◊ **qualify** *verb*
(a) to qualify for = to be in the right position for *or* to be entitled to **berechtigt sein zu;** *he does not qualify for Legal Aid; she qualifies for unemployment pay*
(b) to qualify as = to follow a specialized course and pass examinations so that you can do a certain job **seine Ausbildung zum ... abschließen;** *she has qualified as an accountant; he will qualify as a solicitor next year*
(c) to change *or* to amend **modifizieren, einschränken; the auditors have qualified the accounts** = the auditors have found something in the accounts of the company which they do not agree with, and have noted it **die Wirtschaftsprüfer haben den Jahresabschluß mit einschränkenden Bemerkungen verabschiedet**

◊ **qualified** *adjective*
(a) having passed special examinations in a subject **ausgebildet, qualifiziert;** *she is a qualified solicitor;* **highly qualified** = with very good results in examinations **hochqualifiziert;** *all our staff are highly qualified; they employ twentysix highly qualified legal assistants*
(b) with some reservations *or* conditions **bedingt, mit Einschränkungen;** *qualified acceptance of a bill of exchange; the plan received qualified approval from the board;* **qualified privilege** = protection from being sued for defamation given to someone only if it can be proved that the statements were made without malice **eingeschränkte Indemnität; qualified title** = title to a property which is not absolute because there is some defect **bedingter Rechtstitel**
(c) qualified accounts = accounts which have been noted by the auditors because they contain something with which the auditors do not agree **berichtigter Jahresabschluß**

◊ **qualifying** *adjective*
(a) qualifying period = time which has to pass before something qualifies for a grant *or* subsidy, etc. **Anwartschafts-, Wartezeit;** *there is a six month qualifying period before you can get a grant from the local authority*
(b) qualifying shares = number of shares which you need to own to get a free issue *or* to be a director of a company **Pflichtaktien**

quantify *verb* **to quantify the effect of something** = to show the effect of something in figures **die Auswirkung von etwas quantitativ bestimmen;** *it is impossible* *to quantify the effect of the new legislation on the crime rate*

◇ **quantifiable** *adjective* which can be quantified **quantitativ bestimmbar;** *the effect of the change on the prison population is not quantifiable*

quantity *adjective*
(a) amount *or* number of items **Menge, Quantität, Anzahl;** *a small quantity of illegal drugs; he bought a large quantity of spare parts*
(b) large amount **große Stückzahl/Menge;** *the company offers a discount for quantity purchase*

quantum *noun* amount (of damages) **Schadenhöhe, Entschädigungssumme;** *liability was admitted by the defendants, but the case went to trial because they could not agree the quantum of damages*

◇ **quantum meruit** *Latin phrase meaning* "as much as he has deserved": rule that, when claiming for breach of contract, a party is entitled to payment for work done **angemessene Vergütung (für Teilleistung)**

quarantine
1 *noun* period (originally forty days) when a ship *or* animal *or* person newly arrived in a country has to be kept away from others in case there is danger of carrying diseases **Quarantäne;** *the animals were put in quarantine on arrival at the port; quarantine restrictions have been lifted on imported animals from that country* (NOTE: used without **the: the dog was put in quarantine** *or* **was held in quarantine * was released from quarantine**)
2 *verb* to put in quarantine **unter Quarantäne stellen;** *the ship was searched and all the animals on it were quarantined*

quarter *noun*
(a) period of three months **Quartal, Vierteljahr; first quarter** *or* **second quarter** *or* **third quarter** *or* **fourth quarter** *or* **last quarter** = periods of three months from January to the end of March *or* from April to the end of June *or* from July to the end of September *or* from October to the end of the year **das erste od zweite od dritte od vierte/letzte Quartal;** *the instalments are payable at the end of each quarter; the first quarter's rent is payable in advance;* **quarter day** = day at the end of a quarter, when rents should be paid **Quartalstag**

COMMENT: in England the quarter days are 25th March (Lady Day), 24th June (Midsummer Day), 29th September (Michaelmas Day) and 25th December (Christmas Day)

(b) **Quarter Sessions** = old name for the criminal court replaced by the Crown Court **Quartalgerichte**

◇ **quarterly** *adjective & adverb* happening every three months *or* happening four times a year **vierteljährlich, quartalsweise;** *there is a quarterly charge for electricity; the bank sends us a quarterly statement; we agreed to pay the rent quarterly or on a quarterly basis*

quash *verb* to annul *or* to make something not exist **annullieren, aufheben, für nichtig erklären;** *the appeal court quashed the verdict; he applied for judicial review to quash the order; a conviction obtained by fraud or perjury by a witness will be quashed*

quasi- *prefix* almost *or* which seems like **Quasi-, quasi-;** *a quasi-official body; a quasi-judicial investigation*

◇ **quasi-contract** *noun* = IMPLIED CONTRACT

Queen's Bench Division (QBD)
noun one of the main divisions of the High Court **Abteilung des High Court**

Queen's Counsel *noun* senior British
barrister, appointed by the Lord Chancellor **Anwalt der Krone**
NOTE: abbreviated to **QC**

Queen's evidence *noun* **to turn Queen's evidence** = to confess to a crime and then act as witness against the other criminals involved, in the hope of getting a lighter sentence **als Kron-/Belastungszeuge aussagen**

Queen's Proctor *noun* solicitor acting
for the Crown in matrimonial and probate cases in **Nachlaßdisputen und Scheidungsfällen tätig werdender Kronanwalt**

Queen's Speech *noun* speech made by
the Queen at the opening of a session of Parliament, which outlines the government's plans for legislation **Thronrede, Parlamentseröffnungsrede**

query
1 *noun* question **Frage, Rückfrage;** *the chief accountant had to answer a mass of queries from the auditors*
2 *verb* to ask a question about something *or* to suggest that something may be wrong **sich erkundigen; in Frage stellen, bezweifeln, beanstanden;** *counsel queried the statements of the police witnesses*

question
1 *noun*
(a) words which need an answer **Frage;**

counsel asked the witness questions about his bank accounts; counsel for the prosecution put three questions to the police inspector; the managing director refused to answer questions about redundancies; the market research team prepared a series of questions to test the public's attitude to problems of law and order; **Question Time** = period in the House of Commons when Members of Parliament can put questions to ministers about the work of their departments **Fragestunde**
(b) problem **Problem**; *he raised the question of the cost of the lawsuit; the main question is that of time; the tribunal discussed the question of redundancy payments*
(c) question of fact = fact relevant to a case which is tried at court **Tatfrage; question of law** = law relevant to a case which is tried at court **Rechtsfrage**
2 *verb*
(a) to ask questions **befragen, verhören, vernehmen;** *the police questioned the accounts staff for four hours; she questioned the chairman about the company's investment policy*
(b) to query *or* to suggest that something may be wrong **in Frage stellen, bezweifeln;** *counsel questioned the reliability of the witness' evidence; the accused questioned the result of the breathalyser test*

◊ **questioning** *noun* action of asking someone questions **Befragung, Verhör, Vernehmung;** *the man was taken to the police station for questioning; during questioning by the police, she confessed to the crime; the witness became confused during questioning by counsel for the prosecution*

◊ **questionnaire** *noun* printed list of questions, especially used in market research **Fragebogen;** *to send out a questionnaire to test the opinions of users of the system; to answer or to fill in a questionnaire about problems of inner city violence*

queue
1 *noun*
(a) line of people waiting one behind the other **(Warte)schlange;** *to form a queue or to join a queue; queues formed at the doors of the Crown Court on the morning of the murder trial*
(b) series of documents (such as orders, application forms) which are dealt with in order **Unterlagenstapel; mortgage queue** = list of people waiting for mortgages **Hypotheken-Warteliste**
2 *verb* to form a line one after the other for something **anstehen, Schlange stehen;** *when food was in short supply, people had to queue for bread; we queued for hours to get into the courtroom*

quick *adjective* fast *or* not taking any time **schnell;** *the company made a quick recovery; he is hoping for a quick trial*

◊ **quickie (divorce)** *noun* divorce which is processed rapidly through the court by use of the special procedure **Blitzscheidung**

◊ **quickly** *adverb* without taking much time **schnell;** *the divorce case went through the courts quickly; the accountant quickly looked through the pile of invoices*

quid pro quo *Latin phrase meaning* "one thing for another": action done in return for something done or promised **Gegenleistung**

quiet *adjective* calm *or* not excited **ruhig;** *the prisoner seemed very quiet when the clerk read out the charges;* **on the quiet** = in secret **heimlich;** *he transferred his bank account to Switzerland on the quiet;* **quiet enjoyment** = right of an occupier to occupy property peacefully under a tenancy without the landlord or anyone else interfering with that right **ungestörter Besitz**

quit *verb* to leave a job *or* to leave rented accommodation **kündigen, aufgeben, ausziehen;** *he quit after an argument with the managing director; several of the managers are quitting to set up their own company;* **notice to quit** = formal notice served by a landlord on a tenant before proceedings are started for possession **Kündigung des Mieters; to serve a tenant with notice to quit** = to inform a tenant that he has to leave premises by a certain date **einem Mieter kündigen**
NOTE: **quitting - quit - has quit**

quo *see* STATUS QUO

quorum *noun* minimum number of people who have to be present at a meeting to make it valid **beschlußfähige Anzahl; to have a quorum** = to have enough people present for a meeting to go ahead **beschlußfähig sein;** *do we have a quorum? the meeting was adjourned since there was no quorum*

◊ **quorate** *adjective* having a quorum **beschlußfähig;** *the resolution was invalid because the shareholders' meeting was not quorate; see also* INQUORATE

quota *noun* fixed amount of something which is allowed to be sold *or* bought *or* obtained **Kontingent, Quote; import quota** = fixed quantity of a particular type of goods which the government allows to be imported **Einfuhrkontingent, Importquote;** *the government has imposed a quota on the* *import of cars; the quota on imported cars has been lifted;* **quota system** = system where imports *or* exports *or* supplies are regulated by fixing maximum amounts **Quotensystem, Kontingentierungssystem**

quote *verb*
(a) to repeat words used by someone else; to repeat a reference number **zitieren, anführen; angeben;** *counsel quoted from the statement made by the witness at the police station; she quoted figures from the annual report; in reply please quote this number: PC 1234*
(b) to estimate *or* to say what costs may be **ein Preisangebot/einen Kostenvoranschlag machen, einen Preis nennen;** *to quote a price for supplying stationery; to quote a price in dollars; their prices are always quoted in dollars; he quoted me a price of £1,026; can you quote for supplying 20,000 envelopes?;* **quoted company** = company whose shares are listed on the Stock Exchange **an der Börse notiertes Unternehmen**
◊ **quotation** *noun*
(a) estimate of how much something will cost **Kostenvoranschlag;** *they sent in their quotation for the job; to ask for quotations for building a new courtroom; his quotation was much lower than all the others; we accepted the lowest quotation*
(b) quotation on the Stock Exchange *or* **Stock Exchange quotation** = listing of the price of a share on the Stock Exchange **(Kurs)notierung, Börsenkurs; the company is going for a quotation on the Stock Exchange** = the company has applied to the Stock Exchange to have its shares listed **das Unternehmen hat die Börsennotierung beantragt**

quo warranto *Latin phrase meaning* "by what authority": action which questions the authority of someone **Klage wegen Amtsanmaßung**

q.v. *or* **quod vide** *Latin phrase meaning* "which see" **siehe unten**

Rr

R = REGINA, REX
NOTE: used in reports of cases where the Crown is a party: *R. v. Smith Ltd*

race *noun* group of human beings with similar physical characteristics **Rasse; race relations** = relations between different racial groups in a country **Beziehungen zwischen den Rassen**
◊ **racial** *adjective* referring to race **Rassen-; racial hatred** = violent dislike of someone *or* of a group of people because of race **Rassenhaß; incitement to racial hatred** = offence of encouraging (by words *or* actions *or* writing) people to attack others because of their race **Aufhetzung zum Rassenhaß; racial prejudice** *or* **racial discrimination** = treating people in different ways because of differences in race **Rassenvorurteil; Rassendiskriminierung**

rack rent *noun* (i) full yearly rent of a property let on a normal lease; (ii) very high rent (i) **volle Jahresmiete/Jahrespacht; (ii) überhöhte Miete/Pacht**

racket *noun* illegal deal *or* business which makes a lot of money by fraud **Gaunerei, Betrügerei, Schiebung;** *he runs a cheap ticket racket; see also* PROTECTION
◊ **racketeer** *noun* person who runs a racket **Gauner/-in, Betrüger/-in, Gangster; Erpresser/-in**
◊ **racketeering** *noun* running a racket **organisierte Kriminalität; Schutzgelderpressung**

raid
1 *noun* sudden attack *or* search **Überfall, Angriff; Razzia;** *six people were arrested in the police raid on the club*
2 *verb* to make a sudden attack *or* search **überfallen, angreifen; eine Razzia machen;** *the police have raided several houses in the town; drugs were found when the police raided the club*

raise
1 *noun* US increase in salary **Gehalts-, Lohnerhöhung;** *he asked the boss for a raise; she is pleased - she has had her raise* (NOTE: British English is **rise**)
2 *verb*
(a) to ask a meeting to discuss a question **vorbringen;** *to raise a question or a point at a meeting; in answer to the point of order raised by Mr Smith;* **to raise an objection** = to object to something **einen Einwand erheben;** *the union representatives raised a series of objections to the wording of the agreement*
(b) to increase *or* to make higher **erhöhen, anheben, heraufsetzen;** *the government has raised the penalties for drug smuggling; the company raised its dividend by 10%*
(c) to obtain (money) *or* to organize (a loan) **beschaffen, aufbringen;** *the company is trying to raise the capital to fund its expansion programme; the government*

raises money by taxation; where will he raise the money from to start up his business?

rank

1 level *or* grade in the police force *or* armed services **Rang, Dienstgrad;** *he was promoted to the rank of Chief Superintendent;* **to reduce someone to the ranks** = to punish an officer reducing him to the rank of ordinary soldier **jdn degradieren**
2 *verb* to be level with **gleichrangig sein; rangieren;** *the new shares will rank pari passu with the existing ones*

ransom

1 *noun* money paid to abductors to get back someone who has been abducted **Lösegeld;** *the daughter of the banker was held by kidnappers who asked for a ransom of £1m;* **to hold someone to ransom** = to keep someone secretly until a ransom is paid **jdn bis zur Zahlung eines Lösegeldes gefangenhalten; ransom note** = message sent by kidnappers asking for a ransom to be paid **Lösegeldforderung**
2 *verb* to pay money so that someone is released **frei-, loskaufen;** *she was ransomed by her family*

rape

1 *noun* notifiable offence of forcing a woman (other than one's wife) to have sexual intercourse without her consent **Vergewaltigung, Notzucht;** *he was brought to court and charged with rape; the incidence of cases of rape has increased over the last years*
2 *verb* to force (a woman other than one's wife) to have sexual intercourse without her consent **vergewaltigen**

rata *see* = PRO RATA

rate

1 *noun*
(a) money charged for time worked *or* work completed **Satz, Gebühr, Preis; all-in rate** = price which covers all items in a purchase (such as delivery, tax and insurance, as well as the goods themselves) **Inklusivpreis; fixed rate** = charge which cannot be changed **fester Satz; flat rate** = charge which always stays the same **Pauschale; Grundgebühr; full rate** = full charge, with no reductions **voller Satz; reduced rate** = specially cheap charge **ermäßigter Tarif**
(b) insurance rates = amount of premium which has to be paid per £1,000 of insurance **Versicherungsprämiensatz; interest rate** *or* **rate of interest** = percentage charge for borrowing money **Zinssatz; rate**

of return = amount of interest *or* dividend which comes from an investment, shown as a percentage of the money invested **Rendite**
(c) exchange rate *or* **rate of exchange** = rate at which one currency is exchanged for another **Wechselkurs; forward rate** = rate for purchase of foreign currency at a fixed price for delivery at a later date **Devisenterminkurs; freight rates** = charges for carrying goods **Frachtgebühren; letter rate** *or* **parcel rate** = postage (calculated by weight) for sending a letter *or* a parcel **Briefgebühr; Paketgebühr; night rate** = cheap telephone calls at night **Nachttarif**
(d) amount *or* number *or* speed compared with something else **Rate, Geschwindigkeit; birth rate** = number of children born per 1,000 of the population **Geburtenrate; error rate** = number of mistakes per thousand entries *or* per page **Fehlerquote**
(e) *GB (usually plural)* local tax on property; *entspricht* **Gemeindeabgabe, Grundsteuer;** *the local authority has fixed or has set the rate for next year; our rates have gone up by 25% this year;* **to set a legal rate** = to fix a rate which is within the limits approved by Parliament **die Gemeindeabgabe innerhalb der gesetzlich vorgeschriebenen Grenzen festsetzen**
2 *verb*
(a) to rate someone highly = to value someone *or* to think someone is very good **jdn hoch einschätzen**
(b) highly-rated part of London = part of London with high local taxes **ein Londoner Stadtteil mit hohen Gemeindeabgaben**

◊ **rateable** *adjective* **rateable value** = value of a property as a basis for calculating local taxes **Einheitswert**

◊ **ratepayer** *noun* **domestic ratepayer** = person who pays local taxes on a house *or* flat **privater Gemeindeabgabenzahler; business ratepayer** = business which pays local taxes on a shop *or* factory, etc. **kommerzieller Gemeindeabgabenzahler**

ratify *verb* to approve officially (something which has already been agreed) **ratifizieren, genehmigen;** *the treaty was ratified by Congress; the agreement has to be ratified by the board; although the directors had acted without due authority, the company ratified their actions*

◊ **ratification** *noun* official approval of something which then becomes legally binding **Ratifizierung, Genehmigung**

ratio decidendi *Latin phrase meaning* "reason for deciding": main part of a court judgment setting out the legal principles applicable to the case and forming the binding part of the judgment to which other courts must pay regard **Entscheidungsgrund;** *see also* OBITER DICTA

RD = REFER TO DRAWER

re *preposition* about *or* concerning *or* referring to **betrifft, bezüglich, in Bezugnahme auf;** *re your inquiry of May 29th; re: Smith's memorandum of yesterday; re: the agenda for the AGM;* **in re** = concerning *or* in the case of **in Sachen;** *in re Jones & Co. Ltd*

re- *prefix* again **wieder-**

rea *see* MENS REA

reach *verb* to come to *or* to arrive at **erzielen, kommen zu, gelangen;** *to reach an agreement; the jury was unable to reach a unanimous decision*

reading *noun* **First Reading** *or* **Second Reading** *or* **Third Reading** = the three stages of discussion of a Bill in Parliament **erste od zweite od dritte Lesung**

COMMENT: First Reading is the formal presentation of the Bill; Second Reading is the stage when the Bill is explained by the Minister proposing it and a vote is taken; the Bill is then discussed in Committee and at the Report Stage; Third Reading is the final discussion of the Bill in the whole House of Commons

real *adjective*
(a) true *or* not an imitation **echt;** *his case is made of real leather or he has a real leather case; that car is a real bargain at £300;* **real income** *or* **real wages** = income which is available for spending after tax, etc. has been deducted **Realeinkommen; Reallohn; in real terms** = actually *or* really **Real-, effektiv, in reeller Kaufkraft;** *sales have gone up by 3% but with inflation running at 5% that is a fall in real terms*
(b) real time = time when a computer is working on the processing of data while the problem to which the data refers is actually taking place **Echtzeit, Real-time; real-time system** = computer system where data is inputted directly into the computer which automatically processes it to produce information which can be used immediately **Echtzeitsystem**
(c) referring to things as opposed to persons **dinglich, Sach-; chattels real** = leaseholds **Rechte an einem Grundstück**
(d) referring to land (especially freehold land) **dinglich, unbeweglich; real estate** *or* **real property** = land or buildings considered from a legal point of view **Grundbesitz,** Grundstück, Grund und Boden, Immobilien, unbewegliches Vermögen

realize *verb*
(a) to understand clearly **begreifen, sich klarmachen, sich über etwas im Klaren sein;** *counsel realized the defendant was making a bad impression on the jury; the small shopkeepers realized that the supermarket would take away some of their trade; when he went into the police station he did not realize he was going to be arrested*
(b) to make something become real **verwirklichen, realisieren, durchführen; to realize a project** *or* **a plan** = to put a project *or* a plan into action **einen Plan ausführen**
(c) to sell something to produce money **veräußern, zu Geld machen; erzielen;** *to realize property or assets; the sale realized £100,000*
◊ **realizable** *adjective* **realizable assets** = assets which can be sold for money **leicht realisierbare Aktivposten, flüssige Mittel**
◊ **realization** *noun*
(a) gradual understanding **Erkenntnis;** *the chairman's realization that he was going to be outvoted*
(b) making real **Verwirklichung, Realisierung, Durchführung; the realization of a project** = putting a plan into action **die Ausführung eines Planes;** *the plan moved a stage nearer realization when the contracts were signed*
(c) realization of assets = selling of assets for money **Veräußerung von Vermögenswerten**

realty *noun* property *or* real estate *or* legal rights to land **Grundbesitz, Grundstück, Immobilien; Rechte an Grund und Boden** NOTE: no plural

reapply *verb* to apply again **erneut beantragen; erneut bewerben;** *the company reapplied for an injunction against the union; she reapplied for a maintenance order; when he saw that the job had still not been filled, he reapplied for it*
◊ **reapplication** *noun* second application **erneuter Antrag; erneute Bewerbung**

reason *noun* thing which explains why something has happened **Grund, Motiv, Begründung;** *the defence gave no reason for their objections to the juror; the chairman of the magistrates asked him for the reason why he was late again; the witness was asked for his reasons for returning to the fire*
◊ **reasonable** *adjective*
(a) sensible *or* not annoyed **vernünftig; verständnisvoll;** *the magistrates were very reasonable when she explained that the driving licence was necessary for her work;* **beyond reasonable doubt** = so that no

reasonable person could doubt it (proof needed to convict a person in a criminal case) **ohne jeden (berechtigten) Zweifel;** *the prosecution in a criminal case has to establish beyond reasonable doubt that the accused committed the crime;* **no reasonable offer refused** = we will accept any offer which is not too low **jedes reelle Angebot wird angenommen**
(b) not expensive **angemessen, annehmbar, vernünftig;** *the restaurant offers good food at reasonable prices*

◊ **reasoned** *adjective* carefully thought out and explained **durchdacht;** *after three months, the judge delivered a reasoned judgment*

◊ **reasoning** *noun* thinking which produces a decision **Gedankengang, Argumentation;** *it is difficult to understand the reasoning behind the judge's decision*

rebate *noun* money returned **Rückerstattung; rent rebate** = state subsidy paid to poor people who do not have enough income to pay their rents **Mietbeihilfe**

rebel
1 *noun* person who fights against the government *or* against people in authority **Rebell/-in, Aufständischer;** *anti-government rebels have taken six towns; rebel ratepayers have occupied the town hall*
2 *verb* to fight against authority **rebellieren, sich auflehnen**
NOTE: rebelling - rebelled

◊ **rebellion** *noun* fight against the government *or* against those in authority **Rebellion, Aufruhr, Aufstand;** *the army has crushed the rebellion in the southern province*

rebut *verb* to contradict *or* to go against **widerlegen; ablehnen;** *he attempted to rebut the assertions made by the prosecution witness*
NOTE: rebutting - rebutted

◊ **rebuttal** *noun* act of rebutting **Widerlegung; Ablehnung, Zurückweisung**

recall *verb*
(a) to ask someone to come back **zurückrufen;** *the witness was recalled to the witness box*
(b) to remember **sich erinnern;** *the witness could not recall having seen the accused*

recapture *verb* to capture again **wieder gefangennehmen;** *six prisoners escaped, but they were all quickly recaptured*

recd = RECEIVED

receipt
1 *noun*
(a) paper showing that money has been paid *or* that something has been received **Quittung, Beleg, Empfangsbestätigung;** *customs receipt; rent receipt; receipt for items purchased; please produce your receipt if you want to exchange items;* **receipt book** *or* **book of receipts** = book of blank receipts to be filled in when purchases are made **Quittungsblock**
(b) act of receiving something **Empfang, Eingang, Erhalt;** *goods will be supplied within thirty days of receipt of order; invoices are payable within thirty days of receipt; on receipt of the notification, the company lodged an appeal;* **to acknowledge receipt of a letter** = to write to say that you have received a letter **den Empfang eines Schreibens bestätigen;** *we acknowledge receipt of your letter of the 15th;* **we are in receipt of your letter of** = having received your letter of **wir erhielten Ihr Schreiben vom;** *we are in receipt of a letter of complaint; he was accused of being in receipt of stolen cheques*
(c) receipts = money taken in sales **Einnahmen, Einkünfte;** *to itemize receipts and expenditure; receipts are down against the same period of last year* (NOTE: no plural for (b))
2 *verb* to stamp *or* to sign a document to show that it has been received *or* to stamp an invoice to show that it has been paid **Empfang bestätigen, quittieren**

receive *verb*
(a) to get something which has been delivered **erhalten, empfangen;** *we received the payment ten days ago; the workers have not received any salary for six months; the goods were received in good condition;* **"received with thanks"** = words put on an invoice to show that a sum has been paid **"dankend erhalten"**
(b) to receive stolen goods = crime of taking in and disposing of property which you know to be stolen **Hehlerei begehen**

◊ **receivable** *adjective* which can be received **ausstehend, offen; accounts receivable** = money owed by debtors **Außenstände**

◊ **receivables** *plural noun* money which is owed by debtors **Forderungen**

◊ **receiver** *noun*
(a) person who receives something **Empfänger/-in; receiver of wrecks** = official of the Department of Trade who deals with legal problems of wrecked ships within his area **Strandvogt**
(b) Official Receiver = (i) person who is appointed to administer a company for a period until the person who has appointed him has been paid money due; (ii)

government official who is appointed to administer the liquidation of a limited company after a winding up by the court *or* the affairs of a bankrupt after a receiving order has been made **(i) Zwangsverwalter; (ii) Konkursverwalter;** *the court appointed a receiver for the company; the company is in the hands of the receiver; the Court of Protection appointed a receiver to administer the client's affairs*
(c) person who receives stolen goods and disposes of them **Hehler/-in**

◊ **receivership** *noun* administration by a receiver **Zwangsverwaltung; Konkursverwaltung; the company went into receivership** = the company was put into the hands of a receiver **das Unternehmen hat Konkurs gemacht**
NOTE: no plural

◊ **receiving** *noun*
(a) act of taking something which has been delivered **Empfang, Annahme; receiving clerk** = official who works in a receiving office **Angestellter in der (Waren)annahme; receiving department** = section of a company which deals with goods *or* payments which are received by the company **Warenannahme; receiving office** = office where goods *or* payments are received **Warenannahme; Einzahlungsschalter; receiving stolen property** = crime of taking in and disposing of goods which are known to be stolen **Hehlerei**
(b) receiving order = court order made placing the Official Receiver in charge of a person's assets before a bankruptcy order is made **vorläufiger Konkurseröffnungsbeschluß**

recess *noun* period when Parliament is not sitting **Sitzungspause**

recession *noun* fall in general trade *or* the economy **Rezession, Konjunkturrückgang;** *the recession has put many people out of work; he lost all his money in the recession*

recidivist *noun* criminal who commits a crime again **Gewohnheitstäter, rückfälliger Täter**

recipient *noun* person who receives something **Empfänger/-in;** *the recipient of an allowance from the company*

reciprocal *adjective* given by one country *or* person *or* company to another and vice versa; (arrangement) where each party agrees to benefit the other in the same way **wechsel-, gegenseitig; reciprocal holdings** = situation where two companies own shares in each other to prevent takeover bids **gegenseitige Beteiligung;**

reciprocal trade = trade between two countries **gegenseitiger Handel; reciprocal will** = will where two people (usually man and wife) leave their property to each other **gegenseitiges Testament**

◊ **reciprocate** *verb* to do the same thing to someone as he has just done to you **sich revanchieren, etwas als Gegenleistung tun;** *they offered us an exclusive agency for their cars and we reciprocated with an offer of the agency for our buses*

◊ **reciprocity** *noun* arrangement which applies from one party to another and vice versa **Gegenseitigkeit, Reziprozität**

recitals *plural noun* introduction to a deed *or* conveyance which sets out the main purpose and the parties to it **einleitender Teil**

reckless *adjective* (person) who takes a risk even if he knows that what he does may be dangerous **rücksichtslos, leichtfertig; reckless driving** = offence of driving a car in a wild way where the driver does not think he is causing a risk to other people **rücksichtsloses/grob fahrlässiges Fahren**

COMMENT: causing death by reckless driving is a notifiable offence

◊ **recklessly** *adverb* taking risks, and not caring about the effect on other people **rücksichtslos, leichtfertig;** *the company recklessly spent millions of pounds on a new factory; he was accused of driving recklessly*

◊ **recklessness** *noun* (act of) taking risks, without caring if other people may be harmed **Rücksichtslosigkeit, Leichtfertigkeit, (grobe) Fahrlässigkeit**

reclaim *verb* to claim back money which has been paid earlier **zurückfordern**

recognize *verb*
(a) to know someone *or* something because you have seen *or* heard them before **erkennen, wiedererkennen;** *she recognized the man who attacked her; I recognized his voice before he said who he was; do you recognize the handwriting on the letter?*
(b) to approve something as being legal **anerkennen; to recognize a government** = to say that a government which has taken power in a foreign country is the legal government of that country **eine Regierung anerkennen; the prisoner refused to recognize the jurisdiction of the court** = the prisoner said that he did not believe that the court had the legal right to try him **der Häftling weigerte sich, die Zuständigkeit des Gerichtes anzuerkennen; to recognize a union** = to accept that a union can act on behalf of staff **eine Gewerkschaft anerkennen;** *although*

all the staff had joined the union, the management refused to recognize it; **recognized agent** = agent who is approved by the company for which he acts **zugelassener Vertreter**

◊ **recognition** *noun* act of recognizing **Anerkennung; to grant a trade union recognition** = to recognize a trade union **eine Gewerkschaft anerkennen**

◊ **recognizance** *noun* obligation undertaken by someone to a court that he *or* someone else will appear in court at a later date to answer charges, or if not, he will pay a penalty **Kautionsversprechen für den Fall des Nichterscheinens vor Gericht;** *he was remanded on his own recognizance of £4,000;* **estreated recognizance** = recognizance which is forfeited because the person making it has not come to court **verwirkte Kaution wegen Nichterscheinens vor Gericht**

recommend *verb*
(a) to suggest that something should be done **empfehlen, raten zu;** *the legal adviser recommended applying for an injunction against the directors of the company; we do not recommend bank shares as a safe investment; the Parole Board recommended him for parole; he was sentenced to life imprisonment, the judge recommending that he should serve a minimum of twenty years*
(b) to say that someone *or* something is good **empfehlen;** *I certainly would not recommend Miss Smith for the job; the board meeting recommended a dividend of 10p a share; can you recommend a good hotel in Amsterdam?*
NOTE: you recommend someone **for** a job or you recommend something **to** someone or that someone **should do something**

◊ **recommendation** *noun*
(a) advising that something should be done **Empfehlung;** *he was sentenced to life imprisonment, with a recommendation that he should serve at least twenty years; he was released on the recommendation of the Parole Board or on the Parole Board's recommendation*
(b) saying that someone *or* something is good **Empfehlung;** *we appointed him on the recommendation of his former employer*

reconcile *verb* to make two accounts *or* statements agree **abstimmen;** *to reconcile one account with another; to reconcile the accounts*

◊ **reconciliation** *noun* making two accounts *or* parties *or* statements agree **Abstimmung; Aussöhnung; Ausgleich; reconciliation statement** = statement which explains why two accounts do not agree **Erklärung von Kontenabstimmungsdifferenzen**

reconstruction *noun* new way of organizing **Reorganisation;** the **reconstruction of a company** = restructuring the finances of a company by transferring the assets to a new company **Reorganisation/Sanierung eines Unternehmens**

re-convict *verb* to convict someone again who has previously been convicted of a crime **erneut verurteilen**

◊ **re-conviction** *noun* conviction of someone who has been previously convicted of a crime **erneute Verurteilung;** *the re-conviction rate is rising*

record
1 *noun*
(a) report of something which has happened, especially an official transcript of a court action **Protokoll, Aufzeichnung; Gerichtsakte;** *the chairman signed the minutes as a true record of the last meeting;* **a matter of record** = something which has been written down and can be confirmed **aktenmäßig feststehende Tatsache; for the record** *or* **to keep the record straight** = to note something which has been done **für das Protokoll; on record** = (fact) which has been noted **schriftlich niedergelegt, protokolliert;** *the chairman is on record as saying that profits are set to rise;* **off the record** = unofficially *or* in private **inoffiziell;** *he made some remarks off the record about the rising crime figures*
(b) records = documents which give information **Unterlagen, Aufzeichnungen, Akten;** *the names of customers are kept in the company's records; we find from our records that our invoice number 1234 has not been paid*
(c) description of what has happened in the past **Vorgeschichte;** *the clerk's record of service or service record; the company's record in industrial relations;* **criminal record** = note of previous crimes for which someone has been convicted **Vorstrafe;** *he has a criminal record stretching back twenty years; the court was told she had no previous criminal record;* **track record** = success or failure of someone in the past **Leistungsnachweis;** *he has a good track record as a detective; the company has no track record in the computer market*
(d) result which is better *or* higher than anything before **Rekord; record crime figures** *or* **record losses** *or* **record profits** = crime figures *or* losses *or* profits which are higher than ever before **Rekordzahl an Verbrechen; Rekordverluste; Höchstgewinne;** *1985 was a record year for bankruptcies;*

road accidents in 1983 equalled the record of 1980; the figure for muggings has set a new record or has broken all previous records
2 *verb* to note *or* to report **aufzeichnen, protokollieren; registrieren, verzeichnen;** *the company has recorded another year of increased sales; your complaint has been recorded and will be investigated; the court recorded a plea of not guilty; the coroner recorded a verdict of death by misadventure;* **recorded delivery =** mail service where a receipt for the letter is signed by the person receiving it **Einschreiben**

◊ **recorder** *noun* part-time judge of the Crown Court **nebenberuflicher Richter; Recorder of London =** chief judge of the Central Criminal Court **oberster Richter des Central Criminal Court in London;** *see comment at* JUDGE

◊ **recording** *noun* making of a note **Aufzeichnung, Eintragung; Registrierung;** *the recording of an order or of a complaint*

recours *see* SANS

recourse *noun* **to decide to have recourse to the courts =** to decide in the end to start legal proceedings **die Inanspruchnahme des Gerichts beschließen**

recover *verb*
(a) to get back something which has been lost **zurückbekommen, wiedererlangen;** *he never recovered his money; the initial investment was never recovered; to recover damages from the driver of the car; to start a court action to recover property*
(b) to get better *or* to rise **sich erholen, einen Aufschwung nehmen;** *the market has not recovered from the rise in oil prices; the stock market fell in the morning, but recovered during the afternoon*

◊ **recoverable** *adjective* which can be got back **eintreibbar**

◊ **recovery** *noun*
(a) getting back something which has been lost *or* stolen **Wiederbeschaffung, Wiedererlangung;** *we are aiming for the complete recovery of the money invested; to start an action for recovery of property*
(b) movement upwards of shares *or* of the economy **Aufschwung, Wiederbelebung;** *the economy showed signs of a recovery; the recovery of the economy after a recession*

recruit
1 *noun* new member of a police force *or* other organization **Rekrut/-in, neues Mitglied;** *new recruits have to take a special training course*

2 *verb* to get people to join an organization **rekrutieren, Mitglieder werben;** *twenty-five women were recruited into the local police force*

◊ **recruitment** *noun* action of recruiting **Rekrutierung, Anwerbung von Mitgliedern;** *the recruitment rate is rising*
NOTE: no plural

rectify *verb* to make changes to a document to make it correct *or* to make something correct **berichtigen, korrigieren;** *the court rectified its mistake*

◊ **rectification** *noun* making changes to a document *or* register to make it correct **Berichtigung, Korrektur**

red bag *noun* bag in which a barrister carries his gown, given him by a QC **Tasche des Barristers für seinen Talar;** *see also* BLUE BAG

redeem *verb*
(a) to pay back all the principal and interest on a loan *or* a debt *or* a mortgage **abzahlen, tilgen, ablösen**
(b) **to redeem a bond =** to sell a bond for cash **eine Schuldverschreibung tilgen**

◊ **redeemable** *adjective* which can be sold for cash **einlösbar, rückkaufbar; redeemable preference shares =** preference shares which the company may buy back from the shareholder for cash **rückkaufbare Vorzugsaktien**

redemption *noun*
(a) repayment of a loan **Tilgung, Rückzahlung; redemption date =** date on which a loan, etc., is due to be repaid **Tilgungstermin; redemption before due date =** paying back a loan before the date when repayment is due **Rückzahlung vor Fälligkeit; redemption value =** value of a security when redeemed **Rückkaufswert**
(b) repayment of a debt *or* a mortgage **Tilgung, Rückzahlung; Ablösung; equity of redemption =** right of a mortgagor to redeem the estate by paying off the principal and interest **Auslösungsrecht (des Hypothekenschuldners)**

red tape *noun* (i) red ribbon used to tie up a pile of legal documents; (ii) rules which slow down administrative work **(i) rotes Band (mit dem Dokumente verschnürt werden); (ii) Bürokratismus, Amtsschimmel;** *the application has been held up by red tape*

reduce *verb* to make smaller *or* lower **reduzieren, verringern, herabsetzen, ermäßigen, senken;** *to reduce expenditure on prisons or on crime detection; the Appeal*

Court reduced the fine imposed by the magistrates or reduced the sentence to seven years' imprisonment; we have made some staff redundant to reduce costs; the government's policy is to reduce inflation to 5%

◊ **reduced** *adjective* lower **reduziert, ermäßigt, herabgesetzt, geringer;** *he received a reduced sentence on appeal; prices have fallen due to a reduced demand for the goods*

◊ **reduction** *noun* lowering of prices, etc. Reduzierung, Ermäßigung, Herabsetzung, Verringerung, Senkung; *price reductions; tax reductions; staff reductions; reduction of expenditure; reduction in demand; a reduction in the nominal capital of a limited company requires the leave of a court*

redundancy *noun*

(a) state where someone is no longer employed, because the job is no longer necessary **Arbeitslosigkeit nach Rationalisierung; redundancy payment** = payment made to a worker to compensate for losing his job **Entlassungsabfindung; voluntary redundancy** = situation where the worker asks to be made redundant, usually in return for a payment **freiwillige Arbeitsplatzaufgabe**
(b) person who has lost a job because he is not needed any more **Arbeitsloser;** *the takeover caused 250 redundancies*

◊ **redundant** *adjective*
(a) more than is needed *or* useless; something which is no longer needed **überflüssig, überzählig;** *this law is now redundant; a redundant clause in a contract; the new legislation has made clause 6 redundant*
(b) to make someone redundant = to decide that a worker is not needed any more **jdn entlassen; redundant staff** = staff who have lost their jobs because they are not needed any more **entlassene Arbeitskräfte**

re-entry *noun* going back into a property
Wiedereintritt; right of re-entry = (i) right of a landlord to take back possession of the property if the tenant breaks his agreement; (ii) right of a person resident in a country to go back into that country after leaving it for a time **(i) Recht zur Wiederinbesitznahme; (ii) Recht zur Wiedereinreise**

re-examine *verb (of counsel)* to ask his own witness more questions after the witness has been cross-examined by counsel for the other party **erneut vernehmen**

◊ **re-examination** *noun* asking a witness more questions after cross-examination by counsel for the other party **erneute (Zeugen)vernehmung**

refer *verb*
(a) to mention *or* to deal with *or* to write about something **erwähnen, (sich) beziehen, Bezug nehmen;** *we refer to your letter of May 26th; he referred to an article which he had seen in "The Times"; referring to the court order dated June 4th;* **the schedule before referred to** = the schedule which has been mentioned earlier **der zuvor erwähnte Terminplan**
(b) to pass a problem on to someone else to decide **weiterleiten, verweisen;** *to refer a question to a committee; we have referred your complaint to the tribunal*
(c) the bank referred the cheque to drawer = the bank returned the cheque to person who wrote it because there was not enough money in the account to pay it **die Bank schickte den Scheck an den Aussteller zurück;** **"refer to drawer"** = words written on a cheque which a bank refuses to pay **"vorgelegt und nicht eingelöst", "an den Aussteller zurück"**
NOTE: **referring - referred**

◊ **referee** *noun*
(a) person who can give a report on someone's character *or* ability *or* speed of work, etc. **Referenz;** *to give someone's name as referee; she gave the name of her boss as a referee; when applying please give the names of three referees*
(b) person to whom a problem is passed for a decision **Schiedsrichter; Sachverständiger;** *the question of maintenance payments is with a court-appointed referee;* **official referee** = expert judge appointed by the High Court to try complicated, usually technical, cases where specialist knowledge is required **beauftragter Richter**

◊ **reference** *noun*
(a) passing a problem to a referee for his opinion **Vorlage einer Frage an einen Schiedsrichter od Sachverständigen; terms of reference** = areas which a committee *or* an inspector can deal with **Aufgabenbereich, Zuständigkeit;** *under the terms of reference of the committee, it cannot investigate complaints from the public; the tribunal's terms of reference do not cover traffic offences*
(b) mentioning *or* dealing with **Bezug;** *with reference to your letter of May 25th*
(c) numbers or letters which make it possible to find a document which has been filed **(Akten)zeichen;** *our reference: PC/MS 1234; thank you for your letter (reference 1234); please quote this reference in all correspondence; when replying please quote reference 1234*

(d) written report on someone's character *or* ability, etc. **Referenz, Zeugnis;** *to write someone a reference or to give someone a reference; to ask applicants to supply references;* **to ask a company for trade references** *or* **for bank references** = to ask a company to give names of traders or banks who can report on the company's financial status and reputation **ein Unternehmen um Handelsauskünfte/Bankreferenzen ersuchen; letter of reference** = letter in which an employer or former employer recommends someone for a job **Zeugnis, Referenz**
(e) person who reports on someone's character *or* ability, etc. **Referenz;** *to give someone's name as reference; please use me as a reference if you wish*

referendum *noun* type of vote, where a whole population is asked to vote on a single question **Referendum, Volksentscheid;** *the government decided to hold a referendum on the abolition of capital punishment*
NOTE: plural is **referenda**

reform

1 *noun* change made to something to make it better **Reform;** *they have signed an appeal for the reform of the remand system; the reform in the legislation was intended to make the court procedure more straightforward;* **law reform** = continuing process of revising laws to make them better suited to the needs of society **Rechtsreform**
2 *verb* to change something to make it better **reformieren, verbessern;** *the group is pressing for the prison system to be reformed; the prisoner has committed so many crimes of violence that he will never be reformed*

refrain *verb* **to refrain from something** = to agree not to do something which you were doing previously **etwas unterlassen;** *he was asked to give an undertaking to refrain from political activity*

refresher *noun* fee paid to counsel for the second and subsequent days of a hearing **außerordentliches Anwaltshonorar (bei mehrtägiger Verhandlungsdauer);** *counsel's brief fee was £1,000 with refreshers of £250*

refund

1 *noun* money paid back **Rückerstattung; full refund** *or* **refund in full** = refund of all the money paid **Rückvergütung in voller Höhe**

2 *verb* to pay back money **erstatten, rückerstatten, zurückzahlen;** *to refund the cost of postage; travelling expenses will be refunded to witnesses giving evidence to the tribunal; all money will be refunded if the goods are not satisfactory*

refuse *verb* to say that you will not do something *or* will not accept something **ablehnen, nicht gewähren, verweigern, sich weigern;** *the court refused to allow the witness to speak; the accused refused to take the oath; the bank refused to lend the company any more money; he asked for a rise but it was refused; the loan was refused by the bank; the customer refused the goods or refused to accept the goods*
NOTE: you **refuse to do something** or **refuse something**

◊ **refusal** *noun* saying "No" **Ablehnung, Weigerung, Verweigerung, Absage;** *his request met with a refusal* = his request was refused **auf sein Gesuch bekam er einen abschlägigen Bescheid; to give someone first refusal of something** = to allow someone to be the first to decide if they want something or not **jdm das Vorkaufsrecht einräumen; blanket refusal** = refusal to accept many different items **allgemeine Ablehnung**

regard *noun* **having regard to** *or* **as regards** *or* **regarding** = concerning *or* referring to something **betreffend, was ... anbetrifft, im Hinblick auf;** *having regard to the opinion of the European Parliament; as regards or regarding the second of the accused, the jury was unable to reach a majority verdict*

◊ **regardless** *adverb* **regardless of** = without concerning **ungeachtet, ohne Berücksichtigung;** *such conduct constitutes contempt of court regardless of intent; the court takes a serious view of such crimes, regardless of the age of the accused*

Regina *Latin word meaning* "the Queen": the Crown *or* state, as a party in legal proceedings **die Königin, die Krone, der Staat**
NOTE: in written reports, usually abbreviated to **R: the case of** *R. v. Smith*

register

1 *noun*

(a) official list

Verzeichnis, Liste; *to enter something in a register; to keep a register up to date;* **companies' register** *or* **register of companies** = list of companies, showing their directors and registered addresses, and statutory information kept at Companies House for public inspection **Handelsregister; Gesellschaftsregister; register of charges** = index of charges affecting land **Hypothekenregister; register of debentures** *or* **debenture register** = list of debentures over a company's assets **Verzeichnis der Obligationäre; register of directors** = official list of the directors of a company which has to be sent to the Registrar of Companies **Vorstandsverzeichnis; register of electors** = list of names and addresses of all people in an area who are entitled to vote in local or national elections **Wählerliste; land register** = list of land, showing who owns it and what buildings are on it **Grundbuch; Lloyd's register** = classified list showing details of all the ships in the world **Lloyd's Register; register of members** *or* **of shareholders** *or* **share register** = list of shareholders in a company with their addresses **Aktienbuch, Verzeichnis der Aktionäre**
(b) large book for recording details (as in a hotel, where guests sign in, or in a registry where deaths are recorded) **Eintragungsbuch**
2 *verb*
(a) to write something in an official list *or* record **eintragen, registrieren, eintragen lassen, erfassen;** *to register a company; to register a sale; to register a property; to register a trademark; to register a marriage or a death*
(b) to arrive at a hotel *or* at a conference, sign your name and write your address on a list **sich eintragen/anmelden;** *they registered at the hotel under the name of MacDonald*
(c) to send (a letter) by registered post **als/per Einschreiben schicken;** *I registered the letter, because it contained some money*

◊ **registered** *adjective*
(a) which has been noted on an official list **eingetragen, registriert, angemeldet; registered company** = company which has been properly formed and incorporated **eingetragene Gesellschaft; registered land** = land which has been registered with the land registry **(in das Grundbuch) eingetragener Grundbesitz; a company's registered office** = the address of a company which is officially registered with the Registrar of Companies and to which certain legal documents must normally be sent **der eingetragene Sitz/Hauptsitz der Gesellschaft; registered trademark** = trademark which has been officially recorded **eingetragenes Warenzeichen; registered user** = person *or* company which has been officially given a licence to use a registered trademark **eingetragener Lizenznehmer**
(b) **registered letter** *or* **registered parcel** = letter *or* parcel which is noted by the post office before it is sent, so that compensation can be claimed if it is lost **Einschreibebrief; eingeschriebenes Päckchen;** *to send documents by registered mail or registered post*

◊ **registrar** *noun*
(a) person who keeps official records **Registrator, Registerführer; Standesbeamter; Archivar; Registrar of Companies** = official who keeps a record of all companies which have been incorporated, with details of directors and turnover; *entspricht* **Registerbevollmächtigter; registrar of trademarks** = official who keeps a record of all trademarks **Führer der Warenzeichenrolle**
(b) official of a court who can hear preliminary arguments in civil cases **Gerichtsbeamter; Rechtspfleger**
(c) **district registrar** = official who registers births, marriages and deaths in a certain area **Standesbeamter eines Gerichtsbezirkes**

◊ **Registrar-General** *noun* official who is responsible for registry offices and the registering of births, marriages and deaths **oberster Standesbeamter**

◊ **registration** *noun*
(a) act of having something noted on an official list **Eintragung, Registrierung, Anmeldung, Erfassung;** *registration of a trademark or of a share transaction;* **certificate of registration** *or* **registration certificate** = document showing that an item has been registered **Eintragungsbescheinigung; registration fee** = money paid to have something registered *or* money paid to attend a conference **Anmeldegebühr; registration number** = official number of something which has been registered (such as the number of a car) **Eintragungsnummer, Registrierungsnummer; Kraftfahrzeugkennzeichen**
(b) **land registration** = system of registering land and its owners **Grundbucheintragung**

◊ **registry** *noun*
(a) place where official records are kept **Registratur, Registeramt; Land Registry** = British government office where details of land are kept **Grundbuch-, Katasteramt; probate registry** = court office which deals with the granting of probate **Geschäftsstelle des Nachlaßgerichts; district registry** *or* **registry office** = office where records of births, marriages and deaths are kept **Standesamt**
(b) registering of a ship **Eintragung in das Schiffsregister; certificate of registry** = document showing that a ship has been

officially registered **Schiffsbrief; port of registry** or **registry port** = port where a ship is registered **Heimathafen**

regulate verb
(a) to adjust something so that it works well or is correct **regulieren, einstellen, ordnen**
(b) to change or maintain something by law **(gesetzlich) regeln; prices are regulated by supply and demand** = prices are increased or lowered according to supply and demand **Preise werden durch Angebot und Nachfrage bestimmt; government-regulated price** = price which is imposed by the government **staatlich vorgeschriebener Preis; regulated tenancy** = PROTECTED TENANCY

◊ **regulation** noun act of making sure that something will work well **Regelung, Regulierung;** the regulation of trading practices

◊ **regulations** plural noun
(a) laws or rules made by ministers, which then have to be submitted to Parliament for approval **Satzung, Statuten, Vorschriften;** the new government regulations on standards for electrical goods; safety regulations which apply to places of work; regulations concerning imports and exports; **fire regulations** = local or national regulations which owners of buildings used by the public have to obey in order to be granted a fire certificate **Feuerschutzbestimmungen**
(b) rules laid down by the Commission of the European Communities, which do not have legal force in member countries **Verordnungen**

rehabilitate verb to make (a criminal) fit to become a member of society again **rehabilitieren**

◊ **rehabilitation** noun making someone fit to be a member of society again **Rehabilitierung; rehabilitation of offenders** = principle whereby a person convicted of a crime and being of good character after a period of time is treated as though he had not had a conviction **Resozialisierung von Straftätern**

COMMENT: by the Rehabilitation of Offenders Act, 1974, a person who is convicted of an offence, and then spends a period of time without committing any other offence, is not required to reveal that he has a previous conviction

rehear verb to hear a case again (such as when the first hearing was in some way invalid) **nochmals verhandeln**

◊ **rehearing** noun hearing of a case again **nochmalige Verhandlung, Berufungsverfahren**

reign
1 noun period of time when someone is King or Queen **Herrschaft;** an Act dating back to the reign of Queen Victoria
2 verb
(a) to be King or Queen **herrschen**
(b) to exist **herrschen;** chaos reigned in the centre of town until the police arrived

reimburse verb to pay someone back money which has been spent **erstatten, rückerstatten, vergüten;** witnesses' travelling expenses will be reimbursed

reinsurance noun insurance taken out by one insurer to protect himself in relation to insurance cover he has extended to an insured party **Rückversicherung**

reject
1 noun thing which has been thrown out because it is not of the usual standard **Ausschußware; zweite Wahl;** sale of rejects or of reject items; to sell off reject stock
2 verb to refuse to accept or to say that something is not satisfactory **ablehnen, zurückweisen, verwerfen;** the appeal was rejected by the House of Lords; the union rejected the management's proposals; the magistrate rejected a request from the defendant; **the company rejected the takeover bid** = the directors recommended that the shareholders should not accept the bid **das Unternehmen wies das Übernahmeangebot zurück**

◊ **rejection** noun refusal to accept **Ablehnung, Zurück-, Abweisung;** the rejection of the defendant's request; the rejection of the appeal by the tribunal

rejoinder noun pleading served in answer to a plaintiff's reply **Erwiderung**

relate verb **to relate to** = to refer to or to have a connection with something **sich beziehen auf**

◊ **related** adjective connected or linked or being of the same family **zusammenhängend, verbunden; verwandt;** offences related to drugs or drug-related offences; the law which relates to drunken driving; **related company** = company which is partly owned by another company **Konzerngesellschaft; earnings-related pension** = pension which is linked to the size of the salary **dynamische/lohnbezogene Rente**

◊ **relating to** adverb referring to or connected with **in Zusammenhang mit, in bezug auf;** documents relating to the case

relation *noun*
(a) **in relation to** = referring to *or* connected with **in Zusammenhang mit, in bezug auf;** *documents in relation to the case; the court's powers in relation to children in care*
(b) **relations** = links (with other people *or* other companies) **Beziehungen, Verbindungen; to enter into relations with someone** = to start discussing a business deal with someone **mit jdm in Verbindung treten; to break off relations with someone** = to stop dealing with someone **die Beziehungen zu jdm abbrechen; industrial relations** *or* **labour relations** = relations between management and workers **Arbeitnehmer-Arbeitgeber-Beziehungen, Beziehungen zwischen den Sozialpartnern; public relations** = keeping good links between a company *or* a group and the public so that people know what the company is doing and approve of it **PR-Arbeit, Public Relations, Öffentlichkeitsarbeit; public relations department** = section of a company which deals with relations with the public **PR-Abteilung, Abteilung für Öffentlichkeitsarbeit; public relations officer** = official who deals with relations with the public **Leiter der PR-Abteilung**

◊ **relationship** *noun* connection *or* link with another person *or* company **Beziehung, Verhältnis, Verbindung;** *what is the relationship between the accused and witness?; there is no relationship between the two crimes*

◊ **relatives** *or* **relations** *plural noun* members of a family *or* people with close family links to a certain person **Verwandte, Angehörige**

◊ **relator** *noun* private person who suggests to the Attorney-General that proceedings should be brought (usually against a public body) **Anzeigeerstatter**

release
1 *noun*
(a) setting (someone) free *or* allowing someone to leave prison **Freistellung; Entlassung, Freilassung; release on licence** = allowing a prisoner to leave prison on parole **bedingte Entlassung; day release** = arrangement whereby a company allows a worker to go to college to study for one day each week **Freistellung zur beruflichen Fortbildung**
(b) abandoning of rights by someone in favour of someone else **Verzicht, Aufgabe**
(c) **press release** = sheet giving news about something which is sent to newspapers and TV and radio stations so that they can use the information in it **Pressemitteilung;** *the company sent out or issued a press release about the launch of the new car*

2 *verb*
(a) to free (someone *or* something) *or* to allow (someone) to leave prison **freigeben, freistellen, befreien; entlassen, freilassen;** *the president released the opposition leader from prison; to release goods from customs; the customs released the goods against payment of a fine;* **to release someone from a debt** *or* **from a contract** = to make someone no longer liable for the debt *or* for the obligations under the contract **jdm eine Schuld erlassen; jdn aus einem Vertrag entlassen**
(b) to make something public **veröffentlichen, der Öffentlichkeit zugänglich machen;** *the company released information about the new mine in Australia; the government has refused to release figures for the number of unemployed women*

relevance *noun* connection with a subject being discussed **Relevanz;** *counsel argued with the judge over the relevance of the documents in the case*

◊ **relevant** *adjective* which has to do with what is being discussed **relevant, zuständig;** *the question is not relevant to the case; which is the relevant government department? can you give me the relevant papers?*

reliable *adjective* which can be trusted **zuverlässig, vertrauenswürdig, verläßlich;** *he is a reliable witness or the witness is completely reliable; the police have reliable information about the gang's movements*

◊ **reliability** *noun* being reliable **Zuverlässigkeit, Vertrauenswürdigkeit, Verläßlichkeit;** *the court has to decide on the reliability of the witnesses*
NOTE: no plural

relief *noun*
(a) remedy sought by a plaintiff in a legal action **Klagebegehren;** *the relief the plaintiff sought was an injunction and damages*
(b) help **Hilfe, Unterstützung; ancillary relief** = financial provision *or* adjustment of property rights ordered by a court for a spouse *or* child in divorce proceedings **Unterhaltsregelung; Wohnungs- und Haushaltsregelung; mortgage relief** = allowing someone to pay no tax on the interest payments on a mortgage **Steuervergünstigungen bei Hypothekenzahlungen; tax relief** = allowing someone to pay less tax on certain parts of his income **Steuerermäßigung**

rem *see* ACTION

remain *verb*
(a) to be left **(übrig)bleiben;** *half the stock remained on the shelves; we will sell off the old stock at half price and anything remaining will be thrown away*
(b) to stay **bleiben;** *she remained behind at the office after 6.30 to finish her work*
◇ **remainder**
1 *noun*
(a) things left behind **Rest(bestand);** *the remainder of the stock will be sold off at half price;* **remainders** = new books sold cheaply **Restauflage**
(b) right to an estate which will return to the owner at the end of a lease **Anwartschaftsrecht; contingent remainder** = remainder which is contingent upon something happening in the future **bedingtes Anwartschaftsrecht; interest in remainder** = interest in land which will come into someone's possession when another person's interest ends **Anrecht auf Anwartschaft; vested remainder** = remainder which is vested in someone because the identity of that person has been established **unentziehbares Anwartschaftsrecht;** *see also* REVERSION
2 *verb* **to remainder books** = to sell new books off cheaply **Restauflagen billig verkaufen**

remand
1 *noun* sending a prisoner away for a time when a case is adjourned to be heard at a later date **Zurücksendung in die Untersuchungshaft; prisoner on remand** *or* **remand prisoner** = prisoner who has been told to reappear in court at a later date **Untersuchungsgefangener; remand centre** = special prison for keeping young persons who have been remanded in custody **Jugendstrafanstalt**
2 *verb*
(a) to send (a prisoner) away to reappear later to answer a case which has been adjourned **in die Untersuchungshaft zurückschicken; he was remanded in custody** *or* **remanded on bail for two weeks** = he was sent to prison *or* allowed to go free on payment of bail while waiting to return to court two weeks later **er wurde in die Untersuchungshaft zurückgeschickt; er wurde gegen Kaution zwei Wochen aus der Untersuchungshaft entlassen**
(b) *US* to send a case back to a lower court after a higher court has given an opinion on it **(an die untere Instanz) zurückverweisen**

remedy
1 *noun* way of repairing harm *or* damage suffered **Abhilfe; Rechtsmittel;** *the plaintiff is seeking remedy through the courts*
2 *verb* to help repair harm *or* damage **Abhilfe schaffen, wiedergutmachen**

remember *verb* to bring back into your mind something which you have seen *or* heard *or* read before **sich erinnern, sich entsinnen; denken an;** *do you remember seeing the defendant in the house? she cannot remember where she left the jewels; he remembered the registration number of the car; the last thing he remembered was the sound of the police siren; I remember locking the door of the safe; did you remember to sign the statement?*
NOTE: you **remember doing something** which you did in the past; you **remember to do something** in the future

remind *verb* to make someone remember **erinnern;** *I must remind the court of the details of the defendant's relationship with the plaintiff; can you remind me to lock the safe?*
◇ **reminder** *noun* letter to make a person remember to pay **Mahnung;** *he paid the maintenance after several reminders*

remission *noun* reduction of a prison sentence **Straferlaß;** *he was sentenced to five years, but should serve only three with remission; she got six months' remission for good behaviour*
NOTE: no plural

remit *verb*
(a) to reduce (a prison sentence) **(eine Strafe) erlassen**
(b) to send (money) **überweisen;** *to remit by cheque*
NOTE: **remitting - remitted**
◇ **remittance** *noun* money which is sent **Überweisung;** *please send remittances to the treasurer; the family lives on a weekly remittance from their father in the USA*

remote *adjective* too far to be connected **(weit) entfernt, abgelegen; vage;** *the court decided that the damage was too remote to be recoverable by the plaintiff*
◇ **remoteness** *noun* being too far to be connected **Ferne, Entlegenheit; remoteness of damage** = legal principle that damage that is insufficiently connected *or* foreseeable by a defendant should not make the defendant liable to the plaintiff **Nichtzurechenbarkeit eines Schadens**

remove *verb* to take something away **entfernen, streichen, aufheben;** *we can remove his name from the mailing list; the government has removed the ban on imports from Japan; the minister has removed the embargo on the sale of computer equipment;* **two directors were removed from the board at the AGM** = two directors were dismissed from the board **bei der Jahreshauptversammlung wurden zwei Direktoren aus dem Vorstand ausgeschlosssen**

◊ **removal** *noun*
(a) moving to a new house *or* office **Umzug; removal company** = company which specializes in moving the contents of a house *or* an office to a new building **Spedition(sfirma),Spediteur**
(b) moving an action from one court to another **Verweisung (an ein anderes Gericht)**
(c) sacking someone (usually a director) from a job **Entlassung, Absetzung;** *the removal of the managing director is going to be very difficult*

remuneration *noun* payment for a service **Bezahlung, Lohn, Honorar;** *he receives no remuneration for his work as honorary secretary of the football club*
NOTE: no plural

render *verb* to make (someone *or* something) be **machen;** *failure to observe the conditions of bail renders the accused liable to arrest; the state of health of the witness renders his appearance in court impossible*

renew *verb* to grant something again so that it continues for a further period of time **verlängern, erneuern;** *to renew a bill of exchange or to renew a lease;* **to renew a subscription** = to pay a subscription for another year **ein Abonnement erneuern; to renew an insurance policy** = to pay the premium for another year's insurance **eine Versicherung erneuern**

◊ **renewal** *noun* act of renewing **Verlängerung, Erneuerung;** *renewal of a lease or of a subscription or of a bill; the lease is up for renewal next month; when is the renewal date of the bill?;* **renewal notice** = note sent by an insurance company asking the insured person to renew the insurance **Prämienrechnung; renewal premium** = premium to be paid to renew an insurance **Folgeprämie**

renounce *verb* to give up a right *or* a planned action **aufgeben, verzichten auf;** *the government has renounced the use of force in dealing with international terrorists*

rent
1 *noun* money paid (or occasionally a service provided) for the use of an office *or* house *or* factory for a period of time **Miete, Pacht; high rent** *or* **low rent** = expensive *or* cheap rent **hohe Miete; niedrige Miete;** *to pay three months' rent in advance;* **back rent** = rent owed **Mietrückstand; ground rent** = rent paid by the lessee to the ground landlord;

entspricht **Erbpachtzins; Nutzungsentgelt; nominal rent** = very small rent **Nominalmiete; rent action** = proceedings to obtain payment of rent owing **Klage auf Mietzahlung; rent controls** = government regulation of rents charged by landlords **Mietpreisbindung; income from rents** *or* **rent income** = income from letting office *or* houses, etc. **Mieteinkünfte; rent allowance** *or* **rent rebate** = state subsidy paid to poor people who do not have enough income to pay their rents **Mietbeihilfe, Mietzuschuß; rent tribunal** = court which adjudicates in disputes about rents and awards fair rents **für Mietstreitigkeiten zuständiges Gericht**
2 *verb*
(a) to pay money to hire an office *or* house *or* factory *or* piece of equipment for a period of time **mieten, pachten; leihen;** *to rent an office or a car; he rents an office in the centre of town; they were driving a rented car when they were stopped by the police*
(b) to rent (out) = to own a car *or* office, etc. and let it to someone for money **vermieten, verpachten; verleihen;** *we rented part of the building to an American company*

◊ **rental** *noun* money paid to use an office *or* house *or* factory *or* car *or* piece of equipment, etc., for a period of time **Miete, Pacht; Leihgebühr;** *the telephone rental bill comes to over £500 a quarter;* **rental income** *or* **income from rentals** = income from letting offices *or* houses, etc. **Mieteinkünfte**

◊ **rentcharge** *noun* payment of rental on freehold land **Belastung eines Grundstücks mit regelmäßigen Leistungen**

COMMENT: rare except in the case of covenants involving land

renunciation *noun* act of giving up a right, especially the ownership of shares **Verzicht; letter of renunciation** = form sent with new shares, which allows the person who has been allotted the shares to refuse to accept them and so sell them to someone else **Abtretungsformular für Bezugsrechte**

reopen *verb* to start investigating (a case) again; to start (a hearing) again **wiedereröffnen;** *after receiving new evidence, the police have reopened the murder inquiry; the hearing reopened on Monday afternoon*

reorganize *verb* to organize in a new way **neu organisieren, umorganisieren, umstrukturieren**

◊ **reorganization** *noun* new way of organizing **Neuordnung, Umorganisation, Umstrukturierung;** *the reorganization of a company or a company reorganization* =

restructuring the finances of a company **Unternehmenssanierung**

repair
1 *noun*
(a) mending something which is damaged **Reparatur, Instandsetzung;** *the landlord carried out repairs to the roof; the bill for repairs to the car came to £250*
(b) state of repair = physical condition of something **baulicher Zustand;** *the house was in a bad state of repair when he bought it*
2 *verb* to mend something which is damaged *or* broken **reparieren, instandsetzen; full repairing lease** = lease where the tenant has to pay for all repairs to the property **Miet-/Pachtvertrag, in dem dem Mieter/Pächter die Verpflichtung zu Reparaturen auferlegt wird**
◊ **repairer** *noun* person who repairs **Handwerker, Techniker; repairer's lien** = right of someone who has been carrying out repairs to keep the goods until the repair bill has been paid **Zurückbehaltungs- /Pfandrecht des Handwerkers**

repatriate *verb* to force someone to leave the country he is living in and go back to his own country **repatriieren, wieder einbürgern**
◊ **repatriation** *noun* forcing someone to return to his own country **Repatriierung, Wiedereinbürgerung**

repay *verb* to pay back money borrowed *or* interest on a loan **zurückzahlen, erstatten;** *the loan is to be repaid at the rate of £50 a month*
◊ **repayable** *adjective* which can be repaid **rückzahlbar;** *the loan is repayable over five years*
◊ **repayment** *noun* paying back a loan **Rückzahlung;** *he was unable to meet or to keep up with his mortgage repayments*

repeal
1 *noun* abolishing a law so that it is no longer valid **Aufhebung, Außerkraftsetzung;** *MPs are pressing for the repeal of the Immigration Act*
2 *verb* to abolish *or* to do away with (a law) **aufheben, außer Kraft setzen;** *the Bill seeks to repeal the existing legislation*

repeat *verb*
(a) to say something again **wiederholen;** *he repeated his evidence slowly so that the police officer could write it down; when asked what he planned to do, the chairman of the magistrates repeated "Nothing"*
(b) to repeat an offence = to commit an offence again **eine Straftat wiederholen**

◊ **repetition** *noun* act of repeating something **Wiederholung;** *repetition of a libel is an offence*

replevin *noun* action brought to obtain possession of goods which have been seized, by paying off a judgment debt **Herausgabeklage (zur Wiedererlangung von Pfandgegenständen)**

reply
1 *noun*
(a) answer **Antwort, Erwiderung;** *there was no reply to my letter or to my phone call; in reply to your letter of the 24th; the company's reply to the takeover bid;* **international postal reply coupon** = coupon which can be used in another country to pay the postage of replying to a letter **internationaler Antwortschein; reply paid card** *or* **letter** = card or letter to be sent back to the sender with a reply, the sender having already paid for the return postage **freigemachte/frankierte Antwortkarte**
(b) (i) written statement by a plaintiff in a civil case in answer to the defendant's defence; (ii) speech by prosecution counsel *or* counsel for the plaintiff which answers claims made by the defence **(i) Replik; (ii) Gegenplädoyer des Staatsanwaltes od des Anwaltes des Klägers; right of reply** = right of someone to answer claims made by an opponent **Erwiderungsrecht;** *he demanded the right of reply to the newspaper allegations*
2 *verb*
(a) to answer **antworten, erwidern;** *to reply to a letter; the company has replied to the takeover bid by offering the shareholders higher dividends*
(b) to answer claims made by an opponent; to give an opposing view in a discussion **Stellung nehmen; entgegnen**

report
1 *noun*
(a) statement describing what has happened *or* describing a state of affairs **Bericht;** *to make a report or to present a report or to send in a report; the court heard a report from the probation officer; the chairman has received a report from the insurance company;* **the company's annual report** *or* **the chairman's report** *or* **directors' report** = document sent each year by the chairman of a company or the directors to the shareholders, explaining what the company has done during the year **Geschäftsbericht; Jahresbericht des Aufsichtsratsvorsitzenden; confidential report** = secret document which must not be shown to other than a few named persons **vertraulicher Bericht; Law Reports** =

collection of reports of cases which are legal precedents **Entscheidungs- und Urteilssammlung; progress report =** document which describes what progress has been made **Bericht über den Stand einer Angelegenheit, Fortschrittsbericht; the treasurer's report =** document from the honorary treasurer of a society to explain the financial state of the society to its members **Kassenwartbericht**
(b) a report in a newspaper or **a newspaper report =** article or news item **Zeitungsbericht, Meldung in der Zeitung;** *can you confirm the report that charges are likely to be brought?*
(c) official document from a government committee **amtlicher Bericht, Untersuchungsbericht;** *the government has issued a report on the problems of inner city violence*
2 *verb*
(a) to make a statement describing something **berichten, melden;** *the probation officer reported on the progress of the two young criminals; he reported the damage to the insurance company; we asked the bank to report on his financial status;* **reporting restrictions =** restrictions on information about a case which can be reported in newspapers **Beschränkung der Berichterstattung (über einen Gerichtsfall); reporting restrictions were lifted =** journalists were allowed to report details of the case **die Berichterstattungsbeschränkungen wurden aufgehoben**
(b) to report to someone = to be responsible to or to be under someone **jdm unterstellt sein/unterstehen;** *he reports direct to the managing director*
(c) to go to a place or to attend **sich melden;** *to report for an interview; please report to our London office for training; a condition of bail is that he has to report to the police station once a week*

◊ **reported case** *noun* case which has been reported in the Law Reports because of its importance as a precedent **in die Urteilssammlung aufgenommener Fall**

◊ **Report Stage** *noun* stage in the discussion of a Bill in the House of Commons, where the amendments proposed at Committee Stage are debated by the whole House of Commons **Beratungsstadium einer Gesetzesvorlage**

repossess *verb* to take back an item which someone is buying under a hire-purchase agreement, because the purchaser cannot continue the payments **wieder in Besitz nehmen**

represent *verb*
(a) to state or to show **darstellen, beschreiben;** *he was represented as a man of great honour*
(b) to act on behalf of someone **vertreten, repräsentieren;** *the defendant is represented by his solicitor*
(c) to be the elected representative of an area (in Parliament or on a council) **der Vertreter sein von, vertreten;** *he represents one of the Northern industrial constituencies*

◊ **representation** *noun*
(a) statement, especially a statement made to persuade someone to enter into a contract **Erklärung, Zusicherung, Angabe; false representation =** offence of making a wrong statement which misleads someone **falsche Angabe**
(b) to make representations = to complain **Vorhaltungen machen, Vorstellungen erheben**
(c) being represented by a lawyer **Vertretung; the applicant had no legal representation =** he had no lawyer to represent him in court **der Antragsteller war nicht durch einen Anwalt vertreten**
(d) system where the people of a country elect representatives to a Parliament which governs the country **Volksvertretung; the Representation of the People Act** Act of Parliament which states how elections must be organized **Wahlgesetz; proportional representation =** system of electing representatives where each political party is allocated a number of places which is directly related to the number of votes cast for each party **Verhältniswahl**

◊ **representative** *noun*
(a) person who represents another person **(Stell)vertreter, Repräsentant/-in;** *the court heard the representative of the insurance company;* **personal representative =** person who is the executor of a will or who is the administrator of the estate of a deceased person **Testamentsvollstrecker, Nachlaßverwalter**
(b) *US* member of the lower house of Congress **Abgeordneter; House of Representatives =** lower house of the American Congress **Repräsentantenhaus**
NOTE: a Representative is also referred to as **Congressman**

reprieve
1 *noun* temporarily stopping the carrying out of a sentence or court order **(Straf)vollstreckungsaufschub**
2 *verb* to stop a sentence or order being carried out **(Straf)vollstreckungsaufschub gewähren, die Urteilsvollstreckung aussetzen;** *he was sentenced to death but was reprieved by the president*

reprimand

1 *noun* official criticism **Verweis, Verwarnung, Tadel**; *the police officer received an official reprimand after the inquiry into the accident*

2 *verb* to criticize someone officially **Verweis erteilen, verwarnen**; *he was reprimanded by the magistrate*

reproduce *verb* to make a copy of something **reproduzieren, vervielfältigen**; *the documents relating to the hearings are reproduced in the back of the report*

◊ **reproduction** *noun* making a copy of something **Reproduzierung, Vervielfältigung**; *the reproduction of copyright material without the permission of the copyright holder is banned by law*; **mechanical reproduction rights** = right to make a recording of a piece of music *or* right to make a copy of a printed document by photographing it (against payment of a fee) **Wiedergabe-/Vervielfältigungsrecht auf mechanischem Wege**

repudiate *verb* to refuse to accept **nicht anerkennen**; **to repudiate an agreement** *or* **a contract** = to refuse to perform one's obligations under an agreement *or* contract **eine Vereinbarung/einen Vertrag nicht anerkennen**

◊ **repudiation** *noun* refusal to accept; refusal to perform one's obligations under an agreement *or* contract **Nichtanerkennung; Erfüllungsverweigerung**

reputable *adjective* with a good reputation **angesehen, seriös**; *we use only reputable carriers; a reputable firm of accountants*

◊ **reputation** *noun* opinion of someone *or* something held by other people **Ruf, Ansehen**; *company with a reputation for quality; he has a reputation for being difficult to negotiate with*

request

1 *noun* asking for something **Bitte, Gesuch, Antrag**; *they put in a request for a government subsidy; his request for an adjournment was turned down by the coroner*; **on request** = if asked for **auf Wunsch/Anforderung**; *we will send samples on request or "samples available on request"*

2 *verb* to ask for **bitten, ersuchen, beantragen, anfordern**; *to request assistance from the government; the witness requested permission to give evidence sitting down*

require *verb*

(a) to ask for *or* to demand something **verlangen, fordern, anordnen**; *to require a full*

explanation of expenditure; the law requires you to submit all income to the tax authorities; the Bill requires social workers to seek the permission of the juvenile court before taking action*

(b) to need **brauchen, benötigen, erfordern**; *the document requires careful study; to write the program requires a computer specialist*

◊ **requirement** *noun* what is needed **Erfordernis, Bedarf, Forderung**; **public sector borrowing requirement** = amount of money which a government has to borrow to pay for its own spending **Kreditbedarf der öffentlichen Hand**

requisition

1 *noun* **requisition on title** = asking the vendor of a property for details of his title to the property **Ersuchen um Auskunft über Grundstückseigentumsnachweis**

2 *verb* to take (private property) into the ownership of the state for the state to use **beschlagnahmen, requirieren**; *the army requisitioned all the trucks to carry supplies*

res *Latin word meaning* "thing" *or* "matter" **Gegenstand, Sache**

◊ **res ipsa loquitur** *Latin phrase meaning* "the matter speaks for itself": situation where the facts seem so obvious, that it is for the defendant to prove he was not negligent, rather than for the plaintiff to prove his claim **widerlegbare Vermutung von Fahrlässigkeit**

◊ **res judicata** *Latin phrase meaning* "matter on which a judgment has been given" **rechtskräftig entschiedene Sache**

rescind *verb* to annul *or* to cancel **für nichtig/ungültig erklären, außer Kraft setzen, aufheben**; *to rescind a contract or an agreement*

◊ **rescinding** *or* **rescission** *noun* cancellation of a contract **Nichtigkeits-, Ungültigkeitserklärung, Annullierung, Aufhebung**

reserve

1 *noun*

(a) money from profits not paid as dividend, but kept back by a company in case it is needed for a special purpose **Rücklage**; **bank reserves** = cash and securities held by a bank to cover deposits **Mindest-, Bankreserve**; **cash reserves** = a company's reserves in cash deposits *or* bills kept in case of urgent need **Bar-, Liquiditätsreserven**; **contingency reserve** *or* **emergency reserve** = money set aside in case it is needed urgently **Notfonds, Rückstellung für unvorhergesehene Ausgaben/Eventualverbindlichkeiten**; **reserve for bad debts** = money kept by a company

to cover debts which may not be paid **Rücklagen für uneinbringliche Forderungen; hidden reserves** = illegal reserves which are not declared in the company's balance sheet **stille Reserven; reserve fund** = profits in a business which have not been paid out as dividend but which have been ploughed back into the business **Rücklage(fonds)**
(b) reserve currency = strong currency held by other countries to support their own weaker currencies **Reservewährung; currency reserves** = foreign money held by a government to support its own currency and to pay its debts **Währungsreserven; a country's foreign currency reserves** = a country's reserves in currencies of other countries **die Devisenreserven eines Landes**
(c) in reserve = kept to be used at a later date **in Reserve**
(d) reserve (price) = lowest price which a seller will accept at an auction **Vorbehaltspreis, Mindestgebot;** *the painting was withdrawn when it did not reach its reserve*
2 *verb*
(a) to reserve a room *or* **a table** *or* **a seat** = to book a room *or* table *or* seat *or* to ask for a room *or* table *or* seat to be kept free for you **ein Zimmer od einen Tisch od einen Platz reservieren;** *I want to reserve a table for four people; can your secretary reserve a seat for me on the train to Glasgow?*
(b) to keep back **(sich) vorbehalten, zurückbehalten; to reserve one's defence** = not to present any defence at a preliminary hearing, but to wait until full trial **sich Einwendungen vorbehalten; to reserve judgment** = not to pass judgment immediately, but keep it back until later so that the judge has time to consider the case **die Urteilsverkündung aussetzen; to reserve the right to do something** = to indicate that you consider that you have the right to do something, and intend to use that right in the future **sich das Recht vorbehalten, etwas zu tun;** *he reserved the right to cross-examine witnesses; we reserve the right to appeal against the tribunal's decision*

◊ **reservation** *noun*
(a) booking a room *or* table *or* seat **Reservierung, Buchung;** *he phoned reservations and asked to book a room for four nights*
(b) doubt **Bedenken, Zweifel;** *he expressed reservations about the legality of the action; the plan was accepted by the committee with some reservations*
(c) keeping something back **Einschränkung, Vorbehalt; reservation of title clause** = clause in a contract whereby the seller provides that title to the goods does not pass to the buyer until the buyer has paid for them **Eigentumsvorbehaltsklausel;** *see also* ROMALPA CLAUSE

residence *noun*
(a) place where someone lives **Wohnsitz, Wohnort;** *he has a country residence where he spends his weekends*
(b) act of living *or* operating officially in a country **Aufenthalt; residence permit** = official document allowing a foreigner to live in a country **Aufenthaltsgenehmigung;** *he has applied for a residence permit; she was granted a residence permit for one year*

◊ **resident** *adjective* living or operating in a country **wohnhaft, ansässig;** *the company is resident in France;* **person ordinarily resident in the UK** = person who normally lives in the UK **eine Person mit gewöhnlichem Aufenthalt in Großbritannien; non-resident** = not officially resident in a country **auswärtig, im Ausland ansässig;** *he has a non-resident account with a French bank; she was granted a non-resident visa*

residue *noun* what is left over, especially what is left of an estate after debts and bequests have been made **Rest; restlicher Nachlaß;** *after paying various bequests the residue of his estate was split between his children*

◊ **residual** *adjective* remaining after everything else has gone **übrig(bleibend), restlich**

◊ **residuary** *adjective* referring to what is left **übrig, restlich; residuary devisee** = person who receives the rest of the land when the other bequests have been made **Erbe des restlichen Grundbesitzes; residuary estate** = (i) estate of a dead person which has not been bequeathed in his will; (ii) what remains of an estate after the debts have been paid and bequests have been made **(i) Restnachlaß; (ii) nach Zahlung der Verbindlichkeiten und Auszahlung besonderer Vermächtnisse übrigbleibender Nachlaß; residuary legatee** = person who receives the rest of the personal property after specific legacies have been made **Erbe des Restnachlasses, Nachvermächtnisnehmer**

resign *verb* to leave a job **kündigen, zurücktreten, sein Amt niederlegen;** *he resigned from his post as treasurer; he has resigned with effect from July 1st; she resigned as finance director*

◊ **resignation** *noun* act of giving up a job **Kündigung, Rücktritt, Amtsniederlegung;** *he wrote his letter of resignation to the chairman;* **to hand in** *or* **to give in** *or* **to send in one's resignation** = to resign from a job **seine Kündigung einreichen**

resist *verb* to fight against something *or* not to give in to something **Widerstand leisten, sich wehren, sich widersetzen;** *the* *accused resisted all attempts to make him confess; the company is resisting the takeover bid;* **resisting arrest** = offence of refusing to allow oneself to be arrested **Widerstandsleistung bei der Festnahme**

◊ **resistance** *noun* showing that people are opposed to something **Widerstand;** *there was a lot of resistance from the prison officers to the new plan; the Home Secretary's proposal met with strong resistance from the probation service*

resolution *noun* decision taken at a meeting, especially a meeting of shareholders **Beschluß, Resolution; to put a resolution to a meeting** = to ask a meeting to approve a resolution **einen Beschluß einbringen, über eine Entschließung abstimmen lassen; ordinary resolution** = decision which is taken by a majority vote of shareholders **einfacher/gewöhnlicher Mehrheitsbeschluß; extraordinary** *or* **special resolution** = resolution (such as a change to the articles of a company) which requires the holders of 75% of the shares to vote for it **mit qualifizierter od 3/4 Mehrheit gefaßter Beschluß;** *US* **joint resolution** = Bill passed by both House and Senate, sent to the President for signature to become law **gemeinsame Entschließung/Resolution**

resort
1 *noun* **court of last resort** = highest court from which no appeals are allowed **Gericht letzter Instanz; lender of the last resort** = central bank which lends money to commercial banks **Kreditgeber der letzten Instanz**
2 *verb* **to resort to** = to come to use **etwas anwenden, zu etwas greifen;** *he had to resort to threats of court action to get repayment of the money owing; workers must not resort to violence in industrial disputes*

respect
1 *noun* **with respect to** *or* **in respect of** = concerning **in bezug auf, bezüglich, hinsichtlich;** *his right to an indemnity in respect of earlier disbursements; the defendant counterclaimed for loss and damage in respect of a machine sold to him by the plaintiff*
2 *verb* to pay attention to **anerkennen, berücksichtigen;** *to respect a clause in an agreement; the company has not respected the terms of the contract*

◊ **respectively** *adverb* referring to each one separately **beziehungsweise**

respondeat superior *Latin phrase* meaning "let the superior be responsible": rule that a principal is responsible for

actions of the agent *or* the employer for actions of the employee **Deliktshaftung des Auftraggebers für den Beauftragten od des Arbeitgebers für den Arbeitnehmer**

respondent *noun* (i) the other side in a case which is the subject of an appeal; (ii) person who answers a petition, especially one who is being sued for divorce **(i) Berufungsbeklagter; (ii) (Scheidungs)beklagter;** *see also* CO-RESPONDENT

responsibility *noun*
(a) duty *or* thing which you are responsible for doing **Verpflichtung, Pflicht, Aufgabe;** *he finds the responsibilities of being managing director too heavy; keeping the interior of the building in good order is the responsibility of the tenant*
(b) being responsible **Verantwortung, Verantwortlichkeit;** *there is no responsibility on the company's part for loss of customers' property; the management accepts full responsibility for loss of goods in storage;* **collective responsibility** = doctrine that all members of a group (such as the British cabinet) are responsible together for the actions of that group **Kollektivverantwortung; age of criminal responsibility** = age at which a person is considered to be capable of committing a crime **Strafmündigkeit; diminished responsibility** = state of mind of a criminal (inherited *or* caused by illness or injury) which means that he cannot be held responsible for a crime he has committed **verminderte Zurechnungsfähigkeit**

◊ **responsible** *adjective*
(a) **responsible for** = directing *or* being in charge of *or* being in control of **verantwortlich/zuständig für;** *the tenant is responsible for all repairs to the building; the consignee is held responsible for the goods he has received on consignment; she was responsible for a series of thefts from offices*
(b) **responsible to someone** = being under someone's authority **jdm unterstellt sein;** *magistrates are responsible to the Lord Chancellor*
(c) **a responsible job** = job where important decisions have to be taken *or* where the employee has many responsibilities **eine verantwortungsvolle Stellung**

◊ **responsibly** *adverb* in a responsible way **verantwortungsbewußt;** *the judge congratulated the jury on acting responsibly*

restante *see* POSTE RESTANTE

restitutio in integrum *Latin phrase* meaning "returning everything to the state as it was before" **Wiedereinsetzung in den vorigen Stand, Wiederherstellung des ursprünglichen Zustandes**

restitution *noun*
(a) giving back *or* return (of property) which has been illegally obtained **Herausgabe, Rückgabe;** *the court ordered the restitution of assets to the company;* **restitution order** = court order asking for property to be returned to someone **gerichtliche Verfügung auf Herausgabe, Rückerstattungsbeschluß**
(b) compensation *or* payment for damage or loss **Entschädigung, (Schadens)ersatz**
(c) *(in the EC)* **export restitution** = subsidies to European food exporters **Exporterstattung**

restrain *verb*
(a) to control *or* to hold someone back **zurückhalten, in Schranken halten;** *the prisoner fought and had to be restrained by two policemen*
(b) to tell someone not to do something **verbieten, hindern;** *the court granted the plaintiff an injunction restraining the defendant from breaching copyright*
◊ **restraining order** *noun* court order which tells a defendant not to do something while the court is still taking a decision **einstweilige Verfügung**
◊ **restraint** *noun* control **Be-, Einschränkung; pay restraint** *or* **wage restraint** = keeping increases in wages under control **Politik der Lohnkontrolle; restraint of trade** = (i) situation where a worker is not allowed to use his knowledge in another company if he changes jobs; (ii) attempt by companies to fix prices *or* create monopolies *or* reduce competition, which could affect free trade **(i) Geheimhaltungspflicht; (ii) Wettbewerbsbeschränkung, Konkurrenzverbot**

restrict *verb* to limit *or* to impose controls on **be-, einschränken;** *the agreement restricts the company's ability to sell its products; we are restricted to twenty staff by the size of our offices; to restrict the flow of trade or to restrict imports*
◊ **restriction** *noun* limit *or* act of controlling **Be-, Einschränkung;** *import restrictions or restrictions on imports;* **to impose restrictions on imports** *or* **on credit** = to start limiting imports *or* credit **Importbeschränkungen od Kreditrestriktionen einführen; to lift credit restrictions** to allow credit to be given freely **Kreditrestriktionen aufheben; reporting restrictions** = restrictions on information about a case which can be reported in newspapers **Beschränkung der Berichterstattung (über einen Gerichtsfall); reporting restrictions**

were lifted = journalists were allowed to report details of the case **die Beschränkung der Berichterstattung wurde aufgehoben**
◊ **restrictive** *adjective* which limits **einschränkend, restriktiv; restrictive covenant** = clause in a contract which prevents someone from doing something **vertragsmäßige Einschränkung, Vereinbarung über Unterlassungspflicht in einem Vertrag; restrictive practices** = ways of working which exclude free competition in relation to the supply of goods or labour in order to maintain prices or wages **wettbewerbsbeschränkende Geschäftspraktiken; Restrictive Practices Court** = court which decides in cases of restrictive practices **Kartellgericht, Gericht für Wettbewerbsbeschränkungen**

resume *verb* to start again **wiederaufnehmen;** *the discussions resumed after a two hour break*

résumé *noun US* summary of a person's life story with details of education and work experience **Lebenslauf**
NOTE: GB English is **curriculum vitae**

resumption *noun* starting again **Wiederaufnahme; we expect an early resumption of negotiations** = we expect negotiations will start again soon **wir rechnen mit einer baldigen Wiederaufnahme der Verhandlungen**
NOTE: no plural

retail *noun* sale of small quantities of goods to individual customers **Einzelhandel; retail price** = price to the individual customer **Einzelhandels-, Ladenpreis**
◊ **retailer** *noun* person who runs a retail business, selling goods to the public **Einzelhändler;** *see also* WHOLESALE

retain *verb*
(a) to keep **(ein)behalten, zurückbehalten;** *out of the profits, the company has retained £50,000 as provision against bad debts;* **retained income** = profit not distributed to the shareholders as dividend **nicht ausgeschüttete Gewinne**
(b) to retain a lawyer to act for you = to agree with a lawyer that he will act for you (and pay him a fee in advance) **einen Anwalt nehmen/beauftragen/verpflichten**
◊ **retainer** *noun*
(a) fee paid to a barrister **Anwaltsvorschuß, Anwaltshonorar**
(b) money paid in advance to someone so that he will work for you when required, and not for someone else **Honorarvorschuß;** *we pay him a retainer of £1,000 per annum*

retaliate *verb* to act against someone who has acted against you **sich rächen, Vergeltung üben;** *the court granted an injunction to the workers, and the management retaliated by locking the office doors*

◊ **retaliation** *noun* acting against someone **Rache, Vergeltung, Vergeltungsmaßnahme;** *the robbers fired at the bank staff, and the police fired back in retaliation*

retire *verb*
(a) to stop work and take a pension **sich pensionieren lassen, in Pension gehen, in den Ruhestand treten;** *she retired with a £6,000 pension; the chairman of the company retired at the age of 65; the shop is owned by a retired policeman;* **retiring age** = age at which people retire (in the UK usually 65 for men and 60 for women) **Rentenalter**
(b) to make a worker stop work and take a pension **in den Ruhestand versetzen;** *they decided to retire all staff over 50 years of age*
(c) to come to the end of an elected term of office **ausscheiden, zurücktreten;** *the treasurer retires after six years; two retiring directors offer themselves for re-election*
(d) to go away from a court for a period of time **sich zurückziehen;** *the magistrates retired to consider their verdict; the jury retired for four hours*

◊ **retiral** *noun* *US & Scottish* = RETIREMENT

◊ **retirement** *noun*
(a) act of retiring from work **Pensionierung; to take early retirement** = to leave work before the usual age **vorzeitig in den Ruhestand treten; retirement age** = age at which people retire (in the UK usually 65 for men and 60 for women) **Rentenalter; retirement pension** = pension which someone receives when he retires **Altersversorgung, Altersrente, Altersruhegeld, Pension**
(b) *(of a jury)* going out of the courtroom to consider their verdict **das Sichzurückziehen (der Jury)**

retrial *noun* new trial **erneute Verhandlung, Wiederaufnahmeverfahren;** *the Court of Appeal ordered a retrial*

retroactive *adjective* which takes effect from a time in the past **rückwirkend;** *they received a pay rise retroactive to last January*

◊ **retroactively** *adverb* going back to a time in the past **rückwirkend**

retrospective *adjective* going back in time **retrospektiv, rückwirkend; retrospective legislation** = Act of Parliament which applies to the period before the Act was passed **Gesetz mit rückwirkender Kraft; with retrospective effect** = applying to a past period **mit rückwirkender Kraft;** *the tax ruling has retrospective effect*

◊ **retrospectively** *adverb* in a retrospective way **retrospektiv, rückwirkend;** *the ruling is applied retrospectively*

retry *verb* to try a case a second time **neu verhandeln, wiederaufnehmen;** *the court ordered the case to be retried*

return
1 *noun*
(a) going back *or* coming back **Rückkehr; return journey** = journey back to where you came from **Rückfahrt; return fare** = fare for a journey from one place to another and back again **Preis für eine Rückfahrkarte**
(b) sending back **Rückgabe, Rücksendung; he replied by return of post** = he replied by the next post service back **er antwortete postwendend; return address** = address to send back something **Absender; these goods are all on sale or return** = if the retailer does not sell them, he sends them back to the supplier, and pays only for the items sold **wir haben alle diese Waren auf Kommission**
(c) profit *or* income from money invested **Gewinn, Ertrag, Rendite; return on investment** *or* **on capital** = profit shown as a percentage of money invested **Investitionsrentabilität, Ertrag aus angelegtem Kapital, Kapitalrendite; rate of return** = amount of interest *or* dividend produced by an investment, shown as a percentage **Rendite**
(d) official return = official report *or* statement **amtliche Meldung, öffentliche Erklärung; to make a return to the tax office** *or* **to make an income tax return** = to send a statement of income to the tax office **eine Einkommensteuererklärung abgeben; to fill in a VAT return** = to complete the form showing VAT income and expenditure **eine Mehrwertsteuererklärung ausfüllen; annual return** = form to be completed by each company once a year, giving details of the directors and the financial state of the company **Jahresbericht; nil return** = report showing no sales *or* no income *or* no tax etc. **Fehlanzeige, keinerlei Erträge**
(e) election of an MP **Wahl (eines Parlamentsabgeordneten)**
2 *verb*
(a) to send back **zurückschicken, zurücksenden;** *to return damaged stock to the wholesaler; to return a letter to sender*
(b) to make a statement **erklären, angeben, melden; to return income of £15,000 to the tax authorities** = to notify the tax authorities that you have an income of £15,000 **dem Finanzamt gegenüber sein Einkommen mit £15,000 angeben; returning**

officer = official (usually a High Sheriff *or* mayor) who superintends a parliamentary election in a constituency and announces the result **Wahlleiter;** *(of a jury)* **to return a verdict** = to state the verdict at the end of a trial **das Urteil verkünden;** *the jury returned a verdict of not guilty*
(c) to elect an MP for a constituency **(einen Parlamentsabgeordneten) wählen;** *he was returned with an increased majority*

reus *see* ACTUS REUS

reveal *verb* to show something which was hidden before **enthüllen, aufdecken, offenbaren;** *examination of the bank account revealed that large sums had been drawn out in August; the garden revealed several clues to the murder*

revenue *noun* money earned *or* income **Einnahmen, Einkünfte, Einkommen; Inland Revenue** *or (US)* **Internal Revenue Service** = government department dealing with tax **Finanzamt, Finanzverwaltung;** *to make a declaration to the Inland Revenue;* **revenue officer** = person working in a government tax office **Finanzbeamter**

reversal *noun*
(a) change of a decision **Aufhebung, Abänderung;** *the reversal of the High Court ruling by the Court of Appeal*
(b) change from being profitable to unprofitable **Umschwung, Rückschlag;** *the company suffered a reversal in the Far East*

reverse
1 *adjective* opposite *or* in the opposite direction **umgekehrt, entgegengesetzt; reverse takeover** = takeover of a large company by a small company **gegenläufige Fusion; reverse charge call** = telephone call where the person receiving the call agrees to pay for it **R-Gespräch**
2 *verb*
(a) to change a decision to the opposite one **aufheben, umstoßen;** *the Appeal Court reversed the decision of the High Court*
(b) to reverse the charges = to make a phone call, asking the person receiving it to pay for it **ein R-Gespräch führen**

revert *verb* to go back to the previous state *or* owner **zurückkehren, zurückfallen;** *the property reverts to its original owner in 1998*
◊ **reversion** *noun* return of property to an original owner when a lease expires **Heim-, Rückfall; he has the reversion of the estate** = he will receive the estate when the present lease ends **er hat das Rückfallsrecht auf den Grundbesitz**

◊ **reversionary** *adjective* (property) which passes to another owner on the death of the present one **Anwartschafts-; reversionary annuity** = annuity paid to someone on the death of another person **Rente auf den Überlebensfall; reversionary right** = right of a writer's heir to his copyrights after his death **Anrecht des Erben auf das Urheberrecht;** *see also* REMAINDER

review
1 *noun*
(a) general examination of something again **Überprüfung, Revision;** *to conduct a review of sentencing policy; the coroner asked for a review of police procedures;* **financial review** = examination of an organization's finances **Finanzprüfung; judicial review** = review by a higher court of the actions of a lower court *or* of an administrative body **Revision; gerichtliche Überprüfung (einer Verwaltungsbehörde); wage review** *or* **salary review** = examination of salaries *or* wages in a company to see if the workers should earn more **Gehaltsrevision**
(b) magazine *or* monthly or weekly journal **Zeitschrift**
2 *verb* to examine something generally **überprüfen;** *a committee has been appointed to review judicial salaries; the High Court has reviewed the decision*

revise *verb* to change (a text *or* a decision) after considerable thought **überarbeiten, abändern;** *the revised examination procedures have been published; the judge revised his earlier decision not to consider a submission from defence counsel*
◊ **revision** *noun* act of changing something **Abänderung;** *the Lord Chancellor has proposed a revision of the divorce procedures*

revocandi *see* ANIMUS

revoke *verb* to cancel *or* to annul (a permission *or* right *or* agreement *or* offer *or* will) **aufheben, rückgängig machen, annullieren, widerrufen;** *to revoke a clause in an agreement; the treaty on fishing rights has been revoked*
◊ **revocable** *adjective* which can be revoked **widerruflich**
◊ **revocation** *noun* cancelling *or* annulment (of permission *or* right *or* agreement *or* offer *or* will) **Aufhebung, Annullierung, Widerruf**

revolution *noun* armed rising against a government **Revolution;** *the government was overthrown by a revolution led by the head of the army*

reward *noun* payment given to someone who does a service (especially someone who finds something which has been lost *or* who gives information about something) **Belohnung;** *she offered a £50 reward to anyone who found her watch; the police have offered a reward for information about the man seen at the bank*

Rex *Latin word meaning* "the King": the Crown *or* state, as a party in legal proceedings **der König, die Krone, der Staat** NOTE: in written reports, usually abbreviated to **R**: *the case of R. v. Smith*

rider *noun* additional clause **Zusatzklausel, Anhang;** *to add a rider to a contract*

right *noun*
(a) legal entitlement to something **Recht, Berechtigung, Anrecht, Anspruch;** *right of renewal of a contract; she has a right to the property; he has no right to the patent; the staff have a right to know what the company is doing;* **civil rights** = rights and privileges of each individual according to the law **Grundrechte, bürgerliche Rechte; conjugal rights** = rights of a husband and wife in relation to each other **eheliche Rechte; constitutional right** = right which is guaranteed by the constitution of a country **Grundrecht; foreign rights** = legal entitlement to sell something in a foreign country **Auslandsrechte; human rights** = rights of individual men and women to basic freedoms, such as freedom of speech, freedom of association **Menschenrechte; right to strike** = general right of workers to stop working if they have a good reason for it **Streikrecht; right of way** = legal title to go across someone else's property **Wegerecht;** *see also* BILL OF RIGHTS
(b) rights issue = giving shareholders the right to buy more shares at a lower price than the current market price **Bezugsrechtsausgabe**
◊ **rightful** *adjective* legally correct **rechtmäßig; rightful claimant** = person who has a legal claim to something **Anspruchsberechtigter; rightful owner** = legal owner **rechtmäßiger Besitzer**

rigor mortis *Latin phrase meaning* "stiffening of the dead": state where a dead body becomes stiff some time after death, and which can allow a pathologist to estimate the time of death in some cases **Totenstarre**

ring *noun* group of people who try to fix the prices paid at an auction so as not to compete with each other, so making a large profit by holding a secret auction afterwards with only the members of the group as bidders **Händlerring bei einer Auktion**

riot
1 *noun* notifiable offence when three or more people meet illegally and plan to use force to achieve their aims *or* to frighten the public **Zusammenrottung; Aufruhr, Krawall**
2 *verb* to form an illegal group to use force **sich zusammenrotten; randalieren, Krawall machen**
◊ **rioter** *noun* person who takes part in a riot **Unruhestifter, Aufrührer; Randalierer;** *rioters attacked the banks and post offices*
◊ **riotous assembly** *noun* meeting of people who have come together to use force to achieve their aims *or* to frighten other people **Zusammenrottung**

riparian *adjective* referring to the bank of a river **Ufer-; riparian rights** = rights of people who own land on the bank of a river (usually the right to fish in the river) **Uferanliegerrechte**

rise
1 *noun*
(a) increase *or* growing high **Anstieg, Erhöhung, Zunahme, Steigerung;** *a rise in the crime rate or in interest rates*
(b) increase in salary **Lohn-, Gehaltserhöhung;** (NOTE: US English is **raise**)
2 *verb* to move upwards *or* to become higher **ansteigen, sich erhöhen, zunehmen, steigen, in die Höhe gehen;** *prices are rising faster than inflation; the clear-up rate for crimes of violence has risen by 15%*
NOTE: **rising - rose - has risen**

risk
1 *noun*
(a) possible harm *or* loss *or* chance of danger **Risiko, Gefahr; to run a risk** = to be likely to suffer harm **Gefahr laufen;** *in allowing him to retain his passport, the court runs the risk that the accused may try to escape to the USA;* **at owner's risk** = situation where goods shipped *or* stored are the responsibility of the owner, not of the shipping company or storage company **auf Gefahr des Eigentümers**
(b) loss *or* damage against which you are insured **Gefahr, Risiko; fire risk** = situation *or* goods which could start a fire **Feuergefahr; he is a bad risk** = it is likely that an insurance company will have to pay out compensation as far as he is concerned **bei ihm besteht ein hohes Schadensrisiko, er ist kein gutes Versicherungsobjekt;** *he is likely to*

die soon, so is a bad risk for an insurance company
2 *verb* to put something in danger **riskieren, aufs Spiel setzen;** *he is risking his job by complaining to the police; he risked being arrested* or *he risked arrest by throwing an egg at the Prime Minister*

rob *verb* to steal something from (someone), usually in a violent way **berauben, rauben;** *they robbed a bank in London and stole a car to make their getaway; the gang robbed shopkeepers in the centre of the town*
NOTE: **robbing - robbed.** Note also that you rob someone **of** something

◊ **robber** *noun* person who robs people **Dieb/-in, Räuber/-in**

◊ **robbery** *noun*
(a) offence of stealing something from someone (usually in a violent way) **Raub; robbery with violence** = stealing goods and harming someone at the same time **gewalttätiger Raub**
(b) act of stealing something with violence **Raubüberfall;** *he committed three petrol station robberies in two days*
NOTE: no plural for (a)

roll *noun*
(a) something which has been turned over and over to wrap round itself **Rolle;** *the desk calculator uses a roll of paper*
(b) list of names (which used to be written on a long roll) **Namensliste; Roll of Solicitors** = list of admitted solicitors **Anwaltsliste; he was struck off the roll** = he was banned from practising as a solicitor **von der Anwaltsliste gestrichen werden, disqualifiziert werden; Master of the Rolls** = judge who presides over the Court of Appeal, and is also responsible for admitting solicitors to the Roll of Solicitors **Vorsitzender Richter des Court of Appeal (,der auch für die Zulassung als Anwalt verantwortlich ist)**

◊ **roll over** *verb* **to roll over credit** = to make credit available over a continuing period **bei Fälligkeit einen Kredit erneuern/umschulden**

Romalpa clause *noun* clause in a contract, whereby the seller provides that title to the goods does not pass to the buyer until the buyer has paid for them **Vorbehaltsklausel bis zur vollständigen Zahlung**

COMMENT: called after the case of *Aluminium Industrie Vaassen BV v. Romalpa Ltd*

Roman law *noun* laws which existed in the Roman Empire **römisches Recht**

COMMENT: Roman law is the basis of the laws of many European countries but has had only negligible and indirect influence on the development of English law

root of title *noun* basic title deed which proves that the vendor has the right to sell the property **urkundlicher Eigentumsnachweis von Grundbesitz**

rotation *noun* taking turns **Wechsel, Turnus, Rotation; to fill the post of chairman by rotation** = each member of the group is chairman for a period then gives the post to another member **die Position des Vorsitzenden im Turnus vergeben; two directors retire by rotation** = two directors retire because they have been directors longer than any others, but can offer themselves for re-election **zwei Direktoren scheiden turnusmäßig aus**

rough *adjective*
(a) not very accurate **ungefähr, grob; rough calculation** or **rough estimate** = approximate answer **grobe Berechnung/Schätzung; rough justice** = legal processes which are not always very fair **summarisches Verfahren**
(b) not finished **Roh-; rough copy** = draft of a document which, it is expected, will have changes made to it before it is complete **Konzept, Entwurf**

◊ **roughly** *adverb* more or less **ungefähr, annähernd;** *the turnover is roughly twice last year's; the development cost of the project will be roughly £25,000*

◊ **rough out** *verb* to make a draft or a general design **grob entwerfen;** *the finance director roughed out a plan of investment*

rout *noun* offence of gathering together of people to do some unlawful act **Zusammenrottung, Auflauf**

royal *adjective* referring to a King or Queen **königlich; Royal Assent** = signing of a Bill by the Queen, confirming that the Bill is to become law as an Act of Parliament **königliche Genehmigung; by Royal Command** = by order of the Queen or King **auf Anordnung Ihrer Majestät; Royal Commission** = group of people specially appointed by a minister to examine and report on a major problem **königlicher Untersuchungsausschuß; Royal pardon** = pardon whereby a person convicted of a crime is forgiven and need not serve a sentence **Begnadigung (auf Anordnung Ihrer Majestät)**

royalty *noun* money paid to an inventor *or* writer *or* the owner of land for the right to use his property (usually a certain percentage of sales, or a certain amount per sale) **Lizenz-, Patentgebühren; Tantiemen, Autorenhonorar; Pachtgeld, Nutzungsgebühr;** *oil royalties make up a large proportion of the country's revenue; he is receiving royalties from his invention*

RSVP = REPONDEZ S'IL VOUS PLAIT letters on an invitation showing that a reply is asked for **u.A.w.g.**

rule
1 *noun*
(a) general order of conduct which says how things should be done **Regel, Richtlinie, Vorschrift; company rules (and regulations)** = general way of working in a company **allgemeine Geschäftsbedingungen eines Unternehmens; to work to rule** = to work strictly according to the rules agreed by the company and union, and therefore to work very slowly **Dienst nach Vorschrift tun; Judges' Rules** = informal set of rules governing how the police should act in questioning suspects **Verhörrichtlinien; Rules of the Supreme Court** = rules governing practice and procedure in the Supreme Court **Verfahrensregeln des Supreme Court;** *see also* WHITE BOOK
(b) way in which a country is governed **Herrschaft;** *the country has had ten years of military rule;* **the rule of law** = principle of government that all persons and bodies and the government itself are equal before and answerable to the law and that no person shall be punished without trial **Rechtsstaatlichkeit, Rechtsstaatprinzip**
(c) decision made by a court **gerichtliche Entscheidung; Rule in Rylands v. Fletcher** = rule that when a person brings a dangerous thing (substance *or* animal) to his own land, and the dangerous thing escapes and causes harm, then that person is absolutely liable for the damage caused **gerichtliche Entscheidung im Fall Rylands gegen Fletcher**
2 *verb*
(a) to give an official decision **entscheiden, anordnen, bestimmen;** *we are waiting for the judge to rule on the admissibility of the defence evidence; the commission of inquiry ruled that the company was in breach of contract*
(b) to be in force *or* to be current **gelten;** *prices which are ruling at the moment*
(c) to govern (a country) **herrschen;** *the country is ruled by a group of army officers*
◊ **ruling**
1 *adjective* in operation at the moment *or* current **geltend, laufend;** *we will invoice at ruling prices*

2 *noun* decision (made by a judge *or* magistrate *or* arbitrator, etc.) **Entscheidung;** *the inquiry gave a ruling on the case; according to the ruling of the court, the contract was illegal*

run
1 *noun*
(a) making a machine work **Durchlauf, Maschinenlauf; a cheque run** = series of cheques processed through a computer **Ausstellung von Schecks durch Computer; a computer run** = period of work of a computer **Arbeitsgang/Durchlauf eines Computers; test run** = trial made of a machine *or* a work process **Probelauf**
(b) rush to buy something **Ansturm, starke Nachfrage, Run; a run on the bank** = rush by customers to take deposits out of a bank which they think may close down **Ansturm auf die Bank; a run on the pound** = rush to sell pounds and buy other currencies **Panikverkäufe des Pfundes**
2 *verb*
(a) to be in force **gelten, gültig sein;** *the lease runs for twenty years; the lease has only six months to run;* **a covenant which runs with the land** = covenant which is attached to an estate and has to be obeyed by each new owner of the estate when it changes hands **vertragliche Zusicherung, die mit dem Grundbesitz an den jeweiligen Eigentümer übergeht**
(b) to amount to **sich belaufen, gehen;** *the costs ran into thousands of pounds*
(c) to manage *or* to organize **betreiben, leiten, führen;** *to run a business; she runs a mail-order business from home; they run a staff sports club; he is running a multimillionpound company*
(d) to work on a machine **bedienen, betreiben;** *do not run the copying machine for more than four hours at a time; the computer was running invoices all night*
(e) *(of buses, trains etc.)* to be working **verkehren, fahren;** *there is an evening plane running between London and Paris; this train runs on weekdays*
NOTE: **running - ran - has run**

◊ **runner** *noun (slang)* member of a gang of pickpockets who takes the items stolen and runs away with them to a safe place **Mitglied einer Taschendiebbande, das mit dem Diebesgut davonrennt**

rustle *verb* to steal livestock (especially cows and horses) **Vieh stehlen**

◊ **rustler** *noun* person who steals livestock **Viehdieb;** *a cattle rustler*

◊ **rustling** *noun* crime of stealing cattle *or* horses **Viehdiebstahl**

Ss

sabotage *noun* malicious damage done to machines *or* equipment **Sabotage;** *several acts of sabotage were committed against radio stations*
NOTE: no plural

sack
1 *noun*
(a) large bag made of strong cloth or plastic **Sack;** *the burglars carried a sack of clocks from the shop*
(b) to get the sack = to be dismissed from a job **entlassen/rausgeschmissen werden**
2 *verb* **to sack someone** = to dismiss someone from a job **jdn entlassen/rausschmeißen;** *he was sacked after being late for work*
◊ **sacking** *noun* dismissal from a job **Entlassung, Rausschmiß;** *the union protested against the sackings*

safe
1 *noun* heavy metal box which cannot be opened easily, in which valuable documents, money, etc. can be kept **Safe, Tresor;** *put the documents in the safe; we keep the petty cash in the safe;* **fire-proof safe** = safe which cannot be harmed by fire **feuersicherer Tresor; night safe** = safe in the outside wall of a bank, where money and documents can be deposited at night, using a special door **Nachttresor; wall safe** = safe fixed in a wall **Wandtresor**
2 *adjective*
(a) out of danger **sicher; keep the documents in a safe place** = in a place where they cannot be stolen or destroyed **bewahr die Unterlagen an einem sicheren Ort auf; safe keeping** = being looked after carefully **sichere Verwahrung;** *we put the documents into the bank for safe keeping*
(b) safe investments = shares, etc., which are not likely to fall in value **risikofreie Investitionen, sichere Kapitalanlagen**
◊ **safe deposit** *noun* safe in a bank vault where you can leave jewellery or documents **Tresor, Stahlkammer**
◊ **safe deposit box** *noun* small box which you can rent to keep jewellery or documents in a bank's safe **Bankschließfach**
◊ **safely** *adverb* without being harmed **sicher, wohlbehalten;** *the cargo was unloaded safely from the sinking ship*
◊ **safeguard**
1 *noun* protection **Schutz;** *the proposed legislation will provide a safeguard against illegal traders*

2 *verb* to protect **schützen, sichern;** *the court acted to safeguard the interests of the shareholders*

◊ **safety** *noun*
(a) being free from danger or risk **Sicherheit; Health and Safety at Work Act** = Act of Parliament which regulates what employers must do to make sure that their employees are kept healthy and safe at work **Gesetz zum Schutz der Gesundheit und Unfallverhütung am Arbeitsplatz; safety margin** = time *or* space allowed for something to be safe **Sicherheitsspielraum, Sicherheitsspanne; to take safety precautions** *or* **safety measures** = to act to make sure something is safe **Vorsichtsmaßnahmen/Schutzmaßnahmen ergreifen; safety regulations** = rules to make a place of work safe for the workers **Sicherheitsvorschriften**
(b) fire safety = making a place of work safe for the workers in case of fire **Brandschutz; fire safety officer** = person in a company responsible for seeing that the workers are safe if a fire breaks out **Betriebsfeuerwehrmann**
(c) for safety = to make something safe *or* to be safe **sicherheitshalber;** *put the documents in the cupboard for safety; take a copy of the disk for safety*
NOTE: no plural

sale *noun*
(a) act of selling *or* of transferring an item *or* a property from one owner to another in exchange for a consideration, usually in the form of money **Verkauf, Veräußerung; forced sale** = selling something because a court orders it *or* because it is the only way to avoid insolvency **Zwangsverkauf; sale and lease-back** = situation where a company sells a property to raise cash and then leases it back from the purchaser **Verkauf mit anschließender Vermietung an den Verkäufer; sale or return** = system where the retailer sends goods back if they are not sold, and pays the supplier only for goods sold **Kauf mit Rückgaberecht, Verkauf auf Kommissionsbasis; bill of sale** = (i) document which the seller gives to the buyer to show that a sale has taken place; (ii) document given to a lender by a borrower to show that the lender owns a property as security for a loan **(i) Kaufvertrag;** (ii) **Pfandverschreibung; conditions of sale** *or* **terms of sale** = list of terms under which a sale takes place (such as discounts and credit terms) **Verkaufsbedingungen; Sale of Goods Act** = Act of Parliament which regulates the selling of goods (but not land, copyrights, patents, etc.) **Gesetz über den Warenkauf;** *the*

law relating to the sale of goods is governed by the Sale of Goods Act 1979
(b) for sale = ready to be sold **zu verkaufen; to offer something for sale** *or* **to put something up for sale** = to announce that something is ready to be sold **etwas zum Verkauf anbieten;** *they put the factory up for sale; his shop is for sale; these items are not for sale to the general public*
(c) sales = money received for selling something *or* number of items sold **Umsatz, Absatz; sales conference** *or* **sales meeting** = meeting of sales managers, representatives, advertising staff, etc, to discuss results and plan future sales **Konferenz zur Absatzplanung; sales department** = section of a company which deals in selling the company's products or services **Verkaufsabteilung, Abteilung Verkauf; domestic sales** *or* **home sales** = sales in the home market **Inlandsabsatz; sales figures** = total sales, or sales broken down by category **Verkaufs-, Absatzzahlen; forward sales** = sales (of shares *or* commodities *or* foreign exchange) for delivery at a later date **Terminverkäufe; sales tax** = tax to be paid on each item sold **(allgemeine) Warenumsatzsteuer**
(d) selling of goods at specially low prices **Ausverkauf;** *the shop is having a sale to clear old stock; the sale price is 50% of the normal price;* **half-price sale** = sale of items at half the usual price **Verkauf zum halben Preis; the sales** = period when major stores sell many items at specially low prices **Schlußverkauf**

salvage
1 *noun*
(a) right of a person who saves a ship from being wrecked *or* cargo from a ship which has been wrecked, to receive compensation **Recht auf Bergelohn; salvage agreement** = agreement between the captain of a sinking ship and a salvage crew, giving the terms on which the ship will be saved **Bergungsvertrag; salvage (money)** = payment made by the owner of a ship *or* a cargo to the person who has saved it from being destroyed or wrecked **Bergelohn; salvage vessel** = ship which specializes in saving other ships and their cargoes **Bergungsschiff**
(b) goods saved from a wrecked ship *or* from a fire, etc. **Bergungsgut, geborgenes Gut;** *a sale of flood salvage items* (NOTE: no plural)
2 *verb*
(a) to save goods *or* a ship from being wrecked **bergen, retten;** *we are selling off a warehouse full of salvaged goods*
(b) to save something from loss **retten;** *the company is trying to salvage its reputation after the managing director was sent to prison for fraud; the receiver managed to*

salvage something from the failure of the company

sample
1 *noun* small part of something taken to show what the whole is like **Muster, Probe, Auswahl;** *they polled a sample group of voters;* **blood sample** *or* **urine sample** = small amount of blood *or* urine taken from someone to be tested **Blutprobe; Urinprobe**
2 *verb* to take a small part of something and examine it **testen, Proben entnehmen;** *the suspect's breath was sampled and the test proved positive*

sanction
1 *noun*
(a) official permission to do something **Genehmigung, Zustimmung;** *you will need the sanction of the local authorities before you can knock down the office block; the payment was made without official sanction*
(b) punishment for an act which goes against what is normally accepted behaviour **Sanktion, Strafmaßnahme; (economic) sanctions** = restrictions on trade with a country in order to influence its political situation *or* in order to make its government change its policy **Wirtschaftssanktionen;** *to impose sanctions on a country or to lift sanctions*
2 *verb* to approve *or* to permit (officially) **sanktionieren, genehmigen;** *the board sanctioned the expenditure of £1.2m on the development plan*

sane *adjective* mentally well **geistig gesund;** *was he sane when he made the will?*

◇ **sanity** *noun* being mentally well **normaler Geisteszustand, geistige Gesundheit**

sans recours *French phrase meaning* "with no recourse": used to show that the endorser of a bill (as an agent acting for a principal) is not responsible for paying it **ohne Obligo**

satisfaction *noun*
(a) (i) acceptance of money *or* goods by an injured party who then cannot make any further claim; (ii) payment *or* giving of goods to someone in exchange for that person's agreement to stop a claim **(i) Befriedigung eines Anspruches; (ii) Zufriedenstellung; accord and satisfaction** = payment by a debtor of (part of) a debt *or* performing by a debtor of some act or service which is accepted by the creditor in full settlement, so that the debtor can no longer be sued **vergleichsweise Erfüllung; memorandum of satisfaction** = document

showing that a company has repaid a mortgage or charge **Löschungsbewilligung**
(b) feeling of being happy or good feeling **Zufriedenheit, Befriedigung; job satisfaction** = a worker's feeling that he is happy in his place of work and pleased with the work he does **Zufriedenheit am Arbeitsplatz**
NOTE: no plural

◇ **satisfy** verb
(a) to convince someone that something is correct **überzeugen;** when opposing bail the police had to satisfy the court that the prisoner was likely to try to leave the country
(b) to make someone pleased **zufriedenstellen; to satisfy a client** = to make a client pleased with what he has purchased **einen Kunden zufriedenstellen; a satisfied customer** = a customer who has got what he wanted **ein zufriedener Kunde**
(c) to fulfil or to carry out fully **erfüllen;** has he satisfied all the conditions for parole? the company has not satisfied all the conditions laid down in the agreement; we cannot produce enough to satisfy the demand for the product

save verb
(a) to keep (money) or not to spend (money) **sparen;** he is trying to save money by walking to work; she is saving to buy a house
(b) not to waste or to use less **(ein)sparen;** to save time, let us continue the discussion in the taxi to the airport; the government is encouraging companies to save energy
(c) to store data on a computer disk **sichern;** do not forget to save your files when you have finished correcting them

scaffold noun raised platform on which executions take place **Schafott**

scale
1 noun
(a) system which is classified into various levels **Skala, Tabelle; scale of charges** or **scale of prices** = list showing various prices **Gebührenordnung, Tarife, Preisliste, Preisskala; fixed scale of charges** = rate of charging which does not change **verbindliche Gebührenordnung; scale of salaries** or **salary scale** = list of salaries showing different levels of pay in different jobs in the same company **Gehaltstabelle, Lohn-, Gehaltsordnung**
(b) large scale or **small scale** = working with large or small amounts of investment or staff, etc. **in großem Umfang; in begrenztem Umfang; to start in business on a small scale** = to start in business with a small staff or few products or little investment **ein Geschäft klein anfangen; economies of scale** = making a product more cheaply by

producing it or buying it in large quantities **Größen-, Kostendegression**
2 verb **to scale down** or **to scale up** = to lower or to increase in proportion **verringern, herabsetzen; erhöhen, heraufsetzen**

scam noun US (informal) case of fraud **Betrug**

schedule
1 noun
(a) timetable or plan of time drawn up in advance **Zeitplan, Arbeitsplan, Terminplan; to be ahead of schedule** = to be early **dem Zeitplan voraus/vorzeitig sein; to be on schedule** = to be on time **pünktlich/rechtzeitig fertig sein; to be behind schedule** = to be late **in Verzug sein;** the Bill is on schedule; the Second Reading was completed ahead of schedule; I am sorry to say that we are three months behind schedule; the managing director has a busy schedule of appointments; his secretary tried to fit me into his schedule
(b) additional documents attached to a contract **Anhang;** schedule of markets to which a contract applies; see the attached schedule or as per the attached schedule; the schedule before referred to
(c) list **Verzeichnis, Liste, Aufstellung;** schedule of charges
(d) tax schedules = six types of income as classified in the Finance Acts for British tax **Steuerklassen, Einkommenssteuergruppen; Schedule A** = schedule under which tax is charged on income from land or buildings; **Schedule B** = schedule under which tax is charged on income from woodlands; **Schedule C** = schedule under which tax is charged on profits from government stock; **Schedule D** = schedule under which tax is charged on income from trades or professions, interest and other earnings not derived from being employed; **Schedule E** = schedule under which tax is charged on income from salaries or wages or pensions; **Schedule F** = schedule under which tax is charged on income from dividends **Einkommenssteuergruppen, je nach Art des Einkommens in 6 Gruppen eingeteilt**
2 verb
(a) to list officially **festlegen, aufführen;** scheduled prices or scheduled charges
(b) to plan the time when something will happen **ansetzen, anberaumen;** the building is scheduled for completion in May

scheme of arrangement noun agreement between a company and its creditors, whereby the creditors accept an agreed sum in settlement of their claim

scheme 289 **secondary**

rather than force the company into insolvency **Vergleichsregelung**

scope *noun* limits covered by something **(Geltungs)bereich, Wirkungskreis, Rahmen;** *the question does not come within the scope of the authority's powers; the Bill plans to increase the scope of the tribunal's authority*

screen
1 *noun* glass surface on which computer information *or* TV pictures, etc., can be shown **Bildschirm**
2 *verb* **to screen candidates** = to examine candidates to see if they are completely suitable **Bewerber sieben/aussondern**

◇ **screening** *noun* **the screening of candidates** = examining candidates to see if they are suitable **Aussonderung geeigneter Bewerber**

screw *noun (slang)* prison warder **Schließer**

scrip *noun* certificate showing that someone owns shares in a company **Interims-, Zwischenschein, Scrip; scrip issue** = new shares given free to shareholders **Ausgabe von Gratisaktien**
NOTE: no plural

seal
1 *noun*
(a) piece of wax *or* red paper attached to a document to show that it is legally valid; stamp printed *or* marked on a document to show that it is valid **Siegel; (Beglaubigungs)stempel; common seal** *or* **company's seal** = metal stamp which every company must possess, used to stamp documents with the name of the company to show they have been approved officially **Firmensiegel;** *to attach the company's seal to a document;* **contract under seal** = contract which has been signed and legally approved with the seal of the company *or* the person entering into it **beurkundeter/besiegelter Vertrag**
(b) piece of paper *or* metal *or* wax attached to close something, so that it can be opened only if the paper *or* metal *or* wax is removed *or* broken **Versiegelung, Siegel, Verschluß, Plombe;** *the seals on the ballot box had been tampered with;* **customs seal** = seal attached by customs officers to a box, to show that the contents have passed through the customs **Zollverschluß, Zollsiegel**
2 *verb*
(a) to close something tightly **fest verschließen, zukleben;** *the computer disks were sent in a sealed container;* **sealed envelope** = envelope where the back has

been stuck down to close it **verschlossener Briefumschlag;** *the information was sent in a sealed envelope;* **sealed tenders** = tenders sent in sealed envelopes, which will all be opened together at a certain time **versiegelte Submissionsofferten;** *the company has asked for sealed bids for the warehouse*
(b) to attach a seal *or* to stamp something with a seal **versiegeln; plombieren, verplomben;** *the customs sealed the shipment;* **sealed instrument** = document which has been signed and sealed **gesiegelte Urkunde**

◇ **seal off** *verb* to put barriers across a street *or* an entrance to prevent people from going in or out **absperren, abriegeln;** *police sealed off all roads leading to the town*

search
1 *noun*
(a) examining a place to try to find something **Suche; Durchsuchung; search warrant** = official document signed by a magistrate allowing the police to enter premises and look for persons suspected of being criminals *or* objects which are believed to have been stolen *or* dangerous *or* illegal substances **Durchsuchungsbefehl**
(b) **searches** = examination of records by the lawyer acting for someone who wants to buy a property, to make sure that the vendor has the right to sell it **Einsichtnahme in das Grundbuch, um festzustellen, ob etwaige Rechte Dritter an dem zu kaufenden Grundbesitz bestehen**
2 *verb* to examine a place *or* a person to try to find something *or* to look inside something to see what is there **suchen; durchsuchen;** *the agent searched his files for a record of the sale; all drivers and their cars are searched at the customs post; the police searched the area round the house for clues*

secondary *adjective* second in importance **sekundär, Sekundär-, Neben-, zweitrangig; secondary banks** = companies which provide money for hire-purchase deals **Teilzahlungsinstitute; secondary evidence** = evidence which is not the main proof (such as copies of documents, not the original documents themselves) **indirekter Urkundenbeweis**

COMMENT: secondary evidence can be admitted if there is no primary evidence available

secondary action *or* **secondary picketing** = picketing of another factory *or* place of work, which is not directly connected with a strike, to prevent it supplying a striking factory *or* receiving supplies from it

Bestreikung eines indirekt beteiligten Betriebes

◊ **secondarily** adverb in second place **in zweiter Linie;** the person making a guarantee is secondarily liable if the person who is primarily liable defaults; see also PRIMARY, PRIMARILY

second degree murder noun (US) murder without premeditation and not committed at the same time as rape or robbery **Totschlag**

second mortgage noun further mortgage on a property which is already mortgaged (the first mortgage still has prior claim) **zweite Hypothek**

Second Reading noun (i) detailed presentation of a Bill in the House of Commons by the responsible minister, followed by a discussion and vote;(ii) (US) detailed examination of a Bill in the House, before it is passed to the Senate **(i) & (ii) zweite Lesung**

secret
1 adjective hidden or not known by many people **geheim, Geheim-;** the Chief Constable kept the report secret from the rest of the force; they signed a secret deal with their main competitor
2 noun something hidden **Geheimnis; to keep a secret** = not to tell someone a secret which you know **etwas geheim halten, ein Geheimnis wahren; in secret** = without telling anyone **heimlich, im geheimen;** the gang leader met the detective inspector in secret; he photographed the plan of the bank vault in secret; **official secret** = piece of information which is classified as important to the state, and which it is a crime to reveal **Staatsgeheimnis; Official Secrets Act** = Act of Parliament governing the publication of secrets relating to the state **Gesetz über die Wahrung von Staatsgeheimnissen**

◊ **secretly** adverb without telling anyone **heimlich;** the treaty was signed secretly by the Prime Minister and the President; he offered to copy the plans secretly and sell them to another firm

secretary noun
(a) person who types letters or files documents or arranges meetings, etc. for someone **Sekretär/-in;** secretary and personal assistant; my secretary deals with visitors; his secretary phoned to say he would be late; **legal secretary** = secretary in a firm of solicitors or in the legal

department of a company, etc. **Sekretär in einem Anwaltsbüro od in der Rechtsabteilung**
(b) official of a company or society **Geschäftsführer, Schriftführer; company secretary** = person who is responsible for a company's legal and financial affairs **Manager mit Aufgabenbereich Finanzen und Verwaltung; honorary secretary** = person who keeps the minutes and official documents of a committee or club, but is not paid a salary **ehrenamtlicher Geschäftsführer**
(c) member of the British government in charge of a department **Minister/-in;** Education Secretary; Foreign Secretary; US **Secretary of the Treasury** = senior member of the government in charge of financial affairs **Finanzminister**

◊ **Secretary of State** noun
(a) GB member of the government in charge of a department **Minister/-in**
(b) US senior member of the government in charge of foreign affairs **Außenminister;** see also notes at FOREIGN, MINISTER

◊ **secretarial** adjective referring to the work of a secretary **als Sekretär, Sekretariats-;** she is taking a secretarial course; he is looking for secretarial work; we need extra secretarial help to deal with the mailings; **secretarial college** = college which teaches typing, shorthand and wordprocessing **Sekretärinnenschule**

◊ **secretariat** noun important office and the officials who work in it **Sekretariat; Geschäftsstelle;** the United Nations secretariat

section noun
(a) part **Abteilung; Abschnitt; Absatz; legal section** = department dealing with legal matters in a company **Rechtsabteilung**
(b) part of an Act of Parliament or bylaw **Paragraph;** he does not qualify for a grant under section 2 of the Act

sector noun general area of business **Sektor, Bereich; private sector** = all companies which are owned by private shareholders, not by the state **Privatsektor, Privatwirtschaft; public sector** = nationalized industries and services **öffentlicher Bereich, staatlicher Sektor; public sector borrowing requirement** = amount of money which a government has to borrow to pay for its own spending **Kreditbedarf der öffentlichen Hand**

secure
1 adjective
(a) safe or which cannot change **sicher, gesichert; secure job** = job from which you are not likely to be made redundant **sicherer Arbeitsplatz; secure investment** =

investment where you are not likely to lose money **sichere/risikofreie Investition; secure tenant** = tenant of a local authority who has the right to buy the freehold of the property he rents at a discount **Mieter od Pächter einer der Gemeinde gehörenden Wohnung (oder eines Hauses) mit priviligiertem Vorkaufsrecht (b)** safe *or* not likely to be opened **sicher, geschützt;** *the documents should be kept in a secure place; the police and army have made the border secure*
2 *verb*
(a) to secure a loan = to pledge a property *or* other assets as a security for a loan **ein Darlehen sichern**
(b) to make sure that (something) is done **gewährleisten, erwirken;** *they secured the release of the hostages*

◇ **secured** *adjective* **secured loan** = loan which is guaranteed by the borrower giving valuable property as security **(dinglich) gesichertes Darlehen; secured creditor** = person who is owed money by someone, and holds a mortgage *or* charge on that person's property as security **gesicherter Gläubiger; secured debts** = debts which are guaranteed by assets **gesicherte Verbindlichkeiten**

◇ **securities** *plural noun* investments in stocks and shares; certificates to show that someone owns stock **Wertpapiere, Effekten; gilt-edged securities** *or* **government securities** = British government stock **mündelsichere Staatspapiere; the securities market** = Stock Exchange *or* place where stocks and shares can be bought or sold **Effektenmarkt; securities trader** = person whose business is buying and selling stocks and shares **Effektenhändler**

◇ **security** *noun*
(a) being safe *or* not likely to change **Sicherheit; security of employment** = feeling by a worker that he has the right to keep his job until he retires **Sicherheit des Arbeitsplatzes; security for costs** = guarantee that a party in a dispute will pay costs **Sicherheitsleistung für Prozeßkosten;** *the master ordered that the plaintiff should deposit £2,000 as security for the defendant's costs*

COMMENT: where a foreign plaintiff or a company which may become insolvent brings proceedings against a defendant, the defendant is entitled to apply to the court for an order that the proceedings be stayed unless the plaintiff deposits money to secure the defendant's costs if the plaintiff fails in his action

security of tenure = right to keep a position *or* rented accommodation, provided that certain conditions are met **Kündigungsschutz**

(b) being protected **Schutz, Sicherheit; airport security** = actions taken to protect aircraft and passengers against attack **Flugsicherheit; security guard** = person whose job is to protect money *or* valuables *or* an office against possible theft or damage **Wachmann; office security** = protecting an office against theft of equipment *or* personal property *or* information **Sicherheitsvorkehrungen (gegen Diebstahl) am Arbeitsplatz; top security prison** = prison with very strict security where category "A" prisoners are kept **mit besonderen Sicherungsvorkehrungen versehenes Gefängnis**
(c) being secret **Geheimhaltung, Diskretion; security in this office is nil** = nothing can be kept secret in this office **in diesem Büro kann man nichts geheimhalten; security printer** = printer who prints paper money, secret government documents, etc. **Notenpresse**
(d) social security = money *or* help provided by the government to people who need it **Sozialunterstützung, Sozialhilfe;** *he lives on social security payments*
(e) guarantee that someone will repay money borrowed **Bürgschaft; to stand security for someone** = to guarantee that if the person does not repay a loan, you will repay it for him **für jdn Bürgschaft leisten;** *to give something as security for a debt; to use a house as security for a loan; the bank lent him £20,000 without security*

◇ **Security Council** *noun* permanent ruling body of the United Nations **Sicherheitsrat**

sedition *noun* crime of doing acts *or* speaking or publishing words which bring the royal family or the government into hatred or contempt and encourage civil disorder **Aufwiegelung, Volksverhetzung, staatsgefährdende Propaganda;** (NOTE: no plural)

COMMENT: sedition is a lesser crime than treason

◇ **seditious** *adjective* which provokes sedition **aufrührerisch, hetzerisch, staatsgefährdend; seditious libel** = offence of publishing a libel with seditious intent **staatsgefährdende/aufrührerische Veröffentlichung**

seek *verb*
(a) to ask for **beantragen, erbitten, ersuchen;** *they are seeking damages for loss of revenue; the applicant sought judicial review to quash the order; the Bill requires a social worker to seek permission of the Juvenile Court; a creditor seeking a receiving order under the Bankruptcy Act;* **to seek an interview** = to ask if you can see

someone **um ein Gespräch bitten;** *she sought an interview with the minister*
(b) to look for someone *or* something **suchen;** *the police are seeking a tall man who was seen near the scene of the crime; two men are being sought by the police*
(c) to try to do something **(ver)suchen;** *the local authority is seeking to place the ward of court in accommodation*
NOTE: **seeking - sought - has sought**

seised *adjective* **seised of a property** = being legally in possession of property **im Besitz von etwas sein**

◊ **seisin** *noun* possession of land **Besitz von Grundbesitz**

seize *verb* to take hold of something *or* to take possession of something **einziehen, beschlagnahmen, pfänden;** *the customs seized the shipment of books; his case was seized at the airport; the court ordered the company's funds to be seized*

◊ **seizure** *noun* taking possession of something **Einziehung, Beschlagnahme, Pfändung, Konfiszierung;** *the court ordered the seizure of the shipment or of the company's funds*
NOTE: no plural

select
1 *adjective* of top quality *or* specially chosen **exklusiv, auserwählt, auserlesen;** *our customers are very select; a select group of clients; (in the House of Commons)* **select committee** = special committee (with members representing various political parties) which examines the work of a ministry **Sonderausschuß;** *the Select Committee on Defence or the Defence Select Committee*
2 *verb* to choose **auswählen, aussuchen;** *three members of the committee have been selected to speak at the AGM; he has been selected as a candidate for a Northern constituency*

◊ **selection** *noun* (i) choice; (ii) thing which has been chosen **(i) Auswahl; (ii) Wahl; selection board** *or* **selection committee** = committee which chooses a candidate for a job **Auswahlkomitee, Bewerbungsausschuß; selection procedure** = general method of choosing a candidate for a job **Auswahlverfahren**

self-defence *noun* trying to protect yourself when attacked **Notwehr;** *he pleaded that he had acted in self-defence when he had hit the mugger*
NOTE: no plural

COMMENT: this can be used as a defence to a charge of a crime of violence, where the defendant pleads that his actions were attributable to defending himself rather than to a desire to commit violence

◊ **self-incrimination** *noun* act of incriminating yourself *or* of saying something which shows you are guilty **Selbstbezichtigung; right against self-incrimination** = right not to say anything, when questioned by the police, in case you may say something which could incriminate you **Aussageverweigerungsrecht**

sell *verb* to transfer the ownership of property to another person in exchange for money **verkaufen, veräußern;** *to sell cars or to sell refrigerators; they have decided to sell their house; they tried to sell their house for £100,000; to sell something on credit; her house is difficult to sell; their products are easy to sell;* **to sell forward** = to sell foreign currency, commodities, etc., for delivery at a later date **auf Termin verkaufen**
NOTE: **selling - sold - has sold**

◊ **seller** *noun*
(a) person who sells **Verkäufer;** *there were few sellers in the market, so prices remained high;* **seller's market** = market where the seller can ask high prices because there is a large demand for the product **Verkäufermarkt**
(b) thing which sells **gängiger Artikel;** *this book is a good seller;* **best-seller** = item (especially a book) which sells very well **Bestseller**

◊ **selling** *noun* **direct selling** = selling a product direct to the customer without going through a shop **Direktverkauf; mail-order selling** = selling by taking orders and supplying a product by post **Versandhandel; selling price** = price at which someone is willing to sell **Verkaufspreis**

semble *French word meaning* "it appears": word used in discussing a court judgment where there is some uncertainty about what the court intended **anscheinend**

senate *noun* upper house of a parliament **Senat;** *the Senate of the USA; the Senate Foreign Relations Committee*
◊ **senator** *noun* member of a senate **Senatsmitglied, Senator/-in**

sender *noun* person who sends a letter *or* parcel *or* message **Absender**

senior *adjective* older; more important; (worker) who has been employed longer than another **älter; leitend, übergeordnet,**

höher; dienstälter; **senior manager** *or* **senior executive** = manager *or* director who has a higher rank than others **obere Führungskraft, leitender Angestellter; senior partner** = partner who has a large part of the shares in a partnership **Seniorpartner; John Paine, Senior** = the older John Paine (i.e. the father of John Paine, Junior) **John Paine, senior**

◊ **seniority** *noun* being older *or* more important; being an employee of the company longer **höheres Alter; höherer Dienstrang; höheres Dienstalter; the managers were listed in order of seniority** = the manager who had been an employee the longest *or* the manager with the most important job was put at the top of the list **die Manager wurden entsprechend der Betriebszugehörigkeitsdauer od des Ranges aufgeführt**

sentence

1 *noun* legal punishment given by a court to a convicted person **Strafe, Strafmaß;** *he received a three-year jail sentence; the two men accused of rape face sentences of up to six years in prison;* **to pass sentence on someone** = to give someone the official legal punishment **jdn verurteilen, das Strafurteil über jdn verkünden;** *the jury returned a verdict of manslaughter and the judge will pass sentence next week;* **concurrent sentence** = sentence which takes place at the same time as another **gleichzeitig zu verbüßende Freiheitsstrafe; consecutive sentences** = two sentences which follow one after the other **nacheinander zu verbüßende Freiheitsstrafen; custodial sentence** = sentence which involves sending someone to prison **Freiheitsstrafe**
2 *verb* to give (someone) the official legal punishment **verurteilen, das Urteil sprechen/fällen;** *the judge sentenced him to six months in prison or he was sentenced to six months' imprisonment; the accused was convicted of murder and will be sentenced next week; compare* CONVICT

◊ **sentencer** *noun* person (such as a judge) who can pass a sentence on someone **Strafrichter**

separate

1 *adjective* not together **getrennt, gesondert, einzeln, separat; to send something under separate cover** = to send something in a different envelope **etwas mit getrennter Post schicken**
2 *verb* to divide **trennen, aufteilen;** *the personnel are separated into part-timers and fulltime staff*

◊ **separately** *adverb* not together **getrennt, gesondert, einzeln, separat;** *the two brothers were charged separately*

◊ **separation** *noun*
(a) agreement between a man and his wife to live apart from each other **Trennung, Getrenntleben; judicial** *or* **legal separation** = legal separation of man and wife, ordered by the court, where each becomes separated, but neither is allowed to marry again because they are not divorced **gerichtliche Trennung/Aufhebung der ehelichen Gemeinschaft**
(b) *US* leaving a job (resigning, retiring, or being fired or made redundant) **Aufgabe einer Stellung**

seq *or* **sequenter** *see* ET SEQ

sequester *or* **sequestrate** *verb* to take and keep (property) because a court has ordered it **sequestrieren, konfiszieren, beschlagnahmen**

◊ **sequestration** *noun* taking and keeping of property on the order of a court, especially seizing property from someone who is in contempt of court **Sequestration, Konfiszierung, Beschlagnahme;** *his property has been kept under sequestration*

◊ **sequestrator** *noun* person who takes and keeps property on the order of a court **Sequester, Zwangsverwalter**

sergeant *noun* **(police) sergeant** = rank in the police force above constable and below inspector **Polizeibeamter**

seriatim *Latin word meaning* "one after the other in order" **der Reihe nach**

serious *adjective* bad *or* important **schwer, schlimm; ernsthaft;** *he faces six serious charges; she claims there has been a serious miscarriage of justice*

◊ **seriousness** *noun* being serious **Ernst, Schwere;** *the length of the prison sentence depends on the seriousness of the crime; the Police Commissioner asked for a report on the seriousness of the situation in the centre of town*

Serjeant *see* COMMON SERJEANT

servant *noun*
(a) person who is employed by someone **Bediensteter, Arbeitnehmer; civil servant** = person who works in the civil service **Beamter im öffentlichen Dienst; master and servant** = employer and employee **Dienstherr und Angestellter; the law of master**

and **servant** = employment law **das Arbeitsrecht**
(b) person who is paid to work in someone's house **Diener/-in**

serve *verb*
(a) to spend time in prison following being sentenced to imprisonment **verbüßen;** *he served six months in a local jail; she still has half her sentence to serve*
(b) to deal with (a customer) *or* to do a type of work **bedienen; ausüben; to serve articles** = to work as an articled clerk in a solicitor's office **seine Rechtsreferendarzeit ableisten; to serve a customer** = to take a customer's order and provide what he wants **einen Kunden bedienen; to serve in a shop** *or* **in a restaurant** = to deal with customers' orders **in einem Laden od einem Restaurant bedienen; to serve on a jury** = to be a juror **Geschworener sein**
(c) to serve someone with a writ *or* **to serve a writ on someone** = to give someone a writ officially, so that he has to obey it **jdm eine Ladung od Verfügung zustellen**

◊ **server** *noun* **process-server** = person employed to serve legal documents **Zustellungsbeamter**

service *noun*
(a) service (of process) *or* personal service = delivery of a document (such as a writ *or* summons) to someone in person *or* to his solicitor **Zustellung (der Ladung und der Klageschrift); Zustellung zu eigenen Händen des Beklagten; address for service** = address where court documents (such as pleadings) can be sent to a party in a case **Zustellungsadresse; to acknowledge service** = to confirm that a legal document (such as a writ) has been received **die Zustellung bestätigen; acknowledgement of service** = document in which a defendant confirms that a writ *or* legal document has been received **Zustellungsbestätigung, Zustellungsurkunde**
(b) duty to do work for someone **Dienst, Dienstverhältnis; contract of service** *or* **service contract** = contract between employer and employee showing all conditions of work **Dienst-, Arbeitsvertrag; community service order** = punishment where a convicted person is sentenced to do unpaid work in the local community **Verurteilung zu gemeinnütziger Arbeit; jury service** = duty which each citizen has of serving on a jury if asked to do so **Schöffenamt; service charge** = charge made by a landlord to cover general work done to the property (cleaning of the stairs, collection of rubbish, etc.) *or* charge made in a restaurant for serving the customer **Reinigungskosten; Bedienung(szuschlag)**

(c) civil service = organization and personnel which administers a country under the direction of the government **öffentlicher Dienst, Staatsdienst**

servient tenement *noun* land over which the owner grants an easement to the owner of another property **dienendes Grundstück**

> COMMENT: the grantee of the easement is the dominant tenement

servitude *noun* penal servitude = former punishment by imprisonment with hard labour **Zwangsarbeit; Zuchthaus**

session *noun*
(a) meeting *or* period when a group of people meets **Sitzung;** *the morning session or the afternoon session will be held in the conference room ;* **opening session** *or* **closing session** = first part *or* last part of a conference **Eröffnungssitzung; Schlußsitzung; closed session** = meeting which is not open to the public or to newspaper reporters **nichtöffentliche Sitzung**
(b) period when Parliament is meeting **Sitzungsperiode;** *the government is planning to introduce the Bill at the next session of Parliament*
(c) Court of Session = highest civil court in Scotland **Oberstes Gericht für Zivilsachen**

◊ **sessions** *plural noun* court **Gericht; petty sessions** = Magistrates' Court **summarisches Gericht mit zwei oder mehreren Friedensrichtern; Amtsgericht; special sessions** = Magistrates' Court for a district which is held for a special reason (such as to deal with terrorists) **außerordentliche Sitzung, Sondertermin**

set *verb* to put **stellen, setzen, legen**

◊ **set aside** *verb* to decide not to apply a decision **aufheben, annullieren;** *the arbitrator's award was set aside on appeal*

◊ **set down** *verb* to arrange for a trial to take place by putting it on one of the lists of trials **anberaumen;** *pleadings must be submitted to the court when the action is set down for trial*

◊ **set forth** *verb* to put down in writing **darlegen;** *the argument is set forth in the document from the European Court*

◊ **set-off** *noun* counterclaim by a defendant which should be deducted from the sum being claimed by the plaintiff **Aufrechnung (im Prozeß)**

◊ **set out** *verb*
(a) to put down in writing **darlegen, darstellen;** *the claim is set out in the enclosed*

document; the figures are set out in the tables at the back of the book
(b) to try to do something **sich vornehmen, beabsichtigen;** *counsel for the prosecution has set out to discredit the defence witness*

settle *verb*

(a) to settle an account = to pay what is owed **eine Rechnung bezahlen; ein Konto be-, ausgleichen;** to settle a claim = to agree to pay what is asked for **eine Forderung regulieren;** *the insurance company refused to settle his claim for storm damage;* **the two parties settled out of court** = the two parties reached an agreement privately without continuing the court case **die beiden Parteien haben sich außergerichtlich geeinigt**
(b) to settle property on someone = to arrange for land to be passed to trustees to keep for the benefit of future owners **Grundbesitz nachfolgenden Begünstigten (durch Errichtung eines Trusts) zuwenden**
(c) to write out in final form **(schriftlich) festlegen;** *counsel is instructed to settle the defence*

◇ **settled land** *noun* land which is subject of a settlement **Grundbesitz, der durch erbrechtliche Bestimmungen (vorgenommen in Form eines Trusts) beschränkt wird**

◇ **settlement** *noun*
(a) payment of an account **Bezahlung, Begleichung;** settlement day = day when accounts have to be settled **Abrechnungs-, Verrechnungstag;** *our basic discount is 20% but we offer an extra 5% for rapid settlement* = we take a further 5% off the price if the customer pays quickly **wir geben normalerweise 20% Rabatt, aber wir bieten weitere 5% für prompte Bezahlung;** settlement in cash *or* cash settlement = payment of an invoice in cash, not by cheque **Barzahlung**
(b) agreement after an argument **Beilegung, Schlichtung, Vergleich; to effect a settlement between two parties** = to bring two parties together to make them agree **einen Vergleich zwischen zwei Parteien zustande bringen;** to accept something in full settlement = to accept money *or* service from a debtor and agree that it covers all the claim **etwas zum Ausgleich aller Forderungen akzeptieren**
(c) arrangement where land is passed to trustees to keep for the benefit of future owners **Verfügung über Grundbesitz, der für nachfolgende Begünstigte durch einen Trust verwaltet wird; marriage settlement** = arranging for property to be passed to a person who is getting married **Güterrechtsvertrag über treuhänderische Zuwendung anläßlich der Eheschließung**
(d) convict settlement = prison camp where convicts are sent **Straf-, Sträflingskolonie**

◇ **settle on** *verb* to leave property to someone when you die **vermachen;** *he settled his property on his children*

◇ **settlor** *noun* person who settles property on someone **Testator; Treugeber; Begründer eines Trusts; Errichter eines Trusts;** *(siehe oben unter 'c')*

several *adjective*

(a) more than a few *or* some **einige, mehrere;** *several judges are retiring this year; several of our clients have received long prison sentences*
(b) separate **einzeln, gesondert, getrennt; joint and several liability** = situation where someone who has a claim against a group of people may sue them separately or as a group **gesamtschuldnerische Haftung**

◇ **severally** *adverb* separately *or* not jointly **einzeln, gesondert, getrennt; they are jointly and severally liable** = they are liable both together as a group and as individuals **als Gesamtschuldner/gesamtschuldnerisch haften**

severance *noun*

(a) ending of a joint tenancy **Auflösung des Mitbesitzes/gemeinsamen Eigentums**
(b) ending of a contract of employment **Entlassung; severance pay** = money paid as compensation to someone who is losing his job **Entlassungsabfindung**

severe *adjective* strict *or* not kind **streng, hart;** *the judge passed severe sentences on the rapists*

◇ **severely** *adverb*
(a) in a strict way **streng;** *the police has asked for the gang to be treated severely*
(b) strongly *or* badly **schwer, schlimm;** *he was severely wounded in the battle with the rebel army*

◇ **severity** *noun* being severe **Strenge, Härte;** *the law treats convicted rapists with great severity; the press commented on the severity of the sentences*

sexual *adjective* relating to the two sexes **geschlechtlich, sexuell, Sexual-, Geschlechts-;** sexual intercourse = sexual act between man and woman **Geschlechtsverkehr;** *it is an offence to have sexual intercourse with a girl under sixteen years of age;* sexual offences = criminal acts where sexual intercourse takes place (such as rape, incest) **Sittlichkeits-, Sexualdelikte**

shady *adjective* not honest **zweifelhaft, fragwürdig;** *shady deal*

sham *adjective* false *or* not true **falsch, unecht, nachgemacht, vorgetäuscht, Schein-;** sham marriage = form of marriage arranged for the purpose of acquiring the nationality of the spouse *or* for other reasons **Scheinehe**

share

1 *noun* one of many parts into which a company's capital is divided, owned by shareholders **Aktie;** *he bought a block of shares in Marks and Spencer; shares fell on the London market; the company offered 1.8m shares on the market;* **"A" shares** = ordinary shares with limited voting rights **dividendenberechtigte Aktien mit beschränktem Stimmrecht; "B" shares** = ordinary shares with special voting rights **Aktien mit besonderem Stimmrecht; deferred shares** = shares which receive a dividend only after all other dividends have been paid **Nachzugsaktien; ordinary shares** = normal shares in a company, which have no special benefits or restrictions **Stammaktien; preference shares** = shares (often with no voting rights) which receive their dividend before all other shares and are repaid first (at face value) if the company is liquidated **Vorzugsaktien; share capital** = value of the assets of a company held as shares **Aktienkapital; share certificate** = document proving that someone owns shares **Aktienzertifikat; share issue** = selling new shares in a company to the public **Aktienemission**
2 *verb*
(a) to own *or* use something together with someone else **sich teilen, gemeinsam haben;** *to share a telephone; to share an office*
(b) to divide something among several people **sich teilen, auf-, verteilen;** *three companies share the market; to share computer time; to share the profits among the senior executives;* **to share information** *or* **to share data** = to give someone information which you have **Information/Daten zugänglich machen**

◊ **shareholder** *noun* person who owns shares in a company **Aktionär/-in; shareholders' equity** = ordinary shares owned by shareholders in a company **Eigenkapital; majority** *or* **minority shareholder** = person who owns more than *or* less than half the shares in a company **Mehrheitsaktionär; Minderheitsaktionär;** *the solicitor acting on behalf of the minority shareholders*

◊ **shareholding** *noun* group of shares in a company owned by one person **Aktienbestand; a majority shareholding** *or* **a minority shareholding** = group of shares which are more *or* less than half the total **Mehrheitsbeteiligung; Minderheitsbeteiligung**

sharp *adjective*
(a) sudden **plötzlich, steil;** *sharp rise in*

crimes of violence; sharp drop in prices
(b) sharp practice = way of doing business which is not honest, but not illegal **unsauberes/unlauteres Geschäftsgebaren**

◊ **sharper** *noun* **card sharper** = person who makes a living by cheating at cards **Falschspieler**

◊ **sharply** *adverb* suddenly **plötzlich, steil;** *the number of mugging cases has risen sharply over the last few years*

sheriff *noun*
(a) *US* official in charge of justice in a county **Sheriff, oberster Vollstreckungsbeamter eines County**
(b) (High) Sheriff = official appointed as the government's representative in a county, responsible for executing court decisions, such as sending in bailiffs to seize property and acting as returning officer in parliamentary elections **oberster Verwaltungsbeamter einer Grafschaft mit gerichtlichen Aufgaben**
(c) *(in Scotland)* chief judge in a district **oberster Richter; Sheriff Court** = court presided over by a sheriff; *entspricht* **Amtsgericht**

ship

1 *noun* large boat for carrying passengers and cargo on the sea **Schiff; to jump ship** = to leave the ship on which you are working and not come back **ohne Erlaubnis abheuern**
2 *verb* to send goods (but not necessarily on a ship) **versenden, befördern, transportieren; verschiffen;** *to ship goods to the USA; we ship all our goods by rail; the consignment of cars was shipped abroad last week*

◊ **shipment** *noun* sending of goods *or* goods sent **Versand, Verladung, Transport, Verschiffung; Sendung, Ladung; Schiffsladung; consolidated shipment** = goods from different companies grouped together into a single shipment **Sammelladung; drop shipment** = delivery of a large order from a producer direct to a customer's shop or warehouse, without going through an agent **Direktlieferung**

◊ **shipper** *noun* person who sends goods *or* who organizes the sending of goods for other customers **Spediteur, Ablader, Befrachter**

◊ **shipping** *noun* sending of goods **Versand, Transport; Verschiffung; shipping agent** = company which specializes in the sending of goods **Speditionsfirma; shipping company** *or* **shipping line** = company which owns ships **Reederei; shipping instructions** = details of how goods are to be shipped and delivered **Versandanweisungen; shipping note** = note which gives details of goods being shipped **Verladeschein, Frachtbrief**
NOTE: no plural

◊ **shipwreck** *noun* action of sinking *or* badly damaging a ship **Schiffbruch**

shop

1 *noun*
(a) place where goods are stored and sold (usually to the general public) **Laden, Geschäft;** *a bookshop; a computer shop; an electrical shop; he has bought a shoe shop in the centre of town; she opened a women's wear shop; all the shops in the centre of town close on Sundays;* **retail shop** = shop where goods are sold only to the public **Einzelhandelsgeschäft**
(b) place where goods are made **Werkstatt, Betrieb; machine shop** = place where working machines are kept **Maschinensaal; repair shop** = small factory where machines are repaired **Reparaturwerkstatt**
(c) closed shop = system where a company agrees to employ only union members in certain jobs **gewerkschaftspflichtiger Betrieb**
2 *verb*
(a) to shop (for) something = to look for things in shops **etwas einkaufen**
(b) *slang* to give information about someone to the police **verpfeifen;** *he was shopped to the police by the leader of the other gang*
NOTE: **shopping - shopped**

◊ **shoplifter** *noun* person who steals goods from shops **Ladendieb**

◊ **shoplifting** *noun* offence of stealing goods from shops, by taking them when the shop is open and not paying for them **Ladendiebstahl**

Short Cause List *noun* cases to be heard in the Queen's Bench Division which the judge thinks are not likely to take very long to hear **Terminliste für im Schnellverfahren zu erledigende Sachen**

shorthand *noun* system of taking notes quickly by writing signs instead of letters **Stenographie, Kurzschrift;** *the court proceedings were taken down in shorthand; the reporters could take notes in shorthand;* **shorthand writer** = person who takes down in shorthand evidence *or* a judgment given in court **Stenograph/-in**

shorthold tenancy *noun* protected tenancy for a limited period of less than five years **bis zu fünf Jahren befristeter Miet-od Pachtvertrag**

short sharp shock *noun* type of treatment for young offenders where they are subjected to harsh discipline for a short period in a detention centre **kurze Bestrafung mit harter Disziplin in einem Jugendgefängnis**

short title *noun* usual name by which an Act of Parliament is known **Kurztitel**

show

1 *noun*
(a) exhibition *or* display of goods or services for sale **Ausstellung, Messe;** *motor show; computer show*
(b) show of hands = way of casting votes where people show how they vote by raising their hands **Abstimmung durch Handheben;** *the motion was carried on a show of hands*
2 *verb* to make something be seen **zeigen, aufweisen;** *to show a gain or a fall; to show a profit or a loss;* **to show cause** = to appear before a court to show why an order nisi should not be made absolute **Einwendungen/seine Gründe vorbringen**

SI = STATUTORY INSTRUMENT

sic *noun* used to show that this was the way a word was actually written in the document in question **sic;** *the letter stated: "my legal adviser intends to apply for attack (sic) of earnings"*

sign

1 *noun* advertising board *or* notice which advertises something **Schild, Ladenschild**
2 *verb* to write your name in a special personal way on a document to show that you have written it or approved it **unterschreiben, unterzeichnen;** *to sign a letter or a contract or a document or a cheque; the letter is signed by the managing director; the cheque is not valid if has not been signed by the finance director*

◊ **signatory** *noun* person who signs a contract, etc. **Unterzeichner;** *you have to get the permission of all the signatories to the agreement if you want to change the terms*

◊ **signature** *noun* name written in a special way by someone, which identifies that person **Unterschrift;** *the contract has been engrossed ready for signature; a pile of letters waiting for the managing director's signature; a will needs the signature of the testator and two witnesses; all the company's cheques need two signatures*

silence *noun* not speaking **Schweigen;** *the accused maintained silence throughout the trial;* **right of silence** = right of an accused not to say anything when charged with a criminal offence **Schweigerecht**

silk *noun*
(a) expensive soft material made from

threads made by an insect **Seide; to take silk** = to become a Queen's Counsel **zu einem Queen's Counsel ernannt werden**
(b) *informal* **a silk** = a QC **ein Queen's Counsel**

similiter *Latin word meaning* "similarly" *or* "in a similar way" **ähnlich**

simple *adjective* not complicated *or* not difficult to understand **einfach, unkompliziert;** *the case appears to be a simple one; it was a simple misunderstanding of the government regulations;* **simple interest** = interest calculated on the capital only, and not added to it **einfache Zinsen; simple contract** = contract which is not under seal, but is made orally *or* in writing **einfacher Vertrag;** *see also* FEE

sincerely *adverb* **yours sincerely** *or (US)* **sincerely yours** = words used as an ending to a business letter addressed to a named person; *entspricht* **Mit freundlichen Grüßen**

sine die *Latin phrase meaning* "with no day" **auf unbestimmte Zeit, ohne Anberaumung eines neuen Termins; the hearing was adjourned sine die** = the hearing was put off to a later date without saying when it would start again **die Verhandlung wurde auf unbestimmte Zeit vertagt**

sine qua non *Latin phrase meaning* "without which nothing": condition without which something cannot work **unerläßliche Voraussetzung;** *agreement by the management is a sine qua non of all employment contracts*

sit *verb*
(a) to take place **tagen, eine Sitzung abhalten;** *the court sat from eleven to five o'clock*
(b) to sit on the bench = to be a magistrate **Richter sein**

◊ **sitting** *noun*
(a) meeting of a court *or* of a tribunal **Gerichtssitzung**
(b) sittings = periods when courts sit **Sitzungsperioden**

COMMENT: there are four sittings in the legal year: Michaelmas, Hilary, Easter and Trinity

site *noun* place where something is *or* where something took place **Ort, Schauplatz;** *the judge and jury visited the site of the crime; the planning application includes a photograph of the site*

situation *noun*
(a) state of affairs **Lage, Situation;** *financial situation of a company; the general situation of the economy*
(b) job **Stelle; situations vacant** *or* **situations wanted** = list in a newspaper of vacancies for workers *or* of people wanting work **Stellenangebote; Stellengesuche**
(c) place where something is **Lage;** *the factory is in a very pleasant situation by the sea*

◊ **situate** *or* **situated** *adjective* in a certain place **gelegen;** *a freehold property situate in the borough of Richmond*

slander
1 *noun* untrue spoken statement which damages someone's character **Verleumdung, üble Nachrede; action for slander** *or* **slander action** = case in a law court where someone says that another person had slandered him **Verleumdungsklage**
2 *verb* **to slander someone** = to damage someone's character by saying untrue things about him **jdn verleumden;** *compare* LIBEL

◊ **slanderous** *adjective* which could be slander **verleumderisch, beleidigend;** *he made slanderous statements about the Prime Minister on television*

sleeping partner *noun* partner who has shares in a business but does not work in it **stiller Teilhaber**

slip *noun*
(a) small piece of paper, especially a note of the details of a marine insurance policy **Beleg über die beabsichtigte Seeversicherungspolice; compliments slip** = piece of paper with the name of the company printed on it, sent with documents, gifts, etc., instead of a letter **Kurzmitteilung**
(b) mistake **Versehen, Schnitzer;** *he made a couple of slips in calculating the discount;* **slip rule** = name for one of the Rules of the Supreme Court allowing minor errors to be corrected on pleadings **Regel, nach der unbedeutende Fehler in förmlichen Schriftsätzen berichtigt werden können**

◊ **slip up** *verb* to make a mistake **sich versehen, einen Fehler machen;** *we slipped up badly in not signing the agreement with the Chinese company*

◊ **slip-up** *noun* mistake **Versehen, Fehler, Schnitzer**

small *adjective* not large **klein; small ads** = short private advertisements in a newspaper (selling small items, asking for jobs, etc.) **Kleinanzeigen; small claim** =

claim for less than £500 in the County Court **Bagatellsache; small claims court** = a court which deals with disputes over small amounts of money **Gericht, das für Geldansprüche bis zu einer gewissen Höhe zuständig ist;** *entspricht* **Amtsgericht**

◊ **small-scale** *adjective* (business) working in a small way, with few staff and not much money **in begrenztem Umfang/Rahmen**

smuggle *verb* to take goods into *or* out of a country without declaring them to the customs **schmuggeln;** *they had to smuggle the spare parts into the country*

◊ **smuggler** *noun* person who smuggles **Schmuggler/-in**

◊ **smuggling** *noun* offence of taking goods illegally into *or* out of a country, without paying any tax **Schmuggel;** *he made his money in arms smuggling*
NOTE: no plural

social *adjective* referring to society in general **sozial, Sozial-, gesellschaftlich; social security** = money *or* help provided by the government to people who need it **Sozialunterstützung, Sozialhilfe; social services** = department of a local *or* national government which provides a service for people who need it **Sozialeinrichtungen; social worker** = person who works in a social services department, visiting and looking after people who need help **Sozialarbeiter**

soft *adjective* not hard **weich; soft currency** = currency of a country with a weak economy, which is cheap to buy and difficult to exchange for other currencies **weiche Währung; soft loan** = loan (from a company *or* a government) with no interest payable **zinsloser Kredit**

sole *adjective* only **Allein-, allein, alleinig; sole owner** *or* **sole proprietor** = person who owns a business on his own, with no partners **Alleineigentümer; sole trader** = person who runs a business by himself **Einzelkaufmann;** *see also* FEME

solemn *adjective* **solemn and binding agreement** = agreement which is not legally binding, but which all parties are supposed to obey **förmliches und bindendes Abkommen**

solicit *verb*
(a) to solicit orders = to ask for orders *or* to try to get people to order goods **sich um Aufträge bemühen, Aufträge hereinholen**
(b) to ask for something immoral, especially to offer to provide sexual intercourse for money; *(von Prostituierten)* **anwerben**

◊ **soliciting** *noun* offence of offering to provide sexual intercourse for money **Anwerben von Kunden (zur Prostitution)**

◊ **solicitor** *noun* *(in England and Wales)* lawyer who has passed the examinations of the Law Society and has a valid certificate to practise and who gives advice to members of the public and acts for them in legal matters **(Rechts)anwalt, der nicht plädiert; to instruct a solicitor** = to give orders to a solicitor to act on your behalf **einen Anwalt beauftragen, etwas einem Anwalt übergeben; duty solicitor** = local solicitor who is on duty at a magistrates' court and can be contacted at any time by a party who is appearing in that court *or* who has been taken to a police station under arrest *or* for questioning **abrufbereiter Pflichtverteidiger im Magistrates' Court; the Official Solicitor** = solicitor who acts in the High Court for parties who have no one to act for them, usually because they are under an official disability **Anwalt, der im High Court für Parteien tätig wird, die von niemand anders vertreten werden**

◊ **Solicitor-General** *noun* one of the law officers, a Member of the House of Commons and deputy to the Attorney-General **zweiter Generalstaatsanwalt; Solicitor-General for Scotland** = junior law officer in Scotland **rangniedriger Justizbeamter in Schottland**

solitary confinement *noun* being kept alone in a cell, without being able to see *or* speak to other prisoners **Einzelhaft;** *he was kept in solitary confinement for six months*

solus agreement *noun* agreement where one party is linked only to the other party, especially an agreement where a retailer buys all his stock from a single supplier **Alleinbezugsvertrag**

solve *verb* to find the answer to something **lösen; to solve a crime** = to find out who committed a crime **ein Verbrechen aufklären; to solve a problem** = to find an answer to a problem **ein Problem lösen;** *the loan will solve some of our short-term problems*

solvent *adjective* having enough money to pay debts **zahlungsfähig, solvent;** *when he bought the company it was barely solvent*

◊ **solvency** *noun* being able to pay all debts **Zahlungsfähigkeit, Solvenz**
NOTE: no plural

sought *see* SEEK

sound *adjective* reasonable *or* which can be trusted **solide, stabil, vernünftig, stichhaltig;** *the company's financial situation is very sound; the solicitor gave us some very sound advice; the evidence brought forward by the police is not very sound;* **of sound mind** = sane *or* mentally well **zurechnungsfähig, geistig gesund;** *he was of sound mind when he wrote the will*

◊ **soundness** *noun* being reasonable **Vernünftigkeit**

source *noun* place where something comes from **Quelle, Ursprung;** *source of income; you must declare income from all sources to the Inland Revenue;* **income which is taxed at source** = where the tax is removed before the income is paid **Einkommen mit Quellenbesteuerung**

South-Eastern Circuit *noun* one of the six circuits of the Crown Court to which barristers belong, with its centre in London **Gerichtsbezirk South-East**

sovereign *noun* King *or* Queen **Souverän, Monarch/-in**

◊ **sovereign state** *noun* independent country which governs itself **souveräner Staat**

◊ **sovereignty** *noun* power to govern **Souveränität, Staatshoheit;** **to have sovereignty over a territory** = to have power to govern a territory **Gebietshoheit besitzen** NOTE: no plural

speaker *noun* person who presides over a meeting of a parliament **Vorsitzender, Präsident/-in, Sprecher/-in**

COMMENT: in the House of Commons, the speaker is an ordinary Member of Parliament chosen by the other members; the equivalent in the House of Lords is the Lord Chancellor. In the US Congress, the speaker of the House of Representatives is an ordinary congressman, elected by the other congressmen; the person presiding over meetings of the Senate is the Vice-President

special *adjective* different *or* not normal *or* referring to one particular thing **Sonder-, besonderer, speziell;** *he offered us special terms; the car is being offered at a special price;* **special agent** = (i) person who represents someone in a particular matter; (ii) person who does secret work for a government (i) **Sonderbevollmächtigter;** (ii) **Agent/-in;** **special constable** = part-time policeman who works mainly at weekends or on important occasions **Hilfspolizist;**

special damages = damages awarded by a court to compensate for a quantifiable loss (such as the expense of repairing something) **Schadensersatz für konkreten Schaden;** **special deposits** = large sums of money which banks have to deposit with the Bank of England **Sondereinlagen, Mindestreserven;** **special procedure** = special system for dealing quickly with undefended divorce cases whereby the parties can obtain a divorce without the necessity of a full trial **Scheidung im Einvernehmen der Parteien, einverständliche Scheidung;** **special resolution** = resolution to change the articles of a company, which has to be passed by 75% of the shareholders **Beschluß mit 3/4 Mehrheit;** **special sessions** = magistrates' courts held for a particular reason (such as to deal with terrorists) **außerordentliche Sitzung, Sondertermin**

◊ **specialist** *noun* person *or* company which deals with one particular type of product *or* one subject **Fachmann, Experte/Expertin, Spezialist/-in; Fachhandel;** *you should go to a specialist in divorce cases or to a divorce specialist for advice*

◊ **specialize** *verb* **to specialize in something** = to be particularly interested *or* expert in a certain subject **sich auf etwas spezialisieren;** *this firm of solicitors specializes in divorce cases; a QC who specializes in international contract cases*

◊ **specialty contract** *noun* contract made under seal **gesiegelter Vertrag**

specific *adjective* particular *or* relating to one particular thing **bestimmt, spezifisch;** **specific performance** = court order to a party to carry out his obligations in a contract **Leistung der Vertragsschuld**

◊ **specifically** *adverb* referring to a particular thing **besonders, ausdrücklich;** *the contract specifically excludes the USA; he drafted the will specifically to benefit his grandchildren*

specify *verb* to state clearly what is needed **angeben, einzeln aufführen, spezifizieren;** *to specify full details of the grounds for complaint; the contract specifies that the goods have to be delivered to London*

◊ **specification** *noun* details of what is needed *or* of what is to be supplied **Beschreibung, Spezifikation;** **patent specification** = full details of an invention which is the subject of a patent application **Patentbeschreibung**

specimen *noun* thing which is given as a sample **Muster, Probe, Probeexemplar;** **to give specimen signatures on a bank mandate** = to write the signatures of all people who can sign cheques on an account so that the bank can recognize them **auf einer Kontovollmacht Unterschriftproben geben**

speech *noun*
(a) speaking *or* ability to talk **Sprechen; Sprache; freedom of speech** = being able to say what you want without being afraid of prosecution, provided that you do not break the law **Redefreiheit**
(b) talk given in public **Rede, Ansprache;** *to make a speech in Parliament; counsel's closing speech to the jury;* **Queen's Speech** = speech made by the Queen at the opening of a session of Parliament which outlines the government's plans for legislation **Parlamentseröffnungsrede der Königin**

spend *verb*
(a) to pay money **ausgeben;** *they spent all their savings on buying the shop; the company spends thousands of pounds on research*
(b) to use time **verbringen;** *the tribunal spent weeks on hearing evidence; the chairman spent yesterday afternoon with the auditors;* **spent conviction** = previous conviction for which an accused person has been sentenced in the past and which must not be referred to in open court **gelöschte Vorstrafe**
NOTE: **spending - spent - has spent**

spiritual *adjective* **Lords Spiritual** = archbishops and bishops sitting in the House of Lords **geistliche Mitglieder des Oberhauses**

spoil *verb* to ruin *or* to make something bad **verderben;** *half the shipment was spoiled by water; the company's results were spoiled by the last quarter;* **spoilt ballot paper** = voting paper which has not been filled in correctly by the voter **ungültige Stimme**
NOTE: **spoiling - spoiled** *or* **spoilt**

◊ **spoils of war** *plural noun* goods *or* valuables taken by an army from an enemy **Kriegsbeute**

spouse *noun* husband *or* wife; person who is married to another person **Ehegatte; Ehegattin**

spy
1 *noun* person who tries to find out secrets about another country **Spion/-in;** *he spent many years as a spy for the enemy; he was arrested as a spy*
2 *verb* to try to find out secrets about another country **spionieren, Spionage**

treiben; *she was accused of spying for the enemy*

squad *noun*
(a) special group of police **Kommando, Dezernat; the Fraud Squad** = department of a police force which deals with cases of fraud **Betrugsdezernat; the Homicide Squad** *or* **Murder Squad** = department of a police force which deals with cases of murder **Mordkommission**
(b) special group of soldiers *or* workers **Gruppe, Abteilung; Arbeitstrupp; firing squad** = group of soldiers who execute someone by shooting **Erschießungs-, Exekutionskommando**
◊ **squad car** *noun* police patrol car **(Funk)streifenwagen**

squat *verb* to occupy premises belonging to another person unlawfully and without title *or* without paying rent **unberechtigt ein Haus od eine Wohnung besetzt halten**
NOTE: **squatting - squatted**
◊ **squatter** *noun* person who squats in someone else's property **illegaler Haus- od Wohnungsbesetzer; squatter's rights** = rights of a person who is squatting in another person's property to remain in unlawful possession of premises until ordered to leave by a court **Rechte von Haus- od Wohnungsbesetzern, bis zur Räumungsklage wohnen zu bleiben**

squeal *verb (slang)* to inform the police about other criminals **verpfeifen, singen**

squire *noun* US local legal official, such as a magistrate **Friedensrichter**

stakeholder *noun* person who holds money impartially (such as money deposited by one of the parties to a wager) until he has to give it up to another party **(treuhänderischer) Verwahrer**

stamp
1 *noun*
(a) device for making marks on documents; mark made in this way **Stempel;** *the invoice has the stamp "Received with thanks" on it; the customs officer looked at the stamps in his passport;* **date stamp** = stamp with rubber figures which can be moved, used for marking the date on documents **Datumsstempel; rubber stamp** = stamp made of hard rubber cut to form words **Gummistempel**
(b) small piece of gummed paper which you buy from a post office and stick on a letter *or* parcel to pay for the postage **Briefmarke;** *a postage stamp; a £1 stamp*

(c) stamp duty = tax on legal documents (such as the conveyance of a property to a new owner *or* the contract for the purchase of shares) **Stempelsteuer**

2 *verb*

(a) to mark a document with a stamp **(ab)stempeln;** *to stamp an invoice "Paid"; the documents were stamped by the customs officials*

(b) to put a postage stamp on (an envelope, etc.) **frankieren; stamped addressed envelope** = envelope with your own address written on it and a stamp stuck on it to pay for the return postage **frankierter/freigemachter Rückumschlag**

stand down *verb* to withdraw your name from an election **seine Kandidatur zurückziehen;** *the wife of one of the candidates is ill and he has stood down*

◊ **stand in for** *verb* to take the place of someone **jdn vertreten, für jdn einspringen;** *Mr Smith is standing in for the chairman who is away on holiday*

◊ **stand over** *verb* to adjourn **aufgeschoben/zurückgestellt werden;** *the case has been stood over to next month*

standard

1 *noun* normal quality *or* normal conditions against which other things are judged **Norm, Maßstab, Standard, Niveau; standard of living** *or* **living standards** = quality of personal home life (such as amount of food or clothes bought, size of family car) **Lebensstandard; production standards** = quality of production **Produktionsstandard; up to standard** = of acceptable quality **den Anforderungen genügend; gold standard** = attaching of the value of a currency to value of a quantity of gold **Goldwährung**

2 *adjective* normal *or* usual **Standard-, üblich, normal;** *the standard charge for consultation is £50; we have a standard charge of £25 for a thirty minute session;* **standard agreement** *or* **standard contract** = normal printed contract form **Mustervertrag; standard form contract** = contract which states the conditions of carrying out a common commercial arrangement (such as chartering a ship) **Einheitsvertrag; standard letter** = letter which is sent with only minor changes to various correspondents **Standard-, Formbrief; standard rate** = basic rate of income tax which is paid by most taxpayers *or* basic rate of VAT which is levied on most goods and services **Einheitssteuersatz, Einheitssatz**

standi *see* LOCUS

standing

1 *adjective* permanent **ständig; standing committee** = (i) permanent committee which always examines the same problem; (ii) committee of Members of Parliament which examines in detail Bills which are not passed to other committees **(i) ständiger Ausschuß; (ii) ständiger Parlamentsausschuß;** *see also* AD HOC; **long-standing customer** *or* **customer of long standing** = person who has been a customer for many years **ein treuer/langjähriger Kunde**

2 *noun* good reputation **Ansehen, Ruf;** *the financial standing of a company;* **company of good standing** = very reputable company **eine angesehene Firma**

◊ **standing order** *noun*

(a) order written by a customer asking a bank to pay money regularly to an account **Dauerauftrag;** *I pay my subscription by standing order; compare* DIRECT DEBIT

(b) standing orders = rules *or* regulations which regulate conduct in any body, such as the House of Commons *or* an army camp *or* a police station **Geschäftsordnung**

Star Chamber *noun*

(a) formerly, a royal court which tried cases without a jury **Sternkammer**

(b) cabinet committee which examines the spending proposals of government departments **Kabinettsausschuß, der die geplanten Ausgaben von Ministerien überprüft;** *entspricht* **Haushaltsausschuß des Bundestages**

stare decisis *Latin phrase meaning* "stand by preceding decisions": principle that courts must abide by precedents set by judgments made in higher courts **Grundsatz der bindenden Kraft der Präjudizien**

state

1 *noun*

(a) independent country; semi-independent section of a federal country (such as the USA or FRG) **Staat; Bundesstaat; to turn state's evidence** = to confess to a crime and then act as a witness against the other criminals involved in the hope of getting a lighter sentence **als Kronzeuge/Belastungszeuge aussagen;** *see also* SECRETARY OF STATE

(b) government of a country **Regierung; offence against the state** = act of attacking the lawful government of a country **Staatsschutzdelikt; state enterprise** = company run by the state **Staatsbetrieb, staatliches Unternehmen;** *the bosses of state industries are appointed by the government;* **state ownership** = situation where an industry is nationalized **Staatseigentum**

2 *verb* to say clearly **angeben, festlegen, feststellen;** *the document states that all revenue has to be declared to the tax office;* **case stated** = statement of the facts of a case which has been heard in a lower court, drawn up so that a higher court can decide on an appeal **Revisionsvorlage**

◊ **state-controlled** *adjective* run by the state **unter staatlicher Aufsicht, staatlich gelenkt;** *state-controlled television*

◊ **State Department** *noun* US government department dealing with relations between the USA and other countries **Außenministerium;** *see note at* FOREIGN

◊ **stateless person** *noun* person who is not a citizen of any state **Staatenloser**

◊ **state-owned** *adjective* owned by the state **staatseigen**

statement *noun*
(a) saying something clearly **Angabe, Feststellung, Stellungnahme; to make a statement** = to give details of something to the press *or* to the police **eine Erklärung abgeben; eine Aussage machen; to make a false statement** = to give wrong details **falsche Angaben machen; statement of affairs** = official statement made by a bankrupt *or* an insolvent company, listing its assets and liabilities **Vermögensaufstellung; Konkursbilanz; statement of claim** = pleading containing details of a plaintiff's case and the relief sought against the defendant **Klagebegründung; Statement of Means** = statement showing the financial position of the claimant, attached to an application for Legal Aid **Bedürftigkeitsnachweis, Armenrechtserklärung; bank statement** = written document from a bank showing the balance of an account **Kontoauszug; monthly** *or* **quarterly statement** = statement which is sent every month *or* every quarter by the bank **monatlicher od vierteljährlicher Kontoauszug**
(b) financial statement = document which shows the financial situation of a company **Finanzbericht, Abschluß;** *the accounts department have prepared a financial statement for the shareholders*
(c) statement of account = list of invoices and credits and debits sent by a supplier to a customer at the end of each month **Abrechnung, Rechnungsaufstellung**

station
1 *noun*
(a) police station = building where the police have their local offices **Polizeirevier, Polizeiwache;** *six demonstrators were arrested and taken to the police station; he spent the night in the station cells*

(b) place where trains stop for passengers **Bahnhof;** *the train leaves the Central Station at 14.15*
(c) TV station *or* **radio station** = building where TV or radio programmes are produced **Sender**
2 *verb* to place someone on duty **aufstellen, postieren;** *six police officers were stationed at the door of the courtroom*

stationer *noun* person who makes *or* supplies paper, pens, typewriter ribbons, etc. **Schreibwarenhändler; law stationer** = person who specializes in supplying stationery to legal firms **Händler, der sich auf Schreibwaren für Anwaltsbüros spezialisiert hat**

◊ **stationery** *noun* office supplies for writing, such as paper, typewriter ribbons, pens, etc. **Schreibwaren;** *legal stationery supplier; shop selling office stationery;* **continuous stationery** = paper made as a long sheet used in computer printers **Endlospapier; Her Majesty's Stationery Office (HMSO)** = government office which produces state documents and government stationery **Behörde, die Veröffentlichungen der Regierung und Schreibwaren für die Regierung produziert und verkauft**
NOTE: no plural

status *noun*
(a) importance *or* position in society **Stellung, Rang, Status; loss of status** = becoming less important in a group **Prestigeverlust; status inquiry** = checking on a customer's credit rating **Kreditauskunft**
(b) legal status = legal identity of a person *or* body (such as a company *or* partnership) **rechtliche Stellung, Rechtslage, Rechtsfähigkeit, Rechtspersönlichkeit**
NOTE: no plural

◊ **status quo** *noun* state of things as they are now **status quo, gegenwärtiger Zustand;** *the contract does not alter the status quo;* **status quo ante** = the situation as it was before **status quo ante, vorheriger Zustand**

statute *noun* established written law, especially an Act of Parliament **Gesetz; statute book** = all laws passed by Parliament which are still in force **Gesetzessammlung, Gesetzbuch; statute of limitations** = law which prevents a plaintiff from bringing proceedings after a certain period of time (usually six years) **prozessuales Verjährungsgesetz**

◊ **statute-barred** *adjective* which cannot take place because the time laid down in the statute of limitations has expired **verjährt**

◊ **statutorily** *adverb* by statute **gesetzlich;** *a statutorily protected tenant*

◊ **statutory** *adjective* fixed by law *or* by a statute **gesetzlich, Gesetzes-, gesetzlich vorgeschrieben;** *there is a statutory period of probation of thirteen weeks; the authority has a statutory obligation to provide free education to all children; powers conferred on an authority by the statutory code;* **statutory books** = official registers which a company must keep **gesetzlich vorgeschriebene Geschäftsbücher; statutory declaration** = (i) statement made to the Registrar of Companies that a company has complied with certain legal conditions; (ii) declaration signed and witnessed for official purposes **(i) Anmeldung zum Handelsregister über bestimmte, die Firma betreffende Änderungen; (ii) eidesstattliche Versicherung/Erklärung; statutory duty** = duty which someone must perform and which is laid down by statute **gesetzliche Verpflichtung; statutory holiday** = holiday which is fixed by law **gesetzlicher Feiertag; statutory instrument** = order (which has the force of law) made under authority granted to a minister by an Act of Parliament **Rechts-, Ausführungsverordnung; statutory undertakers** = bodies formed by statute and having legal duties to provide services (such as gas, electricity, water) **Versorgungsbetriebe**

stay

1 *noun*
(a) length of time spent in one place **Aufenthalt;** *the tourists were in town only for a short stay*
(b) temporary stopping of an order made by a court **Aussetzung, Vollstreckungsaufschub; stay of execution** = temporary prevention of someone from enforcing a judgment **vorläufige Einstellung der Zwangsvollstreckung;** *the court granted the company a two-week stay of execution;* **stay of proceedings** = stopping of a case which is being heard **Aussetzung/Einstellung des Verfahrens**
2 *verb*
(a) to stop at a place **bleiben; übernachten;** *the chairman is staying at the Hotel London; inflation has stayed high in spite of the government's efforts to bring it down*
(b) to stop (an action) temporarily **aussetzen, einstellen;** *the defendant made an application to stay the proceedings until the plaintiff gave security for costs*

steal *verb* to take something which does not belong to you **stehlen, entwenden;** *two burglars broke into the office and stole the petty cash; one of our managers left to form his own company and stole the list of our*

clients' addresses; one of our biggest problems is stealing in the wine department;* **stolen goods** = goods which have been stolen **Diebesgut; handling** *or* **receiving stolen goods** = offence of dealing with goods (receiving them *or* selling them) which you know to have been stolen **Hehlerei**
NOTE: **stealing - stole - has stolen.** Note also that you steal things **from** a person *or* company

◊ **stealing** *noun* crime of taking property which belongs to someone else **Stehlen, Diebstahl; going equipped for stealing** = notifiable offence of carrying tools which could be used for burglary **Einbruchswerkzeug bei sich tragen**

stenographer *noun* official person who can write in shorthand and so take records of what is said in court **Stenograph/-in**

step- *prefix* showing a family relationship through a parent who has married again **Stief-; step-father** = man who has married a child's mother, but is not the natural father of the child **Stiefvater**

stiff *adjective* strong *or* difficult **hart, schwierig;** *he received a stiff prison sentence; he had to take a stiff test before he qualified*

stipendiary magistrate *noun* magistrate who is a qualified lawyer and who receives a salary (as opposed to an unpaid Justice of the Peace) **Berufsrichter am Magistrates' Court**

COMMENT: a stipendiary magistrate usually sits alone

stipulate *verb* to demand that a condition be put into a contract **(vertraglich) vereinbaren/festsetzen;** *to stipulate that the contract should run for five years; to pay the stipulated charges; the company failed to pay on the stipulated date or on the date stipulated in the contract; the contract stipulates that the seller pays the buyer's legal costs*

◊ **stipulation** *noun* condition in a contract **Vereinbarung, Bestimmung, Bedingung, Klausel**

stirpes *see* PER STIRPES

stock

1 *noun*
(a) quantity of raw materials **Vorrat;** *we have large stocks of oil or coal; the country's stocks of butter or sugar*
(b) quantity of goods for sale **Waren-, Lagerbestand; opening stock** = details of

stock at the beginning of an accounting period **Eröffnungsbestand; closing stock =** details of stock at the end of an accounting period **Schlußbestand; stock control =** making sure that enough stock is kept and that quantities and movements of stock are noted **Lagersteuerung, Bestandsüberwachung; stock valuation =** estimating the value of stock at the end of an accounting period **Bewertung des Lagerbestandes; to buy a shop with stock at valuation =** to pay for the stock the same amount as its value, as estimated by an independent valuer **ein Geschäft inklusive das Warenbestandes zum Schätzpreis kaufen** (c) **in stock** or **out of stock =** available or not available in the warehouse or store **vorrätig sein; nicht vorrätig/ausverkauft sein** (d) **stocks and shares =** shares in ordinary companies **Effekten, Aktien, Wertpapiere; stock certificate =** document proving that someone owns shares in a company **Aktienzertifikat; debenture stock =** capital borrowed by a company, using its fixed assets as security **Anleihekapital; dollar stocks =** shares in American companies **US-Aktien; government stocks =** government securities **Staatsanleihen; loan stock =** money lent to a company at a fixed rate of interest **festverzinsliche Anleihen;** US **common stock =** ordinary shares in a company giving the shareholders the right to vote at meetings and receive a dividend **Stammaktien** 2 verb to hold goods for sale in a warehouse or store **führen, auf Lager halten**

◊ **stockbroker** noun person who buys or sells stocks and shares for clients **Börsen-, Effektenmakler; stockbroker's commission =** payment to a broker for a deal carried out on behalf of a client **Courtage**

◊ **stockbroking** noun trade of dealing in shares for clients **Effektenhandel, Aktiengeschäft;** a stockbroking firm

◊ **Stock Exchange** noun place where stocks and shares are bought and sold **(Wertpapier)börse;** he works on the Stock Exchange; shares in the company are traded on the Stock Exchange; **Stock Exchange listing =** official list of shares which can be bought or sold on the Stock Exchange **Börsennotierung**

◊ **stockholder** noun person who holds shares in a company **Aktionär/-in**

◊ **stockholding** noun shares in a company held by someone **Aktienbeteiligung**

◊ **stock jobber** noun person who buys and sells shares from other traders on the Stock Exchange **Jobber, Börsenhändler**

COMMENT: stock jobbers are now being replaced by market makers

◊ **stock jobbing** noun buying and selling shares from other traders on the Stock Exchange **Jobbing, Handel an der Börse** NOTE: no plural

◊ **stock market** noun place where shares are bought and sold **Effektenbörse;** stock market price or price on the stock market; **stock market valuation =** value of shares based on the current market price **Aktienbewertung an der Börse**

straight adjective direct or not dishonest **direkt, offen, aufrichtig, ehrlich; to play straight** or **to act straight with someone =** to act honestly with someone **ehrlich zu jdm sein; to go straight =** to stop criminal activities **nicht mehr kriminell sein, keine Straftaten mehr begehen**

strict adjective exact **genau, strikt, präzise;** in strict order of seniority; to follow a strict interpretation of the rules; **strict liability =** total liability for an offence which has been committed (whether you are at fault or not) **unbedingte/verschuldensunabhängige Haftung**

◊ **strictly** adverb exactly **genau, strikt, präzise;** the police ask all drivers to follow strictly the new highway code

strife noun violent public arguments and disorder **Konflikt, Streit, Kampf; civil strife =** trouble when gangs of people fight each other **innere Unruhen**

strike
1 noun
(a) stopping of work by the workers (because of lack of agreement with management or because of orders from a union) **Streik, Ausstand; general strike =** strike of all the workers in a country **Generalstreik; official strike =** strike which has been approved by the union **gewerkschaftlich organisierter Streik; protest strike =** strike in protest at a particular grievance **Proteststreik; token strike =** short strike to show that workers have a grievance **Warnstreik; unofficial strike =** strike by local workers, which has not been approved by the union as a whole **wilder Streik**
(b) **to take strike action =** to go on strike **in den Ausstand treten; strike ballot** or **strike vote =** vote by workers to decide if a strike should be held **Streik-, Urabstimmung; strike call =** demand by a union for a strike **Streikaufruf; no-strike agreement** or **no-strike clause =** (clause in an) agreement where the workers say that they will never strike **Streikverbotsklausel; strike fund =** money collected by a trade union from its members, used to pay strike pay

Streikkasse; **strike pay** = money paid to striking workers by their trade union during a strike **Streikgeld**

(c) **to come out on strike** or **to go on strike** = to stop work **in den Ausstand treten;** *the office workers are on strike for higher pay;* **to call the workers out on strike** = to tell the workers to stop work **zum Streik aufrufen**

2 *verb*

(a) to stop working because there is no agreement with management **streiken;** *to strike for higher wages or for shorter working hours; to strike in protest against bad working conditions;* **to strike in sympathy with the postal workers** = to strike to show that you agree with the postal workers who are on strike **aus Solidarität mit den Postbeamten streiken**

(b) to hit (someone) **schlagen, einen Schlag/Schläge versetzen, treffen;** *two policemen were struck by bottles; he was struck on the head by a cosh*

NOTE: **striking - struck**

◊ **strike off** *verb* to cross off (a name from a list) **streichen; to strike someone off the rolls** = to stop a solicitor from practising by removing his name from the list of solicitors **jdn von der Anwaltsliste streichen**

◊ **strike out** *verb* to cancel an action which has started, because the plaintiff has not appeared or for some other reason **(eine Klage) streichen;** *the statement of claim was struck out because it disclosed no cause of action*

strong *adjective* with a lot of force or strength **stark;** *a strong demand for the abolition of capital punishment; the country needs a strong police force*

◊ **strongbox** *noun* safe or heavy metal box which cannot be opened easily, in which valuable documents, money, etc., can be kept **Stahlkassette**

◊ **strongroom** *noun* special room (in a bank) where valuable documents, money, gold, etc., can be kept **Stahlkammer, Tresorraum**

study

1 *noun* report which examines something carefully **Studie, Untersuchung;** *the government has asked the commission to prepare a study of prison systems in other countries; he has read the government study on inner city crime;* **to carry out a feasibility study on a project** = to examine the costs and possible profits to see if the project should be started **eine Vorstudie zu einem Projekt/eine Projektstudie ausführen**

2 *verb* to examine (something) carefully **sorgfältig untersuchen/prüfen;** *we are studying the possibility of setting up an*

office in New York; the government studied the committee's proposals for two months

sub- *prefix* under or less important **Unter-, unter-, Sub-, sub-; sub-agency** = small agency which is part of a large agency **Untervertretung; sub-agent** = person who is in charge of a sub-agency **Untervertreter; sub-committee** = small committee which reports on a special subject to a main committee **Unterausschuß;** *he is chairman of the Finance Sub-Committee;* **sub-post office** = small post office which is usually on the same premises as a general store **Postzweigstelle**

subcontract

1 *noun* contract between the main contractor for a whole project and another firm who will do part of the work **Untervertrag, Unterauftrag;** *they have been awarded the subcontract for all the electrical work in the new building; we will put the electrical work out to subcontract*

2 *verb* to agree with a company that they will do part of the work for a project **einen Untervertrag abschließen, Arbeit weitervergeben;** *the electrical work has been subcontracted to Smith Ltd*

◊ **subcontractor** *noun* company which has a contract to do work for a main contractor **Subunternehmer**

subject *noun*

(a) what something is concerned with **Gegenstand, Anlaß;** *the subject of the action was the liability of the defendant for the plaintiff's injuries*

(b) person who is a citizen of a country and bound by its laws **Staatsbürger, Staatsangehöriger, Untertan;** *he is a British subject; British subjects do not need visas to visit Common Market countries;* **liberty of the subject** = right of a citizen to be free unless convicted of a crime which is punishable by imprisonment **Bürgerfreiheit**

◊ **subject to**

1 *adjective*

(a) depending on **abhängig von; the contract is subject to government approval** = the contract will be valid only if it is approved by the government **der Vertrag ist vorbehaltlich der Genehmigung der Regierung; agreement** or **sale subject to contract** = agreement or sale which is not legal until a proper contract has been signed **Vereinbarung od Verkauf vorbehaltlich eines Vertragsabschlusses; offer subject to availability** = the offer is valid only if the goods are available **Angebot solange Vorrat reicht**

(b) which can receive **unterworfen; these articles are subject to import tax** = import

tax has to be paid on these articles **auf diese Artikel wird Einfuhrzoll erhoben**
2 *verb* to make someone suffer something **unterwerfen, aussetzen;** *he was subjected to torture; she subjected her husband to bad treatment*

sub judice *Latin phrase meaning* "under the law": being considered by a court (and so not to be mentioned in the media or in Parliament) **noch nicht entschieden, rechtshängig;** *the papers cannot report the case because it is still sub judice*

sublease
1 *noun* lease from a tenant to another tenant **Untervermietung; Unterverpachtung; Untermietvertrag; Unterpachtvertrag**
2 *verb* to lease a leased property from another tenant **untervermieten; unterverpachten;** *they subleased a small office in the centre of town*
◊ **sublessee** *noun* person *or* company which holds a property on a sublease **Untermieter; Unterpächter**
◊ **sublessor** *noun* tenant who lets a leased property to another tenant **Untervermieter; Unterverpächter**
◊ **sublet** *verb* to let a leased property to another tenant **untervermieten; unterverpachten;** *we have sublet part of our office to a financial consultancy*
NOTE: **subletting - sublet - has sublet**

submit *verb*
(a) to put (something) forward to be examined **einreichen, vorlegen;** *to submit a proposal to the committee; he submitted a claim to the insurers*
(b) to plead an argument in court **vortragen, darlegen;** *counsel submitted that the defendant had no case to answer; it was submitted that the right of self-defence can be available only against unlawful attack*
(c) to agree to be ruled by something **(sich) unterwerfen;** *he refused to submit to the jurisdiction of the court*
NOTE: **submitting - submitted**
◊ **submission** *noun* pleading an argument in court **Vortrag, Vorbringen;** *the court heard the submission of defence counsel that there was no case to answer or in the submission of defence counsel there was no case to answer*

subordinate
1 *adjective* less important **untergeordnet; subordinate to** = governed by *or* which depends on **bestimmt durch, abhängig von**
2 *noun* member of staff who is directed by someone **Untergebener;** *his subordinates find him difficult to work with*

subornation of perjury *noun* offence of getting someone to commit perjury **Anstiftung zum Meineid**

subpoena
1 *noun* court order requiring someone to appear in court **Vorladung vor Gericht (unter Strafandrohung); subpoena ad testificandum** = court order requiring someone to appear as a witness **Zeugenladung (unter Strafandrohung); subpoena duces tecum** = court order requiring someone to appear as a witness and bring with him documents relevant to the case **Zeugenladung mit der Auflage (unter Strafandrohung), bestimmte Urkunden vorzulegen**
2 *verb* to order someone to appear in court **(unter Strafandrohung) (vor)laden;** *the finance director was subpoenaed by the prosecution*

subrogation *noun* legal principle whereby someone stands in the place of another person and acquires that person's rights and is responsible for that person's liabilities **Rechtsübertragung, Eintritt in Rechte**

subscribe *verb*
(a) to subscribe to a magazine = to pay for a series of issues of a magazine **eine Zeitschrift abonnieren**
(b) to subscribe for shares = to apply to buy shares in a new company **neue Aktien zeichnen**
◊ **subscriber** *noun* (i) person who subscribes to a magazine; (ii) person who subscribes for shares in a new company **(i) Zeitschriftenabonnent; (ii) Zeichner; subscriber shares** = the first shares issued when a new company is formed **neue/junge Aktien**

subsequent *adjective* which follows because of something **(nach)folgend, anschließend; condition subsequent** = condition which says that a contract will be modified *or* annulled if something is not done **auflösende Bedingung**

subsidiary *adjective* less important than *or* depending on (something) **nebensächlich, Neben-, subsidiär;** *he faces one serious charge and several subsidiary charges arising out of the main charge;* **subsidiary company** = company which is owned by a parent company **Tochtergesellschaft**

subsidize *verb* to help by giving money **subventionieren, durch öffentliche Mittel unterstützen;** *the government has refused to subsidize the car industry;* **subsidized accommodation** = cheap accommodation which is partly paid for by an employer *or* a local authority, etc. **subventionierte Wohnung**
◊ **subsidy** *noun*
(a) money given to help something which is

not profitable **Subvention, Zuschuß;** *the industry exists on government subsidies; the government has increased its subsidy to the car industry*
(b) money given by a government to make a product cheaper **Subvention**

substance *noun*
(a) material **Substanz, Materie, Stoff; dangerous substances** = materials which may cause harm to someone **gefährliche Stoffe**
(b) real basis of a report *or* argument **wesentlicher Inhalt, Substanz;** *there is no substance to the stories about his resignation*

substandard *adjective* not of the necessary quality to meet a standard **unter der Norm, unterdurchschnittlich, minderwertig**

substantial *adjective* large *or* important **beträchtlich, erheblich, stattlich; she was awarded substantial damages** = she received a large sum of money as damages **ihr wurde eine stattliche Schadensersatzsumme zugesprochen; to acquire a substantial interest in a company** = to buy a large number of shares in a company **einen stattlichen Anteil an einem Unternehmen erwerben**

substantive *adjective* real *or* actual **materiell; wirklich, real; substantive law** = all laws including common law and statute law which deal with legal principles (as opposed to procedural law which refers to the procedure for putting law into practice) **materielles Recht; substantive offence** = offence which has actually taken place **vollendete Straftat**

substitute
1 *noun* person *or* thing which takes the place of someone *or* something else **Vertreter/-in, Vertretung, Stellvertreter; Ersatz**
2 *verb* to take the place of something else **ersetzen, austauschen; substituted service** = serving a legal document on someone other than by the legally prescribed method, for example by posting it to the last known address *or* by advertising **Ersatzzustellung**

subtenancy *noun* agreement to sublet a property **Untermiete; Unterpacht**
◊ **subtenant** *noun* person *or* company to which a property has been sublet **Untermieter; Unterpächter**

subversive *adjective* which acts secretly against the government **subversiv, umstürzlerisch;** *the police is investigating*

subversive groups in the student organizations

succeed *verb* to follow, especially to take the place of someone who has retired *or* died **folgen, jds Nachfolger sein; to succeed to a property** = to become the owner of a property by inheriting it from someone who has died **Vermögen erben**
◊ **succession** *noun* acquiring property *or* title from someone who has died **Erbfolge, Erbschaft; law of succession** = laws relating to how property shall pass to others when the owner dies **Erbrecht; intestate succession** = rules which apply when someone dies without having made a will **gesetzliche Erbfolge, Intestaterbfolge**
◊ **successor** *noun* person who takes over from someone **Nachfolger/-in;** *Mr Smith's successor as chairman will be Mr Jones*

sue *verb* to take someone to court *or* to start legal proceedings against someone to get compensation for a wrong **klagen, verklagen, Klage erheben, prozessieren;** *to sue someone for damages; he is suing the company for £50,000 compensation*

sufferance *noun* agreement to something which is not stated, but assumed because no objection has been raised **Duldung;** *he has been allowed to live in the house on sufferance;* **tenant at sufferance** = situation where a previously lawful tenant is still in possession of property after the termination of the lease **(jederzeit kündbarer) geduldeter Mieter od Pächter**

sufficient *adjective* enough **ausreichend, genügend, genug;** *the company has sufficient funds to pay for its expansion programme*

suffrage *noun* right to vote in elections **Wahl-, Stimmrecht; universal suffrage** = right of all citizens to vote **allgemeines Wahlrecht**
NOTE: no plural

suggest *verb* to put forward a proposal **vorschlagen, empfehlen, anregen;** *the chairman suggested (that) the next meeting should be held in October; we suggested Mr Smith for the post of treasurer*
◊ **suggestion** *noun* proposal *or* idea which is put forward **Vorschlag, Empfehlung, Anregung; suggestion box** = place in a company where members of staff can put forward their ideas for making the company more efficient and profitable **Kasten für Verbesserungsvorschläge**

suicide *noun*
(a) act of killing yourself **Selbstmord,**

Selbsttötung; *after shooting his wife, he committed suicide in the bedroom; the police are treating the death as suicide, not murder;* **to commit suicide** = to kill yourself **Selbstmord begehen; suicide pact** = agreement between two or more people that they will all commit suicide at the same time **Selbstmordvereinbarung**
(b) person who has committed suicide **Selbstmörder**

COMMENT: aiding suicide is a notifiable offence

◊ **suicidal** *adjective* likely to commit suicide **selbstmörderisch veranlagt, selbstmordgefährdet;** *the warders should keep close watch on that prisoner - we think he may be suicidal*

sui generis *Latin phrase meaning* "of its own right": (thing) which is in a class of its own **eigener Art**

sui juris *Latin phrase meaning* "in one's own right": (person) who is able to make contracts and sue others *or* be sued himself **geschäftsfähig**

suit *noun* civil legal proceedings *or* lawsuit **Zivilprozeß, Klage, Rechtsstreit, Verfahren;** *US* **class suit** = legal action brought on behalf of several people **Gruppenklage**

suitable *adjective* convenient *or* which fits **passend, geeignet;** *Wednesday is the most suitable day for the hearing; we had to advertise the job again because there were no suitable candidates*

sum
1 *noun*
(a) quantity of money **Betrag;** *a sum of money was stolen from the personnel office; he lost large sums on the Stock Exchange; she received the sum of £500 in compensation;* **the sum insured** = the largest amount which an insurer will pay under the terms of an insurance **die Versicherungssumme; lump sum** = money paid in one payment, not in several small payments **Pauschalbetrag, Pauschale**
(b) total of a series of figures added together **Summe**
2 *verb (of a judge)* **to sum up** = to speak at the end of a trial and review all the evidence and arguments for the benefit of the jury **(für die Geschworenen) die Verhandlung und die Beweisergebnisse zusammenfassen**
NOTE: **summing - summed**

◊ **summing up** *noun* speech by the judge at the end of a trial, where he reviews all the evidence and arguments and notes important points of law for the benefit of the jury **Zusammenfassung der Verhandlung und der Beweisergebnisse (durch den Vorsitzenden) für die Geschworenen**
NOTE: US English is **instructions**

summary
1 *noun* short account of what has happened *or* of what has been written **Zusammmenfassung, Übersicht;** *the chairman gave a summary of his discussions with the German delegation; the police inspector gave a summary of events leading to the raid on the house*
2 *adjective* which happens immediately **Schnell-, beschleunigt; summary arrest** = arrest without a warrant **vorläufige Festnahme; summary conviction** = conviction by a magistrate sitting without a jury **Verurteilung im Schnellverfahren/summarischen Verfahren; summary dismissal** = dismissal of an employee without giving the notice stated in the contract of employment **fristlose Entlassung; summary judgment** = immediate judgment of a case which is applied for by a plaintiff when he believes the defendant cannot put forward any sensible defence **Urteil im beschleunigten Verfahren/ohne streitige Verhandlung; summary jurisdiction** = power of a magistrates' court to try a case without a jury *or* to try a case immediately without referring it to the Crown Court **Recht des Amtsgerichts, einen Fall ohne Schöffen zu verhandeln; Zuständigkeit des Amtsgerichts; summary offence** = minor crime which can be tried only in a magistrates' court **Übertretung, Ordnungswidrigkeit, Bagatellsache**

◊ **summarily** *adverb* immediately **summarisch, beschleunigt;** *magistrates can try a case summarily or refer it to the Crown Court*

◊ **summarize** *verb* to make a short account of something **zusammenfassen;** *the case was summarized in the evening papers*

summon *verb* to call someone to come **herbeirufen, vorladen, laden;** *he was summoned to appear before the committee*

summons *noun* official command from a court requiring someone to appear in court to be tried for a criminal offence *or* to defend a civil action **Vorladung, Ladung;** *he tore up the summons and went on holiday to Spain;* **judgment summons** = summons by a court ordering a judgment debtor to pay or to go to prison **gerichtliche Vorladung (z.B.**

des Vollstreckungsschuldners); **originating summons** = summons whereby a legal action is commenced (usually in the Chancery Division of the High Court in cases relating to land or the administration of an estate) **Klage mit Ladung, Form der Klageerhebung; writ of summons** = document which starts a legal action in the High Court **Klageschrift mit Ladung, Prozeßeröffnungsbeschluß**

sundry

1 *noun* various items **Verschiedenes, Diverses**
2 *adjective* various **verschiedene, diverse; sundry items** *or* **sundries** = small items which are not listed in detail **Verschiedenes**

supergrass *noun (slang)* person (usually a criminal) who gives information to the police about a large number of criminals **Superspitzel**

superintend *verb* to be in charge of **beaufsichtigen, verantwortlich sein für, überwachen;** *he superintends the company's overseas sales*

◇ **superintendent** *noun* person in charge **Leiter/-in, Aufsicht, Aufsichtsbeamter; (police) superintendent** = high rank in a police force, above Chief Inspector and below Chief Superintendent **Polizeichef**

superior

1 *adjective*
(a) better *or* of better quality **besser, überlegen;** *our product is superior to all competing products; their sales are higher because of their superior service*
(b) higher *or* more important **höher;** *the case will be heard in a superior court; he tried to blackmail a superior officer*
2 *noun* more important person **Vorgesetzter;** *each manager is responsible to his superior for accurate reporting of sales*

supersede *verb* to take the place of **an die Stelle treten von, ersetzen;** *the government has published a Bill to supersede the current legislation*

supervise *verb* to watch work carefully to see if it is well done **überwachen, beaufsichtigen;** *the move to the new offices was supervised by the administrative manager; she supervises six girls in the legal department*

◇ **supervision** *noun* being supervised **Aufsicht, Beaufsichtigung;** *new staff work under supervision for the first three months; she is very experienced and can be left to work without any supervision; the cash was* counted under the supervision of the finance director; **supervision order** = court order for a young offender to be placed under the supervision of the probation service **Anordnung, jdn der Aufsicht eines Bewährungshelfers zu unterstellen**
NOTE: no plural

◇ **supervisor** *noun* person who supervises **Aufsicht, Aufsichtsbeamter, Aufseher/-in**

◇ **supervisory** *adjective* as a supervisor **Aufsichts-, Überwachungs-;** *supervisory staff; he works in a supervisory capacity*

supply

1 *noun*
(a) providing something which is needed **Versorgung, Angebot, Lieferung; money supply** = amount of money which exists in a country **Geldvorrat, Geldvolumen; Supply Bill** = Bill for providing money for government requirements **Gesetzesvorlage für den zu beschließenden Etat; supply price** = price at which something is provided **Angebotspreis; supply and demand** = amount of a product which is available at a certain price and the amount which is wanted by customers at that price **Angebot und Nachfrage; the law of supply and demand** = general rule that the amount of a product which is available is related to the needs of the possible customers **das Gesetz von Angebot und Nachfrage**
(b) in short supply = not available in large enough quantities to meet the demand **knapp;** *spare parts are in short supply because of the strike*
(c) stock of something which is needed **Vorrat, Bestand;** *the factory is running short of supplies of coal; supplies of coal have been reduced;* **office supplies** = goods needed to run an office (such as paper, pens, typewriters) **Büromaterial**
(d) supplies = goods *or* services provided **Lieferungen, Zulieferungen, Versorgung; exempt supplies** = sales of goods *or* services which are exempt from VAT **von der Mehrwertsteuer befreite Lieferungen od Dienstleistungen**
2 *verb* to provide something which is needed **liefern, beliefern, versorgen;** *to supply a factory with spare parts; the prosecution supplied the court with a detailed map of the area where the crime took place; details of staff addresses and phone numbers can be supplied by the personnel department*

◇ **supplier** *noun* person *or* company which supplies something **Lieferant, Zulieferer**

support

1 *noun*
(a) giving money to help **Unterstützung, Hilfe;** *the government has provided support to the*

computer industry; we have no financial support from the banks

(b) agreement or encouragement **Unterstützung, Beistand;** the chairman has the support of the committee; **support price** = price (in the EC) at which a government will buy farm produce to stop the price from falling **Stützungspreis**

2 verb

(a) to give money to help **finanziell unterstützen, stützen;** the government is supporting the computer industry to the tune of $2m per annum; we hope the banks will support us during the expansion period

(b) to encourage or to agree with **unterstützen, beistehen, befürworten;** she hopes the other members of the committee will support her; the market will not support another price increase

suppress verb to stop something from being made public **verheimlichen, verschweigen, vertuschen;** the government tried to suppress the news about the prison riot

◊ **suppression** noun act of suppressing **Verheimlichung, Verschweigen, Vertuschung;** the suppression of the truth about the case

suppressio veri Latin phrase meaning "suppressing the truth": act of not mentioning some important fact **Verschweigen der Wahrheit**

supra adverb above or see above **siehe oben**

supreme court noun

(a) Supreme Court (of Judicature) = highest court in England and Wales, consisting of the Court of Appeal and the High Court of Justice **Oberster Gerichtshof für England und Wales**

(b) US highest federal court **Oberstes Bundesgericht**

surety noun

(a) person who guarantees that someone will do something, especially by paying to guarantee that someone will keep the peace **Bürge, Garant;** to stand surety for someone

(b) money or deeds or share certificates, etc., deposited as security for a loan **Sicherheit, Garantie, Bürgschaft, Kaution**

surname noun family name **Nach-, Familienname;** a woman usually takes the surname of her husband when she marries

surrender

1 noun giving up of an insurance policy before the contracted date for maturity

Rückkauf; the contract becomes null and void when these documents are surrendered; **surrender value** = money which an insurer will pay if an insurance policy is given up before it matures **Rückkaufswert**

2 verb

(a) to give in a document or to give up a right **zurückgeben, ausliefern, herausgeben; aufgeben, verzichten;** the court ordered him to surrender his passport; **to surrender a policy** = to give up an insurance **eine Versicherungspolice zum Rückkauf bringen**

(b) to give oneself up to be arrested by the police **sich stellen, sich ergeben;** the hijackers surrendered to the airport security guards

surveillance noun watching someone carefully to get information about what he is doing **Überwachung;** the diplomats were placed under police surveillance; surveillance at international airports has been increased; **surveillance device** = bugging device **Abhörvorrichtung; electronic surveillance** = surveillance using hidden microphones, etc. **elektronische Überwachung**

NOTE: no plural

survive verb to live longer than another person **überleben;** he survived his wife; she is survived by her husband and three children; he left his estate to his surviving relatives = to the relatives who were still alive **er hinterließ seinen überlebenden Verwandten sein Vermögen**

◊ **survivor** noun someone who lives longer than another person **Überlebender, Hinterbliebener**

◊ **survivorship** noun right of the survivor of a joint tenancy to the estate, rather than the heirs of the deceased tenant **Recht des Überlebenden (eines Gesamthandeigentumes), den Anteil des Verstorbenen für sich zu beanspruchen**

SUS law noun law which allows the police to stop and arrest a person whom they suspect of having committed an offence **Recht der Polizei, einen Tatverdächtigen festzunehmen**

suspect

1 noun person whom the police think has committed a crime **Verdächtiger, verdächtige Person, mutmaßlicher Täter;** the police have taken six suspects into custody; the police are questioning the suspect about his movements at the time the crime was committed

2 verb to believe that someone has done something **verdächtigen, den Verdacht haben;** he was arrested as a suspected spy; the police

suspect that the thefts were committed by a member of the shop's staff
NOTE: you suspect someone **of** committing a crime

suspend *verb*

(a) to stop (something) for a time **zeitweilig einstellen, aussetzen, unterbrechen;** *we have suspended payments while we are waiting for news from our agent; the hearings have been suspended for two weeks; work on the preparation of the case has been suspended; the management decided to suspend negotiations;* **suspended sentence** = sentence of imprisonment which a court orders shall not take effect unless the offender commits another crime **zur Bewährung ausgesetzte Freiheitsstrafe**
(b) to stop (someone) working for a time **suspendieren;** *he was suspended on full pay while the police investigations were proceeding*

◊ **suspension** *noun* stopping something for a time **zeitweilige Einstellung, Aussetzung, Aufschub; Suspension;** *suspension of payments; suspension of deliveries*

suspicion *noun* feeling that someone has committed a crime **Verdacht;** *he was arrested on suspicion of being an accessory after the fact*

◊ **suspicious** *adjective* which makes someone suspect **verdächtig;** *the police are dealing with the suspicious package found in the car; suspicious substances were found in the man's pocket*

swear *verb*

to make an oath *or* to promise that what you will say will be the truth **schwören, einen Eid leisten;** *he swore to tell the truth;* "**I swear to tell the truth, the whole truth and nothing but the truth**" = words used when a witness takes the oath in court "**Ich schwöre, daß ich nach bestem Wissen die reine Wahrheit gesagt und nichts verschwiegen habe**"
NOTE: **swearing - swore - has sworn**

◊ **swear in** *verb* to make someone take an oath before taking up a position **vereidigen;** *he was sworn in as a Privy Councillor;* **swearing-in** = act of making someone take an oath before taking up a position **Vereidigung**

swindle

1 *noun* illegal deal in which someone is cheated out of his money **Betrug, Schwindel**
2 *verb* to cheat someone out of his money **betrügen, beschwindeln;** *he made £50,000 by swindling small shopkeepers; the gang swindled the bank out of £1.5m*

◊ **swindler** *noun* person who swindles **Betrüger/-in, Schwindler/-in**

system *noun*

(a) arrangement *or* organization of things which work together **System;** *the British legal system has been taken as the standard for many other legal systems;* **filing system** = way of putting documents in order for easy reference **Ablagesystem; to operate a quota system** = to regulate supplies by fixing quantities which are allowed **ein Quotensystem anwenden**
(b) computer system = set of programs, commands, etc., which make a computer work **Computersystem; control system** = system used to check that a computer system is working correctly **Regelsystem**
(c) systems analysis = using a computer to suggest how a company should work by analyzing the way in which it works at present **Systemanalyse; systems analyst** = person who specializes in systems analysis **Systemanalytiker, Systemberater**

◊ **systematic** *adjective* in order *or* using method **systematisch;** *he ordered a systematic report on the probation service*

Tt

table

1 *noun* list of figures *or* facts set out in lists **Tabelle; Übersicht; table of contents** = list of contents in a book **Inhaltsverzeichnis; actuarial tables** = lists showing how long people of certain ages are likely to live, used to calculate life assurance premiums **Sterbetabellen; Table A, B, C, D, E** = specimen forms for setting up companies, set out in the Companies Act; *see* A, B, C, D, E
2 *verb* to put items of information on the table before a meeting **vorlegen;** *the report of the finance committee was tabled;* **to table a motion** = to put forward a proposal for discussion by putting details of it on the table at a meeting **einen Antrag vorlegen**

tacit *adjective*

agreed but not stated **stillschweigend;** *he gave the proposal his tacit approval; the committee gave its tacit agreement to the proposal*

tack *noun (in Scotland)* lease **Pachtvertrag**

tail *see* FEE

take

1 *noun* money received in a shop **Einnahme(n)**

2 *verb*
(a) to receive *or* to get **nehmen; einnehmen; bekommen;** *(of a lawyer)* **to take instructions** = to ask one's client how he wishes the lawyer to deal with something **Weisungen (des Mandanten) einholen;** *when the defence offered £1,000, the plaintiff's solicitor said he would take his client's instructions*
(b) to do a certain action **unternehmen; durchführen; handeln; to take action** = to do something **Schritte unternehmen;** *you must take immediate action if you want to stop thefts;* **to take the chair** = to be chairman of a meeting **den Vorsitz führen;** *in the absence of the chairman his deputy took the chair;* **to take someone to court** = to sue someone *or* to start civil proceedings against someone **gerichtlich gegen jdn vorgehen, jdn verklagen**
(c) to need (a time *or* a quantity) **brauchen, benötigen;** *it took the jury six hours to reach a verdict or the jury took six hours to reach a verdict; it will take her all morning to type my letters; it took six policemen to hold the burglar*
NOTE: **taking - took - has taken**

◊ **take in** *verb* to trick *or* to swindle (someone) **hereinlegen; täuschen;** *we were taken in by his promise of quick profits*

◊ **take out** *verb* **to take out a patent for an invention** = to apply for and receive a patent **ein Patent für eine Erfindung anmelden; to take out insurance against theft** = to pay a premium to an insurance company, so that if a theft takes place the company will pay compensation **eine Diebstahlversicherung abschließen**

◊ **take over** *verb*
(a) to start to do something in place of someone else **übernehmen;** *Miss Black took over from Mr Jones on May 1st; the new chairman takes over on July 1st;* **the take-over period is always difficult** = the period when one person is taking over work from another **die Übernahmezeit ist immer schwierig**
(b) to take over a company = to buy (a business) by offering to buy most of its shares **ein Unternehmen übernehmen;** *the buyer takes over the company's liabilities; the company was taken over by a large international corporation*

◊ **takeover** *noun* buying a business **Übernahme; takeover bid** *or* **offer** = offer to buy all or a majority of the shares in a company so as to control it **Übernahmeangebot; to make a takeover bid for a company** = to offer to buy most of the shares in a company **eine Übernahmeangebot für ein Unternehmen machen; to withdraw a takeover bid** = to say that you no longer offer to buy most of the shares in a company **ein Übernahmeangebot zurückziehen; the company rejected the**

takeover bid = the directors recommended that the shareholders should not accept the offer **das Unternehmen wies das Übernahmeangebot zurück;** *the disclosure of the takeover bid raised share prices;* **Takeover Panel** = body which supervises and regulates takeovers **Fusionskontrollorgan; contested takeover** = takeover where the board of the company being bought do not recommend the bid, and try to fight it **angefochtene Übernahme**

talaq *noun* Islamic form of divorce, where the husband may divorce his wife unilaterally by an oral declaration made three times **Al-Talak**

tamper *verb* **to tamper with something** = to change something *or* to act in such a way that something does not work **etwas fälschen; an etwas herumhantieren;** *the police were accused of tampering with the evidence; the charges state that he tampered with the wheels of the victim's car*

tangible *adjective* **tangible assets** *or* **property** = property *or* assets which are solid (such as furniture *or* jewels *or* cash) **materielle Vermögenswerte; bilanzierbare Sachwerte**

tariff *noun*
(a) customs tariffs = tax to be paid for importing *or* exporting goods **Zolltarife; tariff barriers** = customs duty intended to make imports more difficult **Zollschranken;** *to impose tariff barriers on or to lift tariff barriers from a product;* **General Agreement on Tariffs and Trade (GATT)** = international treaty which aims to try to reduce restrictions in trade between countries **Allgemeines Zoll- und Handelsabkommen; protective tariff** = tariff which aims to ban imports to prevent competition with local products **Schutzzoll**
(b) rate of charging for electricity, hotel rooms, train tickets, etc. **Preis, Tarif**

tax
1 *noun*
(a) money taken compulsorily by the government *or* by an official body to pay for government services **Steuer; capital gains tax** = tax on capital gains **Veräußerungsgewinnsteuer; capital transfer tax** = tax on the transfer of capital *or* assets from one person to another **Kapitaltransfersteuer; excess profits tax** = tax on profits which are higher than what is thought to be normal **Über-, Mehrgewinnsteuer; income tax** = tax on salaries and wages **Einkommensteuer; land**

tax = tax on the amount of land owned **Grundsteuer; sales tax** = tax paid on each item sold **(allgemeine) Warenumsatzsteuer; Value Added Tax (VAT)** = tax on goods and services, added as a percentage to the invoiced sales price **Mehrwertsteuer (MwSt)** **(b) ad valorem tax** = tax calculated according to the value of the goods taxed **Wertsteuer; back tax** = tax which is owed **Steuerrückstand; basic rate tax** = lowest rate of income tax **Basissteuersatz; to levy a tax** or **to impose a tax** = to make a tax payable **eine Steuer erheben;** *the government has imposed a 15% tax on petrol;* **to lift a tax** = to remove a tax **eine Steuer aufheben; tax adviser** or **tax consultant** = person who gives advice on tax problems **Steuerberater; tax allowances** or **allowances against tax** = part of one's income which a person is allowed to earn and not pay tax on **Steuerfreibetrag; tax avoidance** = trying (legally) to minimize the amount of tax to be paid **legale Steuerumgehung/Steuerverkürzung; tax code** = number given to indicate the amount of tax allowances a person has **Abgabenordnung; tax concession** = allowing less tax to be paid **Steuervergünstigung; tax credit** = part of a dividend on which the company has already paid tax, so that the shareholder is not taxed on it again **Steueranrechnung; tax deductions** = (i) money removed from a salary to pay tax; (ii) *US* business expenses which can be claimed against tax **(i)&(ii) Steuerabzüge; tax deducted at source** = tax which is removed from a salary, interest payment or dividend payment before the money is paid out **Quellensteuer; tax evasion** = illegally trying not to pay tax **Steuerhinterziehung; tax exemption** = (i) being free from payment of tax; (ii) *US* part of income which a person is allowed to earn and not pay tax on **(i) Steuerbefreiung; (ii) Steuerfreibetrag; tax haven** = country where taxes levied on foreigners or foreign companies are low **Steueroase; tax holiday** = period when a new business is exempted from paying tax **Steuerbefreiung; tax inspector** or **inspector of taxes** = official of the Inland Revenue who examines tax returns and decides how much tax someone should pay **Steuerprüfer; Leiter des Finanzamtes; tax loophole** = legal means of not paying tax **Lücke in der Steuergesetzgebung; tax planning** = planning one's financial affairs so that one pays as little tax as possible **Steuerplanung (unter legaler Umgehung belastender Bestimmungen); tax relief** = allowing someone not to pay tax on certain parts of his income **Steuerermäßigung; tax return** or **tax declaration** = completed tax form, with details of income and allowances **Steuererklärung; double tax treaty** = treaty between two countries so that citizens pay tax in one country only **Doppelbesteuerungsabkommen; tax year** = twelve month period on which taxes are calculated (in the UK, 6th April to 5th April of the following year) **Steuerjahr** **2** *verb* **(a)** to make someone pay a tax *or* to impose a tax on something **besteuern, mit einer Steuer belegen;** *to tax businesses at 50%; income is taxed at 29%; these items are heavily taxed* **(b)** to have the costs of a legal action assessed by the court **schätzen; festsetzen;** *the court ordered the costs to be taxed if not agreed;* **taxed costs** = variable amount of costs awarded in legal proceedings by the Taxing Master **festgesetzte Kosten (aus einem Gebührenrahmen)**

◊ **taxable** *adjective* which can be taxed **besteuerbar; steuerpflichtig; taxable items** = items on which a tax has to be paid **steuerpflichtige Objekte; taxable income** = income on which a person has to pay tax **steuerpflichtiges Einkommen**

◊ **taxation** *noun* **(a)** act of taxing **Besteuerung; Veranlagung; direct taxation** = taxes (such as income tax) which are paid direct to the government out of earnings *or* profit **Direktbesteuerung; double taxation** = taxing the same income twice **Doppelbesteuerung; double taxation treaty** = treaty between two countries that citizens pay tax in one country only **Doppelbesteuerungsabkommen** **(b) taxation of costs** = assessment of the costs of a legal action by the Taxing Master **Kostenfestsetzung** NOTE: no plural

◊ **tax-deductible** *adjective* which can be deducted from an income before tax is calculated **steuerlich absetzbar/abzugsfähig;** *these expenses are not tax-deductible* = tax has to be paid on these expenses **diese Ausgaben sind nicht steuerlich abzugsfähig**

◊ **tax-exempt** *adjective* (person *or* organization) not required to pay tax; (income *or* goods) which are not subject to tax **steuerfrei**

◊ **tax-free** *adjective* on which tax does not have to be paid **steuerfrei**

◊ **Taxing Master** *noun* official of the Supreme Court who assesses the costs of a court action **Kostenfestsetzungsbeamter**

◊ **taxpayer** *noun* person *or* company which has to pay tax **Steuerzahler;** *basic taxpayer or taxpayer at the basic rate; corporate taxpayers*

◊ **tax point** *noun* (i) time when goods are supplied and VAT is charged; (ii) time at which a tax begins to be applied **(i)&(ii) Zeitpunkt der Anwendung/des Inkrafttretens bestimmter Steuervorschriften**

technical *adjective* referring to a specific legal point *or* using a strictly legal interpretation **technisch, formal(juristisch);** *nominal damages were awarded as the harm was judged to be technical rather than actual*
◊ **technicality** *noun* special interpretation of a legal point **Formsache;** *the Appeal Court rejected the appeal on a technicality*

teller *noun*
(a) MP who counts the votes in the House of Commons **Stimmenauszähler**
(b) bank clerk **Kassierer/-in**

tem *see* PRO TEM

Temple *see* INNER TEMPLE, MIDDLE TEMPLE

temporary *adjective* which lasts only a short time **vorläufig; einstweilig; vorübergehend; Aushilfs-;** *he was granted a temporary injunction; the police took temporary measures to close the street to traffic; she has a temporary job or temporary post with a firm of solicitors; he has a temporary job as a filing clerk or he has a job as a temporary filing clerk;* **temporary employment** = full-time work which does not last for more than a few days or months **vorübergehende Erwerbstätigkeit; temporary injunction** = injunction which is granted until a case comes to court **einstweilige Verfügung; temporary staff** = staff who are appointed for a short time **Aushilfskräfte**
◊ **temporarily** *adverb* lasting only for a short time **befristet; vorläufig; vorübergehend**

tenancy *noun* (i) agreement by which a person can occupy a property; (ii) period during which a person has an agreement to occupy a property **(i) Miet- od Pachtverhältnis; (ii) Miet- od Pachtdauer; joint tenancy** = situation where two or more persons acquire interests in a property together where, if one of the joint tenants dies, his share goes to the others who survive him **gemeinschaftlich ausgeübtes Miet- od Pachtrecht; several tenancy** = holding of property by several persons, each separately and not jointly with any other person **Einzelbesitzverhältnis; protected tenancy** = tenancy where the tenant is protected from eviction **geschütztes Mietverhältnis mit Mieterschutz; Pachtverhältnis mit Pächterschutz; tenancy in common** = situation where two or more persons jointly hold a property and each can leave his interest to his heirs when he dies **Bruchteilsgemeinschaft; tenancy at will** = situation where the owner of a property

allows a tenant to hold it for as long as either party wishes **jederzeit kündbares Miet- od Pachtverhältnis**

◊ **tenant** *noun* person *or* company which rents a house *or* flat *or* office in which to live or work **Mieter/-in; Pächter/-in;** *the tenant is liable for repairs;* **tenant at will** = tenant who holds a property at the will of the owner **jederzeit kündbarer Mieter od Pächter; tenant for life** = person who can occupy a property for life **lebenslanger Mieter od Pächter; secure tenant** = tenant of a local authority who has the right to buy the freehold of the property he rents at a discount **Mieter od Pächter einer der Gemeinde gehörender Wohnung (oder eines Hauses) mit priviligiertem Kaufrecht; sitting tenant** = tenant who is living in a house when the freehold or lease is sold **unter Mieterschutz stehender Mieter**

tender
1 *noun*
(a) offer to work for a certain price **Angebot; to put a project out to tender** *or* **to ask for** *or* **to invite tenders for a project** = to ask contractors to give written estimates for a job **Angebote für ein Projekt einholen, ein Projekt ausschreiben; to put in a tender** *or* **to submit a tender** = to make an estimate for a job **ein Angebot machen; to sell shares by tender** = to ask people to offer in writing a price for shares **Aktien auf dem Angebotsweg verkaufen; sealed tenders** = tenders sent in sealed envelopes which will all be opened together at a certain time **versiegelte Submissionsofferten**
(b) **legal tender** = coins or notes which can be legally used to pay a debt (small denominations cannot be used to pay large debts) **gesetzliches Zahlungsmittel;** NOTE: no plural for (b)
2 *verb*
(a) **to tender for a contract** = to put forward an estimate of cost for work to be carried out under contract **ein Angebot/eine Offerte unterbreiten;** *to tender for the construction of a hospital*
(b) **to tender one's resignation** = to give in one's resignation **seine Kündigung einreichen**

◊ **tenderer** *noun* person *or* company which tenders for work **Bewerber/-in; Submittent/-in;** *the company was the successful tenderer for the project*

tenement *noun* property which is held by a tenant **Mietwohnung;** *(in Scotland)* building which is divided into rented flats **Mietshaus; dominant tenement** = land which has been granted an easement over another property **herrschendes Grundstück; servient tenement** = land whose owner grants an easement to the owner of the dominant tenement **dienendes Grundstück**

tenens *see* LOCUM

tentative *adjective* not certain **vorläufig; unverbindlich; vorsichtig;** *they reached a tentative agreement over the proposal; we suggested Wednesday May 10th as a tentative date for the next meeting*
◊ **tentatively** *adverb* not sure **zögernd; vorsichtig; unverbindlich; vorläufig;** *we tentatively suggested Wednesday as the date for our next meeting*

tenure *noun*
(a) right to hold property *or* a position **Landbesitzrecht; Innehaben (einer Position); security of tenure** = right to keep a job *or* rented accommodation provided certain conditions are met **Kündigungsschutz; land tenure** = way in which land is held (such as leasehold) **Landbesitzrecht; Pachtverhältnis**
(b) time when a position is held **Amtszeit;** *during his tenure of the office of chairman*
NOTE: no plural

term *noun*
(a) period of time **Dauer, Zeitraum;** *the term of a lease; the term of the loan is fifteen years; to have a loan for a term of fifteen years; during his term of office as chairman;* **term deposit** = money invested for a fixed period which gives a higher rate of interest than normal **Termineinlagen; term insurance** = life assurance which covers a person's life for a fixed period of time **zeitlich begrenzte Lebensversicherung; term loan** = loan for a fixed period of time **befristeter Kredit; term of years** = fixed period of several years (of a lease) **Zeitpacht; term shares** = type of building society deposit for a fixed period of time at a higher rate of interest **Fristeinlagen (bei einer Bausparkasse); fixed term** = period which is fixed when a contract is signed and which cannot be changed afterwards **festgesetzte Dauer (eines Vertrages); short-term** = for a period of months **kurzfristig; long-term** = for a long period of time **langfristig; medium-term** = for a period of one or two years **mittelfristig**
(b) terms = conditions *or* duties which have to be carried out as part of a contract *or* arrangements which have to be agreed before a contract is valid **Bedingungen; Bestimmungen;** *he refused to agree to some of the terms of the contract; by or under the terms of the contract, the company is responsible for all damage to the property;* **terms of payment** *or* **payment terms** = conditions for paying something **Zahlungsbedingungen; terms of sale** = agreed ways in which a sale takes place (such as

discounts and credit terms) **Verkaufsbedingungen; cash terms** = lower terms which apply if the customer pays cash **Barzahlungsbedingungen; implied terms and conditions** = terms and conditions which are not written in a contract, but which are legally taken to be present in the contract **stillschweigende, miteingeschlossene Bestimmungen und Bedingungen; trade terms** = special discount for people in the same trade **Händlerrabatt**
(c) part of a legal *or* university year **Semester;** *the autumn or winter term starts in September*

> COMMENT: the four law terms are Easter, Hilary, Michaelmas and Trinity

(d) terms of employment = conditions set out in a contract of employment **Arbeitsvertrags-, Anstellungsbedingungen; terms of reference** = areas which a committee *or* an inspector can deal with **Aufgabenbereich, Zuständigkeit;** *under the terms of reference of the committee it can only investigate complaints from the public; the tribunal's terms of reference do not cover traffic offences*

terminate *verb* to end (something) *or* to bring (something) to an end *or* to come to an end **(be)enden, lösen, kündigen;** *to terminate an agreement; his employment was terminated; an offer terminates on the death of the offeror*
◊ **terminable** *adjective* which can be terminated **künd-, auflösbar**
◊ **termination** *noun*
(a) bringing to an end **Beendigung, Lösung, Kündigung;** *the termination of an offer or of a lease; to appeal against the termination of a foster order;* **termination clause** = clause which explains how and when a contract can be terminated **Kündigungsklausel**
(b) *US* leaving a job (resigning, retiring, or being fired or made redundant) **Beendigung des Arbeitsverhältnisses; Kündigung**

territory *noun* area of land (ruled by a government) **Gebiet, Territorium;** *their government has laid claim to part of our territory*

◊ **territorial** *adjective* referring to land **territorial, Territorial-, Gebiets-; territorial claims** = claims to own land which is part of another country **Gebietsansprüche; territorial waters** = sea waters near the coast of a country, which is part of the country and governed by the laws of that country **Hoheitsgewässer; outside territorial waters** = in international waters, where a single country's jurisdiction does not run **außerhalb der Hoheitsgewässer**

terrorism *noun* violent action (such as assassination *or* bombing) taken for political reasons **Terrorismus;** *the act of terrorism was condemned by the Minister of Justice*

◊ **terrorist** *noun* person who commits a violent act for political reasons **Terrorist/-in;** *the bomb was planted by a terrorist group or by a group of terrorists; six people were killed in the terrorist attack on the airport*

test
1 *noun*
(a) examination to see if something works well *or* is possible **Test, Prüfung; test certificate** = certificate to show that something has passed a test **Abnahme-, Zulassungsbescheinigung; control test** = test to decide if someone is an employee *or* is selfemployed (used for the purposes of tax assessment) **Kontrollverfahren zur Feststellung der Arbeitnehmereigenschaft; feasibility test** = test to see if something is possible **Durchführbarkeitstest**
(b) test case = legal action where the decision will fix a principle which other cases can follow **Musterprozeß; Präzedenzfall**
2 *verb* to examine something to see if it is working well **testen, prüfen;** *to test a computer system*

testament *noun* **last will and testament** = will *or* document by which a person says what he wants to happen to his property when he dies **Testament**

◊ **testamentary** *adjective* referring to a will **testamentarisch; testamentary capacity** = legal ability of someone to make a will **Testierfähigkeit; testamentary disposition** = passing of property to someone in a will **testamentarische Verfügung**

testate *adjective* having made a will **mit Hinterlassung eines Testaments;** *did he die testate?; see also* INTESTATE

◊ **testator** *noun* man who has made a will **Testator, Erblasser**

◊ **testatrix** *noun* woman who has made a will **Erblasserin**

testify *verb* to give evidence in court **aussagen; bezeugen**

testimonium clause *noun* last section of a will *or* conveyance, etc., which shows how it has been witnessed **Beglaubigungsvermerk**

COMMENT: the testimonium clause usually begins with the words: "in witness whereof I have set my hand"

testimony *noun* oral statement given by a witness in court about what happened **Aussage;** *she gave her testimony in a low voice*
NOTE: no plural

text *noun* written part of something **Text;** *he wrote notes at the side of the text of the agreement;* **text processing** = working with words, using a computer to produce, check and change documents, contracts, reports, letters, etc. **Textverarbeitung**

◊ **textbook** *noun* book of legal commentary which can be cited in court **Gesetzeskommentar**

theft *noun*
(a) crime of stealing *or* of taking of property which belongs to someone else with the intention of depriving that person of it **Diebstahl;** *we have brought in security guards to protect the store against theft; the company is trying to reduce losses caused by theft; to take out insurance against theft;* **petty theft** = stealing small items *or* small amounts of money **Bagatelldiebstahl**
(b) act of stealing **Diebstahl;** *there has been a wave of thefts from newsagents*
NOTE: no plural for (a)

COMMENT: types of theft which are notifiable offences are: theft from the person of another; theft in a dwelling; theft by an employee; theft of mail *or* pedal cycle *or* motor vehicle; theft from vehicles *or* from a shop *or* from an automatic machine or meter

there- *prefix*
NOTE: the following words formed from **there-** are frequently used in legal documents

◊ **thereafter** *adverb* after that **danach, darauf**

◊ **thereby** *adverb* by that **dadurch, damit**

◊ **therefor** *adverb* for that **darum, deshalb**

◊ **therefrom** *adverb* from that **daraus**

◊ **therein** *adverb* in that **darin**

◊ **thereinafter** *adverb* afterwards listed in that document **(weiter) unten, nachstehend**

◊ **thereinbefore** *adverb* before mentioned in that document **(weiter) oben, vorher**

◊ **thereinunder** *adverb* mentioned under that heading **unter**

◊ **thereof** *adverb* of that **davon; in respect thereof** = regarding that thing **unter Berücksichtigung dessen**

◊ **thereto** *adverb* to that **dazu, daran, dafür; darüber hinaus**

◊ **theretofore** *adverb* before that time **zuvor; bis dahin**

◊ **therewith** *adverb* with that **damit**

thief *noun* person who steals *or* who takes property which belongs to someone else **Dieb/-in;** *thieves broke into the office and stole the petty cash;* **petty thief** = person who steals small items *or* small amounts of money **Kleinkrimineller**
NOTE: plural is **thieves**

third *noun* part of something which is divided into three equal parts **Drittel; to sell everything at one third off** = to sell everything at a discount of 33% **alles mit einem Drittel Rabatt verkaufen**

◊ **third party** *noun* any person other than the two main parties involved in proceedings *or* contract; the other person involved in an accident **Dritter, dritte Person; third-party insurance** = insurance which pays compensation if someone who is not the insured person incurs loss or injury **Haftpflichtversicherung; third party notice** = pleading served by a defendant on another party joining that party to an existing court action **Streitverkündung; third party proceedings** = introduction of a third party into a case by the defendant **Streitverkündungsverfahren; the case is in the hands of a third party** = the case is being dealt with by someone who is not one of the main interested parties **mit dem Fall befaßt sich ein Dritter**

◊ **Third Reading** *noun* final discussion and vote on a Bill in Parliament **Dritte Lesung**

threat *noun* words (spoken *or* written) which say that something unpleasant may happen to someone, and which frighten that person **Drohung; Androhung**

◊ **threaten** *verb* to warn someone that unpleasant things may happen to him **androhen; drohen mit; bedrohen;** *he threatened to take the tenant to court or to have the tenant evicted; she complained that her husband threatened her with a knife*

throne *noun* special chair for a King *or* Queen **Thron; speech from the throne** = QUEEN'S SPEECH

throw out *verb*
(a) to reject *or* to refuse to accept **verwerfen;** *the proposal was thrown out by the planning committee; the board threw out the draft contract submitted by the union*
(b) to get rid of (something which is not wanted) **weg-, herauswerfen;** *we threw out the old telephones and put in a computerized system; the AGM threw out the old board of directors*
NOTE: **throwing - threw - has thrown**

thug *noun* man who attacks people **Rowdy, Schläger;** *a group of teenage thugs attacked the couple as they left the shop*

◊ **thuggery** *noun* attacking people **Rowdytum**
NOTE: no plural

time *noun*
(a) period when something takes place (such as one hour, two days, fifty minutes) **Zeit; computer time** = time when a computer is being used (paid for at an hourly rate) **Betriebszeit; real time** = time when a computer is working on the processing of data while the problem to which the data refers is actually taking place **Echtzeit, Realtime; time charter** = agreement to charter a ship for a fixed period **Zeitcharter; time policy** = marine insurance policy which runs for a fixed period of time **zeitlich begrenzte Police; time immemorial** = from before 1189, the date from which events are supposed to be remembered **unvordenkliche Zeit; from time immemorial** from 1189 **seit Urzeiten/Menschengedenken; time summons** = summons issued to apply to the court for more time in which to serve a pleading **Fristverlängerungsantrag, Nachfrist; extension of time** = extra time allowed in which to serve a pleading *or* to take a step in a court action **Fristverlängerung**
(b) hour of the day (such as 9.00, 12.15, ten o'clock at night) **Zeit;** *the time of arrival or the arrival time is indicated on the screen; departure times are delayed by up to fifteen minutes because of the volume of traffic;* **on time** = at the right time **pünktlich;** *the plane was on time; you will have to hurry if you want to get to the hearing on time or if you want to be on time for the hearing*
(c) system of hours on the clock **Zeit, Uhrzeit; Summer Time** *or* **Daylight Saving Time** = system where clocks are set back one hour in the summer to take advantage of the longer hours of daylight **Sommerzeit; Standard Time** = normal time as in the winter months **Normalzeit**
(d) hours worked **Arbeitszeit; he is paid time and a half on Sundays** = he is paid the normal rate with an extra 50% when he works on Sundays **sonntags bekommt er 50% Zuschlag**
(e) period before something happens **Zeitspanne; time limit** = period during which something should be done **Frist; to keep within the time limits** *or* **within the time schedule** = to complete work by the time stated **die Fristen einhalten; time lock** = lock which will open only at a certain time of day (as in a bank vault) **Zeitschloß**

◊ **timetable**
1 *noun*

(a) list showing times of arrivals or departures of buses or trains or planes, etc. **Fahrplan**; *according to the timetable, there should be a train to London at 10.22; the bus company has brought out its new timetable for the next twelve months*
(b) list of appointments or events **Terminkalender, Programm**; *Mr Smith has a very full timetable, so I doubt if he will be able to see you today;* **conference timetable** = list of speakers or events at a conference **Konferenzprogramm**
2 *verb* to make a list of times **einen Zeitplan aufstellen**

tipstaff *noun* official of the Supreme Court who is responsible for arresting persons in contempt of court **Gerichtsdiener, Wachtmeister**

title *noun*
(a) (i) right to hold goods or property; (ii) document proving a right to hold a property **(i) Rechtsanspruch, Eigentumsrecht; (ii)** *entspricht* **urkundlicher Rechtstitel;** *she has no title to the property; he has a good title to the property;* **title deeds** = document showing who is the owner of a property **Grundeigentumsurkunde;** *entspricht* **Grundbucheintrag; to have a clear title to something** = to have a right to something with no limitations or charges **ein unbestrittenes Recht/Anrecht auf etwas haben; good title** = title to a property which gives the owner full rights of ownership **einwandfreier Rechtsanspruch; unbestrittenes Eigentum; possessory title** = title to land acquired by occupying it continuously (usually for a period of twelve years) **Besitztitel; qualified title** = title to a property which is not absolute as there is some defect **bedingter Rechtstitel**
(b) name given to a person in a certain job **Titel, Amtsbezeichnung;** *he has the title "Chief Executive"*
(c) honourable name given to some (such as Lord Smith, Mr Justice Jones) **Titel**
(d) name of a bill which comes before Parliament or name of an Act of Parliament **Titel, Gesetzesbezeichnung; full title** or **long title** = complete title of an Act of Parliament **voller Titel; short title** = usual title of an Act of Parliament **Kurztitel**

token *noun* thing which acts as a sign **Zeichen; Symbol; token charge** = small charge which does not cover the real costs **symbolische Gebühr;** *a token charge is made for heating;* **token payment** = small payment to show that a payment is being made **symbolische Zahlung; token rent** = very low rent payment to show that a rent is being asked **symbolische Miete; token strike** = short strike to show that workers have a grievance **Warnstreik**

toll *noun* payment made for using a road or bridge or ferry **Benutzungsgebühr**

tort *noun* civil wrong done by one person to another and entitling the victim to claim damages **Delikt; action in tort** = action brought by a plaintiff who has suffered damage or harm caused by the defendant **Schadensersatzklage; proceedings in tort** = court action for damages for a tort **Schadensersatzprozeß, Schadensersatzverfahren**
◊ **tortfeasor** *noun* person who has committed a tort **rechtswidrig Handelnder; joint tortfeasors** = two people who together commit a tort **Mittäter**
◊ **tortious** *adjective* referring to a tort **rechtswidrig; unerlaubt; tortious act** = a tort **unerlaubte Handlung; tortious liability** = liability for harm caused by a breach of duty **Deliktshaftung**

torture *verb* to hurt someone badly so as to force him to give information **foltern; quälen**
◊ **torturer** *noun* person who tortures **Folterknecht**

total
1 *adjective* complete or with everything added together **gesamt, Gesamt-** ; **völlig, absolut;** *total amount; total assets; total cost; total expenditure; total income; total output; total revenue;* **the cargo was written off as a total loss** = the cargo was so badly damaged that the insurers said it had no value **die Fracht wurde als Gesamtverlust abgeschrieben**
2 *noun* amount which is complete or with everything added up **Summe, Endbetrag;** *the total of the charges comes to more than £1,000; he was sentenced to a total of twelve years' imprisonment;* **grand total** = final total made by adding several smaller totals **Gesamtsumme, Endbetrag**
3 *verb* to add up to **ergeben, sich belaufen auf;** *costs totalling more than £25,000*
NOTE: **totalling - totalled** but US English **totaling - totaled**
◊ **totally** *adverb* completely **völlig, total;** *the factory was totally destroyed in the fire; the cargo was totally ruined by water*

totiens quotiens *Latin phrase meaning* "as often as necessary"

town *noun* large group of houses and other buildings which is the place where many people live and work **Stadt; Town Clerk =** formerly the title of the person appointed as chief administrator of a town **Stadtdirektor; town planner =** person who supervises the design of a town *or* the way the streets and buildings in a town are laid out and the land in a town used **Stadtplaner; town planning =** supervising the design of a town *or* the use of land in a town **Stadtplanung**

trace *verb* to follow *or* to look for someone *or* something **nachspüren, verfolgen; aufspüren;** *we have traced the missing documents; the police traced the two men to a hotel in London;* **tracing action =** court action begun to trace money *or* proceeds of a sale **Prozeß zur Nachforschung über den Verbleib von Vermögenswerten**

trade

1 *noun*

(a) business of buying and selling **Handel; Gewerbe; export trade** *or* **import trade =** the business of selling to other countries *or* buying from other countries **Exporthandel; Importhandel; home trade =** trade in the country where a company is based **Binnenhandel**

(b) fair trade = international business system where countries agree not to charge import duties on certain items imported from their trading partners **Nichtdiskriminierung im Außenhandel; free trade =** system where goods can go from one country to another without any restrictions **Freihandel; free trade area =** group of countries practising free trade **Freihandelszone; trade agreement =** international agreement between countries over general terms of trade **Handelsabkommen; trade description =** description of a product to attract customers **Warenkennzeichnung; Trade Descriptions Act =** Act of Parliament which limits the way in which products can be described so as to protect customers from wrong descriptions made by the makers of the products **Warenkennzeichnungsgesetz; trade directory =** book which lists all the businesses and business people in a town **Branchenadreßbuch; to ask a company to supply trade references =** to ask a company to give names of traders who can report on the company's financial situation and reputation **ein Unternehmen um Handelsauskünfte ersuchen**

(c) people *or* companies dealing in the same type of product **Branche, Gewerbe;** *he is in the secondhand car trade; she is very well known in the clothing trade;* **trade association =** group which joins together companies in the same type of business

Handels-, Industrie-, Wirtschaftsverband; (NOTE: no plural)

2 *verb* to buy and sell *or* to carry on a business **handeln, Handel treiben;** *to trade with another country; to trade on the Stock Exchange; the company has stopped trading; he trades under the name or as "Eeziphitt"*

◊ **trademark** *or* **trade mark** *or* **trade name** *noun* particular name, design, etc., which identifies the product, has been registered by the maker, and which cannot be used by other makers **Warenzeichen, Handelsmarke;** *you cannot call your beds "Softn'kumfi" - it is a registered trademark*

◊ **trader** *noun* person who does business **Händler/-in, Kaufmann/Kauffrau; commodity trader =** person whose business is buying and selling commodities **Warenterminhändler; free trader =** person who is in favour of free trade **Befürworter des Freihandels; sole trader =** person who runs a business, usually by himself, but has not registered it as a company **Einzelkaufmann**

◊ **trade union** *or* **trades union** *noun* organization which represents workers, who are its members, in discussions about wages and conditions of employment with employers **Gewerkschaft;** *they are members of a trade union or they are trade union members; he has applied for trade union membership or he has applied to join a trade union;* **Trades Union Congress =** central organization for all British trade unions **britischer Gewerkschaftsbund**

NOTE: although **Trades Union Congress** is the official name for the organization, **trade union** is commoner than **trades union**

◊ **trading** *noun* carrying on a business **Handel; fair trading =** way of doing business which is reasonable and does not harm the consumer **lauterer Wettbewerb; Office of Fair Trading =** government department which protects consumers against unfair *or* illegal business practices **Amt für Verbraucherschutz; fraudulent trading =** carrying on the business of a company while knowing that the company is insolvent **betrügerisches Geschäftsgebaren**

traffic

1 *noun* cars *or* vehicles on the road **Verkehr; traffic offences =** offences committed by drivers of vehicles **Verkehrsdelikte; traffic police =** section of the police concerned with problems on the roads **Verkehrspolizei; traffic warden =** official whose duty is to regulate the traffic under the supervision of the police, especially to deal with cars which are illegally parked **Verkehrspolizist ohne polizeiliche Befugnisse;** *(weiblich)* **Politesse**

2 *verb* **to traffic in something** = to buy and sell something illegally **handeln, dealen;** *he was charged with trafficking in drugs or with drug trafficking*

train *verb* to teach someone a skill *or* a profession **ausbilden;** *he is a trained accountant; the director is Americantrained;* **day training centre** = centre where young offenders attend courses as part of their probation **Tagesausbildungsstätte**

◊ **trainee** *noun* young person who is learning a skill; young person who is contracted to work in a solicitor's office for some years to learn the law **Auszubildender; Rechtspraktikant, Rechtsreferendar**

transact *verb* **to transact business** = to carry out a piece of business **Geschäfte abschließen/abwickeln**

◊ **transaction** *noun* **business transaction** = piece of business *or* buying or selling **geschäftliche Transaktion; cash transaction** = transaction paid for in cash **Bargeschäft; a transaction on the Stock Exchange** = purchase *or* sale of shares on the Stock Exchange **eine Börsentransaktion;** *the paper publishes a daily list of Stock Exchange transactions;* **exchange transaction** = purchase *or* sale of foreign currency **Devisengeschäft; fraudulent transaction** = transaction which aims to cheat someone **Schwindelgeschäft**

transcript *noun* record (written out in full) of something noted in shorthand **Abschrift;** *the judge asked for a full transcript of the evidence; transcripts of cases are available in the Supreme Court Library*

transfer
1 *noun* moving someone *or* something to a new place **Transfer; Verlegung; Versetzung; Übertragung; transfer of property** *or* **transfer of shares** = moving the ownership of property *or* shares from one person to another **Eigentumsübertragung; Aktienübertragung; bank transfer** = moving money from a bank account to an account in another country **Banküberweisung; capital transfer tax** = tax on the transfer of capital *or* assets from one owner to another **Kapitaltransfersteuer; credit transfer** *or* **transfer of funds** = moving money from one account to another **Kredittransfer; Geldtransfer; deed of transfer** = agreement which transfers the ownership of shares **Aktienübertragungsurkunde; stock transfer form** = form to be signed by the person transferring shares to another **Formular zur Aktienübertragung**

2 *verb*
(a) to move someone *or* something to a new place **transferieren; verlegen; versetzen; übertragen;** *the accountant was transferred to our Scottish branch; he transferred his shares to a family trust; she transferred her money to a deposit account;* **transferred charge call** = phone call where the person receiving the call agrees to pay for it **R-Gespräch**
(b) to change from one type of travel to another **umsteigen;** *when you get to London airport, you have to transfer onto an internal flight*
NOTE: **transferring - transferred**

◊ **transferable** *adjective* which can be passed to someone else **übertragbar; the season ticket is not transferable** = the ticket cannot be given or lent to someone else to use **die Zeitkarte ist nicht übertragbar; single transferable vote** = voting system in proportional representation where each voter votes for the candidates in order of preference, and his vote is transferred to the next candidate if his first choice is not elected **einfach übertragbare Wahlstimme**

◊ **transferee** *noun* person to whom property *or* goods are transferred **Empfänger/-in**

◊ **transferor** *noun* person who transfers goods *or* property to another **Übertragender**

transit *see* IN TRANSIT

traverse *noun* denial in a pleading by one side in a case that the facts alleged by the other side are correct **Bestreiten (des Vorbringens der klagenden Partei)**

treason *noun* notifiable offence *or* crime of betraying one's country, usually by helping the enemy in time of war **Verrat;** *he was accused of treason; three men were executed for treason; the treason trial lasted three weeks;* **high treason** = formal way of referring to treason **Hochverrat; misprision of treason** = crime of knowing that treason has been committed and not reporting it **strafbares Unterlassen der Anzeige von Hochverrat; treason felony** = notifiable offence of planning to remove a King *or* Queen *or* of planning to start a war against the United Kingdom **Hoch-, Landesverrat**
NOTE: no plural

◊ **treasonable** *adjective* which may be considered as treason **verräterisch; hoch-, landesverräterisch;** *he was accused of making treasonable remarks*

treasure *noun* gold *or* silver *or* jewels, especially when found or stolen **Schatz; Reichtümer;** *thieves broke into the palace* *and stole the king's treasure;* **treasure trove** = treasure which has been hidden by someone in the past and is now discovered **Schatzfund**

COMMENT: treasure which has been found is declared to the coroner, who decides if it is treasure trove. If it is declared treasure trove, it belongs to the state, though the person who finds it will usually get a reward equal to its market value

◊ **treasurer** *noun*
(a) person who looks after the money *or* finances of a club or society, etc. **Finanzverwalter; honorary treasurer** = treasurer who does not receive any fee **ehrenamtlicher Finanzverwalter**
(b) main financial manager of a large company **Finanzmanager**

◊ **treasury** *noun* **the Treasury** = government department which deals with the country's finance **das Finanzministerium; the Treasury Benches** = front benches in the House of Commons where the government ministers sit **die Regierungsbänke; Treasury Bill** = bill of exchange which does not give any interest and is sold by the government at a discount **Schatzwechsel; treasury bonds** = bonds issued by the Treasury of the USA **Schatzobligationen; Treasury counsel** = barrister who pleads in the Central Criminal Court on behalf of the Director of Public Prosecutions **Barrister, der als Staatsanwalt auftritt; Treasury Solicitor** = the solicitor who is head of the Government Legal Service in England and Wales and Legal Adviser to the Treasury, Cabinet Office and other government departments **leitender Rechtsberater des Treasury, Kanzleramts und anderer Ministerien**

treaty *noun*
(a) written legal agreement between countries **Vertrag; Abkommen;** *commercial treaty; cultural treaty;* **Treaty of Accession** = treaty whereby the UK joined the EC **EG-Beitrittsvertrag; Treaty of Rome** = treaty which established the EC in 1957 **Römische Verträge**
(b) agreement between individual persons **Vertrag; to sell (a house) by private treaty** = to sell (a house) to another person not by auction **ein Haus privat verkaufen**

treble *verb* to increase three times **verdreifachen;** *the company's borrowings have trebled*

trend *noun* general way things are going **Trend, Tendenz;** *there is a trend away from old-style policing methods; a downward trend in investment; we notice a general*

trend to sell to the student market; the report points to upwards trends in reported crimes of violence; **economic trends** = way in which a country's economy is moving **ökonomische Trends/Entwicklungen**

trespass
1 *noun* tort of interfering with the land *or* goods of another person **unbefugtes Betreten; trespass to goods** = tort of harming *or* stealing *or* interfering with goods which belong to someone else **Eigentumsstörung; trespass to land** = tort of interfering with *or* going on someone's property *or* putting things *or* animals on someone's property without permission **unbefugtes Betreten; trespass to the person** = tort of harming someone by assault *or* false imprisonment **Verletzung der körperlichen Unversehrtheit und persönlichen Freiheit der Person;** (NOTE: no plural)

COMMENT: trespass on someone's property is not a criminal offence

2 *verb* to offend by going on to property without the permission of the owner **unbefugt betreten**

◊ **trespasser** *noun* person who commits trespass by going on to land without the permission of the owner **jd, der unbefugt fremden Besitz betritt**

triable *adjective* (offence) for which a person can be tried in a court **belangbar; offence triable either way** = offence which can be tried before the Magistrates' Court or before the Crown Court **Vergehen, über das im Magistrates' Court oder im Crown Court gleichermaßen verhandelt werden kann**

trial *noun*
(a) criminal *or* civil court case heard before a judge **Gerichtsverhandlung; Prozeß;** *the trial lasted six days; the judge ordered a new trial when one of the jurors was found to be the accused's brother;* **he is on trial** *or* **is standing trial for embezzlement** = he is being tried for embezzlement **unter Anklage stehen; wegen Unterschlagung angeklagt sein; to commit someone for trial** = to send someone to a court to be tried **jd einem (hohen) Gericht übergeben; trial judge** = judge who is hearing a trial **Verhandlungsrichter**
(b) test to see if something is good **Erprobung; Prüfung; on trial** = (i) being tested; (ii) before a court **(i) zur Prüfung/Probe; (ii) angeklagt;** *the product is on trial in our laboratories;* **trial period** = time when a customer can test a product before buying it **Probezeit; trial sample** = small piece of a product used for testing **Muster; Probestück; free trial** = testing of a machine

or product with no payment involved **kostenlos zur Probe**
(c) trial balance = draft adding of debits and credits to see if they balance **vorläufige Bilanz**

tribunal *noun* a court; especially a specialist court outside the judicial system which examines special problems and makes judgments **Sondergericht; Schiedsgericht; Tribunal; industrial tribunal** = court which can decide in disputes between employers and employees **Arbeitsgericht; Lands Tribunal** = court which deals with compensation claims relating to land **Schiedsstelle für Entschädigungsentscheidungen bei Einteignungen; military tribunal** = court made up of army officers **Militärgericht; rent tribunal** = court which adjudicates in disputes about rents, and can award a fair rent **Schiedsgericht für Mietstreitigkeiten**

trick
1 *noun* clever act to make someone believe something which is not true **Trick; confidence trick** = business where someone gains another person's confidence and then tricks him **Schwindel**
2 *verb* to trick somebody into doing something to get money *or* property by making someone believe something which is not true **jdn mit einem Trick dazu bringen, etwas zu tun;** *the gang tricked the bank manager into giving them the keys of the vault; they tricked the old lady out of £25,000*
◊ **trickster** *noun* **confidence trickster** = person who carries out a confidence trick on someone **Schwindler/-in**

Trinity *noun* one of the four sittings of the law courts; one of the four law terms **Dreieinigkeit (einer der vier traditionellen Sitzungsperioden englischer Gerichte)**
◊ **Trinity House** *noun* body which superintends lighthouses and pilots in some areas of the British coast **Behörde, die für Navigationshilfe vor englischen Küsten zuständig ist**

trip *noun* journey **Trip, Reise; business trip** = journey to discuss business matters with people who live a long way away or overseas **Geschäftsreise**

triplicate *noun* **in triplicate** = with an original and two copies **in dreifacher Ausfertigung;** *to print an invoice in triplicate;* **invoicing in triplicate** = preparing three copies of invoices **Rechnungen in dreifacher Ausfertigung ausstellen**

trouble *noun* problem *or* difficult situation **Schwierigkeiten, Probleme;** *the police are expecting trouble at the football match; there was some trouble in the courtroom after the verdict was announced*
◊ **troubleshooter** *noun* person whose job is to solve problems **Trouble Shooter; Vermittler/-in; Krisenmanager**

trough *noun* low point in the economic cycle **Konjunkturtief, Talsohle**

trove *see* TREASURE

trover *noun* action to recover property which has been converted *or* goods which have been taken *or* passed to other parties **Herausgabeklage**

true *adjective* correct *or* accurate **wahr; true bill** = verdict by a grand jury that an indictment should proceed **begründete (von Geschworenen zugelassene) Anklage; true copy** = exact copy **getreue Kopie;** *I certify that this is a true copy; certified as a true copy*

truly *adverb* **Yours truly** *or (US)* **Truly yours** = ending to a formal business letter where you do not know the person to whom you are writing **Hochachtungsvoll**

trust
1 *noun*
(a) being confident that something is correct, will work, etc. **Vertrauen; we took his statement on trust** = we accepted his statement without examining it to see if it was correct **wir akzeptierten seine Aussage auf Treu und Glauben**
(b) duty of looking after goods *or* money *or* property which someone (the beneficiary) has passed to you (the trustee) **Treuhand(schaft);** *he left his property in trust for his grandchild;* **breach of trust** = failure on the part of a trustee to act properly in regard to a trust **Verletzung von Treuhandpflichten; position of trust** = job where an employee is trusted by his employer to look after money *or* confidential information, etc. **Vertrauensstellung; constructive trust** = trust arising by reason of a person's behaviour **fingiertes Treuhandverhältnis; implied trust** = trust which is implied by the intentions of the parties **stillschweigend zustandegekommenes/als bestehend angenommenes Vertrauens- od Treuhandverhältnis; trust for sale** = trust whereby property is held but can be sold and the money passed to the beneficiaries **Veräußerungstreuhand**

(c) management of money *or* property for someone **Vermögensverwaltung;** *they set up a family trust for their grandchildren; (US)* **trust company** = organization which supervises the financial affairs of private trusts, executes wills, and acts as a bank to a limited number of customers **Treuhandgesellschaft, Trust; trust deed** *or* **instrument** = document which sets out the details of a trust **Treuhandvertrag; trust fund** = assets (money, securities, property) held in trust for the beneficiaries **Treuhandfonds; discretionary trust** = trust where the trustees decide when and how much money is to be paid to the beneficiaries **uneingeschränktes Treuhandverhältnis; investment trust** = company whose shares can be bought on the Stock Exchange and whose business is to make money by buying and selling stocks and shares **Investmenttrust, Kapitalanlagegesellschaft; unit trust** = organization which takes money from investors and invests it in stocks and shares for them under a trust deed **offener Investmentfonds, Unit Trust (d)** *US* group of companies which control the supply of a product **Trust, Syndikat;** NOTE: no plural for (a) and (b)
2 *verb* **to trust someone with something** = to give something to someone to look after **jdm etwas anvertrauen;** *can he be trusted with all that cash?*

◊ **trustee** *noun* person who has charge of money *or* property in trust *or* person who is responsible for a family trust **Vermögensverwalter; Treuhänder;** *the trustees of the pension fund;* **trustee in bankruptcy** = person who is appointed by a court to run the affairs of a bankrupt and pay his creditors **Konkursverwalter; Public Trustee** = official who is appointed as a trustee of a person's property **öffentlich bestellter Treuhänder; Trustee Savings Bank** = bank which takes savings from small savers, and is guaranteed by the government **öffentlich-rechtliches Bankinstitut**

◊ **trusteeship** *noun* position of being a trustee **Treuhänderschaft**

◊ **trustworthy** *adjective* (person) who can be trusted **vertrauenswürdig;** *the staff who deal with cash are completely trustworthy*

◊ **trusty** *noun (slang)* prisoner who is trusted by the prison warders **priviligierter Häftling**

truth *noun* what is true *or* not false **Wahrheit;** *the court is trying to find out the truth about the payments; counsel for the defence said that the plaintiff was not telling the truth; witnesses have to swear to tell the truth*

◊ **truthful** *adjective* true (statement) **wahr; wahrheitsgemäß**

try *verb* to hear a civil *or* criminal trial **verhandeln; vor Gericht stellen;** *he was tried for murder and sentenced to life imprisonment; the court is not competent to try the case*

TUC = TRADES UNION CONGRESS

turn
1 *noun*
(a) movement in a circle *or* change of direction **Drehung**
(b) turn profit *or* commission **Gewinnspanne; Courtage; jobber's turn** = profit made by a stock jobber **Courtage**
2 *verb* to change direction *or* to go round in a circle **(sich) drehen; abbiegen; to turn Queen's evidence** *or* **(US) to turn state's evidence** = to confess to a crime and then act as witness against the other criminals involved in the hope of getting a lighter sentence **eine Aussage als Kronzeuge od Zeuge der Staatsanwaltschaft gegen Zusage der Strafmilderung machen**

◊ **turn down** *verb* to refuse **ablehnen;** *the court turned down his petition; the bank turned down their request for a loan; the application for a licence was turned down*

◊ **turnkey operation** *noun* contract where a company takes all responsibility for building, fitting and staffing a building (such as a school *or* hospital *or* factory) so that it is completely ready for the purchaser to take over **Erfüllung einer geschäftlichen Operation**

◊ **turn over** *verb* to have a certain amount of sales **umsetzen;** *we turn over £2,000 a week*

◊ **turnover** *noun*
(a) *GB* amount of sales **Umsatz;** *the company's turnover has increased by 235%; we based our calculations on last year's turnover*
(b) staff turnover *or* **turnover of staff** = changes in staff, when some leave and others join **Fluktuation**
(c) *US* number of times something is used *or* sold in a period (usually one year), expressed as a percentage of a total **Umschlag(sgeschwindigkeit)**

type
1 *noun* sort *or* kind **Art; Sorte; Kategorie;** *a new type of drug; several types of murder*
2 *verb* to write with a typewriter **(mit der) Schreibmaschine schreiben, tippen;** *he can type quite fast; all his reports are typed on his typewriter*

◊ **typewriter** *noun* machine which prints letters *or* figures on a piece of paper when a key is pressed **Schreibmaschine;** *electronic typewriter*

◊ **typewritten** *adjective* written using a typewriter **maschinengeschrieben;** *he sent in a typewritten job application*

◊ **typing** *noun* writing letters with a typewriter **Schreibmaschineschreiben, Tippen; typing error** = mistake made when using a typewriter **Tippfehler; copy typing** = typing documents from handwritten or typed originals, not from dictation **Abtippen von Dokumenten**
NOTE: no plural

◊ **typist** *noun* person whose job is to write letters using a typewriter **Schreibkraft; copy typist** = person who types documents from handwritten or typed originals, and not from dictation **Schreibkraft ohne Diktat; shorthand typist** = typist who takes dictation in shorthand and then types it **Stenotypist/-in**

Uu

uberrimae fidei *Latin phrase meaning* "of total good faith": state which should exist between parties to certain types of legal relationship (such as partnerships or insurance) **(von) höchste(r) Redlichkeit;** *an insurance contract is uberrimae fidei*

ulterior motive *noun* reason for doing something which is not immediately connected with the action, but is done in anticipation of its result, and so is an act of bad faith **Hintergedanke; niedrige Beweggründe**

ultimate *adjective* last *or* final **letzter; End-; ultimate consumer** = the person who actually uses the product **Endverbraucher; ultimate owner** = real *or* true owner **der eigentliche/wirkliche Besitzer**

◊ **ultimatum** *noun* final demand *or* proposal to someone that unless he does something within a period of time, action will be taken against him **Ultimatum;** *the union officials argued among themselves over the best way to deal with the ultimatum from the management*
NOTE: plural is **ultimatums** or **ultimata**

ultra vires *Latin phrase meaning* "beyond powers" **über die Befugnisse hinausgehend; their action was ultra vires** = they acted in a way which exceeded their legal powers **sie überschritten ihre rechtlichen Befugnisse;** *see* INTRA VIRES

umpire *noun* person called in to decide when two arbitrators cannot agree **Schiedsrichter; Obmann**

unable *adjective* not able **außerstande;** *the court was unable to adjudicate because one side had not finished presenting its evidence*

unanimous *adjective* where everyone votes in the same way **einstimmig;** *there was a unanimous vote against the proposal; they reached unanimous agreement;* **unanimous verdict** = verdict agreed by all the jurors **einstimmiger Richterspruch;** *(GB)* **einstimmiger Geschworenenspruch;** *the jury reached a unanimous verdict of not guilty*

◊ **unanimously** *adverb* with everyone agreeing **einstimmig;** *the proposals were adopted unanimously; the appeal court decided unanimously in favour of the defendant*

unascertained *adjective* not identified **unbestimmt; unermittelt; nicht sicher festgestellt;** *title to unascertained goods cannot pass to the buyer until the goods have been ascertained*

unavoidable *adjective* which cannot be avoided **unvermeidlich; zwangsläufig;** *planes are subject to unavoidable delays*

◊ **unavoidably** *adverb* in a way which cannot be avoided **unvermeidlich; zwangsläufig;** *the hearing was unavoidably delayed*

unbecoming *adjective* (behaviour *or* dress) which is not as decent as it should be **unschicklich**

unborn *adjective* (child) which is still in its mother's body and has not yet been born **ungeboren**

unchallenged *adjective* (evidence) which has not been challenged **unwiderlegt; unbestritten**

unconditional *adjective* with no conditions attached **vorbehaltlos;** *unconditional acceptance of the offer by the board; on the plaintiff's application for summary judgment the master gave the defendant unconditional leave to defend;* **the offer went unconditional last Thursday** = the takeover bid was accepted by the majority of the shareholders and therefore the conditions attached to it no longer apply **das Angebot wurde vorbehaltlos am letzten Donnerstag angenommen**

◊ **unconditionally** *adverb* without imposing any conditions **vorbehaltlos;** *the offer was accepted unconditionally*

unconfirmed *adjective* which has not been confirmed **unbestätigt;** *there are unconfirmed reports that our agent has been arrested*

unconstitutional *adjective* which is in conflict with a constitution *or* which is not allowed by the rules *or* laws of a country *or* organization **verfassungswidrig, nicht verfassungsmäßig;** *the chairman ruled that the meeting was unconstitutional; the Appeal Court ruled that the action of the Attorney-General was unconstitutional*

uncontested *adjective* which is not contested *or* defended **unangefochten; unumstritten;** *an uncontested divorce case or election*

uncontrollable *adjective* which cannot be controlled **unkontrollierbar;** *uncontrollable inflation; he had an uncontrollable impulse to steal*

uncrossed cheque *noun* cheque which may be exchanged for cash anywhere **Barscheck**

undefended *adjective* (case) where the defendant does not acknowledge service and does not appear at the court to defend the case **unwidersprochen; nichtstreitig;** *an undefended divorce case*

under *preposition*
(a) lower than *or* less than **unter;** *the interest rate is under 10%; under 50% of reported crimes are solved*
(b) controlled by *or* according to **nach, gemäß, laut;** *regulations under the Police Act; under the terms of the agreement, the goods should be delivered in October; he is acting under rule 23 of the union constitution; she does not qualify under section 2 of the 1979 Act; a creditor seeking a receiving order under the Bankruptcy Act 1974*

◊ **undercover agent** *noun* secret agent *or* agent acting in disguise **Geheimagent**

◊ **underestimate**
1 *noun* estimate which is less than the actual figure **Unterbewertung;** *the figure of £50,000 in legal costs was a considerable underestimate*
2 *verb* to think that something is smaller *or* not as bad as it really is **unterschätzen; unterbewerten;** *they underestimated the effects of the sanctions on their sales; he*

underestimated the amount of time needed to finish the work

◊ **underlease** *noun* lease from a tenant to another tenant **Untervermietung; Untermiete; Unterverpachtung; Unterpacht**

◊ **underlet** *verb* to let a property which is held on a lease **untervermieten; unterverpachten**

◊ **undermentioned** *adjective* mentioned lower down in a document **untengenannt**

◊ **undersheriff** *noun* person who is second to a High Sheriff and deputizes for him **stellvertretender Polizeichef**

◊ **the undersigned** *noun* person who has signed a letter **der/die Unterzeichnete; we, the undersigned** = we, the people who have signed below **wir, die Unterzeichnenden**
NOTE: can be singular or plural

◊ **understanding** *noun* private agreement **Vereinbarung, Übereinkunft;** *the two parties came to an understanding about the division of the estate;* **on the understanding that** = on condition that *or* provided that **unter der Voraussetzung, daß;** *we accept the terms of the contract, on the understanding that it has to be ratified by the full board*

◊ **undertake** *verb* to promise to do something **übernehmen, sich verpflichten;** *to undertake an investigation of the fraud; the members of the jury have undertaken not to read the newspapers; he undertook to report to the probation office once a month*
NOTE: **undertaking - undertook - has undertaken**

◊ **undertaking** *noun*
(a) business **Unternehmen; Projekt;** *a commercial undertaking*
(b) (legally binding) promise **Zusicherung;** *they have given us a written undertaking that they will not infringe our patent; the judge accepted the defendant's undertaking not to harass the plaintiff*

◊ **undertenant** *noun* person who holds a property on an underlease **Untermieter; Unterpächter**

◊ **underworld** *noun* world of criminals **Unterwelt;** *the police has informers in the London underworld; the indications are that it is an underworld killing*

◊ **underwrite** *verb*
(a) to accept responsibility for **bürgen für; haften; to underwrite a share issue** = to guarantee that a share issue will be sold by agreeing to buy all shares which are not subscribed **eine Wertpapieremission zeichnen/fest übernehmen;** *the issue was underwritten by three underwriting companies;* **to underwrite an insurance policy** = to accept liability for the payment of compensation according to the policy **eine Versicherung übernehmen**

(b) to agree to pay for costs **Haftung übernehmen für;** *the government has underwritten the development costs of the building*
NOTE: **underwriting - underwrote - has underwritten**

◊ **underwriter** *noun*
(a) person who underwrites a share issue **Garant einer Effektenemission**
(b) person who accepts liability for an insurance **Versicherungsträger, Versicherer; Lloyd's underwriter** = member of an insurance group at Lloyd's who accepts to underwrite insurances **Versicherungsträger bei Lloyd's; marine underwriter** = person who insures ships and their cargoes **See(transport)versicherer**

undischarged bankrupt *noun* person who has been declared bankrupt and has not been released from that state **nicht entlasteter Konkursschuldner**

undisclosed *adjective* not identified **ungenannt; undisclosed principal** = principal who has not been identified by his agent **ungenannte Auftraggeber**

COMMENT: the doctrine of the undisclosed principal means that the agent may be sued as well as the principal if his identity is discovered

undue influence *noun* wrong pressure put on someone which prevents that person from acting independently **Einschüchterung, unzulässige Beeinflussung**

unemployed *noun* person with no work **Arbeitsloser; the unemployed** = people with no work **die Arbeits-, Erwerbslosen** *adjective* with no work **arbeitslos**
◊ **unemployment** *noun* absence of work **Arbeitslosigkeit;** *the unemployment figures or the figures for unemployment are rising;* **unemployment benefit** = money paid by the government to someone who is unemployed **Arbeitslosengeld; Arbeitslosenhilfe**

unenforceable *adjective* (contract *or* right) which cannot be enforced **nicht durchsetzbar; nicht anwendbar**

unequivocal *adjective* clear *or* not ambiguous **eindeutig, unmißverständlich**

unfair *adjective* **unfair competition** = trying to do better than another company by using methods such as importing foreign goods at very low prices or by wrongly criticizing a competitor's products

unlauterer Wettbewerb; unfair contract term = term in a contract which is held by law to be unjust **unzulässige Vertragsbedingung; unfair dismissal** = removing someone from a job for reasons which are not fair **ungerechtfertigte Entlassung**

COMMENT: an employee can complain of unfair dismissal to an industrial tribunal

unfit *adjective* **unfit to plead** = not mentally capable of standing trial **prozeßunfähig**

unilateral *adjective* on one side only *or* done by one party only **einseitig; unilateral;** *they took the unilateral decision to cancel the contract*
◊ **unilaterally** *adverb* by one party only **einseitig; unilateral;** *they cancelled the contract unilaterally*

unincorporated association *noun* group of people (such as a club *or* partnership) which is not legally incorporated **nicht eingetragener Verein**

uninsured *adjective* with no valid insurance **nicht versichert;** *the driver of the car was uninsured*

union *noun*
(a) state of being linked together, as the linking of independent states into a federation **Staatenbund; Zusammenschluß; Union;** *the Soviet Union or the Union of Soviet Socialist Republics;* **the States of the Union** = the states joined together to form the United States of America **die Unionsstaaten; State of the Union message** = annual speech by the President of the USA which summarizes the political situation in the country **Jahresrechenschaftsbericht zur Lage der Nation**
(b) trade union *or* **trades union** *or (US)* **labor union** = organization which represents workers who are its members in discussions with management about wages and conditions of work **Gewerkschaft; union agreement** = agreement between a management and a trade union over wages and conditions of work **Tarifvertrag; union dues** *or* **union subscription** = payment made by workers to belong to a union **Gewerkschaftsbeiträge; union recognition** = act of agreeing that a union can act on behalf of staff in a company **Anerkennung der Gewerkschaft**
(c) customs union = agreement between several countries that goods can go between them without paying duty, while

goods from other countries have special duties charged on them **Zollunion**

◊ **unionist** *noun* member of a trade union **Gewerkschaftler/-in; Gewerkschaftsmitglied**

◊ **unionized** *adjective* (company) where the members of staff belong to a trade union **gewerkschaftlich organisiert**

universal *adjective* which applies everywhere *or* to everyone **universal, Universal-; allgemein; universal franchise** *or* **suffrage** = right to vote which is enjoyed by all adult members of the population **allgemeines Wahlrecht**

unjust *adjective* contrary to law *or* not just *or* not fair **ungerecht; unrechtmäßig**

◊ **unjustly** *adverb* not fairly **zu Unrecht;** *she was unjustly accused of wasting police time*

unlawful *adjective* (act) which is against the law **ungesetzlich; gesetzwidrig; unerlaubt;** *unlawful trespass on property; unlawful sexual intercourse ;* **unlawful assembly** = notifiable offence when three or more people come together to commit a breach of the peace or other crime **unerlaubte Versammlung**

◊ **unlawfully** *adverb* illegally *or* in an unlawful way **ungesetzlich; gesetzwidrig; unerlaubt;** *he was charged with unlawfully carrying firearms*

unlimited *adjective* with no limits **unbegrenzt, unbeschränkt;** *the bank offered him unlimited credit;* **unlimited company** = company where the shareholders have no limit as regards liability **Gesellschaft mit unbeschränkter Haftung; unlimited liability** = situation where a sole trader *or* each partner is responsible for all the firm's debts with no limit at the amount each may have to pay **unbeschränkte Haftung**

unliquidated claim *noun* claim for unliquidated damages **Forderung in unbestimmter Höhe**

◊ **unliquidated damages** *plural noun* damages which are not for a fixed amount of money but are awarded by a court as a matter of discretion **nicht festgesetzter Schadensersatzanspruch**

COMMENT: torts give rise to claims for unliquidated damages

unmarried *adjective* (person) who is not married **unverheiratet, ledig**

unofficial *adjective* not official **inoffiziell; unofficial strike** = strike by local workers which has not been approved by the union as a whole **wilder Streik**

◊ **unofficially** *adverb* not officially **inoffiziell;** *the tax office told the company, unofficially, that it would be prosecuted*

unopposed *adjective* (motion) with no one voting against; (proceedings) which have not been opposed **ohne Gegenstimmen;** *the Bill had an unopposed second reading in the House*

unpaid *adjective* (person) who does not receive a salary; (debt *or* bill) which has not been paid **unbezahlt**

unprecedented *adjective* which has no precedent *or* which has not happened before **ohne Präzedenz(fall); beispiellos;** *in an unprecedented move, the tribunal asked the witness to sing a song*

unprofessional conduct *noun* way of behaving which is not suitable for a professional person *or* which goes against the code of practice of a profession **berufswidriges Verhalten**

unquantifiable *adjective* (damage *or* loss) which cannot be quantified **nicht zu beziffern; unbestimmbar**

unreasonable *adjective* (behaviour) which is not reasonable in a normal person **unvernünftig; uneinsichtig;** *his answer to our letter consisted of a number of unreasonable demands for money*

◊ **unreasonably** *adverb* in a way which is not reasonable *or* which cannot be explained **unvernünftig; uneinsichtig;** *approval shall not unreasonably be withheld*

unredeemed pledge *noun* pledge which the borrower has not claimed back by paying back his loan **uneingelöstes Pfand**

unregistered *adjective* (land) which has not been registered **nicht eingetragen/registriert**

unreliable *adjective* which cannot be relied on **unzuverlässig;** *the prosecution tried to show that the driver's evidence was unreliable; the defence called two witnesses and both were unreliable*

unreported *adjective*
(a) not reported to the police **nicht angezeigt/gemeldet;** *there are thousands of unreported cases of theft*

(b) not reported in the Law Reports **nicht berichtet;** *counsel referred the judge to a number of relevant unreported cases*

unsecured *adjective* **unsecured creditor** = creditor who is owed money, but has no mortgage *or* charge over the debtor's property as security **Gläubiger ohne Sicherheiten; unsecured debt** = debt which is not guaranteed by assets **ungesicherte Verbindlichkeit; unsecured loan** = loan made with no security **ungesichertes Darlehen**

unsolicited *adjective* which has not been asked for **unaufgefordert, ungebeten; freiwillig; nicht angefordert;** *an unsolicited gift;* **unsolicited goods** = goods which are sent to someone who has not asked for them, suggesting that he might like to buy them **nicht angeforderte/verlangte Waren**

unsolved *adjective* (crime) which has not been solved **ungelöst**

unsound *adjective* **persons of unsound mind** = people who are not sane **geistesgestörte Personen; nicht zurechnungsfähige Personen**

unsuccessful *adjective* without any success **erfolglos;** *the police carried out an unsuccessful search for the suspect*

unsworn *adjective* which has not been made on oath **uneidlich, unbeeidet; unvereidigt;** *an unsworn statement*

untrue *adjective* not true **unwahr, falsch;** *he made an untrue statement in court*

unwritten *adjective* **unwritten agreement** = agreement which has been reached orally (such as in a telephone conversation) but has not been written down **ungeschriebene (mündliche) Vereinbarung; unwritten law** = rule which is established by precedent **ungeschriebenes Gesetz**

uphold *verb* to keep in good order **halten, wahren; to uphold the law** = to make sure that laws are obeyed **das Gesetz hüten; to uphold a sentence** = to reject an appeal against a sentence **eine Entscheidung/ein Urteil bestätigen;** *the Appeal Court upheld the sentence*
NOTE: **upholding - upheld**

urgent *adjective* which has to be done quickly **dringend; eilig**
◊ **urgently** *adverb* immediately **dringend, dringlich**

urine *noun* waste water from the body **Urin; urine test** = test of a sample of a person's urine to see if it contains drugs *or* alcohol **Urinuntersuchung**

usage *noun*
(a) custom *or* way in which something is usually done **Sitte; Usance**
(b) how something is used **Gebrauch; Anwendung**

use
1 *noun*
(a) land held by the legal owner on trust for a beneficiary **Nutznießung; Nießbrauch; change of use** = order allowing a property to be used in a different way (such as a dwelling house to be used as a business office, a shop to be used as a factory) **Nutzungsänderung; land zoned for industrial use** = land where planning permission has been given to build factories **zur Industrieansiedlung freigebenes Land**
(b) way in which something can be used **Gebrauch, Nutzung; directions for use** = instructions how to run a machine **Gebrauchsanweisungen; to make use of something** = to use something **von etwas Gebrauch machen; items for personal use** = items which a person will use for himself, not on behalf of the company **Gegenstände des persönlichen Gebrauchs; he has the use of a company car** = he has a company car which he uses privately **er hat einen Firmenwagen**
2 *verb* to take a machine *or* a company *or* a process, etc., and work with it **benutzen; verwenden; einsetzen;** *he used the courts to evict his tenants; we use secondclass mail for all our correspondence; the office computer is being used all the time; they use freelance typists for most of their work*
◊ **user** *noun* person who uses something **Benutzer/-in; Anwender/-in; end user** = person who actually uses a product **Endverbraucher; user's guide** *or* **handbook** = book showing someone how to use something **Benutzerhandbuch; registered user** = person *or* company which has been given official permission to use a registered trademark **Lizenznehmer**
◊ **user-friendly** *adjective* which a computer user finds easy to work **benutzerfreundlich;** *these programs are really user-friendly*

usher *noun* person who guards the door leading into a courtroom and maintains order in court **Gerichtsdiener**

usual *adjective* normal *or* ordinary **gewöhnlich, normal, üblich;** *our usual terms or* *usual conditions are thirty days' credit; the usual practice is to have the contract signed by a director of the company; the usual hours of work are from 9.30 to 5.30*

usufruct *noun* right to enjoy the use *or* the profit of the property *or* land of another person **Nießbrauch, Nutznießung**

usurp *verb* to take and use a right which is not yours (especially to take the throne from a rightful king) **usurpieren; sich bemächtigen**

◊ **usurpation** *noun* taking and using a right which is not yours **Usurpation; widerrechtliche Aneignung**

usury *noun* lending money at very high interest **Wucher; Kreditwucher**
NOTE: no plural

utter *verb*
(a) to say **äußern; von sich geben;** *the prisoner did not utter a word when the sentence was read out*
(b) to use a forged document criminally **(gefälschte Urkunden oder Falschgeld) in Umlauf/Verkehr bringen; forgery and uttering** = notifiable offence of forging and then using an official document (such as a prescription for drugs) **Fälschen und in Umlaufbringen**

Vv

v. = VERSUS against **gegen**
NOTE: titles of cases are quoted as *Hills v. The Amalgamated Company Ltd; R. v. Smith*

vacant *adjective* empty *or* not occupied **frei, unbesetzt; unbewohnt; vacant possession** = being able to occupy a property immediately after buying it because it is empty **sofort beziehbar;** *the house is for sale with vacant possession;* **situations vacant** *or* **appointments vacant** = list (in a newspaper) of jobs which are available **Stellenangebote**

vacantia *see* BONA VACANTIA

vacate *verb* to **vacate the premises** = to leave premises, so that they become empty **das Gebäude räumen**
◊ **vacation** *noun*
(a) *GB* period when the courts are closed between sittings *or* period of university holidays **Gerichtsferien; Semesterferien**

(b) *US* holiday *or* period when people are not working **Urlaub**

vagrant *noun* person who goes about with no place to live **Obdachloser, Penner, Land-, Stadtstreicher/-in**
◊ **vagrancy** *noun* being a vagrant **Landstreicherei;** *he was charged with vagrancy*
NOTE: no plural

valid *adjective*
(a) which is acceptable because it is true **begründet, stichhaltig, triftig;** *that is not a valid argument or excuse*
(b) which can be used lawfully **gültig, rechtsgültig;** *the contract is not valid if it has not been witnessed; ticket which is valid for three months; he was carrying a valid passport*
◊ **validate** *verb*
(a) to check to see if something is correct **für gültig erklären, bestätigen;** *the document was validated by the bank*
(b) to make (something) valid **rechtsgültig machen, legalisieren;** *the import documents have to be validated by the customs officials*
◊ **validation** *noun* act of making something valid **Gültigkeitserklärung, Bestätigung**
◊ **validity** *noun* being valid **Gültigkeit, Rechtsgültigkeit; period of validity** = length of time for which a document is valid **Gültigkeitsdauer, Laufzeit**
NOTE: no plural

valorem *see* AD VALOREM

valuable *adjective* which is worth a lot of money **wertvoll, kostbar; valuable consideration** = something of value (such as money) which is passed from one party (the promisee) to another (the promisor) as payment for what is promised **entgeltliche Gegenleistung; valuable property** *or* **valuables** = personal items which are worth a lot of money **Wertgegenstände, Wertsachen**
◊ **valuation** *noun* estimate of how much something is worth **Schätzung, Bewertung;** *to ask for a valuation of a property before making an offer for it;* **stock valuation** = estimating the value of stock at the end of an accounting period **Bewertung des Lagerbestandes**
◊ **value**
1 *noun* amount of money which something is worth **Wert;** *he imported goods to the value of £250; the fall in the value of the dollar; the valuer put the value of the stock at £25,000;* **asset value** = value of a company calculated by adding together all its assets **Vermögenswert; book value** = value

as recorded in the company's accounts **Buch-, Bilanzwert; declared value** = value of goods entered on a customs declaration form **angemeldeter/angegebener Wert; face value** *or* **nominal value** = value written on a coin *or* banknote *or* share **Nominal-, Nennwert; market value** = value of an asset *or* of a product *or* of a company, if sold today **Marktwert; surrender value** = money which an insurer will pay if an insurance policy is given up before maturity date **Rückkaufswert**
2 *verb* to estimate how much money something is worth **schätzen;** *goods valued at £250; he valued the stock at £25,000; we are having the jewellery valued for insurance;* **valued policy** = marine insurance policy where the value of what is insured is stated **Police mit Wertangabe**
◊ **Value Added Tax (VAT)** *noun* tax imposed as a percentage of the invoice value of goods and services **Mehrwertsteuer**
◊ **valuer** *noun* person who values property for insurance purposes **Schätzer, Taxator**

vandal *noun* person who destroys property, especially public property, wilfully **Rowdy;** *vandals have pulled the telephones out of the call boxes*
◊ **vandalism** *noun* wilful destruction of property **vorsätzliche/mutwillige Sachbeschädigung, Rowdytum**
NOTE: no plural
◊ **vandalize** *verb* to destroy property wilfully **vorsätzlich/mutwillig zerstören;** *none of the call boxes work because they have all been vandalized*

vary *verb* to change (the conditions of an order) **abändern**
◊ **variation** *noun* change in conditions **Abänderung;** *the petitioner asked for a variation in her maintenance order*

VAT = VALUE ADDED TAX

vault *noun* underground strongroom usually built under a bank **Tresor, Stahlkammer**

VC = VICE CHANCELLOR

vendor *noun*
(a) person who sells **Verkäufer/-in;** *the solicitor acting on behalf of the vendor*
(b) street vendor = person who sells food or small items in the street **Straßenhändler**

venue *noun* place where a meeting *or* hearing is held **(Tagungs)ort; (zuständiger) Gerichtsort, Gerichtsstand, Verhandlungsort;**

mistake in venue = starting legal proceedings in the wrong court **örtliche Unzuständigkeit**

verbal *adjective* using spoken words, not writing **mündlich; verbal agreement** = agreement which is spoken (such as over the telephone) **mündliche Vereinbarung; verbal warning** = stage in warning a worker that his work is not satisfactory (followed by a written warning, if his work does not improve) **mündliche Verwarnung**
◊ **verbally** *adverb* using spoken words, not writing **mündlich;** *they agreed to the terms verbally, and then started to draft the contract*

verbatim *adjective & adverb* in the exact words **wörtlich, wortgetreu, Wort für Wort;** *a verbatim transcript of the trial*

verdict *noun*
(a) decision of a jury *or* magistrate **Spruch der Geschworenen, Geschworenenspruch; Urteil; to bring in** *or* **to return a verdict** = to state a verdict at the end of a trial **einen Spruch fällen, auf ... erkennen;** *the jury brought in or returned a verdict of not guilty;* **to come to a verdict** *or* **to reach a verdict** = to decide whether the accused is guilty or not **zu einem (Geschworenen)urteil gelangen;** *the jury took two hours to reach their verdict;* **majority verdict** = verdict agreed by at least ten of the jurors **Mehrheitsvotum der Geschworenen**
(b) decision reached by a coroner's court **richterliche Feststellung der Todesursache;** *the court returned a verdict of death by misadventure;* **open verdict** = verdict in a coroner's court which does not decide how a person died **richterliche Feststellung auf unbekannte Todesursache;** *the court recorded an open verdict on the dead policeman*

verify *verb* to check to see if something is correct **(über)prüfen, bestätigen**
◊ **verification** *noun* checking if something is correct **Überprüfung, Bestätigung;** *the shipment was allowed into the country after verification of the documents by the customs*

versa *see* VICE VERSA

version *noun* description of what happened **Darstellung, Version, Fassung;** *she disputed the policeman's version of events* = she argued that the policeman's story of what happened was wrong **sie bestritt die von dem Polizisten gegebene Darstellung der Ereignisse**

versus *preposition* against **gegen**

NOTE: usually abbreviated to **v.** as in **the case of** *Smith v. Williams*

vest *verb* to transfer to someone the legal ownership and possession of land *or* of a right **(Besitz) übertragen, (ein Recht) verleihen; übergehen;** *the property was vested in the trustees*
NOTE: you vest something **in** *or* **on** someone

◊ **vested interest** *noun*
(a) interest in a property which will come into a person's possession when the interest of another person ends **sicher begründetes Recht (auf zukünftigen Besitz)**
(b) special interest in keeping an existing state of affairs **persönliches/festbegründetes Interesse; she has a vested interest in keeping the business working** = she wants to keep the business working because she will make more money if it does **sie hat ein persönliches Interesse am Weiterbestehen des Unternehmens**

◊ **vested remainder** *noun* remainder which is absolutely vested in a person **unentziehbares Anwartschaftsrecht**

◊ **vesting assent** *noun* document which vests settled land on a tenant for life **Grundstücksübertragungsurkunde (des Erbschaftsverwalters)**

◊ **vesting order** *noun* court order which transfers property **gerichtliche Verfügung zur Eigentumsübertragung, gerichtliche Auflassungsverfügung**

vet *verb* to examine someone *or* a document carefully to see if there is any breach of security **überprüfen;** *all applications are vetted by the Home Office;* **positive vetting** = discovery after examination that a person working with classified information may after all not be reliable **Entdeckung, daß jd, der mit geheimen Informationen arbeitet, trotz vorheriger Überprüfung womöglich nicht vertrauenswürdig ist**
NOTE: **vetting - vetted**

veto
1 *noun* ban *or* order not to allow something to become law, even if it has been passed by a parliament **Veto, Einspruch(srecht);** *the President has the power of veto over Bills passed by Congress; the UK used its veto in the Security Council*
2 *verb* to ban something *or* to order something not to become law **verbieten, ein Veto einlegen gegen, Einspruch erheben gegen;** *the resolution was vetoed by the president; the council has vetoed all plans to hold protest marches in the centre of town*

vexatious *adjective* annoying *or* done in order to annoy **ärgerlich; schikanös; vexatious action** *or* **litigation** = case brought in order to annoy the defendant **schikanöse/mutwillige Klage; vexatious litigant** = person who frequently starts legal actions to annoy people and who is barred from bringing actions without leave of the court **Querulant (, der oft Prozesse anfängt)**

viable *adjective* which can work **durchführbar, praktikabel; not commercially viable** = not likely to make a profit **nicht rentabel; viable alternative** = different proposal which may work **brauchbare Alternative**

vicarious *adjective* not direct *or* not personally interested **indirekt, mittelbar, stellvertretend; vicarious performance** = performance of a contract where the work has been done by a third party **Leistung durch einen Dritten; vicarious liability** = liability of one person for torts committed by someone else, especially the liability of an employer for acts committed by an employee in the course of his work **stellvertretende Haftung**

COMMENT: if the employee is on a frolic of his own, the employer may not be liable

◊ **vicariously** *adverb* not directly **indirekt, mittelbar, stellvertretend**

vice- *prefix* deputy *or* second in command **stellvertretend, Vize-;** *he is the vice-chairman of an industrial group; she was appointed to the vice-chairmanship of the committee*

◊ **Vice Chancellor** *noun* senior judge in charge of the Chancery Division of the High Court **Präsident der Chancery Division des High Court**

◊ **Vice-President** *noun* deputy to a president **Vizepräsident**

vice versa *Latin phrase meaning* "reverse position": in the opposite way **umgekehrt;** *the responsibilities of the employer towards the employee and vice versa*

victim *noun* person who suffers a crime *or* a wrong **Opfer;** *the mugger left his victim lying in the road; he was the victim of a con trick; the accident victims* or *victims of the accident were taken to hospital*

vide *Latin word meaning* "see": used in written texts to refer to another reference **siehe, vide**

videlicet *Latin word meaning* "that is" **nämlich, das heißt**
NOTE: usually abbreviated to **viz**

view
1 *noun* way of thinking about something **Ansicht, Meinung; to take a view on something** = to have an opinion about something **zu etwas eine Meinung haben; to take the view that** = to decide that *or* to have the opinion that **die Ansicht vertreten, daß ...** *the court takes the view that the defendant did not publish the defamation maliciously;* **to take the long view** = to plan for a long period before your current investment will become profitable **auf lange Sicht planen; etwas langfristig betrachten; in view of** = because of **angesichts, in Anbetracht;** *in view of the age of the accused the magistrates gave him a suspended sentence*
2 *verb* to look at **betrachten, besichtigen; viewing the scene** = visit by a judge and jury to the place where a crime was committed **Tatortbesichtigung, Lokaltermin**

villain *noun GB (informal)* criminal **Ganove;** *the job of the policeman is to catch villains*
◊ **villainy** *noun* wilful illegal act **Niederträchtigkeit, verbrecherische Handlung**

violate *verb* to break a rule *or* a law **verletzen, übertreten, brechen;** *the council has violated the planning regulations; the action of the government violates the international treaty on commercial shipping*
◊ **violation** *noun* act of breaking a rule **Verletzung, Verstoß, Übertretung;** *the number of traffic violations has increased; the court criticized the violations of the treaty on human rights;* **in violation of a rule** = breaking a rule **unter Verletzung einer Bestimmung;** *the government has acted in violation of its agreement*

violent *adjective* using force **gewalttätig; gewaltsam;** *a violent attack on the police; the prisoner became violent* = the prisoner tried to attack **der Häftling wurde gewalttätig**
◊ **violence** *noun* action using force **Gewalt, Gewalttätigkeit; robbery with violence** = robbery where force is used against people *or* property **gewalttätiger Raub; violence against the person** = one of the types of notifiable offence (such as murder *or* assault) against people **Tätlichkeit, Gewalttätigkeit gegen die Person**
◊ **violently** *adverb* in a violent way **brutal**

vires *see* INTRA VIRES, ULTRA VIRES

virtute officii *Latin phrase meaning* "because of his office" **kraft seines Amtes**

vis major *Latin words meaning* "superior force": force of people *or* of nature (such as a revolution *or* an earthquake) which cannot be stopped **höhere Gewalt**

visa *noun* special document *or* special stamp in a passport which allows someone to enter a country **Visum, Sichtvermerk;** *you will need a visa before you go to the USA; he filled in his visa application form;* **entry visa** = visa allowing someone to enter a country **Einreisevisum; multiple entry visa** = visa allowing someone to enter a country many times **Visum zur mehrmaligen Einreise; tourist visa** = visa which allows a person to visit a country for a short time on holiday **Touristenvisum; transit visa** = visa which allows someone to spend a short time in one country while travelling to another country **Transitvisum**

visitor *noun* person who goes to see someone for a short time **Besucher/-in; prison visitor** = member of a board of visitors appointed by the Home Secretary to visit, inspect and report on conditions in a prison **Gefängnis-Inspekteur/Visitator**

viva voce *Latin phrase meaning* "orally *or* by speaking" **mündlich**

vivos *Latin word meaning* "living people" **Lebende; gift inter vivos** = present given by one living person to another **Schenkung zu Lebzeiten**

viz *see* VIDELICET

void
1 *adjective* not legally valid *or* not having any legal effect **ungültig, nichtig; void marriage** = marriage which is declared not to have had any legal existence **nichtige Ehe; the contract was declared null and void** = the contract was said to be no longer valid **der Vertrag wurde für null und nichtig erklärt**
2 *verb* **to void a contract** = to make a contract invalid **einen Vertrag für ungültig erklären**
◊ **voidable** *adjective* which can be made void **aufhebbar, annullierbar**

COMMENT: a contract is void where it never had legal effect, but is voidable if it is apparently of legal effect and remains of legal effect until one or both parties take steps to rescind it

volenti non fit injuria *Latin phrase meaning* "there can be no injury to a person who is willing": rule that if someone has agreed to take the risk of an injury he cannot sue for it (as in the case of someone injured in a boxing match) **Regel, daß jd nicht Klage erheben kann wegen einer unerlaubten Handlung, der er zugestimmt hat**

volume *noun* large book *or* one book out of a set of books **Band**; *Volume 13 of the Law Reports; look in the 1985 volume of the regulations*

voluntary *adjective*
(a) done without being forced *or* without being paid **freiwillig; unentgeltlich; voluntary confession** = confession made by an accused person without being threatened *or* paid **freiwilliges Geständnis; voluntary disposition** = transfer of property without any valuable consideration **unentgeltliche Verfügung; voluntary liquidation** *or* **winding up** = situation where a company itself decides it must close and sell its assets **freiwillige Liquidation; voluntary redundancy** = situation where a worker asks to be made redundant, usually in return for a payment **freiwillige Arbeitsplatzaufgabe**
(b) without being paid a salary **freiwillig; voluntary organization** = organization which has no paid staff **Wohltätigkeitsorganisation**

◊ **voluntarily** *adverb* without being forced *or* paid **freiwillig; unentgeltlich**; *he voluntarily gave himself up to the police*

volunteer
1 *noun*
(a) person who gives *or* receives property without consideration **unentgeltlicher Eigentumsveräußerer; unentgeltlicher Eigentumserwerber**
(b) person who offers to do something without being forced **Freiwilliger**
2 *verb*
(a) to offer information without being asked **(Information) unaufgefordert geben**; *he volunteered the information that the defendant was not in fact a British subject*
(b) to offer to do something without being forced **sich freiwillig melden**; *six men volunteered to go into the burning house*

vote
1 *noun* marking a paper, holding up your hand, etc., to show your opinion *or* to show who you want to be elected **Abstimmung, Wahl; to take a vote on a proposal** *or* **to put a proposal to the vote** = to ask people present at a meeting to say if they agree or do not agree with the proposal **über einen Vorschlag**

abstimmen lassen; block vote = casting of a large number of votes at the same time (such as of trade union members) by a person who has been delegated by the holders of the votes to vote for them in this way **geschlossene Stimmabgabe; Sammelstimme; casting vote** = vote used by the chairman in the case where the votes for and against a proposal are equal **ausschlaggebende Stimme**; *the chairman has the casting vote; he used his casting vote to block the motion;* **popular vote** = vote of all the people in a country **national abgegebene Stimmen; the president is elected by popular vote** = the president is elected by a majority of all the people in a country **der Präsident wird durch national abgegebene Stimmen gewählt; postal vote** = election where the voters send in their voting papers by post **Briefwahl; vote of censure** *or* **censure vote** = vote which criticizes someone, especially a vote which criticizes the government in the House of Commons **Mißbilligungsvotum; vote of no confidence** = vote to show that a person *or* group is not trusted **Mißtrauensvotum**; *the chairman resigned after the vote of no confidence in him was passed by the AGM*
2 *verb* to show an opinion by marking a paper *or* by holding up your hand at a meeting **abstimmen, wählen**; *the meeting voted to close the factory; 52% of the members voted for Mr Smith as chairman;* **to vote for a proposal** *or* **to vote against a proposal** = to say that you agree *or* do not agree with a proposal **für od gegen einen Vorschlag stimmen; two directors were voted off the board at the AGM** = the AGM voted to dismiss two directors **bei der Jahresversammlung wurden zwei Direktoren des Board of Directors abgewählt; she was voted on to the committee** = she was elected a member of the committee **sie wurde in den Ausschuß gewählt**

◊ **voter** *noun* person who votes **Wähler/-in**

◊ **voting** *noun* act of making a vote **Wahl, Stimmabgabe; voting paper** = paper on which the voter puts a cross to show for whom he wants to vote **Stimmzettel; voting rights** = rights of shareholders to voting at company meetings **Stimmrecht; non-voting shares** = shares which do not allow the shareholder to vote at company meetings **stimmrechtslose Aktien**

vouch for *verb* to state that you believe something is correct *or* to say that you take responsibility for something **etwas bestätigen; bürgen für, einstehen für**; *I cannot vouch for the correctness of the transcript of proceedings*

voucher *noun* paper which entitles the bearer to receive something **Gutschein**

Ww

wager
1 *noun* bet *or* amount deposited when you risk money on the result of a race *or* a game *or* an election **Wette; Einsatz**
2 *verb* to bet *or* to risk money on the possibility of something happening **wetten, setzen auf;** *he wagered £100 on the result of the election*

COMMENT: a wager will not normally be enforced by a court under English law

waive *verb* to give up (a right) **verzichten auf;** *he waived his claim to the estate;* **to waive (a) payment** = to say that payment is not necessary **die Bezahlung erlassen**

◇ **waiver** *noun* voluntarily giving up (a right) *or* removing the conditions (of a rule) **Verzicht, Aufgabe; Verzichterklärung;** *if you want to work without a permit, you will have to apply for a waiver;* **waiver clause** = clause in a contract giving the conditions under which the rights in the contract can be given up **Verzichtklausel**

Wales and Chester Circuit *noun* one of the six circuits of the Crown Court to which barristers belong, with its centre in Cardiff **Gerichtsbezirk Wales und Chester**

walking possession *noun* temporary possession of a debtor's goods taken by a bailiff *or* sheriff until they can be sold to satisfy execution **vorübergehende Aufbewahrung von Pfandstücken durch den Gerichtsvollzieher (bis zur Versteigerung)**

war *noun* situation where one country fights another **Krieg;** *the two countries are at war;* **to declare war on a country** = to state officially that a state of war exists between the two countries **einem Land den Krieg erklären; civil war** = situation inside a country where groups of armed people fight against each other *or* fight against the government **Bürgerkrieg; prisoner of war** = member of the armed forces captured by the enemy in time of war **Kriegsgefangener**

ward
1 *noun*
(a) minor protected by a guardian **Mündel;** *Mr Jones acting on behalf of his ward, Miss Smith*
(b) minor protected by a court **Minderjähriger; ward of court** = minor under the protection of the High Court **Mündel unter Amtsvormundschaft;** *the High Court declared the girl ward of court, to protect her from her uncle who wanted to take her out of the country*
2 *verb* to make a child a ward **jd unter Vormundschaft stellen;** *the court warded the girl*

◇ **wardship** *noun* being in charge of a ward *or* the power of a court to take on itself the rights and responsibilites of parents in the interests of a child **Vormundschaft;** *the judge has discretion to exercise the wardship jurisdiction*
NOTE: no plural

warden *noun* (i) person who is in charge of an institution; (ii) person who sees that rules are obeyed **(i) Leiter/-in; Direktor/-in; (ii) Aufseher/-in; traffic warden** = official whose duty is to regulate the traffic under the supervision of the police, especially to deal with cars which are illegally parked **Verkehrspolizist;** *(weiblich)* **Politesse**

warder *noun* guard in a prison **Vollzugsbeamter, Gefängniswärter**

warehouse
1 *noun* large building where goods are stored **Lagerhaus; bonded warehouse** = warehouse where goods are stored until excise duty has been paid **Zollager**
2 *verb* to store (goods) in a warehouse **lagern, auf Lager bringen od nehmen**

◇ **warehousing** *noun* act of storing goods **Lagerung;** *warehousing costs are rising rapidly;* **warehousing in bond** = keeping imported goods in a warehouse without payment of duty, either to be exported again, or for sale into the country when the duty has been paid **Lagerung unter Zollverschluß**
NOTE: no plural

warn *verb* to say that there is a possible danger **warnen;** *the judge warned the jury that the trial would be long and complicated; the policeman warned the motorist not to exceed the speed limit; he warned the shareholders that the dividend might be cut; the government warned of possible import duties*
NOTE: you warn someone **of** something, or **that** something may happen

◇ **warning** *noun* notice of possible danger **Warnung;** *to issue a warning about* *pickpockets; warning notices were put up around the construction site; he received a warning from the magistrates that for the next offence he might be sent to prison; drivers paid no attention to the warning signs*

warrant

1 *noun* official document from a court which allows someone to do something **Vollmacht; Befugnis; to issue a warrant for the arrest of someone** *or* **to issue an arrest warrant for someone** = to make out and sign an official document which authorizes the police to arrest someone **einen Haftbefehl für jdn ausstellen; bench warrant** = warrant issued by a court for the arrest of an accused person who has not appeared to answer charges **(richterlicher) Haftbefehl; search warrant** = official document signed by a magistrate allowing the police to enter and search premises **Haus-, Durchsuchungsbefehl; warrant of committal** *or* **committal warrant** = court order sending a convicted person to prison **Haftbefehl, Haftanordnung; warrant of execution** = warrant issued by a court which gives the bailiffs *or* sheriffs the power to seize goods from a debtor in order to pay his debts **Vollstreckungsbefehl; Pfändungsauftrag**
2 *verb* to guarantee **garantieren;** *all the spare parts are warranted; the car is warranted in perfect condition*

◊ **warrantee** *noun* person who is given a warranty **Garantieempfänger**

◊ **warrantor** *noun* person who gives a warranty **Garant**

◊ **warranty** *noun*
(a) guarantee **Garantie;** *the car is sold with a twelve-month warranty; the warranty covers spare parts but not labour costs*
(b) contractual term which is secondary to the main purpose of the contract **Gewähr; breach of warranty** = failing to do something which is a part of a contract **Garantieverletzung; Verletzung der Gewährleistungspflicht**
(c) statement made by an insured person which declares that the facts stated by him are true **wahrheitsgemäße Angabe; Gewähr(leistung)**

wastage

noun things which have been wasted **Verlust; Schwund; Verschwendung; natural wastage** = losing workers because they resign or retire, not through redundancies or dismissals **natürliche Fluktuation**

waste

1 *noun* permanent damage done to land which diminishes its value **Einöde**

2 *verb* to use something wrongly *or* to make bad use of something **verschwenden; to waste time** = to spend too much time doing something *or* to use time for purposes which are not relevant **Zeit verschwenden;** *he was accused of wasting the court's time or of wasting police time*

watch

noun group of people who patrol the streets to maintain law and order **Wachkommando; Wache, Wachmannschaft; watch committee** = committee of a local authority which supervises the policing of an area **örtlicher Ausschuß zur Polizeiüberwachung; neighbourhood watch** = system where the residents in an area are encouraged to look out for criminals and help the police **Nachbarschaftsinitiative zur Kriminalitätsbekämpfung**

◊ **watchdog body** *noun* body which watches something (especially government departments *or* commercial firms) to see that regulations are not being abused **Kontrollorgan; Untersuchungsausschuß**

way

noun
(a) right of way = right to go lawfully along a path on another person's land **Wegerecht;** (NOTE: no plural)
(b) manner of doing something **Art (und Weise); Committee of Ways and Means** = committee of the whole House of Commons which examines the Supply Bill **Finanzausschuß**

weak

adjective not strong **schwach; weak case** = criminal case where the evidence against the accused is not strong **Strafverfahren mit ungünstiger Beweislage**

◊ **weakness** *noun* being weak **Schwäche; ungünstige Beweislage;** *the hearing was abandoned because of the weakness of the prosecution case*

weapon

noun dangerous *or* offensive weapon = item (such as a gun *or* knife) which can be used to harm someone physically **gefährliche Waffe, Angriffswaffe; carrying offensive weapons** = offence of holding a weapon *or* something (such as a bottle) which could be used as a weapon **Tragen von gefährlichen Waffen/Angriffswaffen**

wear and tear

noun **fair wear and tear** = acceptable damage caused by normal use **Abnutzungs- und Verschleißerscheinungen;** *the insurance policy covers most damage but not fair wear and tear to the machine*
NOTE: no plural

Weekly Law Reports (WLR) *plural noun* regular reports of cases published by the Council of Law Reporting; *(GB)* **wöchentliche erscheinende, aktuelle Rechtsprechungsübersicht**

welfare *noun* comfort *or* being well cared for **Wohlergehen; Fürsorge;** *it is the duty of the juvenile court to see to the welfare of children in care;* **welfare state** = state which spends a large amount of money to make sure that its citizens are well looked after **Wohlfahrtsstaat**

Western Circuit *noun* one of the six circuits of the Crown Court to which barristers belong, with its centre in Bristol **Gerichtsbezirk West**

whatsoever *adjective* of any sort **was (auch immer); welcher auch (immer);** *there is no substance whatsoever in the report; the police found no suspicious documents whatsoever*
NOTE: always used after a noun and after a negative

where- *prefix*
NOTE: the following words formed from **where-** are frequently used in legal documents

◊ **whereas** *conjunction* as the situation is stated *or* taking the following fact into consideration **da; in Anbetracht der Tatsache, daß;** *whereas the property is held in trust for the appellant; whereas the contract between the two parties stipulated that either party may withdraw at six months' notice*

◊ **whereby** *adverb* by which **wonach; wodurch;** *a deed whereby ownership of the property is transferred*

◊ **wherein** *adverb* in which **worin;** *a document wherein the regulations are listed*

◊ **whereof** *adverb* of which **woraus; dessen; in witness whereof I sign my hand** = I sign as a witness that this is correct **ich bestätige die Richtigkeit durch meine Unterschrift**

◊ **whereon** *adverb* on which **worauf;** *land whereon a dwelling is constructed*

◊ **wheresoever** *adverb* in any place where **wo auch immer;** *the insurance covering jewels wheresoever they may be kept*

whip
1 *noun*
(a) long thin piece of leather, used for beating animals to make them work **Peitsche**
(b) MP who controls the attendance of other MPs of his party at the House of Commons, who makes sure that all MPs vote **Parteimitglied, das die anderen Mitglieder** zu bestimmten Anlässen zusammenruft bzw. den Fraktionszwang aufrechterhält
(c) instruction given by a whip to other MPs **Fraktionsrundschreiben des Whip; three line whip** = strict instructions to MPs to vote as the whips tell them **Fraktionszwang**
2 *verb* to beat with a whip **(aus)peitschen**

White Book *noun* book containing the Rules of the Supreme Court and a commentary on them **Sammlung von Verfahrensregeln des Supreme Court und Kommentare**

◊ **white collar crime** *noun* crimes committed by business people *or* office workers (such as embezzlement, computer fraud, insider dealings) **Wirtschaftsverbrechen**

◊ **White Paper** *noun (GB)* report from the government on a particular problem **Weißbuch**

whole *adjective* complete *or* total **ganz, vollständig; of the whole blood** = relationship whereby a person is related to someone by two common ancestors **von den gleichen Eltern abstammend**

whole-life insurance *or* **whole-life policy** *noun* insurance *or* policy where the insured person pays a fixed premium each year and the insurance company pays a sum when he dies **Lebensversicherung auf den Todesfall**

wholesale *noun & adverb* buying goods direct from the producers and selling in large quantities to traders who then sell in smaller quantities to the general public **(im) Großhandel; wholesale dealer** = person who buys in bulk from producers and sells to retailers **Großhändler**
NOTE: no plural

◊ **wholesaler** *noun* person who buys goods in bulk from producers and sells them to retailers **Großhändler**

wholly-owned subsidiary *noun* company which is owned completely by another company **100%ige Tochtergesellschaft**

widow *noun* woman whose husband has died **Witwe**

◊ **widower** *noun* man whose wife has died **Witwer**

wife *noun* female spouse *or* woman married to a husband **Frau, Ehefrau, Gattin**

wilful *adjective* (person) who is determined to do what he wants *or* (act) which is done because someone wants to do it, regardless of the effect it may have on others **eigensinnig; mutwillig; vorsätzlich; wilful misconduct** = behaviour which may harm someone and which is known to be wrong **vorsätzliches Fehlverhalten; wilful murder** = murder which is premeditated **vorsätzliche Tötung; Mord; wilful neglect** = intentionally not doing something which it is your duty to do **bewußte Unterlassung**

◊ **wilfully** *adverb* done because someone wants to do it, regardless of the effect on others **mutwillig; vorsätzlich;** *he wilfully set fire to the building*

will *noun*
(a) will *or (formal)* **last will and testament** = legal document by which a person gives instructions to his executors as to how his property should be disposed of after he dies **letzter Wille, Testament;** *he wrote his will in 1964; according to her will, all her property is left to her children;* **holograph will** = will, written out by hand, and not necessarily witnessed **handgeschriebenes Testament; nuncupative will** = unwritten will stated in the presence of a witness (such as by a soldier in time of war) **mündliches Zeugentestament;** *see also* BEQUEST, DEVISE, LEGACY

> COMMENT: to make a valid will, a person must be of age and of sound mind; normally a will must be signed and witnessed in the presence of two witnesses who are not interested in the will. In English law there is complete freedom to dispose of one's property after death as one wishes. However, any dependant may apply for provision to be made out of the estate of a deceased under the Inheritance (Provision for Family and Dependants) Act

(b) wishing *or* wanting to do something **Wille; tenancy at will** = situation where the owner of a property allows a tenant to occupy it as long as either party wishes **jederzeit kündbares Miet- od Pachtverhältnis**

wind up *verb*
(a) to end (a meeting) **(be)schließen;** *he wound up the meeting with a vote of thanks to the committee*
(b) to wind up a company = to put a company into liquidation **eine Firma liquidieren/auflösen;** *the court ordered the company to be wound up*
NOTE: **winding - wound - has wound**

◊ **winding up** *noun* liquidation *or* closing of a company and selling its assets **Liquidation, Auflösung; compulsory winding up order** = order from a court saying that a company must be wound up **Zwangsliquidationsbeschluß; voluntary winding up** = situation where a company itself decides it must close down **freiwillige Liquidation; winding up petition** = application to a court for an order that a company be put into liquidation **Konkurseröffnungsantrag**

with costs *adverb* judgment for someone **with costs** = judgment that the party's plea was correct and that all the costs of the case should be paid by the other party **kostenpflichtige Verurteilung**

withdraw *verb*
(a) to take (money) out of an account **abheben;** *to withdraw money from the bank or from your account; you can withdraw up to £50 from any bank on presentation of a banker's card*
(b) to take back (an offer) **zurückziehen; widerrufen; one of the company's backers has withdrawn** = he stopped supporting the company financially **einer der Kapitalgeber der Firma ist ausgeschieden;** *to withdraw a takeover bid*
(c) to take back a charge *or* an accusation *or* a statement **zurücknehmen; widerrufen; fallenlassen;** *the prosecution has withdrawn the charges against him; the opposition MPs forced the minister to withdraw his statement; the chairman asked him to withdraw the remarks he had made about the finance director*
NOTE: **withdrawing - withdrew - has withdrawn**

◊ **withdrawal** *noun* removing money from an account **Abhebung; withdrawal without penalty at seven days' notice** = money can be taken out of a deposit account, without losing any interest, provided that seven days' notice has been given **bei Einhaltung der 7-tägigen Kündigungsfrist entstehen keine Gebühren**

withhold *verb* to keep back *or* not to give (information) **zurückhalten; verschweigen;** *he was charged with withholding information from the police; approval of any loan will not be unreasonably withheld*

within *preposition* inside **in, innerhalb;** *the case falls within the jurisdiction of the court; he was within his rights when he challenged the statement made by the police officer*

without *preposition* **without prejudice** = phrase spoken *or* written in letters when attempting to negotiate a settlement, meaning that the negotiations cannot be referred to in court *or* relied upon by the other party if the discussions fail **ohne**

Verbindlichkeit/Anerkennung **einer Rechtspflicht; without reserve** = sale at an auction where an item has no reserve price **ohne Limit**

witness

1 *noun*
(a) person who sees something happen *or* who is present when something happens **Zeuge/Zeugin; to act as a witness to a document** *or* **a signature** = to sign a document to show that you have watched the main signatory sign it **ein Dokument od eine Unterschrift beglaubigen;** *the contract has to be signed in the presence of two witnesses;* **in witness whereof** = first words of the testimonium clause, where the signatory of the will *or* contract signs **ich bestätige die Richtigkeit (durch meine Unterschrift)**
(b) person who appears in court to give evidence **Zeuge/Zeugin; defence witness** *or* **witness for the defence** = person who is called to court to give evidence which helps the case of the defendant *or* of the accused **Entlastungszeuge; prosecution witness** *or* **witness for the prosecution** = person called by the prosecution side to give evidence against the defendant *or* the accused **Belastungszeuge; adverse witness** = witness whose evidence is not favourable to the side which has called him **Gegenzeuge; expert** *or* **professional** *or* **skilled witness** = witness who is a specialist in a subject and is asked to give his opinion on technical matters **sachverständiger Zeuge; Sachverständiger**
2 *verb* to sign (a document) to show that you guarantee that the other signatures on it are genuine **bezeugen;** *to witness an agreement* or *a signature;* **"now this deed witnesseth"** = words indicating that the details of the agreement follow **im folgenden bezeugt dieser Vertrag**

WLR = WEEKLY LAW REPORTS

Woolsack *noun* seat of the Lord Chancellor in the House of Lords **Sitz des Lordkanzlers im britischen Oberhaus**

word

1 *noun* separate item of speech *or* writing **Wort; word processing** = working with words, using a computer to produce, check and change texts, letters, contracts, etc. **Textverarbeitung; to give one's word** = to promise **sein Wort geben;** *he gave his word that the matter would remain confidential*
2 *verb* to put something into words **formulieren;** *the contract was incorrectly worded*

◊ **wording** *noun* series of words **Wortlaut, Formulierung;** *did you understand the wording of the contract?*
NOTE: no plural

wound

1 *noun* cut done to the skin of a person **Wunde;** *she has a knife wound in her leg*
2 *verb* to injure *or* to hurt someone in such a way that his skin is cut **verwunden, verletzen;** *he was wounded in the fight*

WPC = WOMAN POLICE CONSTABLE

wreck

1 *noun*
(a) (i) action of sinking *or* badly damaging a ship; (ii) ship which has sunk *or* which has been badly damaged and cannot float **(i) Schiffbruch; Verursachung eines Totalschadens; (ii) Wrack;** *they saved the cargo from the wreck; oil poured out of the wreck of the ship*
(b) company which has become insolvent **Konkursfirma, Ruin;** *he managed to save some of his investment from the wreck of the company; investors lost thousands of pounds in the wreck of the investment company*
2 *verb* to damage badly *or* to ruin **zerstören; zum Scheitern bringen;** *they are trying to salvage the wrecked ship; the defence case was wrecked by the defendant's behaviour in court*

writ *noun*
(a) writ (of summons) = legal document which begins an action in the High Court **Prozeßeröffnungsbeschluß; Klageschrift mit Ladung; gerichtliche Verfügung;** *the company issued a writ to prevent the trade union from going on strike; he issued writs for libel in connection with allegations made in a Sunday newspaper;* **to serve someone with a writ** = to give someone a writ officially, so that he has to defend it *or* allow judgment to be taken against him **jdm eine gerichtliche Verfügung zustellen; jdn vorladen; writ of habeas corpus** = writ to obtain the release of someone who has been unlawfully held in prison *or* in police custody *or* to make the person holding a prisoner appear in court to explain why he is being held **gerichtliche Anordnung eines Haftprüfungstermins**
(b) legal action to hold a by-election; *(GB)* **Ausschreibung für eine Nachwahl; to move a writ** = to propose in the House of Commons that a by-election should be held **eine Nachwahl beantragen**

wrong

1 *adjective* not right *or* not correct *or* not

legal **falsch ; unrecht;** *copying computer data is wrong; the total in the last column is wrong; the driver gave the wrong address to the policeman; I tried to phone you, but I got the wrong number*
2 *noun* act against natural justice *or* act which infringes someone else's right **Unrecht; Rechtsverletzung;** *civil wrongs against persons or property are called "torts"*

◇ **wrongdoer** *noun* person who commits an offence **Übeltäter; Rechtsverletzer**

◇ **wrongdoing** *noun* bad behaviour *or* actions which are against the law **Missetat; Vergehen**
NOTE: no plural

◇ **wrongful** *adjective* unlawful **ungesetzlich; unrechtmäßig; wrongful dismissal =** removing someone from a job for a reason which does not justify dismissal and which is in breach of the contract of employment **unrechtmäßige Kündigung**

> COMMENT: an employee can complain of wrongful dismissal to the County Court

◇ **wrongfully** *adverb* in an unlawful way **ungesetzlich; unrechtmäßig;** *he claimed he was wrongfully dismissed; she was accused of wrongfully holding her clients' money*

◇ **wrongly** *adverb* not correctly *or* badly **fälschlicherweise; zu Unrecht;** *he wrongly invoiced Smith Ltd for £250, when he should have credited them with the same amount*

Xx Yy Zz

Yard *noun* **Scotland yard** *or* **the Yard =** headquarters of the Metropolitan Police in London **Scotland Yard**

year *noun* period of twelve months **Jahr; calendar year =** year from January 1st to December 31st **Kalenderjahr; financial year =** the twelve month period for a firm's accounts **Geschäfts-, Rechnungsjahr; fiscal year** *or* **tax year =** twelve month period on which taxes are calculated (in the UK it is April 6th to April 5th of the following year) **Steuerjahr; year end =** the end of the financial year, when a company's accounts are prepared **Jahresabschluß;** *the accounts*

department has started work on the yearend accounts

yellow dog contract *noun* (US) contract of employment where the employee is forbidden to join a trade union **Vertrag, nachdem der Beitritt zu einer Gewerkschaft verboten ist**

yield
1 *noun* money produced as a return on an investment **Ertrag; Rendite**
2 *verb* to produce interest *or* dividend **ein-, erbringen; rentieren;** *the bonds yield 8%*

young offender *noun* person aged between seventeen and twenty years of age who has committed an offence **jugendlicher Straftäter**

◇ **young person** *noun* person over fourteen years of age, but less than seventeen **Jugendlicher, Minderjähriger**

youth *noun* young man *or* young person **Jugendlicher; youth custody order =** sentence sending a young person to detention in a special centre **Verurteilung zum Jugendarrest**

zebra crossing *noun* place in a street marked with white lines, where pedestrians can cross and have right of way **Zebrastreifen**

zero *noun* nought *or* number 0 **Null;** *the code for international calls is zero one zero (010);* **zero inflation =** inflation at 0% **Nullinflation**

◇ **zero-rated** *adjective* (item) which has a VAT rate of 0% **mehrwertsteuerfrei**

◇ **zero-rating** *noun* rating an item at 0% VAT **ohne Mehrwertsteuerpflicht**

zip code *noun* (US) letters and numbers used to indicate a town *or* street in an address on an envelope **Postleitzahl**
NOTE: GB English is **post code**

zone *verb* to order that land in a district shall be used only for one type of building **abstellen erklären (zu);** *the land is zoned for industrial use*

◇ **zoning** *noun* order by a local council that land shall be used only for one type of building **Abstellung; Erklärung (zu)**
NOTE: no plural

Deutsch-Englisches
Register

Aa

a.a.O.: *loc. cit.; op. cit.*
abändern: *alter; amend; revise; vary*
Abänderung: *alteration; amendment; revision; variation*
abbauen: *cut*
Abbaurechte: *mining concession*
Abbau von Kontrollen: *deregulation*
abbiegen: *turn*
abbrechen: *break off; call off*
abbrennen: *burn down*
Abbruch: *derogation*
Abbuchung: *direct debit*
abdecken: *cover*
Abend: spät am ~ *late-night*
abfahren: *depart* **Abfahrt** *departure*
abfassen: *draw up*
abfliegen: *depart* **Abflug** *departure*
Abgabe: *levy* **Abgabenordnung** *tax code*
abgelegen: *remote*
abgemacht: *agreed*
Abgeordnetenimmunität: *Parliamentary privilege*
Abgeordnete(r): *Member of Parliament; representative (US)*
abgesagt: *called off*
abgeworben: er wurde ~ *he was headhunted*
abhaken: *check (US)*
abhalten: *deter; hold*
abhängig von: *depending on; subject to; subordinate to*
abheben: *draw; withdraw* **Abhebung** *withdrawal*
abheften: etwas ~ *to place something on file*
Abhilfe: *remedy* **Abhilfe schaffen** *to remedy*
abholen: *collect*
Abholgebühren: *collection charges or collection rates*
Abholung: *collection*
Abhörgerät: *bugging device*
Abhörvorrichtung: *surveillance device*
abkommandieren: *detail*
Abkommen: *agreement; bond; compact; convention; covenant; deal; treaty*
Ablader: *shipper*
Ablage: *filing basket or tray*
Ablagesystem: *filing system*
Ablauf: *expiration; expiry*
Ablaufdatum: *expiry date*
ablaufen: *expire; lapse; terminate*
Ableben: *decease; demise*
ablegen: *to place something on file*
ablehnen: *challenge; decline; disclaim; object; oppose; rebut; refuse; reject; turn down*
Ablehnung: *challenge; denial; disapproval; rebuttal; refusal; rejection* **allgemeine ~** *blanket refusal* **unbegründete ~** *peremptory challenge*
Ablehnung der Verantwortung: *derogation of responsibility*
ableiten: *derive*

ablösen: *redeem* **Ablösung** *redemption*
Abmachung: *agreement*
Abmachungen: zwischenbetriebliche ~ *intercompany dealings*
abmessen: *measure*
Abnahme: *decline*
Abnahmebescheinigung: *test certificate*
abnehmen: *decrease; diminish*
Abnutzungs- und Verschleißerscheinungen: *fair wear and tear*
ab- od aufgerundet: *in round figures*
Abonnement: ein ~ erneuern *to renew a subscription*
Abordnung: *delegation*
abraten: *advise against*
Abrechnung: *account; statement of account* **spezifizierte ~** *itemized account*
Abrechnungsstelle: *clearing house*
Abrechnungstag: *settlement day*
Abrechnungszeitraum: *accounting period*
Abreise: *departure* **abreisen** *depart*
abriegeln: *to cordon off; seal off*
Abriß: *abstract; outline*
Absage: *cancellation; refusal*
absagen: *call off; cancel*
Absatz: *article; clause; disposal; paragraph; sales; section* **hoher ~** *high sales; high volume (of sales)*
Absatzgebiet *or* **Absatzmarkt:** *market* **begrenzter ~** *limited market*
Absatzzahlen: *sales figures*
abschaffen: *abolish* **Abschaffung** *abolition*
abschätzen: *appraise; evaluate*
Abschätzung: *evaluation*
abschicken: *post*
abschieben: *deport*
Abschiebung: *deportation*
Abschied: *discharge*
abschießen: *fire*
abschlagen: *deny*
Abschlagsdividende: *interim dividend*
Abschlagszahlung: *interim payment*
abschließen: *clinch; conclude; to enter into; lock*
abschließend: *closing; in conclusion*
Abschluß: *bargain; completion; conclusion; deal; financial statement* **zum ~** *in conclusion*
Abschluß-: *closing; final*
Abschluß auf Termin: *forward contract*
Abschlußrechnung nach Vertragsabschluß: *completion statement*
Abschlußtermin: *completion date*
abschneiden: *perform*
Abschnitt: *chapter; paragraph; section*
Abschöpfung: *import*
abschrecken: *deter*
Abschreckung: *deterrence*
Abschreckungsmittel: *deterrent*
Abschrift: *transcript*
Abschwächung: *decline*

Absender: *consignor; return address; sender*

absetzen: *depose; market* **sich** ~ *defect*

Absetzung: *removal*

absichern: *protect*

Absicht: *animus; intent; intention; purpose* **ausdrückliche böse** ~ *express malice* **mit** ~ **übersehen** *to connive at something* **tatsächliche** ~ *intention* **vermutete böse** ~ *implied malice*

absichtlich: *deliberate; intentional; knowingly; on purpose*

Absichtserklärung: *letter of intent*

absolut: *absolute; total*

absperren: *to cordon off; seal off*

Absprache: **geheime** ~ *collusion*

abstammend von: *descended from*

Abstammung: *descent* **direkte** ~ *lineal descent*

Abstand: *key money*

Abstandnahme: *forbearance*

Abstand nehmen von: *to forbear from doing something*

Abstandssumme: *premium*

abstellen: *abate; detail*

abstellen erklären: *zone*

Abstellung: *zoning*

abstempeln: *stamp*

abstimmen: *ballot; reconcile; vote*

abstimmen lassen: *divide*

Abstimmung: *division; poll; reconciliation; vote*

Abstimmung durch Handheben: *show of hands*

abstreiten: *deny; disclaim*

Abteilung: *department; division; section; squad*

Abteilung für Familiengerichtssachen: *Family Division*

Abteilung für Öffentlichkeitsarbeit: *public relations department*

Abteilungsgericht: *divisional court*

Abteilungsleiter: *head of department or department head or department manager*

Abteilungsleiterin: *manageress*

Abteilung Verkauf: *sales department*

Abtippen von Dokumenten: *copy typing*

Abtreibung: *abortion*

abtreten: *assign*

Abtretender: *assignor*

Abtretung: *cession*

Abtretungsempfänger: *assignee*

Abtretungsformular für Bezugsrechte: *letter of renunciation*

Abtretungsurkunde: *deed of assignment*

Abwehr: *defence or defense (US)*

Abweichen von: *departure from*

abweisen: *dismiss*

Abweisung: *rejection*

Abweisungsbegehren: *demurrer*

Abwerben von Arbeitskräften *or* **Gewerkschaftsmitgliedern:** *poaching*

Abwerbung: *enticement*

abwesend: *absent* **Abwesender** *absentee*

Abwesenheit: *absence* **in** ~ *in absentia*

abzahlen: *redeem*

Abzahlungskredit: *consumer credit*

abzeichnen: *initial*

abziehbar: *deductible*

Abziehen: *deduction* **abziehen** *deduct*

Abzug: *hard copy; deduction*

achtlos: *careless; carelessly*

Achtung: *oyez*

adäquat: *adequate*

ad hoc: *ad hoc*

administrativ: *administrative*

adoptieren: *adopt*

Adoption: *adoption*

Adoptionsbeschluß: *adoption order*

Adoptionsverfahren: *adoption proceedings*

Adoptiveltern: *adoptive parents*

Adoptivkind: *adoptive child*

Adreßbuch: *(street) directory*

Adresse: *address*

Adressenliste: *address list; mailing list*

adressieren: *address*

Affaire: *affair*

Affidavit: *affidavit*

affirmativ: *affirmative*

Agent: *agent; special agent*

Agent provocateur: *agent provocateur*

Agentur: *agency*

agieren: *act*

Agio: *exchange premium*

Ahne: *ancestor*

ähnlich: *similiter*

Akkordlohn: **einen** ~ **erhalten** *to be paid at piece-work rates*

akkreditiert: *accredited*

Akkreditiv: *(circular) letter of credit* **unwiderrufliches** ~ *irrevocable letter of credit*

akkumulieren: *accumulate*

Akte: *document; file*

Akten: *records*

Aktenanforderung: *order of certiorari*

Aktenkoffer: *briefcase*

Aktenkopie: *file copy*

Aktenordner: *file* **kastenförmiger** ~ *box file*

Aktenschrank: *filing cabinet*

Aktenzeichen: *reference*

Aktie: *share* **schnell steigende** ~ *high flier*

Aktien: *stocks and shares* **junge** *or* **neue** ~ *subscriber shares* **neue** ~ **zeichnen** *to subscribe for shares* **stimmrechtslose** ~ *non-voting shares* **teilweise eingezahlte** ~ *partly-paid up shares* **voll bezahlte** ~ *fully paid-up shares*

Aktienausgabe: *issue of new shares or share issue*

Aktienbank: *joint-stock bank*

Aktienbesitz: *holding* **wechselseitiger** ~ *cross holdings*

Aktienbestand: *shareholding*

Aktienbeteiligung: *stockholding*

Aktienbuch: *register of members* or *of shareholders* or *share register*

Aktienemission: *share issue*

Aktiengeschäft: *stockbroking*

Aktiengesellschaft: *joint-stock company; public limited company (plc); corporation (US)*

Aktienkapital: *share capital* **teilweise eingezahltes** ~ *partly-paid capital*

Aktienoption: *share option*

Aktienpaket: **lot ein** ~ **plazieren** *to place a block of shares*

Aktienportefeuille: *portfolio*

Aktienübertragung: *transfer of shares*

Aktienübertragungsurkunde: *deed of transfer*

Aktienzertifikat: *share certificate*

Aktienzertifikate verpfänden: *to pledge share certificates*

Aktien zuteilen: *to allot shares*

Aktienzuteilung: *share allocation*

Aktion: *campaign* **geheime** ~ *covert action*

Aktionär: *shareholder; stockholder*

Aktionärsrechte: *shareholders' agreement*

Aktionärsverzeichnis: *list of members*

aktiv: *active; actively*

Aktiva: *asset*

Aktivität: *activity*

Aktivposten: **leicht realisierbare** ~ *realizable assets*

Aktivsaldo: *credit balance*

aktuell: *up to date*

akzeptabel: *acceptable*

Akzeptant: *acceptor*

Akzepthaus: *accepting house*

akzeptieren: *accept*

Akzeptverweigerung: *non-acceptance*

Alarmanlage: *burglar alarm*

Alarmanlagenspezialist: *bellman (slang)*

Alcotest: *breathalyser*

aleatorisch: *aleatory*

alias: *alias*

Alibi: *alibi*

Alkoholschmuggler: *bootlegger*

Alkoholtest: *breath test* **einen** ~ **machen** *breathalyse*

Alleinbezugsvertrag: *solus agreement*

Alleineigentümer: *sole owner* or *proprietor*

alleinig: *sole*

Alleinlizenz: *exclusive licence*

Alleinvertretungsvereinbarung: *exclusive agreement*

Alleinvertrieb: *concession; exclusivity*

allem: **vor** ~ *in particular*

Allerbeste: **das/der/die** ~ *the pick of the group*

Allgefahrendeckung: *comprehensive* or *all-risks policy*

allgemein: *common; general; universal*

allgemeinen: **im** ~ *generally*

Alphabet: *alphabet*

als: *qua*

Al-Talak: *talaq*

Alter: *old age* **höheres** ~ *seniority*

älter: *senior*

Alternative: **brauchbare** ~ *viable alternative*

Altersgrenze: *age limit*

Altersrente or **Altersruhegeld** or **Altersversorgung:** *old age pension; retirement pension* **betriebliche** **Altersversorgung** *occupational pension*

Altersversorgungssystem: *pension plan* or *scheme*

Amnestie: *amnesty*

amnestieren: *amnesty*

Amortisationszeit: *payback period*

Amt: *agency; commission; office* **ererbtes** ~ *hereditary office* **sein** ~ **mißbrauchen** *to abuse one's authority* **sein** ~ **niederlegen** *resign*

Amtes: **kraft seines** ~ *virtute officii* **seines** ~ **entbunden** *functus officio*

Amt für Verbraucherschutz: *Office of Fair Trading*

amtlich: *official*

amtlich eintragen: *incorporate*

Amtmann beim Admiralitätsgericht: *Marshal of the Admiralty Court (GB)*

Amts: **von** ~ **wegen** *ex officio*

Amtsanwalt: *Procurator Fiscal*

Amtsarzt: *medical officer of health (MOH)*

Amtsbezeichnung: *title*

Amtsgericht: *County Court; magistrates' court; local court; petty sessions; Sheriff Court*

Amtsgerichtsbezirk: *petty-sessional division*

Amtsjargon: *officialese*

Amtsniederlegung: *resignation*

Amtspflichtverletzung: *misconduct*

Amtsrichter: *justice of the peace*

Amtsschimmel: *red tape*

Amtstätigkeit gegen Bezahlung: *office of profit (under the Crown)*

Amtsweg: **den** ~ **beschreiten** *to go through official channels*

Amtszeit: *tenure*

Analverkehr: *buggery*

Anarchie: *anarchy*

anarchisch: *anarchical*

anbei: *herewith*

anberaumen: *schedule; set down*

Anbetracht: **in** ~ *in view of*

anbetrifft: **was ...** ~ *having regard to* or *as regards* or *regarding*

anbieten: *offer*

Anbietender: *offeror*

andauern: *continue; last*

andere: **und** ~ *et al.* or *et alia*

anderem: **unter** ~ *inter alia*

Anderkonto: *nominee account*

ändern: *amend; modify*

Änderung: *alteration; amendment; modification* **rechtserhebliche** ~ *material alteration*

andeuten: *imply*

Andeutung: versteckte ~ *innuendo*

androhen: *threaten*

Androhung: *threat*

aneignen: sich ~ *appropriate*

Aneignung: *occupancy* **widerrechtliche** ~ *conversion; usurpation*

anerkennen: *acknowledge; allow; recognize; respect* **nicht** ~ *disallow; repudiate*

anerkennen und bezahlen: *honour (debts)*

Anerkennung: *appreciation; recognition* **in** ~ *in appreciation of*

Anerkennung der Gewerkschaft: *union recognition*

Anfang: von ~ **an** *ab initio*

anfänglich: *initial*

Anfangsbuchstaben: *initials*

anfechten: *challenge; contest; dispute*

Anfechtung: *challenge*

anfordern: *call in; request*

Anforderung: auf ~ *on request* **auf** ~ **bezahlen** *to pay on demand*

Anforderungen: den ~ **genügend** *up to standard*

Anforderungsschreiben: anwaltliches ~ *letter before action*

Anfrage zur Geschäftsordnung: *point of order*

anfügen: *join*

anführen: *cite; head; lead; quote*

Anführer: *principal*

Anführung: *citation*

Angabe: *representation; statement* **falsche** ~ *false representation* **wahrheitsgemäße** ~ *warranty*

Angaben: nähere ~ *particulars*

angeben: *quote; return; specify; state*

angeblich: *ostensible*

Angebot: *bid; supply; tender* **ein** ~ **abgeben** *or* **machen** *to put in a bid for something or to enter a bid for something; to offer; to put in a tender or to submit a tender*

Angebote werden entgegengenommen: *open to offers*

Angebotsempfänger: *offeree*

Angebotspreis: *supply price*

Angebot und Nachfrage: *supply and demand*

angebracht: *proper*

angefordert: nicht ~ *unsolicited*

angehen: *affect; concern*

Angehörige: *relatives or relations*

Angehörigen: *kin*

Angehöriger: finanziell abhängiger ~ *dependant* **nächster** ~ *next of kin*

angeklagt: *on trial*

Angeklagte: der/die ~ *the accused; prisoner at the bar; defendant*

angeklagt sein: *to face a charge*

Angelegenheit: *affair; business; matter*

angemeldet: *registered*

angemessen: *appropriate; proper; reasonable*

angesehen: *reputable*

angesichts: *in view of*

angestellt: *employed*

Angestelltenverhältnis: *employment*

Angestellte(r): *employee; official* **leitende(r)** ~ *senior manager or senior executive* **untere(r)** ~ *junior clerk*

Angestellte(r) außer Haus *or* **im Außendienst:** *outside worker*

Angestellter im Innendienst: *inside worker*

angewandt: nicht mehr ~ *obsolete*

angewiesen sein auf: *to depend on*

angezeigt: nicht ~ *unreported*

angleichen: *adjust; equalize*

Angleichung: *adjustment*

angreifen: *assault; attack; claim (slang); raid*

Angreifer: *attacker*

angrenzen: *adjoin*

angrenzend: *neighbouring*

Angriff: *assault; attack; raid* **tätlicher** ~ *battery*

Angriffswaffe: *dangerous or offensive weapon*

Anhaltspunkt: *clue; lead*

Anhang: *annexe or annex (US); appendix; rider; schedule*

anhängen: *annexe or annex (US); attach*

anhäufen: *accumulate*

anheben: *raise*

Anhörungsausschuß: parlamentarischer ~ *ministerial tribunal*

Anklage: *accusation; charge; information; prosecution* **begründete** ~ *true bill* **die** ~ **vertreten** *prosecute*

Anklagebank: *dock*

Anklagebehörde: *prosecution*

Anklageblatt: polizeiliches ~ *charge sheet*

Anklage erheben: *arraign; indict; prefer charges*

Anklageerhebung: *arraignment; preferment of charges*

Anklagejury: *grand jury (US)*

anklagen: *accuse; charge; indict; prefer charges; prosecute*

Anklagepunkt: *count*

Ankläger: *prosecution* **öffentlicher** ~ *public prosecutor*

Anklageschrift: *indictment*

Anklagevertreter: *prosecution counsel or counsel for the prosecution*

Anklagevertretung: *prosecution*

ankündigen: *announce*

Ankündigung: *announcement*

Anlage: *annexe or annex (US); enclosure; plant*

Anlagegüter: *capital goods*

Anlagekapital: *fixed capital*

Anlagevermögen: *capital or fixed assets*

Anlaß: *occasion; subject*

Anlaß geben zu: *give rise to*

anlegen: *invest*

Anlegestelle: *dock*

Anleihe: festverzinsliche ~ *loan stock* **untilgbare** ~ *irredeemable bond*

Anleihekapital: *debenture capital; loan capital*

Anmeldegebühr: *registration fee*

anmelden: *file* **sich** ~ *register*

anmeldepflichtig: *notifiable*

Anmeldung: *registration*

Anmeldung einer Konkursforderung: *proof of debt*

Anmerkung: *comment*

annähernd: *roughly*

Annahme: *acceptance; adoption; presumption; receiving* **unwiderrufliche** ~ *irrevocable acceptance*

Annahme eines Angebotes: *acceptance of an offer*

annehmbar: *acceptable; reasonable*

annehmen: *accept; adopt; assume; carry; pass; presume*

Annehmer: *acceptor*

annullierbar: *annullable; voidable*

Annullieren: *annulling*

annullieren: *annul; cancel; nullify; quash; revoke; set aside*

Annullierung: *annulment; cancellation; defeasance; invalidation; nullification; rescinding or rescission; revocation*

anordnen: *arrange; direct; order; require; rule*

Anordnung: *fiat; order* **eine** ~ **aufheben** *to countermand an order* **einstweilige** ~ *interim order*

Anordnung der Nachlaßverwaltung: *grant of letters of administration*

Anordnung eines Haftprüfungstermins: *writ of habeas corpus*

Anordnung öffentlicher Fürsorge: *care order*

anormal: *abnormal*

anpassen: *adjust*

Anpassung: *adjustment*

anrechenbar: *chargeable*

Anrecht: *entitlement; interest; right*

Anrecht auf Anwartschaft: *interest in remainder*

Anrecht auf Belegschaftsaktien: *stock option*

anreden: *address*

anregen: *encourage; suggest*

Anregung: *suggestion*

Anreiz: *inducement*

Anruf: *call* **anrufen** *to call*

Anrufer: *caller*

ansammeln: *hoard*

ansässig: *resident*

Anschaffung: *acquisition*

Anschaffungspreis: *purchase price*

Anschein: beim ersten ~ *prima facie*

anscheinend: *semble*

Anschlag: *attempt; notice*

Anschlagbrett: *noticeboard*

anschlagen: *knock*

Anschlagfläche: *display panel*

anschließend: *subsequent*

Anschluß: *extension*

Anschrift: *address*

Ansehen: *reputation; standing*

ansetzen: *schedule*

Ansicht: *opinion; view* **anderer** ~ **sein** *dissent*

ansonsten: *failing; otherwise*

Ansporn: *inducement*

Ansprache: *speech*

Anspruch: *entitlement; right* **obligatorischer** ~ *chose in action*

Anspruchsberechtigter: *rightful claimant*

Anspruchsschreiben: anwaltliches ~ *letter before action*

Anspruchsteller: *claimant*

Anstalt: *institution*

Anstand *or* **Anständigkeit:** *decency*

anständig: *decent*

anstehen: *queue*

anstehend: *pending*

ansteigen: *escalate; increase; rise*

anstellen: *employ; engage*

anstelle von: *in lieu of*

Anstellungsbedingungen: *conditions or terms of employment; conditions of service*

Anstieg: *gain; rise* **prozentualer** ~ *percentage increase*

anstiften: *abet; encourage; incite; induce; procure*

Anstifter: *inciter* **Anstiftung** *incitement*

Anstiftung zum Meineid: *subornation of perjury*

anstößig: *indecent*

Anstößigkeit: *indecency*

Anstoßwirkung: *knock-on effect*

Ansturm: *run*

Anteil: *concern; cut; holding; interest; proportion*

anteilig *or* **anteilmäßig:** *pro rata*

Anteilschein: *share certificate*

Antitrust-: *anti-trust*

Antrag: *application; motion; petition; proposal; request* **auf** ~ *ex parte* **einen** ~ **einbringen** *or* **vorlegen** *to table a motion* **einen** ~ **stellen** *to move or to propose a motion* **erneuter** ~ *reapplication* **verfahrenseinleitender** ~ *originating application*

Antrag auf Aktienzuteilung: *letter of application*

Antrag auf Verfahrenseinstellung: *no case to answer*

Antrag einer Partei: *ex parte application*

Antragsempfänger: *offeree*

Antragsformular: *application form*

Antragsschriftsatz: *notice of motion*

Antragsteller: *claimant; applicant; mover; petitioner*

antreiben: *hurry*

Antrieb: *drive*

Antritt: *accession*

Antworten: ausweichende ~ **geben** *to give evasive answers*

antworten: *answer; reply*

Antwortkarte: frankierte *or* freigemachte ~ reply paid card

Antwortschein: internationaler ~ international postal reply coupon

anvertrauen: jdm etwas ~ to (en)trust someone with something *or* to entrust something to someone

anwachsen: accrue

Anwalt: counsel; solicitor einen ~ beauftragen/verpflichten to instruct/retain a lawyer/solicitor to act for you führender ~ leading counsel; leader

Anwalt der Krone: Queen's Counsel

Anwälte: parliamentary agents die ~ the legal profession

Anwältin: counsel; lawyer; solictor

Anwaltsassistent: paralegal

Anwahltsberuf: the Bar

Anwaltsbüros: chambers

Anwaltschaft: the Bar

Anwaltsgebühren: solicitors' charges

Anwaltsgutachten: counsel's opinion

Anwaltshonorar: retainer außerordentliches ~ refresher

Anwaltskammer: Faculty of Advocates; the Bar Council; Law Society

Anwaltskosten: solicitors' charges; legal costs *or* charges *or* expenses

Anwaltsliste: Roll of Solicitors

Anwaltsreferendar: articled clerk (GB)

Anwaltsreferendarzeit: articles

Anwaltsstand: der ~ the legal profession

Anwalts- und Notarmitarbeiter: legal executive

Anwaltsvertreter: devil

Anwaltsverzeichnis: Law List

Anwaltsvorschuß: retainer

Anwaltszulassung: practising certificate

Anwartschaft: expectancy *or* expectation

Anwartschaftsrecht: bedingtes ~ contingent remainder unentziehbares ~ vested remainder

Anwartschaftszeit: qualifying period

anweisen: direct; instruct

Anweisung: directions

Anweisungen: auf ~ warten to await instructions

anwendbar: nicht ~ unenforceable

anwenden: exercise

Anwender: user

Anwendung: exercise; usage falsche ~ misuse

anwerben: solicit

Anwerben von Kunden: soliciting

Anwerbung von Mitgliedern: recruitment

Anwesen: messuage

anwesend: present

anwesend sein: attend

Anwesenheit: attendance; presence

Anzahl: quantity beschlußfähige ~ quorum

Anzahl der Abschlüsse *or* **der Börsengeschäfte:** bargains done

Anzahlung: advance; deposit; payment on account; down payment eine ~ einbüßen *or* verwirken to forfeit a deposit

Anzeichen: indication

Anzeige: notification

Anzeigeerstatter: relator

anzeigen: indicate jdn ~ to press charges against someone; to inform on someone

Anzeigenblatt: free paper *or* giveaway paper

anzeigepflichtig: notifiable

anziehen: advance

a posteriori: a posteriori **a posteriori-Argument** a posteriori argument

Apparat: extension; instrument; machinery

Appellationstribunal: Employment Appeal Tribunal

appellieren: call on

Appendix: appendix

a priori: a priori **a priori-Argument** a priori argument

Äquivalenz: equivalence

Arbeit: labour *or* labor (US) doppelte ~ duplication of work gemeinnützige ~ community service körperliche ~ manual labour schwere körperliche ~ hard labour während der ~ in the course of employment

arbeitend: employed

Arbeiter: labour *or* labor (US); labourer gewerkschaftlich organisierte ~ organized labour

Arbeiter aussperren: to lock out workers

Arbeitergewerkschaft: labor union (US)

Arbeiter im Innendienst: inside worker

Arbeitgeber: employer

Arbeitgeberanteil: employer's contribution

Arbeitgeber-Arbeitnehmer-Beziehungen: labour relations

Arbeitgeber und Arbeitnehmer: master and servant

Arbeitgeberverband: employers' organization *or* association

Arbeitnehmer: employed; employee; servant gewerkschaftlich organisierte ~ organized labour

Arbeitsablaufdiagramm: flow chart

Arbeitsamt: Job Centre

Arbeitsausschuß: working party

Arbeitsbeschaffungsprogramm: job creation scheme

Arbeitserlaubnis: green card; work permit

Arbeitsfreistellung zur Geburt: paternity leave

Arbeitsgang eines Computers: a computer run

Arbeitsgerät: implement

Arbeitsgericht: Employment Appeal Tribunal; industrial tribunal

Arbeitsgesetze: labour laws

Arbeitsgesetzgebung: labour legislation

Arbeitskampf: industrial dispute *or* labour dispute

Arbeitskraft: ungelernte ~ manual labourer

Arbeitskräfte: labour force; labour *or* labor (US) billige ~ cheap labour entlassene ~ redundant staff ortsansässige ~ local labour

arbeitslos: *unemployed*

Arbeitslosen: die ~ *the unemployed*

Arbeitslosengeld: *unemployment pay*

Arbeitslosenhilfe: *unemployment benefit*

Arbeitsloser: *redundancy; unemployed*

Arbeitslosigkeit: *unemployment*

Arbeitslosigkeit nach Rationalisierung: *redundancy*

Arbeitsplan: *schedule*

Arbeitsplatz: *place of work* **sicherer ~** *secure job*

Arbeitsplatzaufgabe: freiwillige ~ *voluntary redundancy*

Arbeitsplatzbewertung: *job evaluation*

Arbeitsplätze abbauen: *to cut jobs*

Arbeitsplatzsicherheit: *security of employment*

Arbeitsrecht: *labour law* or *labour legislation* **das ~** *the law of master and servant*

Arbeitstrupp: *squad*

Arbeitsunfall: *industrial* or *occupational accident*

Arbeitsverhältnis: *employment*

Arbeitsvermittlungsstelle: *employment office or bureau or agency*

Arbeitsvertrag: *contract of employment* or *employment contract; contract of service* or *service contract*

Arbeitsvertragsbedingungen: *conditions of employment* or *of service; terms of employment*

Arbeit weitervergeben: *subcontract*

Archivar: *registrar*

ärgerlich: *vexatious*

Ärgernis: *nuisance* **öffentliches ~** *public or common nuisance* **öffentliches ~ erregend** *disorderly*

Argumentation: *argument; reasoning*

argumentieren: *argue*

Armenrecht: im ~ *in forma pauperis*

Armenrechtserklärung: *statement of means*

arrangieren: *arrange*

Arrest: *confinement* **dinglicher ~** *attachment; Mareva injunction*

Art: *kind; type; way* **derselben ~** *ejusdem generis* or *eiusdem generis* **eigener ~** *sui generis*

Artikel: *article; chapter; item* **führender ~** *leader* **gängiger ~** *seller*

Arzneimittel: *drug* **patentrechtlich geschütztes ~** *proprietary drug*

Ärzteschaft: die ~ *the medical profession*

ärztlich: *medical*

Assisen: *Assizes or Assize Courts (GB)*

Assistent: persönlicher ~ *personal assistant*

assoziiert: *associate; associated*

Asyl: *asylum*

Atem-Alkoholtest: *breath test*

Attentat: *assassination*

Attentäter: *assassin*

Attest: ärztliches ~ *medical certificate*

Aufarbeitung: *processing*

Aufbewahrung: sichere ~ *safe keeping*

aufbrauchen: *exhaust*

aufbringen: *bring up; raise*

aufdecken: *disclose; expose; reveal*

Aufdeckung: *detection; disclosure; exposure*

aufeinanderfolgend: *consecutive; consecutively*

Aufenthalt: *residence; stay* **gewöhnlicher ~** *habitual residence*

Aufenthaltsgenehmigung: *residence permit*

Aufenthaltsort: gewöhnlicher ~ habitual residence

Aufenthaltsrecht: *right of abode*

auferlegen: *impose*

auffordern: *ask; call on; invite*

Aufforderung: *demand; invitation*

Aufforderungsschreiben: anwaltliches ~ *letter before action*

aufführen: *schedule* **einzeln ~** *detail; itemize; specify*

Aufführungsrecht: *performing right*

Aufgabe: *abandonment; assignment; duty; function; release; responsibility; waiver*

Aufgabe einer Stellung: *separation (US)*

Aufgabe eines Anspruches: *disclaimer*

Aufgabe eines Rechtsanspruchs: *abandonment of a claim*

Aufgabenbereich: *terms of reference*

aufgeben: *abandon; leave; quit; renounce; surrender*

Aufgebot: *banns*

Aufgeld: *premium; exchange premium*

aufgeschoben: *deferred*

aufgrund: *due to*

aufhalten: *hold up* **jdn ~** *delay*

aufhängen: *hang*

aufhebbar: *annullable; voidable*

Aufheben: *annulling*

aufheben: *abolish; cancel; defeat; dissolve; lift; overrule; quash; remove; repeal; rescind; reverse; revoke; set aside*

Aufhebung: *abolition; annulment; cancellation; dissolution; extinguishment; nullification; repeal; rescinding* or *rescission; reversal; revocation*

Aufhebung des Konkursverfahrens: *order of discharge*

Aufhebungsklausel: *defeasance*

Aufhetzung zum Rassenhaß: *incitement to racial hatred*

aufklären: *clear up*

Aufklärungsrate: *clear-up rate*

aufkommen für: *defray*

Auflage: *circulation; condition*

Auflagen: mit ~ *conditional*

Auflagenhöhe: *circulation*

Auflassung: lastenfreie ~ *overreaching*

Auflassungsklausel: *habendum*

Auflassungsverfügung: gerichtliche ~ *vesting order*

Auflauf: *rout*

Auflaufen: *accrual*

auflaufen: *accrue*

auflehnen: sich ~ *rebel*

auflisten: *list*

auflösbar: *terminable*

auflösen: *break; dissolve* sich ~ *break up*

Auflösung: *dissolution; liquidation; winding up* freiwillige ~ *voluntary liquidation*

Auflösung des Parlaments: *dissolution of Parliament*

aufmachen: *open*

aufnehmen: *to enter into; incorporate*

Aufnehmen von Raubdrucken: *bootlegging*

Aufrechnung: *set-off*

aufrechterhalten: *maintain*

Aufrechterhaltung: *maintenance*

aufrichtig: *straight*

aufrufen: *access*

Aufruhr: *civil or public disorder; rebellion; riot*

Aufrührer: *rioter*

aufrührerisch: *seditious*

aufschieben: *defer; postpone; put off*

Aufschlüsselung: *breakdown*

aufschreiben: *book (informal); put down* jdn ~ *to bring someone to book*

Aufschub: *deferment; grace; postponement; suspension*

Aufschub der Urteilsverkündung: *deferment of sentence*

Aufschwung: *recovery*

Aufseher: *custodian; keeper; supervisor; warden*

aufsetzen: *draw up*

Aufsetzen eines Eigentumübertragungsdokuments: *conveyancing*

Aufsicht: *care; control; superintendent; supervision; supervisor* unter staatlicher ~ *government- or state-controlled*

Aufsichtsbeamter: *inspector; superintendent; supervisor*

Aufsichtsbehörde: *inspectorate*

Aufsichtsbehörde des Finanzamts: *the Commissioners of the Inland Revenue*

Aufsichtsrat: *board; directorate*

Aufsichtsratsmitglied: *director*

Aufsichtsratssitzung: *board meeting*

aufspüren: *detect; trace*

Aufstand: *rebellion*

Aufständischer: *rebel*

aufstellen: *nominate; station*

Aufstellung: *nomination; schedule*

aufteilen: *break up; divide; separate; share*

Aufteilung des Nachlasses: *distribution*

Auftrag: *commission; contract (slang); order; purchase order* im ~ von *on behalf of*

Aufträge: unerledigte ~ *back orders; outstanding orders*

Aufträge hereinholen: *to solicit orders*

Auftraggeber: *principal* ungenannte ~ *undisclosed principal*

Auftragnehmer: *contractor*

Auftragsarbeit: *contract work*

Auftragsarbeit vergeben: *to put work out to contract*

Auftragsbuch: *order book*

Auftreten: *appearance* auftreten *to appear*

Auftrittsrecht: *audience*

aufweisen: *show*

Aufwendungen: *expenditure* betriebliche ~ *operating costs or operating expenses*

Aufwiegelung: *sedition*

aufzeichnen: *record*

Aufzeichnung: *record; recording*

Augen: unter vier ~ *in private; privately*

augenblicklich: *present*

Augenzeuge: *eye witness*

Auktion: *auction*

Auktionator: *auctioneer*

ausbezahlen: *disburse*

ausbilden: *train*

Ausbilder: *instructor*

Ausbildungsabgabe: *training levy*

Ausbildungsleiter: *training officer*

Ausbildungsvertrag: *articles of indenture; indentures*

ausborgen: *borrow*

ausbrechen: *escape*

Ausbruch: *escape; jailbreak*

ausbürgern: *expatriate*

Ausbürgerung: *expatriation*

auschlüsseln: *break down*

Ausdruck: *hard copy; printout*

ausdrücken: *express*

ausdrücklich: *explicit; express*

Auseindandersetzung: *argument*

auserlesen: *select*

auserwählt: *select*

Ausfall: *breakdown*

Ausfallbürgschaftserklärung: *letter of indemnity*

ausfallen: *break down*

ausfertigen: *engross*

Ausfertigung: in doppelter *or* zweifacher ~ *in duplicate* in dreifacher ~ *in triplicate* in vierfacher ~ *in quadruplicate*

Ausfertigung (von Urkunden): *engrossment*

ausfindig machen: *detect; discover*

Ausflüchte machen: *prevaricate*

Ausfuhr: *export*

ausführen: *carry out; describe; effect; execute; export; implement*

ausführlich: *detailed*

Ausfuhrlizenz: *export licence*

Ausführung: *execution; implementation; performance*

Ausführungsanzeige: *contract note*

Ausführungsverordnung: *statutory instrument*

Ausgabe: *copy; disbursement; expense; issue; issuance; output*

Ausgabekurs: *issued price*

Ausgaben: *expenditure* **abzugsfähige** ~ *allowable expenses* **öffentliche** ~ *public expenditure*

Ausgabeposten: *item of expenditure*

Ausgabe von Gratisaktien: *bonus or scrip issue*

Ausgabe von Schuldverschreibungen: *debenture issue or issue of debentures*

Ausgang: *output*

Ausgangspunkt: *base*

ausgeben: *disburse; issue; output; spend* **sich** ~ **für** *impersonate*

ausgebildet: *qualified*

ausgedehnt: *extensive*

ausgefallen: *called off*

ausgenommen: *excepted; excluding; exempt*

ausgerichtet sein auf: *cater for*

ausgezeichnet: *excellent*

Ausgleich: *allowance; reconciliation*

ausgleichen: *balance; equalize*

Ausgleichsfonds: *compensation fund*

Aushandeln: *bargaining*

aushandeln: *to bargain*

Aushändigung: *delivery*

aushängen: *display*

Aushilfsarbeit: *casual work*

Aushilfsarbeiter: *casual labour; casual labourer or casual worker*

Aushilfskräfte: *temporary staff*

Ausklarierungsschein: *clearance certificate*

auskommen mit: *get on with*

Auskunft: *information bureau or office; inquiry office*

ausladen: *land*

Auslage: *disbursement*

Auslagefläche: *display panel*

Auslagen: *out-of-pocket expenses*

Ausland: im ~ **ansässig** *non-resident* **im** ~ **Lebender** *expatriate*

Ausländer: *alien; foreigner; non-resident*

ausländisch: *foreign*

Auslandsauftrag: einen ~ **erteilen** *to indent for something*

Auslandsgespräch: *overseas or international call*

Auslandsinvestitionen: *foreign investments*

Auslandsprodukte: *foreign goods*

Auslandsrechte: *foreign rights*

Auslandszahlungsanweisung: *foreign or international or overseas money order*

auslassen: *leave out; omit*

Auslassung: *omission*

auslegen: *construe; interpret*

Auslegung: *interpretation* **falsche** ~ *misinterpretation*

Auslegungsklausel: *interpretation clause*

ausleihen: *lend; loan*

Ausleihung: *lending*

ausliefern: *extradite; surrender*

Auslieferung: *extradition*

Auslieferungsvertrag: *extradition treaty*

Auslösungsrecht: *equity of redemption*

Auslösungsrecht des Hypothekenschuldners: *equity of redemption*

Ausmaß: *extent*

ausmessen: *measure*

Ausnahme: *exception*

Ausnahmebewilligung: *dispensation*

auspeitschen: *whip*

ausreichend: *adequate; sufficient*

Ausrottung: *destruction*

Aussage: *evidence; testimony* **eine** ~ **machen** *to make a statement*

aussagen: *testify*

Aussageverweigerungsrecht: *right against self-incrimination*

Aussageverweigerungsrecht eines Ehegatten: *marital privileges*

Ausschankzeiten: *licensing hours (GB)*

ausscheiden: *retire*

ausschließen: *bar; disqualify; exclude; preclude*

ausschließlich: *excluding; exclusive of*

Ausschluß: *exclusion* **unter** ~ **von** *excluding; to the exclusion of*

Ausschluß der Gewährleistung: *caveat emptor*

Ausschlußgesetz: *prozessuales* ~ *limitation of actions or statute of limitations*

Ausschlußklausel: *exclusion clause*

Ausschuß: *board; commission; committee* **einem** ~ **vorsitzen** *to chair a committee* **gemischter** ~ *joint commission of inquiry or joint committee* **ständiger** ~ *standing committee*

Ausschußmitglied: *commissioner*

Ausschußware: *reject*

Außenhandel: *foreign trade*

Außenminister: *Foreign Secretary; Secretary of State (US)*

Außenministerium: *Foreign (and Commonwealth) Office; State Department*

Außenstände: *accounts receivable; outstanding debts* **nicht einziehbare** ~ *bad debt*

außer: *except; excluding*

außergewöhnlich: *exceptional; extraordinary*

außerhalb: *beyond*

Außerkraftsetzung: *abrogation; repeal*

äußern: utter sich ~ *comment*

außerordentlich: *extraordinary*

außerstande: *unable*

Äußerung: *observation* **beleidigende** ~ *defamatory statement*

aussetzen: *stay; subject to; suspend*

Aussetzung: *stay; suspension*

Aussetzung des Verfahrens: *stay of proceedings*

Aussöhnung: *reconciliation*

Aussonderung geeigneter Bewerber: *the screening of candidates*

Aussperrung: *lockout*

Ausspruch: richterlicher ~ *dictum*

Ausstand: *strike*

ausstehend: *outstanding; receivable*

aussteigen: *get out*

ausstellen: *display; draw; issue*

Aussteller: *drawer*

Aussteller eines Gefälligkeitswechsels: *accommodation maker*

Ausstellung: *show*

Aussteuer: *dowry*

Ausstoß: *output*

ausstreichen: *expunge*

aussuchen: *pick; select*

Austausch: *exchange*

austauschbar: *exchangeable*

austauschen: *substitute*

ausüben: *exercise; practise; serve*

Ausübung: *exercise*

Ausübung einer Option: *exercise of an option*

Ausverkauf: *sale*

ausverkaufen: *clear*

Auswahl: *sample; selection*

auswählen: *pick; select*

Auswahlkomitee: *selection board or committee*

Auswahlverfahren: *selection procedure*

Auswanderer: *emigrant*

auswandern: *emigrate*

Auswanderung: *emigration*

auswärtig: *non-resident*

Auswärtiges Amt: *the Foreign Office*

Ausweichen: *evasion* **ausweichen** *to evade*

ausweichend: *evasive*

Ausweis: *pass*

ausweisen: *deport*

Ausweisung: *deportation*

Ausweisungsbeschluß: *deportation order*

auswirken: sich ~ auf *to affect; to bear on or to have a bearing on*

Auswirkung: *effect; influence*

auszahlen: *disburse; pay off*

Auszahlung: *disbursement*

ausziehen: *quit*

Auszubildender: *trainee*

Auszug: *abstract; extract* **einen ~ machen** *to abstract*

auszuweisen: sich ~ *he was asked for proof of identity*

automatisch: *automatic; ipso facto*

Autopsie: *autopsy*

Autorenhonorar: *royalty*

autorisieren: *authorize*

autorisiert: *accredited; authorized*

Autoverleih(firma): *car hire firm*

Avis: *advice note* **laut ~** *as per advice*

Bb

Bagatelldelikt: *non-arrestable offence*

Bagatelldiebstahl: *petty theft*

bagatellisieren: *minimize*

Bagatellsache: *small claim; summary offence*

Bahnhof: *station*

baldmöglichst: *at your earliest convenience*

Band: *volume*

Bande: *gang*

Bandit: *bandit*

Banditentum: *banditry*

Bank: *bank*

Bank-an-Bank-Kredit: *inter-bank loan*

Bankdarlehen: *bank loan*

Bankdirektor: *bank manager*

Bankenkonzession: *bank charter*

Banker *or* **Bankier:** *banker*

bankfähig: *bankable*

Bankinstitut: öffentlich-rechtliches ~ *Trustee Savings Bank*

Bankkonto: *bank account or banking account (US)*

Bankkredit: *bank loan*

Banknote: *bank note or banknote; bill (US)*

Bankreserve: *bank reserves*

Bankrott: *bankruptcy* **betrügerischer ~** *criminal bankruptcy*

bankrott: *bankrupt*

Bankschließfach: *safe deposit box*

Banktratte: *bank draft or banker's draft*

Banküberweisung: *bank transfer*

Bankvollmacht: *bank mandate*

Bankwechsel: *bank draft or banker's draft*

Barangebot: *cash offer*

Barauszahlung: *"pay cash"*

Barbestand: *balance or cash in hand*

Bargeld: *balance in hand or cash in hand; hard cash; ready money*

Bargeschäft: *cash transaction*

Barposten: *cash items*

Barreserven: *cash reserves*

Barriere: *barrier*

Barrister: *barrister* **einen ~ hinzuziehen** *to instruct a barrister*

Barscheck: *open or uncrossed cheque*

bar zahlen: *to pay cash*

Barzahlung: *settlement in cash or cash settlement*

Barzahlungsbedingungen: *cash terms*

basieren: *base*

Basis: *base; basis* **auf jährlicher ~** *on an annual basis*

Basisjahr: *base year*

Basissteuersatz: *basic rate tax*

Bau: *construction* **im ~ befindlich** *under construction*

bauen: *construct*

Bauernfängerei: *confidence trick or confidence game (US)*

Bauernfänger: *confidence trickster or confidence man (US)*

Baugenehmigung: *building permit; planning permission* **vorläufige ~** *outline planning permission*

Baumaterial: *building materials*
Bauordnungsamt: *planning department*
Bauplatz: *lot (US)*
Bausparkasse: *building society (GB)*
Baustoffe: *building materials*
Bauunternehmen: *construction company*
Bauunternehmer: *property developer*
beabsichtigen: *intend; set out*
Beachtung: *attention*
Beamtendeutsch: *officialese*
Beamtenstelle: feste ~ *established post*
Beamter: *officer; official* **höherer ~** *high official* **richterlicher ~** *magistrate* **unterer ~** *minor official*
Beamtin: *officer; official*
beanspruchen: *claim*
beanstanden: *demur; query*
beantragen: *apply; move; petition; request; seek*
bearbeiten: *handle; process* **etwas ~** *to deal with*
Bearbeitung: *handling*
Bearbeitungsgebühr: *handling charge*
beaufsichtigen: *superintend; supervise*
Beaufsichtigung: *supervision*
beauftragen: *assign; instruct*
Bedarf: *demand; requirement*
Bedenken: *reservation*
bedenken: *consider; deliberate*
bedeutend: *grand; important*
Bedeutung: *importance; intention*
bedienen: *run; serve*
Bediensteter: *servant*
Bedienung: *service charge*
Bedienungszuschlag: *service charge*
bedingt: *conditional; qualified*
bedingt entlassen: *parole*
Bedingung: *condition; stipulation* **auflösende ~** *condition subsequent* **aufschiebende ~** *condition precedent* **unter der ~** *on condition*
Bedingungen: *terms* **günstige ~** *easy terms* **harte ~ stellen** *to drive a hard bargain* **unter normalen ~** *under normal conditions*
Bedingungen aushandeln: *to negotiate terms and conditions or to negotiate a contract*
bedrohen: *threaten*
Bedrohung: *menace*
Bedürftigkeitsnachweis: *statement of means*
beeilen: sich ~ *hurry*
beeinflussen: *govern; influence; lobby*
Beeinflussung: unzulässige ~ *undue influence*
beeinträchtigen: *prejudice*
Beeinträchtigung: *detriment; interference; private nuisance*
beenden: *complete; terminate*
beendigen: *determine*
Beendigung: *completion; termination*
Beendigung des Arbeitsverhältnisses: *termination (US)*
befähigen: *enable*

Befähigung: *capacity*
befangen: *biased; prejudiced*
Befangenheit: *bias*
befassen: sich ~ mit *cater for; concern; to deal with; to be engaged in; handle*
Befehl: *command*
befehlen: *command; order*
befinden für: *find*
befolgen: *keep; obey; observe* **etwas ~** *to comply with something* **nicht ~** *disobey*
Befolgung: *compliance; observance*
befördern: *carry; convey; promote; ship*
Beförderung: *handling; promotion*
Befrachter: *shipper*
Befrachtungsvertrag: *charterparty*
befragen: *canvass; interview; question*
Befragung: *questioning*
befreien: *excuse; exempt; liberate; release* **jdn ~** *to set someone free*
befreit: *exempt*
Befreiung: *discharge; dispensation; exemption*
Befreiungsklausel: *escape clause*
Befriedigung: *satisfaction* **bevorzugte ~** *preferential payment*
Befriedigung eines Anspruches: *satisfaction*
befristet: *temporarily*
Befugnis: *authority; power; warrant*
befugt: *authorized; competent* **nicht ~** *incompetent*
befürworten: *support*
Befürworter des Freihandels: *free trader*
Befürwortung: *advocacy*
begehen: *commit; perpetrate*
Beginn: *commencement*
beginnen: *begin; commence; launch; open* **etwas ~** *to embark on*
beglaubigen: *attest; authenticate; certify*
Beglaubigung: *attestation*
Beglaubigungsstempel: *seal*
Beglaubigungsvermerk: *attestation clause; testimonium clause*
begleichen: *meet*
Begleichung: *discharge; payment; settlement*
Begleichung einer Schuld: *liquidation of a debt*
begleiten: *accompany*
Begleitschreiben: *covering letter or note*
begnadigen: *amnesty; pardon*
Begnadigung: *clemency; pardon* **unbeschränkte ~** *free pardon*
Begnadigungsrecht: *prerogative of mercy*
begreifen: *realize*
begrenzen: *limit*
Begrenzung: zeitliche ~ *time limitation*
Begründer eines Trusts: *settlor*
begründet: *valid*
Begründung: *reason*
begünstigen: *abet; favour or favor (US)*
Begünstigter: *beneficiary; grantee*

behalten: *hold; retain*
Behandlung: bevorzugte ~ *preferential treatment*
behaupten: *allege; assert; aver; claim*
Behauptung: *allegation; assertion; averment*
Behinderte(r): *disabled person*
Behinderung: *disability; obstruction*
Behörde: *agency; council* **örtliche** ~ *local authority*
Behörden: die ~ *the authorities*
bei: *care of*
beifügen: *enclose*
beiheften: *attach*
Beihilfe: *aiding and abetting; benefit; grant*
Beihilfe leisten: *to aid and abet*
Beilage: *enclosure*
beilegen: *enclose*
Beilegung: *settlement*
Beirat: *advisory board*
beiseite: *aside*
Beisitzer: sachverständiger ~ *assessor*
Beispiel: *example* **zum** ~ *for example (e.g.)*
beispiellos: *unprecedented*
Beistand: *support*
beistehen: *support*
beisteuern: *contribute*
Beitrag: *contribution; premium* **einen** ~ **leisten** *contribute*
beitragen zu: *to contribute to*
beitreibbar: nicht ~ *irrecoverable*
Beitritt: *accession*
beiwohnen: *attend*
bejahend: *affirmative; positive*
bekämpfen: *oppose*
Bekämpfung des Terrorismus: *the prevention of terrorism*
Bekanntgabe: *publication*
Bekanntgabe von Urkunden: *discovery*
bekanntgeben: *announce; declare*
Bekanntmachung: *announcement; publication*
Beklagter: *defence or defense (US); defendant; respondent*
bekommen: *get; obtain; take* **zu** ~ *obtainable*
bekräftigen: *confirm*
Bekräftigung: *confirmation*
belagern: *blockade*
belangbar: *actionable; triable*
belanglos: *petty*
belastbar: *debitable*
belasten: *incriminate*
belästigen: *harass; molest*
Belästiger: *molester*
Belästigung: *harassment; molestation* **sexuelle** ~ *importuning*
Belastung: variable ~ *floating charge* **vorrangige** ~ *prior charge*
Belastungszeuge: *prosecution witness or witness for the prosecution* **als** ~ **aussagen** *to turn Queen's evidence or to turn state's evidence (US)*

belaufen: sich ~ **auf** *total; run to*
Beleg: *receipt*
belegen: *occupy*
belegen mit: *impose*
Belegschaft: *labour force; personnel*
Belegung: *occupancy*
beleidigen: *insult*
Beleidigung: *libel; slander*
Beleidigungsklage: *action for libel or slander; libel or slander action*
beliebig: *discretionary*
beliebt: *popular*
beliefern: *furnish; supply*
Belohnung: *bounty; reward*
bemächtigen: sich ~ *usurp*
Bemerkung: *comment; observation*
Bemerkungen: beiläufige ~ *obiter dicta*
benachbart: *neighbouring*
benachrichtigen: *inform*
Benachrichtigung: *notice; notification*
Benehmen: *conduct*
benötigen: *require; take*
benutzen: *use* **Benutzer** *user*
benutzerfreundlich: *user-friendly*
Benutzerhandbuch: *user's guide or handbook*
Benutzungsgebühr: *toll*
Benzinpreis: den ~ **freigeben** *to decontrol the price of petrol*
beobachten: *observe* **Beobachter** *observer*
Beobachtung: *observation*
beraten: *deliberate*
beratend: *advisory; consulting*
Berater: *adviser or advisor; consultant*
Beratung: *consultancy; consultation*
Beratungen: *deliberations*
Beratungsgremium: *advisory board*
Beratungshilfe: *the green form scheme*
Beratungshilfeformular: *green form*
Beratungsstadium einer Gesetzesvorlage: *Report Stage*
Beratungsstelle: öffentliche ~ *Citizens' Advice Bureau*
Beratungs- und Prozeßkostenhilfe: *Legal Aid*
Beratungszimmer: *jury room*
berauben: *mug; rob*
berechnen: *calculate; charge; evaluate*
Berechnung: grobe ~ *rough estimate; rough calculation*
berechtigen: *entitle*
Berechtigte(r): *beneficiary*
berechtigt sein zu: *to qualify for*
Berechtigung: *entitlement; right*
Bereich: *domain; scope; sector* **öffentlicher** ~ *public sector*
bereit: sich ~ **erklären** *to agree to do something*
bereitstellen: *earmark; provide*
Bergbaukonzession: *mining concession*
Bergelohn: *salvage (money)*

bergen: *salvage*
Bergungsgut: *salvage*
Bergungsschiff: *salvage vessel*
Bergungsvertrag: *salvage agreement*
Bericht: *report* **vertraulicher** ~ *confidential report*
berichten: *report*
berichtet: nicht ~ *unreported*
berichtigen: *amend; rectify*
Berichtigung: *corrigendum; rectification*
berücksichtigen: *note; respect* **etwas** ~ *to take something into consideration; to take note of something* **nicht** ~ *override*
Berücksichtigung: ohne ~ *regardless of* **unter** ~ **dessen** *in respect thereof*
Beruf: *occupation; profession* **gefährlicher** ~ *dangerous job*
berufen: *appoint* **sich** ~ **auf** *to pray in aid*
beruflich: *occupational; professional*
Berufsausübung: *practice*
Berufskrankheit: *occupational disease*
Berufsorganisation der Barrister: *the Inns of Court*
Berufspraxis: *practice*
Berufsrichter: *stipendiary magistrate*
Berufsrisiko: *occupational hazards*
Berufsschäden: *industrial injuries*
Berufsstand: *profession*
Berufung: *appeal; appointment*
Berufung einlegen: *appeal*
Berufungsbeklagter: *respondent*
Berufungsgericht: *Appeal Court or Court of Appeal*
Berufungsgerichtsbarkeit: *appellate jurisdiction*
Berufungskläger: *appellant*
Berufungsurkunde: *letters patent*
Berufungsverfahren: *rehearing*
Berühmung: *jactitation*
beschädigen: *to (cause) damage*
Beschädigung: *damage*
beschaffen: *raise*
Beschaffenheit: *nature*
beschäftigen: *employ*
beschäftigt: *busy; employed*
Beschäftigung: *employment*
Beschäftigungsprogramm: *job creation scheme*
Bescheid: *note; notice*
bescheinigen: *attest; certify*
Bescheinigung: *attestation; certificate*
Beschenkter: *donee*
beschimpfen: *abuse*
Beschimpfung: *abuse*
Beschlag: mit ~ **belegen** *arrest*
Beschlagnahme: *attachment; condemnation; confiscation; distress; seizure; sequestration*
beschlagnahmen: *appropriate; attach; confiscate; distrain; impound; requisition; seize; sequester or sequestrate*
Beschlagnahmeverfügung: *charging order*

beschleunigt: *summary; summarily*
beschließen: *decide; fix; hold; wind up*
Beschluß: *decision; resolution* **einen** ~ **einbringen** *to put a resolution to a meeting*
beschlußfähig: *quorate* **nicht** ~ *inquorate*
beschlußfähig sein: *to have a quorum*
Beschlußfassung: *decision making*
beschlußunfähig: *inquorate*
beschränken: *limit; restrict*
beschränkend: *limiting*
beschränkt: *limited*
Beschränkung: *limitation; restraint; restriction*
Beschränkung der Berichterstattung: *reporting restrictions*
beschreiben: *describe; represent*
Beschreibung: *description; specification*
beschuldigen: *accuse; blame; incriminate*
Beschuldigte: der/die ~ *the accused*
Beschuldigung: *accusation; imputation*
beschützen: *guard*
Beschwerde: *complaint; grievance* **leichtfertig erhobene** ~ *frivolous complaint or frivolous action*
Beschwerdebrief: *letter of complaint*
Beschwerdeführer: *complainant*
Beschwerdeverfahren: *complaints or grievance procedure*
beschweren: sich ~ *complain*
beschwerlich: *onerous*
beschwert: *aggrieved*
beschwindeln: *swindle*
beseitigen: *abate*
Beseitigung: *abatement*
besetzen: *occupy*
besetzt: *engaged*
Besetzung: rechtswidrige ~ *adverse possession*
besichtigen: *inspect; view*
Besichtigung: *inspection*
Besichtigungsreise: eine ~ **machen** *to carry out a tour of inspection*
besiegeln: *clinch*
besiegen: *defeat*
Besitz: *occupancy; possession; possessions* **in** ~ **nehmen** *distrain* **mittelbarer or rechtlicher** ~ *possession in law* **unbeschränkter** ~ *freehold* **ungestörter** ~ *quiet enjoyment* **unmittelbarer** ~ *actual possession*
Besitz betrügerisch erwerben: *obtaining property by deception*
Besitz eines Gebäudes: *occupation of a building*
besitzen: *hold; own; possess*
Besitzer: *holder; occupant* **den** ~ **wechseln** *to change hands* **der eigentliche or der wirkliche** ~ *the ultimate owner* **rechtmäßiger** ~ *rightful owner*
Besitzergreifung: *occupancy*
Besitzerin: *proprietress*
Besitzklage: *possessive action*
Besitzrecht: *estate*
besitzrechtlich: *possessory*

Besitzstörung einer Einzelperson: *private nuisance*
Besitztitel: *possessory title*
Besitztümer: *possessions*
Besitzübertragung: *bailment*
Besitz von Angriffswaffen: *carrying offensive weapons*
Besitz von Grundbesitz: *seisin*
Besitz von Rauschgift: *possession of drugs*
besonderer: *particular; special*
besonders: *in particular; specifically*
Besorgnis: *concern*
Besorgnis der Befangenheit: *likelihood of bias*
besprechen: *discuss* **sich ~** *communicate; confer*
Besprechung: *briefing; communication; discussion; meeting*
Besprechungszimmer: *interview room*
Besserungsanstalt: *approved school*
Bestallung: *call*
Bestallungsurkunde: *practising certificate; letter of appointment*
Bestallungsurkunde zum Nachlaßverwalter: *letters of administration*
Bestand: *supply*
Beständigkeit: *permanency*
Bestandsdatei: *master copy of a file*
Bestandsüberwachung: *stock control*
bestätigen: *acknowledge; affirm; attest; authenticate; certify; confirm; corroborate; evidence; validate; verify* **etwas ~** *vouch for*
bestätigend: *corroborative*
Bestätigung: *acknowledgement; attestation; confirmation; corroboration; validation; verification* **erneute gerichtliche ~** *cessate grant* **gerichtliche ~** *probate*
Bestätigungsschreiben: *letter of acknowledgement*
bestechen: *bribe; nobble (slang)*
bestechlich: *corrupt*
Bestechung: *bribery; corruption; graft (informal)*
Bestechungsgeld: *bribe*
Bestechung von Geschworenen: *embracery*
bestehen: *insist; pass*
bestehen auf: *to hold out for*
bestehen aus: *consist of*
Bestellbuch: *order book*
bestellen: *book; order*
bestellt: *on order*
Bestellung: *booking; order; purchase order*
besteuerbar: *taxable*
besteuern: *tax*
Besteuerung: direkte ~ *direct taxation* **hohe ~** *high taxation*
bestimmen: *designate; determine; govern; rule*
bestimmt: *specific*
Bestimmung: *provision; stipulation* **gesetzliche ~** *enactment*
Bestimmung einer Vertragsstrafe: *penalty clause*
Bestimmungen: *terms*

bestrafen: *penalize; punish*
Bestrafung: *punishment*
Bestreiten: *traverse*
bestreiten: *contest; deny; disclaim; dispute*
Bestseller: *best-seller*
Besuch: *call*
besuchen: *call on*
Besucher: *caller; visitor*
Besuchsrecht: *access*
beteiligen: *involve*
Beteiligter: *interested party*
Beteiligung: *holding; interest* **gegenseitige ~** *cross or reciprocal holdings*
Beteiligungen: seine ~ offenlegen *to declare or disclose an interest*
Beteiligungsgesellschaft: *associate company*
beteuern: *assert; aver*
Beteuerung: *assertion; averment*
Betracht: in ~ ziehen *entertain*
betrachten: *deem; view*
betrachten als: *consider*
beträchtlich: *considerable; considerably; substantial*
Betrag: zuviel berechneter ~ *overcharge*
Betragen: ungebührliches ~ *misbehaviour*
betrauen: *assign*
betreffen: *affect; to bear on or to have a bearing on; concern; involve* **etwas ~** *to pertain to*
betreffend: *having regard to or as regards or regarding*
betreiben: *run*
Betreten: entry **unbefugtes ~** *to trespass (to land)*
Betreuung: *care*
Betrieb: *business; establishment; shop* **gewerkschaftspflichtiger ~** *closed shop* **in ~** *operation* **konzessionierter ~** *licensed premises*
betrieblich: *operational*
Betrieb mit Staatsaufträgen: *government contractor*
Betriebsaltersversorgung: *occupational pension scheme*
Betriebsanalyse: *operations review*
Betriebsbudget: *operational budget*
Betriebsfeuerwehrmann: *fire safety officer*
Betriebsgewinn: *operating profit*
Betriebskosten: *business or overhead or general or running expenses; operating costs or expenses; operational costs*
Betriebsplanung: *operational planning*
Betriebsratsgespräch: *joint discussions*
Betriebsrente: *occupational pension*
Betriebsstörung: *breakdown*
Betriebssystem: *operating system*
Betriebsunfall: *industrial accident*
Betriebsverlust: *operating loss*
Betriebswirtschaftsplan: *operating budget*
Betriebszeit: *computer time*
betrifft: *re*

Betrug: *bunco (slang); confidence trick or confidence game (US); deceit or deception; fraud; scam (informal); swindle* **durch ~ erlangen** *obtaining by deception*

betrügen: *cheat; deceive; defraud; swindle*

Betrüger: *cheat; confidence trickster or confidence man (US); deceiver; racketeer; swindler*

Betrügerei: *deceit or deception; racket; fraud*

Betrügereien: *fraud*

betrügerisch: *deceptive; fraudulent*

betrügerisch erwerben: *obtaining by deception*

Betrugsdezernat: *Fraud Squad*

betrunken: *drunk; intoxicated*

Betrunkenheit: *intoxication*

betrunken und unzurechnungsfähig: *drunk and incapable*

beurlauben: sich ~ lassen *to go on leave*

beurlaubt sein: *to be on leave*

Beurlaubung: *leave of absence*

Beurteilung: *measurement*

Beute: *loot; plunder*

Bevölkerung: *community*

bevollmächtigen: *authorize; delegate*

bevollmächtigt: *accredited; authorized*

Bevollmächtigter: *agent; attorney; delegate; managing clerk; plenipotentiary; proxy*

Bevollmächtigung: *agency; delegation*

bevorrechtigt: *privileged*

bevorstehend: *impending*

bevorzugen: *favour or favor (US); prefer*

bevorzugt: *preferential*

bewachen: *guard*

Bewachung: *guard*

Bewaffneter: *gunman*

Bewährung: auf ~ *on probation*

Bewährungshelfer: *probation officer*

bewältigen: zu ~ *manageable*

bewegen: jdn ~ *to prevail upon someone*

Beweggrund: *motive*

Beweggründe: niedrige ~ *ulterior motives*

beweglich: *movable or moveable*

Bewegung: *motion; movement*

Beweis: *evidence; proof* **den ~ antreten** *to discharge a burden of proof* **mündlicher ~ parol** *evidence* **unmittelbarer ~ direct or original evidence*

Beweis antreten: *lead*

beweisbar: *provable*

Beweisen: mangels ~ *not proven*

beweisen: *prove*

Beweis erbringen: *lead*

**Beweisfragen: schriftliche ~ interrogatories*

Beweisführung: *argument*

**Beweislage: ungünstige ~ weakness*

Beweislast: *burden of proof; onus of proof or onus probandi*

**Beweismaterial: primäres ~ best evidence*

Beweismaterial unterschieben: *to plant evidence*

Beweismaterial vorlegen: *to adduce evidence*

Beweismittel: *proof* **originäres ~ original evidence*

Beweismittel erster Ordnung: *primary evidence*

Beweisregeln: *rule of evidence*

Beweisstück: *corpus delicti; exhibit*

Beweis vom Hörensagen: *hearsay evidence*

Bewerber: *applicant; candidate; tenderer*

Bewerber aussondern or sieben: *to screen candidates*

Bewerbung: *application* **erneute ~ reapplication*

Bewerbungsausschuß: *selection board or selection committee*

Bewerbungsformular: *application form*

Bewerbungsschreiben: *letter of application*

bewerten: *appraise*

Bewertung: *valuation*

Bewertung des Lagerbestandes: *stock valuation*

bewilligen: *authorize; grant*

Bewilligender: *grantor*

Bewilligung: *appropriation; authorization; permission*

Bewilligungsausschuß: *appropriations committee*

bewirten: *entertain*

Bewirtungsspesen: *entertainment expenses*

Bewohnen: *occupancy*

bewohnen: *occupy*

Bewohnen eines Gebäudes: *occupation of a building*

Bewohner: *occupant; occupier*

bewußt: *deliberate; deliberately*

bezahlen: ganz ~ *pay up*

Bezahlung: *discharge; payment; remuneration; settlement* **die ~ erlassen** *to waive (a) payment*

Bezahlung in Naturalien: *payment in kind*

bezeugen: *testify; witness*

bezichtigen: *impute*

Bezichtigung: *imputation*

beziehen: *obtain; refer* **sich ~ auf** *to pertain to; to relate to*

Beziehung: *relationship*

Beziehungen: *relations*

beziehungsweise: *respectively*

**beziffern: nicht zu ~ unquantifiable*

Bezirk: *circuit; county; precinct (US)*

Bezirksgericht: *district court (US)*

Bezirksleiter: *area manager*

Bezirksrat: *county council*

Bezirksstaatsanwalt: *district attorney (US)*

Bezogener: *drawee*

Bezug: *reference*

bezug: in ~ auf *relating to; in relation to; with respect to or in respect of*

bezüglich: *re; with respect to or in respect of*

Bezugnahme: in ~ auf *re*

Bezug nehmen: *refer*

Bezugsrechtsausgabe *or*
Bezugsrechtsemission: *rights issue*

Bezugsrechtsklausel: *pre-emption clause*

bezweifeln: *query; question*
bezwingen: *overcome*
bieten: *to bid*
Bietender: *bidder*
Bieter: *bidder*
Bigamie: *bigamy*
Bigamist: *bigamist*
bigamistisch: *bigamous*
Bilanz: *balance sheet* **vorläufige** ~ *trial balance*
Bilanzwert: *book value*
bilateral: *bilateral*
bilden: *establish*
Bildschirm: *monitor; screen*
billig: *equitable*
billigen: *to approve of; endorse*
Billigflagge: *flag of convenience*
Billigkeitsgerichtsbarkeit: *equitable jurisdiction*
Billigkeitsrecht: *equity*
Billigung: *adoption*
binden: *bind*
bindend: *binding; obligatory*
Binnen-: *domestic; inland*
Binnenhandel: *home trade*
Binnenmarkt: *home or domestic market* **der** ~ *the Single Market*
bisher: *heretofore*
bis jetzt: *to date*
Bitte: *request*
bitten: *ask; call on; pray; request*
bitte nachsenden: *please forward*
bittend: *precatory*
Blanko-: *open-ended or open-end (US)*
Blankokredit: *open credit*
Blankoscheck: *blank cheque*
Blankovollmacht: *carte blanche*
Blasphemie: *blasphemy*
bleiben: *remain; stay*
Blitzscheidung: *quickie (divorce)*
Blockade: *blockade* **eine** ~ **verhängen** *blockade*
blockieren: *block; freeze; obstruct*
Blockschrift: *block capitals or block letters*
Blue Chip: *leader*
Blutalkoholgehalt: zu hoher ~ *excess alcohol in the blood*
Blüte: *dud (informal)*
Blutgruppenuntersuchung: *blood grouping test*
Blutprobe: *blood sample; blood sample or urine sample*
Blutschande: *incest*
Blutsverwandtschaft: *blood relationship*
Blutuntersuchung: *blood test*
Bobby: *bobby (GB)*
Boden: *ground*
Bodenschätze: *natural resources*
Bodmerei: *bottomry*
Bodmereibrief: *bottomry bond*
Bona-fide: ein ~ **Angebot** *a bona fide offer*

Bonitätsbestätigung: *letter of comfort or comfort letter*
Bonitätsbeurteilung: *credit rating*
Bord: an ~ **gehen** *board* **über** ~ **werfen** *jettison*
Bordell: *brothel* **ein** ~ **betreiben** *to keep a disorderly house*
Bordkarte: *boarding card or boarding pass; embarkation card*
borgen: *borrow*
Börse: *Stock Exchange; stock market*
Börsengeschäft: *bargain; Stock Exchange operation*
Börsenhändler: *(stock) jobber*
Börsenkapitalisierung: *market capitalization*
Börsenkurs: *quotation on the Stock Exchange or Stock Exchange quotation*
Börsenkurse manipulieren: *to manipulate the market*
Börsenmakler: *stockbroker*
Börsennotierung: *Stock Exchange listing*
Börsentransaktion: *transaction on the Stock Exchange*
bösgläubig: *in bad faith*
böswillig: *with malice aforethought; malicious*
Bote: *messenger*
Botenjunge: *messenger boy*
Boykott: *boycott*
boykottieren: *black; boycott*
Branche: *trade*
Branchenadreßbuch: *commercial or trade directory*
Branchenverzeichnis: *classified directory*
brandmarken: *brand*
Brandmauer: *party wall*
Brandschaden: *fire damage*
Brandschutz: *fire safety*
Brandschutzbescheinigung: *fire certificate*
Brandstifter: *arsonist; fire-raiser*
Brandstiftung: *arson; fire-raising*
Brandversicherung: *fire insurance*
Brauch: *convention; custom*
brauchen: *require; take*
brechen: *break; violate*
bremsen: *check*
Brett: *panel*
Brief: einen ~ **beantworten** *to answer a letter* **einen** ~ **kopieren** *to duplicate a letter* **persönlicher** ~ *private letter*
Briefeschreiber: *correspondent*
Briefgebühr: *letter rate*
Briefkastenadresse: *accommodation address*
Briefkopf: *letter heading or heading on notepaper; letterhead*
Briefkurs: *asking price*
Briefmarke: *stamp*
Briefpost: *letter post*
Briefumschlag: verschlossener ~ *sealed envelope*
Briefwahl: *postal ballot; postal vote*
Briefwechsel: *correspondence*

Briefwerbeaktion: *mail shot; mailing shot*

Bruch des Eheversprechens: *breach of promise*

Bruchschaden: *breakages*

Bruchteilseigentum: *co-ownership*

Bruchteilsgemeinschaft: *tenancy in common*

brutal: *violently*

brutto: *gross*

Bruttoeinnahmen: *gross earnings or gross income; gross receipts*

Bruttogewicht: *gross weight*

Bruttogewinn: *gross profit*

Bruttoinlandsprodukt: *gross domestic product*

Bruttomarge: *gross margin*

Bruttomehrwertsteuer: *output tax*

Bruttosozialprodukt: *gross national product*

Bruttoverdienst: *gross earnings or gross income or gross salary*

Buch: *book*

buchen: *book*

Bücher: *the accounts of a business or a company's accounts* **die ~ abschließen** *to close the accounts* **die ~ schönen** *to manipulate the accounts*

Buchführung: *accounting* **vorsätzlich inkorrekte ~** *false accounting*

Buchgewinn: *paper profit*

Buchhalter: *accountant*

Buchhaltung: *accounting; accounts department*

Buchprüfung: *audit* **ordentliche ~** *general audit*

Buchstabe: *letter*

Buchung: *booking; reservation*

Buchwert: *book value*

Budget: *budget*

Budgetbedarf: *budgetary requirements*

Budgetierung: *budgeting*

Budgetkontrolle: *budgetary control*

Budgetpolitik: *budgetary policy*

Bulle: *cop; copper (informal)*

Bullen: **die ~** *the fuzz (slang)*

Bund: *association*

Bundesgericht: *district court (US); federal court*

Bundeskartellamt: **das ~** *the Monopolies (and Mergers) Commission*

Bundeskriminalamt: *Federal Bureau of Investigation (FBI) (US)*

Bundesrecht: *federal laws*

Bundesstaat: *state*

Bundestagswahlen: *general election*

Bürde: *onus*

Bürge: *bondsman; guarantor; surety*

bürgen für: *underwrite; vouch for*

Bürger: *citizen*

Bürgerfreiheit: *liberty of the subject*

Bürgerkrieg: *civil war*

bürgerlich: *civil*

Bürgerrechte: *civil liberties*

Bürgersteuer: *poll tax*

Bürgin: *guarantor*

Bürgschaft: *bail; guarantee; security; surety*

Büro: *bureau; office*

Büroangestellte: *clerkess (in Scotland)*

Büroangestellte(r): *clerical worker; clerk*

Büroarbeit: *clerical work*

Bürobote: *office messenger*

Bürochef: *chief clerk or head clerk*

Bürogebäude: *office or shop premises*

Bürogehilfe: *junior clerk*

Bürohaus(komplex): *a block of offices or an office block*

Bürohilfe: *office junior*

Bürokratismus: *red tape*

Büromaterial: *office supplies*

Büropersonal: *clerical staff; office staff*

Büroräume: *office space or office accommodation*

Bürostunden: *office hours*

Bürovorsteher: *administrator; chief clerk or head clerk*

Bürozeit: **außerhalb der ~** *outside office hours*

Cc

Casus belli: *casus belli*

Chancengleichheitsplan: *equal opportunities programme*

Chaos: *chaos; mayhem*

chaotisch: *chaotic*

Charakter: *character*

Charter: *charter*

Charterer: *charterer*

Charterflug: *charter flight*

Charterflugzeug: *charter plane*

chartern: *charter*

Charterung: *charter*

Chef: *head; principal*

Chiffre: *box number; code*

chiffrieren: *code*

Chiffrierung: *coding*

chronisch: *chronic*

cif: *c.i.f.*

City: **die ~** *the City*

Clan: *family (slang)*

Clearing-Bank: *clearing bank (GB)*

Clearing-House: *clearing house*

Clubsekretär: **der ~** *the club's membership secretary*

Code Napoléon: *Code Napoleon*

Codes: **maschinenlesbare ~** *machine-readable codes*

College: *college*

Commonwealth: **das ~** *the Commonwealth*

Computer: *computer* **auf ~ umstellen** *computerize*

Computerbetrug: *computer fraud*

Computerdatei: *computer file*

Computerfehler: *computer error*

computerisieren: *computerize*

Computerprogramm: *computer program*
Computerregister: *computer file*
Computersprache: *computer language*
Computersystem: *computer system*
Controller: *controller*
Copyright: *copyright*
Corpus delicti: *corpus delicti*
Corpus legis: *corpus legis*
Coup d'état: *coup (d'état)*
Courtage: *stockbroker's commission; (jobber's) turn*

Dd

da: *whereas*
Dachgesellschaft: *holding or parent company*
dadurch: *thereby*
dafür: *thereto*
dahin: bis ~ *theretofore*
damit: *thereby; therewith*
danach: *thereafter*
"dankend erhalten": *"received with thanks"*
daran: *thereto*
darauf: *thereafter*
daraus: *therefrom*
darin: *therein*
darlegen: *set forth; set out; submit*
Darlehen: *credit; loan* ein ~ sichern *to secure a loan* gesichertes ~ *secured loan* kurzfristiges ~ *accommodation* langfristiges ~ *long-term loan* ungesichertes ~ *unsecured loan* zinsfreies or zinsloses ~ *interest-free credit or loan; soft loan*
Darlehensbetrag: *principal*
darstellen: *constitute; represent; set out*
Darstellung: *version* falsche ~ *misrepresentation*
darüber hinaus: *thereto*
darum: *therefor*
dasselbe: *idem*
Daten: fehlende ~ *lack of data or of information*
Datenabruf: *information retrieval*
Datenbank: *data bank; database*
Dateneingabe: *input*
Daten eingeben: *input*
Datenschutz: *data protection*
Datenverarbeitung: *data processing; data processing or information processing* auf ~ **umstellen** *computerize*
Daten zugänglich machen: *to share information or data*
datieren: *date*
Datum: *date*
Datum des Inkrafttretens: *date of commencement*
Datumsstempel: *date stamp*
Dauer: *life; term* festgesetzte ~ *fixed term* mit unbestimmter ~ *for an indefinite period of time*
Dauerauftrag: *banker's order or standing order*

dauerhaft: *permanent*
Dauerhaftigkeit: *permanency*
dauern: *last*
davon: *thereof*
davonkommen: *get off*
davonkommenlassen: *let off*
dazu: *thereto* die ~ dient *holding charge*
dazubringen: *persuade*
dazwischentreten: *intervene*
dealen: *to traffic in something*
Debatte: *debate; discussion*
debattieren: *debate*
Debet: *debit*
Debetnote: *debit note*
Debetseite: *debit side*
Debetspalte: *debit column; debtor side*
Debet und Kredit: *debit and credit*
Decke: *blanket*
decken: *cover; meet*
Deckname: *alias*
Deckung: zusätzliche ~ *collateral*
Deckungszusage: vorläufige ~ *binder (US); cover note*
Deduktion: *deduction*
Defekt: *defect; fault*
defekt: *defective; faulty*
definieren: *define*
degradieren: jdn ~ *to reduce someone to the ranks*
Deklaration: *declaration*
Dekorationsmaterial: *display material*
Dekret: *fiat*
Delegation: *delegation*
delegieren: *delegate*
Delegierte(r): *delegate*
Delikt: *misfeasance; offence or offense (US); tort*
Deliktshaftung: *tortious liability*
Delinquent: *delinquent*
Delkredereagent: *del credere agent*
Dementi: *denial*
dementsprechend: *accordingly*
Demonstrant: *demonstrator; protester*
Demonstration: *demonstration*
demonstrieren: *demonstrate*
denken an: *remember*
dennoch: *notwithstanding*
Denunziant: *informer*
deponieren: *deposit; lodge*
Deportation: *deportation*
deportieren: *deport*
Depositenquittung: *certificate of deposit*
Depot: *depositary (US)*
Deregulation: *deregulation*
derselbe: *idem*
derzeitig: *current; present*
Deserteur: *deserter*
desertieren: *desert*

Desertion: *desertion*
deshalb: *therefor*
designiert: *designate; -elect*
dessen: *whereof*
Detail: *detail*
detailliert: *in detail; detailed*
detailliert beschreiben: *to detail*
Detektiv: *detective*
Detektivbüro *or* **Detektei:** *detective agency*
deutlich: *clear; explicit*
Deutung: *construction*
Devisen: *foreign currency; foreign exchange*
Devisenbörse: *foreign exchange market*
Devisengeschäft: *exchange transaction*
Devisenhandel: *foreign exchange dealing*
Devisenhändler: *foreign exchange broker or dealer*
Devisenkontrollen: *exchange controls*
Devisenmakler: *foreign exchange broker or dealer*
Devisenmarkt: *foreign exchange market*
Devisenreserven: *foreign exchange reserves*
Devisenterminkurs: *forward (exchange) rate*
Devisentransfer: *foreign exchange transfer*
Dezernat: *squad*
d.h.: *i.e.*
Diagramm: *chart*
-dicht: *-proof*
Dieb: *robber; thief* **kleiner** ~ *pilferer*
Diebesgut: *stolen goods*
Diebstahl: *larceny; stealing; theft* **einfacher** ~ *petty larceny* **erschwerter** ~ *aggravated burglary* **geringfügiger** ~ *pilferage or pilfering* **schwerer** ~ *grand larceny*
Diebstahl geistigen Eigentums: *plagiarism*
Diebstahlsvorsatz: *animus furandi*
Diebstahlversicherung: eine ~ **abschließen** *to take out insurance against theft*
Diener: *servant*
dienlich: *conducive*
Dienst: *duty; service* **öffentlicher** ~ *civil service*
Dienstalter: **höheres** ~ *seniority*
dienstälter: *senior*
Dienstgrad: *rank*
Dienst haben: *to be on duty*
Dienstherr und Angestellter: *master and servant*
Dienstleistungsvertrag: *contract for services*
dienstlich: *official*
Dienstrang: höherer ~ *seniority*
Dienstverhältnis: *employment; service*
Dienstvertrag: *contract of employment or employment contract; contract of service or service contract*
Dienstweg: den ~ **beschreiten** *to go through official channels*
Dienstwohnung: *company flat*
Dienstzeit: *call; office hours*
dieselbe: *idem*
diffamieren: *defame*

Differenz: *balance; disagreement*
differieren: *dissent*
Diktat: *dictation* **ein** ~ **aufnehmen** *to take dictation*
diktieren: *dictate*
Diktiergerät: *dictating machine*
dilatorisch: *dilatory*
Ding: krummes ~ *bent job (slang)*
dinglich: *in rem; real*
Diplomat: *diplomat or diplomatist*
diplomatisch: *diplomatic*
Direktabbuchung: *direct debit*
Direktbesteuerung: *direct taxation*
Direktion: *directorate; head office*
Direktive: *directive*
Direktlieferung: *drop shipment*
Direktor: *director; governor; warden* **geschäftsführender** ~ *company or managing director; chief executive; general manager* **nichtgeschäftsführender** ~ *non-executive director* **unternehmensfremder** ~ *outside director*
Direktorenstelle: *directorship*
Direktorium: *directorate*
Direktverkauf: *direct selling; house-to-house selling*
Direktversand *or* **Direktwerbung:** *direct mail; direct mailing*
Diskette: *disk; diskette*
Diskettenlaufwerk: *disk drive*
diskreditieren: *discredit*
Diskrepanz: *discrepancy*
Diskretion: *security*
Diskriminierung: *discrimination*
Diskussion: *discussion*
diskutieren: *argue; discuss*
Dispache: *average adjustment*
Dispens: *faculty*
Dispo-Kredit: *accommodation*
Disput: einen ~ **schlichten** *to adjudicate or to mediate in a dispute*
disqualifizieren: *disqualify*
Dissens: *dissent*
Distanz: auf ~ *at arm's length*
Disziplinargericht für Bundeswehrangehörige: *court-martial*
disziplinarisch bestrafen: *discipline*
Disziplinarverfahren: *disciplinary procedure*
Diverses: *sundry*
Dividende: eine ~ **ausschütten** *to pay a dividend* **keine** ~ **ausschütten** *to pass a dividend*
Dividendenanspruch: *equity*
Dock: ins ~ **gehen** *to dock*
Dockgebühren: *dock dues*
Doktrin: *doctrine*
Dokument: *document*
dokumentarisch: *documentary*
Dokumentation: *documentation*
Dollar: tausend ~ **grand** *(informal)*
dolmetschen: *interpret*

Dolmetscher: *interpreter*
Doppelbesteuerung: *double taxation*
Doppelbesteuerungsabkommen: *double taxation agreement or treaty*
doppeldeutig: *equivocal*
doppelt: *double; dual*
Dotation: *endowment*
Drang: unwiderstehlicher ~ *irresistible impulse*
Draufgeld: *earnest*
drehen: *turn*
Drehung: *turn*
Dreieinigkeit: *Trinity*
dringend: *pressing; urgent*
dringlich: *urgently*
Drittel: *third*
Dritte Lesung: *Third Reading*
Dritter: *third party*
Drittschuldner: *garnishee*
Drittwiderspruchsklage: *interpleader*
Drogen: gesundheitsgefährdende ~ *dangerous drugs*
Drogenabhängiger *or* **Drogensüchtiger:** *drug addict*
Drogenabhängigkeit *or* **Drogensucht:** *drug addiction*
Drogenmißbrauch: *drug abuse*
drohen mit: *threaten*
Drohung: *menace; threat* **gewaltsame ~** *assault*
Drucksache: *printed matter*
Druckschrift: *block capitals or block letters*
Drucktaste: *key*
dulden: *condone*
Duldung: *sufferance* **stillschweigende ~** *connivance*
Duplikat: *counterpart; duplicate*
durchdacht: *reasoned*
Durcheinander: *disorder*
durchführbar: *viable*
Durchführbarkeitstest: *feasibility test*
durchführen: *carry out; effect; implement; realize*
Durchführung: *implementation; realization*
Durchlauf eines Computers: *a computer run*
durchmachen: *experience*
Durchschlag: *carbon copy*
Durchschnitt: im ~ *on an average*
durchschnittlich: *(on an) average*
durchschnittlich betragen: *average*
durchsetzbar: *enforceable* **nicht ~** *unenforceable*
durchsetzen: *enforce*
Durchsetzung: *enforcement*
durchstreichen: *cross out*
durchsuchen: *frisk; search*
Durchsuchung: *search*
Durchsuchungsbefehl: *search warrant*
Durchsuchung von Häusern: *house-to-house search*
dynamisches Unternehmen: *going concern*

Ee

ebenso: *likewise*
echt: *genuine; real* **für ~ erklären** *authenticate*
Echtheit: *genuineness*
Echtzeit: *real time*
Echtzeitsystem: *real-time system*
Ecklohn: *basic pay or basic wage*
Edikt: *edict*
EDV-Servicebüro: *computer bureau*
Effekt: *effect*
Effekten: *securities; stocks and shares*
Effektenbörse: *stock market*
Effektenhandel: *dealing; Stock Exchange operation; stockbroking* **geordnete ~** *fair dealing*
Effektenhändler: *securities trader*
Effektenmakler: *stockbroker*
Effektenmarkt: *securities market*
effektiv: *actual; effective; in real terms*
effizient: *efficient; efficiently*
EG-Beitrittsvertrag: *Treaty of Accession*
EG Kommissar: *EC commissioner*
EG-Recht: *European Community Law*
Ehe: *marriage; matrimony* **nichtige ~** *void marriage*
Ehe-: *conjugal; marital; matrimonial*
Eheaufhebung: *annulment of marriage*
Ehebetrug: *jactitation of marriage (GB)*
ehebrecherisch: *adulterous*
Ehebruch: *adultery*
Ehefrau: *wife* **mißhandelte ~** *battered wife*
Ehegatte *or* **Ehegattin:** *spouse*
ehelich: *conjugal; legitimate; marital; matrimonial* **für ~ erklären** *legitimate*
ehemalig: *ex*
Ehemann: *husband*
Ehesache: *matrimonial cause*
Eheschließung: durch ~ *by marriage*
Ehestand: *coverture*
Ehrabschneidung: *defamation of character*
ehrenamtlich: *honorary*
Ehrenmitglied: *honorary member*
ehrlich: *in good faith; honest; straight*
Ehrlichkeit: *honesty*
Ehrverletzung: *defamation of character*
Eichmeister: *inspector of weights and measures*
Eid: *oath* **einen ~ leisten** *swear* **unter ~ schwören** *abjure*
Eigenbesitz: freier ~ *fee simple*
eigenhändig: *personally*
Eigenkapital: *shareholders' equity or equity capital*
Eigenmacht: verbotene ~ *deforcement*
eigensinnig: *wilful*
eigentlich: *basic; in fact or in point of fact*
Eigentum: *ownership; possession; property* **bewegliches ~** *goods and chattels* **geistiges ~** *intellectual property* **gemeinschaftliches ~** *joint*

ownership **gewerbliches** ~ *industrial property*
öffentliches ~ *public domain* **unbestrittenes** ~
good title
Eigentümer: *owner; proprietor* **wirtschaftlicher** ~
beneficial owner
Eigentümerin: *proprietress*
Eigentumserwerber: unentgeltlicher ~ *volunteer*
Eigentumsnachweis: *abstract of title*
Eigentumsrecht: *proprietary right; title*
Eigentumsrecht an Grundbesitz: *proprietorship*
Eigentumsstörung: *trespass to goods*
Eigentumsübertragung: *transfer of property* **eine**
~ **abschließen** *to complete a conveyance*
Eigentumsveräußerer: unentgeltlicher ~
volunteer
Eigentumsvorbehaltsklausel: *reservation of title
clause*
Eigentumswohnung: *condominium (US)*
Eigentumsübertragungsverfahren:
conveyancing
Eignung: *capacity; fitness for purpose*
Eil-: *express*
Eile: *hurry* **eilen** *to hurry*
eilig: *urgent*
Einbauten: *fixture*
einbehalten: *dock; retain*
Einbehaltung: *detention*
einberufen: *convene*
einbeziehen: *include; incorporate*
einbrechen: *break in*
einbrechen in: *break into; burglarize (informal);
burgle*
Einbrecher: *burglar; housebreaker*
einbringen: *earn; introduce; promote; yield*
Einbringung: *introduction*
Einbringung eines Gesetzentwurfes:
introduction of a Bill
Einbruch: *break-in (informal); breaking and
entering; burglary; housebreaking*
Einbruchsdiebstahl: *burglary*
Einbruchsdiebstahl begehen: *burglarize
(informal); burgle*
einbürgern: wieder ~ *repatriate*
Einbürgerung: *naturalization*
Einbuße: *loss*
einbüßen: *lose*
eindeutig: *unequivocal*
Eindringen: gewaltsames ~ *forcible entry*
Eindruck: *impression*
einfach: *easy; easily; simple*
Einfluß: *influence*
einfordern: *call in; claim*
einfrieren: *freeze*
Einfuhr: *import*
einführen: *import; introduce*
Einfuhrkontingent: *import quota*
Einfuhrlizenz: *import licence*
Einführung: *introduction*
Einfuhrzoll: *customs or import duty; import levy*

Eingabe: *input*
Eingangsdatum: *date of receipt*
eingeben: *feed*
eingebürgert: *naturalized*
eingehen: *incur*
Eingeständnis: *admission*
eingestehen: *acknowledge*
eingetragen: nicht ~ *unregistered*
eingreifen: *interfere; intervene*
Eingriff: *encroachment; interference; intervention*
Einhalt: *check*
einhalten: *hold to; keep; observe* **etwas** ~ *to
comply with something* **nicht** ~ *break; default*
Einhaltung: *compliance; observance*
einheimisch: *domestic*
Einheitssatz: *flat rate; standard rate*
Einheitssteuersatz: *standard rate*
Einheitsvertrag: *standard form contract*
Einheitswert: *rateable value*
einheizen: jdm ~ *to make things hot for someone*
einkaufen: *purchase* **etwas** ~ *to shop (for)
something*
Einkäufer: *buyer*
Einkaufsleiter: *head buyer*
einklagbar: *actionable; enforceable*
Einkommen: *earnings; income; revenue* **festes** ~
fixed income **steuerpflichtiges** ~ *taxable income*
verfügbares ~ *disposable income*
Einkommen mit Quellenbesteuerung: *income
which is taxed at source*
Einkommensteuer: *income tax*
Einkommensteuererklärung: *declaration of
income* **eine** ~ **abgeben** *to make a return to the tax
office or to make an income tax return*
Einkommensteuergruppen: *tax schedules*
Einkommensteuersatz: niedrigster ~ *basic rate
tax*
Einkommensstufe: *income bracket*
Einkünfte: *earnings; income; receipts; revenue*
einladen: *invite*
Einladung: *invitation*
Einlage: *deposit*
Einlagenbank: *licensed deposit-taker*
Einleger: *depositor*
einleiten: *institute*
einleitend: *opening*
Einleitung: *preamble*
Einleitungsformel: *caption*
einliefern: *commit*
Einlieferung: *commitment*
Einlieferungsbefehl: *committal warrant*
einlochen: *nick (slang)*
einlösbar: *redeemable* **nicht** ~ *irredeemable*
einlösen: nicht ~ *dishonour*
einmischen: sich ~ *interfere; intervene*
Einmischung: *interference; intervention*
Einmütigkeit: *consensus ad idem*
Einnahmen: *receipts; revenue; take*

einnehmen: *take*
Einnehmer: *collector*
Einöde: *waste*
einordnen: *class*
Einräumung: *concession*
einrechnen: *allow for*
Einrede: *exception*
Einrede der Rechtshängigkeit: *lis alibi pendens*
einreichen: *file; prefer; submit*
Einreichung: *filing*
Einreiseerlaubnis: *entry permit*
Einreisekarte: *landing card*
Einreisevisum: *entry visa*
einrichten: *arrange; establish; institute; open*
einrücken: *indent*
Einrückung: *indent*
Einsatz: *input; wager*
Einsatzzentrale: *incident room*
einschätzen: *appraise; evaluate*
Einschätzung: *estimation; evaluation; measurement*
einschiffen: *embark*
Einschiffung: *embarkation*
Einschiffungshafen: *port of embarkation*
einschließen: *include*
einschließlich: *including; inclusive*
einschränken: *limit; qualify; restrict*
einschränkend: *limiting; restrictive*
Einschränkung: *limitation; reservation; restraint; restriction* **vertragsmäßige** ~ *restrictive covenant*
Einschränkungen: mit ~ *qualified*
Einschreibebrief: *registered letter*
Einschreiben: *recorded delivery; registered letter* **per** ~ **schicken** *register*
Einschreiten: *intervention*
einschüchtern: *intimidate*
Einschüchterung: *undue influence; intimidation*
einseitig: *ex parte; unilateral*
einsetzen: *appoint; institute; use* **sich** ~ *campaign*
Einsetzung: *appointment*
Einsicht nehmen: *inspect*
einsparen: *save*
einsperren: *confine; imprison; incarcerate; lock up; pinch (informal); put away*
einspringen: für jdn ~ *stand in for*
Einspruch: *defence or defense (US); veto*
Einspruch einlegen: *to enter a caveat*
Einspruch erheben: *object; oppose*
Einspruch Erhebender: *caveator*
Einspruch erheben gegen: *veto*
Einspruchseinlegung: *notice of opposition*
Einspruchsrecht: *(right of) veto*
einstehen für: *vouch for*
einsteigen: *board; enter*
einstellen: *drop; employ; engage; regulate; stay*
Einstellung: zeitweilige ~ *suspension*
Einstellung des Verfahrens: *stay of proceedings*

Einstellungsschreiben: *letter of appointment*
Einstellungsverfügung: *nolle prosequi*
einstimmig: *unanimous*
einstufen: *classify*
Einstufung: *classification*
einstweilig: *in the interim; interlocutory; temporary*
Eintrag: *entry* **einen** ~ **zurückbuchen** *to contra an entry*
eintragen: *enter; put down; register* **sich** ~ *register*
einträglich: *lucrative; profitable*
Eintragung: *entering; recording; registration* **amtliche** ~ *incorporation*
Eintragung des Urteils: *entry of judgment*
Eintragungsbescheinigung: *certificate of registration; registration certificate*
Eintragungsbuch: *register*
Eintragungsnummer: *registration number*
eintreibbar: *recoverable*
eintreiben: *collect*
Eintreibung: *collection*
Eintreten: *advocacy*
Eintritt: *admission; admission or entry charge; entry*
Eintritt in Rechte: *subrogation*
Eintrittsgebühr: *admission or entry charge*
einverstanden: sich ~ **erklären** *to agree to do something*
Einwand: *demur* **einen** ~ **erheben** *to raise an objection* **rechtshemmender** ~ *estoppel*
Einwanderer: *immigrant*
Einwand erheben: *demur; object*
einwandern: *immigrate*
Einwanderung: *immigration*
Einwanderungsgesetze: *Immigration Laws*
Einweg-: *disposable; non-returnable*
Einweg(ver)packung: *non-returnable packing*
einweisen: *commit*
Einweisung: *commitment*
Einwendung: *exception*
Einwendungen: sich ~ **vorbehalten** *to reserve one's defence* ~ **machen** *demur*
einwilligen: *consent*
Einwilligung: *consent*
Einwilligungsalter: *age of consent*
Einwirkung: *influence*
einzahlen: *deposit*
Einzahler: *depositor*
Einzahlung: *deposit*
Einzahlungsaufforderung: *call*
Einzahlungsschalter: *receiving office*
Einzel-: *individual*
Einzelbesitzverhältnis: *several tenancy*
Einzelblatteinzug: *sheet feed*
Einzelfallrecht: *case law*
Einzelhaft: *solitary confinement*
Einzelhandel: *retail*
Einzelhandelsgeschäft: *retail shop*

Einzelhandelspreis: *retail price*
Einzelhändler: *retailer*
Einzelheit: *detail*
Einzelheiten: *particulars*
Einzelkaufmann: *sole trader*
einzeln: *separate; several*
Einzelperson: *individual*
Einzelrichter ohne Öffentlichkeit: *judge in chambers*
einziehbar: nicht ~ *irrecoverable*
einziehen: *collect; indent; levy; seize*
Einziehung: *collection; seizure*
Einzug: *feed; indent*
Elan: *drive*
elementar: *basic*
Elend: *hardship*
Eltern: leibliche ~ *natural parents*
E-Mail: *electronic mail*
Embargo: ein ~ aufheben *to lift an embargo* **ein ~ verhängen** *embargo* **einem ~ unterliegen** *to be under an embargo*
Emigrant: *emigrant*
Emigration: *emigration*
emigrieren: *emigrate*
Emission: *issue; issuance*
Emission neuer Aktien: *issue of new shares or share issue*
Emissionsbank: *issuing bank or issuing house*
Emissionskurs: *issued price; offer price*
Emissionsprospekt: *prospectus*
Emission von Schuldverschreibungen: *debenture issue or issue of debentures*
emittieren: *issue*
Empfang: *receipt; receiving*
Empfang bestätigen: *receipt*
empfangen: *receive*
Empfänger: *consignee; grantee; receiver; recipient; transferee*
Empfänger einer Jahresrente: *annuitant*
Empfangsbestätigung: *receipt*
Empfangsdatum: *date of receipt*
empfehlen: *advise; recommend; suggest*
Empfehlung: *advice; recommendation; suggestion*
Endbetrag: *(grand) total*
Ende einer Sitzungsperiode: *prorogation*
enden: *terminate*
endgültig: *firm*
Endlospapier: *continuous stationery*
Endlospapiereinzug: *continuous feed*
Endprodukt: *end or final or finished product*
Endverbraucher: *ultimate consumer; end user*
engagieren: *engage*
Engpaß: *bottleneck*
Enquetekommissionsbericht: *Green Paper*
Entblößung: unsittliche ~ *indecent exposure*
entdecken: *detect; discover*
Entdeckung: *detection*
Enteignung: *compulsory purchase; condemnation*

Enteignungsbeschluß *or* **Enteignungsverfügung:** *compulsory purchase order*
enterben: *disinherit*
entfernen: *remove*
entfernt: *remote*
Entfremdung: *alienation of affection*
entführen: *abduct; hijack; kidnap*
Entführer: *abductor; hijacker; kidnapper*
Entführung: *abduction; hijack; hijacking; kidnapping*
entgegengesetzt: *reverse*
entgegnen: *reply*
entgehen: *evade*
Entgelt: für geringes ~ *for a small consideration*
enthalten: *contain; hold; include* **sich ~** *abstain*
Enthaltung: *abstention*
enthaupten: *behead; decapitate*
Enthauptung: *decapitation*
enthüllen: *disclose; divulge; expose; reveal*
Enthüllung: *disclosure; exposure*
Enthüllung vertraulicher Informationen: *disclosure of confidential information*
Entkommen: *escape*
Entlarvung: *detection*
entlassen: *discharge; release* **jdn ~** *to fire someone; to make someone redundant; to sack someone*
entlassen werden: *to get the sack*
Entlassung: *discharge; dismissal; release; removal; sacking; severance* **bedingte ~** *parole; release on licence* **fristlose ~** *summary dismissal* **unbeschränkte ~** *absolute discharge* **ungerechtfertigte ~** *unfair dismissal* **unrechtmäßige** *or* **widerrechtliche ~** *wrongful dismissal*
Entlassungsabfindung: *compensation for loss of office; redundancy payment; severance pay*
Entlassungsentschädigung: *compensation for loss of office*
Entlassungsverfahren: *dismissal procedure*
entlasten: *exonerate*
Entlastung: *exoneration*
Entlastung des Konkursschuldners: *discharge in bankruptcy*
Entlastungszeuge: *defence witness or witness for the defence*
Entlegenheit: *remoteness*
Entleiher: *borrower*
entlocken: *extract*
Entnahmen: *drawings*
entnehmen: *gather*
entschädigen: *compensate; indemnify*
Entschädigung: *compensation; damages; indemnification; indemnity; restitution*
Entschädigungsangebot: schriftliches ~ *offer of amends*
Entschädigungssumme: *quantum*
entscheiden: *adjudicate; decide; hold; judge; rule*

Entscheidung: *adjudication; decision; ruling*
außergerichtliche ~ *award* **gerichtliche** ~ *rule*
Entscheidungsbehörde für Verbrechensopfer: *Criminal Injuries Compensation Board*
Entscheidungsfindung: *decision making*
Entscheidungsgewalt: *discretion; executive power*
Entscheidungsgrund: *ratio decidendi*
Entscheidungsgründe: nicht tragende ~ *obiter dicta*
Entscheidungsprozeß: *decision-making processes*
Entscheidungsträger: *decision maker*
Entscheidungs- und Urteilssammlung: *Law Reports*
entschieden: noch nicht ~ *sub judice*
entschließen: sich ~ *decide*
Entschließung: gemeinsame ~ *joint resolution (US)*
Entschluß: *decision*
entschuldigen: *condone; excuse* **sich** ~ *apologize*
Entschuldigung: *apology; excuse*
entsinnen: sich ~ *remember*
entsprechen: *conform; to correspond with something; meet*
entsprechend: *accordingly; consistent; pursuant to*
Entstehen: im ~ **begriffen** *inchoate*
entstehen: *arise; to come into existence; originate*
entthronen: *depose*
entweichen: *escape*
entwenden: *steal*
entwerfen: *draft; outline*
Entwerfer: *draftsman*
entwickeln: *develop*
Entwicklung: *development*
Entwicklungen: ökonomische ~ *economic trends*
Entwurf: *rough copy; draft; outline; plan*
entziehen: jdm etwas ~ *to deprive someone of something* **sich** ~ *abscond; evade*
Entziehung des Grundbesitzes: *dispossession*
Entziehung eines Vermächtnisses: *ademption*
Entzug der Fahrerlaubnis: *driving disqualification*
Erbe: *beneficiary; heir; inheritance; inheritor* **gesetzlicher** *or* **rechtmäßiger** ~ *heir apparent* **mutmaßlicher** ~ *heir presumptive*
Erbe des Restnachlasses: *residuary legatee*
erben: *inherit*
Erben und Rechtsnachfolger: *heirs and assigns*
Erbfolge: *descent; succession* **gesetzliche** ~ *intestate succession*
Erbin: *beneficiary; heiress; inheritor*
erbitten: *seek*
Erblasser: *testator*
Erblasserin: *testatrix*
erblich: *hereditary*
Erbpachtzins: *ground rent*
Erbrecht: *law of succession*

erbringen: *adduce; yield*
Erbschaft: *inheritance; succession*
Erbschaftssteuer: *death or estate duty; death or estate tax*
Erbschaftsverwalterin: *administratrix*
Erbschein: *grant of probate*
Erbstück: *heirloom*
ereignen: sich ~ *occur*
Ereignis: *event* **kriegsauslösendes** ~ *casus belli* **unvorhergesehenes** ~ *contingency*
ererbt: *hereditary*
erfahren: *experience(d)*
Erfahrung: *experience*
erfassen: *register*
Erfassung: *registration*
erfinden: *invent*
Erfinder: *inventor*
Erfindung: *invention*
erfolglos: *unsuccessful*
Erfolgshonorar: *contingent fee (US)*
erforderlich machen: *entail*
erfordern: *require*
Erfordernis: *requirement*
erfüllen: *carry out; execute; fulfil; meet; perform; satisfy* **nicht** ~ *default* **noch zu** ~ *executory*
Erfüllung: *compliance; execution; performance* **vergleichsweise** ~ *accord and satisfaction*
Erfüllungsort: *place of performance*
Erfüllungsverweigerung: *repudiation*
ergeben: *total* **sich** ~ *arise; surrender*
Ergebnis: *outcome*
Erhalt: *receipt*
erhalten: *get; maintain; obtain; poll; receive*
erhältlich: *available; obtainable*
Erhaltung: *maintenance*
Erhängen: *hanging*
erhärten: *corroborate*
erhärtend: *corroborative*
Erhärtung: *corroboration*
erheben: *file; impose; levy; prefer*
erheblich: *considerable; considerably; substantial*
Erhebung: *filing*
erhöhen: *increase; raise; to scale up* **sich** ~ *rise*
Erhöhung: *increase; rise* **eine** ~ **bekanntgeben** *to post an increase*
erholen: sich ~ *pick up; recover*
erinnern: *remind* **sich** ~ *recall; remember*
erkennen: *recognize*
Erkenntnis: *realization*
Erkennungsmarke: *identity disk*
erklären: *declare; explain; find; return*
erklärend: *explanatory*
erklärt: *declared*
Erklärung: *declaration; explanation; representation; zoning* **eidesstattliche** ~ *affirmation; statutory declaration* **eine** ~ **abgeben** *to make a statement* **einseitige** ~ *deed poll* **öffentliche** ~ *official return*

Erklärung abgeben: *declare*

Erklärung von Kontenabstimmungsdifferenzen: *reconciliation statement*

erkundigen: sich ~ *inquire; query*

Erkundigungen einziehen: *inquire*

erlangen: *derive; gain*

Erlaß: *act; decree; edict; issuance* **königlicher ~** *Order in Council*

Erlaß des Urteils: *entry of judgment*

Erlaß eines Gesetzes: *enactment*

erlassen: *enact; issue; let off; remit*

erlauben: *allow; permit*

Erlaubnis: *leave; licence or license (US); permission; permit* **ohne ~ abheuern** *to jump ship*

Erlaubnisschein: *permit*

erlaubt: *allowable*

erläuternd: *explanatory*

Erläuterung: *gloss*

Erläuterungswerk: *commentary*

erleben: *experience*

erledigen: *handle*

Erledigung: *handling*

Erlös: *profit*

erlöschen: *expire*

Erlöschen: *expiration; expiry; extinction; lapse*

Erlöschen durch Erfüllung: *discharge*

Erlöschen Gläubiger: *discharge*

ermächtigen: *authorize; empower*

Ermächtigung: *authorization; power*

Ermächtigungsgesetz: *enabling legislation or statute*

ermäßigen: *reduce*

ermäßigt: *reduced*

Ermäßigung: *reduction*

Ermessen: *discretion*

ermitteln: *calculate; establish; investigate*

Ermittler: *detective*

Ermittlung: *inquiry; investigation*

Ermittlungsbeamter: *investigator*

Ermittlungskommission: *a fact-finding delegation*

ermöglichen: *enable*

ermutigen: *encourage*

Ernannte(r): *appointee*

ernennen: *appoint; designate*

Ernennung: *appointment*

Ernennungsschreiben or Ernennungsurkunde: *letter of appointment*

erneuern: *renew*

Erneuerung: *novation; renewal*

erneut beantragen/bewerben: *reapply*

erneut vernehmen: *re-examine*

erneut verurteilen: *re-convict*

Ernst: *seriousness*

ernsthaft: *serious*

Ernteertrag: *emblements*

erobern: *capture*

eröffnen: *lead; open*

Eröffnung: *opening*

Eröffnungsbestand: *opening stock*

Eröffnungsbetrag: *opening balance*

Eröffnungsbuchung: *opening entry*

Eröffnungsgebot: *opening bid*

Eröffnungskurs: *opening price*

Eröffnungssitzung: *opening session*

erörtern: *debate; discuss*

Erörterung: *discussion; interlocutory matter; mention*

erpressen: *blackmail; extort*

Erpresser: *blackmailer; extortionist; racketeer*

Erpressung: *blackmail; demanding with menaces; extortion* **verbrecherische ~** *extortion racket*

Erpressung von Schutzgeld: *protection racket*

Erprobung: *trial*

Errichter eines Trusts: *settlor*

Ersatz: *restitution; substitute*

Ersatzteil: *spare part*

Ersatzzustellung: *substituted service*

erscheinen: *appear*

erschießen: *gun down*

Erschießungskommando: *firing squad*

erschließen: *develop*

Erschließung: *development; planning* **industrielle ~** *industrial development*

erschöpfen: *exhaust*

erschwert: *aggravated*

Erschwerung: *aggravation*

ersetzen: *substitute; supersede*

Ersitzung: *prescription*

erstatten: *refund; reimburse; repay*

Erstattung der Anzeige: *laying (an) information*

erstattungsfähig: nicht ~ *non-refundable*

erstehen: *purchase*

Erstgeburt: *primogeniture*

Erstgeburtsrecht: *primogeniture*

Ersthypothek: *first mortgage*

erstklassig: *first-class*

Ersttäter: *first offender*

ersuchen: *pray; request; seek*

ersuchend: *precatory*

Ertrag: *return; yield*

Erträge: keinerlei ~ *nil return*

ertraglos: *dead*

ertragreich: *profitable; profitably*

Erwachsener: *adult*

erwägen: *entertain*

Erwägung: *consideration* **in ~ ziehen** *entertain*

erwählen: *elect*

erwähnen: *mention; name; refer*

erwähnt: wie schon ~ *as aforesaid*

erwarten: *await; expect* **zu ~ probable**

erwartungsgemäß: *duly*

Erwerb: *acquisition; purchase*

erwerben: *acquire; gain; purchase*

Erwerber: *purchaser*
Erwerbslosen: die ~ *the unemployed*
Erwerbstätigkeit: *gainful employment*
vorübergehende ~ *temporary employment*
erwidern: *reply*
Erwiderung: *rejoinder; reply*
Erwiderungsrecht: *right of reply*
erwirken: *obtain; secure*
erwischen: *cop (slang)*
Erzeugnisse: einheimische ~ *home-produced products*
Erzeugung: *production*
Erziehungsanstalt: *borstal*
erzielen: *derive; reach; realize*
erzwingbar: *enforceable*
erzwingen: *enforce; extort*
Erzwingung: *enforcement; extortion*
eskalieren: *escalate*
Etat: den ~ **ausgleichen** *to balance the budget*
Etikette: *etiquette*
europäisch: *European*
Europäische: das ~ **Parlament** *the European Parliament* das ~ **Währungssystem** *the European Monetary System* die ~ **Gemeinschaft** *the European Community*
Europäische Kommission: *Commission of the European Community*
Europäischer Gerichtshof: *European Court of Justice*
Europa-Parlament: das ~ *the Assembly of the EC*
Euthanasie: *euthanasia; mercy killing*
Eventualität: *contingency*
Eventualversicherung: *contingent policy*
Examen: *examination*
Exekutionskommando: *firing squad*
exekutiv: *executive*
Exekutive: die ~ *the Executive (US)*
Exekutivgewalt: *executive powers*
Exekutivorder: *executive order (US)*
exemplarisch: jdn ~ **bestrafen** *to make an example of someone*
Exil: *exile*
Existenz: *existence*
existieren: *exist*
exklusiv: *select*
exklusive: *exclusive of*
Experte: *expert; specialist*
Expertengruppe: *panel of experts*
Expertin: *expert; specialist*
Expertise: *expert's report*
explosiv: *explosive*
Export: *export*
Exporterstattung: *export restitution*
Exportgenehmigung: *export permit*
Exporthandel: *export trade*
exportieren: *export*
Exportlizenz: *export licence*
Express: per ~ *express*

extern: *outside*
Exterritorialität: *extra-territoriality*

Ff

Fabrikarbeiter: *operative*
Facharbeiter: *skilled labour*
Fachhandel: *specialist*
Fachkenntnisse: *know-how*
fachlich: *professional*
Fachmann: *expert; professional; specialist*
fachmännisch: *professional*
Fachmesse: *trade fair*
Fachwissen: *expertise*
Fachzeitschrift: *trade paper*
facto: de ~ *de facto*
Factor: *(debt) factor*
Factoring: *factoring*
fähig: *capable; competent*
fähig sein zu: *capable of*
Fahne: *flag*
Fahnenflucht: *desertion*
Fahnenflüchtiger: *deserter*
fahnenflüchtig werden: *desert*
Fahrbahn: *carriageway*
Fahren: fahrlässiges ~ *careless driving; driving without due care and attention* grob fahrlässiges *or* rücksichtsloses *or* verkehrsgefährdendes ~ *reckless driving*
Fahrkartenschalter: *booking or ticket office*
fahrlässig: *careless; negligent*
Fahrlässigkeit: *negligence; recklessness* grobe ~ *gross negligence* schuldhafte ~ *culpable negligence* strafbare ~ *criminal negligence*
Fahrplan: *timetable*
fair: *equitable; fair; just*
Faksimile: *facsimile (copy)*
Faktor: beitragender ~ *contributory factor* entscheidender ~ *deciding factor*
Faktoren: zyklische ~ *cyclical factors*
Faktum: *fact*
Fakultät: juristische ~ *law school*
fakultativ: *optional*
Fall: *case; instance* der vorliegende ~ *the instant case* ein aussichtsloser *or* unverbesserlicher ~ *a hard case* entschiedener ~ *decided case* zu ~ **bringen** *defeat*
Fallbeil: *guillotine*
Falle: eine ~ **stellen** *frame (informal)* im ~ *in the event of or that*
fallen: *drop; fall*
fallen aus: *to fall outside*
fallenlassen: *withdraw*
fallen unter: *to fall within*
fällig: *due; payable*
Fälligkeitstag: *expiry date*
Fälligkeitstermin: *maturity*

fällig werden: *to fall due or to become due; expire*
Fälligwerden: *expiration*
Fallsammlung: *digest*
falsch: *dud; false; fictitious; incorrectly; sham; untrue; wrong*
falsch auszählen: *miscount*
falsch berechnen: *miscalculate*
falsch darstellen: *misrepresent*
fälschen: *counterfeit; fake; falsify; forge*
Fälschen: *forgery*
fälschlicherweise: *wrongly*
Falschspieler: *card sharper*
Fälschung: *counterfeiting; fake; forgery*
falsch zählen: *miscount*
Familiengesellschaft: *family company*
Familienheim: *homestead (US)*
Familienname: *surname*
Familienrecht: *family law*
Familienunternehmen: *family company*
fassen: *hold*
Fassung: *draft; version*
Fassungsvermögen: *capacity*
FBI: *Federal Bureau of Investigation (FBI) (US)*
Fehlanzeige: *nil return*
Fehlberechnung: *miscalculation*
fehlen an: *lack*
Fehler: *defect; error; failing; fault; imperfection; mistake; slip-up* **sichtbarer** ~ *apparent defect*
fehlerhaft: *defective; faulty; imperfect; incorrect*
fehlerlos: *perfect; perfectly*
Fehlerquote: *error rate*
Fehlverhalten: vorsätzliches ~ *wilful misconduct*
Feierabend machen: *knock off*
Feiertag: *bank holiday; public holiday* **gesetzlicher** ~ *statutory holiday; legal holiday; public holiday*
Feind: zum ~ **überlaufen** *defect*
feindlich *or* **feindselig:** *hostile*
Feingehaltsstempel: *assay mark; hallmark*
Feldfrüchte: *emblements*
Ferne: *remoteness*
Ferngespräch: *trunk call or long-distance call*
Fernhochschule: *correspondence college*
fertigbringen: es ~ *to manage to*
fertigstellen: *complete*
Fertigstellung: *completion*
Fertigstellungstermin: *completion date*
Fertigung: *production*
fertigwerden: *cope*
fest: *firm; fixed; hard; permanent*
Festgeld: *fixed deposit*
Festgenommener: *detainee*
festhalten: *hold*
festhalten an: *hold to*
festigen: sich ~ *firm*
Festkosten: *overhead or general or running expenses*

festlegen: *determine; fix; to lay down; put; schedule; settle; state*
Festlegung: *fixing*
Festnahme: *apprehension* **ungesetzliche** ~ *false imprisonment* **vorläufige** ~ *summary arrest*
Festnahmeanordnung: *warrant of attachment*
festnehmen: *apprehend; arrest; attach; detain; pick up (informal)*
Festplatte: *hard disk*
Festpreis: *firm price*
Festpreisvereinbarung: *fixed-price agreement*
festsetzen: *determine; evaluate; fix; lay down; put; stipulate*
Festsetzung: *evaluation; fixing*
feststellen: *establish; state*
Feststellung: *statement*
Feststellung des Feingehalts: *assay*
Feststellungsurteil: *declaratory judgment*
fest verschließen: *seal*
Feuer: *fire*
Feueralarm: *fire alarm*
Feuer fangen: *to catch fire*
feuerfest: *fireproof*
Feuergefahr: *fire hazard or risk*
Feuerleiter: *fire escape*
Feuermelder: *fire alarm*
feuern: *fire*
Feuerschutzbestimmungen: *fire regulations*
feuersicher: *fireproof*
Feuertreppe: *fire escape*
Feuertür: *fire door*
Feuerversicherung: *fire insurance* **eine** ~ **abschließen** *to take out an insurance against fire*
fiat justicia: *fiat justicia*
Fideikommiß: *entail*
FIFO-Abschreibungsmethode: *first in first out*
fiktiv: *fictitious*
Filiale: *branch (office)*
Filialleiter: *branch manager*
Finanz-: *budgetary; fiscal*
Finanzamt: *Inland Revenue or Internal Revenue Service (US)*
Finanzausschuß: *Committee of Ways and Means*
Finanzbeamter: *revenue officer*
Finanzberater: *financial adviser*
Finanzbericht: *financial statement*
Finanzbuchhalter: *management accountant*
Finanzen: *finance*
Finanzgesetz: *Finance Act (GB)*
Finanzhilfe: *financial assistance*
finanziell: *financial; pecuniary*
finanziell abhängig: *dependent*
finanziell unterstützen: *support*
finanzieren: *finance*
Finanzierungsgesellschaft: *finance company or corporation*
Finanzinstitut: *financial institution*
Finanzmanager: *treasurer*

Finanzminister: *Chancellor of the Exchequer (UK); Secretary of the Treasury (US)*

Finanzministerium: das ~ *the Treasury*

Finanzplanung: *budgeting*

Finanzprüfung: *financial review*

Finanzverwalter: ehrenamtlicher ~ *honorary treasurer*

Finanzverwaltung: *Inland Revenue or Internal Revenue Service (US)*

finden: *find*

Fingerabdruck: *fingerprint* **Fingerabdrücke dabs** *(slang)* **Fingerabdrücke nehmen** *to fingerprint*

fingieren: *fake*

Firma: *company; establishment; firm; Messrs* **eine angesehene** ~ *company of good standing* **eine** ~ **auflösen** *or* **liquidieren** *to wind up a company* **eine** ~ **gründen** *to set up a company*

Firmen-: *corporate*

Firmenansehen: *goodwill*

Firmengründer: *company promoter*

Firmengründung: *promotion of a company*

Firmenname: *business or corporate name*

Firmenregister: *register of companies or companies' register*

Firmensiegel: *common seal or company's seal*

Firmenvorstand: *board*

Fixbelastung: *fixed charge*

Fixkosten: *fixed expenses; fixed costs*

Flächenmaß: *square measure*

Flagge: eine ~ **führen** *to fly a flag*

flagranti: in ~ *in flagrante delicto*

Floppy Disk: *floppy disk*

flüchten: *escape*

flüchtig: *casual; fugitive*

Flüchtiger: *fugitive*

Flugsicherheit: *airport security*

Fluktuation: *staff turnover or turnover of staff* **natürliche** ~ *natural wastage*

Flußdiagramm: *flow chart*

Folge: zur ~ **haben** *entail*

Folge leisten: *obey*

folgen: *follow; succeed*

folgend: *ensuing; subsequent*

folgende: und ~ *et seq. or et sequenter*

folgenden: im ~ *hereafter; hereinafter*

Folgeprämie: *renewal premium*

folgern: *deduce; gather; infer*

Folgerung: *deduction*

Folgeschreiben: *follow-up letter*

Folterknecht: *torturer*

foltern: *torture*

Fonds: *fund*

förderlich: *conducive*

fordern: *ask for; claim; demand; require*

fördern: *encourage; promote*

Forderung: *claim; demand; requirement* **bevorrechtigte** ~ *preferential debt* **eine** ~ **anmelden** *to prove a debt* **eine** ~ **regulieren** *to settle*

a claim **uneinbringliche** ~ *bad or irrecoverable debt*

Forderungen: *receivables* **anmeldbare** ~ *provable debts*

Forderungsberechtigter: *obligee*

Forderungseinziehung: *debt collection or collecting*

Förderungsgebiet: *development area or zone; enterprise zone*

forensisch: *forensic*

Forfaitierung von Aktien: *forfeiture of shares*

forma: pro ~ *pro forma*

Formalität: *formality*

formaljuristisch: *technical*

Formblatt: *form*

Formbrief: *standard (form) letter*

Form der Klageerhebung: *originating summons*

formell *or* **förmlich:** *formal; formally*

Formsache: *technicality*

Formular: *form*

Formular zur Aktienübertragung: *stock transfer form*

Formulieren: *drafting*

formulieren: *formulate; word*

Formulierung: *form of words; wording*

Forschungsinstitut: *research institute*

fortan: *henceforth*

fortfahren: *proceed; pursue*

Fortführung: *continuation*

fortlaufend: *consecutive; continuous*

Fortschreiten: *progress*

Fortschritt: *progress*

Fortschrittsbericht: *progress report*

fortsetzen: *continue; proceed; pursue*

Fortsetzung: *continuation*

Forum: *forum*

Fracht: *freight*

Frachtbrief: *shipping note*

Frachtgebühren: *freight rates*

Frachtkosten: *freight charges or freight rates*

Frachtnachnahme: *carriage forward or freight forward*

Fracht- und Löschungskosten: *landed costs*

Frage: *matter; query; question* **in** ~ **stellen** *challenge; query; question* **zu entscheidende** ~ *point at issue*

Fragebogen: *questionnaire*

fragen: *ask*

Fragestunde: *Question Time*

fragwürdig: *shady*

Fraktionszwang: *three line whip*

Franchise: *franchise*

Franchise-Basis: auf ~ **vergeben** *franchise*

Franchisegeber: *franchiser*

Franchisenehmer: *franchisee*

Franchising: *franchising*

frankieren: *frank; stamp*

Frankiermaschine: *franking machine*

franko: *franco*
Frau: *wife* **gnädige** ~ *Madam* **unverheiratete** ~ **feme sole verheiratete** ~ *feme covert* **Frau Vorsitzende** *Madam Chairman*
frei: *clear; free; at liberty; vacant*
"frei": *"for hire"*
Frei an Bord: *free on board (f.o.b.)*
freiberuflich: *freelance* **freiberuflich tätig sein** *to freelance*
Freigabe: *deregulation*
Freigang: *association*
Freigänger: *category "D" prisoners*
freigeben: *decontrol; release*
Freihafen: *free port*
Freihandel: *free trade*
Freihandelszone: *free trade zone or area*
Freiheit: *freedom; liberty* **in** ~ *at liberty*
Freiheiten: staatsbürgerliche ~ *civil liberties*
Freiheitsberaubung: *false imprisonment*
Freiheitsentzug: *incarceration*
Freiheitsstrafe: *custodial sentence; term of imprisonment* **lebenslängliche** ~ *life imprisonment; life sentence*
freikaufen: *ransom*
freilassen: *discharge; free; release*
Freilassung: *release*
freisprechen: *acquit* **jdn** ~ *to clear someone of charges*
Freispruch: *acquittal*
freistellen: *release*
Freistellung: *release*
freiwillig: *ex gratia; unsolicited; voluntary; voluntarily* **sich** ~ **melden** *volunteer*
Freiwilliger: *volunteer*
Freizeichnungsklausel: *exclusion or exemption clause*
Fremdenverkehrsamt: *information bureau or office*
Fremdkapital: *borrowings; loan capital*
Fremdwährung: *foreign currency*
Frieden: *peace*
Friedenspflicht (bei Arbeitskämpfen): *cooling off period or cooling time (US)*
Friedensrichter: *squire (US)*
frisieren: *fiddle (informal)*
Frist: *time limit* **eine** ~ **einhalten** *to meet a deadline*
Fristeinlagen: *term shares*
Fristen: die ~ **einhalten** *to keep within the time limits or within the time schedule*
Fristverlängerung: *extension of time*
Fristverlängerungsantrag: *time summons*
früher sterben als: *predecease*
frühzeitig: *at an early date; early*
führen: *conduct; handle; keep; lead; manage; run; stock*
führend: *leading*
führen zu: *lead (up) to*
Führer: *leader*

Führer der Warenzeichenrolle: *registrar of trademarks*
Führer des Unterhauses: *Leader of the House*
Führerschein: *driving licence*
Führung: *direction* **gute** ~ *good behaviour*
Führungs-: *managerial*
Führungskraft: *executive* **obere** ~ *senior manager or senior executive*
Führungskräften: nach ~ **suchen** *headhunt*
Führungsnachwuchs: *management trainee*
Fuhrunternehmen: *carrier*
fundamental: *fundamental*
Fünfjahresplan: *Five-Year Plan*
fungieren: *act*
Funkstreifenwagen: *squad car*
Funktion: *function*
funktionieren: *function*
für: *on behalf of; in favour of; pro*
für sich: *per se*
Fürsorge: *care; welfare*
Fürsorgekind: *child in care*
Fürsorgeverfahren: *care proceedings*
Fusion: *merger* **gegenläufige** ~ *reverse takeover*
fusionieren: *merge*
Fusionskontrollorgan: *Takeover Panel*
Fuß: auf freiem ~ *free; at large*
Fußgängerzone: *pedestrian or shopping precinct*

Gg

Galgen: *gallows*
Gangster: *gangster; mobster (US); racketeer*
Ganove: *hoodlum (US); villain (informal)*
ganz: *clear; in full; fully; outright; whole*
Garant: *guarantor; surety; warrantor*
Garant einer Effektenemission: *underwriter*
Garantie: *guarantee; surety; warranty*
Garantieempfänger: *warrantee*
garantieren: *guarantee; warrant*
Garantieschein: *guarantee*
Garantieverletzung: *breach of warranty*
Gaskammer: *gas chamber*
Gaststätte: *public house*
Gattin: *wife*
Gattung: *kind*
Gattungsvermächtnis: **beschränktes** ~ *demonstrative legacy*
Gauner: *crook (slang); racketeer*
Gaunerei: *racket*
Geächteter: *outlaw*
Gebäude: *property* **das** ~ **räumen** *to vacate the premises* **im** ~ *on the premises*
geben: *allow; give* **von sich** ~ *utter*
Gebiet: *district; territory*
Gebietsansprüche: *territorial claims*

Gebietshoheit besitzen: *to have sovereignty over a territory*

Gebietsleiter: *area manager*

Gebot: *bid*

Gebrauch: *usage; use*

gebrauchen: *exercise*

Gebrauchsanweisungen: *directions for use*

Gebrauchsgegenstände: *persönliche* ~ *private effects*

Gebühr: *charge; fee; rate* **symbolische** ~ *token charge*

Gebühr bezahlt Empfänger: *charges forward*

gebührenfrei: *free of charge*

Gebührenordnung: *scale of charges or of prices* **verbindliche** ~ *fixed scale of charges*

gebührenpflichtig: *chargeable*

gebunden: *fixed*

Geburt: *birth*

Geburtenrate: *birth rate*

Geburtstag und Geburtsort: *date and place of birth*

Geburtsurkunde: *birth certificate*

Gedankengang: *reasoning*

geeignet: *suitable*

Gefahr: *danger; hazard; peril; risk*

gefährden: *endanger; jeopardize*

gefährdet sein: *to be in jeopardy*

Gefahrenzulage: *danger money*

Gefahr laufen: *to be in danger of; to be in jeopardy; to run a risk*

gefährlich: *dangerous*

Gefälligkeit: *accommodation* **aus** ~ *as a favour*

Gefälligkeitswechsel: *accommodation bill*

gefälscht: *counterfeit; dud*

Gefangener: *captive; prisoner*

gefangenhalten: *hold; imprison*

gefangennehmen: wieder ~ *recapture*

Gefangenschaft: *captivity*

Gefängnis: *imprisonment; jail or gaol; penitentiary (US); prison* **im** ~ *inside (slang)*

Gefängnisaufseher: *prison officer*

Gefängnisdirektor: *prison governor*

Gefängnis-Inspekteur: *prison visitor*

Gefängnisstrafe: *a term of imprisonment*

Gefängniswärter: *gaoler (GB); jailer; warder*

gefolgert: *implied*

Gegen-: *contra; counter-*

gegen: *against; counter to; v.; versus*

Gegenangebot: *counteroffer*

Gegenanspruch: *counterclaim*

Gegenbuchung: *contra entry* **als** ~ *per contra or as per contra*

Gegenforderung: *counterclaim* **eine** ~ **erheben** *counterclaim*

Gegenkonto: *contra account*

Gegenleistung: *consideration; quid pro quo* **entgeltliche** ~ *valuable consideration* **erbrachte** ~ *executed consideration*

Gegenseite: *opponent*

gegenseitig: *reciprocal*

Gegenseitigkeit: *reciprocity*

Gegenstand: *chose; item; res; subject* **beschädigter** ~ *head of damage* **gekaufter** ~ *purchase*

Gegenstände: vererbbare materielle ~ *corporeal hereditaments*

Gegenstimme: ohne ~ *nemine contradicente or nem con*

Gegenstimmen: ohne ~ *unopposed*

Gegenstück: *counterpart*

Gegenteil: *contrary* **im** ~ *on the contrary*

Gegenversprechen: *counter-promise*

Gegenwart: *presence*

gegenwärtig: *current; instant; present; pro tem or pro tempore*

gegenzeichnen: *countersign*

Gegenzeuge: *adverse witness*

Gegner: *adversary; opponent*

gegnerisch: *adverse*

Gehalt: *compensation (US); content; pay* **ein** ~ **beziehen** *to draw a salary*

Gehaltsaufbesserung or **Gehaltserhöhung:** *(salary) increase; raise (US); rise*

Gehaltspfändung: *attachment of earnings*

Gehaltsrevision: *salary review*

Gehaltsscheck: *pay cheque or paycheck*

Gehaltstabelle: *scale of salaries or salary scale*

geheim: *clandestine; covert; secret* **etwas** ~ **halten** *to keep a secret*

Geheimagent: *secret or undercover agent*

geheimen: im ~ *in secret*

Geheimer Staatsrat: *Privy Council*

Geheimhaltung: *security*

Geheimhaltungspflicht: *restraint of trade*

Geheimnis: *secret* **ein** ~ **wahren** *to keep a secret*

Geheimpolizei: *secret police*

Geheimsache: *classified information*

gehorchen: *obey*

gehören: nicht ~ **zu** *to fall outside*

gehören zu: *to belong to; to belong with; to fall within; to pertain to*

Gehorsam: *obedience*

Geisel: *hostage*

geistesgestört: *insane*

Geistesgestörtheit: *mental disorder; insanity*

geisteskrank: *insane*

Geisteskrankheit: *insanity*

Geisteszustand: normaler ~ *sanity*

geistig: *intellectual; mental; mentally*

geistig gesund: *sane; of sound mind*

geistlich: *clerical; ecclesiastical*

gekürzt sein: *abate*

Gelände: *bebautes* ~ *premises*

gelangen: *reach*

Geld: *billiges* ~ *cheap money* **eingezahltes** ~ *deposit* **heißes** ~ *hot money* **teures** ~ *dear money* **ungedecktes** ~ *fiat money* **zu** ~ **machen** *realize*

Geld anzahlen: *to pay money down*

Gelder: *funds; means; monies* **öffentliche** ~ *public funds*

Gelder veruntreuen: *to convert funds to one's own use*

Geldgeschenk: *gratuity*

Geldhändler: *authorized dealer*

Geldinstitut: *financial institution*

Geldmärkte: *money markets*

Geldmarktsätze: *money rates*

Geldmittel: *finance* **fehlende** ~ *lack of funds*

Geldmittel veruntreuen: *to convert funds to one's own use*

Geldreserve: *money supply*

Geldstrafe: *fine; penalty*

Geldstück: *coin*

Geldtransfer: *credit transfer or transfer of funds*

Geldverleiher: *moneylender*

Geldvolumen *or* **Geldvorrat:** *money supply*

Geldwechsel: *foreign exchange*

gelegen: *situate or situated*

Gelegenheit: *chance; occasion*

Gelegenheitskauf: *bargain*

gelegentlich: *occasional; occasionally*

gelten: *apply; obtain; operate; rule; run*

geltend: *ruling*

Geltungsbereich: *purview; scope*

Geltung verschaffen: *enforce*

gemäß: *according to; as per; pursuant to; under*

Gemeinde: *community; parish*

Gemeindeabgabe: *rate (GB)*

Gemeindeabgabenzahler: kommerzieller ~ *business ratepayer* **privater** ~ *domestic ratepayer*

Gemeindeland: *common land*

Gemeinderat: *borough council or town council*

Gemeindesatzung: *ordinance (US)*

Gemeingut: *public domain*

Gemeinkosten: *fixed costs*

gemeinsam: *collective; common; in common; jointly; mutual*

Gemeinsame: der ~ **Markt** *the Common Market*

gemeinsam haben: *share*

Gemeinschaft: *community* **eheähnliche** ~ *cohabitation; common-law marriage*

gemeinschaftlich: *in common; joint*

Gemeinschaftseigentum: *multiple ownership*

Gemeinschaftsunternehmen: *joint venture or joint adventure (US)*

Gemeinwohl: *public policy*

gemeldet: nicht ~ *unreported*

genannt: *called*

genau: *precise; strict*

genehm: *convenient*

genehmigen: *agree; approve; authorize; permit; ratify; sanction*

genehmigt: *official*

Genehmigung: *approval; authorization; licence or license (US); permission; permit; ratification; sanction* **königliche** ~ *Royal Assent* **mündliche** ~

verbal permission **schriftliche** ~ *written permission*

Genehmigungszertifikat: *certificate of approval*

Generalamnestie: *general amnesty*

Generaldirektor: *managing director*

Generalstaatsanwalt: *Attorney-General (GB); Director of Public Prosecutions (DPP); Lord Advocate; public prosecutor*

Generalstreik: *general strike*

Generation: *generation*

Generationskonflikt: *generation gap*

Genfer Konventionen: *Geneva Convention(s)*

Genossenschaft: *co-operative society*

genötigt: *under duress*

Genozid: *genocide*

Gentleman's Agreement: *gentleman's agreement or gentlemen's agreement (US)*

genügend: *sufficient*

geöffnet: *open*

Gepäckkontrolle: *baggage check*

Gepflogenheit: *practice* **örtliche** ~ *local custom*

geprüft und genehmigt: *acknowledged and agreed*

Gerät: *device; implement; instrument*

Geräteverleih: *equipment hire firm*

Geräte vermieten: *to hire out equipment*

gerecht: *equitable; fair; just*

gerechtfertigt: *justifiable*

Gerechtigkeit: *justice*

Gericht: *court of law or law court* **das** ~ **bitten** *to apply to the Court* **durch das** ~ *per curiam* **erstinstanzliches** ~ *magistrate (GB)* **illegales** ~ *kangaroo court* **unteres** ~ *inferior court* **vor** ~ **in court vor** ~ **gehen** *go to law* **vor** ~ **stellen** *try*

Gericht des Lordkanzlers: *Chancery Court*

Gericht erster Instanz: *court of first instance*

Gericht für Wettbewerbsbeschränkungen: *Restrictive Practices Court*

Gericht letzter Instanz: *court of last resort*

gerichtlich: *judicial*

gerichtlich anordnen: *decree*

gerichtlich vorgehen: *to take legal action; to start legal proceedings*

Gerichtsabteilung: *division*

Gerichtsakte: *record*

Gerichtsbeamter: *registrar*

Gerichtsbeschluß: *court order*

Gerichtsbezirk: *circuit*

Gerichtsdiener: *bailiff (GB); tipstaff; usher*

Gerichtsentscheidung: *adjudication*

Gerichtsferien: *vacation*

Gerichtshof: *court of law or law court*

Gerichtskosten: *costs*

Gerichtsmedizin: *forensic medicine*

Gerichtsort: *venue*

Gerichtsrundschreiben: *pro forma letter*

Gerichtssaal: *courtroom*

Gerichtsschranke: *bar*

Gerichtssitzung: *hearing; sitting*

Gerichtsstand: *forum; venue*

Gerichtsurteil: *judgment or judgement*

Gerichtsverfahren: *court action or case; legal proceedings* **ordentliches** ~ *the due process of the law*

Gerichtsverhandlung: *hearing; trial*

Gerichtsvollzieher: *bailiff (GB)*

Gerichtswesen: *judicature*

geringer: *reduced*

Geringschätzung: *contempt*

gesamt: *total*

Gesamtgebühr: *inclusive sum or inclusive charge*

Gesamthandeigentum: *joint tenancy*

gesamthänderisch: *per my et per tout*

Gesamtpreis: *all-in price*

gesamtschuldnerisch haftbar: *jointly and severally liable*

Gesamtstrafenbildung: bitten um ~ *to ask for other offences to be taken into consideration*

Gesamtsumme: *grand total*

Gesamtvereinbarung: *blanket agreement*

Gesandter: bevollmächtigter ~ *plenipotentiary*

Geschädigte: *injured party*

Geschäft: *affair; bargain; business; deal; operation; shop* **kein gewinnbringendes** ~ *not a commercial proposition* **unabhängiges** ~ *independent trader or independent shop*

Geschäfte abschließen *or* **abwickeln:** *to transact business*

Geschäftemacher: *profiteer*

Geschäftemacherei: *profiteering*

geschäftlich: *commercial* **sich** ~ **durchsetzen** *or* **etablieren** *to establish oneself in business*

Geschäft ohne Wohnräume: *lock-up shop*

Geschäftsbericht: *the company's annual report or the chairman's report or the directors' report*

Geschäftsbesuch: *business call*

Geschäftsbrief: *business letter*

Geschäftsbücher: *the accounts of a business or a company's accounts; a company's books* **gesetzlich vorgeschriebene** ~ *statutory books*

geschäftsfähig: *sui juris*

Geschäftsfähigkeit: *capacity*

Geschäftsführung: gemeinsame ~ *joint management*

Geschäftsgebaren: betrügerisches ~ *fraudulent trading* **unlauteres** *or* **unsauberes** ~ *sharp practice*

Geschäftsgepflogenheiten: *business or industrial or trade practices*

Geschäftsgewinn: *trading profit*

Geschäftsjahr: *financial year*

Geschäftskorrespondenz: *business correspondence*

Geschäftsleben: ins ~ **eintreten** *to go into business*

Geschäftsleiter: *manager*

Geschäftsordnung: *order; standing orders*

Geschäftspraktiken: *business or industrial or trade practices* **wettbewerbsbeschränkende** ~ *restrictive practices*

Geschäftsräume: *business or commercial premises*

Geschäftsreise: *business trip*

Geschäftsschluß: *closing time*

Geschäftsstelle: *agency; branch; office*

Geschäftsstelle des Nachlaßgerichts: *probate registry*

Geschäftsstellenbeamter eines Gerichts: *associate of the Crown Office*

Geschäftsstellenleiter: *branch manager*

Geschäftstätigkeit: *operation*

geschäftsunfähig: *incompetent*

Geschäftsunfähigkeit: *disability; incapacity; incompetency*

Geschäftsviertel: *business centre*

Geschäftswelt: die örtliche ~ *the local business community*

Geschäftszeit: *business or opening hours*

geschehen: *occur*

Geschenk: *gift; present*

geschlagen: sich ~ **geben** *to concede defeat*

geschlechtlich: *sexual*

Geschlechtsverkehr: *sexual intercourse*

geschlossen: *closed*

geschützt: *secure*

Geschwindigkeit: *rate*

Geschworene: *jury (GB)*

Geschworenen: einen ~ **ablehnen** *to object to a juror*

Geschworenenbank: *jury box*

Geschworenenliste: die ~ **aufstellen** *to empanel a jury*

Geschworenenspruch: einstimmiger ~ *unanimous verdict*

Geschworener: *juryman*

Geschworener sein: *to serve on a jury*

Gesellschaft: *association; company; institution* **eine polygame** ~ *a polygamous society* **eingetragene** ~ *registered company*

Gesellschafter: *company member; partner* **beschränkt haftender** ~ *limited partner*

gesellschaftlich: *social*

Gesellschaftsgründung: *incorporation*

Gesellschaftsrecht: *the Companies Act (GB)*

Gesellschaftsregister: *companies' register or register of companies*

Gesellschaftssiegel: *common seal (GB)*

Gesellschaftsvertrag: *articles of association or articles of incorporation (US); articles or deed of partnership*

Gesellschaftszweckbestimmung: *objects clause*

Gesetz: *act; enactment; law; lex; measure; statute* **das** ~ **einhalten** *to keep the law* **das** ~ **hüten** *to uphold the law* **ungeschriebenes** ~ *unwritten law* **zum** ~ **erklären** *enact*

Gesetzbuch: *statute book*

Gesetze erlassen: *legislate*

Gesetzesbestimmungen: *the provisions of a Bill*

Gesetzesbezeichnung: *title*

Gesetzesbrecher: *lawbreaker*

Gesetzesentwurf: *bill* **einen ~ unterstützen** *to back a bill*

Gesetzesfiktion: *fiction of law or legal fiction*

Gesetzeskommentar: *textbook*

Gesetzeskonflikt: *Conflict of Laws*

Gesetzeskraft: die volle ~ *the full power of the law*

Gesetzeslücke: eine ~ finden *to find a loophole in the law*

Gesetzessammlung: *corpus; statute book*

Gesetzessammlung Römischen Rechts: *corpus legis*

Gesetzesübertretung: *law-breaking*

Gesetzesvollzug: *law enforcement*

Gesetzesvorlage: *bill* **gedruckte ~** *engrossed Bill (US)*

Gesetzesvorlage eines Abgeordneten: *Private Member's Bill*

Gesetze von Oleron: *Laws of Oleron*

gesetzgebend: *legislative*

Gesetzgebung: *law-making; legislation*

gesetzlich: *in law; legally; statutorily; statutory*

gesetzlich erlaubt: *licit*

gesetzlich geschützt: *proprietary*

gesetzlich verfügen: *enact*

gesetzlich verpflichtet: *duty bound*

gesetzlich vorgeschrieben: *statutory*

gesetzlos: *lawless*

Gesetzlosigkeit: *lawlessness*

gesetzmäßig: *in law; legitimate*

Gesetzmäßigkeit: *law; legality; legitimacy*

gesetzwidrig: *against the law; illegitimate; lawless; unlawful; unlawfully*

Gesetzwidrigkeit: *illegality; illegitimacy; lawlessness*

gesichert: *secure*

Gesicht: *face*

gesondert: *separate; separately; several; severally*

Gespräch: *call*

Gespräche: produktive ~ *productive discussions*

geständig sein: *confess*

Geständnis: *admission; confession* **freiwilliges ~** *voluntary confession*

gestatten: *allow; permit*

Gestehungskosten: *prime cost*

gesteuert: *controlled*

Gesuch: *application; request*

Gesuchsteller: *petitioner*

gesund: *fit*

Gesundheit: geistige ~ *sanity*

Gesundheits- und Sicherheitsüberprüfung: *medical inspection*

Get: *get or gett*

getrennt: *separate; several*

Getrenntleben: *separation* **gerichtlich angeordnetes ~** *legal separation*

Gewähr: *warranty*

gewähren: *allow; award; extend; grant* **nicht ~** *refuse*

gewährleisten: *secure*

Gewährleistung: *warranty*

Gewahrsam: *custody; detention*

Gewährsmann: *informant*

Gewalt: *violence* **ausübende ~** *executive power* **die vollziehende ~** *the Executive (US)* **höhere ~** *act of God; force majeure; vis major*

Gewaltandrohung: unqualifizierte ~ *common assault*

gewaltsam: *forcible; violent*

gewalttätig: *violent*

Gewalttätigkeit: *violence*

Gewerbe: *business; trade*

Gewerbeaufsichtsamt: *the factory inspectorate*

Gewerbeaufsichtsbeamter: *inspector of factories or factory inspector*

Gewerbegebiet: *industrial or trading estate*

Gewerkschaft: *trade union or trades union or labor union (US)*

Gewerkschaft(l)er: *convenor; unionist*

gewerkschaftlich organisiert: *unionized*

Gewerkschaftsbeiträge: *union dues or subscription*

Gewerkschaftsbund: britischer ~ *Trades Union Congress*

Gewerkschaftsmitglied: *unionist*

Gewicht: falsches ~ *false weight*

Gewichtsschwund *or* **Gewichtsverlust:** *loss in weight*

Gewinn: *gain; profit; return* **nicht realisierter ~** *paper profit*

Gewinn an Erfahrung: *gain in experience*

Gewinnausfall: *lost profits*

gewinnbringend: *profitable; profitably*

Gewinne: nicht ausgeschüttete ~ *retained income*

Gewinn nach Steuern: *profit after tax*

Gewinnspanne: *margin; turn*

Gewinn- und Verlustrechnung: *profit and loss account*

Gewinnverlust: *lost profits*

Gewinn vor Steuern: *profit before tax or pretax profit*

gewiß: *certain*

Gewißheit: *certainty*

Gewohnheit: *practice*

gewohnheitsmäßig: *habitual*

Gewohnheitstäter: *recidivist*

Gewohnheitstrinker: *habitual drunkard*

Gewohnheitsverbrecher: *habitual criminal or habitual offender; persistent offender*

Gift: *poison*

giftig: *noxious*

Girokonto: *cheque or current account*

Glauben: in gutem ~ *bona fides or bona fide; in good faith*

glauben: *believe; deem*

Gläubiger: *creditor; lender* **bevorrechtigter ~** *preferential creditor; preferred creditor* **gesicherter ~** *secured creditor* **nachrangiger ~** *deferred creditor* **ungesicherter ~** *unsecured creditor*

Gläubigerbegünstigung: *fraudulent preference*
Gläubiger ohne Sicherheiten: *unsecured creditor*
Gläubigerversammlung: *creditors' meeting*
gleichermaßen: *equally; likewise*
Gleichgestellter: *peer*
Gleichgewicht: gestörtes psychisches ~ *disturbed balance of mind*
gleichgültig: *carelessly*
Gleichheit: *identity; parity*
gleichkommen: *equal; to be equivalent to*
gleichmäßig: *continuous; equally*
gleichrangig: *pari passu*
Gleichrangigengruppe: *peer group*
Gleichrangiger: *peer*
gleichwertig: *pari passu*
Gleichwertigkeit: *equivalence*
gleichwertig sein: *to be equivalent to*
gleichzeitig: *concurrent; concurrently*
gleichzeitig auslaufend: *coterminous*
Glücksspiel: *game of chance*
GmbH: *plc*
Gnade: *clemency; mercy*
Gnadentod: *mercy killing*
Goldwährung: *gold standard*
Gönner: *benefactor*
Gönnerin: *benefactress*
Goodwill: *goodwill*
Gotteslästerung: *blasphemy*
Gott lästern: *blaspheme*
Gouverneur: *governor*
Grad: *degree (US)*
Grafschaft: *county (GB)*
gratis: *free; gratis; gratuitous*
Gratisprobe: *free sample*
Grausamkeit: *cruelty*
greifbar: nicht ~ *intangible*
greifen: zu etwas ~ *to resort to*
Gremium: *committee*
Grenze: *boundary (line); limit*
grenzen an: *abut (on)*
Grenzkommission: *Boundary Commission*
Grenzmauer: *party wall*
grob: *gross; rough*
grob entwerfen: *rough out*
großartig: *grand*
Größendegression: *economies of scale*
Großfamilie: *extended family*
Großhandel: *wholesale*
Großhändler: *wholesale dealer; wholesaler*
großzügig: *generous*
Grund: *cause; grounds; reason* hinreichender ~ *good cause*
Grundbesitz: *real estate; (real) property; realty* den ~ entziehen *dispossess* eingetragener ~ *registered land* unbeschränkter ~ *freehold property* ungestörter ~ *quiet enjoyment of land* vererbbarer ~ *hereditament* widerrechtlich ~ entziehen *deforce*

Grundbesitzer: *landowner*
Grundbesitz vermachen: *devise*
Grundbestandteil: *element*
Grundbuch: *land or proprietorship register*
Grundbuchamt: *Land Registry*
Grundbuchauszug: *land certificate*
Grundbucheintragung: *land registration*
Grunddienstbarkeit: *easement*
Grunde: im ~ *basically*
Grundeigentümer: *freeholder; ground landlord*
Grundeigentumsurkunde: *title deeds*
gründen: *base; establish; form; institute*
Gründer: *founder*
Gründeraktien: *founder's shares*
Gründe vorlegen: *to show cause*
Grundgebühr: *flat rate*
Grundgehalt: *basic pay or basic salary*
Grundgesetz: *constitution*
Grundkapital: genehmigtes ~ *authorized capital*
Grundlage: *base; basis; element*
Grundlagen: *basics*
grundlegend: *fundamental*
Grundlohn: *basic pay or basic wage*
Grundprodukt: *basic product*
Grundrecht: *constitutional or natural right*
Grundrechte: *civil liberties; civil rights*
Grundsachverhalt: *basics*
Grundsatz: *maxim*
Grundsatzvereinbarung: *agreement in principle*
Grundschuld: *charge on land or charge over property*
Grundsteuer: *land tax*
Grundstoffe: *primary or basic commodities*
Grundstück: *real estate or real property; realty* dienendes ~ *servient tenement* herrschendes ~ *dominant tenement*
Grundstücksbelastung: *encumbrance*
Grundstücksbestandteile: *appurtenances*
Grundstückspacht: *ground lease*
Grundstücksrechte: *chattels real*
Grundstückteilung: *partition*
Grundstücksübertragungsurkunde: *vesting assent*
Grundstücks- und Immobilienfirma: *estate agency*
Grundstücks- und Immobilienmakler: *estate agent*
Grund und Boden: *real estate or real property*
Gründung: *formation or forming*
Gründungserklärung einer Kapitalgesellschaft: *declaration of association*
Gründungskapital: *initial capital*
Gründungsurkunde: *certificate of incorporation; memorandum of association*
Gruppenbuchung: *block booking*
Gruppenklage: *class action or class suit (US)*
Guerilla: *guerilla*
Guillotine: *guillotine*

gültig: *valid* **für ~ erklären** *validate* **nicht mehr ~** *obsolete*

gültig bleiben: *to remain in effect*

Gültigkeit: *validity*

Gültigkeitsdauer: *period of validity*

Gültigkeitserklärung: *validation*

gültig werden: *to become operative*

Gummistempel: *rubber stamp*

günstig: *favourable*

Gut: geborgenes ~ *salvage*

Gutachten: *opinion*

Gutachter: *consultant*

Güter: *goods* **zu verzollende ~** *goods which are liable to duty*

Gütergemeinschaft: *community property*

Güterumlauf: freier ~ *free circulation of goods*

Güterzug: *goods train*

Gütezeichen: *kite mark*

gutheißen: *to approve of*

Gutschein: *voucher*

gutschreiben: *credit*

Gutschriftsanzeige: *credit note*

Gutsverwalter: *land agent (GB)*

Hh

Habe: *possessions* **persönliche ~** *chattels personal; private effects*

Habeaskorpusakte: *habeas corpus*

Haben: *credit*

Habenseite: *credit side*

Hafenanlagen: *the docks*

Hafengebühren: *dock dues or port dues or harbour dues*

Haft: *confinement; detention; imprisonment* **in ~** *under arrest* **in ~ halten** *or* **nehmen** *detain*

Haftanordnung: *committal order; warrant of committal or committal warrant*

Haftanstalt: *lock-up (informal)*

haftbar: *liable (for)*

Haftbefehl: *arrest warrant; bench warrant; detention order; bench warrant; warrant of committal or committal warrant*

haften: *liable (for); underwrite*

Haftentlassung: bedingter ~ *release on licence*

Häftling: *detainee; prisoner* **politischer ~** *political prisoner* **priviligierter ~** *trusty (slang)*

Haftpflichtversicherung: *third-party insurance*

Haftung: *liability* **beschränkte ~** *limited liability* **gesamtschuldnerische ~** *joint and several liability* **stellvertretende ~** *vicarious liability* **unbedingte ~** *strict liability* **unbeschränkte ~** *unlimited liability* **verschuldensunabhängige ~** *strict liability*

Haftungsablehnungserklärung: *disclaimer*

Haftungsausschlußklausel: *disclaimer*

Haftungsbeschränkung: *limitation of liability*

Haftungsklausel: *liability clause*

Haftung übernehmen für: *underwrite*

Hafturlaub: *parole*

Halbjahr: erstes ~ *first half or first half-year*

halbjährlich: *bi-annually*

Hälfte: *moiety* **erste ~** *first half or first half-year*

halten: *deem; hold; keep; last; maintain; uphold* **sich ~ an** *abide by*

halten für: *consider*

Halter: *holder*

Hamsterer: *hoarder*

hamstern: *hoard*

Hand: von ~ *by hand* **von ~ geschrieben** *handwritten* **zur ~** *to hand*

Handel: *affair; bargain; commerce; deal; dealing; trade; trading* **erlaubter ~** *lawful trade* **gegenseitiger ~** *reciprocal trade* **legaler ~** *fair dealing*

Handeln: *bargaining* **rechtmäßiges ~** *lawful practice*

handeln: *act; bargain; take; trade*

Handelnder: rechtswidrig ~ *tortfeasor*

Handelsabkommen: *trade agreement*

Handelsbrauch: *the customs of the trade*

Handelsembargo: ein ~ verhängen *to put an embargo on trade*

Handelsgericht: *Commercial Court (GB)*

Handelsgesellschaft: offene ~ *partnership*

Handelsgesetz: *mercantile law*

Handelsinstitut: *commercial college*

Handelskammer: *Chamber of Commerce*

Handelsmarine: die ~ *the merchant marine*

Handelsmarke: *trademark or trade mark or trade name*

Handelsmesse: *trade fair*

Handelspraktiken: *trade practices*

Handelsrecht: *commercial law; mercantile law or law merchant*

Handelsregister: *companies' register or register of companies*

Handelsverband: *trade association*

Handelsverbot: *trade embargo*

Handelsverkehr: *commerce*

Handel treiben: *trade*

Handfeuerwaffe: *handgun*

Handgeld: *earnest*

handgeschrieben: *handwritten*

handhaben: zu ~ *manageable*

Handhabung: *handling*

Händler: *broker; dealer; trader* **selbständiger ~** *independent trader or independent shop*

Händlerrabatt: *trade terms*

Handlung: *action* **notarielle ~** *notarial act* **offenkundige ~** *overt act* **rechtswidrige ~** *malfeasance* **strafbare ~** *criminal offence* **unerlaubte ~** *tortious act* **verbrecherische ~** *villainy*

Handlungsvollmacht: *power of attorney*

Handschellen: *bracelets (slang); handcuffs* **mit ~ gefesselt** *handcuffed*

Handschrift: *handwriting*

Handwerker: *repairer*
hängen: *hang*
hart: *hard; harsh; heavy; severe; stiff*
Härte: *hardship; harshness; severity*
Hartgeldwährung: *coinage*
hart verhandeln: *to drive a hard bargain*
Haß: *hatred*
häufig: *common*
Häufigkeit: *incidence*
Hauptaktionär: *major shareholder*
Hauptaspekte eines Abkommens: *heads of agreement*
Hauptbüro: *central office*
Hauptgeschäftsstelle: *head office; headquarters*
Hauptkommissar: *Chief Inspector*
Hauptlizenz: *head licence*
Hauptmietvertrag *or* **Hauptpachtvertrag:** *head lease*
hauptsächlich: *basic; primary; primarily*
Hauptsendezeit: *prime time*
Hauptsitz: *headquarters*
Hauptstadt: *capital city*
Hauptsumme: *principal*
Haupttäter: *principal*
Hauptteilhaber: *senior partner*
Haupttitel: *full title*
Hauptverfahren: *full trial*
Hauptvermietung *or* **Hauptverpachtung:** *head lease*
Hauptversammlung: außerordentliche ~ *Extraordinary General Meeting (EGM)* **ordentliche** ~ *general meeting*
Hauptzeuge: *material witness*
Haus: *house* **außer** ~ *outside* **außer** ~ **geben** *put out*
Hausarrest: *house arrest*
Hausbesitz: *house property*
Hausbesitzer: *householder*
Häuserblock: *block*
Häusermakler: *house agent*
Haushalt: *household*
Haushaltsartikel: *household goods*
Haushaltsplan: *budget*
häuslich: *domestic*
Hausmeister: *caretaker*
Haus mit Grund: *premises*
Hausrat: *household effects*
Haussuchungsbefehl: *search warrant*
Havarie: besondere ~ *particular average* **große** ~ *general average*
Hefter: *binder*
hehlen: *fence*
Hehler: *fence (informal); receiver*
Hehlerei: *handling or receiving stolen goods*
Hehlerei begehen: *to receive stolen goods*
Heimathafen: *port of registry or registry port*
Heimatland: *home*
Heimfall: *reversion*

heimlich: *clandestine; on the quiet; in secret; secretly*
Heirat: *marriage; matrimony*
heißt: das ~ *videlicet*
helfen: *assist; help*
hemmen: *check*
Hemmnis: *bar; check*
Henker: *executioner; hangman*
herabgesetzt: *reduced*
herabsetzen: *commute; decrease; minimize; reduce; to scale down*
Herabsetzung: *commutation; reduction*
Herabsetzung des Schadensersatzes: *mitigation of damages*
Herangehensweise: *approach*
herantreten an: *approach*
heraufsetzen: *to raise; to scale up*
herausbringen: *get out*
herausfinden: *discover*
herausfordern: *provoke*
Herausforderung: *provocation*
Herausgabe: *restitution*
Herausgabeklage: *action in detinue; replevin; trover*
herausgeben: *issue; publish; surrender*
Herausgeber: *editor*
herausholen *or* **herauspressen:** *extract*
herausschneiden: *excise*
herauswerfen: *throw out*
herbeirufen: *summon*
Herbstsitzungsperiode: *Michaelmas*
hereinkommen: *enter*
hereinlegen: *con (informal); take in*
Herkunft: *background; origin*
Herkunftsbescheinigung: *certificate of origin*
Herkunftsland: *country of origin*
Herkunftszertifikat: *certificate of origin*
herleiten: *derive*
Herren: *Messrs* **"Meine** ~**"** *or* **"Sehr geehrte** ~**"** *gentlemen*
Herrschaft: *reign; rule*
herrschen: *reign; rule*
Herr Vorsitzender: *Mr Chairman*
Hersteller von Raubdrucken: *pirate*
Herstellung: *production* **serienmäßige** ~ *mass production*
Herstellungskosten: *prime cost*
Herstellungsprozeß: *industrial processes*
herumhantieren: an etwas ~ *to tamper with something*
herunterstufen: *downgrade*
hervorragend: *excellent*
hervorrufen: *give rise to*
hetzerisch: *seditious*
heute: bis ~ *to date*
hierin: *herein*
hiermit: *hereby*
hiervon: *hereof*

Hilfe: *assistance; help; relief; support*
Hilfs-: *ancillary*
Hilfspolizist: *special constable*
hinaufreichen: *hand up*
hinausgehen über: *exceed*
Hinblick: im ~ auf *having regard to or as regards or regarding*
hindern: *prevent; restrain*
Hindernis: *bar; check; obstruction*
Hinderung: *estoppel*
hineingehen: *enter*
Hinfälligkeit: *lapse*
hinhaltend: *dilatory*
hinrichten: *execute*
Hinrichtung: *execution*
hinsichtlich: *with respect to or in respect of*
Hinterbliebener: *survivor*
Hintergedanke: *ulterior motive*
hintergehen: *deceive*
Hintergrund: *background*
hinterher(jagend): *in pursuit*
hinterlassen: *leave*
hinterlegen: *lodge*
Hinterleger: bailor amtlich zugelassener ~ *licensed deposit-taker*
Hinterlegung: *bailment; deposit*
Hinterlegung bei Gericht: *payment in or payment into court*
Hinterlegungsstelle: *depositary (US); depository*
hinwegsetzen: sich ~ über *override*
Hinweis: *clue; indication; lead*
hinweisen auf: *indicate*
hinzuwählen: *to co-opt*
hinzuziehen: *call in*
hoch: jdn ~ einschätzen *to rate someone highly* **zu ~ ansetzen** *overestimate*
Hochachtungsvoll: *yours faithfully; Yours truly or Truly yours (US)*
hochbleiben: *hold up*
hochqualifiziert: *highly qualified*
Hochschule: *college*
Höchstgebot: oder gegen ~ or near offer (o.n.o.)
Höchstgewicht: *weight limit*
Höchstgewinne: *record profits*
Höchststand: *high*
Hochverrat: *high treason; treason felony*
hochverräterisch: *treasonable*
Hoheitsgewässer: außerhalb der ~ *outside territorial waters*
Hohlmaß: *cubic measure*
Holdinggesellschaft: *holding company*
Holzentnahme: *estovers*
Honorar: *fee; remuneration* **freiwillig gezahltes ~** *honorarium*
Honorarvorschuß: *retainer*
honorieren: nicht ~ *dishonour*
hopsnehmen: *pick up (informal)*
hören: *hear*

horten: *hoard*
Horten von Vorräten: *hoarding of supplies*
Hülle: *holder*
Hungerstreik: *hunger strike*
Hürde: *hurdle*
Hypothek: eine ~ abzahlen *to pay off a mortgage* **formlose ~** *equitable mortgage* **nachstehende ~** *puisne mortgage* **zweite ~** *second mortgage*
hypothekarisch belasten: *mortgage*
Hypothekenbestellung: formelle ~ *charge by way of legal mortgage*
Hypothekengläubiger: *chargee; mortgagee*
Hypothekenpfandbrief: *mortgage debenture*
Hypothekenregister: *register of charges*
Hypothekenschulden: *encumbrance*
Hypothekenschuldner: *mortgagor*
Hypothekentilgungen: *mortgage (re)payments*
Hypotheken-Warteliste: *mortgage queue*

Ii

ib. or ibd.: *ibid or ibidem*
identifizieren: *identify*
Identifizierung: *identification*
identisch sein: *on all fours with*
Identität: *identity*
Identitätsnachweis: *proof of identification*
Identitätstäuschung: *personation*
i.e.: *i.e.*
Ihrer: "mit ~ Erlaubnis" *"by your leave"*
illegal: *bootleg; under the counter; illegal*
Illegalität: *illegality*
Imbiß-Stube: *snack bar*
Imitation: *fake; imitation*
imitieren: *imitate*
immateriell: *incorporeal; intangible*
immer mehr: *increasingly*
Immigrant: illegaler ~ *illegal immigrant*
Immobilien: *real estate; immovable property or immovables; (real) property; realty*
Immobilienbesitz verwalten: *to manage property*
Immobiliengesellschaft: *property company*
Immobilienmakler: *house agent; letting agency*
Immunität: absolute ~ *absolute privilege* **diplomatische ~** *diplomatic immunity* **~ des Richters** *judicial immunity*
Impeachment: *impeachment*
implizieren: *imply*
impliziert: *implicit; implied*
Import: *import*
Importbeschränkungen einführen: *to set limits to imports or to impose limits on imports*
Importgenehmigung: *import licence or permit*
Importhandel: *import trade*
importieren: *import*
Importlizenz: *import licence*

Importquote: *import quota*

Impuls: *impulse*

inbegriffen: mit ~ *implicit; implied*

Inbesitzhalten: *holding over*

Inbesitznahme: *distress*

Indemnität: eingeschränkte ~ *qualified privilege*

Indentgeschäft: *indent*

Index: *index*

Indikator: *indicator*

indirekt: *circumstantial; vicarious*

Indiskretion: *leak*

individuell: *individual*

Individuum: *individual*

Indizienbeweis: *circumstantial or presumptive evidence*

Indossament: *endorsement*

Indossant: *endorser*

Indossat: *endorsee*

Industrie: arbeitsintensive ~ *labour-intensive industry*

Industriebetrieb: ein staatseigener ~ *a state-owned industry*

Industriegebiet: *industrial or trading estate*

industriell: *industrial*

Industriepraktiken: *industrial practices*

Industrieverband: *trade association*

Inflationsrate: *rate of inflation or inflation rate*

Informant: *grass (slang); informant*

Information: *information; information bureau or office* **fehlende** ~ *lack of information*

Informationstechnologie: *information technology*

Information zugänglich machen: *to share information*

informell: *informal*

informieren: *advise; brief; inform*

Inhaber: *bearer; holder; keeper; proprietor* **legitimierter** ~ *or* **rechtmäßiger** ~ *holder in due course*

Inhaberscheck: *bearer cheque; negotiable cheque*

Inhaberschuldverschreibung: *bearer bond*

inhaftieren: *imprison; jail or gaol*

Inhaftierter: *detainee*

Inhaftierung: *committal; detainer; detention; imprisonment; incarceration*

Inhalt: *capacity; contents* **wesentlicher** ~ *substance*

Inhaltsbeschreibung: unkorrekte ~ *false description of contents*

Inhaltsvermerk: *endorsement*

Inhaltsverzeichnis: *table of contents*

Initialien: *initials*

Initiative: eine ~ **aufgreifen** *to follow up an initiative*

Inkassobeauftragter: *(debt) collector*

Inkassobüro *or* **Inkassofirma:** *debt collection agency; collecting agency*

Inkassowechsel: *bills for collection*

inklusive: *inclusive*

Inklusivpreis: *all-in rate*

inkompetent: *incompetent*

inländisch: *domestic*

Inlandsabsatz: *domestic or home sales*

Inlandsfrachtkosten: *inland freight charges*

Inlandsmarkt: *home or domestic market*

Inlandsporto: *inland postage*

Inlandsproduktion: *domestic production*

Inlandsverbrauch: *domestic consumption*

Innehaben: *tenure*

Innehabung: *possession*

Innenminister: *Home Secretary*

Innenministerium: *Home Office; Ministry of the Interior or Interior Ministry*

Inneres: *interior*

innerhalb: *inside; within*

inoffiziell: *informal; off the record; unofficial*

insbesondere: *in particular*

Inserat: *ad*

Insiderhandel: *insider dealing or trading*

insolvent: *bankrupt; insolvent*

Insolvenz: *insolvency*

Inspektionskomitee: *board of visitors*

Inspektionstour: eine ~ **machen** *to carry out a tour of inspection*

Installationen und Einbauten: *fixtures and fittings*

Instandhaltung: *maintenance*

instandsetzen: *repair*

Instandsetzung: *repair*

Instandsetzungsvertrag: *covenant to repair*

Institut: *college; institute; institution*

institutionell: *institutional*

Instruktionen: *instructions*

Instrument: *instrument*

integrieren: *incorporate*

intellektuell: *intellectual*

Interesse: *concern; interest* **festbegründetes** ~ *or* **persönliches** ~ *vested interest* **öffentliches** ~ *public policy* **versicherbares** ~ *insurable interest*

Interessenkonflikt: *conflict of interest*

Interims-: *interim; provisional*

Interimsministerpräsident: *caretaker Prime Minister*

Interimsschein: *scrip*

Interimszahlung: *interim payment*

Internationale Anwaltsvereinigung: *International Bar Association*

Internationale Arbeitsorganisation: *International Labour Organization*

Internationaler Gerichtshof: *International Court of Justice*

internieren: *intern*

Internierter: *internee*

Internierung: *internment*

Interpol: *Interpol*

Interpretation: *interpretation* **falsche** ~ *misinterpretation*

interpretieren: *interpret*

intervenieren: *interfere; intervene*
Intervention: *interference; intervention*
Interventionspreis: *intervention price*
interviewen: *interview*
Intestaterbfolge: *intestate succession*
Intimsphäre: *privacy*
investieren: *invest*
Investition: risikofreie ~ *or* **sichere** ~ *secure investment*
Investitionen: *capital expenditure*
Investitionsrentabilität: *return on investment or on capital*
Investmentfonds: offener ~ *unit trust*
Investmentfondsgesellschaft: *mutual funds (US)*
Investmenttrust: *investment trust*
Investor: *contributor of capital; investor*
Inzest: *incest*
irreführen: *mislead*
irreführend: *deceptive*
irreleiten: *misdirect*
Irreleitung: *misdirection*
Irrreführung: *misdirection*
irrtümlich: *by mistake*
islamisch: *Islamic*

Jj

Jagdschein: *game licence*
Jahr: im ~ *per annum* **pro** ~ *per year; per annum* **vorletztes** ~ *the year before last*
Jahre: steuerfreie ~ *tax holiday*
Jahresabschluß: *year end*
Jahresbericht: *annual return*
Jahresbericht des Aufsichtsratsvorsitzenden: *the chairman's report*
Jahresbericht des Verwaltungsrates: *directors' report*
Jahreshauptversammlung: ordentliche ~ *Annual General Meeting (AGM)*
Jahresmiete: volle ~ *rack rent*
Jahresrente: *annuity*
jährlich: *annual*
je nach: *depending on*
jetzig: *present*
Jobber: *(stock) jobber*
Jobbing: *stock jobbing*
Johanni(stag): *Midsummer day*
Joint-venture: *joint venture or joint adventure (US)*
Jugend-: *juvenile*
Jugendarrestanstalt: *attendance centre (GB)*
Jugendgericht: *juvenile court*
jugendlich: *juvenile*
Jugendlicher: *juvenile; young person; youth*
Jugendstrafanstalt: *borstal; detention or remand centre*

Juniorgerichtsanwalt: *junior*
Juniorpartner: *junior partner*
Jura: *jurisprudence*
jure: de ~ *de jure*
Jurisdiktion: *jurisdiction*
Jurist: *parliamentary draftsman; jurist*
juristisch: *juridical; juristic; legal*
Jury: nicht entscheidungsfähige ~ *hung jury*
Justiz: *judicature*
Justiz-: *judicial*
Justizirrtum: *miscarriage of justice*
Justizministerium: *Department of Justice or Justice Department (US)*

Kk

Kabinett: *cabinet*
Kabinettsausschuß: *Star Chamber*
Kadett: *cadet*
Kadi: *beak (slang)*
Kai: dock am ~ **festmachen** *dock*
Kalenderjahr: *calendar year*
Kalendermonat: *calendar month*
Kalkulation: *budgeting; calculation*
kalkulieren: *calculate*
Kammer: *division*
Kampagne: *campaign*
Kampf: *battle; contest; strife*
kämpfen um: *contest*
Kanal: *channel*
Kandidat: *appointee; candidate; nominee*
Kandidatur: seine ~ **zurückziehen** *stand down*
Kanzlei: *office*
Kanzleramt: *Cabinet Office*
Kapazität: *capacity*
Kapital: *capital; principal* **ausgegebenes** ~ *issued capital* **gewinnbringendes** ~ *productive capital* **voll einbezahltes** ~ *fully paid-up capital*
Kapitalanlagegesellschaft: *investment trust*
Kapitalanlagen: festverzinsliche ~ *fixed-interest investments* **sichere** ~ *safe investments*
Kapitalanleger: *investor*
Kapitalertrag: *interest*
Kapital fest anlegen: *to lock up capital*
Kapitalgesellschaft: *corporation; corporation (US)* **eine** ~ **gründen** *incorporate*
Kapitalmarkt: *capital market*
Kapitalrendite: *return on investment or on capital*
Kapitalsammelstellen: *institutional investors*
Kapitalsumme: *principal*
Kapitaltransfersteuer: *capital transfer tax*
Kapitalverbrechen: *capital crime or offence; felony*
Kapitalverkehr: *circulation of capital; movements of capital* **freier** ~ *free movement of capital*
Kapitalverlust: *capital loss*

karitativ: *eleemosynary*

Karteikarte: *filing card*

Kartellgericht: *Restrictive Practices Court*

Kartenhülle: *card holder*

Kasernenarrest haben: *to be confined to barracks*

Kasse: *box office; ticket office*

Kassenbestand: *balance or cash in hand*

Kassenwartbericht: *treasurer's report*

Kassierer: *teller*

Kasten: *box; advertisement panel*

Kasten für Verbesserungsvorschläge: *suggestion box*

Katasteramt: *Land Registry*

Kategorie: *category; class; type*

Kauf: *purchase* **guter** ~ *or* **schlechter** ~ *good buy or bad buy*

Kaufangebot: *offer to buy*

kaufen: *buy; nobble (slang); purchase*

Käufer: *buyer; purchaser* **ernsthafter** ~ *genuine purchaser*

Käufermarkt: *buyer's market*

Kauffrau: *dealer; trader*

käuflich erwerben: *purchase*

Kaufmann: *dealer; trader*

Kauf mit Rückgaberecht: *sale or return*

Kaufoption: *call option; option to purchase*

Kaufpreis: *purchase price*

Kaufsteuer: *purchase tax*

Kaution: *bail; surety*

Kautionsantrag: einen ~ **stellen** *to ask for bail to be granted*

Kautionsurkunde: *bail bond (GB)*

Kenntnis: *knowledge; notice* **gesetzlich unterstellte** *or* **zumutbare** ~ *constructive knowledge; constructive notice* **in** ~ **setzen** *advise; inform* **tatsächliche** ~ *actual notice* **zur** ~ **nehmen** *note*

Kenntnis des Gerichts: *judicial notice*

Kenntnisnahme: *attention*

Kerker: *dungeon*

kidnappen: *kidnap*

Kidnapper: *kidnapper*

killen: *hit (slang)*

Killer: *hit man (slang)*

Kind: *child; issue; offspring* **leibliches** ~ *natural child* **mißhandeltes** ~ *battered child* **uneheliches** ~ *bastard*

Kinder: *issue; offspring*

Kinderheim: kommunales ~ *community home*

Kindesraub: *child stealing*

Kindestötung: *child destruction; infanticide*

Kindestötung durch Abtreibung: *child destruction*

Kirchengericht: *ecclesiastical court*

kirchlich: *ecclesiastical*

Kiste: *case*

klagbar: *actionable*

Klage: *grievance; lawsuit; petition; plaint; suit* **dingliche** ~ *action in rem* **eine** ~ **abweisen** *to*

enter judgment against the plaintiff **eine** ~ **beantworten** *to file a defence* **eine** ~ **zurückziehen** *to abandon an action* **einer** ~ **stattgeben** *to enter judgment for the plaintiff* **leichtfertige erhobene** ~ *frivolous complaint or frivolous action* **obligatorische** ~ *action in personam* **schikanöse** ~ *vexatious action or litigation* **zivilrechtliche** ~ *civil action*

Klageabweisung: *to be nonsuit or nonsuited*

Klageantrag: *prayer*

Klage auf Mietzahlung: *rent action*

Klagebegehren: *claim; relief*

Klagebegründung: *particulars or statement of claim*

Klage erheben: *to take legal action; to start legal proceedings; to sue*

Klageerwiderung: *answer; defence or defense (US); plea*

Klagefrist: *time limitation*

Klagegrund: *cause of action*

Klagehäufung: *joinder*

Klage mit Ladung: *originating summons*

klagen: *go to law; sue*

Kläger: *claimant; complainant; petitioner; plaintiff* **als** ~ **auftreten** *prosecute*

Klagerücknahme: *to be nonsuit or nonsuited*

Klageschrift: *claim; complaint; plaint note*

Klageschrift mit Ladung: *writ (of summons)*

Klageverbindung: *joinder*

Klage wegen Amtsanmaßung: *quo warranto*

klar: *clear; explicit*

klarmachen: sich ~ *realize*

klarstellen: *clarify*

Klarstellung: *clarification*

Klasse: *bracket; category; class*

klassifizieren: *class; classify*

Klassifizierung: *classification*

klauen: *knock off (slang); lift (informal); nick (slang); pilfer; pinch (informal)*

Klausel: *clause; provision; stipulation*

Kleinanzeigen: *small ads*

Kleinkrimineller: *petty thief*

Kleptomane *or* **Kleptomanin:** *kleptomaniac*

Kleptomanie: *kleptomania*

klerikal: *clerical*

Klient: *client*

Klientele: *clientele*

Klinik: psychiatrische ~ *psychiatric hospital*

klug: *clever*

Knacki: *con (slang); jailbird* **alter** ~ *old lag*

knapp: *in short supply*

Knast: *lock-up; porridge (slang)* **im** ~ *inside (slang)*

Knastbruder: *con (slang); jailbird*

Know-how: *know-how*

Knüppel: *cosh*

Koalitionsfreiheit: *freedom of association*

Kodex: *code*

Kodifikation: *consolidation*

kodifizieren: *codify*
Kodifizierungsgesetz: *Consolidating Act*
Kodifizierung von Gesetzen: *codification*
Kodizill: *codicil*
Koffer: *case*
Kohlepapier: *carbon paper*
Kollation: *collation*
Kollege *or* **Kollegin:** *colleague; counterpart*
Kollekte: *collections*
Kollektiveigentum *or* **Kollektivinhaberschaft:** *collective ownership*
Kollektivverantwortung: *collective responsibility*
Kollision: *collision*
Kollisionsrecht: *Conflict of Laws*
Kollusion: *collusion*
Kolonne: *column*
Kombination mehrerer Versicherungsarten: *blanket insurance policy*
Komitee: *committee*
Kommandeur der Polizei: *commissioner of police or police commissioner*
Kommanditgesellschaft: *limited partnership*
Kommando: *squad*
Kommentar: *comment; commentary*
Kommentator: juristischer ~ *legal writer*
kommerzialisieren: *commercialize*
Kommerzialisierung: *commercialization*
kommerziell: *commercial; commercially*
Kommissar: *commissioner*
Kommission: *commission*
Kommissionär: *factor*
Kommissionsware: *goods on consignment*
Kommorienten: *commorientes*
kommunal: *municipal*
Kommunikationsverbindungen: *communications*
Kommunikationswege: neue ~ erschließen *to open up new channels of communication*
kompetent: *competent*
Kompetenzüberschreitung: *excess of jurisdiction*
komplett: *complete* etwas ~ kaufen *to purchase something outright or to make an outright purchase*
Komplex: *complex*
komplex: *complex*
Komplize *or* **Komplizin:** *accessory; accomplice*
kompliziert: *complex; complicated*
Kompromiß: *compromise* einen ~ schließen *compromise*
kompromittieren: *compromise*
Kondition: *condition*
Konferenz: *conference*
Konferenzprogramm: *conference timetable*
Konferenzprotokoll: *conference proceedings*
Konferenz zur Absatzplanung: *sales conference or sales meeting*
konferieren: *confer*
Konfiskation: *forfeiture*

konfiszieren: *confiscate; forfeit; sequester or sequestrate*
Konfiszierung: *confiscation; seizure; sequestration*
Konflikt: *strife*
Kongreß: *Congress*
Kongreß-: *Congressional*
Kongreßabgeordneter: *Congressman*
König: der ~ *Rex*
Königin: die ~ *Regina*
königlich: *royal*
Königliches Hoheitsrecht: *royal prerogative*
Konjunkturindikatoren: staatliche ~ *government economic indicators*
Konjunkturrückgang: *recession*
Konjunkturtief: *trough*
konkludent: *implied*
Konkurrent: *competitor*
Konkurrenz: *competition* die ~ schlagen *to knock the competition*
Konkurrenzverbot: *restraint of trade*
Konkurs: *bankruptcy* betrügerischer ~ *criminal bankruptcy*
Konkursantrag: *bankruptcy petition* einen ~ stellen *to file a petition in bankruptcy*
Konkursanzeige: *bankruptcy notice*
Konkursaufhebung: *discharge in or of bankruptcy*
Konkursaufhebungsbeschluß: *annulment of adjudication*
Konkursbilanz: *statement of affairs*
Konkurseröffnungsantrag: *bankruptcy petition; winding up petition*
Konkurseröffnungsbeschluß: *adjudication order or adjudication of bankruptcy* vorläufiger ~ *receiving order*
Konkursfirma: *wreck*
Konkursforderung: eine ~ anmelden *to prove a debt*
Konkursgericht: *Bankruptcy Court*
Konkursgläubiger: nachrangiger ~ *deferred creditor*
Konkursschuldner: *bankrupt* entlasteter ~ *discharged bankrupt* nicht entlasteter ~ *undischarged bankrupt* rehabilitierter ~ *certificated bankrupt*
Konkursverfahren: *bankruptcy proceedings*
Konkursverwalter: *liquidator; Official Receiver; trustee in bankruptcy* vorläufiger ~ *provisional liquidator*
Konkursverwaltung: *receivership*
Konnossement: *bill of lading* unreines ~ *foul bill of lading*
Konsens: *consensus* durch ~ *consensual*
Konsignatant: *consignor*
Konsignatar: *consignee*
Konsignation: *consignation; consignment*
Konsortium: *concert party; consortium*
Konspiration: *conspiracy*
konspirieren: *conspire*
konstruieren: *construct*

Konstruktion: *construction*
konstruktiv: *constructive*
Konsultation: *consultancy*
konsultieren: *consult*
Konsum: *consumption*
Konsument: *consumer*
Konsumgüter: *consumer goods*
Kontakt aufnehmen: *to contact*
Kontakt(person): *contact*
Kontext: *context*
Kontingent: *quota*
Kontingentierungssystem: *quota system*
kontinuierlich: *continuous*
Konto: ein ~ **auflösen** *to close an account* ein ~ **ausgleichen** *or* **begleichen** *to settle an account* ein ~ **belasten** *to debit an account* **gemeinsames** ~ *joint account* **laufendes** ~ *cheque account; current account* **umsatzloses** ~ *dead or dormant account*
Kontoauszug: *bank statement*
Kontokorrentkonto: *open account*
Kontokorrentkredit: *open credit*
Kontostand: *bank balance*
Kontrolle: *check; control; inspection* **außer** ~ *out of control* **unter** ~ *under control* **unter** ~ **gehalten** *controlled*
Kontrolleur: *inspector*
kontrollieren: *check; inspect; police*
Kontrollorgan: *watchdog body*
Kontrollsiegel: *inspection stamp*
Kontrolltaste: *control key*
Kontroverse: *dispute*
Konvention: *convention*
Konzept: *rough copy; (rough) draft*
Konzern: *concern; group*
Konzernergebnisse: *group results*
Konzerngesellschaft: *related company*
Konzession: *concession; licence or license (US)*
Konzessionär: *concessionnaire*
Konzessions-: *licensing*
Konzessionsinhaber: *licensee*
Konzession zum Alkoholverkauf: *off licence (GB)*
konzipieren: *draft; draw up*
Kooperation: *co-operation*
kooperativ: *co-operative*
Kooperative: *co-operative*
kooperieren: *co-operate*
kooptieren: *to co-opt*
Kopf: pro ~ *per head; per capita*
köpfen: *behead*
Kopfsteuer: *poll tax*
Kopie: *copy; counterpart; duplicate; imitation* **beglaubigte** ~ *certified copy* **getreue** ~ *true copy*
Kopieren: *duplicating*
kopieren: *copy; imitate*
Kopierer: *copier or copying machine*
Kopiergerät: *duplicator; copying or duplicating machine*
körperlich: *bodily; physical* **nicht** ~ *incorporeal*

Körperschaft: *corporation (GB)* **juristische** ~ *corporate personality*
Körperverletzung: *actual bodily harm (ABH); battery; personal injury* **schwere** ~ *grievous bodily harm (GBH)*
Korpus: *corpus*
korrekt: *correct*
Korrektur: *correction; rectification*
Korrespondent: *correspondent*
Korrespondenz: *correspondence*
korrigieren: *correct; rectify*
korrumpieren: *to corrupt*
korrupt: *bent (slang); corrupt*
Korruption: *corruption*
kostbar: *valuable*
Kosten: *charge; cost; expense* **die** ~ **decken** *to cover costs* **die** ~ **tragen** *to pay costs* **erstattungsfähige** ~ *party and party costs* **festgesetzte** *or* **feststehende** ~ *fixed costs* **mit hohen** ~ *at great expense*
kosten: *cost*
Kostendegression: *economies of scale*
Kostenentscheidung: *costs order*
Kostenfestsetzung: *taxation of costs*
Kostenfestsetzungsbeamter: *Taxing Master*
kostenlos: *free (of charge)*
Kostensachbearbeiter: *costs draftsman*
Kostenverteilung: *allocatur*
Kostenvoranschlag: *estimate; quotation*
kostspielig: *dear*
Kraft: *force; power* **außer** ~ **setzen** *abrogate; overrule; repeal; rescind* **in** ~ *in operation* **in** ~ **sein** *to be in force* **in** ~ **treten** *to come into force; to become operative* **mit rückwirkender** ~ *with retrospective effect*
Kraftfahrzeugkennzeichen: *registration number*
Kraftfahrzeugversicherung: *car or motor insurance*
Kraftloserklärung: *invalidation*
Krankenhaus: *hospital*
Krankenhaustrakt: *hospital block*
Krankenurlaub: *sick leave*
Krankenversicherung: *medical insurance*
Krawall: *riot* **Krawall machen** *to riot*
Kredit: *credit; loan* **auf** ~ **kaufen** *to buy on credit* **befristeter** ~ *term loan* **verlängerter** ~ *extended credit* **zinsloser** ~ *soft loan*
Kreditaufnahme: *borrowing*
Kreditauskunft: *status inquiry*
Kreditauskunftei: *credit agency or credit bureau (US)*
Kreditbank: *credit bank*
Kreditfähigkeit: *borrowing power*
Kreditgeber letzter Hand *or* **letzter Instanz:** *lender of the last resort*
Kreditinstitut: *financial institution*
Kreditkarte: *credit card*
Kreditkartenhülle: *credit card holder*
Kreditkarteninhaber: *credit card holder*
Kreditlimit *or* **Kreditlinie:** *credit limit*

Kreditmodalitäten: *credit facilities*
Kreditnehmer: *borrower; debtor*
Kreditnote: *credit note*
Kreditrestriktionen aufheben: *to lift credit restrictions*
Kreditsaldo: *credit balance*
Kreditspalte: *credit column*
Kredittransfer: *credit transfer or transfer of funds*
Kreditvergaben: *bank borrowings*
Kreditwucher: *usury*
Kreis: *circuit*
Kreislauf: *cycle*
Kreistag: *county council*
Kreuz: *mark* **mit** ~ **Unterzeichnender** *marksman*
Kreuzverhör: *cross-examination* **ins** ~ **nehmen** *cross-examine*
Kriegsbeute: *spoils of war*
Kriegsgefangene(r): *prisoner of war*
Kriegsrecht: *martial law*
Kriminalistik: *forensic science*
Kriminalität: *crime; delinquency* **organisierte** ~ *racketeering*
kriminell: *criminal*
Kriminelle(r): *criminal*
Kriminologie: *criminology*
Krisenmanager: *troubleshooter*
Krisenmaßnahmen ergreifen: *to take emergency measures*
Krisenplan: *contingency plan*
Kriterium: *criterion*
Kritik: *criticism* **sachliche** ~ *fair comment*
kritisieren: *criticize*
Kronanwalt: *Queen's Counsel; Crown prosecutor (GB)*
Krone: die ~ *the Crown (GB); Regina; Rex*
Kronrat: *Privy Council*
Kronzeuge: als ~ **aussagen** *to turn Queen's evidence; to turn state's evidence*
krumm: *bent (slang)*
Kulanzzahlung: *an ex gratia payment*
kümmern: sich ~ **um** *attend to*
kündbar: *terminable*
Kunde: *client* **ein langjähriger** ~ *or* **treuer** ~ **a** *long-standing customer or customer of long standing* **ein zufriedener** ~ **a** *satisfied customer*
Kunden: einen ~ **bedienen** *to serve a customer* **einen** ~ **zufriedenstellen** *to satisfy a client*
Kundenkonto: ein ~ **sperren** *to close an account*
Kundenkredit: *consumer credit*
Kundenkreditkonto: *credit account*
kündigen: *leave; quit; resign; terminate*
Kündigung: *notice; resignation; termination* **erzwungene** ~ *constructive dismissal* **seine** ~ **einreichen** *to hand in or to give in or to tender one's resignation* **unrechtmäßige** ~ *wrongful dismissal*
Kündigung des Mieters: *notice to quit*
Kündigungsabsicht: *animus cancellandi*
Kündigungsfrist: *period of notice*
Kündigungsklausel: *termination clause*
Kündigungsschutz: *security of tenure*
Kundin: *client*
Kundschaft: *clientele; custom*
künftig: *henceforth; hereafter*
Kunstfehler: ärztlicher ~ *malpractice*
Kuppelei: *procuring or procurement*
Kuppelei betreiben: *procure*
Kuppler: *procurer*
Kurs: *course; policy*
Kursgewinne: *capital gains*
Kurs-Gewinn-Verhältnis: *price/earnings ratio*
Kursmanipulant: *stock market manipulator*
Kursmanipulation: *stock market manipulation*
Kursnotierung: *quotation on the Stock Exchange or Stock Exchange quotation*
Kursus: *course*
kürzen: *abate; cut; dock*
kürzeren: den ~ **ziehen** *lose out*
kurzfristig: *at short notice; short-term*
Kurzmitteilung: *compliments slip*
Kurzschrift: *shorthand*
Kurztitel: *short title*
Kürzung: *abatement; cut*

Ll

Ladeliste: *manifest*
Laden: *joint (slang); shop*
laden: *summon*
Ladendieb: *shoplifter*
Ladendiebstahl: *shoplifting*
Ladenpreis: *retail price*
Ladenräume: *shop premises*
Ladenschild: *sign*
Ladenschluß: *closing time*
Ladentisch: *counter*
Ladung: *shipment; summons*
Lage: *position; situation*
Lager: auf ~ **halten** *keep; stock*
Lagerbestand: *stock*
Lagerhaus: *warehouse*
Lagerkapazität: *storage capacity*
lagern: *warehouse*
Lagersteuerung: *stock control*
Lagerung: *warehousing*
Lagerung unter Zollverschluß: *warehousing in bond*
Laie: *layman*
Laienbeisitzer: *lay assessor*
Laienrichter: *lay magistrate*
Land: *country; land* **meistbegünstigtes** ~ *most favoured nation*
Landbesitzrecht: *land tenure*
Landegebühren: *landing charges*
landen: *land*
Ländereien der Krone: *Crown Lands*

Landesarbeitsgericht: *Employment Appeal Tribunal*

Landesgesetz: *municipal law*

Landesverrat: *treason felony*

landesverräterisch: *treasonable*

Landstreicher: *vagrant*

Landstreicherei: *vagrancy*

lange: schon ~ **bestehend** *long-standing*

Langfinger: *dip (slang)*

langfristig: *long-term* **etwas** ~ **betrachten** *to take the long view*

Langläufer: *longs*

Langschrift: *longhand*

Lärmbekämpfung: *noise abatement*

lässig: *casual*

Last: *onus*

lästern: Gott ~ **blaspheme**

lästig: *onerous*

Lastschrift: *debit entry*

Lastschriftanzeige: *debit note*

Latein(isch): *Latin*

latent: *latent*

Lauf: im ~ *in the course of*

Laufbursche: *messenger boy*

Laufzeit: *life; period of validity*

laut: *according to; as per; pursuant to*

Leasing: *leasing*

Leben: *life*

Lebenden: unter ~ *inter vivos*

Lebensdauer: *life*

Lebenserwartung: *life expectancy*

Lebenshaltungskosten: *cost of living*

Lebenshaltungskostenindex: *cost-of-living index*

Lebenshaltungskostenzuschuß: *cost-of-living allowance*

lebenslang: *for life*

Lebenslänglicher: *lifer (slang)*

Lebenslauf: *curriculum vitae; résumé (US)*

Lebensstandard: *standard of living*

Lebensversicherung: *life assurance or life insurance* **gemischte** ~ *endowment assurance or endowment policy* **zeitlich begrenzte** ~ *term insurance*

Lebenszeit: auf ~ *for life*

ledig: *unmarried*

leer: *blank*

Leerung: *collection*

legal: *over the counter; legal*

legalisieren: *legalize; validate*

Legalisierung: *legalization; legitimation or legitimization*

Legalität: *legality*

legen: *lay; place; set*

leger: *casual*

legislativ: *legislative*

Legislative: *legislature*

legitim: *legitimate*

Legitimierung: *legitimation or legitimization*

Lehrer: *instructor*

Lehrgang: *course* **kaufmännischer** ~ *commercial course*

Lehrvertrag: *indentures or articles of indenture*

Leibrente: *life annuity or annuity for life*

Leibwächter: *bodyguard; minder (slang)*

Leiche: *cadaver (US); corpse (GB)*

Leichenschau: *inquest*

leichtfertig: *reckless*

Leichtfertigkeit: *recklessness*

Leihen: *borrowing; hire*

leihen: *borrow; loan; rent*

Leihgebühr: *rental*

Leihhaus: *pawnshop*

Leihwagen: *hire car*

leisten: *perform*

Leistung: *benefit; merit; performance*

Leistung der Vertragsschuld: *specific performance*

Leistungsbeurteilung: *merit rating; performance review*

Leistungserfüllung: *discharge by performance*

leistungsfähig: *capable; efficient*

Leistungsklage: *personal action*

Leistungsnachweis: *track record*

Leistungsort: *place of performance*

Leistungsprämie: *merit award or merit bonus*

Leistungsversprechen: wechselseitiges ~ *executory consideration*

Leistungszulage: *merit increase*

Leitartikel: *editorial*

leiten: *conduct; head; manage; run*

Leiter: *director; head; leader; principal; superintendent; warden*

Leiter der Anklagebehörde: *Director of Public Prosecutions (DPP)*

Leiter der Buchhaltung: *controller (US); accounts manager*

Leiter der Haftanstalt: *warden*

Leiter der PR-Abteilung: *public relations officer*

Leiter des Finanzamtes: *inspector of taxes or tax inspector*

Leitsatz: *headnote*

Leitung: *chairmanship; control; direction* **unter neuer** ~ *under new management*

Leitzins: *prime rate*

Lektor: *editor*

Lesung: erste ~ *First Reading* **zweite** ~ *Second Reading*

Leugnen: *denial*

leugnen: *deny*

Leumundsbeweise aufbieten: *to introduce character evidence*

Lichtrecht: *ancient lights (GB)*

Lieferant: *supplier*

Lieferauftrag: *delivery order*

liefern: *deliver; supply*

Lieferschein: *delivery note*

Lieferung: *consignment; delivery; supply* **eine ~ abnehmen** *to take delivery of goods* **zahlbar bei ~** *payable on delivery*

Lieferungen: noch ausstehende ~ *back orders or outstanding orders*

Lieferzeit: *lead time*

Liegegeld: *demurrage*

Liegenschaften: *(real) property*

Liegenschaftsrecht: *law of property*

Liegeplatz: *mooring*

LIFO-Abschreibungsmethode der Vorratsbewertung: *last in first out*

Limit: *limit* **ohne ~** *without reserve*

Linie: *policy* **in erster ~** *primarily* **in zweiter ~** *secondarily*

Linienmanagement: *line management*

Liquidation: *liquidation; winding up* **freiwillige ~** *voluntary liquidation*

Liquidator: *liquidator*

Liquidität: *liquidity*

Liquiditätsreserven: *cash reserves*

Liste: *list; register; schedule* **schwarze ~** *black list*

Listenpreis: *list price*

Lizenz: *licence or license (US)*

Lizenzabkommen: *licensing agreement*

Lizenzgebühren: *royalty*

Lizenzinhaber: *licensee*

Lizenznehmer: eingetragener ~ *registered user*

Lizenzwaren: *goods manufactured under licence*

Lockartikel: *loss-leader*

Lockspitzel: *agent provocateur*

Lohn: *compensation (US); pay; remuneration*

Lohnabzüge: *deductions from salary*

Lohnerhöhung: *raise (US); rise*

Lohnforderung: *wage claim*

Lohnordnung: *scale of salaries or salary scale*

Lohnpfändung: *attachment of earnings*

Lohnrückstand: *back wages or back pay*

Lohnscheck: *pay cheque or paycheck*

Lohn- und Gehaltspaket: *compensation package*

Lohn- und Gehaltspfändung: *attachment of earnings*

Lohn- und Gehaltspfändungsbeschluß: *attachment of earnings order*

Lohnverhandlungen: *pay negotiations or pay talks*

Lohnzulage: *increase*

Lokal: *bar*

lokal: *local*

Lokalblätter: *the local press*

Lokopreis: *spot price*

Londoner: die ~ Polizei *the Metropolitan Police*

Longs: *longs*

Lordkanzler: *Lord Chancellor*

Lordoberrichter: *Lord Chief Justice*

Lordrichter: *Lord Justice*

Lords: *Lords*

Los: *lot*

löschen: *expunge; land*

Löschgebühren und Löschungszölle: *landing charges*

Löschung: *extinguishment*

Löschungsbewilligung: *memorandum of satisfaction*

Lösegeld: *ransom*

Lösegeldforderung: *ransom note*

lösen: *break; solve; terminate*

loskaufen: *ransom*

losschlagen: *to dispose of*

Lösung: *termination*

Losverfahren: *ballot*

Lotterie: *lottery*

Lücke: *blank*

Luftpost: per ~ *by air mail*

Luftpostbrief: *air letter; airmail letter*

lukrativ: *lucrative*

lustlos: *flat*

lynchen: *lynch*

Lynchjustiz: *lynch law*

Mm

Macht: *power*

Machtmißbrauch: *abuse of power*

Mafia: die ~ *the Mafia; mob (US)*

Magazin: *periodical*

Magistratsbeamter: *magistrates' clerk*

Magna Charta: *Magna Carta*

Magnetband: *magnetic tape or mag tape (informal)*

Mahnbescheid: *default summons*

Mahnbrief or Mahnschreiben: *letter of demand*

Mahnung: letzte ~ *final demand*

Mahnverfahren: *default action*

Majorität: *majority*

Makler: *agent; broker*

Maklergebühr: *commission*

Management: *management* **mittleres ~** *middle management* **unteres ~** *junior management* **zielorientiertes ~** *management by objectives*

Management-Ausbildung: *management training*

Managementkurs: *management course*

Management-Team: *management team*

Managerin: *manageress*

Mandant: *client*

Mangel: *defect; imperfection; lack*

mangeln an: *lack*

mangels: *failing*

Manipulation der Wahlresultate: *ballot-rigging*

manipulieren: *fiddle (informal)*

Mappe: *binder* **kastenförmige ~** *box file*

Marge: *margin*

Mariä Verkündigung: *Lady Day*

Marineministerium: britisches ~ *Admiralty*

Marke: *brand*

Marken-: *proprietary*
Markenartikel: *branded goods*
Markenname: *brand name*
Markenpirat: *pirate*
Markenpiraterie: *piracy*
Market-maker: *market maker*
markieren: *brand; mark*
Markierung: *mark*
Markt: *market* den ~ **beherrschen** *monopolize* **geschlossener** ~ *closed market* **offener** ~ *open market; market overt*
Markterschließung: *a market opening*
Marktführer: *market leader*
Marktpreis: *market price*
Markttag: *market day*
Marktwert: *market value*
Marktwirtschaft: **freie** ~ *free market economy*
Maschine: **eine** ~ **bedienen** *to operate a machine*
Maschinenanlage: *plant*
Maschinencode: *machine code*
maschinengeschrieben: *typewritten*
Maschinenlauf: *run*
Maschinensaal: *machine shop*
Maschinensprache: *machine language*
Maschinerie: *machinery*
Maschinist: *operative*
Maß: *measure*
Maße: *measurements* **in gewissem** ~ *to a certain extent*
Massenausbruch: *mass jailbreak*
Massenproduktion: *mass production*
maßgebend: *leading*
Maßnahmen: **steuerpolitische** ~ *fiscal measures*
Maßstab: *standard*
Materie: *substance*
materiell: *substantive*
Matrizenpapier: *duplicating paper*
maximal-: *maximum*
Maxime: *maxim*
Maximum: *maximum*
Medikament: *drug*
Medizin: *medicine*
medizinisch: *medical*
Meeres-: *marine*
mehrdeutig: *ambiguous*
Mehrdeutigkeit: *ambiguity* **versteckte** ~ *latent ambiguity*
mehrfach: *multiple*
Mehrgewinn: *excess profits*
Mehrgewinnsteuer: *excess profits tax*
Mehrheit: *majority* **ohne** ~ *hung*
Mehrheitsaktionär: *majority shareholder*
Mehrheitsbeschluß: *majority vote or majority decision* **einfacher** ~ *ordinary resolution* **gewöhnlicher** ~ *ordinary resolution*
Mehrheitsbeteiligung: *majority shareholding or interest*

Mehrheitsvotum der Geschworenen: *majority verdict*
Mehrwertsteuer: *output tax; Value Added Tax (VAT)*
Mehrwertsteuererklärung: *VAT declaration* **eine** ~ **ausfüllen** *to fill in a VAT return*
mehrwertsteuerfrei: *zero-rated*
Meineid: *perjury*
meineidig werden: *to perjure oneself*
Meinung: *view* **anderer** ~ **sein** *differ; dissent; to have a division of opinion* **der** ~ **sein** *to be of the opinion* **öffentliche** ~ *public opinion*
Meinungsforscher: *canvasser; pollster*
Meinungsforschung: *canvassing*
Meinungsumfrage: *opinion poll or research*
Meinungsverschiedenheit: *dissent* **eine** ~ **haben** *to have a division of opinion*
Meistbegünstigungsklausel: *most-favoured-nation clause*
Meistbietender: *highest bidder*
meistern: *overcome*
melden: *report; return*
meldepflichtig: *notifiable*
Meldeschein: *certificate of registration*
Meldung: *amtliche* ~ *official return*
Menschengedenken: **seit** ~ *from time immemorial*
Menschenraub: *kidnapping*
Menschenrechte: *human rights*
menschlich: *human*
Messe: *show*
messen: *measure*
Meuterei: *mutiny*
Meuterer: *mutineer*
meutern: *mutiny*
Michaelis(tag): *Michaelmas*
Mietbeihilfe: *rent rebate*
Miete: *rent(al)* **nominelle** ~ *peppercorn rent* **symbolische** ~ *token rent* **überhöhte** ~ *rack rent*
Mieteinkünfte: *rental income or income from rentals*
Mieten: *chartering; hire*
mieten: *charter; lease; rent; hire*
Mieter: *charterer; hirer; lessee; tenant* **einem** ~ **kündigen** *to give a tenant notice to quit or to serve a tenant with notice to quit*
Mieterschutzgesetz: *the Landlord and Tenant Act*
Miet- od Pachtdauer *or* **Miet- od Pachtverhältnis:** *tenancy*
Mietpreisbindung: *rent controls*
Mietrückstand: *back rent*
Mietshaus: *tenement*
Mietverhältnis mit Mieterschutz: *protected tenancy*
Mietvertrag: *lease*
Mietvorauszahlung: *key money*
Mietwagen: *hire car*
Mietwohnung: *tenement*

Mietzuschuß: *rent allowance*
Mikrofiche: *microfiche*
Mikrofilm: *microfilm*
mild: *lenient*
Milde: *clemency*
mildern: *commute; mitigate*
Milderung: *commutation; mitigation* **zur** ~ **von** *in extenuation of something*
Militärgericht: *court-martial (GB); military tribunal*
Militärgerichtsprozeß: *court-martial*
militärisch: *martial*
Militärpolizei: *military police*
Minderheit: *minority*
Minderheitsaktionär: *minority shareholder*
Minderheitsbeteiligung: *minority shareholding or minority interest*
Minderjähriger: *infant; minor; ward; young person*
Minderjährigkeit: *minority*
minderwertig: *inferior; substandard*
Mindestbetrag: *minimum payment*
Mindestdividende: *minimum dividend*
Mindestgebot: *reserve (price)*
Mindestlohn: *minimum wage*
Mindestpreis: garantierter ~ *intervention price*
Mindestreserven: *bank reserves or special deposits*
Mindeststrafe: *minimum sentence*
Minister: *minister; Secretary of State (GB)*
Ministerium: *Department of State; ministry*
Minister ohne Geschäftsbereich: *Minister without Portfolio*
Ministerpräsident: *Prime Minister*
Ministerrat: *Council of Ministers*
Minna: grüne ~ *Black Maria (informal)*
Minorität: *minority*
mißachten: *flout*
Mißachtung der Parlamentshoheit: *contempt of Parliament or contempt of the House*
Mißachtung des Gerichts: *contempt of court*
mißbilligen: *disapprove*
Mißbilligung: *disapproval*
Mißbilligungsvotum: *vote of censure or censure vote*
Mißbrauch: *abuse; misuse*
mißbrauchen: *abuse*
Mißerfolg: kommerzieller ~ *commercial failure*
Missetat: *wrongdoing*
mißhandeln: *abuse*
Mißhandlung: *abuse; battery; cruelty*
mißinterpretieren: *misinterpret*
Mißtrauensvotum: *vote of no confidence*
Mißverständnis: *misunderstanding*
mißverstehen: *misinterpret*
Mißwirtschaft: *maladministration; mismanagement*
Mit-: *co-; joint*
Mitarbeiter: *associate* **freier** ~ *freelance*
Mitbeklagter: *co-defendant; co-respondent*

Mitdirektor: *co-director*
Miteigentum: *common ownership; co-ownership; joint ownership; ownership in common*
Miteigentümer: *co-owner; co-proprietor*
Miterbe: *joint heir*
Mit freundlichen Grüßen: *yours faithfully*
Mitgift: *dowry*
Mitglied: *member* **neues** ~ *recruit* **ordentliches** ~ *ordinary member*
Mitglied des Kronrates: *Privy Councillor*
Mitglied des Oberhauses: *peer*
Mitglied des Unterhauses: *Member of Parliament (GB)*
Mitglieder des Oberhauses: *Lords*
Mitglieder werben: *recruit*
Mitgliedschaft: *membership*
Mitinhaber: *co-owner*
Mitinhaberschaft: *co-ownership*
mitrechnen: *count*
Mittäter: *accessory; accomplice; joint tortfeasors*
mitteilen: *inform*
Mitteilung: *communication; memorandum; note; notice* **laut** ~ *as per advice*
Mitteilung der Nichthonorierung *or* **der Nichtzahlung:** *notice of dishonour*
Mittel: *funds; means* **flüssige** ~ *liquid assets; ready money; realizable assets* **öffentliche** ~ *public funds*
Mittel-: *mesne; middle*
mittelbar: *vicarious*
mittelfristig: *medium-term*
Mittelwert: *average*
Mitverschulden: *contributory negligence*
Mitversicherung: *co-insurance*
mitzählen: *count*
Möbelabteilung: *furniture department*
Möbellager: *furniture depository*
Mobiliar: *goods and chattels*
Mobiliarhypothek: *chattel mortgage (US)*
Mobilien: *movable property; movables*
möblieren: *furnish*
Modell: *example*
modifizieren: *modify; qualify*
Modifizierung: *modification*
Modus operandi: *modus operandi*
Möglichkeit: *chance*
mohammedanisch: *Muslim*
Monarch: *sovereign*
Monat: jeden zweiten ~ *bi-monthly* **vorletzten** ~ *the month before last*
monatlich: *monthly*
Monitor: *monitor*
Monogamie: *monogamy*
Monopol: staatliches ~ *public monopoly or state monopoly* **unumschränktes** ~ *absolute monopoly*
monopolisieren: *monopolize*
Monopolisierung: *monopolization*
Moral: *morals* **jds** ~ **korrumpieren** *or* **verderben** *to corrupt someone's morals*

moralisch: *moral*
Moratorium: *moratorium*
Mord: *assassination; homicide; murder* **vorsätzlicher ~** *first degree murder*
morden: *murder*
Mörder: *assassin; killer; murderer* **gedungener ~** *hired killer; hit man (slang)*
Mörderin: *murderess*
mörderisch veranlagt: *homicidal*
Mordkommission: *Homicide or Murder Squad*
Mordversuch: *attempted murder*
moslemisch: *Muslim*
Motiv: *motive; reason*
Mr. X: *Mr Big (informal)*
Mündel: *ward*
Mündelkonto: *nominee account*
Mündel unter Amtsvormundschaft: *ward of court*
mündlich: *oral; parol; verbal; viva voce*
Münze: *coin*
Muster: *example; sample; specimen* **gemäß dem ~** *as per sample*
Musterbuch: *pattern book*
Musterprozeß: *test case*
Mustervertrag: *standard agreement or standard contract*
Muttergesellschaft: *parent company*
Muttermord: *matricide*
Mutterschaftsurlaub: *maternity leave*
mutwillig: *wilful; wilfully*
mutwillig zerstören: *vandalize*

Nn

nach-: *post-*
Nachahmung: *imitation*
Nachbar: *neighbour*
Nachbarschaft: *neighbourhood*
Nachbarschaftsinitiative zur Kriminalitätsbekämpfung: *neighbourhood watch*
Nachdruck: unerlaubter ~ *piracy*
Nacheile: *hot pursuit*
nachfassen: *follow up*
Nachfaßschreiben: *follow-up letter*
nachfolgend: *ensuing; subsequent*
Nachfolger: successor jds ~ sein *succeed*
Nachfrage: *demand*
Nachfragemonopol: *monopsony*
Nachfrist: *extension of time; grace; time summons*
nachgeboren: *posthumous*
nachgehen: *follow up*
nachgemacht: *sham*
Nachkomme: *descendant* **Nachkommen** *issue; offspring*
nachkommen: *obey*
Nachlaß: *allowance; estate* **beweglicher ~** *personal estate or property* **restlicher ~** *residue*

nachlassen: *knock off*
nachlässig: *negligent*
Nachlässigkeit: *negligence*
Nachlaßverwalter: *administrator*
Nachlösegebühr: *excess fare*
nachmachen: *imitate*
nachmittags: *p.m. or post meridiem*
Nachnahme: gegen ~ *cash on delivery*
Nachname: *surname*
Nachrede: üble ~ *defamatory statement; slander*
Nachricht: *communication*
Nachrichten: *news*
Nachrichtenagentur: *news agency*
Nachricht zum Strafantritt: *committal warrant*
nachschicken: jdm etwas ~ *to forward something to someone*
Nachsicht: *connivance*
nachsichtig: *lenient*
nachspüren: *trace*
nachstehend: *hereafter; hereinafter; puisne; thereinafter*
Nachtdienst: *night duty*
Nachteil: *disadvantage*
nachteilig: *adverse; detrimental*
Nachttarif: *night rate*
Nachttresor: *night safe*
Nachvermächtnisnehmer: *residuary legatee*
Nachwahl: *by-election*
nachweisbar: *provable*
Nachweis der Identifizierung: *proof of identification*
Nachweis des Eigentumtitels: *deducing title*
Nachweis einer Konkursforderung: *proof of debt*
nachweisen: *establish; evidence; prove*
Nachwuchsmanager: *junior executive or junior manager*
Nachzahlung: *back payment*
Nachzugsaktien: *deferred stock or shares*
nähern: sich ~ *approach*
Nahverkehrszug: *commuter train*
Namen: in ~ von *on behalf of* **unter dem ~** *under the name of*
namens: *pro*
Namensliste: *roll*
nämlich: *videlicet*
Nation: *nation*
national: *national*
Nationalität: *nationality*
Natur: *nature*
Naturfasern: *natural fibre*
Naturrecht: *natural justice; natural right*
Nebenanschluß: *extension*
Nebenanwalt: *junior*
Nebenausgaben: *incidental expenses*
Nebenbeschuldigung: *holding charge*
Nebenfrage: *collateral issue*
Nebenintervenient: *intervener*
Nebenkläger: *intervener*

nebensächlich: *incidental; subsidiary*
Nebenvertrag: *collateral contract*
negativ: *negative*
nehmen: auf sich ~ *incur*
nennen: *name*
Nennwert: *denomination; face value; nominal value*
Nervenheilanstalt: *asylum; mental hospital*
Nettogewinn: *net profit*
Nettopreis: *net price*
Nettoverdienst: *take-home pay*
Neubeginn: *departure*
Neuemission: *new issue*
Neuordnung: *reorganization*
Nichtanerkennung: *repudiation*
Nichtanerkennung der Menschenrechte: *denial of human rights*
Nichtansässiger: *non-resident*
Nichtbezahlung einer Verpflichtung: *non-payment of a debt*
Nichtdiskriminierung im Außenhandel: *fair trade*
nichtehelich: *illegitimate*
Nichtehelichkeit: *illegitimacy*
Nichteinhaltung: *failure; non-conformance*
Nichterfüllung: *default*
Nichthonorierung: *dishonour*
nichtig: *invalid; null; void* **für ~ erklären** *annul; nullify; quash; rescind*
Nichtigkeit: *invalidity; nullity*
Nichtigkeitserklärung: *rescinding or rescission*
nichtöffentlich: *closed*
Nichts: *nil*
Nichtschuldvermutung: *presumption of innocence*
nichtstreitig: *undefended*
Nichtvollzug der Ehe: *non-consummation of marriage*
Nichtzahlung: *default*
Nichtzurechenbarkeit eines Schadens: *remoteness of damage*
Niederlage: *defeat*
Niederlassung: *branch (office)*
Niederlassungsrecht: *right of establishment*
Niederträchtigkeit: *villainy*
niedriger einstufen: *downgrade*
Nießbrauch: *beneficial interest; use; usufruct*
Nießbrauchberechtigter: *beneficial occupier*
Niveau: *standard*
nochmals verhandeln: *rehear*
Nominalkapital: *nominal capital*
Nominalmiete: *nominal rent*
Nominalwert: *face or nominal value*
nominell: *nominal*
nominieren: *nominate*
Nominierte(r): *nominee*
Nominierung: *nomination*
Norm: *standard* **unter der ~** *substandard*
normal: *normal; ordinary; standard; usual*

normalerweise wohnhaft: *ordinarily resident*
Normalzeit: *Standard Time*
Normenkontrolle: *judicial review*
Not: *hardship*
Notar: *notary public*
Notariats-: *notarial*
notariell: *notarial*
Notenbank: *central bank*
Notenpresse: *security printer*
Notfall: *emergency*
Notfonds: *contingency fund or contingency reserve; emergency reserves*
notieren: *note*
Notierung: *Stock Exchange quotation*
nötig: *necessary*
nötigen: *molest*
Nötiger: *molester*
Nötigung: *coercion; duress; molestation* **durch ~** *under duress*
Nötigung zur Unzucht: *indecent assault*
Notiz: *note*
Notizblock: *notepad*
Notizbuch: *notebook*
Notlage: *hardship*
Notstand: *emergency*
Notstandsermächtigung: *emergency powers*
Notwehr: *self-defence*
notwendig(erweise): *necessarily; of necessity*
Notwendiges: *necessaries*
Notwendigkeit: *necessity*
Notzucht: *rape*
Novellierung: *amendment*
Null: *nil; zero*
Nullinflation: *zero inflation*
Nullsatz eintragen: *to make a nil return*
Nutzen: *benefit*
Nutznießer: *beneficiary*
Nutznießung: *use; usufruct*
Nutzung: *use*
Nutzungsänderung: *change of use*
Nutzungsrecht: *beneficial interest* **lebenslanges ~** *life interest* **unbeschränktes ~** *beneficial use*
Nutzungsrecht auf Lebensdauer: *life interest*

Oo

Obdachloser: *vagrant*
Obduktion: *post mortem*
oben: *thereinbefore*
Oberhaus: *House of Lords*
Oberhausmitglieder: geistliche ~ *Lords Spiritual* **weltliche ~** *Lords Temporal*
Oberrichter: *Chief Justice (US)*
Oberster Gerichtshof: *Supreme Court (of Judicature)*

Oberster Marinestaatsanwalt: *Judge Advocate of the Fleet (GB)*

Oberster Militärstaatsanwalt: *Judge Advocate-General*

Oberstes Bundesgericht: *supreme court (US)*

Oberstes Strafgericht: *High Court of Justiciary*

Oberstes Zivilgericht: *High Court (of Justice)*

Obhut: *care*

Objekt: *chose*

Objekte: steuerpflichtige ~ *taxable items*

objektiv: *objective*

Objektivität: *impartiality*

obliegt: es ~ **ihm** *it is incumbent upon him*

Obligation: *(debenture) bond*

Obligationär: *debenture holder*

Obligationsinhaber: *bondholder*

obligatorisch: *compulsory; mandatory; obligatory*

Obligo: ohne ~ *sans recours*

Obmann: *foreman of the jury; umpire*

obszön: *obscene*

Obszönität: *obscenity*

offenbaren: *reveal*

offenkundig: *flagrant; manifest; overt*

Offenlegung von Urkunden: *discovery*

offensichtlich: *a fortiori; apparent; patent*

Offensivwaffe: *offensive weapon*

offenstehend: *open; owing*

öffentlich: *public*

Öffentlichkeit: die ~ *the (general) public* **in der** ~ *in public*

Öffentlichkeitsarbeit: *public relations (PR)*

öffentlich verleumden: *libel*

Offerent: *offeror*

öffnen: *open*

Öffnungszeit: *opening hours*

Ombudsmann: *ombudsman; Parliamentary Commissioner*

Opfer: *victim*

Oppositionsführer: *Leader of the Opposition*

Oppositionspartei: *opposition*

Option: eine ~ **ausüben** *to exercise an option*

Optionsgeschäfte *or* **Optionshandel:** *option dealing or option trading*

Optionsrecht: sein ~ **ausüben** *to take up an option or to exercise an option*

Optionsrecht auf Kauf: *option to purchase*

Optionsrecht auf Verkauf: *option to sell*

Optionsvertrag: *option contract*

Order: *order* **durch königliche** ~ *by Royal Command*

ordnen: *arrange; order; regulate*

Ordnung: *order* **öffentliche** ~ *public order*

ordnungsgemäß: *due; duly; proper* **nicht** ~ *irregular*

ordnungswidrig: *disorderly*

Ordnungswidrigkeit: *summary offence*

Organisation: *organization* **karitative** ~ *charity*

Organisationsplan: *organization chart*

organisieren: *organize* **neu** ~ *reorganize*

Original: *top copy; master; original*

original: *original*

Ort: *locus; place; site; venue* **am angegebenen** ~ *loc. cit.; op. cit.* **am selben** ~ *ibid or ibidem*

öffentlicher ~ *public place*

örtlich: *local*

Ortsgespräch: *local call*

Ortsnetzkennzahl: *area code*

Output: *output*

Pp

Pacht: *leasehold; rent(al)*

pachten: *lease; rent*

Pächter: *leaseholder; lessee; tenant*

Pachtgeld: *royalty*

Pachtverhältnis: *land tenure*

Pachtverhältnis mit Pächterschutz: *protected tenancy*

Pachtvertrag: *lease; tack*

Päckchen: eingeschriebenes ~ *registered parcel*

Paket: *block*

Paketgebühr: *parcel rate*

Paketpost: *parcel post*

Panikverkäufe des Pfundes: *a run on the pound*

Papier: auf dem ~ *on paper* **bankfähiges** ~ *bankable paper* **liniertes** ~ *lined paper*

Papiere: *papers*

Papiereinzug: *paper feed*

Papiergeld: *paper money*

Papier mit Briefkopf: *headed paper*

Papiervorschub: *paper feed*

Paragraph: *article; clause; section*

paralegal: *paralegal*

paraphieren: *initial*

Parität: *parity*

Parlament: *parliament* **das** ~ **auflösen** *to dissolve Parliament*

parlamentarisch: *parliamentary*

Parlament ohne Mehrheit: *hung parliament*

Parlamentsausschuß: ständiger ~ *standing committee*

Parlamentseröffnungsrede der Königin: *Queen's Speech*

Parlamentsgebäude: die ~ *the Houses of Parliament*

Parlamentsgesetz: *Act of Parliament*

Parlamentsprotokoll: offizielles ~ *Hansard*

Parlamentswahl: *general election*

Partei: *party* **geschädigte** ~ *injured party* **politische** ~ *political party* **seitens einer** ~ *ex parte*

Parteiausführungen: *pleadings*

Parteien: die beteiligten ~ *the parties hereto*

Parteiengleichheit: *identity of parties*

parteiisch: *biased; partial*

Parteilichkeit: *bias*

partiell: *partial*

Partnerschaft: eine ~ auflösen *to dissolve a partnership* **jederzeit kündbare ~ partnership** *at will*

Paß: abgelaufener ~ *lapsed passport*

Passagierliste: *passenger manifest*

passend: *appropriate; convenient; proper; suitable*

Passierschein: *pass*

Paßinhaber: *passport holder*

Pate: *baron (slang); godfather (slang)*

Patent: ein ~ anmelden *to file a patent application* **ein ~ verletzen** *to infringe a patent*

Patentamt: *patent office*

Patent angemeldet: *patent applied for or patent pending*

Patentanwalt: *patent agent*

Patentbeschreibung: *patent specification*

Patentgebühren: *royalty*

patentiert: *patented*

Patentinhaber: *patent holder; patentee*

Patentnummer: *patent number*

Patentprüfer: *patent examiner*

Patentrecht: *patent rights* **ein ~ verletzen** *to infringe a patent*

patentrechtlich geschützt: *patented*

Patenturkunde: *letters patent*

Patentverletzung: *infringement of patent or patent infringement*

Pathologe *or* **Pathologin:** *pathologist*

Pathologie: *pathology*

Patrouille: *patrol*

patrouillieren: *patrol*

Pauschalarrangement: *package deal*

Pauschalbetrag: *lump sum*

Pauschale: *inclusive sum or inclusive charge; flat rate; lump sum*

Pauschalpreis: *all-in price*

Pauschalsatz: *flat rate*

Pause: *break*

PC: *personal computer*

Peer auf Lebenszeit: *life peer*

Peeress: *peeress*

Peitsche: *whip*

peitschen: *to whip*

pekuniär: *pecuniary*

Pendant: *counterpart*

pendeln: *commute*

Pendler: *commuter*

Pendlerzug: *commuter train*

Penner: *vagrant*

Pension: *pension* **in ~ gehen** *to retire*

pensionieren: sich ~ lassen *retire*

Pensionierung: *retirement*

Pensionsalter: *pensionable age*

pensionsberechtigt: *pensionable*

perfektionieren: *perfect*

Periode: *period*

periodisch erscheinend: *periodic or periodical*

Person: dritte ~ *third party* **juristische ~** *legal or artificial person* **natürliche ~** *natural person* **pro ~ per head** **unerwünschte ~** *persona non grata* **verdächtige ~** *suspect*

Personal: *personnel*

Personalausweis: *identity card or ID card*

Personalbestand: *establishment*

Personalchef: *personnel officer*

Personal-Computer: *personal computer*

Personal einstellen: *to hire staff*

Personalreferent: *personnel officer*

Personal unterbringen *or* **vermitteln:** *to place staff*

Persona non grata: *persona non grata*

Personen: ausgenommene ~ *excepted persons* **geistesgestörte ~** *or* **nicht zurechnungsfähige ~** *persons of unsound mind*

Personengesellschaft: *close company or close(d) corporation (US)*

Personenschaden: *personal injury*

Personenstandsunterdrückung: *concealment of birth*

Personenverwechslung: *mistaken identity*

persönlich: *in person; personal(ly)*

pervers: *perverse*

Petition: *petition*

Pfand: pledge ein ~ auslösen *to take something out of pawn* **ein ~ einlösen** *to redeem a pledge* **uneingelöstes ~** *unredeemed pledge*

Pfandbrief: *mortgage bond*

Pfandbriefinhaber: *bondholder; debenture holder*

pfänden: *attach; seize*

Pfandgeber: *pledger*

Pfandleihanstalt: *pawnshop*

Pfandleiher: *pawnbroker*

Pfandnehmer: *pledgee*

Pfandrecht: lien allgemeines ~ *general lien*

Pfandrecht des Handwerkers: *repairer's lien*

Pfandsache: *pledge*

Pfandschein: *pawn ticket*

Pfändung: *attachment; seizure*

Pfändungsauftrag: *warrant of execution*

Pfändungs- und Überweisungsbeschluß: *garnishee order*

Pfandverkauf: *distress sale*

Pfandverschreibung: *bill of sale*

Pflege: in ~ nehmen *foster*

Pflegeeltern: *fosterparents*

Pflegeheim: *foster home*

Pflegekind: *foster child*

Pflegemutter: *foster mother*

Pflegevater: *foster father*

Pflicht: *duty; responsibility*

Pflichtaktien: *qualification or qualifying shares*

Pflichtverletzung: *breach or dereliction of duty*

Pfund: pound tausend ~ *grand (informal)*

Phantombild: *identikit picture*

physikalisch: *physically*

physisch: *physical; physically*

Pirat: *pirate*
Piratensender: *pirate radio station*
Piraterie: *piracy*
plädieren: *plead*
Plädieren: *pleading*
Plädoyer: *pleading*
Plagiat: *piracy; plagiarism*
Plagiator: *pirate*
plagiieren: *pirate; plagiarize*
Plakatwand: *advertisement hoarding*
Plan: *arrangement; plan* **einen ~ ausführen** *to realize a project or a plan*
planen: *organize; plan*
Planer: *planner*
Planstelle: *established post*
Planung: *organization; planning*
Planungsanhörung: *planning inquiry*
Planungsbehörde: *planning authority*
Planwirtschaft: *planned economy*
Platz: *place*
platzen: *bounce*
Plausibilität: *likelihood*
Plenarausschuß: *Committee of the Whole House*
Plombe: *seal*
plombieren: *seal*
Plünderer: *looter*
plündern: *loot; plunder*
Plünderung: *looting*
Polente: **die ~** *the law (informal)*
Police: **untaxierte ~** *open policy* **zeitlich begrenzte ~** *time policy*
Police mit Wertangabe: *valued policy*
Police ohne Wertangabe: *open policy*
Politesse: *traffic warden*
Politik: *policy*
Politik der Lohnkontrolle: *pay or wage restraint*
Politik des Miteinander: *consensus politics*
politisch: *political*
Polizei: *police force; police* **berittene ~** *mounted police*
Polizeibeamter: *detective; police officer*
Polizeibeamter vom Dienst: *duty sergeant*
Polizeibehörde: *police authority*
Polizeibezirk: *police precinct (US)*
Polizeichef: *(police) superintendent* **stellvertretender ~** *undersheriff*
Polizeieinheit: *police force*
Polizeikette or **Polizeikordon:** *police cordon*
Polizeikommissar: *(police) inspector*
polizeilich überwachen: *to police*
Polizeipräsident: **stellvertretender ~** *Assistant or Deputy Chief Constable*
Polizeipräsidium: *police headquarters*
Polizeirevier: *police precinct (US); police station*
Polizeirichter: *magistrate*
Polizeischutz: *police protection*
Polizeistreife: *police patrol*
Polizeiwache: *police station*

Polizist: *police constable; lawman (US); police officer; policeman* **korrupter ~** *bent copper (slang)*
Polizist im Streifendienst: *patrolman (US)*
Polizistin: *policewoman*
polygam: *polygamous*
Polygamie: *polygamy*
populär: *popular*
Pornographie: *pornography*
Porto: *postage*
portofrei: *franco; post free*
Portokasse: *petty cash*
Position: **eine ~ abdecken** *to cover a position*
positiv: *positive*
possessorisch: *possessory*
Post: *mail; post* **elektronische ~** *electronic mail* **mit gewöhnlicher ~** *by surface mail* **per ~** *by mail*
Postanweisung: *money order*
Postdienst: *postal service*
Posten: *item; office; post* **einen ~ buchen** *to post an entry* **einmalige ~** *non-recurring items*
Postfach: *box*
Postgebühren: *postage*
postieren: *station*
Postleitzahl: *post code or zip code (US)*
Postpaket: *postal packet*
Poststelle: *post room*
postum: *posthumous*
Postverkehr: *postal service*
Postversand: *mail-order*
postwendend antworten: *to send a reply by return of post*
Postwurfsendung: *mailing piece*
Postzustellung: *postal service*
Postzweigstelle: *sub-post office*
Post(amt): *post office*
Präambel: *preamble*
PR-Abteilung: *public relations department*
praktikabel: *viable*
praktisch: *convenient*
praktizieren: *practise*
Prämie: *premium*
Prämienrechnung: *renewal notice*
Prämienzuschlag: *additional premium*
PR-Arbeit: *public relations (PR)*
Prärogative: *prerogative*
Präsentation: *presentation; presentment*
Präsenz: *presence*
Präsident: *president*
Präsident der Familiengerichtsabteilung: *President of the Family Division*
präventiv: *preventive*
Präventivhaft: *preventive detention*
Praxis: *practice* **in der ~** *in practice*
Präzedenz: **ohne ~** *unprecedented*
Präzedenzfall: *(judicial) precedent; test case* **bindender ~** *binding precedent* **einem ~ folgen** *to follow a precedent* **einen ~ schaffen** *to set a*

precedent **nicht bindender** ~ *persuasive precedent*
ohne ~ *unprecedented*
Präzedenzfälle: *leading cases*
Präzedenzfallrecht: *case law*
präzis: *precise*
Preis: *cost; price; rate; tariff* **angemessener** ~ *fair price* **einen** ~ **festsetzen** *price* **einen** ~ **nennen** *quote* **fairer** ~ *fair price* **geforderter** ~ *asking price* **staatlich vorgeschriebener** ~ *government-regulated price* **vereinbarter** ~ *agreed price*
Preis ab Lager: *price ex warehouse*
Preisabsprache: *common pricing; price fixing*
Preis ab Werk: *price ex works or ex factory*
Preisanstieg *or* **Preiseskalation:** *escalation of prices*
Preisbindung: *price controls*
Preise: erschwingliche ~ *popular prices*
Preisfestsetzung: *pricing*
Preisgabe: *disclosure*
preisgeben: *betray; disclose; divulge*
Preisgleitklausel: *escalator clause*
Preiskalkulation: *pricing*
Preiskontrollen: *price controls*
Preisnachlaß: *discount*
Preispolitik: *pricing policy*
Preisskala *or* **Preisliste:** *scale of charges or scale of prices*
Preistreiberei: *profiteering*
Preisüberwachung: *price controls*
Prellerei: *bilking*
Premierminister: *Prime Minister*
Presse: *press* **die überregionale** ~ *the national press*
Pressefreiheit: *freedom of the press*
Pressekonferenz: *press conference*
Pressemitteilung: *press release*
Pressenotiz: *news release*
Presserat: *Press Council*
Pressereferent: *information officer*
Prestigeverlust: *loss of status*
primär: *primary*
Prime Rate: *prime rate*
Primogenitur: *primogeniture*
Prinzip: *doctrine; principle* **im** ~ *in principle*
prinzipiell: *in principle*
Priorität: *priority*
Prise: *prize*
privat: *personal; private*
Privatangelegenheit: *private business*
Privatbesitz: *private property*
Privatbetrieb: *private business*
Privatdetektiv: *private detective or private eye (informal)*
Privateigentum: *private ownership*
Privateinkommen: *personal income*
Privatentnahmen: *personal drawings or withdrawals*
Privatgrundstück: *private property*
Privathaus: *domestic premises*

Privatklage: *private prosecution*
Privatkunde: *private client or customer*
Privatleben: *privacy*
Privatrecht: *private law*
Privatsekretär: *personal assistant*
Privatsektor: *private sector*
Privatvermögen: bewegliches ~ *personal assets; personal chattels or chattels personal; personalty*
Privatvertrag: durch ~ *by private contract*
Privatwirtschaft: *private sector*
Privatwohnung: *domestic premises*
Privileg: *privilege*
privilegiert: *privileged*
pro: *per*
Probe: *sample; specimen* **auf** ~ *on probation; probationary* **auf** ~ **Angestellte(r)** *probationer* **kostenlos zur** ~ *free trial* **zur** ~ *on approval; on trial*
Probeexemplar: *specimen*
Probelauf: *test run*
Proben entnehmen: *sample*
Probestück: *trial sample*
Probezeit: *probation; trial period*
Problem: *matter; problem; question* **ein** ~ **lösen** *to solve a problem*
Problembereich: *problem area*
Produkthaftung: *product liability*
Produktion: *output; production* **die** ~ **zurückschrauben** *to cut (back) production*
Produktionsfaktoren: *factors of production*
Produktionsleistung: *rate of production or production rate*
Produktionsstandard: *production standards*
produktiv: *productive*
professionell: *professional*
Profit: *gain; profit*
Profitabilität: *profitability*
profitieren von: *to benefit from or by (something)*
Proforma-Rechnung: *pro forma (invoice)*
Prognose: langfristige ~ *long-term forecast*
Programm: *timetable* **bezuschußtes** ~ *or* **subventioniertes** ~ *grant-aided scheme*
programmieren: *program*
Programmiersprache: *computer or programming language*
Projekt: *undertaking* **ein** ~ **ausschreiben** *to put a project out to tender or to ask for or to invite tenders for a project*
Pro-Kopf-Ausgaben: *per capita expenditure*
Pro-Kopf-Einkommen: *average income per capita or per capita income*
Prokura: per ~ *per pro*
Prolongation: *extension*
prolongieren: *extend*
prompt: *immediate; prompt*
Propaganda: staatsgefährdende ~ *sedition*
proportional: *proportional*
Prospekt: *prospectus*
Prostituierte: *prostitute*

Prostitution: *prostitution*
Protest: *protest* aus ~ gegen *in protest at*
protestieren: *object*
Protestierende(r): *protester*
Protestmarsch: *protest march*
Proteststreik: *protest strike*
Protokoll: *minutes; protocol; record* für das ~ *for the record or to keep the record straight* zu ~ nehmen *minute*
Protokollbuch: *minutebook*
Protokoll führen: *to take the minutes*
protokollieren: *minute; record*
protokolliert: *on record*
Provenienz: *origin*
Provision: *commission* außerordentliche ~ *overrider or overriding commission* geheime ~ *kickback*
Provisionsagent: *commission agent*
provisorisch: *provisional*
Provokation: *provocation*
provozieren: *provoke*
Prozent: *per cent; percentage*
Prozentpunkt: ein ~ *a percentage point*
Prozentsatz: *percentage*
Prozeß: *court action; court case; litigation; legal proceedings; process; trial* einem ~ beitreten *intervene*
Prozeßeröffnungsbeschluß: *writ (of summons)*
prozeßfähig: *fit to plead*
Prozeßführender: *litigant*
Prozeßgegner: *adversary*
prozessieren: *litigate; sue*
Prozeßkosten: *costs; party and party costs*
Prozeßkostenhilfe: *the green form scheme*
Prozeßkostenhilfeformular: *green form*
Prozeßliste: *docket (US)*
Prozeß mit Verfahrensmängeln: *mistrial*
Prozeßpartei: *litigant*
Prozeßpfleger: *guardian ad litem; next friend*
prozeßsüchtig: *litigious*
prozessual: *procedural*
prozeßunfähig: *unfit to plead*
Prozeßunfähiger: *person under a disability*
prüfen: *examine; inspect; test; verify*
Prüfer: *examiner; inspector*
Prüfung: *examination; inspection; test; trial* zur ~ on trial
prügeln: *batter*
Prügelstrafe: *corporal punishment*
Psychiater: *psychiatrist*
Psychiatrie: *psychiatry*
psychiatrisch: *psychiatric*
Public Relations-Abteilung: *public relations department*
Public Relations-Fachmann: *public relations officer*
Publikation: *publication*
Punkt: *item; point* strittiger ~ *point at issue*

pünktlich: *promptly; on time*
pünktlich fertig sein: *to be on schedule*

Qq

quälen: *torture*
Qualifikation: *eligibility; qualification*
Qualifikationen: fachliche ~ *professional qualifications*
qualifiziert: *qualified*
Quantität: *quantity*
quantitativ bestimmbar: *quantifiable*
Quarantäne: *quarantine* unter ~ stellen *quarantine*
Quarantäneattest: *bill of health*
Quartal: erstes ~ *first quarter* letztes ~ *last quarter*
Quartalgerichte: *Quarter Sessions*
Quartalstag: *quarter day*
quartalsweise: *quarterly*
Quartalszahltag: *Michaelmas*
Quelle: *source*
Quellenabzugssystem: *pay as you earn or pay-as-you-go (US)*
Quellensteuer: *tax deducted at source*
Querulant: *vexatious litigant*
quittieren: *receipt*
Quittung: ordnungsgemäße ~ *receipt in due form*
Quittungsblock: *receipt book or book of receipts*
Quittungsduplikat: *duplicate (of a) receipt*
Quote: *quota*
Quotensystem: *quota system* ein ~ anwenden *to operate a quota system*

Rr

Rabatt: *discount*
Rache: *retaliation*
rächen: sich ~ *retaliate*
Rahmen: *scope* in begrenztem ~ *small-scale*
randalieren: *riot*
Randalierer: *rioter*
Rang: *rank; status*
rangieren: *rank*
Rasse: *race*
Rassendiskriminierung: *racial discrimination*
Rassenhaß: *racial hatred*
Rassenvorurteil: *racial prejudice*
Rat: *advice; council*
Rate: *instalment; rate* zu ~ ziehen *consult*
Raten: in ~ zahlen *to pay in instalments*
raten: *advise*
Ratenkauf: *hire purchase*
Ratenzahlung: *deferred payment; installment plan (US)*

raten zu: *recommend*
Ratgeber: *adviser or advisor*
ratifizieren: *approve; ratify*
Ratifizierung: *ratification*
Ratsmitglied: *councillor*
Raub: *robbery* **gewalttätiger** ~ *robbery with violence*
Raubdruck: *piracy*
rauben: *plunder; rob*
Räuber: *bandit; mugger; robber*
Raubüberfall: *heist (slang); holdup; robbery* **bewaffneter** ~ *blag (slang)*
Rauchverbot: das ~ **aufheben** *to lift the ban on smoking*
Rauchverbot erlassen: *to impose a ban on smoking*
räumen: *clear*
Räumung: *ejection* **zur** ~ **zwingen** *eject; evict*
Räumungsklage: *action of ejectment*
Raumverteilungsplan: *floor plan*
Rauschgiftdezernat: *the Drug Squad*
Rauschgifte: *drugs*
Rauschgifthandel: *drug trafficking*
rausgeschmissen werden: *to get the sack*
rausschmeißen: jdn ~ *to sack someone*
Rausschmiß: *sacking*
Razzia: *raid* **eine** ~ **machen** *raid*
real: *substantive*
Realeinkommen: *real income*
realisierbar: *convertible*
realisieren: *convert; realize*
Realisierung: *realization*
Reallohn: *real wages*
Real-time: *real time*
Realwert: *actual value*
Rebell: *mutineer; rebel*
rebellieren: *mutiny; rebel*
Rebellion: *mutiny; rebellion*
Rechenfehler: *miscount*
Rechenmaschine: *calculator*
Rechenschaft ablegen: *to account for*
Rechenzentrum: *computer bureau*
rechnen: *calculate; count*
rechnen mit: *count on*
Rechner: *computer*
Rechnerprogramm: *computer program*
Rechnung: *bill; invoice; note of costs* **detaillierte** ~ *detailed account* **die** ~ **begleichen** *or* **bezahlen** *to foot the bill* **eine** ~ **bezahlen** *to settle an account* **eine** ~ **vordatieren** *to date an invoice forward* **in** ~ **stellen** *bill* **laut** ~ *as per invoice* **ordnungsgemäße** ~ *receipt in due form* **spezifizierte** ~ *detailed account*
Rechnungen: dringende ~ *pressing bills* **fällige** ~ *bills for collection*
Rechnungsaufstellung: *statement of account*
Rechnungsbetrag: fälliger ~ *balance due*
Rechnungsjahr: *financial year*
Rechnungslegungsklage: *action for an account*

Rechnungsprüfer: *auditor; comptroller* **betriebsinterner** ~ *internal auditor* **unabhängiger** ~ *external auditor*
Rechnungsprüfer des Rechnungshofes: *Comptroller and Auditor General (GB)*
Rechnungsprüfung: *audit* **betriebsinterne** ~ *internal audit* **unabhängige** ~ *external or independent audit*
Rechnungsprüfungen vornehmen: *audit*
Rechnungsprüfungsausschuß: *Public Accounts Committee*
Rechnungswesen: *accounting*
Recht: *interest; jus; law; right* **bürgerliches** ~ *civil law* **internationales** ~ *international law* **islamisches** ~ *Islamic Law* **kanonisches** ~ *canon law* **materielles** ~ *substantive law* **nichtkodifiziertes** ~ *common law* **öffentliches** ~ *public law* **römisches** ~ *Roman law* **unangreifbares** *or* **unverletziches** ~ *indefeasible right* **vollkommenes** ~ *perfect right*
Recht auf Bergelohn: *salvage*
Recht des Amtsgerichts: *summary jurisdiction*
Recht des Gerichtsortes *or* **Gerichtsstandes:** *lex fori*
Recht des Handlungsortes: *lex loci actus*
Recht des Tatortes: *lex loci delicti*
Recht des Überlebenden: *survivorship*
Recht des Vertragsortes: *lex loci contractus*
Rechte: auf ~ **hinweisen** *caution* **eheliche** ~ *conjugal rights* **(staats)bürgerliche** ~ *civil rights* **vorrangige** ~ *overriding interest*
rechtfertigen: *justify*
Rechtfertigung: *justification* **zur** ~ *in justification*
Rechtfertigungsgrund: absoluter ~ *absolute privilege*
rechtlich: *de jure; juridical; legal*
rechtmäßig: *lawful; legal; proper; rightful* **für** ~ **erklären** *legitimate*
Rechtmäßigkeit: *legitimacy*
Rechts: von ~ **wegen** *de jure*
Rechtsabteilung: *legal department or legal section*
Rechtsanspruch: *legal claim; title* **einwandfreier** ~ *good title*
Rechtsanwalt: *advocate; attorney (US); barrister; counsellor (US); lawyer; solicitor*
Rechtsausschuß: ständiger ~ *Law Commission (GB)*
Rechtsausschuß des Kronrates: *Judicial Committee of the Privy Council*
Rechtsausschuß des Oberhauses: *Judicial Committee of the House of Lords*
Rechtsbeistand: *advocate (US)*
Rechtsbeistandberatung: *Law Centre*
Rechtsbelehrung erteilen: *direct*
Rechtsbelehrung (der Geschworenen): *directions*
Rechtsberater: *counsellor (US); legal adviser*
Rechtsberater der Krone: *Advocate General*
Rechtsberater des Staates: *Law Officers*

Rechtsberatungsstelle: *Law Centre (GB); Legal Aid Centre*

Rechtsbeugung: *miscarriage of justice*

Rechtsfähigkeit: *capacity; legal status*

Rechtsfall: *cause* **erstmaliger** ~ *case of first impression*

Rechtsfiktion: *fiction of law or legal fiction*

Rechtsfrage: *matters of law; point of law; question of law*

Rechtsgebiet: *branch (of law)*

rechtsgültig: *in due form; valid*

Rechtsgültigkeit: *validity*

rechtsgültig machen: *validate*

Rechtsgutachten: *counsel's advice or opinion*

rechtshängig: *sub judice*

Rechtslage: *legal status*

Rechtsmittel: *remedy* **außerordentliches** ~ *prerogative order or writ*

Rechtsmittelbelehrung: *caution*

Rechtsmittelkammer: *divisional court*

Rechtsnachfolger: *assigns*

Rechtspersönlichkeit: *legal personality; legal status*

Rechtspflege: *judicature*

Rechtspfleger: *master; Practice Master*

Rechtspraktikant: *trainee*

Recht sprechen: *to administer or to dispense justice*

Rechtsprechung: *dispensation*

Rechtsprechungsübersicht: aktuelle ~ *Weekly Law Reports (WLR) (GB)*

Rechtsreferendar: *trainee*

Rechtsreferendarzeit: seine ~ **ableisten** *to serve articles*

Rechtsreform: *law reform*

Rechtsschutzversicherung: *legal expenses insurance*

Rechtsstaatlichkeit *or* **Rechtsstaatprinzip:** *the rule of law*

Rechtsstreit: *cause; lis; litigation; suit* **anhängiger** ~ *lis pendens; pending action* **für den** ~ *ad litem*

Rechtssubjekt: *entity*

Rechtstitel: bedingter ~ *qualified title* **einwandfreier** ~ *good title*

Rechtsträger: *entity*

Rechtstreit: einem ~ **beizutreten** *to join someone to an action*

Rechtsübertragung: *subrogation*

Rechtsungültigkeit: *invalidity*

rechtsunwirksam: *invalid*

Rechtsverdreher: *brief (slang)*

Rechtsverfolgung: böswillige ~ *malicious prosecution*

Rechtsverletzer: *wrongdoer*

Rechtsverletzung: *wrong*

Rechtsverordnung: *enactment; statutory instrument*

Rechtsverordnungen: *orders*

Rechtsverweigerung: *denial of justice*

Rechtsverwirkung: *estoppel*

Rechtsweg: *judicial process*

rechtswidrig: *illegal; tortious*

Rechtswidrigkeit: *illegality*

Rechtswissenschaft: *jurisprudence* **vergleichende** ~ *comparative law*

Rechtswissenschaftler: *jurist*

rechtswissenschaftlich: *juristic*

rechtzeitig fertig sein: *to be on schedule*

Recht zur Wiedereinreise: *right of re-entry*

Recht zur Wiederinbesitznahme: *right of re-entry*

Redakteur: *editor*

Redaktion: *editorial board*

redaktionell: *editorial*

Redaktionskomitee: *editorial board*

Rede: *speech*

Redefreiheit: *freedom of speech*

Rederecht: *audience*

redlich: *in good faith; honest*

Redlichkeit: *good faith* **(von) höchste(r)** ~ *uberrimae fidei*

reduzieren: *cut; decrease; reduce*

reduziert: *reduced*

Reduzierung: *reduction*

Reederei: *shipping company or shipping line*

REFA-Studie: *time and motion study*

Referendum: *referendum*

Referenz: *(letter of) reference; referee*

Reform: *reform*

reformieren: *reform*

Regel: *rule*

Regeln: *code*

regeln: *regulate*

Regelsystem: *control system*

Regelung: *regulation*

regieren: *govern*

Regierung: *administration; government* **eine** ~ **anerkennen** *to recognize a government*

Regierungsvorlagen: *Command papers*

Register: *index*

Registeramt: *registry*

Registerführer *or* **Registrator:** *registrar*

Registratur: *registry*

registrieren: *record; register* **etwas** ~ *file*

registriert: nicht ~ *unregistered*

Registrierung: *recording; registration*

Registrierungsnummer: *registration number*

Regreßverzichtsvereinbarung: gegenseitige ~ *knock-for-knock agreement*

regulieren: *regulate*

Regulierung: *regulation*

rehabilitieren: *rehabilitate*

Rehabilitierung: *rehabilitation*

Reichtümer: *treasure*

Reihe: der ~ **nach** *seriatim*

Reihenfolge: alphabetische ~ *alphabetical order* **chronologische** *or* **zeitliche** ~ *chronological order* **zahlenmäßige** ~ *numerical order*

reingelegt: er wurde ~ *he has been framed (informal)*

Reingewinn: *clear profit*

Reinigungskosten: *service charge*

Reinschrift: *fair copy*

Reise: *trip*

Reisechecks: *traveller's cheques*

Reisespesen: *travelling expenses*

Reitweg: *bridleway*

Reklame machen: *promote*

Reklametafel: *advertisement hoarding*

Rekordverluste: *record losses*

Rekordzahl an Verbrechen: *record crime figures*

Rekrut: *recruit*

rekrutieren: *recruit*

Rekrutierung: *recruitment*

Rektapapier: *non-negotiable instrument*

relevant: *relevant*

Relevanz: *relevance*

Rendite: *(rate of) return; yield*

rentabel: *profitable* **nicht** ~ *not commercially viable*

Rentabilität: *profitability*

Rentabilitätsberechnung: *measurement of profitability*

Rente: *pension* **lohnbezogene** ~ *earnings-related pension*

Rentenalter: *pensionable or retiring or retirement age*

Rentenanspruch: *pension entitlement*

Rentenbeiträge: *pension contributions*

rentenberechtigt: *pensionable*

Rentenempfänger: *old age pensioner*

Rentenfonds: *pension fund*

Rentensystem: gestaffeltes ~ *graduated pension scheme*

Rentenversicherung: beitragsfreie ~ *non-contributory pension scheme* **beitragspflichtige** ~ *contributory pension plan or scheme* **private** ~ *personal pension plan*

Rentenversicherungsbeiträge: *pension contributions*

Rentenversicherungssystem: *pension plan or pension scheme*

rentieren: *yield*

Rentner: *(old age) pensioner*

Reorganisation: *reconstruction*

Reparatur: *repair*

Reparaturwerkstatt: *repair shop*

reparieren: *fix; repair*

repatriieren: *repatriate*

Repatriierung: *repatriation*

Replik: *answer; reply*

Repräsentant: *representative*

Repräsentantenhaus: *House of Representatives*

repräsentieren: *represent*

Reproduktionsrechte: *reproduction rights*

reproduzieren: *reproduce*

Reproduzierung: *reproduction*

requirieren: *requisition*

Reserve: in ~ *in reserve*

Reserven: stille ~ *hidden assets or reserves*

Reservewährung: *reserve currency*

reservieren: *book*

Reservierung: *booking; reservation*

Resolution: eine ~ **annehmen** *to pass a resolution* **gemeinsame** ~ *joint resolution (US)*

Resozialisierung von Straftätern: *rehabilitation of offenders*

Respektlosigkeit: *disrespect*

Ressort: *portfolio*

Rest: *remainder; residue*

Restauflage: *remainders*

Restbestand: *remainder*

Restbetrag: *balance*

restlich: *residual; residuary*

Restnachlaß: *residuary estate*

restriktiv: *restrictive*

Resultat: *outcome*

retrospektiv: *ex post facto; retrospective*

retten: *salvage*

revanchieren: sich ~ *reciprocate*

Revier: *beat*

Revision: *appeal; audit; (judicial) review* **betriebsinterne** ~ *internal audit* **unabhängige** ~ *external or independent audit*

Revision einlegen: *to give notice of appeal*

Revisions-: *appellate*

Revisionsgericht: *Appeal Court or Court of Appeal*

Revisionskläger: *appellant*

Revisionsvorlage: *case stated*

Revisor: betriebsinterner ~ *internal auditor* **unabhängiger** ~ *external auditor*

Revolution: *revolution*

Rezession: *recession*

Reziprozität: *mutuality; reciprocity*

R-Gespräch: *collect call (US); reverse charge call; transferred charge call* **ein** ~ **führen** *to reverse the charges*

Richter: *judge; justice* **beauftragter** ~ *official referee* **erstinstanzlicher** ~ *Lord Ordinary* **nebenberuflicher** ~ *recorder*

Richterbank: *bench*

richterlich: *judicial; juridical*

Richterschaft: *judiciary; justiciary*

Richterspruch: einstimmiger ~ *unanimous verdict*

Richterstuhl: *bench*

Richterzimmer: *chambers*

richtig: *correct; proper*

Richtlinie: *directive; rule*

Richtlinien: *code of practice; guidelines*

Richtlinien eines Grafschaftsgerichts: *County Court Rules (GB)*

Richtung: *direction*

Ringbuch: *ring binder*
Risiko: *danger; hazard; peril; risk* **ein ~ decken** *to cover a risk*
Risikoübernahme: *assumption of risks*
Risikoversicherung: *contingent policy*
riskant: *dangerous*
riskieren: *risk*
Robe: *gown*
Roheinnahmen: *gross receipts*
Rohentwurf: *rough draft*
Rohgewicht: *gross weight*
Rohgewinn: *gross profit*
Rohstoffe: *raw materials*
Rolle: *roll*
Römische Verträge: *Treaty of Rome*
Rotation: *rotation*
Rowdy: *hooligan; thug; vandal*
Rowdytum: *thuggery; vandalism*
Rubrum: *caption*
rückerstatten: *refund; reimburse*
Rückerstattung: *rebate; refund*
Rückerstattungsbeschluß: *restitution order*
Rückfahrt: *return journey*
Rückfall: *reversion*
Rückforderung: *clawback*
Rückfrage: *query*
Rückgabe: *restitution; return*
Rückgang: *decline; drop*
rückgängig machen: *defeat; go back on; revoke*
Rückkauf: *surrender*
rückkaufbar: *redeemable*
Rückkaufswert: *redemption or surrender value*
Rückkehr: *return*
rückkgängig machen: *annul*
Rücklage: *provision; reserve*
Rücklagefonds: *reserve fund*
Rückschlag: *reversal*
Rückseite: *back*
Rückseitenvermerk: *indorsement*
Rückseitenvermerken: mit ~ versehen *indorse*
Rücksendung: *return*
rücksichtslos: *reckless(ly)*
Rücksichtslosigkeit: *recklessness*
Rückstand: im ~ *in arrears*
Rückstände: *arrears*
Rückstellung: *provision*
Rücktritt: *resignation*
Rücktrittsfrist: *cooling off period or cooling time (US)*
Rücktrittsklausel: *cancellation clause; escape clause; let-out clause*
Rückumschlag: frankierter or freigemachter ~ *stamped addressed envelope*
Rückversicherung: *reinsurance*
rückwirkend: *ex post facto; retroactive; retrospective*
rückzahlbar: *repayable* **nicht ~** *irredeemable*

Rückzahlung: *payback; back payment; redemption; repayment*
Rückzahlungsklausel: *payback clause*
Rückzahlung vor Fälligkeit: *redemption before due date*
Ruf: *reputation; standing* **schlechter ~** *disrepute*
Rufschädigung: *injurious or malicious falsehood*
rügen: *censure*
Ruhe: die ~ stören *to disturb the peace*
Ruhegehalt: *pension*
ruhend: *dormant*
Ruhe! Ruhe!: *order ! order!*
Ruhestörung: *disturbance*
Ruhe und Ordnung: *law and order*
ruhig: *quiet*
Ruin: *wreck*
ruinieren: *bankrupt*
Rundschreiben: *circular (letter); mail shot; mailing shot*
Rundschreiben verschicken: *circularize*

Ss

Sabotage: *sabotage*
Sachbearbeiter: *clerk*
Sachbearbeiterin: *clerkess (in Scotland)*
Sachbeschädigung: böswillige ~ *malicious damage* **mutwillige or vorsätzliche ~** *vandalism* **strafbare ~** *criminal damage*
Sache: *affair; business; cause; matter; res* **bewegliche ~** *chose in possession* **rechtskräftig entschiedene ~** *res judicata*
Sachen: bewegliche ~ *personal property* **in ~ in** *re* **vertretbare ~** *fungible goods or fungibles* **"herrenlose" ~** *bona vacantia*
Sachenrecht: *law of property*
Sachherrschaft: *possession*
Sachkenntnis: *expertise*
sachkundig: *experienced*
Sachleistung: *payment in kind*
sachlich: *objective*
Sachverhaltsdarstellung: zusammenfassende ~ *headnote*
Sachverständigenausschuß: *panel of experts*
Sachverständigengutachten: *expert's report*
Sachverständiger: *expert; referee; expert or professional or skilled witness* **juristischer ~** *legal expert*
Sachwerte: bilanzierbare ~ *tangible assets*
Sack: *sack*
Safe: *safe*
Safeknacker: *cracksman (slang)*
saldieren: *balance*
Saldo: *balance*
Saldovortrag: *balance brought forward or carried forward*
Sammelladung: *consolidated shipment*

sammeln: *gather*

Sammelstimme: *block vote*

Sammlung: *collection*

Sanierung eines Unternehmens: *the reconstruction of a company*

Sanktion: *sanction*

sanktionieren: *sanction*

Satz: fester ~ *fixed rate* **voller** ~ *full rate*

Satzung: *articles of association or articles of incorporation (US); constitution; regulations*

satzungsgemäß: *constitutional*

Saugpostpapier: *duplicating paper*

Schachtel: *box*

Schaden: *damage; detriment; harm; prejudice* **bezifferter** ~ *liquidated damages* **sichtbarer** ~ *apparent defect*

schaden: *harm; hurt*

Schaden anrichten: *to cause damage*

Schaden erleiden: *to suffer damage*

Schadenfreiheitsrabatt: *no-claims bonus*

Schadenhöhe: *quantum*

Schaden nehmen: *to suffer damage*

Schadenregulierer: *average adjuster or loss adjuster*

Schadensansprüche stellen: *to put in a claim*

Schadensbearbeitung der Versicherung: *the processing of a claim for insurance*

Schadensbemessung: *measure of damages*

Schadensersatz: *compensation for damage; damages; indemnification; restitution* **allgemeiner** ~ *general damages* **ausgleichender** ~ *compensatory damages* **erhöhter** ~ *aggravated damages* **genereller** ~ *general damages* **geringer or nomineller** ~ *nominal damages* **verschärfter** ~ *exemplary damages*

Schadensersatzanspruch: einen ~ **stellen** *to put in a claim for damage or loss* **nicht festgesetzter** ~ *unliquidated damages*

Schadensersatzklage: *action in tort*

Schadensersatz leisten: *indemnify; make amends*

Schadensersatzprozeß *or* **Schadensersatzverfahren:** *proceedings in tort*

Schadensformular: *claim form*

Schadenssachverständiger: *adjuster*

Schadensteilungsvereinbarung: *knock-for-knock agreement*

Schaden verursachen: *to cause damage*

Schaden zufügen: *hurt*

schadhaft: *damaged; defective*

schädigen: *prejudice*

schädlich: *detrimental; injurious; noxious*

Schadloshaltungserklärung: *letter of indemnity*

schaffen: *create; establish* **es** ~ *to manage to*

Schaffung: *creation*

Schafott: *scaffold*

Schalterstunden: *business hours*

Schankkonzession: *licence to sell liquor or liquor licence*

Schankkonzession im Hause: *on licence*

Scharfrichter: *executioner*

Scharfschütze: *marksman*

Schattenwirtschaft: *black economy*

Schatz: *treasure*

schätzen: *appreciate; assess; calculate; estimate; tax; value* **zu** ~ **wissen** *appreciate*

Schätzer: *appraiser; estimator; valuer*

Schatzfund: *treasure trove*

Schatzkanzler: *Chancellor of the Exchequer (UK)*

Schatzobligationen: *treasury bonds*

Schätzung: *assessment; estimate; valuation* **bei vorsichtiger** ~ *at a conservative estimate* **grobe** ~ *rough calculation or estimate*

Schatzwechsel: *Treasury Bill*

Schauplatz: *site*

Scheck: bestätigter ~ *certified cheque or certified check (US)* **einen** ~ **einlösen** *to clear a cheque* **einen** ~ **girieren** *or* **indossieren** *to endorse a cheque* **einen** ~ **stornieren** *to cancel a cheque* **einen** ~ **unterschreiben** *to sign a cheque* **mit** ~ **bezahlen** *to pay by cheque* **ungedeckter** ~ *dud cheque*

Scheckinhaber: *holder*

scheiden: sich ~ **lassen** *divorce*

Scheidung: *divorce; get or gett* **einverständliche** ~ *special procedure*

Scheidungsantrag *or* **Scheidungsklage:** *divorce petition*

Scheidungsbeklagter: *respondent*

Scheidungsurteil: *decree absolute* **vorläufiges** ~ *decree nisi*

Schein: *bank note or banknote; bill (US)*

Scheinaktiva: *fictitious assets*

scheinbar: *ostensible*

Scheinehe: *sham marriage or marriage of convenience*

scheinen: *appear*

Scheingericht: *kangaroo court*

Scheingesellschafter: *ostensible partner*

Scheitern: *breakdown; failure* **zum** ~ **bringen** *wreck*

scheitern: *break down; fail*

Schema: übliches ~ *pattern*

schenken: *gift; give; present*

Schenkung: *donation*

Schenkungsempfänger: *donee*

Schenkungsgeber: *donor*

Schenkung zu Lebzeiten: *gift inter vivos*

schicken: *mail; post*

Schiebung: *fiddle (informal); racket*

Schiedsgericht: *tribunal*

Schiedsgericht für Mietstreitigkeiten: *rent tribunal*

Schiedsrichter: *referee; umpire*

Schiedsspruch: *award; arbitration award*

Schiedsvertrag: *arbitration agreement*

schießen: *fire*

Schiffahrts-: *maritime*

Schiffbruch: *shipwreck; wreck*

Schiffsbrief: *certificate of registry*

Schiffshypothek: *bottomry*
Schiffsladung: *shipment*
Schiffspfandrecht: *maritime lien*
Schikane: *harassment*
schikanieren: *harass*
schikanös: *vexatious*
Schild: *sign*
schildern: *describe*
Schilderung: *description*
Schlag: einen ~ versetzen *strike*
schlagen: *batter; beat; defeat; strike*
Schläger: *heavy (slang); thug*
Schlägerei: *affray*
Schlange: *queue* ~ stehen *to queue*
schlau: *clever*
schlechthin: *per se*
schlecht verwalten: *mismanage*
Schleuderpreisen: zu ~ verkaufen *to sell at giveaway prices*
schlichten: *arbitrate*
Schlichter: *adjudicator; arbitrator; official mediator*
Schlichtung: *arbitration; conciliation; settlement*
Schlichtungsausschuß: *arbitration board*
Schlichtungskommission: *adjudication tribunal*
Schlichtungs- und Schiedsgerichtsdienst: *the Advisory Conciliation and Arbitration Service (ACAS) (GB)*
schließen: *close; close down; conclude; deduce; gather; infer; wind up*
Schließer: *screw (slang)*
schließlich: *finally*
Schließung: *closing; closure*
Schloß: *lock*
Schluß: *close; conclusion; deduction* zum ~ in *conclusion*
Schlußbestand: *closing stock*
Schlußdividende: *final dividend*
Schlüssel: *key*
schlußfolgern: *conclude*
Schlußfolgerung: *conclusion*
schlüssig: *conclusive(ly)*
Schlußkurs: *closing price*
Schlußplädoyer: *closing speech*
Schlußsitzung: *closing session*
Schlußverkauf: *the sales*
Schmiergeld: *kickback*
Schmuggel: *smuggling*
schmuggeln: *smuggle*
Schmuggelware: *contraband (goods); prohibited goods*
Schmuggler: *smuggler*
Schnäppchen: *bargain*
schnappen: *cop (slang)*
Schneeballeffekt: *knock-on effect*
Schnitzer: *slip; slip-up*
Schöffe: *juror; juryman*
Schöffen: *jury; "Members of the jury"*

Schöffenamt: *jury service*
Schöffenbank: *jury box*
Schöffengerichtsverhandlung: *trial by jury or jury trial*
Schöffenüberprüfung: *jury vetting (GB)*
Schöffin: *juror*
Schrank: *cabinet*
Schranke: *barrier*
Schranken: in ~ halten *restrain*
Schreibarbeit: *clerical work or paperwork*
Schreibfehler: *clerical error*
Schreibkraft: *typist*
Schreibkräfte: *clerical staff*
Schreibkraft ohne Diktat: *copy typist*
Schreibmaschine: *typewriter*
Schreibmaschinenpapier: *typing paper*
Schreibmaschineschreiben: *typing*
Schreibmaschine schreiben: *to type*
Schreibschrift: normale ~ *longhand*
Schreibwaren: *stationery*
Schreibwarenhändler: *stationer*
Schrift: *publication*
Schriftführer: *secretary*
schriftlich niedergelegt: *on record*
schriftlich verleumden: *libel*
Schriftsachverständiger: *handwriting expert*
Schriftsätze: *pleadings*
Schriftwechsel: *correspondence*
Schritte unternehmen: *to take action*
Schuld: *blame; fault; guilt; obligation* eine ~ begleichen *to discharge or to honour or to liquidate a debt* eine ~ beitreiben *to enforce a debt* eine ~ zurückzahlen *to pay back a debt*
Schulden: *debt; indebtedness; liabilities* aufgenommene ~ *borrowings*
schulden: *owe*
Schulden begleichen: *to pay off a debt*
Schuldenbegleichung: *clearing of a debt*
Schulden eintreiben: *to collect a debt*
Schuldeneintreibung: *debt collection or collecting*
Schulden einziehen: *to collect a debt*
Schuldeneinziehung: *debt collection*
schuldenfrei sein: *to be out of debt*
Schulden haben: *to be in debt*
Schulden machen: *to get into debt; to incur debts*
Schulden tilgen: *to pay off a debt*
Schuldentilgung: völlige ~ in *full discharge of a debt*
schuldhaft: *culpable*
schuldig: *blameworthy; guilty* jdn ~ sprechen *to find someone guilty or to return a verdict of guilty or to return a guilty verdict* nicht ~ *innocent* sich ~ bekennen *to plead guilty*
Schuldiger: *culprit*
schuldig sprechen: *condemn*
Schuldner: *debtor* säumiger ~ *defaulter; slow payer*
Schuldnerland: *debtor nation*
Schuldposten: *debit*

Schuldrecht: *contract law or law of contract*
Schuldschein: *bond; debenture; note of hand; IOU; promissory note*
Schuldscheininhaber: *holder*
Schuldspruch: einen ~ verkünden *to find someone guilty or to return a verdict of guilty or to return a guilty verdict*
Schuldunfähigkeit: *automatism*
Schuldverschreibung: *bond; debenture bond; debenture* **eine ~ tilgen** *to redeem a bond*
Schuß: *gunshot*
Schußwaffe: *firearm; gun* **mit vorgehaltener ~** *at gunpoint*
Schutz: *protection; safeguard; security*
schützen: *guard; protect; safeguard*
Schutzgelderpressung: *extortion racket; racketeering*
Schutzmaßnahmen ergreifen: *to take safety precautions or safety measures*
Schutzzoll: *protective tariff*
Schwäche: *failing; weakness*
schwanger: *pregnant*
Schwangerschaft: *pregnancy* **eine ~ abbrechen** *to terminate a pregnancy*
Schwangerschaftsabbruch: *abortion*
Schwarzarbeit: *moonlighting (informal)*
schwarzarbeiten: *to moonlight (informal)*
Schwarzarbeiter: *moonlighter (informal)*
Schwarzbrennen: *bootlegging*
Schwarzbrenner: *bootlegger*
Schwarzbrennerei: *bootlegging*
Schwarzes Brett: *noticeboard*
schwarz gebrannt: *bootleg*
Schwarzhändler: *bootlegger*
Schwarzmarkt: *black market*
Schwarzmarkthändler: *black marketeer*
Schwarzmarktpreise bezahlen: *to pay black market prices*
schwebend: *pending*
Schweigegeld: *hush money (informal)*
Schweigen: *silence*
Schweigerecht: *right of silence*
Schwere: *seriousness*
Schwierigkeiten: *trouble*
Schwindel: *bunco (slang); con (informal); confidence trick or confidence game (US); swindle*
Schwindelgeschäft: *fraudulent transaction*
Schwindler: *confidence trickster or confidence man (US); swindler*
schwören: *swear*
Schwund: *wastage*
Schwung: *drive*
Scotland Yard: *Scotland Yard or the Yard*
Scrip: *scrip*
sechsmal jährlich: *bi-monthly*
See: hohe ~ *high seas*
See-: *marine; maritime*
Seegericht: *Admiralty Court (GB)*
Seehandel: *maritime trade*

Seeräuber: *pirate*
Seeräuberei: *piracy*
Seerecht: *Admiralty law; maritime law or the law of the sea*
Seerisiken: *perils of the sea or maritime perils*
Seetransportversicherer: *marine underwriter*
Seetransportversicherung: *marine insurance*
Seeweg: auf dem ~ *by sea mail*
Sehr geehrte(r): *dear*
Seide: *silk*
Seite: zur ~ *aside*
Sekretär: *secretary* **als ~** *secretarial*
Sekretariat: *secretariat*
Sekretärinnenschule: *secretarial college*
Sektor: staatlicher ~ *public sector*
sekundär: *secondary*
selbständig: *self-employed*
Selbständigen: die ~ *the self-employed*
Selbstbehalt: *excess*
Selbstbezichtigung: *self-incrimination*
Selbstmord: *suicide*
Selbstmord begehen: *to commit suicide*
Selbstmörder: *suicide*
selbstmörderisch veranlagt *or* **selbstmordgefährdet:** *suicidal*
Selbstmordvereinbarung: *suicide pact*
Selbsttötung: *suicide*
selbstverständlich: *of course*
Semester: *term*
Semesterferien: *vacation (GB)*
Senat: *senate*
Senator or Senatsmitglied: *senator*
Sender: *TV or radio station*
Sendung: *shipment; broadcast*
Seniorpartner: *senior partner*
senken: *cut; lessen; reduce*
Senkrechtstarter: *high flier*
Senkung: *cut; reduction*
separat: *separate(ly)*
Sequester: *sequestrator*
Sequestration: *sequestration*
sequestrieren: *sequester or sequestrate*
Serienfertigung: *mass production*
seriös: *reputable*
setzen: *place; put; set*
setzen auf: *wager*
Sexualdelikte: *sexual offences*
sexuell: *sexual*
Sheriff: *sheriff (US)*
Shifttaste: *shift key*
sic: *sic*
sicher: *certain; firm; safe; secure* **nicht ~ festgestellt** *unascertained*
-sicher: *-proof*
Sicherheit: *cover; guarantee; safety; security; surety* **zusätzliche ~** *collateral*
Sicherheit des Arbeitsplatzes: *security of employment*

sicherheitshalber: *for safety*
Sicherheitsleistung des Nachlaßverwalters: *administration bond*
Sicherheitsleistung für Prozeßkosten: *security for costs*
Sicherheitsrat: *Security Council*
Sicherheitsspanne *or* **Sicherheitsspielraum:** *safety margin*
Sicherheitsverwahrung: *preventive detention*
Sicherheitsvorkehrungen: *safety measures; safety precautions*
Sicherheitsvorkehrungen am Arbeitsplatz: *office security*
Sicherheitsvorschriften: *safety regulations*
sicherhöhen: *increase*
sichern: *cover; safeguard; save*
Sicherungspfandrecht: *equitable lien*
Sicht: auf lange ~ *in the long term*
sichtbar: *apparent*
Sichttratte: *sight draft*
Sichtvermerk: *visa*
Sichtwechsel: *demand bill; sight draft*
Siegel: *seal*
siehe: *vide*
siehe oben: *supra*
singen: *squeal (slang)*
Sinken: *decline*
Sinn: *effect; intention*
Sitte: *convention; custom; usage*
Sittlichkeit: *decency*
Sittlichkeitsdelikte: *sexual offences*
Situation: *position; situation*
Sitz: *base; domicile* **eingetragener** ~ *registered office*
Sitzstreik: *sit-down protest*
Sitzung: *hearing; meeting; session* **außerordentliche** ~ *special sessions* **eine** ~ **abhalten** *sit* **eine** ~ **eröffnen** *to open a meeting; to call a meeting to order* **eine** ~ **leiten** *to conduct a meeting* **eine** ~ **schließen** *to close a meeting* **geheime** ~ *privileged meeting* **geschlossene** *or* **nichtöffentliche** ~ *closed session*
Sitzungskalender: *calendar (US)*
Sitzungspause: *recess*
Sitzungsperiode: session eine ~ **beenden** *prorogue*
Sitzungsperioden: *sittings*
Sitzungsprogramm: *order paper*
Skala: *scale*
skizzieren: *outline*
Sodomie: *buggery*
sofort beziehbar: *with immediate occupancy; vacant possession*
sofortig: *instant; prompt*
Solidargläubiger: *co-creditor*
solide: *copper-bottomed; sound*
Soll: *debit*
Sollbuchung: *debit entry*
Sollsaldo: *debit balance*

Sollspalte: *debtor side*
Soll und Haben: *debit and credit*
solvent: *solvent*
Solvenz: *solvency*
Sommerferien: *the summer holidays*
Sommersemesterferien: *Long Vacation*
Sommersonnenwende: *Midsummer day*
Sommerurlaub: *the summer holidays*
Sommerzeit: *Summer Time or Daylight Saving Time*
Sonderangebot: *bargain offer; special offer*
Sonderausgaben: unvorhergesehene ~ *contingent expenses*
Sonderausschuß: *select committee*
Sonderbevollmächtigter: *special agent*
Sondereinlagen: *special deposits*
Sonderfonds: *contingency fund or contingency reserve*
Sondergericht: *tribunal*
Sonderkonzession: *occasional licence*
Sonderposten: *exceptional or extraordinary items*
Sonderrecht: *privilege*
Sondertermin: *special sessions*
sondieren: *explore*
Sonntag: geschäftsfreier ~ *Sunday closing*
Sonntagsgesetze: *blue laws (US)*
sonst: *failing that; otherwise*
Sorge: *concern*
sorgen: für jdn ~ *to provide for someone*
Sorgepflicht: *care and control*
Sorgerecht: *custody*
Sorgfalt: wegen mangelnder ~ *per incuriam*
sorgfältig prüfen *or* **untersuchen:** *study*
Sorgfaltspflicht: *duty of care*
Sorgfaltspflichtverletzung: *malpractice*
Sorte: *kind; type*
Souverän: *sovereign*
Souveränität: *sovereignty*
Sozialarbeiter: *social worker*
Sozialeinrichtungen: *social services*
Sozialhilfe *or* **Sozialunterstützung:** *social security*
Sozialleistungen: außergewöhnliche ~ *exceptional needs payment*
Sozialversicherung: *National Insurance*
Sozialversicherungsbeiträge: *National Insurance contributions*
Sozietät: *partnership*
Spalte: *column*
Spareinlagen: zinstragende ~ *interest-bearing deposits*
sparen: *save*
Sparkampagne: *economy drive*
Sparkonto: *deposit account*
Sparmaßnahme: *economy measure*
Sparprämienanleihe: *premium bond*
Sparsamkeit: *economy*
Sparsystem: britisches ~ *National Savings*
Spediteur: *shipper*

Spediteurpfandrecht: *carrier's lien*
Spedition: *carrier*
Speditionsfirma: *removal company; shipping agent*
speisen: *feed*
Spende: *donation*
Spendenempfänger: *donee*
Spender: *donor*
Sperre: *barrier*
sperren: *freeze*
Sperrgebiet: *exclusion zone*
Sperrung eines Kunden(kredit)kontos: *closing of an account*
Spesen: *expenses*
Spesenkonto: *expense account*
Spezialist: *specialist*
speziell: *particular; special*
Spezifikation: *specification*
spezifisch: *specific*
spezifizieren: *break down; itemize; specify*
Spezifizierungen im Schriftsatz: *particulars*
Spiel: aufs ~ setzen *risk*
Spielen: *gaming*
Spion: *spy*
Spionage: *espionage*
Spionageabwehr: *counter-intelligence*
spionieren: *spy*
Spitze: *head*
Spitzel: *grass (slang); informer; nark (slang)*
Spitzenreiter: *leader*
Spitzenwert: *leader*
Spottpreise: *knockdown prices*
Sprache: *language; speech* **zur ~ bringen** *bring up*
Sprechen: *speech*
sprechen zu: *address*
Sprecher: *foreman of the jury; speaker*
Sprengkörper: *explosive device*
Sprengstoff: *explosive*
Spruch: einen ~ fällen *to bring in or to return a verdict*
Spruch der Geschworenen: *verdict*
Spur: *clue; lead*
Staat: *country; state* **der ~ Regina; Rex souveräner ~** *sovereign state*
Staatenbund: *union*
Staatenloser: *stateless person*
staatlich: *government; governmental; public*
staatlich gelenkt: *government-controlled; state-controlled*
Staatsangehöriger: *subject*
Staatsangehörigkeit: doppelte ~ *dual nationality*
Staatsanleihen: *government stocks*
Staatsanwalt: *Director of Public Prosecutions (DPP); district attorney (US); Procurator Fiscal; Crown or public prosecutor*
Staatsanwaltschaft: *prosecution*
Staatsausgaben: *public expenditure*

Staatsbeamter: *civil servant*
Staatsbesitz: *public ownership*
Staatsbetrieb: *state enterprise*
Staatsbürger: *citizen; national; subject*
Staatsbürgerschaft: *citizenship*
Staatsdienst: *civil service*
staatseigen: *state-owned*
Staatseigentum: *public or state ownership*
Staatsfinanzen: *public finance*
staatsgefährdend: *seditious*
Staatsgeheimnis: *official secret*
Staatshaushalt: der ~ *the Budget*
Staatshoheit: *sovereignty*
Staatsminister: *Minister of State*
Staatspapiere: mündelsichere ~ *gilt-edged securities or gilts; government securities*
Staatsschutzdelikt: *offence against the state*
Staatssiegel: *Great Seal*
Staatssiegelbewahrer: *Keeper of the Great Seal*
Staatsstreich: *coup (d'état)*
stabil: *firm; sound*
Stabilität: *firmness*
Stadt: *city; town*
Stadtdirektor: *Town Clerk*
Stadtgemeinde: *borough*
städtisch: *municipal*
Stadtplan: *street plan or town plan*
Stadtplaner: *town planner*
Stadtplanung: *town planning*
Stadtplan (mit Index): *street directory*
Stadtrat: *borough or town council*
Stadtstreicher: *vagrant*
Stadtteil: *district*
Stadtverwaltung: *municipality*
Stahlkammer: *safe deposit; strongroom; vault*
Stahlkassette: *strongbox*
Stammaktien: *equities; ordinary shares; common stock (US)*
Stammaktionär: *ordinary shareholder*
Stammdatei: *master copy of a file*
Stämmen: nach ~ *per stirpes*
Standard: *standard*
Standardbrief: *standard (form) letter*
Standesamt: *district registry or registry office*
Standesbeamter: oberster ~ *Registrar-General*
Standesbeamter eines Gerichtsbezirkes: *district registrar*
ständig: *continual; permanent; standing*
Standmiete: *market dues*
Standort: *base*
Stärke: *power*
starten: *launch*
Startkapital: *initial capital*
stationieren: *base*
stattfinden: *hold; to take place*
stattlich: *substantial*

Status: *status*

status quo ante: *status quo ante*

Statuten: *regulations*

stehenbleiben: *break down*

Stehlen: *stealing*

stehlen: *pilfer; steal*

steigen: *advance; appreciate; increase; rise*

steigern: *increase*

Steigerung: *increase; rise*

Steigerung der Lebenshaltungskosten: *increase in the cost of living*

steil: *sharp; sharply*

Stelle: *place; position; post; situation* **an ~ von** *pro* **eine ~ innehaben** *to occupy a post* **undichte ~** *leak*

Stellen: *freie ~ job openings*

stellen: *place; set* **sich ~** *surrender*

Stellenangebote: *situations or appointments vacant*

Stellenausschreibung: **juristische ~** *legal appointments vacant*

Stellengesuche: *situations wanted*

Stellenvermittlung: *Job Centre; employment office or bureau or agency*

Stellung: *place; position; post; status* **eine verantwortungsvolle ~** *a responsible job* **hohe amtliche ~** *high office* **rechtliche ~** *legal status*

Stellungnahme: *opinion; statement*

Stellung nehmen: *reply*

stellvertretend: *vicarious; vice-*

Stellvertreter: *agent; deputy; locum (tenens); representative; substitute*

Stellvertreter des Sheriffs: *bailiff (US); deputy (US)*

Stellvertretung: *agency*

Stempel: *seal; stamp*

Stempelgebühr: *stamp duty*

stempeln: *stamp*

Stempelsteuer: *stamp duty*

Stenograph: *shorthand writer; stenographer*

Stenographie: *shorthand*

Stenotypist: *shorthand typist*

Sterbegeld: *death benefit; death grant*

sterben vor: *predecease*

Sterbetabellen: *actuarial or mortality tables*

Sterbeurkunde: *death certificate*

Sternkammer: *Star Chamber*

Steuer: *duty; levy; tax* **eine ~ aufheben** *to lift a tax* **eine ~ erheben** *to levy or to impose a tax*

Steuer-: *fiscal*

Steuerabzüge: *tax deductions*

Steueranrechnung: *tax credit*

Steuerbefreiung: *exemption from tax or tax exemption; tax holiday*

Steuerberater: *tax adviser or tax consultant*

Steuereinnehmer: *exciseman*

Steuererklärung: *tax return or tax declaration*

Steuerermäßigung: *tax relief*

steuerfrei: *exempt from tax or tax-exempt; free of tax or tax-free; non-taxable*

Steuerfreibetrag: *tax allowances or allowances against tax; tax exemption* **persönlicher ~** *personal allowances*

Steuer hinterziehen: *to evade tax*

Steuerhinterziehung: *tax evasion*

Steuerjahr: *fiscal year; tax year*

Steuerklasse: *tax bracket*

Steuerklassen: *tax schedules*

steuerlich: *fiscal*

steuerlich absetzbar *or* **abzugsfähig:** *tax-deductible*

steuern: *control*

Steueroase: *tax haven*

steuerpflichtig: *taxable*

Steuerplanung: *tax planning*

Steuerprüfer: *inspector of taxes or tax inspector*

Steuerrückstand: *back tax(es)*

Steuerumgehung: *legale ~ tax avoidance*

Steuerungssysteme: *control systems*

Steuervergünstigung: *tax concession*

Steuervergünstigungen **bei Hypothekenzahlungen:** *mortgage relief*

Steuerverkürzung: *legale ~ tax avoidance*

Steuerzahler: *taxpayer*

stichhaltig: *sound; valid*

Stichprobe: *check sample*

Stichtag: *deadline*

Stiefvater: *step-father*

Stifter: *donor*

Stiftung: *donation; endowment* **gemeinnützige ~** *charitable trust or charitable corporation (US)*

Stiftungsaufsichtsamt: *the Charity Commissioners*

still: *dormant*

stillegen: *close down*

stillschweigend: *tacit*

stillschweigend angenommen: *implied*

Stillstand: *deadlock* **zum ~ kommen** *deadlock*

Stimmabgabe: *voting* **geschlossene ~** *block vote*

Stimme: *ausschlaggebende ~ casting vote* **eine ~ abgeben** *to cast a vote* **entscheidende ~ casting vote* **ungültige ~ spoilt ballot paper*

Stimmen: *national abgegebene ~ popular vote*

Stimmenauszähler: *teller*

Stimmrecht: *suffrage; voting rights*

Stimmrechtsvertreter: *proxy*

Stimmzettel: *ballot paper; voting paper*

Stoff: *substance*

Stoffe: *gefährliche ~ dangerous substances*

Störer im Gerichtssaal: *contemnor*

Stornierungsabsicht: *animus cancellandi*

Störung einer Einzelperson: *private nuisance*

stoßen: *knock*

Straf-: *criminal; penal*

Strafanstalt: *bridewell (slang); custodial establishment or institution; penal institution; penitentiary (US)*

Strafanzeige: *complaint; information*

Strafaussetzung: bedingte ~ *conditional discharge*

Strafaussetzung zur Bewährung: *probation (order)*

strafbar: *criminal; felonious; guilty; punishable*

Strafbarkeit: *culpability; guilt*

Strafe: penalty; punishment; sentence abschreckende ~ *deterrent sentence* **exemplarische ~** *exemplary sentence* **verlängerte ~** *extended sentence*

strafen: *punish*

Strafentlassener auf Bewährung: *probationer*

Straferlaß: *licence or license (US); pardon; remission*

Strafgefangene(r): *convict*

Strafgericht: *Criminal Court or Civil Court*

Strafgesetz: *penal laws*

Strafgesetzbuch: *penal code*

Strafklausel: *penalty clause*

Strafkolonie: *penal colony*

Sträflingskolonie: *convict settlement*

Strafmaß: sentence auf ~ plädieren *to cop a plea*

Strafmaßnahme: *sanction*

Strafmilderung: auf ~ plädieren *plead in mitigation*

strafmündig: *doli capax*

Strafmündigkeit: *age of criminal responsibility*

Strafrecht: *criminal law; penal laws*

strafrechtlich: *penal*

strafrechtlich verfolgen: *prosecute*

Strafrechtssystem: *the penal system*

Strafrichter: *sentencer*

Straftat: crime; offence or offense (US) eine ~ begehen *offend* **eine ~ wiederholen** *to repeat an offence* **vollendete ~** *substantive offence*

Straftaten: einleitende or unvollendete ~ *inchoate offences*

Straftäter: flüchtiger ~ *fugitive offender* **jugendlicher ~** *juvenile delinquent; juvenile or young offender* **verurteilter ~** *convicted criminal*

Straftatsbestände: *outstanding offences*

strafunmündig: *doli incapax*

Strafurlaub: *parole*

Strafverfahren: *criminal action*

Strafverfolgung: *prosecution*

Strafvollstreckungsaufschub: *reprieve*

Strafvollstreckungsaufschub gewähren: *to reprieve*

Strafvollzugsanstalt: penal institution; prison offene ~ *open prison*

Strafvollzugsbeamter: *prison officer*

Strafvollzugswissenschaft: *penology*

Strafzeit: *term of imprisonment*

Strafzeit verbüßen: *to do time or porridge (slang)*

Strafzettel: einen ~ verpassen *book (informal)*

Strandgut: *flotsam*

Strandvogt: *receiver of wrecks*

Straße: *highway*

Straßenhändler: *street vendor*

Straßenraub: *mugging*

Straßenverkehrsordnung: *the Highway Code*

Streckengeschäft: *drop shipment*

streichen: cross off; cut; delete; expunge; remove; strike off; strike out

Streife: *patrol*

Streife gehen: *patrol*

Streifengang: auf ~ *on foot patrol*

Streifenpolizist: *constable on the beat*

Streifenwagen: *patrol car; squad car*

Streik: gewerkschaftlich organisierter ~ *official strike* **wilder ~** *unofficial strike* **zum ~ aufrufen** *to call (workers) out on strike*

Streikabstimmung: *strike ballot or strike vote*

Streikaufruf: *strike call*

Streikbrecher: *blackleg*

streiken: *strike*

Streikgeld: *strike pay*

Streikkasse: *strike fund*

Streikposten: *picket*

Streikpostenkette: *picket line*

Streikpostenstehen: *picketing*

Streikrecht: *right to strike*

Streikverbotsklausel: *no-strike clause*

Streit: *argument; dispute; strife*

streiten: *argue*

Streitfrage or Streitpunkt: *issue*

streitig: *contentious*

Streitverkündung: *third party notice*

Streitverkündungsverfahren: *third party proceedings*

streng: *harsh; severe*

Strenge: *harshness; severity*

strikt: *strict; strictly*

strittig: *contentious*

Struktur: *pattern*

Stückelung: *denomination*

Stückzahl: große ~ *quantity*

Studie: *study*

Stufe: *bracket*

Stuhl: elektrischer ~ *electric chair or the chair*

Stunde: pro ~ *per hour*

stundenweise bezahlt werden: *to be paid by the hour*

Sturmschaden: *storm damage*

Sturz: *drop*

stürzen: *drop*

stützen: *support*

Stützungspreis: *support price*

Submissionsofferten: versiegelte ~ *sealed tenders*

Submittent: *tenderer*

subsidiär: *subsidiary*

Subskriptionsprospekt: *prospectus*

Substanz: *substance*

Subunternehmer: *subcontractor*

Subvention: *bounty; grant; subsidy*

subventionieren: *subsidize*

subversiv: *subversive*
Suche: *hunt; search*
suchen: *hunt; search; seek*
Suggestivfrage: *leading question*
Suggestivfragen stellen: *lead*
summarisch: *summarily*
Summe: *figure; sum; total*
Superspitzel: *supergrass (slang)*
suspendieren: *suspend*
Suspension: *suspension*
Symbol: *token*
Syndikat: *syndicate; trust (US)*
Systemanalyse: *systems analysis*
Systemanalytiker *or* **Systemberater:** *systems analyst*
systematisch: *systematic*

Tt

Tabelle: *scale; table*
Tadel: *reprimand*
tadeln: *censure*
Tafel: *panel*
Tag: *pro* ~ *per day; per diem*
Tag des Inkrafttretens: *date of commencement; effective date*
Tagebuch: *blotter (US); diary*
tagen: *sit*
Tagesausbildungsstätte: *day training centre*
Tagesgeld: *money at call or money on call or call money*
Tagesordnung: *agenda* **schriftliche** ~ *order paper*
Tagesordnung!: **zur** ~ *order ! order!*
Tagesordungspunkt: *matters arising*
täglich: *day-to-day*
Tagungsort: *venue*
Taktik: *policy*
Talar: *gown*
Talsohle: *trough*
Tantiemen: *royalty*
Tarif: *tariff* **ermäßigter** ~ *reduced rate*
Tarife: *scale of charges or scale of prices*
Tarifverhandlungen: *collective bargaining* **autonome** ~ *free collective bargaining*
Tarifvertrag: *union agreement*
Tasche: **aus eigener** ~ *out of pocket*
Taschendieb: *dip (slang); pickpocket; picker (slang)*
Taschenrechner: *calculator*
Tastatur: *keyboard*
Tat: **auf frischer** ~ *in flagrante delicto*
Tatbestand: *actus reus*
Tatbestände: *matters of fact*
Täter: *culprit; offender; perpetrator* **flüchtiger** ~ *fugitive offender* **jugendliche** ~ *young offenders* **jugendlicher** ~ *juvenile delinquent* **mutmaßlicher**

~ **suspect** **nicht vorbestrafter** ~ *first offender* **rückfälliger** ~ *recidivist*
Tatfrage: *matter or point or question of fact*
Tätigkeit: *occupation; operation*
tätig sein: *to be engaged in*
Tätlichkeit: *violence (against the person)*
Tatortbesichtigung: *viewing the scene of the crime*
Tatsache: *fact* **aktenmäßig feststehende** ~ *a matter of record*
Tatsachen: *matters of fact*
Tatsachenermittlung: *fact-finding*
tatsächlich: *actual; in fact or in point of fact*
tatsächlich vorhanden: *in esse*
tauglich: *fit*
Tauglichkeit: *fitness*
Tausch: *exchange*
tauschen: *convert; exchange*
täuschen: *deceive; take in*
täuschend: *deceptive*
Täuschung: *deceit or deception* **arglistige** ~ *fraudulent misrepresentation*
Taxator: *valuer*
Techniker: *repairer*
technisch: *technical*
Teil: *cut; part; proportion* **einleitender** ~ *recitals* **zum größten** ~ *largely* **zum** ~ *in part; partly*
teilen: *divide* **sich** ~ *share*
Teilerfüllung: *part performance*
Teilhaber: *associate; co-partner; partner* **geschäftsführender** ~ *active or working partner* **stiller** ~ *sleeping or dormant partner*
Teilhaberschaft: *co-partnership; partnership*
Teilleistung: *part performance*
Teilschaden *or* **Teilverlust:** *partial loss*
teilweise: *to a certain extent; in part; partial; partly*
Teilzahlung: *part payment*
Teilzahlungsfinanzierungsgesellschaft: *hire-purchase company*
Teilzahlungsinstitute: *secondary banks*
Teilzahlungskauf: *hire purchase*
Teilzahlungskaufvertrag: *hire purchase agreement*
Teilzahlungssystem: *installment plan (US)*
Telefonbuch: *(tele)phone book; telephone directory*
Telefonzelle: *call box*
Tendenz: *trend*
Termin: *appointment; deadline* **auf** ~ **verkaufen** *to sell forward*
Termine: *engagements* **dringende** ~ *pressing engagements*
Termineinlagen: *term deposit*
Termingeschäfte: *forward dealings; futures*
Terminkalender: *appointments book; cause list; diary; timetable*
Terminkauf: *forward buying or buying forward*
Terminlieferung: *future delivery*

Terminmarkt: *forward market*
Terminplan: *schedule*
Terminverkäufe: *forward sales*
territorial: *territorial*
Territorium: *territory*
Terrorismus: *terrorism*
Terrorist: *terrorist*
Testament: *last will and testament* **gegenseitiges ~** *reciprocal will* **handgeschriebenes ~** *holograph will*
testamentarisch: *testamentary*
Testamente: gegenseitige ~ *mutual wills*
Testamentsbestätigung: gerichtliche ~ *probate*
Testamentsnachtrag: *codicil*
Testamentsvollstrecker: *executor; personal representative*
Testamentsvollstreckerin: *executrix*
Testator: *settlor; testator*
testen: *sample; test*
Testierfähigkeit: *testamentary capacity*
teuer: *dear*
Teuerungszulage: *cost-of-living increase*
teurer werden: *to increase in price*
Textverarbeitung: *word or text processing*
Theaterkasse: *box office*
theoretisch: *on paper*
Thron: *throne*
Thronbesteigung: *accession to the throne*
Thronrede: *Queen's Speech*
Ticket: offenes ~ *open ticket*
tilgen: *pay off; redeem*
Tilgung: *discharge; redemption*
Tilgungsrate: letzte ~ *final discharge*
Tilgungsrecht des Hypothekenschuldners: *equity of redemption*
Tilgungssumme: *payoff*
Tilgungstermin: *redemption date*
Tilgungszeitraum: *payback period*
Tippen: *typing*
tippen: *type*
Tippfehler: *typing error*
Titel: voller ~ *full or long title*
Tochtergesellschaft: *subsidiary company; division* **eine hundertprozentige ~** *a wholly-owned subsidiary*
Tod: *death; decease; demise*
Todesstrafe: *capital punishment; death penalty*
Todesvermutung: *presumption of death*
Todeszelle: *condemned cell*
tödlich: *fatal*
Toleranz: *allowance*
tot: *dead*
total: *outright; totally*
Totalverlust: *dead loss*
töten: *kill*
Totenschein: *death certificate*
Totenstarre: *rigor mortis*

Totschlag: *culpable homicide; second degree murder; manslaughter*
Totschläger: *cosh; life preserver (slang)*
Tötung: *destruction; homicide* **fahrlässige ~** *involuntary manslaughter* **vorsätzliche ~** *voluntary manslaughter; wilful murder*
Touristenvisum: *tourist visa*
tragen: *bear; defray*
Traktorenhersteller: *tractor company*
Transaktion: geschäftliche ~ *business transaction*
Transfer: *transfer*
transferieren: *transfer*
Transitgüter: *goods in transit*
Transitvisum: *transit visa*
Transport: *carriage; shipment; shipping*
transportieren: *ship*
Transportschaden *or* **Transportverlust:** *loss in transport*
Transportunternehmen: *carrier* **öffentliches ~** *common carrier* **privates ~** *private carrier*
Trassant: *drawer*
Trassat: *drawee*
Tratte: *bill (of exchange); draft*
Treffen: *consultation*
treffen: *meet; strike*
Treffpunkt: *meeting place*
Treibgut: *flotsam*
Trend: *trend*
trennen: *separate*
Trennung: *separation*
Tresen: *counter*
Tresor: *safe deposit; vault* **feuersicherer ~** *fireproof safe*
Tresorraum: *strongroom*
Treueeid: *oath of allegiance*
Treuepflicht: *allegiance*
Treugeber: *settlor*
Treuhand: *trust*
Treuhänder: *bailee; fiduciary; trustee* **öffentlich bestellter ~** *Public Trustee*
treuhänderisch: *fiduciary*
treuhänderisch hinterlegt: *in escrow*
Treuhänderschaft: *trusteeship*
Treuhandfonds: *trust fund*
Treuhandgesellschaft: *trust company (US)*
Treuhandkonto: *escrow account (US)*
Treuhandschaft: *trust*
Treuhandverhältnis: fingiertes ~ *constructive trust* **uneingeschränktes ~** *discretionary trust*
Treuhandvertrag: *trust deed or instrument*
Tribunal: *tribunal*
Trick: *con (informal); device; trick*
Trickbetrügerei: *bunco (slang)*
Trickserei: *fiddle (informal)*
Trieb: unwiderstehlicher ~ *irresistible impulse*
triftig: *valid*
Trinker: *drunkard*
Trip: *trip*

Trockenmaß: *dry measure*
Trottel: *mug*
trotz(dem): *notwithstanding*
Trouble Shooter: *troubleshooter*
Trunkenheit: *intoxication*
Trunkenheit am Steuer: *drunken driving*
tüchtig: *efficient*
Turnus: *rotation*

Uu

u.A.w.g.: *RSVP*
übel: *noxious*
Übeltäter: *wrongdoer*
überarbeiten: *revise*
Überblick: *outline*
überblicken: *overlook*
Überbringer: *bearer*
Überbringerscheck: *bearer cheque*
Überbrückungskredit: *bridging loan*
übereignen: *assign*
Übereignung: *assignment*
Übereignungsurkunde: *deed of assignment*
Übereinkunft: *understanding*
übereinstimmen: *concur; to correspond with something* **nicht** ~ *differ; disagree; dissent*
übereinstimmend: *compliant; ad idem* **nicht** ~ **mit** *not compliant with*
Übereinstimmung: *concurrence; conformance; consensus* **grundsätzliche** ~ *agreement in principle* **in** ~ **mit** *in accordance with; ad idem; in conformity with*
Überfall: *attack; raid*
überfallen: *attack; hijack; hold up; raid*
überfällig: *overdue*
überflüssig: *redundant*
Überführung: *conviction*
Übergabe: *delivery*
Übergangs-: *interim*
Übergangsministerpräsident: *caretaker Prime Minister*
übergeben: *hand over; present*
Übergeber: *bailor*
übergehen: *vest*
übergeordnet: *senior*
Übergewinnsteuer: *excess profits tax*
Übergriff: *encroachment*
überholt: *obsolete*
überleben: *survive*
Überlebende(r): *survivor*
überlegen: *consider; deliberate; superior*
Überlegung: *consideration; premeditation* **nach reiflicher** ~ *after due consideration*
übermäßig: *excessive*
übernachten: *stay*
Übernahme: *accession; assumption; takeover* **angefochtene** ~ *contested takeover*

Übernahmeangebot: *takeover bid or offer*
übernehmen: *assume; defray; incur; take over; undertake*
überprüfen: *check; examine; go into; investigate; review; verify; vet*
Überprüfung: *check; checking; control test; investigation; review; verification* **gerichtliche** ~ *judicial review*
überqueren: *cross*
überreden: *persuade*
Überredung zum Vertragsbruch: *inducement to break contract*
überreichen: *give; hand over; present*
überschätzen: *overestimate*
überschreiten: *exceed; overrun*
Überschrift: *heading*
Überschuß: *excess*
übersehen: *overlook*
Übersicht: *summary*
übersteigen: *exceed*
überstellen: *commit*
Überstellung: *commitment; committal*
überstimmen: *outvote*
Überstunden: *overtime*
Überstundenlohn: *overtime pay*
Überstunden machen: *to work overtime*
Überstundenverbot: *overtime ban*
übertragbar: *transferable* **nicht** ~ *inalienable; "not negotiable"*
Übertragbarkeit: *negotiability*
übertragen: *assign; attorn; confer; transfer; vest*
Übertragender: *transferor; grantor*
Übertragung: *alienation; assignment; delegation; delivery; transfer; grant*
Übertragungsurkunde: *assignment; conveyance; deed of transfer*
übertreten: *break; contravene; infringe; violate*
Übertretung: *breach; contravention; infringement; misdemeanour; summary offence; violation*
überwachen: *monitor; superintend; supervise*
Überwachung: *control; surveillance* **elektronische** ~ *electronic surveillance* **polizeiliche** ~ *policing*
überweisen: *remit*
Überweisung: *remittance*
überwinden: *overcome*
überzählig: *redundant*
überzeugen: *convince; satisfy*
Überzeugung: *conviction*
überziehen: *overrun*
üblich: *normal; standard; usual*
übrig: *residual; residuary*
übrigbleiben: *remain*
übrigbleibend: *residual*
Uferanliegerrechte: *riparian rights*
Uhrzeit: *time*
Ultimatum: *ultimatum*
Umfang: *extent* **in begrenztem** ~ *small-scale* **in großem** ~ *large scale*
umfangreich: *extensive*

umfassend: *comprehensive; extensive*
umgehen: *avoid; get round*
umgehend: *forthwith; out of hand; immediate(ly)*
Umgehung: *avoidance; evasion*
umgekehrt: *reverse; vice versa*
Umlauf: *circulation* **in** ~ **bringen** *circulate*
Umlaufvermögen: *current assets*
umlegen: *hit (slang)*
Umorganisation: *reorganization*
umorganisieren: *reorganize*
Umsatz: *sales; turnover (GB)*
Umschalttaste: *shift key*
Umschlag: *handling*
Umschlagsgeschwindigkeit: *turnover (US)*
Umschlagspesen: *handling charges*
Umschreibung: *alienation*
Umschwung: *reversal*
umsetzen: *turn over*
umsonst: *gratis*
Umstand: fördernder ~ *contributory factor*
Umstände: *circumstances* **mildernde** ~
extenuating or mitigating circumstances or factors
mitverursachende ~ *contributory causes*
Umstände bereiten: *inconvenience*
umsteigen: *transfer*
umstoßen: *reverse*
umstrukturieren: *restructure*
Umstrukturierung: *restructuring*
umstürzlerisch: *subversive*
umtauschbar: *exchangeable*
umtauschen: *exchange*
umwandelbar: *convertible*
umwandeln: *commute; convert*
Umwandlung: *commutation*
Umwandlungsklausel: *let-out clause*
umziehen: *move*
Umzug: *removal*
unabhängig: *independent(ly)*
unangefochten: *uncontested*
Unannehmlichkeit: *inconvenience*
Unannehmlichkeiten bereiten: *to inconvenience*
unanständig: *indecent*
Unanständigkeit: *indecency*
unaufgefordert: *unsolicited*
unausgefüllt: *blank*
unbedeutend: *minor; nominal; petty* **nicht** ~ *not negligible*
unbedingt: *necessarily*
unbedingt notwendig: *essential*
unbeeidet: *unsworn*
unbefristet: *open-ended or open-end (US)*
unbefugt betreten: *trespass*
unbegrenzt: *indefinite; unlimited*
unbeschränkt: *open-ended or open-end (US); unlimited*
unbesetzt: *free; vacant*
unbestätigt: *unconfirmed*

unbestimmbar: *unquantifiable*
unbestimmt: *indefinite; unascertained*
unbestritten: *unchallenged*
unbeweglich: *immovable*
unbewohnbar: für ~ **erklären** *condemn*
unbewohnt: *vacant*
unbezahlt: *outstanding; unpaid*
unecht: *sham*
unehelich: *illegitimate*
Unehelichkeit: *illegitimacy*
unehrlich: *dishonest(ly)*
uneidlich: *unsworn*
Uneinigkeit: *disagreement*
uneinsichtig: *unreasonable*
unentgeltlich: *gratuitous; voluntary*
unerheblich: *negligible*
unerläßlich: *essential*
unerlaubt: *illicit; tortious; unlawful*
unerlaubt nachdrucken: *pirate*
unermittelt: *unascertained*
unerschwinglich: *prohibitive*
unfähig: *incapable; incompetent*
Unfähigkeit: *incapacity*
Unfall: accident durch ~ *accidental*
Unfallgeld: *injury benefit*
Unfalltod: *death by misadventure*
Unfallversicherung: *accident insurance*
Unfallversicherungspolice: *accident policy*
unfertig: *inchoate*
unfreiwillig: *involuntary; involuntarily*
Unfug: grober ~ *public or common nuisance*
ungeachtet: *notwithstanding; regardless of*
ungebeten: *unsolicited*
ungeboren: *unborn*
ungebunden: *independent*
ungefähr: *rough(ly)*
ungehindert: *without let or hindrance*
Ungehorsam: bürgerlicher *or* **ziviler** ~ *civil disobedience*
Ungelegenheit: *inconvenience*
ungelöst: *unsolved*
ungenannt: *undisclosed*
ungenau: *incorrect(ly)*
ungerecht: *unjust*
Ungerechtigkeit: *injustice*
ungesetzlich: *illegal; unlawful; wrongful* **für** ~ **erklären** *outlaw*
Ungesetzlichkeit: *illegality*
ungestraft: *with impunity*
Unglück: *accident; misadventure*
ungültig: *defective; invalid; null; void* **für** ~ **erklären** *invalidate; rescind*
Ungültigkeit: *invalidity; nullity*
Ungültigkeitserklärung: *invalidation; rescinding or rescission*
unheilbar: *irreconcilable; irretrievable*
unilateral: *unilateral(ly)*

Unionsstaaten: die ~ *the States of the Union*
Unit Trust: *unit trust*
universal: *universal*
Universalversicherungspolice: *comprehensive or all-risks policy*
Unkenntnis: *ignorance*
unklar: *equivocal*
unkompliziert: *simple*
unkontrollierbar: *uncontrollable*
Unkosten: *expenses* **abzugsfähige** ~ *allowable expenses* **allgemeine** ~ *overhead or general or running expenses* **sich** ~ **aufladen** *to incur costs*
unmißverständlich: *unequivocal*
unmittelbar: *direct(ly)*
unmöglich: *impossible*
Unmöglichkeit der Erfüllung *or* **der Leistung:** *impossibility of performance*
Unordnung: *disorder*
unparteiisch: *impartial(ly)*
Unparteilichkeit: *impartiality*
unpassend: *improper*
unpersönlich: *impersonal*
unproduktiv: *dead*
Unrecht: *injustice; wrong* **zu** ~ *unjustly; wrongly*
unrecht: *wrong*
unrechtmäßig: *illegal; illegitimate; unjust; wrongful*
Unrechtmäßigkeit: *illegitimacy*
unredlich: *dishonest(ly)*
Unregelmäßigkeit: *irregularity*
unrentabel: *not commercially viable*
unrichtig: *improper(ly)*
Unruhen: *civil or public disorder or public disorders; disturbance* **innere** ~ *civil strife*
Unruhestifter: *rioter*
unschicklich: *unbecoming*
unschlüssig sein: *hesitate*
Unschuld: *innocence*
unschuldig: *innocent*
Unschuldvermutung: *presumption of innocence*
unstatthaft: *irregular*
Untat: *misdeed*
untätig: *dormant*
untengenannt: *undermentioned*
untenstehend: *hereunder*
Unterauftrag: *subcontract*
Unteraufträge vergeben: *to put work out to contract*
Unterausschuß: *sub-committee*
unterbewerten: *underestimate*
Unterbewertung: *underestimate*
unterbrechen: *suspend*
Unterbringung: *placement*
unterdrücken: *conceal*
Unterdrückung: *concealment*
unterdurchschnittlich: *substandard*
Untergebener: *subordinate*
untergeordnet: *puisne; subordinate*

Unterhalt: *maintenance; palimony*
unterhalten: *entertain; maintain*
Unterhaltsberechtigter: *dependant*
Unterhaltsregelung: *ancillary relief*
Unterhaltsurteil: *maintenance order*
Unterhaltsverfügung: *affiliation order*
Unterhaltszahlung: *alimony* **vorläufige** ~ *alimony pending suit or pendente lite; maintenance pending suit*
Unterhändler: *official mediator; negotiator*
Unterhaus: *House of Commons*
Unterkunft: **möblierte** ~ *furnished accommodation*
Unterlagen: *information; papers; records*
Unterlagen abheften: *to file documents*
unterlassen: *fail; forbear; omit* **etwas** ~ *to refrain from something*
Unterlassung: *default; failure; forbearance; neglect; omission* **bewußte** *or* **vorsätzliche** ~ *wilful neglect* **pflichtwidrige** ~ *nonfeasance*
Unterlassungsfall: **im** ~ *by default*
unterliegen: *liable to*
Untermiete: *subtenancy; underlease*
Untermieter: *sublessee; subtenant; undertenant*
Untermietvertrag: *sublease or underlease*
Unternehmen: *business; company; corporation; enterprise; establishment; firm; undertaking* **börsenfähiges** ~ *listed company* **ein** ~ **auflösen** *or* **liquidieren** *to put a company into liquidation; to liquidate a company* **ein** ~ **übernehmen** *to take over a company* **gemeinnütziges** ~ *non profit-making organization or non-profit corporation (US)* **rentables** ~ *going concern* **staatliches** ~ *state enterprise* **unabhängiges** ~ *independent company*
unternehmen: **etwas** ~ *to take action*
Unternehmensberater: *management consultant*
Unternehmens-Fixkosten: *establishment charges*
Unternehmensforschung: *operational research*
Unternehmensführung: *management*
Unternehmensführung mit Zielvorgabe: *management by objectives*
Unternehmensgewinne: *corporate profits*
Unternehmensleitung: *management*
Unternehmensplanung: *corporate planning*
Unternehmensrecht: *company law*
Unternehmenssanierung: *the reorganization of a company*
Unternehmensspitze: *top management*
Unternehmen zu verkaufen: *business for disposal*
Unternehmer: **selbständiger** ~ *independent contractor*
Unternehmertum: **freies** ~ *free enterprise*
Unterpacht: *subtenancy; underlease*
Unterpächter: *sublessee; subtenant; undertenant*
Unterpachtvertrag: *sublease or underlease*
unterrichten: *advise; brief; inform*
untersagen: *bar; prohibit*
Untersagung: *prohibition*
unterschätzen: *underestimate*

unterscheiden: *distinguish*
Unterscheidung: *distinction*
Unterschied: *difference; distinction*
unterschiedlich: *different*
unterschlagen: *defraud; embezzle; misappropriate*
Unterschlagung: *defalcation; embezzlement; misappropriation*
Unterschlupf gewähren: *harbour*
unterschreiben: *sign*
Unterschrift: *signature* seine ~ einlösen *to honour a signature*
unterstellen: *impute*
unterstellt: jdm ~ sein *to report to someone; to responsible to someone*
Unterstellung: *imputation*
unterstützen: *assist; encourage; help; support* jdn ~ *to back someone*
Unterstützung: *assistance; help; relief; support* finanzielle ~ *financial assistance*
untersuchen: *examine; explore; go into; inspect; investigate*
Untersuchung: *examination; inquiry; inspection; investigation; study* gerichtliche ~ *(coroner's) inquest*
Untersuchungsausschuß: *fact-finding delegation* gemischter ~ *joint commission of inquiry or joint committee* königlicher ~ *Royal Commission*
Untersuchungsbeamter: *investigator*
Untersuchungsbericht: *report*
Untersuchungsgefangene(r): *prisoner on remand or remand prisoner*
Untersuchungsgericht: *coroner's court*
Untersuchungshaft: *(remand in) custody*
Untersuchungshaft anordnen: *bind over (US)*
Untersuchungsrichter: *examining justice or magistrate*
Untertan: *subject*
untervermieten *or* unterverpachten: *sublease; sublet; underlet*
Untervermieter *or* Unterverpächter: *sublessor*
Untervermietung *or* Unterverpachtung: *sublease or underlease*
Untervertrag: *subcontract* einen ~ abschließen *subcontract*
Untervertreter: *sub-agent*
Untervertretung: *sub-agency*
Unterwelt: *underworld; gangland*
unterwerfen: *subject to; submit*
unterworfen: *liable to; subject to*
unterzeichnen: *sign*
Unterzeichnenden: die ~ *(we,) the undersigned*
Unterzeichner: *signatory*
Unterzeichnete: der/die ~ *the undersigned*
Unterzeichnung des Kaufvertrages: *exchange of contracts*
untilgbar: *irredeemable*
untragbar: *prohibitive*
unüberbrückbar: *irreconcilable*
unumstritten: *uncontested*

ununterbrochen: *continual(ly); continuous(ly)*
unverantwortlich: *irresponsible*
Unverantwortlichkeit: *irresponsibility*
unveräußerlich: *inalienable*
unverbindlich: *tentative(ly)*
unvereidigt: *unsworn*
unverheiratet: *unmarried*
unverkäuflich: *not negotiable*
unvermeidbar *or* unvermeidlich: *inevitable; unavoidable*
unvernünftig: *unreasonable*
unversöhnlich: *irreconcilable*
unverzüglich: *out of hand*
unvollständig: *inchoate*
unvordenklich: *immemorial*
unvoreingenommen: *impartial*
Unvoreingenommenheit: *impartiality*
unwahr: *untrue*
Unwahrheit: *falsehood*
unwesentlich: *negligible*
unwichtig: *minor; petty*
unwiderbringlich: *irretrievable*
unwiderlegt: *unchallenged*
unwiderruflich: *irrevocable*
unwidersprochen: *undefended*
unwiderstehlich: *irresistible*
Unwissenheit: *ignorance*
Unzucht: *indecency* gewerbsmäßige ~ *prostitution* schwere ~ *gross indecency* schwere ~ begehen *to commit an act of gross indecency*
unzüchtig: *indecent; obscene*
unzulänglich: *defective; incompetent*
unzulässig: *illegitimate; inadmissible*
unzurechnungsfähig: *non compos mentis*
Unzuständigkeit: *excess of jurisdiction* örtliche ~ *mistake in venue*
unzutreffend: *improper*
unzuverlässig: *unreliable*
unzweifelhaft: *beyond reasonable doubt*
Urabstimmung: *strike ballot or strike vote*
Urheberrecht: *copyright* ein ~ verletzen *to infringe a copyright*
Urheberrecht der Krone: *Crown copyright (GB)*
urheberrechtlich geschützt: *copyright; copyrighted*
urheberrechtlich schützen: *copyright*
Urheberrechtsgesetz: *Copyright Act*
Urheberrechtsinhaber: *copyright owner*
Urheberrechtsvermerk: *copyright notice*
Urin: *urine*
Urinprobe: *urine sample*
Urinuntersuchung: *urine test*
Urkunde: *certificate; charter; copy; document; engrossment; instrument* eigenhändig geschriebene ~ *holograph* einseitige ~ *deed poll* gesiegelte ~ *deed; sealed instrument* unvollständige ~ *inchoate instrument* vorliegende ~ *these presents*

Urkundenbeweis: *documentary evidence or proof*
indirekter ~ *secondary evidence*
Urkundeneinsicht: *inspection*
Urkundenpapier: *engrossment or judicature paper*
Urkundenverfasser: *draftsman*
urkundlich: *documentary*
Urlaub: *holiday; leave; vacation (US)*
Urlaubsanspruch: *holiday entitlement*
Urlaubsgeld: *holiday pay*
Ursache: *cause*
Ursprung: *source*
ursprünglich: *originally*
Ursprungswohnsitz: *domicile of origin*
Urteil: *decision; findings; verdict* **abweichendes** ~ *dissenting judgment* **das** ~ **fällen** *or* **sprechen** *sentence; adjudicate* **das** ~ **verkünden** *to return a verdict* **ein** ~ **eintragen** *to enter or take judgment* **rechtskräftiges** ~ *final judgment* **vorläufiges** ~ *interlocutory judgment*
Urteil auf Schadensersatz: *compensation order*
Urteilsschrift: *certificate of judgment*
Urteilsspruch: *findings*
Urteils- und Entscheidungssammlung: *Law Reports (GB)*
Urteilsverkündung: die ~ **aussetzen** *to reserve judgment*
Urteilsvollstreckung: die ~ **aussetzen** *reprieve*
Urzeiten: seit ~ *from time immemorial*
US-Aktien: *dollar stocks*
Usance: *the customs of the trade; usage*
US-Bundesanwaltskammer: *American Bar Association*
Usurpation: *usurpation*
usurpieren: *usurp*
usw.: *etc. or etcetera*

Vv

vage: *remote*
Vater: mutmaßlicher ~ *putative father*
Vatermord: *patricide*
Vaterschaftsprozeß: *affiliation proceedings; paternity action or suit*
Vaterschaftstest: *blood test or blood grouping test*
VB: *or near offer (o.n.o.)*
Vehaltenskodex: *code of conduct*
Verabredung: eine ~ **einhalten** *to keep an appointment*
verabreichen: *administer*
verabschieden: *pass*
Verachtung: *contempt*
veraltet: *obsolete*
verändern: *alter*
veranlagen: *assess*
Veranlagung: *taxation*

veranlassen: *induce; occasion; procure* **jdn** ~ *to join someone to an action; to prevail upon someone (to do something)*
verantwortlich: *accountable; answerable*
verantwortlich für: *responsible for*
Verantwortlichkeit: *accountability; responsibility*
verantwortlich machen: *blame*
Verantwortung: *responsibility*
verantwortungsbewußt: *responsibly*
verantwortungslos: *irresponsible*
Verantwortungslosigkeit: *irresponsibility*
Verarbeitung: *processing*
veräußern: *to dispose of; realize; sell*
Veräußerung: *disposal; sale*
Veräußerungsgewinne: *capital gains*
Veräußerungsgewinnsteuer: *capital gains tax*
Veräußerungstreuhand: *trust for sale*
Veräußerung von Vermögenswerten: *realization of assets*
Verband: *association; federation*
verbannen: *banish; exile*
Verbannte(r): *exile*
Verbannung: *banishment; exile*
verbergen: *conceal*
verbessern: *correct; reform*
Verbesserung: *correction*
verbieten: *ban; bar; forbid; outlaw; prohibit; proscribe; restrain; veto*
verbinden: *connect; consolidate; join*
verbindlich: *binding; compulsory*
Verbindlichkeit: *obligation* **eine** ~ **erfüllen** *to discharge a debt* **ungesicherte** ~ *unsecured debt*
Verbindlichkeiten: *accounts payable; liabilities* **gesicherte** ~ *secured debts* **kurzfristige** ~ *current liabilities* **langfristige** ~ *long-term liabilities or debts* **seinen** ~ **nachkommen** *to discharge one's liabilities; to meet one's obligations*
Verbindung: *connection; consolidation; contact; relationship*
Verbindung aufnehmen: *contact*
Verbindungen: *relations*
verborgen: *hidden; latent*
Verbot: *ban; interdict; prohibition* **ein** ~ **umgehen** *to beat a ban*
Verbote: *mala prohibita*
verboten: *illicit*
Verbrauch: *consumption*
Verbraucher: *consumer*
Verbraucherberatung: *consumer council*
Verbraucherschutz: *consumer protection*
Verbraucherschutzgesetze: *consumer legislation*
Verbrauchsgüter: *consumer goods*
Verbrauchssteuer: *excise duty or tax*
Verbrechen: *crime; misdeed* **ein** ~ **aufklären** *to solve a crime* **organisiertes** ~ *organized crime* **politisches** ~ *political crime* **schweres** ~ *arrestable offence*
Verbrechenswelle: *crime wave*

Verbrecher: *gangster*
Verbrecherfoto: *mug shot*
verbrecherisch: *felonious*
Verbreitung: *circulation; dissemination*
verbrennen: *burn*
verbringen: *spend*
verbunden: *incidental; related* **mit etwas** ~ *incident to something*
verbürgen: sich ~ *guarantee*
verbüßen: *serve*
Verdacht: *suspicion* **den** ~ **haben** *suspect*
verdächtig: *suspicious*
verdächtigen: *suspect*
Verdächtige(r): *suspect*
verdeckt: *hidden*
verderben: *deprave; spoil*
verdienen: *earn*
Verdienst: *merit*
Verdienstausfallentschädigung: *compensation for loss of earnings*
Verdienstmöglichkeit: *earning power*
verdoppeln: *double*
verdrehen: *pervert*
verdreifachen: *treble*
vereidigen: *to administer an oath; swear in*
Vereidigung: *swearing-in*
Verein: nicht eingetragener ~ *unincorporated association*
vereinbaren: *agree; stipulate*
vereinbart: *agreed*
Vereinbarung: *agreement; engagement; stipulation; understanding* **eine** ~ **beeinträchtigen** *to derogate from something which has been agreed* **einschränkende** ~ *restrictive covenant* **frühere** ~ *prior agreement* **mündliche** ~ *verbal agreement* **ungeschriebene** ~ *unwritten agreement*
vereinfachen: *consolidate*
Vereinigung von Gesetzen: *codification*
Vereinsfreiheit: *freedom of association*
Vereinsschriftführer: *club's membership secretary*
vereiteln: *block; frustrate*
Vereitelung: *frustration*
vererbbar: *hereditary*
vererben: *bequeath; hand down*
Verfahren: *procedure; process; suit* **familienrechtliches** ~ *domestic proceedings* **ordnungsgemäßes** ~ *the due process of the law* **summarisches** ~ *rough justice*
Verfahrensanweisungen: *practice direction*
Verfahrensaufschub: *arrest of judgment*
Verfahrensformeln: *judicial process*
Verfahrensfrage: *procedural problem or question*
Verfahrensmißbrauch: *abuse of process*
Verfahrensrecht: *code of practice; procedural law*
verfahrensrechtlich: *procedural*
Verfahrensweise: *practice; process*
Verfall: *expiry; forfeit; lapse*
verfallen: *lapse*

Verfallsdatum: *expiry date*
Verfallserklärung: endgültige ~ *foreclosure order absolute* **vorläufige** ~ *foreclosure order nisi*
Verfallsklausel: *forfeit clause*
Verfassen: *drafting*
Verfasser: *drafter*
Verfassung: *constitution*
verfassungsgemäß *or* **verfassungsmäßig:** *constitutional* **nicht** ~ *unconstitutional*
Verfassungsrecht: *constitutional law*
verfassungswidrig: *unconstitutional*
Verfehlung: *misconduct*
verfolgen: *trace*
Verfolgung: sofortige ~ *fresh pursuit* **strafrechtliche** ~ *criminal action*
Verfolgungsrecht: *hot pursuit*
verfügbar: *available*
verfügen: *decree*
Verfügung: *disposition; order* **einstweilige** ~ *interim or interlocutory or provisional or temporary injunction; interdict* **gerichtliche** ~ *court order* **testamentarische** ~ *testamentary disposition* **unentgeltliche** ~ *voluntary disposition* **zur** ~ **in hand**
Verfügungen: prozeßleitende ~ *directions*
Verfügungsentwurf: *minutes of order*
Verfügung über Grundbesitz: *settlement*
Vergangenheit: rechtlich erfaßte ~ *legal memory*
vergeben: *give away; put out*
Vergehen: *breach; delinquency; misdemeanour; misfeasance; misprision; offence or offense (US); petty crime; wrongdoing* **anzeigepflichtiges** ~ *notifiable offence* **schweres** ~ *indictable offence*
vergehen: *elapse*
Vergeltung(smaßnahme): *retaliation*
Vergeltung üben: *retaliate*
vergessen: *forget*
vergewaltigen: *rape*
Vergewaltigung: *rape*
vergiften: *poison*
Vergleich: *arrangement; collation; comparison; composition; settlement* **einen** ~ **schließen** *compound*
vergleichbar: *comparable*
vergleichen: *compare*
vergleichend: *comparative*
Vergleichsregelung: *scheme of arrangement*
Vergleichsvereinbarung *or* **Vergleichsvertrag:** *deed of arrangement*
Vergnügen: zum eigenen ~ *frolic of his own*
Vergünstigung: *concession*
vergüten: *reimburse*
Vergütung: *compensation (US)* **angemessene** ~ *quantum meruit*
verhaften: *arrest; attach; claim (slang); pinch (informal)*
Verhalten: *conduct* **beleidigendes** ~ *insulting behaviour* **berufswidriges** *or* **standeswidriges** ~ *unprofessional conduct; professional misconduct* **verkehrswidriges** ~ *jaywalking*

Verhaltenskodex: *code of conduct*
Verhaltensmaßregeln: *instructions*
Verhältnis: *affair; relationship* **im** ~ **zu** *in proportion to*
verhältnismäßig: *proportionately*
Verhältnisse: *background*
Verhältniswahl: *proportional representation*
verhandeln: *hear; try* **mit jdm** ~ *to negotiate with someone* **neu** ~ *retry*
Verhandelnde(r): *negotiator*
Verhandlung: *hearing; negotiation* **erneute** ~ *retrial* **in öffentlicher** ~ *in open court* **nochmalige** ~ *rehearing* **öffentliche** ~ *open court*
Verhandlungen: die ~ **abbrechen** *to break off negotiations* **die** ~ **wiederaufnehmen** *to resume negotiations*
Verhandlungen aufnehmen: *to enter into or start or open negotiations*
Verhandlungen führen: *to conduct negotiations*
Verhandlungsausschuß: *negotiating committee*
Verhandlungsführer: *negotiator*
Verhandlungsliste: *cause list*
Verhandlungsniederschrift: *protocol*
Verhandlungsort: *venue*
Verhandlungspaket: *package deal*
Verhandlungsposition: *bargaining position*
Verhandlungsrichter: *trial judge*
Verhandlungssache: *matter for negotiation*
Verhandlungsstärke: *bargaining power*
verhängen: *impose*
Verhängung: *imposition*
verheimlichen: *suppress*
Verheimlichung: *suppression*
verhindern: *prevent*
Verhinderung: *prevention*
Verhör: *examination; interrogation; questioning*
verhören: *interrogate; question*
Verhörrichtlinien: *Judges' Rules*
verhüten: *prevent*
verhütend: *preventive*
Verhütung: *prevention*
Verhütung von Bestechung: *prevention of corruption*
verjährt: *statute-barred*
Verjährung: *time limitation*
Verjährungsgesetz: prozessuales ~ *limitation of actions or statute of limitations*
Verkauf: *disposal; sale*
Verkauf auf Kommissionsbasis: *sale or return*
Verkäufe: ungesetzliche ~ *under-the-counter sales*
verkaufen: *market; sell* **zu** ~ *for sale*
Verkäufer: *seller; vendor*
Verkäufermarkt: *seller's market*
Verkauf im Freiverkehr: *over-the-counter sales*
Verkaufsabteilung: *sales department*
Verkaufsangebot: *offer to sell*
Verkaufsbedingungen: *conditions or terms of sale*
Verkaufserlös: *proceeds of a sale*

Verkaufsoption: *option to sell; put option*
Verkaufspreis: *selling price*
Verkaufszahlen: *sales figures*
Verkehr: *traffic* **einverständlicher** ~ *consensual acts* **in** ~ **bringen** *utter*
verkehren: *associate; run*
Verkehrsdelikte: *traffic offences*
Verkehrsdienst: *point duty*
Verkehrsmittel: öffentliche ~ *public transport*
Verkehrspolizei: *traffic police*
Verkehrspolizist: *traffic warden*
Verkehrssünder: *jaywalker*
Verkehrsunternehmen: öffentliches ~ *common carrier*
verklagen: *sue* **jdn** ~ *to bring a lawsuit or proceedings against someone; to take someone to court or to law; to proceed against someone*
Verkleidung: *disguise*
verkleinern: *lessen*
verkleinert: *lesser*
verkuppeln: *procure*
Verladeschein: *shipping note*
Verladung: *shipment*
Verlag: *publisher*
verlagsrechtlich geschützt: *copyrighted*
verlangen: *ask for; charge; demand; require*
verlängern: *extend; renew*
Verlängerung: *extension; renewal*
Verlassen: *abandonment; desertion*
verlassen: *abandon; desert; leave* **sich** ~ **auf** *count on*
verläßlich: *reliable*
Verläßlichkeit: *reliability*
Verlauf: *direction; progress* **im** ~ *in the course of*
verlegen: *move; publish; transfer*
Verleger: *publisher*
Verlegung: *transfer*
verleihen: *confer; lend; loan; to rent (out); vest*
Verleihung: *lending*
Verleihung des Wahlrechts: *enfranchisement*
verleiten: *entice; incite*
Verleitung: *incitement*
verletzen: *break; infringe; injure; violate; wound*
verletzend: *injurious*
Verletzung: *breach; infringement; injury; violation*
Verletzung der Anzeigepflicht: *concealment of birth*
Verletzung der Gewährleistungspflicht: *breach of warranty*
Verletzung der Privatsphäre: *invasion of privacy*
Verletzung des Parlamentsfriedens: *breach of parliamentary privilege*
Verletzung des Urheberrechts: *infringement of copyright or copyright infringement*
Verletzung von Treuhandpflichten: *breach of trust*
verleumden: *defame; libel; slander*
Verleumder: *libeller; slanderer*

verleumderisch: *libellous; slanderous*
Verleumdung: *libel; slander* **schriftliche** ~ *libel* **strafbare** ~ *criminal libel*
Verleumdungsklage: *action for libel or libel action; action for slander or slander action*
verlieren: *lose*
Verlies: *dungeon*
Verlockung: *enticement*
Verlust: *loss; wastage* **mit** ~ *at a loss* **nicht realisierter** ~ *paper loss*
Verluste: seine ~ **verringen** *to cut one's losses*
Verluste hinnehmen müssen: *lose out*
vermachen: *bequeath; settle on*
Vermächtnis: *bequest; legacy* **hinfällig gewordenes** ~ *lapsed legacy*
Vermächtnisnehmer: *legatee*
vermeiden: *avoid*
Vermeidung: *avoidance*
Vermerk: *indorsement*
vermerken: *endorse; note*
vermessen: *measure*
vermieten: *lease; let; to rent (out)*
Vermieter: *landlord; lessor*
Vermieterin: *landlady*
vermindern: *decrease; diminish; lessen*
vermindert: *lesser*
vermitteln: *mediate*
Vermittler: *intermediary; troubleshooter*
Vermittlung: *mediation*
Vermögen: *power* **bewegliches** ~ *movable property* **unbewegliches** ~ *immovable property or immovables* **zukünftiges** ~ *future estate*
Vermögen erben: *to succeed to a property*
Vermögensanlage: *investment*
Vermögensaufstellung: *statement of affairs*
Vermögensdelikt: *offence against property*
Vermögensgegenstand: *property*
Vermögensgegenstände: materielle vererbbare ~ *corporeal hereditaments*
Vermögenssteuer: *capital levy*
Vermögensverschleierung: *concealment of assets*
Vermögensverwalter: *trustee*
Vermögensverwaltung: *trust*
Vermögenswert: *asset (value)*
Vermögenswerte: blockierte or eingefrorene ~ *frozen assets* **immaterielle vererbbare** ~ *incorporeal hereditaments* **immaterielle** ~ *intangible assets; incorporeal chattels* **materielle** ~ *tangible assets*
vermuten: *presume*
vermutlich: *probably*
Vermutung: *presumption*
vernachlässigen: *neglect*
Vernachlässigung: *neglect*
vernehmen: *interrogate; question*
Vernehmung: *examination; interrogation; questioning* **erneute** ~ *re-examination*
Vernehmungsbeamter: *interrogator*

Vernehmungsrichtlinien: *Judges' Rules*
verneinend: *negative*
Vernichtung: *destruction*
vernünftig: *reasonable; sound*
Vernünftigkeit: *soundness*
veröffentlichen: *publish; release*
Veröffentlichung: *publication* **aufrührerische or staatsgefährdende** ~ *seditious libel* **pornographische** ~ *obscene publication*
verordnen: *decree*
Verordnung: *decree; ordinance* **örtliche or städtische** ~ *bylaw or byelaw or by-law or bye-law; ordinance (US)*
verpachten: *lease; to rent (out)*
Verpächter: *lessor*
Verpachtung: *demise*
verpfänden: etwas ~ *to put something in pawn*
Verpfänder: *pledger*
Verpfändung: *pawn; pledge*
verpfeifen: *shop (slang); squeal (slang); grass (slang)*
verpflichten: bind sich ~ *undertake*
verpflichtend: *obligatory*
verpflichtet: sich ~ **fühlen** *to be under an obligation to do something*
Verpflichteter: *obligor*
verpflichtet sein: *to be obligated to do something (especially US)*
Verpflichtung: *engagement; obligation; responsibility* **gesetzliche** ~ *statutory duty*
Verpflichtungen: *commitments* **finanzielle** ~ *financial commitments* **seinen** ~ **nachkommen** *to meet one's obligations*
verplomben: *seal*
Verrat: *treason*
verraten: *betray*
verräterisch: *treasonable*
Verrats: wegen ~ **anklagen** *impeach*
Verrechnungsscheck: *crossed cheque*
Verrechnungstag: *settlement day*
verringern: *diminish; reduce; to scale down*
Verringerung: *reduction*
Versagen: *failure*
Versalien: *block capitals or letters; capital letters*
versammeln: sich ~ *assemble*
Versammlung: *assembly; meeting* **obligatorische** ~ *mandatory meeting* **unerlaubte** ~ *unlawful assembly*
Versammlungsfreiheit: *freedom of assembly or of meeting*
Versand: *consignment; consignment; shipment; shipping*
Versandanweisungen: *forwarding or shipping instructions*
Versandanzeige: *advice note; consignment note*
Versandhandel: *mail-order selling*
Versandhaus: *mail-order business or firm or house*
Versandhauskatalog: *mail-order catalogue*
Versandliste: *mailing list*

Versandvorschriften: *forwarding or shipping instructions*

versäumen: *neglect; omit*

Versäumnis: *default; misprision; neglect; omission*

Versäumnisurteil: *judgment by default or default judgment*

verschärft: *aggravated*

Verschärfung: *aggravation*

verschenken: *give away*

Verschicken: *mailing*

verschicken: *mail*

verschieben: *defer; hold over; postpone; put off*

verschieden: *different; miscellaneous*

verschiedene: *sundry*

Verschiedenes: *any other business (AOB); sundry items or sundries*

verschiffen: *ship*

Verschiffung: *shipment; shipping*

verschließen: *lock*

Verschluß: *seal*

verschlüsseln: *code*

Verschlüsselung: *coding*

Verschlußsache: *classified information*

Verschulden: *fault*

verschulden: sich ~ *to get into debt*

verschuldet: *indebted*

Verschuldung: *state of indebtedness*

Verschweigen: *suppression*

verschweigen: *conceal; suppress; withhold*

Verschweigen der Wahrheit: *suppressio veri*

verschwenden: *waste*

Verschwendung: *wastage*

verschwören: sich ~ *conspire*

Verschwörung: *conspiracy*

Versehen: *slip; slip-up* **aus ~** *by mistake*

versehen: sich ~ *slip up*

versehentlich: *by mistake*

Versenden: *consignation; consignment; mailing*

versenden: *ship*

Versender: *consignor*

versetzen: *transfer*

Versetzung: *transfer*

versicherbar: *insurable*

Versicherer: *insurer; underwriter*

versichern: *assure; aver; insure*

versichert: nicht ~ *uninsured*

Versicherte: der/die ~ *the (life) assured; the (life) insured; person named in the policy*

Versicherung: *assurance; averment; insurance* **eidesstattliche ~** *statutory declaration* **eine ~ erneuern** *to renew an insurance policy* **eine ~ übernehmen** *to underwrite an insurance policy*

Versicherung abschließen: *insure*

Versicherungsanspruch: *insurance claim*

Versicherungsantrag: *proposal form*

versicherungsfähig: *insurable*

Versicherungsgesellschaft: *insurance company*

Versicherungskarte: grüne ~ *green card*

Versicherungsmathematiker: *actuary*

versicherungsmathematisch: *actuarial*

Versicherungsnachtrag: *endorsement*

Versicherungsnehmer: *policy holder*

Versicherungspolice: *insurance policy* **verfallene ~** *lapsed (insurance) policy*

Versicherungsprämie: *insurance premium*

Versicherungsprämiensatz: *insurance rates*

Versicherungsschutz: *insurance cover; coverage (US)* **vollen ~ haben** *to be fully covered* **voller ~** *full cover*

Versicherungssumme: *sum insured*

Versicherungsträger: *assurer or assuror; insurer; underwriter*

Versicherungsverein auf Gegenseitigkeit: *friendly society; mutual (insurance) company*

Versicherungsvertreter: *insurance broker*

versiegeln: *seal*

Versiegelung: *seal*

Version: *version*

versorgen: *furnish; supply*

Versorgung: *supply; supplies*

Versorgungsbetriebe: *statutory undertakers*

verspäten: sich ~ *delay*

verspätet: *late*

Verspätung: *delay*

versperren: *obstruct*

Versprechen: *promise* **ein ~ brechen** *to go back on a promise* **ein ~ halten** *to keep a promise* **unentgeltliches ~** *gratuitous promise*

versprechen: *promise*

versprechend: *promissory*

Versprechen der Schadloshaltung: *indemnity*

Versprechen ohne Verpflichtung: *gratuitous promise*

Versprechensempfänger: *promisee*

Versprechensgeber: *promisor*

Versprechensurkunde: *deed of covenant*

verstaatlichen: *nationalize*

Verstaatlichung: *nationalization*

Verstand: bei gesundem ~ *compos mentis*

verständigen: sich ~ *communicate*

Verständigung: *communication*

verständnisvoll: *reasonable*

versteckt: *covert; hidden*

verstehen: *apprehend* **sich ~ mit** *get on with* **zu ~ geben** *imply*

versteigern: *auction*

Versteigerung: *auction*

Versterbende: gleichzeitig ~ *commorientes*

verstorben: *dead; deceased*

Verstorbene(r): *deceased*

Verstoß: *breach; contravention; violation*

Verstöße: *irregularities*

verstoßen: *contravene; to be in contravention of; disobey*

verstreichen: *elapse*

Verstümmelung: *mayhem*

Versuch: *attempt*

versuchen: *attempt; seek*

versuchsweise: *on approval*

vertagen: *adjourn; defer; hold over; postpone*

Vertagung: *adjournment; deferment; postponement*

verteidigen: *defend*

Verteidiger: *defence or defense (US); defence counsel*

Verteidigung: *defence or defense (US); justification; plea*

Verteidigungsvorbringen: *defence or defense (US)*

verteilen: *distribute; share*

Verteilung des Nachlasses *or* **Vermögens:** *distribution of assets*

Verteilungsanordnung der Nachlaßverwalter: *administration order*

Vertrag: *compact; contract; covenant; treaty* **aleatorischer** ~ *aleatory contract* **besiegelter** *or* **beurkundeter** ~ *contract under seal* **durch** ~ *contractually* **einen** ~ **aushandeln** *to negotiate a contract* **einfacher** ~ *simple contract* **formloser** ~ *parol agreement or contract* **gesiegelter** ~ *specialty contract* **rechtswidriger** *or* **sittenwidriger** ~ *illegal contract* **unter** ~ **stehen** *under contract*

vertraglich: *contractual(ly)* **sich** ~ **verpflichten** *contract*

vertraglich gebunden sein: *under contract*

Vertragsangebot: *offer*

Vertragsbedingung: **unzulässige** ~ *unfair contract term*

Vertragsbedingungen: die ~ **prüfen** *to consider the terms of a contract*

Vertragsbeendigung: **einverständliche** ~ *discharge by agreement*

Vertragsbeziehung: *privity of contract*

Vertragsbruch: *breach of contract* **schwerer** ~ *fundamental breach*

Vertragshaftung: *contractual liability*

vertragsmäßig: *contractual*

Vertragspartner: *contracting party*

Vertragsrecht: *contract law or law of contract*

Vertragsurkunde: *deed of covenant; indenture* **treuhänderisch hinterlegte** ~ *escrow*

Vertragsvereinbarung: **ausdrückliche** ~ *express term*

Vertragsverhältnis: **unmittelbares** ~ *privity of contract*

Vertragsverlängerung: *extension of a contract*

Vertragsverletzung: *default; discharge* **vorweggenommene** ~ *anticipatory breach*

Vertrag wird verhandelt: *contract under negotiation*

Vertrauen: *confidence; trust*

Vertrauensbruch: *betrayal of trust; breach of confidence*

Vertrauensmann: *fiduciary*

Vertrauensstellung: *position of trust*

Vertrauensvotum: *confidence vote or vote of no confidence*

vertrauenswürdig: *reliable; trustworthy*

Vertrauenswürdigkeit: *reliability*

vertraulich: *in confidence; confidential*

Vertraulichkeit: *confidentiality*

vertretbar: *justifiable*

vertreten: *represent* **jdn** ~ *to deputize for someone; stand in for*

Vertreter: *canvasser; deputy; representative; substitute* **gesetzlicher** ~ *attorney* **zugelassener** ~ *recognized agent*

Vertreterbesuche: *canvassing*

Vertreter der Anklage: *prosecutor*

Vertretung: *representation; substitute* **in** ~ *per procurationem; per pro*

vertuschen: *suppress*

Vertuschung: *suppression*

verüben: *perpetrate*

veruntreuen: *embezzle; misappropriate*

Veruntreuer: *embezzler*

Veruntreuung: *defalcation; embezzlement; misappropriation*

Veruntreuung von Geldern: *conversion of funds*

verursachen: *cause; occasion*

Verursachung eines Totalschadens: *write-off*

Verursachung strafbarer Sachbeschädigung: *causing criminal damage*

verurteilen: *condemn; sentence*

Verurteilung: *con (slang); condemnation; conviction* **erneute** ~ *re-conviction* **kostenpflichtige** ~ *judgment for someone with costs*

Verurteilung zum Jugendarrest: *youth custody order*

vervielfältigen: *reproduce*

Vervielfältigung: *duplication; reproduction*

Vervielfältigungsapparat *or* **Vervielfältigungsgerät:** *copying or duplicating machine*

vervollkommnen: *perfect*

Verwahrer: *bailee; depositary (US); depository; keeper; stakeholder*

verwahrlosen lassen: *neglect*

verwahrlost: *neglected*

Verwahrlosung: *neglect*

Verwahrung: *safe keeping* **gerichtliche** ~ *impounding* **in** ~ **geben** *deposit* **sichere** ~ *safe keeping*

verwalten: *administer*

Verwalter: *administrator*

Verwaltung: *administration* **öffentliche** ~ *public administration* **örtliche** ~ *local government* **schlechte** ~ *maladministration*

Verwaltungsbezirk: *precinct (US)*

Verwaltungsgericht: *administrative tribunal*

Verwaltungsrat: *directorate*

Verwaltungsratsmitglied: **außerordentliches** ~ *associate director*

Verwaltungsrecht: *administrative law*

verwaltungstechnisch: *administrative*

Verwandschaft: *kin*

Verwandschaftsgrade: verbotene ~ *prohibited degrees*
verwandt: *related*
Verwandte: *relatives or relations*
Verwandten: *kin*
verwanzen: *bug*
verwarnen: *caution; reprimand*
Verwarnen mit Strafvorbehalt: *bind over (GB)*
Verwarnung: *caution; reprimand* **mündliche ~** *verbal warning*
verweigern: *deny; refuse*
Verweigerung: *abstention (US); denial; refusal*
Verweis: *caution; reprimand*
verweisen: *advert; refer*
Verweis erteilen: *reprimand*
Verweisung: *removal*
verwenden: *use*
verwerfen: *reject; throw out*
verwickeln: *involve*
verwirken: *forfeit*
verwirklichen: *realize*
Verwirklichung: *realization*
Verwirkung: *defeasance; estoppel; forfeit; forfeiture*
Verwirkungsklausel: *forfeit clause; defeasance*
verwunden: *wound*
verzählen: sich ~ *miscount*
verzeichnen: *record*
Verzeichnis: *docket; index; list; register; schedule*
Verzeichnis der Aktionäre: *register of shareholders or share register*
Verzeichnis der Grundstückseigentümer: *proprietorship register*
Verzeichnis der Obligationäre: *debenture register or register of debentures*
Verzeihung: *condonation*
verzerren: *pervert*
Verzicht: *release; renunciation; waiver*
verzichten: surrender zu ~ *abjure*
verzichten auf: *renounce; waive*
Verzichterklärung: *waiver*
Verzichtklausel: *waiver clause*
Verzichtleistung unter Eid: *abjuration*
verzögern: hold up sich ~ *delay*
verzögernd: *dilatory*
Verzögerung: *delay; hold-up*
Verzögerungsantrag: *dilatory motion*
Verzug: *delay* **in ~ geraten** *default* **in ~ sein** *to be behind schedule*
Veschweigung: *concealment*
Veto: *veto*
vide: *vide*
Viehdieb: *rustler*
Viehdiebstahl: *rustling*
Vieh stehlen: *rustle*
vielfach: *multiple*
Vierteljahr: *quarter*
vierteljährlich: *quarterly*

Visage: *mug*
Visitator: *prison visitor*
Visum: *visa*
Vitrine: *cabinet*
Vizepräsident: *Vice-President*
Völkermord: *genocide*
Völkerrecht: *international law*
Volksentscheid: *referendum*
Volksverhetzung: *sedition*
Volksvertretung: *representation*
voll bezahlen: *pay up*
Vollindossament: *special indorsement*
Volljährigkeit: *legal age (US); majority*
vollkommen: *completely; perfect*
Vollkosten: *full costs*
Vollmacht: *authority; faculty; mandate; power; warrant* **in ~** *per procurationem; per pro*
Vollmacht erteilen: *delegate; empower*
Vollmachtsbescheinigung: *letter of attorney*
Vollmachtsurkunde: *proxy*
vollständig: *complete; in full; fully; outright; whole*
vollständig abbezahlen: *pay off*
vollstreckbar: *enforceable*
vollstrecken: *enforce*
Vollstreckung: *enforcement; fieri facias*
Vollstreckungsaufschub: *stay of execution; reprieve*
Vollstreckungsaufschub gewähren: *reprieve*
Vollstreckungsbeamten: *law enforcement officers*
Vollstreckungsbeamter: *marshal (US)*
Vollstreckungsbefehl: *warrant of execution; writ of fieri facias*
Vollstreckungsgläubiger: *judgment creditor*
Vollstreckungsschuldner: *judgment debtor*
Vollstreckungsvereitelung durch Eigentumsübertragung: *fraudulent conveyance*
Vollstreckungsverfahren: *judgment summons*
vollziehen: *implement* **noch zu ~** *executory*
vollziehend: *executive*
Vollzug: *consummation; implementation*
Vollzugsanordnung: *executive order (US)*
Vollzugsbeamter: *managing clerk; warder*
von selbst: *per se*
vorab: *in advance; advance*
Vorabentscheidung: *preliminary ruling*
Voranfragen: *preliminary inquiries*
vorangehen: *precede*
Vorangehendes: *premises*
vorankommen mit: *get on with*
Voranschlag der Ausgaben: *estimate of expenditure*
voraus: im ~ *in advance; advance; beforehand; forward* **im ~ bezahlen** *to pay in advance* **im ~ urteilen** *prejudge* **im ~ zahlbar** *payable in advance*
vorausgehend: *preliminary; prior*
vorausgesetzt: *provided that or providing*
Voraussehbarkeit: *foreseeability*

voraussehen: *foresee*

Voraussetzung: unerläßliche ~ *sine qua non* **unter der** ~ *on the understanding that*

Vorbedacht: *premeditation* **mit** ~ *premeditated*

Vorbedingung: *condition precedent*

Vorbehalt: *proviso; reservation* **unter** ~ *conditional(ly)* **unter** ~ **annehmen** *to give a conditional acceptance*

vorbehalten: *reserve*

vorbehaltlos: *unconditional(ly)*

Vorbehaltsklausel: *proviso*

Vorbehaltspreis: *reserve (price)*

vorbeigehen *or* **vorbeikommen:** *call in*

vorbereitend: *preliminary*

Vorbesprechung: *preliminary discussion or meeting*

Vorbestellungen: *dues*

vorbestraft sein: *to have a criminal record*

vorbeugend: *preventive*

vorbildlich: *exemplary*

Vorbringen: *allegation; submission*

vorbringen: *allege; plead; prefer; raise*

vordatieren: *postdate*

Vordruck: *form*

voreingenommen: *partial; prejudiced*

vorenthalten: jdm etwas ~ *to deprive someone of something*

Vorenthaltung: *detention*

Vorenthaltung (von Besitz): *detinue*

Vorfahr: gemeinsamer ~ *common ancestor*

Vorfall: *event; incident*

vorführen: *demonstrate*

Vorführung: *presentation*

Vorgänger: *predecessor*

vorgeben: *pretend*

Vorgehen: *(course of) action; procedure* **gerichtliches** ~ *court action*

vorgehen: *override; to have priority over or to take priority over something*

Vorgeschichte: *record*

Vorgesetzte(r): *principal; superior*

vorgetäuscht: *sham*

vorhaben: *intend; propose to*

Vorhaltungen machen: *to make representations*

Vorhand: *first option*

vorher: *heretofore; previously; thereinbefore*

vorher erwähnt: *aforementioned; aforesaid*

vorhergehend: *previous*

vorhersehen: *foresee*

vorig: *previous*

Vorkaufsrecht: *pre-emption*

Vorkehrungen: *precautions*

Vorkehrungen treffen für: *to make provision for*

vorkommen: *occur*

vorladen: *cite; summon; subpoena* **jdn** ~ *to serve someone with a writ*

Vorladung: *citation; process; summons*

Vorladung vor Gericht: *subpoena*

Vorlage: *filing; presentation; presentment; production* **bei** ~ **von** *on production of*

vorläufig: *interim; interlocutory; provisional; temporary; tentative*

Vorleben: *antecedents*

vorlegen: *adduce; file; get out; present; produce; submit*

Vorlegung: *presentment*

Vormerkung: *caution* **eine** ~ **eintragen** *to lodge caution*

Vormerkungsbegünstigter: *cautioner*

vormittags: *a.m.* *or ante meridiem*

Vormund: *guardian*

Vormundschaft: *guardianship; wardship*

Vormundschaftsbeschluß: *guardianship order*

vornehmen: sich ~ *set out*

Vorrang: *prerogative; priority*

Vorrang haben: *to have priority*

vorrangig: etwas ~ **behandeln** *to give something top priority*

Vorrat: *stock; supply*

vorrätig: *in hand* **nicht** ~ **sein** *out of stock* **vorrätig sein** *in stock*

Vorrecht: *prerogative*

vorsagen: *prompt*

Vorsatz: *animus; intent; intention*

vorsätzlich: *deliberate; intentional; premeditated; wilful* **nicht** ~ *involuntary*

vorsätzlich zerstören: *vandalize*

vorschießen: *advance*

Vorschlag: *proposal; suggestion*

vorschlagen: *propose; suggest*

vorschnell: im ~ **urteilen** *prejudge*

Vorschrift: rule laut ~ *in accordance with or according to instructions*

Vorschriften: *code; regulations*

vorschriftsmäßig: *in due form; duly; in accordance with or according to instructions* **nicht** ~ *improper(ly)*

vorschriftswidrig: *irregular*

Vorschriftswidrigkeit: *irregularity*

Vorschub: *feed*

Vorschuß: *advance*

vorsehen: *earmark* **sich** ~ *beware*

vorsichtig: *tentative(ly)*

Vorsichtsmaßnahme: als ~ *as a precautionary measure*

Vorsichtsmaßnahmen ergreifen: *to take safety precautions or safety measures*

Vorsitz: *chair; chairmanship* **den** ~ **führen** *preside; to take the chair*

Vorsitzende(r): *chairman; chairwoman; chairperson; president; speaker*

Vorsitzender Amtsrichter: *chairman of the justices*

Vorsitzender des Aufsichtsrates: *chairman of the board*

Vorsorge treffen für: *to make provision for*

Vorspiegelung falscher Tatsachen: *false pretences*

Vorstand: *board of directors; chairman of the board*

Vorstandsmitglied: *director*

Vorstandssitzung: *board meeting*

Vorstandsverzeichnis: *register of directors*

Vorstandsvorsitzender: *chairman*

vorstehen: *head*

Vorstehendes: *premises*

vorstellen: *introduce*

Vorstellung: *introduction*

Vorstellungen erheben: *to make representations*

Vorstellungsgespräch: ein ~ führen *interview*

Vorsteuer: *input tax*

Vorstrafe: *criminal record* **gelöschte ~** *spent conviction*

vortäuschen: *fake; pretend*

Vortäuschung der Ehe: *jactitation of marriage (GB)*

Vorteil: *advantage; benefit*

vorteilhaft: *favourable*

Vortrag: *submission*

vortragen: *submit*

vorübergehend: *pro tem or pro tempore; temporary; temporarily*

Voruntersuchung: *preliminary hearing or investigation* **gerichtliche ~** *committal proceedings*

Vorurteil: *prejudice*

vorurteilslos: *impartial; impartially*

Vorverfahren: *interlocutory matter or proceedings; pretrial review*

Vorverkaufsstelle: *booking office*

vorverlegen: *advance; bring forward*

Vorwahl: *area code*

vorweggenommen *or* **vorwegnehmend:** *anticipatory*

Vorwegnahme: *anticipation*

Vorzeigen: *production*

vorzeigen: *produce*

vorzeitig: *early* **jdn ~ pensionieren** *to pension someone off*

vorziehen: *prefer*

Vorzug: *preference*

vorzüglich: *excellent*

Vorzugsaktien: *preference shares; preferred shares or preferred stock (US)* **kumulative ~** *cumulative preference shares* **rückkaufbare ~** *redeemable preference shares*

Vorzugsaktienbesitzer: *preference shareholders*

Vorzugsfahrpreis: *concessionary fare*

Vorzugskonditionen: *preferential terms*

Vorzugstarif: *preferential tariff*

Vorzugszoll: *preferential duty*

Votum: einheitliches ~ *block vote*

Ww

Wache: *nick (slang); watch*

Wachkommando: *watch*

Wachmann: *(security) guard*

Wachmannschaft: *watch*

wachsen: *increase*

wachsend: *increasing*

Wachstumsmarkt: *growth market*

Wächter: *custodian; (security) guard*

Wachtmeister: *tipstaff*

Waffe: gefährliche ~ *dangerous or offensive weapon*

Waffenschein: *firearms certificate*

Wagen vermieten: *to hire out cars*

Wahl: *ballot; election; pick; poll; preference; return; selection; vote; voting* **eine ~ abhalten** *ballot* **geheime ~** *secret ballot* **zur ~ gehen** *to go to the polls* **zweite ~** *reject*

Wahlausschuß: *electoral college*

wählbar: *eligible*

Wählbarkeit: *eligibility*

wählen: *elect; return; vote*

Wähler: *elector; voter*

Wählerliste: *register of electors*

Wählerschaft: *electorate*

Wahlgesetz: *the Representation of the People Act*

Wahlhelfer: *canvasser*

Wahlkreis: *constituency*

Wahlleiter: *returning officer*

Wahlmännergremium: *electoral college*

Wahlrecht: *franchise; suffrage* **allgemeines ~** *universal franchise or suffrage* **das ~ entziehen** *disenfranchise or disfranchise* **das ~ verleihen** *enfranchise*

Wahlstimme: einfach übertragbare ~ *single transferable vote*

Wahlurne: *ballot box*

wahlweise: *optional*

Wahlwerbung: *canvassing*

Wahlwerbung betreiben: *canvass*

Wahlzettel: *ballot paper*

wahr: *true; truthful*

wahren: *uphold*

Wahrheit: *truth*

wahrheitsgemäß: *truthful*

wahrscheinlich: *probable; probably*

Wahrscheinlichkeit: *likelihood*

Währung: frei konvertierbare ~ *free currency* **gesetzliche ~** *legal currency* **harte ~** *hard currency* **weiche ~** *soft currency*

Währungsausgleichsfonds: *Exchange Equalization Account (GB)*

Währungsreserven: *currency reserves*

Waise(nkind): *orphan*

Wandelanleihe: *convertible loan stock*

Wandtresor: *wall safe*

Wanze: *bug*

Ware: *article; commodity* **unverkaufte ~** *goods left on hand*

Wunde: *wound*
Wunsch: auf ~ *on request* **auf** ~ **erhältlich** *optional*
Würdigung: *appreciation*

Zz

Zahl: *figure*
zahlbar: *payable*
zahlen: *pay*
zählen: *count*
Zahlen aufbereiten: *to process figures*
Zahlenfolge: *numerical order*
Zahlenwerk: *figures*
Zahler: *payer*
Zahltag: *pay day*
Zahlung: *payment* **aufgeschobene** ~ *deferred payment* **bevorrechtigte** ~ *preferential payment* **eine** ~ **leisten** *to effect a payment* **symbolische** ~ *token payment*
Zahlungen: regelmäßig wiederkehrende ~ *periodical payments*
Zahlungsanweisung: *order*
Zahlungsaufforderung: *call; letter of demand*
Zahlungsaufschub: *moratorium*
Zahlungsbedingungen: *terms of payment or payment terms*
Zahlungsbefehl für Kommunalsteuern: *precept*
Zahlungsempfänger: *payee*
Zahlungserleichterungen: *easy terms*
zahlungsfähig: *solvent*
Zahlungsfähigkeit: *solvency*
Zahlungsmittel: gesetzliches ~ *legal tender*
Zahlungstermin: letzter ~ *final date for payment*
zahlungsunfähig: *insolvent*
Zahlungsunfähigkeit: *insolvency*
Zahlungsversprechen: ein ~ *a promise to pay*
Zahlungsverzug: bei ~ *in default of payment* **in** ~ **geraten** *default*
z.B.: *e.g.*
Zebrastreifen: *zebra crossing*
Zeichen: *indication; mark; reference; token*
zeichnen: *apply*
Zeichner: *applicant; subscriber*
Zeichnung: *application*
Zeichnungsangebot: *tender*
zeigen: *display; indicate; show*
Zeit: *period; time* **auf unbestimmte** ~ *sine die* **für unbegrenzte** ~ *for an indefinite period of time* **unvordenkliche** ~ *time immemorial* **zur** ~ *currently; pro tem or pro tempore*
Zeitcharter: *time charter*
Zeitpacht: *term of years*
Zeitplan: *schedule* **einen** ~ **aufstellen** *timetable*
Zeitraum: *period; term*
Zeitschloß: *time lock*

Zeitschrift: *periodical; review* **eine** ~ **abonnieren** *to subscribe to a magazine*
Zeitschriftenabonnent: *subscriber*
Zeitspanne: *lapse of time; period*
Zeit- und Bewegungsstudie: *time and motion study*
Zeitung: *paper*
Zeitungsbericht: *a report in a newspaper or a newspaper report*
Zeit verschwenden: *to waste time*
zeitweilig einstellen: *suspend*
Zelle: *cell*
Zellen: *bridewell (slang)*
Zellengenosse: *cellmate*
zensieren: *censor*
Zensor: *censor*
Zensur: *censorship*
zentral: *central*
Zentralbank: *central bank*
Zentrale: *central or general or head or main office; headquarters*
zentralisieren: *centralize*
Zentralisierung: *centralization*
Zentralregierung: *central government*
Zentralstrafgericht: *Central Criminal Court*
Zentrum: *centre*
Zerrüttung der Ehe: *irretrievable breakdown of a marriage*
zerstören: *wreck*
Zerstörung: *destruction*
Zertifikat: *certificate*
Zession: *cession*
Zeuge: *witness* **als** ~ **hiervon** *as witness hereto* **aussagepflichtiger** ~ *a compellable witness* **sachverständiger** ~ *expert or professional or skilled witness* **vereidigter** ~ *deponent*
Zeugenaussage: mündliche ~ *oral evidence* **schriftliche** ~ *deposition*
Zeugenaussagen: widersprüchliche ~ *conflicting evidence*
Zeugen beeinflussen: *to interfere with witnesses*
Zeugenladung: *subpoena ad testificandum*
Zeugenstand: *witness box*
Zeugentestament: mündliches ~ *nuncupative will*
Zeugenvernehmung: erneute ~ *re-examination*
Zeugin: *witness*
Zeugnis: *(letter of) reference*
Ziel: *object; objective; purpose*
Zielsetzung: kurzfristige ~ *short-term objective* **langfristige** ~ *long-term objective*
Ziffer: *figure*
Zinsbelastung: *interest charges*
Zinsen: aufgelaufene ~ *accrued interest* **einfache** ~ *simple interest* **feste** ~ *fixed interest*
Zinsen zahlen: *to pay interest*
Zinseszins(en): *compound interest*
Zinsfuß *or* **Zinssatz:** *interest rate or rate of interest*
Zinsrückstand: *back interest*

Zinsthesaurierung: *accrual of interest*
zirkulierend: *circulating*
zirkulieren lassen: *circulate*
Zitat: *citation*
zitieren: *cite; quote*
Zivil-: *civil; plainclothes*
Zivilgericht: *Civil Court*
Zivilprozeß: *civil action; lawsuit*
Zivilrecht: *civil law*
Zivilsache: streitige ~ *contentious business*
zögern: *hesitate; hold back*
zögernd: *tentatively*
Zoll: *customs* or *Customs and Excise* den ~ passieren *to go through customs*
Zollabfertigung: *customs clearance*
Zollabfertigungsschein: *clearance certificate*
Zollager: *bonded warehouse*
zollamtlich abfertigen lassen: *to effect customs clearance*
Zollbeamter: *customs officer* or *official*
Zollbehörde: *customs* or *Customs and Excise*
Zolldeklaration or **Zollerklärung:** *customs declaration*
Zollformalitäten: *customs formalities*
zollfrei: *free of duty* or *duty-free*
Zollkontrolle: *customs examination*
Zollpassierschein: *landing order*
Zollschranke: *customs barrier*
Zollsiegel: *customs seal*
Zolltarife: *customs tariffs*
Zollunion: *customs union*
Zollverschluß: *customs seal* unter ~ *bonded*
Zuchthaus: *bridewell (slang); penal servitude*
Züchtigung: körperliche ~ *corporal punishment*
zufallsbedingt: *aleatory*
Zufriedenheit: *satisfaction*
Zufriedenheit am Arbeitsplatz: *job satisfaction*
zufriedenstellen: *satisfy*
Zufriedenstellung: *satisfaction*
Zugang: *access*
zugeben: *admit; concede*
zugehörig: *appurtenant*
zugelassen: nicht ~ *inadmissible*
Zugeständnis: *concession*
zugestehen: *allow; concede*
zugreifen auf: *access*
Zuhälter: *pimp; procurer*
Zuhälterei: *procuring* or *procurement* von ~ leben *living off immoral earnings*
Zuhause: *home*
zukleben: *seal*
Zukunft: *future* in ~ *hereafter*
zukünftig: *future*
zulassen: *admit; call*
zulässig: *admissible; allowable; licit*
Zulässigkeit: *admissibility*
Zulassung: *call*

Zulassungsbescheinigung: *test certificate*
Zulassungsfrist: *period of qualification*
zuletzt: *last*
Zulieferer: *supplier*
Zulieferungen: *supplies*
zumessen: *apportion*
Zumessung: *apportionment*
Zunahme: *gain; increase; rise*
zunehmen: *increase; rise*
Zuneigung: *affection*
zurechnungsfähig: *of sound mind*
Zurechnungsfähigkeit: mens rea **verminderte** ~ *diminished responsibility* or *diminished capacity (US)*
zurechtkommen: *cope*
Zurkenntnisbringung: *publication*
zurückbehalten: *reserve; retain*
Zurückbehaltungsrecht: *lien*
Zurückbehaltungsrecht des Handwerkers or **von Reparaturwerkstätten:** *repairer's lien*
Zurückbehaltungsrecht von Aktien: *lien on shares*
zurückbekommen: *get back; recover*
zurückdatieren: *antedate; backdate*
zurückfallen: *revert*
zurückfordern: *claim back; claw back; reclaim*
zurückgeben: *surrender*
zurückgehen: *decrease; drop*
zurückhalten: *hold back; restrain; withhold*
zurückholen: sich ~ *claw back*
zurückkaufen: *buy back*
zurückkehren: *revert*
zurücknehmen: *go back on; withdraw*
zurückrufen: *recall*
zurückschicken or **zurücksenden:** *return*
zurückstellen: *defer*
Zurückstellung: *deferment*
zurücktreten: *resign; retire*
zurückverweisen: *remand (US)*
zurückweisen: *disallow; reject*
Zurückweisung: *rebuttal; rejection*
zurückzahlen: *pay back; refund; repay*
zurückziehen: withdraw sich ~ *retire*
Zusage: *promise*
zusagen: *promise*
zusammen: *jointly*
Zusammenarbeit: *collaboration; co-operation*
zusammenarbeiten: *collaborate; co-operate*
Zusammenbruch: kommerzieller ~ *commercial failure*
zusammenfassen: *to bracket* or *to group together; summarize*
Zusammenfassung: *consolidation*
Zusammenhang: *context* **im** ~ **mit** *in connection with; relating to; in relation to*
Zusammenhänge: *background*
zusammenhängend: *related*
zusammenpacken: *gather*

zusammenrotten: sich ~ *riot*
Zusammenrottung: *riot; riotous assembly; rout*
zusammenrufen: *convene*
zusammenschließen: *merge*
Zusammenschluß: *merger; union*
zusammensetzen: sich ~ **aus** *consist of*
Zusammenstoß: *collision*
zusammentragen: *assemble*
zusammenzählen: *count*
Zusammmenfassung: *summary*
zusammmensammeln: *gather*
Zusatzklausel: *endorsement; rider*
zusätzlich: *collateral*
Zuschlag: *premium*
zuschlagen: jdm etwas ~ *to knock something down (to a bidder)*
zuschreiben: *attribute; impute*
Zuschuß: *allowance; grant; subsidy*
Zusicherung: *representation; undertaking*
zuspielen: *leak*
zusprechen: *award*
Zustand: *condition; order* **baulicher** ~ *state of repair* **besitzloser** ~ *abeyance* **gegenwärtiger** ~ *status quo* **vorheriger** ~ *status quo ante*
zuständig: *competent; relevant*
zuständig für: *responsible for*
Zuständigkeit: *jurisdiction*
Zuständigkeit des Amtsgerichts: *summary jurisdiction*
zustellen: *deliver*
Zusteller: *process-server*
Zustellung: *service (of process)* **die** ~ **bestätigen** *to acknowledge service* **persönliche** ~ *personal service*
Zustellungsadresse: *address for service*
Zustellungsbeamter: *process-server*
Zustellungsbestätigung: *acknowledgement of service*
Zustellungsnachweis: *proof of service*
Zustellungsurkunde: *acknowledgement of service*
zustimmen: *agree; concur; endorse*
zustimmend: *affirmative; positive*
Zustimmung: *acceptance; assent; concurrence; sanction*
zuteilen: *allocate; allot; apportion*
Zuteilung: *allocation; allotment; apportionment*
Zuteilungsanzeige: *letter of allotment or allotment letter*
zuträglich sein: *help*
Zutritt: *access; admission*
Zutritt gewähren: *admit*
zuverlässig: *reliable*
Zuverlässigkeit: *reliability*
zuversichtlich: *confident*
zuviel berechnen: *overcharge*
zuvor: *theretofore*
zuvorkommen: *pre-empt*
Zuwachs: *accrual; gain; increase*

zuweisen: *allocate; allot*
Zuweisung: *allocation; appropriation*
Zuwendung: testamentarische ~ *bequest*
zuzuschreiben: jdm ~ **sein** *to be attributable to somebody*
Zwang: *coercion; compellability; duress* **unter** ~ *under duress*
Zwangsarbeit: *hard labour*
Zwangsernährung: *forcible feeding*
zwangsläufig: *unavoidable; unavoidably*
Zwangsliquidation: *compulsory liquidation or winding up*
Zwangsliquidationsbeschluß: *compulsory winding up order*
zwangsräumen: *eject; evict*
Zwangsräumung: *ejection; eviction; ouster*
Zwangsräumung durchführen: *eject*
Zwangsverkauf: *forced sale*
Zwangsverwalter: *Official Receiver; sequestrator*
Zwangsverwaltung: *receivership*
zwangsvollstrecken lassen: *foreclose*
Zwangsvollstreckung: *foreclosure*
Zweck: *intention; object; purpose* **zu diesem** ~ *ad hoc*
Zweckdienlichkeit: *fitness for purpose*
Zweckentfremdung: *misuse*
Zweckheirat: *sham marriage or marriage of convenience*
zweideutig: *ambiguous; equivocal*
Zweideutigkeit: *ambiguity*
zweifach: *double*
Zweifel: *doubt; reservation* **jeden** ~ **ausschließend** *or* **ohne jeden** ~ *beyond reasonable doubt*
zweifelhaft: *shady*
Zweigstelle: *branch*
Zweigstelle der Post: *sub-post office*
Zweikammersystem: *bicameralism*
zweimal jährlich: *bi-annually*
zweimal monatlich: *bi-monthly*
zweiseitig: *bilateral*
zweistellig: *in double figures*
Zweithypothek: *second mortgage*
zweitklassig: *inferior*
zweitrangig: *secondary*
Zweitschrift: *duplicate*
zwingen: *compel; force*
zwingend: *conclusive; conclusively*
Zwischen-: *inter-; interim; interlocutory; mesne*
Zwischenbericht: *interim report*
Zwischendividende: *interim dividend*
Zwischenfall: *incident*
Zwischenschein: *scrip*
Zwischenverfahren: *interlocutory proceedings; mesne process*
Zwischenzeit: in der ~ *in the interim*
zyklisch: *cyclical*
Zyklus: *cycle*

Anhang

c. 29 1

ELIZABETH II

Enduring Powers of Attorney Act 1985

1985 CHAPTER 29

An Act to enable powers of attorney to be created which will survive any subsequent mental incapacity of the donor and to make provision in connection with such powers. [26th June 1985]

B E IT ENACTED by the Queen's most Excellent Majesty, by and with the advice and consent of the Lords Spiritual and Temporal, and Commons, in this present Parliament assembled, and by the authority of the same, as follows:—

Enduring powers of attorney

1.—(1) Where an individual creates a power of attorney which is an enduring power within the meaning of this Act then—

    (*a*) the power shall not be revoked by any subsequent mental incapacity of his ; but

    (*b*) upon such incapacity supervening the donee of the power may not do anything under the authority of the power except as provided by subsection (2) below or as directed or authorised by the court under section 5 unless or, as the case may be, until the instrument creating the power is registered by the court under section 6 ; and

Enduring power of attorney to survive mental incapacity of donor.

A 2

Statutory Instrument

S T A T U T O R Y   I N S T R U M E N T S

1986 No. 636 (L.3)

COUNTY COURTS

PROCEDURE

The County Court (Amendment) Rules 1986

| *Made* - - - - | 26*th March* 1986 |
| *Coming into force* | 28*th April* 1986 |

Citation and interpretation

1.—(1) These Rules may be cited as the County Court (Amendment) Rules 1986.

(2) In these Rules, unless the context otherwise requires, an Order referred to by number means the Order so numbered in the County Court Rules 1981**(a)** and Appendix A, B or C means Appendix A, B or C to those Rules.

Service of documents through document exchanges

2. After the definition of "defendant" in Order 1, rule 3, there shall be inserted the following definition:—

" 'document exchange' means any document exchange for the time being approved by the Lord Chancellor;".

3. After Order 2, rule 5(1), there shall be inserted the following new paragraph:—

"(1A) References in paragraph (1) to the conduct of business by post and to the sending of documents by prepaid post shall include in any case where the court is a member of a document exchange and the party is represented by a solicitor references to the conduct of business and to the sending of documents through a document exchange.".

4. For Order 7, rule 1(1)(*b*), there shall be substituted the following sub-paragraph:—

"(*b*) if the person to be served is acting by a solicitor:—

(i) by delivering the document at, or sending it by first-class post to, the solicitor's address for service, or

(ii) where the solicitor's address for service includes a numbered box at a document exchange, by leaving the document at that document exchange or at a document exchange which transmits documents daily to that document exchange.".

(a) S.I. 1981/1687; the relevant amending instruments are S.I. 1982/436, 1140, 1794, 1983/1716, 1984/576, 878, 1985/566 and 1269.

Bill

A

B I L L

T O

Establish a legally enforceable right to interest on late
payment of debts.

B^{E IT ENACTED} by the Queen's most Excellent Majesty, by and A.D. 1986.
with the advice and consent of the Lords Spiritual and
Temporal, and Commons, in this present Parliament
assembled, and by the authority of the same, as follows:—

5   **1.** The High Court or the County Court is empowered to Right to
award simple interest on late payment of debts subject to the Interest.
provisions of section 2 below.

   2.—(1) Subject to the Rules of Court, in proceedings (whenever Conditions
instituted) before the High Court or a County Court for the relating to
10 recovery of simple interest, the Court shall give judgement, at right to
such rate as the Court thinks fit, or the rules of Court may provide, Interest.
for the period between the date when the cause of action arose
and the date of payment.

   (2) The cause of action shall arise 30 days after notice in
15 writing is given of the intention to claim simple interest on a debt.

   (3) The Rules of Court may provide for a rate of interest by
reference to the rate specified in section 17 of the Judgements 1838 c. 110.
Act 1838 as that section has effect from time to time or by reference
to a rate for which any other enactment provides.

   [Bill 127]   49/3

2   *Right to Interest*

(4) Interest in respect of a debt shall not be awarded under this section for a period during which, for whatever reason, interest on the debt already runs.

(5) Interest under this section may be calculated at different rates in respect of different periods.   5

Short title and commencement.

3.—(1) This Act may be cited as the Right to Interest Act 1986.

(2) This Act shall come into force at the end of the period of two months beginning with the day on which it is passed.

Right to Interest

A
BILL

To establish a legally enforceable right to interest on late payment of debts.

Ordered to be brought in by Mr. Richard Ottaway, Mr. Patrick Nicholls, Mr. Andrew Rowe, Mr. Michael Grylls, Mr. Michael Fallon, Mr. Michael Forsyth and Mr. Michael Knowles.

Ordered, by The House of Commons, to be Printed, 8 April 1986.

[Bill 127]   (312767)   49/3

LONDON
Printed and published by
Her Majesty's Stationery Office
Printed in England at St Stephen's
Parliamentary Press
45p net

ISBN 0 10 312786 0

Notice of the European Parliament

III

(Notices)

EUROPEAN PARLIAMENT

NOTICE

(86/C 116/03)

GENERAL PROVISIONS GOVERNING OPEN COMPETITIONS

Open competitions organized for the recruitment of officials of the European Communities shall, in accordance with the provisions of the Staff Regulations, be preceded by a notice of competition published in the *Official Journal of the European Communities*. Competitions may be organized both to fill a certain number of vacancies and to draw up a reserve list.

I. General conditions

To be eligible for appointment as an official in an institution of the European Communities, the candidate shall, pursuant to the provisions of the Staff Regulations:

1. be a national of one of the Member States of the Communities (¹), unless an exception is authorized by the appointing authority, and enjoy his full rights as citizen;

2. have fulfilled any obligations imposed on him by the laws concerning military service;

3. produce the appropriate character references as to his suitability for the performance of his duties;

4. have passed a competition based on either qualifications or tests, or both qualifications and tests;

5. be physically fit to perform his duties;

6. have a thorough knowledge of one of the official languages of the Communities (²) and a satisfactory knowledge of another official language of the Communities to the extent necessary for the performance of his duties.

(¹) The Member States are Belgium, Denmark, France, the Federal Republic of Germany, Greece, Ireland, Italy, Luxembourg, the Netherlands, Portugal, Spain and the United Kingdom.

(²) The official Community languages are Danish, Dutch, English, French, German, Greek, Italian, Portuguese and Spanish.

Regulation of the Commission of the European Communities

COMMISSION REGULATION (EEC) No 1399/86
of 12 May 1986
amending Regulation (EEC) No 1146/86 laying down protective measures, in respect of imports of sweet potatoes

THE COMMISSION OF THE EUROPEAN COMMUNITIES,

Having regard to the Treaty establishing the European Economic Community,

Having regard to Council Regulation (EEC) No 2727/75 of 29 October 1975 on the common organization of the market in cereals (¹), as last amended by Regulation (EEC) No 3793/85 (²), and in particular Article 20 (2) thereof,

Whereas, in accordance with Commission Regulation (EEC) No 1146/86 (³), the issue of import licences for sweet potatoes falling within subheading 07.06 B of the Common Customs Tariff has been suspended since 19 April 1986;

Whereas this is the first time that the issue of import licences has been suspended for such products and this has occured in the middle of a period of shipment; whereas the special situation of products which were being loaded or shipped by sea on 19 April 1986 should be taken into account;

Whereas, with a view to control and administrative management, the term of validity of licences issued in compliance with this Regulation should be limited,

HAS ADOPTED THIS REGULATION:

Article 1

The following three subparagraphs are added to Article 1 of Regulation (EEC) No 1146/86:

'This Regulation shall not apply to products which are shown to be in shipment on the date of publication of this Regulation, or to have left the supplying country by that date.

The parties concerned shall prove to the satisfaction of the competent authority that the conditions laid down in the second subparagraph are fulfilled.

The term of validity of licences issued in compliance with this Article shall be limited to 30 June 1986.'

Article 2

This Regulation shall enter into force on the day of its publication in the *Official Journal of the European Communities.*

It shall apply from 19 April 1986.

This Regulation shall be binding in its entirety and directly applicable in all Member States.

Done at Brussels, 12 May 1986.

For the Commission
Frans ANDRIESSEN
Vice-President

(¹) OJ No L 281, 1. 11. 1975, p. 1.
(²) OJ No L 367, 31. 12. 1985, p. 19.
(³) OJ No L 103, 19. 4. 1986, p. 58.

BRITISH COURT SYSTEM

CIVIL	Appeals	CRIMINAL
County Court (minor cases)	*from* County Court *to* Court of Appeal	Magistrates' Court (minor cases, or cases for committal to Crown Court)
	from Magistrates' Court *to* Crown Court *or to* Queen's Bench Divisional Court	
High Court (major cases)	*from* High Court *to* Court of Appeal	Crown Court (major cases)
	from Crown Court *to* Queen's Bench Divisional Court *or to* Court of Appeal	
	from Court of Appeal *to* House of Lords	
	from Court of Appeal *and* Queen's Bench Divisional Court *to* House of Lords	
	from House of Lords *to* European Court of Justice	

Action in the High Court: a Writ

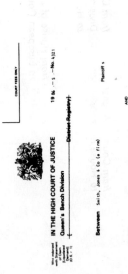

Writ endorsed
with Statement
(Updated
General)
(O.6, r.1)

IN THE HIGH COURT OF JUSTICE 19 86. — S .— No. 531

Queen's Bench Division ~~District Registry~~

Between Smith, Jones & Co (a Firm)

Plaintiff s

AND

Flybynite Limited

Defendants

(1) insert name To the Defendant(¹) Flybynite Limited

(2) insert address of² whose registered office is at Flybynite House, 7 High Street, Newtown, Essex.

This Writ of Summons has been issued against you by the above-named Plaintiff in respect of the claim set out on the back.

Within 14 days after the service of this Writ on you, counting the day of service, you must either satisfy the claim or return to the Court Office mentioned below the accompanying Acknowledgment of Service stating therein whether you intend to contest these proceedings.

If you fail to satisfy the claim or to return the Acknowledgment within the time stated, or if you return the Acknowledgment without stating therein an intention to contest the proceedings, the Plaintiffs may proceed with the action and judgment may be entered against you forthwith without further notice.

Issued from the (³) [Central Office] ~~District Registry~~
of the High Court this 16th day of November 1986.

NOTE.—This Writ may not be served later than 12 calendar months beginning with that date unless renewed by order of the Court.

IMPORTANT

Directions for Acknowledgment of Service are given with the accompanying form.

Statement of Claim

The Plaintiffs' claim is for the sum of £6,900, the price of goods sold and delivered by the Plaintiffs to the Defendants at their request in or about the month of July 1986.

Particulars

Date of Invoice	Invoice No.	Goods	Amount
30th August 1986	12490	Building materials	£6,900

AND THE PLAINTIFFS CLAIM:-

(1) the sum of £6,9000.00

(2) Interest thereon from 30th September 1986 to the date hereof (41 days) at 15% per annum pursuant to section 35A Supreme Court Act 1981, namely £116.44.

(3) Further interest thereon from the date hereof until judgement or payment at 15% per annum pursuant of section 35A Supreme Court Act 1981 at a daily rate of £2.85.

(Signed) Simmonds & Baxter

If, within the time for returning the Acknowledgment of Service, the Defendant pays   the amount claimed and £ 118.50   for costs and, if the Plaintiffs obtain   an order for substituted service, the additional sum of £ 30.00   further proceedings will be stayed. The money must be paid to the Plaintiffs', their Solicitors or Agent¹s.

(¹) [(2) The space] [One of the causes] of action in respect of which the Plaintiff claim ~~relief in this action arose wholly or in part~~
~~in the District or the District Registry named overleaf.~~

(¹) If this Writ was issued out of a District Registry this indorsement as to place where the cause of action arose should be completed.
(2) Delete as necessary.
(4) For proceedings of this indorsement where the Plaintiff sues in person, see Supreme Court Practice vol 2, para 1.

(³) This Writ was issued by Simonds & Baxter
of 14 New Street, London WC1

[Agent for
[—]
of.

Solicitor's   for the said Plaintiffs whose address   (³) [is] [are]
24 New Street, London WC1

(4) Complete and delete as necessary

OYEZ The Solicitors' Law Stationery Society, plc Oyez House, 237 Long Lane, London SE1 4PU.   1486 3.85
* * * * *   High Court A2A

Action in the High Court: Acknowledgement of Service

Notes for Guidance

1. Each Defendant (if there are more than one) is required to complete an Acknowledgement of Service and return it to the appropriate Court Office.

[2] For the purpose of calculating the period of 14 days for acknowledging service, a writ served on the Defendant personally is treated as having been served on the day it was delivered to him and a writ sent by post or by insertion through the Defendant's letter-box is treated as having been served on the seventh day after the date of posting or insertion.]

3. Where the Defendant is sued in a name different from his own, the form must be completed by him with the addition in paragraph 1 of the words 'sued as (the name stated on the Writ of Summons)'.

4. Where the Defendant is a FIRM and a Solicitor is not instructed, the form must be completed by a PARTNER by name, with the addition in paragraph 1 of the description 'partner in the form of ( )' after his name.

5. Where the Defendant is sued as an individual TRADING IN A NAME OTHER THAN HIS OWN, the form must be completed by him with the addition in paragraph 1 of the description 'trading as ( )' after his name.

6. Where the Defendant is a LIMITED COMPANY the form must be completed by a Solicitor or by someone authorised to act on behalf of the Company, but the Company can take no further step in the proceedings without a Solicitor acting on its behalf.

7. Where the Defendant is a MINOR or a MENTAL Patient, the form must be completed by a Solicitor acting for a guardian ad litem.

8. A Defendant acting in person may obtain help in completing the form either at the Central Office of the Royal Courts of Justice or at any District Registry of the High Court or any Citizens' Advice Bureau.

9. A Defendant who is NOT a Limited Company or a Corporation may be entitled to Legal Aid. Information about the Legal Aid Scheme may be obtained from any Citizens' Advice Bureau and from most forms of Solicitors.

10. These notes deal only with the more usual cases. In case of difficulty a Defendant in person should refer to paragraphs 8 and 9 above.

* Not applicable if the Defendant is a Company served at its Registered Office

---

Acknowledgement of Service of Writ of Summons (Queen's Bench)

The Judgment heading should be completed by the Plaintiff

IN THE HIGH COURT OF JUSTICE 1986 ---S.---No. 4321

Queen's Bench Division [District Registry]

Between   Smith, Jones & Co (a firm)   Plaintiffs

AND

Flybynite Limited   Defendants

Defendant 5

If you intend to instruct a Solicitor to act for you, give him this form IMMEDIATELY. Please complete in black ink.

IMPORTANT Read the accompanying directions and notes for guidance carefully before completing this form. If any information required is omitted or given wrongly, THIS FORM MAY HAVE TO BE RETURNED. Delay may result in judgment being entered against a Defendant whereby he or his solicitor may have to pay the costs of applying to set it aside.

See Notes 1, 3, 4 and 5

1. State the full name of the Defendant by whom or on whose behalf the service of the Writ is being acknowledged:
   FLYBYNITE LIMITED

See Direction 2

2. State whether the Defendant intends to contest the proceedings (tick appropriate box)   X yes   no

See Direction 3

3. If the claim against the Defendant is for a debt or liquidated demand, AND he does not intend to contest the proceedings, state if the Defendant intends to apply for a stay of execution against any judgment entered by the Plaintiff (tick box)   yes

See Direction 4

4. If the Writ of Summons was issued out of a District Registry and
   (a) the Defendant's residence, place of business or registered office (if a limited company) is NOT within the district of that District Registry AND
   (b) there is no indorsement on the Writ that the Plaintiff's cause of action arose wholly or in part within that district,
   state if the Defendant applies for the transfer of the action (tick box)   yes

If YES, state—   to the Royal Courts of Justice, London
OR
(tick appropriate box)   to the*   District Registry

*State which Registry

Service of the Writ is acknowledged accordingly

(Signed) [signature]

† [Solicitor] [Agents]

Address for service (See notes overleaf)

9 Court Road, Liverpool

†Where words appear between brackets delete if inapplicable. Insert Defendant in Person if appropriate

Please complete overleaf

Action in the High Court: Acknowledgement of Service

Indorsement by Plaintiff's solicitor (or by Plaintiff if suing in person) of his name, address and reference, if any, in the box below.

Simmonds & Baxter
24 New Street
London WC1

Tel: 01-999 0022 Ref: SB

Notes as to Address for Service

Solicitor. Where the Defendant is represented by a Solicitor, state the business or place of business in England or Wales. If the Solicitor is the Agent of another Solicitor, state the name and the place of business of the Solicitor for whom he is acting.

Defendant in person. Where the Defendant is acting in person, he must give his residence OR, if he does not reside in England or Wales, an address in England or Wales where communications for him should be sent. In the case of a limited company, 'residence' means its registered or principal office.

Indorsement by Defendant's solicitor (or by Defendant if suing in person) of his name, address and reference, if any, in the box below.

HAXBYS
9 COURT ROAD
LIVERPOOL

Tel: 051-232 9876 Ref: H/2

Acknowledgement
of Service
of Writ
(Queen's Bench)
(O. 12, r. 3)

(*) Insert address

Directions for Acknowledgment of Service

1. The accompanying form of **ACKNOWLEDGMENT OF SERVICE** should be detached and completed by a Solicitor acting on behalf of the Defendant or by the Defendant if acting in person. After completion it must be delivered or sent by post to the District Registrar (*)

2. A Defendant who states in his Acknowledgment of Service that he intends to contest the proceedings **MUST ALSO SERVE A DEFENCE** on the Solicitor for the Plaintiff (or on the Plaintiff if acting in person)

If a Statement of Claim is indorsed on the Writ (i.e. the words "Statement of Claim" appear at the top of the back of the first page), the Defence must be served within 14 days after the time for acknowledging service of the Writ, unless in the meantime a summons for judgment is served on the Defendant

If a Statement of Claim is not indorsed on the Writ, the Defence need not be served until 14 days after a Statement of Claim has been served on the Defendant. If the Defendant fails to serve his defence within the appropriate time, the Plaintiff may enter judgment against him without further notice.

3. **A STAY of EXECUTION** against the Defendant's goods may be applied for where the Defendant is unable to pay the money for which any judgment is entered. If a Defendant to an action for debt or liquidated demand (i.e. a fixed sum) who does not intend to contest the proceedings states, in answer to Question 3 in the Acknowledgment of Service, that he intends to apply for a stay, execution will be stayed for 14 days after his Acknowledgment, but he must, within that time, **ISSUE A SUMMONS** for a stay of execution, supported by an affidavit of his means. The affidavit should state any offer which the Defendant desires to make for payment of the money by instalments or otherwise.

4. **IF THE WRIT IS ISSUED OUT OF A DISTRICT REGISTRY** but the Defendant does not reside or carry on business within the district of the registry and the writ is not indorsed with a statement that the Plaintiff's cause of action arose in that district, the Defendant may, in answer to Question 4 in the Acknowledgment of Service, apply for the transfer of the action to some other District Registry or to the Royal Courts of Justice.

See over for Notes for Guidance

OYEZ The Solicitors' Law Stationery Society plc, Oyez House, 237 Long Lane, London SE1 4PU

High Court E22 (DR)

Action in the High Court: a Summons

IN THE HIGH COURT OF JUSTICE 19 86 — S — No. 4321

Queen's Bench Division

Master Archer   Master in Chambers

Between Smith, Jones & Co (a firm)

                                  Plaintiffs

AND

Flybynite Limited

                                  Defendants

Let all parties concerned attend the Master in Chambers, in Room No. 96
Central Office, Royal Courts of Justice, Strand, London on the 13th day,
the (19th) day of January 19 87, at 11 00 o'clock in
the fore noon on the hearing of an application on the part of the Plaintiff for final
judgment in this action against(¹)

(1) The Defendant
(or if against one
or some of several
Defendants insert
names)

                the defendants

(2) Or as the case
may be, setting
out the nature of
the claim.

for the amount claimed in the statement of claim with interest, if any (²)

and costs

Take Notice that a party intending to oppose this application or to apply for a stay of
execution should send to the opposite party or his solicitor, to reach him not less than
three days before the date above-mentioned, a copy of any affidavit intended to be
used.

Dated the 28th day of November 19 86

This Summons was taken out by Simmonds & Baxter
of 14 New Street, London WC1

[Agent for
of

Solicitor s for the Plaintiff s

To M essrs Haxbys

Solicitor s or Agent for the Defendants

IN THE HIGH COURT OF JUSTICE
Queen's Bench Division

19 86 — S — No. 4321

Dated 28th November   19 86

Returnable 10th January   19 87

Smith, Jones & Co (a firm)

v.

Flybynite Ltd

Summons

Under Order 14 for Whole Claim

Simmonds & Baxter
14 New Street,
London WC1

Agent for the
of

Solicitor for the Plaintiff s

OYEZ The Solicitors' Law Stationery Society plc, Oyez House
237 Long Lane, London SE1 4PU

High Court S3 (PR)

Action in the High Court: an Affidavit

IN THE HIGH COURT OF JUSTICE
Queen's Bench Division

Between

Smith, Jones & Co (a firm)   Plaintiffs

AND

Flybynite Limited   Defendants

I, John Jones, builder,

of 24 New Street, London WC1

(¹) make oath and say as follows:—

1. The Defendant s, Flybynite Limited
    (²) were   and (³) are   at the commencement of this action,
    justly and truly indebted to (⁴) the Plaintiffs

    in the sum of £ 6,900.00, the   for the price of building materials £
    supplied by the Plaintiffs to the Defendants at their request.

    The particulars of the said claim appear by the indorsement on the Writ of
    Summons in this action.

2. It is within my own knowledge that the said debt was incurred and is still
    due and owing as aforesaid.   (£)
                                    or
(² I am informed by (⁴)   (£)

    that the said debt was incurred and is still due and owing as aforesaid.]

3. I verily believe that there is no defence to this action.

4. I am duly authorised by the Plaintiff to make this affidavit. (⁵)

Sworn at 41 Old Street, London WC2

the 30th day of November 19 86.

Before me. Peter Higgins   John Jones

                        A Commissioner for Oaths

            This affidavit is filed on behalf of the Plaintiff

---

IN THE HIGH COURT OF JUSTICE
Queen's Bench Division

Sworn the 30th   day of November 19 86.

Smith, Jones & Co
(a firm)   **Affidavit**

                under   Order   14,
                        Rule 2,
v.   by or on behalf
Flybynite Ltd   of Plaintiff

Filed on behalf of the Plaintiff

Simmonds & Baxter,
14 New Street,
London WC1

                Plaintiffs Solicitors

OYEZ The Solicitors' Law Stationery Society Ltd Oyez House

High Court B34 (PR)

Action in the High Court: Judgment

Judgment under Order 14 (fixed or fixed Costs) O 14 r 3, O 42 r 1)

IN THE HIGH COURT OF JUSTICE

Queen's Bench Division

19 86 — S. — No. 431

Between

Smith, Jones & Co (a firm)   Plaintiffs

AND

Flybynite Limited   Defendants

The 10th   day of   January   1987

The Defendant having given notice of intention to defend herein and the Court having under Order 14, Rule 3, ordered that judgment as hereinafter provided be entered for the Plaintiff against the Defendant
IT IS THIS DAY ADJUDGED that the Defendant

(1) do pay the Plaintiffs

[margin: (1) or, do give the Plaintiff possession of the land described in the writ of summons (or statement of claim) as]

£4,900.00 together with interest from the due date of payment to the date of issue of the writ at 15% per annum pursuant to section 35A Supreme Court Act 1981 namely £116.44 and further interest from the date of issue to the date hereof at 15% per annum pursuant to section 35A Supreme Court Act 1981 amounting to £176.08 a total of £7,192.52

and £ 178.50   costs [or costs to be taxed].

The above costs have been taxed and allowed at £   as appears by a taxing officer's certificate dated the   day of   19

Plaintiff's Solicitor

---

19 86 — S. — No. 431

IN THE HIGH COURT OF JUSTICE

Queen's Bench Division

Dated 10th January   1986

Smith, Jones & Co (a firm)

v

Flybynite Ltd

Judgment

Under Order 14, Rule 3

Simmonds & Baxter
14 New Street,
London WC1

Plaintiff's Solicitors

OYEZ The Solicitors' Law Stationery Society plc, Oyez House
237 Long Lane, London SE1 4PU

High Court D5

High Court Injunction

IN THE HIGH COURT OF JUSTICE   1986 -A- No. 1390
QUEEN'S BENCH DIVISION

The Honourable Mr Justice Good   Judge in Chambers

BETWEEN

     ACME ADVERTISING LIMITED   Plaintiffs

     and

     SIMON SLY   Defendant

_____

ORDER

_____

UPON HEARING Counsel for the Plaintiffs and the Defendant in person and upon reading the affidavit of Adrian Acme sworn herein

And the Plaintiffs by their said Counsel undertaking to abide by any Order this Court may make as to damages in case this Court shall hereafter be of opinion that the Defendant shall have sustained any by reason of this Order which the Plaintiffs ought to pay

IT IS ORDERED and directed that the Defendant be restrained and an injunction is hereby granted restraining him until 15th October, 1987, directly or indirectly, whether for himself, any other person, firm, company or otherwise from soliciting or seeking orders for advertising from any person, firm or company within the Greater London area who were customers of the Plaintiffs on 16th October 1986

AND IT IS ORDERED that the Defendant do deliver up forthwith to the Plaintiffs' solicitors any books, records, customer lists or other documents, the property of the Plaintiffs, or any copies thereof which are in his possession or control

AND IT IS ORDERED that the costs of this application be costs in the cause.

DATED the 30th day of October 1986

Guarantee

To:

XYZ (Supplies) Limited,
9 Old Street,
London EC7.

Dear Sirs,

In consideration of your agreeing at my request to refrain from taking proceedings to recover payment of the debt of £6,497.50 owed to you by Simon Baxter Ltd, we jointly and severally guarantee payment of it (or of such part of it as remains unpaid after 2nd December 1986) on the understanding that all sums received by you from Simon Baxter Ltd. or for the credit of their account with you shall be first applied by you in reduction of that debt.

This guarantee is not to be impaired by any time or indulgence which you may grant. Moreover, our right to be subrogated to you in respect of payments received from, or from the resources of, Simon Baxter Ltd is not to attach until you have received the full amount of your claim to which this guarantee relates.

Yours faithfully,

Simon Baxter

John Baxter

Simon Baxter

John Baxter

Contract of Sale

CONTRACT OF SALE
The National Conditions of Sale, Twentieth Edition

Vendor **JOHN PETER SMITH and MAUREEN ANNE SMITH** both of
12 Sherborne Avenue Norwood Green Southall Middlesex

Purchaser **ROBERT FRANK GREEN and LINDA GREEN** both of
291 Finchley Road London NW3

Registered Land		Purchase price	£ 100,000	00
District Land Registry: HARROW		Deposit	£ 10,000	00
Title Number: NGL 227147		Balance payable	£ 90,000	00
Agreed rate of interest:		Price fixed for chattels or valuation money (if any)	£ 7,000	00
4½ per annum above base rate at Midland Bank plc for the time being in force.		Total	£ 97,000.00	

Property and interest therein sold

ALL THAT freehold property situate at and known as
12 Sherborne Avenue Southall in the London
Borough of Ealing as the same is registered
at H M Land Registry with Title Absolute.

Vendor sells as   Beneficial Owners   Completion date:

AGREED that the Vendor sells and the Purchaser buys as above, subject to the Special Conditions
endorsed hereon and to the National Conditions of Sale Twentieth Edition so far as the latter Conditions
are not inconsistent with the Special Conditions.

* Signed

Date   19

* This is a form of legal document. Neither the form nor the National Conditions of Sale which the form embodies, were produced or drafted for use, without technical assistance, by persons unfamiliar with the law and practice of conveyancing.

SPECIAL CONDITIONS OF SALE

A.   The sale is with vacant possession on completion.

B.   The deposit shall be paid by way of bankers draft, Building Society cheque or Solicitors' client account cheque to the Vendors Solicitors as Stakeholders.

C.   The Purchaser hereby acknowledges that, save for replies to enquiries made of the Vendors Solicitors by the Purchasers Solicitors :-

  i.   No statement or representation made to the Purchaser or to anyone concerned on his behalf by or on behalf of the Vendors whether orally or in writing induced him to enter into this contract.

  ii. Any such statement or representation does not form part of this contract.

  iii. Any liability of the Vendors and any remedy of the Purchaser at law or in equity in respect of any such statement or representation is excluded to the extent authorised by the Unfair Contract Terms Act 1977.

D.   If the Vendors Solicitors receive the monies due on completion after 2.30pm the following working day shall be deemed the date of actual completion And where completion is by post, all deeds and documents shall be posted at the Purchasers risk.

E.   On completion the Vendors will sell and the Purchaser will buy the following additional items for the price of Seven thousand pounds (£7,000):

All carpets   Wardrobes in bedroom 2 and small bedroom
All curtains   Tumbledryer
All blinds   Fridge/Freezer
Chandeliers   Cooker

— 1981

OYEZ

THE SOLICITORS' LAW STATIONERY SOCIETY plc
Oyez House 237 Long Lane London SE1 4PU

Transfer of Property

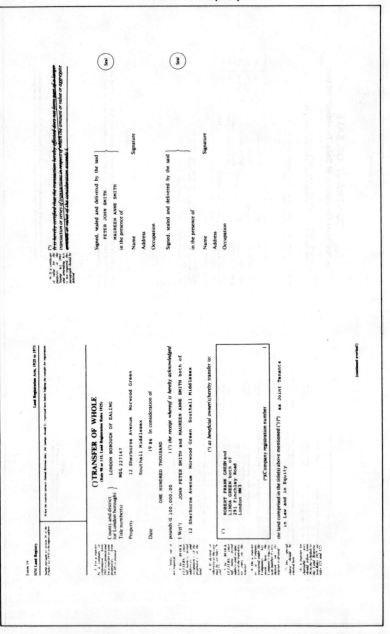

Form 19

HM Land Registry

Land Registration Acts, 1925 to 1971

Insert paragraph l or a, section 24 or the Finance Act 1931 in the appropriate place

When the register attracts limited Revenue duty, the stamps should be impressed here before lodging the transfer for registration

( )TRANSFER OF WHOLE

(Rule 98 or 115, Land Registration Rules 1925)

County and district (or London borough) } LONDON BOROUGH OF EALING

Title number(s): NGL 227147

Property: 12 Sherborne Avenue Norwood Green
Southall Middlesex

Date 19 86 In consideration of

pounds (£ 100,000.00) ONE HUNDRED THOUSAND

I We(*) JOHN PETER SMITH and MAUREEN ANNE SMITH both of

12 Sherborne Avenue Norwood Green Southall Middlesex

(*) the receipt whereof is hereby acknowledged

(*) as beneficial owner(s) hereby transfer to:

(*)
ROBERT FRANK GREEN and
LINDA GREEN both of
291 Finchley Road
London NW3

(*)Company registration number

the land comprised in the title(s) above mentioned(*)(*) as Joint Tenants
in Law and in Equity

(continued overleaf)

Signed, sealed and delivered by the said
PETER JOHN SMITH

MAUREEN ANNE SMITH

in the presence of   Signature   ⎰ Seal

Name

Address

Occupation

Signed, sealed and delivered by the said

in the presence of   Signature   ⎰ Seal

Name

Address

Occupation

Will

I, <u>JOHN HENRY BROWN</u> of 22 New Grove, Wincham, Suffolk, hereby revoke all former testamentary dispositions made by me.

1. I give all my real and personal property whatsoever and wheresoever (including any property over which I may have a general power of appointment or disposition by will) to my wife Emily Jane Brown absolutely and appoint her the sole executrix of this my will.

2. If my wife shall not survive me for the period of one month then I declare that the foregoing clause shall not have effect and in lieu thereof I give all my said property including the income accruing from the date of my death until the death of my wife to Robert Black of 9 The Elms Littleton in the County of Kent absolutely and appoint him the sole executor of this my will.

IN WITNESS whereof I have hereunto set my hand this 10th day of October 1972

SIGNED by the above-named   )
John Henry Brown as his last)
will in the presence of us   )
present at the same time   )   *John H. Brown.*
who at his request in his   )
presence and in the presence)
of each other have hereunto   )
subscribed our names as   )
witnesses   )

Nigel Day
Accountant
10 Oak Way
Wincham
Suffolk

Ronald Henderson
Teacher
16 New Grove
Wincham
Suffolk

Particulars of Claim in the County Court

IN THE KINGSTON-UPON-THAMES   **COUNTY COURT**

CASE No. 86036541

Between   Smith's Shoe Shop Ltd

                                                    Plaintiff

              Jack Robinson   **AND**

                                                  Defendant

	£
The Plaintiff's claim is for the sum of £63.75, the price of two pairs of shoes sold by the Plaintiffs to the Defendant on 7th June 1986 from their shop in South Street, Kingston-upon-Thames.	
The following are the particulars:—	
1 pair of men's shoes £40.00	
1 pair of ladies' shoes £23.75	63.75
AND the Plaintiff claims the sum of **£**	63.75

Dated this   10th   day of   September   19 86

(Signed)   *John Smith*

~~*Plaintiff's solicitor, who will accept service of all proceedings at*~~

~~at~~

~~on behalf of the Plaintiff.~~

To the above-named Defendant

Particulars of claim (general)
O 6, r 1

Defence to Claim in the County Court

In the KINGSTON-UPON-THAMES County Court

CASE No. 86036541

SMITH'S SHOE SHOP LTD v JACK ROBINSON

ADMISSION

Read the instructions on the back of the summons carefully before completing this form. Immediately after you have filled in this form send it by post or take it to the Court Office as stated on the summons. PLEASE USE BLACK INK.

1. Do you admit the plaintiff's claim in full — ~~YES~~/NO

2. Do you admit part of the plaintiff's claim — YES/~~NO~~

   If so, how much do you admit? £ 40.00
   (Put your reasons for disputing the balance overleaf)

3. If you wish the court to consider whether to make an instalment order answer the following questions:—

PAY AND MEANS

(a) What is your occupation? lorry driver

(b) What is the name and address of your employer?

   H.G.V. LORRY COMPANY
   RICHMOND ROAD
   KINGSTON ON THAMES

(c) What is your pay before deductions? £ 120.00 per week/month

(d) What overtime, bonuses, fees, allowances, or commissions do you receive? £ 20.00 per week/month

(e) What is your usual take home pay? £ 113.00 per week/month

(f) Do you receive
   (i) a pension? £ No per week/month
   (ii) any state benefits? £ No per week/month
   (iii) any other income? £ No per week/month

(g) What contributions, if any, are made by any member of your household?

   NONE

LIABILITIES

(a) What persons, if any, are financially dependent on you? Please give details including the ages of any dependent children:—

   My wife and 2 children ages 4 and 7

(b) What rent or mortgage instalments are you liable to pay? £ 25.00 per week/month

   What amount do you actually pay? £ 25.00 per week/month

(c) What rates are you liable to pay? £ 12.00 per week/month

   What amount do you actually pay? £ 12.00 per week/month

(d) Do you have to pay under any Court Orders? Please give details including name of court and case number, the amount still owing and the instalments you are paying.

   Judgement for arrears of rates in this court which I am paying at £5 per month. I still have £25 to pay.

(e) What other regular payments do you have to make?

   H.P. on car £30 per month. Maintenance to my former wife and children £10 per month.

(f) Have you any other liabilities which you would like the Court to take into account? Please give details:—

   No.

WHAT OFFER OF PAYMENT DO YOU MAKE?

Payment in full on the ___ day of ___ 19___

Address to which notices about this case should be sent to you: 13 Black Street Kingston on Thames

OR by instalments of £ 3.00 per month

SIGN HERE J. Robinson

DATE 14th September 1986

N9 Form of Admission, Defence and Counterclaim to accompany form N1, 2, 3 and 4
Order 3 Rule 3(2)(c)

MCR 341637/1/F24336 9m 3/85 TL

Defence to Claim in the County Court

In the KINGSTON-UPON-THAMES County Court

CASE No. 86036541

SMITH'S SHOE SHOP LTD .... v. .... JACK ROBINSON

DEFENCE	COUNTERCLAIM
1. Do you dispute the plaintiff's claim or any part of it?	1. Do you wish to make a claim against the plaintiff?
YES/NO	YES/NO
2. If so, how much do you dispute and what are your reasons?	2. If so, for how much? £ ....
	3. What is the nature of the claim?

I returned the shoes I
bought for £23.75 2 days
after I bought them
because they fell apart.

TO BE COMPLETED WHERE THE SUM CLAIMED OR AMOUNT INVOLVED EXCEEDS £500

If you dispute the plaintiff's claim or wish to make a claim against him do you want the proceedings referred to arbitration?   YES/NO

NOTES:

1. Any claim for £500 or less which is defended will be referred to arbitration automatically, but the reference may be rescinded on application.

2. When a defended claim is arbitrated the right of appeal against the arbitrator's award is very limited.

3. If your claim against the plaintiff is bigger than his claim against you, you may have to pay a fee before it can be dealt with. You can find out whether a fee is payable by enquiring at any county court office.

Address to which notices about this case should be sent to you: 17 Black Street
Kingston on thames

SIGN HERE J. Robinson

DATE 14th September 1986

N9 Form of Admission, Defence and Counterclaim to accompany forms N1, 2, 3 and 4
Order 3 Rule 3(2)(c)

In the _____ **County Court***

_____ **Divorce Registry***

No of matter 1472 of 1986

IN THE MATTER of the Petition of

JEAN BROOKS Petitioner

and

JOHN BROOKS Respondent

Divorce Petition

(Wife against Husband)

(Behaviour)

Note 22

Simmonds & Baxter,
14 New Street,
London WC1

OYEZ The Solicitors' Law Stationery Society plc, Oyez House,
237 Long Lane, London SE1 4PU

Divorce 2(W)

Wife's Petition (Behaviour)

**MATRIMONIAL
CAUSES RULES**

Rule 9
Appendix 2

The Notes for
guidance in
drawing the
petition are on
a separate sheet

IN THE _____

_____ **COUNTY COURT***
DIVORCE REGISTRY*

No of matter 1472 of 1986

The Petition of Jean Brooks (née Smith)

Shows that

Note 1
1   On the 10th   day of June   19 72   the Petitioner
Jean Brooks (née Smith)   was lawfully
married to John Brooks
(hereinafter called the Respondent) at St. John's Church in Oldtown in the
County of Sussex.

Note 2
2   The Petitioner and the Respondent last lived together as husband and
wife at 14 Chaucer Crescent, London N2

Note 3
3   The Petitioner is domiciled in England and Wales.

Note 4
the Petitioner is a   dress designer   and resides at
14 Chaucer Crescent, London N2
and the Respondent is a   unemployed   and resides
at 9 Acacia Grove, Bromley, Kent.

Note 5
4   There are/are] two   children of the family now living
James Brooks born on 14th February 1974,
Sarah Brooks born on 9th July 1977

Note 6
5   No other child now living has been born to the Petitioner during the
marriage

Note 7
6   There are or have been no other proceedings in any court in England
and Wales or elsewhere with reference to the marriage (or to any children of the
family) or between the Petitioner and the Respondent with reference to any

Divorce Petition

property of either or both of them.

Note 8

7 There are no proceedings continuing in any country outside England and Wales which relate to the marriage or are capable of affecting its validity or subsistence.

Note 9

8 The said marriage has broken down irretrievably.

Note 10

9 The Respondent has behaved in such a way that the Petitioner cannot reasonably be expected to live with the Respondent.

Note 11

10 (a) The Respondent throughout the marriage has drunk to excess and in spite of the Petitioner's requests refuses to seek medical or other assistance.

Note 13

(b) When drunk the Respondent is abusive to the Petitioner and the children of the family causing them distress.

(c) As a result of the Respondent's excessive drinking the Respondent has failed to keep any employment and thus has been unable adequately or at all to contribute to the maintenance of the family, the full burden of which has fallen on the Petitioner.

Note 14
Note 15
Note 16

The Petitioner therefore prays —

(1) That the said marriage may be dissolved.

Note 17

(2) That she may be granted the custody of James Brooks and Sarah Brooks;

Note 18

(3) That the Respondent may be ordered to pay the costs of this suit

Note 19

(4) That she may be granted the following ancillary relief —

Note 20

(i) an order for maintenance pending suit

(ii) a periodical payments order } for herself

(iii) a secured periodical payments order }

(iv) a lump sum order

(v) a periodical payments order } for the children

(vi) a secured periodical payments order } of the family

(vii) a lump sum order

(viii) a property adjustment order

Simmonds & Baxter (Signed)

Note 21

The names and addresses of the persons who are to be served with this Petition are —

Note 22

John Brooks
9 Acacia Grove, Bromley, Kent

Note 23

The Petitioner's address for service is —
c/o Messrs Simmonds & Baxter, 4 New Street, London WC1
Dated this 14th day of September 1986

Address all communications for the Court to: The Registrar, County Court

(or to the Divorce Registry, Somerset House, Strand, London WC2R 1LP).
The Court Office is open from 10 a.m. to 4 p.m. (4.30 p.m. at the Divorce Registry) on Mondays to Fridays only.

Notizen

Notizen